The GALE ENCYCLOPEDIA of CHILDREN'S HEALTH

INFANCY THROUGH ADOLESCENCE

The GALE ENCYCLOPEDIA *of* CHILDREN'S HEALTH

INFANCY THROUGH ADOLESCENCE

VOLUME

A-C

KRISTINE KRAPP AND JEFFREY WILSON, EDITORS

Detroit • New York • San Francisco • San Diego • New Haven, Conn. • Waterville, Maine • London • Munich

THOMSON
GALE

The Gale Encyclopedia of Children's Health: Infancy through Adolescence

Product Manager
Kate Millson

Project Editors
Kristine M. Krapp, Jeffrey J. Wilson

Editorial
Donna Batten, Shirelle Phelps, Erin Watts

Editorial Support Services
Luann Brennan, Andrea Lopeman, Mark Springer

Rights Acquisition Management
Margaret Abendroth, Ann Taylor

Imaging
Randy Bassett, Lezlie Light, Dan Newell, Christine O'Bryan, Robyn Young

Product Design
Michelle DiMercurio, Tracey Rowens

Composition and Electronic Prepress
Evi Seoud, Mary Beth Trimper

Manufacturing
Wendy Blurton, Dorothy Maki

Indexing
Synapse Corp. of Colorado

LIBRARY OF CONGRESS CATALOGING-IN-PUBLICATION DATA

The Gale encyclopedia of children's health : infancy through adolescence / Kristine Krapp and Jeffrey Wilson, editors.
p. cm.
Includes bibliographical references and index.
ISBN 0-7876-9241-7 (set hardcover : alk. paper) –
ISBN 0-7876-9427-4 (v. 1) – ISBN 0-7876-9428-2 (v. 2) –
ISBN 0-7876-9429-0 (v. 3) – ISBN 0-7876-9430-4 (v. 4)
1. Children–Health and hygiene–Encyclopedias.
2. Children–Diseases–Encyclopedias. 3. Pediatrics–Encyclopedias. [DNLM: 1. Pediatrics–Encyclopedias–English. 2. Pediatrics–Popular Works. 3. Child Welfare–Encyclopedias–English. 4. Child Welfare–Popular Works. 5. Infant Welfare–Encyclopedias–English. 6. Infant Welfare–Popular Works. WS 13 G1515 2005]
I. Title: Encyclopedia of children's health. II. Krapp, Kristine M. III. Wilson, Jeffrey, 1971- IV. Gale Group.

RJ26.G35 2005
618.92'0003–dc22   2005003478

This title is also available as an e-book
ISBN 0-7876-9425-8 (set)
Contact your Gale sales representative for ordering information.
ISBN 0-7876-9241-7 (set)
0-7876-9427-4 (Vol. 1)
0-7876-9428-2 (Vol. 2)
0-7876-9429-0 (Vol. 3)
0-7876-9430-4 (Vol. 4)
Printed in Canada
10 9 8 7 6 5 4 3 2 1

CONTENTS

LIST OF ENTRIES

A

Abandonment
Abdominal wall defects
Acetaminophen
Acne
Acromegaly and gigantism
Acting out
Adaptive behavior scales for infants and early childhood
Addiction
Adenoid hyperplasia
Adenovirus infections
Adjustment disorders
Adolescence
Adoption
Aggressive behavior
Albinism
Alcoholism
Allergic purpura
Allergic rhinitis
Allergies
Allergy shots
Allergy tests
Allowance and money management
Alopecia
Alpha-fetoprotein test
Alternative school
Amblyopia
Amenorrhea
Amniocentesis
Anabolic steroids
Analgesics
Anaphylaxis
Anatomical age
Anemias

Angelman's syndrome
Animal bite infections
Anorexia nervosa
Antenatal testing
Antepartum testing
Antiacne drugs
Antiasthmatic drugs
Antibiotics
Antibiotics, topical
Antidepressants
Antiepileptics
Antihistamines
Antisocial behavior
Antisocial personality disorder
Antiviral drugs
Anxiety
Apgar testing
Apnea of infancy
Appendicitis
Arteriovenous fistula
Asphyxia neonatorum
Assessment
Asthma
Ataxia telangiectasia/chromosome breakage disorders
Atopic dermatitis
Atrial septal defect
Attachment between infant and caregiver
Attention-deficit/Hyperactivity disorder (AD/HD)
Audiometry
Auditory discrimination test
Autism

B

Babysitters
Battered child syndrome
Bayley Scales of Infant Development
Bed-wetting
Beery-Buktenica test
Bejel
Bell's palsy
Biliary atresia
Bilingualism/Bilingual education
Bilirubin test
Binge eating disorder
Bipolar disorder
Birth order
Birthmarks
Bites and stings
Blood sugar tests
Bonding
Botulism
Brachial plexopathy, obstetric
Breast development
Breath holding spells
Breech birth
Bronchiolitis
Bronchitis
Bruises
Bruton's agammaglobulinemia
Bulimia nervosa
Bullies
Burns

Fear
Febrile seizures
Fetal alcohol syndrome
Fetal hemoglobin test
Fever
Fever of unknown origin
Fifth disease
Fine motor skills
Fingertip injuries
Flu vaccine
Fluoridation
Folic acid
Food allergies and sensitivities
Food poisoning
Foreign objects
Foster care
Fractures
Fragile X syndrome
Friedreich's ataxia
Frostbite and frostnip

G

Galactosemia
Gangs
Gastroenteritis
Gastroesophageal reflux disease
Gender constancy
Gender identity
Gross motor skills
Growth hormone tests

H

Handedness
Hand-eye coordination
Hand-foot-mouth disease
Head injury
Head Start programs
Headache
Hearing impairment
Heart murmurs
Heat disorders
Heavy metal poisoning
Heimlich maneuver

Hemophilia
Hemophilus infections
Hepatitis A
Hepatitis B
Hepatitis B vaccine
Hereditary fructose intolerance
Hereditary hemorrhagic
    telangiectasia
Hernia
Herpes simplex
Hib vaccine
High-risk pregnancy
Hirschsprung's disease
Histiocytosis X
HIV infection and AIDS
Hives
Home schooling
Homosexuality and bisexuality
Hospitalization
Human bite infections
Hydrocephalus
Hyperglycemia
Hyperhidrosis
Hyper-IgM syndrome
Hypertension
Hyperthyroidism
Hypoglycemia
Hypogonadism
Hypospadias
Hypothyroidism
Hypotonia

I

Idiopathic thrombocytopenic
    purpura
Ileus
Immobilization
Immune system development
Immunodeficiency
Immunoglobulin deficiency
    syndromes
Impetigo
Impulse control disorders
Inclusion conjunctivitis
Infant massage

Infant mortality
Infectious mononucleosis
Influenza
Insect sting allergy
Intelligence
Intermittent explosive disorder
Intersex states
Intestinal obstructions
Intrauterine growth retardation
Intravenous rehydration
Iron deficiency anemia
Irritable bowel syndrome
Itching

J

Jaundice
Juvenile arthritis

K

Kawasaki syndrome
Klinefelter syndrome

L

Labyrinthitis
Lactation
Lactose intolerance
Language delay
Language development
Language disorders
Laxatives
Lead poisoning
Learning disorders
Leukemias, acute
Leukemias, chronic
Lice infestation
Lipidoses
Lisping
Listeriosis
Lying
Lyme disease
Lymphadenitis

M

Macrocephaly
Magnetic resonance imaging
Malnutrition
Malocclusion
Marfan syndrome
Massage therapy
Mastoiditis
Masturbation
Maxillofacial trauma
Measles
Meningitis
Meningococcal meningitis
    vaccine
Meningococcemia
Menstruation
Mental retardation
Methylphenidate
Mineral deficiency
Mineral toxicity
Minerals
Minnesota Multiphasic Personality
    Inventory
Minority health
Mitochondrial disorders
MMR vaccine
Moles
Mood disorders
Moral development
Motion sickness
Movement disorders
Mucopolysaccharidoses
Multicultural education/curriculum
Multiple endocrine neoplasia
    syndromes
Multiple pregnancy
Mumps
Munchausen syndrome
Muscle spasms and cramps
Muscular dystrophy
Mutism
Myers-Briggs Type Indicator
Myopathies
Myopia
Myotonic dystrophy
Myringotomy and ear tubes

N

Nail-patella syndrome
Narcolepsy
Narcotic drugs
Nasal trauma
Nausea and vomiting
Near-drowning
Necrotizing enterocolitis
Neonatal jaundice
Neonatal reflexes
Neurofibromatosis
Neurologic exam
Night terrors
Nightmares
Nonsteroidal anti-inflammatory
    drugs
Nosebleed
Numbness and tingling
Nursemaid's elbow
Nutrition
Nystagmus

O

Obesity
Obsessive-compulsive disorder
Oligomenorrhea
Oppositional defiant disorder
Oral contraceptives
Oral hygiene
Orthodontics
Osteochondroses
Osteogenesis imperfecta
Osteopetroses
Otitis externa
Otitis media
Overhydration

P

Pacifier use
Pain
Pain management
Parent-child relationships

Patau syndrome
Patent ductus arteriosus
Peer acceptance
Peer pressure
Penicillins
Perforated eardrum
Perinatal infection
Periodontal disease
Peroxisomal disorders
Personality development
Personality disorders
Pervasive developmental disorders
Phenylketonuria
Phobias
Pica
Piercing and tattoos
Pinta
Pinworms
Pituitary dwarfism
Pityriasis rosea
Platelet count
Play
Pneumonia
Poison ivy, oak, and sumac
Poisoning
Polio
Polio vaccine
Polydactyly and syndactyly
Porphyrias
Post-concussion syndrome
Prader-Willi syndrome
Precocious puberty
Prematurity
Premenstrual syndrome
Prenatal development
Prenatal surgery
Preschool
Prickly heat
Protein-energy malnutrition
Psoriasis
Psychological tests
Psychosocial personality disorders
Puberty
Pulmonary function tests

PLEASE READ—IMPORTANT INFORMATION

The Gale Encyclopedia of Children's Health is a medical reference product designed to inform and educate readers about a wide variety of health issues related to children, ranging from prenatal to adolescence. Thomson Gale believes the product to be comprehensive, but not necessarily definitive. It is intended to supplement, not replace, consultation with a physician or other healthcare practitioner. While Thomson Gale has made substantial efforts to provide information that is accurate, comprehensive, and up-to-date, Thomson Gale makes no representations or warranties of any kind, including without limitation, warranties of merchantability or fitness for a particular purpose, nor does it guarantee the accuracy, comprehensiveness, or timeliness of the information contained in this product. Readers should be aware that the universe of medical knowledge is constantly growing and changing, and that differences of medical opinion exist among authorities. They are also advised to seek professional diagnosis and treatment for any medical condition, and to discuss information obtained from this book with their healthcare provider.

INTRODUCTION

The Gale Encyclopedia of Children's Health: Infancy Through Adolescence (GECH) is a one-stop source for medical information that covers common and rare diseases and medical conditions, immunizations and drugs, procedures, and developmental issues. It particularly addresses parents' concerns about their children's health from before birth through age 18. The book avoids medical jargon, making it easier for the layperson to use. *The Gale Encyclopedia of Children's Health* presents authoritative, balanced information and is more comprehensive than single-volume family medical guides.

SCOPE

Approximately 600 full-length articles are included in *The Gale Encyclopedia of Children's Health.* Articles follow a standardized format that provides information at a glance. Rubrics include:

Diseases/Disorders
- Definition
- Description
- Demographics
- Causes and symptoms
- Diagnosis
- Treatment
- Prognosis
- Prevention
- Parental concerns
- Resources
- Key terms

Procedures
- Definition
- Purpose
- Description
- Risks
- Normal results

- Parental concerns
- Resources
- Key terms

Immunizations/Drugs
- Definition
- Description
- General use
- Precautions
- Side effects
- Interactions
- Parental concerns
- Resources
- Key terms

Development
- Definition
- Description
- Common problems
- Parental concerns
- Resources
- Key terms

A preliminary list of diseases, conditions, procedures, drugs, and developmental issues was compiled from a wide variety of sources, including professional medical guides and textbooks, as well as consumer guides and encyclopedias. The advisory board, composed of seven doctors with specialties in pediatric medicine, evaluated the topics and made suggestions for inclusion. Final selection of topics to include was made by the medical advisors in conjunction with Thomson Gale editors.

INCLUSION CRITERIA

A preliminary list of diseases, conditions, procedures, drugs, and developmental issues was compiled from a wide variety of sources, including professional medical guides and textbooks, as well as consumer guides and encyclopedias. The advisory board, composed of seven doctors with specialties in pediatric medicine, evaluated the topics and made suggestions for inclusion. Final selection of topics to include was made by the medical advisors in conjunction with Thomson Gale editors.

ABOUT THE CONTRIBUTORS

The essays were compiled by experienced medical writers, including healthcare practitioners and educators, pharmacists, nurses, and other healthcare professionals. *GECH* medical advisors reviewed all of the completed essays to insure that they are appropriate, up-to-date, and medically accurate.

HOW TO USE THIS BOOK

The Gale Encyclopedia of Children's Health has been designed with ready reference in mind:
- Straight **alphabetical arrangement** allows users to locate information quickly.
- Bold faced terms function as *print hyperlinks* that point the reader to related entries in the encyclopedia.
- A list of **key terms** is provided where appropriate to define unfamiliar words or concepts used within the

context of the essay. Additional terms may be found in the **glossary**.

- **Cross-references** placed throughout the encyclopedia direct readers to where information on subjects without their own entries can be found. Synonyms are also cross-referenced.
- A **Resources section** directs users to sources of further medical information.
- An appendix of updated **growth charts** from the U.S. Centers for Disease Control for children from birth through age 20 is included.
- An appendix of **common childhood medications** is arranged alphabetically and includes descriptions of each drug and important information about their uses.
- A comprehensive **general index** allows users to easily target detailed aspects of any topic, including Latin names.

GRAPHICS

The Gale Encyclopedia of Children's Health is enhanced with approximately 300 full-color images, including photos, tables, and customized line drawings.

ADVISORY BOARD

An advisory board made up of prominent individuals from the medical community provided invaluable assistance in the formulation of this encyclopedia. They defined the scope of coverage and reviewed individual entries for accuracy and accessibility. The editors would therefore like to express our appreciation to them.

CONTRIBUTORS

Margaret Alic, PhD
Medical Writer
Eastsound, WA

Kim Saltel Allan, R.D., BHEcol
Clinical Dietitian
Winnipeg, Manitoba, Canada

Linda K. Bennington, MSN, CNS, RNC
Lecturer, School of Nursing
Old Dominion University
Norfolk, VA

Mark A. Best, MD, MBA, MPH
Pathologist
Eastview, KY

Rosalyn Carson-Dewitt, M.D.
Medical Writer
Durham, NC

Angela Costello
Medical Editor
Cleveland, OH

L. Lee Culvert
Medical Writer
Alna, ME

Tish Davidson, MA
Medical Writer
Fremont, CA

L. Fleming Fallon, Jr., MD, DrPH
Professor of Public Health
Bowling Green University
Bowling Green, OH

Paula Ford-Martin, MA
Medical Writer
Warwick, RI

Janie Franz
Medical Writer
Grand Forks, ND

Rebecca J. Frey, PhD
Medical Writer
New Haven, CT

Clare Hanrahan
Medical Writer
Asheville, NC

Crystal H. Kaczkowski, MSc.
Medical Writer
Chicago, IL

Christine Kuehn Kelly
Medical Writer
Havertown, PA

Monique Laberge, Ph.D.
Medical Writer
Philadelphia, PA

Aliene S. Linwood, BSN, DPA, FACHE
Medical and Science Writer
Athens, Ohio

Mark Mitchell, M.D.
Medical Writer
Seattle, WA

Deborah L. Nurmi, M.S.
Medical Writer, Public Health Researcher
Atlanta, GA

Martha Reilly, OD
Clinical Optometrist
Madison, WI

Joan M. Schonbeck, RN
Medical Writer
Marlborough, MA

Stephanie Dionne Sherk
Medical Writer
Ann Arbor, MI

Judith Sims, MS
Science Writer
Logan, UT

Jennifer E. Sisk, M.A.
Medical Writer
Philadelphia, PA

Genevieve Slomski, Ph.D.
Medical Writer
New Britain, CT

Deanna M. Swartout-Corbeil, RN
Medical Writer
Thompsons Station, TN

Samuel Uretsky, PharmD
Medical Writer
Wantagh, NY

Ken R. Wells
Freelance Writer
Laguna Hills, CA

Abandonment

Definition

Abandonment is a legal term describing the failure of a non-custodial parent to provide support to his or her children according to the terms approved by a court of law. In common use, abandonment refers to the desertion of a child by a parent.

Description

Legal abandonment is an persistent issue that has received increasing attention since the 1970s. It refers to non-custodial parents who do not fulfill court-ordered financial responsibilities to their children, regardless of their involvement in their children's lives in other ways. Lack of such support is blamed for substantial poverty among **single-parent families**.

In 2002 it was estimated that up to 30 percent (19.8 million) of children in the United States, representing 11.9 million families, lived in single-parent households. While the number of single mothers has remained constant in recent years at 9.9 million, the number of single fathers has grown from 1.7 million in 1995 to 2 million in 2002, according to data from the U.S. Census Bureau. In 2002, some 19.8 million children lived with one parent. Of these, 16.5 million lived with their mother and 3.3 million with their father.

Fewer than half of single-parent children under the age of 18 received any financial support from the non-custodial parent. The income of more than a third of these households fell below the poverty level. The term "deadbeat dads" is often used in discussions about abandonment because most of the parents involved are fathers.

An increasing **divorce** rate and a rise in the number of infants born to unmarried mothers were in large part responsible for forcing the abandonment issue into public consciousness in the 1970s. Typically during the twentieth century, mothers involved in divorce or unwed births were routinely given physical custody of children, while fathers were granted visitation rights and ordered to pay a certain amount of money to help care for the children's needs. Many men ignored this financial responsibility, forcing some women to get jobs or to seek government support.

States have always taken on the main responsibility for ensuring the welfare of abandoned children. Federal involvement came as early as 1935, when the Social Security Act established the Aid to Dependent Children (ADC) program, primarily to assist widows. Over subsequent years, federal provisions strengthened the states' mandate. During the early 1970s, when the government's financial burden grew as more and more women turned to welfare, the U.S. Congress began to call for even stronger child-support enforcement provisions.

Enforcement laws vary from state to state. Garnishing wages, attacking bank accounts, and foreclosing on real estate are all used to force payment to affected children. All state enforcement systems are automated, allowing more efficient monitoring of payment and better tracking of violating parents. Some states have begun to deny drivers' and professional licenses to known delinquent parents. For example, in California, licenses for real estate salespersons, brokers, and appraisers can be revoked, suspended, or denied to applicants who are delinquent in child support payments. "Wanted" posters and other forms of advertising are more unconventional methods used occasionally to locate such parents.

Most states give priority to finding parents whose children, lacking parental support, are receiving government assistance. Some families with independent incomes turn to lawyers or private collection agencies to find offenders and bring them to court for nonpayment. In the late 1990s and early 2000s, hundreds of agencies specializing in child support collection, some of them unscrupulous, have been formed to meet the demand forced by overburdened state agencies. They sometimes charge extremely high retainer or contingency fees, substantially reducing the size of the payment recovered by the **family**.

In the 1990s, the federal government adopted measures to further assist states in the support-collection effort. Military personnel files have become more available, and a program to confiscate federal tax refunds has contributed to keeping the issue in the spotlight. The 1992 Child Support Recovery Act allows courts to impose criminal penalties on parents who cross state lines to avoid child support payments.

Some support exists for consolidating child-support enforcement through the Internal Revenue Service (IRS) rather than the states. Proponents argue that only the IRS can efficiently confiscate deadbeat parents' income and return it to children. Opponents contend that the involvement of the federal bureaucracy would more likely add inefficiency to the enforcement process and only aggravate an already growing problem.

Abandonment can take on a broader form than just legal abandonment. The term is used to refer to the abandonment of a child by one or both parents, either through desertion, divorce, or death. Although death is not legally abandonment, many children experience feelings and **fear** of abandonment following the death of one or both parents.

Abandonment is about the loss of love and a loss of connectedness. To the abandoned adolescent, it involves feelings of betrayal, guilt, loneliness, and lack of **self-esteem**. Abandonment is a core fear in humans, and this fear is intensified in adolescents.

The abandonment of children is an extreme form of child neglect stemming from many causes. Some include family breakdown, irresponsible fatherhood or motherhood, premature motherhood, birth out of wedlock, or the death of one or both parents.

The problem is not new. In the nineteenth century, "ragamuffins" were a familiar part of London's urban scene, and parents in Paris abandoned their children at the rate of 20 percent of the live births in the city. In his 1987 book, *Children of the Sun* Morris West tells of the survival of street children in Naples in the 1950s. What is new, rather, is the growing scale of the problem. The United Nations estimates 60 million children and infants have been abandoned by their families and live on their own or in orphanages in the world. In the United States, more than 7,000 children are abandoned each year.

Infancy and toddlerhood

Children in this stage of development understand little, if anything, about abandonment. However, they are aware of the emotional climate of the family. For the remaining parent, it is important to cuddle and care for the infant or toddler warmly, frequently, and consistently. The parent-child relationship continues to be central to the child's sense of security and independence.

Preschool

Preschoolers tend to have a limited and mistaken perception of abandonment. They are highly self-centered with a strict sense of right and wrong. So when bad things happen to them, they usually blame themselves by assuming they did something wrong. Children this age often interpret the departure of a parent as a personal rejection. Youngsters are likely to deny the reality of the abandonment and wish intently for the parent to return. They can also regress to behaviors such as **thumb sucking**, bed wetting, temper **tantrums**, and clinging to a favorite blanket or toy. They also fear abandonment by the other parent. They generally become afraid of the dark and of being alone.

School age

By the time children reach the early school years, ages six to nine, they can no longer deny the reality of the abandonment. They are extremely aware of the pervasive **pain** and sadness. Boys, especially, mourn the loss of their fathers, and their anger is frequently directed at their mothers. Crying, daydreaming, and problems with friends and in school are common abandonment behaviors in children of this age.

In the age group of nine to 12, adolescents usually react to abandonment with anger. They may also resent the additional household duties expected of them. There is also a significant disruption in the child's ability to learn. **Anxiety**, restlessness, inability to concentrate, and intrusive thoughts about the abandonment take a toll and can lead to a drop in school performance and difficulties with classmates.

Feelings of sadness, loneliness, guilt, lack of self worth, and self-blame are common in nine to 12-year-olds. They also tend to have concerns about family life, worry about finances, and feel they are a drain on the remaining parent's resources.

In children ages 13 to 18, the feelings are usually the same as with the younger groups except more pronounced. They become concerned about their own futures. **Truancy** is high, school performance is low, and they have a distorted view of themselves. In this popula-

KEY TERMS

Contingencies—Naturally occurring or artificially designated reinforcers or punishers that follow a behavior.

Deadbeat dad—A father who has abandoned his child or children and does not pay child custody as required by a court.

Deadbeat parent—A mother or father who has abandoned his or her child or children and does not pay child custody as required by a court.

Non-custodial parent—A parent who does not have legal custody of a child.

Promiscuous—Having many indiscriminate or casual sexual relationships.

Ragamuffins—A term used in nineteenth-century London to describe neglected or abandoned children who lived on the streets.

Retainer—A fee paid in advance to secure legal services.

tion there is a high incidence of drug and alcohol abuse and **aggressive behavior**.

The teen may also withdraw from all relationships, including those with friends, family, and classmates, and become extremely dependent on the remaining parent. Teens may also react by becoming sexually promiscuous at an early age, sometimes to the point of **addiction**. Sometimes, however, the child makes valuable decisions about their own future and values.

Common problems

Problems to watch for include trouble sleeping, crying, aggression, deep anger and resentment, feelings of betrayal, difficulty concentrating, chronic fatigue, and problems with friends or at school.

Parental concerns

The remaining parent should be aware of the effects of the abandonment on the child and above all, reassure the child that the remaining parent will not abandon them.

When to call the doctor

Medical help may be needed if the abandoned child inflicts self-injury. Psychological counseling may also be needed to help the child understand and cope with the abandonment. This is especially true if any of the common reactions lasts for an unusual amount of time, intensifies over time, or if the child talks about or threatens **suicide**.

Resources

BOOKS

Anderson, Susan. *The Journey from Abandonment to Healing*. New York: Berkley Books, 2000.

Lyster, Mimi E. *Child Custody*. Berkeley, CA: Nolo Press, 2003.

Peterson, Marion, and Diane Warner. *Single Parenting for Dummies*. New York: Wiley & Sons, 2003.

Teyber, Edward. *Helping Children Cope with Divorce*. New York: Jossey-Bass, 2001.

PERIODICALS

Anderson, Susan. "Recovering from Abandonment: Surviving Through the Five Stages that Accompany the Loss of Love." *Share Guide* (January-February 2002): 14–16.

Fields-Meyer, Thomas. "Home Safe: New Laws Allow Women to Leave Newborns with Authorities—No Questions Asked—Possibly Saving their Lives. But Is Legal Abandonment a Good Thing?" *People Weekly* (March 17, 2003): 94+.

Pollack, William S. "Relational Psychoanalytic Treatment for Young Adult Males." *Journal of Clinical Psychology* (November 2003): 1205–13.

Wolchik, Sharlene A., et al. "Fear of Abandonment as a Mediator of the Relations Between Divorce Stressors and Mother-Child Relationship Quality and Children's Adjustment Problems." *Journal of Abnormal Child Psychology* (August 2002): 401–18.

ORGANIZATIONS

American Bar Association (ABA) Center on Children and the Law. 740 15th St., NW, Washington, DC 20005. Web site: <www.abanet.org/child/home.html>.

Children's Rights Council. 6200 Editors Park Drive, Suite 103, Hyattsville, MD 20782. Web site: <www.gocrc.com/>.

WEB SITES

"Child Custody: An Overview." *Legal Information Institute*, 2004. Available online at <www.law.cornell.edu/topics/child_custody.html> (accessed October 9, 2004).

"Children, Youth, and Family Consortium." *Family Relationships and Parenting*. Nov. 21, 2003. Available online at <www.cyfc.umn.edu/family/index.html> (accessed October 9, 2004).

Ken R. Wells

Abdominal wall defects

Definition

Abdominal wall defects are birth (congenital) defects that allow the stomach or intestines to protrude.

Description

Many unexpected events occur during the development of a fetus inside the womb. The stomach and intestines begin development outside the baby's abdomen and only later does the abdominal wall enclose them. Occasionally, either the umbilical opening is too large or it develops improperly, allowing the bowels or stomach to remain outside or squeeze through the abdominal wall. This results in one of two conditions, gastroschisis and omphalocele. Gastroschisis occurs when the abdominal wall does not close completely and the stomach and the small and large intestines appear outside the infant's body. In omphalocele, some of the internal organs protrude through the abdominal muscles in the area around the umbilical cord. Omphalocele may be minor, involving only a small portion of the intestines, or it may be severe with most of the abdominal organs, such as the intestines, liver, and spleen, outside the body.

Demographics

Abdominal wall defects, specifically gastroschisis and omphalocele, are rare and occur in only once in every 5000 births. Both boys and girls have these defects in equal numbers. While infants with gastroschisis rarely have defects other than those affecting the intestines, of children with omphalocele, 50 percent to 75 percent have associated congenital anomalies and 20 percent to 35 percent have chromosomal abnormalities.

Causes and symptoms

There are many causes for birth defects that still remain unclear. As of 2004, the causes of abdominal wall defects remained unknown. Any symptoms the mother may have had to indicate that the defects are present in the fetus are nondescript.

Diagnosis

At birth, the problem is obvious, because the base of the umbilical cord at the navel will bulge or, in worse cases, contain internal organs. Before birth, an ultrasound examination may detect the problem. It is always

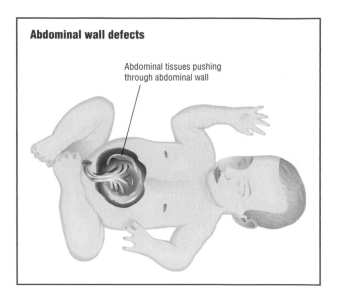

Abdominal wall defects

Abdominal tissues pushing through abdominal wall

Illustration of an omphalocele, or umbilical hernia, in a newborn. *(Illustration by GGS Information Services.)*

necessary in children with abdominal wall defects to look for other birth defects, because multiple anomalies are more likely to occur in these children.

Treatment

Abdominal wall defects are effectively treated with surgical repair. Unless there are accompanying anomalies, the surgical procedure is not overly complicated. However, if the defect is large, it may be difficult to fit all the organs into the small abdominal cavity.

Prognosis

If there are no other defects, the prognosis after surgical repair of this condition is relatively good. However, 10 percent of those with more severe or additional abnormalities die from it. The organs themselves are fully functional; the difficulty lies in fitting them inside the abdomen. The condition is, in actuality, a **hernia** requiring only replacement and strengthening of the passageway through which it occurred. However, after surgery, increased pressure in the stretched abdomen can compromise the function of the organs inside.

Prevention

Some, but by no means all, birth defects are preventable by early and attentive prenatal care, good **nutrition**, supplemental **vitamins**, and other elements of a healthy lifestyle, along with the diligent avoidance

KEY TERMS

Congenital—Present at birth.

Hernia—A rupture in the wall of a body cavity, through which an organ may protrude.

Umbilical—Refers to the opening in the abdominal wall where the blood vessels from the placenta enter.

of all unnecessary drugs and chemicals—especially tobacco.

Parental concerns

Most children with abdominal wall defects require immediate and intensive medical care. Some of these infants may have multiple surgeries, and serious complications such as feeding problems and infections may persist long term. Parents will need to work closely with a team of physicians during the treatment of their child. Children with abdominal wall defects may need additional services, especially those with omphalocele and associated chromosomal abnormalities and birth defects. These children require long-term treatment for both the physical and developmental difficulties they face. Parents may need support services in addition to the services provided by the healthcare team. They can contact the hospital's social work department to learn more about available resources.

Resources

BOOKS

Key, Doneen. *Do You Want to Take Her Home: Trials and Tribulations of Living Life as a Handicapped Person Due to Multiple Birth Defects*. Lancaster, CA: Empire Publishing, 2001.

Moore, Keith L., et al. *Before We Are Born: Essentials of Embryology and Birth Defects*. Kent, UK: Elsevier, Health Sciences Division, 2002.

WEB SITES

"Birth Defects." *National Center on Birth Defects and Developmental Disabilities*. Available online at <www.cdc.gov/ncbddd/bd/> (accessed October 15, 2004).

"Fetal Diagnoses: Omphalocele." *The Center for Fetal Diagnosis and Treatment*. Available online at <www.fetalsurgery.chop.edu/omphalocele.shtml> (accessed October 15, 2004).

"Gastroschisis." *The Center for Fetal Diagnosis and Treatment*. Available online at

<www.fetalsurgery.chop.edu/gastroschisis.shtml> (accessed October 15, 2004).

J. Ricker Polsdorfer, MD
Deborah L. Nurmi, MS

Abuse, child *see* **Child abuse**

Accessory digits *see* **Polydactyly and syndactyly**

Acetaminophen

Definition

Acetaminophen is a medicine used to relieve **pain** and reduce **fever**.

Description

Acetaminophen is used to relieve many kinds of minor aches and pains: headaches, muscle aches, backaches, toothaches, menstrual cramps, arthritis, and the aches and pains that often accompany colds.

Description

This drug is available without a prescription. Acetaminophen is sold under various brand names, including Tylenol, Panadol, Aspirin Free Anacin, and Bayer Select Maximum Strength **Headache** Pain Relief Formula. Many multi-symptom cold, flu, and sinus medicines also contain acetaminophen.

Studies have shown that acetaminophen relieves pain and reduces fever about as well as aspirin. But differences between these two common drugs exist. Acetaminophen is less likely than aspirin to irritate the stomach. However, unlike aspirin, acetaminophen does not reduce the redness, stiffness, or swelling that accompany arthritis.

Precautions

Most of the precautions for acetaminophen apply to adults rather than children but may apply to some teenagers.

The primary precaution in children's therapy is to watch the dosage carefully and follow the label instructions only. Acetaminophen for children comes in two strengths. Children's acetaminophen contains low concentrations of the drug, 160 milligrams in a teaspoonful of solution. The infant drops contain a much higher concentration of acetaminophen, 100 milligrams in 20 drops, equal to 500 milligrams in a teaspoonful. The infant drops should never be given by the teaspoonful.

Parents should never give their child more than the recommended dosage of acetaminophen unless told to do so by a physician or dentist.

Patients should not use acetaminophen for more than 10 days to relieve pain (five days for children) or for more than three days to reduce fever, unless directed to do so by a physician. If symptoms do not go away or if they get worse, a physician should be contacted. Anyone who drinks three or more alcoholic beverages a day should check with a physician before using this drug and should never take more than the recommended dosage. A risk of liver damage exists from combining large amounts of alcohol and acetaminophen. People who already have kidney or liver disease or liver infections should also consult with a physician before using the drug. Women who are pregnant or breastfeeding should do the same.

Side effects

Acetaminophen causes few side effects. The most common one is lightheadedness. Some people may experience trembling and pain in the side or the lower back. Allergic reactions do occur in some people, but they are rare. Anyone who develops symptoms such as a rash, swelling, or difficulty breathing after taking acetaminophen should stop taking the drug and get immediate medical attention. Other rare side effects include yellow skin or eyes, unusual bleeding or bruising, weakness, fatigue, bloody or black stools, bloody or cloudy urine, and a sudden decrease in the amount of urine.

Overdoses of acetaminophen may cause **nausea**, **vomiting**, sweating, and exhaustion. Very large overdoses can cause liver damage. In case of an overdose, parents should get immediate medical attention for their child.

Interactions

Acetaminophen may interact with a variety of other medicines. When this happens, the effects of one or both of the drugs may change or the risk of side effects may be greater. Among the drugs that may interact with acetaminophen are the following:

- alcohol
- nonsteroidal anti-inflammatory drugs (NSAIDs) such as Motrin
- oral contraceptives

- the antiseizure drug phenytoin (Dilantin)
- the blood-thinning drug warfarin (Coumadin)
- the cholesterol-lowering drug cholestyramine (Questran)
- the antibiotic Isoniazid
- zidovudine (Retrovir, AZT)

Check with a physician or pharmacist before combining acetaminophen with any other prescription or nonprescription (over-the-counter) medicine.

Acetaminophen is generally safe when taken as directed. Acetaminophen is commonly mixed with other ingredients as part of combinations intended for colds, **influenza**, and other conditions. Parents should read the labels carefully in order to avoid giving an overdose of acetaminophen to their child. They need to be particularly cautious about liquid medicines that contain acetaminophen and alcohol.

Parental concerns

Acetaminophen is very safe when used properly. While most precautions are intended to reduce the risk of overdose, parents should not try to reduce the risk by giving a lower than normal dose. Children should not suffer pain if it can be safely treated.

See also Analgesics; Pain management.

Resources

BOOKS

Beers, Mark H., and Robert Berkow, eds. *The Merck Manual*, 2nd home ed. West Point, PA: Merck & Co., 2004.

Mcevoy, Gerald, et al. *AHFS Drug Information 2004.* Bethesda, MD: American Society of Healthsystems Pharmacists, 2004.

Siberry, George K., and Robert Iannone, eds. *The Harriet Lane Handbook*, 15th ed. Philadelphia: Mosby Publishing, 2000.

PERIODICALS

Burillo-Putze G., et al. "Changes in pediatric toxic dose of acetaminophen." *American Journal of Emergency Medicine* 22, no. 4 (July 2004): 323.

Evered, L. M. "Evidence-based emergency medicine/ systematic review abstract. Does acetaminophen treat fever in children?" *American Journal of Emergency Medicine* 41, no. 5 (May 2003): 741–3.

Goldman, Ran D., and D. Scolnik. "Underdosing of acetaminophen by parents and emergency department utilization." *Pediatric Emergency Care* 20, no. 2 (February 2004): 89–93.

Kociancic T., et al. "Acetaminophen intoxication and length of treatment: how long is long enough?" *Pharmacotherapy* 23, no. 8 (August 2003): 1052–9.

Losek, Joseph D. "Acetaminophen dose accuracy and pediatric emergency care." *Pediatric Emergency Care* 20, no. 5 (May 2004): 285–8.

ORGANIZATIONS

American Pain Society. 4700 W. Lake Ave., Glenview, IL 60025. Web site: <www.ampainsoc.org/>.

WEB SITES

"Acetaminophen." *MedlinePlus.* Available online at <www.nlm.nih.gov/medlineplus/druginfo/medmaster/a681004.html> (accessed October 15, 2004).

Nancy Ross-Flanigan
Samuel Uretsky, PharmD

Acne

Definition

Acne is a skin disorder that leads to an outbreak of lesions called pimples or "zits." The most common form of the disease is called acne vulgaris—the rash that affects many adolescents. Acne vulgaris is triggered by the hormonal changes that occur in **puberty**.

Description

Acne is a condition in which pimples appear on the face, chest, and back. In teenagers, acne usually appears on the forehead, nose, and chin. It is caused by the overproduction of sebum. Sebum is an oily substance that forms in glands just under the surface of the skin called sebaceous glands. Sebum normally flows out hair follicles onto the skin to act as a natural skin moisturizer. The glands are connected to hair follicles that allow the sebum, or oil, to empty onto the skin through a pore.

If hair follicles become blocked by sebum, dead skin cells, and bacteria, acne is the result. The sebaceous gland units are most commonly found on the face, neck, and back.

During puberty, there are increased levels of the male hormone androgen. High levels of androgen cause excess sebum to form. Sometimes the sebum combines with dead, sticky skin cells and bacteria called *Propionibacterium acnes (P. acnes)* that normally live on the skin. The mixture of oil and cells allows the bacteria to grow in the plugged follicles. When this happens, a hard plug called a comedo can form. A comedo is an enlarged hair follicle. It can take the following forms:

• a blackhead, which is a comedo that reaches the skin's surface and looks black

• a whitehead, which is a comedo that is sealed by keratin, the fibrous protein produced by the skin cells and looks like a white bump.

In addition, pimples can form on the skin. Types of pimples include:

• papules, which are small, red bumps that may be tender to the touch

• pustules, which are pus-filled lesions that are often red at the base

• nodules, which are large, painful lesions deep in the skin

• cysts, which are painful pus-filled lesions deep in the skin that can cause scarring

Pimples form when the follicle is invaded by the *P. acnes* bacteria. The damaged follicle weakens and bursts open, releasing sebum, bacteria, skin cells, and white blood cells into surrounding tissues. Scarring happens when new skin cells are created to replace the damaged cells. The most severe type of acne includes both nodules and cysts.

Demographics

Acne affects as many as 17 million people in the United States, making it the most common skin disease. Acne usually begins at puberty and worsens during **adolescence**. Nearly 85 percent of people develop acne at some point between ages 12 to 25. As many as 20 million teens have the condition. Acne may appear as early as age 10, and even may be found in some newborns. Some people may continue to be affected by acne after age 30.

Causes and symptoms

The exact cause of acne is as of 2004 not known. There are several risk factors that make acne more likely to occur:

• Age. Adolescents are more likely to have acne.

• Disease. Certain hormonal disorders such as polycystic ovarian syndrome make acne more likely.

- Hormonal changes. Acne can flare up before **menstruation**. An increase in the male hormone androgen during puberty (seen in both males and females) causes the sebaceous glands to overproduce androgen. Boys have more severe acne than girls.

- Heredity. Some individual are genetically more susceptible to acne.

- Drugs. Steroids and performance enhancing drugs, **oral contraceptives**, **antibiotics**, **antidepressants**, and tranquillizers such as lithium are known to cause acne.

- Cosmetics. Oily cosmetics can plug up hair follicles.

Other factors can worsen acne or cause it to flare up:

- Environmental irritants. Air pollution and high humidity can worsen acne, as can exposure to greasy environments such as working in a fast food restaurant.

- Friction. Rubbing the skin vigorously or exposure to constant friction from backpacks or tight collars can worsen acne.

- Personal hygiene. Picking at pimples or scrubbing the skin too hard can result in worsened acne.

Factors that do not cause acne include:

- chocolate and greasy foods
- stress

When to call the doctor

A healthcare provider should be contacted under the following circumstances:

- Painful nodules and cysts are present.
- Over-the-counter medications have not been effective.
- Acne lesions are causing scarring.
- Acne is causing dark skin to have darker patches when lesions heal.
- Acne is causing embarrassment or self-consciousness.
- Acne is creating emotional upset.

Acne may be treated by the **family** doctor. More severe cases may be referred to a dermatologist (skin doctor) or an endocrinologist (doctor who treats hormonal/glandular disorders).

Diagnosis

Acne can be diagnosed by physical examination and a medical history of acne. The physician will take a medical history, including information about skin care, diet, medications, factors that can cause flare-ups, and prior treatment. Blood tests are not usually necessary unless a hormonal disorder is suspected.

Physical examination will include the face, neck, shoulders, back, and other affected areas. Using specialized lighting, the physician will examine the affected areas to see the following:

- what type and how many lesions are present
- how deep the lesions are
- whether they are inflamed
- whether scarring or skin discoloration is present

Treatment

Acne treatment consists of reducing the sebum production, removing dead skin cells, and killing bacteria with oral medication and drugs used on the skin (topical). The treatment depends on the severity of the condition.

Drugs

TOPICAL (SKIN) MEDICATION Treatment for mild noninflammatory acne consists of reducing the formation of new comedones with medications including topical tretinoin, benzoyl peroxide, adapalene, or salicylic acid. Tretinoin is especially effective because it increases turnover and replacement of skin cells. If lesions are inflamed, **topical antibiotics** may be added to the treatment regimen. Improvement is usually seen in two to four weeks.

Topical medications are available as cream, gel, lotion, or pad preparations of varying strengths. They include antibiotics (to kill bacteria) such as erythromycin, clindamycin (Cleocin-T), and meclocycline (Meclan); and comedolytics (agents that loosen hard plugs and open pores) such as the vitamin A acid tretinoin (Retin-A), salicylic acid, adapalene (Differin), resorcinol, and sulfur. Drugs that act as both comedolytics and antibiotics, such as benzoyl peroxide, azelaic acid (Azelex), or benzoyl peroxide plus erythromycin (Benzamycin), are also used. These drugs may be used for months to years to achieve disease control.

After the person washes with mild soap, the drugs are applied alone or in combination, once or twice a day over the entire affected area of skin. Possible side effects include mild redness, peeling, irritation, dryness, and an increased sensitivity to sunlight that requires use of a sunscreen.

ORAL DRUGS Oral antibiotics are taken daily for two to four months. The drugs used include tetracycline, erythromycin, minocycline (Minocin), doxycycline, clindamycin (Cleocin), and trimethoprim-sulfamethoxazole (Bactrim, Septra). Possible side effects include allergic reactions, stomach upset, vaginal yeast infections, **dizziness**, and tooth discoloration.

The goal of treating moderate acne is to decrease inflammation and prevent new comedones from forming. One effective treatment is topical tretinoin, used along with a topical or oral antibiotic. A combination of topical benzoyl peroxide and erythromycin is also very effective. Improvement is normally seen within four to six weeks, but treatment is maintained for at least two to four months.

A drug reserved for the treatment of severe acne, oral isotretinoin (Accutane), reduces sebum production and cell stickiness. It is the treatment of choice for severe acne with cysts and nodules and is used with or without topical or oral antibiotics. Taken for four to five months, it provides long-term disease control in up to 60 percent of patients. If the acne reappears, another course of isotretinoin may be needed by about 20 percent of patients, while another 20 percent may do well with topical drugs or oral antibiotics. However there are significant side effects, including temporary worsening of the acne; dry skin; nosebleeds; vision disorders; and elevated liver enzymes, blood fats, and cholesterol. The drug also causes benign intracranial **hypertension** (pseudotumor cerebri) and mood changes. This drug must not be taken during pregnancy since it causes birth defects. Sexually active young women being treated with isotretinoin must use a reliable contractive, and they need to use **contraception** for up to one month after stopping use of the drug.

Anti-androgens, drugs that inhibit androgen production, are used to treat women who are unresponsive to other therapies. Certain types of oral contraceptives (for example, Ortho-Tri-Cyclen) and female sex hormones (estrogens) reduce hormone activity in the ovaries. Other drugs (for example, spironolactone and corticosteroids) reduce hormone activity in the adrenal glands. Improvement may take up to four months.

Oral corticosteroids, or anti-inflammatory drugs, are the treatment of choice for an extremely severe, but rare type of destructive inflammatory acne called acne fulminans, found mostly in adolescent males. Acne conglobata, a more common form of severe inflammation, includes numerous, deep, inflammatory nodules that heal with scarring. It is treated with oral isotretinoin and corticosteroids.

Other treatments

Several surgical or medical treatments are available to alleviate acne or the resulting scars:

- Comedone extraction. The comedo is removed from the pore with a special tool.
- Chemical peels. Glycolic acid is applied to peel off the top layer of skin to reduce scarring.
- Dermabrasion. The affected skin is frozen with a chemical spray and removed by brushing or planing.
- Punch grafting. Deep scars are excised and the area repaired with small skin grafts.
- Intralesional injection. Corticosteroids are injected directly into inflamed pimples.
- Collagen injection. Shallow scars are elevated by collagen (protein) injections.

Alternative treatment

Alternative treatments for acne focus on self care: proper cleansing to keep the skin oil-free; eating a well-balanced diet high in fiber, zinc, and raw foods; and avoiding alcohol, dairy products, tobacco, **caffeine**, sugar, processed foods, and foods high in iodine, such as salt.

Supplementation with herbs such as burdock root (*Arctium lappa*), red clover (*Trifolium pratense*), and milk thistle (*Silybum marianum*), and with nutrients such as essential fatty acids, vitamin B complex, zinc, vitamin A, and chromium is also recommended. Chinese herbal remedies used for acne include cnidium seed (*Cnidium monnieri*) and honeysuckle flower (*Lonicera japonica*). Holistic physicians or nutritionists can recommend the proper amounts of these herbs.

Nutritional concerns

Acne is not caused or worsened by eating chocolate or oily foods.

Prognosis

Acne is not curable, although it can be controlled by proper treatment. Improvement can take two or more months. Long-term control is achieved in up to 60 percent of patients with severe acne who are treated with the drug isotretinoin. Acne tends to reappear when treatment stops, but spontaneously improves over time. Acne usually improves after adolescence, although some individuals continue to have lesions after age 30. Inflammatory acne may leave scars that require further treatment.

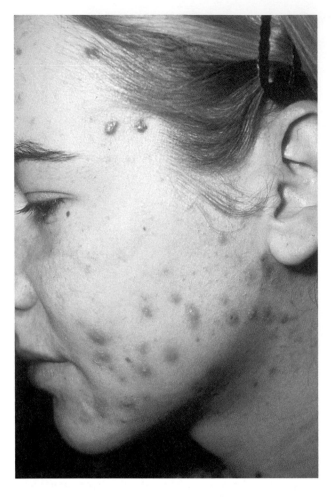

Teenage girl with acne. *(Photograph by Biophoto Associates. National Audubon Society Collection/Photo Researchers, Inc.)*

Prevention

There are no sure ways to prevent acne, but the following steps may be taken to minimize flare-ups:

- gentle washing of affected areas once or twice every day
- avoiding abrasive cleansers
- using noncomedogenic (does not clog pores) makeup and moisturizers
- shampooing often and wearing hair off the face
- eating a well-balanced diet, avoiding foods that trigger flare-ups
- unless told otherwise by the healthcare provider, giving dry pimples a limited amount of sun exposure
- not picking or squeezing blemishes

Parental concerns

Acne comes at a difficult time, during the adolescent years. While mild acne can be treated with over-the-counter medications, more severe acne needs medical attention. Experts advise against a wait-and-see attitude. Treatment options can help control acne and avoid scarring.

See also Antiacne drugs.

Resources

BOOKS

Ceaser, Jennifer. *Everything You Need to Know about Acne.* New York: Rosen Publishing Group, 2003.

KEY TERMS

Androgens—Hormones (specifically testosterone) responsible for male sex characteristics.

Antiandrogen—A substance that blocks the action of androgens, the hormones responsible for male characteristics.

Antibiotics—Drugs that are designed to kill or inhibit the growth of the bacteria that cause infections.

Comedo—A hard plug composed of sebum and dead skin cells, also called a blackhead. The mildest type of acne.

Comedolytic drugs—Medications that break up comedones and open clogged pores.

Corticosteroids—A group of hormones produced naturally by the adrenal gland or manufactured synthetically. They are often used to treat inflammation. Examples include cortisone and prednisone.

Estrogen—Female hormone produced mainly by the ovaries and released by the follicles as they mature. Responsible for female sexual characteristics, estrogen stimulates and triggers a response from at least 300 tissues. After menopause, the production of the hormone gradually stops.

Isotretinoin—A powerful vitamin A derivative used in the treatment of acne.

Noncomedogenic—A substance that does not contribute to the formation of blackheads or pimples on the skin.

Sebaceous follicle—A structure found within the skin where a sebaceous gland opens into a hair follicle.

Sebum—An oily skin moisturizer produced by sebaceous glands.

Tretinoin—A drug, used in the treatment of acne, that works by increasing the turnover (death and replacement) of skin cells.

Papadopoulos, Linda, et al. *Understanding Skin Problems: Acne, Eczema, Psoriasis, and Related Conditions.* New York: John Wiley and Sons, 2003.

Preston, Lydia, et al. *Breaking Out: A Woman's Guide to Coping with Acne.* New York: Simon & Schuster, 2004.

ORGANIZATIONS

American Academy of Dermatology. 930 E. Woodfield Rd., Schaumburg, IL 60168. Web site: <www.aad.org/>.

WEB SITES

"Questions and Answers about Acne." *National Institute of Arthritis and Musculoskeletal and Skin Diseases (NIAMS) Information Clearinghouse*, October 2001. Available online at <www.niams.nih.gov/hi/topics/acne/acne.htm> (accessed October 15, 2004).

"Treating Acne in Skin of Color." *AcneNet* 2002. Available online at <www.skincarephysicians.com/acnenet/update.htm> (accessed October 15, 2004).

"What Can I Do About Pimples?" *American Family Physician, Information from Your Family Doctor Handout*, January 15, 2000. Available online at <www.aafp.org/afp/20000115/20000115a.html> (accessed October 15, 2004).

Christine Kuehn Kelly

Acromegaly and gigantism

Definition

Acromegaly is a disease in which an abnormality in the pituitary gland leads to an oversecretion of growth hormone. In adults, this condition results in an enlargement of bones; in children, the abnormality results in excessive height and is called gigantism.

Description

Acromegaly is a disorder in which the abnormal release of a particular chemical from the pituitary gland in the brain causes increased growth in bone and soft tissue, as well as a variety of other disturbances throughout the body. This chemical released from the pituitary gland is called growth hormone (GH). The body's ability to process and use nutrients like fats and sugars is also altered. In children whose bony growth plates have not closed, the chemical changes of acromegaly result in exceptional growth of long bones. This variant is called gigantism, with the additional bone growth causing unusual height. When the abnormality occurs after bone growth stops, i.e. in adults, the disorder is called acromegaly.

Demographics

Acromegaly is a relatively rare disorder, occurring in approximately 50 out of every 1 million people. Gigantism occurs even more rarely, with reported cases in the United States numbering only about 100 by 2004. Males and females are similarly affected. Onset of gigantism is usually at **puberty**, although some cases of toddlers and young children with gigantism have been reported.

Causes and symptoms

The pituitary is a small gland located at the base of the brain, which releases certain hormones that are important to the functioning of other organs or body systems. The pituitary hormones travel throughout the body and are involved in a large number of activities, including the regulation of growth and reproductive functions. The cause of acromegaly can be traced to the pituitary's production of GH.

Under normal conditions, the pituitary receives input from another brain structure, the hypothalamus, located at the base of the brain. This input from the hypothalamus regulates the pituitary's release of hormones. For example, the hypothalamus produces growth hormone-releasing hormone (GHRH), which directs the pituitary to release GH. Input from the hypothalamus should also direct the pituitary to stop releasing hormones.

In acromegaly, the pituitary continues to release GH and ignores signals from the hypothalamus. In the liver, GH causes production of a hormone called insulin-like growth factor 1 (IGF-1), which is responsible for growth throughout the body. When the pituitary refuses to stop producing GH, the levels of IGF-1 also reach abnormal peaks. Bones, soft tissue, and organs throughout the body begin to enlarge, and the body changes its ability to process and use nutrients like sugars and fats.

The most common cause of acromegaly and gigantism is the development of a noncancerous tumor within the pituitary, called a pituitary adenoma. In the case of pituitary adenomas, the tumor itself is the source of the abnormal release of GH. As these tumors grow, they may press on nearby structures within the brain, causing headaches and changes in vision. As the adenoma grows, it may disrupt other pituitary tissue, interfering with the release of other hormones. These disruptions may be responsible for changes in the menstrual cycle and abnormal production of breast milk in women or delayed development of reproductive organs. In rare cases, acromegaly is caused by the abnormal production of GHRH, which leads to the increased production of GH. Certain tumors in the pancreas, lungs, adrenal glands, thyroid, and intestine can produce GHRH, which in turn triggers production of an abnormal quantity of GH.

In acromegaly, an individual's hands and feet begin to grow, becoming thick and doughy. The jaw line, nose, and forehead also grow, and facial features are described as coarse. The tongue grows larger, and because the jaw is larger, the teeth become more widely spaced. Due to swelling within the structures of the throat and sinuses, the voice becomes deeper and sounds hollower, and patients may develop loud snoring. Children and adolescents with gigantism show a characteristic lengthening and enlargement of bones, principally of the limbs. Some symptoms caused by various hormonal changes are as follows:

- heavy sweating

- oily skin

- increased coarse body hair

- improper processing of sugars in the diet (and sometimes actual diabetes)

- high blood pressure

- increased calcium in the urine (sometimes leading to kidney stones)

- increased risk of gallstones

- swelling of the thyroid gland

People with acromegaly have more skin tags, or outgrowths of tissue, than normal. This increase in skin tags is also associated with the development of growths, called polyps, within the large intestine that may eventually become cancerous. Patients with acromegaly often suffer from headaches and arthritis. The various swellings and enlargements throughout the body may press on nerves, causing sensations of local **tingling** or burning and sometimes result in muscle weakness.

When to call the doctor

Because early diagnosis and treatment of acromegaly and gigantism can often lead to the avoidance of more serious symptoms, a healthcare professional should be contacted if a child develops any of the early symptoms of the disease, such as a marked increase in height or height that is excessive for his or her age.

Diagnosis

Because acromegaly produces slow changes, diagnosis is often significantly delayed. In fact, the characteristic coarsening of the facial features is often not recognized by **family** members, friends, or long-time family physicians. Often, the diagnosis is suspected by a new physician who sees the patient for the first time and is struck by the patient's characteristic facial appearance. Comparing old photographs from a number of different periods often increases suspicion of the disease. By contrast, the effects of gigantism are typically dramatic, with remarkable changes over a short period of time.

Because the quantity of GH produced varies widely under normal conditions, demonstrating high levels of GH in the blood is not sufficient to merit a diagnosis of acromegaly. Instead, laboratory tests measuring an increase of IGF-1 (three to ten times above the normal level) are useful. These results, however, must be carefully interpreted because normal laboratory values for IGF-1 vary when the patient is pregnant, is pubescent, is elderly, or is severely malnourished. Normal patients will show a decrease in GH production when given a large dose of sugar (glucose). Patients with acromegaly will not show this decrease and will often show an increase in GH production. **Magnetic resonance imaging** (MRI) is useful for viewing the pituitary gland and for identifying and locating an adenoma. When no adenoma can be located, the search for a GHRH-producing tumor in another location begins.

Treatment

The first step in treatment of acromegaly is removal of all or part of the pituitary adenoma. Removal usually requires surgery, usually performed by entering the skull through the nose. While this surgery can cause rapid improvement of many acromegaly symptoms, most patients will also require additional treatment with medication. Bromocriptine (Parlodel) is a medication that can be taken by mouth, while octreotide (Sandostatin) must be injected every eight hours. Both of these medications are helpful in reducing GH production but must often be taken for life and produce their own unique side effects.

Alternative treatment

Some patients who cannot undergo surgery are treated with radiation therapy to the pituitary in an attempt to shrink the adenoma. Radiating the pituitary may take up to ten years, however, and may also injure or destroy other normal parts of the pituitary.

KEY TERMS

Adenoma—A type of noncancerous (benign) tumor that often involves the overgrowth of certain cells found in glands. These tumors can secrete hormones or cause changes in hormone production in nearby glands.

Gland—A collection of cells whose function is to release certain chemicals (hormones) that are important to the functioning of other, sometimes distantly located, organs or body systems.

Hormone—A chemical messenger secreted by a gland or organ and released into the bloodstream. It travels via the bloodstream to distant cells where it exerts an effect.

Hypothalamus—A part of the forebrain that controls heartbeat, body temperature, thirst, hunger, body temperature and pressure, blood sugar levels, and other functions.

Pituitary gland—The most important of the endocrine glands (glands that release hormones directly into the bloodstream), the pituitary is located at the base of the brain. Sometimes referred to as the "master gland," it regulates and controls the activities of other endocrine glands and many body processes including growth and reproductive function. Also called the hypophysis.

Nutritional concerns

Individuals with acromegaly or gigantism who have diabetes or diabetes-like symptoms should maintain a diet that helps normalize blood sugar levels.

Prognosis

Without treatment, patients with acromegaly are likely to die early because of the disease's effects on the heart, lungs, brain, or due to the development of **cancer** in the large intestine. With treatment, however, a patient with acromegaly may be able to live a normal lifespan.

Prevention

The initial onset of acromegaly or gigantism cannot as of 2004 be prevented. Once a pituitary adenoma has been removed, radiotherapy and/or medication may be recommended to prevent a recurrence of the tumor.

Parental concerns

In the great majority of children of tall stature, genetics and **nutrition** are the cause of the greater-than-average height, and linear growth ceases with the end of puberty. In individuals with gigantism who are not treated, linear growth can continue unchecked for several decades. It is important that a child with the symptoms of gigantism be assessed medically so that treatment can be implemented and abnormal linear height as well as potentially serious symptoms such as heart disease or colon cancer be minimized or avoided.

Resources

BOOKS

Cohen, Pinchas. "Hyperpituitarism, Tall Stature, and Overgrowth Syndromes." In *Nelson Textbook of Pediatrics*, 17th ed. Edited by Richard E. Behrman et al. Philadelphia: Saunders, 2004.

Melmed, Shlomo, and David Kleinberg. "Acromegaly." In *Williams Textbook of Endocrinology*, 10th ed. Edited by P. Reed Larson et al. Philadelphia: Saunders, 2003.

PERIODICALS

Melmed, Shlomo, et al. "Consensus Guidelines for Acromegaly Management." *Journal of Clinical Endocrinology and Metabolism* 87, no. 9 (September 1, 2002): 87–95.

ORGANIZATIONS

Pituitary Network Association. PO Box 1958, Thousand Oaks, CA 91358. Web site: <www.acromegaly.org>.

WEB SITES

Shim, Melanie, and Pinchas Cohen. "Gigantism and Acromegaly." *eMedicine*, July 29, 2004. Available online at <www.emedicine.com/ped/topic2634.htm> (accessed December 23, 2004).

Rosalyn Carson-DeWitt, MD
Stephanie Dionne Sherk

Acting out

Definition

Acting out is defined as the release of out-of-control aggressive or sexual impulses in order to gain relief from tension or **anxiety**. Such impulses often result in antisocial or delinquent behaviors. The term is also sometimes used in regard to a psychotherapeutic release of repressed feelings, as occurs in psychodrama.

Description

Infants and toddlers

The earliest acting out behaviors are often referred to as temper **tantrums**. These behaviors are usually first observed in infants between the ages of 12 and 18 months of age. At that point, temper tantrums can be considered a normal part of growth and development. These early tantrums are simply an infant's attempt to communicate feelings of dissatisfaction or extreme disappointment. Observed behaviors in infants trying to express their anger or frustration usually include patently angry-sounding crying, kicking hands and feet, and possibly even trying to strike out. For toddlers, such violent outbursts of temper often include hitting, kicking, and biting others; and possibly self-injurious behaviors such as head-banging. The child's reaction to the supposed cause of the tantrum is often markedly disproportionate to the precipitating incident. An example would be the child who is told that he or she cannot have a lollipop and then proceeds to violently attack the mother, hitting and kicking her, while screaming as loudly as possible.

Acting out conduct can include any highly emotional, disruptive, and unacceptable outburst that appears to be the child's reaction to unmet needs or wishes. A primary reason for such emotional lack of control in a child, especially above the age of three or four, is having not learned how to cope with their own frustration. Such temper tantrums usually peak between the ages of two and three. Because under normal circumstances the child has learned the necessary lessons in how to deal with disappointment by the time he or she has reached the age of four, there is then a noticeable decrease in this sort of acting out behavior.

Preschool and school age children

When no medical or psychological determination is discovered for acting out behaviors in young children above the age of four, the assumption can be made that the temper tantrums are a learned behavior. Toddlers and **preschool** children very rapidly learn the effectiveness of such acting out. If parents or other caregivers acquiesce to the child's wishes each time to avoid the occurrence of a tantrum, it quickly becomes obvious to the child that this is the most successful means of getting his or her wishes fulfilled. Acting out quickly becomes a time-honored response to the word "No."

More critical negative behaviors including aggressive or abusive actions toward other children, animals, adults, or even themselves are usually a more serious and longer-lasting form of acting out. These are usually related to more momentous causes including mental ill-

ness or pathological conditions in the child's life, either in the home or in some other facet of the child's environment. Such negative childhood conduct is often seen in children who have been the victims of physical and/or sexual abuse or of severe neglect. Such acting out for this group of children is often referred to among mental health professionals as "a cry for help." Though certainly significant problems, acting out in the form of various rebellious behaviors that are not self-injurious or life-threatening is considered the less serious form of this "cry for help." These actions include disobeying parents and teachers, non-life-threatening alcohol or drug use, promiscuity, and exercising poor judgment in relationships and activities.

Common problems

High-profile crimes such as the Columbine High School shootings have made most people much more acutely aware of the potential danger involved in young people acting out in a highly antisocial manner. In 2000, the National Institute of Mental Health (NIMH) began to study child and adolescent violence in the United States. One of NIMH's initial findings indicates that though youth violence is indeed a serious problem, events such as Columbine are a rare occurrence. On average across the United States, every day six to seven young people are murdered by their peers. The overwhelming majority of these homicides occur within the confines of inner cities, and the average victim is a member of a minority group. These teenagers' deaths for the most part do not occur on school grounds. Moreover, many factors other than those that cause acting out may contribute to these crimes.

The NIMH found in its research that causes for serious acting out include the following:

- weak **bonding** with parents, caused by parents being physically or emotionally unavailable to the child
- impotent parenting as manifested by failing to watch over children, by being excessively strict, or by providing harsh and inconsistent discipline
- a home environment that exposes children to violence and supports and models aggressive and violent behaviors
- the impact of rejection by or competition with peers in early school years (In some cases this experience results in children who do not succeed socially or academically banding together to act out. This tendency to band together appeared to be true of the Columbine High School perpetrators.)
- gender (From approximately the age of four years, boys were found by the NIMH study to be more likely

than girls to engage in aggressive, acting out behaviors.)

- child psychopathology (The NIMH study suggests that children with behavioral difficulties are likely to have two or more psychological problems such as conduct or anxiety disorders or depression.)

- lower socioeconomic status (A correlation between low **family** income and antisocial acting out has been repeatedly noted.)

- heredity (Perhaps the most surprising factor of the NIMH study has been the possibility that genes may indeed influence behaviors. Exactly how genetics affects personality and mental illness is not clearly understood. How the environment interacts with this genetic component also remains a mystery. However, in 2004 this genetic ingredient in acting out behaviors was a topic of study for the NIMH.)

A 2001 Carleton University (Ottawa, Canada) study published in the *Journal of Research in Childhood Education* attempted to look at means of predicting which preschool children would be more apt to act out or experience academic or social difficulties in school. The study entitled "Solitary-Active **Play** Behavior: A Marker Variable for Maladjustment in the Preschool?" concluded that young children who play alone in a very active and boisterous manner were more likely to have adjustment problems in school.

Problems identified for this group of children include the following:

- exhibiting a lower attention span

- being more difficult to comfort

- being more timid and bashful

- showing more aggression and acting out

- doing poorer on academic testing for early skills

- showing a less positive response to being in school

- showing less ability to form positive relationships with other children

The Carleton study asserted two points: first, their research gave no evidence that these children had less learning ability than other children, but rather that they simply experienced problems with adjusting to school; second, it is normal for preschool age children to engage in solitary play. However it is the mode in which a child plays alone—in an overly boisterous, hyperactive manner—that seems to provide the marker for potential acting out problems later. The Canadian researchers undertook this study not to merely identify future acting out children, but to find those children who could benefit from specialized and comprehensive educational programs that address both academic and social needs.

Parental concerns

When to call the doctor

The parent whose child exhibits the negative behaviors called "acting out" probably wonders what is normal and what is not. Well-meaning friends and family may assure them that the child "will grow out of it" when the acting out behaviors are clearly not a normal part of growth and development. Some people consider acting out behaviors as simply part of the learning process for young children not requiring professional help. The results of appropriate parental intervention may suggest the real severity of the behavior. For example, the child who ceases having temper tantrums once he or she realizes that the tantrum will not get him or her the desired result has both identified the severity of the problem and resolved the identified problem for their parents.

Temper tantrums after the age of four or in children younger than four when very frequent and/or prolonged (that is, lasting longer than a half hour) should be evaluated by a healthcare professional as there may be a other medical or psychological causes. Any type of acting out behavior that can be termed unsafe, damaging to others, or self-injurious will probably need to be evaluated by the child's healthcare provider.

Among the forms of acting out behavior seen in children and teens that warrant professional attention are the following:

- pathological lying

- bullying others

- self-injury, such as cutting self or head-banging

- alcohol or drug abuse

- truancy

- **running away**

- participating in unsafe sexual activities

- getting into fights

- assault

- vandalism

- fire-setting

- stealing

- rape

- homicide

Coping with acting out in toddlers

For toddlers, most childcare professionals recommend that parents make it obvious that temper tantrums are not an appropriate way to handle disappointment. Giving a "time out," having the child go to his or her room or another quiet area for a set period of time or until able to interact in a socially acceptable manner, is an effective means of dealing with this form of acting out. Though small children often do not appear able to hear or comprehend reason, it is perfectly appropriate for parents to note that they understand the child's disappointment or frustration but that the child's negative behavior will not alter the situation. Some parents combine time outs with the message, "Deal with it." As time has gone on, the time outs become less necessary, and the direction "Deal with it" is enough for the child to regain self-control. The child learns that people do not always get what they want.

A research program under the auspices of NIMH has as of 2004 two decades of experience in the prevention of serious childhood acting out. The Nurse Home Visitation Program operates in Colorado, New York, and Tennessee. Nurses visit high-risk families beginning during a pregnancy and continuing through the child's second birthday. The selected families are considered at-risk because they have low income and/or a single parent. The goals of the visits are to improve the outcome in **childbirth**, promote the child's health and development, and aid in increasing the family's financial self-sufficiency. Follow-up of these children to the age of 15 show them to have fewer behavioral problems than comparable 15-year-olds without the service. Behavioral problems studied included use of drugs and alcohol, running away, sexual acting out, and arrests and convictions for crimes.

Coping with acting out in preschool and school age children

The Administration on Children, Youth, and Families (ACYF) has collaborated with NIMH in developing several **assessment** tools to identify children at risk for behavioral problems. Many of these tools are designed to pinpoint even preschool children at risk, and are provided within such programs as Head Start. It is now known that 70 to 80 percent of all children provided services for mental health problems in United States schools have these services delivered by the school system itself, by school guidance counselors and psychologists. Several recent initiatives by the NIMH have as their goal working with the child, classmates, parents, and teachers to reduce disruptive behavior. The Families and Schools Together (FAST) Track Program currently

KEY TERMS

Antisocial—Actions described as impulsively aggressive, sometimes violent, that do not comply with established social and ethical codes.

Anxiety disorder—A mental disorder characterized by prolonged, excessive worry about circumstances in one's life. Anxiety disorders include agoraphobia and other phobias, obsessive-compulsive disorder, post-traumatic stress disorder, and panic disorder.

Attention deficit hyperactivity disorder (ADHD)—A condition in which a person (usually a child) has an unusually high activity level and a short attention span. People with the disorder may act impulsively and may have learning and behavioral problems.

Conduct disorder—A behavioral and emotional disorder of childhood and adolescence. Children with a conduct disorder act inappropriately, infringe on the rights of others, and violate societal norms.

Delinquent—A term applied to young people who behave in a manner in defiance of established social and ethical codes.

Depression—A mental condition in which a person feels extremely sad and loses interest in life. A person with depression may also have sleep problems and loss of appetite and may have trouble concentrating and carrying out everyday activities.

Psychodrama—A specific form of role play that focuses on acting out "scripts" of unresolved issues within the family, or helping family members adopt new approaches and understanding of one another.

Psychopathology—The study of mental disorders or illnesses, such as schizophrenia, personality disorder, or major depressive disorder.

Psychotherapy—Psychological counseling that seeks to determine the underlying causes of a patient's depression. The form of this counseling may be cognitive/behavioral, interpersonal, or psychodynamic.

operates in North Carolina, Pennsylvania, Tennessee, and Washington. FAST Track has studied aggressive children from the age of six on for several years now, providing intervention as necessary. Follow-up studies have shown that those FAST Track Program children who received intervention required less **special educa-**

tion services by grade 3 than children that did not participate in the program.

The Coping with Stress Course is a group educational program as of 2004 provided to adolescents in Maryland, Ohio, and Oregon. Its purpose is help young people develop strategies for coping positively with their negative thinking, tendencies toward depression, and acting out behaviors. Initial results from this course have shown successful outcomes for course participants. Among teens who did not take the course, symptoms of depression were reported twice as often. Adolescents taking the Coping with Stress Course showed a reduction in depressive symptoms and an increase in overall positive adjustment. However, it appears that time reduced the potency of this learning experience. Research over a longer period showed less difference between the two groups.

The NIMH study of acting out concluded that it is a multi-faceted problem involving the interactions between the child and his or her family, friends, classmates, school, and community. Children who have a warm, loving, and supportive childhood are far less likely to act out as a cry for help or to act out in a violent manner. Two types of teen **antisocial behavior** have been identified by NIMH: life course persistent and **adolescence** limited. Teens with life course persistent behaviors act out in violent ways from early childhood on, in a variety of situations. They are considered to have psychopathology, often including attention deficit hyperactivity disorder (ADHD). They usually continue with negative behaviors into adulthood. Those young people with adolescence limited behaviors typically act out in specific defined social situations and usually stop acting out behaviors before reaching adulthood.

See also Antisocial behavior.

Resources

BOOKS

Kelly, Kate. *The Baffled Parent's Guide to Stopping Bad Behavior.* New York: McGraw-Hill, 2003.

Swanson, Noel. *Good Child Guide: Putting an End to Bad Behavior.* London: Aurum Press, 2000.

WEB SITES

Association for Childhood Educational International (ACIE). Available online at <www.acei.org> (accessed October 15, 2004).

National Institute of Mental Health. Available online at <www.nimh.nih.gov.htm> (accessed October 15, 2004).

Joan Schonbeck, R.N.

Adaptive behavior scales for infants and early childhood

Definition

Adaptive behavior scales are standardized tests used to describe and evaluate the behavior of infants, toddlers, and preschoolers, especially those at risk for communication delays and behavior impairments.

Purpose

Adaptive behaviors are learned. They involve the ability to adapt to and manage one's surroundings to effectively function and meet social or community expectations. Infants learn to walk, to talk, and to eat with a spoon. Older children learn to cross the street, to go to the store, and to follow a great variety of rules while interacting with people, such as when to say please and thank you. Good adaptive behavior promotes independence at home, at school, and in the community. Undesirable or socially unacceptable behaviors that interfere with the acquisition of desired skills and with the performance of everyday activities are classified as maladaptive behaviors, or more commonly, behavior problems. Maladaptive behavior interferes with child's achievement of independence because the child requires more supervision and assistance in order to learn how to behave appropriately.

Problems in developing adaptive skills can occur in children of any age. For example, difficulties can develop in mastering basic functional skills (such as talking, walking, or toileting), in learning academic skills and concepts, or in making social and vocational adjustments. Adaptive behavior scales are evaluation tools designed to help care providers improve their assessments of the abilities and needs of infants and children who have disabilities or are at risk for developmental delays.

Description

Many different adaptive behavior scales are used in the United States for **assessment** purposes. The most widely used are the Developmental Profile II (DPII), the Early Coping Inventory (ECI), the **Bayley Scales of Infant Development** (BSID), the Scales of Independent Behavior—Revised (SIB-R), the Vineland Adaptive Behavior Scales (VABS), and the Adaptive Behavior Scales (ABS).

Developmental Profile II (DPII)

The DP-II behavior scale is used to screen for developmental delays and compare a child's development to that of other children who are in the same age group. This scale is a check-off list of 186 skills. A parent or therapist who knows the child well simply indicates whether the child has mastered the skill in question. The DPII, which can be administered from infancy to age nine, assesses development in the following areas:

- Physical development: Large and small muscle coordination, strength, stamina, flexibility, and sequential motor skills.

- Self-help development: Ability to cope independently with the environment, for example, to eat, dress, and take care of self and others.

- Social development: Interpersonal abilities, emotional needs, and how the child relates to friends, relatives, and other adults.

- Academic development: Intellectual abilities and skills required for academic achievement; IQ (intellectual quotient) score.

- Communication development: Expressive and receptive **communication skills**, including written, spoken, and body language.

Early Coping Inventory (ECI)

The ECI measures adaptive behavior. It is based on observation and is used to assess the coping-related behaviors that are used by infants and toddlers in everyday living. Analysis of a child's scores provides information about level of effectiveness, coping style, and specific coping strengths and weaknesses. The findings can then be used to plan educational and therapeutic interventions. The ECI can also be used to involve parents in its use as a means of increasing knowledge of the child. The ECI, which can be administered to infants aged four to 36 months or to children with disabilities, has 48 test items that are divided into three broad coping clusters:

- Sensorimotor organization: According to the famous developmental psychologist, Jean Piaget, infants learn, from birth to approximately age two, to coordinate all their sensory experiences (sights, sounds, etc.) with their motor behaviors. At this stage of development, children start to explore and understand the world around them by doing things like sucking, grasping, and **crawling**. This part of the ECI tests the child's level of sensorimotor skills: visual attention, reaction to touch, self-regulation of basic body functions, tolerance for various body positions, and activity level depending on various situations.

- Reactive behavior: This behavior includes a child's capacity to accept emotional warmth and support from other people and to react to the feelings and moods of

others. The ECI can assess reactive behavior, including tolerance of frustration, ability to "bounce back" after stressful events, and capacity to adapt to changes in the environment.

- Self-initiated behavior: This part of the ECI tests the ability of a child to initiate action in order to communicate needs, to try new behaviors, to achieve a goal, as well as problem-solving abilities and level of persistence during activities.

Bayley Scales of Infant Development (BSID)

The BSID are used extensively to assess the development of infants from one to three years of age. The test is given on an individual basis and takes from 45 to 60 minutes to complete. It is administered by examiners who are experienced clinicians specifically trained in BSID test procedures. The examiner presents a series of test materials to the child and observes the child's responses and behaviors. The test also contains items designed to identify young children at risk for **developmental delay**. BSID evaluates three scales:

- Mental scale: This part of the evaluation assesses several types of abilities: sensory/perceptual acuities, discriminations, and response; memory-learning and problem-solving; vocalization and range of verbal communication; basis of abstract thinking; development of habits.

- Motor scale: This part of the BSID assesses the degree of body control, large muscle coordination, finer manipulatory skills of the hands and fingers, dynamic movement, postural imitation, and the ability to recognize objects by sense of touch (stereognosis).

- Behavior rating scale: This scale provides information that can be used to supplement information gained from the mental and motor scales. This 30-item scale rates the child's relevant behaviors and measures attention/arousal, orientation/engagement, emotional regulation, and motor quality.

Scales of Independent Behavior—Revised (SIB-R)

Children with developmental disabilities or who become handicapped through accident or illness often need special assistance at home and at school. The SIB-R assesses adaptive and maladaptive behavior to determine the type and amount of special assistance that children with disabilities may need. The SIB-R is widely used in **preschool** and **special education** programs for diagnosis, for intervention planning, and for assessing outcomes. The SIB-R evaluation can be completed by a teacher, psychologist, or social worker directly or with the help of special interview materials that involve par-

KEY TERMS

Adaptive behavior—The ability to do things on one's own without getting into trouble and to adapt to and manage one's surroundings.

Asperger syndrome—A developmental disorder of childhood characterized by autistic behavior but without the same difficulties acquiring language that children with autism have.

Autism—A developmental disability that appears early in life, in which normal brain development is disrupted and social and communication skills are retarded, sometimes severely.

Behavior—A stereotyped motor response to an internal or external stimulus.

Body language—Communication without words, also sometimes referred to as "non-verbal communication"; conscious or unconscious bodily movements and gestures that communicate to others a person's attitudes and feelings.

Fine motor skill—The abilities required to control the smaller muscles of the body for writing, playing an instrument, artistic expression and craft work. The muscles required to perform fine motor skills are generally found in the hands, feet and head.

Gross motor skills—The abilities required to control the large muscles of the body for walking, running,

sitting, crawling, and other activities. The muscles required to perform gross motor skills are generally found in the arms, legs, back, abdomen and torso.

Maladaptive behavior—Undesirable and socially unacceptable behavior that interferes with the acquisition of desired skills or knowledge and with the performance of everyday activities.

Motor skills—Controlled movements of muscle groups. Fine motor skills involve tasks that require dexterity of small muscles, such as buttoning a shirt. Tasks such as walking or throwing a ball involve the use of gross motor skills.

Sensorimotor—Relating to the combination of sensory and motor coordination.

Sensory—Refers to network of nerves that transmit information from the senses to the brain.

Sequential motor skill—Ability to coordinate different motor skills in sequence, such as running followed by a jump.

Socialization—The process by which new members of a social group are integrated in the group.

Stereognosis—The ability to recognize objects by sense of touch.

---

ents. The SIB-R contents provide opportunity for team discussion, often eliciting information and opinions that parents might not otherwise bring up on their own.

The SIB-R adaptive behavior items include 14 sub-scales grouped into four clusters: motor skills, social interaction and communication skills, personal living skills, and community living skills. Each SIB-R adaptive behavior item is a statement of a task. (For example, "Child washes, rinses, and dries hair.") The examiner rates the child being assessed regarding each task, using a scale from zero to three:

• 0—never or rarely performs the task (even if asked)

• 1—does the task but not well or about 25 percent of the time (may need to be asked)

• 2—does the task fairly well or about 75 percent of the time (may need to be asked)

• 3—does the task very well always or almost always (without being asked)

The Vineland Adaptive Behavior Scales (VABS)

The VABS are designed to assess the personal and social self-sufficiency of individuals from birth to early adulthood. The scales are equally applicable to handicapped and non-handicapped children. The VABS assessment provides the information required for the diagnosis or evaluation of a wide range of disabilities, including **mental retardation**, developmental delays, functional skills impairment, and speech/language impairment. Vineland has also been proven to be an accurate resource for predicting **autism** and Asperger syndrome, among other diagnoses. The Vineland measures adaptive behavior in four domains:

• Communication: Vineland evaluates expressive and written communication skills, as well as the ability to listen.

• Daily living skills: These skills are assessed on a personal basis, in the **family** setting and in the wider community.

- Socialization: VABS evaluate interpersonal relationships, **play** and leisure time activities, and interpersonal coping skills.

- Motor skills: The test also evaluates both gross and fine motor skills.

The Adaptive Behavior Scales—School (ABS-S)

The ABS-S scale was developed to assess the personal independence of school-age children. Like other scales, it evaluates the personal and social skills used for everyday living. It is most frequently used to assess the current functioning of children being evaluated for evidence of mental retardation, for evaluating adaptive characteristics in autistic children, and for distinguishing behavior-disordered children who require special education assistance from those who can be educated in a regular school setting. The ABS-S is divided into two parts:

- ABS Part One: This part focuses on personal independence and is designed to evaluate coping skills considered important for developing personal independence and responsibility in daily living. The skills within Part One are grouped into nine behavior domains: independent functioning, physical development, economic activity, **language development**, numbers and time, prevocational/vocational activity, self-direction, responsibility, and socialization.

- ABS Part Two: This part evaluates social maladaptation. The behaviors assessed are assigned to seven domains that are measures of those adaptive behaviors that may lead to personality and behavior disorders: social behavior, conformity, trustworthiness, stereotyped and hyperactive behavior, self-abusive behavior, social engagement, and disturbing interpersonal behavior.

Precautions

Since behavior is socially defined, a child's performance must be considered within the context of the cultural environments and social expectations that affect his or her functioning.

Preparation

Before performing an adaptive behavior test, the examiner explains to the parents the purpose of the test. If the parents are required to provide the answers, they are reminded that accuracy is the best way to achieve a result that may help the child. If the test is given directly to the child, the examiner describes what will happen during the test procedure and the parents are asked not to talk to the child during the test to avoid skewing results.

Risks

There are no risks associated with adaptive behavior tests.

Parental concerns

Parental involvement in the developmental assessment of their children is very important. First, because parents are more familiar with their child's behavior, their assessment may indeed be more indicative of the child's developmental status than an assessment that is based on limited observation in an unfamiliar clinical setting. The involvement of parents in their child's development testing also improves their knowledge of child development issues and their subsequent participation in required intervention programs, if any.

See also Autism; Bayley Scales of Infant Development; Emotional development; Personality development; Personality disorders.

Resources

BOOKS

Frieman, Jerome L. *Learning and Adaptive Behavior.* Florence, KY: Wadsworth Publishing, 2002.

Porter, Louise. *Young Children's Behavior: Practical Approaches for Caregivers and Teachers*, 2nd ed. Baltimore, MD: Paul H. Brookes Publishing Co., 2003.

Sattker, Jerome M. *Assessment of Children: Behavioral and Clinical Applications*, 4th ed. Lutz, FL: Psychological Assessment Resources Inc., 2001.

Wetherby, Amy, et al. *Communication and Symbolic Behavior Scales: Developmental Profile.* Baltimore, MD: Paul H. Brookes Publishing Co., 2002.

PERIODICALS

Fenton, G., et al. "Vineland adaptive behavior profiles in children with autism and moderate to severe developmental delay." *Autism* 7, no. 3 (September 2003): 269–87.

Hall, J. R., et al. "Criterion-related validity of the three-factor model of psychopathy: personality, behavior, and adaptive functioning." *Assessment* 11, no. 1 (March 2004): 4–16.

Ladd, G. W. "Probing the adaptive significance of children's behavior and relationships in the school context: a child by environment perspective." *Advances in Child Development Behavior* 31 (2003): 43–104.

Matson, J. L., et al. "A system of assessment for adaptive behavior, social skills, behavioral function, medication side-effects, and psychiatric disorders." *Research in Developmental Disabilities* 24, no. 1 (January-February 2003): 75–81.

ORGANIZATIONS

American Academy of Child & Adolescent Psychiatry (AACAP). 3615 Wisconsin Ave., NW, Washington, DC 20016–3007. Web site: <www.aacap.org>.

American Academy of Pediatrics (AAP). 141 Northwest Point Boulevard, Elk Grove Village, IL 60007–1098. Web site: <www.aap.org>.

American Psychological Association (APA). 750 First Street, NE, Washington, DC 20002–4242. Web site: <www.apa.org>.

Child Development Institute (CDI). 3528 E Ridgeway Road, Orange, CA 92867. Web site: <www.childdevelopmentinfo.com>.

WEB SITES

"Early Child Assessment Measures." *New Assessments: Early Childhood Resource.* Available online at <www.newassessment.org> (accessed November 8, 2004).

SIB-R User's Group Home Page. Available online at <www.cpinternet.com/~bhill/sibr/> (accessed November 8, 2004).

Monique Laberge, Ph.D.

ADD *see* **Attention deficit/Hyperactivity disorder**

Addiction

Definition

Addiction is a physical or mental dependence on a behavior or substance that a person feels powerless to stop.

Description

Addiction is one of the most costly public health problems in the United States. It is a progressive syndrome, which means that it increases in severity over time unless it is treated. The term has been partially replaced by the word "dependence" for substance abuse. Addiction has been extended, however, to include mood-altering behaviors or activities. Some researchers speak of two types of addictions: substance addictions (for example, **alcoholism**, drug abuse, and **smoking**); and process addictions (for example, gambling, spending, shopping, eating, and sexual activity). There was as of 2004 a growing recognition that many addicts are addicted to more than one substance or process. Substance abuse is characterized by frequent relapse or return to the abused substance. Substance abusers often make repeated attempts to quit before they are successful.

The National Survey on Drug Use and Health (NSDUH) is conducted annually by the Substance Abuse and Mental Health Services Administration (SAMHSA) of the U.S. Department of Health and Human Services. Among the findings of the 2003 study are the following:

- In 2003, an estimated 19.5 million Americans, or 8.2 percent of the population aged 12 or older, were current illicit drug users. Current illicit drug use means use of an illicit drug during the month prior to the survey interview. The numbers did not change from 2002.

- The rate of illicit drug use among youths aged 12–17 did not change significantly between 2002 (11.6%) and 2003 (11.2%), and there were no changes for any specific drug. The rate of current marijuana use among youths was 8.2 percent in 2002 and 7.9 percent in 2003. There was a significant decline in lifetime marijuana use among youths, from 20.6 percent in 2002 to 19.6 percent in 2003. There also were decreases in rates of past year use of LSD (1.3 to 0.6%), ecstasy (2.2 to 1.3%), and methamphetamine (0.9 to 0.7%).

- About 10.9 million persons aged 12–20 reported drinking alcohol in the month prior to the survey interview in 2003 (29.0 percent of this age group). Nearly 7.2 million (19.2%) were binge drinkers and 2.3 million (6.1%) were heavy drinkers. The 2003 rates were essentially the same as those from the 2002 survey.

- An estimated 70.8 million Americans reported current (past month) use of a tobacco product in 2003. This is 29.8 percent of the population aged 12 or older, similar to the rate in 2002 (30.4%). Young adults aged 18–25 reported the highest rate of past month cigarette use (40.2%), similar to the rate among young adults in 2002. An estimated 35.7 million Americans aged 12 or older in 2003 were classified as nicotine dependent in the past month because of their cigarette use (15% of the total population), about the same as for 2002.

Demographics

In 2003, the rate of substance dependence or abuse was 8.9 percent for youths aged 12–17 and 21 percent for persons aged 18–25. Among persons with substance dependence or abuse, illicit drugs accounted for 58.1

percent of youths and 37.2 percent of persons aged 18–25. In 2003, males were almost twice as likely to be classified with substance dependence or abuse as females (12.2% versus 6.2%). Among youths aged 12–17, however, the rate of substance dependence or abuse among females (9.1%) was similar to the rate among males (8.7%). The rate of substance dependence or abuse was highest among Native Americans and Alaska Natives (17.2%). The next highest rates were among Native Hawaiians and other Pacific Islanders (12.9%) and persons reporting mixed ethnicity (11.3%). Asian Americans had the lowest rate (6.3%). The rates among Hispanics (9.8%) and whites (9.2%) were higher than the rate among blacks (8.1%).

Rates of drug use showed substantial variation by age. For example, in 2003, some 3.8 percent of youths aged 12 to 13 reported current illicit drug use compared with 10.9 percent of youths aged 14 to 15 and 19.2 percent of youths aged 16 or 17. As in other years, illicit drug use in 2003 tended to increase with age among young persons, peaking among 18 to 20-year-olds (23.3%) and declining steadily after that point with increasing age. The prevalence of current alcohol use among adolescents in 2003 increased with increasing age, from 2.9 percent at age 12 to a peak of about 70 percent for persons 21 to 22 years old. The highest prevalence of both binge and heavy drinking was for young adults aged 18 to 25, with the peak rate of both measures occurring at age 21. The rate of binge drinking was 41.6 percent for young adults aged 18 to 25 and 47.8 percent at age 21. Heavy alcohol use was reported by 15.1 percent of persons aged 18 to 25 and 18.7 percent of persons aged 21. Among youths aged 12 to 17, an estimated 17.7 percent used alcohol in the month prior to the survey interview. Of all youths, 10.6 percent were binge drinkers, and 2.6 percent were heavy drinkers, similar to the 2002 numbers.

Rates of current illicit drug use varied significantly among the major racial-ethnic groups in 2003. The rate of illicit drug use was highest among Native Americans and Alaska Natives (12.1%), persons reporting two or more races (12%), and Native Hawaiians and other Pacific Islanders (11.1%). Rates were 8.7 percent for African Americans, 8.3 percent for Caucasians, and 8 percent for Hispanics. Asian Americans had the lowest rate of current illicit drug use at 3.8 percent. The rates were unchanged from 2002. Native Americans and Alaska Natives were more likely than any other racial-ethnic group to report the use of tobacco products in 2003. Among persons aged 12 or older, 41.8 percent of Native Americans and Alaska Natives reported using at least one tobacco product in the past month. The lowest current tobacco use rate among racial-ethnic groups in

2003 was observed for Asian Americans (13.8%), a decrease from the 2002 rate (18.6%).

Young adults aged 18 to 25 had the highest rate of current use of cigarettes (40.2%), similar to the rate in 2002. Past month cigarette use rates among youths in 2002 and 2003 were 13 percent and 12.2 percent, respectively, not a statistically significant change. However, there were significant declines in past year (from 20.3% to 19%) and lifetime (from 33.3% to 31%) cigarette use among youths aged 12 to 17 between 2002 and 2003. Among persons aged 12 or older, a higher proportion of males than females smoked cigarettes in the past month in 2003 (28.1% versus 23%). Among youths aged 12 to 17, however, girls (12.5%) were as likely as boys (11.9%) to smoke in the past month. There was no change in cigarette use among boys aged 12 to 17 between 2002 and 2003. However, among girls, cigarette use decreased from 13.6 percent in 2002 to 12.5 percent in 2003.

Causes and symptoms

Addiction to substances results from the interaction of several factors.

Drug chemistry

Some substances are more addictive than others, either because they produce a rapid and intense change in mood or because they produce painful withdrawal symptoms when stopped suddenly.

Genetics

Some people appear to be more vulnerable to addiction because their body chemistry increases their sensitivity to drugs. Some forms of **substance abuse and dependence** seem to run in families; a correlation that may be the result of a genetic predisposition, environmental influences, or a combination of the two.

Brain structure and function

Using drugs repeatedly over time changes brain structure and function in fundamental and long-lasting ways. Addiction comes about through an array of changes in the brain and the strengthening of new memory connections. Evidence suggests that those long-lasting brain changes are responsible for the distortions of cognitive and emotional functioning that characterize addicts, particularly the compulsion to use drugs. Although the causes of addiction remain the subject of ongoing debate and research, many experts as of 2004 considered addiction to be a brain disease, a condition caused by persistent changes in brain structure and function. However, having this brain disease does not absolve the addict of responsibility for his or her behavior, but it does explain why many addicts cannot stop using drugs by sheer force of will alone.

Social learning

Social learning is considered the most important single factor in causing addiction. It includes patterns of use in the addict's **family** or subculture, **peer pressure**, and advertising or media influence.

Availability

Inexpensive or readily available tobacco, alcohol, or drugs produce marked increases in rates of addiction. Increases in state taxes on alcohol and tobacco products have not resulted in decreased use.

Personality

Before the 1980s, the so-called addictive personality was used to explain the development of addiction. The addictive personality was described as escapist, impulsive, dependent, devious, manipulative, and self-centered. Many doctors in the early 2000s believe that these character traits develop in addicts as a result of the addiction, rather than the traits being a cause of the addiction.

When to call the doctor

The earlier one seeks help for their teen's behavioral or drug problems, the better. How is a parent to know if their teen is experimenting with or moving more deeply into the drug culture? Above all, a parent must be a careful observer, particularly of the little details that make up a teen's life. Overall signs of dramatic change in appearance, friends, or physical health may signal trouble. If parents believe their child may be drinking or using drugs, they should seek help through a substance abuse recovery program, family physician, or mental health professional.

Diagnosis

In addition to noting a preoccupation with using and acquiring the abused substance, the diagnosis of addiction focuses on five criteria:

- loss of willpower
- harmful consequences
- unmanageable lifestyle
- increased tolerance or escalation of use
- withdrawal symptoms on quitting

Treatment

According to the American Psychiatric Association, there are three goals for the treatment of persons with substance use disorders: (1) the patient abstains from or reduces the use and effects of the substance; (2) the patient reduces the frequency and severity of relapses; and (3) the patient develops the psychological and emotional skills necessary to restore and maintain personal, occupational, and social functioning.

In general, before treatment can begin, many treatment centers require that the patient undergo detoxification. Detoxification is the process of weaning the patient from his or her regular substance use. Detoxification can be accomplished "cold turkey," by complete and immediate cessation of all substance use, or by slowly decreasing (tapering) the dose that a person is taking, to minimize the side effects of withdrawal. Some substances must be tapered because cold-turkey methods of detoxification are potentially life threatening. In some cases, medications may be used to combat the unpleasant and threatening physical and psychological symptoms of withdrawal. For example, methadone is used to help patients adjust to the tapering of heroin use.

The most frequently recommended social form of outpatient treatment is the 12-step program. Such programs are also frequently combined with psychotherapy. According to the American Psychological Association (APA), anyone, regardless of his or her religious beliefs or lack of religious beliefs, can benefit from participation in 12-step programs such as Alcoholics Anonymous (AA) or Narcotics Anonymous (NA). The number of visits to 12-step self-help groups exceeds the number of visits to all mental health professionals combined. There are 12-step groups for all major substance and process addictions.

Alternative treatment

Acupuncture and homeopathy have been used to treat withdrawal symptoms. Meditation, **yoga**, and reiki healing have been recommended for process addictions; however, the success of these programs has not been well documented through controlled studies.

Prognosis

The prognosis for recovery from any addiction depends on the substance or process, the individual's circumstances, and underlying personality structure. People who have multiple substance dependencies have the worst prognosis for recovery. It is not uncommon for someone in a treatment program to have a relapse, but the success rate increases with subsequent treatment programs.

Teenager smoking crystal methamphetamine, known to cause a very strong psychological addiction to the drug. (© *Houston Scott/Corbis Sygma.*)

cation programs are also widely used to inform young people of the harmfulness of substance abuse.

Parental concerns

Parents and guardians need to be aware of the power they have to influence the development of their kids throughout the teenage years. **Adolescence** brings a new and dramatic stage to family life. The changes that are required are not just the teen's to make; parents need to change their relationship with their teenager. It is best if parents are proactive about the challenges of this life stage, particularly those that pertain to the possibility of experimenting with and using alcohol and other drugs. Parents should not be afraid to talk directly to their kids about drug use, even if they have had problems with drugs or alcohol themselves. Parents should give clear, no-use messages about smoking, drugs, and alcohol. It is important for kids and teens to understand that the rules and expectations set by parents are based on parental love and concern for their well being. Parents should also be actively involved and demonstrate interest in their teen's friends and social activities. Spending quality time with teens and setting good examples are essential. Even if problems such as substance abuse already exist in the teen's life, parents and families can still have a positive influence on their teen's behavior.

Recovery from substance use is notoriously difficult, even with exceptional treatment resources. Although relapse rates are difficult to accurately obtain, the National Institute on Alcohol Abuse and Alcoholism cites evidence that 90 percent of alcohol dependent users experience at least one relapse within four years after treatment. Relapse rates for heroin and nicotine users are believed to be similar. Certain pharmacological treatments, however, have been shown to reduce relapse rates. Relapses are most likely to occur within the first 12 months of having discontinued substance use. Triggers for relapses can include any number of life stresses (problems in school or on the job, loss of a relationship, death of a loved one, financial stresses), in addition to seemingly mundane exposure to a place or an acquaintance associated with previous substance use.

Prevention

The most effective form of prevention appears to be a stable family that models responsible attitudes toward mood-altering substances and behaviors. Prevention edu-

Resources

BOOKS

Haugen, Hayley Mitchell. *Teen Smoking*. Minneapolis, MN: Sagebrush Bound, 2004.

Raczek, Linda Theresa. *Teen Addiction*. San Diego, CA: Lucent Books, 2003.

Stevens, Sally J., and Andrew R. Morral. *Adolescent Substance Abuse Treatment in the United States: Exemplary Models from a National Evaluation Study.* Binghamton, NY: Haworth Press, 2002.

Townsend, John. *Drugs—Teen Issues.* Chicago, IL: Raintree, 2004.

PERIODICALS

Johnson, Kate. "Tobacco Dependence: Even Minimal Exposure Can Cause Rapid Onset; Daily Smoking Not Necessary." *Family Practice News* (June 15, 2004): 66.

Kaminer, Yifah, and Chris Napolitano. "Dial for Therapy: Aftercare for Adolescent Substance Use Disorders." *Journal of the American Academy of Child and Adolescent Psychiatry* (September 2004): 1171.

"SAMHSA Reveals State Estimates of Substance Use for the First Time: Washington, D.C. Ranks Highest in Illegal Drug Use." *Alcoholism & Drug Abuse Weekly* (August 16, 2004): 31.

"Sexually Active Friends Can Signal Increase in Teen's Substance Abuse Risk." *Obesity, Fitness & Wellness Week* (September 18, 2004): 410.

Sherman, Carl. "Early Disorders Often Precede Substance Abuse." *Clinical Psychiatry News* (June 2004): 34.

ORGANIZATIONS

Alateen. 1600 Corporate Landing Parkway, Virginia Beach, VA 23454. Web site: <www.al-anon.alateen.org>.

National Academy of Child & Adolescent Psychiatry. 3615 Wisconsin Ave. NW, Washington, DC 20016. Web site: <www.aacap.org>.

WEB SITES

"Fact Sheet: Addiction (Substance Dependence)." *New York Presbyterian Hospital.* Available online at <www.noah-health.org/english/illness/mentalhealth/cornell/conditions/substdep.html> (accessed November 8, 2004).

"National Youth Anti-Drug Media Campaign." *Parents: The Anti-Drug.* Available online at <www.theantidrug.com> (accessed November 8, 2004).

Bill Asanjo, MS, CRC
Ken R. Wells

Adenoid hyperplasia

Definition

Adenoid hyperplasia is an enlargement of the lymph glands located above the back of the mouth.

Description

Located at the back of the mouth above and below the soft palate are two pairs of lymph glands. The tonsils below are clearly visible behind the back teeth; the adenoids lie just above them and are hidden from view by the palate. Together these four arsenals of immune defense guard the major entrance to the body from foreign invaders, the germs we breathe and eat. In contrast to the rest of the body's tissues, lymphoid tissue reaches its greatest size in mid-childhood and recedes thereafter. In this way children are best able to develop the immunities they need to survive in a world full of infectious diseases.

Beyond its normal growth pattern, lymphoid tissue grows excessively (hypertrophies) during an acute infection, as it suddenly increases its immune activity to fight off the invaders. Often it does not completely return to its former size. Each subsequent infection leaves behind a larger set of tonsils and adenoids. To make matters worse, the sponge-like structure of these hypertrophied glands can produce safe havens for germs where the body cannot reach and eliminate them. Before **antibiotics** and the reduction in infectious childhood diseases over the last few generations of the twentieth century, tonsils and adenoids caused even greater health problems.

Demographics

The true incidence of adenoid hyperplasia is difficult to assess. What is clear, however, is that tonsillectomy and adenoidectomy (T and A), the surgical treatment for the condition, is the most frequently performed major surgical procedure in the United States. Information current in 2004 on the exact number of these procedures performed was difficult to obtain because they are routinely performed in outpatient settings. Adenoid hypertrophy does not appear to affect any gender or racial group more than another.

Causes and symptoms

Most tonsil and adenoid hypertrophy is simply caused by the normal growth pattern for that type of tissue. Less often, the hypertrophy is due to repeated throat infections by cold viruses, **strep throat**, mononucleosis, and in the past, **diphtheria**. The acute infections are usually referred to as **tonsillitis**, the adenoids getting little recognition because they cannot be seen without special instruments. Symptoms include painful, bright red, often ulcerated tonsils, enlargement of lymph nodes (glands) beneath the jaw, **fever**, and general discomfort.

After the acute infection subsides, symptoms are generated simply by the size of the glands. Extremely large tonsils can impair breathing and swallowing, although that is quite rare. Large adenoids can impair nose breathing and require a child to breathe through the mouth. Because they encircle the only connection between the middle ear and the eustachian tube, hypertrophied adenoids can also obstruct the tube and cause middle ear infections.

Diagnosis

A simple depression of the tongue allows an adequate view of the tonsils. Enlarged tonsils may have deep pockets (crypts) containing dead tissue (necrotic debris). Viewing adenoids requires a small mirror or fiberoptic scope. A child with recurring middle ear infections may well have large adenoids. A **throat culture** or mononucleosis test usually reveals the identity of the germ.

Treatment

It used to be standard practice to remove tonsils and/or adenoids after a few episodes of acute throat or ear infection. The surgery is called tonsillectomy and adenoidectomy (T and A). Medical opinions changed as it was realized that this tissue is beneficial to the development of immunity. For instance, children without tonsils and adenoids produce only half the immunity to oral **polio vaccine**. In addition, treatment of ear and throat infections with antibiotics and of recurring ear infections with surgical drainage through the eardrum (tympanostomy) has greatly reduced the incidence of surgical removal of these lymph glands.

Alternative treatment

There are many botanical/herbal remedies that can be used alone or in formulas to locally assist the tonsils and adenoids in their immune function at the opening of the oral cavity and to tone these glands. Keeping the eustachian tubes open is an important contribution to optimal function in the tonsils and adenoids. **Food allergies** are often the culprits for recurring ear infections, as well as tonsillitis and adenoiditis. Identification and removal of the allergic food(s) can greatly assist in alleviating the cause of the problem. Acute tonsillitis also benefits from warm saline gargles.

Prognosis

Hypertrophied adenoids are a normal part of growing up and should be respected for their important role in the development of immunity. Only when their size causes problems by obstructing breathing or middle ear drainage do they demand intervention.

KEY TERMS

Eustachian tube—A thin tube between the middle ear and the pharnyx. Its purpose is to equalize pressure on either side of the ear drum.

Hyperplastic—Refers to an increase in the size of an organ or tissue due to an increase in the number of cells.

Hypertrophy—An increase in the size of a tissue or organ brought about by the enlargement of its cells rather than cell multiplication.

Strep throat—An infection of the throat caused by *Streptococcus* bacteria. Symptoms include sore throat, chills, fever, and swollen lymph nodes in the neck.

Ulcerated—Characterized by the formation of an ulcer.

Prevention

Prevention can be directed toward prompt evaluation and appropriate treatment of sore throats to prevent overgrowth of adenoid tissue. Avoiding other children with acute respiratory illness also reduces the spread of these common illnesses.

Parental concerns

Adenoid hypertrophy is a relatively common childhood condition. If a child has repeated ear infections, a physician, usually an ear, nose, and throat (ENT) specialist, will recommend treatment options. To alleviate the discomfort experienced by the child and to prevent secondary complication such as delayed speech that can occur if the child's hearing is compromised because of the accompanying ear infections, frequently a surgery called an adenoidectomy is performed.

When to call the doctor

Following an adenoidectomy, parents should call the doctor if any of the following occurs:

- unexpected bright red bleeding
- fever over 101°F (38°C)
- **pain** that is not relieved by pain medications

See also Tonsillitis.

Resources

WEB SITES

McClay, John E. "Adenoidectomy." *eMedicine*. Available online at <www.emedicine.com/ent/topic316.htm> (accessed November 8, 2004).

"Tonsils and Adenoids." *Healthy Kids and Pediatrics*. Available online at <www.medicinenet.com/ adenoids_and_tonsils/article.htm> (accessed November 8, 2004).

"What are tonsils and adenoids?" Available online at <www.itonsils.com> (accessed November 8, 2004).

J. Ricker Polsdorfer, MD
Deborah L. Nurmi, MS

Adenovirus infections

Definition

Adenoviruses are small infectious agents that cause upper respiratory tract infections, **conjunctivitis**, and other infections in humans.

Description

Adenoviruses were discovered in 1953. By 2004 about 49 different types had been identified, and about half of those were believed to cause human diseases. Adenovirus infections can occur throughout the year, unlike the seasonality associated with other respiratory viruses.

In children, adenoviruses most often cause acute upper respiratory infections with **fever** and runny nose. Adenovirus types 1, 2, 3, 5, and 6 are responsible for most of these infections. Occasionally more serious lower respiratory diseases, such as **pneumonia** or **bronchitis**, may occur. Adenoviruses can also cause acute **diarrhea** in young children, characterized by fever and watery stools. This condition is caused by adenovirus types 40 and 41 and can last as long as two weeks.

As much as 51 percent of all hemorrhagic **cystitis** (inflammation of the bladder and of the tubes that carry urine to the bladder from the kidneys) in American and Japanese children can be attributed to adenovirus infection. A child who has hemorrhagic cystitis has bloody urine for about three days, and invisible traces of blood can be found in the urine a few days longer. The child will feel the urge to urinate frequently but find it difficult to do so, for about the same length of time.

Other illnesses associated with adenovirus include:

- **encephalitis** (inflammation of the brain) and other infections of the central nervous system (CNS)
- **gastroenteritis** (inflammation of the stomach and intestines), which sometimes leads to enlarged lymph nodes in the intestines and rarely intussusception
- acute pharyngoconjunctival fever (inflammation of the lining of the eye [conjunctivitis] with fever)
- acute mesenteric **lymphadenitis** (inflammation of lymph glands in the abdomen)
- chronic interstitial fibrosis (abnormal growth of connective tissue between cells)
- intussusception (a type of intestinal obstruction)
- pneumonia that does not respond to antibiotic therapy
- **whooping cough** syndrome when *Bordetella pertussis* (the bacterium that causes classic whooping cough) is not found

Transmission

Specific adenovirus infections can be traced to particular sources and produce distinctive symptoms. In general, however, adenovirus infection is transmitted by the following:

- inhaling airborne viruses
- getting the virus in the eyes by swimming in contaminated water, using contaminated eye solutions or instruments, wiping the eyes with contaminated towels, or rubbing the eyes with contaminated fingers
- not washing the hands after using the bathroom and then touching the mouth or eyes

Infections often occur in situations in which individuals are in close contact with one another, such as the military, cruise ships, or college dormitories. Outbreaks among children are frequently reported at boarding schools and summer camps.

Most children have been infected by at least one adenovirus by the time they reach school age. Most adults have acquired immunity to multiple adenovirus types due to infections they had as children.

Demographics

Adenoviruses are responsible for 3 to 5 percent of acute respiratory infections in children. Most adenovirus infections occur between the ages of six months and five years. The incidence of adenovirus infection does not appear to differ among males and females or individuals of different race.

Causes and symptoms

In one mode of adenovirus infection (called lytic infection because it destroys large numbers of cells), adenoviruses kill healthy cells and replicate up to 1 million new viruses per cell killed, of which 1 to 5 percent are infectious. People with this kind of infection feel sick. In chronic or latent infection, a much smaller number of viruses are released, and healthy cells can multiply more rapidly than they are destroyed. People who have this kind of infection do not exhibit symptoms.

Children who have normal immune systems usually experience only minor symptoms when infected with adenovirus. The course of infection tends to be more serious in children who are immunocompromised, such as those undergoing **chemotherapy** or those who have a disease that disrupts normal immune response (e.g. human **immunodeficiency** syndrome [HIV]). In such children, the virus more often affects organs such as the lungs, liver, and kidneys, and the risk of fatality increases.

Symptoms common to respiratory illnesses caused by adenovirus infection include cough, fever, runny nose, **sore throat**, and watery eyes. In children with gastroenteritis caused by the adenovirus, symptoms may include diarrhea, fever, **nausea**, **vomiting**, and respiratory symptoms. Children with acute pharyngoconjunctival fever usually show signs of conjunctivitis, fever, sore throat, runny nose, and inflammation of the lymph glands in the neck (certical adenitis). More rarely, if the virus infects the lining of the brain and spinal cord (meninges) or the brain itself, **meningitis** or encephalitis may result; symptoms include fever, stiff or painful neck, irritability, changes in personality, or seizures.

When to call the doctor

Parents should contact a healthcare provider if the following applies to the infected child:

- The child is under three months of age.

- The child has symptoms that continue to worsen after one week.

- The child has difficulty breathing.

- The child shows symptoms of meningitis or encephalitis.

- The child has eye redness and swelling that becomes painful.

- The child shows signs of infection and is immunocompromised.

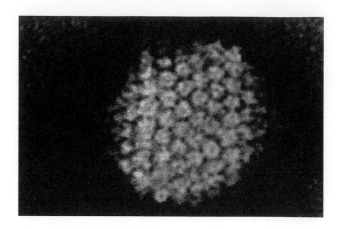

Magnification of an adenovirus. (© Hans Gelderblom/Visuals Unlimited.)

Diagnosis

Although symptoms may suggest the presence of adenovirus, distinguishing these infections from other viruses can be difficult. A definitive diagnosis is based on culture or detection of the virus in eye secretions, sputum, urine, or stool.

The extent of infection can be estimated from the results of blood tests that measure increases in the quantity of antibodies the immune system produces to fight it. Antibody levels begin to rise about a week after infection occurs and remain elevated for about a year.

Treatment

Treatment of adenovirus infections is usually supportive and aimed at relieving symptoms of the illness. Bed rest may be recommended along with medications to reduce fever and/or **pain**. (Aspirin should not be given to children because it is associated with Reye's syndrome.) Eye infections may benefit from topical corticosteroids to relieve symptoms and shorten the course of the disease. **Hospitalization** is usually required for severe pneumonia in infants and for keratoconjunctivitis (to prevent blindness). No effective **antiviral drugs** had been developed as of 2004.

Nutritional concerns

Because a child can become easily dehydrated if suffering from vomiting or diarrhea, it is important caregivers provide adequate fluid intake. Fluids such as water, breast milk or formula (if applicable), electrolyte replacement drinks, diluted juice, or clear broths should be encouraged. Drinks with **caffeine** should be avoided because of caffeine's diuretic effects (i.e. causes water to be lost through urine).

Prognosis

In otherwise healthy children, adenovirus infections are rarely fatal, and most patients recover fully. Immunocompromised children have a greater chance of serious side effects and death, with fatality rates as high as 50 to 69 percent (depending on the cause and extent of immunodeficiency).

Prevention

Practicing good personal hygiene and avoiding contact with people with infectious illnesses can reduce the risk of developing adenovirus infection. Proper hand washing can prevent the spread of the virus by oral-fecal transmission. Sterilization of instruments and solutions used in the eye can help prevent the spread of EKC, as can adequate chlorination of swimming pools.

A vaccine containing live adenovirus types 4 and 7 has been used to control disease in military recruits, but it is not recommended or available for civilian use. A recent resurgence of the adenovirus was found in a military population as soon as the **vaccination** program was halted. Vaccines prepared from purified subunits of adenovirus were as of 2004 under investigation.

Parental concerns

In the home setting, frequent hand washing should be encouraged, and children's **toys** and shared belongings should be frequently cleaned. Children who suffer from adenovirus infection should be kept home from school or daycare until they no longer show symptoms.

Resources

BOOKS

Demmler, Gail J. "Adenoviruses." In *Principles and Practice of Pediatric Infectious Diseases*. Edited by Sarah S. Long. New York: Churchill Livingstone, 2003.

Treanor, John J., and Frederick G. Hayden. "Adenovirus." *Textbook of Respiratory Medicine*. Edited by John F. Murray and Jay A. Nadel. Philadelphia: Saunders, 2000.

PERIODICALS

Evans, Jeff. "Viral Gastroenteritis On Board." *Internal Medicine News* (January 15, 2003): 44.

"Guard against Pertussis." *Contemporary Pediatrics* (February 2003): 87.

ORGANIZATIONS

American Academy of Pediatrics. 141 Northwest Point Blvd., Elk Grove Village, IL 60007-1098. Web site: <www.aap.org>.

National Center for Infectious Diseases, Center for Disease Control and Prevention. Mailstop C-14, 1600 Clifton Rd., Atlanta, GA 30333. Web site: <www.cdc.gov/ncidod>.

WEB SITES

"Adenoviruses." *Centers for Disease Control and Prevention, Respiratory and Enteric Viruses Branch*, August 11, 2003. Available online at <www.cdc.gov/ncidod/dvrd/revb/respiratory/eadfeat.htm> (accessed December 23, 2004).

Gompf, Sandra G., and Wendy Carter. "Adenoviruses." *eMedicine*, July 19, 2004. Available online at <www.emedicine.com/med/topic57.htm> (accessed December 23, 2004).

Maureen Haggerty
Teresa G. Odle
Stephanie Dionne Sherk

ADHD *see* **Attention deficit/Hyperactivity disorder**

Adjustment disorders

Definition

Adjustment disorder is an umbrella term for several mental states characterized by noticeable behavioral and/ or emotional symptoms. In order to be classified as an adjustment disorder, these symptoms must be shown to be a response to an identifiable stressor that has occurred within the past three months.

Description

The American Psychiatric Association (APA), in its *Diagnostic and Statistical Manual of Mental Disorders (DSM-IV)*, states that the behavioral and/or emotional signs observed must appear excessive for the stressor involved or have significant impact on the child's social and school functioning. The cause of the stress may be a single event affecting only the child, such as starting daycare or school, or an event that involves the entire **family**, such as a **divorce**. Multiple simultaneous stressors are also possible, such as starting daycare and having an abusive caretaker at the daycare or a divorce complicated by parental substance abuse. Chronic medical conditions of the child or parents, such as childhood leukemia or **cancer**, can also be a cause of stress.

Adjustment disorder, in some ways, is a hopeful diagnosis. Many mental health professionals consider it one of the less severe mental illnesses. It is normally a time-limited condition with manifestations arriving almost immediately after the appearance of the pressure-causing event and resolving within six months of the elimination of the stressor. However, the exception to this would be the duration of symptoms related to long-term stressors such as chronic illness or even the fall-out from divorce. Though these may appear within three months of the event, resolution may also take longer than six months.

Demographics

The diagnosis of adjustment disorder is a very common one for both children and teens, with a higher incidence among children than adults. Nearly one third (32%) of all adolescents are estimated to suffer from adjustment disorders during teenage years as opposed to a rate of occurrence of only 10 percent among adults. There is no identified difference between adjustment disorder rates between girls or boys. What provides the precipitating event and the symptoms manifested can vary, according to the culture in which a child lives. However, generally across all cultures, children and adolescents are more apt to experience **conduct disorder** symptoms manifested by **acting out** behaviors, while adults are more apt to experience depressive symptoms.

Causes and symptoms

Few descriptions of any mental illness specify its cause as precisely as the description of adjustment disorders does. An explicit incident or incidents causing stress for the child is always the precipitant. The cause of the stress seen in adjustment disorders can be events that for many children would be within the parameters of normal experience. These incidents are usually not the severe traumas associated with more serious stress-related illnesses such as post-traumatic stress disorder (PTSD). Though adjustment disorder precipitants are usually more "normal" events that can typically occur in the lives of most children, these events are still changes from everyday events. Especially for children, change is often the precursor of stress. For example, for a child who has always had daycare or **babysitters**, having caregivers other than his or her mother is a normal occurrence, so having a caregiver is not likely to be terribly stressful. However, a child who has never been separated from his or her mother may find going to daycare or kindergarten an extremely traumatic event.

Other examples of such childhood stressors include:

- divorce or separation of parents
- moving to a new place
- birth of a sibling
- natural disasters such as hurricanes or tornadoes
- illness of either the child or another loved one
- loss of a pet
- problems in school
- family conflict
- sexuality issues
- witnessing or being involved in an incidence of violence

Some psychological theorists and researchers consider adjustment disorders in adolescents less of an illness than a stage in establishing an identity. Adolescents may develop adjustment disorders as part of a defense mechanism meant to break their feelings of dependence on parents. This psychological maneuver may precipitate problems in families as adolescents begin seeking individuals outside the family as replacements for their parents. This behavior can be particularly destructive when these feelings of dependence are transferred to involvement with **gangs** or cults. However, it should be noted that the APA does classify adjustment disorder as a mental illness.

DSM-IV divides adjustment disorders into subgroups, based upon the symptoms manifested most prominently. These subgroups include:

- Adjustment disorder with depressed mood. This is characterized by feelings of sadness or hopelessness of varying degrees. However depression usually interferes with the child's ability to function, i.e. attending school or playing with friends. The sad feelings are sometimes accompanied by feelings of anger or frustration. It is important to note that though depressed mood adjustment disorder is less common among children, when it does occur, suicidal thoughts and even **suicide** attempts can be one of the symptoms. This symptom requires careful monitoring and the involvement of a mental health professional.

- Adjustment disorder with **anxiety**. This form typically includes agitation or nervous behavior and/or obsessive worrying. The child may feel or express **fear** of being separated from parents.

- Adjustment disorder with mixed anxiety and depressed mood. This condition combines the symptoms seen in both adjustment disorders with depression and with anxiety.

- Adjustment disorder with disturbance of conduct. Behavioral signs of this adjustment disorder include primarily actions that show a disregard for rules, laws, and the rights of others, such as picking fights, vandalism, **truancy**, and reckless driving for teens.

- Adjustment disorder with mixed disturbance of emotions and conduct. This condition combines depression and anxiety symptoms with those of disturbance of conduct.

- Unspecified adjustment disorders. This phrase is the catch-all term to describe any adjustment disorder not showing a predominance of any one set of the above-listed symptoms.

When to call the doctor

In order to even establish a diagnosis of adjustment disorder, a mental health professional needs to meet and evaluate the child or teen. As this illness can be debilitating, making it quite difficult for the child to function, that evaluation should take place as soon as possible after symptoms are observed. As noted above, suicidal ideation can be a potential facet of depressed mood adjustment disorders, and untreated adjustment disorder with depressed mood can lead to more serious mental illness, including major depression. These two facts give additional impetus to quickly involving a psychiatrist or psychologist.

Diagnosis

One of the primary measurements used in diagnosing adjustment disorder is the occurrence of the stress-causing event within the past three months. The only usual life-stressor not considered a possible cause for adjustment disorder is bereavement. Adjustment disorders are also differentiated from other reactions to stress such as PTSD by both symptoms and the relative severity of the causative event. Adjustment disorders can be caused by almost any stressor and manifest a wide variety of symptoms, while PTSD is normally associated with severe stress-causing life events and has a more specific set of symptoms.

The child being evaluated for an adjustment disorder needs to meet the following criteria in order to confirm the diagnosis:

- has had a psychological evaluation
- has experienced a psychological stressor within the past three months
- shows symptoms that appear disproportionate to the stressful event
- does not appear to be suffering from any other underlying mental or physical illness

Treatment

The most important goal in the treatment of adjustment disorder is relieving the symptoms a child or teen experiences so that they can return to the same level of functioning they possessed prior to the onset of illness. Treatment depends upon the age and overall health of the child as well as the severity of the symptoms. Medication is only ordered on an extremely limited basis or not ordered at all because psychotropic medications have been shown to have little efficacy in treating adjustment disorders. Age-appropriate cognitive-behavioral individual psychotherapy, focusing on problem solving, communication, impulse control, and stress and anger-management is a usual component of treatment. **Family therapy** to improve communication between the child or teen and parents and siblings is often helpful, as is group therapy with peers (other children also suffering from adjustment disorder).

Prognosis

Early detection and treatment of adjustment disorders in children has been shown to appreciably reduce the severity of symptoms and improve their quality of life. Most recoveries from adjustment disorder uncomplicated by other mental illness are both rapid and complete returns to the child's former level of functioning.

KEY TERMS

Anxiety—Worry or tension in response to real or imagined stress, danger, or dreaded situations. Physical reactions, such as fast pulse, sweating, trembling, fatigue, and weakness, may accompany anxiety.

Cognitive-behavioral therapy—A type of psychotherapy in which people learn to recognize and change negative and self-defeating patterns of thinking and behavior.

Defense mechanisms—Indirect strategies used to reduce anxiety rather than directly facing the issues causing the anxiety.

Depression—A mental condition in which a person feels extremely sad and loses interest in life. A person with depression may also have sleep problems and loss of appetite and may have trouble concentrating and carrying out everyday activities.

Post-traumatic stress disorder (PTSD)—A disorder that occurs among survivors of extremely stressful or traumatic events, such as a natural disaster, an airplane crash, rape, or military combat. Symptoms include anxiety, insomnia, flashbacks, and nightmares. Patients with PTSD are unnecessarily vigilant; they may experience survivor guilt, and they sometimes cannot concentrate or experience joy.

Psychological evaluation—Examination of a patient by a psychologist through interviews, observation of behavior, and psychological testing with the goal of determining personality adjustment, identifying problems, and helping to diagnose and plan treatment for a mental disorder.

Psychotherapy—Psychological counseling that seeks to determine the underlying causes of a patient's depression. The form of this counseling may be cognitive/behavioral, interpersonal, or psychodynamic.

Psychotropic drug—Any medication that has an effect on the mind, brain, behavior, perceptions, or emotions. Psychotropic medications are used to treat mental illnesses because they affect a patients moods and perceptions.

Stressor—A stimulus, or event, that provokes a stress response in an organism. Stressors can be categorized as acute or chronic, and as external or internal to the organism.

Prevention

The National Institute for Mental Health (NIMH) notes that there is no way to predict who will develop an adjustment disorder given the appearance of certain life-situation stressors. Since there is also no known way to prevent the occurrence of these stressors, prevention seems impossible. However, it is known that understanding and support from family and friends can help.

Resources

BOOKS

Bell, Susan Givens, et al. *Mosby's Pediatric Nursing Reference*, 5th ed. Kent, UK: Elsevier Science, 2003.

ORGANIZATIONS

American Academy of Child and Adolescent Psychiatry. 3615 Wisconsin Avenue, NW Washington, DC 20016–3007. Web site: <www.aacap.org>.

Federation of Families for Children's Mental Health. 1021 Prince Street, Alexandria, VA 22314–2971. Web site: <www.ffcmh.org>.

WEB SITES

"Adjustment Disorder." *National Institute of Mental Health.* Available online at <www.nimh.nih.gov.htm> (accessed October 16, 2004).

Franklin, Donald. "Adjustment Disorders." *Psychology Information Online.* Available online at <www.psychologyinfo.com> (accessed October 16, 2004).

Joan Schonbeck, R.N.

Adolescence

Definition

Sometimes referred to as teenage years, youth, or **puberty**, adolescence is the transitional period between childhood and maturity, occurring roughly between the ages of 10 and 20.

Description

The word adolescence is Latin in origin, derived from the verb *adolescere,* which means "to grow into adulthood." Adolescence is a time of moving from the immaturity of childhood into the maturity of adulthood. There is no single event or boundary line that denotes the end of childhood or the beginning of adolescence. Rather, experts think of the passage from childhood into and through adolescence as composed of a set of transitions that unfold gradually and that touch upon many aspects of the individual's behavior, development, and relationships. These transitions are biological, cognitive, social, and emotional.

Puberty

The biological transition of adolescence, or puberty, is perhaps the most observable sign that adolescence has begun. Technically, puberty refers to the period during which an individual becomes capable of sexual reproduction. More broadly speaking, however, puberty is used as a collective term to refer to all the physical changes that occur in the growing girl or boy as the individual passes from childhood into adulthood.

The timing of physical maturation varies widely. In the United States, menarche (onset of **menstruation**) typically occurs around age 12, although some youngsters start puberty when they are only eight or nine, others when they are well into their teens. The duration of puberty also varies greatly: 18 months to six years in girls and two to five years in boys.

The physical changes of puberty are triggered by hormones, chemical substances in the body that act on specific organs and tissues. In boys a major change incurred during puberty is the increased production of testosterone, a male sex hormone, while girls experience increased production of the female hormone estrogen. In both sexes, a rise in growth hormone produces the adolescent growth spurt, the pronounced increase in height and weight that marks the first half of puberty.

Perhaps the most dramatic changes of puberty involve sexuality. Internally, through the development of primary sexual characteristics, adolescents become capable of sexual reproduction. Externally, as secondary sexual characteristics appear, girls and boys begin to look like mature women and men. In boys primary and secondary sexual characteristics usually emerge in a predictable order, with rapid growth of the testes and scrotum, accompanied by the appearance of pubic hair. About a year later, when the growth spurt begins, the penis also grows larger, and pubic hair becomes coarser, thicker, and darker. Later still comes the growth of facial and body hair, and a gradual lowering of the voice. Around mid-adolescence internal changes begin making a boy capable of producing and ejaculating sperm.

In girls, sexual characteristics develop in a less regular sequence. Usually, the first sign of puberty is a slight elevation of the breasts, but sometimes this is preceded by the appearance of pubic hair. Pubic hair changes from sparse and downy to denser and coarser. Concurrent with these changes is further **breast development**. In teenage girls, internal sexual changes include maturation of the uterus, vagina, and other parts of the reproductive system. Menarche, the first menstrual period, happens relatively late in puberty. Regular ovulation and the ability to carry a baby to full term usually follow menarche by several years.

Cognitive transition

A second element of the passage through adolescence is a cognitive transition. Compared to children, adolescents think in ways that are more advanced, more efficient, and generally more complex. This is evident in five distinct areas of cognition.

First, during adolescence individuals become better able than children to think about what is possible, instead of limiting their thought to what is real. Whereas children's thinking is oriented to the here and now (i.e., to things and events that they can observe directly), adolescents are able to consider what they observe against a backdrop of what is possible—they can think hypothetically.

Second, during the passage into adolescence, individuals become better able to think about abstract ideas. For example, adolescents find it easier than children to comprehend the sorts of higher-order, abstract logic inherent in puns, proverbs, metaphors, and analogies. The adolescent's greater facility with abstract thinking also permits the application of advanced reasoning and logical processes to social and ideological matters. This is clearly seen in the adolescent's increased facility and interest in thinking about interpersonal relationships, politics, philosophy, religion, and morality—topics that involve such abstract concepts as friendship, faith, democracy, fairness, and honesty.

Third, during adolescence individuals begin thinking more often about the process of thinking itself, or metacognition. As a result, adolescents may display increased introspection and self-consciousness. Although improvements in metacognitive abilities provide important intellectual advantages, one potentially negative byproduct of these advances is the tendency for adolescents to develop a sort of egocentrism, or intense preoccupation with the self. Acute adolescent egocentrism sometimes leads teenagers to believe that others are constantly watching and evaluating them. Psychologists refer to this as the imaginary audience.

A fourth change in cognition is that thinking tends to become multidimensional, rather than limited to a single issue. Whereas children tend to think about things one aspect at a time, adolescents describe themselves and others in more differentiated and complicated terms and find it easier to look at problems from multiple perspectives. Being able to understand that people's personalities are not one-sided, or that social situations can have different interpretations, depending on one's point of view, permits the adolescent to have far more sophisticated and complicated relationships with other people.

Finally, adolescents are more likely than children to see things as relative, rather than absolute. They are more likely to question others' assertions and less likely to accept "facts" as absolute truths. This increase in relativism can be particularly exasperating to parents, who may feel that their adolescent children question everything just for the sake of argument.

Emotional transition

Adolescence is also a period of emotional transition, marked by changes in the way individuals view themselves and in their capacity to function independently. As adolescents mature intellectually and undergo cognitive changes, they come to perceive themselves in more sophisticated and differentiated ways. Compared with children, who tend to describe themselves in relatively simple, concrete terms, adolescents are more likely to employ complex, abstract, and psychological self-characterizations. As individuals' self-conceptions become more abstract and as they become more able to see themselves in psychological terms, they become more interested in understanding their own personalities and why they behave the way they do.

For most adolescents, establishing a sense of autonomy, or independence, is as important a part of the emotional transition out of childhood as is establishing a sense of identity. During adolescence, there is a movement away from the dependency typical of childhood toward the autonomy typical of adulthood. For example, older adolescents do not generally rush to their parents whenever they are upset, worried, or in need of assistance. They do not see their parents as all-knowing or all-powerful, and often have a great deal of emotional energy wrapped up in relationships outside the **family**. In addition, older adolescents are able to see and interact with their parents as people, not just as their parents.

Many parents find, for example, that they can confide in their adolescent children, something that was not possible when their children were younger, or that their adolescent children can easily sympathize with them when they have had a hard day at work.

Being independent, however, means more than merely feeling independent. It also means being able to make decisions and to select a sensible course of action. This is an especially important capability in contemporary society, where many adolescents are forced to become independent decision makers at an early age. In general, researchers find that decision-making abilities improve over the course of the adolescent years, with gains continuing well into the later years of high school.

Many parents wonder about the susceptibility of adolescents to **peer pressure**. In general, studies that contrast parent and peer influences indicate that in some situations, peers' opinions are more influential, while in others, parents' are more influential. Specifically, adolescents are more likely to conform to their peers' opinions when it comes to short-term, day-to-day, and social matters—styles of dress, tastes in music, and choices among leisure activities. This is particularly true during junior high school and the early years of high school. When it comes to long-term questions concerning educational or occupational plans, however, or values, religious beliefs, and ethical issues, teenagers are influenced in a major way by their parents.

Susceptibility to the influence of parents and peers changes during adolescence. In general, during childhood, boys and girls are highly oriented toward their parents and less so toward their peers; peer pressure during the early elementary school years is not especially strong. As they approach adolescence, however, children become somewhat less oriented toward their parents and more oriented toward their peers, and peer pressure begins to escalate. During early adolescence, conformity to parents continues to decline and conformity to peers and peer pressure continues to rise. It is not until middle adolescence that genuine behavioral independence emerges, when conformity to parents as well as peers declines.

Social transition

Accompanying the biological, cognitive, and emotional transitions of adolescence are important changes in the adolescent's social relationships. Developmentalists have spent considerable time charting the changes that take place with friends and with family members as the individual moves through the adolescent years.

One of the most noteworthy aspects of the social transition into adolescence is the increase in the amount of time individuals spend with their peers. Although relations with age-mates exist well before adolescence, during the teenage years they change in significance and structure. For example, there is a sharp increase during adolescence in the sheer amount of time individuals spend with their peers and in the relative time they spend in the company of peers versus adults. In the United States, well over half of the typical adolescent's waking hours are spent with peers, as opposed to only 15 percent with adults, including parents. Second, during adolescence, peer groups function much more often without adult supervision than they do during childhood, and more often involve friends of the opposite sex.

Finally, whereas children's peer relationships are limited mainly to pairs of friends and relatively small groups—three or four children at a time, for example—adolescence marks the emergence of larger groups of peers, or crowds. Crowds are large collectives of similarly stereotyped individuals who may or may not spend much time together. In contemporary American high schools, typical crowds are "jocks," "brains," "nerds," "populars," "druggies," and so on. In contrast to cliques, crowds are not settings for adolescents' intimate interactions or friendships, but instead serve to locate the adolescent (to himself and to others) within the social structure of the school. As well, the crowds themselves tend to form a sort of social hierarchy or map of the school, and different crowds are seen as having different degrees of status or importance.

The importance of peers during early adolescence coincides with changes in individuals' needs for intimacy. As children begin to share secrets with their friends, loyalty and commitment develop. During adolescence, the search for intimacy intensifies, and self-disclosure between best friends becomes an important pastime. Teenagers, especially girls, spend a good deal of time discussing their innermost thoughts and feelings, trying to understand one another. The discovery that they tend to think and feel the same as someone else becomes another important basis of friendship.

One of the most important social transitions that takes place in adolescence concerns the emergence of sexual and romantic relationships. In contemporary society, most young people begin dating sometime during early adolescence. Dating during adolescence can mean a variety of different things, from group activities that bring males and females together (without much actual contact between the sexes); to group dates, in which a group of boys and girls go out jointly (and spend part of the time as couples and part of the time in large groups); to casual dating as couples; and to serious involvement with a steady boyfriend or girlfriend. More adolescents have experience in mixed-sex group activities like parties or dances than dat-ing, and more have experience in dating than in having a serious boyfriend or girlfriend.

Most adolescents' first experience with sex falls into the category of "autoerotic behavior," sexual behavior that is experienced alone. The most common autoerotic activities reported by adolescents are erotic fantasies and **masturbation**. By the time most adolescents are in high school, they have had some experience with sexual behaviors in the context of a relationship. The Youth Risk Behavior Surveillance System (YRBSS), a self-reported survey of a national representative sample of high school students in grades nine to 12, indicated that in 2003, 46.7 percent of the students reported having had sex. By grade level, the rates were 32.8 percent for ninth grade, 44.1 percent for tenth grade, 53.2 percent for eleventh grade, and 61.6 percent for twelfth grade.

Common problems

Generally speaking, most young people are able to negotiate the biological, cognitive, emotional, and social transitions of adolescence successfully. Some adolescents, however, are at risk of developing certain problems, such as:

- eating disorders such as **anorexia nervosa**, bulimia, or obesity
- drug or alcohol use
- depression or suicidal ideation
- violent behavior
- anxiety, stress, or **sleep** disorders
- unsafe sexual activities

Parental concerns

Many parents dread the onset of adolescence, fearing that their child will become hostile and rebellious and begin to reject his or family. Although it is incorrect to characterize adolescence as a time when the family ceases to be important, or as a time of inherent and inevitable family conflict, adolescence is a period of significant change and reorganization in family relationships. Family relationships change most around the time of puberty, with increasing conflict and decreasing closeness occurring in many parent-adolescent relationships. Changes in the ways adolescents view family rules and regulations may contribute to increased disagreement between them and their parents. Family conflict during this stage is more likely to take the form of bickering over day-to-day issues than outright fighting. Similarly, the diminished closeness is more likely to be manifested in increased privacy on the part of the adolescent and diminished physical affection between teenagers and parents, rather than any serious

KEY TERMS

Anorexia nervosa—An eating disorder marked by an unrealistic fear of weight gain, self-starvation, and distortion of body image. It most commonly occurs in adolescent females.

Bulimia nervosa—An eating disorder characterized by binge eating and inappropriate compensatory behavior, such as vomiting, misusing laxatives, or excessive exercise.

Hormone—A chemical messenger secreted by a gland or organ and released into the bloodstream. It travels via the bloodstream to distant cells where it exerts an effect.

Menarche—The first menstrual cycle in a girl's life.

Metacognition—Awareness of the process of cognition.

loss of love or respect between parents and children. Research suggests that this distancing is temporary, and that family relationships may become less conflicted and more intimate during late adolescence.

When to call the doctor

Although changes—biologically, cognitively, emotionally, and socially—are to be expected during adolescence, certain inappropriate behaviors, drastic changes in personality or physical appearance, or abnormal sexual development may warrant a phone call to a physician or counselor. These include:

- extreme changes in weight (loss or gain) or excessive dieting
- sleep disturbances
- social withdrawal or loss of interest in activities
- sudden personality changes
- signs of alcohol or drug use
- talk or threats of suicide
- violent or aggressive behavior
- atypical (early or late) onset of puberty; in girls, failure to menstruate by the age of 16

See also Puberty.

Resources

BOOKS

Steinberg, L. *Adolescence*, 4th ed. New York: McGraw-Hill, 1996.

PERIODICALS

Blondell, Richard D., Michael B. Foster, and Kamlesh C. Dave. "Disorders of Puberty." *American Family Physician* 60 (July 1999): 209-24.

Department of Health and Human Services, Centers for Disease Control and Prevention. "Youth Risk Behavior Surveillance: United States, 2003." *Morbidity and Mortality Weekly Report* 53, no. SS-2 (May 21, 2004): 12-20.

ORGANIZATIONS

American Academy of Child & Adolescent Psychiatry. 3615 Wisconsin Ave. NW, Washington, DC 20016-3007. (202) 966-7300. Web site: <www.aacap.org>.

Society for Research on Adolescence, 3131 S. State St., Suite 302, Ann Arbor, MI 48108-1623. Web site: <www.s-r-a.org>.

WEB SITES

Paulu, Nancy. "Helping Your Child through Adolescence." *U.S. Department of Education.* August 2002 [cited December 31, 2004]. Available online at: <www.ed.gov/parents/academic/help/adolescence/index.html>.

Rutherford, Kim. "A Parent's Guide to Surviving Adolescence." *KidsHealth.* June 2002 [cited December 31, 2004]. Available online at: <kidshealth.org/parent/growth/growing/adolescence.html>.

Laurence Steinberg, Ph.D.
Stephanie Dionne Sherk

Adoption

Definition

Adoption is the practice in which an adult assumes the role of parent for a child who is not the adult's biological offspring. The process usually involves some legal paperwork.

Description

The ancient practice of adoption was a way of ensuring male heirs to childless couples in order to preserve **family** lines and religious traditions. In the 1850s the Children's Aid Society of New York City began to move dependent children out of city institutions. Between 1854 and 1904 orphan trains carried an estimated 100,000 children to families on farms in the Midwest; these children were to provide farm work in exchange for care.

Modern U.S. adoption laws are designed with the best interests of the child in mind, not the best interests of the adult who intends to adopt. Throughout most of the twentieth century, adoptions were conducted in secret, and records were often sealed to protect those involved from the social stigma of birth out of wedlock. After World War I, the advent of commercial formula facilitated raising babies without their being fed by breast. Adults were trained in parenting, and childless couples became interested in adopting. Because of the rapidly increasing interest in infant adoptions, many state laws demanded investigations of prospective adoptive parents and court approval before the adoption could be completed.

In the early 2000s, state laws on adoption vary. Adoptions can be conducted privately between individuals, between independent agencies and individuals, and between public agencies (such as a state's child protective services) and individuals. Adoptees may be infants or older children, they may be adopted singly or as sibling groups, and they may come from the local area or from other states or countries. Adoptive parents may be married couples, single men or women, or nontraditional couples. Adoptive parents may be childless or have other children.

Demographics

In the 1990s, roughly 120,000 children were adopted annually in the United States. This number remained proportionate to the U.S. population throughout that decade and into the early 2000s. During this period, nearly 10,000 children were adopted from abroad.

Types of adoptions

PUBLIC ADOPTIONS In 2000 and 2001, about 127,000 children were adopted annually in the United states. Since 1987, the number of adoptions annually has remained relatively constant, ranging from 118,000 to 127,000. Adoptions through publicly funded child welfare agencies accounts for about 40 percent of all adoptions. More than 50,000 public agency adoptions in each year (2000 and 2001) accounted for 40 percent of adoptions, up from 18 percent in 1992 for 36 states that reported public agency adoptions in that year.

PRIVATE ADOPTIONS In a private adoption, children are placed in non-relative homes through a non-profit agency licensed by the state in which it operates. In an independent or non-agency adoption, children are placed in non-relative homes directly by the birthparents or through the services of a licensed or unlicensed facili-

tator, certified medical doctor, member of the clergy, or attorney.

About 40 percent of the 127,000 adoptions in 2000 and 2001 were primarily private agency, kinship, or tribal adoptions. There were 58,420 adoptions (46%) private adoptions reported in 2000–2001. With the available data, it is not possible to separate figures within this group for types of adoptions. However, in 1992, for example, stepparent adoptions (a form of kinship adoption) alone accounted for 42 percent of all adoptions.

Informal adoptions occur when a relative or stepparent assumes permanent parental responsibilities without court involvement. However, legally recognized adoptions need a court or other government agency to award permanent custody of a child to adoptive parents.

The U.S. Department of Health and Human Services, Administration for Children and Families Interim Estimates for 2000 as of August 2002 reports 30,939 foster parent adoptions and 10,612 relative adoptions through the foster parent system. (Relatives who were also foster parents were counted as relatives.)

The U.S. Census is the principal source of data on adopted children and their families on a national level. The report for 2000 presents information on 2.1 million adopted children and 4.4 million stepchildren of householders, as estimated from the census sample, which collected from approximately one out of every six households. Together, these children represented approximately 8 percent of the 84 million sons and daughters of householders. In 2000 there were more than twice as many stepchildren as adopted children in U.S. households, with stepchildren representing 5 percent of children in the household. While these data are non-specific, it is safe to say that a significant number of the stepchildren were neither kinship nor stepparent adoptions. Since almost all adoptions by related applicants are independent, it is likely that most independent adoptions were by relatives.

TRANSRACIAL In transracial adoptions, children are placed with an adoptive family of another race. These adoptions may be through public and private agencies or be independent, but most transracial adoptions take place through the public child welfare system. The civil rights movement of the 1960s led to an increase in transracial adoptions involving black children and white parents. This practice peaked in 1971, and one year later the National Association of Black Social Workers issued a statement opposing transracial adoption. The association argued that white families were unable to foster the growth of psychological and cultural identity in black children.

An estimated 15 percent of the 36,000 adoptions of foster children in 1998 were transracial or transcultural adoptions. Many Americans continue to be troubled by these adoptions. The National Association of Black Social Workers called them a form of cultural genocide. That point aside, there are in fact not enough African American adults willing to adopt to fill the need of African American children in need of adoption.

INTRANATIONAL AND INTERNATIONAL In response to a shortage of healthy, Caucasian infants, prospective adoptive white parents started adopting children from Japan and Europe. In 2003, approximately 21,616 children were adopted through international adoption. International adoptions accounted for more than 15 percent of all U.S. adoptions, an increase from 5 percent between 1992 and 2001. This practice showed a dramatic increase between the mid-1990s and the early 2000s.

Between 1999 and 2004, international adoptions grew in popularity in the United States as more families recognized the global humanitarian need to provide homes for waiting children. Besides this pressing need, international adoptions have proven to be safe and successful, so they provide an attractive option for people who have been trying without success to adopt within the United States.

Though U.S. citizens adopted children from 106 different countries in 2001, nearly three-fourth of all children came from only five countries: China (25%), Russia (22%), South Korea (10%), Guatemala (8%), and Ukraine (6%). The Chinese government's population control policy, which penalizes families who have more than one child, and the greater value placed on male heirs in Chinese culture have led many families to abandon female Chinese infants. These babies constituted a bountiful source of adoption candidates for American families. In 2003, U.S. interest in adopting from Kazakhstan also grew as many U.S. families reported a fast, smooth adoption experience there. Americans adopt children from Peru, Colombia, El Salvador, Mexico, and the Philippines. Some adoptions come from Vietnam. Adoption from India, however, is difficult for non-Indian parents. In 2002, Cambodia and Romania stopped international adoptions.

SINGLE PARENT According to the United States Department of Health and Human Services, 33 percent of adoptions from **foster care** are by single parents. Most of these single parents are women. Single women are more likely to adopt an older child than an infant. Single men adopted some children, and unmarried couples adopted some children in the same period. As one-parent households increase in number and become more acceptable, adoptions in these households also become more common. More than one half of African-American children, nearly one third of Hispanic children, and one fifth of Caucasian children live with a single parent because of **divorce** and unmarried mothers. This prevalence gives adoption agencies a more open-minded approach toward single parent adoptions. Also, the issue of personal finances and single income families has become less important since adoption subsidies are available nationwide.

Treatment of adoption information

Through most of the nineteenth century and into the twentieth century, adoptions were often informal and unofficial. Agencies, counselors, doctors, and private attorneys were generally not involved. If a young woman was pregnant out-of-wedlock, the baby's adoption might be arranged by the mother's parents with the help of the head of her extended family. Some family member or close friend took in the child. The child might refer to the adoptive parents as aunt and uncle, but people in the immediate social circle might know the child's biological parent.

In the early twentieth century, as governmental and independent agencies became involved with adoption, information about the individuals involved tended to be restricted. Decisions about who could adopt which baby were often made solely by agency personnel. In closed adoptions, mothers gave up parental rights immediately after birth. They did not see or hold their babies.

In the later twentieth century and in the early 2000s, information about adoptions is open to the participants. The birth mother may room in with the baby in the hospital. The birth mother and adoptive parents may have a contract before delivery and a formal or informal agreement about shared responsibility for the baby. The birth parent may have visitation rights after adoption takes place. This arrangement often occurs between a teenage birth parent and grandparents who become the legal parents through adoption. Open adoptions may also take place between surrogate and adopting parents.

Fraud by adoption agencies

Adoption fraud may involve the misrepresentation and fraudulent concealment of a child's pre-adoption history. Some state laws require full disclosure in good faith of information pertaining to the child's health. This information helps adopting parents anticipate any special needs the child may have. Full disclosure by

Parents with their adopted children. *(Photograph by John Hart. AP/Wide World Photos.)*

the adoption agency facilitates the child's receiving appropriate intervention and treatment as needed.

Parental concerns

Adoptions are expensive. Most of the financial expenses are attorney or court fees, and the cost of preparing the home for a new child. Expense results from parents' lost wages for time off to meet with social agencies or to have their homes inspected. Adoptions are emotionally taxing as well. The adoptive parents deal with uncertainty, and if there are other children in the household already, the parents deal with those children's responses and feelings as everyone involved prepares for the possibility of a new family member. Time must be spent with a social worker whose task it is to evaluate the home.

In some cases, the adoptive child is placed in the adoptive home before the legal termination of parental rights has freed the child for adoption. In these cases, child protective services are fairly certain the courts will decide in favor of the adoptive placement, but this tentative situation imposes a potentially uncomfortable arrangement on the adoptive family and their household.

Adoption is challenging for the adopting parents, for other children if they have them, and for the adopted child. Soon after the new child arrives, the adoptive parents should schedule a medical exam. Adopted children from other countries may be at greater risk for certain illnesses or conditions related to possible substandard care they received before their arrival in their new home. Medical evaluation may identify special needs the adoptive parents can then address.

Adopted children should be told early that they are adopted. Knowing from early childhood of the adoption is better for children than learning about it later. Three-year-old children can understand the story of their adoption.

Adolescents may have questions about identity that are connected to their not knowing their biological parents. It is common for them to spend time tracing records and trying to find their birth parents. This activity does not

KEY TERMS

Abandonment—Legally, the refusal to provide adequate financial support for one's dependent child; the failure to maintain a parental relationship with one's dependent child.

Adoptee—A person who has been adopted.

Adoption subsidy—A short-term or long-term financial payment, either in the form of cash or services, to help an adoptive family provide for the on-going care of an adopted child. A subsidy can be medical insurance for the child, counseling services for the family, respite care for the adoptive parents; or a monthly cash allowance to help cover other extraordinary expenses and services associated with the adoption.

Birth parents—The biological parents of a child.

Custody—The care, control, and maintenance of a child, which in abuse and neglect cases can be awarded by the court to an agency or in divorce to

parents. Foster parents do not have legal custody of the children who are in their care.

Disclosure—Release of information.

Relinquishment—Giving up parental rights to a child, so someone else can adopt the child.

Severance of parental rights—The end of parental rights; the involuntarily removal of parental rights of a parent that has abandoned a child; has without just cause failed to support a child; has neglected or abused a child or has stood by and allowed others to neglect or abuse a child; or who because of extended incarceration in prison, is unavailable to parent or nurture the child. Once the parental rights of both parents of a child are removed the child will become available for adoption by another family.

Trans-racial adoptions—Adoption in which a family of one race adopts a child of another race.

necessarily constitute a rejection of the adopting parents. Children seek out their birth parents because they need information about themselves in order to shape a sense of who they are and where they belong in the world.

Sometimes the adopted child will feel loss, **abandonment**, and resentment toward the birth parent and the adopting parents. For a period, the adoptive family may not be able to compensate the child who faces the loss of the birth family.

Parenting the adopted child

Adopting parents who intuitively understand the sense of loss and **separation anxiety** experienced by an adopted child and communicate with their child about the adoption can develop closeness. Even tiny infants have a bond with their mother before birth. A child knows his mother and instinctively wants to be with her. Even babies may experience loss of the natural mother and a sense of confusion regarding the stranger who assumes the role of mother. Parental separation from the child can also be traumatic. The adoptive parents need to be attuned to the child's emotional responses to loss.

In the absence of genetic markers (facial features, gestures, body language, basic personality, interests, and talents) both adoptive parents and the adopted child must learn how to communicate. The adopted child may have trouble fitting into the adoptive family when genetic traits are not mirrored or reflected.

There are many ways for adoptive parents to help an older child deal with sorrow, anger, **anxiety**, and low **self-esteem** caused by separation from the biological parents:

- Celebrate birthdays a week or so before the birthday, if the birthday is really the date of separation from the natural parent.

- Take extra time to prepare the child for changes in routine, a new school, and family life.

- Listen more and talk less to the adopted child.

- Respond to painful feelings with support, rather than by discounting them in any way.

- Respect and value the differences between the child and other members of the family.

- Encourage the child's talents and interests, even if they are different from the adoptive family.

Parenting an adopted child is parenting plus. But with intuition, information, understanding, and empathy, it can be a rewarding experience.

Resources

BOOKS

Adamec, Christine. *The Complete Idiot's Guide to Adoption.* East Rutherford, NJ: Penguin Group, 2005.

Rothman, Barbara Katz. *Weaving a Family: Untangling Race and Adoption.* Boston, MA: Beacon Press, 2005.

Volkman, Toby Alice. *Cultures of Transnational Adoption.* Durham, NC: Duke University Press, 2005.

Wolfe, Jaymie Stuart. *The Call to Adoption: Making Your Child Your Own.* Boston, MA: Pauline Books & Media, 2005.

WEB SITES

Craft, Carrie. "Developmental Grieving." Available online at <adoption.about.com/cs/legalissues/a/Holiday_strugl_p.htm> (accessed December 12, 2004).

—— "Teaching Foster/Adoptive Children How to Respond to Common Questions." Available online at <adoption.about.com/od/fostering/a/coverstories_p.htm> (accessed December 12, 2004).

Rapport, Bruce M. "Open Adoption History." *Independent Adoption Center (IAC).* Available online at <www.adoptionhistory.org/> (accessed December 12, 2004).

Schlossberg, Patty D. "Helping Your Older Child Adjust." Available online at <adoption.about.com/cs/olderchildren/a/adjust_p.htm> (accessed December 12, 2004).

U.S. Department of Health and Human Services, Administration for Children and Families. Available online at <www.acf.hhs.gov/programs/cb> (accessed December 16, 2004).

Aliene S. Linwood, R.N., DPA, FACHE

Adrenoleukodystrophy *see* **Peroxisomal disorders**

AFP test *see* **Alpha-fetoprotein test**

Aggressive behavior

Definition

Aggressive behavior is reactionary and impulsive behavior that often results in breaking household rules or the law; aggressive behavior is violent and unpredictable.

Description

Aggression can a problem for children with both normal development and those with psychosocial disturbances. Aggression constitutes intended harm to another individual, even if the attempt to harm fails (such as a bullet fired from a gun that misses its human target). There is no single theory about the causes of aggressive behavior in humans. Some believe aggression is innate or instinctive. Social theorists suggest the breakdown in commonly shared values, changes in traditional **family** patterns of child-rearing, and social isolation lead to increasing aggression in children, adolescents, and adults. Aggression in children correlates with family unemployment, strife, criminality, and psychiatric disorders.

Differences exist between levels of aggression in boys and girls in the same families. Boys are almost always more aggressive than girls. Larger children are more aggressive than smaller ones. Active and intrusive children are also more aggressive than passive or reserved ones.

Aggressive behavior may be intentional or unintentional. Many hyperactive, clumsy children are accidentally aggressive, but their intentions are compassionate. Careful medical evaluation and diagnostic assessments distinguish between intentional behaviors and the unintentional behaviors of emotionally disturbed children.

Children in all age groups learn that aggressive behavior is a powerful way to communicate their wishes or deal with their likes and dislikes.

Infancy

Infants are aggressive when they are hungry, uncomfortable, fearful, angry, or in **pain**. Parents can tell what babies need by the loudness and pitch of crying and the flailing of arms and legs. Crying is an infant's defense, the way to communicate feelings and needs.

Toddlers

Children between two and four years of age show aggressive outbursts such as temper **tantrums** and hurting others or damaging **toys** and furniture because they are frustrated. Usually the aggression in this age group is expressed toward parents as a way to get their compliance with the child's wishes. Verbal aggression increases as vocabulary increases.

Preschool

Children between four and five years of age can be aggressive toward their siblings and peers. Because of greater social interaction, children need to learn the differences between real and imaginary insults, as well as the difference between standing up for their rights and attacking in anger.

School-age and adolescence

Aggressive boys between three to six years of age are likely to carry their behavior style into **adolescence**. In extreme cases, they may show aggression by purse snatching, muggings, or robbery, or in less overt ways by persistent **truancy**, **lying**, and vandalism. Girls younger than six years of age who have aggressive styles toward their peers do not tend to continue being aggressive when they are older, and their earlier aggression does not correlate with adult competitiveness.

Common problems

Frustration is a response to conditions that keep children from achieving goals important to **self-esteem**. Frustration and aggression are closely associated. If children learn that being aggressive when frustrated is tolerated or gives them special treatment, the behavior is reinforced and may be repeated. Aggression may be a way for children to face obstacles or solve problems. It is important not to attribute malice to children who are responding to **anxiety**, feelings of incompetence, or a sense of low self-esteem.

Through the media, including film, the U.S. culture reinforces violence and aggressive behavior in children. Police brutality, crime-based television programs, and governmental reliance on military aggression to solve political and economic differences all create a climate in which violence is presented to children as a legitimate solution to problems.

Violent behavior in children and adolescents

CULTURAL VIOLENCE Violence includes a wide range of behaviors: explosive temper tantrums, physical aggression, fighting, and threats or attempts to hurt others (including homicidal thoughts). Violent behaviors also include the use of weapons, cruelty toward animals, setting fires, and other intentional forms of destruction of property.

PREDISPOSITION TO VIOLENCE Some children are supersensitive, easily offended, and quick to anger. Many children are tense and unusually active, even as infants. They are often more difficult to soothe and settle as babies. Beginning in the **preschool** years, they are violent toward other children, adults, and even animals. They often lash out suddenly, sometimes for no obvious reason. When they hurt someone in their anger, they tend not to be sorry and may tend not to take responsibility for their actions. Instead, they blame others for their own actions. Parent should give this behavior serious attention and take measures to correct it.

Children may go through a brief period of aggressive behavior if they are worried, tired, or stressed. If the behavior continues for more than a few weeks, parents should talk to the pediatrician. If it becomes a daily pattern for more than three to six months, it could be a serious problem.

Factors that increase risk of violent behavior

Parents and teachers should be careful not to play down aggressive behaviors in children. In fact, certain factors put some children at risk for developing violent behaviors as adults. These factors include the following:

• being the victim of physical and sexual abuse

• exposure to violence in the home and community

• exposure to violence in media (TV, movies)

• use of drugs and alcohol

• presence of firearms in home

• combination of stressful family socioeconomic factors (poverty, severe deprivation, marital breakup, single parenting, unemployment, loss of support from extended family)

• brain injury

Parents can teach children nonviolence by controlling their own tempers. If parents express anger in quiet, assertive ways, children may follow their parent's example. Children need to understand when they have done something wrong so they can learn to take responsibility for their actions and learn ways to make amends. Responsible parenting does not to tolerate violence or use it in any way.

Violence prevention strategies

Efforts should be directed at dramatically decreasing the exposure of children and adolescents to violence in the home, community, and through the media. Clearly, violence leads to violence. Parents can use the following strategies to reduce or prevent violent behavior:

• prevent **child abuse** in the home

• provide sex education and parenting programs for adolescents

• provide early intervention programs for violent youngsters

• monitor children's TV programs, videos, and movies

The most important step that parents can take with aggressive children is to set firm, consistent limits and be sure that everyone caring for the children acts in accord with the parents' rules and expectations.

Parents should know the importance of helping children find ways to deal with anger without resorting to violence. Children can learn to say no to their peers, and they can learn how to settle differences with words instead of physical aggression. When children control their violent impulses, they should be praised.

KEY TERMS

Anxiety—Worry or tension in response to real or imagined stress, danger, or dreaded situations. Physical reactions, such as fast pulse, sweating, trembling, fatigue, and weakness, may accompany anxiety.

Consequences—Events that occur immediately after the target behavior.

Misbehavior—Behavior outside the norms of acceptance within the group.

Time-out—A discipline strategy that entails briefly isolating a disruptive child in order to interrupt and avoid reinforcement of negative behavior.

Parental concerns

All children have feelings of anger and aggression. Children need to learn positive ways to express these feelings and to negotiate for what they want while maintaining respect for others. Parents can help their children develop judgment, self discipline, and the other tools children need to express feelings in more acceptable ways and to live with others in a safe way.

Understanding the aggressive child

When children lose their sense of connection to others, they may feel tense, frightened, or isolated. These are the times when they may unintentionally lash out at other children, even children to whom they are close. Parents should be careful not to let children think aggression is acceptable.

When children are overcome with feelings of isolation or despair, they may run for the nearest safe person and begin to cry. They immediately release the terrible feelings, trusting that they are safe from danger and criticism. Effective parents listen and allow the child to vent without becoming alarmed.

Disciplining aggressive behavior

Parents can control the aggressive child in various ways. They should intervene quickly but calmly to interrupt the aggression and prevent the their child from hurting another child. Younger children may need a time-out to calm down and before rejoining a group. Simple rules about appropriate behavior are easier for a child to understand than lengthy explanations. Parents can affirm feelings while stressing that all feelings cannot be acted upon.

Parents can reach older children with eye contact, a stern voice, and physical contact. Older children can be told that they need to learn a better way to handle conflicts. Parents can suggest that, for instance, the child ask an adult to intervene before lashing out at a classmate. Any disciplinary measures should be explained as a simple consequence to the child's aggression.

When parents arrive after conflict occurs, it may be useful to listen to the child's explanation. Having a parent listen can encourage the child to develop trust in the parent.

Parents should not expect the aggressive child to be reasonable when he or she is upset. The child may need time to calm down. Sometimes the child may feel trapped and may need adult support. Parents should encourage the aggressive child to come to them when they are upset, hopefully before violence occurs.

Resources

BOOKS

Davis, Jean Q. *Anger, Aggression, and Adolescents*. New York: Pantheon Books, 2004.

Delfos, Martine F. *Anxiety, ADHD, Depression, and Aggression in Childhood: Guidelines for Diagnostics and Treatment*. Herndon, VA: Jessica Kingsley Publishers, 2003.

Valkenburg, Pattie M. *Children's Responses to the Screen: A Media Psychological Approach*. Mahwah, NJ: Lawrence Erlbaum Associates, 2004.

ORGANIZATIONS

Parents Leadership Institute. PO Box 1279, Palo Alto, CA 94302. Web site: <www.parentleaders.org>.

WEB SITES

"Understanding Violent Behavior in Children and Adolescents." *American Academy of Child and Adolescent Psychiatry*, March 2001. Available online at <www.aacap.org/publications/factsfam/behavior.htm> (accessed December 12, 2004).

Aliene S. Linwood, RN, DPA, FACHE

AIDS *see* HIV infection and AIDS

Albinism

Definition

Albinism is an inherited condition that is present at birth. It is characterized by a lack of melanin, the pigment that normally gives color to the skin, hair, and eyes. Many types of albinism exist, all of which involve lack of pigment in varying degrees. The condition, which is found in all races, may be accompanied by eye problems and may ultimately lead to skin **cancer**.

Description

The most common type of albinism is oculocutaneous albinism, which affects the eyes, hair, and skin. In its most severe form, hair and skin remain completely white throughout life. People with a less severe form are born with white hair and skin that turn slightly darker as they age. Everyone with oculocutaneous albinism experiences abnormal flickering eye movements (**nystagmus**) and sensitivity to bright light. There may be other eye problems as well, including poor vision and crossed or "lazy" eyes (**strabismus**).

The second most common type of the condition is known as ocular albinism, in which only the eyes lack color; skin and hair are normal. Some types of ocular albinism cause more problems, especially eye problems, than others.

Albinism is also referred to as hypopigmentation.

Demographics

Albinism is a rare disorder found in fewer than five people per 100,000 in the United States and Europe. Although albinism can affect all races, other parts of the world have a much higher rate; for example, albinism is found in about 20 out of every 100,000 people in southern Nigeria. The parents of most children with albinism have normal hair and eye color for their ethnic background and do not have a **family** history of albinism.

Causes and symptoms

Albinism is an inherited problem caused by an alteration in one or more of the genes that are responsible for directing the eyes and skin to produce or distribute melanin, which is a photoprotective pigment that absorbs ultraviolet (UV) light coming from the sun so that the skin is not damaged. Sun exposure normally produces a tan, which is an increase in melanin pigment in the skin. Many people with albinism do not have melanin pigment in their skin, do not tan with exposure to the sun, and as a result develop **sunburn**. Over time, people with albinism may develop skin cancers if they do not adequately protect their skin from sun exposure.

Melanin is also important in the eyes and brain, but it is not known what role melanin plays in those areas.

Parts of the retina do not develop correctly if melanin pigment is not present during development. Also nerve connections between the retina and brain are altered if melanin is not present in the retina during development.

Albinism is a autosomal recessive disease, which means that a person must have two copies of the defective gene to exhibit symptoms of the disease. The child therefore inherits one defective gene responsible for making melanin from each parents. Because the task of making melanin is complex, there are many different types of albinism, involving a number of different genes.

It is also possible to inherit one normal gene and one albinism gene. In this case, the one normal gene provides enough information to make some pigment, and the child has normal skin and eye color. The child has one gene for albinism. About one in 70 people are albinism carriers, with one defective gene but no symptoms; they have a 50 percent chance of passing the albinism gene to their child. However, if both parents are carriers with one defective gene each, they have a one in four chance of passing on both copies of the defective gene to the child, who will have albinism. There is also a type of ocular albinism that is carried on the X chromosome and occurs almost exclusively in males because they have only one X chromosome and, therefore, no other gene for the trait to override the defective one.

People with albinism may experience a variety of eye problems, including one or more of the following:

- They may be very far-sighted or near-sighted and may have other defects in the curvature of the lens of the eye (astigmatism) that cause images to appear unfocused.

- They may have a constant, involuntary movement of the eyeball called nystagmus.

- They may have problems in coordinating the eyes in fixing and tracking objects (strabismus), which may lead to an appearance of having "crossed eyes" at times.

- They may have reduced depth perception due to altered nerve connections from the retina to the brain.

- Their eyes may be very sensitive to light (photophobia) because their irises allow stray light to enter their eyes. It is a common misconception that people with albinism should not go outside on sunny days, but wearing sunglasses can make it possible to go outside quite comfortably.

One of the myths about albinism is that it causes people to have pink or red eyes. In fact, people with

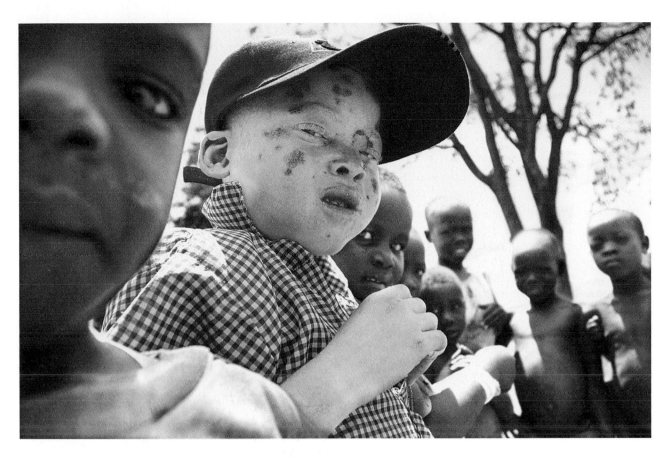

African child with albinism surrounded by normally pigmented friends. *(© Silvia Morara/Corbis.)*

albinism can have irises varying from light gray or blue to brown. (The iris is the colored portion of the eye that controls the size of the pupil, the opening that lets light into the eye.) If people with albinism seem to have reddish eyes, it is because light is being reflected from the back of the eye (retina) in much the same way as happens when people are photographed with an electronic flash. In addition, albinism does not cause blindness.

In addition to characteristically light skin and eye problems, people with a rare form of albinism called Hermansky-Pudlak syndrome (HPS) also have a greater tendency to have bleeding disorders, inflammation of the large bowel (colitis), lung (pulmonary) disease, and kidney (renal) problems.

When to call the doctor

The doctor should be called when a person with albinism exhibits symptoms such as photophobia that cause discomfort. Also the doctor should be consulted if there are any skin changes that might be an early sign of skin cancer.

The parent of a child with albinism should also call the doctor if the child bruises easily or has unusual bleeding, such as repeated nosebleeds or bloody **diarrhea**. The child may have the rare Hermansky-Pudlak syndrome, which requires additional medical care.

Diagnosis

It is not always easy to diagnose the exact type of albinism a person has. The specific type is sometimes determined by developing a thorough family history and by examining the patient and several close relatives. In the early 2000s, a blood test has been developed that can identify carriers of the gene for some types of albinism; a similar test during **amniocentesis** can diagnose some types of albinism in an unborn child. A chorionic villus sampling test during the fifth week of pregnancy may also reveal some types of albinism.

There are also two tests available that can identify two types of the condition. The hairbulb pigmentation test is used to identify carriers by incubating a piece of the person's hair in a solution of tyrosine, a substance in

KEY TERMS

Amino acid—An organic compound composed of both an amino group and an acidic carboxyl group. Amino acids are the basic building blocks of proteins. There are 20 types of amino acids (eight are "essential amino acids" which the body cannot make and must therefore be obtained from food).

Astigmatism—An eye condition in which the cornea doesn't focus light properly on the retina, resulting in a blurred image.

Carrier—A person who possesses a gene for an abnormal trait without showing signs of the disorder. The person may pass the abnormal gene on to offspring. Also refers to a person who has a particular disease agent present within his/her body, and can pass this agent on to others, but who displays no symptoms of infection.

DNA—Deoxyribonucleic acid; the genetic material in cells that holds the inherited instructions for growth, development, and cellular functioning.

DOPA—The common name for a natural chemical (3,4-dihydroxyphenylalanine) made by the body during the process of making melanin.

Enzyme—A protein that catalyzes a biochemical reaction without changing its own structure or function.

Gene—A building block of inheritance, which contains the instructions for the production of a particular protein, and is made up of a molecular sequence found on a section of DNA. Each gene is found on a precise location on a chromosome.

Hairbulb—The root of a strand of hair from which growth and coloration of the hair develops.

Hermansky-Pudlak syndrome—A rare type of albinism, most common in the Puerto Rican community, which can cause pigment changes, lung disease, intestinal disorders, and blood disorders.

Melanin—A pigment that creates hair, skin, and eye color. Melanin also protects the body by absorbing ultraviolet light.

Nystagmus—An involuntary, rhythmic movement of the eyes.

Strabismus—A disorder in which the eyes do not point in the same direction. Also called squint.

Tyrosinase—An enzyme in a pigment cell which helps change tyrosine to dopa during the process of making melanin.

Tyrosine—An amino acid synthesized by the body from the essential amino acid phenylalanine. It is used by the body to make melanin and several hormones, including epinephrine and thyroxin.

---

food which the body uses to make melanin. If the hair turns dark, it means the hair is making melanin (a positive test); light hair means there is no melanin. This test is the source of the names of two types of albinism: "ty-pos" and "ty-neg."

The tyrosinase test is more precise than the hairbulb pigmentation test. It measures the rate at which hair converts the amino acid tyrosine into another chemical (3,4-dihydroxyphenylalanine, or DOPA), which is then made into pigment. The hair converts tyrosine with the help of an enzyme called tyrosinase. In some types of albinism, a genetic defect in tyrosinase means that the amino acid tyrosine cannot be converted by tyrosinase into melanin.

Treatment

There is no treatment that can replace the lack of melanin that causes the symptoms of albinism. In addition, doctors can only treat, but not cure, the eye problems that often accompany the lack of skin color.

Glasses or corrective lenses and low vision aids, for example, magnifiers, monoculars (handheld telescopes used with only one eye), or bioptics (glasses with small telescopic lenses mounted in the standard lenses) can improve vision but usually cannot correct vision to 20/20. The lenses can be tinted to ease **pain** from too much sunlight. For reading, children with albinism may or may not need materials with large print text, depending on the severity of their vision problems. There is no cure for involuntary eye movements (nystagmus), and treatments for focusing problems (surgery or **contact lenses**) are not effective in all cases.

Crossed eyes (strabismus) can be treated during infancy by using eye patches, surgery, or medicine injections. Treatment may improve the appearance of the eye, but it can do nothing to cure the underlying condition.

Patients with albinism should avoid excessive exposure to the sun, especially between 10 a.m. and 2 p.m., and should wear long sleeves and pants if possible. If exposure cannot be avoided, they should use a UVA-UVB sunblock with an SPF rating at least 30.

Most children with albinism function satisfactorily in a mainstream classroom as long as the school provides classroom assistance for their vision needs. The child's eye doctor, the classroom teacher, and the school's vision resource teacher should work as a team with the parents to determine what classroom modifications and vision aids will best help the child. The local school district or the state agency for the blind should be contacted during the child's infancy or during **preschool** years to determine what assistive services might be available for the child. Early intervention allows parents and teachers to develop an educational plan for the child.

Prognosis

In the United States, people with this condition can expect to have a normal lifespan. However, one of the greatest health hazards for people with albinism is excessive exposure to sun without protection, which may lead to skin cancer. Wearing opaque clothes and sunscreen with at least an SPF rating of 30, people with albinism can safely work and **play** outdoors even during the summer.

Prevention

Genetic counseling should be considered for individuals with a family history of albinism.

Parental concerns

Children with albinism may experience complex social problems because of their unusual appearance, especially when a member of a normally dark-skinned ethnic group has albinism. The eyes of children with albinism may move rapidly and not focus together, and the children may have to squint, tilt their heads, and hold reading materials close in order to see. These behaviors may result in the child being treated badly by peers. Modifications made for the children in the classroom and in physical education classes to compensate for low vision may make them feel even more isolated. Parents often feel that teasing and name-calling, insensitivity, and ignorance are the greatest challenges that they face with regards to their child's albinism. The support and love of these families of children with albinism are essential to helping the children understand and accept themselves. Support groups for the children and for their families, as well as counseling, may be useful for developing means of coping with the social effects of albinism.

Resources

BOOKS

Albinism: A Medical Dictionary, Bibliography, and Annotated Research Guide to Internet References. San Diego, CA: Icon Health Publications, 2003.

Edwards, Lee G. *Too White to Be Black and Too Black to Be White: Living with Albinism.* Bloomington, IN: AuthorHouse, 2001.

Mitchell, Elizabeth Tromsness. *Albinism in the Family: Albinismo en la Familia.* Bloomington, IN: AuthorHouse, 2004.

ORGANIZATIONS

Albinism World Alliance. Web site: <www.albinism.org/awa.html>.

American Foundation for the Blind. 11 Penn Plaza, Suite 300 New York, NY 10001. Web site: <www.afb.org/>.

Hermansky-Pudlak Syndrome Network Inc. One South Road, Oyster Bay, NY 11771–1905. Web site: <www.hpsnetwork.org/HTML/frame.html>.

National Organization for Albinism and Hypopigmentation (NOAH). PO Box 959, East Hampstead, NH 03826–0959. Web site: <www.albinism.org>.

WEB SITES

King, Richard A., et al. "Facts about Albinism." *International Albinism Center, University of Minnesota.* Available online at <www.cbc.umn.edu/iac/facts.htm> (accessed November 8, 2004)

Judith L. Sims
Carol A. Turkington

Alcoholism

Definition

Alcoholism, or alcohol dependence, is described in the *Diagnostic and Statistical Manual of Mental Disorders (DSM-IV)* as "A maladaptive pattern of alcohol use, leading to clinically significant impairment or distress."

That maladaptive pattern is manifested, according to the *DSM-IV*, by the following behaviors occurring any time within one 12-month period:

• tolerance for alcohol

• withdrawal from alcohol

- alcohol taken in larger amounts and over a longer period of time than was intended

- persistent desire or unsuccessful efforts to cut down or control alcohol use

- much time spent in activities necessary to obtaining alcohol

- various important activities, for example, in socializing or at work, are given up or reduced because of alcohol use

- alcohol use continued regardless of the pattern of physical or psychological problems that it causes or worsens

Alcohol abuse has the same definition but is manifested by one (or more) of the following behaviors occurring within the same 12-month period:

- repeated alcohol use leading to failure to fulfill major role obligations at work, school, or home

- repeated alcohol use in situations in which it is physically hazardous

- repeated alcohol-related legal problems

- persistent alcohol use despite its causing social and interpersonal problems or exacerbating them

This definition and the criteria established by *DSM-IV* apply to both adults and children. The American Academy of Pediatrics (AAP) states that the pattern of use and abuse of alcohol in children and adolescents is not observably different from what is manifested in young people using marijuana or cocaine.

Description

The AAP divides the progression into childhood alcoholism into three stages:

- Stage 1: Experimentation with alcohol. Normally there is no change noted in physical status or behavior, and the drinking usually occurs only on weekends during social occasions with peers, making it the least detectable of the three. **Peer pressure** to use alcohol "just for fun."

- Stage 2: Actively trying to obtain alcohol. Alcohol use happens during the week to provide relief when stress is felt or to "feel good" when depressed.

- Stage 3: Preoccupation with alcohol. The child or adolescent has nearly lost the capacity for controlling alcohol use. Setting limits results in withdrawal symptoms, including depression, moodiness, or irritability. Severe withdrawal can result in serious medical problems, including delirium tremens.

Demographics

Prevalence and severity of the problem

Based on findings mostly coming from the 1990s, the National Council on Alcohol and Drug Dependence (NCAAD) cites the following in its fact sheet *Youth, Alcohol and Other Drugs*:

- Approximately 10.4 million Americans ages 12 to 20 have at least one drink per month. One fifth of these (2.1 million) are heavy drinkers who have five or more drinks on a minimum of five different occasions. More than half of these (6.8 million) are considered binge drinkers who have five or more drinks on a single occasion.

- Eighty percent of all high school seniors have tried alcohol.

- Eight percent of eighth graders, 24 percent of tenth graders, and 32 percent of high school seniors have been intoxicated from alcohol in the past month.

- Children who begin **smoking** tobacco before the age of 13 are significantly more at risk for alcohol problems.

- Among high school seniors, alcohol use is more prevalent among Caucasian and Hispanic students than among African American students.

- Junior, middle, and senior high school students consume 35 percent of all wine coolers sold in the United States as well as 1.1 billion cans of beer.

- A Southern Illinois University study showed that students with overall grades of D or F drank on average three times as much alcohol as students with overall grades of A.

- A United States Department of Justice survey showed that nearly one third of children below the age of 18 incarcerated in juvenile institutions are under the influence of alcohol at the time of their arrest.

- More than half (56%) of children and teens in grades five through 12 report that alcohol advertising encourages them to drink.

- Thirty percent of children in grades four through six state that they have received pressure from peers to drink beer.

- Two thirds of teenagers who drink report that they are able to make their own alcohol purchases.

- The total cost of alcohol use by young people, including automobile crashes, violent crime, alcohol **poisoning**, **burns**, drowning, **suicide** attempts, and **fetal alcohol syndrome** is more than 58 billion dollars each year.

- Eighty percent of teenagers do not know that a 12-ounce can of beer has the same amount of alcohol as a shot of whiskey or a five-ounce glass of wine.

Causes and symptoms

In their article "Early Identification and Intervention for Adolescent Alcohol Use," Mark Werner and Hoover Adjer Jr., both fellows at the American Academy of Pediatrics (AAP), state that attitudes regarding alcohol use are developed quite early in life, usually by the age of eight. Parental attitudes regarding alcohol and behaviors related to alcohol use have a major impact on how children and young adults view drinking alcohol. Not every child or teen who experiments with alcohol becomes an alcoholic, but NCADD studies have shown that children who drink before the age of 15 are four times more likely to become alcoholic than those who begin drinking after the age of 21. Some evidence supports a genetic component to this disease. Parents who are themselves alcoholic or problem drinkers are more likely to have children who develop alcohol dependence. Statistically, one in five children who have an alcoholic parent becomes an alcoholic, too.

Physical symptoms seen in adult alcoholics, such as gastritis, pancreatitis, hepatitis, or even cirrhosis, usually are absent in childhood alcoholics. Such physical damage normally takes longer to develop and is more typical of long-term adult alcoholics. More often in potential childhood alcoholics, behavioral symptoms provide the most significant clues.

These behavioral warning signs, according to the AAP, typically include the following:

- decline in school functioning, decreased attendance, poorer grades, and/or general deterioration in social functioning in school
- increased isolation outside school; rejection of usual long-term friendships in favor of new or different friends
- frequent arguments or less communication with **family** members; being more secretive
- marked changes in grooming and clothing styles
- noticeable increase in unexplained injuries and fights
- running away from home
- depressive symptoms such as weight loss, **sleep** problems, lethargy, feelings of hopelessness, mood swings, suicidal feelings, or suicide attempts
- evidence of the presence of risk-taking behaviors such as either driving while under the influence of alcohol or driving with others who are intoxicated, engaging in violent behaviors such as fights, or participating in unsafe sex

When to call the doctor

It is worth noting that these behavioral warning flags can appear in non-alcoholic children or teens and also are usually not observed before the second or third stage of childhood alcoholism. Parents observing some or all of these warning signs need professional help to both clarify diagnosis and plan treatment. Individual and family denial is considered a large portion of any alcohol problem. Parents need objectivity and open and honest communication with their children in order to deal effectively with childhood alcoholism and to know when to seek help.

Diagnosis

As noted, behavioral symptoms help to determine the diagnosis, but not usually until the second and third stage of the disease. There are assessments available that can provide both earlier identification and intervention for childhood alcoholism.

Diagnostic assessments for alcoholism, according to the APA, include:

- CAGE, a mnemonic that points to four key questions by highlighting key words: "Cut down," "Annoyed," "Guilty," and "Early" (see below)
- Alcohol Use Disorders Inventory Test (AUDIT)
- Personal Experience Screening Questionnaire (PESQ)
- Problem Oriented Screening Instrument for Teenagers (POSIT)

CAGE is an assessment guide containing the following four questions:

- C: Have you ever felt the need to *cut down* on your drinking?
- A: Do you get *annoyed* at criticism by others about your drinking?
- G: Have you ever felt *guilty* about your drinking or something you have done while drinking?
- E: Have you ever felt the need for a drink *early* in the morning?

Treatment

Once assessment has led to a diagnosed problem with alcohol, its severity determines the treatment needed. In "Early Identification and Intervention for Adolescent Alcohol Use," Werner and Adjer divide problem teen drinkers into three groups:

- The first category includes those teens who are using alcohol occasionally but still doing well emotionally and developmentally and who are not drinking and driving. The treatment objectives for this group are to encourage abstinence and re-enforce **safety** by fostering the continuation of not driving while drinking and not driving with others who are drinking.

- The second category includes those teens who are more at-risk because while they are maintaining stability in physical, developmental, and emotional status, they are also drinking and driving. Professionals dealing with members of this group may not be able to maintain confidentiality, and people in this group may benefit from an introduction to organizations such as Students Against Drunk Driving (SADD).

- The third category includes those showing serious signs of impairment, including inability to follow through on obligations at school or on a job, alcohol-related encounters with police or the justice system, and mental health problems such as **anxiety**, depression, or oppositional-defiant behavior. These children may experience frequent acute intoxication or withdrawal symptoms, medical complications, or an inability to stop or reduce their alcohol intake. Werner and Adjer suggest that professionals dealing with members of this group probably need to set aside confidentiality in order to involve parents in the treatment process. Treatment may include detoxification in an in-patient facility and/or rehabilitation in a youth-centered substance abuse program.

Treatment options

The following key issues should be considered in determining which treatment option is appropriate:

- severity of the problem and evidence to suggest other mental health problems (e.g. depression, suicide attempts)

- staff credentials of those treating the child or teen, and what forms of therapy (e.g., family, group, medications) are to be used

- nature of family involvement

- how education is to be continued during treatment

- if an in-patient program is necessary, what length it should be

- what aftercare is to be provided following discharge

- what portion of treatment is to be covered by health insurance and what needs to be paid out of pocket

Alcoholics Anonymous

Since its inception in the 1930s, Alcoholics Anonymous (AA) has been an important non-medical means of treating alcoholism with millions of members worldwide, many of whom are teenagers. It is a spiritual but non-religious program that fosters abstinence from alcohol based upon a belief that the person suffering from alcoholism is "powerless" over their **addiction**. AA suggests that people can stay free of alcohol by using an attitude that focuses on "one day at a time" and that consciously seeks spiritual support from "a power greater than themselves." AA is generally a part of most in-patient treatment and rehabilitation programs.

Prognosis

Prevention provides the best possible prognosis for alcohol abuse and dependence. The National Council on Alcoholism and Drug Dependence estimates that parents who talk with their children regularly about the danger from drugs (including alcohol) have children who are 42 percent less likely to use these substances. Once alcoholism is present, abstinence is the only known completely successful treatment. Children suffering from alcohol dependence continue for the rest of their lives to be at risk for problems with alcohol if they again drink. The prognosis is excellent for young alcoholics who remain alcohol-free and who do not substitute other drugs for alcohol, sometimes called "chewing their booze" in AA.

Prevention

Alcohol use and abuse has been a feature of Western culture for centuries, a facet of American life since Europeans arrived in North America, literally arriving with the pilgrims on the Mayflower. It is typically part of U.S. celebrations and even some American-observed religious rites. Because alcohol overuse and abuse has been so much a part of Western experience, there is clearly a tremendous need–among children and adults—for better education about both alcohol consumption and alcoholism. The statistics indicate that parents, teachers, and healthcare professionals need to begin educating children as early as possible regarding the risks involved in alcohol use. Parents who provide the example of limiting their own alcohol and other drug use can help their children inestimably. It should never be inferred that difficult situations can be better coped with by having a drink or that getting drunk is either helpful or amusing. Moreover, parents and other adults need to set the example by not driving a car or operating machinery while they are drinking or under the influence of alcohol.

The APA suggests the following as the most effective ways that parents can aid their children in resisting drinking:

- Provide children with self-confidence by building **self-esteem** and not engaging in constant criticism. Good self-esteem is the best defense against peer pressure to drink.

- Listen to children. Parents who listen attentively and provide support during difficult times give their children invaluable aid in coping with pressures.

- Get to know the children's friends.

- Provide supervision and discourage teens from attending parties where alcohol is served or parents are absent, and band together with other parents to arrange alcohol-free social events for children.

- Be available and encourage children and teens to call home for a ride rather than drive with someone who has been drinking; assure children there will be no recrimination, as SADD recommends.

- Teach therapeutic coping mechanisms by modeling how to handle stress, **pain**, or tension in healthy ways, by exercising, using **yoga** and meditation, and talking about feelings.

- Understand the tremendous importance of child and adolescent issues, including alcohol and other drug use and acceptance by peers; be ready and able to discuss these subjects with children.

- Encourage and participate in enjoyable, worthwhile activities with children; be reassuring that there is time enough for both work and fun.

- Be willing to learn about alcohol abuse; attend, along with their children, programs offered by schools, churches, and other groups providing information about the prevention of alcohol abuse.

- Maintain healthy lines of communication with children; remember the saying, "You are only as sick as the secrets you keep."

Nutritional concerns

Most childhood alcoholics do not reach the serious state of **malnutrition** that chronic adult alcoholics can reach. However, severe cases of alcohol abuse and dependence may result in a child or teen not eating normally, resulting in weight loss and vitamin deficiencies (B-vitamins particularly). Resumption of normal eating habits and possible addition of vitamin supplements can help in regaining normal **nutrition**.

Parental concerns

Parents of alcoholic children often encounter persistent and highly traumatic worries regarding serious physical, emotional, social, and legal problems for the affected child as well as the terrifying possibility of that child's death or serious injury. Clearly, these concerns can take a huge toll in a family. The denial mentioned earlier is often a complicating factor. The notion of "Not my son or daughter!" can actually hinder treatment and recovery for a child. Parents are also often embarrassed by their child's alcohol abuse and may believe that it is somehow their fault. It is not uncommon for parents to feel isolated and to feel as if they are the only ones with this problem. High school programs such as the earlier-described SADD can address some of the fear regarding drunk driving. Parental support groups such as *Tough Love* programs and twelve-step groups such as Al Anon can help parents to better understand the problem they facing and can help make them aware that they not alone and that they have options.

Al Anon is a twelve-step program (that is, a program based on the twelve steps employed by Alcoholics Anonymous) that provides support and spiritual recovery for the families and loved ones of alcoholics. This program was begun in the early 1940s by the wives of some of AA's earliest members and founders, including Lois Wilson, wife of AA founder Bill Wilson. Twelve-step programs have spun off over the years to meet the needs of specific populations, including adult children of alcoholics and teens who are alcoholics.

Because parents of alcoholic children often believe they are responsible for their child's drinking, the *Three C's* that Al Anon offers its participants may be particularly helpful. These *Three C's* state:

- "I didn't cause anyone else's alcoholism."

- "I can't control anyone else's alcoholism."

- "I can't cure anyone else's alcoholism."

Tough Love, a program begun by Phyllis and David York, co-authors of a book by the same title, is designed to help families and especially parents cope with a variety of problems, including alcoholism and drug abuse, that often affect children and ultimately the whole family. *Tough Love*'s approach is different from that of Al Anon. The ten beliefs listed below form the basis for this program and show clearly the difference in philosophy:

- Parents are people too.

- Parents' material and emotional resources are limited.

- Parents and kids are not equal.

- Blaming keeps people helpless.

KEY TERMS

Alcohol Use Disorders Inventory Test (AUDIT)—A test for alcohol use developed by the World Health Organization (WHO). Its ten questions address three specific areas of drinking over a 12-month period: the amount and frequency of drinking, dependence upon alcohol, and problems that have been encountered due to drinking alcohol.

Binge drinking—Consumption of five or more alcoholic drinks in a row on a single occasion.

CAGE—A four-question assessment for the presence of alcoholism in both adults and children.

Delirium tremens—A complication that may accompany alcohol withdrawal. The symptoms include body shaking (tremulousness), insomnia, agitation, confusion, hearing voices or seeing images that are not really there (hallucinations), seizures, rapid heart beat, profuse sweating, high blood pressure, and fever.

Detoxification—The process of physically eliminating drugs and/or alcohol from the system of a substance-dependent individual.

Personal Experience Screening Questionnaire (PESQ)—A questionnaire for alcoholism.

Problem Oriented Screening Instrument for Teenagers (POSIT)—A questionnaire used specifically for teenagers to assess alcohol and drug use.

Students against Drunk Driving (SADD)—An organization that offers a "Contract for Life" that asks teens to discuss substance use with parents, to call home for a ride if safe transportation is needed, and to wear a seat belt. Parents in turn promise to arrange for that safe transportation home "regardless of the time or circumstances," without discussion of the incident until both teens and parents are calm.

Tolerance—A condition in which an addict needs higher doses of a substance to achieve the same effect previously achieved with a lower dose.

Twelve-step programs—Several programs to assist in breaking addictions, offering either support to addicted people or to friends and loved ones of addicted people. These programs are spiritual but not religious and are based on the twelve steps that are the basis of Alcoholics Anonymous (AA). Programs include AA, Narcotics Anonymous (NA), Al-Anon, Adult Children of Alcoholics (ACOA), Alateen, and Co-Dependence Anonymous (CODA).

Withdrawal—The characteristic withdrawal syndrome for alcohol includes feelings of irritability or anxiety, elevated blood pressure and pulse, tremors, and clammy skin.

• Kids' behavior affects parents. Parents' behavior affects kids.

• Taking a stand precipitates a crisis.

• From a controlled crisis comes the possibility of positive change.

• Families need to give and get support in their own community in order to change.

• The essence of family life is cooperation, not togetherness.

Al Anon and *Tough Love* are offered in a variety of formats to the families of alcoholic children through treatment centers, churches, and other community services. It is clear that there are dramatic differences between these two philosophies. But perhaps the best way for parents to decide which approach makes sense to them is to take the advice Al Anon offers all newcomers: "Take what you like and leave the rest."

Resources

BOOKS

Egendorf, Laura K. *Teen Alcoholism.* Farmington Hills, MI: Gale, 2001.

Greenleaf, Victoria C. G. *Fighting the Good Fight: One Family's Struggle against Adolescent Alcoholism.* Fort Bragg, CA: Cypress House, 2002.

Shannon, Joyce Brennflech. *Alcohol Information for Teens: Health Tips about Alcohol and Alcoholics.* Detroit, MI: Omnigraphics, 2004.

ORGANIZATIONS

Alcoholics Anonymous. (See white pages of local telephone book for area groups.) Web site: <www.alcoholics-anonymous.org>.

National Council on Alcoholism and Drug Dependence. 20 Exchange Place, Suite 2902, New York, NY 10005. Web site: <www.ncadd.org>.

National Institute on Alcohol Abuse and Alcoholism (NIAAA),National Institute of Health, Willco Building, 6000 Executive Blvd., Bethesda, MD 20892–7003. Web site: <www.niaaa.nih.gov>.

Students Against Drunk Driving (SADD). Marlborough, MA. 01752. Web site: <www.saddonline.com>.

WEB SITES

Al-Anon and Alateen. Available online at <www.al-anon.alateen.org> (accessed October 16, 2004).

Alcoholics Anonymous. Available online at <www.alcoholics-anonymous.org> (accessed October 16, 2004).

"Alcohol Use and Abuse: A Pediatric Concern." *American Academy of Pediatrics, Committee on Substance Abuse.* Available online at <http://pediatrics.aappublications.org/cgi> (accessed October 16, 2004).

Werner, Mark J., and Hoover Adjer. "Early Identification and Intervention for Adolescent Alcohol Use." *American Academy of Pediatrics.* Available online at <www.aap.org/advocacy/chm98ado.htm> (accessed October 16, 2004).

"Youth, Alcohol, and Other Drugs: An Overview." *National Council on Alcoholism and Drug Dependence.* Available online at <www.ncadd.org/facts/youthalc.html> (accessed October 16, 2004).

Joan Schonbeck, R.N.

Allergic purpura

Definition

Allergic purpura (AP), a form of vasculitis (inflammation of the blood vessels), is a disease characterized by inflammation of the small arterial vessels (capillaries) in the skin, kidneys, and intestinal tract. Symptoms include a purple spotted skin rash, abdominal **pain**, gastrointestinal upsets, and joint inflammation, swelling, and pain. Although the exact cause of the disease is unknown, it often develops following a recent viral or bacterial infection of the respiratory tract and is an abnormal reaction of the immune system to the infection.

Description

AP may occur suddenly, or it may develop slowly over a period of weeks. The characteristic rash is always present in the disease. The rash begins as areas of redness and as small **hives**, which may develop anywhere on the body, but especially on the legs and buttocks, and may itch. The rash is caused by inflamed capillaries rupturing, allowing small amounts of blood to accumulate in the surrounding tissues. Through time the rash changes color from red to a bruised, purple color. Each rash spot will last about five days, and the rash can reoccur several times. The skin rash is the most obvious symptom of AP but is not the most serious, for the joints, gastrointestinal tract, and kidneys may also be affected.

Joint inflammation (arthritis), especially of the knees and ankles, occurs in two-thirds of the children affected by AP. The joints become swollen, tender, and painful with movement; the pain may be debilitating. However, the arthritis usually clears up with no permanent damage.

Gastrointestinal symptoms are a result of inflammation and bleeding of the capillaries in the gastrointestinal tract, including the mouth, esophagus, stomach, and intestines. Most children with AP experience severe abdominal pain, **vomiting** (possibly with blood), and bloody stools.

The most serious complication of AP is kidney inflammation (nephritis), which occurs in almost half of older affected children. Symptoms include blood and protein in the urine. Most children whose kidneys are affected recover fully, but about 10 percent later develop more serious chronic kidney disease. In 80 percent of those with kidney involvement, the kidney disease develops within the first four weeks of illness.

Children younger than three years who contract AP have a shorter, milder course of the disease with fewer recurrences. Older children are more likely to have more serious symptoms.

AP is also called Henoch-Schonlein purpura, named after the two German physicians who first recognized and described it in the 1880s. AP is also referred to as anaphylactoid purpura or vascular purpura.

Demographics

AP is the most common acute vasculitis affecting children. In the United States, the prevalence of AP is approximately 14 to 15 cases per 100,000 population.

Approximately 75 percent of cases occur in children between the ages of two and 11, with peak prevalence in children aged five years. AP is rare in infants and younger children. Boys are affected more often than girls (the female-to-male ratio is 1.5-2:1). Most cases occur in late fall and winter. Adults can also develop the disease.

Causes and symptoms

Causes

AP is caused by reactions of antibodies binding with foreign proteins, called antigens. In some cases, the antigen-antibody complexes become too large to remain suspended in the bloodstream. When this occurs, they precipitate out and become lodged in the capillaries, which can cause the capillary to burst, resulting in a local hemorrhage.

The source of the antigens that cause AP is unknown. Antigens may be introduced by bacterial or viral infection, because more than 75 percent of children with AP report having had an infection of the throat, upper respiratory tract, or gastrointestinal system several weeks before the onset of AP. AP may also be caused by allergens, which are otherwise harmless substances that stimulate an immune reaction. Drug allergens that may cause AP include penicillin, ampicillin, erythromycin, and quinine. Vaccines possibly linked to AP include those for typhoid, **measles**, cholera, and yellow fever. Food allergens, cold exposure, and insect **bites** have also been associated with AP.

Symptoms

The onset of AP may be preceded by a **headache**, fever, and loss of appetite. Most children first develop an itchy skin rash. The rash is red, either flat or raised, and may be small and freckle-like. The rash may also be larger, resembling a bruise. **Rashes** become purple and then rust-colored over the course of a day, and fade after several weeks. Rashes are most common on the buttocks, abdomen, and lower extremities. Rashes higher on the body may also occur, especially in younger children.

Joint pain and swelling is common, especially in the knees and ankles. Abdominal pain occurs in almost all children with AP, along with blood in the stools. About half of all affected children show blood in the urine, low urine volume, or other signs of kidney involvement. Kidney failure may occur due to widespread obstruction of the capillaries in the filtering structures called glomeruli. Kidney failure develops in about 2–5 percent of all affected children and in 15 percent of those with elevated blood or protein in the urine.

Less common symptoms include prolonged headache, fever, and pain and swelling of the scrotum, scalp, eyelids, lips, ears, backs of the hands and feet, and perineum. Involvement of other organ systems may lead to heart attack (myocardial infarction), inflammation of the pancreas (pancreatitis), intestinal obstruction, bowel perforation, or acute intussusception (a twisting inversion of the lining of the bowel).

Diagnosis

Diagnosis of AP is based on the symptoms and their development, a careful medical history, and blood and urine tests. **X rays** or computed tomography (CT) scans may be performed to assess complications in the bowel or other internal organs. In some cases a renal biopsy may be useful to determine the extent of kidney involvement.

When to call the doctor

A doctor should be consulted if a child exhibits symptoms of AP. After a child has had an episode of AP, the doctor should be called if the child experiences sudden increases in abdominal pain, which may indicate a bowel infarction or perforation, or if the child exhibits decreased urine output, indicating kidney disease.

Treatment

Most cases of AP resolve completely without treatment. Nonetheless, a hospital stay with supportive treatment is usually required because of the possibility of serious complications. Non-aspirin pain relievers may be given for joint pain. Corticosteroids (such as prednisone) are sometimes used to alleviate gastrointestinal tract inflammation but have not been shown to be effective for associated kidney problems. Kidney involvement requires monitoring and correction of blood fluids and electrolytes. Salt intake should be restricted. A child with AP should be monitored until abnormal urinary findings subside.

Children with severe kidney complications may require a kidney biopsy so that tissue can be analyzed. Even after all other symptoms subside, elevated levels of blood or protein in the urine may persist for months and require regular long-term monitoring. **Hypertension** or kidney failure may develop months or even years after the acute phase of the disease. Kidney failure requires dialysis or transplantation.

Surgery may be necessary to correct acute intussusception of the bowel.

KEY TERMS

Capillaries—The tiniest blood vessels with the smallest diameter. These vessels receive blood from the arterioles and deliver blood to the venules. In the lungs, capillaries are located next to the alveoli so that they can pick up oxygen from inhaled air.

Glomerulus—Plural, glomeruli; a network of capillaries located in the nephron of the kidney where wastes are filtered from the blood.

Prognosis

AP may be mild, lasting only two or three days. However, for those children with moderate to severe symptoms, AP may last for four to six weeks, with relapses in about half of all children within six weeks, especially if the child contracts another respiratory infection or is exposed to the allergic agent. Relapses can occur up to seven years after the initial disease. Full recovery occurs in most cases without kidney involvement. However, one fourth of children who have kidney symptoms still have detectable problems years later. There is a higher likelihood of permanent renal damage with a higher number of recurrences.

Prevention

If the initiating trigger for a case of AP is identified in an affected child, everything possible should be done to ensure that the child is not exposed to that substance again. If the cause is thought to be a bacterial infection, such as **strep throat**, prophylactic antibiotic treatment is sometimes given once the infection has been treated to prevent recurrence.

Parental concerns

Parents should be vigilant regarding recurrence of symptoms after their child has had AP. Parents should also realize that although severe kidney involvement is rare, if it does occur, it may require aggressive treatment and long-term care. If the child does have long-term kidney problems, the stress of the illness can often be mitigated by parents joining a support group in which members share common experiences and problems.

Resources

BOOKS

Henoch-Schonlein Purpura: A Medical Dictionary, Bibliography, and Annotated Research Guide to Internet References. San Diego, CA: Icon Health Publications, 2004.

ORGANIZATIONS

National Kidney Foundation. 30 East 33rd St., Suite 1100, New York, NY 10016. Web site: <www.kidney.org>.

WEB SITES

Scheinfeld, Noah S., et al. "Henoch-Schoenlein Purpura." *emedicine*, October 8, 2004. Available online at <www.emedicine.com/ped/topic3020.htm> (accessed November 28, 2004).

Judith Sims
Richard Robinson

Allergic rhinitis

Definition

Allergic **rhinitis**, more commonly referred to as hay fever, is an inflammation of the nasal passages caused by allergic reaction to airborne substances.

Description

Allergic rhinitis (AR) is the most common allergic condition and one of the most common of all minor afflictions. AR affects up to 20 percent of children and 15 to 30 percent of adolescents in the United States. **Antihistamines** and other drugs used to treat allergic rhinitis make up a significant fraction of both prescription and over-the-counter drug sales each year.

There are two types of allergic rhinitis: seasonal and perennial. Seasonal AR occurs in the spring, summer, and early fall, when airborne plant pollens are at their highest levels. In fact, the term hay fever is really a misnomer, since allergy to grass pollen is only one cause of symptoms for most children. Perennial AR occurs all year and is usually caused by airborne pollutants in the home and other places. A child can be affected by one or both types. Symptoms of seasonal AR are worst after being outdoors, while symptoms of perennial AR are worst after spending time indoors.

Both types of **allergies** can develop at any age, although onset in childhood through early adulthood is most common. Although allergy to a particular substance is not inherited, increased allergic sensitivity may be genetic (inherited). While allergies can improve on their own over time, they can also become worse over time.

Demographics

AR affects up to 20 percent of children and 15 to 30 percent of adolescents. Boys are twice as likely to get allergic rhinitis as girls. Half of children develop the condition before age 10, and half after that time. Some regions of the country are more likely to have the pollens that cause AR, so those areas will have more children with the condition. Other risk factors include having a mother with **asthma** or having asthma oneself, having others in the **family** with AR, being the oldest in the family, having a family dog, being breast fed for more than a month and having a higher socioeconomic level.

Causes and symptoms

Causes

Allergic rhinitis is a type of immune reaction. Normally, the immune system responds to foreign microorganisms, or particles like pollen or dust, by producing specific proteins, called antibodies. Antibodies are capable of binding to identifying molecules (antigens) on the foreign particle. This reaction between antibody and antigen sets off a series of reactions designed to protect the body from infection. Sometimes this same series of reactions is triggered by harmless, everyday substances. This is the condition known as allergy, and the offending substance is called an allergen.

Like all allergic reactions, AR involves a special set of cells in the immune system known as mast cells. Mast cells, found in the lining of the nasal passages and eyelids, display a special type of antibody called immunoglobulin type E (IgE) on their surfaces. Inside, mast cells store reactive chemicals in small packets called granules. When the antibodies encounter allergens, they trigger release of the granules, which spill out their chemicals onto neighboring cells, including blood vessels and nerve cells. One of these chemicals, histamine, binds to the surfaces of these other cells, through special proteins called histamine receptors.

Interaction of histamine with receptors on blood vessels causes neighboring cells to become leaky, leading to the fluid collection, swelling, and increased redness characteristic of a runny nose and red, irritated eyes. Histamine also stimulates **pain** receptors, causing the itchy, scratchy nose, eyes, and throat common in allergic rhinitis.

The number of possible airborne allergens is enormous. Seasonal AR is most commonly caused by grass and tree pollens, since their pollen is produced in large amounts and is dispersed by the wind. Showy flowers like roses or lilacs that attract insects produce a sticky pollen that is less likely to become airborne. Different plants release their pollen at different times of the year, so seasonal AR sufferers may be most affected in spring, summer, or fall, depending on which plants provoke a response. The amount of pollen in the air is reflected in the pollen count, often broadcast on the daily news during allergy season. Pollen counts tend to be lower after a good rain that washes the pollen out of the air and higher on warm, dry, windy days.

Virtually any type of tree or grass may cause AR. A few types of weeds that tend to cause the most trouble include the following:

- ragweed
- sagebrush
- lamb's-quarters
- plantain
- pigweed
- dock/sorrel
- tumbleweed

Perennial AR is often triggered by house dust, a complicated mixture of airborne particles, many of which are potent allergens. House dust contains some or all of the following:

- House mite body parts. All houses contain large numbers of microscopic insects called house mites. These harmless insects feed on fibers, fur, and skin shed by the house's larger occupants. Their tiny body parts easily become airborne.
- Animal dander. Animals constantly shed fur, skin flakes, and dried saliva. Carried in the air, or transferred from pet to owner by direct contact, dander can cause allergy in many sensitive people.
- Mold spores. Molds live in damp spots throughout the house, including basements, bathrooms, air ducts, air conditioners, refrigerator drains, damp windowsills, mattresses, and stuffed furniture. Mildew and other molds release airborne spores that circulate throughout the house.

Other potential causes of perennial allergic rhinitis include the following:

- cigarette smoke
- perfume
- cosmetics
- cleansers
- copier chemicals
- industrial chemicals
- construction material gases

Symptoms

Inflammation of the nose, or rhinitis, is the major symptom of AR. Inflammation causes **itching**, sneezing, runny nose, redness, and tenderness. Sinus swelling can constrict a child's eustachian tube that connects the inner ear to the throat, causing a congested feeling and "ear popping." The drip of mucus from the sinuses down the back of the throat, combined with increased sensitivity, can also lead to throat irritation and redness. AR usually also causes redness, itching, and watery eyes. Fatigue and **headache** are also common.

When to call the doctor

AR that is not successfully treated by over-the-counter medication will benefit from an evaluation and treatment by a healthcare professional.

Diagnosis

Diagnosing seasonal AR is usually easy and can often be done without a medical specialist. When a child's symptoms appear in spring or summer and disappear with the onset of cold weather, seasonal AR is almost certainly the culprit. Other causes of rhinitis, including infection, can usually be ruled out by a physical examination and a nasal smear, in which a sample of mucus is taken on a swab for examination.

Along with a runny nose and reddened eyes, other symptoms may include dark circles under the eyes caused by nasal congestion, the "alleric salute" in which a child rubs a hand along the side of the nose, mouth breathing, sleepiness during the day, and learning problems caused by inability to concentrate during school.

Allergy tests including skin testing and provocation testing can help identify the precise culprit, but may not be done unless a single source is suspected and subsequent avoidance is possible. Skin testing involves placing a small amount of liquid containing a specific allergen on the skin and then either poking, scratching, or injecting it into the skin surface to observe whether redness and swelling occurs. Provocation testing involves challenging an individual with either a small amount of an inhalable or ingestible allergen to see if a response is elicited.

Perennial AR can also usually be diagnosed by careful questioning about the timing of exposure and the onset of symptoms. Specific allergens can be identified through allergy skin testing.

Treatment

Avoidance of the allergens is the best treatment, but this is often not possible. When it is not possible to avoid one or more allergens, there are two major forms of medical treatment: drugs and immunotherapy. Always read the package label for directions or consult your doctor or pharmacist before treating children with over-the-counter medications. Children are not small adults, but have different physiology. They are more susceptible than adults to the effects of certain medicines and may have unexpected reactions.

Drugs

ANTIHISTAMINES Antihistamines block the histamine receptors on nasal tissue, decreasing the effect of histamine release by mast cells. They may be used after symptoms appear, though they may be even more effective when used preventively, before symptoms appear. A wide variety of antihistamines are available.

Older (first generation) antihistamines often produce drowsiness as a major side effect. Such antihistamines include the following:

- Diphenhydramine (Benadryl and generics). May be used for children age 2 and up, depending on the type of delivery (capsule, liquid).
- Chlorpheniramine (Chlor-trimeton and generics). May be used for children age 6 and up.
- Brompheniramine (Dimetane and generics). May be used for children age 2 and up.
- Clemastine (Tavist and generics). May be used for children age 12 and up.

Newer antihistamines (second generation) that do not cause drowsiness are available by prescription or over-the-counter include the following:

- Loratidine (Claritin). May be used for children age 2 and up.
- Cetirizine (Zyrtec). May be used for children age 2 and up.
- Fexofenadine (Allegra). May be used for children age 6 and up.
- Azelastin HCl (Astelin). May be used for children age 5 and up.

DECONGESTANTS **Decongestants** constrict blood vessels to counteract the effects of histamine. Nasal sprays are available that can be applied directly to the nasal lining and oral systemic preparations are available. Decongestants are stimulants and may cause increased heart rate and blood pressure, headaches, and agitation. Use of topical decongestants for longer than several days can cause loss of effectiveness and rebound congestion, in which nasal passages become more severely swollen than before treatment.

TOPICAL CORTICOSTEROIDS Topical corticosteroids reduce mucous membrane inflammation and are available by prescription. Allergies tend to become worse as the season progresses because the immune system becomes sensitized to particular antigens and can produce a faster, stronger response. Topical corticosteroids are especially effective at reducing this seasonal sensitization because they work more slowly and last longer than most other medication types. As a result, they are best started before allergy season begins. Side effects are usually mild, but may include headaches, nosebleeds, and unpleasant taste sensations.

However, a larger skin surface area to body weight ratio may make children more susceptible to adrenal gland problems such as growth retardation and delayed weight gain. Topical corticosteroids administration to children should be limited to the least amount possible to achieve therapeutic effect.

MAST CELL STABILIZERS Cromolyn sodium prevents the release of mast cell granules, thereby preventing release of histamine and the other chemicals contained in them. It acts as a preventive treatment if it is begun several weeks before the onset of the allergy season. It can be used for perennial AR as well. Cromolyn sodium is so low in side effects that it is recommended for children as young as two years of age.

Immunotherapy

Immunotherapy, also known as desensitization or **allergy shots**, alters the balance of antibody types in the body, thereby reducing the ability of IgE to cause allergic reactions. Immunotherapy is preceded by allergy testing to determine the precise allergens responsible. Injections involve very small but gradually increasing amounts of allergen, over several weeks or months, with periodic boosters. Full benefits may take up to several years to achieve and are not seen at all in about one in five patients. Individuals receiving all shots will be monitored closely following each shot because of the small risk of **anaphylaxis**, a condition that can result in difficulty breathing and a sharp drop in blood pressure. Allergy shots can be given to children as young as five years.

Alternative treatment

Alternative treatments for AR often focus on modulation of the body's immune response, and frequently center around diet and lifestyle adjustments. Chinese herbal medicine can help rebalance a person's system, as can both acute and constitutional homeopathic treatment. Vitamin C in substantial amounts can help stabilize the mucous membrane response. For symptom relief, western herbal remedies including eyebright (*Euphrasia officinalis*) and nettle (*Urtica dioica*) may be helpful. Bee pollen may also be effective in alleviating or eliminating AR symptoms.

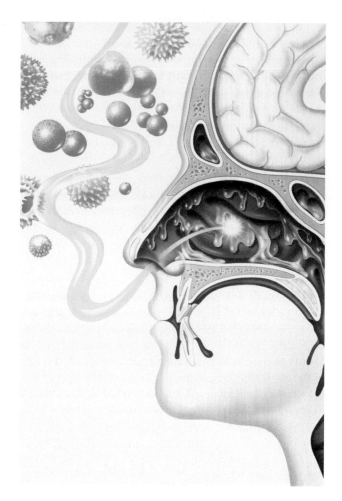

Illustration depicting excessive mucus production in the nose after inhalation of airborne pollen. *(Photograph by John Bavosi. Photo Researchers, Inc.)*

Prognosis

Most children with AR can achieve adequate relief with a combination of preventive strategies and treatment. While allergies may improve over time, they may also get worse or expand to include new allergens. Early treatment can help prevent an increased sensitization to other allergens.

Prevention

Reducing exposure to pollen may improve symptoms of seasonal AR. Strategies include the following:

- staying indoors with windows closed during the morning hours, when pollen levels are highest
- keeping car windows up
- avoiding uncut fields

- learning which trees are producing pollen in which seasons, and avoiding forests at the height of pollen season
- washing clothes and hair after being outside
- cleaning air conditioner filters in the home regularly
- using electrostatic filters for central air conditioning

Moving to a region with lower pollen levels is rarely effective, since new allergies often develop in children.

Preventing perennial AR requires identification of the responsible allergens.

Mold spores:

- keeping the house dry through ventilation and use of dehumidifiers
- using a disinfectant such as dilute bleach to clean surfaces such as bathroom floors and walls
- having heating/air conditioning ducts cleaned and disinfected
- cleaning and disinfecting air conditioners and coolers
- throwing out moldy or mildewed books, shoes, pillows, or furniture

House dust:

- vacuuming frequently, and changing the bag regularly (Use a bag with small pores to catch extra-fine particles.)
- cleaning floors and walls with a damp mop
- installing electrostatic filters in heating and cooling ducts, and changing all filters regularly

Animal dander:

- avoiding contact if possible
- washing hands after contact
- vacuuming frequently
- keeping pets out of the child's bedroom, and off furniture, rugs, and other dander-catching surfaces
- having pets bathed and groomed frequently

Parental concerns

AR can lead to daytime sleepiness in school and affect school performance.

Resources

BOOKS

Allergic and Non-Allergic Rhinitis: Clinical Aspects. Editted by N. Mygind and R. M. Naclerio. Philadelphia: W. B. Saunders Co.,1993.

Lawlor, G. J. Jr., T. J. Fischer, and D. C. Adelman. *Manual of Allergy and Immunology.* Boston: Little, Brown and Co., 1995.

Novick, N. L. *You Can Do Something About Your Allergies.* New York: Macmillan, 1994.

Weil, A. *Natural Health, Natural Medicine: A Comprehensive Manual for Wellness and Self-Care.* New York: Houghton Mifflin,1995.

WEB SITES

"Allergic Rhinitis." *The Children's Hospital of Philadelphia.* September 2003. [cited August 13, 2003]. <http://

www.chop.edu/consumer/jsp/division/
generic.jsp?id=76995.>

"Allergic Rhinitis in Children." *Medical College
of Wisconsin.* 2001. [cited August 13, 2003].
<http://healthlink.mcw.edu/article/992530573.html>.

Christine Kuehn Kelly

Allergies

Definition

Allergies are abnormal reactions of the immune system that occur in response to otherwise harmless substances.

Description

Allergies are among the most common of medical disorders. It is estimated that 60 million Americans, or more than one in every five people, suffer from some form of allergy, with similar proportions throughout much of the rest of the world. Allergy is the single largest reason for school absence and is a major source of lost productivity in the workplace.

Allergies are a type of immune reaction. Normally, the immune system responds to foreign microorganisms, or particles, like pollen or dust, by producing specific proteins, called antibodies, that are capable of binding to identifying molecules, or antigens, on the foreign particle. This reaction between antibody and antigen sets off a series of reactions designed to protect the body from infection. When this same series of reactions is triggered by harmless, everyday substances, it is called an allergy. The substance that causes the allergy is called an allergen.

All allergic reactions involve a special set of cells in the immune system known as mast cells. Mast cells, found in the lining of the nasal passages and eyelids, display a special type of antibody, called immunoglobulin type E (IgE), on their surface. Inside, mast cells store reactive chemicals in small packets, called granules. When the antibodies encounter allergens, they trigger release of the granules, which spill out their chemicals onto neighboring cells, including blood vessels and nerve cells. One of these chemicals, histamine, binds to the surfaces of these other cells, through special proteins called histamine receptors. Interaction of histamine with receptors on blood vessels causes neighboring cells to become leaky, leading to the fluid collection in the body's tissues, swelling, and increased redness characteristic of a runny nose and red, irritated eyes. Histamine also stimulates

pain receptors, causing the itchy nose, eyes, and throat common in **allergic rhinitis**. In the gastrointestinal tract, these reactions lead to swelling and irritation of the intestinal lining, which causes the cramping and **diarrhea** typical of food allergy. Allergens that enter the circulation may cause **hives**, angioedema, **anaphylaxis**, or **atopic dermatitis**. Allergens on the skin usually cause a delayed hypersensitivity reaction. This type of allergic response may develop over several days following contact with the allergen, and symptoms may persist for a week or more.

Demographics

According to the National Institute of Allergy and Infectious Diseases, annually, more than 50 million Americans suffer from allergic diseases, with approximately 36 million suffering from allergic **rhinitis**. Up to 6 percent of the general population suffers from an allergy to latex, and children with **spina bifida** who have had multiple surgical procedures are at higher risk for allergic reactions to latex. Atopic **dermatitis** is one of the most common skin conditions and occurs commonly in infants and children. Prevalence in the United States is about 10 percent. **Food allergies** occur in 8 percent of children aged six years and younger. Peanut or other nut allergies affect about 3 million Americans and produce the most severe reactions. Acute allergic hives affect from 10 percent to 20 percent of Americans at some time during their lifetime, and half of those affected have symptoms for more than six months. Allergies to stinging insects occur in about 3.5 percent of Americans. According to the American Academy of Allergy, **Asthma**, and Immunology, if one parent has an allergic disease, a child has a 48 percent risk of developing allergies. If both parents have allergies, risk increases to 70 percent.

Causes and symptoms

Allergens enter the body through four main routes: the airways, the skin, the gastrointestinal tract, and the circulatory system.

Airborne allergens cause the sneezing, runny nose, and itchy, bloodshot eyes of allergic rhinitis (hay fever). Airborne allergens can also affect the lining of the lungs, causing asthma, or the conjunctiva of the eyes, causing allergic **conjunctivitis**. The most common airborne allergens are the following:

- plant pollens
- animal fur and dander
- body parts and excrement from dust mites (microscopic creatures found in all houses)

- excrement from cockroaches
- house dust
- mold spores
- cigarette smoke
- solvents
- cleaners

Allergens in food can cause **itching** and swelling of the lips and throat, cramps, and diarrhea. When absorbed into the bloodstream, they may cause hives (urticaria) or more severe reactions involving recurrent, non-inflammatory swelling of the skin, mucous membranes, organs, and brain (angioedema). Some food allergens may cause anaphylaxis, a potentially life-threatening condition marked by tissue swelling, airway constriction, and drop in blood pressure. Common food allergens include the following:

- nuts, especially peanuts, walnuts, and brazil nuts
- fish, mollusks, and shellfish
- eggs
- wheat
- milk
- food additives and preservatives

In contact with the skin, allergens can cause reddening, itching, and blistering, called **contact dermatitis**. Skin reactions can also occur from allergens introduced through the airways or gastrointestinal tract. This type of reaction is known as atopic dermatitis. Dermatitis may arise from an allergic response (such as from **poison ivy**) or exposure to an irritant causing nonimmune damage to skin cells (such as soap, cold, and chemical agents). Injection of allergens, from insect **bites and stings** or drug administration, can introduce allergens directly into the circulation, where they may cause system-wide responses (including anaphylaxis), as well as the local ones of swelling and irritation at the injection site.

Common causes of contact dermatitis include the following:

- poison ivy, oak, and sumac
- nickel or nickel alloys
- latex

Insects and other arthropods whose **bites** or **stings** typically cause allergy include the following:

- bees, wasps, and hornets
- mosquitoes
- fleas

The following types of drugs commonly cause allergic reactions:

- penicillin or other **antibiotics**
- flu vaccines
- tetanus toxoid vaccine
- gamma globulin

Children and adolescents with allergies are not equally sensitive to all allergens. Some may have severe allergic rhinitis but no food allergies, for instance, or be extremely sensitive to nuts but not to any other food. Allergies may get worse over time. For example, childhood ragweed allergy may progress to year-round dust and pollen allergy. On the other hand, a child may outgrow allergic sensitivity. Infant or childhood atopic dermatitis disappears in almost all people. More commonly, what seems to be loss of sensitivity is instead a reduced exposure to allergens or an increased tolerance for the same level of symptoms.

Symptoms depend on the specific type of allergic reaction. Allergic rhinitis is characterized by an itchy, runny nose, sneezing, and often a scratchy or irritated throat due to postnasal drip. Inflammation of the thin membrane covering the eye (allergic conjunctivitis) causes redness, irritation, and increased tearing in the eyes. Asthma causes wheezing, coughing, and shortness of breath. Symptoms of food allergies depend on the tissues most sensitive to the allergen and whether the allergen spread systemically by the circulatory system. Gastrointestinal symptoms may include swelling and tingling in the lips, tongue, palate or throat; **nausea**; cramping; diarrhea; and gas. Contact dermatitis is marked by red, itchy, weepy skin blisters, and an eczema that is slow to heal. It sometimes has a characteristic pattern from the object containing the allergen, such as a glove allergy with clear demarcation on the hands, wrist, and arms where the gloves are worn, or on the earlobes by wearing earrings.

Whole-body or systemic reactions may occur from any type of allergen but are more common following ingestion or injection of an allergen. Skin reactions include the raised, red, and itchy patches called hives that characteristically blanch with pressure and resolve within 24 hours. A deeper and more extensive skin reaction, involving more extensive fluid collection and pain, is called angioedema. This response usually occurs on the extremities, fingers, toes, and parts of the head, neck, and face. Anaphylaxis is marked by airway constriction, blood pressure drop, widespread tissue swelling, heart rhythm abnormalities, and in some cases, loss of consciousness. Other symptoms may include **dizziness**, weakness, seizures, coughing, flushing, or cramping. The symptoms may begin within five minutes after exposure to the allergen up to one hour or more later. Commonly, this is associated with allergies to medications, foods, and insect venoms. In some individuals, anaphylaxis can occur with **exercise**, plasma exchange, hemodialysis, reaction to insulin, radiocontrast media used in certain types of medical tests, and on rare occasions during the administration of local anesthetics.

When to call the doctor

Parents should consult a physician when a child has repeated and prolonged symptoms. Allergic rhinitis may be mistaken for a cold or other upper respiratory infection. Usually, a fever indicates an infection. Food allergies and allergies to insect stings or medications can be especially dangerous, causing anaphylactic reactions that require emergency treatment.

Diagnosis

Allergies can often be diagnosed by a careful medical history, matching the onset of symptoms to the exposure to possible allergens. Allergy is suspected if the symptoms presented are characteristic of an allergic reaction, and this occurs repeatedly upon exposure to the suspected allergen. **Allergy tests** can also be conducted to determine allergens.

Skin tests

Skin tests are performed by administering a tiny dose of the suspected allergen by pricking, scratching, puncturing, or injecting the skin. The allergen is applied to the skin as an aqueous extract, usually on the back, forearms, or top of the thighs. Once in the skin, the allergen may produce a classic immune wheal and flare response (a skin lesion with a raised, white, compressible area surrounded by a red flare). The tests usually begin with prick tests or patch tests that expose the skin to small amounts of allergen to observe the response. A positive reaction occurs on the skin even if the allergen is at levels normally encountered in food or in the airways. Reactions are usually evaluated approximately 15 minutes after exposure. Intradermal skin tests involve injection of the allergen into the dermis of the skin. These tests are more sensitive and are used for allergies associated with risk of death, such as allergies to antibiotics. Skin testing may be painful for children.

Provocation tests

These tests involve the administration of allergen to elicit an immune response. Provocation tests, most commonly done with airborne allergens, present the allergen directly through the route normally involved. Delayed

<table>
<tr><td colspan="2">**Common childhood allergies**</td></tr>
<tr><td>**Type of allergy**</td><td>**Common triggers**</td></tr>
<tr><td>Food allergies</td><td>Eggs, dairy products, peanuts, soy, wheat</td></tr>
<tr><td>Allergic rhinitis and asthma</td><td>Pollens, molds, dust mites, animal dander, cigarette smoke</td></tr>
<tr><td>Atopic dermatitis (eczema)</td><td>Food allergy (see above), irritating laundry or body soaps, scratchy fabrics, rubbing of fabric on skin, overheating</td></tr>
<tr><td>Other allergies</td><td>Insect stings, medications, latex (for children who are often exposed in a medical setting), poison ivy, oak, and sumac</td></tr>
</table>

(Table by GGS Information Services.)

allergic contact dermatitis diagnosis involves similar methods by application of a skin patch with allergen to induce an allergic skin reaction. Food allergen provocation tests require abstinence from the suspect allergen for two weeks or more, followed by ingestion of a measured amount of the test substance administered as an opaque capsule along with a placebo control. Provocation tests are not used if anaphylaxis is a concern given the patient's medical history.

Treatment

Avoiding allergens is the first line of defense to reduce the possibility of an allergic attack. However, complete environmental control is often difficult to accomplish; hence, therapeutic interventions are usually necessary. A large number of prescription and over-the-counter drugs are available for treatment of immediate hypersensitivity reactions. Most of these products work by decreasing the ability of histamine to provoke symptoms. Other drugs counteract the effects of histamine by stimulating other systems or reducing immune responses in general.

Antihistamines

Antihistamines are drugs used to treat the symptoms of allergic rhinitis by blocking the action of histamine, a chemical released by the immune system in allergic reactions. Antihistamines are available as prescription and over-the-counter tablets, topical gels or creams, nasal sprays, and eye drops.

Commonly used antihistamines include the following:

- diphenhydramine (Benadryl)
- loratadine (Claritin)
- cetirizine (Zyrtec)

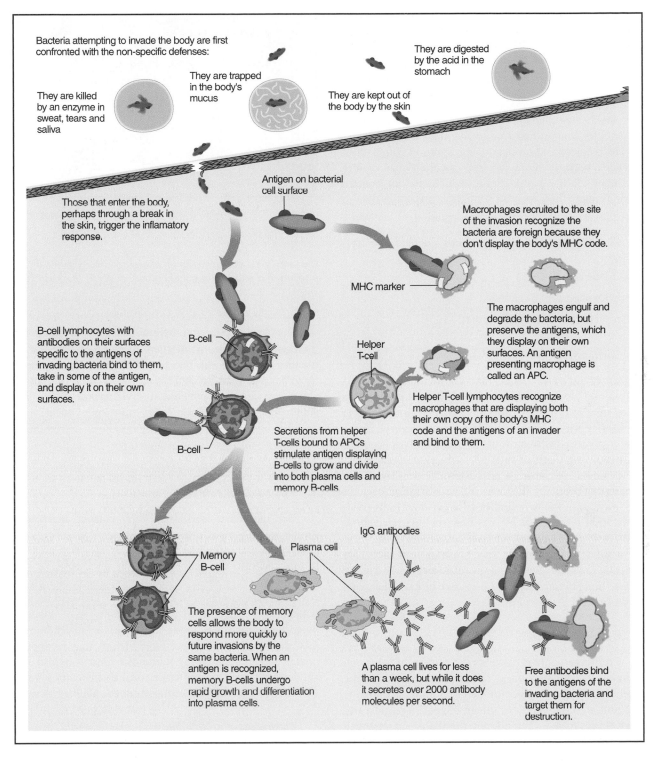

Bacteria attempting to invade the body are first confronted with the non-specific defenses:

They are trapped in the body's mucus

They are digested by the acid in the stomach

They are killed by an enzyme in sweat, tears and saliva

They are kept out of the body by the skin

Antigen on bacterial cell surface

Those that enter the body, perhaps through a break in the skin, trigger the inflamatory response.

Macrophages recruited to the site of the invasion recognize the bacteria are foreign because they don't display the body's MHC code.

MHC marker

The macrophages engulf and degrade the bacteria, but preserve the antigens, which they display on their own surfaces. An antigen presenting macrophage is called an APC.

B-cell lymphocytes with antibodies on their surfaces specific to the antigens of invading bacteria bind to them, take in some of the antigen, and display it on their own surfaces.

B-cell

Helper T-cell

Helper T-cell lymphocytes recognize macrophages that are displaying both their own copy of the body's MHC code and the antigens of an invader and bind to them.

B-cell

Secretions from helper T-cells bound to APCs stimulate antigen displaying B-cells to grow and divide into both plasma cells and memory B-cells.

IgG antibodies

Plasma cell

Memory B-cell

The presence of memory cells allows the body to respond more quickly to future invasions by the same bacteria. When an antigen is recognized, memory B-cells undergo rapid growth and differentiation into plasma cells.

A plasma cell lives for less than a week, but while it does it secretes over 2000 antibody molecules per second.

Free antibodies bind to the antigens of the invading bacteria and target them for destruction.

Flow chart depicting a response to an allergen introduced into the body, causing an allergic response. *(Illustration by Hans & Cassidy.)*

- fexofenadine (Allegra)
- clemastine fumarate (Tavist)
- chlorpheniramine (Chlor Trimeton)
- brompheniramine (Dimetapp)

Decongestants

Decongestants dry up nasal passage tissues and reduce swollen nasal membranes so as to relieve congestion. Decongestants are available as nasal sprays or drops, oral tablets, or syrups. Decongestants are stimulants and may cause increased heart rate and blood pressure, headaches, and agitation. Use of nasal spray decongestants for longer than four to five days can cause loss of effectiveness and rebound congestion, in which nasal passages become more severely swollen than before treatment. Saline nasal sprays, which do not contain decongestants, may be used for longer periods of time to help congestion and nasal passage irritation.

Commonly used decongestants include the following:

- oxymetazoline (Afrin)
- pseudoephedrine (Sudafed)
- phenylephrine (Neo Synephrine)

Corticosteroids

Corticosteroids reduce mucous membrane inflammation and are available by prescription and taken as a series of oral tablets. Corticosteroids are also available as nasal sprays. Allergies tend to become worse as the season progresses because the immune system becomes sensitized to particular antigens and can produce a faster, stronger response. Corticosteroids are especially effective at reducing this seasonal sensitization because they work more slowly and last longer than most other medication types. Side effects may include headaches, nosebleeds, and unpleasant taste sensations. Long-term use of oral corticosteroids may cause more serious side effects, such as weight gain, cataracts, weakening bones, high blood pressure, elevated blood sugar, and easy bruising.

Mast cell stabilizers

Cromolyn sodium prevents the release of mast cell granules, thereby preventing release of histamine and the other chemicals contained in them. Cromolyn sodium is available in nasal sprays or via an inhaler. It is most frequently prescribed when allergic rhinitis is accompanied by asthma.

Immunotherapy

Immunotherapy, also known as desensitization therapy or **allergy shots**, alters the balance of antibody types in the body, thereby reducing the ability of IgE to cause allergic reactions. Immunotherapy is preceded by allergy testing to determine the precise allergens

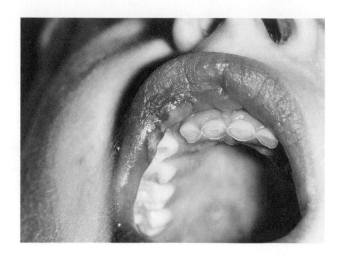

Close-up view of a boy with an allergic reaction on his lip as a result of contact with a latex glove. (© Dr. P. Marazzi/Photo Researchers, Inc.)

responsible. Injections involve very small but gradually increasing amounts of allergen, over several weeks or months, with periodic boosters. Full benefits may take up to several years to achieve and are not seen at all in about one in five patients. Individuals receiving all shots are monitored closely following each shot because of the small risk of anaphylaxis, a condition that can result in difficulty breathing and a sharp drop in blood pressure.

Treatment of contact dermatitis

An individual suffering from contact dermatitis should initially take steps to avoid possible sources of exposure to the offending agent. Calamine lotion applied to affected skin can reduce irritation somewhat, as can cold-water compresses. Topical antihistamine and corticosteroid sprays, gels, and creams are available to reduce itching. Side effects of topical agents may include overdrying of the skin. In the case of acute contact dermatitis, short-term oral corticosteroid therapy may be appropriate. Moderately strong corticosteroids can also be applied as a wrap for 24 hours. Healthcare workers are especially at risk for hand eruptions due to latex glove use.

Treatment of anaphylaxis

The emergency condition of anaphylaxis is treated with injection of adrenaline, also known as epinephrine. Children and adolescents who are prone to anaphylaxis because of food or insect allergies often carry an Epi-pen containing adrenaline in a hypodermic needle. Other medications may be given to aid the action of the Epi-pen. Prompt injection can prevent a more serious reaction from developing. Particular care should be taken to assess the affected child's airway status, and he or she should be placed in a recumbent pose and vital signs determined. Emergency treatment may be required for severe reactions.

Nutritional concerns

For children and adolescents with food allergies, all foods must be monitored to make sure that the allergen is not an ingredient or was not used during preparation. In individuals with severe food allergies to peanuts, peanut oil used to fry foods, or even the fumes produced during cooking with peanut oil have been known to cause anaphylactic shock.

Parents whose children have allergies to foods, like milk and gluten, which are common ingredients in many other foods, can purchase gluten-free foods and lactose-free foods in most grocery stores. Cookbooks dealing with allergies to these foods are also available.

Prognosis

Allergies can improve over time, although they often worsen. While anaphylaxis and severe asthma are life threatening, other allergic reactions are not. Learning to recognize and avoid allergy-provoking situations allows most children and adolescents with allergies to lead normal lives.

Prevention

Avoiding allergens is the best means of limiting allergic reactions. For food allergies, there is no effective treatment except avoidance. By determining the allergens that are causing reactions most people can learn to avoid allergic reactions from food, drugs, and contact allergens such as poison ivy or latex. Airborne allergens are more difficult to avoid. Preventive measures for airborne allergens include the following:

- staying indoors with windows closed during the morning hours, when pollen levels are highest
- keeping car windows up while driving
- using a surgical face mask when outside
- avoiding uncut fields
- learning which trees are producing pollen in which seasons and avoiding forests at the height of pollen season
- washing clothes and hair after being outside
- regularly cleaning air conditioner filters in the home
- using electrostatic filters for central air conditioning

For mold spores, the following steps will help:

- keeping the house dry through ventilation and use of dehumidifiers
- using a disinfectant such as diluted bleach to clean surfaces such as bathroom floors and walls
- having air ducts cleaned and disinfected
- cleaning and disinfecting air conditioners and coolers
- throwing out moldy or mildewed books, shoes, pillows, or furniture

For house dust, the following steps will help:

- vacuuming frequently and changing the bag regularly; using a bag with small pores to catch extra-fine particles
- cleaning floors and walls with a damp mop
- installing electrostatic filters in heating and cooling ducts and changing all filters regularly

For animal dander, the following steps will help:

- avoiding contact if possible
- washing hands after contact
- vacuuming frequently
- keeping pets out of the bedroom and off furniture, rugs, and other dander-catching surfaces
- bathing and grooming pets frequently

Parents may find it helpful to keep an allergy journal for their child to track occurrence of allergic responses. For seasonal allergic rhinitis, they may use a calendar to note when symptoms begin and end. Documenting the level of seasonal allergens at the time can help determine when seasonal allergies tend to occur and what allergens affect the child. Local weather reports on television and on Web sites provide detailed allergen maps of pollen and mold/mildew spores. Antihistamines can then be taken as a preventive measure before symptoms begin each season. For children with allergies to foods, keeping a journal of foods eaten can help identify specific food allergens.

Parental concerns

For children who resist taking pills, many antihistamines are available as flavored chewable tablets, tablets that easily dissolve on the tongue, or flavored syrups. Because many over-the-counter allergy medicines contain multiple drugs, parents should be sure to read the prescribing and dosage information for any antihistamine their children are taking to ensure safe use.

Parents of children and adolescents with severe food and insect sting allergies that might result in sudden ana-

KEY TERMS

Allergen—A foreign substance that provokes an immune reaction or allergic response in some sensitive people but not in most others.

Allergic rhinitis—Swelling and inflammation of the nasal membranes caused by sensitivity to airborne matter like pollen or cat hair.

Anaphylaxis—Also called anaphylactic shock; a severe allergic reaction characterized by airway constriction, tissue swelling, and lowered blood pressure.

Angioedema—Patches of circumscribed swelling involving the skin and its subcutaneous layers, the mucous membranes, and sometimes the organs frequently caused by an allergic reaction to drugs or food. Also called angioneurotic edema, giant urticaria, Quincke's disease, or Quincke's edema.

Antibody—A special protein made by the body's immune system as a defense against foreign material (bacteria, viruses, etc.) that enters the body. It is uniquely designed to attack and neutralize the specific antigen that triggered the immune response.

Antigen—A substance (usually a protein) identified as foreign by the body's immune system, triggering the release of antibodies as part of the body's immune response.

Asthma—A disease in which the air passages of the lungs become inflamed and narrowed, causing wheezing, coughing, and shortness of breath.

Atopic dermatitis—An intensely itchy inflammation often found on the face, in the bend of the elbow, and behind the knees of people prone to allergies. In infants and young children, this condition is called infantile eczema.

Conjunctivitis—Inflammation of the conjunctiva, the mucous membrane covering the white part of the eye (sclera) and lining the inside of the eyelids also called pinkeye.

Contact dermatitis—Skin inflammation as a result of contact with a foreign substance.

Granules—Small packets of reactive chemicals stored within cells.

Histamine—A substance released by immune system cells in response to the presence of an allergen. It stimulates widening of blood vessels and increased porousness of blood vessel walls so that fluid and protein leak out from the blood into the surrounding tissue, causing localised inflammation of the tissue.

Immune hypersensitivity reaction—An allergic reaction that is mediated by mast cells and occurs within minutes of allergen contact.

Mast cells—A type of immune system cell that is found in the lining of the nasal passages and eyelids. It displays a type of antibody called immunoglobulin type E (IgE) on its cell surface and participates in the allergic response by releasing histamine from intracellular granules.

---

phylactic reactions should make sure that their children and any other **family** members and caregivers fully understand the severity of the allergic response and the need for immediate administration of epinephrine. Parents should consider having children with these severe allergies wear a medical alert bracelet.

Children with severe food allergies to whole food groups, such as milk or wheat, may require dietary management by a dietitian or nutritionist to ensure they receive the proper nutrients and a well-balanced diet. Breastfeeding mothers of highly allergic infants may need to eliminate suspected food allergens from their diets, because food proteins ingested by a mother can be transferred to the infant via breast milk. Special formulas are available for infants sensitive to breast milk, cow's milk, and soy milk.

Resources

BOOKS

Borrel, Marie. *60 Tips: Allergies*. London: Hachette Illustrated, 2004.

Cross, Linda. *How to Manage Your Child's Life-Threatening Food Allergies*. Lake Forest, CA: Plumtree Press, 2004.

Dadamo, Peter J. *Eat Right for Your Type Allergies*. East Rutherford, NJ: Penguin Group, 2005.

Ford, Jean. *Breathe Easy: A Teen's Guide to Allergies and Asthma*. Broomall, PA: Mason Crest Publishers, 2005.

Taylor, R., et al. *Allergy Relief and Prevention*, 3rd. ed. Vancouver: Hartley and Marks, 2000.

PERIODICALS

Ansel, K. "Working with the Food-Allergic Child. *Today's Dietitian*. 4 (November 2002): 36–39.

ORGANIZATIONS

Allergy and Asthma Network. 3554 Chain Bridge Road, Suite 200. Web site: <www.aanma.org>.

American Academy of Allergy, Asthma, and Immunology. 611 East Wells St, Milwaukee, WI 53202. Web site: <www.aaaai.org>.

Asthma and Allergy Foundation of America. 1125 15th Street NW, Suite 502, Washington, DC 20005. Web site: <www.aafa.org/>.

WEB SITES

"All About Allergies." *Nemours Foundation.* Available online at <www.kidshealth.org/parent/medical/allergies/allergy.html> (accessed October 26, 2004).

Jennifer E. Sisk, MA

Allergy elimination diet *see* **Elimination diet**

Allergy medication *see* **Antihistamines**

▌ Allergy shots

Definition

Allergy shots, also called immunotherapy, are a form of treatment that reduces a person's allergic reaction to a particular allergen. Allergy shots can reduce symptoms of **allergic rhinitis** (hay fever) and allergic **asthma**. Allergy shots are less effective against molds and are not a useful method for treating **food allergies**.

Description

Allergy shorts are a series of injections with a solution containing the allergens that cause an allergic reaction. Treatment begins with a weak solution given once or twice a week. The strength of the solution gradually increases with each dose. The incremental increases of the allergen cause the child's immune system to become less sensitive to the substance by producing a "blocking" antibody. Once the strongest dose is reached, the child's sensitivity has decreased, and the injections are given monthly to control allergic symptoms.

General use

The term allergy refers to a person's immunologic sensitivity to any substance that causes an allergic reaction. Allergies can become obvious in the first few months of life in the form of nasal congestion, **cough**, rash, or **diarrhea** following food intake. Allergies affect all races and occur in all parts of the world.

Depending on the severity and nature of the allergies, allergen avoidance and allergy medications alone may not effectively manage symptoms in children. Allergens that doctors most commonly use in immunotherapy treatments for allergic **rhinitis**, allergic **conjunctivitis**, and allergic asthma include extracts of inhalant allergens from tree, grass, and weed pollens; mold spores; and dust mites. The doctor selects the treatment based on the patient's particular patterns of allergic response.

Allergy shots are not recommended for food allergies. However, if these allergies are left untreated, infants and children may be more likely to develop chronic allergies, asthma, and respiratory infections later in life. Furthermore, knowing and managing the child's sensitivities to food help in isolating the antigens that respond to immunotherapy. Parents can follow a few simple steps to reduce the child's risk to allergies:

• Pay attention to symptoms that persist, like eczema, earaches, or runny nose. See the pediatrician for treatment.

• Review the **family** history. If allergies run in the family, the child is likely to have them too.

• Minimize exposure to new foods in the first year. Avoid cow's milk until after the first birthday, eggs until the second birthday, and peanut butter or fish until age three. Introduce new foods in small servings.

• Eliminate from the child's diet foods suspected of being an allergy trigger and see if the symptom diminishes. Gradually reintroduce the food to see if the symptom returns. If a reaction recurs, avoid the food in the future.

• A simple blood test can help determine if the infant has allergies to certain foods and other substances. As children often outgrow allergies, they should have a second blood test to see if the allergies persist.

When to use immunotherapy

Parents considering allergy shots for their child should be referred to a board certified allergist. An allergist will follow specific steps to determine if allergy shots are necessary. The allergist will consider the child's age and general health status in deciding to start allergy treatments. The allergist will also inquire as to the child's environment (indoor and outdoor) and related symptoms to decide if testing is necessary. Allergy testing provides convincing evidence of specific antibodies to which the child is reacting. A pediatric allergist can diagnose the specific cause of the allergic reaction and provide the correct allergen extracts. He or she may also consider the following factors when deciding whether a child would benefit from allergy shots:

- The child's particular allergen may be difficult or impossible to avoid because of exposure to environment.

- Expensive medications producing side effects that adversely affect the child's health and quality of life are necessary to manage allergy symptoms. If the child's deterioration in health and the cost of allergy drugs outweigh their benefits, allergy shots may be appropriate.

- A parental commitment to see the child through the therapy is necessary for immunotherapy to work. The treatments demand a significant investment of parental time and support.

Allergy shots are also effective in treating allergic asthma. Allergy shots can help relieve the allergic reactions that trigger asthma episodes and decrease the need for asthma medications.

Skin testing

The allergist may decide to conduct skin testing on a child to determine the specific allergen that is causing a reaction in the child. In a skin test, a small dose of suspect antigens is injected under the skin. The physician looks at the injected area 20 minutes later; if it is red, with a raised area (wheal) in the center, the reaction is positive.

Skin testing should only be performed under the supervisions of a board certified allergist. The child should be followed closely during a skin test, because occasionally skin testing causes a severe reaction. This condition is unusual, since the amount of allergen used is small; however, it can happen if the child is highly sensitive to the allergen.

Preparing the shot

Once the testing is finished, the allergist prepares an allergen abstract (serum) specially for the child. If the child is sensitive to multiple allergens, the physician may mix similar abstracts in one vial. Preparing the vials in combination extracts ensures that the child receives only one shot for each group of extracts, thus reducing the number of injections needed for effective therapy.

INJECTIONS The first intramuscular injection (shot) is important because based on this experience the parent and child build an attitude toward future injections. If the child is old enough to understand, the nurse or physician will explain why the child must receive the injection. The procedure should be explained in simple terms, and should proceed quickly and as gently as possible. The child should be allowed to express his **fear** and resentment of needles.

Although the healthcare professional will record the allergy shot in the medical record, the parent may want to keep an updated record of the treatment for quick reference during emergencies and when the child is traveling.

INJECTION SITES The following injections sites are recommended for children:

- Infants: Outer front thigh. The parent should place the child in a secure position to prevent movement of the extremity. The parent should hold and cuddle the infant following the injection.

- Toddlers and school-age children: Buttocks, upper outer side. The buttocks do not develop until the child begins to walk, so this site is used only when the child has been walking for one year or more.

- Older children: Upper portion of the buttocks. This site provides a dense muscle mass in older children, which eliminates the possibility of injuring the nervous and vascular organs. The disadvantage of this site is that it is visible to the child who may become apprehensive when the injection is given. Older children can also receive shots in the upper arm and in the upper outer part of the thigh.

After the injection, the parent and nurse should take time to praise the child for his cooperation. Infants and small children should be cuddled and given affection for a few minutes so they do not associate the experience only with the **pain**. A small child may be given a toy to divert attention. Older children may be allowed to select the site for the injection. In addition, nasal sprays are in the early 2000s being developed as a painless alternative to injection delivery.

Precautions

Strict adherence is essential to an effective immunotherapy program for children. Parents should maintain as exactly as possible the injection schedule that the allergist prescribes. They should also report immediately to their healthcare provider any adverse reactions to the treatment.

Children who receive allergy shots may develop serum sickness or other problems in reaction to the treatment. Serum sickness, an allergic reaction to serum contained in the allergy shot, may occur with the first injection or as a delayed reaction. Children may have a

KEY TERMS

Allergen—A foreign substance that provokes an immune reaction or allergic response in some sensitive people but not in most others.

Allergic conjunctivitis—Inflammation of the membrane lining the eyelid and covering the eyeball; congestion of the conjunctiva, with mucus secretion.

Allergic reaction—An immune system reaction to a substance in the environment; symptoms include rash, inflammation, sneezing, itchy watery eyes, and runny nose.

Anaphylaxis—Also called anaphylactic shock; a severe allergic reaction characterized by airway constriction, tissue swelling, and lowered blood pressure.

Antibody—A special protein made by the body's immune system as a defense against foreign material (bacteria, viruses, etc.) that enters the body. It is uniquely designed to attack and neutralize the specific antigen that triggered the immune response.

Antigen—A substance (usually a protein) identified as foreign by the body's immune system, triggering the release of antibodies as part of the body's immune response.

Asthma—A disease in which the air passages of the lungs become inflamed and narrowed, causing wheezing, coughing, and shortness of breath.

Desensitization—A treatment for phobias which involves exposing the phobic person to the feared situation. It is often used in conjunction with relaxation techniques. Also used to describe a technique of pain reduction in which the painful area is stimulated with whatever is causing the pain.

Leukotriene antagonist—An agent or class of drugs which exerts an action opposite to that of another.

Pediatric allergist—A board certified physician specializing in the diagnosis and treatment of allergic conditions in children.

Rhinitis—Inflammation and swelling of the mucous membranes that line the nasal passages.

Urticaria—An itchy rash usually associated with an allergic reaction. Also known as hives.

---

moderate fever, local redness and **itching**, or pain at the site of injection and a generalized skin eruption, most commonly urticaria (**hives**) associated with severe itching. The child may be uncomfortable but not seriously ill. A more severe and less common variety of serum sickness includes several of the following symptoms: malaise, protein in the urine, joint pains, swelling of mucous membranes with hoarseness and cough, vertigo, **nausea**, and **vomiting**. A rare and still more severe variety of serum illness produces extreme weakness approaching collapse; the child's temperature may be subnormal and the pulse weak. The rarest and most severe reaction, called **anaphylaxis**, produces immediate shock and can be fatal.

The symptoms of serum disease, particularly urticaria, may occur when a child acquires sensitivity to several drugs. Penicillin is the most frequent and important offender, and in these circumstances the symptoms are often delayed until days or even weeks after the penicillin therapy begins. Any of the symptoms of serum sickness may be mimicked. Immediate severe reactions to penicillin are almost unknown in children but can occur in adults.

There is an increased risk of a reaction with a variation of allergy shots which "rushes" the first phase of the treatment. In this treatment, steadily increasing doses of allergen extract are given every few hours instead of every few days or weeks. Rush immunotherapy should only be performed in a hospital under close supervision. Also, children who take medication that contain beta blockers for unstable heart conditions should not be given allergy shots unless the allergist thinks the benefits of starting immunotherapy outweigh the risks associated with suspending cardiac inhibitors.

Parental concerns

The goal shared by both physicians and parents in treating childhood asthma and allergies is to minimize medication side effects while maximizing the chance for children to lead normal lives. Parents can take the following steps to increase their child's comfort:

- Remove carpet, launder bed linens in hot water, and keep windows closed at night and in the early morning hours to minimize exposure to outdoor allergens.

- Avoid exposure to perfume and tobacco, or other forms of smoke.

- Monitor weather and seasonal changes in an effort to minimize exposure to pollen.

- Schedule outdoor playtime or **exercise** at non-peak pollen periods, such as afternoons or early evening.

- Have the child wear a mask when helping in the garden or cutting the lawn, vacuuming, or dusting.

- Involve the allergist in decisions regarding child's lifestyle.

Resources

BOOKS

Berger, William E. *Allergies and Asthma for Dummies.* New York: John Wiley & Sons, 2000.

Lockey, Richard F., et al. *Allergen Immunotherapy.* New York: Marcel Dekker Inc., 2004.

PERIODICALS

Dozor, Allen J. "Kids Health and Safety: Baby Allergy Alert." *Parents* (September 2004): 94.

WEB SITES

"Allergy." *Healthology.* Available online at <www.healthology.com> (accessed December 13, 2004).

"Immunotherapy (Allergy Shots)." *American College of Allergy, Asthma, and Immunology (ACAAI)*, March 4, 2000. Available online at <www.allergy.mcg.edu/advice/it.html> (accessed December 13, 2004).

"Immunotherapy (Allergy Shots)." *Medfacts.* Available online at <www.njc.org/medfacts/shots.html> (accessed December 13, 2004)

Aliene Linwood, RN, DPA

Allergy tests

Definition

Allergy tests evaluate levels of allergic sensitivity to commonly encountered allergens, which may be foods, pollen, chemicals, or other substances in the environment.

Purpose

When recurring symptoms in children indicate sensitivity to certain substances in the environment, allergy testing can be used to identify the particular allergens that my be triggering reactions. Using special testing techniques, the child will be exposed to small amounts of specific allergens to determine which of these might provoke a reaction or a "positive" result. Laboratory tests may also be conducted to identify allergens that react with allergy-related substances in the child's blood serum. Positive results from any allergy test may be used to narrow candidates for the allergen responsible for the reaction. Identification of the allergen may help parents avoid exposing their child to the substance and thereby reduce allergic reactions. In addition, allergy testing may be done on children with **asthma**, eczema, or skin **rashes** to determine if an allergy is causing the condition or making another condition worse. Allergy tests may also be done before allergen desensitization treatments to ensure the safety of additional exposure.

Description

Allergy is the reaction of the immune system to substances foreign to the body. It is normal for the immune system to respond to foreign microorganisms and particles, like pollen or dust, by producing antibodies against those substances. Antibodies are specific proteins the immune system manufactures to bind to corresponding molecules (antigens) on the cell surfaces of foreign organisms in an attempt to render them harmless. This antigen/antibody reaction is the body's way of protecting itself from invasion by harmful substances and the allergic responses or possible illness that may follow. In some sensitive individuals, excessive antibody production can be triggered by seemingly harmless, everyday substances in the environment. This reactive condition is commonly known as allergy, and the offending substance is called an allergen. Allergic disease arises in the sensitive child from either acute or chronic exposure to certain allergens by inhaling, ingesting, or touching them. Allergic reactions may be dose dependent; that is, longer exposure or exposure to larger amounts of the offending allergen may cause a greater response of the immune system and result in a stronger reaction. Common inhaled allergens include pollen, dust, cat dander, and insect parts from tiny house mites. Common food allergens, all protein-based, include nuts, shellfish, and milk. Allergic reactions can also be triggered by insect **bites**, molds and fungi, certain prescription drugs, plants such as **poison ivy** and **poison oak**, and irritating or toxic substances released into the air.

Allergic reactions involve a special set of cells in the immune system known as mast cells. Mast cells serve as guards in the tissues where the body meets the outside world: the skin; the mucous membranes of the eyes (conjunctiva), nose and throat (nasal and oral mucosa); and the linings of the respiratory and digestive (gastrointestinal) systems. Mast cells produce a special class of antibody, immunoglobulin E (IgE), that coats cell surfaces. Inside the mast cells are reactive chemicals in small packets or granules. When the antibodies encounter allergens, mast cells release granules, which spill out their chemicals onto the cells of nearby tissues, including blood vessels and nerves. Histamine is the most notable of these chemicals, binding quickly to histamine receptors on cell surfaces. Interaction of histamine with receptors on blood vessel, nerve, and tissue cells causes inflammation and the accumulation of intracellular fluid released by the cells. The characteristic swelling and redness that accompanies **allergies** are the result, seen especially in an irritated nose and throat, a runny nose, and red, irritated eyes. Histamine also stimulates **pain** receptors, causing the itchy, scratchy nose, eyes, and throat common in **allergic rhinitis**.

Allergy tests may be performed on the skin or using blood serum in a test tube. During skin tests, potential allergens are placed on the skin and the reaction is observed. In radio-allergosorbent allergy testing (RAST), blood serum is combined with a specific concentration of potential allergens in a test tube, and the mixture is tested for antibody/antigen reactions. Provocation testing involves direct exposure to a likely allergen, either through inhalation or ingestion. It is sometimes performed to determine if symptoms develop on exposure to allergens identified in skin or RAST tests.

The range of allergens used for allergy testing is chosen to reflect possible sources in the environment and may include the following:

• pollen from a variety of trees, common grasses, and weeds

• mold and fungus spores

• house dust

• house mites

• animal skin cells (dander) and saliva

• food extracts

• antibiotics

• insect venoms

Skin testing is the most common type of allergy test. There are two forms of skin tests: percutaneous and intradermal. In percutaneous or prick testing, a drop of each allergen to be tested is placed on the skin, usually on the forearm or the back. A typical battery of tests may involve two dozen allergen drops, including a drop of saline solution that should never provoke a reaction (negative control) and a drop of histamine that should always provoke a reaction (positive control). A small needle is inserted through the drop to prick the skin below. A new needle is used for each prick. The sites are examined over the next 20 minutes for evidence of swelling and redness, indicating a positive reaction. In some

instances, a tracing of the set of reactions may be made by placing paper over the tested area. Scratch testing, in which the skin is scratched instead of punctured, is used less often, but the principle is the same.

Intradermal testing involves directly injecting allergen solutions into the skin. Separate injections are made for each allergen tested. Observations are made over the next 20 minutes. As in percutaneous tests, a reddened, swollen spot develops at the injection site for each substance to which the child is sensitive. Skin reactivity can be seen for allergens whether they usually affect the skin. In other words, airborne and food allergens that are inhaled or ingested are capable of causing skin reactions when contact is made with mast cells.

Radio-allergosorbent testing (RAST) is a laboratory test performed on those who may be too sensitive to risk exposure to allergens through skin testing or when medications or skin conditions make testing unreliable. RAST testing involves obtaining a blood sample, usually venous blood from a vein in the arm. The sample will be centrifuged in the laboratory to separate the antibody-containing serum from the blood cells. The serum is then exposed to allergens bound to a solid-phase medium. If antibodies against a particular allergen are present, those antibodies will bind to the solid medium and remain attached after being rinsed. The antigen/antibody complex can be detected in the laboratory by adding specific immunoglobulins that are linked with a radioactive dye. The test is read by locating radioactive spots on the solid-phase medium, and a positive result is reported in each test in which reactive allergens are found.

Testing for **food allergies** is usually done through diet by a process of elimination, that is, by removing the suspect food from the diet for two weeks and then eating a single portion of the suspect food, followed by careful monitoring for symptoms. A slightly different method is to eat a simple, bland, prescribed diet for a period of two weeks, removing all possible food allergens. Suspect foods are then added to the diet one at a time and the individual is observed for reactions.

Provocation testing is done in some cases to confirm associations between exposure to certain allergens and the subsequent development of symptoms when skin testing or RAST tests have indicated possible sensitivity. In provocation challenges, the skin, nasal and oral mucosa, and lining of the lungs and gastrointestinal tract are exposed to suspected allergens. A purified preparation of the allergen is inhaled or ingested in increasing concentrations to determine if it will provoke symptoms. Oral food challenges with foods are more tedious than inhalation testing, since full passage through the digestive system may take a day or more. The test involves gradual ingestion of increasing amounts of the suspect food, usually at timed intervals. The test is discontinued with a particular food when either gastrointestinal symptoms occur or it becomes clear that the food is tolerated. In bronchial provocation challenges, the individual inhales increasingly concentrated solutions of a particular allergen prepared in a nebulizer. Each inhalation is followed by measuring the exhalation capacity with a measuring tool called a spirometer. Only one allergen is tested per day. Because provocation tests may actually provoke an allergic reaction in sensitized individuals, treatment medications such as **antihistamines** are typically available during and following the tests, for administration as needed.

Precautions

While allergy tests are quite safe for most people, the testing involves additional exposure to allergens. The possibility of causing an exaggerated allergic response, a dangerous condition known as **anaphylaxis**, does exist. Anaphylaxis can result in difficulty breathing and a sharp drop in blood pressure. Individuals who have had prior anaphylactic episodes should inform the testing clinician. Skin tests should never include a substance to which the individual has had severe allergic reactions or that has previously caused anaphylaxis.

Provocation tests may provoke an allergic reaction by exposing the individual to reactive allergens. Treatment medications such as injectable antihistamines should, therefore, be available during and following the tests, to be administered if needed.

Preparation

Skin testing is preceded by a brief examination of the skin. The patient should refrain from using anti-allergy drugs for at least 48 hours before testing. Prior to inhalation testing, children with asthma who can tolerate it may be asked to stop asthma medications. Testing for food allergies usually requires the child to avoid all suspect food for at least two weeks before testing.

The RAST test will usually require that a venous blood sample be drawn to obtain sufficient serum for the test. Parents can explain the procedure briefly to the child ahead of time to help reduce fears and encourage cooperation.

Aftercare

Skin testing does not usually require any aftercare. A generalized redness and swelling may occur in the test area, but it will usually resolve within a day or two.

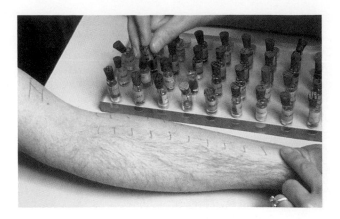

A scratch test is used to identify reactions to allergens. *(Custom Medical Stock Photo Inc.)*

Inhalation tests may cause delayed asthma attacks, even if the antigen administered in the test initially produces no response. Severe initial reactions may justify close professional observation for at least 12 hours after testing.

If a blood sample has been drawn for RAST testing, a bandage may be applied to the venipuncture site to help keep it clean and to stop slight bleeding that may occur. Unusual bleeding or bruising of the site should be reported to the pediatrician.

Children should be observed closely for signs of allergic reactions after allergy testing using skin tests, inhalation tests, or provocation tests.

Risks

Intradermal testing may inadvertently result in the injection of the allergen into the circulation, with an increased risk of adverse reactions. Inhalation tests may provoke an asthma attack. Exposure to new or unsuspected allergens in any test carries the risk of anaphylaxis. Because patients are monitored following allergy testing, an anaphylactic reaction is usually recognized and treated promptly to reverse the condition. Occasionally, a delayed anaphylactic response can occur that requires immediate care. It is critical that physicians provide education about how to recognize anaphylaxis and tell patients what to do if it occurs at home.

Normal results

Lack of redness or swelling on a skin test indicates no allergic response. In an inhalation test, the exhalation capacity should remain unchanged. In a food challenge, no symptoms should occur.

KEY TERMS

Allergen—A foreign substance that provokes an immune reaction or allergic response in some sensitive people but not in most others.

Anaphylaxis—Also called anaphylactic shock; a severe allergic reaction characterized by airway constriction, tissue swelling, and lowered blood pressure.

Antibody—A special protein made by the body's immune system as a defense against foreign material (bacteria, viruses, etc.) that enters the body. It is uniquely designed to attack and neutralize the specific antigen that triggered the immune response.

Antigen—A substance (usually a protein) identified as foreign by the body's immune system, triggering the release of antibodies as part of the body's immune response.

Antihistamine—A drug used to treat allergic conditions that blocks the effects of histamine, a substance in the body that causes itching, vascular changes, and mucus secretion when released by cells.

Histamine—A substance released by immune system cells in response to the presence of an allergen. It stimulates widening of blood vessels and increased porousness of blood vessel walls so that fluid and protein leak out from the blood into the surrounding tissue, causing localised inflammation of the tissue.

Immunoglobulin G (IgG)—Immunoglobulin type gamma, the most common type found in the blood and tissue fluids.

Intradermal—An injection into a deep layer of skin.

Mast cells—A type of immune system cell that is found in the lining of the nasal passages and eyelids. It displays a type of antibody called immunoglobulin type E (IgE) on its cell surface and participates in the allergic response by releasing histamine from intracellular granules.

Abnormal results

Presence of redness or swelling, especially over 5 mm (0.25 inch) in diameter, indicates an allergic response. This reaction does not mean the substance actually causes the child's symptoms, however, since he or she may have no regular exposure to the allergen. In fact, the actual allergen may not have been included in the test array.

Following allergen inhalation, reduction in exhalation capacity of more than 20 percent, and for at least 10 to 20 minutes, indicates a positive reaction to the allergen and the sensitivity of the individual being tested.

Gastrointestinal symptoms within 24 hours following the ingestion of a suspected food allergen indicates a positive response and sensitivity to that food allergen.

Parental concerns

Parents who are already confronted with their child's allergies may be reluctant to have the child undergo testing. Physicians and medical personnel can assure parents that careful observation is involved in testing procedures and that allergens to which the child may have had severe reactions will be avoided. Appropriate medications will be available to treat the child immediately if a reaction is provoked by testing. It is important for parents to tell the child how the tests will be done so that the child is not anxious or apprehensive, which in some cases may increase the likelihood of false positive reactions.

See also Asthma; Allergic rhinitis; Drug allergies/sensitivities.

Resources

BOOKS

Gordon, Susan, et al. *Allergy Methods and Protocols.* Totowa, NJ: Humana Press, 2004.

Kemp, Stephen F., and Richard F. Lockey, eds. *Diagnostic Testing of Allergic Disease.* NY: Marcel Dekker Inc., 2000.

WEB SITES

"Allergies." *Harvard Medical School Consumer Information.* Available online at <http://www.intelihealth.com> (accessed October 10, 2004).

"ImmunoCAP Specific IgE Blood Test." *Quest Diagnostics.* Available online at <www.questdiagnostics.com/hcp/topics/immunocap/immunocap.html> (accessed October 10, 2004).

L. Lee Culvert
Richard Robinson

Allowance and money management

Definition

An allowance is money earned or given to a child at regular intervals to teach the child how to manage money.

Purpose

Parents differ in their opinions about giving allowances to their children. Some parents believe that they should provide for the material needs of their children, and there is no reason a child should have to manage money until they are old enough to understand the working world and mature enough to make responsible purchases. Other parents feel that giving their children allowances is a good way to teach them about money and financial responsibility. If parents decide to give their children allowances, there are several ways to do it. How much they receive, how often they receive it, what they may spend it on, and whether the children must earn their allowance by completing chores at home are all questions for parents to consider.

Description

School-age children are starting to develop the cognitive skills necessary to understand basic monetary ideas, such as identifying coins, counting change, and matching small amounts of money to items they want to buy. Apart from introducing children to basic economics, money lessons have other benefits. Money illustrates parental values and teaches children about the relative worth of things, time, and effort.

When to start an allowance

Children younger than five are not mature enough to understand money management. They usually resist saving money and tend to spend money right way. Older children are more likely to take responsibility for their money. As they learn math skills, children are more able to calculate expenses. They can begin to figure how much they need to save for a item or how much they will have left over after buying something.

By the time children are five or six years old, they may be responsible enough to handle small amounts of money. Before starting an allowance, parents may discuss budgets with children and what children want to buy. They may shop with their children in stores on online and discuss prices.

The amount of allowance is a personal choice for parents. Young children may be given one or two dollars, while teenagers may be given ten dollars or more. Some families will give close-in-age siblings the same amount of allowance, but general practice is to give older children more money than younger children.

Young children may be given enough money to buy small items such as trading cards, hair clips, or ice-cream bars. The next time parents go shopping, the children can bring their own money if they think they might want to buy something. If they have already spent their allowance, then they have to wait for the next allowance before buying something else.

Building financial skills

Parents may want to reinforce lessons the children learn in school by making a chart that shows basic money equivalents. They may choose to post it on the refrigerator or in the child's room. Playing store and putting price tags on things around the house teach children relative worth of items.

Like adults, children may have trouble saving money. If a child wants to buy an item that costs more than his or her allowance, parents may choose to be flexible. They can allot the child an extra allowance or help the child figure out how long it would take to save the amount from future allowances. Parents may offer to provide matching funds, contributing a dollar for every dollar the child saves.

Some parents devise a category system to help their children manage their allowances. The first category is short-term expenses, money the child may spend right away on whatever he or she wants. The second category is savings, money put in a special jar, where its gradual accumulation is visible. This money is used for items the child wants that cost more than the weekly allowance. The third category is charity, money for church donation or a local cause, for example, or for gifts. The parents may decide how a younger child's allowance should be divided among the three categories, or the budgeting may be left up to an older child.

Allowances and chores

Many people believe that child's allowance should not be tied to household chores. Children should help out around the house because they are part of the **family**, not because they are paid. Allotting children chores that are proper to their abilities teaches responsibility and makes them feel the worth of their contribution to the family. The sense of belonging and empowerment gained by being an inherent part of a family team is important for children. Children learn to contribute something valuable and realize that others depend on them to do their part. This relationship raises **self-esteem** and allows children to see themselves as active and valuable participants in others' lives.

Guidelines for spending the allowance

If parents expect children to pay for their needs, such as school clothes, **sports** gear, music lessons, or a comic book collection, or services the parents would otherwise pay for, the allowance has to be large. These items should be in the budget developed with the children's help.

Children need to learn that they can increase the money they have by saving it or working for it. Parents may create a list of jobs children can do above and beyond their regular chores, listing the amount of money the parents are willing to pay for these jobs.

Parental concerns

Some parents stop giving allowances to their teenagers at a certain age and encourage them to get a part-time job. Although teenagers may earn money from jobs outside the home, they may still need parental guidance to develop correct spending habits. They need to know how to save money and give to charity as well.

Parents can be authoritative without being dictatorial in teaching their children how to manage money. They can invite suggestions from the teenager about what he or she should buy and how much money to spend on it. Teenagers may be asked to buy gas for the family car when they drive it to work or to social events. They may be asked to use their earnings to pay their telephone service if they own a cell phone and to buy gifts with their own money for their friends and for the family.

Some families put teenagers in charge of all their own expenses, so they learn to budget. But some parents also maintain that teenagers should not take large sums of money from their account to make important purchases such as a car or motorcycle without parental permission. Money can become a difficult issue between parents and children of any age, and learning to be flexible can help each member of the family become more financially responsible.

Money management

Children's financial education extends throughout childhood. It occurs as they listen to parents talk about money; in their parents' wage earning patterns;

---

and in their increasing experience with earning and spending.

Children can absorb a lot of knowledge from their parents about money management. Parent can **play** money games with them, using mail-order catalogs and price tags in stores, to teach values. When children are old enough, parents can discuss banking and investments. Rather than let children keep their financial gifts in a piggy bank in the house, parents can help children open a passbook savings account or a mutual fund and let them file the receipts for these accounts. Parents can also discuss with their children the impact of advertisement on personal spending habits and introduce their children to consumer advocacy publications such as *Consumers Report*.

Resources

BOOKS

McCurrach, David. *The Allowance Workbook: For Kids and Their Parents.* Franklin, TN: Kids' Money Press, 2000.

———. *Kids' Allowances: How Much, How Often, and How Come.* Franklin, TN: Kids' Money Press, 2000.

Orman, Suze. *The 9 Steps to Financial Freedom.* New York: Three River Press, 2000.

Aliene S. Linwood, RN, DPA, FACHE

Alopecia

Definition

Alopecia is the partial or complete loss of hair—especially on the scalp—either in patches (alopecia areata), on the entire head (alopecia totalis), or over the entire body (alopecia universalis).

Description

A basic understanding of hair biology and normal hair development is essential in distinguishing normal versus abnormal hair loss in children and adolescents.

Hair consists of the shaft and the root, which is anchored into a follicle beneath the epidermis. Hair is formed by rapid divisions of cells at the base of the follicle. Except for a few growing cells at the base of the root, hair, which is composed of keratin and other proteins, is dead tissue.

An individual hair follicle has a long growth phase, producing steadily growing hair for two to six years. About 80 percent to 90 percent of hair follicles are involved in this active growing period called the anagen phase. Next is a brief transitional phase (of about three weeks' duration)—the catagen phase—during which the hair follicle degenerates. About 5 percent of follicles are involved in the catagen phase.

Then a dormant period known as the telogen phase occurs. About 10 percent to 15 percent of hairs are involved in this phase, which lasts for approximately three months. Following the telogen phase, the growth phase begins again, and the growth cycle repeats.

Each person has about 100,000 hairs on their scalp. Although it is normal to lose between 25 and 100 hairs per day, any disruption of the hair growth cycle may cause abnormal hair loss.

Demographics

It is estimated that alopecia affects several million children in the United States and that hair loss is responsible for about 3 percent of all pediatric office visits.

Alopecia areata affects both sexes and all ages but is most common in children five to 12 years old. About one per 1000 children has alopecia areata. Approximately 5 percent of children with alopecia areata go on to develop alopecia totalis, and some of these children may develop alopecia universalis.

Tinea capitis (**ringworm**) affects an estimated 10 percent to 20 percent of susceptible children, and although the demographics are sketchy, telogen effluvium is the most common type of alopecia in both children and adults.

Causes and symptoms

Although in children and adolescents, hair loss may be caused by a wide variety of factors, most children experience hair loss as a result of one of four major causes:

- fungal infections
- alopecia areata
- trauma to the hair shaft
- telogen effluvium

A fungal infection called tinea capitis, which is similar to athlete's foot, is a common cause of hair loss, particularly among toddlers and early school-aged children. Tinea capitis, which affects the hair root, is a highly contagious condition and is often transmitted when a child uses the comb, brush, hat, or bed linen of an infected child. Tinea capitis seldom occurs after **puberty**.

Children with this condition usually have patchy hair loss with some broken hairs visible just above the surface of the scalp. The patches of hair loss are usually round or oval but are sometimes irregular in shape. When broken off at the surface, the hairs resemble small black dots on the scalp. Occasionally gray flakes or scales are present.

Alopecia areata, or localized baldness, is the sudden appearance of sharply defined circular or oval patches of hair loss, most often on the scalp. These patches are smooth and without inflammation, scaling, or broken hairs and may appear overnight or over the course of a few days. This condition may affect scalp hair, the eyebrows, eyelashes, genital area, and occasionally the underarms. The hair loss is not accompanied by other visible evidence of scalp disease, and the condition is not contagious.

In alopecia areata, immune system cells (white blood cells) attack the rapidly growing cells in the hair follicles that produce hair. The affected hair follicles decrease in size and hair production slows drastically. Because the stem cells that continually supply the follicles with new cells do not appear to be affected, the follicle retains the potential to regrow hair.

Although it is uncertain why the hair follicles undergo these changes, it is thought that a combination of genes may predispose some children and adults to the disease. In those who are genetically predisposed, some type of trigger—perhaps a virus or something in the child's environment—brings on the attack against the hair follicles.

Trauma to the hair shaft is another common cause of hair loss in children. Often the trauma is caused by traction resulting from, for example, tight braids, ponytails, or by friction (hats, hair bands, or rubbing against a bed). Trauma may also be caused by chemicals or **burns**.

Another important cause of hair trauma is called tri-chotillomania—a habit similar to thumb-sucking or nail-biting—of twirling or pulling out the hair. **Trichotillomania** is generally considered to be a nervous habit and may include the pulling of eyebrows and eyelashes.

The hair loss associated with trichotillomania is patchy and is characterized by broken hairs of varying length. Within the patches, hair loss is not complete. If the hair trauma is not severe or chronic enough to cause scarring, the child's hair usually regrows when the trauma ceases.

Telogen effluvium, another common cause of hair loss, affects both children and adults. This condition is responsible for more hair loss than any other cause except adult male-pattern baldness. In telogen effluvium, there is a physiologic basis to the hair loss; something happens to interrupt the hair's normal growth cycle and to drive many or all of the hairs into the telogen phase. Between six and 16 weeks later, partial or complete baldness occurs.

Many factors can cause telogen effluvium, including the following:

- high fever
- medications, including chemotherapy
- crash diets
- excessive vitamin A
- emotional stress
- surgery
- severe injury

In the telogen phase, a child's hair undergoes growth spurts and pauses. During the rest phase between spurts, the bulb at the end of the hair root decreases in volume and the hair loosens. Although exaggerated during **adolescence**, particularly in girls (due the influence of female hormones), even preadolescents may experience excessive hair loss on a daily basis. The scalp hair, however, appears normal in this condition.

When to call the doctor

It is important to consult a dermatologist or pediatrician if a child sheds hair in large amounts (more than 100 hairs per day for longer than four weeks) after combing, brushing, or shampooing or if the hair becomes significantly thinner. Also, if a child's scalp show signs of infection (redness, swelling, tenderness, warmth), consulting a physician is advised.

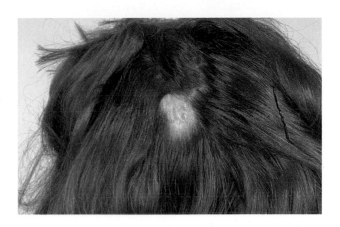

Bald spot on the scalp from the effects of alopecia. *(© Mediscan/Visuals Unlimited.)*

If children are observed pulling out their hair, eyelashes, or eyebrows, parents should consult a physician in order to determine the underlying cause of the habit.

Diagnosis

Because hair loss is caused by a variety of conditions, a physician diagnoses the cause of the child's hair loss based on medical history, **family** history of hair loss, medications (including **vitamins**), nutritional status, hair-care habits, and a physical examination.

If the physician suspects a fungal infection of the scalp, a hair sample may be tested by microscopic examination in the laboratory. Microscopic examination of a hair plucked at the periphery of the hair loss area often reveals a characteristic disruption of the integrity of the hair shaft. The infection may be confirmed by culturing the scalp for fungal organisms.

Blood tests or a scalp biopsy may be required if a medical condition—such as lupus erythematosus, thyroid dysfunction, iron deficiency, or hormonal imbalance—is suspected.

Treatment

Treatment varies with the cause of the hair loss. In some cases, early treatment is important in restoring the hair. Often congenital and hereditary hair loss and hair shaft abnormalities, however, have no effective treatment.

For fungal infections such as tinea capitis, treatment usually requires a systemic approach with an oral antifungal prescription medication such as griseofulvin (Fulvicin). This medication, which must be taken for four to eight weeks, is very effective in curing the infection and restoring the hair. Early treatment is important in preventing possible permanent hair loss.

Topical creams or antifungal shampoos containing 2 percent ketoconazole are often used two to three times per week for eight weeks. Although shampoos and topical antifungal creams may decrease scaling, the infection usually returns because these products do not penetrate the hair follicle deeply enough to eradicate the infection.

A wide variety of treatments are available for alopecia areata. There has been some success with use of medications that suppress the immune system, including dinitrochlorobenzene (DNCB) and diphenylcyclopropenone (DPCP). The side effects of these drugs, however, may outweigh the benefits for a disease that most often resolves on its own.

In addition, topical creams or lotions such as minoxidil, cortisone (also injected into the scalp), or anthralin are sometimes used. Because such treatment triggers hair growth in bald patches but does not eradicate the disease, however, new bald patches can occur in other parts of the scalp even if new growth occurs.

Hair loss resulting from telogen effluvium or drug side effects usually requires no treatment. Hair loss from poor **nutrition** or medical illness usually stops with the adoption of a healthy diet and treatment of the underlying medical condition. Once the stressful event is over, complete hair growth usually occurs within six months.

Alternative treatment

There is some evidence to suggest that aromatherapy is a safe and effective treatment for alopecia areata. Aromatherapy involves rubbing scented essential oils into the skin to treat localized and systemic disease.

Massaging the essential oils of rosemary, lavender, sage, thyme, and cedar into the scalp is believed to increase circulation and reduce stress. About three to six drops of essential oil are added to 1 tablespoon of jojoba or grape seed oil and massaged into the scalp.

In addition to aromatherapy, stress reduction techniques such as **yoga**, meditation, or creative visualization may increase blood flow to the scalp and stimulate hair growth.

Prognosis

The prognosis for children with alopecia varies with the cause of hair loss. Certain types of alopecia respond more readily to treatment. For example, hair loss in telogen effluvium usually occurs over several weeks to months, then stops. Hair then grows back over the next several months.

Overall, the outlook for children with alopecia areata is good. Alopecia areata usually resolves with time, although alopecia totalis is less likely to remit. With appropriate treatment, from 60 percent to 95 percent of children regrow all of their hair within one year.

Early treatment and the proper antifungal medications can cure tinea capitis, although patience is required because the condition may take several months to resolve.

Prevention

Although it may not be possible to prevent all types of alopecia—such as alopecia areata or hair loss associated with medical conditions—certain forms of hair loss may be prevented. Highly contagious fungal infections such as tinea capitis, for example, may be prevented by keeping hair clean and by teaching children not to share hats, combs, or hair brushes. In addition, adolescent girls should be cautioned not to share makeup.

It is important to teach children and adolescents to handle their hair with care, especially when shampooing, drying, brushing, combing, braiding, and using chemical processes. Hair is more fragile when it is wet, so vigorous towel drying and rough combing and brushing should be avoided. Wide-toothed combs and brushes with smooth tips are recommended.

Nutritional concerns

Children may experience hair loss or excessive thinning as a result of certain nutritional deficiencies. To prevent such hair loss, it is essential to include B-6, biotin, and folic acid—either in the diet or in supplement form.

It has been found that certain **minerals**, including magnesium, sulfur, silica, and zinc are also important for maintaining healthy hair. Beta-carotene, which is converted to vitamin A in the body, is also essential to healthy skin, hair, and nails. Beta-carotene is found in green and yellow vegetables and fruits.

Because hair is composed of protein, a diet that is too low in protein may cause hair thinning or a disruption of the growth cycle. Thus eating a protein-rich diet often results in improved hair growth. In addition to lean meat, good food sources of protein include fish, eggs, dairy products, and beans.

Parental concerns

Because society has placed so much emphasis on appearance, hair loss, particularly if it is severe, may be emotionally devastating to children and adolescents. Hair loss can lead to embarrassment, low **self-esteem**, and depression. Thus it is important for parents to consult a physician as soon as possible to minimize not only the physical but also the emotional impact of hair loss on their child.

See also Dermatitis; Malnutrition; Trichotillomania.

Resources

BOOKS

"Disorders of Hair." In *Nelson Textbook of Pediatrics*, 17th ed. Edited by Richard E. Behrman, Robert M. Kliegman, and Hal B. Jenson. Philadelphia: Saunders, 2004.

Powell, Jennifer, Natalie Stone, and Rodney P. R. Dawber. *An Atlas of Hair and Scalp Diseases.* Carnforth, UK: Parthenon, 2000.

PERIODICALS

Usatine, Richard P. "Bald Spots on a Young Girl." *Journal of Family Practice* 53, no. 1 (January 2004): 33–36.

ORGANIZATIONS

American Academy of Dermatology. PO Box 4014, Schaumburg, IL 60168–0050. Web site: <www.aad.org>.

American Hair Loss Council. 125 Seventh Street, Suite 625, Pittsburgh, PA 15222. Web site: <www.ahlc.org>.

National Alopecia Areata Foundation. PO Box 150760, San Rafael, CA 94915–0760. Web site: <http://www.naaf.org>.

WEB SITES

Brodell, Robert T., and Giorgio Vescera. "Black Dot Tinea Capitis." *Postgraduate Medicine Online* 111, no. 4 (April 2002). Available online at <www.postgraduatemedicine.com/issues/2002/04_02/pd_brodell.htm> (accessed October 10, 2004).

Genevieve Slomski, Ph.D.

Alpha-fetoprotein test

Definition

The alpha-fetoprotein (AFP) test is a blood test that is performed during pregnancy to screen the fetus for certain conditions; it is also used to screen for certain diseases in infants and children. The screening test measures the level of AFP in the mother's blood and indicates the probability that the fetus has one of several serious birth defects. The level of AFP can also be determined by analyzing a sample of amniotic fluid. This screening test cannot diagnose a specific condition; it only indicates the increase of risk for several birth defects. In infants and children, the AFP test is used to detect liver disease, certain cancerous tumors, and to monitor the progress of **cancer** treatment.

Purpose

Alpha-fetoprotein is a substance produced by the liver of a fetus, by tumors of the liver, by testes and ovaries, and by certain other diseases of the liver. The exact function of this protein was as of 2004 unknown. After birth, the infant's liver stops producing AFP; an adult liver contains only trace amounts. During pregnancy, the fetus excretes AFP in urine, and some of the protein crosses the fetal membranes to enter the mother's blood. The level of AFP can then be determined by analyzing a sample of the mother's blood.

By analyzing the amount of AFP found in a blood or amniotic fluid sample, doctors can determine the probability that the fetus is at risk for certain birth defects. It is very important that the doctor know precisely how old the fetus is when the test is performed, because the AFP level changes over the length of the pregnancy. AFP screening is used as an indicator of risk and then an appropriate line of testing (like **amniocentesis** or ultrasound) follows, based on the results.

Abnormally high AFP may indicate that the fetus has an increased risk of a neural tube defect, the most common and severe type of disorder associated with increased AFP. These types of defects include spinal column defects (**spina bifida**) and anencephaly (a severe and usually fatal brain abnormality). If the tube that becomes the brain and spinal cord does not close correctly during fetal development, AFP may leak through this abnormal opening and enter the amniotic fluid. This leakage creates abnormally high levels of AFP in amniotic fluid and in maternal blood.

Other fetal conditions that can raise AFP levels above normal include: cysts at the end of the spine, blockage in the esophagus or intestines, some liver diseases, defects in the abdominal wall, kidney or urinary tract defects or disease, and brittle bone disease.

Levels may also be high if there is too little fluid in the amniotic sac around the fetus, more than one developing fetus, or a pregnancy that is farther along than estimated. For unknown reasons, abnormally low AFP may indicate that the fetus has an increased risk of **Down syndrome**. Down syndrome is a condition that includes **mental retardation** and a distinctive physical appearance linked to an abnormality of chromosome 21 (called trisomy 21). If the maternal screening test indicates an abnormally low AFP, amniocentesis is used to diagnosis the problem. Abnormally low levels of AFP can also occur when the fetus has died or when the mother is overweight.

AFP is often part of a triple-check blood test that analyzes three substances as risk indicators of possible birth defects: AFP, estriol, and human chorionic gonadotropin (HCG). When all three substances are measured in the mother's blood, the accuracy of the test results increases. Although AFP in human blood gradually disappears after birth, it never disappears entirely. It may reappear in liver disease, or tumors of the liver, ovaries, or testicles. The AFP test is used to screen people at high risk for these conditions. After a cancerous tumor is removed, an AFP test can monitor the progress of treatment. Continued high AFP levels suggest the cancer is growing.

Description

The AFP maternal screening test is usually performed at week 16 of pregnancy. In both pregnant mothers (whose fetus is being screened) and in children, blood is drawn from a vein, usually on the inside of the elbow. For a fetus, AFP can also be measured in the sample of amniotic fluid taken at the time of amniocentesis. Test results are usually available after about one week.

Precautions

It is very important that the doctor know precisely how old the fetus is when the test is performed, because the AFP level considered normal changes over the length of the pregnancy. Errors in determining the age of the fetus lead to errors when interpreting the test results. Since an AFP test is only a screening tool, more specific tests must follow to make an accurate diagnosis. An abnormal test result does not necessarily mean that the fetus has a birth defect. The test has a high rate of abnor-

mal results (either high or low) in order to prevent missing a fetus that has a serious condition.

Preparation

There is no specific physical preparation for the AFP test.

Aftercare

Other than making sure the bleeding stops from the needle puncture site and watching for any signs of infection at the needle site, there is no specific aftercare involved with this blood test.

Risks

The risks associated with drawing blood are minimal but may include bleeding from the puncture site, feeling faint or lightheaded after the blood is drawn, or blood accumulating under the puncture site (hematoma).

Normal results

Alpha-fetoprotein is measured in nanograms per milliliter (ng/mL) and is expressed as a probability. The probability 1:100, for example, translates into the chance that the fetus has a one in 100 chance, for example, of having the defect. An AFP level less than or equal to 50 ng/mL is considered normal.

Abnormal results

The doctor inform the mother of the fetus about the specific increased risk as compared to the normal risk of a standard case. If the risk of Down syndrome is greater than the standard risk for women who are 35 years old or older (1:270), then amniocentesis is recommended. Again, the test has a high rate of showing an abnormal AFP level in order to prevent missing a fetus that has Down syndrome. This screening test only predicts risk; appropriate diagnostic testing follows an abnormal screening result. In neonatal liver disease testing, an AFP level greater than 40 ng/mL is considered abnormal. An AFP level greater than 20 ng/mL may be associated with tumors of the ovary or testes.

Parental concerns

A parent might be concerned about drawing blood from a child, but the **pain** from the needle puncture only lasts a moment.

When to call a doctor

If there is excess bleeding from the needle puncture site, or if hours to days later, the puncture site looks infected (red and swollen), then a doctor should be contacted.

Resources

BOOKS

Henry, John. *Clinical Diagnosis and Management by Laboratory Methods*, 20th ed. Philadelphia: Saunders, 2001.

Wallach, Jacques. *Interpretation of Diagnostic Tests*, 7th ed. Philadelphia: Lippincott, Williams, and Wilkins, 2000.

ORGANIZATIONS

March of Dimes Birth Defects Foundation. 1275 Mamaroneck Ave., White Plains, NY 10605. Web site: <www.modimes.org>.

National Cancer Institute. Building 31, Room 10A31, 31 Center Drive, MSC 2580, Bethesda, MD 20892–2580. Web site: <www.nci.nih.gov>.

Mark A. Best

Alternative school

Definition

An alternative school is an educational setting designed to accommodate educational, behavioral, and/or medical needs of children and adolescents that cannot be adequately addressed in a traditional school environment.

Purpose

Alternative schools have been established since about the 1970s to meet the needs of children and adolescents who cannot learn effectively in a traditional school environment (i.e., conventional public or parochial schools) due to learning disabilities, certain medical conditions, psychological and behavioral issues, or advanced skills. In general, alternative schools have more comprehensive educational and developmental objectives than conventional schools. They often have curriculum elements that focus on improving student **self-esteem**, fostering growth of individuality, and enhancing social skills. Alternative schools are more flexible in their organization and administration, which allows for more variety in educational programs.

Once available primarily for disruptive students and those at risk for dropping out of a traditional school environment, alternative schools have expanded significantly in function as educators, parents, and wider communities recognize that many children cannot learn effectively in a traditional school environment. For children and adolescents with psychological and behavioral issues, such as **personality disorders**, substance use and abuse, depression, and violence, alternative schools can provide a safer therapeutic environment and more individualized attention than traditional schools. For children and adolescents with learning disabilities and certain medical conditions, such as attention deficit hyperactivity disorder (ADHD), **dyslexia**, and Asperger's syndrome, alternative schools can provide integrated education and clinical services in one place to facilitate learning.

Description

Alternative school structure and curriculum varies depending on the educational goals and desired student population. Alternative schools may be available and accessible locally or may require additional daily travel or boarding by the student. Usually, local alternatives to public schools do not require tuition, while private schools do require parents to pay tuition for student attendance.

A number of different types of alternative schools exist, including the following:

- local alternatives to public schools, for example, charter schools, magnet schools, at-risk programs
- special-needs day schools
- independent private schools
- therapeutic wilderness programs
- emotional growth boarding schools

For parents who desire a local alternative to traditional public and parochial schools, several charter and magnet schools may be available, especially in urban areas. Charter schools are independent, publicly funded schools run by teachers, parents, or foundations that are often formed to meet local community needs as an alternative to public schools. Charter schools may have a special focus, such as technical skills or music. As of 2004, virtual charter schools have been formed that offer all courses via the Internet or other distance learning methods for students who need to remain at home or whose parents wish them to remain at home. Magnet schools are public schools that offer specialized programs designed to attract students wishing to enhance particular skills. Magnet schools were originally formed in the 1960s and 1970s to promote voluntary racial desegregation in urban school districts. Magnet schools often advertise themselves as "centers of excellence" in a certain area, such as performing arts, science, or mathematics. Both charter and magnet schools generally have smaller classes and enhanced extracurricular offerings.

For children and adolescents identified as "at-risk" by the public school district, alternative programs may be available. Usually, at-risk alternative programs are offered at a special location within the public school district or at a location that is accessible to and serves multiple public schools (e.g., a county-wide program). At-risk students usually have undergone school psychological and behavioral evaluation that identifies them as requiring specialized attention not available in the traditional school environment. Suitable programs can include emotionally disturbed, oppositional, and disruptive students and offer smaller classes, specially trained staff, and closer supervision. Some programs may be dedicated to serving a particular group of at-risk students, such as pregnant teens and teen mothers. Researchers have estimated that more than 280,000 at-risk students in the United States are in alternative programs offered by school districts or private boarding schools (see below).

Special-needs day schools focus on **special education** programs to meet the needs of children and adolescents with learning disabilities and learning challenges. Students with severe ADHD, moderate-to-severe physical or behavioral obstacles, and other specialized educational needs receive customized instruction with individualized lesson plans, special counseling, adaptive physical education, speech therapy, and other supportive services to ensure that they can learn despite educational barriers caused by a medical condition or learning disability.

Independent private schools are privately funded schools controlled by an individual or non-government organization. Private schools may be day schools or boarding schools. Private schools require that parents pay tuition and usually have a competitive admissions process requiring students to complete an application and interview. Private schools usually emphasize academic and/or athletic achievement, and student acceptance is based on academic and athletic potential, as well as enthusiasm for being active in school community life. Private schools have smaller classes, a more structured learning environment, a variety of **extracurricular activities**, and individualized opportunities for developing student **creativity** and intellect.

Therapeutic wilderness programs involve group and individual therapy in an outdoor adventure setting. Depending on the program, academics may or may not be included. Usually, therapeutic wilderness programs do not run for a full school year and thus are not alternative schools per se; however, these programs generally run for a full summer or school semester (six to eight weeks) and may, therefore, be considered alternative education. Therapeutic wilderness programs use the outdoors to rapidly influence adolescents with at-risk behaviors through physical and emotional challenges that help them understand unhealthy behaviors and gain a more positive sense of self and responsibility. Group therapy employed in a wilderness setting helps adolescents learn how to successfully interact with peers. Therapeutic wilderness programs are appropriate for adolescents who have exhibited extreme defiance; who have a history of **running away**, substance abuse, sexual promiscuity, poor school performance (failing), and violence; and have not responded to other treatment programs. Therapeutic wilderness programs often serve as a transition to long-term therapeutic placement in a residential treatment center or emotional growth boarding school, depending on the needs of the adolescent.

Emotional growth boarding schools integrate therapeutic programs with academics to provide for students whose emotional, psychological, and behavioral issues prevent them from learning effectively in a traditional school environment. Therapeutic components of these schools include daily and weekly group and individual therapy, highly structured learning and living environments, experiential learning, and individualized academic programming. Because the root of many emotional and behavioral problems is low self-esteem and a negative perception of self, emotional growth programs focus on helping students permanently change negative self-perceptions, discovering and healing emotional trauma, and identifying and changing negative behaviors. Emotional growth boarding schools usually offer rolling admission; that is, students are accepted year-round and academics are available year-round. This type of operation helps parents whose children need emergency placement. Candidates for emotional growth boarding schools are enrolled from therapeutic wilderness programs or undergo psychological and educational testing to determine their academic and therapeutic needs. Poor academic performance, a symptom of many emotional problems, is expected, and trained staff, counselors, and teachers provide support to improve student performance. While emotional growth boarding schools use different therapeutic models, depending on the school, most programs do use incentive-based learning and therapy, wilderness therapy, and intensive counseling to improve student decision-making, interpersonal skills, academic performance, and emotional coping skills. These schools also use **sports**, the arts, and interaction with animals as part of therapy.

Precautions

Parents considering alternative schools should thoroughly investigate the school's credentials, staff training, available curriculum, student support services, and student population to make sure that the needs of their child will be met.

There are a number of wilderness programs available for different types of students, and not all have a therapeutic component. In addition, some wilderness programs employ "boot camp" methods that may be unsafe for children and adolescents. A therapeutic wilderness program should have trained and/or certified wilderness counselors and medical support services, as well as provide training in wilderness skills for participants.

Preparation

Making the decision to place a child in an alternative school can be difficult and involves a number of factors. For independent private schools and schools that focus on a specific skill or talent, interviews and applications may be necessary, and advanced students and students with special talents have to complete an often-rigorous application process. Parents and students should be prepared to visit all schools under consideration and participate in interviews with school staff.

For children with special medical needs, clinical care may need to be coordinated with current physicians and clinical staff at the new alternative school. Parents and students should be prepared to undergo additional medical and educational testing to determine the student's needs for individualized lesson plans.

Schools that accept at-risk children and adolescents require psychological and educational testing, as well as references or recommendations from a professional (usually a psychologist, psychiatrist, or therapist). In some situations where the child or adolescent is a danger to himself/herself and/or others, emergency transport services to the therapeutic school are available; specially trained individuals escort the student from their home to the school, even via air travel, to ensure the child's **safety**. Parents of at-risk children and adolescents should be prepared emotionally to handle such situations and also to participate in regular **family therapy** sessions during the alternative program.

Public schools are obligated to provide access to a free and safe education for students, and if their curriculum and support services cannot handle the needs of a particular student, the public school may also be obligated to financially support the student in an alternative school that can better address the student's needs. To prepare for obtaining such financial support, parents of children whose needs are not being met in the public school should request an official evaluation by a school psychologist and the formulation of an individualized education plan (IEP), which should detail how the public school will meet the child's needs. Having an independent psychologist or psychiatrist complete testing as well can provide a second opinion. If the IEP does not address the child's problems, parents can request that the school find and pay for an alternative school program. An educational consultant and attorney specializing in educational issues can help guide parents through this process.

Aftercare

Students graduating or transferring from alternative schools may continue to require special support, such as counseling, group therapy, or medical care. Support and encouragement from **family** members is important.

Parental concerns

Choosing an alternative school is often difficult, particularly for parents of at-risk children and adolescents. Parents who feel that their local school district is not adequately addressing the educational needs of their child should consider an alternative school. Reasons for choosing an alternative school vary, depending on the child, who may:

- be unusually gifted or motivated
- have a special talent or interest, such as music or science, that cannot be further developed in the present school
- be an underachiever or failing and require more individualized attention

KEY TERMS

Asperger syndrome—A developmental disorder of childhood characterized by autistic behavior but without the same difficulties acquiring language that children with autism have.

Attention deficit hyperactivity disorder (ADHD)—A condition in which a person (usually a child) has an unusually high activity level and a short attention span. People with the disorder may act impulsively and may have learning and behavioral problems.

Dyslexia—A type of reading disorder often characterized by reversal of letters or words.

Individualized educational plan (IEP)—A detailed description of the educational goals, assessment methods, behavioral management plan, and educational performance of a student requiring special education services.

• have special needs due to a learning disability or medical condition

• be exhibiting behaviors such as substance abuse, inappropriate sexual activity, **acting out**, and oppositional defiance

• have engaged in petty criminal behaviors and is becoming more self-destructive

• have been diagnosed with emotional and/or psychological problems that require a more structured therapeutic environment

An educational consultant can help parents choose an alternative school. Educational consultants usually have visited any school they recommend and will consider the student's psychological evaluations and other test results to determine the alternative school that will best meet their needs. An attorney specializing in educational issues can help parents obtain financial support for alternative therapeutic programs from the public school.

At-risk children and adolescents involved in an emotional growth school require significant involvement and support from family members, since many psychological and behavioral issues are rooted in family dynamics and history (e.g., bitter **divorce**). Hence, parents may need to take family medical leave from their work or make significant changes in their family lifestyle to support therapy for their child. Joining a parent support group can help, and most emotional growth schools have parent networks. Alternative schools for at-risk children and adolescents may seem too structured and too rigor-

ous with regard to emotional therapy for some parents. However, outcomes research for these types of schools has shown a high success rate; more than 85 percent of students completing such programs have improved family and peer relationships, attend a college or find a job, and remain free from substance use.

Resources

BOOKS

Conley, B. E. *Alternative Schools: A Reference Handbook.* Santa Barbara, CA: ABC-CLIO, 2002.

Mottaz, Carole. *Breaking the Cycle of Failure: How to Build and Maintain Quality Alternative Schools.* Blue Ridge Summit, PA: Rowman & Littlefield Publishers, 2002.

Neumann, Richard. *Sixties Legacy: A History of the Public Alternative Schools Movement, 1967–2001.* New York: Peter Lang Publishers, 2003.

PERIODICALS

Rimer, S. "Desperate Measures: Parents of Troubled Youths are Seeking Help at any Cost." *New York Times* September 10, 2001.

Spear, H. J. "Reading, Writing, and Having Babies: A Nurturing Alternative School Program." *Journal of School Nursing* 18 (October 1, 2002): 293–300.

ORGANIZATIONS

Advisory Service on Private Schools and Camps. Web site: <www.asops.com>.

Independent Educational Consultants Association. Web site: <www.iecaonline.org>.

Magnet Schools of America. 733 15th Street NW, Suite 330, Washington, DC 20005. Web site: <www.magnet.edu>.

National Association of Therapeutic Schools and Programs. 126 North Marina, Prescott, AZ 86301. Web site: <www.natsap.org/>.

National Association of Therapeutic Wilderness Camps. 698 Dinner Bell—Ohiopyle Road, Ohiopyle PA 15470. Web site: <www.natwc.org/>.

WEB SITES

"Being an Advocate for Your School-Aged Child." *National Center for Learning Disabilities.* Available online at <www.ncld.org/LDInfoZone/ InfoZone_FactSheet_Advocate_SchoolAged.cfm> (accessed October 24, 2004).

Emotional Growth Boarding Schools: National Youth Network. Available online at <www.nationalyouth.com/ emotionalgrowthboardingschool.html> (accessed October 24, 2004).

Emotional Growth Outdoor Programs: National Youth Network. Available online at <www.nationalyouth.com/wildernessandoutdoor.html> (accessed October 24, 2004).

Grunbaum, J. A., et al. "Youth Risk Behavior Surveillance—2003." *MMWR Surveillance Summary* 53 (May 21, 2004): 1–96. Available online at <www.cdc.gov/mmwr/preview/mmwrhtml/ss5302a1.htm> (accessed October 24, 2004).

Jennifer E., Sisk, M.A.

Ambiguous genitalia *see* **Intersex states**

Amblyopia

Definition

Amblyopia refers to diminished vision in either one or both eyes, for which no cause can be discovered upon examination of the eye. Amblyopia is the medical term used when the vision in one of the eyes is reduced because the eye and the brain are not working together properly. The eye itself looks normal, but it is not being used normally because the brain is favoring the other eye. This condition is also sometimes called lazy eye.

Description

Lazy eye is a common non-medical term used to describe amblyopia because the eye with poorer vision does not seem to be doing its job of seeing. Amblyopia is the most common cause of impaired vision in childhood. It affects approximately two or three out of every 100 children. Vision is a combination of the clarity of the images of the eyes (visual acuity) and the processing of those images by the brain. If the images produced by the two eyes are substantially different, the brain may not be able to fuse the images. Instead of seeing two different images or double vision (diplopia), the brain suppresses the blurrier image. This suppression can lead to amblyopia. During the first few years of life, preferring one eye over the other may lead to poor visual development in the blurrier eye. Unless it is treated successfully in early childhood, amblyopia usually persists into adulthood and is the most frequent cause of monocular (one eye) visual impairment among children.

Demographics

The prevalence of amblyopia is difficult to assess, with estimates ranging from 1.0 to 3.5 percent in healthy children to 4.0 to 5.3 percent in children with other vision problems. It is seen in similar numbers in both sexes and in all races.

Causes and symptoms

Amblyopia may be caused by any condition that adversely affects normal visual development or use of the eyes. All babies are born with poor eyesight. As babies grow, however, their eyesight usually progresses. Good eyesight needs a clear, focused image that is the same in both eyes. If the image is not clear in one eye, or if the image is not the same in both eyes, the vision pathways will not develop as they should. In fact, the pathways may actually worsen. Anything that blurs the vision or causes the eyes to be crossed during childhood may cause amblyopia. Some of the major causes of amblyopia are as follows:

- **Strabismus**. A misalignment of the eyes is the most common cause of functional amblyopia. The two eyes are looking in two different directions at the same time. The eyes may turn in, out, up, or down. Strabismus may be diagnosed at birth, or it may develop later in childhood. The brain is sent two different images and this creates confusion. Images from the misaligned or "crossed" eye are turned off to avoid double vision.

- Anisometropia. A difference of refractive states exists between the two eyes (in other words, a difference in prescription between the two eyes). For example, one eye may be more nearsighted than the other eye, or one eye may be farsighted and the other eye nearsighted. Because the brain cannot fuse the two images, the brain suppresses the blurrier image, causing the eye to become amblyopic.

- Cataract. Clouding of the lens of the eye causes the image to be blurrier than the other eye. The brain prefers the clearer image, and the eye with the cataract may become amblyopic.

- Ptosis. If light cannot enter the eye because of the drooping lid, the eye is essentially going unused, which can lead to amblyopia. However, ptosis is rarely related to the development of amblyopia, unless the droopy eyelid completely obscures the pupil.

Barring the presence of strabismus or ptosis, children may or may not show signs of amblyopia. Children may position their heads at an angle while trying to favor the eye with normal vision. They may have difficulty seeing or reaching for things when approached from the side of the amblyopic eye. Parents should see if one side of approach is preferred by the child or infant. If an infant's good eye is covered, the child may cry.

When to call the doctor

Parents should call the doctor if their child demonstrates any signs associated with amblyopia, including the appearance of crossed eyes, lazy eye, a drooping eyelid, difficulty seeing, or if the child seems to favor one side of approach over the other. However, since children do not always show symptoms of amblyopia, it is important to get their eyes examined at or before the age of three and no later than age five, while the disorder is more easily treated.

Diagnosis

It is not easy to recognize amblyopia. A child may not be aware of having one strong eye and one weak eye. Unless the child has a misaligned eye or other obvious abnormality, there is often no way for parents to tell that something is wrong. Because children with outwardly normal eyes may have amblyopia, it is important to have regular vision screenings performed for all children. While there is some disagreement regarding the age children should have their first vision examination, their eyes can, in actuality, be examined at any age, even on the first day of life.

Some people recommend that children have their vision checked by their pediatrician, **family** physician, ophthalmologist, or optometrist at or before six months of age. Others recommend testing by at least the child's fourth birthday. There may be a critical period in the development of vision, and amblyopia may not be treatable after age eight or nine. The earlier amblyopia is found, the better chance there is for a positive outcome. Most physicians test vision as part of a child's medical examination. If there is any sign of an eye problem, they may refer a child to an eye specialist.

There are objective methods, such as retinoscopy, by which to measure the refractive status of the eyes. This form of examination can help diagnose anisometropia. In retinoscopy, a hand-held instrument is used to shine a light in the child's (or infant's) eyes. While the doctor uses hand-held lenses, he can obtain a rough prescription. Visual acuity can be determined using a variety of methods. Many different eye charts are available (e.g. tumbling E, pictures, or letters). In amblyopia, single letters are easier to recognize than when a whole line is shown. This is referred to as the "crowding effect" and helps in diagnosing amblyopia. Neutral density filters may also be held over the eye to aid in the diagnosis. Sometimes visual fields to determine defects in the area of vision will be performed. Color vision testing may also be done. Again, it must be emphasized that amblyopia is a diagnosis of exclusion.

Boy wearing eye patch used to treat amblyopia. The patch is worn over the stronger eye to build the weaker one's strength. (*© Mark Clarke/Photo Researchers, Inc.*)

Various medical problems can also cause a decrease in vision. An examination of the eyes and visual system is very important when there is an unexplained decrease in vision.

Treatment

Amblyopia treatment is most effective when done early in the child's life, usually before age seven. It is important that any anisometropia and refractive problems be treated initially, because sometimes amblyopia can be resolved with glasses alone.

The next step is to make the child use the eye with the reduced vision (weaker eye). As of 2004, there are two ways to do this:

- Patching. An opaque, adhesive patch is worn over the stronger eye for weeks to months. This therapy forces the child to use the eye with amblyopia. Patching stimulates vision in the weaker eye and aids the section of

KEY TERMS

Anisometropia—An eye condition in which there is an inequality of vision between the two eyes. There may be unequal amounts of nearsightedness, farsightedness, or astigmatism, so that one eye will be in focus while the other will not.

Cataract—A condition in which the lens of the eye turns cloudy and interferes with vision.

Occulsion therapy—A type of treatment for amblyopia in which the good eye is patched for a period of time, thus forcing the use of the weaker eye.

Visual acuity—Sharpness or clearness of vision.

the brain that manages vision to develop more completely. Patching may be part-time or full-time. Studies in the early 2000s have shown that less time patching the eye may be as effective as more. In the case of moderate amblyopia, two hours of daily patching for four months gave the same benefit as six hours of daily patching for the same period of time. Compliance with the patching regimen was also improved with the shorter daily patching time. The treatment plan should be discussed with the doctor to determine how long the patch should be worn. When the child is wearing the patch, prescribed eye exercises may force the amblyopic eye to focus and work. This is called vision therapy or vision training. Even after the child's vision has been restored in the weak eye, part-time patching may be required over a period of years to maintain the improvement.

- Atropine. This therapy is generally reserved for children who will not wear a patch or where compliance may be an issue. A drop of a drug called atropine is placed in the stronger eye once a day to temporarily blur the vision so that the child will prefer to use the eye with amblyopia. Treatment with atropine also stimulates vision in the weaker eye and helps the part of the brain that manages vision to develop more fully.

Prognosis

The younger the child, the better the chance for improvement with occlusion and vision therapy. Success in the treatment of amblyopia also depends on the amblyopia's severity, its specific type, and the child's compliance with treatment. It is important to diagnose and treat amblyopia early because significant vision loss

can occur if it is left untreated. The best outcomes result from early diagnosis and treatment.

Prevention

Early recognition and treatment of amblyopia in children can help to prevent permanent visual deficits. All children should have a complete eye examination at least once between age three and five to avoid the risk of allowing unsuspected amblyopia to go beyond the age where it can be treated successfully.

Nutritional concerns

There are some rarer forms of amblyopia caused by various nutritional deficiencies. In these cases, the doctor recommends the proper diet and perhaps supplementation in order to resolve the problem.

Parental concerns

It is vital that parents bring their child for an eye exam sometime between the ages of three and five to prevent amblyopia from becoming untreatable.

Resources

BOOKS

Barber, Anne. *Infant and Toddler Strabismus and Amblyopia, Vol. 41, No. 2: Behavioral Aspects of Vision Care.* Santa Ana, CA: Optometric Extension Program Foundation, 2000.

Fielder, Alistair, et al. *Amblyopia: A Multidisciplinary Approach.* Kent, UK: Elsevier—Health Sciences Division, 2002.

Pratt-Johnson, John A., et al. *Management of Strabismus and Amblyopia: A Practical Guide.* New York: Thieme Medical Publishers, 2000.

PERIODICALS

Dutton, Gordon N., and Marie Cleary. "Should We Be Screening for and Treating Amblyopia? Evidence Shows Some Benefit." *British Medical Journal* 327, no. 7426 (November 29, 2003): 1242–44.

Finn, Robert. "Less Patching Fine for Amblyopia in Young Children: Two Studies." *Family Practice News* 34, no. 9 (May 1, 2004): 70–71.

ORGANIZATIONS

American Association for Pediatric Ophthalmology and Strabismus. PO Box 193832, San Francisco, CA 94119–3832. Web site: <www.aapos.org>.

National Eye Institute. 31 Center Drive MSC 2510, Bethesda, MD 20892–2510. Web site: <www.nei.nih.gov>.

Prevent Blindness America. 500 E. Remington Road, Schaumburg, IL 60173. Web site: <www.preventblindness.org>.

WEB SITES

"Amblyopia." *National Eye Institute*, June 2004. Available online at <www.nei.nih.gov/health/amblyopia> (October 16, 2004).

Deanna M. Swartout-Corbeil, RN
Lorraine Steefel, RN

Amenorrhea

Definition

Amenorrhea is the medical term for the absence of **menstruation**. There are two types of amenorrhea, primary and secondary. Primary amenorrhea refers to delayed menarche (the first menstrual period) and is defined as any one of three conditions:

- the absence of menarche by age 16 in a girl with otherwise normal pubertal development (development of breasts and/or pubic hair)
- the absence of menarche by age 14 combined with delayed pubertal development
- the absence of menarche two years after **puberty** is otherwise completed

Secondary amenorrhea is defined as the absence of menstruation after menarche has taken place. Although it is not uncommon for a girl's menstrual periods to be irregular during early **adolescence**, most girls' periods usually become regular within 18 months after the first one. After that time, it is considered abnormal for an adolescent to miss three consecutive periods.

Description

Normal menstrual periods are the result of proper functioning and synchronization of the hypothalamus, pituitary gland, and ovaries. The hypothalamus is the part of the brain that controls body temperature, cellular metabolism, and such basic functions as appetite for food, the sleep/wake cycle, and reproduction. The hypothalamus also secretes hormones that regulate the pituitary gland. The pituitary gland in turn produces hormones that stimulate the ovaries to secrete two hormones known as estradiol and progesterone. These ovarian hormones encourage the growth of the endometrium, which is the tissue that lines the uterus. If pregnancy does not occur, the endometrium breaks down and the uterus sheds the extra tissue during the next menstrual period.

Amenorrhea can result from an interruption at any of several points in the normal cycle:

- The hypothalamus and pituitary may fail to produce enough hormone to stimulate the ovaries to produce their hormones.
- The ovaries may fail to produce enough estradiol to stimulate the growth of the endometrium.
- There may be structural abnormalities in the uterus, cervix, or vagina that prevent the shed tissue from leaving the body.

Demographics

Secondary amenorrhea is more common in females in North America than primary amenorrhea. One study estimates that about 5 percent of menstruating women have an episode of secondary amenorrhea each year.

The average age for the onset of the menses in girls in the United States and Canada is 12.77 years. There is no evidence as of the early 2000s that the incidence of either primary or secondary amenorrhea is related to race or ethnic background.

Causes and symptoms

Causes

There are a number of possible causes of amenorrhea:

- Pregnancy: An adolescent with amenorrhea most likely does not have a serious underlying medical problem. All teenagers with amenorrhea should seek medical care, and an adolescent who has had sexual intercourse even once and then missed a period should assume she is pregnant until a reliable pregnancy test proves otherwise. It should be noted that spotting or even bleeding is not unusual during early pregnancy. In addition, it is possible for a girl to conceive before she has had even one period.
- Disorders of the hypothalamus or the pituitary gland: These problems may be associated with brain tumors.
- Ovarian disorders: These disorders may include premature ovarian failure or may be the side effects of **chemotherapy** or radiation therapy for **cancer**. Premature ovarian failure accounts for about 10 percent of cases of secondary amenorrhea.
- Hyperandrogenism: The overproduction of male hormones (androgens) by the girl's body can interrupt menstruation. Male hormones are produced in small quantities

by all women, but some individuals produce excessive amounts, leading to such conditions as polycystic ovarian syndrome (PCOS), hirsutism (excessive growth of body hair), or abnormalities of the external genitalia. PCOS in adolescents is often triggered by **obesity**.

- Genetic disorders: Some genetic disorders that affect the X chromosome, such as Turner's syndrome, prevent normal sexual maturation in girls.
- Psychiatric disorders: Depression, **obsessive-compulsive disorder**, eating disorders, and **schizophrenia** can all cause disturbances of the menstrual cycle.
- Abuse of alcohol or other drugs: Excessive alcohol intake can lead to **malnutrition**, while cocaine and opioids (narcotics) can affect the menstrual cycle directly.
- **Immunodeficiency** disorders or conditions.
- Emotional stress: This disturbance can interfere with the brain's hormonal signals to the ovaries. It is not uncommon for a girl's period to be delayed when she is having problems with school, work, or relationships. A change in environment (the first year of college or taking a new job, for example) can also cause a young woman's period to be late.
- Female athlete triad: Female athletes at the high school or college level are at increased risk for a triad of disorders: excessive dieting or disordered eating, amenorrhea, and loss of bone **minerals** leading to osteoporosis. The triad was first formally named in 1993 but had been known to doctors for decades before. Girls who are involved in **sports** that emphasize weight control or a slender body build (gymnastics, track and field, cheerleading) are at greater risk than those who **play** field hockey, basketball, softball, or other sports that emphasize strength.

Symptoms

Amenorrhea may be associated with the symptoms of other disorders; for example, girls with an eating disorder will often have eroded tooth enamel, tiny pinpoint hemorrhages around the eyes, an abnormal heart rhythm, low blood pressure, and other signs of frequent **vomiting**. Girls whose amenorrhea is part of the female athlete triad may have a record of bone **fractures** or other evidence of bone mineral loss. Hot flashes and night sweats may indicate premature ovarian failure. Headaches or visual disturbances may suggest a brain tumor.

When to call the doctor

Girls who have not had a menstrual period by age 16 or who have not shown any signs of **breast development** or other indications of puberty by age 14 should be examined for causes of primary **dysmenorrhea**. Girls who have begun to menstruate and have missed three periods should be evaluated for secondary amenorrhea. If they are sexually active, they should have a pregnancy test after missing even one period.

Diagnosis

History and physical examination

The first part of diagnosing amenorrhea is a careful history, including a record of medications and any surgical procedures involving the abdomen or genitals. The doctor will ask detailed questions about stress, dieting, sexual activity, and athletic participation, as well as questions about chronic diseases or disorders of the central nervous system. **Family** history should be taken into consideration in any adolescent with primary amenorrhea, as mothers who started to menstruate late will often have daughters who also menstruate late.

In the case of female athletes, the doctor may need to establish a relationship of trust with the patient before asking about such matters as diet, practice and workout schedules, and the use of such drugs as steroids or ephedrine. The presence of stress fractures in young women should be investigated. In some cases, the doctor may give the patient the Eating Disorder Inventory (EDI) or a similar screening questionnaire to help determine whether the patient is at risk for developing anorexia or bulimia.

The doctor will then perform a physical examination to evaluate the patient's weight in proportion to her height as well as her general nutritional status; to check for breast development, pubic hair, and other signs of normal female sexual development; to make sure the heart rhythm, blood pressure, and other vital signs are normal; and to palpate (feel) the thyroid gland for evidence of swelling. The physical examination may include a pelvic examination to check for abnormalities in the structure of the vagina or cervix.

Laboratory tests

To rule out specific causes of amenorrhea, the doctor may order a pregnancy test in sexually active young women as well as blood tests to check the level of thyroid hormone. Based on the initial test results, the doctor may want to perform additional tests to determine the level of other hormones that play a role in reproduction. A special type of blood test called a karyotype may be done to analyze the girl's chromosomes if the doctor suspects Turner's syndrome or another genetic disorder.

One way to determine whether a teenager's ovaries and uterus are functioning is a progesterone challenge test. In this test, an amenorrheic teenager is given a dose of progesterone either orally or as an injection. If her ovaries are producing estrogen and her uterus is responding normally, she should have a menstrual period within a few days of the progesterone dose. This challenge indicates that the ovaries and uterus are functioning normally, and the cause of the amenorrhea is probably in the brain.

Imaging studies

In some cases the doctor may order an ultrasound study of the pelvic region to check for anatomical abnormalities or **x rays** or a bone scan to check for bone fractures. In some cases the doctor may order an MRI to rule out tumors affecting the hypothalamus or pituitary gland.

Psychiatric interview

Teenagers whose amenorrhea may be related to depression, family stress, eating disorders, or other mental health issues may be referred to a psychiatrist for further evaluation.

Treatment

The most frequent risk associated with amenorrhea is osteoporosis (thinning of the bone) caused by low estrogen levels. Because osteoporosis can begin as early as adolescence, hormone replacement therapy is sometimes recommended for teenagers with chronic amenorrhea.

Amenorrhea associated with hormonal, genetic, psychiatric, or immunodeficiency disorders may require a variety of different medications and other treatments administered by specialists. Tumors of the hypothalamus and the pituitary gland or abnormalities of the reproductive organs usually require surgery.

Alternative treatment

As with conventional medical treatments, alternative treatments are based on the cause of the condition. If a hormonal imbalance is revealed by laboratory testing, hormone replacements that are more natural for the body (including tri-estrogen and natural progesterone) are recommended. Glandular therapy can assist in bringing about a balance in the glands involved in the reproductive cycle, including the hypothalmus, pituitary, thyroid, ovarian, and adrenal glands.

Since homeopathy and acupuncture work on deep energetic levels to rebalance the body, these two forms of therapy may be helpful in treating amenorrhea. Western and Chinese herbal medicines also can be very effective. Herbs used to treat amenorrhea include dong quai (*Angelica sinensis*), black cohosh (*Cimicifuga racemosa*), and chaste tree (*Vitex agnus-castus*). Herbal preparations used to bring on the menstrual period are known as emmenagogues. For some adolescents, meditation, guided imagery, and visualization can play a key role in the treatment of amenorrhea by relieving emotional stress.

Nutritional concerns

Diet and adequate **nutrition**, including adequate protein, essential fatty acids, whole grains, and fresh fruits and vegetables are important for every female past puberty, especially if deficiencies are present or if she regularly exercises very strenuously. Girls who are abusing alcohol or other drugs should be evaluated for possible malnutrition as part of treatment for substance abuse.

Female athletes at the high school or college level should consult a nutritionist to make sure that they are eating a well-balanced diet that is adequate to maintain a healthy weight for their height. Girls participating in dance or in sports that emphasize weight control or a slender body type (gymnastics, track and field, swimming, and cheerleading) are at higher risk of developing eating disorders than those that are involved in such sports as softball, weight lifting, or basketball. In some cases the athlete may be given calcium or vitamin D supplements to lower the risk of osteoporosis.

Prognosis

The prognosis of either primary or secondary amenorrhea depends on the underlying cause.

Prevention

Amenorrhea related to pregnancy, the female athletic triad, drug or alcohol abuse, or eating disorders is preventable insofar as these are lifestyle choices. Primary or secondary amenorrhea associated with genetic mutations or other systemic diseases or disorders is not preventable.

Parental concerns

Amenorrhea is a fairly dramatic symptom of menstrual dysfunction that often causes parents to consult a doctor about a girl's health. Parental concerns about

KEY TERMS

Anorexia nervosa—An eating disorder marked by an unrealistic fear of weight gain, self-starvation, and distortion of body image. It most commonly occurs in adolescent females.

Emmenagogue—A type of medication that brings on or increases a woman's menstrual flow.

Endometrium—The mucosal layer lining the inner cavity of the uterus. The endometrium's structure changes with age and with the menstrual cycle.

Female athlete triad—A combination of disorders frequently found in female athletes that includes disordered eating, osteoporosis, and oligo- or amenorrhea. The triad was first officially named in 1993.

Hyperandrogenism—The excessive secretion of androgens.

Menarche—The first menstrual cycle in a girl's life.

Osteoporosis—Literally meaning "porous bones," this condition occurs when bones lose an excessive amount of their protein and mineral content, particularly calcium. Over time, bone mass and strength are reduced leading to increased risk of fractures.

Turner syndrome—A chromosome abnormality characterized by short stature and ovarian failure caused by an absent X chromosome. It occurs only in females.

amenorrhea, however, should be directed to the underlying cause. Amenorrhea related to emotional stress, dieting, or excessive **exercise** usually goes away when the stress is relieved or when the girl makes appropriate lifestyle adjustments. On the other hand, amenorrhea associated with glandular disturbances, tumors, genetic or anatomical abnormalities, diabetes, or other systemic disorders is part of a larger and more worrisome picture. Parents should discuss their concerns about the long-term effects of amenorrhea on the girl's health, whether she will be able to have children in adult life, and how they can help her manage her condition with the doctors, nutritionists, and other healthcare professionals who are treating her.

See also Anorexia nervosa; Bulimia nervosa; Menstruation; Oligomenorrhea; Sports.

Resources

BOOKS

Diagnostic and Statistical Manual of Mental Disorders, 4th edition, Text Revision. Washington, DC: American Psychiatric Association, 2000.

"Menstrual Abnormalities and Abnormal Uterine Bleeding." Section 18, Chapter 235 in *The Merck Manual of Diagnosis and Therapy*, edited by Mark H. Beers and Robert Berkow. Whitehouse Station, NJ: Merck Research Laboratories, 2002.

Pelletier, Kenneth R. "CAM Therapies for Specific Conditions: Menstrual Symptoms, Menopause, and PMS." In *The Best Alternative Medicine*, Part II. New York: Simon and Schuster, 2002.

PERIODICALS

Gordon, C. M., and L. M. Nelson. "Amenorrhea and Bone Health in Adolescents and Young Women." *Current Opinion in Obstetrics and Gynecology* 15 (October 2003): 377–84.

Khalid, A. "Irregular or Absent Periods: What Can an Ultrasound Scan Tell You?" *Best Practice and Research: Clinical Obstetrics and Gynaecology* 18 (February 2004): 311.

Seidenfeld, Marjorie E. K., and Vaughn J. Rickert. "Impact of Anorexia, Bulimia and Obesity on the Gynecologic Health of Adolescents." *American Family Physician* 64 (August 1, 2001): 445–50.

Warren, M. P., and L. R. Goodman. "Exercise-Induced Endocrine Pathologies." *Journal of Endocrinological Investigation* 26 (September 2003): 873–78.

ORGANIZATIONS

American Academy of Child and Adolescent Psychiatry. 3615 Wisconsin Avenue, NW, Washington, DC 20016–3007. Web site: <www.aacap.org>.

American College of Obstetricians and Gynecologists (ACOG). 409 12th Street, SW, PO Box 96920, Washington, DC 20090–6920. Web site: <www.acog.org>.

American College of Sports Medicine (ACSM). 401 West Michigan Street, Indianapolis, IN 46202–3233. Web site: <www.acsm.org>.

WEB SITES

Barrow, Boone. "Female Athlete Triad." *eMedicine*, June 17, 2004. Available online at <www.emedicine.com/sports/topic163.htm> (accessed November 8, 2004).

Chandran, Latha. "Menstruation Disorders." *eMedicine*, August 9, 2004. Available online at <www.emedicine.com/ped/topic2781.htm> (accessed November 8, 2004).

Nelson, Lawrence M., et al. "Amenorrhea." *eMedicine*, August 9, 2004. Available online at <www.emedicine.com/med/topic117.htm> (accessed November 8, 2004).

Gail Slap, MD

Amniocentesis

Definition

Amniocentesis is a procedure used to diagnose fetal defects in the early second trimester of pregnancy. A sample of the amniotic fluid, which surrounds a fetus in the womb, is collected through a pregnant woman's abdomen using a needle and syringe. Tests performed on fetal cells found in the sample can reveal the presence of many types of genetic disorders, thus allowing doctors and prospective parents to make important decisions about early treatment and intervention.

Purpose

Since the mid-1970s, amniocentesis has been used routinely to test for **Down syndrome**, by far the most common, nonhereditary, genetic birth defect, afflicting about one in every 1,000 babies. By 1997, approximately 800 different diagnostic tests were available, most of them for hereditary genetic disorders such as **Tay-Sachs disease**, **sickle cell anemia**, **hemophilia**, **muscular dystrophy**, and **cystic fibrosis**.

Amniocentesis, often called amnio, is recommended for women who will be older than 35 on their due-date. It is also recommended for women who have already borne children with birth defects, or when either of the parents has a **family** history of a birth defect for which a diagnostic test is available. Another reason for the procedure is to confirm indications of Down syndrome and certain other defects which may have shown up previously during routine maternal blood screening.

The risk of bearing a child with a nonhereditary genetic defect such as Down syndrome is directly related to a woman's age—the older the woman, the greater the risk. Thirty-five is the recommended age to begin amnio testing because that is the age at which the risk of carrying a fetus with such a defect roughly equals the risk of miscarriage caused by the procedure–about one in 200. At age 25, the risk of giving birth to a child with this type of defect is about one in 1,400; by age 45 it increases to about one in 20. Nearly half of all pregnant women over

35 in the United States undergo amniocentesis and many younger women also decide to have the procedure. Notably, some 75% of all Down syndrome infants born in the United States each year are to women younger than 35.

One of the most common reasons for performing amniocentesis is an abnormal alpha-fetoprotein (AFP) test. Alpha-fetoprotein is a protein produced by the fetus and present in the mother's blood. A simple blood screening, usually conducted around the 15th week of pregnancy, can determine the AFP levels in the mother's blood. Levels that are too high or too low may signal possible fetal defects. Because this test has a high false-positive rate, another test such as amnio is recommended whenever the AFP levels fall outside the normal range.

Amniocentesis is generally performed during the 16th week of pregnancy, with results usually available within three weeks. It is possible to perform an amnio as early as the 11th week, but this is not usually recommended because there appears to be an increased risk of miscarriage when done at this time. The advantage of early amnio and speedy results lies in the extra time for decision making if a problem is detected. Potential treatment of the fetus can begin earlier. Important, also, is the fact that elective abortions are safer and less controversial the earlier they are performed.

Precautions

As an invasive surgical procedure, amnio poses a real, although small, risk to the health of a fetus. Parents must weigh the potential value of the knowledge gained, or indeed the reassurance that all is well, against the small risk of damaging what is in all probability a normal fetus. The serious emotional and ethical dilemmas that adverse test results can bring must also be considered. The decision to undergo amnio is always a matter of personal choice.

Description

The word amniocentesis literally means "puncture of the amnion," the thin-walled sac of fluid in which a developing fetus is suspended during pregnancy. During the sampling procedure, the obstetrician inserts a very fine needle through the woman's abdomen into the uterus and amniotic sac and withdraws approximately one ounce of amniotic fluid for testing. The relatively painless procedure is performed on an outpatient basis, sometimes using local anesthesia.

The physician uses ultrasound images to guide needle placement and collect the sample, thereby minimizing the risk of fetal injury and the need for repeated needle insertions. Once the sample is collected, the woman can return home after a brief observation period. She may be instructed to rest for the first 24 hours and to avoid heavy lifting for two days.

The sample of amniotic fluid is sent to a laboratory where fetal cells contained in the fluid are isolated and grown in order to provide enough genetic material for testing. This takes about seven to 14 days. The material is then extracted and treated so that visual examination for defects can be made. For some disorders, like Tay-Sachs, the simple presence of a telltale chemical compound in the amniotic fluid is enough to confirm a diagnosis. Depending on the specific tests ordered, and the skill of the lab conducting them, all the results are available between one and four weeks after the sample is taken.

Cost of the procedure depends on the doctor, the lab, and the tests ordered. Most insurers provide coverage for women over 35, as a follow-up to positive maternal blood screening results, and when genetic disorders run in the family.

An alternative to amnio, now in general use, is chorionic villus sampling, or CVS, which can be performed as early as the eighth week of pregnancy. While this allows for the possibility of a first trimester abortion, if warranted, CVS is apparently also riskier and is more expensive. The most promising area of new research in prenatal testing involves expanding the scope and accuracy of maternal blood screening as this poses no risk to the fetus.

Preparation

It is important for a woman to fully understand the procedure and to feel confident in the obstetrician performing it. Evidence suggests that a physician's experience with the procedure reduces the chance of mishap. Almost all obstetricians are experienced in performing amniocentesis. The patient should feel free to ask questions and seek emotional support before, during and after the amnio is performed.

Aftercare

Necessary aftercare falls into two categories, physical and emotional.

PHYSICAL AFTERCARE   During and immediately following the sampling procedure, a woman may experience **dizziness**, **nausea**, a rapid heartbeat, and cramping. Once past these immediate hurdles, the physician will send the woman home with instructions to rest and to report any complications requiring immediate treatment, including:

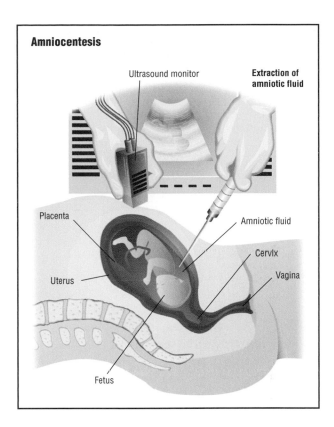

Amniocentesis

Ultrasound monitor

Extraction of amniotic fluid

Placenta

Amniotic fluid

Cervix

Uterus

Vagina

Fetus

To perform amniocentesis, a physician uses an ultrasound monitor to visualize the fetus while inserting a syring to extract amnniotic fluid for analysis. (Illustration by GGS Information Services.)

- Vaginal bleeding. The appearance of blood could signal a problem.

- Premature labor. Unusual abdominal **pain** and/or cramping may indicate the onset of premature labor. Mild cramping for the first day or two following the procedure is normal.

- Signs of infection. Leaking of amniotic fluid or unusual vaginal discharge, and **fever** could signal the onset of infection.

EMOTIONAL AFTERCARE   Once the procedure has been safely completed, the anxiety of waiting for the test results can prove to be the worst part of the process. A woman should seek and receive emotional support from family and friends, as well as from her obstetrician and family doctor. Professional counseling may also prove necessary, particularly if a fetal defect is discovered.

Risks

Most of the risks and short-term side effects associated with amniocentesis relate to the sampling procedure and have been discussed above. A successful amnio

KEY TERMS

Alpha fetoprotein (AFP)—A substance produced by a fetus' liver that can be found in the amniotic fluid and in the mother's blood. Abnormally high levels of this substance suggests there may be defects in the fetal neural tube, a structure that will include the brain and spinal cord when completely developed. AFP may also be found at elevated levels in the blood of adults with liver, testicular, and ovarian cancer.

Anencephaly—A genetic defect resulting in the partial to complete absence of the brain and malformation of the brainstem.

Chorionic villus sampling—A procedure used for prenatal diagnosis at 10–12 weeks gestation. Under ultrasound guidance a needle is inserted either through the mother's vagina or abdominal wall and a sample of the chorionic membrane. These cells are then tested for chromosome abnormalities or other genetic diseases.

Chromosome—A microscopic thread-like structure found within each cell of the human body and consisting of a complex of proteins and DNA. Humans have 46 chromosomes arranged into 23 pairs. Chromosomes contain the genetic information necessary to direct the development and functioning of all cells and systems in the body. They pass on hereditary traits from parents to child (like eye color) and determine whether the child will be male or female.

Down syndrome—A chromosomal disorder caused by an extra copy or a rearrangement of chromosome 21. Children with Down syndrome have varying degrees of mental retardation and may have heart defects.

Genetic—Refers to genes, the basic units of biological heredity, which are contained on the chromosomes.

Hereditary—Something which is inherited, that is passed down from parents to offspring. In biology and medicine, the word pertains to inherited genetic characteristics.

Maternal blood screening—Screening that is normally done early in pregnancy to test for a variety of conditions. Abnormal amounts of certain proteins in a pregnant woman's blood raise the probability of fetal defects. Amniocentesis is recommended if such a probability occurs.

Tay-Sachs disease—An inherited disease caused by a missing enzyme that is prevalent among the Ashkenazi Jewish population of the United States. Infants with the disease are unable to process a certain type of fat which accumulates in nerve and brain cells, causing mental and physical retardation, and, finally, death.

Ultrasonography—A medical test in which sound waves are directed against internal structures in the body. As sound waves bounce off the internal structure, they create an image on a video screen. Ultrasonography is often used to diagnose fetal abnormalities, gallstones, heart defects, and tumors. Also called ultrasound imaging.

---

sampling results in no long-term side effects. Risks include:

- Maternal/fetal hemorrhaging. While spotting in pregnancy is fairly common, bleeding following amnio should always be investigated.

- Infection. Infection, although rare, can occur after amniocentesis. An unchecked infection can lead to severe complications.

- Fetal injury. A very slight risk of injury to the fetus resulting from contact with the amnio needle does exist.

- Miscarriage. The rate of miscarriage occurring during standard, second trimester amnio appears to be approximately 0.5%. This compares to a miscarriage rate of 1% for CVS. Many fetuses with severe genetic defects miscarry naturally during the first trimester.

- The trauma of difficult family-planning decisions. The threat posed to parental and family mental health from the trauma accompanying an abnormal test result can not be underestimated.

Normal results

Negative results from an amnio analysis indicate that everything about the fetus appears normal and the pregnancy can continue without undue concern. A negative result for Down syndrome means that it is 99% certain that the disease does not exist.

An overall "normal" result does not, however, guarantee that the pregnancy will come to term, or that the fetus does not suffer from some other defect. Laboratory tests are not 100% accurate at detecting targeted conditions, nor can every possible fetal condition be tested for.

Abnormal results

Positive results on an amnio analysis indicate the presence of the fetal defect being tested for, with an accuracy approaching 100%. Prospective parents are then faced with emotionally and ethically difficult choices regarding treatment options, the prospect of dealing with a severely affected newborn, and the option of elective abortion. At this point, the parents need expert medical advice and counseling.

Parental concerns

There is a risk of miscarrage with this procedure.

When to call a doctor

If there is excess bleeding, a doctor should be contacted.

Resources

BOOKS

Hassold, Terry and Schwartz, Stuart. "Chromosome Disorders." In *Harrison's Principles of Internal Medicine*, ed. Eugene Braunwald, et al. Philadelphia: McGraw-Hill, 2001.

Miesfeldt, Susan and Jameson, J. Larry. "Screening, Counseling, and Prevention of Genetic Disorders." In *Harrison's Principles of Internal Medicine*, ed. Eugene Braunwald, et al. Philadelphia: McGraw-Hill, 2001.

Wallach, Jacques. *Interpretation of Diagnostic Tests,*7th ed. Philadelphia, PA: Lippincott Williams & Wilkens, 2000.

ORGANIZATIONS

American College of Obstetricians and Gynecologists. 409 12th St., S.W., P.O. Box 96920, Washington, DC 20090-6920. <http://www.acog.org>.

ORGANIZATIONS

National Institutes of Health. <http://www.nlm.nih.gov/medlineplus/encyclopedia.html>.

Mark A. Best

Amoxicillin *see* **Penicillins**

Amphetamines *see* **Stimulant drugs**

Amputation *see* **Traumatic amputations**

Anabolic steroids

Definition

Anabolic steroids are compounds, derived from testosterone, which promote tissue growth and repair. Because they have been used improperly by body builders and other athletes, they are controlled substances under United States federal law.

Description

As of 2004, there are four anabolic steroids available:

- nandrolone
- oxandrolone
- oxymetholone
- stanzolol

Although these products have different labeled uses, they are very similar in action and side effects and may be used interchangeably, subject to differences in route of administration and duration of action.

General use

Anabolic steroids are used for the following conditions:

- catabolic states such as chronic infections, extensive surgery, **burns**, or severe trauma
- anemia associated with renal insufficiency, **sickle cell anemia**, aplastic anemia, and bone marrow failure
- angioedema
- growth failure, including the short stature associated with Turner's syndrome

Precautions

Anabolic steroids are not recommended for young children because the drugs may cause an early end to the growth of long bones, which results in short stature. Anabolic steroids should be used with great care in girls, because the drugs have masculinizing properties. The drugs should be reserved for situations in which the benefits outweigh the risk. Anabolic steroids have been associated with liver **cancer**, and they have psychological effects, such as contributing to rage attacks.

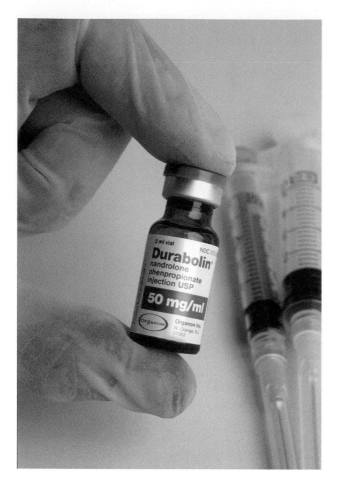

Bottle of the injectable anabolic steroid, Durabolin. *(Custom Medical Stock Photo, Inc.)*

Side effects

Anabolic steroids cause masculinization of females, including hair growth or loss, enlargement of the clitoris, and deepening of the voice. These effects are not reversible, even when the drug is promptly discontinued. In males past the age of **puberty**, side effects include increased urinary frequency, breast tenderness and enlargement, and frequent erections. In both males and females, anabolic steroids cause swelling of the feet, liver problems, and stomach upset.

This list of side effects is incomplete; many additional effects have been reported. Specialized drug references maintain for a complete list for each individual drug, including analysis of psychological effects of these drugs that contribute to rage attacks.

Interactions

Anabolic steroids have an anticoagulant effect. They should be used with care in combination with other drugs that have the same effect, including warfarin, **nonsteroidal anti-inflammatory drugs** (NSAIDs), and aspirin. Simultaneous use of anabolic steroids and corticosteroids will increase the risk of foot and ankle swelling. The combination is very likely to cause **acne**. Anabolic steroids may also lower blood glucose levels. They should be used with extreme care in patients taking insulin or other antidiabetic drugs. Other drug interactions have also been reported.

Parental concerns

Because of the nature of the adverse effects of anabolic steroids, their use should be restricted to cases where the benefits clearly outweigh the risks. Regular blood testing for blood counts and liver function is essential. Parents should observe the patient carefully for signs of liver damage, including **headache**, unpleasant breath odor, and black tarry stools.

Resources

BOOKS

Anabolic Steroids: A Medical Dictionary, Bibliography, and Annotated Guide to Internet References. San Diego, CA: Icon Group International, 2003.

Taylor, William N. *Anabolic Steroids and the Athlete.* Jefferson, NC: McFarland & Co., 2002.

WEB SITES

"Anabolic Steroids." *MedlinePlus.* Available online at <www.nlm.nih.gov/medlineplus/druginfo/uspdi/202035.html>.

"Steroids (Anabolic-Androgenic.)" *National Institute on Drug Abuse*. Available online at <www.nida.nih.gov/Infofax/steroids.htm/> (accessed December 18, 2004).

Samuel Uretsky, PharmD

Analgesics

Definition

Analgesics are medicines that relieve **pain**.

Description

Analgesics are those drugs whose primary purpose is pain relief. The primary classes of analgesics are the narcotics, including additional agents that are chemically based on the morphine molecule but have minimal abuse potential; **nonsteroidal anti-inflammatory drugs** (NSAIDs) including the salicylates; and **acetaminophen**. Other drugs, notably the tricyclic **antidepressants** and anti-epileptic agents, such as gabapentin, have been used to relieve pain, particularly neurologic pain, but are not routinely classified as analgesics. Analgesics provide symptomatic relief but have no effect on causation, although clearly the NSAIDs, by virtue of their dual activities as pain relievers and anti-inflammatories, may be beneficial in both regards.

Description

Pain has been classified as "productive" and "non-productive." While this distinction has no physiologic meaning, it may serve as a guide to treatment. Productive pain has been described as a warning of injury and so may be both an indication of need for treatment and a guide to diagnosis. Non-productive pain by definition serves no purpose either as a warning or diagnostic tool.

Although pain syndromes may be dissimilar, the common factor is a sensory pathway from the affected organ to the brain. Analgesics work at the level of the nerves, either by blocking the signal from the peripheral nervous system or by distorting the interpretation by the central nervous system. Selection of an appropriate analgesic is based on consideration of the risk-benefit factors of each class of drugs, based on type of pain, severity of pain, and risk of adverse effects. Traditionally, pain has been divided into two classes, acute and chronic, although severity and projected patient survival are other factors that must be considered in drug selection.

Acute pain

Acute pain is self limiting in duration and includes post-operative pain, pain of injury, and **childbirth**. Because pain of these types is expected to be short term, the long-term side effects of analgesic therapy may routinely be ignored. Thus, these patients may safely be treated with narcotic analgesics without concern for their addictive potential, or NSAIDs with only limited concern for their ulcerogenic (ulcer-causing) risks. Drugs and doses should be adjusted based on observation of healing rate, switching patients from high to low doses and from narcotic analgesics to non-narcotics when circumstances permit.

An important consideration of **pain management** in severe pain is that patients should not be subject to the return of pain. Analgesics should be dosed adequately to assure that the pain is at least tolerable and frequently enough to avoid the anxiety that accompanies the anticipated return of pain. Generally analgesics should not be dosed on an as-needed basis but should be administered often enough to assure constant blood levels of analgesic. This applies to both the narcotic and non-narcotic analgesics.

Chronic pain

Chronic pain, pain lasting over three months and severe enough to impair function, is more difficult to treat, since the anticipated side effects of the analgesics are more difficult to manage. In the case of narcotic analgesics this means the **addiction** potential, as well as respiratory depression and **constipation**. For the NSAIDs, the risk of gastric ulcers may be dose limiting. While some classes of drugs, such as the narcotic agonist/antagonist drugs bupronophine, nalbuphine, and pentazocine, and the selective COX-2 inhibitors celecoxib and rofecoxib represent advances in reduction of adverse effects, they are still not fully suitable for long-term management of severe pain. Generally, chronic pain management requires a combination of drug therapy, life-style modification, and other treatment means.

Narcotic analgesics

The narcotic analgesics, also termed opioids, are all derived from opium. The class includes morphine, codeine, and a number of semi-synthetics including meperidine (Demerol), propoxyphen (Darvon), and others. The narcotic analgesics vary in potency, but all are effective in treatment of visceral pain when used in adequate doses. Adverse effects are dose related. Because these drugs are all addictive, they are controlled under federal and state laws. A variety of dosage forms are available, including oral solids, liquids, intravenous and intrathecal injections, and transcutaneous patches.

NSAIDs are effective analgesics even at doses too low to have any anti-inflammatory effects. There are a number of chemical classes, but all have similar therapeutic effects and side effects. Most are appropriate only for oral administration; however, ketorolac (Toradol) is appropriate for injection and may be used in moderate to severe pain for short periods.

Three new NSAIDs, celecoxib, rofecoxib, and valdecoxib may reduce the risk of gastric ulcers in long-term use for adults and have been widely advertised. As of 2004 these drugs had not been properly tested in children, and even in adults, their advantages were not well established. These drugs should not be given to infants and are not well documented for use in older children.

Acetaminophen is a non-narcotic analgesic with no anti-inflammatory properties. It is appropriate for mild to moderate pain. Although the drug is well tolerated in normal doses, it may have significant toxicity at high doses. Because acetaminophen is largely free of side effects at therapeutic doses, it has been considered the first choice for mild pain, including that of osteoarthritis.

General use

Appropriate dosage varies by drug and should consider the type of pain, as well as other risks associated with patient age and condition. For example, narcotic analgesics should usually be avoided in patients with a history of substance abuse but may be fully appropriate in patients with **cancer** pain. Similarly, because narcotics are more rapidly metabolized in patients who have used these drugs for a long period, higher than normal doses may be needed to provide adequate pain management.

Precautions

Narcotic analgesics may be contraindicated in patients with poor respiratory function. NSAIDS should be used with care in patients with insufficient kidney function or **coagulation disorders**. NSAIDs are contraindicated in patients who are allergic to aspirin.

Side effects

Parents of children taking analgesics should review adverse effects of each drug individually. Drugs within a class may vary in their frequency and severity of adverse effects.

The primary adverse effects of the narcotic analgesics are addiction, constipation, and poor respiratory function. Because narcotic analgesics stimulate the production of enzymes that cause the metabolism of these drugs, patients on narcotics for a prolonged period may require increasing doses. This physical tolerance is not the same thing as addiction and is not a reason for withholding medication from patients in severe pain.

NSAIDs may cause kidney problems. Gastrointestinal discomfort is common, although in some cases, these drugs may cause ulcers without the prior warning of gastrointestinal distress. NSAIDs may cause blood to clot less readily, although not to the same extent as if seen with aspirin.

Interactions

Parents should study information on interactions for specific drugs their children are taking.

Analgesics will interact with other drugs that have similar side effects. Nonsteroidal anti-inflammatory drugs should be used with care with other drugs that may cause stomach upset, such as aspirin. Narcotic analgesics should be used with care when taken in combination with drugs that inhibit respirations, such as the benzodiazepines.

Parental concerns

Regarding acetaminophen, parents should never confuse baby formulations, which are high concentration, with children's formulas. The infant formulas are meant to be given by the drop, never by the teaspoonful. Children's liquids are for teaspoonful dosing. Parents must read labels carefully and use the appropriate measure.

Aspirin should never be given to children under the age of 16 who have **chickenpox** or **influenza**, because children who have received aspirin for these conditions seem to have a higher than expected frequency of developing **Reye's syndrome**. High dose aspirin may be given to children for treatment of rheumatism, but this should only be done under medical supervision.

Regarding narcotics, although addiction is a concern when narcotic analgesics are used, this concern is not a problem when the medications are given appropriately. When a child is in severe pain, these pain relievers should not be withheld.

KEY TERMS

Acute pain—Pain in response to injury or another stimulus that resolves when the injury heals or the stimulus is removed.

Anodyne—A medicinal herb or other drug that relieves or soothes pain.

Chronic pain—Pain that lasts over a prolonged period and threatens to disrupt daily life.

Inflammation—Pain, redness, swelling, and heat that develop in response to tissue irritation or injury. It usually is caused by the immune system's response to the body's contact with a foreign substance, such as an allergen or pathogen.

Juvenile arthritis—A chronic inflammatory disease characterized predominantly by arthritis with onset before the sixteenth birthday.

Osteoarthritis—A noninflammatory type of arthritis, usually occurring in older people, characterized by degeneration of cartilage, enlargement of the margins of the bones, and changes in the membranes in the joints. Also called degenerative arthritis.

See also Acetaminophen; Nonsteroidal anti-inflammatory drugs; Pain management.

Resources

BOOKS

Beers, Mark H., and Robert Berkow, eds. *The Merck Manual*, 2nd home ed. West Point, PA: Merck & Co., 2004.

Mcevoy, Gerald, et al. *AHFS Drug Information 2004.* Bethesda, MD: American Society of Healthsystems Pharmacists, 2004.

Siberry, George K., and Robert Iannone, eds. *The Harriet Lane Handbook*, 15th ed. Philadelphia: Mosby, 2000.

PERIODICALS

Losek, J. D. "Acetaminophen dose accuracy and pediatric emergency care." *Pediatric Emergency Care* 20 (May 2004): 285–8.

Rupp, T., and K. A. Delaney. "Inadequate analgesia in emergency medicine." *Annual Emergency Medicine* 43 (April 2004): 494–503.

ORGANIZATIONS

American Academy of Pediatrics. 141 Northwest Point Boulevard Elk Grove Village, IL 60007-1098. Web site: <www.aap.org>.

American Pain Society. 47000 W. Lake Ave., Glenview, IL 60025. Web site: <www.ampainsoc.org/>.

WEB SITES

"Pediatric Chronic Pain." *American Pain Society*, January-February 2001. Available online at <www.ampainsoc.org/pub/bulletin/jan01/posi1.htm> (accessed December 19, 2004).

OTHER

Pediatric Pain [Internet links]. Available online at <www.painandhealth.org/pediatric links.htm> (accessed December 19, 2004).

Samuel Uretsky, PharmD

Anaphylaxis

Definition

Anaphylaxis is a severe, sudden, and potentially fatal allergic reaction to a foreign substance or antigen that affects multiple systems of the body.

Description

Anaphylaxis is a severe, whole-body allergic reaction. After initial exposure to a substance such as wasp sting toxin, the allergic child's immune system becomes sensitized to that allergen. On a subsequent exposure to the specific allergen, an allergic reaction, which can involve a number of different areas of the body, occurs. Anaphylaxis is thought to result from antigen-antibody interactions on the surface of mast cells, connective tissue cells that are believed to contain a number of regulatory, or mediator, chemicals. Specifically, an immunoglobulin antibody protein, IgE, is produced in response to the presence of the allergen. IgE binds to the mast cells, causing them to suddenly release a number of chemicals, including histamine, heparin, serotonin, and bradykinin. Once released, these chemicals produce the bodily reactions that characterize anaphylaxis: constriction of the airways, causing wheezing and difficulty in breathing; and gastrointestinal symptoms, such as abdominal **pain**, cramps, **vomiting**, and **diarrhea**. Shock can occur when the released histamine causes the blood vessels to dilate, which lowers blood pressure; histamine also causes fluids to leak from the bloodstream

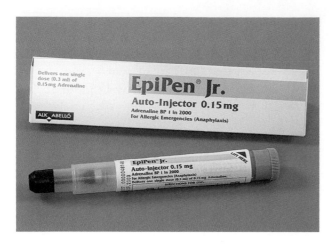

EpiPen Jr., a syringe containing a child's dosage of adrenaline, is used for the emergency treatment of anaphylactic shock. *(© Mark Thomas/Photo Researchers, Inc.)*

into the tissues, lowering the blood volume. Pulmonary edema can result from fluids leaking into the alveoli (air sacs) of the lung.

Substances that can trigger an anaphylactic reaction include:

- insect **stings** from hornets, wasps, yellow jackets, honey bees, or fire ants
- medications, including penicillin, cephalosporin, anesthetics, streptokinase, and others
- foods (ingesting even tiny amounts or simply being near the offending food), including peanuts, tree nuts (such as walnuts or almonds), fish, shellfish, eggs, milk, soy, and wheat
- vaccines, including **allergy shots** and egg- and gelatin-based vaccines
- hormones, including insulin and possibly progesterone
- rubber latex products
- animal and human proteins, including seminal fluid and horse serum (which is used as snake anti-venom)

Anaphylactoid (meaning "anaphylactic-like") reactions are similar to those of true anaphylaxis but do not require an IgE immune reaction. These are usually caused by direct stimulation of the mast cells. The same chemicals as with anaphylaxis are released, with the same effects, so the symptoms are treated the same way. However, an anaphylactoid reaction can occur on initial exposure to an allergen as well as on subsequent exposures, since no sensitization is required.

There is also a rare kind of food allergy, called exercise-induced allergy, that is caused by eating a specific food and then exercising. It can produce **itching**, light-

headedness, **hives**, and anaphylaxis. The offending food does not cause a reaction without **exercise**, and, alternately, exercise does not cause a reaction without ingesting the food beforehand.

Demographics

Although likely an underestimate, about 10,000 cases of anaphylaxis occur per year in North America, with about 750 fatalities a year. The exact prevalence of anaphylaxis is unknown, because milder reactions may be attributed to **asthma** attacks or sudden cases of hives, and more serious or fatal episodes might be reported as heart attacks, as the initial symptoms of hives, asthma, and swollen throat can fade quickly.

Causes and symptoms

The symptoms of anaphylaxis may occur within seconds of exposure, or be delayed 15 to 30 minutes and sometimes even an hour or more later, if the allergen is aspirin or other similar drugs. The sooner the symptoms occur after exposure, the more severe the anaphylactic reaction is likely to be.

The first symptoms of an anaphylactic reaction are associated with the skin: flushing (warmth and redness), itching (often in the groin or armpits), and hives. These symptoms are often accompanied by **anxiety**; a rapid, irregular pulse; and a sense of impending doom. Then the throat and tongue swell, the voice becomes hoarse, and swallowing and breathing become labored. Symptoms of **rhinitis** or asthma may also occur, causing a runny nose, sneezing, wheezing, and abnormal high-pitched breathing sounds, further worsening the breathing problems. Gastrointestinal effects may also develop, including vomiting, diarrhea, and stomach cramps. The child may be confused and have slurred speech. In about 25 percent of the cases, the chemicals flooding the blood stream will cause a generalized opening of capillaries (tiny blood vessels), resulting in a drop in blood pressure, lightheadedness, and even a loss of consciousness, which are typical symptoms of anaphylactic shock. The child may exhibit blueness of the skin (cyanosis), lips, or nail beds.

After the original symptoms occur, there are three possible outcomes:

- The symptoms may be mild and fade spontaneously or be quickly ended by administering emergency medication. The anaphylactic episode is over for that particular exposure.
- After initial improvement, the symptoms may reoccur after four to 12 hours (a late phase recurrent reaction)

and require additional treatment and monitoring. Late phase reactions occur in about 10 percent of cases.

- The reaction may be persistent and severe, requiring extensive medical treatment and **hospitalization**. This condition occurs in about 20 percent of cases.

When to call the doctor

The child should be given immediate emergency care, if possible, and then taken to the emergency room or the local emergency number (e.g., 911) should be called if symptoms of anaphylaxis develop.

Diagnosis

A child having an anaphylactic reaction will exhibit typical symptoms of anaphylaxis, such as hives and swelling of the eyes or face, blue skin from lack of oxygen, or pale skin from shock. The airway may be blocked, and the child may be wheezing as well as confused and weak. The pulse will be rapid and the blood pressure may be low. Anaphylaxis is an emergency condition that requires immediate professional medical attention.

Once a child has had an anaphylactic reaction, an allergist should be consulted to identify the specific allergen that caused the reaction. The allergist will take a detailed medical history and use blood or skin tests to identify the allergen. The allergist will ask about activities that the child participated in before the event, food and medications the child may have ingested, and whether the child had contact with any rubber products.

Treatment

Because of the severity of these reactions, treatment must begin immediately. The most common emergency treatment involves injection of epinephrine (adrenaline) to stop the release of histamines and relax the muscles of the respiratory tract. The injection is given in the outer thigh and can be administered through light fabric such as trousers, skirts, or stockings. Heavier clothing may have to be removed prior to the injection. After the injection, emergency services or 911 should be called immediately. A child with known severe allergic reactions should be carrying an allergy kit with epinephrine; if not, treatment will have to be delayed until emergency personnel can provide the required medication. For reactions to insect stings or allergy shots, a tourniquet should be placed between the puncture site and the heart; the tourniquet should be released every 10 minutes. If the child is conscious, he or she should lie down and elevate

the feet. If trained, the parents or others present should administer CPR if the child stops breathing or does not have a pulse. After 10 to 15 minutes, if symptoms are still significant, another dose of epinephrine can be injected. Even after the reaction subsides, the child should still be taken to the emergency room immediately and monitored for three to four hours, since symptoms can redevelop. Other treatments may be given by medical personnel, including oxygen, intravenous fluids, breathing medications, and possibly more epinephrine. The epinephrine may make the child feel shaky and have a rapid, pounding pulse, but these are normal side effects and are only dangerous to those with heart problems. Steroids and **antihistamines** may also be given but are usually not as helpful initially as epinephrine. However, they may be useful in preventing a recurrent delayed reaction.

If the child is being treated with beta blocker medications commonly used to treat high blood pressure, angina, thyroid disorders, migraines, or glaucoma, it may be difficult to reverse an anaphylactic reaction.

Prognosis

Anaphylaxis is a severe disorder that has a poor prognosis without prompt treatment. Symptoms are usually resolved with appropriate therapy; therefore, immediate emergency care is essential.

Prevention

For children with known reactions to **antibiotics**, foods, insect stings, specific foods, or any of the allergens that can induce an anaphylactic reaction, avoidance of the symptom-inducing agent is the best form of prevention.

Specific avoidance measures that are recommended include:

Drugs/medications:

- Parents should advise healthcare personnel of the childs **allergies**.
- Parents should ask the doctor whether prescribed medications could contain the drug(s) to which the child is allergic.
- The child should take all medications by mouth, if possible, since the risk of anaphylaxis is greater with injections.
- Any child should stay in a doctors office or near medical care for a period of time after receiving injections of an antibiotic or vaccine.

Insect stings:

- The child should avoid areas where insects breed and live.
- The child should not wear bright clothing, perfume, hair spray, or lotions that might attract insects.
- If possible the child should wear long sleeves, long trousers, and shoes when out of doors.

Food:

- The child must be instructed to never again eat that kind of food that causes an anaphylactic reaction.
- Parents should carefully read all ingredient labels of foods that the child might eat and be aware of the different terms used for various foods, such as caseinate for milk or albumin for eggs.
- Parents should ask about ingredients in foods while eating out with the child, bring safe substitutes from home, and bring an allergy kit.
- Parents should be aware of possible cross-contamination, such as when an ice cream scoop is used for Rocky Road ice cream, which contains peanuts, and then for vanilla ice cream.
- School kitchen personnel should be notified of the childs condition.
- The child should avoid eating foods that might cross-react with foods that the child is allergic to, for example, if the child is allergic to shrimp, the child may also be allergic to crab or lobster.
- When traveling to other countries, parents should learn the appropriate words for foods that trigger their childs allergy; in addition, parents can request that air carriers serve peanut-free snacks to all passengers when their child is traveling; also the child should avoid eating airline meals.

Latex:

- The child should avoid all latex rubber products.
- If the child has to be hospitalized, the parents should alert the hospital personnel to the childs allergy to latex.
- A child with a latex allergy may also have allergies to kiwi fruit, passion fruit, papayas, bananas, avocados, figs, peaches, nectarines, plums, tomatoes, celery, and chestnuts.

In addition, children with a history of allergic reactions should carry an emergency kit containing injectable epinephrine and chewable antihistamine and be instructed in its use. A child who is not prepared to deal with an anaphylactic reaction is at an increased risk of dying. The allergy kit should include simple instructions on when and how to use the kit; sterilizing swabs to cleanse the skin before and after the injection; epinephrine in a preloaded syringe, as prescribed by the childs doctor in doses appropriate for children; and antihistamine tablets. The expiration date on the medications in the allergy kit should be checked and medications replaced as needed. Also, the epinephrine solution should be clear; if it is pinkish brown, it should be discarded and replaced.

There are many brands of allergy kits. The simplest kit to use is the Ana-kit, which contains a sterile syringe preloaded with two doses of epinephrine with a stop between. Another commonly used kit is the Epi-Pen, which carries a single self-injecting, spring-loaded syringe of epinephrine. Two Epi-Pen kits should be carried, so that two doses are available. Allergy kits should be kept at home, school, and **day care**; and the school administrator, teachers, and friends should be made aware of the childs allergies. Adults associated with the child should be trained in giving an injection and have a plan to transport the child to the hospital. Older children should be taught to give self-injections. Children at risk for anaphylaxis should also wear a Medic Alert bracelet or necklace or carry a medical emergency card with them at all times that clearly describes their allergy.

A consultation with an allergist can help to identify the substances that trigger the reaction; the allergist can also provide information on how to best avoid the triggering substance. The allergist may also be able to give allergy shots to children with wasp, yellow jacket, hornet, honey bee, or fire ant allergies. These shots provide 90 percent protection against the first four insect reactions, but less protection against fire ant reactions. Premedication is also helpful in preventing anaphylaxis from x-ray dyes; also there may be alternative dyes available for use that are less likely to cause reactions. Desensitization to medications has also been successful in some cases. The process involves gradually increasing the amount of medication given under controlled conditions. The procedure has worked for sensitivities to penicillin, sulfa drugs, and insulin.

The risk of anaphylaxis sometimes diminishes over time if there are no repeated exposures or reactions. However, the child at risk should also expect the worst and be prepared with preventive medication.

Parental concerns

Parents caring for children who are at risk for life-threatening anaphylactic reactions may experience high stress levels, for they have to maintain vigilance in order to protect the child while creating a sense of normalcy as

KEY TERMS

Allergen—A foreign substance that provokes an immune reaction or allergic response in some sensitive people but not in most others.

Allergy—A hypersensitivity reaction in response to exposure to a specific substance.

Epinephrine—A hormone produced by the adrenal medulla. It is important in the response to stress and partially regulates heart rate and metabolism. It is also called adrenaline.

Immunoglobulin E (IgE)—A type of protein in blood plasma that acts as an antibody to activate allergic reactions. About 50% of patients with allergic disorders have increased IgE levels in their blood serum.

the child grows up. Parents can reduce their stress by using social support groups, accepting their childs condition, and maintaining a positive attitude.

See also Allergies.

Resources

BOOKS

Barber, Marianne S. *The Parents Guide to Food Allergies: Clear and Complete Advice from the Experts on Raising Your Food-Allergic Child.* New York: Owl Books, 2001.

Coss, Linda Marienhoff. *How to Manage Your Childs Life-Threatening Food Allergies: Practical Tips for Daily Life.* Lake Forest, CA: Plumtree Press, 2004.

Jevon, Philip. *Anaphylaxis: A Practical Guide.* London, UK: Butterworth-Heinemann, 2004.

Smith, Nicole. *Allie the Allergic Elephant: A Childrens Story of Peanut Allergies.* San Francisco: Jungle Communications, 2002.

ORGANIZATIONS

American Academy of Allergy, Asthma, and Immunology. 611 E. Wells Street, Milwaukee, WI 53202. Web site. <www.aaaai.org>

Food Allergy and Anaphylaxis Network. 10400 Eaton Place, Suite 107, Fairfax, VA 220302208. Web site: <www.foodallergy.org>

WEB SITES

American College of Allergy, Asthma, and Immunology. Available online at <http://allergy.mcg.edu> (accessed October 10, 2004).

Judith Sims

Anatomical age

Definition

Anatomical age is the numerical **assessment** of a child's physical growth in relation to the statistical average based on the child's chronological age.

Description

Using statistical data, the American Academy of Pediatrics and the National Institutes of Health in the United States have developed tables to illustrate the growth patterns of children. These tables describe the population of all children of a certain age, with ranges for weight, height, and other physical characteristics. For most children, anatomical age—based on weight and height measurements—is the same as chronological age—based on the number of months or years since birth. However, when a child's physical growth falls outside the range of his chronological age, the child's age is determined by his growth. For example, if a six-year-old's height and weight falls within the range for five-year-olds, his anatomical age will be given as five, not six years.

Anatomical age has been used as a determination of chronological age by immigration and **adoption** agencies when no birth certificates have been available. This has been crucial for refugee children in particular. However, prolonged **malnutrition** can cloud actual age assessments. That is why radiographs, or **x rays**, of a child's bones have been taken and read by osteologists (doctors who special in the skeletal system) and radiologists.

William Walter Greulich and S. Idell Pyle's atlas of **skeletal development** and Tanner and White's method are the two major assessment tools for wrist radiography. X rays of a child's left wrist are compared visually with a series of x rays of wrists of children of various ages. A computerized system has been developed based on Tanner and Whitehouse's model, which uses pattern recognition like finger print databases. This technique greatly speeds up the diagnostic process.

In addition, an ultrasound version of the Greulich-Pyle Atlas has proven to be as effective as wrist x rays. This method does not expose children to radiation.

Common problems

Standardized growth charts and wrist radiographs can assess normal skeletal growth and determine whether there are problems concerning growth that is too fast or too slow. Anatomical age assessment can also reveal other conditions. Because bone growth is affected by calcium regulating hormones, sex steroids, and thyroid hormones, disturbances in the endocrine system, which controls hormones, can be detected.

Parental concerns

Determining anatomical age can give parents an indication of their children's future growth and can help them work with their doctors to determine treatment if there seem to be growth problems.

When to call the doctor

Usually, the child sees the doctor for immunizations, school physical exams, or childhood illnesses. At these times, the doctor may discuss findings about anatomical age with parents. If parents have concerns about their children's growth, they can bring them up at these visits.

See also X rays.

Resources

BOOKS

Hochberg, Ze'ev. *Endocrine Control of Skeletal Maturation.* Farmington, CT: S. Karger Publishers, 2002.

PERIODICALS

Flores-Mir, C., et al. "Use of Skeletal Maturation Based on Hand-Wrist Radiographic Analysis as a Predictor of Facial Growth: A Systematic Review." *Angle Orthodontia* 74, no. 1 (February 2004): 118–24.

Janie Franz

Anemias

Definition

Anemia is a blood disorder characterized by abnormally low levels of healthy red blood cells (RBCs) or reduced hemoglobin (Hgb), the iron-bearing protein in red blood cells that delivers oxygen to tissues throughout the body. Reduced blood cell volume (hematocrit) is also considered anemia. The reduction of any or all of the three blood parameters reduces the oxygen-carrying capability of the blood, causing reduced oxygenation of body tissues, a condition called hypoxia.

Description

All tissues in the human body need a regular supply of oxygen to stay healthy and perform their functions. RBCs contain Hgb, a protein pigment that allows the cells to carry oxygen (oxygenate) tissues throughout the body. RBCs live about 120 days and are normally replaced in an orderly way by the bone marrow, spleen, and liver. As RBCs break down, they release Hgb into the blood stream, which is normally filtered out by the kidneys and excreted. The iron released from the RBCs is returned to the bone marrow to help create new cells. Anemia develops when either blood loss, a slow-down in the production of new RBCs (erythropoiesis), or an increase in red cell destruction (hemolysis) causes significant reductions in RBCs, Hgb, iron levels, and the essential delivery of oxygen to body tissues.

Anemia can be mild, moderate, or severe enough to lead to life-threatening complications. More than 400 different types of anemia have been identified. Many of them are rare. Most are caused by ongoing or sudden blood loss. Other causes include vitamin and mineral deficiencies, inherited conditions, and certain diseases that affect red cell production or destruction.

Anemia in newborn infants is noted when hemoglobin levels are lower than expected for the birth weight and postnatal age. Premature or low birth-weight infants may have lower hemoglobin levels. The normal newborn Hgb is 16.8 dL, which may be 1 to 2 dL lower if birth weight is abnormally low. Anemia may be the first sign of certain disorders in the newborn, such as blood loss that has occurred from transplacental hemorrhage, a condition in which the infant's blood bleeds back into the mother's circulation; bleeding from ruptures in the liver, spleen, adrenals, or kidneys; or hemorrhage within the brain (intracranial hemorrhage). Anemia can also be caused by the destruction of red blood cells or reduced red blood cell production. Newborns may also have low red blood cell volume (hematocrit or Hct) if they were born by **cesarean section**. It must be noted, however, that hemoglobin decreases naturally (physiologic decrease) in infants by eight to 12 weeks of age, leveling at a normal value of 11 g/dL or better.

Iron-deficiency anemia

Iron deficiency anemia is the most common form of anemia worldwide. In the United States, it affects thousands of toddlers between one and two years of age and more than 3 million women of childbearing age. This condition is less common in older children and in adults over 50 and rarely occurs in teenage boys and young men.

The onset of iron deficiency anemia is gradual and may not have early symptoms. The deficiency begins when the body loses more iron than it derives from food and other sources. Because depleted iron stores cannot meet the red blood cell's needs, fewer red blood cells develop. In this early stage of anemia, the red blood cells look normal, but they are reduced in number. Then the body tries to compensate for the iron deficiency by producing more red blood cells, which are characteristically small in size (spherocytosis). Symptoms of anemia, especially weakness and fatigue, develop at this stage. Individuals may be given iron preparations by injection or advised to take oral iron supplements. It sometimes helps to take vitamin C along with oral iron supplementation to encourage better absorption of the iron. Taking iron supplements can result in **diarrhea**, cramps, or **vomiting**.

Folic acid deficiency anemia

Folic acid deficiency anemia is the most common type of megaloblastic anemia, arising from a problem with the synthesis of deoxyribonucleic acid (DNA) within the cells of the body. It is characterized by RBCs that are larger than normal and is caused by a deficiency of folic acid, a vitamin that the body needs to produce normal cells and normal DNA.

Folic acid anemia is especially common in infants and teenagers. This condition usually results from a dietary deficiency but may also be due to an inability to absorb (malabsorption) folic acid. Folic acid is available in many foods, such as cheese, eggs, fish, green vegetables, meat, milk, mushrooms, and yeast. **Smoking** raises the risk of developing this condition by interfering with the absorption of vitamin C, which the body needs to absorb folic acid. Folic acid anemia can be a complication of pregnancy, when a woman's body needs eight times more folic acid than it does otherwise. Folic acid deficiency in pregnant women may lead to birth defects in their children. Supplementation of folic acid is recommended during pregnancy.

Vitamin B$_{12}$ deficiency anemia

Less common in the United States than folic acid anemia, vitamin B$_{12}$ deficiency anemia is another type of megaloblastic anemia that develops when the body does not absorb enough of this nutrient. Necessary for the creation of healthy RBCs, B$_{12}$ is found in meat, eggs, whole grains, and most vegetables. Large amounts of B$_{12}$ are stored in the body, so this condition may not become apparent until up to four years after B$_{12}$ absorption stops or slows down. The resulting drop in RBC production can cause loss of muscle control; loss of sensation in the legs, hands, and feet; soreness, slickness, or burning of the tongue; weight loss; or yellow-blue **color blindness**. Confusion, depression, and memory loss may also be associated with the deficiency.

Pernicious anemia is the most common form of B$_{12}$ deficiency. Since most people who eat meat or eggs get enough B$_{12}$ in their diets, a deficiency of this vitamin usually means that the body is not absorbing it properly. This condition can be found in those who do not produce adequate amounts of a chemical secreted by the stomach lining that combines with B$_{12}$ to help its absorption in the small intestine. Pernicious anemia is diagnosed more often in adults between ages 50 and 60 than in children or young people, although there is the possibility of inheriting the condition, with symptoms not appearing until later in life.

Vitamin C deficiency anemia

Anemia due to vitamin C deficiency is a rare disorder that causes the bone marrow to manufacture abnormally small red blood cells. Vitamin C deficiency anemia results from a severe, long-standing dietary deficiency or malabsorption of this essential vitamin. It is usually easily corrected with supplementation.

Hemolytic anemia

Hemolytic anemia can be present at birth (congenital hemolytic anemia or spherocytosis) or acquired later in life. It is the result of either infection or the presence of antibodies that destroy RBCs more rapidly than bone marrow can replace them. Hemolytic anemia can enlarge the spleen, an organ that also produces red blood cells when necessary. Production of cells by the spleen will increase to meet the demands of accelerated RBC destruction (hemolysis). Complications of hemolytic anemia in older children or adults include **pain**, gallstones, and other serious health problems.

Hemolytic disease of the newborn is a specific variation of hemolytic anemia in which an incompatibility exists between antigens on the cells of the mother and baby, causing antibodies to develop in the mother's circulation. The antibodies are produced as an immune response to what the body views as foreign antigens on the surface of the infant's RBCs. Several specific antigens are responsible for the incompatibilities: Rh type incompatibility, ABO blood group incompatibility, and other incompatibilities involving antigens known as Kell, Duffy, M, N, and P, among many others. Hemolytic disease of the newborn and the anemia that results is detectable within the first few days after birth. Depending on the strength of the antibody, the anemia may clear up on its own or exchange transfusions may be necessary to replace the newborn's blood.

Thalassemia

An inherited form of hemolytic anemia, **thalassemia** comes from the production of abnormal hemoglobin. It is characterized by low hemoglobin and unusually small and fragile RBCs (microcytosis), although the RBC count may be normal. Thalassemia has several types that involve imbalances in the four chains of amino acids that comprise hemoglobin (alpha- and beta-globins). In thalassemia minor or thalassemia trait (heterozygous thalassemia), also called alpha-thalassemia, there is an imbalance in the production of the alpha chain of amino acids. In thalassemia minor, fetal hemoglobin (HbF), the hemoglobin form that circulates in the fetus, does not decrease normally after birth and may remain high in later life. A child may inherit thalassemia trait when only one parent has the genes responsible for it. It is usually not treated and does not have serious consequences. Thalassemia major (homozygous thalassemia or Cooley's anemia) occurs in children in whom both parents pass on the genes responsible. It is known as beta-thalassemia, because of an imbalance in the beta chain amino acids of hemoglobin. It also involves the persistence of HbF with larger than normal amounts appearing in the child's circulation. Alpha-thalassemias occur most commonly in African Americans; beta-thalassemias most commonly affect people of Mediterranean or middle-Eastern ancestry and Southeast Asians. Hemoglobin H disease is another form of thalassemia in which three of the four beta-globin genes are missing.

Sickle cell anemia

Sickle cell anemia is an inherited, chronic, incurable blood disorder that causes the body to produce defective hemoglobin, the abnormal HgbS, which occurs primarily in African Americans. The condition is characterized by abnormal, crescent-shaped RBCs. Unlike normal oval cells, fragile sickle cells cannot hold enough hemoglobin to nourish body tissues. The deformed shape makes it hard for sickle cells to pass through narrow blood vessels. When capillaries become obstructed, a life-threatening condition called sickle cell crisis is likely to occur. A child who inherits the sickle cell gene from each parent will have the disease. A child who inherits the sickle cell gene from only one parent carries the sickle cell trait but does not have the disease.

Aplastic anemia

Sometimes curable by bone marrow transplant, but potentially fatal, aplastic anemia is characterized by decreased production of red and white blood cells and platelets (disc-shaped cells that are a key component of blood coagulation). This disorder may be inherited or acquired as a result of the following:

- recent severe illness
- long-term exposure to industrial chemicals
- chemotherapy, use of anticancer drugs, and certain other medications

Anemia of chronic disease

Cancer, chronic infection or inflammation, and kidney and liver disease often cause mild or moderate anemia. Chronic liver failure generally produces the most severe symptoms because the production of RBCs is directly affected.

Causes and symptoms

Anemias do not all stem from the same causes. Anemia can be the result of injuries, chronic or acute illnesses, complications of surgery or **childbirth**, metabolic disturbances or deficiencies, and adverse response to drug therapy administered for other conditions. Causes may include sudden or ongoing loss of blood, nutritional deficiencies, decreased red blood cell production, or increased red blood cell destruction. **Malnutrition** or malabsorption of nutrients can contribute to vitamin deficiency anemia and iron deficiency anemias. Although red cell destruction and replacement is an ongoing process in the body, hereditary disorders and certain diseases can accelerate blood cell destruction, resulting in anemia. However, excessive bleeding is the most common cause of severe anemia, and the speed with which blood loss occurs has a significant effect on the severity of symptoms. Chronic blood loss may be a consequence of the following:

- cancer
- gastrointestinal tumors
- diverticulosis
- polyposis
- heavy or frequent menstrual flow
- hemorrhoids
- nosebleeds

- stomach ulcers
- long-standing alcohol abuse

Acute blood loss may occur as a result of injury, a ruptured blood vessel, or a complication of surgery or childbirth. When a lot of blood is lost within a short time, blood pressure and the amount of oxygen in the body drop suddenly, sometimes leading to heart failure or death. Loss of even one third of the body's blood volume in the space of several hours can be fatal. Gradual blood loss is less threatening, because the body has time to replace RBCs and blood volume.

Symptoms

Weakness, fatigue, and a run-down feeling may be the first signs of anemia. Pasty or sallow skin color, or the absence of color in the gums, nail beds, creases of the palm, or lining of the eyelids are other signs of anemia. Individuals who appear to be weak, easily tired, often out of breath, and who may feel faint or dizzy on movement may be severely anemic.

Other symptoms of anemia may include the following:

- unusual cravings for ice (chewing on ice cubes), paint, or earth (actually eating dirt)
- headache
- inability to concentrate, memory loss
- inflammation of the mouth (**stomatitis**) or tongue (glossitis)
- insomnia
- irregular heartbeat
- loss of appetite
- dry, brittle, or ridged nails
- rapid breathing
- sores in the mouth, throat, or rectum
- perspiration, especially around the head and neck
- swelling of hands and feet
- constant thirst
- ringing in the ears (tinnitus)
- unexplained bleeding or bruising
- angina pectoris, i.e., chest pain accompanied by a **choking** sensation that may provoke anxiety

Demographics

Acquired anemias affect about 4 million individuals in the United States, and over 50 percent of these are under age 45, although less than 10 percent of cases occur in children and adolescents. In the United States, iron deficiency anemia is the most prevalent type of anemia, affecting about 240,000 toddlers between one and two years of age and 3.3 million women of childbearing age. Anemia due to gradual blood loss is more common in women than in men, particularly pregnant women or women of menstruating age. Pernicious anemia is more common in women and in African Americans and is less common in other racial groups. Folate deficiency is not common in young people who eat an adequate diet and is usually associated with malnutrition, pregnancy, and **alcoholism**. Sickle cell anemia is more frequently diagnosed than thalassemias and occurs most often among African Americans. Thalassemia occurs in four out of 100,000 individuals in the United States, particularly among those of Mediterranean, Asian, or middle Eastern descent.

When to call the doctor

When a child exhibits weakness, **dizziness**, listlessness, or fatigue, it may be the first sign of anemia. The pediatrician should be consulted if the child is also extremely pale or has little or no color in the gums, nail beds, creases of the palm, or lining of the eyelids. Any prolonged bleeding or sudden blood loss requires examination by a physician and testing for anemia.

Diagnosis

The child's medical history will be taken, including the child's age, symptoms, illnesses, and general state of health, and a **family** history of ancestry and known inherited anemias will be noted. Symptoms noticed in children by their parents may include fatigue, weight loss, inability to concentrate, loss of appetite, and light-headedness when standing up. The physical examination may reveal paleness, lack of color in the creases of the palm, gums, and the linings of the eyelids. The child's breathing rate may be increased and, in advanced cases, the spleen or liver may be enlarged when palpated. If anemia is due to chronic disease, there may be evidence of infection or inflammation. Urine output may be reduced in severe anemia.

Diagnostic testing begins with a complete blood count (CBC) and differential to reveal the RBC count, white blood cell (WBC) count, hemoglobin (Hgb), and hematocrit (Hct); any of these counts can be altered, and in most anemias the RBC and hemoglobin will be reduced. The mean corpuscular volume (MCV) will be measured to compare the size of RBCs with normal RBCs. A reticulocyte (young RBCs) count will help determine if anemia is caused by impaired RBC production or increased RBC destruction. Iron, vitamin C, vitamin B_{12}, and folate levels will be measured to evaluate and identify possible deficiencies. Diagnosing thalassemia and sickle cell anemia, both of which involve disorders of hemoglobin, will require measuring the different types of hemoglobin through a laboratory testing method called hemoglobin electrophoresis. In some anemias, a bone marrow sample will be removed (bone marrow biopsy) for microscopic examination, especially to confirm iron deficiency anemia or the megaloblastic anemias. Kidney function tests, coagulation tests, and stool examinations for occult blood may also be performed.

Treatment

Surgery may be necessary to correct blood losses caused by injury or hemorrhage (nose bleeds, aneurysm, cerebral hemorrhage, bleeding ulcer) or childbirth. Transfusions of packed red blood cells or whole blood may also be used to replace blood volume and to stimulate the body's own production of red blood cells. Medication or surgery may also be necessary to control heavy menstrual flow or to remove polyps (growths or nodules) from the bowels.

Anemia due to nutritional deficiencies can usually be treated with iron replacement therapy, specific vitamin supplements, or self-administered injections of vitamin B$_{12}$. People with folic acid anemia may be advised to take oral folic acid.

Vitamin B$_{12}$ deficiency anemia requires a life-long regimen of B$_{12}$ shots to maintain vitamin levels and control symptoms of pernicious anemia. The patient may be advised to limit physical activity until treatment restores strength and balance.

Anemia resulting from chronic disease is typically corrected by treating the underlying illness. This type of anemia rarely becomes severe. If it does, transfusions or hormone treatments to stimulate red blood cell production may be given.

Thalassemia minor is typically not treated. Thalassemia major may be treated with regular transfusions, surgical resection of the spleen to avoid its removal of RBCs from circulation, and sometimes iron chelation therapy. Symptoms are treated as they occur. Children or young adults with thalassemia major may require periodic **hospitalization** to receive blood transfusions or, in some cases, bone marrow transplants.

Sickle cell anemia will be monitored by regular eye examinations and diagnostic blood work. Immunizations for **pneumonia** and infectious diseases are part of treatment along with prompt treatment for sickle cell crises and infections of any kind. Psychotherapy or counseling may help older children deal with the emotional symptoms characteristic of this condition.

Children with aplastic anemia are especially susceptible to infection. Treatment for aplastic anemia may involve blood transfusions and bone marrow transplantation to replace malfunctioning cells with healthy ones.

Hemolytic anemia of the warm-antibody type may be treated with large doses of intravenous and oral corticocosteroids (cortisone). Individuals who do not respond to medical therapy, may undergo surgery to remove the spleen, which controls the anemia in some individuals by helping to add more RBCs to the circulation. Immune-system suppressants are prescribed when surgery is not successful. There is no specific treatment for cold-antibody hemolytic anemia.

Treatment of newborn anemia depends on the severity of symptoms, the level of Hgb, and the presence of any other diseases that may affect oxygen delivery, such as lung or heart disease or hyaline membrane disease. Transfusions may be given in certain situations or exchange transfusions if hemolytic disease of the newborn is not quickly resolved. The risk of transfusion (such as transfusion reactions, potential toxins, and infections such as HIV or hepatitis) are carefully weighed against the severity of the anemia in the infant.

Alternative treatment

Vitamin C is noted for helping to absorb iron and folate supplements. Cooking in a cast iron skillet may leach small amounts of absorbable iron into the diet. Folic acid can be readily absorbed from raw salad greens such as lettuce, spinach, arugula, alfalfa sprouts, and others. Blackstrap molasses is a good source of iron and B **vitamins**. Herbal supplements that will benefit individuals who have anemia include bilberry, dandelion, goldenseal, mullein, nettle, Oregon grape root, red raspberry, and yellow dock. Herbs are available as tinctures and teas or in capsules.

Nutritional concerns

The diet is a ready source of nutrients that prevent and treat anemia. Children with anemia can include more of these nutrients in their diet by eating a broad variety of whole grains, fruits and vegetables, beans, lean meat, poultry and fish, and supplementing the diet regularly with vitamins, **minerals**, and iron (as recommended). Pediatricians should be consulted before iron supplements are taken, however, because of the difficulty in absorbing non-food sources of iron. Vitamin C can stimulate iron absorption. Good food sources of iron

KEY TERMS

Erythropoiesis—The process through which new red blood cells are created; it begins in the bone marrow.

Hematocrit—A measure of the percentage of red blood cells in the total volume of blood in the human body.

Hemoglobin—An iron-containing pigment of red blood cells composed of four amino acid chains (alpha, beta, gamma, delta) that delivers oxygen from the lungs to the cells of the body and carries carbon dioxide from the cells to the lungs.

Hemolysis—The process of breaking down of red blood cells. As the cells are destroyed, hemoglobin, the component of red blood cells which carries the oxygen, is liberated.

Hypoxia—A condition characterized by insufficient oxygen in the cells of the body

Megaloblast—A large erythroblast (a red marrow cell that synthesizes hemoglobin).

Reticulocyte—An early, immature form of a red blood cell. Over time, the reticulocyte develops to become a mature, oxygen-carrying red blood cell.

include: almonds, broccoli, dried beans, raisins, dried apricots, seaweed (as soup stock), whole-grain breads and cereals, brown rice, lean red meat, liver, potatoes, poultry, and shellfish.

Because light and heat destroy folic acid, fruits and vegetables should be eaten raw or cooked as little as possible to help assimilation of folic acid. Folic acid can also be taken as a supplement.

Prognosis

Most anemias can be treated or managed. The prognosis for anemias generally depends upon the severity of the anemia, the type of anemia, and the response to treatment. The hereditary anemias, such as the thalassemias and sickle cell anemia, may require life-long treatment and monitoring whereas other types of anemia, once treated, are apt not to recur. Thalassemia major may cause deformities and may shorten life expectancy. Severe anemia may lead to other serious conditions, particularly if oxygen delivery is compromised for long periods of time or RBC destruction is more rapid than can be controlled by normal RBC replacement or specific

treatment. Severe blood loss or prolonged anemia can result in life-threatening complications.

Prevention

Safety is the primary preventive measure for blood loss by injury. A wholesome, balanced diet rich in nutrients can help prevent dietary deficiencies that lead to anemia. Hereditary anemias cannot be prevented; parents can seek genetic testing and counseling if they are concerned about inherited anemias noted in their families or ethnic background.

Nutritional concerns

Sources of iron such as liver, red meat, whole grains, and poultry may help maintain hemoglobin levels and reduce the likelihood of deficiency-related anemias. Vitamin C is noted for helping to improve assimilation of iron taken as supplements.

Parental concerns

Parents may be particularly concerned about the possibility of inherited anemias. Genetic testing is available to address their doubts. **Nutrition** education is readily available from public health sources, books, and the reliable Internet sources for parents who are concerned about providing essential nutrients for children who may be susceptible to deficiency anemias. Regular physical examinations can help evaluate a child's overall health and reveal possible signs or symptoms of anemia.

Resources

BOOKS

"Blood Disorders." *The Merck Manual of Medical Information*, 2nd Home ed. Edited by Mark H. Beers et al. White House Station, NJ: Merck & Co., 2003.

Hill, Shirley, A. *Managing Sickle Cell Disease in Low-Income Families.* Philadelphia: Temple University Press, 2003.

Lande, Bruce. *Aplastic Anemia and Other Autoimmune Diseases: Help Your Body Heal Itself.* Syracuse, NY: Action Enterprises, 2003.

Ross, Allison J. *Everything You Need to Know about Anemia.* New York: Rosen Publishing Group, 2001.

Wick, M., et al. *Iron Metabolism, Anemias, Clinical Aspects and Laboratory.* New York: Springer, 2003.

ORGANIZATIONS

National Heart, Lung, and Blood Institute (NHLBI). 6701 Rockledge Drive, PO Box 30105, Bethesda, MD 20824–0105. Web site: <http://www.nhlbi.nih.gov>.

WEB SITES

"Anemia." *KidsHealth.* Available online at <http://kidshealth.org/parent/medical/heart/anemia.html> (accessed October 10, 2004).

"Understanding Anemia: Your Life May Depend on It." *Anemia Lifeline.* Available online at <www.anemia.com> (accessed October 10, 2004).

L. Lee Culvert
Maureen Haggerty

Angelman's syndrome

Definition

Angelman's syndrome is a relatively rare genetic disorder that causes a variety of neurological problems, including **developmental delay**, seizures, speech impairment, and problems with movement and balance.

Description

Angelman's syndrome was first described in 1965 by Harold Angelman, who noted that a group of children in his medical practice had flat heads, made jerky movements, held their tongues in a protruding way, and had curious bouts of laughter.

Demographics

Angelman's syndrome is relatively rare. As of the early 2000s there were only about 1,000 to 5,000 known cases of the syndrome in the United States. There is no predilection for either sex or for any particular ethnicity.

Causes and symptoms

Most cases of Angelman's syndrome can be traced to a genetic abnormality inherited from a maternal chromosome (15). A particular area of genes that should control the production and function of a protein called ubiquitin is either absent or ineffective. A minority of cases of Angelman's syndrome are due to new mutations in this same area of genes.

Children with Angelman's syndrome have an abnormally small, flat appearance to their skull. By one to two months of age, infants with the syndrome develop feeding difficulties. By six to 12 months, developmental delay is usually noted. Most children develop seizures by three years of age. Other characteristics of the syndrome

include abnormally decreased muscle tone, fair skin and hair, protruding jaw, hyperactivity, episodes of uncontrollable laughter, difficulty sleeping, and severe problems with movement and balance. The disorder is sometimes called "happy puppet syndrome," because many children with the disorder have jerky, flapping movements of the arms; a stiff, jerky style of walking (gait); a happy, excited demeanor; and regular episodes of uncontrollable laughter.

Diagnosis

Diagnosis is made by noting the characteristic cluster of symptoms. Careful chromosomal study can reveal abnormalities on chromosome 15 that are consistent with those identified in Angelman's syndrome.

Treatment

As of 2004 there is no cure for Angelman's syndrome. Treatments attempt to ameliorate the symptoms in order to improve the quality of life. Treatments may include anti-seizure medications, physical and occupational therapy, and speech and language therapy.

Prognosis

Most children with Angelman syndrome are severely developmentally delayed. They never acquire normal speech, and they require care and supervision throughout their lives.

Prevention

There are no methods to prevent Angelman syndrome. However, if the disorder is known to run in a **family**, genetic counseling may help parents evaluate their level of risk for having a child with this disorder. Specialized testing of chromosome 15 will be required; the usual tests done during **amniocentesis** or chorionic villi sampling will not reveal the specific, small genetic flaw that causes Angelman syndrome.

Parental concerns

Caring for a child with Angelman syndrome constitutes a complex challenge. Parents should be encouraged to seek out parental and sibling support groups and respite care in order to help them face these challenges.

Resources

BOOKS

Hall, Judith G. "Chromosomal Clinical Abnormalities." In *Nelson Textbook of Pediatrics.* Edited by Richard E. Behrman, et al. Philadelphia: Saunders, 2004.

Jankovic, Joseph. "Movement Disorders." In *Textbook of Clinical Neurology.* Edited by Christopher G. Goetz. Philadelphia: Saunders, 2003.

PERIODICALS

Didden, R. "Sleep problems in individuals with Angelman syndrome." In *American Journal of Mental Retardation* 109 (July 2004): 275–84.

Oliver, C. "Effects of environmental events on smiling and laughing behavior in Angelman syndrome." In *American Journal of Mental Retardation* 107 (May 2002): 194–200.

Peters, S. U. "Cognitive and adaptive behavior profiles of children with Angelman syndrome." In *American Journal of Medical Genetics* 128A (July 2004): 110–3.

ORGANIZATIONS

American Academy of Pediatrics. 141 Northwest Point Blvd., Elk Grove Village, IL 60007-1098. Web site: <www.aap.org>.

WEB SITES

"Angelman Syndrome: Just because I can't talk doesn't mean I don't have anything to say." Available online at <www.armyofangels.org/> (accessed December 19, 2004).

"Facts about Angelman Syndrome: Information for Families [Internet links]." Available online at <www.asclepius.com/angel/asinfo.html> (accessed December 19, 2004).

Rosalyn Carson-DeWitt, MD

Animal bite infections

Definition

Animal bite infections develop in humans when an animal's teeth break the skin and introduce saliva containing disease organisms below the skin surface. The saliva of dogs, cats, ferrets, and rabbits is known to contain a wide variety of bacteria. According to one study, bacteria or other pathogens show up in about 85 percent of animal **bites**. These microorganisms may grow within the wound and cause an infection. The consequences of infection from these bites range from mild discomfort to life-threatening complications.

Description

Animal bites may occur in a variety of circumstances, ranging from unprovoked attacks in the wild by rabid or naturally aggressive animals to injuries inflicted by household pets who do not feel well, are frightened, are interrupted during their meal, or are annoyed by a child's teasing or overly rough play. The bite may be a simple warning to back off (as in most household cats), an assertion of dominance and control (as in many dogs), or an intention to seriously injure or kill (as in a few breeds of dogs and some wild animals). Animal bites can range from small injuries that barely break the skin to severe **wounds** that can cause a person to lose the use of a hand, eye, or foot or even bleed to death.

Demographics

The number of animal bites that occur in the United States each year is difficult to estimate because many of these injuries are treated successfully at home. Still, U.S. figures range from 1 million to 4.5 million animal bites each year. About 1 percent of these bites requires hospital inpatient treatment. Cat and dog bites result in 334,000 emergency room visits per year, which represents approximately 1 percent of all emergency hospital visits, at an annual cost of $100 million dollars in healthcare expenses and lost income. Children are the most frequent victims of dog bites, with five to nine year-old boys having the highest incidence. The average age of a dog bite victim is 13, whereas the average age of a cat bite victim is 19 or 20. Men are more often bitten by dogs than are women (3:1), whereas women are more often bitten by cats (3:1).

Children are more likely than adults to suffer dog bites on the face and neck, partly because they are shorter than adults. Cat bites in children as well as adults are far more likely to injure the hands or lower arms rather than other parts of the body.

Dog bites make up 80 to 85 percent of all reported animal bites in the United States and Canada. Cats account for about 10 percent of reported bites, and other animals (including rats, hamsters, ferrets, rabbits, horses, sheep, raccoons, bats, skunks, and monkeys) make up the remaining 5 to 10 percent. Cat bites, however, become infected more frequently than dog bites. A dog's mouth is rich in bacteria, but only 15 to 20 percent of dog bites become infected. In contrast, approximately

30 to 50 percent of cat bites become infected because a cat's teeth can penetrate more deeply than a dog's and carry bacteria deeper into a wound.

Figures on bite injuries from animals other than cats and dogs are difficult to obtain, although bites from pet hamsters and ferrets have been reported more frequently since the late 1990s. Rat bites are becoming more common, particularly in large cities where the rat population has been increasing in the early 2000s. Bites from such wild animals as mountain lions and bears are also reported more frequently as humans explore or move into their natural habitats.

Causes and symptoms

Causes

Many factors contribute to the risk of infection from an animal bite, including the type of wound inflicted, the location of the wound, pre-existing health conditions in the bitten person, the extent of delay before treatment, compliance with treatment, and the presence of a foreign body in the wound. Dogs usually inflict crush injuries because they have rounded teeth and strong jaws; thus, the bite of an adult dog can exert up to 200 pounds per square inch of pressure. This pressure usually results in a crushing injury, causing damage to such deep structures as bones, blood vessels, tendons, muscles, and nerves. The canine teeth are sharp and strong, often inflicting lacerations. Cats, with their needle-like incisors and carnassial teeth, typically cause puncture wounds. Puncture wounds appear innocuous on the surface, but the underlying injury goes deep. The teeth of a cat essentially inject bacteria deep within the bite, and the deep, narrow wound is difficult to clean. Persons with impaired immune systems—for example, individuals with HIV infection—are especially vulnerable to infection from cat bites.

The bacterial species most commonly found in animal bite wounds include *Pasteurella multocida*, *Staphylococcus aureus*, *Pseudomonas sp.*, and *Streptococcus sp.*, *P. multocida*, the root cause of pasteurellosis, is especially prominent in cat bite infections. Other infectious diseases from animal bites include **cat-scratch disease**, **tetanus**, and **rabies**.

Doctors are increasingly aware of the importance of checking animal bite wounds for anaerobic organisms, which are microbes that can live and multiply in the absence of air or oxygen. A study published in 2003 reported that about two-thirds of animal bite wounds contain anaerobes. These organisms can produce such complications as septic arthritis, tenosynovitis, **meningitis**, and infections of the lymphatic system.

With regard to the most common types of domestic pets, it is useful to note that biting and other **aggressive behavior** has different causes in dogs and cats. To some extent these differences are rooted in divergent evolutionary pathways, but they have also been influenced by human interference through selective breeding. Dogs were first domesticated by humans as early as 10,000 B.C. for hunting and as guard or attack dogs. Many species travel in packs or groups in the wild, and many human fatalities resulting from dog bites involve a large group of dogs attacking one or two persons. In addition, dogs typically relate to humans according to a hierarchical model of dominance and submission, and many of the techniques of dog training are intended to teach the dog to respect human authority. Certain breeds of dogs are much more likely to attack humans than others; those most often involved in fatal attacks are pit bulls, Rottweilers, German shepherds, huskies, and mastiffs. According to the Centers for Disease Control (CDC), there are between 15 and 20 fatal dog attacks on humans in the United States each year. There are several assessment or evaluation scales that veterinarians or animal trainers can use to score individual dogs and screen them for dominant or aggressive behavior.

Unlike dogs, cats were not domesticated until about 3000 B.C., and were important to ancient civilizations as rodent catchers and household companions rather than as protectors or hunters of wild game. Biologists classify cats as solitary predators rather than as pack or herd animals; as a result, cats do not relate to humans as authority figures in the same way that dogs do, and they do not form groups that attack humans when threatened or provoked. In addition, domestic cats have been selectively bred for appearance rather than for fierceness or aggression. Most cat bites are the result of **fear** on the cat's part (as when being placed in a carrier for a trip to the vet) or a phenomenon known as petting-induced aggression. Petting-induced aggression is a behavior in which a cat that has been apparently enjoying contact with a human suddenly turns on the human and bites. This behavior appears to be more common in cats that had no contact with humans during their first seven weeks of life. In other cats, this type of aggression appears to be related to a hypersensitive nervous system; petting or cuddling that was pleasurable to the cat for a few seconds or minutes becomes irritating, and the cat bites as a way of indicating that it has had enough. In older cats, petting-induced aggression is often a sign that the cat feels **pain** from touching or pressure on arthritic joints in its neck or back.

General signs of infection

The most common sign of infection from an animal bite is inflammation, which usually develops within eight to 24 hours following the bite. The skin around the wound is red and feels warm, and the wound may ooze pus or a whitish discharge. Nearby lymph glands may be swollen, and there may be red streaks running up the arm or leg from the wound toward the center of the body. Complications can arise if the infection is not treated and spreads into deeper structures or into the bloodstream. Complications are more likely to develop if the bite is deep or occurs on the hand or at a joint.

Live disease-causing bacteria within the bloodstream and tissues may cause complications far from the wound site. Such complications include meningitis, brain abscesses, **pneumonia** and lung abscesses, and heart infections, among others. These complications can be fatal. Deep bites or bites near joints can damage joints and bones, causing inflammation of the bone and bone marrow or septic arthritis.

Cat-scratch fever

Cat-scratch disease is caused by *Bartonella henselae*, a bacterium that is carried in cat saliva; infection may be transmitted by a bite or scratch. Approximately 22,000 cases are reported each year in the United States; worldwide, nine out of every 100,000 individuals become infected. More than 80 percent of reported cases occur in persons under the age of 21. The disease is not normally severe in individuals with healthy immune systems. Symptoms may become serious, however, in immunocompromised individuals, such as those with acquired immune deficiency syndrome (**AIDS**) or those undergoing **chemotherapy**. Common symptoms include an inflamed sore in the area of the bite or scratch, swollen lymph nodes, **fever**, fatigue, and rash.

Rabies

Rabies is caused by a virus that is transmitted through the bite of an animal that is already infected. It is classified as a zoonosis, which is a term that refers to any disease of animals that can be transmitted to humans. More than 90 percent of animal rabies cases occur in such wild animals as skunks, bats, and raccoons, with such domestic animals as dogs and cats accounting for fewer than 10 percent of cases. The World Health Organization (WHO) estimates that between 35,000 and 50,000 individuals worldwide die each year as a result of rabies. The highest incidence of rabies occurs in Asia where, in 1997, over 33,000 deaths were noted, most occurring in India. Rabies is in the early 2000s rare in the United States, as a result of good animal control practices. Onset is delayed, usually weeks to months after the person has been bitten. Early symptoms of rabies include fever, **headache**, and flu-like symptoms. These conditions progress to **anxiety**, hallucinations, **muscle**

spasms, partial paralysis, fear of water (hydrophobia), and other neurological symptoms as the virus spreads to the central nervous system. Medical treatment must be sought soon after exposure because death invariably follows once the infection becomes established.

Most deaths from rabies in the United States in the late twentieth and early twenty-first centuries have resulted from bat rather than dog bites; one victim was a man in Iowa who died in September 2002.

When to call the doctor

Minor animal bites and scratches (those that just break the surface of the skin) can be treated satisfactorily at home. The American Academy of Family Practice (AAFP) recommends the following steps:

- Wash the bite with soap and water, and rinse well.
- Apply pressure with a clean towel or cloth to stop the bleeding.
- Cover the wound with a sterile dressing or bandage.
- Hold the injured area above the level of the heart to lower the risk of tissue swelling and infection.
- Apply antibiotic ointment to the bite twice a day until it heals.
- Report the incident to the local animal control authority or police.

Parents should, however, take their child to a doctor or the emergency room in any of the following circumstances:

- The bite was inflicted by a cat.
- The child was bitten by a dog on the hand, foot, head, or neck.
- The wound is deep or gaping.
- The child has an **immunodeficiency** disease, **cancer**, diabetes, a kidney or liver disorder, or any other condition that affects the body's ability to fight off infection.
- The wound already shows signs of infection.
- The bleeding does not stop after 15 minutes of pressure.
- The child has a broken bone, nerve damage, injury to the skull, or other serious injury in addition to the bite.
- The child has not had a tetanus shot or booster within the past five years.

Diagnosis

Most animal bites that cannot be treated at home are examined by a doctor in the emergency room of a hospital. The medical examination involves taking the history of the injury and assessing the type of wound and damage. The child's record of tetanus immunization and general health status are checked. An x ray may be ordered to assess bone damage and to check for **foreign objects** in the wound. Wound cultures are done for infected bites if the victim is at high risk for complications or if the infection does not respond to treatment. If the child was bitten severely on the head, the emergency room doctor will call in a neurologist for consultation, particularly if the eyes, ears, or neck were injured or the skull was penetrated. The doctor may also consult a plastic surgeon if the bites are extensive, if large pieces of tissue have been lost, or if the functioning or appearance of the affected part of the body is likely to be affected.

Evaluation of possible exposure to rabies is also important. A biting animal suspected of having rabies is usually caught and restrained, tested, and observed for a period of time for evidence of pre-existing infection.

Treatment

Treatment depends on the wound type, its site, and risk factors for infection. All wounds from animal bites are cleaned and disinfected as thoroughly as possible. The doctor begins by injecting a local anesthetic in order to examine the wound thoroughly without causing additional pain to the child. The next step is to remove dead tissue, foreign matter, and blood clots, all of which can become sources of infection. This removal is called debridement. After debriding the wound, the doctor will cut away the edges of the tissue, as clean edges heal faster and are less likely to form scar tissue. The doctor then irrigates, or flushes, the wound with saline solution forced through a syringe under pressure. Irrigation is highly effective in lowering the risk of infection from animal bites; in one study of 45 children with a total of 145 dog bite wounds on the face, pressure irrigation combined with trimming the edges of the wounds resulted in an infection rate of 0.4 percent.

Bites to the head and face usually receive sutures, as do severe lacerations elsewhere. Puncture wounds are left open. If an abscess forms, the physician may perform an incision in order to drain the abscess.

If infection does occur, the doctor will prescribe antibiotic medications. **Antibiotics** may also be used for infection prevention. Since a single bite wound may contain many different types of bacteria, no single antibiotic is always effective. Commonly prescribed antibiotics are penicillin or a combination of amoxicillin and clavulanate potassium (Augmentin). Aztreonam

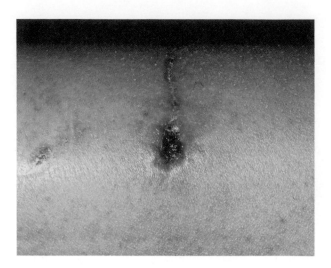

View of an infected animal bite. *(Photograph by Dr. P. Marazzi. Science Photo Library/Custom Medical Stock Photo, Inc.)*

(Azactam) has been reported to be effective in treating infections caused by *P. multocida*. In most cases, antibiotics taken by mouth are sufficient; however, some deep bites may require treatment with intravenous antibiotics.

Because rabies is caused by a virus, antibiotics are not effective against it. In addition, there is no known cure for the disease as of 2004 once symptoms become apparent. People with a high risk of contracting the disease should receive preexposure **vaccination**. Individuals bitten by an unknown or potentially rabid animal should receive postexposure vaccination, also called postexposure prophylaxis (PEP). The PEP regimen consists of one dose of vaccine given at the initial visit as well as one dose of human immune globulin. Additional doses of vaccine are given on days three, seven, 14, and 28.

Prognosis

Once a bacterial infection is halted, the bite victim usually recovers fully. There is no known cure for rabies once symptoms become evident and death is almost certain. WHO reports that 114 rabies deaths occurred in the Americas in 1997, with only four deaths occurring that year in the United States, thus emphasizing the importance of good animal control practice and postexposure prophylaxis.

The prognosis for restoring the function or appearance of a hand or other body part following a severe bite depends on the location of the bite, the promptness of treatment, and the availability of specialized surgical repair.

Prevention

Preventing bites obviously prevents subsequent infections. With regard to domestic pets, parents should inform themselves about the aggression level and other characteristics of a particular breed before bringing a purebred pet dog into the family and consider having a specific dog evaluated by a veterinarian or animal behaviorist before adopting it. In addition, parents should make sure that the dog has been neutered or spayed, since intact dogs of either sex are more likely to bite than those that have been altered. Cat bites can often be prevented by learning about a cat's body language and recognizing the signs of petting-induced aggression. These include dilating pupils, a low growl, stiffening of the body, twitching of the tail, and flattening the ears backward against the head.

Children under 12 years of age are at a higher risk for bites due to their small size and their inexperience with animals; therefore, they should be supervised with animals and taught to act appropriately around them. In particular, children should be taught not to tease a dog by pulling its fur or tail; to leave a dog alone while it is eating; and to avoid running or screaming in the presence of a dog, as the animal is more likely to chase a moving object. Direct eye contact with a threatening dog should be avoided, as the dog may interpret that as aggression. It is best to stand still if at all possible, with feet together and arms against the chest; most dogs will lose interest in an object that is not moving and will eventually go away.

A wild animal that is unusually aggressive or behaving strangely (e.g. a raccoon or bat that is active during the daytime or is physically uncoordinated) should be avoided and reported to the local animal control authorities; it may be infected with the rabies virus. Wild animals should not be taken in as pets, and garbage or pet food that might attract wild animals should not be left outside the home or campsite. People should also avoid trying to break up fights between animals and should as a rule approach unknown cats and dogs very cautiously, especially on their territory. Finally, animals should not be trained to fight.

Domestic pets should be vaccinated against rabies; people should consult a veterinarian for advice about the frequency of booster vaccinations for the area in which they live. In addition, families planning to travel to countries where rabies is endemic should consider vaccination before leaving the United States. The AAFP frequently posts updated travel advisories for rabies immunizations.

KEY TERMS

Anaerobic—An organism that grows and thrives in an oxygen-free environment.

Canines—The two sharp teeth located next to the front incisor teeth in mammals that are used to grip and tear. Also called cuspids.

Carnassials—The last upper premolar teeth in the mouths of cats and other carnivores, adapted to shear or puncture food. Carnassial teeth often cause puncture wounds when a cat bites a human.

Culture—A test in which a sample of body fluid is placed on materials specially formulated to grow microorganisms. A culture is used to learn what type of bacterium is causing infection.

Debridement—The surgical removal of dead tissue and/or foreign bodies from a wound or cut.

Irrigation—Cleansing a wound with large amounts of water and/or an antiseptic solution. Also refers to the technique of removing wax (cerumen) from the ear canal by flushing it with water.

Microorganism—An organism that is too small to be seen with the naked eye, such as a bacterium, virus, or fungus.

Pasteurellosis—A bacterial wound infection caused by *Pasteurella multocida*. Pasteurellosis is characterized by inflammation around the wound site and may be accompanied by bacteria in the bloodstream and infection in tissues and organs.

Pathogen—Any disease-producing microorganism.

Postexposure prophylaxis—Any treatment given after exposure to a disease to try to prevent the disease from occurring. In the case of rabies, postexposure prophylaxis involves a series of vaccines given to an individual who has been bitten by an unknown animal or one that is potentially infected with the rabies virus.

Tenosynovitis—Inflammation of a tendon and its enveloping sheath, usually resulting from overuse injury.

Zoonosis—Any disease of animals that can be transmitted to humans. Rabies is an example of a zoonosis.

Parental concerns

Given prompt treatment, most animal bites are not cause for major concern; as has been mentioned, minor bites can be treated at home without a visit to the doctor.

Some children bitten by large dogs, however, may become extremely fearful of dogs in general and may require counseling, particularly if the bite was severe or had long-term effects on the child's health. Fear of cats following a bite is much less common. Parents may also need to talk with or comfort their child if it is necessary to give up a family pet that cannot be retrained. In many cases, however, a qualified animal behaviorist can assess the reasons for a pet's biting or other aggressive behavior and suggest appropriate treatments.

See also Cat-scratch disease; Human bite infections; Rabies.

Resources

BOOKS

"Central Nervous System Viral Diseases: Rabies (Hydrophobia)." Section 13, Chapter 162 in *The Merck Manual of Diagnosis and Therapy*, edited by Mark H. Beers and Robert Berkow. Whitehouse Station, NJ: Merck Research Laboratories, 2002.

Dodman, Nicholas H. *If Only They Could Speak: Stories about Pets and Their People*. New York: Norton, 2002. Contains several useful appendices about aggression in various dog breeds and a sample assessment form for evaluating a dog's potential for biting.

PERIODICALS

Brook, I. "Microbiology and Management of Human and Animal Bite Wound Infections." *Primary Care* 30 (March 2003): 25–39.

Downing, N. D., et al. "A Rare and Serious Consequence of a Rat Bite." *Annals of the Royal College of Surgeons of England* 83 (July 2001): 279–80.

Fooks, A. R., et al. "Risk Factors Associated with Travel to Rabies Endemic Countries." *Journal of Applied Microbiology* 94, Supplement (2003): 31S–36S.

"Human Rabies: Iowa, 2002." *Morbidity and Mortality Weekly Report* 52 (January 24, 2003): 47–8.

Lamps, L. W., and M. A. Scott. "Cat-Scratch Disease: Historic, Clinical, and Pathologic Perspectives." *American Journal of Clinical Pathology* 121, Supplement (June 2004): S71–S80.

Le Moal, G., et al. "Meningitis Due to *Capnocytophaga canimorsus* after Receipt of a Dog Bite: Case Report and Review of the Literature." *Clinical Infectious Diseases* 36 (February 1, 2003): 42–6.

Messenger, S. L., et al. "Emerging Pattern of Rabies Deaths and Increased Viral Infectivity." *Emerging Infectious Diseases* 9 (February 2003): 151–54.

Ojukwu, I. C., and C. Christy. "Rat-Bite Fever in Children: Case Report and Review." *Scandinavian Journal of Infectious Diseases* 34 (June 2002): 474–77.

Presutti, R. John. "Prevention and Treatment of Dog Bites." *American Family Physician* 63 (April 15, 2001): 1567–74.

Sacks, Jeffrey J., et al. "Special Report: Breeds of Dogs Involved in Fatal Human Attacks in the United States between 1979 and 1998." *Journal of the American Veterinary Medical Association* 217 (September 15, 2000): 836–40.

Weiss, R. A. "Cross-Species Infections." *Current Topics in Microbiology and Immunology* 278 (2003): 47–71.

Zepf, Bill. "Update on Rabies Vaccination in World Travelers." *American Family Physician* 66 (February 15, 2004): 22.

ORGANIZATIONS

American Academy of Emergency Medicine (AAEM). 555 East Wells Street, Suite 1100, Milwaukee, WI 53202. Web site: <www.aaem.org>.

American Veterinary Medical Association (AVMA). 1931 North Meacham Road, Suite 100, Schaumburg, IL 60173–4360. Web site: <www.avma.org>.

Centers for Disease Control and Prevention. 1600 Clifton Rd., NE, Atlanta, GA 30333. Web site: <www.cdc.gov>.

WEB SITES

"Cat and Dog Bites." *American Academy of Family Physicians (AAFP)*, September 2002. Available online at <www.familydoctor.org/x1827.xml> (accessed November 9, 2004).

Fisher, Donna J. "Rabies." *eMedicine*, January 29, 2004. Available online at <www.emedicine.com/ped/topic1974.htm> (accessed November 9, 2004).

Friedman, Allan D. "Catscratch Disease." *eMedicine*, July 17, 2003. Available online at <www.emedicine.com/ped/topic333.htm> (accessed November 9, 2004).

Stump, Jack. "Bites, Animal." *eMedicine*, August 23, 2004. Available online at <www.emedicine.com/emerg/topic60.htm> (accessed November 9, 2004).

OTHER

National Association of State Public Health Veterinarians, Inc. "Compendium of Animal Rabies Prevention and Control, 2003." In *Morbidity and Mortality Weekly Report Recommendations and Reports* 52, (RR-5) (March 21, 2003): 16.

Julia Barrett
Rebecca Frey, PhD

Anorexia nervosa

Definition

Anorexia nervosa is an eating disorder characterized by self-starvation, unrealistic **fear** of weight gain, and conspicuous distortion of body image.

Description

The term anorexia nervosa comes from two Latin words that mean "nervous inability to eat." Anorexics have the following characteristics in common:

- inability to maintain weight at or above what is normally expected for age or height
- intense fear of becoming fat
- distorted body image
- in females who have begun to menstruate, the absence of at least three menstrual periods in a row, a condition called **amenorrhea**

There are two subtypes of anorexia nervosa: a restricting type, characterized by strict dieting and **exercise** without binge eating; and a binge-eating/purging type, marked by episodes of compulsive eating with or without self-induced **vomiting** and/or the use of **laxatives** or enemas. A binge is defined as a time-limited (usually under two hours) episode of compulsive eating in which the individual consumes a significantly larger amount of food than most people would eat in similar circumstances.

Demographics

Anorexia nervosa was not officially classified as a psychiatric disorder until the third edition of *Diagnostic and Statistical Manual of Mental Disorders (DSM)* in 1980. It is, however, a growing problem in the early 2000s among adolescent females. Its incidence in the United States has doubled since 1970. The rise in the number of reported cases reflects a genuine increase in the number of persons affected by the disorder and not simply earlier or more accurate diagnosis. Estimates of the incidence of anorexia range between 0.5 percent and 1 percent of Caucasian female adolescents. Over 90 percent of patients diagnosed with the disorder as of 2001 are female. The peak age range for onset of the disorder is 14 to 18 years. In the 1970s and 1980s, anorexia was regarded as a disorder of upper- and middle-class women, but that generalization is as of 2004 also changing. Studies indicate that anorexia is increasingly common among females of all races and social classes in the United States.

Causes and symptoms

While the precise cause of the disease is not known, anorexia is a disorder that results from the interaction of cultural and interpersonal as well as biological factors.

Social influences

The rising incidence of anorexia is thought to reflect the present idealization of thinness as a badge of upper-class status as well as of female beauty. In addition, the increase in cases of anorexia includes "copycat" behavior, with some patients developing the disorder from imitating other girls.

The onset of anorexia in **adolescence** is attributed to a developmental crisis caused by girls' changing bodies coupled with society's overemphasis on female appearance. The increasing influence of the mass media in spreading and reinforcing gender stereotypes has also been noted.

Occupational goals

The risk of developing anorexia is higher among adolescents preparing for careers that require attention to weight and/or appearance. These high-risk groups include dancers, fashion models, professional athletes (including gymnasts, skaters, long-distance runners, and jockeys), and actresses.

Genetic and biological influences

Girls whose biological mothers or sisters have or have had anorexia nervosa appear to be at increased risk of developing the disorder.

Psychological factors

A number of theories have been advanced to explain the psychological aspects of the disorder. No single explanation covers all cases. Anorexia nervosa has been given the following interpretations:

- Overemphasis on control, autonomy, and independence: Some anorexics come from achievement-oriented families that stress physical fitness and dieting. Many anorexics are perfectionists who are driven about schoolwork and other matters in addition to weight control.
- Evidence of **family** dysfunction: In some families, a daughter's eating disorder serves as a distraction from marital discord or other family tensions.

- A rejection of female sexual maturity: This rejection is variously interpreted as a desire to remain a child or as a desire to resemble males.

- A reaction to sexual abuse or assault.

- A desire to appear as fragile and nonthreatening as possible: This hypothesis reflects the idea that female passivity and weakness are attractive to males.

- Inability to interpret the body's hunger signals accurately due to early experiences of inappropriate feeding.

Male anorexics

Although anorexia nervosa largely affects females, its incidence in the male population is rising in the early 2000s. Less is known about the causes of anorexia in males, but some risk factors are the same as for females. These include certain occupational goals and increasing media emphasis on external appearance in men. Homosexual males are under pressure to conform to an ideal body weight that is about 20 pounds lighter than the standard attractive weight for heterosexual males.

When to call the doctor

A healthcare professional should be contacted if a child or adolescent is suspected of having anorexia nervosa or displays early signs of the disorder, such as the following:

- fear of gaining weight

- distorted body image

- recent weight loss

- restrictive or abnormal eating patterns such as skipping meals or eliminating once-liked foods

- preoccupation with food and dieting

- compulsive exercising

- purging behaviors such as vomiting or using laxatives

- withdrawal from friends and family

- wearing baggy clothes to hide weight loss

Diagnosis

Diagnosis of anorexia nervosa is complicated by a number of factors. One is that the disorder varies somewhat in severity from patient to patient. A second factor is denial, which is regarded as an early sign of the disorder. Many anorexics deny that they are ill and are usually brought to treatment by a family member.

Anorexia nervosa is a serious public health problem not only because of its rising incidence, but also because

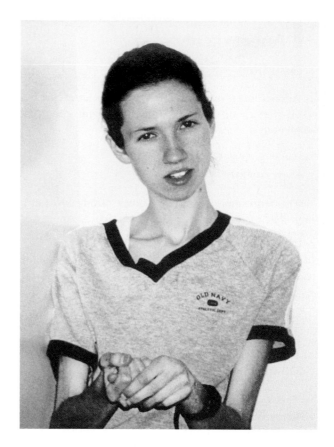

Extreme weight loss in an anorexic adolescent. (© Ed Quinn/ Corbis.)

it has one of the highest mortality rates of any psychiatric disorder. Moreover, the disorder may cause serious long-term health complications, including congestive heart failure, sudden death, growth retardation, dental problems, **constipation**, stomach rupture, swelling of the salivary glands, anemia and other abnormalities of the blood, loss of kidney function, and osteoporosis.

Most anorexics are diagnosed by pediatricians or family practitioners. Anorexics develop emaciated bodies, dry or yellowish skin, and abnormally low blood pressure. There is usually a history of amenorrhea in female patients, and sometimes of abdominal **pain**, constipation, or lack of energy. The patient may feel chilly or have developed lanugo, a growth of downy body hair. If the patient has been self-inducing vomiting, she may have eroded tooth enamel or Russell's sign (scars on the back of the hand). The second step in diagnosis is measurement of the patient's weight loss. *DSM-IV* specifies a weight loss leading to a body weight 15 percent below normal, with some allowance for body build and weight history.

Anorexia nervosa

Criteria

1. Refusal to maintain body weight at or above a minimally normal weight for age and height. Body weight is less than 85 percent of what is expected.

2. Intense fear of gaining weight or becoming fat, even though patient is underweight.

3. Undue influence of body weight or shape on self-evaluation, or denial of the seriousness of current underweight condition.

4. Absence of at least three consecutive menstrual cycles in previously menstruating females.

Restricting type: No regular episodes of binge-eating or purging (self-induced vomiting or misuse of laxatives, diuretics, or enemas).

Binge-eating/purging type: Regular episodes of binge-eating or purging (self-induced vomiting or misuse of laxatives, diuretics, or enemas).

SOURCE: *Diagnostic and Statistical Manual of Mental Disorders IV.*

(Table by GGS Information Services.)

The doctor will need to rule out other physical conditions that can cause weight loss or vomiting after eating, including metabolic disorders, brain tumors (especially hypothalamus and pituitary gland lesions), diseases of the digestive tract, and a condition called superior mesenteric artery syndrome. Persons with this condition sometimes vomit after meals because the blood supply to the intestine is blocked. The doctor will usually order blood tests, an electrocardiogram, urinalysis, and bone densitometry (bone density test) in order to exclude other diseases and to assess the patient's nutritional status.

The doctor will also need to distinguish between anorexia and other psychiatric disorders, including depression, **schizophrenia**, social phobia, **obsessive-compulsive disorder**, and body dysmorphic disorder. Two diagnostic tests that are often used are the Eating Attitudes Test (EAT) and the Eating Disorder Inventory (EDI).

Treatment

Treatment of anorexia nervosa includes both short- and long-term measures and requires **assessment** by dietitians and psychiatrists as well as medical specialists. Therapy is often complicated by the patient's resistance or failure to carry out a treatment plan.

Hospital treatment

Hospitalization is recommended for anorexics with any of the following characteristics:

- weight of 40 percent or more below normal or weight loss over a three-month period of more than 30 lbs (13.6 kg)
- severely disturbed metabolism
- severe binging and purging
- signs of psychosis
- severe depression or risk of **suicide**
- family in crisis

Hospital treatment includes individual and group therapy as well as refeeding and monitoring of the patient's physical condition. Treatment usually requires two to four months in the hospital. In extreme cases, hospitalized patients may be force-fed through a tube inserted in the nose (nasogastric tube) or into a vein (hyperalimentation).

Outpatient treatment

Anorexics who are not severely malnourished can be treated by outpatient psychotherapy. The types of treatment recommended are supportive rather than insight-oriented and include behavioral approaches as well as individual or group therapy. **Family therapy** is often recommended when the patient's eating disorder is closely tied to family dysfunction. Self-help groups are often useful in helping anorexics find social support and encouragement. Psychotherapy with anorexics is a slow and difficult process; about 50 percent of patients continue to have serious psychiatric problems after their weight has stabilized.

Medications

Anorexics have been treated with a variety of medications, including **antidepressants**, antianxiety drugs, selective serotonin reuptake inhibitors, and lithium carbonate. The effectiveness of medications in treatment regimens is as of 2004 debated. However, at least one study of fluoxetine (Prozac) showed it helped the patient maintain weight gained while in the hospital.

Nutritional concerns

A key focus of treatment for anorexia nervosa is teaching the principles of healthy eating and improving disordered eating behaviors. A dietician or nutritionist plays an important role in forming a **nutrition** plan for the patient; such plans are individualized and ensure that the patient is consuming enough food to gain or maintain weight as needed and stabilize medically. The anorexic's weight and food intake are closely monitored to ensure that the plan is being followed.

KEY TERMS

Amenorrhea—The absence or abnormal stoppage of menstrual periods.

Binge—A pattern of eating marked by episodes of rapid consumption of large amounts of food; usually food that is high in calories.

Body dysmorphic disorder—A psychiatric disorder marked by preoccupation with an imagined physical defect.

Hyperalimentation—A method of refeeding anorexics by infusing liquid nutrients and electrolytes directly into central veins through a catheter.

Lanugo—A soft, downy body hair that covers a normal fetus beginning in the fifth month and usually shed by the ninth month. Also refers to the fine, soft hair that develops on the chest and arms of anorexic women. Also called vellus hair.

Purging—The use of vomiting, diuretics, or laxatives to clear the stomach and intestines after a binge.

Russell's sign—A scraped or raw area on the patient's knuckles, caused by self-induced vomiting.

Superior mesenteric artery syndrome—A condition in which a person vomits after meals due to blockage of the blood supply to the intestine.

Prognosis

Figures for long-term recovery vary from study to study, but reliable estimates are that 40 to 60 percent of anorexics make a good physical and social recovery, and 75 percent gain weight. The long-term mortality rate for anorexia is estimated at around 10 percent, although some studies give a lower figure of 3 to 4 percent. The most frequent causes of death associated with anorexia are starvation, electrolyte imbalance, heart failure, and suicide.

Prevention

Short of major long-term changes in the larger society, the best strategy for prevention of anorexia is the cultivation of healthy attitudes toward food, weight control, and beauty (or body image) within families. Early treatment such as counseling may help to prevent early signs of disordered eating from progressing into more serious behaviors.

Parental concerns

There are many strategies that parents can undertake to help encourage healthy attitudes toward weight, food, and exercise in their children. These include the following:

- teaching children the importance of healthy eating and exercise

- avoiding using food as a punishment or reward

- instilling healthy eating and exercise habits by example

- being a good role model by promoting healthy body image and encouraging children and adolescents to find role models in the media who do the same

- encouraging children or teens who wish to diet to talk to a healthcare professional about healthy strategies to lose weight

See also Binge eating disorder; Bulimia nervosa.

Resources

BOOKS

"Anorexia Nervosa." In *The Merck Manual of Diagnosis and Therapy*, 17th ed. Edited by Mark H. Beers and Robert Berkow. Whitehouse Station, NJ: Merck & Co. Inc., 2004.

Knowles, Jarol B. "Eating Disorders." In *Textbook of Primary Care Medicine*, 3rd ed. Edited by John Noble. St. Louis: Mosby Inc., 2001.

Litt, Iris F. "Anorexia Nervosa and Bulimia." In *Nelson Textbook of Pediatrics*, 17th ed. Edited by Richard E. Behrman, Robert M. Kliegman, and Hal B. Jenson. Philadelphia: Saunders, 2004.

Smith, Delia. "The Eating Disorders." In *Cecil Textbook of Medicine*, 21st ed. Edited by Lee Goldman and J. Claude Bennett. Philadelphia: Saunders, 2000.

PERIODICALS

American Academy of Pediatrics Committee on Adolescence. "Identifying and Treating Eating Disorders." *Pediatrics* 111, no. 1 (January 1, 2003): 204–11.

Pritts, Sarah D., and Jeffrey Susman. "Diagnosis of Eating Disorders in Primary Care." *American Family Physician* 67, no. 2 (January 15, 2003): 297–304.

Rome, E. S. "Eating Disorders." *Obstetrics and Gynecology Clinics of North America* 30, no. 2 (June 1, 2003): 353–77.

Rosen, David S. "Eating Disorders in Children and Young Adolescents: Etiology, Classification, Clinical Features, and Treatment." *Adolescent Medicine* 14, no. 1 (February 1, 2003): 49–59.

———. "Eating Disorders in Adolescent Males." *Adolescent Medicine* 14, no. 3 (October 1, 2003): 677–89.

Sigman, Gary S. "Eating Disorders in Children and Adolescents." *Pediatric Clinics of North America* 50, no. 5 (October 2003): 1139–77.

ORGANIZATIONS

American Anorexia/Bulimia Association. 418 East 76th St., New York, NY 10021. Telephone: 212/734–1114.

National Association of Anorexia Nervosa and Associated Disorders. Web site: <www.anad.org>.

National Institute of Mental Health Eating Disorders Program. Building 10, Room 3S231. 9000 Rockville Pike, Bethesda, MD 20892. Telephone: 301/496–1891.

Rebecca J. Frey, PhD
Stephanie Dionne Sherk

Antenatal testing

Definition

Antenatal testing describes procedures performed during pregnancy to detect health problems in the growing fetus; establish characteristics such as fetal age, sex, or weight; or diagnose any material conditions that may affect fetal development.

Purpose

Antenatal tests and exams are important tools for protecting the health of a pregnant woman and her developing child. Various tests are administered over the course of pregnancy to determine if the mother has any health conditions that may interfere with normal development of the fetus or if the fetus has any health conditions that may affect the baby's quality of life. Often, families will use information provided by the tests to prepare for the baby's birth and make arrangements for special care if needed or make the decision to terminate the pregnancy. Physicians also use antenatal tests to determine various characteristics of the fetus, such as gestational age, size, and position in the uterus, or to verify the presence of multiple fetuses.

Description

Women who become pregnant may undergo tests at any stage in their pregnancy: during the first trimester (weeks one through 12), second trimester (weeks 13–26), or third trimester (weeks 27–40+). What tests are ordered depends on the stage of pregnancy, the age and health of the mother, the medical history of both parents, and the family's background or ethnicity. There are two distinct types of antenatal tests:

- Screening tests tend to be less invasive and indicate the possibility of a certain genetic disorder or birth defect but do not determine with certainty that the abnormality exists.

- Diagnostic tests tend to more invasive but are able to determine with more certainty that a fetus will be born with a certain condition.

Blood and urine tests

In the early stages of pregnancy, physicians may order blood or urine tests to screen for possible disorders or infections that could affect the growing fetus. The tests may also be ordered in later stages if the pregnant woman comes in contact with an infectious agent or develops symptoms of infection. In many cases, complications can be avoided if early diagnosis is made and treatment initiated. Examples of conditions that are commonly screened for with blood and/or urine tests include:

- Rh factor: About 15 percent of people lack a certain blood protein called Rh factor and are called Rh negative. Complications may arise if an Rh-negative mother is carrying an Rh-positive child. These can be avoided if the mother is given a substance called Rh immune globulin (RhIg) at approximately 28 weeks into the pregnancy and again within 72 hours after the baby is born.

- Anemia: If there is too little of a substance called hemoglobin in a pregnant woman's red blood cells, a condition called anemia may result. If a blood test reveals low hemoglobin, supplementation with iron may be recommended.

- Human **immunodeficiency** virus: HIV can be transmitted from mother to child, although treatment of the disease during pregnancy can greatly reduce the risk of transmission. Because it is possible for individuals to be infected without exhibiting symptoms and because unprotected sex is a major risk factor for contracting the virus, the American Academy of Pediatrics recommended in 1999 that a screening test for HIV be routinely offered. A second test later in pregnancy may be recommended if the pregnant woman is considered to be at high risk of becoming infected with HIV.

- Syphilis: If transmitted from mother to child during pregnancy, syphilis leads to death of the fetus or newborn in approximately 40 percent of cases. The goal of syphilis screening is to diagnose and treat infections before transmission occurs. Syphilis is treated with **antibiotics**.

- **Rubella** (German **measles**): Although the majority of women in the United States are immune to rubella because of prior immunization or infection, serious complications to the fetus (such as deafness, blindness, or heart defects) can arise if a woman becomes infected during pregnancy. If a woman is found to not have immunity, it will be recommended that she avoid contact with infected individuals during her pregnancy and receive a **vaccination** against rubella after she gives birth.

- Group beta strep (GBS): GBS is a type of bacteria commonly found in the vagina and rectum. GBS can be present in a person's body without causing any symptoms, so many women do not realize they are infected with it. Newborns who are exposed to GBS, however, can develop serious complications such as **meningitis**, **pneumonia**, blindness, deafness, and death is possible. Doctors test for the presence of GBS in urine or in samples collected from the vagina or rectum. This test is usually performed late in pregnancy, at 35 to 37 weeks of gestation. If a woman is found to be infected with GBS, physicians generally administer antibiotics to the mother so the baby is not born with the infection.

A multiple marker test or triple screen is used to determine if a fetus is at an increased risk of having certain congenital abnormalities. The test has a high rate of false-positives; as few as 10 percent of women with abnormal results go on to have babies with congenital defects. The purpose of the test is to determine if further testing (such as ultrasound or **amniocentesis**) is warranted. The test requires a sample of maternal blood, typically taken during the fifteenth and twentieth week of pregnancy, and measures the level of certain pregnancy hormones.

Ultrasound

Ultrasound is a device that records sound waves as they bounce off the developing fetus and create an image that is projected onto a large computer screen. A physician may order an ultrasound scan to listen for a fetal heartbeat, determine a woman's precise due date, or check for **twins**, among other uses. Also known as a sonogram, the procedure takes only a few minutes, is safe and painless, and usually is covered by health insurance.

During the procedure, an ultrasound technician asks the pregnant woman to remove her clothes and change into a gown. The technician may rub some gel on the woman's fundus (lower abdomen), which helps the hand-held device pick up sound waves. In certain cases, the technician may insert a plastic probe into the woman's vaginal canal to get a clearer picture of the fetus. Early in pregnancy, the test may need to be done with a full bladder.

Pregnant women will often have their first ultrasound between eight and 12 weeks of gestation. In normal cases, the technician is able to identify a fetal heartbeat, which appears as a flashing light on the screen. Closer to the due date, physicians use ultrasound to make sure the fetus is in the correct head-first position to exit the birth canal, to assess the fetus for certain birth defects, and to determine the sex of the fetus if the parents desire.

Between ten and 14 weeks of gestation, ultrasonography may be used to measure a small collection of fluid beneath the skin at the back of the neck. Called nuchal translucency, the measurement tends to be larger in fetuses with genetic abnormalities such as **Down syndrome**, trisomy 13, trisomy 18, **Turner syndrome**, and triploidy. A particular neck measurement combined with maternal age as an indicator (e.g. the incidence of the disorder increases in proportion to the age of the mother) has been shown to correctly diagnose Down syndrome in 75 to 80 percent of cases; this number increases to 90 percent if the procedure is combined with the multiple marker test.

Amniocentesis

Amniocentesis is a more invasive test that carries a higher risk of complications than blood tests or ultrasonography, but is able to determine more precisely the presence of certain birth defects. It is also used to determine the level of maturity of the baby's lungs, of particular interest if the baby will be delivered prematurely. During amniocentesis, a doctor inserts a thin needle through a woman's abdomen and into the uterus. Using ultrasound as a guide, the doctor uses the needle to withdraw a sample of fluid from the amniotic sac. Afterward, tiny cells shed by the fetus can be studied in the laboratory; scientists can analyze the samples to determine if the fetus has certain genetic conditions. Amniocentesis is typically performed during the second trimester of pregnancy and particularly in mothers over the age of 40.

Chorionic villus sampling

Chorionic villus sampling (CVS) is a procedure that allows for prenatal diagnosis during the first trimester (generally between ten and 12 weeks of gestation, during the embryonic stage of development). The test involves

KEY TERMS

Alpha fetoprotein test—A screening blood test that can be done after the sixteenth week of pregnancy to evaluate the possibility of spina bifida and other neural tube defects in the fetus.

Amniocentesis—A procedure performed at 16–18 weeks of pregnancy in which a needle is inserted through a woman's abdomen into her uterus to draw out a small sample of the amniotic fluid from around the baby for analysis. Either the fluid itself or cells from the fluid can be used for a variety of tests to obtain information about genetic disorders and other medical conditions in the fetus.

Breech position—The foot-down or bottom-down position of a fetus just before delivery.

Group B streptococcus—A serotype of streptococcus, *Streptococcus agalactiae*, which is beta hemolytic and can cause neonatal sepsis, pneumonia, or meningitis if present in the birth canal at the time of delivery especially when the delivery is difficult.

Hemoglobin—An iron-containing pigment of red blood cells composed of four amino acid chains (alpha, beta, gamma, delta) that delivers oxygen from the lungs to the cells of the body and carries carbon dioxide from the cells to the lungs.

Meningitis—An infection or inflammation of the membranes that cover the brain and spinal cord. It is usually caused by bacteria or a virus.

Ultrasonography—A medical test in which sound waves are directed against internal structures in the body. As sound waves bounce off the internal structure, they create an image on a video screen. Ultrasonography is often used to diagnose fetal abnormalities, gallstones, heart defects, and tumors. Also called ultrasound imaging.

taking a small sample of cells from the placenta with a needle through the abdominal wall or a small tube (catheter) through the cervix. The procedure is guided by ultrasound. The cells are then analyzed in a laboratory for the presence of genetic abnormalities.

Risks

The risks associated with antenatal testing depend on the specific procedure being performed:

- Blood tests: The risks associated with blood testing are minimal and include discomfort, bleeding from the puncture site, hematoma (collection of blood under the skin), and infection.

- Ultrasound: As of 2004 there is no recognized risk for ultrasonography.

- Amniocentesis: The risk of miscarriage associated with amniocenteses performed between 15 and 20 weeks is less than 0.5 percent. The other risks are maternal infection, injuries to the fetus, and premature labor.

- Chorionic villus sampling: The risk of miscarriage associated with CVS performed between nine and 11 weeks is less than 2 percent. The risks are similar to those associated with amniocentesis.

Parental concerns

Impending parenthood is often accompanied by concerns that the baby may be born with defects or other health problems that would affect the quality of life of the baby and the **family**. That worry is often weighed against the **anxiety** associated with antenatal tests and their risks. Parents should be encouraged to educate themselves on the benefits and risks associated with the various antenatal screening procedures and work with their obstetrician to formulate an individualized prenatal care plan.

Resources

BOOKS

Seashore, Margretta R. "Genetic Counseling." In *Cecil Textbook of Medicine.* Edited by Lee Goldman and J. Claude Bennett. Philadelphia: Saunders, 2000.

Simpson, Joe Leigh. "Diagnostic Procedures for Prenatal Genetic Diagnosis." In *Obstetrics: Normal and Problem Pregnancies.* Edited by Steve G. Gabbe et al. New York: Churchill Livingstone, 2002.

PERIODICALS

Andrews, Janet I., Daniel J. Diekema, and Jerome Yankowitz. "Prenatal Testing for Infectious Disease." *Clinics in Laboratory Medicine* 23, no. 2 (June 2003): 295–315.

Bubb, Jennifer A., and Anne L. Matthews. "What's New in Prenatal Screening and Diagnosis?" *Primary Care* 31, no. 3 (September 2002): 561.

ORGANIZATIONS

American College of Obstetricians and Gynecologists. 409 12th St., SW, PO Box 96920, Washington, DC 20090–6920. Web site: <www.acog.org>.

March of Dimes Birth Defects Foundation. 275 Mamaroneck Ave., White Plains, NY 10605. Web site. <www.modimes.org>.

WEB SITES

Singh, Daljit, Jai Rup Singh, and Vanita Kumar. "Prenatal Diagnosis for Congenital Malformations and Genetic Disorders." *eMedicine*, July 29, 2004. Available online at <www.emedicine.com/oph/topic485.htm> (accessed December 23, 2004).

Stephanie Dionne Sherk
Melissa Knopper

Antepartum testing

Definition

Antepartum testing involves the use of **electronic fetal monitoring** (EFM) or ultrasound (US) to assess fetal well-being as determined by the fetal heart rate (FHR) and other characteristics during the antepartal period, which is the period spanning from conception to labor. Antepartum tests include the nonstress test (NST), modified biophysical profile (MBPP), contraction stress test (CST), oxytocin contraction stress test (OCT), biophysical profile (BPP), doppler flow studies, **amniocentesis**, cordocentesis, and fetal echocardiography.

Purpose

Antepartum testing can start as early as 24 weeks but usually begins after 32 weeks of pregnancy depending on the mother's physical status. It provides a means for the physician and pregnant woman to identify any problems and be alert to any changes that may necessitate additional testing or interventions. The testing results reflect how well the placenta is functioning in its ability to adequately supply blood and, therefore, oxygen to the fetus.

The testing is done for pregnancies at risk for maternal and/or fetal complications. Some of these risks include:

- any chronic illness in the mother, such as high blood pressure, diabetes, or autoimmune diseases, including systemic lupus erythematosus (SLE)
- problems with previous pregnancies, such as a history of unexplained stillbirth
- fetal complications, such as intrauterine growth restriction (IUGR) (growth in the fetus below the tenth percentile), birth defects, **twins**, or other multiple gestations in which a growth discrepancy occurs, such as twin-to-twin transfusion syndrome
- problems in current pregnancy, including pregnancy-induced **hypertension** (frequently referred to as preeclampsia); gestational diabetes (diabetes caused by pregnancy) requiring the use of insulin; premature rupture of the membranes (PROM); too little or too much amniotic fluid (the liquid surrounding the fetus) called oligohydramnios and polyhydramnios, respectively; vaginal bleeding; placental abnormalities, i.e., partial abruption (a portion of the placenta pulls away from the wall of the uterus), or placenta previa (a condition in which the placenta is covering the cervix instead of near the top of the uterus)

Antepartum testing is also used in low-risk pregnancies to evaluate decreased fetal activity, a lag in fundal height (as measured from top of the pubic area to the highest point in the midline at the top of the uterus), and postdates or post-term pregnancy. A normal pregnancy is 40 weeks and testing should begin at 41 weeks to assess the status of the placenta, which may no longer be capable of meeting the baby's needs. This can be indicated by the FHR pattern, amniotic fluid status, and fetal movement patterns.

Description

The spectrum of fetal **assessment** includes fetal movement (FM) counting, nonstress test (NST), modified biophysical profile (MBPP), contraction stress test (CST), oxytocin contraction stress test (OCT), biophysical profile (BPP), doppler flow studies, amniocentesis, cordocentesis, and fetal echocardiography. Fetal movement should be determined on a daily basis by all pregnant women regardless of risk status. The woman should be instructed to monitor fetal movement by selecting a consistent time of day to document how long it takes to feel 10 fetal movements. She should call her healthcare provider if there are fewer than 10 movements in a 10-hour period or immediately if there are no movements in any 10-hour period. She should also be instructed to report significant decreases in fetal activity from the baby's normal pattern. This daily monitoring of FM by all pregnant women is the least expensive and easiest of all antepartum tests to perform.

Non-stress test (NST)

The NST is performed with an electronic fetal monitor (EFM) that traces the fetal heart rate (FHR) and the presence of any contractions on a monitor strip. The mother reclines with a slight pelvic tilt to prevent compression of the large blood vessels by the pregnant uterus. The EFM is applied to her abdomen by two straps: one is to listen to the FHR by means of a transducer, and the other is to pick up any contractions by pressure on a tocodynameter. The NST indirectly provides information about fetal status by the observation of FHR accelerations that occur with fetal movement. If a fetus is not receiving adequate oxygen from the placenta, the FHR will not accelerate, but if the oxygen supply is sufficient, accelerations will be noted. If it is difficult to obtain fetal movements, a vibroacoustic stimulator (VAS) is sometimes used to provide a loud noise to awaken the fetus and produce the desired results. The minimum amount of time required for an NST is 20 minutes. During those 20 minutes, there must be two accelerations in the FHR that are 15 beats above the baseline FHR and last for 15 seconds, often called the 15 by 15 rule. Depending upon the conditions, however, it may sometimes take up to 60 to 90 minutes to obtain definitive results.

Modified biophysical profile (MBPP)

The MBPP is performed in the same manner as the NST with a limited ultrasound (US) performed to assess the amount of amniotic fluid, which is reported as the amniotic fluid index (AFI). Following the NST, an US is done to observe the amount of amniotic fluid present in four quadrants, which are divided along the umbilicus midline and perpendicular to the midline. There must be no fetal parts or any umbilical cord present in any of these pockets of fluid in order to be counted.

Contraction stress test (CST) and oxytocin contraction stress test (OCT)

The contraction stress test (CST) is similar to the NST except the FHR is evaluated for accelerations, 15 beats higher than baseline lasting 15 seconds, and in response to contractions as well. A CST requires the presence of three uterine contractions (UCs) within a 10-minute period lasting at least 40 seconds and of moderate intensity. During a contraction, the blood flow to the baby is temporarily restricted, which provides a form of "stress" to the baby. The baby's response to this stressor reveals significant information regarding available oxygen stores. If contractions are not spontaneously present, the pregnant woman will be instructed on the use of nipple stimulation to produce contractions through the release of natural oxytocin, or oxytocin can be administered through an intravenous infusion (IV) called pitocin to produce contractions. When oxytocin is administered IV, it is called an oxytocin contraction stress test (OCT). The CST/OCT is generally used after an abnormal NST is obtained in order to verify if there are problems present. Many clinicians require their diabetic patients to have at least one CST/OCT a week to assure fetal well-being. Maternal blood pressure is taken with each test.

Biophysical profile (BPP)

The biophysical profile (BPP) is performed by an ultrasound exam over a 30-minute period. The ultrasonographer/examiner looks for gross fetal movement, i.e., kicking and moving around; fetal tone, i.e., making a fist; breathing movements (which the mother can often perceive as hiccoughs); and amniotic fluid volume. A score of 0 or 2 points is assigned to each observation with the results of the NST also adding 2 points for a total possible score of 10 points.

Doppler flow studies, amniocentesis, cordocentesis, and fetal echocardiography

A physician or specially trained ultrasonographer performs Doppler flow studies, which examines the blood flow in the umbilical artery and the baby's middle cerebral artery. An experienced obstetrician/perinatologist performs the amniocentesis or the cordocentesis. For the amniocentesis, an US is used to determine an appropriate place to insert a needle and withdraw amniotic fluid for testing. In a similar manner, US is used with cordocentesis, but in this procedure a needle is guided into the umbilical cord to withdraw fetal blood for testing. Fetal echocardiography is a specialized ultrasound of a baby's heart. Since it detects most congenital heart defects, it is recommended if a baby is at a higher risk for a defect than the risk in the general population. The majority of health insurance companies do cover a portion, if not all, of the tests' costs.

Precautions

Clinicians should only prescribe these tests if they are ready to intervene when faced with worrying results. A fetus is considered viable at 24 weeks since that is the minimum gestational age for sufficient lung development. There are no significant risks to the mother or the fetus from the nonstress test (NST), modified biophysical profile (MBPP), or the biophysical profile (BPP). Ultrasound waves utilized in detecting the FHR and for the BPP are painless and safe because this method employs no harmful radiation. There is no evidence that sound waves cause any harm to the mother or the baby.

Aftercare

If the test results are acceptable, the pregnant woman is instructed to continue following her current medical regimen and return for additional testing on the dates prescribed. For NSTs/MBPPs/CSTs, the time period between tests should be no longer than three to four days under high-risk conditions with fetal movement counting taking place in between testing dates. Ultrasounds should be rescheduled as the need dictates per the physician.

Electronic fetal monitoring occurs after an amniocentesis or cordocentesis to assure fetal well-being.

Risks

There are no complications per se from the tests themselves with the exception of unfavorable test results or supine (lying horizontality on the back) hypotension secondary to a pregnant woman lying on her back for an ultrasound. When a pregnant woman lies on her back, the vena cava (one of two large veins that return blood from peripheral circulation to the heart) can become compressed from the pressure of the pregnant uterus such that blood flow to the heart is significantly reduced. There are potential complications from an amniocentesis, i.e., preterm labor, spontaneous rupture of membranes, fetal or placental injury; and the clinician performing the procedure should explain what these are prior to the procedure. There are similar risks and potential complications from cordocentesis as well which should be explained.

Normal results

Usually, a report of normal results for NSTs provides reassurance that the fetus is healthy and should remain so for three to four days, at which time repeat testing will be necessary. A normal NST is reported as being reactive, which means the fetal heart is "reacting" to movement such that the FHR is accelerating 15 beats per minute above the baseline FHR for 15 seconds twice within a 20-minute period of time. A non-reactive NST is one that fails to meet this criterion within an 80 to 90 minute period of time. For an extremely preterm fetus, a normal NST is reported as being reactive for gestational age, which indicates the FHR demonstrated two accelerations of 10 beats per minute above baseline for 10 seconds over a 20–30 minute period. Typically, the central nervous system is not completely mature until approximately 32 weeks gestational age, and a report of reactive for gestational age takes this into consideration. It is important to remember that a normal result does not guarantee that no problems are present. Although very rare in occurrence, false normal results can be observed.

The CST results are reported as reactive/negative, reactive/suspicious, reactive/positive (a very unlikely result), or non-reactive/negative, non-reactive/suspicious, non-reactive/positive. The reactive/non-reactive part of the test report refers to the presence or absence of accelerations. The negative part refers to no decelerations being present with uterine contractions (UCs). "Suspicious" refers to the presence of some decelerations with UCs, and "positive" refers to the presence of

decelerations more than 50 percent of the time with UCs. A suspicious or positive result requires further evaluation, i.e., prolonged EFM monitoring or a BPP. A normal BPP report without an NST is 8 points and 10 points with a reactive NST. Six points is suspicious and requires either a CST or a repeat BPP within 24 hours. A total of 4 points is not reassuring and requires immediate evaluation by prolonged EFM.

All results are given to the primary physician who must then make a decision as to the appropriate course of action. Abnormal CST results generally indicate the baby is not receiving sufficient oxygen and may not be capable of withstanding the stress of labor and subsequent vaginal delivery. If this is the case, a **cesarean section** may be performed. The final outcome depends on the mother's individual circumstances. Severe pregnancy-induced hypertension may require immediate delivery via cesarean section. In some cases, medications such as betamethasone may be given to the mother to speed up the lung maturity of the baby. If the mother's cervix is favorable for induction, labor may be induced.

Parental concerns

The healthcare provider should give a complete explanation to the pregnant woman and her partner regarding the tests, i.e., what to expect, how long the test may take, what it means, and why it is being done. It frequently helps if the pregnant woman has eaten prior to undergoing the test. Pregnant women should know that every test is not compulsory, and that if the results of the test do not matter to the parents, it may not have to be performed.

See also High-risk pregnancy.

Resources

BOOKS

Freeman, Roger, et al. *Fetal Heart Rate Monitoring*, 3rd ed. Philadelphia: Lippincott Williams & Wilkins, 2003.

Gabbe, Steven, et al. *Obstetrics*, 4th ed. London: Churchill Livingstone, 2001.

Neilson, J. P., and Z. Alfirevic. "Doppler ultrasound for fetal assessment in high risk pregnancies (Cochrane Review)." In *The Cochrane Library*, vol. 3. Chichester, UK: John Wiley & Sons, Ltd., 2004.

Pattison, N., and L. McCowan. "Cardiotocography for antepartum fetal assessment (Cochrane Review)." In *The Cochrane Library*. Chichester, UK: John Wiley & Sons, Ltd., 2004.

Tucker, Susan. *Pocket Guide to Fetal Monitoring and Assessment*, 4th ed. St. Louis, MO: Mosby, 2000.

ORGANIZATIONS

American College of Obstetricians and Gynecologists. 409 12th Street, SW, PO Box 96920, Washington, DC 20090. Web site: <www.acog.org>.

Association of Women's Health, Obstetric, and Neonatal Nursing. 2000 L Street, NW, Suite 740, Washington, DC 20036. Web site: <www.awhonn.org/>.

Linda K. Bennington, RNC, MSN, CNS

Antiacne drugs

Definition

Acne is a skin disorder that leads to an outbreak of lesions called pimples or "zits." The most common form of the disease in adolescents is called acne vulgaris. Antiacne drugs are the medicines that help clear up the pimples, blackheads, whiteheads, and more severe forms of lesions that occur when a teen has acne.

Different types of antiacne drugs are used for different treatment purposes, depending on the severity of the condition. For example, lotions, soaps, gels, and creams containing substances called benzoyl peroxide or treti-

noin may be used to clear up mild to moderately severe acne. Isotretinoin (Accutane) is an oral drug that is prescribed only for very severe, disfiguring acne.

Acne is caused by the overproduction of sebum during **puberty** when high levels of the male hormone androgen cause excess sebum to form. Sebum is an oily substance that forms in glands just under the surface of the skin called sebaceous glands. Sebum normally flows out hair follicles onto the skin to act as a natural skin moisturizer. The glands are connected to hair follicles that allow the sebum, or oil, to empty onto the skin through a pore.

Sometimes the sebum combines with dead, sticky skin cells and bacteria called *Propionibacterium acnes (P. acnes)* that normally live on the skin. The mixture of oil and cells allows the bacteria to grow in the follicles. When this happens, a hard plug called a comedo can form. A comedo is an enlarged hair follicle. It can appear on the skin as a blackhead, which is a comedo that reaches the skin's surface and looks black, or as a whitehead, which is a comedo that is sealed by keratin, the fibrous protein produced by the skin cells and looks like a white bump.

In addition, pimples can form on the skin. Types of pimples include:

- papules, which are small, red bumps that may be tender to touch

- pustules, which are pus-filled lesions that are often red at the base

- nodules, which are large, painful lesions deep in the skin

- cysts, which are painful pus-filled lesions deep in the skin that can cause scarring

Pimples form when the follicle is invaded by the *P. acnes* bacteria. The damaged follicle weakens and bursts open, releasing sebum, bacteria, skin cells, and white blood cells into surrounding tissues. Scarring happens when new skin cells are created to replace the damaged cells. The most severe type of acne includes both nodules and cysts.

Description

Acne cannot be cured, but antiacne drugs can help clear the skin and reduce the chance of scarring. The goal of treating moderate acne is to decrease inflammation and prevent new comedones from forming. Benzoyl peroxide and tretinoin work by mildly irritating the skin. This encourages skin cells to slough off, which helps open blocked pores. Benzoyl peroxide also kills bacteria, which helps prevent whiteheads and blackheads from turning into pimples. Isotretinoin shrinks the glands that produce sebum. It is used for severe acne lesions and must be carefully monitored because of its side effects. **Antibiotics** also may be prescribed to kill bacteria and reduce inflammation.

General use

Benzoyl peroxide is found in many over-the-counter acne products that are applied to the skin, such as Benoxyl, Neutrogena Acne, PanOxyl, and some formulations of Clean & Clear, Clearasil, and Oxy. Some benzoyl peroxide products are available without a physician's prescription; others require a prescription. Acne treatments that can dry the skin should be used with caution by people with skin of color.

Tretinoin (Retin-A) is available only with a physician's prescription. It comes in liquid, cream, and gel forms, which are applied to the skin. Isotretinoin (Accutane), which is taken by mouth in capsule form, is available only with a physician's prescription. Only physicians experienced in diagnosing and treating severe acne, such as dermatologists, should prescribe isotretinoin.

Recommended dosages

The recommended dosage depends on the type of antiacne drug. These drugs usually come with written directions for patients and should be used only as directed by the prescribing physician. Teens who have questions about how to use the medicine should check with their physician or pharmacist.

Patients who use isotretinoin usually take the medicine for a few months, then stop for at least two months. Their acne may continue to improve even after they stop taking the medicine. If the condition is still severe after several months of treatment and a two-month break, the physician may prescribe a second course of treatment.

Precautions

Isotretinoin

Isotretinoin can cause serious birth defects, including **mental retardation** and physical deformities. This medicine should not be used during pregnancy. Females who are able to bear children should not use isotretinoin unless they have very severe acne that has not cleared up with the use of other antiacne drugs. In that case, a woman who uses this drug must have a pregnancy test two weeks before beginning treatment and each month she is taking the drug. Another pregnancy test must be

done one month after treatment ends. The woman must use an effective birth control method for one month before treatment begins and must continue using it throughout treatment and for one month after treatment ends. Females who are able to bear children and who want to use this medicine should discuss this information with their healthcare providers. Before using the medicine, they will be asked to sign a consent form stating that they understand the danger of taking isotretinoin during pregnancy and that they agree to use effective birth control.

People using this drug should not donate blood to a blood bank while taking isotretinoin or for 30 days after treatment with the drug ends. This will help reduce the chance of a pregnant woman receiving blood containing isotretinoin, which could cause birth defects.

Isotretinoin may cause a sudden decrease in night vision. If this happens, users should not drive or do anything else that could be dangerous until vision returns to normal. They should also let the physician know about the problem.

This medicine may also make the eyes, nose, and mouth dry. Ask the physician about using special eye drops to relieve eye dryness. To temporarily relieve the dry mouth, chew sugarless gum, suck on sugarless candy or ice chips, or use saliva substitutes, which come in liquid and tablet forms and are available without a prescription. If the problem continues for more than two weeks, check with a physician or dentist. Mouth dryness that continues over a long time may contribute to **tooth decay** and other dental problems.

Isotretinoin may increase sensitivity to sunlight. Patients being treated with this medicine should avoid exposure to the sun and should not use tanning beds, tanning booths, or sunlamps until they know how the drug affects them.

In the early stages of treatment with isotretinoin, some people's acne seems to get worse before it starts getting better. If the condition becomes much worse or if the skin is very irritated, they should check with the physician who prescribed the medicine.

Benzoyl peroxide and tretinoin

When applying antiacne drugs to the skin, people should be careful not to get the medicine in the eyes, mouth, or inside the nose. They should not put the medicine on skin that is wind burned, sunburned, or irritated, and not apply it to open **wounds**.

Because antiacne drugs such as benzoyl peroxide and tretinoin irritate the skin slightly, users should avoid doing anything that might cause further irritation. They should wash the face with mild soap and water only two or three times a day, unless the physician says to wash it more often. They should also avoid using abrasive soaps or cleansers and products that might dry the skin or make it peel, such as medicated cosmetics, cleansers that contain alcohol, or other acne products that contain resorcinol, sulfur, or salicylic acid.

If benzoyl peroxide or tretinoin make the skin too red or too dry or cause too much peeling, the user should check with a physician. Using the medicine less often or using a weaker strength may be necessary. Benzoyl peroxide can irritate the skin of people with skin of color and cause darkened spots called hyperpigmentation on the skin. Benzoyl peroxide may discolor hair or colored fabrics.

ORAL DRUGS Oral antibiotics are taken daily for two to four months. The drugs used include tetracycline, erythromycin, minocycline (Minocin), doxycycline, clindamycin (Cleocin), and trimethoprim-sulfamethoxazole (Bactrim, Septra). Possible side effects include allergic reactions, stomach upset, vaginal yeast infections, **dizziness**, and tooth discoloration.

The goal of treating moderate acne is to decrease inflammation and prevent new comedones from forming. One effective treatment is topical tretinoin, used along with a topical or oral antibiotic. A combination of topical benzoyl peroxide and erythromycin is also very effective. Improvement is normally seen within four to six weeks, but treatment is maintained for at least two to four months.

Special conditions

People who have certain medical conditions or who are taking certain other medicines may have problems if they use antiacne drugs. Before using these products, the physician should be informed about any of the following conditions.

ALLERGIES Anyone who has had unusual reactions to etretinate, isotretinoin, tretinoin, vitamin A preparations, or benzoyl peroxide in the past should let the physician know before using an antiacne drug. The physician should also be told about any **allergies** to foods, dyes, preservatives, or other substances.

PREGNANCY Teens who are pregnant or who may become pregnant should check with a physician before using tretinoin or benzoyl peroxide. Isotretinoin causes birth defects in humans and must not be used during pregnancy.

OTHER MEDICAL CONDITIONS Before using antiacne drugs applied to the skin, people with any of these medical problems should make sure their physicians are aware of their conditions:

- Eczema. Antiacne drugs that are applied to the skin may make this condition worse.
- Sunburn or raw skin. Antiacne drugs that are applied to the skin may increase the **pain** and irritation of these conditions.

In people with certain medical conditions, isotretinoin may increase the amount of triglyceride (a fatty substance) in the blood. This may lead to heart or blood vessel problems. Before using isotretinoin, adolescents with any of the following medical problems should make sure their physicians are aware of their conditions:

- alcoholism or heavy drinking, currently or in the past
- diabetes or **family** history of diabetes (Isotretinoin may change blood sugar levels.)
- family history of high triglyceride levels in the blood
- severe weight problems

Using antiacne drugs with certain other drugs may affect the way the drugs work or may increase the chance of side effects.

Side effects

Conditions caused by isotretinoin

Minor discomforts such as dry mouth or nose, dry eyes, dry skin, or **itching** usually go away as the body adjusts to the drug and do not require medical attention unless they continue or are bothersome.

Other side effects should be brought to a physician's attention. These include:

- burning, redness, or itching of the eyes
- nosebleeds
- signs of inflammation of the lips, such as peeling, burning, redness or pain

Bowel inflammation is not a common side effect, but it may occur. If any of the following signs of bowel inflammation occur, stop taking isotretinoin immediately and check with a physician:

- pain in the abdomen
- bleeding from the rectum
- severe diarrhea

Conditions caused by benzoyl peroxide and tretinoin

The most common side effects of antiacne drugs applied to the skin are slight redness, dryness, peeling, and stinging, and a warm feeling to the skin. These problems usually go away as the body adjusts to the drug and do not require medical treatment.

Other side effects should be brought to a physician's attention. Check with a physician as soon as possible if any of the following side effects occur:

- blistering, crusting, or swelling of the skin
- severe burning or redness of the skin
- darkening or lightening of the skin (This effect will eventually go away after treatment with an antiacne drug ends.)
- skin rash

Other side effects are possible with any type of antiacne drug. Anyone who has unusual symptoms while using antiacne drugs should get in touch with his or her physician.

Interactions

Patients using antiacne drugs on their skin should tell their physicians if they are using any other prescription or nonprescription (over-the-counter) medicine that they apply to the skin in the same area as the antiacne drug.

Isotretinoin may interact with other medicines. When this happens, the effects of one or both drugs may change or the risk of side effects may be greater. Anyone who takes isotretinoin should let the physician know about all other medicines being used and should ask whether the possible interactions can interfere with drug therapy. Among the drugs that may interact with isotretinoin are listed below:

- Etretinate (Tegison), used to treat severe **psoriasis**. Using this medicine with isotretinoin increases side effects.
- Tretinoin (Retin-A, Renova). Using this medicine with isotretinoin increases side effects.
- Vitamin A or any medicine containing vitamin A. Using any vitamin A preparations with isotretinoin increases side effects. Do not take vitamin supplements containing vitamin A while taking isotretinoin.
- Tetracyclines (used to treat infections). Using these medicines with isotretinoin increases the chance of swelling of the brain. Make sure the physician knows if

KEY TERMS

Acne—A chronic inflammation of the sebaceous glands that manifests as blackheads, whiteheads, and/or pustules on the face or trunk.

Bacteria—Singular, bacterium; tiny, one-celled forms of life that cause many diseases and infections.

Bowel—The intestine; a tube-like structure that extends from the stomach to the anus. Some digestive processes are carried out in the bowel before food passes out of the body as waste.

Cyst—An abnormal sac or enclosed cavity in the body filled with liquid or partially solid material. Also refers to a protective, walled-off capsule in which an organism lies dormant.

Eczema—A superficial type of inflammation of the skin that may be very itchy and weeping in the early stages; later, the affected skin becomes crusted, scaly, and thick.

Noncomedogenic—A substance that does not contribute to the formation of blackheads or pimples on the skin. Jojoba oil is noncomedogenic.

Pimple—A small, red swelling of the skin.

Psoriasis—A chronic, noncontagious skin disease that is marked by dry, scaly, and silvery patches of skin that appear in a variety of sizes and locations on the body.

Pus—A thick, yellowish or greenish fluid composed of the remains of dead white blood cells, pathogens, and decomposed cellular debris. It is most often associated with bacterial infection.

Triglyceride—A substance formed in the body from fat in the diet. Triglycerides are the main fatty materials in the blood. Bound to protein, they make up high- and low-density lipoproteins (HDLs and LDLs). Triglyceride levels are important in the diagnosis and treatment of many diseases including high blood pressure, diabetes, and heart disease.

tetracycline is being used to treat acne or another infection.

Parental concerns

Acne comes at a difficult time, the adolescent years. While mild acne can be treated with over-the-counter medications, more severe acne needs medical attention. Experts advise against a wait-and-see attitude. Treatment options can help control acne and avoid scarring.

Isotretinoin can cause serious birth defects, including mental retardation and physical deformities. This medicine should not be used during pregnancy. Sexually active adolescent females who are able to bear children should not use isotretinoin unless they have very severe acne that has not cleared up with the use of other antiacne drugs. In addition, acne treatments that can dry the skin should be used with caution by people with skin of color.

See also Acne.

Resources

BOOKS

McNally, Robert A. *Skin Health Information for Teens: Health Tips about Dermatological Concerns and Skin Cancer Risks.* Detroit, MI: Omnigraphics, 2003.

Simons, Rae. *For All to See: A Teen's Guide to Healthy Skin.* Broomall, PA: Mason Crest, 2005.

ORGANIZATIONS

American Academy of Dermatology. 930 E. Woodfield Rd., Schaumburg, IL 60168. Web site: <www.aad.org/pamphlets/acnepamp.html>.

WEB SITES

"Accutane." *American Osteopathic College of Dermatology.* Available online at <http://aocd.org/skin/dermatologic_diseases/accutane.html> (accessed October 16, 2004).

"Questions and Answers about Acne." *National Institute of Arthritis and Musculoskeletal and Skin Diseases (NIAMS) Information Clearinghouse*, October 2001. Available online at <www.niams.nih.gov/hi/topics/acne/acne.htm> (accessed October 16, 2003).

"Treating Acne in Skin of Color." *AcneNet*, 2002. Available online at <www.skincarephysicians.com/acnenet/update.htm> (accessed October 16, 2004).

"'What Can I Do about Pimples?'" *American Family Physician, Information from Your Family Doctor Handout*, January 15, 2000. Available online at <www.aafp.org/afp/20000115/20000115a.html> (accessed October 15, 2004).

Christine Kuehn Kelly

▌Antiasthmatic drugs

Definition

Antiasthmatic drugs are medicines that treat or prevent **asthma** attacks.

Description

Three types of drugs are used in treating and preventing asthma attacks:

- Bronchodilators relax the smooth muscles that line the airway. This makes the airways open wider, letting more air pass through them. These drugs are used mainly to relieve sudden asthma attacks or to prevent attacks that might come on after **exercise**. They may be taken by mouth, injected, or inhaled.

- Corticosteroids block the inflammation that narrows the airways. Used regularly, these drugs help prevent asthma attacks. Those attacks that do occur will be less severe. However, corticosteroids cannot stop an attack that is already underway. These drugs may be taken by mouth, injected, or inhaled.

- Cromolyn also is taken regularly to prevent asthma attacks and may be used alone or with other asthma medicines. It cannot stop an attack that already has started. The drug works by preventing certain cells in the body from releasing substances that cause allergic reactions or asthma symptoms. One brand of this drug, Nasalcrom, comes in capsule and nasal spray forms and is used to treat hay fever and other **allergies**. The inhalation form of the drug, Intal, is used for asthma. It comes in aerosol canisters, in capsules that are inserted into an inhaler, and in liquid form that is used in a nebulizer.

General use

All three types of drugs may be used in combination with each other.

Cromolyn is a common but not invariable first choice for children who have asthma. It reduces the frequency of asthmatic attacks and is suitable for long-term use. Cromolyn may not be needed when attacks are mild and infrequent.

Bronchodilators should be used to treat attacks once they begin. They may also be taken on a regular basis to prevent attacks.

Corticosteroids are valuable, but some have serious long-term side effects. Except in patients whose conditions cannot be managed with cromolyn and brochodilators, corticosteroids should be reserved for emergency room use. In patients who require ongoing use of steroids, alternate day dosing or inhalation of some of the newer corticosteroids may minimize the adverse effects of this class of drugs.

A young girl suffering from asthma uses an inhaler to assist her breathing. (© Alan Towse; Ecoscene/Corbis.)

Precautions

Using antiasthmatic drugs properly is important. Because bronchodilators provide quick relief, some people may be tempted to overuse them. However, with some kinds of bronchodilators, doing so can lead to serious and possibly life-threatening complications. In the long run, patients are better off using bronchodilators only as directed and also using corticosteroids, which eventually will reduce their need for bronchodilators.

Parents whose children are using their antiasthmatic drugs correctly but feel their asthma is not under control should see consult their child's physicians. The physician can either increase the dose, switch to another medicine, or add another medicine to the regimen.

Corticosteroids are powerful drugs that may cause serious side effects when used over the long term. However, these problems are much less likely with the inha-

lant forms than with the oral and injected forms. While the oral and injected forms generally should be used only for one to two weeks, the inhalant forms may be used for long periods.

When used to prevent asthma attacks, cromolyn must be taken as directed every day. The drug may take as long as four weeks to start working. Unless told to do so by a physician, patients should not stop taking the drug just because it does not seem to be working. When symptoms do begin to improve, patients should continue taking all medicines that have been prescribed, unless a physician directs otherwise.

Side effects

Inhalant forms of antiasthmatic drugs may cause dryness or irritation in the throat, dry mouth, or an unpleasant taste in the mouth. To help prevent these problems, patients can gargle and rinse the mouth or take a sip of water after each dose.

More serious side effects are not common when these medicines are used properly. However, parents whose children have unusual or bothersome symptoms after taking an antiasthmatic drug should get in touch with the child's physician.

Interactions

There are many drugs that are used in treatment of asthma. Interactions should be reviewed on an individual basis.

Drugs which decrease blood levels of aminophylline (which opens bronchial passages) and may require a dose increase are:

• carbamazepine

• isoprenolol

• phenobarbital

• phenytoin

• rifampin

Parental concerns

All health professionals with responsibility for an asthmatic's drug therapy should have an up-to-date list of the drugs and doses being used by the child. Asthmatic children should wear a suitable identification bracelet with a list of drugs being used, in case of an emergency room admission. Children using inhalers should be knowledgeable on the use of these devices.

See also Asthma.

Resources

BOOKS

Beers, Mark H., and Robert Berkow, eds. *The Merck Manual,* 2nd home ed. West Point, PA: Merck & Co., 2004.

Mcevoy, Gerald, et al. *AHFS Drug Information 2004.* Bethesda, MD: American Society of Healthsystems Pharmacists, 2004.

Raskin, Lauren. *Breathing Easy: Solutions in Pediatric Asthma.* Washington, DC: Georgetown University, 2000.

Siberry, George K., and Robert Iannone, eds. *The Harriet Lane Handbook,* 15th ed. Philadelphia: Mosby Publishing, 2000.

PERIODICALS

Allen, D. B. "Systemic effects of inhaled corticosteroids in children." *Current Opinion in Pediatrics* 4 (August 16, 2004): 440–4.

Berger, W. E., and G. G. Shapiro. "The use of inhaled corticosteroids for persistent asthma in infants and young children." *Annual Allergy Asthma Immunology* 92 (April 2004): 387–99.

ORGANIZATIONS

American Academy of Allergy, Asthma, & Immunology. 555 East Wells St., Suite 1100, Milwaukee, WI 53202-3823. Web site: <www.aaai.org>.

WEB SITES

"Pediatric Asthma." *MedlinePlus.* Available online at <www.nlm.nih.gov/medlineplus/ency/article/000990.htm> (accessed December 19, 2004).

Nancy Ross-Flanigan
Samuel Uretsky, PharmD

Antibiotics

Definition

Antibiotics are used for treatment or prevention of bacterial infection. They may be informally defined as the subgroup of anti-infectives that are derived from bacterial sources and are used to treat bacterial infections. Other classes of drugs, most notably the **sulfonamides**, may be effective antibacterials. Similarly, some antibiotics may have secondary uses, such as the use of demeclocycline (Declomycin, a tetracycline derivative) to treat the syndrome of inappropriate antidiuretic hormone (SIADH) secretion. Other antibiotics may be useful in treating protozoal infections.

Description

Classifications

Although there are several classification schemes for antibiotics, based on bacterial spectrum (broad versus narrow) or route of administration (injectable versus oral versus topical), or type of activity (bactericidal versus bacteriostatic), the most useful is based on chemical structure. Antibiotics within a structural class will generally show similar patterns of effectiveness, toxicity, and allergic potential.

PENICILLINS The **penicillins** are the oldest class of antibiotics and have a common chemical structure that they share with the cephalosporins. Classed as the beta-lactam antibiotics, the two groups are generally bactericidal, which means that they kill bacteria rather than simply inhibit its growth. The penicillins can be further subdivided. The natural penicillins are based on the original penicillin G structure; penicillinase-resistant penicillins, notably methicillin and oxacillin, are active even in the presence of the bacterial enzyme that inactivates most natural penicillins. Aminopenicillins such as ampicillin and amoxicillin have an extended spectrum of action compared with the natural penicillins; extended spectrum penicillins are effective against a wider range of bacteria. These generally include coverage for *Pseudomonas aeruginosa.*

CEPHALOSPORINS Cephalosporins and the closely related cephamycins and carbapenems, like the penicillins, contain a beta-lactam chemical structure. Consequently, there are patterns of cross-resistance and cross-allergenicity among the drugs in these classes. The "cepha" drugs are among the most diverse classes of antibiotics and are themselves subdivided into first, second, and third generations. Each generation has a broader spectrum of activity than the one before. In addition, cefoxitin, a cephamycin, is highly active against anaerobic bacteria, which offers utility in treatment of abdominal infections. The third generation drugs, cefotaxime, ceftizoxime, ceftriaxone, and others, cross the blood-brain barrier and may be used to treat **meningitis** and **encephalitis**. Cephalosporins are the usually preferred agents for surgical prophylaxis.

FLUOROQUINOLONES The fluoroquinolones are synthetic antibacterial agents and not derived from bacteria. They are included here because they can be readily interchanged with traditional antibiotics. An earlier, related class of antibacterial agents, the quinolones, drugs that were not well absorbed, could be used only to treat urinary tract infections. The fluoroquinolones, which are based on the older group, are broad-spectrum bacteriocidal drugs that are chemically unrelated to the penicillins or the cephalosporins. They are well distributed into bone tissue and so well absorbed that in general they are as effective by the oral route as by intravenous infusion.

TETRACYCLINES **Tetracyclines** got their name from the fact that they share a chemical structure that has four rings. They are derived from a species of *Streptomyces* bacteria. Broad-spectrum bacteriostatic agents, the tetracyclines may be effective against a wide variety of microorganisms, including rickettsia and amoebic parasites.

MACROLIDES The macrolide antibiotics are derived from *Streptomyces* bacteria. Erythromycin, the prototype of this class, has a spectrum and use similar to penicillin. Newer members of the group, azithromycin and clarithromycin, are particularly useful for their high level of lung penetration. Clarithromycin has been widely used to treat *Helicobacter pylori* infections, the cause of stomach ulcers.

OTHERS Other classes of antibiotics include the aminoglycosides, which are particularly useful for their effectiveness in treating *Pseudomonas aeruginosa* infections, and the lincosamide drugs clindamycin and lincomycin, which are highly active against anaerobic pathogens. There are other, individual drugs which may have utility in specific infections.

General use

Antibiotics are used for treatment or prevention of bacterial infections. In most cases, they are prescribed for a short period of time to treat a specific infection. This period may range from three days to 10 days or more. More serious infections may require longer periods of treatment, up to several months or longer. Lower doses may be used over a long period of time to prevent the return of a serious infection.

Precautions

All antibiotics should be used as prescribed. These drugs will degrade over time and lose their potency. Not completing a prescribed course of treatment increases the probability that drug-resistant strains of organisms will develop.

Side effects

All antibiotics cause risk of overgrowth by non-susceptible bacteria. Manufacturers list other major hazards by class; however, the healthcare provider should review each drug individually to assess the degree of risk. Generally, breastfeeding may be continued while taking antibiotics, but nursing mothers should always check with their physician first. Excessive or inappropriate use may promote growth of resistant pathogens.

Hypersensitivity to penicillins may be common, and cross allergenicity with cephalosporins has been reported. (That is, those who are allergic to penicillin may also be allergic to cephalosporins.) Penicillins are classed as category B during pregnancy.

Several cephalosporins and related compounds have been associated with seizures. Cefmetazole, cefoperazone, cefotetan, and ceftriaxone may be associated with problems in poor blood clotting. Pseudomembranous colitis (an intestinal disorder) has been reported with cephalosporins and other broad spectrum antibiotics. Some drugs in this class may cause kidney toxicity. Cephalosporins are classed as category B during pregnancy.

Regarding fluoroquinolones, lomefloxacin has been associated with increased sensitivity to light. All drugs in this class have been associated with convulsions. Fluoroquinolones are classed as category C during pregnancy.

Of the tetracyclines, demeclocycline may cause increased photosensitivity. Minocycline may cause **dizziness**. Healthcare providers do not prescribe tetracyclines in children under the age of eight, and they specifically avoid doing so during periods of tooth

KEY TERMS

Bacteria—Singular, bacterium; tiny, one-celled forms of life that cause many diseases and infections.

Bacterial spectrum—The number of bacteria an antibiotic is effective against. Broad-spectrum antibiotics treat many different kinds of bacteria. Narrow-spectrum antibiotics treat fewer kinds.

Inflammation—Pain, redness, swelling, and heat that develop in response to tissue irritation or injury. It usually is caused by the immune system's response to the body's contact with a foreign substance, such as an allergen or pathogen.

Meningitis—An infection or inflammation of the membranes that cover the brain and spinal cord. It is usually caused by bacteria or a virus.

Microorganism—An organism that is too small to be seen with the naked eye, such as a bacterium, virus, or fungus.

Organism—A single, independent unit of life, such as a bacterium, a plant, or an animal.

Pregnancy category—A system of classifying drugs according to their established risks for use during pregnancy. Category A: Controlled human studies have demonstrated no fetal risk. Category B: Animal studies indicate no fetal risk, but no human studies, or adverse effects in animals, but not in well-controlled human studies. Category C: No adequate human or animal studies, or adverse fetal effects in animal studies, but no available human data. Category D: Evidence of fetal risk, but benefits outweigh risks. Category X: Evidence of fetal risk. Risks outweigh any benefits.

development. Oral tetracyclines bind to anions such as calcium and iron. Although doxycycline and minocycline may be taken with meals, people must be advised to take other tetracycline antibiotics on an empty stomach and not to take the drugs with milk or other calcium-rich foods. Expired tetracycline should never be administered. These drugs have a pregnancy category D. Use during pregnancy may cause alterations in fetal bone development.

Of the macrolides, erythromycin may aggravate the weakness of people with myasthenia gravis. Azithromycin has, rarely, been associated with allergic reactions, including angioedema (swelling), **anaphylaxis**, and severe skin reactions. Oral erythromycin may be highly irritating to the stomach and when given by injection

may cause severe phlebitis (inflammation of the veins). These drugs should be used with caution in people with liver dysfunction. Azithromycin and erythromycin are pregnancy category B. Clarithromycin, dirithromycin, and troleandomycin are pregnancy category C.

The aminoglycosides class of drugs causes kidney and ear problems. These problems can occur even with normal doses. Dosing should be based on kidney function, with periodic testing of both kidney function and hearing. These drugs are pregnancy category D.

Parental concerns

Parents should be sure to follow all dosage and label directions. This includes using all of a prescription at the time it is prescribed. Parents should also ensure that children cannot ingest any prescription medications by accident.

Resources

BOOKS

Antibiotics: A Medical Dictionary, Bibliography, and Annotated Research Guide to Internet References. San Diego, CA: ICON Health Publications, 2003.

Archer, Gordon, and Ronald E. Polk. "Treatment and Prophylaxis of Bacterial Infections." In *Harrison's Principles of Internal Medicine*, 15th ed. Edited by Eugene Braunwald, et al. New York: McGraw-Hill, 2001, pp. 867-81

Diasio, Robert B. "Principles of Drug Therapy." In *Cecil Textbook of Medicine*, 22nd ed. Edited by Lee Goldman, et al. Philadelphia: Saunders, 2003, pp. 124-34.

Scott, Geoffrey M. *Handbook of Essential Antibiotics.* New York: Gordon & Breach Publishing Group, 2004.

Sherman, Josepha. *War against Germs.* New York: Rosen Publishing Group, 2004.

PERIODICALS

Ashworth, M., et al. "Why has antibiotic prescribing for respiratory illness declined in primary care?" *Journal of Public Health (Oxford)* 26, no. 3 (2004): 268–74.

Carrat, F., et al. "Antibiotic treatment for influenza does not affect resolution of illness, secondary visits or lost workdays." *European Journal of Epidemiology* 19, no. 7 (2004): 703-5.

Dancer, S. J. "How antibiotics can make us sick: the less obvious adverse effects of antimicrobial chemotherapy." *Lancet Infectious Diseases* 4, no. 10 (2004): 611–9.

Simoes, J. A., et al. "Antibiotic resistance patterns of group B streptococcal clinical isolates." *Infectious Diseases in Obstetrics and Gynecology* 12, no. 1 (2004): 1–8.

ORGANIZATIONS

American Academy of Family Physicians. 11400 Tomahawk Creek Parkway, Leawood, KS 66211-2672. Web site: <www.aafp.org/>.

American Academy of Pediatrics. 141 Northwest Point Blvd., Elk Grove Village, IL 60007-1098. Web site: <www.aap.org/>.

American College of Emergency Physicians. PO Box 619911, Dallas, TX 75261-9911. Web site: <www.acep.org/>.

WEB SITES

"Antibiotic Guide." *Johns Hopkins Point of Care Information Technology.* Available online at <http://hopkins-abxguide.org/> (accessed December 19, 2004).

"Antibiotics: When They Can and Can't Help." *American Academy of Family Physicians.* Available online at <http://familydoctor.org/x2250.xml> (accessed December 19, 2004).

L. Fleming Fallon, Jr., MD, DrPH

Antibiotics, topical

Definition

Topical **antibiotics** are medicines applied to the skin to kill bacteria.

Description

Some topical antibiotics are available without a prescription and are sold in many forms, including creams, ointments, powders, and sprays. Some widely used topical antibiotics are bacitracin, neomycin, mupirocin, and polymyxin B. Among the products that contain one or more of these ingredients are Bactroban (a prescription item), Neosporin, Polysporin, and triple antibiotic ointment or cream.

General use

Topical antibiotics help prevent infections caused by bacteria that get into minor cuts, scrapes, and **burns**. Treating minor **wounds** with antibiotics allows quicker healing. If the wounds are left untreated, the bacteria will multiply, causing **pain**, redness, swelling, **itching**, and oozing. Untreated infections can eventually spread and become much more serious.

Different kinds of topical antibiotics kill different kinds of bacteria. Many antibiotic first-aid products contain combinations of antibiotics to make them effective against a broad range of bacteria.

When treating a wound, it is not enough to simply apply a topical antibiotic. The wound must first be cleaned with soap and water and patted dry. After the antibiotic is applied, the wound should be covered with a dressing, such as a bandage or a protective gel or spray. It is best to keep wounds clean and moist while they heal. The covering should still allow some air to reach the wound, however.

Precautions

The recommended dosage depends on the type of topical antibiotic. Parents should follow the directions on the package label or ask a pharmacist for directions before dressing their child's wound.

In general, topical antibiotics should be applied within four hours after injury. More than the recommended amount should not be used, and the antibiotic should not be applied more often than three times a day.

In the early 2000s many people are concerned about antibiotic resistance, a problem that can develop when antibiotics are overused. Over time, bacteria develop new defenses against antibiotics that once were effective against them. Because bacteria reproduce so quickly, these defenses can be rapidly passed on through generations of bacteria until almost all are immune to the effects of a particular antibiotic. The process happens faster than new antibiotics can be developed. To help control this development, many experts advise people to use topical antibiotics only for short periods, that is, until the wound heals, and only as directed. For the topical antibiotic to work best, it should be used only to prevent infection in a fresh wound, not to treat an infection that has already started. Wounds that are not fresh may need the attention of a physician in order to prevent complications such as blood poisoning.

Topical antibiotics are meant to be used only on the skin and only for only a few days at a time. If the wound has not healed in five days, the antibiotic should be discontinued and a doctor called.

Topical antibiotics should not be used on large areas of skin or on open wounds. These products should not be used to treat **diaper rash** in infants or incontinence rash in adults.

Only minor cuts, scrapes, and burns should be treated with topical antibiotics. Certain kinds of injuries may need medical care and should not be self-treated with topical antibiotics. These include:

- large wounds
- deep cuts

KEY TERMS

Bacteria—Singular, bacterium; tiny, one-celled forms of life that cause many diseases and infections.

Conception—The union of egg and sperm to form a fetus.

Fungal—Caused by a fungus.

Fungus—A member of a group of simple organisms that are related to yeast and molds.

Incontinence—A condition characterized by the inability to control urination or bowel functions.

Inflammation—Pain, redness, swelling, and heat that develop in response to tissue irritation or injury. It usually is caused by the immune system's response to the body's contact with a foreign substance, such as an allergen or pathogen.

- cuts that continue bleeding
- cuts that may need stitches
- burns any larger than a few inches in diameter
- scrapes imbedded with particles that will not wash away
- animal bites
- deep puncture wounds
- eye injuries

Regular topical antibiotics should never be used in the eyes. Special prescription antibiotic products are available for treating eye infections.

Although topical antibiotics control infections caused by bacteria, they may allow fungal infections to develop. The use of other medicines to treat the fungal infections may be necessary. Parents should check with the physician or pharmacist.

Some people may be allergic to one or more ingredients in a topical antibiotic product. If an allergic reaction develops, the product should be discontinued immediately and a physician called.

As of 2004, no harmful or abnormal effects had been reported in babies whose mothers used topical antibiotics while pregnant or nursing. However, pregnant women generally are advised not to use any drugs during the first three months after conception. A woman who is pregnant or breastfeeding or who plans to become pregnant should check with her physician before using a topical antibiotic.

Unless a parent is so advised by the childs' physician, topical antibiotics should not be used on children under two months of age.

Side effects

The most common minor side effects of topical antibiotics are itching or burning. These problems usually do not require medical treatment unless they do not go away or they interfere with normal activities.

If any of the following side effects occur, a doctor should be called as soon as possible:

- rash
- swelling of the lips and face
- sweating
- tightness or discomfort in the chest
- breathing problems
- fainting or dizziness
- low blood pressure
- nausea
- diarrhea
- hearing loss or ringing in the ears

Other rare side effects may occur. Anyone who has unusual symptoms after using a topical antibiotic should get in touch with the physician who prescribed or the pharmacist who recommended the medication.

Parental concerns

Using certain topical antibiotics at the same time as hydrocortisone (a topical corticosteroid used to treat inflammation) may hide signs of infection or allergic reaction. People should not use these two medicines at the same time unless told to do so by a healthcare provider.

Anyone who is using any other type of prescription or nonprescription (over-the-counter) medicine on the skin should check with a doctor before using a topical antibiotic.

Resources

BOOKS

Antibiotics: A Medical Dictionary, Bibliography, and Annotated Research Guide to Internet References. San Diego, CA: Icon Health Publications, 2003.

Archer, Gordon, and Ronald E. Polk. "Treatment and Prophylaxis of Bacterial Infections." In *Harrison's Principles of Internal Medicine*, 15th ed. Edited by

Eugene Braunwald et al. New York: McGraw-Hill, 2001, pp. 867-81.

Diasio, Robert B. "Principles of Drug Therapy." In *Cecil Textbook of Medicine*, 22nd ed. Edited by Lee Goldman et al. Philadelphia: Saunders, 2003, pp. 124-34.

Scott, Geoffrey M. *Handbook of Essential Antibiotics.* New York: Gordon & Breach Publishing Group, 2004.

Sherman, Josepha. *War against Germs.* New York: Rosen Publishing Group, 2004.

PERIODICALS

Chung, I., and V. Buhr. "Topical ophthalmic drugs and the pediatric patient." *Optometry* 71, no. 8 (2004): 511–8.

Haider, A., and J. C. Shaw. "Treatment of acne vulgaris." *Journal of the American Medical Association* 292, no. 6 (2004): 726–35.

ORGANIZATIONS

American Academy of Dermatology. 930 N. Meacham Road, PO Box 4014, Schaumburg, IL 60168-4014. Web site: <www.aad.org/>.

American Academy of Family Physicians. 11400 Tomahawk Creek Parkway, Leawood, KS 66211-2672. Web site: <www.aafp.org/>.

American Academy of Pediatrics. 141 Northwest Point Blvd., Elk Grove Village, IL 60007-1098. Web site: <www.aap.org/>.

WEB SITES

"Antibiotic Guide." *Johns Hopkins Point of Care Information Technology.* Available online at <http://hopkins-abxguide.org/> (accessed December 19, 2004).

"The Role of Topical Antibiotics in Dermatologic Practice." *Medscape,* June 25, 2003. Available online at <http://www.medscape.com/viewprogram/2501> (accessed December 19, 2004).

"Topical Antibiotics Are Effective in Bacterial Conjunctivitis." *University of Michigan Department of Pediatrics.* Available online at <www.med.umich.edu/pediatrics/ebm/cats/conjunctivitis.htm> (accessed December 19, 2004).

L. Fleming Fallon, Jr., MD, DrPH

Antidepressants

Definition

An antidepressant is a medication used primarily in the treatment of depression. Depression can occur if some of the chemicals called neurotransmitters in the brain are not functioning effectively. There are three specific chemicals that can affect a person's mood: serotonin, norepinephrine, or dopamine. Antidepressants affect one or more of these chemicals in different ways to help stabilize the chemical imbalance often seen in depression. Antidepressant drugs are not happy pills, and they are not a panacea. They are prescription-only drugs that come with risks as well as benefits and should only be taken under a doctor's supervision. Because children and adolescents experience depression just as adults do, they are sometimes prescribed antidepressants by their physician.

Description

Antidepressants are medicines used to help people who have depression. Antidepressant medications may be indicated for those children and adolescents with bipolar depression, psychotic depression, depression with severe symptoms that prevent effective psychotherapy or counseling, and depression that does not respond to psychotherapy. However, given the psychosocial dynamics that often coexist with depression, antidepressants are usually insufficient as the only treatment for children who have the disorder. Psychotherapy is often recommended as an adjunct treatment along with the prescribed antidepressant. The use of antidepressants among children has been growing steadily since the late 1980s.

All antidepressant medications have a slow onset of action, typically three to five weeks. Although side effects may be observed as early as the first dose, significant therapeutic improvement is always delayed. Most antidepressants are believed to work by slowing the removal of certain chemicals from the brain. These chemicals are called neurotransmitters, which are needed for normal brain function. Antidepressants help people with depression by making these natural chemicals more available to the brain. There are many different kinds of antidepressants, including the ones listed below.

Monoamine oxidase (MAO) inhibitors

MAO inhibitors work by blocking the action of a chemical substance known as monoamine oxidase in the nervous system. Studies done in animals suggest that MAO inhibitors may slow growth in children. Little information on the use of MAO inhibitors in children under 16 years old was available as of 2004.

Tricyclics

Tricyclics have been used to treat depression for a long time. They include amitriptyline, desipramine, imipramine, nortriptyline, and trimipramine. Tricyclic antidepressants work by shoring up the brain's supply of norepinephrine and serotonin, chemicals that are abnormally low in depressed patients. This effect allows the flow of nerve impulses to return to normal. The tricyclics do not act by stimulating the central nervous system or by blocking monoamine oxidase.

Selective serotonin reuptake inhibitors (SSRIs)

SSRIs are a group of antidepressants that includes drugs such as citalopram (Celexa), fluoxetine (Prozac), paroxetine (Paxil), sertraline (Zoloft), and escitalopram (Lexapro). In the early 2000s SSRIs have replaced tricyclic antidepressants as the drugs of choice in the treatment of **depressive disorders**, primarily because of their improved tolerability and safety if taken in overdose. These medicines tend to have fewer side effects than the tricyclics.

Others

There are several antidepressants available as of 2004 that, because they are not chemically structured like the other types of antidepressants, are grouped into the category "other" or miscellaneous. Bupropion (Wellbutrin), mirtazapine (Remeron), and venlafaxine (Effexor) are among those in this category.

General use

SSRIs

Selective serotonin reuptake inhibitors (SSRIs) are considered an improvement over older antidepressants because they are better tolerated and are safer if taken in an overdose. The prescription of SSRIs has risen dramatically in the past several years in children and adolescents age 10 to 19. Some research points out that this increase has coincided with a significant decrease in **suicide** rates in this age group, but it is unknown if SSRIs are directly responsible for this improvement. As of 2004, fluoxetine (Prozac) was the only SSRI that the Food and Drug Administration (FDA) has approved for the treatment of children's depression. Fluoxetine (Prozac), sertraline (Zoloft), and fluvoxamine (Luvox) are approved by the FDA for the treatment of **obsessive-compulsive disorder** because studies have shown they are safe and effective medicines for adolescents with this disorder. An early 2000s study showed that citalopram (Celexa) significantly reduced symptoms of major depression in children and adolescents. Sertraline (Zoloft) was also found in studies

to be effective with youths, slightly more so for adolescents than younger children. Physicians may frequently prescribe many of the SSRI antidepressants besides fluoxetine (Prozac) for children to treat depression, even though they have not been approved for this use by the FDA. This is called "off-label" use. Off-label refers to the use by doctors of FDA-approved drugs for purposes other than those approved by the agency.

Tricyclics

Tricyclic antidepressants (TCAs) are primarily used to treat depression in adults. The most commonly used ones are nortriptyline (Pamelor), desipramine (Elavil), and imipramine (Tofranil). They function similarly and have similar risks and side effects. They are not as effective in treating depression in children who have not reached **puberty**, and for these children should only be used as a second line agent. There is marginal evidence to support the use of tricyclics in the treatment of depression in adolescents, but the effect is likely to be moderate. Although they are actually not very effective as antidepressants with children, they can be quite helpful for a variety of other problems, including attention deficit disorder, enuresis (**bed-wetting**), and obsessive-compulsive disorder. The American Academy of Child and Adolescent Psychiatry (AACAP) does not recommend TCAs as a first-line treatment for youths requiring medicine for depressive disorders. However, the AACAP acknowledges that some young people with depression may respond better to TCAs than to other antidepressants.

MAO inhibitors

Studies on MAO inhibitors have only been performed on adult patients, and there is as of 2004 no specific information comparing the use of MAO inhibitors in children with use in other age groups. However, animal studies have shown that these medicines may slow growth in young children and are therefore not generally recommended for use in children. Parents should be sure to speak with the doctor regarding whether the use of these medicines is appropriate before giving a monoamine oxidase inhibitor to their child.

Others

Bupropion (Wellbutrin) seems to be a better antidepressant for children than the tricyclic antidepressants. Again, as of 2004 bupropion has not been approved for this use by the FDA. It has also proven to be an effective treatment for children diagnosed with attention deficit disorder. The manufacturer of venlafaxine (Effexor) has issued a statement that the drug is not effective in treating depression in children and teenagers and is recommending that venlafaxine (Effexor) not be used in pediatric patients. Early 2000s studies have found increased reports of thinking about suicide and self-harm, among children and teens taking venlafaxine (Effexor). Mirtazapine (Remeron) must be used with caution in children with depression. Studies have shown occurrences of children thinking about suicide or attempting suicide in clinical trials for this medicine.

Precautions

In 2004, the FDA issued a health advisory recommending close observation for worsening depression in both adults and children treated with certain antidepressants. The FDA requested that a warning of a possible association between the use of SSRIs and **suicidal behavior** be inserted in the labeling of these medications. Studies have found no direct link between these antidepressants and worsening depression or increased suicide in children. In fact, no suicide has been reported among the more than 4,100 people studied who take SSRIs. However, the FDA continues to study this issue. Some believe the increased risk of suicide is not related to the SSRIs themselves, but a phenomenon seen when the symptoms of depression first begin to improve. This phenomenon occurs when the depressed person starts to gain more energy but is not yet fully relieved of the depressive symptoms. The drugs under review include bupropion (Wellbutrin), citalopram (Celexa), fluoxetine (Prozac), mirtazapine (Remeron), nefazodone (Serzone), paroxetine (Paxil), sertraline (Zoloft), escitalopram (Lexapro) and venlafaxine (Effexor). It should be again noted that the only drug that has received approval for use in children with major depressive disorder is fluoxetine (Prozac). Several of these drugs, including sertraline (Zoloft) and fluoxetine (Prozac) are approved for the treatment of obsessive-compulsive disorder in pediatric patients. The drug escitalopram (Lexapro) does not appear to help depressed children and adolescents, according to one clinical study.

Side effects

MAO inhibitors

MAO inhibitors have largely been supplanted in therapy because of their high risk of significant side effects, most notably severe, possibly fatal high blood pressure, if foods or alcoholic beverages containing tyramine are consumed. Other side effects include **dizziness**, fainting, **headache**, tremors, muscle twitching, confusion, memory impairment, **anxiety**, agitation, insomnia, weakness, drowsiness, chills, blurred vision, and heart palpitations. Treatment with MAO inhibitors should never be halted abruptly, and should not be stopped without first consulting a physician.

Tricyclics

Although TCAs have been shown to be effective in many clinical situations, their use is associated with potentially serious side effects. The most important of these is the potential for an irregular heartbeat, which can at times (though rarely) be fatal. The vast majority of TCA-related deaths happen when an overdose is taken. Physician will likely monitor blood levels, as well as perform echocardiograms to monitor heart functioning. Other side effects include dry mouth, **constipation**, difficulty urinating, blurred vision, sedation, weight gain, central nervous system and cardiovascular toxicity, delirium, and risk of suicide by overdose. The risk of side effects can be reduced with careful prescribing practices.

SSRIs

Several side effects are possible with SSRIs. Special care should be paid in the first few weeks of taking the prescribed drug. Should nervousness, agitation, irritability, mood instability, or sleeplessness emerge or worsen during treatment with SSRIs, parents should obtain a prompt evaluation by their doctor. Some of the side effects that can be caused by SSRIs include dry mouth, **nausea**, nervousness, insomnia, and headache. Those taking fluoxetine (Prozac) might also have a feeling of being unable to sit still. Children already on any of the SSRIs should remain on the drug if it has been helpful, but they should also be carefully monitored by a physician for evidence of side effects. Once begun, treatment with these medications should not be abruptly stopped, because the child may experience further agitation and restlessness. Families should not discontinue treatment without consulting their physician.

Others

Bupropion (Wellbutrin) has several side effects, including drowsiness, lightheadedness, headache, constipation, dry mouth, nausea, and **vomiting**. Occasionally patients may experience tiredness, muscle twitching, weight loss, blurred vision, and trouble sleeping. The main side effect is appetite suppression. In some children this may also lead to **hypoglycemia** (low blood sugar). It is recommended that children on Wellbutrin should eat mid-morning, mid-afternoon, and bedtime snacks in addition to the usual three meals in a manner similar to that of diabetics. The main risk of Wellbutrin is that it increases the likelihood of seizures, though the incidence is rare. Some of these seizures may be related to hypoglycemia and so may be prevented by sticking to the diet as described

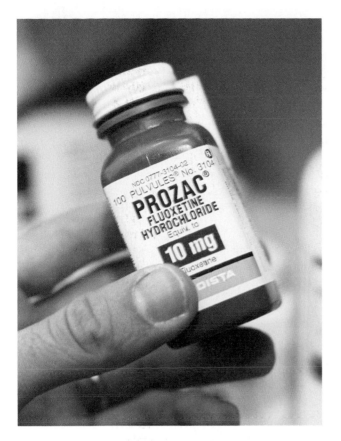

The antidepressant Prozac is used to treat depressive disorders. *(© David Butow/Corbis Saba.)*

above. The drug should not be used when there is a past history of seizures or a **family** history of epilepsy.

Interactions

MAO inhibitors

MAO inhibitors have many dietary restrictions, and people taking them need to follow the dietary guidelines and physician's instructions very carefully. A rapid, potentially fatal increase in blood pressure can occur if foods or alcoholic beverages containing tyramine are ingested by a person already taking MAO inhibitors. Foods containing tyramine include sour cream; parmesan, mozzarella, cheddar and other cheeses; beef or chicken liver; cured meats; game meat; caviar; dried fish; bananas; avocados; raisins; soy sauce; fava beans; and caffeine-containing products like colas, coffee and tea, and chocolate. Beverages to be avoided include beer, red wine, other alcoholic beverages, non-alcoholic and reduced alcohol beer, and red wine products.

SSRIs

SSRIs should not be used with any drug that increases serotonin concentrations, including MAO inhi-

bitors, tramadol, sibutramine, meperidine, sumatriptan, lithium, St. John's wort, ginkgo biloba, and some antipsychotic agents. A "serotonin syndrome" may occur, where mental status changes and where agitation, sweating, shivering, tremors, **diarrhea**, and uncoordination, and **fever** may develop. This syndrome may be life-threatening. SSRIs interact with a number of other drugs that act on the central nervous system. Care should be used in combining SSRIs with major or minor tranquilizers or with anti-epileptic agents such as phenytoin (Dilantin) or carbamazepine (Tegretol).

Tricyclics

Tricyclic antidepressants should not be taken with the gastric acid inhibitor cimetidine (Tagamet), since this increases the blood levels of the tricyclic compound. TCAs have many interactions, and specialized references should be consulted. Specifically, it is best to avoid other drugs with anticholinergic effects. Tricyclics should not be taken with the **antibiotics** grepafloxacin and sprafloxacin, since the combination may cause serious heart arrythmias.

Others

Alcohol, phenothiazines, and benzodiazepines may all increase the likelihood of seizures if consumed with bupropion (Wellbutrin).

Parental concerns

Major depression in children and adolescents is a serious condition that should be treated in a way that includes careful follow-up and monitoring. If the physician determines that medication is indicated, parents should ensure their child continues to receive ongoing assessment. Selection of an antidepressant for their child is done on an individual basis, as drugs may work differently for different people. What is effective for some may not be effective for others. If one antidepressant is ineffective, then there is probably another one that can be tried. All potentially effective treatments can be associated with side effects. A careful weighing of risks and benefits, with appropriate follow-up to help reduce risks, is the best that can be recommended.

See also Depression.

Resources

BOOKS

Mondimore, Francis Mark. *Adolescent Depression.* Baltimore, MD: Johns Hopkins University Press, 2002.

PERIODICALS

Ables, Adrienne Z., and Otis L. Baughman III. "Antidepressants: Update on New Agents and Indications." *American Family Physician* 67, no. 3 (February 1, 2003): 547–54.

ORGANIZATIONS

National Alliance for the Mentally Ill. Colonial Place Three, 2107 Wilson Blvd., Suite 300, Arlington, VA 22201–3042. Web site: <www.nami.org>.

National Mental Health Association. 2001 N. Beauregard Street, 12th Floor, Alexandria, Virginia 22311. Web site: <www.nmha.org>.

WEB SITES

National Institute of Mental Health. Available online at <www.nimh.nih.gov/> (accessed October 16, 2004).

National Mental Health Association. Available online at <www.mentalhealth.org> (accessed October 16, 2004).

Deanna M. Swartout-Corbeil, RN

Antiepileptics

Definition

Antiepileptic drugs are medicines that reduce the frequency of epileptic seizures.

This class of drugs includes some drugs that have other uses as well. Phenobarbital is a barbiturate. Barbiturates were once widely used as sleeping pills and are still used in anesthesia for surgery. Clonazepam, clorazepate, and diazepam are members of the benzodiazepine group of drugs and are best known for their use as tran-

quilizers. Phenytoin is used both to control epileptic seizures and to control irregular heart beats.

Description

There are several different types of epilepsy. Different drugs work best on different types of epilepsy. Following is a list of some of the drugs and their uses:

- topamax (Topiramate), keppra, and ACTH: for infantile spasms (IS)
- ativan: for status epilepticas
- phenobarbital: widely used for tonic-clonic but effective in all forms of epilepsy
- phenytoin (Dilantin): used in tonic-clonic and psychomotor epilepsy
- ethosuximide (Zarontin): used to treat absence seizures
- methsuximide (Celontin): used to treat absence seizures
- zonisamide (Zonegran): used to treat partial seizures
- clonazepam (Klonopin): a benzodiazepine, used to treat absence, myoclonic, and akinetic seizures
- clorazepate (Tranxene): a benzodiazepine used to treat partial seizures
- diazepam (Valium): a benzodiazepine used for treatment of status epilepticus but effective against all forms of epilepsy
- primidone (Mysoline, Myidone, Sertan): useful for tonic-clonic, psychomotor, and focal epilepsy
- valproic acid and sodium valproate (Depakene, Depakote): used to treat all types of generalized seizures
- carbamazepine (Carbatrol, Tegretol): used in treatment of tonic-clonic, mixed, and psychomotor seizures
- felbamate (Felbatol): used primarily in adults but may be used to treat seizures associated with Lennox-Gastaut syndrome
- oxcarbazepine (Trileptal): for treatment of complex-partial, simple-partial, and focal seizures
- lamotrigine (Lamictal): used primarily in adults to treat simple and complex partial seizures but may be used to treat seizures associated with Lennox-Gastaut syndrome in children

General use

Although epilepsy is a collective term for a variety of different types of seizures, all forms of epilepsy start with a random discharge of nerve impulses into the brain. Antiepileptic drugs act by either raising the seizure threshold or by limiting the spread of impulses from one nerve to another inside the brain. As of 2004 the exact mechanism of action is not understood, but there are theories about how some of these drugs work.

Phenobarbital appears to act by slowing down all parts of the brain.

Hydantoins, the class that includes phenytoin, mephenytoin, and ethotoin, seem to work by reducing the flow of sodium into and out of nerve cells. This makes the cells less likely to send out spontaneous impulses, which are the beginning of an epileptic seizure.

Succinimides (ethosuximide, methsuximide, phensuximide) elevate the seizure threshold and make it harder for a nerve impulse to spread from one nerve to another.

Zonisamide may work in a manner similar to the hydantoins, by restricting sodium flow, but some studies contradict this theory.

Benzodiazepines may work by stimulating some brain chemicals that normally slow down nerve function, but the exact mechanism is not known.

Felbamate is similar to the tranquilizer meprobamate (Equanil, Miltown) and may work by blocking the effects of some of the brain chemicals that stimulate the nervous system.

Precautions

Anticpileptic drugs have a large number of side effects and possible adverse effects. To work best, the blood levels of drugs must be kept within a fairly narrow range. Patients should be seen by a qualified physician on a regular basis and, if required, have their blood tested routinely. Too high a blood level of these drugs is likely to cause toxic reactions, while a level that is too low may lead to seizures.

Side effects

Most anticonvulsant medications cause some drowsiness and stomach upset. The following list gives some of the common adverse effects of the various classes of drugs. Parents should consult specific references for more comprehensive lists.

Barbiturates cause the following side effects:

- clumsiness
- dizziness
- constipation
- depression
- faintness

Benzodiazepines cause the following side effects:

- fatigue
- abnormal behavior which can include hallucinations and agitation
- slowed breathing and slowed heart rate
- increased or decreased appetite
- rash and itching

Hydantoins cause the following side effects:

- confusion
- dizziness
- growth of the gums
- severe skin reactions
- stuttering and trembling

Succinimides cause the following side effects:

- dizziness and loss of balance
- severe skin reactions
- depression
- headache
- aggressive behavior

Valproic acid and sodium valproate cause the following side effects:

- stomach and intestinal discomfort
- weight gain or loss
- hair loss
- menstrual bleeding changes
- trembling

Interactions

These drugs have many interactions. People should consult specific references for full information regarding the interactions of all drugs that may be used to treat epilepsy.

Phenobarbital and the hydantoins have a large number of other interactions, but most of the drugs involved are not commonly used in patients under the age of 18 years. The succinimides have no significant drug interactions.

Valproic acid and sodium valproate interact with many of the other drugs used to treat epilepsy. If valproates are added to an existing anti-epileptic drug regimen or other drugs are added to a regimen that contains valproate, additional dose adjustments will usually be needed.

Absence seizure—A brief seizure with an accompanying loss of awareness or alertness. Also known as a petit mal seizure.

Lennox-Gastaut syndrome—A severe form of epilepsy that is characterized by the onset in early childhood of frequent seizures of multiple types and by developmental delay.

Seizure threshold—The amount of stimulation required to induce a seizure.

Sodium—An element; sodium is the most common electrolyte found in animal blood serum.

Tonic-clonic seizure—This is the most common type of seizure among all age groups and is categorized into several phases beginning with vague symptoms hours or days before an attack. These seizures are sometimes called grand mal seizures.

Cimetidine (Tagamet) increases the effects of diazepam, clonazepam, and clorazepate.

Interaction prevention

Because antiepileptic drugs have large numbers of adverse effects and drug interactions, they should be prescribed only by physicians who are experienced in their use. Parents should consult specific references for complete information on the drugs related to their child's case.

Best effects and lowest toxicity are achieved when the blood levels of these drugs are kept constant. Maintaining that constant level requires taking the drugs at the same time each day.

Excessive gum growth associated with the hydantoins can normally be prevented or minimized by good dental care.

Patients taking antiepileptic drugs should not receive additional medications without checking with a physician or pharmacist for possible drug interactions. This precaution includes over-the-counter remedies.

Parental concerns

For liquid dosage forms, parents should always use a medicinal teaspoon or calibrated teaspoon. These are designed to deliver an exact amount of medication. Household teaspoons vary in size and should not be used for measuring medication.

Different dosage forms of the same drug may vary in their onset and duration of action. This fact is particularly relevant to phenytoin, which comes in liquid, chewable tablets, short-acting capsules and long-acting capsules. Patients should not switch from one dosage form to another without consulting their physician.

Because children may not be able to describe some of the symptoms associated with some of the adverse effects of these drugs, any evidence of change in behavior or activity should be discussed with the physician who prescribed the drug.

See also Seizure disorder.

Resources

BOOKS

Beers, Mark H., and Robert Berkow, eds. *The Merck Manual*, 2nd home ed. West Point, PA: Merck & Co., 2004.

Mcevoy, Gerald, et al. *AHFS Drug Information 2004*. Bethesda, MD: American Society of Healthsystems Pharmacists, 2004.

Siberry, George K., and Robert Iannone, eds. *The Harriet Lane Handbook*, 15th ed. Philadelphia: Mosby Publishing, 2000.

PERIODICALS

Dutta, S., et al. "Divalproex-ER pharmacokinetics in older children and adolescents." *Pediatric Neurology* 30 (May 2004): 330–7.

ORGANIZATIONS

American Neurological Association. 5841 Cedar Lake Road, Suite 204, Minneapolis, MN 55416. Web site: <www.aneuroa.org>.

Epilepsy Foundation. 4351 Garden City Drive, Landover, MD 20785-7223. Web site: <www.efa.org>.

WEB SITES

"Epilepsy." *MedlinePlus.* Available online at <www.nlm.nih.gov/medlineplus/epilepsy.html> (accessed December 20, 2004).

Samuel Uretsky, PharmD

Antihistamines

Definition

Antihistamines are drugs used to treat the symptoms of **allergies** and **allergic rhinitis** by blocking the action of histamine, a chemical released by the immune system in allergic reactions.

Description

Antihistamines are used to treat the sneezing, runny nose, and itchy eyes of allergies and allergic **rhinitis**, as well as allergic skin reactions and anaphylactic reactions to insect **stings** and certain foods. Antihistamines are available as prescription and over-the-counter tablets, topical preparations, nasal sprays, and eye drops.

Antihistamines work by blocking the effects of histamine, a chemical released by mast cells during an allergic response to an allergen. Histamine irritates and inflames the airways to produce sneezing and mucus production. Antihistamines attach to the areas on cells that histamines attach to, thereby blocking the allergic response.

Antihistamines are most effective when taken before exposure to an allergen. When used over time as an allergy treatment, antihistamines reduce the amount of histamine released by cells and decrease the likelihood that an allergic reaction will occur.

General use

Antihistamines are prescribed or recommended for infants, children, and adolescents with allergies and allergic rhinitis. Depending on the type of allergy, oral antihistamines may be taken regularly or seasonally to combat responses to allergens. Common allergens include dog and cat hair, dust mites, grass and tree pollen, and molds and mildew. For allergies that produce nasal symptoms, an antihistamine nasal spray may be used. For itchy eyes, antihistamine eye drops may be used.

Antihistamine tablets and topical creams, gels, sprays, or ointments are used to treat skin **hives** related to **food allergies** and **itching** and hives associated with allergic **contact dermatitis** and insect **bites and stings**.

In addition to treating allergies, some antihistamines have side effects that are used to treat other conditions. The strong sedating effect of some antihistamines is used to treat insomnia and difficulties in falling asleep. Some antihistamines also help inhibit **nausea and vomiting** and reduce **motion sickness**.

Commonly used antihistamines include the following:

- diphenhydramine (Benadryl)
- loratadine (Claritin)
- cetirizine (Zyrtec)
- fexofenadine (Allegra)
- clemastine fumarate (Tavist)
- chlorpheniramine (Chlor Trimeton)
- brompheniramine (Dimetapp)

Precautions

Some antihistamines produce drowsiness, although clinical studies have shown that children are less susceptible to antihistamine-induced drowsiness than adults. Some nonsedating antihistamines can act as stimulants in children and produce hyperactivity and sleeplessness.

Children with certain medical conditions may not be able to take antihistamines. The following are absolute or relative contraindications to use of antihistamines. The significance of the contraindication will vary with the drug and dose.

- glaucoma
- hyperthyroidism (overactive thyroid)
- high blood pressure
- heart disease
- ulcers or other stomach problems
- stomach or intestinal blockage
- liver disease
- kidney disease
- bladder obstruction
- diabetes

Side effects

The frequency and severity of adverse effects will vary depending on the antihistamine.

Central nervous system reactions include drowsiness, sedation, **dizziness**, faintness, disturbed coordination, lassitude, confusion, restlessness, excitation, tremor, seizures, **headache**, insomnia, euphoria, blurred vision, hallucinations, disorientation, disturbing dreams/nightmares, schizophrenic-like reactions, weakness, vertigo, nerve **pain**, and convulsions.

Gastrointestinal problems include increased appetite, decreased appetite, **nausea**, **vomiting**, **diarrhea**, and **constipation**.

Hematologic reactions are rare but may be severe. These include anemia, or breakdown of red blood cells; reduced platelets; reduced white cells; and bone marrow failure.

A large number of additional reactions have been reported. Not all apply to every drug, and some reactions may not be drug related. Some of the other adverse effects are chest tightness; wheezing; nasal stuffiness;

dry mouth, nose, and throat; **sore throat**; respiratory depression; sneezing; and a burning sensation in the nose.

Interactions

Drug interactions vary with the chemical class of antihistamine. In general, antihistamines increase the effects of other sedatives, including alcohol.

Monoamine oxidase inhibitor **antidepressants** may prolong and increase the effects of some antihistamines.

Parental concerns

For children who resist taking pills, many antihistamines are available as flavored chewable tablets, tablets that easily dissolve on the tongue, and in flavored syrups. Because many over-the-counter allergy medicines contain multiple drugs, parents should be sure to read the prescribing and dosage information for any antihistamine their children are taking to ensure safe use.

Resources

BOOKS

Simms, F. Estelle. *Histamine and Ill-Antihistamines in Allergic Disease.* New York: Marcel Dekker Incorporated, 2002.

Taylor, R., J. Krohn, and E. M. Larson. *Allergy Relief and Prevention*, 3rd ed. Vancouver: Hartley and Marks, 2000.

ORGANIZATIONS

Allergy and Asthma Network: Mothers of Asthmatics. 2751 Prosperity Ave., Suite 150, Fairfax, VA 22031. Web site: <www.aanma.org>.

American Academy of Allergy, Asthma, and Immunology. 611 East Wells St., Milwaukee, WI 53202. Web site: <www.aaaai.org>.

WEB SITES

"All about Allergies." *Nemours Foundation.* Available online at <www.kidshealth.org/parent/medical/allergies/allergy.html> (accessed October 24, 2004).

Jennifer E. Sisk, MA

Antisocial behavior

Definition

Antisocial behaviors are disruptive acts characterized by covert and overt hostility and intentional aggression toward others. Antisocial behaviors exist along a severity continuum and include repeated violations of social rules, defiance of authority and of the rights of others, deceitfulness, theft, and reckless disregard for self and others. Antisocial behavior can be identified in children as young as three or four years of age. If left unchecked these coercive behavior patterns will persist and escalate in severity over time, becoming a chronic behavioral disorder.

Description

Antisocial behavior may be overt, involving aggressive actions against siblings, peers, parents, teachers, or other adults, such as verbal abuse, bullying and hitting; or covert, involving aggressive actions against property, such as theft, vandalism, and fire-setting. Covert antisocial behaviors in early childhood may include noncompliance, sneaking, **lying**, or secretly destroying another's property. Antisocial behaviors also include drug and alcohol abuse and high-risk activities involving self and others.

Demographics

Between 4 and 6 million American children have been identified with antisocial behavior problems. These disruptive behaviors are one of the most common forms of psychopathology, accounting for half of all childhood mental health referrals.

Gender differences in antisocial behavior patterns are evident as early as age three or four. There has been far less research into the nature and development pattern of antisocial behavior in girls. Pre-adolescent boys are far more likely to engage in overtly aggressive antisocial behaviors than girls. Boys exhibit more physical and verbal aggression, whereas antisocial behavior in girls is more indirect and relational, involving harmful social manipulation of others. The gender differences in the way antisocial behavior is expressed may be related to the differing rate of maturity between girls and boys. Physical aggression is expressed at the earliest stages of development, then direct verbal threats, and, last, indirect strategies for manipulating the existing social structure.

Antisocial behaviors may have an early onset, identifiable as soon as age four, or late onset, manifesting in middle or late **adolescence**. Some research indicates that girls are more likely than boys to exhibit late onset antisocial behavior. Late onset antisocial behaviors are less persistent and more likely to be discarded as a behavioral strategy than those that first appear in early childhood.

As many as half of all elementary school children who demonstrate antisocial behavior patterns continue these behaviors into adolescence, and as many as 75 percent of adolescents who demonstrate antisocial behaviors continue to do so into early adulthood.

Causes and symptoms

Antisocial behavior develops and is shaped in the context of coercive social interactions within the **family**, community, and educational environment. It is also influenced by the child's **temperament** and irritability, cognitive ability, the level of involvement with deviant peers, exposure to violence, and deficit of cooperative problem-solving skills. Antisocial behavior is frequently accompanied by other behavioral and developmental problems such as hyperactivity, depression, learning disabilities, and impulsivity.

Multiple risk factors for development and persistence of antisocial behaviors include genetic, neurobiological, and environmental stressors beginning at the prenatal stage and often continuing throughout the childhood years.

Genetic factors are thought to contribute substantially to the development of antisocial behaviors. Genetic factors, including abnormalities in the structure of the prefrontal cortex of the brain, may play a role in an inherited predisposition to antisocial behaviors.

Neurobiological risks include maternal drug use during pregnancy, birth complications, low birth weight, prenatal brain damage, traumatic **head injury**, and chronic illness.

High-risk factors in the family setting include the following:

- parental history of antisocial behaviors
- parental alcohol and drug abuse
- chaotic and unstable home life
- absence of good parenting skills
- use of coercive and corporal punishment
- parental disruption due to **divorce**, death, or other separation
- parental psychiatric disorders, especially maternal depression
- economic distress due to poverty and unemployment

Heavy exposure to media violence through television, movies, Internet sites, **video games**, and even cartoons has long been associated with an increase in the likelihood that a child will become desensitized to violence and behave in aggressive and antisocial ways. However, research relating the use of violent video games with antisocial behavior is inconsistent and varies in design and quality, with findings of both increased and decreased aggression after exposure to violent video games.

Companions and peers are influential in the development of antisocial behaviors. Some studies of boys with antisocial behaviors have found that companions are mutually reinforcing with their talk of rule breaking in ways that predict later delinquency and substance abuse.

When to call the doctor

Parents and teachers who notice a pattern of repeated lying, cheating, **stealing**, bullying, hitting, noncompliance, and other disruptive behaviors should not ignore these symptoms. Early screening of at-risk children is critical to deterring development of a persistent pattern of antisocial behavior. Early detection and appropriate intervention, particularly during the **preschool** years and middleschool years, is the best means of interrupting the developmental trajectory of antisocial behavior patterns. Serious childhood antisocial behaviors can lead to diagnoses of **conduct disorder** (CD) or **oppositional defiant disorder** (ODD). Children who exhibit antisocial behaviors are at an increased risk for alcohol use disorders (AUDs).

Diagnosis

Systematic diagnostic interviews with parents and children provide opportunity for a thorough assessment of individual risk factors and family and societal dynamics. Such assessment should include parent-adolescent relationships; peer characteristics; school, home, and community environment; and overall health of the individual.

Various diagnostic instruments have been developed for evidence-based identification of antisocial behavior in children. The onset, frequency, and severity of antisocial behaviors such as stealing, lying, cheating, sneaking, peer rejection, low academic achievement, negative attitude, and aggressive behaviors are accessed to determine appropriate intervention and treatment.

Treatment

Enhanced parent-teacher communications and the availability of school psychologists and counselors trained in family intervention within the school setting are basic requirements for successful intervention and treatment of childhood antisocial behaviors.

School-based programs from early childhood onward that teach conflict resolution, emotional literacy, and anger management skills have been shown to interrupt the development of antisocial behavior in low-risk students. Students who may be at higher risk because of difficult family and environmental circumstances will benefit from more individualized prevention efforts, including counseling, academic support, social-skills training, and behavior contracting.

Academic settings with the capacity to deliver professional parental support and provide feedback in a motivating way can help parents to develop and hone effective parenting skills that may interrupt further progression of antisocial behavior patterns in their children. Access to written and video information on parenting skills and information about community family resources, as well as promotion of parent-support groups, are effective intervention strategies for changing family dynamics that shape antisocial behavior in the children.

Older students who already exhibit a persistent pattern of antisocial behavior can be helped with intensive individualized services that may involve community mental health agencies and other outside intervention.

KEY TERMS

Alcohol use disorder (AUD)—The repetitive, long-term ingestion of alcohol in ways that impair psychosocial functioning and health, leading to problems with personal relationships, school, or work. Alcohol use disorders include alcohol dependence, alcohol abuse, alcohol intoxication, and alcohol withdrawal.

Coercive behavior—Maladaptive behaviors engaged in as a means of avoiding or escaping aversive events. Coercive behavior may include whining, noncompliance, and lying.

Conduct disorder—A behavioral and emotional disorder of childhood and adolescence. Children with a conduct disorder act inappropriately, infringe on the rights of others, and violate societal norms.

Oppositional defiant disorder (ODD)—A persistent disruptive behavior that includes three or more of the following types of antisocial behaviors occurring frequently over a six-month period: loss of temper; arguments with adults; defiance or refusal to comply with adult's requests/rules; annoying others deliberately and being easily annoyed;, blaming others with unwillingness to accept responsibility for mistakes or behavior; angry, resentful, spiteful, and vindictive behaviors.

Community-based programs, including youth centers and recreational programs with trained therapists, can provide additional support for at-risk children.

Prognosis

The longer antisocial behavior patterns persist, the more intractable they become. Early-onset conduct problems left untreated are more likely to result in the development of chronic antisocial behavior than if the disruptive behavior begins in adolescence. Though it is never too late to intervene, researchers warn that if by age eight a child has not learned ways other than coercion to meet his social goals, he has a high chance of continuing with antisocial behavior throughout his lifetime.

Longitudinal studies have found that as many as 71 percent of chronic juvenile offenders had progressed from childhood antisocial behaviors through a history of early arrests to a pattern of chronic law breaking.

Prevention

Healthy **nutrition** and prenatal care, a safe and secure family and social environment, early **bonding** with an emotionally mature and healthy parent, role models for prosocial behaviors, non-coercive methods of parenting, peer relationships with prosocial individuals, and early intervention when problems first appear are all excellent means of assuring development of prosocial behaviors and reducing and extinguishing antisocial behaviors in children.

Parental concerns

Parents may hesitate to seek help for children with antisocial behavior patterns out of **fear** of the child being negatively labeled or misdiagnosed. Almost all children will engage in some form of antisocial behavior at various stages of development. Skilled parents will be able to lovingly confront the child and help the child recognize that certain behaviors are unacceptable. However if these conduct disturbances persist and worsen, they should be taken seriously as precursors to more serious problems. Early intervention is important for the sake of the child and the entire family system.

Resources

BOOKS

Coloroso, Barbara. *The Bully, the Bullied, and the Bystander.* New York: Harper Collins, 2003.

Connor, Daniel F. *Aggression and Antisocial Behavior in Children and Adolescents.* New York: Guilford Press, 2002.

Reid, John B., et al. *Antisocial Behavior in Children and Adolescents.* Washington, DC: American Psychological Association, 2002.

Walker, Hill M., et. al. *Antisocial Behavior in School*, 2nd ed. Belmont, CA: Wadsworth/Thomson Learning, 2004.

WEB SITES

Clark, Duncan B., et al., "Childhood Antisocial Behavior and Adolescent Alcohol Use Disorders." *National Institute on Alcohol Abuse and Alcoholism*, November 2002. Available online at <www.niaaa.nih.gov/publications/arh26-2/109-115htm> (accessed October 11, 2004).

Wood, Derek. "What is Antisocial Personality Disorder?" *Mental Health Matters.* Available online at <www.mental-health-matters.com/articles/print.php?artID=51> (accessed October 11, 2004).

Clare Hanrahan

Antisocial personality disorder

Definition

Antisocial behavior is that which is verbally or physically harmful to other people, animals, or property, including behavior that severely violates social expectations for a given environment. Antisocial personality disorder in adults is also referred to as sociopathy or psychopathy.

Description

Antisocial behavior can be broken down into two components: the presence of antisocial (i.e., angry, aggressive, or disobedient) behavior and the absence of prosocial (i.e., communicative, affirming, or cooperative) behavior. Most children exhibit some antisocial behavior during their development, and different children demonstrate varying levels of prosocial and antisocial behavior. Some children—for example, the popular but rebellious child—may exhibit high levels of both antisocial and prosocial behaviors. Others—for example, the withdrawn, thoughtful child—may exhibit low levels of both types of behaviors.

High levels of antisocial behavior are considered a clinical disorder. Young children may exhibit hostility towards authority, and be diagnosed with oppositional-defiant disorder. Older children may lie, steal, or engage in violent behaviors, and be diagnosed with **conduct disorder**. A minority of children with conduct disorder whose behavior does not improve as they mature will go on to develop adult antisocial personality disorder.

A salient characteristic of antisocial children and adolescents is that they appear to have no feelings. They demonstrate no care for others' feelings or remorse for hurting others, and tend not to show their own feelings except for anger and hostility, and even these are communicated through aggressive acts and are not necessarily expressed through affect. One analysis of antisocial behavior is that it is a defense mechanism that helps children avoid painful feelings, or avoid the **anxiety** caused by lack of control over the environment.

Antisocial behavior may also be a direct attempt to alter the environment. Social learning theory suggests that negative behaviors are reinforced during childhood by parents, caregivers, or peers. In one formulation, a child's negative behavior (e.g., whining, hitting) initially serves to stop the parent from behaving in ways that are aversive to the child (the parent may be fighting with a partner, yelling at a sibling, or even crying). The child will apply the learned behavior at school, and a vicious cycle sets in: he or she is rejected, becomes angry and attempts to force his will or assert his pride, and is then further rejected by the very peers from whom he might learn more positive behaviors. As the child matures, "mutual avoidance" sets in with the parent(s), as each party avoids the negative behaviors of the other. Consequently, the child receives little care or supervision and, especially during **adolescence**, is free to join peers who have similarly learned antisocial means of expression.

Demographics

Mental health professionals agree, and rising rates of serious school disciplinary problems, delinquency, and violent crime indicate, that antisocial behavior in general is increasing. Thirty to 70% of childhood psychiatric admissions are for disruptive behavior disorders, and diagnoses of behavior disorders are increasing overall. A small percentage of antisocial children (about 3% of males and 1% of females) grow up to become adults with antisocial personality disorder, and a greater proportion suffer from the social, academic, and occupational failures resulting from their antisocial behavior.

Causes and symptoms

Factors that contribute to a particular child's antisocial behavior vary, but they usually include some form of **family** problems (e.g., marital discord, harsh or inconsistent disciplinary practices or actual **child abuse**, frequent changes in primary caregiver or in housing, learning or cognitive disabilities, or health problems). Attention deficit/hyperactivity disorder is highly correlated with antisocial behavior.

A child may exhibit antisocial behavior in response to a specific stressor (such as the death of a parent or a **divorce**) for a limited period of time, but this is not considered a psychiatric condition. Children and adolescents with antisocial behavior problems have an increased risk of accidents, school failure, early alcohol and substance use, **suicide**, and criminal behavior. The elements of a moderate to severely antisocial personality are established as early as kindergarten. Antisocial children score high on traits of impulsiveness, but low on anxiety and reward-dependence—the degree to which they value, and are motivated by, approval from others. Yet underneath their tough exterior, antisocial children have low **self-esteem**.

Although antisocial personality disorder is only diagnosed in people over age 18, the symptoms are similar to those of conduct disorder, and the criteria for diagnosis include the onset of conduct disorder before the age of 15. According to the *Diagnostic and Statistical Manual of Mental Disorders, 4th Edition Text Revision (DSM-IV-TR)*, people with antisocial personality disorder demonstrate a pattern of antisocial behavior since age 15.

The adult with antisocial personality disorder displays at least three of the following behaviors:

- fails to conform to social norms, as indicated by frequently performing illegal acts, and pursuing illegal occupations
- is deceitful and manipulative of others, often in order to obtain money, sex, or drugs
- is impulsive, holding a succession of jobs or residences
- is irritable or aggressive, engaging in physical fights
- exhibits reckless disregard for the **safety** of self or others, misusing motor vehicles, or playing with fire
- is consistently irresponsible, failing to find or sustain work or to pay bills and debts
- demonstrates lack of remorse for the harm his or her behavior causes others

An adult diagnosed with antisocial personality disorder will demonstrate few of his or her own feelings beyond contempt for others. Authorities have linked antisocial personality disorder with abuse, either physical or sexual, during childhood, neurological disorders (which are often undiagnosed), and low IQ. Those with a parent with an antisocial personality disorder or substance abuse problem are more likely to develop the disorder. The antisocially disordered person may be poverty-stricken, homeless, a substance abuser, or have an extensive criminal record. Antisocial personality disorder is associated with low socioeconomic status and urban settings.

When to call the doctor

When symptoms of antisocial behavior appear, a child should be taken to his or her health care provider as soon as possible for evaluation and possible referral to a mental health care professional. If a child or teen reveals at any time that he/she has had recent thoughts of self-injury or suicide, or if he/she demonstrates behavior that compromises personal safety or the safety of others, professional assistance from a mental health care provider or care facility should be sought immediately.

Diagnosis

Antisocial behavior and childhood antisocial disorders such as conduct disorder may be diagnosed by a family physician or pediatrician, social worker, school counselor, psychiatrist, or psychologist. A comprehensive evaluation of the child should ideally include interviews with the child and parents, a full social and medical history, review of educational records, a cognitive evaluation, and a psychiatric exam.

One or more clinical inventories or scales may be used to assess the child, including the Youth Self-Report, the School Social Behavior Scales (SSBS), the Overt Aggression Scale (OAS), Behavioral **Assessment** System for Children (BASC), Child Behavior Checklist (CBCL), the Nisonger Child Behavior Rating Form (N-CBRF), Clinical Global Impressions scale (CGI), and Diagnostic Interview Schedule for Children (DISC). The tests are verbal and/or written and are administered in both hospital and outpatient settings.

Treatment

The most important goals of treating antisocial behavior are to measure and describe the individual child's or adolescent's actual problem behaviors and to effectively teach him or her the positive behaviors that should be adopted instead. In severe cases, medication will be administered to control behavior, but it should not be used as a substitute for therapy. A child who experiences explosive rage may respond well to medication. Ideally, an interdisciplinary team of teachers, social workers, and guidance counselors will work with parents or caregivers to provide services to help the child in all aspects of his or her life: home, school, work, and social contexts. In many cases, parents themselves need intensive training on modeling and reinforcing appropriate behaviors in their child, as well as in providing appropriate **discipline** to prevent inappropriate behavior.

A variety of methods may be employed to deliver social skills training, but especially with diagnosed antisocial disorders, the most effective methods are systemic therapies which address **communication skills** among the whole family or within a peer group of other antisocial children or adolescents. These probably work best because they entail actually developing (or redeveloping) positive relationships between the child or adolescent and other people. Methods used in social skills training include modeling, role-playing, corrective feedback, and token reinforcement systems. Regardless of the method used, the child's level of cognitive and emotional development often determines the success of treatment. Adolescents capable of learning communication and problem-solving skills are more likely to improve their relations with others.

Unfortunately, conduct disorders, which are the primary form of diagnosed antisocial behavior, are highly resistant to treatment. Few institutions can afford the comprehensiveness and intensity of services required to support and change a child's whole system of behavior. In most cases, for various reasons, treatment is terminated (usually by the client) long before it is completed. Often, the child may be fortunate to be diagnosed at all. Schools are frequently the first to address behavior problems, and regular classroom teachers only spend a limited amount of time with individual students. **Special education** teachers and counselors have a better chance at instituting long-term treatment programs—if the student stays in the same school for a period of years. One study showed teenage boys with conduct disorder had had an average of nine years of treatment by 15 different institutions. Treatments averaged seven months each.

Studies show that children who are given social skills instruction decrease their antisocial behavior, especially when the instruction is combined with some form of supportive peer group or **family therapy**. But the long-term effectiveness of any form of therapy for antisocial behavior has not been demonstrated. The fact that peer groups have such a strong influence on behavior suggests that schools that employ collaborative learning and the mainstreaming of antisocial students with regular students may prove most beneficial to the antisocial child. Because the classroom is a natural environment, learned skills do not need to be transferred. By dividing the classroom into groups and explicitly stating procedures for group interactions, teachers can create opportunities for positive interaction between antisocial and other students.

Prognosis

Early and intensive intervention is the best hope for children exhibiting antisocial behaviors or diagnosed conduct disorder. For those who grow into adults with antisocial personality disorder, the prognosis is not promising; the condition is difficult to treat and tends to be chronic. Although there are medications available that could quell some of the symptoms of antisocial personality disorder, noncompliance or abuse of the drugs prevents their widespread use. The most successful treatment programs are long-term, structured residential settings in which the patient systematically earns privileges as he or she modifies behavior.

Prevention

A supportive, nurturing, and structured home environment is believed to be the best defense against antisocial behavioral problems. Children with learning disabilities and/or difficulties in school should get appropriate academic assistance. Addressing these problems

KEY TERMS

Attention deficit hyperactivity disorder (ADHD)—A condition in which a person (usually a child) has an unusually high activity level and a short attention span. People with the disorder may act impulsively and may have learning and behavioral problems.

Major depressive disorder—A mood disorder characterized by profound feelings of sadness or despair.

Modeling—A type of teaching method used in social skills training. Therapists who use this method may offer positive and negative examples of the behaviors that make up a social skill.

Prosocial behavior—Actions that promote communication, cooperation, and other positive interactions with peers and family members.

when they first appear helps to prevent the frustration and low self-esteem that may lead to antisocial issues later.

Parental concerns

A child with antisocial behavioral problems can have a tremendous impact on the home environment and on the physical and emotional welfare of siblings and others sharing the household, as well as their peers at school. While seeking help for their child, parents must remain sensitive to the needs of their other children. This may mean avoiding leaving siblings alone together, getting assistance with childcare, or even seeking residential or hospital treatment for the child if the safety and well-being of other family members is in jeopardy. Parents should also maintain an open dialog with their child's teachers to ensure that their child receives appropriate educational assistance and that classmates are not put at risk.

See also Aggression; Conduct disorder; Oppositional defiant disorder.

Resources

BOOKS

American Psychiatric Association. *Diagnostic and Statistical Manual of Mental Disorders,* 4th ed., text revision (DSM-IV-TR). Washington, DC: American Psychiatric Press, Inc., 2000.

Connor, Daniel. *Aggression and Antisocial Behavior in Children and Adolescents: Research and Treatment.* New York: Guilford Press, 2002.

Eddy, J. Mark. *Conduct Disorders: The Latest Assessment and Treatment Strategies.* Kansas City, MO: Compact Clinics, 2003.

PERIODICALS

Cellini, Henry R. "Biopsychological Treatment of Antisocial and Conduct-Disordered Offenders." *Federal Probation* 66, no. 2 (September 2002): 78+.

Connor, Daniel F. "Aggression and Antisocial Behavior in Youth." *Brown University Child & Adolescent Behavior Letter* 18, no. 9 (September 2002): 1+.

ORGANIZATIONS

The American Academy of Child and Adolescent Psychiatry. 3615 Wisconsin Ave., N.W., Washington, D.C. 20016-3007. (202) 966-7300. Web site: <www.aacap.org>

WEB SITES

The National Mental Health Association. <www.nmha.org>.

NYU Child Study Center. *Changing the Face of Child Mental Health.* <www.aboutourkids.org>.

Paula Ford-Martin

Antiviral drugs

Definition

Antiviral drugs act against diseases caused by viruses.

Description

Viruses represent a large group of infective agents that are composed of a core of nucleic acids, either RNA or DNA, surrounded by a layer of protein. They are not really living organisms according to general understanding, since they lack the cell membrane that is associated with living cells. Viruses can reproduce only inside a living cell, and they cause many diseases. Viruses are not normally affected by **antibiotics** but a small number of viruses can either be destroyed or have their growth stopped by drugs.

The drugs as of 2004 available for treatment of viral diseases in children are:

- Acyclovir (Zovirax), used for treatment of diseases caused by the **herpes simplex** virus and herpes zoster virus. Although it is approved only for children over the age of six months, the drug has been used for newborn infants with **encephalitis**. This drug is most reliable when given intravenously.

- Amantidine (Symmetrel), used to prevent or treat infections of the **influenza** virus type A. It is recommended for patients who cannot or should not receive influenza virus vaccine. As of 2004 it has not been studied in children below the age of one year.

- Foscarnet (Foscavir), is not recommended for young children but may be given to adolescents. It is used to treat cytomegalovirus infections of the eye, and for herpes simplex infections that are resistant to other drugs.

- Ganciclovir (Cytovene), used to treat cytomegalovirus infections of the eye. Although the manufacturer does not recommend use of ganciclovir in patients below the age of 12 years, the drug is recommended by standard pediatric references for children as young as three months.

- Oseltamivir (Tamiflu), used for treatment of influenza virus infections of children over the age of 13 years. In adults, oseltamivir has also been used for prevention if influenza, but this use has not been studied in children.

- Ribavirin (Rebetol, Virazol), used for treatment of hospitalized infants and young children with severe lower respiratory tract infections caused by respiratory syncytial virus (RSV), but its value is controversial.

- Rimantidine (Flumadine), used to protect against the influenza virus type A.

- Valacyclovir (Valtrex), used for treatment of diseases caused by the herpes simplex virus and herpes zoster virus. This drug is converted to acyclovir inside the body and is more reliable for oral use. Although the manufacturer says that safety and efficacy in children have not been established, valacyclovir is recommended for use in standard pediatric resources.

- Vidarabine (Vira-A), used to treat severe herpes infections in the newborn, but its primary value is in the form of an eye ointment to treat herpes infections of the eye.

- Zanamivir (relenza), used to treat influenza infections caused by viruses types A and B in adults and children over the age of seven.

In addition to the above drugs, there are drugs which treat retrovirus infections. Retroviruses are composed of RNA molecules instead of DNA, and the only treatable one is the one that causes acquired immune deficiency syndrome (**AIDS**). The drugs in this group that are appropriate for treatment of children are as follows:

- abacavir (Ziagen)

- amprenavir (Agenerase), for children above the age of four

- didanosine (Videx)

- efavirenz (Sustiva), for children over the age of three

- indinavir (Crixavan), according to the manufacturer safety and efficacy of which in children has not been established, but the drug has been recommended in standard pediatric references

- lamivudine (Epivir), for treatment of **hepatitis B** as well as for AIDS

- lopinavir/Ritonavir fixed combination (Kaletra), used in children as young as six months

- stavudine (Zerit)

- nelfinavir (Viracept), the manufacturer of which does not recommend use of this drug for children younger than two, but it has been studied with some success in children as young as newborns

- ritonavir (Norvir)

- saquinavir (Fortovase, Invirase)

- zalcitabine (Hivid)

- zidovudine (Retrovir)

Other drugs for treatment of HIV disease are marketed, but there have been neither sufficient studies not clinical experience to recommend their use in children.

General use

The antiviral drugs are used to prevent or treat the diseases listed above. These drugs are specific for individual viruses and offer no benefit for conditions caused by other viruses.

Precautions

Each of the drugs listed has specific warnings. See specific drugs references or ask a pediatrician.

Side effects

Each of the drugs listed has its own side effects. See specific drugs references or ask a pediatrician.

Indinavir (Crixivan) has the unique adverse effects of causing changes in patterns of fat distribution. This has been called Crix belly and may be more distressing to the patient than more serious side effects caused by other drugs since these effects are clearly visible. As of 2004 it is not clear whether this effect can be reversed when the drug is discontinued. Antiretroviral drugs should not be discontinued unless there is an alternative antiretroviral regimen to adopt.

KEY TERMS

Herpes virus—A family of viruses including herpes simplex types 1 and 2, and herpes zoster (also called varicella zoster). Herpes viruses cause several infections, all characterized by blisters and ulcers, including chickenpox, shingles, genital herpes, and cold sores or fever blisters.

Influenza virus type—The nature of the proteins in the outer coat of an influenza virus. Depending on the proteins, influenza viruses may be classified as A, B, or C.

Retrovirus—A family of RNA viruses containing a reverse transcriptase enzyme that allows the viruses' genetic information to become part of the genetic information of the host cell upon replication. Human immunodeficiency virus (HIV) is a retrovirus.

Virus—A small infectious agent consisting of a core of genetic material (DNA or RNA) surrounded by a shell of protein. A virus needs a living cell to reproduce.

Interactions

See specific drugs references or ask a pediatrician about interactions for an antiviral drug that has been prescribed.

Patients should use these drugs exactly as directed. With regard to the AIDS drugs in particular, the drugs should not be discontinued without consultation with the prescriber. AIDS drugs are normally prescribed in combinations of two and three drugs used together, and discontinuing any single drug may lead to the virus developing resistance to the other agents.

Parental concerns

Liquid dosage forms must always be measured with a calibrated teaspoon or dropper, never with a household teaspoon. Household teaspoons vary in the volume they deliver and may result in inadvertent overdose or under dose.

Anti-influenza drugs should be used only for patients who cannot receive vaccinations. Annual **vaccination** remains the preferred method of preventing influenza.

Antiretroviral drugs are routinely given in combinations of three to four drugs at a time. In some cases, fixed combinations of medications are the most practical way to administer these drugs, since they require the lowest number of doses each day.

Some antiviral drugs, particularly the antiretroviral agents, have potentially severe adverse effects. They should be prescribed only by qualified professionals experienced in their use. These drugs must be routinely monitored. Regular laboratory testing is essential for safe and effective use. Adverse effects and side effects must be reported to the prescriber as soon as they are observed.

Antiherpetic drugs may have only a limited value in reducing the severity or duration of herpes attacks. They are more important for their effect in reducing the period of viral shedding, the period of time in which a person infected with herpes virus can infect other people. For this reason, continued use of the drugs is important to **family** members and those in close proximity to the patient. The drugs should not be discontinued, even if there is no observed benefit.

See also Herpes simplex; HIV infection and AIDS; Influenza.

Resources

BOOKS

Beers, Mark H., and Robert Berkow, eds. *The Merck Manual*, 2nd home ed. West Point, PA: Merck & Co., 2004.

Mcevoy, Gerald, et al. *AHFS Drug Information 2004*. Bethesda, MD: American Society of Healthsystems Pharmacists, 2004.

PERIODICALS

Bell, G. S. "Highly active antiretroviral therapy in neonates and young infants." *Neonatal Netword: The Journal of Neonatal Nursing* 23, no. 2 (March-April 2004: 55–64.

Eksborg, S. "The pharmacokinetics of antiviral therapy in pediatric patients." *Herpes* 10, no. 3 (December 2003): 66–71.

Fraaij, Pieter L., et al. "Therapeutic drug monitoring in children with HIV/AIDS." *Therapeutic Drug Monitoring* 26, no. 2 (April 2004): 122–6.

Feder, Henry M., Jr., and Diane M. Hoss. "Herpes zoster in otherwise healthy children." *Pediatric Infectious Diseases Journal* 23, no. 5 (May 2004): 451–7.

Jaspan, H. B., and R. F. Garry. "Preventing neonatal HIV: a review." *Current HIV Research* 1, no. 3 (July 2003): 321–7.

Kamin, D., and C. Hadigan C. "Hyperlipidemia in children with HIV infection: an emerging problem." *Expert Reviews in Cardiovascular Therapy* 1, no. 1 (May 2003): 143–50.

Maggon, Krishan, and Sailen Barik. "New drugs and treatment for respiratory syncytial virus." *Reviews in Medical Virology* 14, no. 3 (May-June 2004): 149–68.

Rakhmanina, Natella Y., et al. "Therapeutic drug monitoring of antiretroviral therapy." *AIDS Patient Care and STDS* 18, no. 1 (January 2004): 7–14.

Whitley, Richard. "Neonatal herpes simplex virus infection." *Current Opinion in Infectious Diseases* 17, no. 3 (June 2004): 243–6.

ORGANIZATIONS

Elisabeth Glaser Pediatric AIDS Foundation. 1140 Connecticut Avenue NW, Suite 200, Washington, DC 20036. Web site: <www.charitywire.com/charity60/>.

WEB SITES

National Institute of Allergy and Infectious Diseases. Available online at <www.niaid.nih.gov/default.htm> (accessed October 17, 2004).

National Institute of Child Health & Human Development. Available online at <www.nichd.nih.gov/> (accessed October 17, 2004).

National Pediatric AIDS Network. Available online at <www.npan.org/> (accessed October 17, 2004).

The Pediatric AIDS Clinical Trials Group. Available online at <http://pactg.s-3.com/> (accessed October 17, 2004)

"Pediatric Antiretroviral Drug Information." Available online at <http://aidsinfo.nih.gov/guidelines/pediatric%5CSUP_PED_012004.html> (accessed October 17, 2004).

Samuel Uretsky, PharmD

Anxiety

Definition

Anxiety is a condition of persistent and uncontrollable nervousness, stress, and worry that is triggered by anticipation of future events, memories of past events, or ruminations over day-to-day events, both trivial and major, with disproportionate fears of catastrophic consequences.

Description

Stimulated by real or imagined dangers, anxiety affects people of all ages and social backgrounds. When it occurs in unrealistic situations or with unusual intensity, it can disrupt everyday life. Some researchers believe anxiety is synonymous with **fear**, occurring in varying degrees and in situations in which people feel threatened by some danger. Others describe anxiety as an unpleasant emotion caused by unidentifiable dangers or dangers that, in reality, pose no threat. Unlike fear, which is caused by realistic, known dangers, anxiety can be more difficult to identify and alleviate.

A small amount of anxiety is normal in the developing child, especially among adolescents and teens. Anxiety is often a realistic response to new roles and responsibilities, as well as to sexual and identity development. When symptoms become extreme, disabling, and/or when children or adolescents experience several symptoms over a period of a month or more, these symptoms may be a sign of an anxiety disorder, and professional intervention may be necessary. Two common forms of childhood anxiety are general anxiety disorder (GAD) and **separation anxiety** disorder (SAD), although many physicians and psychologists also include panic disorder and **obsessive-compulsive disorder**, which tend to occur more frequently in adults. Anxiety that is the result of experiencing a violent event, disaster, or physical abuse is identified as post-traumatic stress disorder (PTSD). Most adult anxiety disorders begin in **adolescence** or young adulthood and are more common among women than men.

Demographics

According to the U.S. surgeon general, 13 percent, or over 6 million children, suffer from anxiety, making it the most common emotional problem in children. Among adolescents, more girls than boys are affected. About half of the children and adolescents with anxiety disorders also have a second anxiety disorder or other mental or behavioral disorder, such as depression.

Causes and symptoms

A child's genetics, biochemistry, environment, history, and psychological profile all seem to contribute to the development of anxiety disorders. Most children with these disorders seem to have a biological vulnerability to stress, making them more susceptible to environmental stimuli than the rest of the population.

Emotional and behavioral symptoms of anxiety disorders include tension; self-consciousness; new or recurring fears (such as fear of the dark, fear of being alone, or fear of strangers); self-doubt and questioning; crying and whining; worries; constant need for reassurance (clinging to parent and unwilling to let the parent out of sight); distractibility; decreased appetite or other changes in eating habits; inability to control emotions; feeling as if one is about to have a heart attack, die, or go insane;

nightmares; irritability, stubbornness, and anger; regression to behaviors that are typical of an earlier developmental stage; and unwillingness to participate in **family** and school activities. Physical symptoms include rapid heartbeat; sweating; trembling; muscle aches (from tension); dry mouth; **headache**; stomach distress; **diarrhea**; **constipation**; frequent urination; new or recurrent bedwetting; **stuttering**; hot flashes or chills; throat constriction (lump in the throat); **sleep** disturbances; and fatigue. Many of these anxiety symptoms are very similar to those of depression, and as many as 50 percent of children with anxiety also suffer from depression. Generally, physiological hyperarousal (excitedness, shortness of breath, the fight or flight response) characterizes anxiety disorders, whereas underarousal (lack of pleasure and feelings of guilt) characterizes depression. Other signs of anxiety problems are poor school performance, loss of interest in previously enjoyed activities, obsession about appearance or weight, social **phobias** (e.g., fear of walking into a room full of people), and the persistence of imaginary fears after ages six to eight. Children with anxiety disorders are often perfectionists and are concerned about "getting everything right," but rarely feel that their work is satisfactory.

Shyness does not necessarily indicate a disorder, unless it interferes with normal activities and occurs with other symptoms. A small proportion of children do experience social anxiety, incapacitating shyness that persists for months or more, which should be treated. Similarly, performance anxiety experienced before athletic, academic, or theatrical events does not indicate a disorder, unless it significantly interferes with the activity.

Separation anxiety disorder (SAD) is the most common anxiety disorder among children, affecting 2 to 3 percent of school-aged children. SAD involves extreme and disproportionate distress over day-to-day separation from parents or home and unrealistic fears of harm to self or loved ones. Approximately 75 to 85 percent of children who refuse to go to school have separation anxiety. Normal separation fears are outgrown by children by the ages of five or six, but SAD usually starts between the ages of seven and 11.

When to call the doctor

A qualified mental health professional should be consulted if a child's anxiety begins to affect his or her ability to perform the three main responsibilities of childhood: to learn, to make friends, and to have fun. Often fears and anxieties come and go with time and age. However, in some children, anxiety becomes severe, excessive, unreasonable, and long-lasting (usually considered as long-lasting if the child experiences the elevated level of anxiety for a month or more), interferes with the child's ability to function normally, and causes the child to be distraught and easily upset, thus necessitating professional intervention.

Diagnosis

Diagnosing children with an anxiety disorder can be very difficult, since anxiety often results in disruptive behaviors that overlap with other disorders such as attention-deficit hyperactivity. Children showing signs of an anxiety disorder should first get a physical exam to rule out any possible illness or physical problem. Diagnosis of normal versus abnormal anxiety depends largely upon the degree of distress and its effect on a child's functioning. The degree of abnormality must be gauged within the context of the child's age and developmental level. The specific anxiety disorder is diagnosed by the pattern and intensity of symptoms using various psychological diagnostic tools.

Treatment

Depending on the severity of the problem, treatments for anxiety include school counseling, **family therapy**, and cognitive-behavioral or dynamic psychotherapy, sometimes combined with antianxiety drugs. Therapies generally aim for support by providing a positive, entirely accepting, pressure-free environment in which to explore problems; by providing insight through discovering and working with the child or adolescent's underlying thoughts and beliefs; and by exposure through gradually reintroducing the anxiety-producing thoughts, people, situations, or events in a manner so as to confront them calmly. Relaxation techniques, including meditation, may be employed in order to control the symptoms of physiological arousal and provide a tool the child can use to control his or her response.

Creative visualization, sometimes called rehearsal imagery by actors and athletes, may also be used. In this technique, the child writes down (or draws pictures of) each detail of the anxiety-producing event or situation and imagines his or her movements in performing the activity. The child also learns to perform these techniques in new, unanticipated situations.

In severe cases of diagnosed anxiety disorders, antianxiety and/or antidepressant drugs may be prescribed in order to enable therapy and normal daily activities to continue. Previously, narcotics and other sedatives, drugs that are highly addictive and interfere with cognitive capacity, were prescribed. With pharmacological advances and the development of synthetic drugs, which act in specific ways on brain chemicals, a more refined set of antianxiety drugs became available. Studies have found that generalized anxiety responds well to these drugs (benxodiazepines are the most common), which serve to quell the physiological symptoms of anxiety. Other forms of anxiety such as panic attacks, in which the symptoms occur in isolated episodes and are predominantly physical (and the object of fear is vague, fantastic, or unknown), respond best to the antidepressant drugs. Childhood separation anxiety is thought to be included in this category. Psychoactive drugs should only be considered as a last treatment alternative, and extra caution should be used when they are prescribed for children.

Prognosis

Studies consistently report that anxiety disorders can be debilitating and impinge seriously on a person's quality of life. Despite their common occurrence, little is understood about the natural course of anxiety disorder. Adults experiencing anxiety disorders often report that they have felt anxious all of their lives, with one half of adults with general anxiety disorder reporting that the onset of the condition occurred during childhood or adolescence. Anxiety disorders can be chronic, and the severity of symptoms can fluctuate significantly, with symptoms being more severe when stressors are present. Without treatment, extended periods of remission are not likely.

Prevention

Parents can help their child respond to stress by taking the following steps:

- providing a safe, secure, familiar, and consistent home life
- being selective in the types of television programs that children watch (including news shows), which can produce fears and anxieties
- spending calm and relaxed time with their child
- encouraging questions and expressions of fears, worries, or concerns
- listening to the child with encouragement and affection and without being critical
- rewarding (and not punishing) the child for effort rather than success
- providing the child with opportunities to make choices; with more control over situations, the child has a better response to stress
- involving the child in activities in which he or she can succeed and limiting events and situations that are stressful for the child

---

KEY TERMS

Psychological—Pertaining to the mind, its mental processes, and its emotional makeup.

Psychotherapy—Psychological counseling that seeks to determine the underlying causes of a patient's depression. The form of this counseling may be cognitive/behavioral, interpersonal, or psychodynamic.

Shyness—The feeling of insecurity when among people, talking with people, or asking somebody a favor.

Stress—A physical and psychological response that results from being exposed to a demand or pressure.

- developing an awareness of the situations and activities that are stressful for the child and recognizing signs of stress in the child
- keeping the child informed of necessary and anticipated changes (e.g., moving, change of school) that may cause the child to be stressed
- seeking professional help or advice when the symptoms of stress do not decrease or disappear

The child should also be encouraged to use various techniques to reduce stress, including the following strategies:

- talking about problems to parents or others whom the child trusts
- relaxing by listening to music, taking a warm bath, meditating, practicing breathing exercises, or participating in a favorite hobby or activity
- exercising
- respecting themselves and others
- avoiding the use of drugs and alcohol
- feeling free to ask for help if he or she is having difficulties with stress management

Parental concerns

Parenting an anxious child is difficult and can create stress within the entire family. Parents need to help the child learn and apply techniques to manage his or her anxiety. The use of support groups and professional assistance is recommended.

Parents of children with anxiety disorders may exhibit anxiety symptoms themselves and should also seek professional assistance.

See also Fear; Separation anxiety.

Resources

BOOKS

Chansky, Tamar E. *Freeing Your Child from Anxiety: Powerful, Practical Solutions to Overcome Your Child's Fears, Worries, and Phobias.* New York: Broadway Books, 2004.

Dacey, John S., and Lisa B. Fiore. *Your Anxious Child: How Parents and Teachers Can Relieve Anxiety in Children.* New York: John Wiley & Sons, 2001.

Fox, Paul. *The Worried Child: Recognizing Anxiety in Children and Helping Them Heal.* Alameda, CA: Hunter House Publishers, 2004.

Rapee, Ron, Sue Spence, and Ann Wignall. *Helping Your Anxious Child.* Oakland, CA: New Harbinger Publications, 2000.

Spencer, Elizabeth, Robert L. Dupont, and Caroline M. Dupont. *The Anxiety Cure for Kids: A Guide for Parents.* New York: John Wiley & Sons Inc., 2003.

Wagner, Aureen Pinto *Worried No More: Help and Hope for Anxious Children.* Rochester, NY: Lighthouse Press Inc., 2002.

ORGANIZATIONS

Anxiety Disorders Association of America. 8730 Georgia Avenue, Suite 600, Silver Spring, MD 20910. Web site: <www.adaa.org>.

National Institute of Mental Health (NIMH), Office of Communications. 6001 Executive Boulevard, Room 8184, MSC 9663, Bethesda, MD 20892-9663. Web site: <www.nimh.nih.gov/>.

WEB SITES

The Child Anxiety Network. <www.childanxiety.net/> (accessed October 11, 2004).

Judith Sims

Apgar testing

Definition

The Apgar scoring system evaluates the physical condition of the newborn at one minute after birth and again at five minutes after birth. The newborn receives a total score (Apgar score) that ranges from 0 to 10 based on rating color, heart rate, respiratory effort, muscle tone, and reflex irritability.

Purpose

Virginia Apgar specialized in anesthesiology and **childbirth**. She developed the Newborn Scoring System, later called the Apgar score, in 1949 for practitioners to use in deciding whether or not a newborn needed resuscitation. This score provides a uniform method of observation and evaluation of a newborn infant's need for resuscitation immediately after delivery at one minute and again at five minutes. The score is significant because one person in the delivery room evaluates the infant using five signs in an objective, standard and measurable manner. Research published in *The New England Journal of Medicine* in 2001 concluded that the Apgar scoring system remains as relevant for the prediction of neonatal survival in the early 2000s as it was in 1949.

Description

Five factors are considered in the evaluation of a newborn and the word Apgar can be used as a mnemonic to remember them, i.e., A = Activity (or muscle tone); P = Pulse; G = Grimace (or reflexes to stimuli); A = Appearance (or skin color), and R = Respiration. Scores are given as follows:

- Activity: Limpness, no movement at all = 0; some flexion of the limbs = 1; active movement, vigorous movements of arms and legs = 2.

- Pulse: No pulse = 0; pulse below 100 beats per minute (bpm) = 1; pulse over 100 per minute = 2. This is the most important assessment and can be determined by auscultation with a stethoscope or palpation at the junction of the umbilical cord and skin. A newborn heart rate of less than 100 bpm indicates the need for immediate resuscitation.

- Grimace: No response to stimuli = 0; some response, a slight cry or grimace = 1; active response, coughing, sneezing, or vigorously crying = 2. The stimuli used to evoke a response can be the use of nasal suctioning, stroking the back to assess for spinal abnormalities, having the foot tapped.

- Appearance: The whole body is blue, gray, or very pale = 0; acrocyanosis, i.e., trunk and head have a pink skin color and hands and feet are blue = 1; pink all over = 2. Newborns with naturally darker skin color will not be pink, but pallor is still noticeable and especially in the soles of the feet and palms of the hands. Skin color is related to the newborn's ability to oxygenate its body and extremities and is dependent on heart rate and respirations.

- Respiration: No breathing, apnea = 0; slow and irregular respiration = 1; good regular respiration, especially accompanied by crying = 2. Respirations are best assessed by watching the rise and fall of the neonate's abdomen since infants are diaphragmatic breathers.

Preparation

Essentially no preparation is needed to determine an Apgar score. Clinicians have suctioning equipment available and may use it during the birth process for nasal and oral suctioning to remove mucus and amniotic fluid. This is usually performed when the head of the newborn is safely delivered while the mother rests for her final push. The Apgar score should not be performed by the individual doing the delivery, but by the labor and delivery nurse or nursery nurse.

Aftercare

The Apgar score is primarily observational in nature and its only purpose is to alert the healthcare provider that the baby may need immediate assistance or prolonged observation in the nursery. It provides a means of monitoring the effectiveness of interventions and a process of determining which interventions are valuable.

Normal results

It is important to note that an Apgar score is strictly used to determine a newborn's immediate condition at birth and that it does not necessarily reflect the future health of a baby. The maximum obtainable score is 10 and the minimum is zero. It is quite rare to receive a true 10 as some acrocyanosis is considered normal and not a cause for concern. A score of 7 to 10 is considered normal, and these infants are expected to have an excellent outcome. A score of 4, 5, or 6 requires immediate intervention, usually in the form of oxygen and respiratory assistance or in the form of suctioning if breathing has been obstructed by mucus. A source of oxygen referred to as "blow-by" may be placed near but not directly over the nose and mouth of the neonate during suctioning. A score in the 4–6 range indicates that the neonate is having difficulty adapting to extrauterine life, which in some cases may be related to medications given to the mother during labor, **prematurity**, or a rapid delivery.

A low Apgar score provides a warning signal that the baby may have hidden health problems, such as breathing difficulties or internal bleeding. With a score of 0–3, the newborn is unresponsive, pale, limp, and may not have a pulse; therefore, an infant with a score of

0–3 needs immediate resuscitation. An ongoing evaluation is continued during resuscitation and documented again at five minutes. In the event of a difficult resuscitation, the Apgar score is done at 10, 15, and 20 minutes as well. A newborn with an Apgar score in this range generally requires advanced medical care and emergency measures, such as assisted breathing, administration of fluids or medications, and observation in a neonatal intensive care unit (NICU) by a neonatologist. An Apgar score of 0–3 at 20 minutes of age, for example, is indicative of high rates of morbidity (disease) and mortality (death).

Risks

There are no risks involved with the Apgar scoring process. It is an evaluation of the baby at birth to determine if any resuscitation procedures are needed.

Parental concerns

Parental concerns may be addressed if the Apgar score is low at five minutes and then again at 10 minutes. The healthcare provider should address the possible risks associated with a low score and advise the parents as to follow-up care. A persistently low Apgar score could indicate neurological problems and the parents would want to obtain additional treatment for the baby to ensure appropriate development. Children with **cerebral palsy** often have neurological damage at birth and the use of physical therapy or speech therapy enhances their outcome.

Resources

BOOKS

Olds, Sally, et al. *Maternal-Newborn Nursing & Women's Health Care*, 7th ed. Saddle River, NJ: Prentice Hall, 2004.

Tappero, Ellen, and Mary Honeyfield. *Physical Assessment of the Newborn*, 3rd ed. Santa Rosa, CA: NICU Ink Book Publishers, 2003.

PERIODICALS

Casey, B. M., et al. "The Continuing Value of Apgar Score for the Assessment of Newborn Infants." *New England Journal of Medicine* 334 (February 15, 2000): 467–71.

ORGANIZATIONS

Association of Women's Health, Obstetric, and Neonatal Nursing. 2000 L Street, NW, Suite 740, Washington, DC 20036. Web site: <www.awhonn.org>.

National Association of Neonatal Nurses. 4700 W. Lake Avenue, Glenview, IL 60025–1485. Web site: <www.nann.org>.

WEB SITES

"APGAR Scoring for Newborns." Available online at <www.childbirth.org/articles/apgar.html> (accessed November 28, 2004).

"What is the Apgar Score?" *KidsHealth.* Available online at <http://kidshealth.org/parent/pregnancy_newborn/medical_care/apgar.html> (accessed November 28, 2004).

Linda K. Bennington, RNC, MSN, CNS

Apnea of infancy

Definition

Apnea is a temporary cessation of breathing. Among children, this is most common in newborns.

Description

Babies born prematurely (before 34 weeks of gestation) usually lack a fully developed central nervous system. A component of this temporary deficit is inadequate control of their breathing reflex. The more premature a baby is born, the greater is the likelihood of apnea. Episodes of apnea are also more problematic for smaller than for larger babies. A small baby stores a smaller amount of oxygen, so the effects of oxygen deprivation are more severe. Apnea usually appears within the first several days after the baby is born.

Mild apnea causes no ill effects. The breathing pause is short (10–15 seconds), and the baby starts breathing again on his or her own. In a severe episode, though, breathing may cease for 20 seconds or longer. The infant begins to turn blue (cyanosis) because of the lack of oxygen in the blood. The baby retains carbon dioxide and may lapse into unconsciousness unless stimulated to breathe. Rubbing the infant with a finger or striking the soles of the feet may be all that is needed to end a short episode of apnea. If the baby has become unconscious, however, he or she may need to be revived with an oxygen mask. If apnea is frequent or severe, the baby's doctor may decide to treat it by altering conditions in the incubator, such as lowering the temperature, increasing oxygen, or placing the infant in a rocking incubator. Blood transfusions and medication may also be necessary.

Premature babies are also at higher risk for "late apnea," which occurs when the infant is older than six weeks. Late apnea can also affect full-term babies and may be a sign of an underlying problem such as **congenital heart disease**, infection, anemia, **meningitis**, or seizures. The baby usually recovers from apnea as the underlying disease is treated. Even if no underlying cause is found, late apnea is usually outgrown by the time the baby turns one year old.

Demographics

Apnea usually occurs during **sleep** and is primarily a disorder of premature infants. Sleep apnea before the early 2000s was thought to be a disease of older adults, but it can occur in children as well.

Causes and symptoms

In apnea of newborns, breathing stops and begins again automatically after a few seconds; it can also cause a prolonged pause which requires that the baby be resuscitated. Babies born before 34 weeks of gestation do not have a fully developed central nervous system, and they often do not have adequate control of the breathing reflex.

There are no specific measures for preventing apnea. It seems to be a sign of developmental immaturity, and it subsides as the baby grows older. Usually a premature baby in an incubator is continually monitored, and hospital staff can easily detect apnea. With late apnea, parents may not notice that a child has stopped breathing while sleeping. If apnea is suspected or diagnosed, parents may install a home monitor until the condition is outgrown. Undiagnosed late apnea can be fatal and is associated with **sudden infant death syndrome** (SIDS). Parents of premature babies need to be apprised of the possibility of apnea and should be instructed on how to resuscitate their infant if it occurs. Those particularly worried about late apnea may also wish to be trained in infant first aid. Since apnea usually occurs during sleep, parents may decide to sleep near the baby.

When to call the doctor

Parents of a newborn who have taken the baby home should call the child's pediatrician if they notice the baby has episodes of not breathing during sleep. This especially true if the child was born prematurely or has other medical conditions.

Diagnosis

Diagnosis of sleep apnea of newborns is made by observation of the baby by a physician. Premature babies who are still in the hospital under neonatal care are monitored by machines that will alert staff when a baby stops breathing.

Treatment

Sleep apnea in infants is treated by gently stimulating the children by stroking their bodies. Touching them this way induces them to resume breathing. In severe cases, giving the baby oxygen or medication may be necessary.

Prognosis

If apnea is diagnosed, it will probably recur, but most premature babies outgrow the condition by the time they reach their normal due date.

Prevention

Premature babies are usually kept in an incubator, where their breathing and heart rate are monitored. A drop in the baby's heart rate or respiratory rate will sound an alarm, and a nurse can stimulate the baby to resume breathing, if necessary.

> ## KEY TERMS
>
> **Cyanosis**—A bluish tinge to the skin that can occur when the blood oxygen level drops too low.
>
> **Sudden infant death syndrome (SIDS)**—The general term given to "crib deaths" of unknown causes.

Parental concerns

Parents should monitor the breathing patterns of infants who are born prematurely. Doing so is especially important during the first few weeks of life or until the infant reaches an age commensurate with full-term gestation.

Resources

BOOKS

Apnea: A Medical Dictionary, Bibliography, and Annotated Research Guide to Internet References. San Diego, CA: Icon Health Publications, 2004.

Lavie, Peretz, and Anthony Berris. *Restless Nights: Understanding Snoring and Sleep Apnea.* New Haven, CT: Yale University Press, 2003.

Phillipson, Eliot A. "Sleep Apnea." In *Harrison's Principles of Internal Medicine*, 15th ed. Edited by Eugene Braunwald et al. New York: McGraw-Hill, 2001, pp. 1520–2.

Rosen, Carol L., et al. "Obstructive Sleep Apnea and Hypoventilation." In *Nelson Textbook of Pediatrics*, 17th ed. Edited by Richard E. Behrman et al. Philadelphia: Saunders, 2003, pp. 1397–1400.

Sleep Apnea: A Medical Dictionary, Bibliography, and Annotated Research Guide to Internet References. San Diego, CA: ICON Health Publications, 2004.

Strohl, Kingman P. "Obstructive Sleep Apnea: Hypopnea Syndrome." In *Cecil Textbook of Medicine*, 22nd ed. Edited by Lee Goldman et al. Philadelphia: Saunders, 2003, pp. 576–9.

PERIODICALS

Hoban, T. F. "Sleep and its disorders in children." *Seminars in Neurology* 24, no. 3 (2004): 327–40.

Schiffman, P. H., et al. "Mandibular dimensions in children with obstructive sleep apnea syndrome." *Sleep* 27, no. 5 (2004): 959–65.

ORGANIZATIONS

American Academy of Sleep Medicine. 6301 Bandel Road NW, Suite 101, Rochester, MN 55901. Web site. <www.asda.org/>.

American Sleep Apnea Association. 1424 K Street NW, Suite 302, Washington, DC 20005. Web site: <www.sleepapnea.org/>.

WEB SITES

A.P.N.E.A. Network. *The Apnea Patient's News, Education & Awareness Network.* Available online at <www.apneanet.org/> (accessed December 20, 2004).

"Sleep Apnea." *American Academy of Family Physicians.* Available online at <http://familydoctor.org/212.xml> (accessed December 20, 2004).

"Sleep Apnea." *American Sleep Foundation.* Available online at <www.sleepfoundation.org/publications/sleepap.cfm> (accessed December 20, 2004).

"Sleep Apnea." *MedlinePlus.* Available online at <www.nlm.nih.gov/medlineplus/sleepapnea.html> (accessed December 20, 2004).

L. Fleming Fallon Jr., MD, DrPH

Appendicitis

Definition

Appendicitis is an inflammation of the appendix, which is the small, finger-shaped pouch attached to the beginning of the large intestine on the lower-right side of the abdomen. Appendicitis is a medical emergency, and if left untreated, the appendix may rupture and cause a potentially fatal infection.

Description

In children, appendicitis is the most common abdominal medical emergency and most common pediatric emergency surgical procedure. Although the appendix has no known function, it can become inflamed and diseased. This condition, called appendicitis, can rapidly evolve into a life-threatening or fatal infection of the abdominal cavity (peritonitis) if not treated immediately. Appendicitis usually involves emergency consultation with a physician and evaluation in a hospital emergency department.

Demographics

Appendicitis is the most common abdominal emergency found in children and young adults. One person in 15 develops appendicitis in his or her lifetime. The incidence is highest among males aged 10 to 14, and among females aged 15 to 19. More males than females develop appendicitis between **puberty** and age 25. It is rare in infants and children under the age of two. In the United States, appendicitis occurs in four out of 1,000 children.

Causes and symptoms

Appendicitis is usually caused by a blockage of the inside of the appendix, which is called the lumen. Most often, the lumen is blocked by fecal material. Lymphoid tissue, which is present in mucosal lining of the appendix and intestines to help fight bacterial and viral infections, can swell and lead to obstruction of the appendix. This condition, called lymphoid hyperplasia, may also be associated with a variety of inflammatory and infectious diseases, such as Crohn's disease, **gastroenteritis**, respiratory infections, mononucleosis, and **measles**. Appendicitis can also be caused by foreign bodies (e.g., intrauterine device or something swallowed), traumatic abdominal injury, or tumors. In addition, genetics may play a role in appendicitis; some children may inherit genes that make them more susceptible to blockage of the appendiceal lumen. Having **cystic fibrosis** also increases a child's risk for appendicitis.

Blockage of the appendix then causes inflammation, increased pressure, and restricted blood flow, leading to abdominal **pain** and tenderness in the right lower quadrant of the abdomen. If the appendix is not removed, bacteria and inflammation within the appendix rapidly expand, the wall of the appendix stretches, and perforation can occur. Once the appendix is perforated, bacteria-filled fluid is released into the abdominal cavity and peritonitis then develops. Perforation is more common in younger children. Perforation can occur as soon as 48 to 72 hours after symptoms first begin and can become life-threatening.

Classic symptoms of appendicitis include the following:

- abdominal pain, first around the navel then moving to the lower right quadrant of the abdomen
- **nausea**
- **vomiting**
- loss of appetite
- **diarrhea**, **constipation**, and/or inability to pass gas
- **fever** beginning after other symptoms
- abdominal swelling and tenderness

Other possible symptoms are pain on urination, inability to urinate, or frequent urge to urinate if the swollen appendix is near the urinary tract and bladder. When perforation occurs, abdominal pain becomes more intense and involves the whole abdominal area, and fever may be very high.

Symptoms of appendicitis vary, and not every child will have all the symptoms. In children younger than age two years, the most common symptoms are vomiting and a bloated or swollen abdomen. Toddlers with appendicitis may have difficulty eating and may seem very tired. Children may have constipation, but may also have small stools that contain mucus. Although infants and children younger than two years may also have abdominal pain and other symptoms, they are too young to effectively communicate their symptoms to adults, who may then miss the symptoms of appendicitis.

When to call the doctor

Appendicitis is a medical emergency. A doctor should be called immediately if appendicitis is suspected so that children can receive prompt medical treatment before perforation occurs. Parents who suspect that their child has appendicitis should not give the child any pain medication because it may interfere with the results of a doctor's physical examination for appendicitis. In addition, parents should not give their child anything to eat or drink in case surgery is required immediately.

Symptoms in combination that require a doctor's immediate attention include significant abdominal pain, fever, diarrhea, **nausea and vomiting**, swollen or bloated abdomen, and loss of appetite. If abdominal pain begins before nausea and vomiting, rather than after, appendicitis rather than intestinal infection is more likely.

Diagnosis

Appendicitis is diagnosed by physical examination, laboratory tests, and imaging tests. During a physical examination, the doctor palpates the abdomen to find tender and painful spots. A physical examination can also include a rectal examination, examination of the genitals in boys, and a gynecologic examination in girls, because other conditions, such as **testicular torsion** and ectopic pregnancy may have symptoms similar to appendicitis. Laboratory tests involve an analysis of white blood cell count to determine whether infection is present, urinalysis to rule out urinary tract or kidney infection, and other tests, such as pregnancy and liver function tests, to rule out other causes of abdominal pain. Imaging tests can include abdominal x rays, ultrasound, and **computed tomography** (CT).

In 2004, a new imaging technique that uses nuclear medicine imaging and an injection of an imaging agent called NeutroSpec was introduced for the diagnosis of

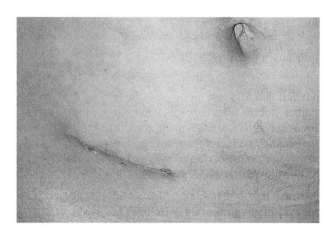

Appendectomy scar on the right side of the patient's abdomen. (© Dr. P. Marazzi/Science Photo Library/Photo Researchers, Inc.)

appendicitis. This technique provides images of infected areas and may help physicians decide which children are candidates for surgery to remove the appendix. Up to 20 percent of appendectomies are performed on infants and children with a normal appendix.

Abdominal pain is a common complaint in children, and making a timely diagnosis of appendicitis before perforation is often difficult. Up to 30 percent of children with appendicitis are misdiagnosed, even by experienced physicians. In infants, diagnosis is often not possible and not made until after perforation. Appendicitis is most often misdiagnosed as gastroenteritis or respiratory infection.

Treatment

Appendicitis is treated by immediate surgery to remove the appendix, called an appendectomy. Appendectomy is the most common emergency surgery performed by pediatric surgeons. In an open appendectomy, the appendix is removed through a standard abdominal incision. In laparoscopic appendectomy, surgeons insert a small scope through tiny abdominal incisions to remove the appendix. A laparoscopic appendectomy results in less postoperative pain and fewer surgical incision infections. However, the procedure is longer and requires specialized surgical experience in operating on pediatric patients. In female teen patients, laparascopy has the added benefit of being able to diagnose and treat gynecologic conditions and ectopic pregnancy during the appendectomy if the appendix is found to be normal.

Preoperative **antibiotics** are given to children with suspected appendicitis and stopped after surgery if there is no perforation. Antibiotic treatment kills bacteria, and

KEY TERMS

Appendectomy—Surgical removal of the appendix.

Appendix—The worm-shaped pouch attached to the cecum, the beginning of the large intestine.

Computed tomography (CT)—An imaging technique in which cross-sectional x rays of the body are compiled to create a three-dimensional image of the body's internal structures; also called computed axial tomography.

Ectopic pregnancy—A pregnancy that develops outside of the mother's uterus, such as in the fallopian tube. Ectopic pregnancies often cause severe pain in the lower abdomen and are potentially life-threatening because of the massive blood loss that may occur as the developing embryo/fetus ruptures and damages the tissues in which it has implanted.

Laparoscopy—A surgical procedure in which a small incision is made, usually in the navel, through which a viewing tube (laparoscope) is inserted. This allows the doctor to examine abdominal and pelvic organs. Other small incisions can be mad to insert instruments to perform procedures. Laparoscopy is done to diagnose conditions or to perform certain types of surgeries.

Peritonitis—Inflammation of the peritoneum. It is most often due to bacterial infection, but can also be caused by a chemical irritant (such as spillage of acid from the stomach or bile from the gall bladder).

Testicular torsion—A condition involving the twisting of the spermatic cord inside the testicle that shuts off its blood supply and can seriously damage the testicle.

Ultrasonography—A medical test in which sound waves are directed against internal structures in the body. As sound waves bounce off the internal structure, they create an image on a video screen. Ultrasonography is often used to diagnose fetal abnormalities, gallstones, heart defects, and tumors. Also called ultrasound imaging.

stronger and longer courses of antibiotics are required if peritonitis occurs.

If the appendix is removed before perforation occurs, the hospital stay is usually two to three days. A child with a perforated appendix and peritonitis must remain in the hospital up to a week.

Prognosis

Appendicitis is usually treated successfully by appendectomy, and unless there are complications, children should recover without further problems. The mortality rate in cases without complications is less than 0.1 percent. Perforated and ruptured appendix, as well as peritonitis, occur at higher rates among children. When the appendix has ruptured or a severe infection has developed, the likelihood for developing complications is higher, and recovery is longer. Peritonitis is a life-threatening condition, and death occurs in about 1 percent of cases.

Prevention

In general, appendicitis cannot be prevented. The incidence of appendicitis is lower in cultures where people eat more daily dietary fiber, which is thought to decrease the viscosity of feces, decrease bowel transit time, and discourage formation of fecaliths, which predispose individuals to obstructions within the appendix.

Parental concerns

Because the appendix is more likely to perforate in children than adults, parents should not hesitate to call the doctor if their child develops symptoms that may indicate appendicitis. Parents should feel free to ask their doctor and other medical staff questions about any medical tests or treatments their child receives.

Resources

BOOKS

Majumdar, P. C. *Appendicitis.* New Delhi, India: B. Jain, 2003.

Tilden, J. H. *Appendicitis: The Etiology, Hygienic, and Dietetic Treatment.* Pahrump, NV: Library of New Atlantis, 2003.

Harvard Medical School. *Medical Tests: A Practical Guide to Common Tests.* Boston, MA: Harvard Health Publications, 2004.

PERIODICALS

Kosloske, A. M., et al. "The Diagnosis of Appendicitis in Children: Outcomes of a Strategy Based on Pediatric Surgical Evaluation." *Pediatrics* 113 (January 2004): 29–34.

McCullough, M. "Targeting Appendicitis: A New Tool Offers Wider Promise." *Philadelphia Inquirer* (July 7, 2004).

Zitsman, J. L. "Current Concepts in Minimal Access Surgery for Children." *Pediatrics* 111 (June 2003): 1239–52.

ORGANIZATIONS

American College of Emergency Physicians. Web site: <www.acep.org>.

American College of Radiology. Web site: <www.acr.org>.

WEB SITES

"Appendicitis." Available online at <http://kidshealth.org/parent/infections/stomach/appendicitis.html> (accessed October 24, 2004).

"Appendicitis." *National Digestive Diseases Information Clearinghouse.* Available online at <http://digestive.niddk.nih.gov/ddiseases/pubs/appendicitis/> (accessed October 24, 2004).

Trevino, M. "CT for Appendicitis Diagnosis in Children Gains Popularity." Available online at <www.dimag.com/dinews/2003050901.shtml> (accessed October 24, 2004).

Tucker, J. "Pediatrics: Appendicitis." *Emedicine.* Available online at <www.emedicine.com/emerg/topic361.htm> (accessed October 24, 2004).

Jennifer E. Sisk, M.A.

Arachnodactyly *see* **Marfan syndrome**

Arnold-Chiari malformation *see* **Chiari malformation**

Art *see* **Drawings**

Arteriovenous fistula

Definition

An arteriovenous fistula is an abnormal channel or passage between an artery and a vein.

Description

An arteriovenous fistula is a disruption of the normal blood flow pattern. Normally, oxygenated blood flows to the tissue through arteries and capillaries. Following the release of oxygen in the tissues, the blood returns in veins to the heart. An arteriovenous fistula is an abnormal connection of an artery and a vein. The blood bypasses the capillaries and tissues and returns to the heart. Arterial blood has a higher blood pressure than blood in veins. Although both the artery and the vein retain their normal connections, the new opening between the two causes some arterial blood to shunt (be diverted) into the vein because of the blood pressure difference. As a result, the vein swells.

Demographics

Congenital arteriovenous fistula is rare. Acquired arteriovenous fistula is also uncommon in children. When it occurs, it is most likely to be found in the arms or legs.

Causes and symptoms

There are two types of arteriovenous fistulas, congenital and acquired. A congenital arteriovenous fistula is a rare birth defect that formed during fetal development. In congenital fistulas, blood vessels of the lower extremity are more frequently involved than other areas of the body. An acquired arteriovenous fistula is one that develops after a person is born. It usually occurs when an artery and vein that are side-by-side are damaged, and the healing process results in the two becoming linked. For example, after catheterizations, arteriovenous fistulas may occur as a complication of the arterial puncture in the leg or arm. Fistulas also form without obvious cause. In the case of patients on hemodialysis, physicians perform surgery to create a fistula. These patients receive many needle sticks to flush their blood through dialysis machines and for routine blood analysis testing. The veins used may scar and become difficult to access. Surgery is used to connect an artery and vein so that arterial blood pressure and flow rate widens the vein and decreases the chance of blood clots forming inside the vein.

The main symptoms of arteriovenous fistulas near the surface of the skin are bulging and discolored veins. In some cases, the bulging veins can be mistaken for varicose veins. Other fistulas can cause more serious problems without obvious symptoms, depending on their location and the blood vessels involved.

When to call the doctor

If the child has veins that appear to be varicose, the doctor should be consulted.

Diagnosis

Using a stethoscope, a physician can detect the sound of a pulse in the affected vein (bruit). The sound is a distinctive to-and-fro sound. Dye injected into the blood vessels can be tracked by x ray to confirm the presence of a fistula.

Treatment

Small arteriovenous fistulas can be corrected by surgery. Fistulas in the brain or eye are very difficult to treat. If surgery is not possible or is very difficult, injection therapy may be used. Injection therapy, also called sclerotherapy, is the injection of an irritating chemical that causes scaring at the site of the injection. In the case of an arteriovenous fistula, this procedure should stop the passage of blood from the artery to the vein. Surgery is the most common method of treating acquired fistulas.

Prognosis

The prognosis for treated acquired arteriovenous fistula is usually very good. Congenital arteriovenous fistula is not usually treated quite as successfully, but it can also be treated in such a way as to minimize further problems.

Prevention

As of 2004, there is no known way to prevent arteriovenous fistula.

Parental concerns

If not treated, arteriovenous fistulas can be very dangerous. Tissues below the fistula may not get enough blood and may die. If too much blood is diverted through the fistula, heart complications may occur.

Resources

BOOKS

Steiger, Hans-Jacob, et al. *Neurosurgery of Arteriovenous Malformations and Fistulas: A Multimodal Approach.* New York: Springer-Verlag, 2002.

PERIODICALS

Hung, Po-Cheng, and Huei-Shyong Wang. "Successful endovascular treatment of cerebral arteriovenus fistula." *Pediatric Neurology* 27 (October 2002): 300–03.

"'Gigantic' Coronary Arteriovenous Fistula Closed in Neonate." *Medical Devices & Surgical Technology Week* (February 1, 2004): 85.

Nakayama, Hideki, et al. "Multiple cerebral arteriovenous fistulas and malformations in the neonate." *Pediatric Neurology* 25 (September 2001): 236–39.

ORGANIZATIONS

American Heart Association. 7272 Greenville Avenue Dallas, TX 75231. Web site: <www.americanheart.org>.

WEB SITES

Morasch, Mark D., and Dipen Maun. "Arteriovenous Fistulas." *eMedicine.com*, October 23, 2003. Available online at < www.emedicine.com/med/topic169.htm> (accessed November 16, 2004).

Tish Davidson, A.M.
John T. Lohr, PhD

Arthritis *see* **Juvenile arthritis**

"Asleep" body parts *see* **Numbness and tingling**

Asperger's syndrome *see* **Pervasive developmental disorders**

Asphyxia neonatorum

Definition

Asphyxia neonatorum is respiratory failure in the newborn, a condition caused by the inadequate intake of oxygen before, during, or just after birth.

Description

Asphyxia neonatorum, also called birth or newborn asphyxia, is defined as a failure to start regular respiration within a minute of birth. Asphyxia neonatorum is a neonatal emergency as it may lead to hypoxia (lowering of oxygen supply to the brain and tissues) and possible brain damage or death if not correctly managed. Newborn infants normally start to breathe without assistance and usually cry after delivery. By one minute after birth most infants are breathing well. If an infant fails to establish sustained respiration after birth, the infant is diagnosed with asphyxia neonatorum. Normal infants have good muscle tone at birth and move their arms and legs actively, while asphyxia neonatorum infants are completely limp and do not move at all. If not correctly managed, asphyxia neonatorum will lead to hypoxia and possible brain damage or death.

Demographics

According to the National Center for Health Statistics (NCHS), in 2002, **infant mortality** caused by asphyxia neonatorum amounted to 14.4 deaths per 100,000 live births in the United States, representing the tenth leading cause of infant mortality. Worldwide, more than 1 million babies die annually from complications of birth asphyxia. According to the World Health Organization, asphyxia neonatorum is one of the leading causes of newborn deaths in developing countries, in which 4 to 9 million cases of newborn asphyxia occur each year, accounting for about 20 percent of the infant mortality rate.

Causes and symptoms

There are many causes of asphyxia neonatorum, the most common of which include the following: prenatal hypoxia (a condition resulting from a reduction of the oxygen supply to tissue below physiological levels despite adequate perfusion of the tissue by blood), umbilical cord compression during **childbirth**, occurrence of a preterm or difficult delivery, and maternal anesthesia (both the intravenous drugs and the anesthetic gases cross the placenta and may sedate the fetus). High-risk pregnancies for asphyxia neonatorum include:

- maternal age of less than 16 years old or over 40 years old
- low socioeconomic status
- maternal illnesses, such as diabetes, **hypertension**, Rh-sensitization, severe anemia
- mothers with previous abortions, stillbirths, early neonatal deaths, or preterm births
- lack of prenatal care
- abnormal fetal presentation or position
- alcohol abuse and **smoking** by the mother
- severe fetal growth retardation
- preterm labor

The symptoms of asphyxia neonatorum are bluish or gray skin color (cyanosis), slow heartbeat (bradycardia), stiff or limp limbs (**hypotonia**), and a poor response to stimulation.

When to call the doctor

Pregnant women who are at high risk of delivering newborns with asphyxia neonatorum should arrange for a close follow-up of their pregnancy with their obstetrician.

Diagnosis

Diagnosis can be objectively assessed using the Apgar score—a recording of the physical health of a newborn infant, determined after examination of the adequacy of respiration, heart action, muscle tone, skin color, and reflexes. Normally, the Apgar score is of 7 to 10. Infants with a score between 4 and 6 have moderate depression of their vital signs while infants with a score of 0 to 3 have severely depressed vital signs and are at great risk of dying unless actively resuscitated.

Treatment

The treatment for asphyxia neonatorum is resuscitation of the newborn. All medical delivery rooms have adequate resuscitation equipment should an infant not breathe well at delivery. Between 1970 and 2000, neonatal resuscitation has evolved from disparate teaching methods to organized programs. The most widely used procedure is the Neonatal Resuscitation Program, supported by the American Academy of Pediatrics (AAP) and the American Heart Association (AHA).

If stimulation fails to initiate regular respiration in the newborn, the attending physician attempts resuscitation. He may decide first to gently suction the oropharynx—the area of the throat at the back of the mouth, with a soft catheter. When stimulation and a clear airway do not result in adequate respiration, the physician may give 100 percent oxygen via a face mask. If the infant is still not breathing, some form of artificial ventilation is then required. The usual method is to use mask ventilation with a resuscitator. The mask is applied tightly to the infant's face. If this procedure fails, the infant can be intubated with a endotracheal tube to which the resuscitator can then be connected. The more severe the fetal asphyxia, the longer it will take before the infant starts to breathe spontaneously. If the infant does not breathe despite adequate ventilation, or if the heart rate remains below 80 beats per minute, the physician can give an external cardiac massage using two fingers to depress the lower sternum at approximately 100 times a minute while continuing with respiratory assistance. Adrenaline may also be administered to increase cardiac output. Once the infant starts breathing, he or she is transferred to a nursery for observation and further assessment. Temperature, pulse and respiratory rate, color, and activity are recorded, and blood glucose levels checked for at least four hours.

Treatment may also include the following:

- giving the mother extra amounts of oxygen before delivery

KEY TERMS

Adrenaline—Another name for epinephrine, the hormone released by the adrenal glands in response to stress. It is the principal blood-pressure raising hormone and a bronchial and intestinal smooth muscles relaxant.

Anemia—A condition in which there is an abnormally low number of red blood cells in the bloodstream. It may be due to loss of blood, an increase in red blood cell destruction, or a decrease in red blood cell production. Major symptoms are paleness, shortness of breath, unusually fast or strong heart beats, and tiredness.

Anesthesia—Treatment with medicine that causes a loss of feeling, especially pain. Local anesthesia numbs only part of the body; general anesthesia causes loss of consciousness.

Apgar score—The results of an evaluation of a newborn's physical status, including heart rate, respiratory effort, muscle tone, response to stimulation, and color of skin.

Asphyxia—Lack of oxygen.

Asphyxia neonatorum—Respiratory failure in the newborn.

Bradycardia—A slow heart rate, usually under 60 beats per minute.

Cyanosis—A bluish tinge to the skin that can occur when the blood oxygen level drops too low.

Hemoglobin—An iron-containing pigment of red blood cells composed of four amino acid chains (alpha, beta, gamma, delta) that delivers oxygen from the lungs to the cells of the body and carries carbon dioxide from the cells to the lungs.

Hypotonia—Having reduced or diminished muscle tone or strength.

Hypoxia—A condition characterized by insufficient oxygen in the cells of the body

Neonatal—Refers to the first 28 days of an infant's life.

Oropharynx—One of the three regions of the pharynx, the oropharynx is the region behind the mouth.

Respiratory failure—Inability to rid the body of CO_2 or establish an adequate blood oxygen level.

Resuscitation—Bringing a person back to life or consciousness after he or she was apparently dead.

- medications to support the baby's breathing and sustain blood pressure

- extracorporeal membrane oxygenation (ECMO)

ECMO is a technique similar to a heart-lung bypass machine, which assists the infant's heart and lung functions with use of an external pump and oxygenator.

Alternative treatment

If an inadequate supply of oxygen from the placenta is detected during labor, the infant is at high risk for asphyxia, and an emergency delivery may be attempted either using forceps or by cesarean section.

Prognosis

The prognosis for asphyxia neonatorum depends on how long the newborn is unable to breathe. For example, clinical studies show that the outcome of babies with low five-minute Apgar scores is significantly better than those with the same scores at 10 minutes. With prolonged asphyxia, brain, heart, kidney, and lung damage can result and also death, if the asphyxiation lasts longer than 10 minutes.

Prevention

Anticipation is the key to preventing asphyxia neonatorum. It is important to identify fetuses that are likely to be at risk of asphyxia and to closely monitor such high-risk pregnancies. High-risk mothers should always give birth in hospitals with neonatal intensive care units where appropriate facilities are available to treat asphyxia neonatorum. During labor, the medical team must be ready to intervene appropriately and to be adequately prepared for resuscitation.

Parental concerns

Women at risk for asphyxia neonatorum pregnancies should receive focused prenatal care from an obstetrician skilled at preventing and detecting problems such as anemia that may contribute to asphyxia neonatorum. While prenatal care will not necessarily prevent newborn asphyxia, it can help ensure that both the mother and her baby are as healthy as possible at the time of birth.

See also Hypotonia.

Resources

BOOKS

Birth Asphyxia and the Brain: Basic Science and Clinical Implications. Edited by Steven M. Donn et al. Malden, MA: Futura Publishing Co., 2002.

PERIODICALS

Cheung, P. Y., and C. M. Robertson. "Predicting the outcome of term neonates with intrapartum asphyxia." *Acta Paediatrica* 89, no. 3 (March 2000): 262–264.

Clark, R., and J. A. Carcillo. "Is it time to revisit a role for antithrombotic therapy in asphyxia neonatorum?" *Pediatric Critical Care Medicine* 5, no. 2 (March 2004): 198–199.

Wiswell, T. E. "Neonatal resuscitation." *Respiratory Care* 48, no. 3 (March 2003): 288–294.

ORGANIZATIONS

American Academy of Pediatrics (AAP). 141 Northwest Point Blvd., Elk Grove Village, IL, 60007. Web site: <www.aap.org>

WEB SITES

Dave Woods. "Neonatal resuscitation." *International Association for Maternal and Neonatal Health.* Available online at <www.gfmer.ch/Medical_education_En/PGC_RH_2004/Neonatal_asphyxia.htm> (accessed October 11, 2004).

Monique Laberge, Ph.D.

▌Assessment

Definition

Assessment is a process of gathering and documenting information about the achievement, skills, abilities, and personality variables of an individual.

Description

Assessment is used in both an educational and psychological setting by teachers, psychologists, and counselors to accomplish a range of objectives. These include the following:

- to learn more about the competencies and deficiencies of the individual being tested
- to identify specific problem areas and/or needs
- to evaluate the individual's performance in relation to others
- to evaluate the individual's performance in relation to a set of standards or goals
- to provide teachers with feedback on effectiveness of instruction
- to evaluate the impact of psychological or neurological abnormalities on learning and behavior
- to predict an individual's aptitudes or future capabilities

In the early 2000s standardized tests are increasingly used to evaluate performance in U.S. schools. Faced with declining test scores by American students when compared to others around the world, state governments and the federal government have sought ways to measure the performance of schools and bring a measurable accountability to the educational process. Thus, states and the federal government have adopted standardized tests for evaluating knowledge and skills on the assumption that testing is an effective way to measure outcomes of education. One prominent program has been the No Child Left Behind Act that requires schools to meet certain performance standards annually, for their students as a group and also for individual ethnic and racial subgroups. The use of this type of standardized tests is controversial. Many educators feel that it limits the **creativity** and effectiveness of the classroom teacher and produces an environment of "teaching to the test."

Educational assessments

The choice of an assessment tool depends on the purpose or goal of the assessment. Assessments might be made to establish rankings among individual students, to determine the amount of information students have retained, to provide feedback to students on their levels of achievement, to motivate students by recognizing and rewarding good performances, to assess the need for remedial education, and to evaluate students for class placement or ability grouping. The goal of the assessment should be understood by all stakeholders in the process: students, parents, teachers, counselors, and outside experts. An assessment tool that is appropriate for one goal is often inappropriate for another, leading to misuse of data.

Assessment tools fall broadly into two groups. Traditional assessments rely on specific, structured procedures and instructions given to all test-takers by the test administrator (or to be read by the test-takers themselves). These tests are either norm-referenced or criterion-referenced tests. Standardized tests allow researchers to compare data from large numbers of students or subgroups of students. Alternative assessments are often handled on an individual basis and offer students the opportunity to be more closely involved with the recognition of their progress and to discover what steps they can take to improve.

NORM-REFERENCED ASSESSMENTS In norm-referenced assessments, one person's performance is interpreted in relation to the performance of others. A norm-referenced test is designed to discriminate among individuals in the area being measured and to give each individual a rank or relative measure regarding how he or she performs compared to others of the same age, grade, or other subgroup. Often the mean, or average score, is the reference point, and individuals are scored on how much above or below the average they fall. These tests are usually timed. Norm-referenced tests are often used to tell how a school or school district is doing in comparison to others in the state or nation.

CRITERION-REFERENCED ASSESSMENTS A criterion-referenced assessment allows interpretation of a test-taker's score in relation to a specific standard or criterion. Criterion-referenced tests are designed to help evaluate whether a child has met a specific level of performance. The individual's score is based not on how he or she does in comparison to how others perform, but on how the individual does in relation to absolute expectations about what he or she is supposed to know. An example of a criterion-referenced test is a timed arithmetic test that is scored for the number of problems answered correctly. Criterion-referenced tests measure what information an individual has retained and they give teachers feedback on the effectiveness of their teaching particular concepts.

PERFORMANCE ASSESSMENT Performance assessment can be used to evaluate any learning that is skill-based or behavioral. Performance assessment requires the test-taker to perform a complex task that has to do with producing a certain product or performing a specific task. Performance assessments can be either individual or group-oriented and may involve application of real-life or workplace skills (for example, making a piece of furniture in wood shop).

AUTHENTIC ASSESSMENT Authentic assessment derives its name from the idea that it tests students in skills and knowledge needed to succeed in the real world. Authentic assessment focuses on student task performance and is often used to improve learning in practical areas. An advantage of authentic assessment is that students may be able to see how they would perform in a practical, non-educational setting and thus may be motivated to work to improve.

PORTFOLIO ASSESSMENT Portfolio assessment uses a collection of examples of the actual student's work. It is designed to advance through each grade of school with the student, providing a way for teachers and others to evaluate progress. One of the hallmarks of portfolio assessment is that the student is responsible for selecting examples of his or her own work to be placed in the portfolio. The portfolio may be used by an individual classroom teacher as a repository for work in progress or for accomplishments. Portfolios allow the teacher to evaluate each student in relation to his or her own abilities and learning style. The student controls the assessment samples, helping to reinforce the idea that he or she is responsible for learning and should have a role in choosing the data upon which he or she is judged. Portfolios are often shared by the student and teacher with parents during parent-teacher conferences.

INTERVIEW ASSESSMENT The assessment interview involves a one-on-one or small group discussion between the teacher and student, who may be joined by parents or other teachers. Standardized tests reveal little about the test-taker's thought process during testing. An interview allows the teacher or other administrator to gain an understanding of how the test-taker reached his or her answer. Individual interviews require a much greater time commitment on the part of the teacher than the administration of a standardized test to the entire class at one time. Thus, interviews are most effective when used to evaluate the achievements and needs of specific students. To be successful, interviews require both the teacher and the student to be motivated, open to discussion, and focused on the purpose of the assessment.

JOURNALS Journals have been used as part of the English curriculum since at least the 1980s. In assessment, the journal allows the student to share his or her thoughts on the learning process. A journal may substitute for or supplement a portfolio in providing a student-directed assessment of achievement and goals.

ATTITUDE INVENTORY Attitude is one component of academic success that is rarely measured objectively. An attitude inventory is designed to reveal both positive and negative (or productive and unproductive) aspects of a student's outlook toward school and learning. However, this type of assessment may be of limited use if the student's negative attitude makes him or her unwilling to actively participate in the assessment. By demonstrating a sincere interest in addressing student concerns that affect attitude, a school can improve the effectiveness of attitude inventory assessments.

COMPUTER-AIDED ASSESSMENT Computer-aided assessment is increasingly employed as a supplement to other forms of assessment. A key advantage in the use of computers is the capability of an interactive assessment to provide immediate feedback on responses. Students must be comfortable with computers and reading on a computer screen for these assessments to be successful.

Psychological assessments

Psychological assessment of children is used for a variety of purposes, including diagnosing learning disabilities and behavioral and attention problems. Psychologists can obtain information about a child in three general ways: observation, verbal questioning or written questionnaires, and assignment of tasks. The child's pediatrician, parents, or teacher may ask for psychological assessment to gain a greater understanding of the child's development and needs. There are many different **psychological tests**, and the psychologist must choose the ones that will provide the most relevant and reliable information in each situation. Often multiple tests are performed. However, most psychological assessments fall into one of three categories: observational methods, personality inventories, or projective techniques.

OBSERVATIONAL ASSESSMENT Observations are made by a trained professional either in a familiar setting (such as a classroom or playroom), an experimental setting, or during an office interview. **Toys**, dolls, or other items are often included in the setting to provide stimuli. The child may be influenced by the presence of an observer. However, researchers report that younger children often become engrossed in their activities and thus are relatively unaffected by the presence of an observer. Sometimes, for example, if attention deficit is suspected, several people are asked to observe the child under different circumstances: the teacher at school, the parent at home, and the psychologist in an office setting. Observational assessments are usually combined with other types of educational or psychological assessments when learning needs and behavioral problems are being evaluated.

PERSONALITY INVENTORIES A personality inventory is a questionnaire used with older children and adults that contains questions related to the subject's feelings or reactions to certain scenarios. One of the best-known personality inventories for people over age 16 is the **Minnesota Multiphasic Personality Inventory** (MMPI), a series of over 500 questions used to assess personality traits and psychological disturbances. Interviews or verbal questionnaires for personality assessment may be structured with a specific series of questions or be unstructured, allowing the subject to direct the discussion. Interviewers often use rating scales to record information during interviews.

PROJECTIVE TESTS A projective test asks the test-taker to interpret ambiguous situations. It requires a skilled, trained examiner to administer and interpret a projective test. The reliability of these tests with children is difficult to establish due to their subjective nature, with results varying widely among different examiners. One well-known projective test is the Rorschach Psycho-

diagnostic Test, or inkblot test, first devised by the Swiss psychologist Hermann Rorschach in the 1920s. Another widely used projective test for people ages 14 to 40 is the **Thematic Apperception Test** (TAT), developed at Harvard University in the 1930s. In this test, the subject is shown a series of pictures, each of which can be interpreted in a variety of ways, and asked to construct a story based on each one. An adaptation administered to children aged three to ten is the **Children's Apperception Test** (CAT). Apperception tests are administered to children individually by a trained psychologist to assess personality, maturity, and psychological health.

ASSIGNMENT OF TASK ASSESSMENT Assignment of tasks is an assessment method involving the performance of a specific task or function. These tests are designed to inform the test administrator about attributes such as the test-taker's abilities, perceptions, and motor coordination. They can be especially helpful in assessing if there is a physical or neurological component that needs to be addressed medically or with occupational, speech, or physical therapy.

Common problems

Assessment of children is challenging given the rapid changes in growth they experience during childhood. In childhood, it is difficult to ensure that the test-taker's responses will be stable for even a short time. Thus, psychologists, educators, and other test administrators are careful to take the stage of childhood into account when interpreting a child's test scores.

Traditional standardized tests rely on specific, structured procedures, which with young children presents some problems. Young children (**preschool** and early elementary years) do not have past experience and familiarity with tests and have limited understanding of the expectations of testing procedures. With young test-takers, the test administrator represents a significant factor that influences success. The child must feel comfortable with the test administrator and feel motivated to complete the test exercise. The administrator helps support the test-taker's attention to the test requirements. The testing environment affects all test-takers but may represent a more significant variable for the youngest test-takers.

One shortcoming of standardized testing is that it assumes that the same instrument can evaluate all students. Because most standardized tests are norm-referenced and measure a student's test performance against the performance of other test-takers, students and educators focus their efforts on the test scores, and schools develop curricula to prepare students to take the test.

KEY TERMS

Authentic task assessment—Evaluation of a task performed by a student that is similar to tasks performed in the outside world.

Criterion-referenced test—An assessment that measures the achievement of specific information or skills against a standard as opposed to being measured against how others perform.

Halo effect—An observer bias in which the observer interprets a child's actions in a way that confirm the observer's preconceived ideas about the child.

Norm-referenced test—A test that measures the performance of a student against the performance of a group of other individuals.

Portfolio—A student-controlled collection of student work products that indicates progress over time.

Standardized test—A test that follows a regimented structure, and each individuals scores may be compared with those of groups of people. In the case of the Cognistat, test taker's scores can be compared to groups of young adults, middle-aged adults, the geriatric, and people who have undergone neurosurgery.

Task—A goal directed activity used in assessment.

Other criticisms of standardized tests are that they are culturally insensitive and that they may not accurately represent the abilities of children in the United States for whom English is not their first language or who are not a part of mainstream American culture. Finally, in middle and high school settings, disgruntled students may inconspicuously sabotage their tests since these scores do not affect the students' own grades but reflect rather upon the competency of the teacher and the school administration.

Alternative assessments are subject to other concerns. Observer biases and inconsistencies have been identified through study of the assessment procedures. In the halo effect, the observer evaluates the child's behavior in a way that confirms his general previous impression of the child. For example, the observer believes a particular child is happy and loving. If, when the observer assesses that child, the child lays a doll face down on the table, the observer interprets this act as parenting behavior. On the other hand, if the observer believes the child is angry and hostile, when this child is observed laying the doll face down on the table, the observer may interpret the action as aggression. The expectations of the observer conveyed directly or through body language and other subtle cues may also influence how the child performs and how the observer records and interprets his or her observations. This observer bias can influence the outcome of an assessment.

Parental concerns

Parents are justifiably concerned that their child be evaluated fairly and appropriately. They have the right to understand the purpose of the assessment, how it will be performed, how the information will be used, who will see the assessment results, and how the privacy of their child will be protected. Any professional performing an educational or psychological assessment should be willing discuss these concerns and to share the results of the assessment and their implications with the parent. Parents should be willing to share with examiners any information that might alter interpretation of the assessment results (for example, medical problems, cultural concerns).

When to ask for an assessment

Parents should request an assessment from the teacher whenever necessary to understand their child's progress, both in relation to expected grade-level expectations and performance in relation to other children in the class. Most schools and teachers offer parents many opportunities to discuss the assessment of their child. When teacher assessment indicates that a child has special needs or problems, the parent should request an evaluation by the school's child study team or an outside expert. Parents may also want to discuss appropriate assessments with their child's pediatrician and ask for an referral to a child psychologist or psychiatrist.

See also California Achievement Tests (CAT); Children's Apperception Test (CAT); Development tests.

Resources

BOOKS

Carter, Phillip, and Ken Russell. *Psychometric Testing: 1000 Ways to Assess Your Personality, Creativity, Intelligence, and Lateral Thinking.* New York: Wiley & Sons, 2001.

Groth-Marnat, Gary. *Handbook of Psychological Assessment,* 4th ed. New York: Wiley & Sons, 2003.

Joint Committee on Standards for Educational Evaluation. *The Student Evaluation Standards.* Thousand Oaks, CA: Corwin Press, 2003.

ORGANIZATIONS

Evaluation Center. 4405 Ellsworth Hall, Western Michigan University, Kalamazoo, MI 49008–5237. Web site: <www.wmich.edu/evalctr/jc>.

National Association for the Education of Young Children. 1509 16th Street, NW Washington, DC 20036. Web site: <www.naeyc.org>.

Tish Davidson, A.M.

Asthma

Definition

Asthma is a chronic (long-lasting) inflammatory disease of the airways. In people susceptible to asthma, this inflammation causes the airways to narrow periodically. This narrowing, in turn, produces wheezing and breathlessness that sometimes causes the patient to gasp for air. Obstruction to air flow either stops spontaneously or responds to a wide range of treatments, but continuing inflammation makes the airways hyper-responsive to stimuli such as cold air, **exercise**, dust mites, pollutants in the air, and even stress and **anxiety**.

Description

The changes that take place in the lungs of people with asthma make the airways (the "breathing tubes," or bronchi and the smaller bronchioles) hyper-reactive to many different types of stimuli that do not affect healthy lungs. In an asthma attack, the muscle tissues in the walls of the bronchi go into spasm, and the cells lining the airways swell and secrete mucus into the air spaces. These two actions cause the bronchi to become narrowed (bronchoconstriction). As a result, a person with asthma has to make a much greater effort to breathe.

Cells in the bronchial walls, called mast cells, release certain substances that cause the bronchial muscles to contract and stimulate mucus formation. These substances, including histamine and a group of chemicals called leukotrienes, also bring white blood cells into the area, which play a key role in the inflammatory response. Many patients with asthma are prone to react to such "foreign" substances as pollen, house dust mites, or animal dander. These are called allergens. An acute asthma attack can begin immediately after exposure to a trigger or several days or weeks later.

When asthma begins in childhood, it often affects a child who is likely, for genetic reasons, to become sensi-

tized to common "allergens" in the environment (atopic person). When these children are exposed to house dust mites, animal proteins, fungi, or other potential allergens, they produce a type of antibody that is intended to engulf and destroy the foreign materials. This makes the airway cells sensitive to particular materials. Further exposure can rapidly lead to an asthmatic response.

Demographics

Asthma affects about 17 million Americans, including nearly five million children. Asthma usually begins in childhood or **adolescence**, but it also may first appear in adulthood. Asthma is the leading cause of chronic illness in children, accounting for 14 million missed school days annually. It is the third-ranking cause of **hospitalization** among children under age 15.

Asthma affects as many as 10–12 percent of children in the United States and the number has been steadily increasing. Since 1980, asthma has increased by 160 percent among children at least four years of age. Asthma is becoming more frequent, and—despite modern drug treatments—it is more severe than in the past. Some experts suggest this is due to increased exposure to allergens such as dust, air pollution, second-hand smoke, and industrial components.

Asthma can begin at any age, but most children experience their first symptoms by the time they are five years old. Boys have a higher incidence of asthma than girls, and the disease is more prevalent in African American children. Children living in inner cities, low-income populations, and minorities have disproportionately higher morbidity and mortality due to asthma.

Causes and symptoms

Causes

About 80 percent of childhood asthma cases are caused by **allergies**. In most cases, inhaling an allergen sets off the chain of biochemical and tissue changes leading to airway inflammation, bronchoconstriction, and wheezing characteristic of asthma. Because avoiding (or at least minimizing) exposure is the most effective way of treating asthma, it is vital to identify the allergen or irritant that is causing symptoms in a particular child.

Once asthma is present, symptoms can be triggered or made worse if the child also has **rhinitis** (inflammation of the lining of the nose) or **sinusitis**. **Gastroesophageal reflux disease** (GERD), a condition that causes stomach acid to pass back up the esophagus, can worsen asthma. Many pulmonary infections in early childhood, including those due to *Chlamydia pneumoniae,*

Mycoplasma pneumoniae, and respiratory syncytial virus, have been linked with an increased risk for wheezing and asthma. Aspirin and a class of drugs called beta-blockers (often used to treat high blood pressure) can also worsen the symptoms of asthma. Foggy and cloudy environments have been noted to aggravate asthma, and **obesity** facilitates asthma, but does not cause it.

The most important inhaled allergens and triggers contributing to attacks of asthma are:

- animal dander
- mites in house dust
- fungi (molds) that grow indoors
- mold spores that grow outdoors
- cockroach allergens
- tree, grass, and weed pollen
- occupational exposure to chemicals, fumes, or particles of industrial materials in the air
- strong odors, such as from perfume
- wood smoke

Inhaling tobacco smoke (from secondhand smoke or **smoking**) can irritate the airways and trigger an asthmatic attack. Air pollutants can have a similar effect.

There are three important factors that regularly produce attacks in certain patients with asthma, and they may sometimes be the sole cause of symptoms. They are:

- humidity and temperature changes, especially inhaling cold air
- exercise (in certain children, asthma is caused simply by exercising, and is called exercise-induced asthma)
- stress, strong emotions, or a high level of anxiety

Risk factors

There are many risk factors for childhood asthma, including:

- presence of allergies
- **family** history of asthma and/or allergies
- frequent respiratory infections
- low birth weight
- mother's exposure to tobacco smoke during pregnancy and/or child's exposure after birth
- wheezing with upper respiratory infections

Symptoms

Wheezing is often very obvious, but mild asthmatic attacks may be confirmed when the physician listens to the patient's chest with a stethoscope. Wheezing is often loudest when the child breathes out, in an attempt to expel used air through the narrowed airways. Besides wheezing and shortness of breath, the child may **cough** and experience **pain** or pressure in the chest. The child may have **itching** on the back or neck at the start of an attack. Infants may have feeding problems and may grunt while sucking or feeding. Tiring easily or becoming irritated are other common symptoms.

Some children with asthma are free of symptoms most of the time, but may occasionally experience brief periods during which they are short of breath. Others spend much of their days (and nights) coughing and wheezing, until the asthma is properly treated. Crying or even laughing may bring on an attack. Severe episodes, which are less common, may be seen when the patient has a viral respiratory tract infection or is exposed to a heavy load of an allergen or irritant. Asthmatic attacks may last only a few minutes or can go on for hours or even days (a condition called status asthmaticus).

Asthma symptoms can be classified as:

- Mild intermittent: Symptoms occur twice a week or less; nighttime symptoms occur twice a month or less; symptoms are brief and last a few hours to a few days; no symptoms occur between more severe episodes.
- Mild persistent: Symptoms occur more than twice a week but not every day; nighttime symptoms occur more than twice a month; episodes are severe and sometimes affect activity.
- Moderate persistent: Symptoms occur daily; nighttime symptoms occur more than once a week; quick-relief medication is used daily; symptoms affect daily activities; severe episodes occur twice a week or more and last for days.
- Severe persistent: Symptoms occur continually throughout the day and frequently at night; symptoms affect daily activities and cause the patient to limit activities.

Shortness of breath may cause a patient to become very anxious, sit upright, lean forward, and use the neck or chest wall muscles to help with breathing. These symptoms require emergency attention. In a severe attack that lasts for some time, some of the air sacs in the lung may rupture so that air collects within the chest. This makes it even harder to breathe in adequate amounts of air.

Almost always, even patients with the most severe attacks will recover completely.

When to call the doctor

If a child has the following symptoms, the parent should contact the child's pediatrician:

- inability to participate in normal activities
- missed school due to asthma symptoms
- symptoms that do not improve about 15 minutes after initial treatment with medication
- signs of infection such as increased fatigue or weakness, **fever** or chills, **sore throat**, coughing up mucus, yellow or green mucus, sinus drainage, nasal congestion, headaches, or tenderness along the cheekbones

If the parent is unsure about what action to take to treat the child's symptoms, he or she should call the child's doctor.

The parent or caregiver should seek emergency care by calling 911 in most areas when the child has these symptoms or conditions:

- bluish skin tone
- bluish coloration around the lips, fingernail beds, and tongue
- severe wheezing
- uncontrolled coughing
- very rapid breathing
- inability to catch his or her breath
- tightened neck and chest muscles due to breathing difficulty
- inability to perform a peak expiratory flow
- feelings of anxiety or panic
- pale, sweaty face
- difficulty talking
- difficulty walking
- confusion
- dizziness or fainting
- chest pain or pressure

Diagnosis

Early diagnosis is critical to proper asthma treatment and management. Asthma may be diagnosed by the child's primary pediatrician or an asthma specialist, such as an allergist.

The diagnosis of asthma may be strongly suggested when the typical symptoms and signs are present, including coughing, wheezing, shortness of breath, rapid breathing, or chest tightness. The physician will question the child (if old enough to provide an accurate history of symptoms) or parent about his or her physical health (the medical history), perform a physical examination, and perform or order certain tests to rule out other conditions.

The medical and family history help the physician determine if the child has any conditions or disorders that might be the cause of asthma. A family history of asthma or allergies can be a valuable indicator of asthma and may suggest a genetic predisposition to the condition. The physician will ask detailed questions about the child's symptoms, including when they first occurred, what seems to cause them, the frequency and severity, and how they are being managed.

During the physical exam, the pediatrician will listen to the patient's chest with a stethoscope to evaluate distinctive breathing sounds. He or she also will look for maximum chest expansion during inhalation. Hunched shoulders and contracting neck muscles are signs of narrowed airways. Nasal polyps or increased amounts of nasal secretions are often noted in patients with asthma. Skin changes, like **atopic dermatitis** or eczema, may demonstrate that the patient has allergic problems.

When asthma is suspected, the diagnosis can be confirmed using certain respiratory tests. Spirometry is a test that measures how rapidly air is exhaled and how much air is retained in the lungs. Usually the child should be at least five years of age for this test to be successful. During the test, the child exhales and the spirometer measures the airflow, comparing lung capacity to the normal range for the child's age and race. The child then inhales a drug that widens the air passages (a short-acting bronchodilator) and the doctor takes another measurement of the lung capacity. An increase in lung capacity after taking this medication often indicates the asthma symptoms are reversible (a very typical finding in asthma). The spirometer is similar to the peak flow meter that patients use to keep track of asthma severity at home.

Often, it is difficult to determine what is triggering asthma attacks. Allergy skin testing may be performed, especially if the doctor suspects the child's symptoms are persistent. An allergic skin response does not always mean that the allergen being tested is causing the asthma. Also, the body's immune system produces an antibody to fight off the allergen. The amount of antibody can be measured by a blood test that will show how sensitive the patient is to a particular allergen. If the diagnosis is still in doubt, the patient can inhale a suspect allergen while using a spirometer to detect airway narrowing. Spirometry can also be repeated after a bout of exercise if exercise-induced asthma is a possibility. A chest x ray will help rule out other disorders.

Treatment

Once asthma is diagnosed, a treatment plan should be initiated as quickly as possible to manage asthma symptoms.

In most cases, asthma treatment is managed by the child's pediatrician. Referral to an asthma specialist should be considered if:

- There has been a life-threatening asthma attack or severe, persistent asthma.

- Treatment for three to six months has not met its goals.

- Some other condition, such as nasal polyps or chronic lung disease, complicates the asthma.

- Special tests, such as allergy skin testing or an allergen challenge, are needed.

- Intensive steroid therapy has been necessary.

The first step in bringing asthma under control is to reduce or avoid exposure to known allergens or triggers as much as possible. Treatment goals for all patients with asthma are to prevent troublesome symptoms, maintain lung function as close to normal as possible, avoid emergency room visits or hospitalizations, allow participation in normal activities—including exercise and those requiring exertion—and improve the quality of life.

Medications

The best drug treatment plan will control asthmatic symptoms while causing few or no side effects. The child's doctor will work with the parent to determine the drugs that are most appropriate and may be the most effective, based on the severity of symptoms. Age and the presence of other medical conditions may affect the drugs selected.

Two types of asthma medications include short-acting, quick relief, medications and long-acting, controller, medications. Quick relief medications are used to treat asthma symptoms when they occur. They relieve symptoms rapidly and are usually taken only when needed. Long-acting medications are preventative and are taken daily to help a patient achieve and maintain control of asthma symptoms.

Asthma treatment guidelines may be based on these symptom classifications:

- Mild intermittent: No daily medication is needed but a short-acting beta2 agonist may be used when needed to treat symptoms.

- Mild persistent: Daily long-term medication may be prescribed.

- Moderate persistent: Two medications may be prescribed, including a long-term medication to control inflammation and a short-acting medication to use when symptoms are more severe.

- Severe persistent: Multiple long-term control medications are required.

When asthma symptoms worsen, medication is increased. When asthma symptoms are controlled, less medication is needed. It is very important to discuss any desired changes to the medication schedule with the doctor. The medication dose should never be changed without the doctor's approval. The condition can worsen if certain medications are not taken.

Inhaled medications have a special inhaler that meters the dose. The inhaler may have a spacer that holds the burst of medication until it is inhaled. Patients will be instructed on how to properly use an inhaler to ensure that it will deliver the right amount of medication.

A home nebulizer, also known as a breathing machine, may be used to deliver asthma medications at home. The nebulizer changes medication from liquid form to a mist. The child wears a face mask to breathe in the medications. Nebulizer treatments generally take seven to 10 minutes.

Quick relief medications include short-acting, inhaled beta2 agonists and anticholinergics. Long-acting medications include leukotriene modifiers, mast cell stabilizers, inhaled and oral corticosteroids, long-acting beta2 agonists, and methylxanthines.

SHORT-ACTING BETA-2 AGONISTS These drugs, which are bronchodilators, open the airways by relaxing the muscles around the airways that have tightened (bronchospasm). The short-acting forms of beta-receptor agonists are the best choice for relieving sudden attacks of asthma and for preventing attacks triggered by exercise. These drugs generally start acting within minutes, but their effects last only four to six hours (although longer-acting forms are being developed). They may be taken by mouth, inhaled, or injected.

ANTICHOLINERGICS Anticholinergics are medications that open the airways by relaxing the muscle bands that tighten around the airways. They also suppress mucus production. They do not provide immediate relief, but can be used to control severe attacks when added to an inhaled beta-receptor agonist.

LEUKOTRIENE MODIFIERS Leukotriene modifiers, also called antileukotrienes, can be used in place of steroids for older children who have a mild degree of asthma that persists. They work by counteracting leukotrienes, substances released by white blood cells in the lung that cause the air passages to constrict and promote mucus secretion.

MAST CELL STABILIZERS Available only in inhaled form, mast cell stabilizers, such as cromolyn and nedocromil, prevent asthma symptoms. These anti-inflammatory drugs are often given to children as the initial treatment to prevent asthmatic attacks over the long term. They can also prevent attacks when given before exercise or when exposure to an allergen cannot be avoided. They are not effective until three to four weeks after therapy is started. These medications need to be taken two to four times a day.

STEROIDS These drugs, which resemble natural body hormones, block inflammation. Steroids are extremely effective in relieving asthma symptoms and can control even severe cases over the long term while maintaining good lung function. When steroids are taken by inhalation for a long period, asthma attacks become less frequent as the airways become less sensitive to allergens. Besides being inhaled, steroids may be taken by mouth or injected, to rapidly control severe asthma. Steroids are the strongest class of asthma medications and can cause numerous side-effects, including bleeding from the stomach, loss of calcium from bones, cataracts in the eye, and a diabetes-like state. Patients using steroids for lengthy periods also may have problems with wound healing, weight gain, and mental disorders. In children, growth may be slowed. To prevent serious side effects, the child will have periodic monitoring tests.

LONG-ACTING BETA-2 AGONISTS Long-acting beta-2 agonists are used for better control—not relief—of asthma symptoms. The medications take longer to work and the effects last longer, up to 12 hours.

METHYLXANTHINES Theophylline is the chief methylxanthine drug. It may exert some anti-inflammatory effect, and is especially helpful in controlling nighttime symptoms of asthma. If a patient cannot use an inhaler to maintain long-term control, sustained-release theophylline is a good alternative. The blood levels of the drug must be measured periodically, as too high of a dose can cause an abnormal heart rhythm or convulsions.

OTHER DRUGS Some inhalers contain a combination of two different medications that can be delivered together to shorten treatment times and decrease the number of inhalers that need to be purchased. Clinical trials are continuously evaluating new asthma medications.

IMMUNOTHERAPY If a patient's asthma is caused by an allergen that cannot be avoided, or if medications have not been effective in controlling symptoms, immunotherapy (also called **allergy shots**) may be considered. Immunotherapy is helpful when symptoms tend to occur throughout all or most of the year. Typically, increasing amounts of the allergen are injected over a period of three to five years, so that the body can build up an effective immune response. There is a risk that this treatment may cause the airways to become narrowed and bring on an asthmatic attack.

An international conference, Immunotherapy in Allergic Asthma, hosted by the American College of Allergy, Asthma, and Immunology (ACAII) in 2000 concluded that immunotherapy is an effective treatment for allergic asthma and can prevent the onset of asthma in children with **allergic rhinitis**. The Preventive Allergy Treatment study, published in 2002, confirmed the ACAII conference conclusions, documenting that immunotherapy reduces the risk of developing asthma and reduces lung airway inflammation in children with hay fever, a condition that predisposes them to asthma.

Managing asthmatic attacks

Urgent measures to control asthma attacks and ongoing treatment to prevent attacks are equally important. No matter how severe a person's asthma, quick-relief medications must be readily available to treat acute symptoms. If the patient's asthma symptoms are present most of the time, an anti-inflammatory medication should be used regularly.

A severe asthma attack should be treated as quickly as possible. It is most important for a patient suffering an acute attack to be given extra oxygen. Rarely, it may be necessary to use a mechanical ventilator to help the patient breathe. A beta-receptor agonist is inhaled repeatedly or continuously. A steroid is given if the patient's symptoms do not improve promptly and completely. Steroids also may help if a viral infection caused severe asthmatic symptoms. A course of steroid therapy, given after the attack is over, will make a recurrence less likely.

Starting treatment at home, rather than in a hospital, minimizes delays and helps the patient gain a sense of control over the disease. When deciding whether a patient should be hospitalized, the past history of acute attacks, severity of symptoms, current medication, and availability of adequate support at home must be taken into account.

Maintaining control

Children with asthma should follow up with their doctor every one to six months, depending on the frequency of attacks. During the follow-up visits, the child's lung function should be measured by spirometry to make sure treatment goals are being met. Once asthma has been controlled for several weeks or months, the child's physician may adjust the medication dosage. If there is no clear improvement with the current treatment plan, another treatment plan should be established.

All patients with asthma should learn how to monitor their symptoms so that they will know when an attack is starting. Symptoms can be monitored with a peak flow meter (also called a peak expiratory flow meter). To effectively follow the instructions for using a peak flow meter, the child should be at least five years old. The peak flow meter measures the child's airflow when he or she blows into it quickly and forcefully. The peak flow meter can be used to determine when to call the doctor or seek emergency care.

Knowing the child's allergens or triggers will help parents reduce exposure by making improvements in the home environment. Specific guidelines may include reducing indoor humidity, using allergen-impermeable bedding covers, minimizing the use of carpet and upholstered furniture, and minimizing pet exposure. For more information, see the Prevention section.

All patients with asthma should have a written action plan to follow if symptoms suddenly become worse, including how to adjust medication and when to seek medical help. A Northwestern University study indicates that asthma symptoms and the need for emergency medications in children can be greatly reduced by using a planned-care method. This method involves regularly scheduled visits with specially trained nurses to help the patient and family learn how to anticipate and improve the management of asthma symptoms.

The health care provider should write out an asthma treatment plan for the child's school personnel or care providers. The plan should detail the early warning signs of an asthma attack, what medications the student uses and how they are taken, and when to contact the doctor or seek emergency care. Children with asthma often need medication at school to control acute symptoms or to prevent exercise-induced attacks. Proper management will usually allow a child to take part in play activities. Only as a last resort should activities be limited.

Alternative treatment

Alternative and complementary therapies include approaches considered to be outside the mainstream of traditional health care. Alternative treatments for asthma include **yoga** to control breathing and relieve stress and acupuncture to reduce asthma attacks and improve lung function. Biofeedback, which teaches patients how to direct mental thoughts to influence physical functions, may be helpful for some patients. For example, learning to increase the amount of air inhaled may help some patients reduce **fear** and anxiety. Some Chinese traditional herbs, such as *ding-chan tang*, have been thought to help decrease inflammation and relieve bronchospasm.

Before learning or practicing any particular technique, it is important for the parent or caregiver and child to learn about the therapy, its safety and effectiveness, potential side effects, and the expertise and qualifications of the practitioner. Although some practices are beneficial, others may be harmful to certain patients.

Relaxation techniques and dietary supplements should not be used as a substitute for medical therapies prescribed by a doctor. Parents should discuss these alternative treatments with the child's doctor to determine the techniques and remedies that may be beneficial.

Nutritional concerns

Some children have reportedly experienced improved symptoms by limiting dairy products and sugar in the diet. Some studies show that vitamin C helps improve asthma symptoms.

Food additives may trigger asthma symptoms in some children, although this is rare. If the parent suspects that certain foods trigger asthma symptoms in the child, the pediatrician may recommend keeping a food diary for a few weeks to identify problematic foods. Allergy skin testing may be recommended to rule out foods that may trigger asthma symptoms.

Prognosis

Although there is no cure for asthma, it can be treated and managed. Most patients with asthma respond well and are able to lead relatively normal lives when the best drug or combination of drugs is found. Asthma should not be a progressive, disabling disease; a child with asthma can have normal or near-normal lung function with the proper treatment.

Some children stop having attacks as they grow and their airways get bigger. About 50 percent of children have less frequent and less severe attacks as they grow older. However, symptoms can recur when the child reaches his or her thirties or forties.

KEY TERMS

Acute—Refers to a disease or symptom that has a sudden onset and lasts a relatively short period of time.

Allergen—A foreign substance that provokes an immune reaction or allergic response in some sensitive people but not in most others.

Allergy—A hypersensitivity reaction in response to exposure to a specific substance.

Alveoli—The tiny air sacs clustered at the ends of the bronchioles in the lungs in which oxygen-carbon dioxide exchange takes place.

Anti-inflammatory—A class of drugs, including nonsteroidal anti-inflammatory drugs (NSAIDs) and corticosteroids, used to relieve swelling, pain, and other symptoms of inflammation.

Atopy—A state that makes persons more likely to develop allergic reactions of any type, including the inflammation and airway narrowing typical of asthma.

Bronchial tubes—The major airways to the lungs and their main branches.

Bronchioles—Small airways extending from the bronchi into the lobes of the lungs.

Bronchospasm—The tightening of the muscle bands that surround the airways, causing the airways to narrow.

Dander—Loose scales shed from the fur or feathers of household pets and other animals. Dander can cause allergic reactions in susceptible people.

Dust mites—Tiny insects, unable to be seen without a microscope, that are present in carpet, stuffed animals, upholstered furniture, and bedding, including pillows, mattresses, quilts, and other bed covers. Dust mites are one of the most common asthma triggers. They grow best in areas with high humidity.

Hypersensitivity—A condition characterized by an excessive response by the body to a foreign substance. In hypersensitive individuals even a tiny amount of allergen can cause a severe allergic reaction.

Inflammation—Pain, redness, swelling, and heat that develop in response to tissue irritation or injury. It usually is caused by the immune system's response to the body's contact with a foreign substance, such as an allergen or pathogen.

Peak flow measurement—Measurement of the maximum rate of airflow attained during a forced vital capacity determination.

Pollen—A fine, powdery substance released by plants and trees; an allergen.

Spirometry—A test using an instrument called a spirometer that measures how much and how fast the air is moving in and out of a patient's lungs. Spirometry can help a physician diagnose a range of respiratory diseases, monitor the progress of a disease, or assess a patient's response to treatment.

Trigger—Any situation or substance that causes asthma symptoms to start or become worse.

A small number of patients will have progressively more difficulty breathing. These patients have an increased risk of respiratory failure, and they must receive intensive treatment. Asthma can be a deadly disease if it is not managed properly; an estimated 5,000 people die each year from asthma or its complications.

Prevention

Prolonged breastfeeding in infants for six to 12 months has been shown to reduce the child's likelihood for developing persistent asthma.

Minimizing exposure to allergens

There are a number of ways parents can reduce or prevent a child's exposure to the common allergens and irritants that provoke asthmatic attacks:

- If the child is sensitive to a family pet, the pet should be removed or kept out of the child's bedroom (with the bedroom door closed). The pet should be kept away from carpets and upholstered furniture. All products made from feathers should be removed. An air filter should be used on air ducts in the child's room.

- To reduce exposure to house dust mites, wall-to-wall carpeting should be removed, humidity should be kept down, and special pillow and mattress covers should be used. The number of stuffed **toys** should be reduced, and they should be washed in hot water weekly. Bedding should also be washing weekly in hot water, and dried in a dryer on the hot setting. The child should not be allowed to **sleep** on upholstered furniture. Carpets should be removed from the child's bedroom.

- If cockroach allergen is causing asthma attacks, the roaches should be killed (using poison, traps, or boric acid rather than chemicals). Food or garbage should not be exposed.

- Indoor air may be kept clean by vacuuming carpets once or twice a week (with the child absent), avoiding humidifiers, and using air conditioning during warm weather (so that windows remain closed).

- To reduce exposure to mold, indoor humidity should be decreased to less than 50 percent, leaky faucets and pipes should be repaired, and vaporizers avoided.

- Family members should quit smoking and others should not be allowed to smoke in the house or near the child.

- The child should not exercise outdoors when air pollution levels are high.

Parental concerns

Parents should take an open and honest approach when explaining asthma to their child. They should explain that asthma does not define or limit the child. The success of the child's treatment plan will depend on parental guidance and support. As a child ages, the responsibility for personal asthma management can be increased. For example, toddlers can mimic treatment on a toy or doll; preschoolers can help parents in peak flow monitoring and discuss symptoms with them; school-aged children can begin to take medications on their own (while supervised); and adolescents can be nearly independent in following the structured management plan.

Parents should stress the consequences of improper symptom management with their child. The main concern with older children is **peer pressure** and the desire to fit in; therefore, symptoms may not be reported accurately and medications may not be taken to avoid comments from peers or appearing different. Parents may want to counteract peer pressure by offering a contract that outlines the management plan and lists specific rewards and consequences.

Parents should work with school personnel to foster a supportive environment that so the child's symptoms can be managed properly. A specific action plan can be developed for school by the child's doctor. Parents should inform school personnel about the child's specific allergens and asthma triggers so steps can be taken to help the child avoid them at school. Students who are able to recognize symptoms requiring medication and know how to use their inhaler properly should be permitted to keep the medication with them. For younger children, parents must ensure that school personnel know how to administer the child's medications.

Asthma should not be used as an excuse to avoid exercise. Sometimes children with asthma avoid school activities because they are afraid of being embarrassed if symptoms occur. Parents should encourage athletic or physical activity participation and talk to gym teachers or coaches to ensure they understand the child's symptoms and treatment protocol. They should make sure the child knows what to do if exercise causes symptoms. Swimming is generally well-tolerated by many people with asthma because it is usually performed in a warm, moist environment. Other activities that involve brief, intermittent periods of exertion, such as volleyball, gymnastics, baseball, walking, and wrestling are usually well-tolerated. Cold-weather **sports**, such as skiing, ice skating, or hockey, may be not be tolerated as well. The child's doctor can provide specific exercise recommendations and guidelines.

See also Allergy shots.

Resources

BOOKS

American Medical Association. *The American Medical Association Essential Guide for Asthma (Better Health for 2003)* Pocket, 2000.

Fanta, Christopher H., et al. *The Harvard Medical School Guide to Taking Control of Asthma.* New York, NY: Free Press, 2003.

Wolf, Rauol. *Essential Pediatric Allergy, Asthma, and Immunology.* New York, NY: McGraw-Hill Professional, 2004.

ORGANIZATIONS

Allergy and Asthma Network/Mothers of Asthmatics America, Inc. 2751 Prosperity Ave., Suite 150, Fairfax, VA 22031. (800) 878-4403. Web site: <www.aanma.org.>.

American Academy of Allergy, Asthma and Immunology (AAAAI). 611 E. Wells St., Milwaukee, WI 53202. (800) 822-ASTHMA or (414) 272-6071. Web site: <www.aaaai.org>.

American College of Asthma, Allergy and Immunology (AACI). 85 W. Algonquin Rd., Suite 550, Arlington Hts., IL 60005. (800) 842-7777. Web site: <www. aaci.org.>.

American Lung Association. 1740 Broadway, New York, NY 10019. (800) 586-4872. Web site: <www.lungusa.org.>.

Asthma and Allergy Foundation of America. 1233 20th Street, NW, Suite 402, Washington, DC 20036. (800) 727-8462 or (202) 466-7643. Web site: <www.aafa.org>.

National Asthma Education Program. National Heart, Lung and Blood Institute Information Center. P.O. Box 30105, Bethesda, MD 20824-0105. (301) 592-8573. Web site: <www.nhlbi.nih.gov/about/naepp/>.

National Institute of Allergy and Infectious Diseases. NIAID Office of Communications and Public Liaison, Building 31, Room 7A-50, 31 Center Dr., MSC 2520, Bethesda, MD 20892-2520. Web site: <www.niaid.nih.gov>.

David A. Cramer, M.D.
Angela M. Costello

Ataxia *see* **Movement disorders**

Ataxia telangiectasia/chromosome breakage disorders

Definition

Ataxia telangiectasia (A-T), also called Louis-Bar syndrome or cerebello-oculocutaneous telangiectasia, is a rare, inherited disease that attacks the neurological and immune systems of children. A-T is a recessive disorder, meaning that it affects children who carry two copies of a defective (mutated) A-T gene, one copy from each parent. A-T affects the brain and many parts of the body and causes a wide range of severe disabilities.

Description

Ataxia means poor coordination, and the telangiectasia are tiny, red spider blood vessels which develop in A-T patients, especially on the whites of the eyes and on the surface of the ears. A-T is a progressive disease that affects the cerebellum (the body's motor control center) and, in about 70 percent of cases, weakens the immune system as well, leading to respiratory disorders. The weakening of the immune system (**immunodeficiency**) resulting from A-T has been traced to defects in both B-cells and T-cells, the specialized white blood cells (lymphocytes) that defend the body against infection, disease, and foreign substances. In A-T children, B-cell responses are very weak, and levels of immunoglobulins, the proteins that B-cells make to fight infection by specific recognition of invading organisms, may also be low. T-cells are few and weak, and the thymus gland is immature. This is why A-T is also considered an immunodeficiency disease. A-T first shows itself in early childhood, usually at the toddler stage. The characteristic symptoms are lack of balance, slurred speech, and perhaps a higher-than-normal number of infections. All children at this age take a little while to develop good walking skills, coherent speech, and an effective immune system, so it often takes a few years before A-T is correctly diagnosed. Other features of the disease may include mild diabetes, premature graying of the hair, difficulty swallowing, and delayed physical and sexual development. Children with A-T usually have normal or above normal **intelligence**, but some cases of **mental retardation** have been reported.

Transmission

A-T is genetically transmitted by parents who are carriers of the gene responsible for A-T. The A-T mode of inheritance is autosomal recessive (AR) and requires two copies of the predisposing gene—one from each parent—for the child to have the disease. Parents do not exhibit symptoms, but they each carry a recessive gene that may cause A-T in their offspring. In AR families, there is one chance in four that each child born to the parents will have the disorder. Every healthy sibling of an A-T patient has a 66 percent chance of being a carrier, like the parents.

Demographics

According to the National **Cancer** Institute, the incidence of A-T is between one out of 40,000 and one out of 100,000 persons worldwide, and for Caucasians it is about three per million, so the disorder is very rare. In the United States, there are about 500 children with A-T with both males and females equally affected. An estimated 1 percent (2.5 million) of the general population carries one of the defective A-T genes. Carriers of one copy of this gene do not develop A-T but have a significantly increased risk of cancer (over 38 percent of children with A-T develop cancer).

Causes and symptoms

A-T is a genetic disorder, meaning that it is caused by a defect in a gene that is present in a person at birth. All people have genes that contain a few mistakes or variations that do not result in a disorder. Disorders result when the gene variations are significant enough to affect the function a gene controls. Variations that cause disease are called mutations and A-T results from a defective gene, the ATM gene (for ataxia telangiectasia, mutated), first identified in 1995. The ATM gene is located on the long arm of chromosome 11 at position 11q22-23. It encodes for (controls) the production of a protein that plays a role in regulating cell division following DNA damage. The various symptoms seen in A-T reflect the main role of this protein, which is to induce several cellular responses to DNA damage. The protein made by the ATM gene is located in the nucleus of the cell and normally functions to control the rate at which the cell grows. The ATM protein does this by sending signals and modifying other proteins in the cell, which then changes the function of the proteins. The ATM protein also interacts with other special proteins when DNA is damaged as a result of exposure to some type of radiation. If the strands of DNA are broken, the ATM protein coordinates DNA repair by activating repair proteins, which helps to maintain the stability of cells. Mutations in ATM prevent cells from repairing DNA damage, which may lead to cancer. Mutations can also signal cells in the brain to die inappropriately, causing the movement and coordination problems associated with A-T.

A-T affects several different organs in the body. The most important symptoms are as follows:

- Neurologic abnormalities resulting in poor coordination and an unsteady gait (ataxia). Shortly after learning to walk, children with A-T begin to stagger. They tend to sway when they stand or sit and wobble when they walk. Jerking and tremors are present in about 25 percent of patients. This symptom results from neurologic abnormalities affecting the cerebellum that controls balance. Writing is affected by seven or eight years of age.

- Dilated blood vessels (telangiectasia). Telangiectasias usually occur on the white portion of the eye or on the ears, neck and extremities.

- Variable immunodeficiency resulting in increased vulnerability to infections. This symptom is a major feature in some individuals. The infections most commonly involve the lungs and sinuses and are usually of bacterial or viral origin. About 10 percent of patients have severe immunodeficiency.

- Predisposition to certain types of cancer. At least 10 percent of all A-T patients, including adults, develop cancer. Most of these are cancers of the lymphoid tissues (leukemias and lymphomas), but one fifth of the cancers occur in the stomach, brain, ovary, skin, liver, larynx, parotid gland, and breast.

Additional clinical symptoms include the following:

- autosomal recessive inheritance of the ATM gene
- involuntary, rapid, rhythmic movement of the eyeball (nystagmus)
- impaired ability to coordinate certain types of eye movements (oculomotor apraxia)
- squint of ocular muscles
- speech defect (dysarthria)
- slow, writhing motions (choreoathetosis)
- lack of T-lymphocytes (thymic aplasia)
- albinism of hair

- decreased to absent deep tendon reflexes
- multiple skin changes including eczema and "coffee-with-milk"x colored spots
- incomplete development of tonsils, lymph nodes, and spleen (hypoplasia)
- seizures (any type)
- abnormal ovaries
- small testes
- high blood sugar levels (hyperglycemia)

When to call the doctor

A-T children appear normal as infants. The decreased coordination of movements (ataxia) associated with A-T first becomes apparent when a child begins to walk, typically between 12 and 18 months of age. Toddlers with A-T are usually wobbly walkers. In their **preschool** years, children with A-T begin to stumble and fall, and drooling is frequent. Parents should contact their pediatrician if they observe any A-T signs or symptoms in their child. Telangiectasias are another typical warning sign. They become apparent after the onset of the ataxia, often between two and eight years of age.

Diagnosis

Establishing a diagnosis for ataxia telangiectasia is most difficult in very young children, primarily because the full-blown syndrome is not yet apparent. As of 2004, the A-T diagnosis is usually based on the characteristic clinical findings and supported by laboratory tests that point to a defect of DNA (genes and chromosomes) and to an inability to repair some types of damage to DNA. Laboratory tests are helpful but not as important as the individual patient's symptoms and signs, **family** history, and complete neurological evaluation including a **magnetic resonance imaging** (MRI) scan of the brain. The cerebellum atrophies early in the disease, being visibly smaller on MRI examination by seven or eight years of age. Diagnosis is more difficult before the disorder has fully developed, when the child is still uncertain on his/her feet. The most difficult time to diagnose A-T is during the period when neurologic symptoms start to appear (early childhood) and the typical telangiectasias have not yet appeared. During this period, a history of recurrent infections and typical immunologic findings can suggest the diagnosis. Four tests are used to help establish the A-T diagnosis:

- Increased alpha-fetoprotein levels in blood. Alpha-fetoproteins are fetal proteins that are usually produced during fetal development but may persist at high blood levels after birth. The vast majority of A-T patients (more than 95 percent) have elevated levels of serum alpha-fetoprotein. This test is considered good but yields similar results for other conditions.

- Decreased immunoglobulin levels (Iga, IgG, IgM). Approximately 30 percent of patients with A-T have immunodeficiency. The drawback of this test is that immunoglobulin levels are not always low for A-T, and they are also low in other conditions.

- Sequence analysis. Sequence analysis of the ATM coding region is available on a clinical basis. Sequencing detects more than 95 percent of ATM sequence alterations but significant difficulties exist in distinguishing normal variations from A-T-causing mutations.

- Increased chromosome breaks and rearrangements. Individuals with A-T have an increased frequency of spontaneous breaks in their chromosomes as well as an increased frequency of chromosomal rearrangements. These chromosomal abnormalities often occur close to genes that control the function of white blood cells, such as immunoglobulins and T-lymphocytes. The frequency of chromosomal breaks is increased when T-lymphocytes are exposed to **x rays** in the laboratory, and this sensitivity to ionizing irradiation forms the basis for a specialized A-T diagnostic test.

The ionizing irradiation sensitivity test is the most useful test for diagnosing A-T. However, it can only be carried out in specialized centers and takes much longer than the other tests.

Because of its variable symptoms, A-T is often misdiagnosed as a form of **cerebral palsy** or as slow development.

Treatment

As of 2004, there is no cure for ataxia telangiectasia, thus specific therapy is not available, and treatment is largely supportive. Patients are encouraged to participate in as many activities as possible. Children are encouraged to attend school on a regular basis and receive support to maintain as normal a lifestyle as possible. The following are some types of interventions have been shown to help those with the disorder:

- Exercise and physiotherapy. These programs help prevent the development of stiffness in muscles and help maintain functional mobility, showing A-T patients how to best use muscle control and stretch muscles and ligaments.

- Antibiotics, immunoglobulins, vaccinations. For patients who have normal levels of immunoglobulins and normal antibody responses to vaccines, immunization with **influenza** and pneumococcal vaccines may

be helpful. For patients with total IgG deficiencies or patients who have problems making normal antibody responses to vaccines, therapy with gammaglobulin may be indicated.

- Speech therapy. Speech therapy can significantly improve diction, especially in the second decade of the disorder.

- Orthopedic referral/assessment. Corrective procedures can be helpful for joint or postural problems, particularly in the lower limbs or spine.

Because cells from patients with A-T are 30 percent more sensitive to ionizing radiation than the cells of normal individuals, any required radiotherapy or **chemotherapy** should be reduced or monitored carefully; conventional doses are contraindicated and are potentially lethal.

Alternative treatment

No single alternative medicine or herbal remedy can help people with A-T. The use of thymic transplants and hormones has not led to improvement. Similarly, there is no scientific evidence as of 2004 that any specific supplemental nutritional therapy is beneficial.

Concerning drug therapy, most drugs which act on the nervous system can cause problems in A-T. Some people have found Benzhexol beneficial, but others have suffered reactions to it. Drug therapy for A-T remains in 2004 experimental and accordingly requires highly specialized A-T clinical teams.

Since the 1995 isolation of the ATM gene, scientists have worked very hard to understand how the ATM protein is activated or turned on following damage to a cell's DNA. This knowledge is in turn being used to develop A-T treatment approaches. The following are among the most promising:

- Gene therapy: Scientists are starting to test the efficiency of gene therapy protocols in mice and are simultaneously developing a new gene therapy protocol for A-T which would allow for stable, long-term production of the ATM protein.

- Neural stem cells: Researchers have demonstrated a significant therapeutic effect by using neural stem cells in mice that have a pattern of neurodegeneration similar to A-T.

- Bone marrow transplantation: Significant progress has been made in the development of a successful bone marrow transplantation protocol in mice with A-T. Researchers are testing how effectively this protocol prevents immune abnormalities and immune-related cancers in these mice.

Albinism—An inherited condition that causes a lack of pigment. People with albinism typically have light skin, white or pale yellow hair, and light blue or gray eyes.

Allele—One of two or more alternate forms of a gene.

Ataxia—A condition marked by impaired muscular coordination, most frequently resulting from disorders in the brain or spinal cord.

Atrophy—The progressive wasting and loss of function of any part of the body.

B-cell (B lymphocyte)—A small white blood cell from bone marrow responsible for producing antibody and serving as a precursor for plasma cells.

Carrier—A person who possesses a gene for an abnormal trait without showing signs of the disorder. The person may pass the abnormal gene on to offspring. Also refers to a person who has a particular disease agent present within his/her body, and can pass this agent on to others, but who displays no symptoms of infection.

Central nervous system—Part of the nervous system consisting of the brain, cranial nerves, and spinal cord. The brain is the center of higher processes, such as thought and emotion and is responsible for the coordination and control of bodily activities and the interpretation of information from the senses. The cranial nerves and spinal cord link the brain to the peripheral nervous system, that is the nerves present in the rest of body.

Cerebellum—The part of the brain involved in the coordination of movement, walking, and balance.

Chromosome—A microscopic thread-like structure found within each cell of the human body and consisting of a complex of proteins and DNA. Humans have 46 chromosomes arranged into 23 pairs. Chromosomes contain the genetic information necessary to direct the development and functioning of all cells and systems in the body. They pass on hereditary traits from parents to child (like eye color) and determine whether the child will be male or female.

Diabetes—A disease characterized by an inability to process sugars in the diet, due to a decrease in or total absence of insulin production.

DNA—Deoxyribonucleic acid; the genetic material in cells that holds the inherited instructions for growth, development, and cellular functioning.

Fetal proteins—Proteins that are usually produced during fetal development but may persist at high blood levels in some conditions (such as A-T) after birth. The vast majority of A-T patients (more than 95%) have elevated levels of serum alpha-fetoprotein.

Gene—A building block of inheritance, which contains the instructions for the production of a particular protein, and is made up of a molecular sequence found on a section of DNA. Each gene is found on a precise location on a chromosome.

Immune response—A physiological response of the body controlled by the immune system that involves the production of antibodies to fight off specific foreign substances or agents (antigens).

Immune system—The system of specialized organs, lymph nodes, and blood cells throughout the body that work together to defend the body against foreign invaders (bacteria, viruses, fungi, etc.).

Immunodeficiency—A condition in which the body's immune response is damaged, weakened, or is not functioning properly.

Immunoglobulin G (IgG)—Immunoglobulin type gamma, the most common type found in the blood and tissue fluids.

Leukemia—A cancer of the blood-forming organs (bone marrow and lymph system) characterized by an abnormal increase in the number of white blood cells in the tissues. There are many types of leukemias and they are classified according to the type of white blood cell involved.

Lymphocyte—A type of white blood cell that participates in the immune response. The two main groups are the B cells that have antibody molecules on their surface and T cells that destroy antigens.

Lymphocytic leukemia—An acute form of childhood leukemia characterized by the development of abnormal cells in the bone marrow.

Lymphoma—A diverse group of cancers of the lymphatic system characterized by abnormal growth of lymphatic cells. Two general types are commonly recognized–Hodgkin's disease and non-Hodgkin's lymphoma.

Magnetic resonance imaging (MRI)—An imaging technique that uses a large circular magnet and radio waves to generate signals from atoms in the body. These signals are used to construct detailed images of internal body structures and organs, including the brain.

KEY TERMS (contd.)

Motor skills—Controlled movements of muscle groups. Fine motor skills involve tasks that require dexterity of small muscles, such as buttoning a shirt. Tasks such as walking or throwing a ball involve the use of gross motor skills.

Neurodegenerative disease—A disease in which the nervous system progressively and irreversibly deteriorates.

Nystagmus—An involuntary, rhythmic movement of the eyes.

Progressive—Advancing, going forward, going from bad to worse, increasing in scope or severity.

Recessive disorder—Disorder that requires two copies of the predisposing gene one from each parent for the child to have the disease.

Stem cell—An undifferentiated cell that retains the ability to develop into any one of a variety of cell types.

T cell—A type of white blood cell that is produced in the bone marrow and matured in the thymus gland. It helps to regulate the immune system's response to infections or malignancy.

Telangiectasia—Abnormal dilation of capillary blood vessels leading to the formation of telangiectases or angiomas.

Thymic aplasia—A lack of T lymphocytes, due to failure of the thymus to develop, resulting in very reduced immunity.

- High throughput drug screening: Testing methods are also being developed to help scientists screen large numbers of already-approved drugs as well as new compounds to see if they are useful for treating A-T.

- Transplants of thymus tissue: The new approaches that medical researchers are testing also include transplants of thymus tissue to boost the immune system.

Clinical trials

Parents may consider enrolling their A-T diagnosed child in a NIH-approved clinical trial. The first-ever A-T clinical treatment study took place at Children's Hospital in Philadelphia, with a second trial that started in 2000. In 2004, the A-T Clinical Center at Johns Hopkins Hospital in Baltimore also started a clinical study. Children who participate in these clinical trials receive complete immunological and neurological evaluations as part of being enrolled in the study. Many patients also receive nutritional evaluations and consultations as well.

Nutritional concerns

Some A-T patients have impaired swallowing function. Patients who aspirate or have food and liquids reaching their lungs have been shown to improve when thin liquids are removed from their diet. In some individuals, a tube from the stomach to the outside of the abdomen (gastrostomy tube) may be required to eliminate the need for swallowing large volumes of liquids and to decrease the risk of aspiration. Vitamin E supplements are often recommended, although the vitamin has not been formally tested for efficacy in patients with A-T.

Prognosis

Generally, the prognosis for individuals with A-T is poor. Those with the disease are frequently wheelchair-bound by their teens and usually die in their teens or early 20s. However, the course of the disease can be quite variable, and it is difficult to predict the outcome for any given individual as A-T varies considerably from patient to patient. Even within families, in which the specific genetic defect should be the same, some children have mostly neurologic problems while others have recurrent infections, and still others have neither neurologic problems nor recurrent infections.

There was no cure for A-T as of 2004. The cloning and sequencing of the ATM gene has opened several avenues of research with the goal of developing better treatment, including gene therapy and the design of drugs for more effective treatments. Research is also leading to a greater understanding of AT, increased awareness, and more genetic counseling.

Prevention

In the past, A-T carriers were identified because they were parents of a child diagnosed with A-T. But the cloning of the ATM gene responsible for A-T as of 2004 allows physicians or cancer genetics professionals to conduct genetic testing, analyzing patients' DNA to look for A-T mutations in the ATM gene. Thus, prenatal diagnosis can be carried out in most families. Genetic counseling is also of benefit to prospective parents with a family history of ataxia-telangiectasia. Parents of a child diagnosed with A-T may have a slight increased risk of cancer. They should have genetic counseling and more intensive screening for cancer.

Parental concerns

Any family touched by ataxia telangiectasia is forever affected. Old assumptions have to be discarded and new, often very difficult, realities need to be accepted, including the uncertainty of the A-T outcome. Significant adjustments, both physical and psychological, are required, many of them agonizingly difficult. A-T support groups have been organized by all major A-T organizations, such as the Ataxia Telangiectasia Children's Project, the National Ataxia Foundation (NAF), and the Ataxia Telangiectasia Medical Research Foundation. These organizations are dedicated to improving the lives of families affected by A-T. They also provide the latest news on A-T research, information on coping with A-T, and personal accounts of living with A-T.

See also Immunodeficiency; Magnetic resonance imaging.

Resources

BOOKS

Key, Doneen. *Do You Want to Take Her Home?: Trials and Tribulations of Living Life as a Handicapped Person Due to Multiple Birth Defects.* Lancaster, CA: Empire Publishing, 2001.

Parker, J. N., and P. M. Parker, eds. *The Official Parent's Sourcebook on Ataxia Telangiectasia: A Revised and Updated Directory for the Internet Age.* San Diego, CA: Icon health Publications, 2002.

PERIODICALS

Farr, A. K., et al. "Ocular manifestations of ataxia-telangiectasia." *American Journal of Ophthalmology* 134, no. 6 (December 2002): 891–96.

McKinnon, P. J. "ATM and ataxia telangiectasia." *EMBO Reports* 5, no. 8 (August 2004): 772–76.

Nowak-Wegrzyn, A., et al. "Immunodeficiency and infections in ataxia-telangiectasia." *Journal of Pediatrics* 144, no. 4 (April 2004): 505–11.

Perlman, S., et al. "Ataxia-telangiectasia: diagnosis and treatment." *Seminars in Pediatric Neurology* 10, no. 3 (September 2003): 173–82.

Shiloh, Y., et al. "In search of drug treatment for genetic defects in the DNA damage response: the example of ataxia-telangiectasia." *Seminars in Cancer Biology* 14, no. 4 (August 2004): 295–305.

Sun, X., et al. "Early diagnosis of ataxia-telangiectasia using radiosensitivity testing." *Journal of Pediatrics* 140, no. 6 (June 2002): 724–31.

ORGANIZATIONS

Ataxia Telangiectasia (A-T) Children's Project. 668 South Military Trail, Deerfield Beach, FL 33442–3023. Web site: www.atcp.org>.

Ataxia Telangiectasia (A-T) Medical Research Foundation. 5241 Round Meadow Road, Hidden Hills, CA 91302. Web site: <www.gspartners.com/at/>.

National Ataxia Foundation (NAF). 2600 Fernbrook Lane, Suite 119, Minneapolis, MN 55447–4752. (763) Web site: <www.ataxia.org>.

National Institute of Child Health and Human Development (NICHD). 31 Center Drive, Rm. 2A32, MSC 2425, Bethesda, MD 20892–2425. Web site: <www.nichd.nih.gov>.

National Organization for Rare Disorders (NORD). PO Box 1968, 55 Kenosia Avenue, Danbury, CT 06813–1968. (203) 744–0100.

WEB SITES

"What is ataxia?" *National Ataxia Foundation.* Available online at <www.ataxia.org> (accessed November 22, 2004).

"Questions and Answers: Ataxia Telangiectasia." *National Cancer Institute.* Available online at <www.cancer.gov/newscenter/ATMQandA> (accessed November 22, 2004).

Monique Laberge, Ph.D.

Atopic dermatitis

Definition

Atopic **dermatitis** (AD) is a chronic skin disorder associated with biochemical abnormalities in the patient's body tissues and immune system. It is characterized by inflammation, **itching**, weepy skin lesions, and an individual or **family** history of **asthma**, hay fever, **food allergies**, or similar allergic disorders. Atopic dermatitis is also known as infantile eczema or atopic eczema. The word atopic comes from *atopy*, which is derived from a Greek word that means "out of place." Atopy is a genetic predisposition to type I (immediate) hypersensitivity reactions to various environmental triggers. It includes bronchial asthma and food **allergies** as well as atopic dermatitis.

Description

AD varies in severity but in general is characterized by red, weeping, crusted patches of inflamed skin that itch constantly. The distribution of the skin lesions depends on the child's age. In infants, the skin lesions are usually found on the face, scalp, diaper area, body folds, hands, and feet, and tend to be exudative (oozing fluid that has escaped from blood vessels as a result of inflammation). Infants old enough to crawl may have patches of inflamed skin on the neck and trunk as well. In older children, the affected areas are usually located on the wrists, ankles, back of the neck, insides of the elbows, and the backs of the knees. The skin lesions in older children are more likely to be lichenified than exudative. Lichenification is the medical term for a leather- or bark-like thickening of the outermost layer of skin cells (the epidermis) as a result of long-term scratching or rubbing of itching lesions. In addition, the normal markings of the skin are exaggerated in lichenification.

The lesions of AD are accompanied by intense pruritus, which is the medical term for itching. Children with atopic dermatitis often have a lowered threshold of sensitivity to itching, which means that they feel itching sensations more intensely than children without the disorder. The pruritus often creates a vicious cycle of itching and scratching, which leads to more widespread rash, which leads to more itching. The child may scratch the affected skin only intermittently during the day, however. It is common for children with AD to do more scratching in the early evening and at night; moreover, disruptions of normal **sleep** patterns are common in these children.

Transmission

Atopic dermatitis is not contagious but may affect several members of the same family at the same time.

Demographics

Atopic dermatitis is a very common condition in the general population. According to the National Institute of Arthritis and Musculoskeletal and Skin Diseases (NIAMS), about 15 million people in the United States have one or more symptoms of the disease. It accounts for 15 to 20 percent of all visits to dermatologists (doctors who specialize in treating diseases of the skin). About 20 percent of infants develop symptoms of atopic dermatitis. Moreover, the proportion of people affected by AD is increasing; the American Academy of Allergy, Asthma, and Immunology (AAAAI) began a long-term study in 1999 that indicates that a larger percentage of children are affected by AD than was the case in the

1980s. This rise in prevalence is true of all developed countries, not just the United States and Canada. People who immigrate to Europe or North America from underdeveloped countries have increased rates of atopic dermatitis, which suggests that environmental factors play a role in the development or triggering of the disorder.

Atopic dermatitis begins early in life; about 65 percent of patients with AD develop symptoms during the first 12 months of life, with 90 percent showing symptoms before five years of age. The most common age for the onset of symptoms in infants is between six and 12 weeks of age. It is unusual for adults over the age of 30 to develop AD for the first time.

There is some disagreement among researchers with regard to race or ethnicity as risk factors for atopic dermatitis. Some studies indicate that all races and ethnic groups are equally at risk, while others suggest that Asians and Caucasians have slightly higher rates of AD than African Americans or Native Americans. Some skin lesions typical of AD may be more difficult to evaluate in African Americans because of the underlying skin pigmentation. With regard to sex, males and females appear to be equally at risk.

Atopic dermatitis is a major economic burden on families with children affected by the disorder. One researcher in Australia stated that the stresses on families with children diagnosed with moderate or severe AD are greater than the burdens on families with children with type 1 diabetes. These stresses include loss of sleep, loss of employment for the parents, time taken for direct care of the skin disorder, and the financial costs of treatment. The National Institutes of Health (NIH) estimates that atopic dermatitis costs U.S. health insurance companies more than $1 billion every year.

Causes and symptoms

Causes

The causes of atopic dermatitis were not completely understood as of 2004 but are thought to be a combination of genetic susceptibility, damaged skin barrier function, and abnormal responses of the child's immune system to environmental triggers. With regard to genetic factors, the disorder has been tentatively linked to loci on chromosomes 11 and 13. A child with one parent with AD has a 60 percent chance of developing the disorder; if both parents are affected, the risk rises to 80 percent. Nearly 40 percent of newly diagnosed children have at least one first-degree relative with atopic dermatitis.

In addition to genetic susceptibility, AD is the end result of a complex inflammatory process involving abnormalities in the child's skin and immune system. Some researchers have noted that the skin of people with AD contains lower levels of fatty acids, which may cause the skin to lose moisture more readily and become more sensitive to chemicals and other irritants. Others point to decreased production of a hormone in the immune system called interferon-gamma that ordinarily helps to regulate the body's response to allergens. People with AD may be hypersensitive to irritants because they have abnormally low levels of interferon-gamma in their systems.

About 80 to 90 percent of children with AD also have unusually high levels of an antibody called IgE in their blood. Antibodies are specialized proteins produced by the immune system that seek out and destroy bacteria, viruses, and other invaders. The high levels of IgE in the blood of AD patients are produced by hyperactive T helper 2 cells reacting against antigens in the environment. Although the role of increased IgE production in the development of atopic dermatitis was not fully understood as of 2004, measuring the level of this antibody in a sample of blood serum may be done to help distinguish AD from other skin diseases with similar symptoms.

Symptoms

The basic symptoms of AD have already been described. Dermatologists classify the lesions of AD into three basic categories:

- Acute lesions: These include extremely itchy reddened papules (small solid eruptions resembling pimples) and vesicles (small blister-like elevations in the skin surface that contain tissue fluid) over erythematous (reddened) skin. Acute lesions produce a watery exudate and are often accompanied by exfoliation (scaling or peeling of layers of skin) and erosion (destruction of the skin surface).

- Subacute lesions: These are characterized by reddening, peeling, and scaling but are less severe than acute lesions and do not produce an exudate.

- Chronic lesions: These are characterized by thickened plaques of skin, lichenification, and fibrous papules.

It is possible for a child or adolescent with chronic atopic dermatitis to have all three types of lesions at the same time.

Associated symptoms and disorders

Children and adolescents with AD frequently develop one or more of the following disorders or problems:

- Asthma: About 50 percent of children diagnosed with AD eventually develop asthma.

- **Allergic rhinitis**: Between 70 and 75 percent of children with AD eventually develop a nasal allergy. Allergic **rhinitis**, which is sometimes called atopic rhinitis, may be either seasonal (hay fever or rose fever) or nonseasonal (caused by dust, mold spores, pet dander, cigarette smoke, and other household allergens).

- Eye complications: These include such disorders as **conjunctivitis** (inflammation of the tissue that lines the eyelid), keratoconus (a cone-shaped distortion of the cornea of the eye), and cataracts. Although cataracts are usually associated with older adults, between 4 and 12 percent of children with AD develop rapidly maturing cataracts that may begin to interfere with vision as early as age 20. About 1 percent develop keratoconus.

- Ichthyosis, xerosis (dry skin), lichenification, and other skin abnormalities not caused by infections: Children with AD are likely to develop other skin problems.

- Secondary skin infections: Children and adolescents with AD frequently develop infections from bacteria that live on the skin and multiply when the child's scratching causes breaks or open sores in the skin. Most of these secondary infections are caused by *Staphylococcus aureus* and *Streptococcus pyogenes*.

- Psychosocial problems: Children with atopic dermatitis may withdraw socially if the lesions are extensive or otherwise noticeable. In addition, children with severe cases may have frequent absences from school. Adolescents may suffer depression or **anxiety** related to concerns about their appearance or the need to avoid participating in **sports** in order to minimize sweating.

When to call the doctor

Atopic dermatitis is rarely a medical emergency and can often be treated by the child's pediatrician. Parents should, however, consider consulting a dermatologist, allergist, or immunologist under any of the following circumstances:

- The child's AD has been diagnosed as severe. This classification means that 20 percent of the body's skin surface has been affected or 10 percent of the skin area in addition to involvement of the eyes, hands, and body folds.

- There is extensive exfoliation (peeling and scaling) of the skin.

- The child has eye complications.

- The child has recurrent secondary bacterial infections.

- The child is frequently absent from school, has developed psychosocial complications, or has impaired quality of life. In many cases the entire family's quality of life is affected by the stresses and frustrations of coping with the disease, and other family members' reactions may in turn upset the child with AD.

- The child has had to be hospitalized for treatment of the AD.

- The child has had to take more than one course of oral steroid drugs.

- The diagnosis is uncertain.

Diagnosis

History and physical examination

Diagnosis of atopic dermatitis begins with a history-taking and physical examination by the child's doctor. In the case of infants or very young children, the doctor will ask the parents for information about a family history of atopic disorders as well as information about the onset of the symptoms. The doctor will then examine the child's skin and assess the following factors:

- physical appearance of the lesions and their distribution on the child's body

- timing, which includes seasonal variations in the severity of the rash as well as its chronic or recurrent nature

- environmental factors, which includes foods as well as such common triggers of AD as dust, pet dander, household cleaning agents, plastics, nail polish remover, and other cosmetics or chemicals

- presence of such other conditions associated with AD as eye complications or bacterial infections of the skin

The doctor will ask older children and adolescents directly whether their skin lesions are affected by such factors as pets in the household; **smoking**; using perfumes, shampoos, deodorants, or other personal care products; taking certain prescription medications; wearing wool or other rough-textured fabrics; using laundry detergents or fabric softeners; being exposed to extremes of temperature or humidity; athletic activity; emotional stress; and (in females past **puberty**) hormonal changes related to **menstruation**.

There are no laboratory tests that can confirm the diagnosis of AD; in some cases, the doctor may need to examine the child more than once in order to distinguish between atopic and **seborrheic dermatitis**. In most cases, the doctor will make the diagnosis on the basis of criteria established by the AAAAI in the 1990s. To be considered atopic dermatitis, the child's symptoms must at total at least three major and three minor symptom criteria.

There are four major criteria for AD:

- pruritus
- typical form and distribution of skin lesions
- chronic or recurrent dermatitis
- a personal or family history of atopic disorders

There are about two dozen minor criteria for atopic dermatitis. The most common minor characteristics are early age of onset, food intolerance, wool intolerance, susceptibility to skin infections, immediate type I response to skin test, elevated total serum IgE, eczema of the nipples, xerosis or dry skin, dermatitis of the hands and feet, recurrent conjunctivitis, sensitivity to emotional stress, and ichthyosis.

Family practitioners often refer patients with AD to an allergist for consultation, particularly if the child has developed asthma or has acute reactions to foods.

Laboratory tests

In addition to a general physical examination, the doctor may order a blood test to look for the presence of elevated IgE levels in the blood serum. The doctor may also test tissue fluid or smears from the child's lesions to rule out skin parasites or infections that mimic atopic dermatitis, such as bacterial infections, **scabies**, or herpesvirus infections.

The doctor may recommend skin prick testing to determine whether certain specific substances or foods trigger the child's AD. These tests are usually given only to children with moderate or severe cases of atopic dermatitis. The child must discontinue taking oral antihistamine medications for one week before the tests and discontinue using topical steroid creams for two weeks. The test is performed by pricking the surface of the skin with a thin needle containing a small amount of a suspected allergen.

Treatment

The AAAAI recommends a four-part approach to the treatment of atopic dermatitis. Children with AD should take the following steps:

- Avoid foods or other factors that trigger symptoms, avoid such irritating fabrics as wool and synthetic fibers, wear 100 percent cotton underwear, trim fingernails short to minimize damage to the skin from scratching, keep the skin moist with proper use of emollient creams or oils after bathing, avoid the use of fabric softeners or scented detergents when laundering clothes and rinse clothes completely, and try to reduce emotional stress.

- Use appropriate medications as prescribed. The types of medications used vary depending on the severity of the child's symptoms and the presence of other infections. Most children are given both oral and topical (applied to the skin) medications. Topical medications include corticosteroid creams (Aristocort, Kenalog, Halog, Topicort, and many other brand names) and ointments containing immunomodulators, usually tacrolimus (Protopic) or pimecrolimus (Elidel). Corticosteroid creams are used to suppress inflammation, while the immunomodulator creams work by reducing the reactivity of the child's immune system. Although the corticosteroid creams have been used in both prescription-strength and over-the-counter (OTC) formulations for many years to treat AD, they may cause such side effects as thinning of the skin or stretch marks when used for long periods. They may also make skin infections worse. For these reasons, doctors recommend using the least powerful corticosteroid creams that control the symptoms. With regard to oral medications, **antihistamines** are often prescribed to stop itching at night so that the child can sleep. Oral or injected corticosteroids are sometimes used for short-term treatment of severe cases of AD that have not responded to topical medications; however, these drugs often have severe side effects, including stunted growth, thinning or weakening of the bones, high blood sugar levels, infections, and an increased risk of cataracts. Children with skin infections are usually given oral rather than **topical antibiotics**, most commonly penicillin or a cephalosporin.

- Regarding asthma or allergic rhinitis, the child should be evaluated for immunotherapy.

- The child's family and friends need to be educated about the condition, and the child needs to maintain a schedule of regular follow-ups. In addition to follow-up visits with the pediatrician and allergist, the child should have regular eye examinations as a safeguard against cataracts or other eye complications.

Other treatments that are sometimes used for atopic dermatitis are tar preparations and ultraviolet light therapy (phototherapy). Tar preparations are messy but were still as of 2004 considered useful for treating patients with chronic lichenified areas of skin. Phototherapy with ultraviolet A or B light waves, or a combination of both, may be used to treat older children or adolescents with mild or moderate atopic dermatitis; it is not suitable for infants or younger children. Some patients who do not respond to ultraviolet light alone benefit from a combi-

nation of phototherapy and an oral medication known as psoralen, which makes the skin more sensitive to the light. Phototherapy has two potential side effects from long-term use: premature aging of the skin and an increased risk of skin **cancer**.

Children or adolescents with AD must use extra care when bathing or showering. The doctor may recommend a non-soap skin cleanser, as standard bath soaps tend to dry and irritate the skin. If soaps are used, they should never be applied directly to broken or eroded areas of skin. The water should be lukewarm rather than hot, and the skin should be allowed to air-dry or be gently patted with a towel; brisk rubbing or the use of bath brushes must be avoided. After the skin has dried, the patient should apply a skin lubricant to seal moisture in the skin and create a barrier against further dryness or irritation.

Children with AD should also avoid unnecessary exposure to extremely hot, cold, moist, or dry outdoor environments. They should take care to avoid getting sunburned and should avoid participating in sports that involve physical contact or cause heavy perspiration.

Alternative treatment

There are a number of different complementary and alternative (CAM) approaches that have been used to treat atopic dermatitis, in part because the disorder is so widespread among children. In fact, infantile eczema is one of the most common conditions for which parents seek help from alternative practitioners. Most alternative therapies for atopic dermatitis fall into one of the following groups.

NATUROPATHY Naturopathy is a commonly used form of alternative treatment for AD; in one British study it was found effective for 19 out of 46 children in the subject group. Naturopaths favor food elimination diets as a way of managing AD, as well as lowering the child's overall intake of animal products. They recommend adding fish oil, flaxseed oil, or evening primrose oil to the child's diet to improve the condition of the skin, as many naturopaths believe that deficient intake of essential fatty acids is a major cause of AD. With regard to botanical products, a naturopath may suggest herbal preparations taken by mouth as well as topical creams made from herbs. Oral preparations may include extracts of hawthorn berry, blackthorn, or licorice root, while topical preparations to relieve itching typically include licorice or German chamomile. One German study found that a cream made with an extract of St. John's wort relieved the symptoms of AD better than a placebo, but the herbal preparation had not as of 2004 been compared to a standard corticosteroid cream.

HOMEOPATHY Homeopathy is the single most common CAM approach to atopic dermatitis in Europe, although it is frequently used in the United States as well. One German study followed a group of 2800 adults and 1130 children diagnosed with AD who were treated by homeopathic practitioners. The researchers found that over 600 different homeopathic remedies were recommended for the patients, although *Sepia, Lycopodium, Sulphur,* and *Natrum muriaticum* were the remedies most frequently prescribed. Most homeopathic practitioners in the United States as well as Europe consider AD a chronic condition that should be treated by constitutional homeopathic prescribing rather than by what is known as acute prescribing. In constitutional prescribing, the remedy is selected for long-term treatment of the patient's underlying susceptibility or constitutional weakness rather than short-term relief of present symptoms.

TRADITIONAL SYSTEMS OF MEDICINE According to Kenneth Pelletier, the former director of the alternative medicine program at Stanford University School of Medicine, both traditional Chinese remedies and Ayurvedic medicines benefit some people with atopic dermatitis. The British study of the use of CAM treatments in children with AD found that parents of Indian or Afro-Caribbean background were more likely to use these traditional approaches than Caucasian parents.

MIND/BODY APPROACHES Because flare ups of AD are often related to increased emotional stress, some researchers have hypothesized that alternative approaches to lowering stress might help in treating the disorder. There is disagreement, however, about the effectiveness of such treatments as hypnosis or autogenic training. While some studies have reported that self hypnosis, biofeedback, or autogenic training helped children with AD to manage their skin lesions with lower levels of steroid medications, other studies have reported that there is no conclusive evidence of the effectiveness of mind/body approaches in treating atopic dermatitis.

Nutritional concerns

Children and adolescents should avoid foods that trigger their AD. The most common offenders in flare-ups are peanuts and peanut butter, eggs and milk, seafood, soy, and chocolate. Long-term food elimination diets as a strategy for controlling AD are discussed below.

Children with moderate or severe AD often develop eroded areas or open cracks in the skin around the mouth from licking their lips or from allergic reactions to specific foods. They should apply a thin layer of petroleum jelly around the mouth before a meal to avoid irritation from citrus fruits, tomatoes, and other highly acidic foods.

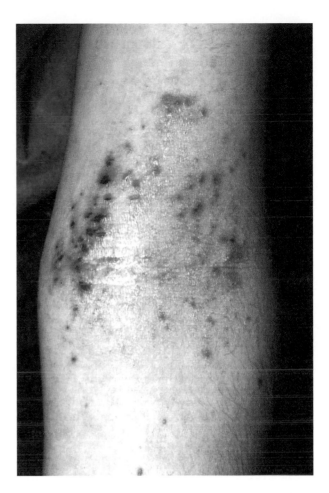

Close-up view of atopic dermatitis in the crook of the elbow of a 12-year-old patient. *(SPL/Custom Medical Stock Photo, Inc.)*

Prognosis

As of the early 2000s, there is no cure for atopic dermatitis. People diagnosed with AD have highly individual combinations of symptoms that may vary greatly in severity over time. A significant percentage of children diagnosed with the condition, however, remain atopic into adulthood; one source states that 20 to 40 percent of children with infantile eczema continue to be affected, while NIAMS gives a figure of 60 percent. Some children included in these figures, however, outgrow the more severe forms of atopic dermatitis and suffer flare-ups in adult life only when they are exposed to high stress levels, chemical irritants, or other triggers in the environment. Other children may have only mild symptoms of AD until **adolescence**, when changes in hormone levels may cause a sudden worsening of symptoms.

Prevention

While atopic dermatitis in children cannot be completely prevented, NIAMS offers the following tips to

KEY TERMS

Allergen—A foreign substance that provokes an immune reaction or allergic response in some sensitive people but not in most others.

Atopy—A state that makes persons more likely to develop allergic reactions of any type, including the inflammation and airway narrowing typical of asthma.

Autogenic training—A form of self-hypnosis developed in Germany that appears to be beneficial to migraine sufferers.

Conjunctivitis—Inflammation of the conjunctiva, the mucous membrane covering the white part of the eye (sclera) and lining the inside of the eyelids also called pinkeye.

Dander—Loose scales shed from the fur or feathers of household pets and other animals. Dander can cause allergic reactions in susceptible people.

Dermatologist—A physician that specializes in diseases and disorders of the skin.

Eczema—A superficial type of inflammation of the skin that may be very itchy and weeping in the early stages; later, the affected skin becomes crusted, scaly, and thick.

Erythema—A diffuse red and inflamed area of the skin.

Exfoliate—To shed skin. In skin care, the term exfoliate describes the process of removing dead skin cells.

Exudation—Leakage of cells, proteins, and fluids through the blood vessel wall into the surrounding tissue.

Ichthyosis—A group of congenital skin disorders of keratinization characterized by dryness and scaling of the skin.

Keratin—A tough, nonwater-soluble protein found in the nails, hair, and the outermost layer of skin. Human hair is made up largely of keratin.

Keratoconus—An eye condition in which the central part of the cornea bulges outward, interfering with normal vision. Usually both eyes are affected.

Lichenification—Thickening of the outer layer of skin cells caused by prolonged scratching or rubbing and resulting in a leathery or bark-like appearance of the skin.

Papule—A solid, raised bump on the skin.

Pruritus—The symptom of itching or an uncontrollable sensation leading to the urge to scratch.

Rhinitis—Inflammation and swelling of the mucous membranes that line the nasal passages.

Scabies—A contagious parasitic skin disease caused by a tiny mite and characterized by intense itching.

Vesicle—A bump on the skin filled with fluid.

Xerosis—The medical term for dry skin. Many children diagnosed with atopic dermatitis have a history of xerosis even as newborns.

---

parents as they try to help control the severity and frequency of flare-ups:

• Keep the child from scratching or rubbing the affected areas whenever possible.

• Avoid dressing the child in rough or scratchy fabrics and protect his or her skin from high levels of moisture.

• Keep the house at a cool, stable temperature with a consistent humidity level, using a humidifier during the heating season in colder climates.

• Quit smoking and do not allow others to smoke inside the house.

• Limit the child's exposure to dust, pollen, and animal dander. Some doctors recommend installing special filters in the house to remove dust and pollen from the air, removing carpets from the floors, or encasing mattresses and pillows with special covers to control dust mites.

• Recognize when the child is under stress and lower the stress level in the household if possible.

Nutritional concerns

The doctor may suggest a food challenge in order to identify a food or foods that may be triggering the child's skin rash. In a food challenge, a particular food is eliminated from the child's diet for a few weeks and then reintroduced. In some cases, a child with AD may benefit from a longer-term diet that eliminates problem foods entirely. In these cases, however, the child's height and weight should be carefully monitored to make sure that the diet is nutritionally adequate, and the diet itself should be reevaluated every four to six months. The doctor may recommend vitamin supplements or a consultation with a dietitian.

Parental concerns

Parental concerns about atopic dermatitis extend to the possible long-term consequences of the disorder as well as the child's present discomfort and sleeping problems. Depending on the severity and location of the skin rash, the child may withdraw from social activities to avoid teasing or resent restrictions on athletic or other outdoor activities. In addition to such possible complications of AD as eye disorders and skin infections, parents must also be attentive to signs of long-term side effects caused by medications or other forms of treatment for the AD. To cope with the impact of AD on other family members, parents may find counseling and support groups helpful. Because atopic dermatitis is so widespread in the general population, many support groups have been formed, particularly in the larger cities.

See also Allergic rhinitis; Allergies; Asthma.

Resources

BOOKS

"Atopic Dermatitis." Section 10, Chapter 111 in *The Merck Manual of Diagnosis and Therapy*, edited by Mark H. Beers and Robert Berkow. Whitehouse Station, NJ: Merck Research Laboratories, 2002.

"Hypersensitivity Disorders." Section 12, Chapter 148 in *The Merck Manual of Diagnosis and Therapy*, edited by Mark H. Beers and Robert Berkow. Whitehouse Station, NJ: Merck Research Laboratories, 2002.

Pelletier, Kenneth R. "CAM Therapies for Specific Conditions: Eczema." In *The Best Alternative Medicine*, Part II. New York: Simon & Schuster, 2002.

PERIODICALS

Ernst, E., et al. "Complementary/Alternative Medicine in Dermatology: Evidence-Assessed Efficacy of Two Diseases and Two Treatments." *American Journal of Clinical Dermatology* 3 (2002): 341–48.

Johnston, G. A., et al. "The Use of Complementary Medicine in Children with Atopic Dermatitis in Secondary Care in Leicester." *British Journal of Dermatology* 149 (September 2003): 566–71.

Kemp, A. S. "Cost of Illness of Atopic Dermatitis in Children: A Societal Perspective." *Pharmacoeconomics* 21 (2003): 105–13.

Leung, D. Y., et al. "New Insights into Atopic Dermatitis." *Journal of Clinical Investigation* 113 (March 2004): 651–57.

Ross, S. M. "An Integrative Approach to Eczema (Atopic Dermatitis)." *Holistic Nursing Practice* 17 (January February 2003): 56–62.

Schempp, C. M., et al. "Topical Treatment of Atopic Dermatitis with St. John's Wort Cream: A Randomized, Placebo-Controlled, Double-Blind Half-Side Comparison." *Phytomedicine* 10 (2003), Supplement 4: 31–7.

ORGANIZATIONS

American Academy of Allergy, Asthma, and Immunology (AAAAI). 611 East Wells Street, Milwaukee, WI 53202. Web site: <www.aaaai.org>.

American Academy of Dermatology (AAD). PO Box 4014, Schaumburg, IL 60168–4014. Web site: <www.aad.org>.

National Institute of Arthritis and Musculoskeletal and Skin Diseases (NIAMS). 1 AMS Circle, Bethesda, MD 20892–3675. Web site: <www.niams.nih.gov>.

WEB SITES

Krafchik, Bernice R. "Atopic Dermatitis." *eMedicine*, January 23, 2002. Available online at <www.emedicine.com/derm/topic38.htm> (accessed November 22, 2004).

OTHER

"Handout on Health: Atopic Dermatitis". NIH Publication No. 03–4272. *National Institute of Arthritis and Musculoskeletal and Skin Diseases (NIAMS).* Bethesda, MD: NIAMS, 2003.

Rebecca Frey, PhD

Atrial septal defect

Definition

An atrial septal defect (ASD) is an abnormal opening in the muscular wall separating the left and right upper chambers (atria) of the heart.

Description

During normal development of the fetal heart, there is an opening in the wall (septum) separating the left and right upper chambers of the heart. Normally, the opening closes before birth, but if it does not, the child is born with a hole between the left and right atria. This abnormal opening is called an atrial septal defect and causes blood from the left atrium to flow (or "shunt") across the hole into the right atrium.

Different types of atrial septal defects occur, and they are classified according to where in the separating wall they are found. The most commonly found atrial septal defect, called secundum atrial septal defect, occurs in the middle of the atrial septum and accounts for about 70 percent of all atrial septal defects.

Abnormal openings also form in the upper part of the atrial septum (called sinus venosus ASD) where the superior vena cava and right atrium join, and lower parts of the atrial septum (called primum ASD). A sinus venosus ASD usually involves the right upper pulmonary vein, while a primum ASD often occurs along with an abnormality in the mitral valve and/or tricuspid valve, and causes some blood leakage (regurgitation) back through the valves.

Atrial septal defects can occur alone or in combination with other congenital heart disorders, such as ventricular septal defect. They can be as small as a pinpoint or as large as the space where the entire septum should be located.

Demographics

Atrial and ventricular septal defects are the most common congenital heart defects. Atrial septal defect accounts for 4–10 percent of all cases of **congenital heart disease** in the United States. Abnormal openings in the atrial septum are twice as common in females as in males.

Causes and symptoms

Causes

Abnormal openings in the atrial septum occur during fetal development. These abnormalities can go unnoticed if the opening is small and produces no abnormal symptoms. If the defect is large, oxygen-rich blood from the left atrium flows back into the right atrium and gets pumped back to the lungs again, causing more work for the heart and lungs. The right atrium may swell or enlarge to hold the extra blood.

In some cases, an atrial septal defect can allow blood clots from the body to enter the brain and cause a **stroke**. Untreated atrial septal defect can lead to pulmonary **hypertension**, chest infection, Eisenmenger's syndrome, atrial fibrillation, atrial flutter, stroke, or right-sided heart failure.

Symptoms

A person born with an atrial septal defect may have no symptoms in childhood, and the condition may go undetected into adulthood. Stunted growth may be a symptom of atrial septal defect. Other symptoms that might develop over time include:

- shortness of breath

- fainting
- irregular heart beats or palpitations (abnormal heart beats that feel like fluttering in the chest)
- inability to **exercise** without becoming over-tired
- difficulty breathing with exercise or activity

By age 50, most people with atrial septal defects experience symptoms that interfere with activities of daily living.

When to call the doctor

The parent or caregiver should call the child's pediatrician or cardiologist when the child has these symptoms or conditions:

- swelling in the ankles or feet
- swollen abdomen
- poor exercise tolerance
- recurrent chest colds and respiratory infections
- abnormal blood pressure
- signs of infection, including **sore throat**, general body aches, or **fever**

The parent or caregiver should seek emergency treatment by calling 911 in most areas when the child has these symptoms or conditions:

- breathing difficulties or rapid breathing
- dizziness or fainting
- uncontrolled coughing or coughing with blood
- bluish skin tone or bluish coloration around the lips, fingernail beds, and tongue
- irregular heart beats or palpitations (abnormal heart beats that feel like fluttering in the chest)
- chest **pain** (rare in children)

Diagnosis

The medical and **family** history help the physician determine if the child has any conditions or disorders that might contribute to or cause the heart defect. A family history of heart defects may suggest a genetic predisposition to the condition.

During the physical exam, the child's blood pressure is measured, and a stethoscope is used to listen to sounds made by the heart and blood flowing through the arteries. Some **heart murmurs** (abnormal heart sounds) can indicate an atrial septal defect. The child's pulse, reflexes, height, and weight are checked and recorded. The child's blood oxygen level can be measured using a pulse oximeter, a sensor placed on the fingertip or earlobe. Internal organs are palpated, or felt, to determine if they are enlarged.

A chest x ray, electrocardiogram (ECG, EKG), echocardiogram (echo), or **magnetic resonance imaging** (MRI) can confirm the presence of an atrial septal defect. A chest x ray evaluates the size, shape, and location of the heart and lungs.

An electrocardiogram helps the physician evaluate the electrical activity of the heart. During an EKG, small electrode patches are attached to the skin on the chest. The electrodes are connected to a computer that measures the heart's electrical impulses and records them in a zigzag patter on a moving strip of paper.

An echocardiogram uses ultrasound, or high-frequency sound waves, to display an image of the heart's internal structures. It can detect valve and other heart problems. A Doppler echo uses sound waves to measure blood flow.

Magnetic resonance imaging is a scanning method that uses magnetic fields and radio waves to create three-dimensional images of the heart, which reveal how blood flows through the heart and how the heart is working.

In some cases, cardiac catheterization, a more invasive diagnostic procedure, may be performed to diagnose atrial septal defect. This procedure should be performed by a specially trained physician and diagnostic team in a well-equipped heart center. During the procedure, a long, slender tube called a catheter is inserted into a vein or artery and slowly directed to the heart, using x ray guidance. To better view the heart and blood vessels, contrast material (dye) is injected through the catheter and viewed and recorded on an x ray video as it moves through the heart. This imaging technique is called angiography. The catheter measures the amount of oxygen present in the blood within the heart. If the heart has an opening between the atria, oxygen-rich blood from the left atrium enters the right atrium. The cardiac catheterization can help doctors detect the higher-than-normal amount of oxygen in the heart's right atrium and right ventricle, and in the large blood vessels that carry blood to the lungs, where the blood would normally collect its oxygen.

Treatment

Twenty percent of atrial septal defects in children correct themselves without medical treatments by the time a child is two years old. If the opening does not close on its own, it needs to be repaired to prevent the pulmonary arteries from becoming thickened and blocked due to increased blood flow. If this condition (pulmonary vascular obstructive disease) is left untreated, it can increase the risk of death by 25 percent.

Treatment should be provided by a pediatric cardiologist, a specialist trained to diagnose and treat congenital heart disease. Surgery should be performed by a pediatric cardiovascular surgeon. A catheter-based cardiac implant should be done by an interventional cardiologist skilled in performing this procedure on children.

Surgery

There are two types of surgical repair for atrial septal defects: primary closure in which the opening is repaired with sutures alone if the defect is small; or secondary closure in which a patch closes the opening if the defect is large. The secondary closure may involve sewing a synthetic patch made of Dacron material over the opening, or wrapping the patient's own tissue (often from the fluid-filled sac around the heart called the pericardium) to close the opening.

During traditional atrial septal defect surgery, the heart is exposed through an incision made in the chest or between the ribs. A heart-lung bypass machine pumps blood for the heart while the heart is stopped and the wall defect is being repaired. Recuperation from surgery involves three to five days in the hospital and four to six weeks recovering at home. When possible, minimally-invasive surgical techniques that use smaller incisions (3–4 inches [7–10 cm]) may be performed, depending on the size and location of the defect. Minimally invasive surgery results in a much shorter hospital stay, reduced scarring, and a faster recovery than traditional surgery.

Surgical repair in asymptomatic children is usually recommended before the child begins grade school. Earlier surgical treatment is recommended when the child develops symptoms or has stunted growth.

Catheter-based cardiac implant procedure

A catheter-based cardiac implant procedure is less invasive than surgical repair, requires smaller incisions, does not require a heart-lung bypass machine, and results in a much shorter hospital stay, reduced scarring, and a more rapid recovery. The child usually stays in the hospital less than 24 hours after the procedure and returns to normal activities within one to two weeks.

The catheter-based cardiac implant procedure involves the implantation of a closure device that seals the defect. Closure devices cannot be used to treat all atrial septal defects, especially if the defect is large, if it is not centrally located within the atrial septum, or if there is not enough nearby tissue to adequately support the closure device. Other situations that prevent the use of a closure device include: very narrow blood vessels that will not allow the catheter-based system to be inserted; abnormalities of the heart valves; venous drainage from the lungs; and the presence of blood clots, bleeding disorders, active infections, or aspirin intolerance.

The procedure starts with a cardiac catheterization to determine the size and location of the defect. If the cardiac catheterization indicates that a closure device would be an effective treatment, an anticoagulant medication, is given intravenously to reduce the risk of blood clot. The closure device is placed through a specially designed catheter and guided to the location of the heart wall defect. The closure device stays in place permanently to stop the abnormal flow of blood between the atria. Over time, the heart tissue grows over the implanted closure device, becoming part of the heart. Although the device remains the same size, the heart tissue covering the device grows with the child.

Within 24 hours after the closure device implant procedure, a chest x ray, electrocardiogram, and echocardiogram are performed to ensure that the device is properly placed.

Medications

Patients who undergo the cardiac implant procedure take a daily anticoagulant medication such as aspirin or warfarin (Coumadin) for three to six months after the procedure. This medication reduces the risk of blood clot formation around the closure device.

Diuretics may be prescribed if the atrial septal defect was diagnosed later in life and is causing fluid build-up. Diuretics aid the excretion of water and salts and help remove excess fluid from tissues. A potassium supplement may be prescribed with some diuretics to remove potassium from the body along with excess fluid. Other medications include Digoxin, which strengthens the contraction of the heart, slows the heartbeat, and removes fluid from tissues, and antihypertensive medications that treat high blood pressure.

Nutritional concerns

Infants and children with atrial septal defects may gain weight more slowly. The most common reason for poor growth is inadequate caloric or nutrient intake. Other factors that may interfere with growth include:

- rapid heart beat and increased breathing rate
- poor appetite

- decreased food intake due to rapid breathing and fatigue
- frequent respiratory infections
- poor absorption of nutrients from the digestive tract
- decreased oxygen in the blood

Babies with atrial septal defects tire quickly when they eat, making frequent feedings necessary. Feedings should be on-demand and may need to be as often as every two hours in the first few months. Some babies have difficulty feeding from a regular bottle nipple; parents may need to try different brands. If medications are prescribed, they should be given before a feeding. Medications should not be mixed in the formula or breast milk unless the doctor advises otherwise.

The pediatrician will advise when to introduce solid foods, usually around six months of age. Fat should not be restricted in the diet, especially in the first two years. High-calorie foods and snacks can play an important role in providing good **nutrition** and helping the child grow at a healthy rate.

In children older than two years of age, the following low-fat dietary guidelines are recommended:

- total fat intake should comprise 30 percent or less of total calories consumed per day
- calories consumed as saturated fat should equal no more than 8–10 percent of total calories consumed per day
- total cholesterol intake should be less than 300 mg/dl per day

A gradual transition to a heart-healthy diet can help decrease a child's adulthood risk of coronary artery disease and other health conditions. Foods high in fat should be replaced by grains, vegetables, fruits, lean meat, and other foods low in fat and high in complex carbohydrates and protein. Salt should not be added to foods while cooking; highly processed foods, which are usually high in sodium should be avoided. These items include fast foods, canned foods, boxed mixes, and frozen meals.

Follow-up care

Children with atrial septal defects require lifelong monitoring, even after a successful surgery or procedure to close the defect. Along with routine medical care and standard immunizations, periodic heart check-ups are necessary. Usually, heart check-up appointments are scheduled more frequently just after the diagnosis or following the treatment procedure. Additional immunizations, such as the **influenza** vaccine, may be recommended.

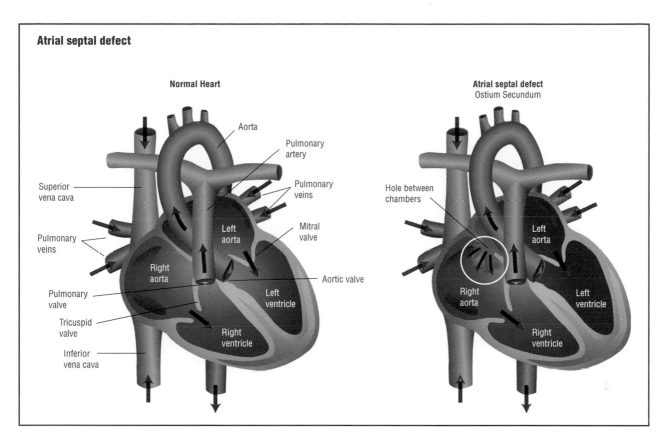

Atrial septal defect

Normal Heart

Aorta

Pulmonary artery

Pulmonary veins

Superior vena cava

Mitral valve

Pulmonary veins

Left aorta

Right aorta

Aortic valve

Pulmonary valve

Left ventricle

Tricuspid valve

Right ventricle

Inferior vena cava

Atrial septal defect
Ostium Secundum

Hole between chambers

Left aorta

Right aorta

Left ventricle

Right ventricle

A normal heart (left) and one affected by atrial septal defect. The defect is a hole in the wall that separates the chambers of the heart, resulting in the mixing of oxygenated and unoxygenated blood. *(Illustration by GGS Information Services.)*

Medical identification

In case of emergency, a medical identification bracelet or necklace should be worn to alert all health care providers of the child's heart condition.

Prognosis

The outlook for children with atrial septal defects has improved markedly in the past two decades. Individuals with small defects can live a normal life, but larger defects require surgical correction. Less than 1 percent of people younger than age 45 die from corrective surgery. Five to ten percent of patients can die from the surgery if they are older than 40 and have other heart-related problems. There is a 25 percent lifetime risk of death if the atrial septal defect is not repaired. When an atrial septal defect is corrected within the first 20 years of life, there is an excellent chance for the child to live a normal and productive life.

Prevention

Atrial septal defects cannot be prevented. However, to protect patients with atrial septal defects and those with

implanted closure devices from heart infections (endocarditis), the American Heart Association recommends regular dental check-ups to prevent infections of the mouth, as well as the preventive use of **antibiotics**. Preventive antibiotics should be taken before surgery, invasive tests or procedures, and all routine dental cleanings and procedures. A 2003 study reported that preventive antibiotics are underused in people with congenital heart conditions, possibly because they do not understand their increased risk of developing bacterial endocarditis.

Parental concerns

If the child needs surgery or a catheter-based cardiac implant, it is important for him or her to be as healthy as possible for the procedure. If the child has a fever, **cough**, or cold, the parent should inform the medical team to determine whether the procedure should be delayed. The medical team can help parents prepare the child for the procedure, and can instruct them on how to explain the procedure based on the child's age, ability to understand, and emotions. Once an atrial septal defect has been closed, it is unlikely that more surgery will be needed. Rarely, a patient may have a residual hole that may require further treatment, depending upon its size.

KEY TERMS

Atrial—Referring to the upper chambers of the heart.

Atrial fibrillation—A type of heart arrhythmia in which the upper chamber of the heart quivers instead of pumping in an organized way. In this condition, the upper chambers (atria) of the heart do not completely empty when the heart beats, which can allow blood clots to form.

Cardiac catheterization—A procedure to passes a catheter through a large vein into the heart and its vessels for the purpose of diagnosing coronary artery disease, assessing injury or disease of the aorta, or evaluating cardiac function.

Congenital—Present at birth.

Dacron—A synthetic polyester fiber used to surgically repair damaged sections of heart muscle and blood vessel walls.

Echocardiogram—A record of the internal structures of the heart obtained from beams of ultrasonic waves directed through the wall of the chest.

Eisenmenger's syndrome—A condition in which high pressures in the pulmonary arteries cause them to thicken. To compensate, the right side of the heart works harder, causing it to stretch and weaken. Eisenmenger's syndrome is a serious condition that leads to heart failure and can result in death by age 40 if left untreated.

Electrocardiagram (ECG, EKG)—A record of the electrical activity of the heart, with each wave being labeled as P, Q, R, S, and T waves. It is often used in the diagnosis of cases of abnormal cardiac rhythm and myocardial damage.

Heart failure—A condition in which the heart is unable to pump enough blood to supply the needs of the body

Pericardium—The thin, sac-like membrane that surrounds the heart and the roots of the great vessels. It has two layers: the inner, serous (or visceral) pericardium and the outer, fibrous (or parietal) pericardium.

Pulmonary hypertension—A disorder in which the pressure in the blood vessels of the lungs is abnormally high.

Septal—Relating to the septum, the thin muscle wall dividing the right and left sides of the heart. Holes in the septum are called septal defects.

Septum—A wall or partition. Often refers to the muscular wall dividing the left and right heart chambers or the partition in the nose that separates the two nostrils. Also refers to an abnormal fold of tissue down that center of the uterus that can cause infertility.

Ventricles—The lower pumping chambers of the heart. The ventricles push blood to the lungs and the rest of the body.

Most children with atrial septal defects can be fully active and are encouraged to exercise. An American Heart Association scientific statement advises children and teens with genetic heart conditions to seek advice from their doctors about the types of physical activities that are safe. The statement was intended to help doctors counsel patients who have an increased risk of sudden cardiac death during physical activity. Certain athletic activities such as competitive **sports** may be limited, depending on the child's type of defect and medical condition. A child with an atrial septal defect may tire more easily than other children; frequent breaks and rest periods should be encouraged as needed during activities. Parents should obtain a doctor's note to explain their child's specific exercise limitations to teachers and coaches.

A child with an atrial septal defect has a greater risk of having a child with a heart defect. The frequency of the condition increases from less than 1 percent in the general population to 2–20 percent when a parent is affected. Genetic counseling and further testing, such as chromosome analysis before pregnancy, or **amniocentesis** during pregnancy, may be recommended in adults with atrial septal defects.

Treatment and care for a child with an atrial septal defect can be costly, and some health insurance plans may not cover all expenses associated with a child's **hospitalization** or surgery. Help is available to cover medical expenses. The parents can discuss financial aid with the hospital. Some organizations, including The Heart of a Child Foundation and Little Hearts on the Mend Fund, provide financial assistance to children in need of heart surgery.

Caring for a child with an atrial septal defect is demanding. Support groups are available to help parents and caregivers cope with the challenges of providing care for children with special medical needs. It is important for parents to take care of themselves, too, by eating properly, exercising regularly, maintaining personal hygiene, keeping in contact with friends and family members for support, and managing stress by practicing relaxation techniques.

See also Congenital heart disease.

Resources

BOOKS

Bellenir, Karen, and Peter D. Dresser, eds. "If Your Child Has A Congenital Heart Defect" In *Heart Diseases and Disorders Sourcebook.* 2nd ed. Detroit, MI: Omnigraphics, Inc., 2000.

Friedman, William F., and John S. Child. "Disorders of the Cardiovascular System." In *Harrison's Principles of Internal Medicine.* Dennis L. Kasper, et al., eds. New York: McGraw Hill, 2004.

McGoon, Michael D., ed. and Bernard J. Gersh, M.D. *Mayo Clinic Heart Book: The Ultimate Guide to Heart Health.* 2nd ed. New York: William Morrow and Co., Inc., 2000.

Topol, Eric J., M.D. "Pediatric and Congenital Heart Diseases." In *Cleveland Clinic Heart Book: The Definitive Guide for the Entire Family from the Nation's Leading Heart Center.* New York: Hyperion, 2000.

Trout, Darrell, and Ellen Welch. *Surviving with Heart: Taking Charge of Your Heart Care.* Colorado: Fulcrum Publishing, 2002.

Wild, C. L., and M. J. Neary. *Heart Defects in Children: What Every Parent Should Know.* Minneapolis, MN: Chronimed Publishing, 2000.

PERIODICALS

"New Insight Offered into the Genetics of Congenital Heart Disease." *Heart Disease Weekly* (Oct.12, 2003): 3.

ORGANIZATIONS

Adult Congenital Heart Association (ACHA). 1500 Sunday Dr., Suite 102, Raleigh NC 27607-5151. (919) 861-4547. Web site: <www.achaheart.org>.

American College of Cardiology. Heart House. 9111 Old Georgetown Rd., Bethesda, MD 20814-1699. (800) 253-4636 ext. 694 or (301) 897-5400. Web site: <www.acc.org>.

American Heart Association. 7320 Greenville Ave., Dallas, TX 75231-4596. (214) 373-6300 or (800) 242-8721. Web site: <www.americanheart.org/children>.

Children's Heart Services. P.O. Box 8275, Bartlett, IL 60108-8275. (630) 415-0282. Web site: <www.childrensheartservices.org>.

The Cleveland Clinic Heart Center. The Cleveland Clinic Foundation. 9500 Euclid Ave., F25, Cleveland, Ohio, 44195. (800) 223-2273 ext. 46697 or (216) 444-6697. Web site: <www.clevelandclinic.org/heartcenter>.

Congenital Heart Disease Information and Resources. 1561 Clark Dr., Yardley, PA 19067. Web site: <www.tchin.org>.

The Heart of a Child Foundation and Little Hearts on the Mend Fund. Provides financial assistance to children in need of heart surgery. 26710 Fond Du Lac Rd., Rancho Palos Verdes, CA 90275. (310) 375-6617. Web sites: <www.heartofachild.org> and <www.littleheartsonthemend.org>.

Heart Support of America. 4873 N. Broadway, Knoxville, TN 37918. Web site: <www.heartsupport.com>.

International Children's Heart Foundation. 1750 Madison, Suite 100, Memphis, TN 38104. (877) 869-4243. Web site: <www.babyhearts.com>.

Mended Little Hearts. Support program for parents of children with heart defects. (888)-HEART99. Web site: <www.mendedhearts.org/MLH/mlh.htm>.

National Heart, Lung and Blood Institute. P.O. Box 30105, Bethesda, MD 20824-0105. (301) 251-1222. Web site: <www.nhlbi.nih.gov>.

Texas Heart Institute. Heart Information Service. P.O. Box 20345, Houston, TX 77225-0345. Web site: <www.tmc.edu/thi>.

WEB SITES

HeartCenterOnline. Available online at: <http://www.heartcenteronline.com>.

The Heart: An Online Exploration. Developed by The Franklin Institute Science Museum with support from Unisys Corporation. The Franklin Institute Science Museum. 222 N. 20th St., Philadelphia, PA, 19103. (215) 448-1200. Available online at: <www.sln2.fi.edu/biosci/heart.html>.

Heart Information Network. Available online at: <www.heartinfo.org>.

Dominic De Bellis, Ph.D.
Angela M. Costello

Attachment between infant and caregiver

Definition

Infant attachment is the deep emotional connection that an infant forms with his or her primary caregiver, often the mother. It is a tie that binds them together, endures over time, and leads the infant to experience pleasure, joy, **safety**, and comfort in the caregiver's company. The baby feels distress when that person is absent. Soothing, comforting, and providing pleasure are primary elements of the relationship. Attachment theory holds that a consistent primary caregiver is necessary for a child's optimal development.

Description

Attachment theory originated in the early 1950s with John Bowlby, a child psychiatrist, and Mary Ainsworth, a psychologist, who both became interested in young children's responses to experiencing loss. They began studying the realms of attachment and **bonding**. Their theory was developed and integrated over the following 60 years by researchers around the world. (For attachment as it pertains to **adoption**, readers can consult the entry in this encyclopedia on adoption.)

Attachment theory is based on the idea that the bond between an infant and his or her primary caregiver is the crucial and primary influence in infant development and as such forms the basis of coping, the development of relationships, and the formation of personality. If the mother is absent or not available, a primary caregiver serves the role usually assumed by the mother. Attachment refers to a relationship that emerges over time from a history of caregiver-infant interactions. As adults nurture and interact with infants during the first year of life, infants organize their behavior around these caregivers. Attachment is a phenomenon involving physiological, emotional, cognitive, and social processes. The baby displays instinctual attachment behaviors that are activated by cues or signals from the caregiver. Therefore, the process of attachment is defined as a mutual regulatory system, in which the baby and the caregiver have an influence on one another over time. The caregiver's presence provides a feeling of safety and security for the infant. Once this relationship is established, the preference tends to remain stable, and a shift of attachment behavior to a new or strange person becomes more difficult.

Some theorists believe that the attachment system evolved to ensure that infants and caregivers remain physically close, and that the infant is protected. Thus, in order to survive, an infant must become attached to the primary caregiver, who is stronger and wiser regarding the dangers of the world. The caregiver is a safe refuge, a source of comfort and protection, and serves as a secure base from which the infant can explore.

Research has shown that babies and caregivers demonstrate an instinct to attach. Babies instinctively reach out for the safety and security of the safe haven they have with their primary caregiver, while parents usually instinctively protect and nurture their children. Children who start their lives with the essential basis of secure attachment fare better in all aspects of functioning as their development progresses.

Attachment and behavior

From a behavioral perspective, attachment is represented by a group of instinctive infant behaviors that serve to form the attachment bond, protect the child from **fear** and harm, and aid in the infant's protected exploration of the world. These behaviors include:

- reaching
- crying
- grasping
- smiling
- vocalizing
- clinging
- sucking
- moving

All of these behaviors assist in facilitating the maximum physical and emotional development of the child. These particular behaviors may vary from one culture or society to others, but the attachment relationship appears to be universal.

Attachment and emotions

From an emotional perspective, attachment is the development of a mutual bond in which the primary caregiver positively influences infant development through the interactions and relationship that person has with the child. Babies are unable to regulate themselves and become overwhelmed by their emotional states, including those of fear, pleasure, and sadness. Babies are unable to keep themselves in a state of equilibrium, as they lack the skills to control either the intensity or the duration of those emotions. In an attached relationship, babies rely on their primary caregiver to help them navigate the world. The primary caregiver serves as a secure base that is used for exploration and learning. At the same time, the infant forms the necessary skills of self-protection and intimacy.

Other important functions that a secure attachment between an infant and his or her caregiver serves for the developing child include the following:

- learning basic trust, which serves as a basis for all future emotional relationships

- exploring the environment with feelings of safety and security, which leads to healthy intellectual and social development
- developing the ability to control behavior, which results in effective management of impulses and emotions
- creating a foundation for the development of identity, which includes a sense of capability, self-worth, and a balance between dependence and independence
- establishing a moral framework that leads to empathy, compassion, and conscience
- generating a core set of beliefs
- providing a defense against stress and trauma

Children will display distinct attachment styles, which can be loosely defined as either secure or insecure. Secure styles show a child consistently connected to the primary caregiver, with a firmly established sense of trust and a nurturing response; however, insecure styles of attachment have features of instability.

Infancy

Several milestones occur over the course of their first year as infants form an attached relationship with their primary caregiver. These milestones include the following:

- In the first two months of life, even though infants show little observable preference for a particular caregiver, the warm, sensitive, and reliable responses of the caregiver to the child set the stage for the developing attachment relationship.
- From two to seven months, infants tend to interact differently with primary caregivers than they do with strangers but in general still do not display solid preferences.
- By four to six months of age, infants begin to develop expectations of how their primary caregiver will respond to them when they are distressed.
- Between seven months and one year, infants show a definite preference for their primary caregiver. They start to exhibit a wariness of strangers and symptoms of **separation anxiety**.

Toddlerhood

From 12 to 18 months, as they start to walk and crawl, children use their attachment figure as a secure base from which to go out and discover the world and as a safe haven to which to return when frightened or alarmed. Children with secure histories have been shown

to be more determined, enthusiastic, and competent in problem-solving as toddlers.

Preschool

During this time, the attachment relationship is characterized by an increased tolerance for separation and an ability to cooperate with others. The child is learning to balance his or her need for independence, self-discipline, and exploration and the need for love and protection from the primary caregiver. However, as **preschool** approaches, children are still susceptible to a variety of dangers. Therefore, attachment behaviors, such as wanting to stay close to the primary caregiver and displaying occasional separation anxiety are adaptive processes, not regressive ones. Western culture has often portrayed this type of behavior as controlling or attention-seeking. Attachment theorists believe this is inaccurate, as these behaviors help serve to ensure the child's survival and socialization.

School age

School-age children with a history of secured attachment histories demonstrate an ability to be more goal-oriented and often display positive leadership skills. Numerous long-term studies have shown that in the following areas securely attached children do better as they grow older:

- self-esteem
- autonomy
- ability to manage impulses and feelings
- long-term friendships
- positive relationships with parents, caregivers, and other authority figures
- effective coping skills
- trust, intimacy, and affection
- positive and hopeful belief systems
- academic success in school

Common problems

Insecure attachment develops when a primary caregiver does not consistently respond in ways that are warm, affectionate, loving, dependable, and sensitive to the infant's needs. The three primary insecure types are resistant attachment, avoidant attachment, and disorganized attachment.

Resistant attachment

This pattern is characterized by an emotional ambivalence in the child and a physical resistance to the primary caregiver. The infant is often hesitant to separate from the caregiver and is quick to display anxiety and distress in an unfamiliar setting. This classification is often referred to as anxious-ambivalent because the child will demonstrate anger towards the caregiver at the same time they are expressing their need for comforting. This type of insecure attachment may be an indicator of risk for the development of emotional, social, and behavioral problems in childhood and later in life.

Avoidant attachment

The key behavior in this type of insecure attachment is an active avoidance of the primary caregiver when the infant is upset. These babies readily separate from their primary caregivers in order to explore and may be more affectionate with strangers than their own mother. They exhibit little preference for and appear emotionally distant from the primary caregiver.

Disorganized attachment

In this type of insecure attachment, infants show a variety of confused and contradictory behaviors. For example, during a reunion with the primary caregiver, the child may look away or even display a blank stare when being held. Other babies may exhibit confusing patterns such as crying unexpectedly after being held or displaying odd, dazed expressions.

Parental concerns

Healthy attachment is the key to healthy babies, and healthy babies are the key to healthy adults. It is crucial for parents, however, to understand that each parent faces times when things do not function flawlessly. What is important in the development of secure attachment is that the primary caregiver is available emotionally to the child and sensitive to the infant's needs.

When to call the doctor

Parents should call their doctor if their child exhibits any of the behaviors of an insecure attachment.

See also Adoption.

Resources

BOOKS

Blackman, James A. *Infant Development and Mental Health in Early Intervention*. Austin, TX: PRO-ED Incorporated, 2005.

Bremner, J. Gavin, et al. *The Blackwell Handbook of Infant Development*. Oxford, UK: Blackwell Publishing, 2004.

Lerner, Claire, et al. *Bringing Up Baby: Three Steps to Making Good Decisions in Your Child's First Years*. Washington, DC: Zero to Three Press, 2004.

Spitz, Rene A. *First Year of Life: A Psychoanalytic Study of Normal and Deviant Behavior*. Madison, CT: International Universities Press, 2005.

PERIODICALS

Carlson, Elizabeth A., Megan C. Sampson, and L. Alan Stroufe. "Implications of Attachment Theory and Research for Developmental-Behavioral Pediatrics." *Journal of Developmental & Behavioral Pediatrics* 24, no. 5 (October 2003): 364+.

ORGANIZATIONS

Attachment Parenting International. 2906 Berry Hill Drive, Nashville, TN 37204. Web site: <www.attachmentparenting.org>.

WEB SITES

Palmer, Linda F. "The Chemistry of Attachment." *API News* 5, no. 2 (2002). Available online at <www.attachmentparenting.org/artchemistry.shtml> (accessed October 11, 2004).

Porter, Lauren Lindsey. "The Science of Attachment: The Biological Roots of Love-Family Living." *Mothering* (July-August 2003). Available online at <www.findarticles.com/p/articles/mi_m0838/is_119/ai_105515898/> (accessed October 11, 2004).

Thurber, Christopher A. "Roots and Wings: how attachment and temperament shape development—Revolutionary Studies in Child Psychology." *Camping Magazine* (March-April 2003). Available online at <www.findarticles.com/p/articles/mi_m1249/is_2_76/ai_98953747/> (accessed October 11, 2004).

Deanna M. Swartout-Corbeil, RN

Attempted suicide *see* **Suicide and suicidal behavior**

Attention-deficit/Hyperactivity disorder (AD/HD)

Definition

Attention-deficit/hyperactivity disorder (AD/HD) is a neurobiological disorder characterized by hyperactivity, impulsive behavior, and the inability to remain focused on tasks or activities.

Description

AD/HD, also known as hyperkinetic disorder (HKD) outside of the United States, is estimated to affect 3–7 percent of school-aged children, and seems to afflict boys more often than girls. However, the prevalence in boys may be cited because often girls are not diagnosed until later in age. Although difficult to assess in infancy and toddlerhood, signs of AD/HD may begin to appear as early as age two or three, but visible symptoms change as **adolescence** approaches. Many symptoms, particularly hyperactivity, diminish in early adulthood, while impulsivity and inattention problems often continue.

First documented in 1902, AD/HD has been called minimal brain dysfunction, hyperkinetic reaction, and attention-deficit disorder (ADD). The name AD/HD reflects the various behaviors of inattention, hyperactivity, and impulsiveness that characterize the disorder. Its more precise classification is a result of the *Diagnostic and Statistical Manual, fourth edition (DSM-IV)* system for characterizing and diagnosing mental and behavioral disorders.

Children with AD/HD have difficulties with inattention that can be manifest as a lack of concentration, an easily distracted focus, and an inability to know when and how long to focus. The characteristics of inattention vary with each AD/HD child; however, all most often translate into poor grades and difficulties in school and other social arenas. AD/HD children act impulsively, taking action first and thinking later. They are constantly moving, running, climbing, squirming, and fidgeting. Yet, they often have trouble with gross and **fine motor skills** and, as a result, they may be physically clumsy and awkward. Their clumsiness may also extend to their social skills. They are sometimes shunned by peers due to their impulsive and intrusive behavior.

Demographics

Of the 3–7 percent of school-aged children with AD/HD, some will have a reduction of symptoms as they reach adulthood. However, 65 percent of AD/HD children will continue to display characteristics of AD/HD through adulthood. Until recently, it was believed that boys were three times more likely to have AD/HD; however, that gap has been narrowed. It is more likely that the presence of AD/HD is distributed equally between boys and girls. The reason for the discrepancy was, in part, because young boys tend to more readily and overtly manifest the characteristics of AD/HD, making diagnosis easier. In addition, the inattentive form affects girls more than the hyperactive form; as a result, girls may be less likely to be diagnosed.

Causes and symptoms

The causes of AD/HD are not specifically known. However, it is a neurologically based disease that may be genetic. Children with an AD/HD parent or sibling are more likely to develop the disorder themselves. Although the exact cause of AD/HD is not known, an imbalance or deficiency of certain neurotransmitters—the chemicals in the brain that transmit messages between nerve cells—is believed to be the mechanism behind AD/HD symptoms.

A widely publicized study conducted by Dr. Ben Feingold in the early 1970s suggested that **allergies** to certain foods and food additives caused the characteristic hyperactivity of AD/HD children. By eliminating the food allergen, the premise was that AD/HD characteristics would disappear. Although some children may have adverse reactions to certain foods and food additives that can affect their behavior, carefully controlled follow-up studies have uncovered no link between **food allergies** and AD/HD. Another popularly held misconception about food and AD/HD is that the consumption of sugar causes the hyperactive behavior in an AD/HD child. Again, studies have shown no link between sugar intake and AD/HD. (In a recent study conducted by the National Institute of Mental Health, the level of glucose use in the brain was actually lower in individuals with AD/HD. Since glucose is the main source of fuel for the brain, this is a significant finding.) Finally, parenting style is not a cause for AD/HD. While certain parenting skills and/or deficiencies can affect the environment of an AD/HD child and, as a result, exasperate or help manage the characteristics of AD/HD, it appears that neurological issues are the primary causal agents at play.

In order to diagnose AD/HD, psychologists and other mental health professionals typically use the criteria listed in the *DSM-IV. DSM-IV* requires the presence of at least six of the following symptoms of inattention, or six or more symptoms of hyperactivity and impulsivity combined.

Inattention:

- fails to pay close attention to detail or makes careless mistakes in schoolwork or other activities
- has difficulty sustaining attention in tasks or activities
- does not appear to listen when spoken to
- does not follow through on instructions and does not finish tasks
- has difficulty organizing tasks and activities
- avoids or dislikes tasks that require sustained mental effort (e.g., homework)
- is easily distracted
- is forgetful in daily activities

Hyperactivity:

- fidgets with hands or feet or squirms in seat
- does not remain seated when expected to
- runs or climbs excessively when inappropriate (in adolescence and adults, feelings of restlessness)
- has difficulty playing quietly
- is constantly on the move
- talks excessively

Impulsivity:

- blurts out answers before the question has been completed
- has difficulty waiting for his or her turn
- interrupts and/or intrudes on others

Of those symptoms, AD/HD can be categorized further by three subtypes. Each subtype exhibits particular behaviors that make up the general symptoms of a child with AD/HD. They are:

AD/HD predominantly inattentive type (AD/HD-I)

- is disorganized
- is easily distracted
- is forgetful
- has unsustained attention
- has difficulty following instructions
- appears to have poor listening skills
- makes careless mistakes

AD/HD predominantly hyperactive-impulsive type (AD/HD-HI)

- fidgets
- is unable to engage in quiet activity

- is interruptive or intrusive
- cannot remain seated
- speaks out of turn
- climbs or runs about inappropriately
- talks excessively

AD/HD combined type (AD/HD-C) is a combination of the symptoms exhibited by the other two subtypes (inattentive type and hyperactive-impulsive type). Also, for a complete diagnosis, *DSM-IV* requires that some symptoms develop before age seven, and that they significantly impair functioning in two or more settings (e.g., home and school) for a period of at least six months.

Diagnosis

AD/HD cannot be diagnosed with a laboratory test. Diagnosis is difficult and it takes into consideration many aspects of the child's behavior. Often the child's teacher is the one to bring the first signs to the attention of the parents. However, the first step in determining if a child has AD/HD is to consult with a pediatrician. The pediatrician can make an initial evaluation of the child's developmental maturity compared to other children in his or her age group. The physician should also perform a comprehensive physical examination to rule out any organic causes of AD/HD symptoms, such as an overactive thyroid or vision or hearing problems.

If no organic problem can be found, a psychologist, psychiatrist, neurologist, neuropsychologist, or learning specialist is typically consulted to perform a comprehensive AD/HD **assessment**. A complete medical, **family**, social, psychiatric, and educational history is compiled from existing medical and school records and from interviews with parents and teachers. Interviews may also be conducted with the child, depending on his or her age. Along with these interviews, several clinical inventories may also be used, such as the Conners' Rating Scales (Teacher's Questionnaire and Parent's Questionnaire), Child Behavior Checklist (CBCL), and the Achenbach Child Behavior Rating Scales. These inventories provide valuable information on the child's behavior in different settings and situations.

Other disorders such as depression, **anxiety** disorder, and **learning disorders** can cause symptoms similar to AD/HD. A complete and comprehensive psychiatric assessment is critical to differentiate AD/HD from other possible mood and behavioral disorders. **Bipolar disorder**, for example, may be misdiagnosed as AD/HD.

Public schools are required by federal law to offer free AD/HD testing upon request. A pediatrician can also provide a referral to a psychologist or pediatric specialist for AD/HD assessment. Parents should check with their insurance plans to see if these services are covered.

Treatment

Despite similar behavioral characteristics, AD/HD must be treated individually by developing an approach combining various types of treatment. The use of medication in combination with behavioral interventions, classroom accommodations, and proactive parents provide the best treatment option.

Psychostimulants and their effects have been studied in approximately 6,000 children and the positive results of their use have been documented. Such psychostimulants as dextroamphetamine (Dexedrine, Dextrostat), pemoline (Cylert), **methylphenidate** (Ritalin, Concerta, Metadate, Focalin), and mixed salts of a single-entity amphetamine product (Adderall, Adderall XR) are commonly prescribed to control hyperactive and impulsive behavior as well as to increase attention. They work by stimulating the production of certain neurotransmitters in the brain. Generally, short-acting medication lasts for four hours, while long-lasting preparations will last for six to eight hours. Some medication is effective for 10–12 hours. Specific dosages depend upon the patient and that is determined by trial and error in conjunction with close monitoring by a physician in order to find the most beneficial strength. Possible side effects of stimulants include nervous **tics**, irregular heartbeat, loss of appetite, and insomnia. However, the medications are usually tolerated and safe in most cases. In fact, 70–80 percent of AD/HD children respond well to psychostimulants.

In children who do not respond well to stimulant therapy, nonstimulant medications are prescribed. In 2002, the Food and Drug Administration (FDA)approved atomoxetine (Strattera) for the treatment of AD/HD. Unlike the stimulant medications, atomoxetine is not a controlled substance and can be prescribed with refills. (With the use of stimulant medication, the physician must write prescriptions each month of treatment.) Atomoxetine usually takes three to four weeks of use until its effect is evident. In January 2005 the FDA warned that evidence of atleast two cases of liver problems in an adult and teenage patient taking atomoxetine were reported. In both cases, the individuals fully recovered. The manufacturer of atomoxetine (Strattera) planned to notify users of the new FDA warning; however, the company, Eli Lilly & Co., believed that the risk-benefit analysis during trials of the drug was still positive. Such tricyclic **antidepressants** as desipramine (Norpramin,

Pertofane) and amitriptyline (Elavil) are frequently recommended as well. Reported side effects of these drugs include persistent dry mouth, sedation, disorientation, and cardiac arrhythmia (particularly with desipramine).

Other medications prescribed for AD/HD therapy include buproprion (Wellbutrin), an antidepressant; fluoxetine (Prozac), an SSRI antidepressant; and carbamazepine (Tegretol, Atretol), an anticonvulsant drug. Clonidine (Catapres), an antihypertensive medication, has also been used to control aggression and hyperactivity in some AD/HD children, although it should not be used in combination with Ritalin.

A child's response to medication will change with age and maturation, so AD/HD symptoms should be monitored closely and prescriptions adjusted accordingly.

Behavior interventions are also crucial to AD/HD treatment. In a Nation Institute of Mental Health (NIMH) study conducted on 579 children over the course of 14 months it was observed that the children receiving AD/HD medication or both medication and behavioral interventions were more likely to see the most relief from their symptoms than those children that only received community aid. The use of a reward system to reinforce good behavior and task completion can be implemented both in the classroom and at home. A chart system may be used to visually illustrate the child's progress and encourage continued success with the use of larger rewards after a certain number of daily rewards are achieved. The reward system stays in place until the appropriate behavior becomes second nature to the child.

A variation of this technique, cognitive-behavioral therapy, works to decrease impulsive behavior by getting the child to recognize the connection between thoughts and behavior, and to change behavior by changing negative thinking patterns.

Individual psychotherapy can help an AD/HD child build **self-esteem**, give them a place to discuss their worries and anxieties, and help them gain insight into their behavior and feelings. **Family therapy** may also be beneficial in helping family members develop coping skills and in working through feelings of guilt or anger parents may be experiencing.

AD/HD children perform better within a familiar, consistent, and structured routine with an emphasis on positive reinforcements for good behavior and minimal use of punishments. When a negative behavior must be acknowledged and corrected, "time outs" give the child with AD/HD an opportunity to regroup without negative reinforcement. Family, friends, and caretakers should all be educated on the special needs and behaviors of the AD/HD child.

Alternative treatment

A number of alternative treatments exist for AD/HD; however, there are very few studies to prove their efficacy. When choosing a treatment option, it is important to investigate authoritative sources that provide a basis through documented studies for the validity of the treatment. AD/HD is not a disorder that can be cured but rather it is one that is managed by a variety of treatment options. Some of the more popular alternative treatments include:

- EEG (electroencephalograph) biofeedback. By measuring brainwave activity and teaching the AD/HD patient which type of brainwave is associated with attention, EEG biofeedback attempts to train patients to generate the desired brainwave activity. This treatment has been in use for over 25 years and it has had positive response from parents. However, no consistent medical studies are available.

- Chelation therapy focuses on removing excess lead within the body. This treatment is based on the idea that excessive lead in animals causes hyperactivity; yet, not enough medical studies have been done. A physician should be consulted when this approach is considered.

- Intractive metronome training uses a similar instrument as the metronome used by musicians to keep time in order to train individuals to develop their motor and timing skills through repetitively tapping the beat.

- Nutritional supplements claiming to be a cure for AD/HD are not regulated by the Food and Drug Administration (FDA) and should not be considered a treatment option without consultation with a medical doctor.

There are many advertised alternative and complementary treatment options for AD/HD. Only a few are listed here; however, it is always necessary to consult a physician to develop a fine-tuned treatment plan specific to each child's needs.

Nutritional concerns

As mentioned, links between **nutrition** and AD/HD have not been confirmed through medical studies. However, it is important to note that a nutritionally balanced diet is important for normal development in all children.

Prognosis

Untreated, AD/HD negatively affects a child's social and educational performance and can seriously damage his or her self-esteem. Children with AD/HD have impaired relationships with their peers, and may be looked upon as social outcasts. They may be perceived as slow learners or troublemakers in the classroom. Siblings and even parents may develop resentful feelings towards the AD/HD child.

Some AD/HD children also develop a **conduct disorder**. For those adolescents who have both AD/HD and a conduct disorder, up to 25 percent go on to develop **antisocial personality disorder** and the criminal behavior, substance abuse, and high rate of **suicide** attempts that are symptomatic of it. Children diagnosed with AD/HD are also more likely to have a learning disorder, a mood disorder such as depression, or an anxiety disorder.

Approximately 70–80 percent of AD/HD patients treated with stimulant medication experience significant relief from symptoms, at least in the short-term. Approximately half of AD/HD children seem to "outgrow" the disorder in adolescence or early adulthood; the other half will retain some or all symptoms of AD/HD as adults. With early identification and intervention, careful compliance with a treatment program, and a supportive and nurturing home and school environment, children with AD/HD can flourish socially and academically.

Parental concerns

Because AD/HD is often indicated when the AD/HD child is in school, parents are extremely concerned about their child's academic progress. Communication between parents and teachers is especially critical to ensure an AD/HD child has an appropriate learning environment. Educational interventions under Individuals with Disabilities Education Act (IDEA) and Section 504 of the Rehabilitation Act of 1973 mandate that AD/HD children will be served within the public school system. This means that upon request the public school is required to test the child for AD/HD as well as other learning disabilities if they are suspected. In addition, **special education** services are mandated for those children with AD/HD that need extra help and accommodation. It is important that parents assume a positive relationship with their child's educator and school in order to develop the best possible teaching strategies and learning environment for their AD/HD child.

Development of self-esteem is another particular concern for parents of AD/HD children. Because they often have difficulty in school and in social relationships, low self-esteem can be a factor that leads the school aged children toward dangerous or destructive behaviors as they reach adolescence. Finding one activity that the child excels at is essential in fostering a positive self-

KEY TERMS

Conduct disorder—A behavioral and emotional disorder of childhood and adolescence. Children with a conduct disorder act inappropriately, infringe on the rights of others, and violate societal norms.

Nervous tic—A repetitive, involuntary action, such as the twitching of a muscle or repeated blinking.

Oppositional defiant disorder—An emotional and behavioral disorder of children and adolescents characterized by hostile, deliberately argumentative, and defiant behavior towards authority figures that lasts for longer than six months.

image. Often parents look to **sports** as an appropriate outlet. Individual sports such as karate, swimming, tennis, etc. are less socially demanding than team sports; yet they provide an opportunity for the child to thrive in a competitive activity.

AD/HD is a chronic condition. Parents can feel overwhelmed when they have to deal with AD/HD characteristics on a daily basis. Parent should face the issues honestly and directly while fostering a positive relationship with their AD/HD child. The best advocate the AD/HD child has is a parent so it is important that parents be proactive and keep up to date on the latest research. Learning about AD/HD and the various treatment options helps parents cope with their own concerns at the same time they are helping their child.

Resources

BOOKS

Alexander-Roberts, Colleen. *The ADHD Parenting Handbook: Practical Advice for Parents from Parents.* Dallas: Taylor Publishing Co., 1994.

American Psychiatric Association. *Diagnostic and Statistical Manual of Mental Disorders.* 4th ed. Washington, DC: American Psychiatric Press, Inc., 1994.

Barkley, Russell A. *Taking Charge of ADHD.* Revised Edition. New York: Guilford Press, 2000.

Hallowell, Edward M., and John J. Ratey. *Driven to Distraction: Recognizing and Coping with Attention Deficit Disorder from Childhood Through Adulthood.* New York: Touchstone, 1995.

Osman, Betty B. *Learning Disabilities and ADHD: A Family Guide to Living and Learning Together.* New York: John Wiley & Sons, 1997.

PERIODICALS

Foley, Kevin. "Experiencing Nature May Quell ADHD in Kids." *Pediatric News* 38 (Nov. 2004).

Franklin, Deeanna. "FDA Issues Warning for ADHD Drug." *Pediatric News* 39 (Jan. 2005):42.

Glicken, Anita D. "Attention Deficit Disorder and the Pediatric Patient: A Review." *Physician Assistant* 21, no. 4 (Apr. 1997):101-11.

Hallowell, Edward M. "What I've Learned from A.D.D." *Psychology Today* 30, no. 3 (May/June 1997): 40-6.

Swanson, J. M., et al. "Attention-deficit Hyperactivity Disorder and Hyperkinetic Disorder." *The Lancet* 351 (7 Feb. 1997): 429-33.

ORGANIZATIONS

American Academy of Child and Adolescent Psychiatry. (AACAP). 3615 Wisconsin Ave. NW, Washington, DC 20016. (202) 966-7300. Web site: <http://www.aacap.org>

Children and Adults with Attention Deficit Disorder (CH.A.D.D.). 8181 Professional Place, Ste. 150, Landover, MD 20785. (800) 233-4050. (305) 306-7070.

National Attention Deficit Disorder Association. (ADDA). 9930 Johnnycake Ridge Road, Suite 3E, Mentor, OH 44060. (800) 487-2282. Web site: <http://www.add.org>

WEB SITES

Schwablearning.org: A Parent's Guide to Helping Kids with Learning Difficulties (cited March 8, 2005). Available online at: <www.schwablearning.org>.

Jacqueline L. Longe
Paula A. Ford-Martin

Audiometry

Definition

Audiometry encompasses those procedures used to measure hearing thresholds.

Purpose

The purpose of audiometry is to establish an individual's range of hearing. It is most often performed when hearing loss is suspected. Audiometry can establish the extent as well as the type of a hearing loss. Audiometric techniques are also used when an individual has vertigo or **dizziness**, since many hearing and vestibular or balance problems are related. Since those with facial paralysis may also have hearing loss, audiologic testing may be performed on these individuals as well.

Description

The primary purpose of audiometry is to determine the frequency and intensity at which sounds can be heard. Humans can hear sounds in the frequency or pitch range of 20 to 20,000 Hertz (Hz), but most conversations occur between 300 and 3000 Hz. Audiometric testing is done between 125 and 8000 Hz. The intensity levels or degree of loudness at which sounds can be heard for most adults is between 0 and 20 decibels (dB).

Both air conduction and bone conduction of sounds are evaluated by audiometry. Air conduction establishes the extent of sound transmission through the bones of the middle ear. The results of a bone conduction test determine how soft a sound an individual can hear over several frequencies or pitches. Bone conduction audiometry determines the extent to which there is neurosensory hearing loss. An individual with a neurosensory loss may be able to hear sounds but not understand them. Since those with hearing losses often cannot hear sounds at normal decibel levels, intensities as high as 115 dB are used to assess the extent of air conduction loss and as high as 70 dB for bone conduction loss. The difference between bone conduction loss and neurosensory hearing loss is called the air-bone gap.

The most common method of assessing hearing ability is with the audiometer. Audiometric testing with the audiometer is performed while the patient sits in a soundproof booth and the examiner outside the booth communicates to the patient with a microphone. The patient wears headphones when air conduction is tested and a vibrating earpiece behind the ear next to the mastoid bone or along the forehead when bone conduction is tested. One ear is tested at a time, and a technique called masking, in which noise is presented to the ear not being tested, assures the examiner that only one ear is tested at a time. Through the headphones or earpiece pure sounds in both frequency and intensity are transmitted to the patient and the threshold at which the patient can hear for each frequency is established. The patient signals an ability to hear a sound by raising a hand or finger.

When the child is capable of understanding and responding to words, speech discrimination is also assessed as part of audiometry. Speech discrimination establishes one's ability to understand consonant sounds.

In speech discrimination testing, two syllable words are read to and then repeated by the patient. This is an important part of audiometry, since much of a child's learning depends on the ability to discriminate speech. Older children of ten to 12 years of age have speech recognition comparable to adults and do well with speech discrimination testing. To insure that speech discrimination only is being assessed, this part of the hearing test is done at decibel levels of 30 to 40 decibels, higher than that of everyday conversation. By age five most children can do some type of speech discrimination testing.

Speech discrimination in the child of three to six years of age may be tested by having the child look at pictures of common objects as a monosyllabic word is read to him or her. The child indicates comprehension of the word by pointing to the corresponding object.

When evaluating infants, rather than testing of threshold levels, the examiner establishes the minimum response level at which the child responds to auditory stimuli. The minimum intensity level at which a neonate responds to sound is 25 dBs. This minimum level gradually decreases through infancy and at 36 months most children respond to sound intensities of less than 10 dBs.

For the young infant under four months of age, audiologists employ behavioral observation audiometry (BOA). The audiologist observes startle responses and motor reflex changes in the child as various noisemakers are employed to elicit these responses. The difficulty with this test is that the noises used are not standardized in frequency or intensity.

Visual reinforcement audiology (VRA) testing evaluates the hearing of infants from six months to two years. Sounds of varying intensity are presented to one of two speakers as the child sits on a parent's lap. If a sound is heard by the child, then he or she turns toward the appropriate speaker and is rewarded by a visual stimulus, such as an animated toy or a flashing light, although video images have been used for older children.

As the child gets older, condition play audiometry (CPA) is useful. The child is instructed to listen for a sound and to respond when a sound is heard by doing varying tasks, such as placing a ball in a cup or placing a peg in a pegboard, when the auditory stimulus is heard. Headphones may be worn by the child for this type of testing.

Because a reliable subjective response is difficult or impossible in a young patient electrophysiological testing is often performed. Electrophysiological testing is a reliable and nonbehavioral method to assess hearing loss in infants and young children and can be done while the child is either sleeping or under sedation. Some electro-

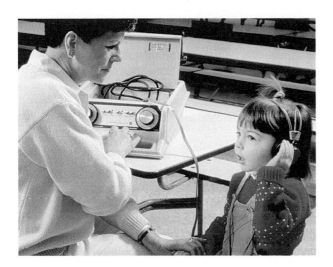

Technician testing a young girl's hearing with an audiometer.
(Photograph by Jon Meyer. Custom Medical Stock Photo, Inc.)

physiological tests are the auditory brainstem response (ABR) test, auditory steady-state response (ASSR) testing, electroencephalic audiometry (EEG) test, and otoacoustic emission testing (OAE).

To perform the auditory brainstem response (ABR) test, headphones are placed on the infant or child and electrophysiological responses from the scalp and ears are recorded in response to tones sent through the headphones. A computer compiles the findings into a waveform that gives the examiner information about the location of a hearing problem anywhere along this pathway from the ear canal to the brainstem. This test is also called the brainstem auditory evoked response.

Auditory steady-state response (ASSR) testing also involves monitoring recorded responses from the scalp of tones at varying frequencies. This test is a more sensitive test than the ABR and can also measure residual hearing better. The EEG or electroencephalic audiometry test measures tone loss but cannot locate the site of a hearing loss. Otoacoustic emission testing (OAE) records spontaneous emissions from the ear and can detect middle ear problems. It is simpler than ABR, and it can be used to screen infants for severe hearing losses, since if hearing loss of greater than 40 dBs exist, no emission will be recorded.

An adjunct test of audiometry is acoustic immitance testing which assesses the facility with which sound can travel from the external ear to the cochlea inside the ear. The most familiar of this type of testing is the tympanogram, which determines if fluid has built up behind the eardrum.

Precautions

Audiometry is a safe procedure to which there are rarely contraindications.

Preparation

For most audiometric testing no special preparation is required, although the first time that hearing testing is done on a child the procedure should be explained as clearly as possible. If ABR or ASSR testing is done under sedation, then the child may not eat for several hours prior to administration of the drugs.

Aftercare

Audiometric testing, except when sedation is involved, requires no special aftercare.

Risks

If the ABR is used under sedation then the side effects of sedatives must be considered. Otherwise there are no risks associated with audiometry.

Parental concerns

Audiometry should be performed on all infants and children since unidentified hearing loss can delay speech and language skills. The earlier that a child with a hearing problem can be identified, the sooner the child's **communication skills** will develop. The audiometry available as of 2004 can determine the type and extent of a hearing loss as well as identify the location of the hearing problem. The results of audiometric testing can help determine if a hearing aid or cochlear implant may help a child. Audiometric testing can also be an adjunct to diagnosis of more serious problems related to hearing loss such a related syndrome or a tumor.

Parents of a child diagnosed with a hearing loss must be prepared to bring the child back for follow-up evaluations to monitor the hearing loss every three months for the first year after diagnosis and at least annually through the remainder of childhood. As the child gets older, more extensive audiometry testing can be performed.

Resources

BOOKS

Beasley, Donald J., and Ronald G. Amedee. "Hearing Loss." In *Expert Guide to Otolaryngology*, edited by Karen H. Calhoun. Philadelphia: American College of Physicians, 2001.

Miller, Andre J., and Gernard J. Gianoli. "Dizziness." In *Expert Guide to Otolaryngology*, edited by Karen H. Calhoun. Philadelphia: American College of Physicians, 2001.

Turkington, Carol, and Allen E. Sussman. *Deafness and Hearing Disorders*, 2nd ed. New York: Facts On File, 2004.

PERIODICALS

Firszt, Jill B., et al. "Auditory Sensitivity in Children Using the Auditory Steady-State Response." *Archives of Otolaryngology—Head & Neck Surgery* 130 (May 2004): 536–40.

Schmida, Milton J., et al. "Visual Reinforcement Audiometry Using Digital Video Disc and Conventional Reinforcers." *American Journal of Audiology* 12, no. 1 (June 2003): 35–40

Martha Reilly, OD

Auditory discrimination test

Definition

An auditory discrimination test is a screening or diagnostic **assessment** tool designed to identify and diagnose deficits in auditory discrimination.

Purpose

Auditory discrimination is a central auditory processing skill that involves the ability to differentiate among phonemes—the smallest significant units of sound in a language. Phonemes are combined into words. For example the word "goes" is made up of three phonemes: "g," "oh," and "zzz." Auditory discrimination is part of phonology which, in turn, is one of the five components of language.

Auditory discrimination tests (ADTs) are one type of auditory analysis tests, which are used to measure how well a child understands speech and the spoken word. ADTs are designed to measure a child's phonological awareness—the ability to focus on and manipulate phonemes within spoken words. Phonological awareness skills include the ability to do the following:

- compare and contrast speech sounds
- separate and blend phonemes
- identify phonemes within spoken words
- combine phonemes into spoken words

ADTs measure a child's ability to detect subtle similarities and differences between speech sounds. Two of the most commonly used ADTs are Wepman's Auditory Discrimination Test (WADT) and the Goldman-Fristoe-Woodcock Test of Auditory Discrimination.

Auditory discrimination skills are very important in the classroom. Activities that require auditory discrimination skills include the following:

- following directions
- reading
- writing
- spelling

Auditory discrimination ability or phonological awareness skills have long been correlated with reading ability. Some specialists believe that ADTs should be a component of all reading programs and that poor auditory discrimination can be a major factor in children's failure to reach reading targets. The WADT is used to evaluate **communication skills** in general, as well to identify potential reading difficulties and to predict certain types of speech defects. Because it requires a child to recognize small differences between phonemes, the WADT is widely used to measure a child's readiness for reading instruction using a phonic method.

Some underachieving but gifted children have learning disabilities that are caused by deficits in central auditory skills, including auditory discrimination. The WADT commonly is used to test for an auditory discrimination deficit in such children. Deficits in auditory discrimination are also believed to be one of the causes of central auditory processing disorder (CAPD). There are various methods for addressing auditory discrimination problems in children.

Description

Auditory discrimination is one component of central auditory processing skills or auditory perception. The other components are as follows:

- auditory memory: the ability to recall a sequence of auditory stimuli or phonemes
- auditory blending: the ability to perceive separate phenomes, divide a word into phenomes, and combine phenomes into words
- auditory comprehension: the ability to comprehend and interpret information that is presented orally

The WADT

The WADT, first published in 1958 and revised in 1973, is designed to measure the ability of children aged four to eight to recognize small differences between English phonemes. The test consists of 40 pairs of words. The words in a pair are of equal length. In ten of the pairs the words are identical. In the remaining 30 pairs the words differ by a single phoneme. The test requires the child to differentiate between the following:

- 13 word-pairs differing in their initial consonant, such as "coast" and "toast"
- four word pairs differing in their medial vowels, such as "pat" and "pet"
- 13 word-pairs differing their final consonant, such as "lease" and "leash"
- 10 identical word-pairs or false choices, such as "jam" and "jam"

Often the WADT is administered by a **special education** teacher or a speech/language pathologist. The test is administered orally to an individual child who is seated such that neither the examiner's mouth nor the words on the test form are visible to the child. The examiner reads each word-pair only once, and the child indicates whether the word-pair consists of different or identical words. The test requires about five to 10 minutes to administer. The performance rating scale ranges from "very good development" for the child's age to "below adequate" for the child's age. Two equivalent forms of the test are provided so that children can be retested if their initial scores are questionable or if the test is needed for evaluating the effectiveness of subse-

quent remedial instruction. The WADT is widely considered to be both reliable and valid, with norms based on the scores of 2,000 children.

The WADT is considered to be a fast, inexpensive means of screening children for auditory discrimination deficits and for identifying children who are slower than average in developing auditory discrimination skills. It also is used to identify children who may have difficulty learning the phonics that are necessary for learning to read. The WADT often is used as a component of formal reading assessments.

Other ADTs

Other ADTs include the following tests:

- Goldman-Fristoe-Woodcock (G-F-W) Test of Auditory Discrimination, which includes visual stimuli
- Goldman-Fristoe-Woodcock (G-F-W) Diagnostic Auditory Discrimination Test
- auditory word discrimination subtest of the Test of Auditory Perceptual Skills (TAPS); the subtest uses only auditory stimuli
- Auditory Discrimination and Attention Test
- Schonell Auditory Discrimination Test which, like the WADT, is a component of some formal reading assessments

In one type of ADT the test administrator says a word and the child is asked to repeat the word, leaving out a syllable or sound. For example the examiner says "outdoor" and tells the child to say the word but to not say "out." The correct answer is "door." Children's responses are graded according to the following:

- The child gives the correct answer quickly.
- The child takes more than five seconds to give the correct answer.
- The child answers incorrectly.

The child's auditory discrimination skill is assigned a grade level:

- a kindergartner told to repeat the word "cucumber" without the "cu (q)" should easily answer "cumber"
- a first-grader told to repeat "please" without the "zzz" sound should easily answer "plea"
- a second-grader told to repeat "clay" without the "k" should easily answer "lay"
- a third-grader told to repeat "smock" without the "mmm" sound should be able to easily answer "sock"

The Sheshore Measures of Musical Talent is a widely used standardized test for measuring musical abilities in students applying to music programs, conservatories, and colleges and universities. It tests the listener's auditory discrimination abilities with regard to the following:

- pitch
- volume
- rhythm
- sound duration
- tonal quality or timbre
- tonal memory

Electrophysiological tests

Sometimes electrophysiological techniques are used to assess various types of central auditory processing including auditory discrimination. These techniques measure auditory evoked potentials (AEPs), which are changes in the brain's neural-electrical activity in response to the reception of auditory signals. AEPs are recorded via electrodes on the child's scalp. During auditory discrimination decisions, which involve various processes including attention and recognition, a large positive peak called P300 appears at about 200 milliseconds after the presentation of the word or other auditory stimulus. The electrical signals that contribute to P300 come from various parts of the brain. The most common way of measuring auditory discrimination with P300 is the oddball paradigm, in which a series of low-frequency auditory stimuli is randomly interspersed with high-frequency stimuli. The child attempts to count the number of high-frequency pitches. Significant differences in the appearance of the P300 peak have been found between poorly achieving gifted children and highly achieving gifted children.

Precautions

ADTs can give confusing or false negative results. Many children do well on the auditory word discrimination subtest of TAPS, which uses auditory stimuli, but perform poorly on the G-F-W Test of Auditory Discrimination, which uses visual stimuli. Such children may have good auditory discrimination skills but poor auditory-visual integration discrimination.

Risks

In the early 2000s research suggests that auditory discrimination and other perceptual processes may not be primary factors in predicting reading ability and learning disabilities. Thus some children may be falsely

labeled with a learning disability because of their results on ADTs. Other children might fail to be identified as candidates for early intervention for reading or other learning difficulties on the basis of their ADT scores.

Normal results

ADTs are standardized by testing large numbers of children to determine the normal range of scores for children of a given age. The vast majority of children have ADT scores within the normal range. Children who score significantly below the normal range may be referred for additional assessment. Early intervention for children with low ADT scores may include exercises and activities designed to improve auditory discrimination.

Parental concerns

ADTs are short, simple tests that do not require preparation on the part of the child. However parents should be aware of the normal developmental milestones of speech and **language development**. Although no two children reach these milestones at precisely the same age, a significant lag may indicate the need for assessment of auditory discrimination and/or other components central auditory processing. Typical milestones include:

- producing vowel sounds within the first six months of life

- understanding certain words by six to 12 months of age

- speaking first words at 12–18 months

- combining words by 18–24 months of age

- understandable speech and the use of consonant sounds by two to three years

- speaking faster and with longer and more varied sentences by three to four years

- a vocabulary of more than 1,500 words, sentences averaging five words, and the ability to modify speech by four to five years of age

Resources

ORGANIZATIONS

American Speech-Language-Hearing Association. 10801 Rockville Pike, Rockville, MD 20852. Web site: <http://asha.org>.

International Listening Association. Web site: <www.listen.org>.

WEB SITES

Burk, Rickie W. "Interview with Dorothy Kelly." *MSHA News.* Mississippi Speech-Language-Hearing Association. <www.mshausa.org/kelly.html> (accessed November 9, 2004).

Troost, B. Todd, and Melissa A. Walker. "Diagnostic Principals in Neuro-otology: The Auditory System." Available online at <www.bgsm.edu/neurology/Rosenberg/audio1.html> (accessed November 9, 2004).

Margaret Alic, PhD

Autism

Definition

Autism is a severely incapacitating developmental disorder of brain function characterized by three major types of symptoms: impaired social interaction, problems with verbal and nonverbal communication, and unusual or severely limited activities and interests.

Description

Autism is a complex developmental disability with symptoms that typically appear during the first three years of childhood and continue throughout life. It is the most severe disorder within a group of developmental disorders called autism spectrum disorders (ASDs) or **pervasive developmental disorders** (PDDs) that cover a wide range of behaviors and symptoms, all related to a lesser or greater extent to impaired social and **communication skills**.

In its most severe form, autism may include extreme self-injurious, repetitive, highly unusual, and aggressive behaviors.

Demographics

According to the Center for Disease Control and Prevention, PDDs were estimated to occur in two to six per 1,000 births in 2003 with autism being the most common PDD, affecting an estimated one in 250 births. As of 2004, as many as 1.5 million Americans are were believed to have some form of autism. The disorder is four times more prevalent in boys than girls and is not associated with any specific racial or ethnic background. **Family** income, lifestyle, and educational levels also do not affect the chance of the disorder's occurrence.

The Autism Society of America (ASA) warns that autism is on the rise. Based on statistics from the U.S. Department of Education and other governmental agencies, the ASA estimates that the disorder is growing at a rate of 10 to 17 percent per year, which could lead to 4 million Americans being affected by autism between 2005 and 2015.

Causes and symptoms

While understanding of autism grew tremendously since it was first described by Leo Kanner in 1943, no known single cause for autism as of 2004 was yet identified, although research has shown that it results from specific abnormalities in brain structure or function. For example, brain scans show that the shape and structure of the brain in autistic children are different from those of non-autistic children. Researchers investigated several theories and established a firm link between heredity, genetics, and medical problems, while also establishing that no known psychological factors in the development of the child have been shown to cause autism.

The genetic link is supported by observations showing that, in many families, there seems to be a pattern of autism or ASDs. While no one gene was identified as causing autism as of 2004, researchers are searching for irregular segments of genetic code that autistic children may have inherited.

Autism has also been shown to occur more frequently among individuals who have certain medical conditions, including **fragile X syndrome**, **tuberous sclerosis**, congenital **rubella** syndrome, and untreated **phenylketonuria**.

Toxins and pollution in the environment have also been associated with autism. The Center for the Study of Autism and other agencies documented a high prevalence of autism in certain communities, for example, in the small town of Leomenster, Massachusetts, and in Brick Township, New Jersey, and attempted to uncover the reason.

The symptoms of autism occur in a wide variety of combinations, from mild to severe and are caused by physical disorders of the brain. According to the ASA, they may include any combination of the following in varying degrees of severity:

- insistence on sameness; resistance to change
- difficulty in expressing needs; using gestures or pointing instead of words
- repeating words or sentences instead of using normal, responsive language (echolalia)
- laughing, crying, showing distress for reasons not apparent to others
- aloof behavior, seeking solitude
- tantrums
- refusal to cuddle or be cuddled
- little or no eye contact
- unresponsiveness to normal teaching methods
- sustained odd **play**
- inappropriate attachments to objects
- apparent over-sensitivity or under-sensitivity to **pain**
- no **fear** of danger
- uneven gross/fine motor skills
- not responsive to verbal cues; acts as if deaf although hearing tests in normal range

When to call the doctor

The characteristic behaviors of autism may or may not be apparent in infancy (18 to 24 months) but usually become obvious during early childhood (two to six years).

The National Institute of Child Health and Human Development (NICHD) lists the five following behaviors as signals that medical evaluation is needed:

- does not babble or coo by 12 months
- does not gesture (point, wave, grasp) by 12 months
- does not say single words by 16 months
- does not say two-word phrases on his or her own by 24 months
- loss of any language or social skills at any age

The presence of any of these five behaviors does not mean that a child has autism, but because the characteristics of the disorder vary so much, a child should be evaluated by a multidisciplinary team that may include a neurologist, psychologist, developmental pediatrician, speech/language therapist, learning consultant, or other professionals knowledgeable about autism.

Diagnosis

There are no medical tests for diagnosing autism. An accurate diagnosis must be based on observation of the individual's communication, behavior, and developmental level. A diagnosis of autistic disorder is usually made when an individual displays six or more of 12 symptoms listed across three major areas: social interaction, communication, and behavior. Several screening procedures have been developed for use in diagnosing autism, among which are the following:

- Childhood Autism Rating Scale (CARS). CARS is based on observed behavior. Using a 15-point scale, professionals evaluate a child's relationship to people, body use, adaptation to change, listening response, and verbal communication.
- Checklist for Autism in Toddlers (CHAT). CHAT is used to screen for autism at 18 months of age. The screening tool uses a short questionnaire with two sections, one prepared by the parents, the other by the child's family doctor or pediatrician.
- Autism Screening Questionnaire (ASQ). The ASQ is a 40-item screening scale used with children four and older to help evaluate communication skills and social functioning.
- Screening Test for Autism in Two-Year Olds. This test uses direct observations to study behavioral features in children under two. It is focused on three skills areas, play, motor imitation, and joint attention, that are associated with autism.

Treatment

There is as of 2004 no cure for autism, but appropriate treatment may promote relatively normal development and lower the incidence of undesirable behaviors. Doctors also may prescribe a variety of drugs to reduce the symptoms of autism, such as **antidepressants** and tranquilizers. Educational/behavioral therapies emphasize highly structured and often intensive skill-oriented training, and they are comparatively the most effective treatments available.

The importance of early treatment is well established among professionals. Researchers have proposed that there is a critical period during which the young, developing brain is highly modifiable. For some children with autism, the repeated, active interaction provided by intensive educational/behavioral therapy may modify their neural circuitry before it goes too much awry, correcting it before autism becomes permanent.

A wide spectrum of educational/behavioral therapies were developed during the last decades of the twentieth century under the umbrella of applied behavior analysis (ABA), the science of human behavior. ABA is the process of systematically applying interventions based upon the principles of learning theory to improve socially significant behaviors to a meaningful degree. ABA methods treat autism with particular strategies: using reinforcement procedures to increase on-task behavior and social interactions; teaching new skills (functional life skills, communication skills, or social skills); maintaining desirable behaviors (teaching self-control and self-monitoring procedures to maintain social skills); transferring behavior from one situation or response to another (from completing assignments in the resource room to performing as well in the mainstream classroom); reducing interfering behaviors (e.g., self-injury).

Specific educational/behavioral therapy programs for the treatment of autism include, for example, the following:

- The Miller Method. Developed at the Language and **Cognitive Development** Center (LCDC) in Boston, MA. The LCDC is a Massachusetts Chapter 766-approved day school, serving students with autism or PDD ages three to 14. The LCDC specializes in a particular approach to teaching children with autism. The Miller Method extensively uses adaptive equipment, including platforms (to elevate the child so as to help increase eye contact), large swinging balls (to expand the child's reality system) and Swiss cheese boards (to teach motor planning, as well as to increase the child's understanding of his or her relation to environment and space).

- Discrete Trial Training (DTT). DTT methodology has been likened to controlling the river of information and interaction that typically confronts the child with autism such that it is presented one drop at a time. This control manages learning opportunities so that skills are more easily mastered by the child. Learning occurs in small steps. Simple skills must be mastered before new learning opportunities are presented, in which the

Therapy for autistic children may include working on jigsaw puzzles. (© Michael Macor/San Francisco Chronicle/Corbis.)

child then builds upon the mastered skill toward a more complex one.

- Treatment and Education of Autistic and Communication Handicapped Children (TEACCH). TEACCH is a statewide program in North Carolina that tries to respond to the needs of autistic people by using the best available approaches and methods. The TEACCH approach includes a focus on the person with autism and development of a program around this person's skills, interests, and needs. The major priorities include centering on the individual, understanding autism, adopting appropriate adaptations, and a broadly based intervention strategy building on existing skills and interests.

Alternative treatment

Some alternative treatments have been proposed for autism. They include:

- The Son-Rise program. The Son-Rise program was created by Barry and Samahria Lyte Kaufman in the 1970s, as a means to teach their own son, who was diagnosed with autism and **mental retardation**. The program ranges from one week to six months and is designed to

KEY TERMS

Antidepressant drug—A medication prescribed to relieve major depression. Classes of antidepressants include selective serotonin reuptake inhibitors (fluoxetine/Prozac, sertraline/Zoloft), tricyclics (amitriptyline/Elavil), MAOIs (phenelzine/Nardil), and heterocyclics (bupropion/Wellbutrin, trazodone/Desyrel).

Asperger syndrome—A developmental disorder of childhood characterized by autistic behavior but without the same difficulties acquiring language that children with autism have.

Congenital rubella syndrome (CRS)—Viral illness caused by a togavirus of the genus *Rubivirus*. When rubella infection occurs during pregnancy, fetal infection is likely and often causes congenital rubella syndrome (CRS), resulting in miscarriages, stillbirths, and severe birth defects. Up to 20 percent of the infants born to mothers infected during the first half of pregnancy have CRS. The most common congenital defects are cataracts, heart disease, deafness, and mental retardation.

Echolalia—Involuntary echoing of the last word, phrase, or sentence spoken by someone else.

Fragile X syndrome—A genetic condition related to the X chromosome that affects mental, physical, and sensory development. It is the most common form of inherited mental retardation.

Pervasive developmental disorder—A category of childhood disorder that includes Asperger syndrome and Rett's disorder. The PDDs are sometimes referred to collectively as autistic spectrum disorders.

Phenylketonuria (PKU)—A rare, inherited, metabolic disorder in which the enzyme necessary to break down and use phenylalanine, an amino acid necessary for normal growth and development, is lacking. As a result, phenylalanine builds up in the body causing mental retardation and other neurological problems.

Tranquilizer—A medication that has a calming effect and is used to treat anxiety and mental tension.

Tuberous sclerosis—A genetic condition that affects many organ systems including the brain, skin, heart, eyes, and lungs. Benign (non-cancerous) growths or tumors called hamartomas form in various parts of the body, disrupting their normal function.

teach parents, professionals, and support staff of children with a wide range of disabilities how to implement home-based programs based upon the Kaufmans' theories of learning. There have been no studies of the Son-Rise Program's effectiveness, and the method has not been subjected to scientific evaluation.

- Megavitamin therapy. Some studies have shown that vitamin B_6 improves eye contact and speech and lessens tantrum behavior. Vitamin B_6 causes fewer side effects than other medications and is considered safe when used in appropriate doses. However, not many health practitioners advocate its use in the treatment of autism, citing that the studies showing its benefit were flawed.

Nutritional concerns

Dimethylglycine (DMG) is a compound available in many health food stores, that is legally classified as a food, not a vitamin or drug. Some researchers claim that it improves speech in children with autism. Those who respond to this treatment usually do so within a week. Many doctors, however, do not feel that the studies are adequate to promote DMG in the diet of autistic individuals.

Prognosis

People with autism have normal life expectancies. Symptoms in many children improve with treatment, or as the children grow up, some eventually are able to lead normal or near-normal lives. **Adolescence** can worsen behavior problems in some children, and treatment should be adjusted for the child's changing needs. According to the National Institute of Neurological Disorders and **Stroke** (NINDS), about one third of children with ASDs eventually develop epilepsy. The risk is highest in children with severe cognitive impairment and motor deficits.

Prevention

Since the cause of the brain anomalies associated with autism is not known, prevention is not possible.

Parental concerns

Following a diagnosis of autism, parents need to work with health and education professionals for the child's benefit. Specifically, they need to take the following steps:

- Be informed. Parents should learn as much as they can about autism so that they can be involved in determining care.

- Be prepared. Parents should prepare for meetings with doctors, therapists, and school personnel. They should ask questions and communicate their concerns regarding treatment issues and the impact of the diagnosis on the family.

- Be organized. Many parents find it useful to keep a notebook detailing their child's diagnosis, treatment, and the meetings they have with professionals.

- Communicate effectively. Open communication is very important. If parents disagree with a professional's recommendation, for example, they should communicate specifically why they disagree.

See also Fragile X syndrome; Pervasive developmental disorders; Phenylketonuria.

Resources

BOOKS

Barron, Judy, and Sean Barron. *There's a Boy in Here.* Arlington, TX: Future Horizons, 2002.

Boushey, Ann. *Parent to Parent: Information and Inspiration for Parents Dealing with Autism and Asperger's Syndrome.* Herndon, VA: Jessica Kingsley Publishers, 2004.

Buten, Howard. *Through the Glass Wall: Journeys into the Closed-off Worlds of the Autistic.* New York: Bantam Books, 2005.

Coleman, Mary. *The Neurology of Autism.* Oxford, UK: Oxford University Press, 2005.

Griffin, Elizabeth. *Fragile X, Fragile Hope: Finding Joy in Parenting a Special Needs Child.* Lynnwood, WA: Emerald Books, 2004.

Hamilton, Lynn M. *Facing Autism: Giving Parents Reasons for Hope and Guidance for Help.* New York: Waterbrook Press, 2000.

Harris, Sandra L., and Lara Delmolino. *Motivating People with Autism Spectrum Disorders to Learn and Gain Independence.* Bethesda, MD: Woodbine House, 2004.

PERIODICALS

Barrett, S., et al. "Children on the borderlands of autism: differential characteristics in social, imaginative, communicative, and repetitive behavior domains." *Autism* 8, no. 1 (March 2004): 61–87.

Lord, C., et al. "Regression and word loss in autistic spectrum disorders." *Journal of Child Psychology and Psychiatry* 45, no. 5 (July 2004): 936–55.

Lewis, W. "Play and language in children with autism." *Autism* 7, no. 4 (December 2003): 391–99.

Muhle, R., et al. "The genetics of autism." *Journal of Pediatrics* 113, no. 5 (May 2004): 472–86.

Nader, R., et al. "Expression of pain in children with autism." *Clinical Journal of Pain* 20, no. 2 (March-April 2004): 88–97.

Pinto-Martin, J., and S. E. Levy. "Early Diagnosis of Autism Spectrum Disorders." *Current Treatment Options in Neurology* 6, no. 5 (September 2004): 391–400.

Whitaker, P. "Supporting families of preschool children with autism: what parents want and what helps." *Autism* 6, no. 4 (December 2002): 411–16.

Williams, K. R., and J. G. Wishart. "The Son-Rise Program intervention for autism: an investigation into family experiences." *Journal of Intellectual Disabilities Research* 47, Pt. 4–5 (May-June 2003): 291–99.

ORGANIZATIONS

Association for Science in Autism Treatment (ASAT). PO Box 7468, Portland, ME 04112–7468. Web site: <www.asatonline.org>.

Autism Network International (ANI). PO Box 35448, Syracuse, NY 13235–5448. Web site: <http://ani.autistics.org>.

Autism Research Institute (ARI). 4182 Adams Ave., San Diego, CA 92116. Web site: <www.autismresearchinstitute.com>.

Autism Society of America. 7910 Woodmont Avenue, Suite 300, Bethesda, MD 20814–3067. Web site: <www.autism-society.org>.

Families for Early Autism Treatment. PO Box 255722, Sacramento, CA 95865–5722. Web site: <www.feat.org>.

MAAP Services for Autism, Asperger's, and PDD. PO Box 524, Crown Point, IN 46308. Web site: <www.maapservices.org>.

National Alliance for Autism Research (NAAR). 99 Wall Street, Research Park, Princeton, NJ 08540. Web site: <www.naar.org>.

National Autism Hotline. Autism Services Center, 605 Ninth St., Huntington, WV 25710. Web site: <www.autismservicescenter.org>.

National Institute of Child Health and Human Development (NICHD). 31 Center Drive, Rm. 2A32, MSC 2425, Bethesda, MD 20892–2425. Web site: <www.nichd.nih.gov>.

National Institute of Mental Health (NIMH). 6001 Executive Blvd., Rm. 8184, MSC 9663, Bethesda, MD 20892–9663. Web site: <www.nimh.nih.gov>.

WEB SITES

"Different Roads to Learning: The resource dedicated to helping children with autism learn and grow." Available online at <www.difflearn.com> (accessed October 11, 2004.)

Monique Laberge, Ph.D.

Autoeroticism *see* **Masturbation**

B

Babysitters

Definition

A babysitter is someone who provides occasional child care for a few hours at a time. Teenage babysitters often provide babysitting services for a few hours at a time. However, in-home sitters range from nannies who may have training in child development and first aid to women who, although not trained formally, have had many years of experience caring for children, including their own. Parents might prefer an au pair, a young person, usually a woman in her early twenties, often from abroad, who lives with the **family** to provide child care.

Purpose

In order to give themselves time off from parenting, parents hire babysitters. However, time away from home is enjoyable only when parents are secure in knowing that their child is well cared for. Some parents join a babysitters' club, for example, a group of mothers may agree to take turns caring for each others' children so that each of them can have some time away from their children and know their children are in excellent hands.

Babysitter course

The American Red Cross provides a certification course for babysitters. Young people over age 11 are eligible to enroll in the eight-hour training course, offered at various community organizations and schools. Some organizations underwrite the cost of the course and offer it free to participants; others charge a fee. The course provides instruction in supervision of children, planning activities for children of all ages, accident prevention, emergency response techniques (including what to do in a **choking** emergency), and job-hunting strategies.

Description

Babysitters should understand that parents often have ambivalent feelings about leaving their children with a babysitter. The primary goal of parents is to provide safe and competent babysitting without feeling a need for substitute parents. No matter how conscientious the sitter, she or he will not care for the child in precisely the same way as a parent, and it is unreasonable to expect a carbon-copy parent. Once convinced the sitter is a decent and kind individual, parents will allow the young person to be herself (within the outline of the family's needs and rules) and to use her own judgments.

Most families provide the babysitter with general guidelines about bedtime, acceptable activity and behavior during the parents' absence, and instructions on who to contact if case of an emergency. In addition, young people who want to be babysitters may take the American Red Cross course. Books and videotapes also outline techniques and strategies for safe and successful babysitting. The teenage babysitter must be able to answer lots of questions in an extensive interview with conscientious parents.

Finding a sitter

Parents advertise for a nanny or sitter in the local paper, on the church or community bulletin boards, or with an agency. Word-of-mouth is often the best source. Parents ask other parents for recommendations. Good sources for sitters who are no longer needed by a family are local preschools and nursery schools. Many parents post their names and numbers in these locations as soon as they anticipate needing a sitter.

Interviewing the sitter

Parents interview interested applicants and request and examine references. This meeting provides an opportunity for direct exchange of ideas between the sitter and the parents. Questions pertain to rules regarding food and methods for handling **discipline** problems and fees the parents will pay. The sitter and the child(ren) should meet to get to know each other a bit.

Potential babysitters need to prepare for interviews with parents. The sitters should be ready to answer specific questions. They need to provide proof of identity (such as a driver's license or social security card) and supply names, addresses, and phone numbers for three to five references.

During the interview parents may want to address the following concerns:

- Is the teenage babysitter mature, well-groomed, and disciplined?

- What childcare experience does she/he have? What were the sitter's best and worst experiences?

- How does the sitter handle issues of discipline? What would the sitter do if the baby cried for an hour or more? What if the toddler was defiant or inattentive to the sitter's directions? What if the child broke the sitter's watch or destroyed other prized possessions?

- How does the sitter feel about TV? Would the sitter watch TV while the child was playing or napping? What kinds of programs do children and teenagers watch in her home? Would the sitter offer television as regular entertainment for the child?

- How much time does the sitter spend with other sitters and friends? Does the sitter enjoy taking the children outside to **play** in the backyard or to the neighborhood playground?

- What does she know about good **nutrition**? Does she limit snacks to healthy foods?

- Does the sitter drive a car, have a cellular telephone, or have a need to spend time talking on the phone while working?

- What would the teenager do in an emergency such as a sudden illness for the child or if the sitter became ill suddenly? What would the sitter do if there was a fire and other emergency?

The interview is the proper time to discuss hourly or evening rates. Some sitters request a higher rate after midnight. This is also the time to discuss travel arrangements. Does the sitter drive and have a car or does the sitter need to be picked up and returned home?

Paying the babysitter

Babysitter pay rates consider the age and number of children, the age of the babysitter, the type of care expected from the sitter, and the time of day (or night), and whether the sitter drives or not. The distance traveled to the job also dictates the pay rate. For teenagers the base rate is $4.00 to $5.00 an hour for a baby sitter who cares for two children and drives to and from the job. The pay increases with the number of children to perhaps $10.00 an hour for three children.

The going rate varies by geographical location and over time in any one area. Urban rates may range from $3.50 to $10.00 depending on age and experience, the number of children, and the lateness of the hour when the parents return home. In general, fees are higher for younger children.

Babysitter checklist

Parents should leave emergency information for the sitter, most often near the telephone or on the refrigerator, where it can be found easily. The information may include the following:

- 911, as the emergency number to call

- family name, home address, and phone number (Sitters may "blank out" while trying to give this critical information over the telephone to the 911 operator.)

- telephone numbers of the family doctor or pediatrician

- telephone numbers, including cellular phones, for reaching parents

- children's full names and dates of birth

- name, address, and phone numbers of neighbors who have agreed to be on call in case of an emergency and numbers of back-up friends or relative

- time parents are expected to come home

- parents' full names, cell phone or pager numbers

- special activities for children and any food restriction for each child

- child's routine, including approved snacks, toileting habits, bedtime, and comfort objects needed for bedtime

- guidelines for the babysitter's personal behavior, such as personal telephone calls or friends visiting

- safety and security procedures, such as what to say when answering the telephone and how to secure all doors

Parental concerns

Children should be told in advance that their parents are going out and the babysitter will be staying with them. Even if they are initially accepting, it is not unusual for young children to cry when they realize that their parents are leaving. The tears will dry when the parents leave; in response to children's tears, it is useful to minimize the problem and leave happily, assuring young children about the parents' return. The babysitter can use this time to comfort the children. She can distract them by engaging them in conversation or mentioning the next activity.

Parents should plan to stay in the house for at least 15 to 20 minutes after the sitter arrives to give general information about the kids and specific instructions about the home. If the family lives in an apartment building, the parent should point out emergency exits or fire escapes and leave candles and flashlight handy in case of a possible power failure. They should review simple first-aid, where to find bandages and home remedies for bumps or **bruises**. However, juvenile sitters should not be asked to dispense medications to children.

Sitters should know the household routines, approved television programs, recommended bedtime stories, and bedtime. They should be prepared for behaviors that are problematic, such as temper **tantrums**. In all, the sitter's job is to keep the children safe and as happy as possible within the guidelines set by the parents.

Resources

BOOKS

Dayee, Frances S., et al. *Babysitting*. Danbury, CT: Scholastic Library Publishing, 2001.

Lansky, Vicky. *Dear Babysitter Handbook: A Handy Guide for Your Child's Sitter*. Reno, Nevada: Group West, 2001.

Murkoff, Heidi, and Sharon Mazel. *What to Expect Baby-Sitter's Handbook*. New York: Workman Publishing Company, 2004.

Williams, Joseph L., et al. *About Babysitting Our Children: A Personalized Information Resource for Your Babysitter*. Farmington Hills, MI: Petit Pois, 2000.

Wolf, Jerri L. *Redbook's Nannies, Au Pairs & Babysitters: How to Find and Keep the Right In-Home Child Care for Your Family*. New York: Sterling Publishing Company Inc., 2001.

ORGANIZATIONS

National Institute on Early Childhood Development and Education. Office of Educational Research and Improvement, U.S. Department of Education, 555 New Jersey Ave, NW Washington, DC 20208. Web site: <www.ed.gov/offices/OER/ECI>.

WEB SITES

"A Guide to the Business of Babysitting." *University of Illinois Extension.* Available online at <www.urbanext.uiuc.edu/babysitting> (accessed December 13, 2004).

Aliene Linwood, RN, DPA

Bacillary dysentery *see* **Shigellosis**

Bariatric surgery *see* **Obesity**

Bath therapy *see* **Therapeutic baths**

Battered child syndrome

Definition

Battered child syndrome (BCS) refers to non-accidental injuries sustained by a child as a result of physical abuse, usually inflicted by an adult caregiver.

Description

Internal injuries, cuts, **burns**, **bruises**, and broken or fractured bones are all possible results of battered child syndrome. Because adults are so much larger and stronger than children are, an abused can suffer severe injury or death without the abuser intentionally causing such an injury. Shaking an infant can cause bleeding in the brain (**subdural hematoma**), resulting in permanent brain damage or death. Emotional damage to a child is also often the byproduct of **child abuse**, which can result in the child exhibiting serious behavioral problems such as substance abuse or the physical abuse of others.

BCS is alternatively referred to as child physical abuse or non-accidental trauma (NAT).

Demographics

The total abuse rate of children is 25.2 per 1,000 children, with physical abuse accounting for 5.7 per 1,000, sexual abuse 2.5 per 1,000, emotional abuse 3.4

per 1,000, and neglect accounting for 15.9 per 1,000 children. These categories overlap, with sexual and physical abuse often occurring together; physical abuse or neglect seldom occur without emotional abuse. These numbers may be underestimates due to underreporting of the problem or failure of diagnosis by medical personnel.

In 1996, more than 3 million victims of alleged abuse were reported to child protective services in the United States; reports were substantiated in more than one million cases. Parents were abusers in 77 percent of the confirmed cases; other relatives in 11 percent. More than 1,000 children died from abuse in 1996.

Causes and symptoms

Causes

Battered child syndrome (BCS) is found at every level of society, although the incidence may be higher in lower-income households, where adult caregivers may suffer greater stress and social difficulties and have a greater lack of control over stressful situations. Other risk factors include lack of education, single parenthood, and **alcoholism** or other drug addictions. The child abuser most often injures a child in the heat of anger or during moments of stress. Common trigger events that may occur before assaults include incessant crying or whining of infants or children; perceived excessive "fussiness" of an infant or child; a toddler's failed **toilet training**; and exaggerated perceptions of acts of "disobedience" by a child. Sometimes cultural traditions may lead to abuse, including beliefs that a child is property, that parents (especially males) have the right to control their children any way they wish, and that children need to be toughened up to face the hardships of life. Child abusers were often abused as children themselves and do not realize that abuse is not an appropriate disciplinary technique. Abusers also often have poor impulse control and do not understand the consequences of their actions.

Symptoms

Symptoms may include a delayed visit to the emergency room with an injured child; an implausible explanation of the cause of a child's injury; bruises that match the shape of a hand, fist or belt; cigarette burns; scald marks; bite marks; black eyes; unconsciousness; lash marks; bruises or choke marks around the neck; circle marks around wrists or ankles (indicating twisting); separated sutures; unexplained unconsciousness; and a bulging fontanel in small infants.

Emotional trauma may remain after physical injuries have healed. Early recognition and treatment of these emo-

tional "bruises" is important to minimize the long-term effects of physical abuse. Abused children may exhibit:

- a poor self-image
- sexual acting out
- an inability to love or trust others
- aggressive, disruptive, or illegal behavior
- anger, rage, **anxiety**, or **fear**
- self-destructive or self-abusive behavior
- suicidal thoughts
- passive or withdrawn behavior
- fear of entering into new relationships or activities
- school problems or failure
- sadness or other symptoms of depression
- flashbacks or nightmares
- drug or alcohol abuse

Sometimes emotional damage of abused children does not appear until **adolescence** or even later, when abused children become abusing parents who may have trouble with physical closeness, intimacy, and trust. They are also at risk for anxiety, depression, substance abuse, medical illnesses, and problems at school or work. Without proper treatment, abused children can be adversely affected throughout their life.

When to call the doctor

Anyone should call a health care provider or child protective services if they suspect or know that a child is being abused. Reporting child abuse to authorities is mandatory for doctors, teachers, and childcare workers in most states as a means to prevent continued abuse.

Diagnosis

Battered child syndrome is most often diagnosed by an emergency room physician or pediatrician, or by teachers or social workers. Physical examination will detect injuries such as bruises, burns, swelling, retinal hemorrhages (bleeding in the back of the eye), internal damage such as bleeding or rupture of an organ, **fractures** of long bones ore spiral-type fractures that result from twisting, and fractured ribs or skull. **X rays**, and other imaging techniques, such as MRI or scans, may confirm or reveal other internal injuries. The presence of injuries at different stages of healing (i.e., having occurred at different times) is nearly always indicative of BCS. Establishing the diagnosis is often hindered by the excessive cautiousness of caregivers or by actual concealment of the true origin of the child's injuries, as a result of fear, shame and avoidance or denial mechanisms.

Treatment

Medical treatment for battered child syndrome will vary according to the type of injury incurred. Counseling and the implementation of an intervention plan for the child's parents or guardians are necessary. The child abuser may be incarcerated, and/or the abused child removed from the home to prevent further harm. Decisions regarding placement of the child with an outside caregiver or returning the child to the home will be determined by an appropriate government agency working within the court system, based on the severity of the abuse and the likelihood of recurrence. Both physical and psychological therapy are often recommended as treatment for the abused child. If the child has siblings, the authorities should determine where they have also been abused, for about 20 percent of siblings of abused children are also shown to exhibit signs of physical abuse.

Prognosis

The prognosis for battered child syndrome will depend on the severity of injury, actions taken by the authorities to ensure the future **safety** of the injured child, and the willingness of parents or guardians to seek counseling for themselves as well as for the child.

Prevention

Recognizing the potential for child abuse and the seeking or offering of intervention, counseling, and training in good parenting skills before battered child syndrome occurs is the best way to prevent abuse. The use of educational programs to teach caregivers good parenting skills and to be aware of abusive behaviors so that they seek help for abusive tendencies is critical to stopping abuse. Support from the extended **family**, friends, clergy, or other supportive persons or groups may also be effective in preventing abuse. Signs that physical abuse may occur include parental alcohol or substance abuse; high stress factors in the family life; previous abuse of the child or the child's siblings; history of mental or emotional problems in parents; parents abused as children; absence of visible parental love or concern for the child; and neglect of the child's hygiene.

Parental concerns

Parents who are in danger of abusing their children (for example, when they find themselves becoming inap-

KEY TERMS

Child protective services (CPS)—The designated social services agency (in most states) to receive reports, investigate, and provide intervention and treatment services to children and families in which child maltreatment has occurred. Frequently this agency is located within larger public social service agencies, such as Departments of Social Services.

Fontanelle—One of several "soft spots" on the skull where the developing bones of the skull have yet to fuse.

Multiple retinal hemorrhages—Bleeding in the back of the eye.

Subdural hematoma—A localized accumulation of blood, sometimes mixed with spinal fluid, in the space between the middle (arachnoid) and outer (dura mater) membranes covering the brain. It is caused by an injury to the head that tears blood vessels.

propriately or excessively angry in response to a child's behavior) should seek professional counseling. Parents may also call the National Child Abuse Hotline (800-4-A-Child; 800-422-4453, a nationwide 24-hour telephone hotline), where they will be counseled through a parenting or caretaking crisis and offered guidance about how to better handle the situation.

Parents should also exercise caution in arranging for or hiring **babysitters** and other caretakers. If they suspect abuse, they should immediately report those suspicions to the police or to their local child protective services agency. They should also teach their children to report abuse to a trusted adult.

Resources

BOOKS

Besharov, Douglas J. *Recognizing Child Abuse: A Guide for the Concerned.* New York, NY: Free Press, 1990.

Crosson-Tower, Cynthia. *Understanding Child Abuse and Neglect. 5th Edition.* New York, NY: Allyn & Bacon, 2001.

Feinen, Cynthia, Winifred Coleman, Margaret C. Ciocco, et al., eds. *Child Abuse: A Quick Reference Guide.* Long Branch, New Jersey: Vista Publishing, 1998.

Giardino, Angelo P., and Giardino, Eileen. *Recognition of Child Abuse for the Mandated Reporter,* 3rd ed. St. Louis, MO: G.W. Medical Publishing, 2002.

Lukefahr, James L. *Treatment of Child Abuse.* Baltimore, MD: Johns Hopkins University Press, 2000.

Monteleone, James A. *A Parent's & Teacher's Handbook on Identifying and Preventing Child Abuse: Warning Signs Every Parent and Teacher Should Know.* St. Louis, MO: G.W. Medical Publishing, 1998.

Reece, Robert, and Stephen Ludwig. *Child Abuse: Medical Diagnosis and Management,* 2nd ed. Baltimore, MD: Lippincott, Williams, and Wilkins, 2001.

ORGANIZATIONS

National Child Abuse Hotline. 800-4-A-Child (800-422-4453).

National Clearinghouse on Child Abuse and Neglect Information. P.O. Box 1182, Washington, DC 20013-1182. 800-394-3366. Web site: <http://nccanch.acf.hhs.gov>.

Prevent Child Abuse America. 200 South Michigan Avenue, 17th Floor, Chicago, IL 60604. (312) 663-3520. Web site: <http://preventchildabuse.org>.

National Parents Anonymous. 675 West Foothill Blvd., Suite 220m Claremont, CA 91711. (909) 621-6184. Web site: <http://www.parentsanonymous.org/pahtml/paNPLTabout.html>.

WEB SITES

Child Abuse: Types, Symptoms, Causes, and Help. Available online at: <http://www.helpguide.org/mental/child_abuse_physical_emotional_sexual_neglect.htm>.

"State by State Abuse Hotline & Organization Directory." *The Broken Spirits Network.* Available online at: <http://www.brokenspirits.com/directory>.

Judith Sims
Mary Jane Tenerelli, MS

Bayley Scales of Infant Development

Definition

The Bayley Scales of Infant Development (BSID) measure the mental and motor development and test the behavior of infants from one to 42 months of age.

Purpose

The BSID are used to describe the current developmental functioning of infants and to assist in diagnosis and treatment planning for infants with developmental delays or disabilities. The test is intended to measure a child's level of development in three domains: cognitive, motor, and behavioral.

Cognitive development

Cognition can be defined as a process by which knowledge is gained from perceptions or ideas. **Cognitive development** refers to how an infant perceives, thinks, and gains an understanding of the world. Within the history of developmental psychology, the work of Jean Piaget (1896–1980), the Swiss psychologist, has had the greatest impact on the study of cognitive development. Piaget's theory is focused on the processes of cognitive development and states that the child is born with an innate curiosity to interact with and understand his/her environment. It is through interaction with others that the child actively constructs his/her development.

Motor development

During the first two years of life, infants grow and develop in many ways. Two types of motor development occur at this stage. Cephalocaudal development occurs in the following sequence: head before arms and trunk and arms and trunk before legs. Proximodistal development occurs as follows: head, trunk, arms before hands and fingers. Motor development has a powerful impact on the social relationships, thinking, and language of infants. Large motor development allows infants to have more control over actions that help them move around their environment, while small motor development gives them more control over movements that allow them to reach, grasp, and handle objects. The sequence of these developments is similar in most children; however, the rate of growth and development varies by individual.

Behavioral development

Temperament is the set of genetically determined traits that organize the child's approach to the world. They are instrumental in the development of the child's distinct personality and behavior. This behavioral style appears very early in life—within the first two months after birth—and undergoes development, centered on features such as intensity, activity, persistence, or emotionality.

Besides measuring normal cognitive, motor, and behavioral developmental levels, the BSID are also used in cases in which there are significant delays in acquiring certain skills or performing key activities in order to qualify a child for special interventions. Specifically, they are also used to do the following:

• identify children who are developmentally delayed

• chart a child's progress after the initiation of an intervention program

- teach parents about their infant's development

- conduct research in developmental psychology

Description

The BSID were first published by Nancy Bayley in *The Bayley Scales of Infant Development* (1969) and in a second edition (1993). The scales have been used extensively worldwide to assess the development of infants. The test is given on an individual basis and takes 45–60 minutes to complete. It is administered by examiners who are experienced clinicians specifically trained in BSID test procedures. The examiner presents a series of test materials to the child and observes the child's responses and behaviors. The test contains items designed to identify young children at risk for **developmental delay**. BSID evaluates individuals along three scales:

- Mental scale: This part of the evaluation, which yields a score called the mental development index, evaluates several types of abilities: sensory/perceptual acuities, discriminations, and response; acquisition of object constancy; memory learning and problem solving; vocalization and beginning of verbal communication; basis of abstract thinking; habituation; mental mapping; complex language; and mathematical concept formation.

- Motor scale: This part of the BSID assesses the degree of body control, large muscle coordination, finer manipulatory skills of the hands and fingers, dynamic movement, postural imitation, and the ability to recognize objects by sense of touch (stereognosis).

- Behavior rating scale: This scale provides information that can be used to supplement information gained from the mental and motor scales. This 30-item scale rates the child's relevant behaviors and measures attention/arousal, orientation/engagement, emotional regulation, and motor quality.

The BSID are known to have high reliability and validity. The mental and motor scales have high correlation coefficients (.83 and .77 respectively) for test-retest reliability.

Precautions

BSID data reflect the U.S. population in terms of race, ethnicity, infant gender, education level of parents, and demographic location of the infant. The BSID was standardized on 1,700 infants, toddlers, and preschoolers between one and 42 months of age. Norms were established using samples that did not include disabled, premature, and other at-risk children. Corrected scores are sometimes used to evaluate these groups, but their use remains controversial.

The BSID has poor predictive value, unless the scores are very low. It is considered a good screening device for identifying children in need of early intervention.

Preparation

Before giving the BSID test to a child, the examiner explains to the parents what will happen during the test procedure. This is to allow the examiner to establish a focused rapport with the child once the procedure has started and avoid diverting attention from the child to the parents during the test. The parents are also asked not to talk to the child during the BSID test to avoid skewing results.

Risks

There are no risks associated with the BSID test.

Parental concerns

As of 2004 it was recognized that parental involvement in the developmental **assessment** of their children is very important. First, because parents are more familiar with their child's behavior, their assessment may indeed be more indicative of the child's developmental status than an assessment that is based on limited observation in an unfamiliar clinical setting. The involvement of parents in their child's development testing also improves their knowledge of child development issues and their subsequent participation in required intervention programs, if any. In cases of developmental problems, parents should bear in mind that the scoring and interpretation of the test results is a highly technical matter that requires years of training and experience. Besides the BSID, parents should be aware that three other infant development scales are commonly used:

- Brazelton Neonatal Behavioral Assessment Scale: This scale tests an infant's neurological development, interactive behavior, and responsiveness to the examiner, and need for stimulation. This test is administered during the newborn period only.

- Gesell Developmental Schedules: These schedules test for fine and **gross motor skills**, language behavior, adaptive behavior including eye-hand coordination, imitation, object recovery, personal-social behavior such as reaction to persons, initiative, independence, and **play** response.

- Denver Developmental Screening Test: This test is used to identify problems or delays that should be more carefully evaluated. It measures four types of development: personal/social, fine-motor/adaptive, language, and gross motor skills.

KEY TERMS

Behavior—A stereotyped motor response to an internal or external stimulus.

Cephalocaudal development—Motor development which occurs in the first two years of life: head before arms and trunk, arms and trunk before legs.

Cognition—The act or process of knowing or perceiving.

Cognitive—The ability (or lack of) to think, learn, and memorize.

Motor skills—Controlled movements of muscle groups. Fine motor skills involve tasks that require dexterity of small muscles, such as buttoning a shirt. Tasks such as walking or throwing a ball involve the use of gross motor skills.

Proximodistal development—Motor development which occurs in the first two years of life: head, trunk, arms before hands and fingers.

Stereognosis—The ability to recognize objects by sense of touch.

Temperament—A person's natural disposition or inborn combination of mental and emotional traits.

See also Cognitive development; Personality development; Personality disorders.

Resources

BOOKS

Amiel-Tison, Claudine, et al. *Neurological Development from Birth to Six Years: Guide for Examination and Evaluation.* Baltimore, MD: Johns Hopkins University Press, 2001.

Sattker, Jerome M. *Assessment of Children: Behavioral and Clinical Applications*, 4th ed. Lutz, FL: Psychological Assessment Resources Inc., 2001.

———. *Assessment of Children: Cognitive Applications*, 4th ed. Lutz, FL: Psychological Assessment Resources Inc., 2001.

PERIODICALS

Glenn, S. M., et al. "Comparison of the 1969 and 1993 standardizations of the Bayley Mental Scales of Infant Development for infants with Down's syndrome." *Journal of Intellectual Disability Research* 45, no. 1 (February 2001): 55–62.

Provost, B., et al. "Concurrent validity of the Bayley Scales of Infant Development II Motor Scale and the Peabody Developmental Motor Scales in two-year-old children." *Physical and Occupational Therapy in Pediatrics* 20, no. 1 (2000): 5–18.

Voigt, R. G., et al. "Concurrent and predictive validity of the cognitive adaptive test/clinical linguistic and auditory milestone scale (CAT/CLAMS) and the Mental Developmental Index of the Bayley Scales of Infant Development." *Clinical Pediatrics (Philadelphia)* 42, no. 5 (June 2003): 427–32.

ORGANIZATIONS

American Academy of Child & Adolescent Psychiatry (AACAP). 3615 Wisconsin Ave., N.W., Washington, DC. 20016–3007. Web site: <www.aacap.org>.

American Academy of Pediatrics (AAP). 141 Northwest Point Boulevard, Elk Grove Village, IL 60007–1098. Web site: <www.aap.org>.

American Psychological Association (APA). 750 First Street, NE, Washington, DC 20002–4242. Web site: <www.apa.org>.

Child Development Institute (CDI). 3528 E. Ridgeway Road, Orange, CA 92867. Web site: <www.childdevelopmentinfo.com>.

WEB SITES

"Assessments for Young Children." *LD Online.* Available online at <www.ldonline.org/ld_indepth/early_identification/assessment_devareas.html> (accessed November 23, 2004).

Monique Laberge, Ph.D.

Bed-wetting

Definition

Bed-wetting, also called enuresis, is the unintentional discharge of urine during **sleep**. Although most children between the ages of three and five begin to stay dry at night, the age at which children are physically and emotionally ready to maintain complete bladder control varies.

Description

Most children wet the bed occasionally, and definitions of the age and frequency at which bed-wetting becomes a medical problem vary somewhat. The word enuresis is derived from a Greek word meaning "to make water." Enuresis is defined as the repeated voiding of urine into the bed or clothes at least twice a week for at least three consecutive months in a child who is at least five years of age. It can be nocturnal (occurring at night) or diurnal (occurring during the day). Enuresis is a fairly common condition in children. It can be a stressful condition as well for both parents and children. Some children find bed-wetting extremely embarrassing. Parents sometimes become both frustrated and angry.

Enuresis is divided into two classes. A child with primary enuresis has never been consistently dry through the night. A child with secondary enuresis begins to wet after a prolonged dry period. Some children have both nocturnal and diurnal enuresis.

Demographics

The prevalence of bedwetting gradually declines throughout childhood. Of children aged five years, 23 percent have nocturnal enuresis. During elementary school years, the problem remains common, with 20 percent of seven-year-old children and 4 percent of ten-year-old children still experiencing nighttime bedwetting. Nocturnal enuresis is more common in males. It occurs in boys aged seven and ten years at 9 percent and 7 percent, respectively, compared to 6 percent and 3 percent, respectively, in girls.

Causes and symptoms

The causes of bed-wetting are not entirely known. It tends to run in families. Most children with primary enuresis have a close relative—a parent, aunt, or uncle who also had the disorder. Over 70 percent of children with two parents who wet the bed will also wet the bed. Twin studies have shown that both of a pair of identical **twins** experience enuresis more often than both of a pair of fraternal twins.

Sometimes bed-wetting can be caused by a serious medical problem like diabetes, sickle-cell anemia, or epilepsy. Snoring and episodes of interrupted breathing during sleep (sleep apnea) occasionally contribute to bed-wetting problems. Enlarged adenoids can cause these conditions. Other physiological problems, such as urinary tract infection, severe **constipation**, or **spinal cord injury**, can cause bed-wetting.

Children who wet the bed frequently may have a smaller than normal functional bladder capacity. Functional bladder capacity is the amount of urine a person can hold in the bladder before feeling a strong urge to urinate. When functional capacity is small, the bladder will not hold all the urine produced during the night. Tests have shown that bladder size in these children is normal. Nevertheless, they experience frequent strong urges to urinate. Such children urinate often during the daytime and may wet several times at night.

Although a small functional bladder capacity may be caused by a **developmental delay**, it may also be that the child's habit of voiding frequently slows bladder development.

Parents often report that their bed-wetting child is an extremely sound sleeper and difficult to wake. However, several research studies found that bed-wetting children have normal sleep patterns and that bed-wetting can occur in any stage of sleep.

In the early 2000s medical research has found that many children who wet the bed may have a deficiency of an important hormone known as antidiuretic hormone (ADH). ADH helps to concentrate urine during sleep hours, meaning that the urine contains less water and, therefore, takes up less space. This decreased volume of water usually prevents the child's bladder from overfilling during the night, unless the child drinks a lot just before going to bed. Testing of many bed-wetting children has shown that these children do not have the usual increase in ADH during sleep. Children who wet the bed, therefore, often produce more urine during the hours of sleep than their bladders can hold. If they do not wake up, the bladder releases the excess urine and the child wets the bed.

Research demonstrates that in most cases bed-wetting does not indicate that the child has a physical or psychological problem. Children who wet the bed usually have normal-sized bladders and have sleep patterns that are no different from those of non-bed-wetting children. Sometimes emotional stress, such as the birth of a sibling, a death in the **family**, or separation from the family, may be associated with the onset of bed-wetting in a previously toilet-trained child. Daytime wetting, however, may indicate that the problem has a physical cause.

While most children have no long-term problems as a result of bed-wetting, some children may develop psychological problems. Low **self-esteem** may occur when these children, who already feel embarrassed, are further humiliated by angry or frustrated parents who punish them or who are overly aggressive about **toilet training**. The problem can by aggravated when playmates tease or when social activities such as sleep-away camp are avoided for **fear** of teasing.

When to call the doctor

Parents should contact their child's doctor if the child has started wetting the bed after a sustained period of time staying dry. Parents should also notify the physician if their child over the age of five begins to have urinary incontinence during the day, as this may be caused by a physical disorder.

Diagnosis

If a child continues to wet the bed after the age of six, parents may feel the need to seek evaluation and diagnosis by the family doctor or a children's specialist (pediatrician). Typically, before the doctor can make a diagnosis, a thorough medical history is obtained. Then the child receives a physical examination, appropriate laboratory tests, including a urine test, and if necessary, radiologic studies (such as **x rays**).

If the child is healthy and no physical problem is found, which is the case 90 percent of the time, the doctor may not advise treatment but rather may provide the parents and the child with reassurance, information, and advice.

Treatment

Occasionally a doctor will determine that the problem is serious enough to require treatment. Standard treatments for bed-wetting include bladder training exercises, motivational therapy, drug therapy, psychotherapy, and diet therapy.

Bladder training exercises are based on the theory that those who wet the bed have small functional bladder capacity. Children are told to drink a large quantity of water and to try to prolong the periods between voiding. These exercises are designed to increase bladder capacity but are only successful in resolving bed-wetting in a small number of patients.

In motivational therapy, parents attempt to encourage the child to combat bed-wetting, but the child must want to achieve success. Positive reinforcement, such as praise or rewards for staying dry, can help improve self-image and resolve the condition. Punishment for wet nights hamper the child's self-esteem and compound the problem.

The following motivational techniques are commonly used:

- Behavior modification: This method of therapy is aimed at helping children take responsibility for their nighttime bladder control by teaching new behaviors. For example, children are taught to use the bathroom before bedtime and to avoid drinking fluids after dinner. While behavior modification generally produces good results, it is long-term treatment.

- Alarms: This form of therapy uses a sensor placed in the child's pajamas or in a bed pad. This sensor triggers an alarm that wakes the child at the first sign of wetness. If the child is awakened, he or she can then go to the bathroom and finish urinating. The intention is to condition a response to awaken when the bladder is full. Bed-wetting alarms require the motivation of both

parents and children. They were considered the most effective form of treatment available as of 2004.

A number of drugs are also used to treat bed-wetting. These medications are usually fast acting; children often respond to them within the first week of treatment. Among the drugs commonly used are a nasal spray of desmopressin acetate (DDAVP), a substance similar to the hormone that helps regulate urine production; and imipramine hydrochloride, a drug that helps to increase bladder capacity. Studies show that imipramine is effective for as many as 50 percent of patients. However, children often wet the bed again after the drug is discontinued, and it has some side effects. Some bed-wetting with an underlying physical cause can be treated by surgical procedures. These causes include enlarged adenoids that cause sleep apnea, physical defects in the urinary system, or a spinal tumor.

Psychotherapy is indicated when the child exhibits signs of severe emotional distress in response to events such as a death in the family, the birth of a new child, a change in schools, or **divorce**. Psychotherapy is also indicated if a child shows signs of persistently low self-esteem or depression.

In rare cases, **allergies** or intolerances to certain foods—such as dairy products, citrus products, or chocolate—can cause bed-wetting. When children have **food sensitivities**, bed-wetting may be helped by discovering the substances that trigger the allergic response and eliminating these substances from the child's diet.

Prognosis

Occasional bed-wetting is not a disease, and it does not have a cure. If the child has no underlying physical or psychological problem that is causing the bed-wetting, in most cases he or she will outgrow the condition without treatment. About 15 percent of bed-wetters become dry each year after age six. If bed-wetting is frequent, accompanied by daytime wetting, or falls into the American Psychiatric Association's diagnostic definition of enuresis, a doctor should be consulted. If treatment is indicated, it usually successfully resolves the problem. Marked improvement is seen in about 75 percent of cases treated with wetness alarms.

Prevention

Although preventing a child from wetting the bed is not always possible, parents can take steps to help the child keep the bed dry at night. These steps include:

- encouraging and praising the child for staying dry instead of punishing when the child wets

- reminding the child to urinate before going to bed, if he or she feels the need

- limiting liquid intake at least two hours before bedtime

Parental concerns

Bed-wetting often leads to behavioral problems because of the embarrassment and guilt the child may feel. Parents should not attempt to make their child feel guilty about wetting the bed. They should let the child know that bedwetting is not their fault. Punishment is an inappropriate response to enuresis and will not resolve the problem.

Resources

BOOKS

Mercer, Renee. *Seven Steps to Nighttime Dryness: A Practical Guide for Parents of Children with Bedwetting.* New York: Brookville Media: 2003.

PERIODICALS

"Summary of the Practice Parameter for the Assessment and Treatment of Children and Adolescents with Enuresis." *Journal of the American Academy of Child and Adolescent Psychiatry* 43 (January 2004): 1, 123–125.

ORGANIZATIONS

National Kidney Foundation. 30 East 33rd St., New York, NY 10016. Web site: <http://kidney.org>.

WEB SITES

"Enuresis (Bed-wetting)." *FamilyDoctor.org*, October 2003. Available online at <http://familydoctor.org/366.xml> (accessed January 11, 2005).

Deanna M. Swartout-Corbeil, RN
Genevieve Slomski, Ph.D.

Bee sting *see* **Bites and stings**

Bee sting allergy *see* **Insect sting allergy**

Beery-Buktenica test

Definition

The Beery-Buktenica visual-motor integration test is a neuropsychological test that analyzes visual construction skills. It identifies problems with visual perception, motor coordination, and visual-motor integration such as **hand-eye coordination**.

Purpose

The Beery-Buktenica Test, also known as Developmental Test of Visual-Motor Integration or VMI, is designed to identify deficits in visual perception, **fine motor skills**, and hand-eye coordination. It may be used to diagnose **cognitive development** disorders in young children through an analysis of visual construction skills. It can be administered to individuals from age two through young adulthood and can also be used to test adults of all ages, particularly those who have been disabled by **stroke**, injury, or Alzheimer's disease.

The Beery-Buktenica VMI test is used by physicians, psychologists, neuropsychologists, learning disability specialists, counselors, educators, and other professionals. It can be effectively used for the following purposes:

- to identify individuals who are having visual-motor difficulties

- to help diagnose visual-motor deficits

- to make referrals to specific professionals or services

- to test individual learning levels and educational programs

- to monitor the progress of individuals with known visual-motor or developmental difficulties

Description

One of the basic aspects of an individual's ability to think and know (cognition) is how one is able to perceive certain stimuli. Assessing perception skills—observing how individuals may respond to things they see, hear, and touch—is, therefore, a basic part of assessing cognitive function. Children with possible **developmental delay** may be tested for their perception of visual, auditory, and tactile stimuli, not just to understand their ability to see, hear, and touch, but to understand how they perceive stimuli and what conclusions they make as a result. This information can help pediatricians and child psychologists evaluate the child's nervous system (neurological) functioning and psychological development. Visual testing may include color perception, object recognition, visual organizational abilities, and the ability to differentiate figures from the background against which they appear. It also includes visual construction tests. Some visual construction tests are designed to test memory by asking the child to draw a familiar object. Others, such as the Beery-Buktenica test, are designed to test visual motor skills as a factor of visual perception and integration.

Visual-motor integration or VMI can be evaluated as a factor in child development by providing the child with geometric designs ranging from simple line **drawings** to more complex figures and asking that the designs be copied. The construction skills used in the test have been shown to indicate visual motor impairment, such as problems with fine motors skills of the hand and hand-eye coordination. The developers of the test, Keith E. Beery and Norman A. Buktenica, have established adequate norms for visual motor performance by children in various age groups. The test is considered especially useful to help evaluate children with other disabilities or disabling conditions. It can also be used for the evaluation of motor skills such as handwriting.

The Beery-Buktenica test is usually administered individually but can also be given in groups. The child is given a booklet containing increasingly complex geometric figures and asked to copy them without any erasures and without rotating the booklet in any direction. The test is given in two versions: the Short Test Form containing 15 figures is used for ages three through eight; the Long Test Form, with 24 figures, is used for older children, adolescents, and adults with developmental delay. A raw score based on the number of correct copies is converted based on norms for each age group, and results are reported as converted scores and percentiles. The test is untimed but usually takes 10–15 minutes to administer.

Precautions

There are no precautions involved in visual motor testing.

Preparation

More successful testing is achieved when no preparatory steps are taken. The test can be explained briefly to the child beforehand.

Aftercare

No particular care is recommended after administration of the test. Further testing may be recommended as

well as specific intervention to help correct any deficits noted. Depending upon the specific deficits found, intervention may include occupational therapy, physical therapy, counseling, behavior modification, **play** therapy, and medication for certain neuropsychological disorders.

Risks

There are no risks associated with taking the Beery-Buktenica VMI test.

Normal results

Children who perform well on VMI testing may still have visual perception or motor coordination deficits. Visual conceptualization and motor coordination should be evaluated separately to confirm the results.

Children who do not perform well on VMI testing may have impairment of visual-motor skills including the following types:

- visual analysis and visual spatial ability

- motor coordination (MC)

- visual conceptualization (VC)

- visual motor integration

Parental concerns

Parents may be apprehensive about the performance of their child in the Beery-Buktenica testing process. Results are carefully analyzed, and parents are advised not to judge the child's skills until they have discussed the test with the pediatrician, neurologist, or psychologist who will use the results in conjunction with other developmental tests in order to make a diagnosis or recommendations for therapy.

See also Cognitive development; Fine motor skills.

Resources

ORGANIZATIONS

National Institute of Neurological Disorders and Stroke. National Institutes of Health, Bethesda, MD 20892. Web site: <http//www.nindsnih.gov>.

WEB SITES

"Beery-Buktenica Development Test of Visual-Motor Integration." *Psychological Assessment Resources Inc. (PAR).* Available online at <www.parinc.com> (accessed October 28, 2004).

"Beery VMI." *Pearson Assessments.* Available online at <www.pearsonassessments.com/tests/vmi htm> (accessed October 28, 2004).

L. Lee Culvert

Bejel

Definition

Bejel, also known as endemic syphilis, is a chronic but curable disease that is seen mostly in children in dry regions, such as parts of Africa (Sudan, southern Rhodesia, and South Africa), parts of the Middle East (among nomadic/Bedouin tribes of Saudi Arabia, Iraq, and Syria), and parts of Asia (Turkey, southeast Asia, and the western Pacific). Unlike venereal syphilis, endemic syphilis is not sexually transmitted. Similar to venereal syphilis, however, it begins with skin sores and has a latent period followed by a more severe stage, which includes bone infections and additional skin lesions.

Demographics

Bejel occurs predominately in children aged two to 15 years. Twenty-five percent of the cases occur in those younger than six years of age, and 55 percent of the cases occur before the age of 16 years. The remaining 20 percent of the cases occur in adults who are in close contact with infected children. Bejel is only rarely reported in the United States and then usually among immigrants and people arriving from areas where the disease is common. Both sexes are equally susceptible to bejel.

Description

Bejel has many other names depending on the locality, including siti (Gambia), njovera (southern Rhodesia), therlijevo (Croatia), and frenjak (Balkans). Bejel is related to yaws and **pinta**, and together the three diseases are referred to as treponematoses. Yaws, which also affects the skin and bones, occurs in the humid equatorial countries, while pinta, which only affects the skin, is common among the native peoples of Mexico, Central America, and South America.

Transmission

Treponema pallidum subspecies *endemicum*, the bacteria that causes bejel, is very closely related to the one that causes the sexually transmitted form of syphilis, but the method of transmission is different. In bejel, transmission is by direct contact, with broken skin or contaminated hands, or indirectly by sharing drinking vessels and eating utensils. *T. pallidum* subspecies *endemicum* is passed on mostly among children living in poverty in unsanitary environments and with poor hygiene.

Causes and symptoms

The skin, bones, and mucous membranes are all affected by bejel. The disease begins with slimy patches on the inside of the mouth, followed by blisters on the trunk, arms, and legs. Bone infections, mainly in the legs, develop later and cause **pain** deep within the bones. Eventually, the bones may become deformed because of bone and cartilage destruction. In later stages, soft gummy lesions may form in the nasal passages, destroying nasal cartilage and in the roof of the mouth, even breaking through the mouth palate. The lesions associated with bejel are destructive and may leave disfiguring scars.

Diagnosis

T. pallidum subspecies *endemicum* can be detected by microscopic study of samples taken from the sores or lymph fluid. However, since antibody tests do not distinguish between the types of syphilis, specific diagnosis of

KEY TERMS

Endemic disease—An infectious disease that occurs frequently in a specific geographical locale. The disease often occurs in cycles.

Lymph fluid—Clear, colorless fluid found in lymph vessels and nodes. The lymph nodes contain organisms that destroy bacteria and other disease causing organisms (also called pathogens).

Syphilis—This disease occurs in two forms. One is a sexually transmitted disease caused by A systemic infection caused by the spirochete *Treponema pallidum*. It is most commonly transmitted by sexual contact.

the type of syphilis depends on the child's history, symptoms, and environment.

When to call the doctor

The doctor should be called if symptoms of bejel develop in a child. Travel information is invaluable in diagnosis of the disease.

Treatment

Large doses of benzathine penicillin G given by injection into the muscle can cure this disease in any stage, although it may take longer and require additional doses in later stages. If penicillin cannot be given, alternative **antibiotics** are chloramphenicol and tetracycline. Since tetracycline can permanently discolor new teeth that are still forming, it is usually not prescribed for children unless no viable alternative is available.

Prognosis

Bejel is usually completely curable with antibiotic treatment. Death from bejel is uncommon. Follow-up care is recommended to detect treatment failures and reinfection.

Prevention

The World Health Organization (WHO) has worked with many countries to prevent this and other diseases, and the number of cases of bejel has been reduced somewhat. Widespread use of penicillin has been responsible for reducing the number of existing cases, but the only way to eliminate bejel is by improving living and sanitation conditions and through continuing health education.

Since the disease is very contagious, public health personnel must seek out and treat infected children and their contacts in order to prevent additional cases.

Parental concerns

When traveling in areas where bejel is endemic, parents should ensure that their children avoid contact with children with lesions and avoid shared drinking and eating utensils.

See also Pinta.

Resources

ORGANIZATIONS

National Organization for Rare Disorders Inc. 55 Kenosia Ave, PO Box 1968, Danbury, CT 06813–1968. Web site: <www.rarediseases.org>.

WEB SITES

"Endemic syphilis." *eMedicine*, October 28, 2004. Available online at <www.emedicine.com/derm/topic117.htm> (accessed December 6, 2004).

Judith Sims
Jill S. Lasker

Bell's palsy

Definition

The National Institute of Neurological Disorders and Stroke (NINDS), a part of the National Institute of Health (NIH), defines Bell's palsy as "a form of facial paralysis resulting from damage to the seventh (facial) cranial nerve." This condition is considered to be normally a transient phenomenon and not permanently disabling. It is named for Sir Charles Bell, a Scottish surgeon who, over two hundred years ago, did much of the earliest research regarding the anatomy and pathology of the cranial nerves.

Description

There are 12 sets of bilateral cranial nerves originating in the posterior portion of the brain stem, called the pons. These nerves control various functions in the upper portion of the body, especially within the face and head. The seventh cranial nerve enters the facial region through a small opening in the bony area behind the ear called the stylomastoid foramen. From the stylomastoid foramen, the nerve enters the parotid gland and divides into an estimated 7,000 nerve fibers that control a wide range of facial and neck activity. Seventh cranial nerve endings control neck, eyelid, and forehead muscles; are responsible for facial expression, the secretion of saliva, the volume at which sound is perceived; and a myriad of other functions.

The taste sensations for the front two-thirds of the tongue are sent to the brain via the seventh cranial nerve. In Bell's palsy, this nerve becomes compressed due to swelling and inflammation that is a part of the body's reaction to an infectious disease process. This compression results in weakness or paralysis that normally occurs on one side of the face only. However, though highly unusual (occurring in only 1 percent of all incidences), it is also possible to have bilateral Bell's palsy, that is, paralysis on both sides of the face at the same time, caused by compression of both seventh cranial nerves.

Transmission

Bell's palsy, in itself, is not contagious. Many of the agents that cause it, however, are conditions that have already caused an infection in the body.

Demographics

In the past, Bell's palsy was thought to be a highly uncommon occurrence. It is now known that this nerve disorder is the most common cause of one-sided facial weakness for children. It affects on average approximately one in every five thousand people worldwide, and nearly 40,000 Americans each year. Because diseases that compromise the immune system such as **HIV infection** or sarcoidosis can also result in Bell's palsy, there are geographical variations in the incidence of the disease. Bell's palsy is seen more commonly in areas where **AIDS** or sarcoidosis are more prevalent, but its incidence overall throughout the world remains constant.

The majority of Bell's palsy sufferers are adults. This disorder is much more likely to occur in old age or in the last trimester of pregnancy than in childhood. Diabetics are four times more apt to contract Bell's palsy than non-diabetics. Though children are considered far less likely than adults to contract Bell's palsy, they are not immune from it. There is no difference in the incidence of Bell's palsy between males and females, nor does race seem to be a factor. In addition to incidence, severity of symptoms and recovery rates appear to be equal across both gender and racial lines. The number of children that contract left-sided Bell's palsy is no different from the number that get the right-sided form.

Causes and symptoms

As noted previously, Bell's palsy occurs as a manifestation of the body's reaction to microbial infection of the structures surrounding the seventh cranial nerve. The most commonly responsible germs are viruses that are members of the herpes family. The herpes family of viruses share some common characteristics, including the capacity for long life, going into a dormant phase that in some cases can literally last decades following infection, having an affinity for nerve tissue. Herpes viruses are the cause of infections as diverse as **sexually transmitted diseases**, chickenpox and cold sores. As early as 1970, a study by researcher Shingo Murakami identified HSV-1 as the primary cause of Bell's palsy. Several subsequent studies have consistently verified Murakami's research. HSV-1, also known as herpes simplex and the usual cause of cold sores, has been shown to be the infecting agent in at least 60–70 percent of all Bell's palsy cases.

HSV-1 is a herpes virus that nearly all of the human race has been exposed to, with exposure beginning in early childhood. It is spread through kissing, sharing towels, and/or sharing eating and drinking utensils. It is now known that HSV-1 often infects children but does not always manifest itself by the creation of cold sores. (In fact, only 15 percent of people exposed to HSV-1 develop cold sores.) Because the virus becomes dormant following its initial infection of the body, a large number of HSV-1 carriers are thus produced, most often without the infected person or others even being aware that HSV-1 is present. Other herpes viruses such as Epstein-Barr, responsible for mononucleosis as well as the viruses causing the **common cold**, **influenza** (the flu) are all potential culprits for causing this condition. The bacterial infection involved in **Lyme disease** has also been demonstrated as causing some cases of Bell's palsy. The same causative agents infect both adults and children.

Impairment of the immune system has been unquestionably determined to be the reason why Herpes Viruses are reactivated from a dormant state and re-infect children causing Bell's palsy. Such a weakening of the immune system can be long-term, caused by chronic disease such as leukemia or autoimmune disorders such as lupus, or short-term. The most common causes for short-term or temporary impaired immunity are:

- stress created by difficult situations for the child either at home or at school

- lack of sleep

- non-life-threatening illness such as upper respiratory infection (URI)

- physical trauma

It is also worth noting that in 2004, the World Health Organization (WHO) Global Advisory Committee on Vaccine Safety reported that in October of 2000 an increased incidence of Bell's palsy in Switzerland was observed following the initiation of an internasal **flu vaccine**. Due to this adverse effect, the vaccine manufacturer discontinued research and production. In 2003, another internasal flu vaccine was licensed in the United States, and this vaccine has so far shown no increased occurrence of Bell's palsy. However, the Global Advisory Committee on Vaccine Safety continues to monitor these vaccines, and the use of internasal vaccines should be discussed with the family healthcare provider.

Clearly the overwhelming majority of children that contract mononucleosis, cold sores, Lyme disease, cold or flu do not develop Bell's palsy. But for some, a reaction of their immune system to viral, or in some cases bacterial, infection causes the production of antibodies which in turn produces inflammation and swelling. In Bell's palsy, this process typically occurs after the seventh cranial nerve's passage through the stylomastoid foramen into a tiny bony tube called the fallopian canal. If the inflammation within the fallopian canal is severe enough, it will exert sufficient pressure on the seventh cranial nerve to make it impossible for the nerve to carry messages to and from the brain.

As noted previously, such messages normally carried by healthy seventh cranial nerves control the actions of several facial muscles, each side acting in synchronization to "tell" eyelids to close, tears to form, saliva to be created within the mouth, or the mouth to turn up in a smile. When the nerve is unable to transmit the message to facial muscles to relax or contract, facial muscles quickly become paralyzed or weakened. Such paralysis normally lasts only for the period of time that the nerve is unable to transmit messages. Because this swelling and infection usually affects only the seventh cranial nerve on one side of the head, the resultant paralysis normally occurs solely on one side of the face and affects only the facial areas that the seventh cranial nerve transmits to.

Because there is a wide variance in the severity of symptoms, signs of Bell's palsy may not be immediately noticed by parents. However, classical symptoms of Bell's palsy include:

- Though not always present, the child may complain of **headache** or **pain** behind or in front of the ear a few days prior to the onset of Bell's palsy.

- One side of the face droops, feels stiff or numb. (Though one side of the face is always affected, there are varying degrees of severity of this facial paralysis. Some children have only very mild weakness of facial muscles while others may be totally unable to move that side of their face.)

- An over-all droopy appearance of the child's facial expression.

- Swelling of the child's face.

- The child has a continually runny or stuffy nose.

- The child has either excessive or reduced production of saliva.

- The child is having difficulty speaking.

- The child is unable to blink or completely close one eye.

- Drooping of one side of the child's mouth is noted.

- The child has either excessive tears or marked dryness and inability to make tears in one eye.

- There are problems with the child holding food or fluids in the affected side of the mouth, resulting in drooling or difficulty swallowing.

- The child complains of either diminished, distorted or complete inability to taste food or drink.

- The child is experiencing *Hyperacusis*, or hearing sounds as seeming louder than they really are.

- The child is experiencing photosensitivity, or sensitivity to light.

- The child complains of dizziness.

When to call the doctor

Signs and symptoms of Bell's palsy typically manifest themselves within 14 days after a child has had a viral or bacterial infection. There is usually a very rapid onset once facial paralysis or weakness makes an appearance, and Bell's palsy normally reaches its peak symptoms within 48 hours of onset. In some rare cases, symptoms may take longer than this, but have very seldom been shown to take longer than two weeks to develop. It is of tremendous importance to clarify the diagnosis, and assure that it is truly Bell's palsy that a child is suffering from as soon as possible. This is because there are several other, far more serious and even life-threatening possible causes for facial paralysis in children.

These possible causes include:

- head trauma such as blunt force injuries, including temporal bone **fractures** or damage to the brain stem

- brain pathology, including neuromas, brain tumors, or cysts

- otitis media

- mastoiditis

- abcess of the temporal bone

- accidental surgical injury

- less likely causes such as congenital conditions, lupus, diabetes, or thyroid conditions

These conditions are considerably more dangerous to a child or teen than Bell's palsy and will require immediate, possibly emergency treatment as quickly as feasible. It is important to remember that paralysis in any other part of the body than the face is definitely not Bell's palsy and should be evaluated by a medical professional as soon as possible. As the facial paralysis of Bell's palsy is usually perceived correctly by parents to be a neurological condition, neurologists are often consulted. However, pediatricians and otolaryngologists (ENT—ear, nose and throat specialists) also treat Bell's palsy.

Diagnosis

Reaching a diagnosis of Bell's palsy is a process of ruling out other possible causes for the child's complaints and the observed symptoms. As noted previously, other, more serious possible causes of facial paralysis need to be eliminated before diagnosis can be made. Paralysis located in any other part of the body than the face definitely rules out Bell's palsy, and should be considered a more serious potential problem. A detailed history, including queries about recent injuries or falls; as well as various imaging tests such as **magnetic resonance imaging** (MRI), **computed tomography** (CT) scans, **x rays**, and electromyography (EMG) assure that the correct diagnosis is made.

Ramsey-Hunt syndrome

Another differential cause of facial paralysis similar to Bell's palsy is Ramsey-Hunt Syndrome. Ramsey-Hunt's chief differences from Bell's palsy are both its causative agent and the severity of some symptoms. It has been conclusively proven that another herpes virus—varicella zoster virus (VZV), the cause of both chickenpox and shingles—is the culprit for Ramsey-Hunt syndrome. This syndrome is usually an adult disease whose incidence increases after the age of 50. However, children and young adults found to have Ramsey-Hunt syndrome are considered at risk for, and in need of evaluation for, having autoimmune diseases.

Some of the symptoms that differentiate Ramsey-Hunt syndrome from Bell's palsy include:

- shingles, or painful skin eruptions, that last for two to five weeks

- more severe ear pain, often located inside of the ear

- more severe and longer-lasting dizziness

- loss of hearing (This occurs because Ramsey-Hunt syndrome also affects the eighth cranial nerve that is responsible for hearing.)

- swollen, painful lymph nodes near the area involved

Treatment

General treatment

Though most nerve compression in Bell's palsy is mild and temporary for children, the primary goal is to assure that no further damage to the seventh cranial nerve occurs. Careful monitoring is necessary, and in some cases aggressive treatment may include eliminating the swelling and inflammation that is compressing the nerve as quickly as possible. Typically the ideal time for reducing this inflammation is within the first seven days after diagnosis. A 2001 NINDS study showed steroids such as prednisone and the antiviral medication acyclovir offer some relief of these symptoms, but are considered a more controversial treatment by some health care professionals when prescribed for children. Mild **analgesics** such as **acetaminophen** (Tylenol) may be ordered if there is pain. Because of changes in saliva production and difficulty swallowing, extra care in **oral hygiene** for the child may be necessary. As in any infection or injury, rest and good **nutrition** is of paramount importance in allowing the body to heal itself.

Monitoring the state of, and providing care to the affected eye is very important. Tears may not be produced at all, or if produced, run out without actually lubricating the eye. This can cause a stinging or burning sensation in the child's eye due to dryness. Under normal circumstances, we protect our eyes by blinking every five to seven seconds. This provides moisture by moving tears across the eye and stops the entrance of debris from the external world. When the eye is unable to produce tears or close completely or to blink, as often occurs in Bell's palsy, there is danger of doing permanent damage to the cornea of the eye. Children with Bell's palsy who are old enough to follow instructions and are showing eye symptoms should be taught to manually "blink" the eye by holding the lid shut every few minutes with one finger, especially when the eye feels dry. Artificial tear products may be ordered by the pediatrician or specialist. Tinted **eyeglasses** or sunglasses may be helpful. A patch and eye ointment can be necessary at night if the child is unable to close an eye. If the eye is seriously affected, an ophthalmologist should be consulted to develop the best means of protection for the eye.

When facial paralysis persists

Though most cases of Bell's palsy resolve uneventfully in children, some do not. It is possible that rehabilitation, including retraining the brain through facial **exercises**, or even surgical correction for weakened facial muscles can be necessary in extreme cases. In the early stage of Bell's palsy, when facial muscles are the most flaccid, it is desirable to allow the muscles to simply rest and recover on their own. Gentle massage and moist warmth may provide pain relief and improve circulation, but stronger interventions should wait. Usually facial exercises will not be necessary for children with Bell's palsy unless the paralysis does not resolve itself and there is long-term damage to nerves. However facial exercises such as wrinkling the forehead, flaring and sniffling the nostrils, curling and puckering the lips, and several others may be used to retrain the brain's messages to facial muscles. Even younger children can often be taught to do these exercises, and they can be presented by parents or therapists as playing a game—making faces in the mirror. Sessions of facial exercise should be brief and performed two to three times a day. A surgical procedure involving decompression of the facial nerve through extremely delicate microsurgery has, in severe cases, also been done. But its effectiveness in Bell's palsy remains at issue among child health-care providers. Benefits of this surgery are considered by some child health specialists to be insufficient compared to the risks involved.

Nutritional concerns

Because compromise of the immune system is so often a facet of children contracting Bell's palsy, good nutrition is necessary to rebuild and strengthen that immune system. This involves following the American Dietetic Association (ADA) nutritional guidelines for children, and possibly the addition of a multivitamin if the pediatrician feels it is advisable. Semi-solid foods such as yogurt, jello, pudding, or ice cream may be easier to take in than liquids if the child is experiencing swallowing difficulty.

ADA nutritional guidelines for children include:

• Grain group: Six servings per day. Includes, per serving, one slice of bread, one-half cup cooked rice or pasta, one-half cup cooked cereal or 1 oz (28 g) of ready-to-eat cereal.

• Vegetable group: Three servings per day. Includes, per serving, one-half cup of chopped raw or cooked vegetables, one cup of raw, leafy vegetables.

• Fruit group: Two servings per day. Includes, per serving, one piece of fruit or melon wedge, three-quarters cup of fruit juice, one-half cup of canned fruit, one-quarter cup of dried fruit.

• Milk group: Two servings per day. Includes, per serving, one cup of milk or yogurt, or 2 oz (57 g) of cheese.

• Meat group: Two servings per day. Includes, per serving, 2–3 oz (57–85 g) of cooked lean meat, poultry or fish, one-half cup of cooked dry beans, one egg, or two tablespoons of peanut butter.

• Fats and sweets group: Should be limited as much as possible.

Prognosis

The potential outcome from Bell's palsy is quite hopeful. NINDS notes that the majority of all Bell's palsy sufferers improve dramatically, with or without treatment, within two weeks. The Bell's Palsy Information Site notes that half of all people contracting this condition recover completely within "a short time," and another 35 percent have "good recoveries within a year." The outlook for children is better. Eighty-five percent of children with this disease recover completely. Ten percent of the children who contract Bell's palsy will have mild weakness remaining afterward, and 5 percent will have severe residual facial weakness. Statistically, 7 percent of all children that develop Bell's palsy will have a recurrent episode in the future.

Prevention

Because of the prevalence of HSV-1, the primary cause of Bell's palsy, it is extremely difficult to prevent children from coming in contact with it. Teaching children to routinely wash their hands, and to not share towels, face-cloths, cups, or silverware can be helpful. However none of these will probably stop a visiting relative or friend from kissing a child or teen, passing along the HSV-1 virus that this friend or relative may carry. Assuring that children get sufficient rest and do not become fatigued can help in maintaining and building up an immune system that can fight off these infecting agents. This strengthening or maintenance of the immune system is even more important following any childhood illness.

Parental concerns

Clearly the notion of a child having permanent facial paralysis can be quite frightening for parents as well as the child suffering from Bell's palsy. The realization of looking different—not being able to smile,

KEY TERMS

Autoimmune disorder—One of a group of disorders, like rheumatoid arthritis and systemic lupus erythematosus, in which the immune system is overactive and has lost the ability to distinguish between self and non-self. The body's immune cells turn on the body, attacking various tissues and organs.

Cornea—The clear, dome-shaped outer covering of the eye that lies in front of the iris and pupil. The cornea lets light into the eye.

Dormant—The biological state of being relatively inactive or in a resting state in which certain processes are slowed down or suspended.

Electrooculography (EOG)—A diagnostic test that records the electrical activity of the muscles that control eye movement.

Herpesvirus—A family of viruses including herpes simplex types 1 and 2, and herpes zoster (also called varicella zoster). Herpes viruses cause several infections, all characterized by blisters and ulcers, including chickenpox, shingles, genital herpes, and cold sores or fever blisters.

Human immunodeficiency virus (HIV)—A transmissible retrovirus that causes AIDS in humans. Two forms of HIV are now recognized: HIV-1, which causes most cases of AIDS in Europe, North and South America, and most parts of Africa; and HIV-2, which is chiefly found in West African patients. HIV-2, discovered in 1986, appears to be less virulent than HIV-1 and may also have a longer latency period.

Lyme disease—An acute, recurrent, inflammatory disease involving one or a few joints, and transmitted by the bite of ticks carrying the spiral-shaped bacterium *Borrelia burgdorferi*. The condition was originally described in the community of Lyme, Connecticut, but has also been reported in other parts of the United States and other countries. Knees and other large joints are most commonly involved with local inflammation and swelling.

Mastoiditis—An inflammation of the bone behind the ear (the mastoid bone) caused by an infection spreading from the middle ear to the cavity in the mastoid bone.

Mononucleosis—An infection, caused by the Epstein-Barr virus, that causes swelling of lymph nodes, spleen, and liver, usually accompanied by extremely sore throat, fever, headache, and intense long-lasting fatigue. Also called infectious mononucleosis.

Neurological disorders—Pathological conditions relating to the brain and/or nervous system.

Neuromas— Usually benign tumors affecting nerve tissue.

Otitis media—Inflammation or infection of the middle ear space behind the eardrum. It commonly occurs in early childhood and is characterized by ear pain, fever, and hearing problems.

Sarcoidosis—A chronic disease that causes the formation of granulomas, masses resembling small tumors composed of clumps of immune cells, in any organ or tissue. Common sites include the lungs, spleen, liver, mucous membranes, skin, and lymph nodes.

Shingles—An disease caused by an infection with the *Herpes zoster* virus, the same virus that causes chickenpox. Symptoms of shingles include pain and blisters along one nerve, usually on the face, chest, stomach, or back.

Temporal bones—The compound bones that form the left and right sides of the skull and contain various cavities associated with the ear.

---

close an eye or even hold fluids in the mouth properly is highly upsetting to parents, and embarrassing and frustrating for the child. Once the diagnosis of Bell's palsy is made, parents can feel reasonably optimistic that this is a condition that normally resolves itself within a set period of time, usually a matter of days or weeks. When Bell's palsy is understood, parents can generally feel some personal reassurance and transmit a sense of comfort and hope to the child. As noted previously, the paramount concern is reaching the correct diagnosis as other causes of facial or any other bodily paralysis can be of a much more serious nature. When the diagnosis has been verified by a health-care professional, accurate information about Bell's palsy can greatly alleviate further fears. The Bell's Palsy Information website <http://www.bellspalsy.ws> provides

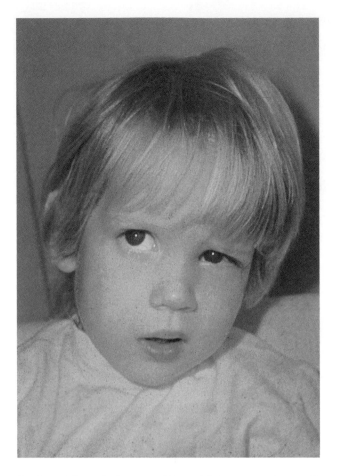

Boy's facial paralysis caused by a tick-borne meningoradicultis. *(Photo Researchers, Inc.)*

extensive information regarding all aspects of this disease, including measures that parents can take, and even products that can be helpful in making the child more comfortable.

Resources

BOOKS

Bell, Susan Givens, Joan Calandra, and Linda Sowden. *Mosby's Pediatric Nursing Reference, 5th ed.* Elsevier Science, 2003.

Markel, Howard, MD. *Practical Pediatrician.* New York: H. Freeman & Co., 1996.

Taubman, Bruce, MD. *Your Child's Symptoms: A Parent's Guide to Understanding Pediatric Medicine.* New York: Simon & Schuster, 1992.

WEB SITES

Bell's Palsy Information. Available online at: <http://www.bellspalsy.ws>.

Bell's Palsy. Available online at <http://www.kidshealth.org>.

National Institute of Neurological Disorders and Stroke. *Bell's Palsy Information Page.* Available online at <http://www.ninds.nih.gov/health_and_medical/disorders/bells_doc.htm>.

Joan Schonbeck, RN

Benzoyl peroxide *see* **Antiacne drugs**

Biliary atresia

Definition

Biliary atresia is the congenital failure of a fetus to develop an adequate pathway for bile to drain from the liver to the intestine.

Description

Biliary atresia is the congenital absence or closure of the ducts that drain bile from the liver. Bile is a liquid mixture of cholesterol, bile salts, and waste products, including bilirubin, which the liver excretes through thousands of tiny biliary ducts to the intestine, where the bile aids in the digestive process of dietary fats. These ducts merge into larger and larger channels, like streams flowing into rivers, until they all pour into a single duct that empties into the duodenum (first part of the small intestine). Between the liver and the duodenum this duct has a side channel connected to the gall bladder. The gall bladder stores bile and concentrates it, removing much of its water content. Then when food enters the stomach, the gall bladder contracts and empties its contents.

If bile cannot get out because the ducts are absent or blocked, it backs up into the liver (referred to as biliary stasis) and eventually into the rest of the body. The major pigment in bile is a chemical called bilirubin, which is yellow. Bilirubin is a breakdown product of hemoglobin (the red chemical in blood that carries oxygen). If the body accumulates an excess of bilirubin, it turns yellow (jaundiced). Bile also turns the stool brown; without it, stools are pale gray-, white- or fawn-colored. Bile trapped within the liver causes damage and scarring to the liver cells (cirrhosis of the liver). Scarring of the liver can cause portal **hypertension** (high blood pressure in the portal vein, which is the main vein carrying blood from the intestine to the liver). Portal hypertension may result in the development of fragile veins in the intestinal lining, stomach, or esophagus, which can bleed and require emergency medical attention.

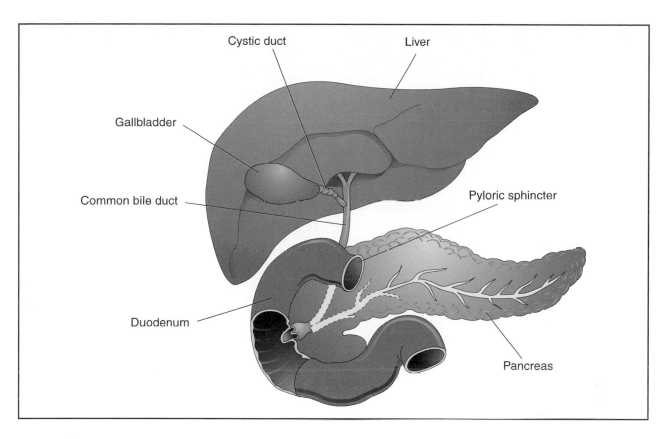

Cystic duct

Liver

Gallbladder

Common bile duct

Pyloric sphincter

Duodenum

Pancreas

Biliary atresia is a congenital condition in which the pathway for bile to drain from the liver to the intestine is undeveloped. It is the most common lethal liver disease in children. *(Illustration by Electronic Illustrators Group.)*

Demographics

Biliary atresia is the most common lethal liver disease in children, occurring once every 10,000 to 15,000 live births. In the United States, approximately 300 cases of biliary atresia are diagnosed each year. Females are affected slightly more often than males. The incidence of biliary atresia is highest in Asian populations. The disorder also occurs in black infants at a rate approximately two times higher than that in white infants.

Causes and symptoms

The cause of biliary atresia is unknown. However, there are indications that viral infections or autoimmune mechanisms may be responsible for the development of biliary atresia. About 10 percent of children with biliary atresia also have other associated congenital defects in blood vessels, heart, spleen, or intestines.

The affected infant appears normal at birth and during the newborn period. After about two to three weeks, the infant develops **jaundice**. The infant has yellow eyes and skin and dark yellow or brown urine due to build-up of bilirubin, and the stools are probably light colored. The child's abdomen begins to swell because of a firm, enlarged

liver, and the infant gets progressively more ill. Weight loss and irritability will increase as the effects of jaundice increase. Some infants may develop intense **itching** (pruritis), which makes them even more uncomfortable. Nearly all untreated children die of liver failure within two years.

When to call the doctor

The doctor should be called if an infant older than two weeks of age exhibits jaundice or has other symptoms typical of biliary atresia.

If, after surgery for biliary atresia, an infant becomes jaundiced, has a high temperature for more than 24 hours, or if there is a change in the color of the stools or urine. Also after surgery, the infant may experience an abnormal collection of fluid in the abdomen, referred to as ascites, so the doctor should be consulted if the infant's stomach is distended.

If a child has black stools, pallor, or **vomiting** of blood due to the development of portal hypertension, emergency medical attention is required to treat the bleeding.

Diagnosis

The persistence or development of jaundice beyond the second week in a newborn who also has light-colored stools indicates obstruction to the flow of bile. An immediate evaluation that includes blood tests and imaging of the biliary system (through ultrasound, specialized x-ray techniques, or radioactive screens of the liver) are required to confirm the diagnosis. Other liver diseases that cause symptoms similar to biliary atresia must be ruled out through the testing process. In addition, in most cases, a liver biopsy or a surgical exploration of the infant's abdomen is necessary for a definitive diagnosis.

Treatment

Surgery is the only means to treat biliary atresia. The surgeon must create an adequate pathway for bile to escape the liver into the intestine. The altered anatomy of the biliary system is different in every case, calling upon the surgeon's skill and experience to select and execute the most effective among several options. If the obstruction is only between the gall bladder and the intestine, it is possible to attach a piece of intestine directly to the gall bladder.

If the upper biliary system is also inadequate, the surgeon will attach a piece of intestine directly to the liver using the Kasai procedure, named after Morio Kasai, the Japanese surgeon who developed the procedure. The tiny bile ducts in that part of the liver where the surgery is performed discharge their bile directly into the intestine, and the channels will gradually enlarge. A possible complication after the Kasai operation is an infection in the bile ducts (cholangitis). This infection must be treated immediately with intravenous **antibiotics**. If the child develops ascites (abnormal build-up of fluid in the abdomen), treatment consists of medications and alteration of the diet to maintain calorie intake but to reduce salt and fluid intake.

The operation is most successful in infants under the age of eight weeks. However, in many cases, liver damage may continue to occur, and without further intervention, cirrhosis of the liver and associated complications may develop. Continued problems often develop because there are also obstructed ducts within the liver that cannot be surgically treated. In these cases, liver transplantation is required. Improved techniques of liver transplantation, which allow transplantation in children of any age, and development of drugs that help overcome the problems of organ rejection offer significant hope to children with biliary atresia who are not successfully treated with surgical techniques.

Nutritional concerns

A low- or modified-fat diet with supplementary **vitamins** is often required after surgery, since the absorption of fats and vitamins can be impaired. Postoperative breastfeeding is encouraged whenever possible, as breast milk contains lipases and bile salts to aid in digestion. Infants who are formula-fed should use special

---

KEY TERMS

Cirrhosis—A chronic degenerative disease of the liver, in which normal cells are replaced by fibrous tissue and normal liver function is disrupted. The most common symptoms are mild jaundice, fluid collection in the tissues, mental confusion, and vomiting of blood. Cirrhosis is associated with portal hypertension and is a major risk factor for the later development of liver cancer. If left untreated, cirrhosis leads to liver failure.

Duodenum—The first of the three segments of the small intestine. The duodenum is about 10 in (25 cm) long and connects the stomach and the jejunum.

Hemoglobin—An iron-containing pigment of red blood cells composed of four amino acid chains (alpha, beta, gamma, delta) that delivers oxygen from the lungs to the cells of the body and carries carbon dioxide from the cells to the lungs.

Jaundice—A condition in which the skin and whites of the eyes take on a yellowish color due to an increase of bilirubin (a compound produced by the liver) in the blood. Also called icterus.

---

formulas (Alimentum, Pregestimil) that contain chemicals to enhance digestion of dietary fats. Extra calories may also be required to help the infant gain weight. A dietary expert should be consulted to guide in the development of feeding requirements for an infant who has been treated surgically for biliary atresia.

Prognosis

Early diagnosis of biliary atresia is essential, for if left untreated, few children survive beyond the age of two years. If surgery is performed before the infant is two months old, success is much more likely, while after three months of age, the success rate is much poorer. Unfortunately for many infants, surgery is not a cure, and complications of cirrhosis of the liver may develop gradually, and the child eventually requires liver transplantation to avoid an early death. Transplantation as of 2004 achieves up to 80 to 90 percent one-year survival rates and promises to prevent the chronic disease that used to accompany earlier surgical procedures.

Prevention

Since the specific cause of this birth defect is unknown, there is no way known as of 2004 to prevent biliary atresia. However, it is not a hereditary condition.

Parental concerns

Parents of children with biliary atresia require help in coping with the strain of this chronic illness as well as the stress associated with waiting for a liver transplant. Parents may also feel guilty because they feel that they may have in some way contributed to the development of biliary atresia, although as of 2004, there is no known way to prevent the disease. The American Liver Foundation organizes and coordinates mutual help groups to provide emotional support for families, to make referrals to specialists as needed, and keep parents aware of research developments.

Resources

BOOKS

Kelly, Deirdre A., and Sheila Sherlock. *Diseases of the Liver and Biliary System in Children*, 2nd ed. Oxford, UK: Blackwell Publishers, 2004.

ORGANIZATIONS

American Liver Foundation. 75 Maiden Lane, Suite 603, New York, NY 10038. Web site: <www.liverfoundation.org/>.

Children's Liver Association for Support Services. 27023 McBean Parkway #126, Valencia, CA 91355. Web site: <www.classkids.org/>.

WEB SITES

Biliary Atresia Network. Available online at <http://health.groups.yahoo.com/group/biliaryatresianetwork/> (accessed December 6, 2004).

"Patient Information about Biliary Atresia." Available online at <www.pediatriconcall.com/fordoctor/DiseasesandCondition/Faqs/biliaryArt.asp> (accessed December 6, 2004).

Judith Sims
J. Ricker Polsdorfer, MD

Bilingualism/Bilingual education

Definition

Bilingualism is the ability to communicate in two different languages. Bilingual education is the use of two different languages in classroom instruction.

Description

Languages are learned most readily during the toddler and **preschool** years and, to a lesser extent, during elementary school. Therefore, children growing up in bilingual homes and/or receiving bilingual education easily acquire both languages. Throughout much of the world, bilingualism is the norm for both children and adults. In the past, immigrants to the United States often began learning and using English in their homes as soon as possible. In the early 2000s, however, many immigrants choose to maintain their native language at home. Bilingual children are at an advantage in this increasingly multilingual nation.

Bilingual language development

Language acquisition is very similar for monolingual and bilingual children, although some experts view bilingualism as a specialized case of **language development**. Children growing up in homes where two different languages are spoken usually acquire both languages simultaneously. Although their acquisition of each language may be somewhat slower than that of children who are acquiring a single language, their development in the two languages combined is equivalent to that of monolingual children. Bilingual language learners proceed through the same patterns of language and speech development as children acquiring a single language. Their first words usually are spoken at about one year of age, and they begin stringing two words together at about age two. Even if the two languages do not share similarities in pronunciation, children eventually master them both.

There are two major patterns of bilingual language development, both occurring before the age of three. Simultaneous bilingualism occurs when a child learns both languages at the same time. In the early stages of simultaneous bilingual language development, a child may mix words, parts of words, and inflections from both languages in a single sentence. Sometimes this occurs because a child knows a word in one language but not in the other. Some bilingual children initially resist learning words for the same thing in two languages. Children also may experiment with their two languages for effect. During the second stage of bilingual language development, at age four or older, children gradually begin to distinguish between the two languages and use them separately, sometimes depending on where they are. One language may be used less formally to talk about home and **family**, whereas the other language may be used more formally, perhaps for relating events that took place outside the home. Often children find it easier to express a specific idea in one language rather than the other. Bilingual children also go through periods when one language is used more than the other. Some children may begin to prefer one language over the other, particularly if that language is spoken more frequently in their home or school. Bilingual children usually are not equally skilled in both languages. Often they understand more in one language but speak more in the other.

Sequential bilingualism occurs when children use their knowledge of and experience with a first language to rapidly acquire a second language. The first language may influence the way in which they learn and use their second language. Learning the second language is easier for children if the sounds, words, and vocabulary of the languages are similar.

Bilingual language development usually proceeds more smoothly when both languages are introduced early and simultaneously. When the parents each use a different language with their child, the child is less likely to experience language confusion.

Research indicates that there are numerous advantages to bilingualism. Bilingualism has been reported to improve the following skills:

• verbal and linguistic abilities

• general reasoning

• concept formation

• divergent thinking

• metalinguistic skills, the ability to analyze and talk about language and control language processing

These abilities are important for reading development in young children and may be a prerequisite for later learning to read and write in a new language.

Types of bilingual education

Bilingual education is common throughout the world and involves hundreds of languages. In the United States bilingualism is assumed to mean English and another language, often Spanish. More than 300 languages are spoken in the United States. In New York City schools, classroom instruction is given in 115 different languages. Bilingual education includes all teaching methods that are designed to meet the needs of English-language learners (ELLs), also referred to as "limited English proficient" (LEP) students.

There are numerous approaches to bilingual education, although all include English as a second language (ESL). ESL is English language instruction that includes little or no use of a child's native language. ESL classes often include students with many different primary languages. Some school districts use a variety of approaches to bilingual education, designing individual programs based on the needs of each child.

A common approach is transitional bilingual education (TBE). TBE programs include ESL; however, some or all academic classes are conducted in children's primary languages until they are well-prepared for English-only classes. Even children who converse well in English may not be ready to learn academic subjects in English. Often these children spend part of the school day in an intensive ESL program and the remainder of the day receiving instruction in their primary language. Bilingual teachers may help students improve their primary language skills. Bilingual/bicultural programs include instruction in the history and culture of a student's ethnic heritage. Studies have shown that children who receive several years of instruction in their native language learn English faster and have higher overall academic achievement levels that those who do not.

Two-way bilingual or dual-language programs use both English and a second language in classrooms made up of both ELLs and native English speakers. The goal is for both groups to become bilingual. Children in two-way bilingual education programs have been found to outperform their peers academically.

Many educators—and a segment of the public—believe in the English immersion approach, even if ELLs do not understand very much in the classroom. In this approach nearly all instruction is in English, and there is little or no use of other languages. If the teacher is bilingual, students may be allowed to ask questions in their native language, but the teacher answers them in English. Some schools employ structured English immersion or sheltered English, in which teachers use pictures, simple reading words, and other techniques to teach ELLs both English and academic subjects.

History of bilingual education

Although bilingual education has been used in the United States for more than 200 years, the 1968 Title VII amendment to the 1965 Elementary and Secondary Education Act (ESEA) instituted federal grants for bilingual education programs. This legislation led to the development of appropriate teaching and learning materials and training for teachers of bilingual students.

In 1974 the U.S. Supreme Court ruled that the San Francisco school system had violated the Civil Rights Act of 1964 by not providing English-language instruction for Chinese-speaking students. All school districts were directed to serve ELLs adequately, and bilingual education quickly spread throughout the United States. In the 1980s a group called Asian Americans United filed a class-action lawsuit charging that Asian Americans were not being provided with an equitable education because they were not offered bilingual classes. The result of this suit was the creation of sheltered ESL, in which ESL students take all of their classes together.

The No Child Left Behind (NCLB) Act of 2001—President George W. Bush's major education initiative—reauthorized the ESEA. It also imposed penalties on schools that did not raise the achievement levels of ELLs for at least two consecutive years. Although most research indicates that it often takes seven years for ELLs to attain full English fluency, the new federal law allows these children only three years before they must take standardized tests in English. Schools with large numbers of children speaking many different languages are particularly disadvantaged under the law. A 2003 survey by the National Education Association found that 22,000 schools in 44 states failed to make the required yearly progress on standardized tests, primarily because of low test scores by ELLs and disabled students. The National Association for Bilingual Education claims that NCLB sets arbitrary goals for achievement and uses "invalid and unreliable assessments." Furthermore, although the NCLB requires teachers to be qualified, as of 2004 there is a severe shortage of qualified teachers for ELLs. Some communities have developed early-intervention programs for Spanish-speaking parents and preschoolers to help children develop their Spanish language skills in preparation for entering English-only schools.

In May of 2004, the U.S. Department of Education and faith-based community leaders launched an initiative to inform Hispanic, Asian, and other parents of ELLs about the NCLB. It featured the "Declaration of Rights for Parents of English Language Learners under No Child Left Behind."

As of 2004 American public schools include about 11 million children of immigrants. Approximately 5.5 million students—10 percent of the public school enrollment—speak little or no English. Spanish speakers account for 80 percent of these children. About one-third of children enrolled in urban schools speak a primary language other than English in their homes. Between 2001 and 2004, 19 states reported increases of 50 to 200 percent in Spanish-speaking students. ELLs are the fastest-growing public school population in kindergarten through twelfth grade. Between 2000 and 2002, nationwide ELL enrollment increased 27 percent. About 25 percent of California public school children are ELLs. However, there is a profound shortage of bilingual and ESL teachers throughout the United States. Although 41 percent of U.S. teachers have ELLs in their classrooms, only about 2.5 percent of them have degrees in ESL or bilingual education. The majority of these teachers report that they are not well-prepared for teaching ELLs. About 75 percent of ELLs are in poverty schools, where student turnover is high and many teachers have only emergency credentials.

Opposition to bilingual education

In 1980 voters in Dade County, Florida, made English their official language. In 1981 California Senator S. I. Hayakawa introduced a constitutional amendment to make English the country's official language. In 1983 Hayakawa founded U.S. English, Inc., which grew to include 1.8 million members by 2004. U.S. English argues the following premises:

- The unifying effect of the English language must be preserved in the United States.

- Bilingual education fails to adequately teach English.

- Learning English quickly in English-only classrooms is best for ELLs, both academically and socially.

- Any special language instruction should be short-term and transitional.

In 1986 California voters passed Proposition 63 that made English the state's official language. Other states did the same. In 1998 Californians passed Proposition 227, a referendum that attempted to eliminate bilingual education by allowing only one year of structured English immersion, followed by mainstreaming. Similar initiatives have appeared on other state ballots. However, only 9 percent of the California children attained English proficiency in one year, and most remained in the immersion programs for a second year. Prior to the new law only 29 percent of California ELLs were in bilingual programs, in part because of a shortage of qualified teachers. Since the law allowed parents to apply for waivers, 12 percent of the ELLs were allowed to remain in bilingual classes.

In January of 2004, as part of a lawsuit settlement, the California State Board of Education was forced to radically revise the implementation of their "Reading First" program. Previously California had withheld all of the $133 million provided by NCLB from ELLs enrolled in alternative bilingual programs.

Common problems

Language delay

Language and learning difficulties occur with the same frequency in monolingual and bilingual children. However, as the number of bilingual children in the United States increases, it becomes increasingly important for parents and pediatricians to understand the normal patterns of bilingual language development in order to recognize abnormal language development in a bilingual child.

If a bilingual child has a speech or language problem, it should be apparent in both languages. However detecting language delays or abnormalities in bilingual children can be difficult. Signs of possible **language delay** in bilingual children include the following:

- not making sounds between two and six months of age

- fewer than one new word per week in children aged six to 15 months

- fewer than 20 words in the two languages combined by 20 months of age

- limited vocabulary without word combinations in children aged two to three years of age

- prolonged periods without using speech

- difficulty remembering words

- missing normal milestones of language development in the first language of a sequentially bilingual child

Language development in bilingual children can be assessed by a bilingual speech/language pathologist or by a professional who has knowledge of the rules and structure of both languages, perhaps with the assistance of a translator or interpreter.

English-only education

ELLs in English-only programs often fall behind academically. Many ELLs who are assessed using traditional methods are referred for **special education**. Such children often become school drop-outs.

Parental concerns

Parents in bilingual households can help their children by taking the following steps:

- speaking the language in which they are most comfortable

- being consistent regarding how and with whom they use each language

- using each language's grammar in a manner that is appropriate for the child's developmental stage

- keeping children interested and motivated in language acquisition

See also Language development.

Resources

BOOKS

Bhatia, Tej K., and William C. Ritchie, eds. *The Handbook of Bilingualism.* Malden, MA: Blackwell, 2004.

Cadiero-Kaplan, Karen. *The Literacy Curriculum and Bilingual Education: A Critical Examination.* New York: P. Lang, 2004.

Calderon, Margarita, and Liliana Minaya-Rowe. *Designing and Implementing Two-Way Bilingual Programs: A Step-by-Step Guide for Administrators, Teachers, and Parents.* Thousand Oaks, CA: Corwin Press, 2003.

Crawford, James. *Educating English Learners: Language Diversity in the Classroom.* Los Angeles, CA: Bilingual Educational Services, 2004.

Genesee, Fred, et al. *Dual Language Development and Disorders: A Handbook on Bilingualism and Second Language Learning.* Baltimore, MD: Paul H. Brookes, 2004.

KEY TERMS

Elementary and Secondary Education Act (ESEA)—The 1965 federal law that is reauthorized and amended every five years.

English as a second language (ESL)—English language instruction for English language learners (ELLs) that includes little or no use of a child's native language; a component of all bilingual education programs.

English language learner (ELL)—A student who is learning English as a second language; also called limited English proficient (LEP).

Immersion—A language education approach in which English is the only language used.

Limited English proficient (LEP)—Used to identify children who have insufficient English to succeed in English-only classrooms; also called English language learner (ELL).

Metalinguistic skills—The ability to analyze language and control internal language processing; important for reading development in children.

No Child Left Behind (NCLB) Act—The 2001 reauthorization of the ESEA, President George W. Bush's major education initiative.

Sequential bilingualism—Acquiring first one language and then a second language before the age of three.

Sheltered English—Structured English immersion; English instruction for ELLs that focuses on content and skills rather than the language itself; uses simplified language, visual aids, physical activity, and the physical environment to teach academic subjects.

Sheltered ESL—Bilingual education in which ESL students attend all of their classes together.

Simultaneous bilingualism—Acquiring two languages simultaneously before the age of three.

Structured English immersion—Sheltered English; English-only instruction for ELLs that uses simplified language, visual aids, physical activity, and the physical environment to teach academic subjects.

Transitional bilingual education (TBE)—Bilingual education that includes ESL and academic classes conducted in a child's primary language.

Two-way bilingual education—Dual language programs in which English and a second language are both used in classes consisting of ELLs and native-English speakers.

Santa Ana, Otto, ed. *Tongue-Tied: The Lives of Multilingual Children in Public Education.* Lanham, MD: Rowman & Littlefield, 2004.

San Miguel Jr., Guadalupe. *Contested Policy: The Rise and Fall of Federal Bilingual Education in the United States, 1960–2001.* Denton, TX: University of North Texas Press, 2004.

PERIODICALS

Dillon, Sam. "School Districts Struggle with English Fluency Mandate." *New York Times* November 5, 2003.

Gutiérrez-Clellen, Vera F., et al. "Verbal Working Memory in Bilingual Children." *Journal of Speech, Language, and Hearing Research* 47, no. 4 (August 2004): 863–76.

Hamers, Josiane F. "A Sociocognitive Model of Bilingual Development." *Journal of Language and Social Psychology* 23, no. 1 (March 2004): 70.

Hammer, Carol Scheffner, et al. "Home Literacy Experiences and Their Relationship to Bilingual Preschoolers' Developing English Literacy Abilities: An Initial Investigation." *Language, Speech, and Hearing Services in Schools* 34 (January 2003): 20–30.

ORGANIZATIONS

American Speech-Language-Hearing Association. 10801 Rockville Pike, Rockville, MD 20852. Web site: <http://asha.org>.

National Association for Bilingual Education. 1030 15th St., NW, Suite 470, Washington, DC 20005. Web site: <www.nabe.org>.

National Association for Multicultural Education. 733 15th St., NW, Suite 430, Washington, DC 20005. Web site: <http://nameorg.org>.

National Clearinghouse for English Language Acquisition. Office of English Language Acquisition, Language Enhancement & Academic Achievement for Limited English Proficient Students, U.S. Department of Education, George Washington University Graduate School of Education and Human Development, 2121 K St., NW, Suite 260, Washington, DC 20037. Web site: <www.ncela.gwu.edu>.

U.S. English Inc. 1747 Pennsylvania Ave., NW, Suite 1050, Washington, DC 20006. Web site: <www.us-english.org>.

WEB SITES

"Children and Bilingualism." *American Speech-Language-Hearing Association.* Available online at <www.asha.org/public/speech/development/Bilingual-Children.htm> (accessed December 6, 2004).

"Immigrant Children Enrolled in Some of the State's Poorest School Districts Will Now Have Access to Millions of Dollars to Help Them Learn to Read." *hispanic vista,* January 29, 2004. Available online at <www.latinobeat.net/html4/013104be.htm> (accessed December 6, 2004).

Jehlen, Alain. "English Lessons." *National Education Association,* May 2002. Available online at <www.nea.org/neatoday/0205/cover.html> (accessed December 6, 2004).

"Language Development in Bilingual Children." *KidsGrowth.com.* Available online at <www.kidsgrowth.com/resources/articledetail.cfm?id=1229> (accessed December 6, 2004).

"What is Bilingual Education?" *National Association for Bilingual Education,* 2001. Available online at <www.nabe.org/faq_detail.asp?ID=20> (accessed December 6, 2004).

"What's the Score on English-Only?" *National Education Association,* May 2002. Available online at <www.nea.org/neatoday/0205/cover.html> (accessed December 6, 2004).

Margaret Alic, PhD

Bilirubin test

Definition

A bilirubin test is a diagnostic blood test performed to measure levels of bile pigment in an individual's blood serum and to help evaluate liver function.

Purpose

The bilirubin test is an important part of routine newborn (neonatal) diagnostic screening tests. The level of bilirubin in a newborn's blood serum is measured to determine if the circulating level of bilirubin is normal or abnormal. Bilirubin is a yellow-orange bile pigment produced during the breakdown of hemoglobin, the iron-bearing and oxygen-carrying protein in red blood cells. All individuals produce bilirubin daily as part of the normal turnover of red cells. A higher than normal (elevated) bilirubin test can reflect accelerated red blood cell destruction or may indicate that bilirubin is not being excreted as it should be, suggesting that liver function problems or other abnormalities may be present. Neonatal bilirubin screening often reveals an elevated bilirubin (hyperbilirubinemia). The bilirubin test will determine if hyperbilirubinemia is present and, along with other diagnostic tests, help determine if the condition is relatively normal (benign) or possibly related to liver function problems or other conditions.

Description

Usually all newborns (neonates) delivered in the hospital will have total serum bilirubin (TSB) measured in the

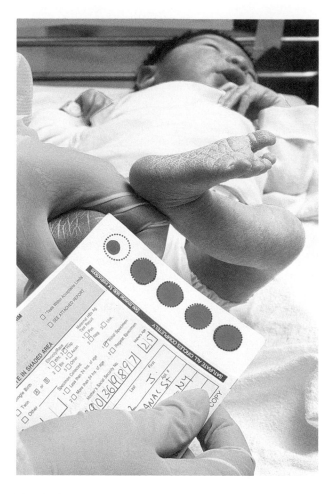

Blood taken from the heel of a newborn to test the level of bilirubin. (© Ted Horowitz/Corbis.)

clinical laboratory on one or more blood samples as requested by attending pediatricians. To obtain a blood sample for TSB, a phlebotomist takes blood from the infant's tissue (usually the heel) rather than from a vein, as the veins of newborns are extremely small and easily damaged. After sterilizing the surface of the site with alcohol and/or an antibacterial solution such as betadine, a heel puncture is made and blood from the puncture is drawn into a tiny capillary tube about 2 inches (5 cm) long that is stoppered at each end when full. This tube is spun down in a special centrifuge in the laboratory to separate serum, the liquid part of blood, from red cells. In the TSB test, spectrophotometry is used to identify and quantify the amount of bilirubin in a specific amount of serum by measuring the amount of ultraviolet light absorbed by bilirubin pigment in the sample. The test method requires only minutes and a very small amount of blood serum to produce accurate results, measuring the results in milligrams per deciliter (mg/dL). The amount of total bilirubin in circulating blood can be calculated from the results of a single biliru-

bin test. Results are compared to known normal values to determine if the individual has normal or abnormal levels.

All newborn infants begin to destroy fetal red blood cells (RBCs) in their first few days of life, replacing them with new red blood cells. The rapid destruction of red blood cells and subsequent release of fetal hemoglobin into the bloodstream results in the production of bilirubin. As a waste product, bilirubin is filtered out of blood (cleared) by the liver and excreted in bile, eliminated normally in stool produced by the large intestine. However, immediately after birth, more bilirubin is produced than the infant's immature liver can handle, and the excess remains circulating in the blood. This situation results in **jaundice** in over 60 percent of newborns, usually due to the presence of fetal hemoglobin released into the blood during the normal destruction of fetal red blood cells. Even healthy infants may appear to have a yellow stain in their skin (physiological jaundice or icterus) and the whites of the eyes (sclerae) in the first week after birth. This may first be noticed by pediatric nurses as they care for the infant. Visual evaluation of jaundice is not considered a reliable way, however, to determine its cause or the risk of continued rising of bilirubin and possible complications. Performing bilirubin tests is the first step in making sure that normal degrees of jaundice do not become more severe and that liver dysfunction or other causative conditions, if present, are identified and treated early.

Besides normal red cell destruction after birth, neonatal hyperbilirubinemia may also be caused by the following:

- low birth weight

- feeding or **nutrition** problems

- glucose 6-phospho-dehydrogenase (G6PD) deficiency

- insufficient intestinal bacteria

- incompatibility of major blood groups (ABO) between mother and baby

- blood type (Rh) incompatibility (rare due to treatment of Rh negative mothers)

- genetic abnormalities linked to a history of jaundice among siblings

- liver dysfunction

From 8 to 9 percent of newborns develop severe hyperbilirubinemia. Severe hyperbilirubinemia is of great concern to pediatricians because it may lead to bilirubin-related brain damage (kernicterus). Persistent elevated levels of bilirubin in the body can place infants at risk of neurotoxicity or bilirubin-induced neurologic dysfunction (BIND). The risk of liver dysfunction has been shown to be higher in infants who were born before term (less than

37 weeks' gestation) or who have other abnormalities in addition to an elevated total serum bilirubin.

Some pediatricians order bilirubin tests at defined times within 24 to 48 hours after birth to monitor the rate of increase of bilirubin and to help determine associated risks on an individual basis. Infants with a low rate of rise in bilirubin (less than 17mg/dL per hour) are considered lower risk and are likely to be discharged without further testing or treatment. Those who show visual jaundice at birth or within several hours after birth and whose rate of bilirubin rises more rapidly are considered at higher risk for severe hyperbilirubinemia and associated kernicterus, especially if the bilirubin level is still rising at time of discharge.

Some newborns are placed under special lamps (phototherapy) to help correct the jaundice caused by elevated bilirubin levels and to bring down the bilirubin level. Supervision of breastfeeding and supplemental nutritional support may be needed to help infants who are not getting their nutritional needs met. Exchange transfusions may be given for high-risk infants, especially those with blood group (ABO) or type (Rh positive infants born to Rh negative mothers) incompatibilities. Additional tests may be required to evaluate G6PD deficiency, genetic abnormalities, or liver function.

After discharge from the hospital, about 25 percent of otherwise healthy infants who are still showing signs of jaundice may continue to be tested for bilirubin levels. An elevated bilirubin usually goes down on its own if the hyperbilirubinemia is benign; if liver dysfunction or other abnormalities exist, bilirubin levels may remain elevated or continue to rise, indicating that further diagnostic testing, clinical evaluation, and treatment are needed.

Precautions

Performance of the bilirubin test itself is a precaution against the serious consequences that can occur when bilirubin levels continue to rise in jaundiced infants. Visual jaundice present at birth may predict rapid rises in bilirubin and risk of liver dysfunction or other abnormalities.

Preparation

No preparation is needed before performing bilirubin tests on infants' blood samples. Proper identification and careful handling of the infant are important when a blood sample is being obtained for testing. A site, usually on the infant's heel, is chosen by the phlebotomist who draws the infant's blood sample. The area is prepared by wrapping the baby's foot in a warm cloth for a few minutes to bring blood to the surface and allow it to flow more easily. The heel is then wiped with alcohol and/or an antibacterial solution such as betadine to sterilize the surface. The heel is then punctured with a lancet, avoid-

ing the center of the heel, in order to prevent inflammation of the bone. The blood sample is drawn in tiny capillary tubes, properly labeled, and taken to the laboratory for testing. In rare instances, a phlebotomist is not able to draw sufficient blood from a heel puncture, and a physician may draw venous blood from a femoral vein in the groin area, which is larger than veins in an infant's arms.

Aftercare

The site from which blood is withdrawn must be kept clean after the procedure and must be checked regularly for bleeding. A small adhesive patch may be used to protect the site.

Risks

The performance of bilirubin tests carries no significant risk. Drawing blood for the test may involve light bleeding or bruising at the site of puncture, or blood may accumulate under the puncture site (hematoma), requiring that a new location be found for subsequent tests. Not performing bilirubin tests, however, may have significant risks for some infants. Infants with rising bilirubin levels are at risk of neurotoxicity and developing kernicterus, making the monitoring of bilirubin in the first week of life critical for these infants.

Normal results

At birth, a newborn's TBS is normally 1 or 2 mg/dL, peaking at 6 mg/dL in three or four days. In 10 days to two weeks, a healthy infant's TBS is expected to be less than 0.3 mg/dL.

During the first seven days of the infant's life, TBS results are rated for risk of bilirubin toxicity or bilirubin-related brain damage within percentile ranges representing degrees of hyperbilirubinemia. TBS values less than 20 mg/dL are lower-risk percentile ranges below the 95th percentile, with an incidence of one in nine infants. TBS values greater than 20 mg/dL are in the 98th percentile, with an incidence of one in 50 infants; greater than 25 mg/dL are in the 99.9 percentile, with an incidence of one in 700 infants; and TBS values greater than 30 ng/dL are at the highest level of risk at 99.99 percentile, indicating almost certain neurotoxicity. One in 10,000 infants are in the 99.99 percentile.

Parental concerns

Parents will usually be informed by the pediatrician about any risks associated with an elevated bilirubin, such as liver dysfunction or possible kernicterus. Parents concerned about these risks can be made aware that bilirubin levels usually return to normal in most infants (more than 60%) and the related jaundice goes away gradually. Testing after the baby is discharged is sometimes necessary (in 25% of infants) and is a preventive measure rather than a cause for concern. Repeat testing is necessary to monitor bilirubin levels. Parents should be aware that, although the baby's heel may be bruised, elevated bilirubin levels can cause serious complications, and testing is critical to help prevent them.

See also Neonatal jaundice.

Resources

BOOKS

Maisels, M. Jeffrey. *Neonatal Jaundice.* London: CRC Press, 2000.

WEB SITES

"Jaundice." *MedicineNet*, March 2001. Available online at <www.medicinenet.com/jaundice/article.htm> October 28, 2004).

"Newborn Jaundice." *Caring for Your Baby.* Available online at <www.march ofdimes.com/pnhec/298_9545.asp> (accessed October 28, 2004).

L. Lee Culvert

Binge eating disorder

Definition

Binge eating disorder (BED) is characterized by loss of control over eating behaviors. The binge eater consumes unnaturally large amounts of food in a short time period, but unlike a bulimic, does not regularly engage in any inappropriate weight-reducing behaviors such as excessive **exercise**, induced **vomiting**, or taking **laxatives** following the binge episodes.

Description

BED typically strikes individuals sometime between **adolescence** and the early twenties. Because of the nature of the disorder, most BED patients are overweight or obese. Studies of weight loss programs have shown that an average of 30 percent of individuals enrolling in these programs report binge eating behavior.

Demographics

Binge eating affects an equal numbers of females and males. Although there are no good statistics on how many children suffer from the condition, an estimated 1 to 2 million Americans of all ages are binge eaters. Many of them report that their condition started in childhood.

Causes and symptoms

Binge eating episodes may act as a psychological release for excessive emotional stress. Other circumstances that may make a child or adolescent more likely to engage in binge eating include heredity and certain psychological affective disorders such as major depression. BED patients are also more likely to have a comorbid (co-existing) diagnosis of impulsive behaviors such as compulsive buying, post-traumatic stress disorder (PTSD), panic disorder, or **personality disorders**.

Individuals who develop BED often come from families who put an extreme emphasis on the importance of food as a source of comfort in times of emotional distress. Children with BED may have been taught to clean their plates regardless of their satiety or that their finishing a meal makes them a "good" girl or boy. Cultural attitudes towards beauty and thinness may also be a factor in whether a person binges.

During binge episodes, BED patients experience a definite loss of control over their eating. They eat quickly and to the point of discomfort even if they are not hungry. They typically binge alone two or more times a week and often feel depressed and guilty when the episode concludes.

Diagnosis

Binge eating disorder is usually diagnosed and treated by a psychiatrist and/or a psychologist. In addition to an interview with the child, personality and behavioral inventories, such as the **Minnesota Multiphasic Personality Inventory** (MMPI), may be administered as part of the **assessment** process. One of several clinical inventories, or scales, may also be used to assess depressive symptoms, including the Hamilton Depression Scale (HAM-D) or Beck Depression Inventory (BDI). These tests may be administered in an outpatient or hospital setting.

Treatment

Many BED individuals binge after long intervals of excessive dietary restraint; therapy helps normalize this pattern. The initial goal of BED treatment is to teach the patient to gain control over the eating behavior by focusing on eating regular meals and avoiding snacking. Cognitive-behavioral therapy (learning new behavior), group therapy, or interpersonal psychotherapy may be employed to uncover the emotional motives, distorted thinking, and behavioral patterns behind the binge eating.

Because the prevalence of depression in BED patients is high, treatment with **antidepressants** may also be prescribed. Once the binge eating behavior is curbed and depressive symptoms are controlled, the physical symptoms of BED can be addressed. The overweight BED patient may be placed on a moderate exercise program and a nutritionist may be consulted to educate the patient on healthy food choices and strategies for weight loss.

Prognosis

If left unchecked, the poor dietary habits and **obesity** that are symptomatic of BED can lead to serious health problems, such as high blood pressure, heart attacks, and type 2 diabetes. BED is a chronic condition that requires ongoing medical and psychological management. Some of these conditions such as diabetes can occur in young people. To bring long-term relief to the

---

KEY TERMS

Bulimia nervosa—An eating disorder characterized by binge eating and inappropriate compensatory behavior, such as vomiting, misusing laxatives, or excessive exercise.

Cognitive-behavioral therapy—A type of psychotherapy in which people learn to recognize and change negative and self-defeating patterns of thinking and behavior.

BED patient, it is critical to address the underlying psychological causes for binge eating behaviors. It appears that up to 50 percent of BED patients stop bingeing with cognitive behavioral therapy.

Parental concerns

Binge eating can lead to excessive weight, a risk for serious current and future diseases including heart disease, type 2 diabetes, and **cancer**. Overweight children also suffer from psychological distress, particularly when teased or shunned by peers. Parents should be aware that antidepressant drugs used to treat BED as of 2004 contain a warning that recommends close observation of pediatric patients treated with the drugs. In some cases, worsening depression or emergence of suicidal tendencies may occur.

See also Bulimia nervosa.

Resources

BOOKS

Gay, Kathlyn. *Eating Disorders: Anorexia, Bulimia, and Binge Eating.* Berkeley, NJ: Enslow Publishers, 2003.

Matthews, Dawn D. *Eating Disorders Sourcebook: Basic Consumer Health Information about Eating Disorders . . .* Detroit, MI: Omnigraphics, 2001.

Parker, James N., et al. *The 2002 Official Parent's Sourcebook on Binge Eating Disorders.* Boulder, CO: netLibrary, 2002.

ORGANIZATIONS

American Psychiatric Association. 1400 K Street NW, Washington DC 20005. Web site: <www.psych.org>.

American Psychological Association (APA). 750 First St. NE, Washington, DC 20002–4242. Web site: <www.apa.org>.

Eating Disorders Awareness and Prevention. 603 Stewart St., Suite 803, Seattle, WA 98101. Web site: <www.edap.org>.

National Eating Disorders Association (NEDA). 603 Stewart St., Suite 803, Seattle, WA 98101. Web site: <www.nationaleatingdisorders.org>.

Overeaters Anonymous World Service Office. 6075 Zenith Ct. NE, Rio Rancho, NM 87124. Web site: <www.overeatersanonymous.org>.

Christine Kuehn Kelly

Bipolar disorder

Definition

Bipolar, or manic-depressive disorder, is a mood disorder that causes radical emotional changes and mood swings, from manic highs to depressive lows. The majority of bipolar individuals experience alternating episodes of mania and depression.

Description

The Diagnostic and Statistical Manual of Mental Disorders, fourth edition (*DSM-IV*), the diagnostic standard for mental health professionals in the United States, defines four separate categories of bipolar disorder: bipolar I, bipolar II, cyclothymia, and bipolar not-otherwise-specified (NOS).

Bipolar I disorder is characterized by manic episodes, the "high" of the manic-depressive cycle. A person with bipolar disorder experiencing mania often has feelings of self-importance, elation, talkativeness, increased sociability, and a desire to embark on goal-oriented activities, coupled with the characteristics of irritability, impatience, impulsiveness, hyperactivity, and a decreased need for **sleep**. Usually this manic period is followed by a period of depression, although a few bipolar I individuals may not experience a major depressive episode. Mixed states, where both manic or hypomanic symptoms and depressive symptoms occur at the same time, also occur frequently with bipolar I patients (for example, depression with the racing thoughts of mania). Also, dysphoric mania is common (mania characterized by anger and irritability).

Bipolar II disorder is characterized by major depressive episodes alternating with episodes of hypomania, a milder form of mania. Bipolar depression may be difficult to distinguish from a unipolar major depressive episode. Patients with bipolar depression tend to have extremely low energy, retarded mental and physical processes, and more profound fatigue (for example, hypersomnia, a sleep disorder marked by a need for excessive sleep or sleepiness when awake) than unipolar depressives.

Cyclothymia refers to the cycling of hypomanic episodes with depression that does not reach major depressive proportions. One third of patients with cyclothymia develop bipolar I or II disorder later in life.

A phenomenon known as rapid cycling occurs in up to 20 percent of bipolar I and II patients. In rapid cycling, manic and depressive episodes must alternate frequently, at least four times in 12 months, to meet the diagnostic definition. In some cases of "ultra-rapid cycling" the patient may bounce between manic and depressive states several times within a 24-hour period. This condition is very hard to distinguish from mixed states.

Bipolar NOS is a category for bipolar states that do not clearly fit into the bipolar I, II, or cyclothymia diagnoses.

Demographics

According to the American Academy of Child and Adolescent Psychiatry, up to one third of American children and adolescents diagnosed with depression develop early onset bipolar disorder. The average age of onset of bipolar disorder is from **adolescence** through the early twenties. However, because of the complexity of the disorder, a correct diagnosis can be delayed for several years or more. In a survey of bipolar patients conducted by the National Depressive and Manic Depressive Association (MDMDA), one half of respondents reported visiting three or more professionals before receiving a correct diagnosis, and over one third reported waiting ten years or more before they were correctly diagnosed.

Causes and symptoms

The cause of bipolar disorder had not as of 2004 been clearly defined. Because two thirds of bipolar patients have a **family** history of affective or emotional disorders, researchers have searched for a genetic link to the disorder. Several studies have uncovered a number of possible genetic connections to the predisposition for bipolar disorder. A 2003 study found that **schizophrenia** and bipolar disorder could have similar genetic causes that arise from certain problems with genes associated with myelin development in the central nervous system. (Myelin is a white, fat-like substance that forms a sheath around nerve fibers.) Another possible biological cause under investigation is the presence of an excessive calcium build-up in the cells of bipolar patients. Dopamine and other neurochemical transmitters appear to be implicated in bipolar disorder, and these are under investigation as well.

Over one-half of patients diagnosed with bipolar disorder have a history of substance abuse, which may be an issue in adolescent patients. There is a high rate of association between cocaine abuse and bipolar disorder. Some studies have shown up to 30 percent of abusers meet the criteria for bipolar disorder. The emotional and physical highs and lows of cocaine use correspond to the manic depression of the bipolar patient, making the disorder difficult to diagnose.

For some bipolar patients, manic and depressive episodes coincide with seasonal changes. Depressive episodes are typical during winter and fall, and manic episodes are more probable in the spring and summer months.

Symptoms of bipolar depressive episodes include low energy levels, feelings of despair, difficulty concentrating, extreme fatigue, and psychomotor retardation (slowed mental and physical capabilities). Manic episodes are characterized by feelings of euphoria, lack of inhibitions, racing thoughts, diminished need for sleep, talkativeness, risk taking, and irritability. In extreme cases, mania can induce hallucinations and other psychotic symptoms such as grandiose delusions.

When to call the doctor

When symptoms of bipolar disorder are present, a child should be taken to a qualified medical healthcare professional as soon as possible for evaluation. If a child or teen diagnosed with bipolar disorder reveals at any time that they have had recent thoughts of self-injury or **suicide**, or if they demonstrate behavior that compromises their **safety** or the safety of others, professional assistance from a mental healthcare provider or care facility should be sought immediately.

Diagnosis

Bipolar disorder usually is diagnosed and treated by a psychiatrist and/or a psychologist. In addition to an interview with the child and her parents, several clinical inventories or scales may be used to assess the patient's mental status and determine the presence of bipolar symptoms. These include the Children's Global **Assessment** Scale (C-GAS), General Behavior Inventory (GBI), Beck Depression Inventory (BDI), **Minnesota Multiphasic Personality Inventory** Adolescent (MMPI-A), the Youth Inventory (YI-4), and the Young Mania Rating Scale (YMRS). The tests are verbal and/or written and are administered in both hospital and outpatient settings.

Bipolar symptoms often present differently in children and adolescents. Manic episodes in these age groups are typically characterized by more psychotic features than in adults, which may lead to a misdiagnosis of schizophrenia. Children and adolescents also tend to demonstrate irritability and aggressiveness instead of the elation of mania in adults. Further, symptoms tend to be chronic, or ongoing, rather than acute, or episodic. Bipolar children are easily distracted, impulsive, and hyperactive, which can lead to a misdiagnosis of attention deficit hyperactivity disorder

(ADHD). Their aggression can lead to violence, which may be misdiagnosed as a **conduct disorder**.

Psychologists and psychiatrists typically use the criteria listed in the *Diagnostic and Statistical Manual of Mental Disorders,* fourth edition (*DSM-IV*) as a guideline for diagnosis of bipolar disorder and other mental illnesses. *DSM-IV* describes a manic episode as an abnormally elevated or irritable mood lasting a period of at least one week that is distinguished by at least three of the mania symptoms: inflated **self-esteem**, decreased need for sleep, talkativeness, racing thoughts, distractibility, increase in goal-directed activity, or excessive involvement in pleasurable activities that have a high potential for painful consequences. If the mood of the patient is irritable and not elevated, four of the symptoms are required.

Although many clinicians find the criteria too rigid, a hypomanic diagnosis requires a duration of at least four days with at least three of the symptoms indicated for manic episodes (four if mood is irritable and not elevated). *DSM-IV* notes that unlike manic episodes, hypomanic episodes do not cause a marked impairment in social or occupational functioning, do not require **hospitalization**, and do not have psychotic features. In addition, because hypomanic episodes are characterized by high energy and goal-directed activities and often result in a positive outcome or are perceived in a positive manner by the patient, bipolar II disorder can go undiagnosed.

Substance abuse can mask or mimic the presence of bipolar disorder and can make diagnosis more difficult in adolescents. When substance abuse or **addiction** is present, a patient must ordinarily undergo a period of detoxification and abstinence before a mood disorder can be accurately diagnosed.

Treatment

The manic and depressive symptoms of bipolar disorder are usually controlled by a combination of prescription medications, including lithium, antipsychotics, anticonvulsants, and **antidepressants**.

Lithium

Lithium (Cibalith-S, Eskalith, Lithane, Lithobid, Lithonate, Lithotabs) is one of the oldest and most frequently prescribed drugs available for the treatment of adult bipolar mania and depression. Because the drug takes four to ten days to reach a therapeutic level in the bloodstream, it sometimes is prescribed in conjunction with neuroleptics and/or benzodiazepines to provide more immediate relief of a manic episode. Lithium also has been shown to be effective in regulating bipolar depression, but is not recommended for mixed mania. Lithium may not be an effective long-term treatment option for rapid cyclers, who typically develop a tolerance for it, or may not respond to it. Possible side effects of the drug include weight gain, thirst, **nausea**, and hand tremors. Prolonged lithium use also may cause **hyperthyroidism**.

Antipsychotics

Clozapine (Clozaril) is an atypical antipsychotic medication used to control manic episodes in adult patients who have not responded to typical mood stabilizing agents. The drug has also been a useful prophylactic, or preventative treatment, in some bipolar patients. Common side effects of clozapine include tachycardia (rapid heart rate), hypotension, **constipation**, and weight gain. Agranulocytosis, a potentially serious but reversible condition in which the white blood cells that typically fight infection in the body are destroyed, is a possible side effect of clozapine. Patients treated with the drug should undergo weekly blood tests to monitor white blood cell counts.

Risperidone (Risperdal) is another atypical antipsychotic that has been successful in controlling mania in several clinical trials when low doses were administered. The side effects of risperidone are mild compared to many other antipsychotics (constipation, coughing, **diarrhea**, dry mouth, **headache**, heartburn, increased length of sleep and dream activity, nausea, runny nose, **sore throat**, fatigue, and weight gain).

Olanzapine (Zyprexa) was approved in 2003 for use in combination with lithium or valproate for treatment of acute manic episodes associated with bipolar disorder. In 2004 it received additional approval for long-term maintenance of bipolar disorder. Possible side effects include drowsiness, **dizziness**, weight gain, dry mouth, rapid heartbeat, nausea, and muscle weakness.

Quetiapine (Seroquel) was approved by the FDA in 2004 for the treatment of acute mania associated with bipolar disorder. Potential side effects of the drug include dizziness, sleepiness, dry mouth, weight gain, and constipation.

Ziprasidone (Geodon) is a schizophrenia drug that is often prescribed to treat bipolar mania. Common side effects associated with ziprasidone include dizziness, fatigue, constipation, and rash. Unlike the other antipsychotic drugs, however, it does not promote weight gain.

Atypical antipsychotics have been associated with **hyperglycemia** (high blood sugar) and diabetes in some patients. Their use may be contraindicated (i.e., not recommended) in children and teens with type 1 or type 2 diabetes.

Anticonvulsants

Valproate (divalproex sodium, or Depakote; valproic acid, or Depakene) is one of the few drugs available that has been proven effective in treating rapid cycling bipolar and mixed states patients. It is also approved for the treatment of mania. Valproate is prescribed alone or in combination with carbamazepine and/or lithium. Stomach cramps, indigestion, diarrhea, hair loss, appetite loss, nausea, and unusual weight loss or gain are some of the common side effects of valproate. A 2003 study found that the risk of suicide from death is about two and one half times higher in people with bipolar disorder taking divalproex than those taking lithium.

Gabapentin (Neurontin) has been prescribed by some physicians for the treatment of bipolar disorder, although there is no conclusive clinical evidence as to its effectiveness.

Carbamazepine (Tegretol, Atretol) is an anticonvulsant drug usually prescribed in conjunction with other mood stabilizing agents. The drug often is used to treat bipolar patients who have not responded well to lithium therapy. Blurred vision and abnormal eye movement are two possible side effects of carbamazepine therapy. Clinical trials continue as of 2004 in an attempt to obtain FDA approval of carbamazepine for use in bipolar treatment.

Lamotrigine (Lamictal, or LTG), an anticonvulsant medication, is often used in patients with a history of rapid cycling and antidepressant-induced mania. A University of Cincinnati one-year study of the drug in patients with bipolar I disorder found that it provided sustained relief of depressive symptoms. Lamotrigine may be used in conjunction with divalproex (divalproate) and/or lithium. Possible side effects of lamotrigine include skin rash, dizziness, drowsiness, headache, nausea, and **vomiting**.

Antidepressants

Because antidepressants may stimulate manic episodes in some bipolar children and teens, their use is typically short-term. Some researchers have hypothesized that the use of antidepressants for depression may even trigger bipolar disorder in children who are genetically predisposed.

When antidepressants are prescribed for episodes of bipolar depression, they are usually selective serotonin reuptake inhibitors (SSRIs) or, less often, monoamine oxidase inhibitors (MAO inhibitors). Tricyclic antidepressants used to treat unipolar depression may trigger rapid cycling in bipolar patients and are, therefore, not a preferred treatment option for bipolar depression.

SSRIs, such as fluoxetine (Prozac), sertraline (Zoloft), and paroxetine (Paxil) regulate depression by regulating levels of serotonin, a neurotransmitter. **Anxiety**, diarrhea, drowsiness, headache, sweating, nausea, sexual problems, and insomnia are all possible side effects of SSRIs.

MAOIs such as tranylcypromine (Parnate) and phenelzine (Nardil) block the action of monoamine oxidase (MAO), an enzyme in the central nervous system. Patients taking MAOIs must cut foods high in tyramine (found in aged cheeses and meats) out of their diet to avoid hypotensive side effects.

Bupropion (Wellbutrin) is a heterocyclic antidepressant. The exact neurochemical mechanism of the drug is not known, but it has been effective in regulating bipolar depression in some patients. Side effects of bupropion include agitation, anxiety, confusion, tremor, dry mouth, fast or irregular heartbeat, headache, and insomnia.

In 2004, 10 antidepressant drugs (including fluoxetine, sertraline, paroxetine, and bupropion) came under scrutiny when the FDA issued a public health advisory and announced it was requesting the addition of a warning statement in drug labeling that outlined the possibility of worsening depression and increased suicide risk. These developments were the result of several clinical studies that found that some children taking these antidepressants had an increased risk of suicidal thoughts and actions. The FDA announced at the time that the agency would embark on a more extensive analysis of the data from these clinical trials and decide if further regulatory action was necessary.

Electroconvulsive therapy

Electroconvulsive therapy (ECT) has a high success rate for treating both unipolar and bipolar depression and mania. However, because of the convenience of drug treatment and the stigma sometimes attached to ECT therapy, ECT usually is employed after all pharmaceutical treatment options have been explored. ECT is given under anesthesia, and patients are given a muscle relaxant medication to prevent convulsions. The treatment consists of a series of electrical pulses that move into the brain through electrodes on the patient's head. Although the exact mechanisms behind the success of ECT therapy are not known, it is believed that this electrical current alters the electrochemical processes of the brain, consequently relieving depression. Headaches, muscle soreness, nausea, and confusion are possible side effects immediately following an ECT procedure. Temporary memory loss has also been reported in ECT patients. In bipolar patients, ECT is often used in conjunction with drug therapy.

Adjunct therapies

Other drugs that may be use as adjunct therapies (i.e., in addition to regular treatment) to treat manic episodes include the following:

- Calcium channel blockers: Nimodipine (Nimotop, Admon) and verapamil (Calan, Covera, Isoptin), typically used to treat angina and hypotension, have been found effective in a few small studies, for treating rapid cyclers.

Calcium channel blockers stop the excess calcium build up in cells that is thought to be a cause of bipolar disorder. They usually are used in conjunction with other drug therapies such as carbamazepine or lithium.

- Long-acting benzodiazepines: Lorazepam (Ativan), clonazepam (Klonapin), and alprazolam (Xanax) are used for rapid treatment of manic symptoms to calm and sedate patients until mania or hypomania have waned and mood stabilizing agents can take effect. Sedation is a common effect, and clumsiness, lightheadedness, and slurred speech are other possible side effects of benzodiazepines.

- Neuroleptics: Chlorpromazine (Thorazine) and haloperidol (Haldol) are also used to control mania while a mood stabilizer such as lithium or valproate takes effect. Because the side effects of these drugs can be severe (difficulty in speaking or swallowing, paralysis of the eyes, loss of balance control, **muscle spasms**, severe restlessness, stiffness of arms and legs, tremors in fingers and hands, twisting movements of body, and weakness of arms and legs), benzodiazepines are generally preferred over neuroleptics.

Because bipolar disorder is thought to be biological in nature, therapy and/or counseling is recommended as a companion to, but not a substitute for, pharmaceutical treatment of the disease. Psychotherapy, such as cognitive-behavioral therapy, can be a useful tool in helping patients and their families adjust to the disorder, in encouraging compliance to a medication regimen, and in reducing the risk of suicide. A 2003 report revealed that people on medication for bipolar disorder had better results if they also participated in family-focused therapy.

Alternative treatment

General recommendations include maintaining a calm environment, avoiding overstimulation, getting plenty of rest, regular **exercise**, and proper diet. Biofeedback may be effective in helping some children and adolescents control symptoms such as irritability, poor self control, racing thoughts, and sleep problems. A diet low in vanadium (a mineral found in meats and other foods) and high in vitamin C may be helpful in reducing depression.

Repeated transcranial magnetic stimulation (rTMS) is a new and still experimental treatment for the depressive phase of bipolar disorder. In rTMS, a large magnet is placed on the patient's head and magnetic fields of different frequency are generated to stimulate the left front cortex of the brain. Unlike ECT, rTMS requires no anesthesia and does not induce seizures.

Prognosis

While most children show some positive response to treatment, response varies widely, from full recovery to

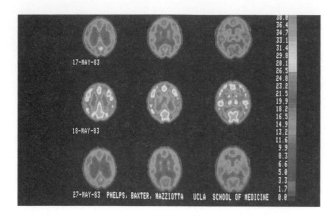

Bipolar disorder shown in a series of positron emission tomography (PET) scans. *(Dr. Michael E. Phelps.)*

a complete lack of response to all drug and/or ECT therapy. Drug therapies frequently need adjustment to achieve the maximum benefit for the patient. Bipolar disorder is a chronic recurrent illness in over 90 percent of those afflicted, and one that requires lifelong observation and treatment after diagnosis. Patients with untreated or inadequately treated bipolar disorder have a suicide rate of 15 to 25 percent and a nine-year decrease in life expectancy. With proper treatment, the life expectancy of the bipolar patient will increase by nearly seven years and work productivity increases by 10 years.

According to the American Psychiatric Association, bipolar children and adolescents experiencing a manic episode have a one-year recovery rate of 37.1 percent and a relapse rate of 38.3 percent. Discontinuing lithium treatment too early may increase the risk of relapse in adolescents with bipolar disorder. In one 1990 study, 92 percent of adolescents hospitalized for mania who stopped taking the drug experienced a relapse of symptoms within 18 months of discharge, compared to 37 percent of those who stayed on lithium therapy.

Children and teens with bipolar disorder are at a greater risk for substance abuse than their non-bipolar peers, and substance abuse can worsen or complicate bipolar treatment. In a 1999 two-year follow-up study of adolescents hospitalized for manic episodes, patients who had ongoing drug or alcohol abuse problems had more manic episodes and poorer functioning than those patients who were not substance abusers. In addition, some studies have indicated that children who develop bipolar disorder in adolescence are more likely to develop a substance abuse problem than those who have early-onset of bipolar disorder in childhood.

Prevention

The ongoing medical management of bipolar disorder is critical for preventing relapse, or recurrence, of manic episodes. Even in carefully controlled treatment programs, bipolar patients may experience recurring episodes of the disorder. Education in the form of psychotherapy or self-help groups is crucial for training bipolar patients and their caregivers to recognize signs of mania and depression and to take an active part in their treatment program.

Parental concerns

Children with bipolar disorder may require special accommodations in the classroom. Section 504 of the Rehabilitation Act of 1973 enables parents to develop both a Section 504 plan (which describes a child's medical needs) and an individualized education plan (IEP), which describes what special accommodations a child requires to address those needs. The IEP may cover issues such as allowing extra time on tests, modifying assignments, and providing home tutoring or a classroom aide when necessary.

Children who are diagnosed with bipolar disorder should be reassured that the condition is due to factors beyond their control (i.e., genetics, neurochemical imbalance) rather than any fault of their own. For those children and teens who feel stigmatized or self-conscious about their diagnosis, arranging psychotherapy sessions outside school hours may lessen their burden. Any child on prescription medication for bipolar disorder should be carefully monitored for any sign of side effects, and these should be reported to their physician when they do occur. A dosage adjustment or medication change may be warranted if side effects are disruptive or potentially dangerous.

See also Depressive disorders; Minnesota Multiphasic Personality Inventory.

Resources

BOOKS

American Psychiatric Association. *Diagnostic and Statistical Manual of Mental Disorders* 4th edition, Text Revision (DSM-IV-TR). Washington, DC: American Psychiatric Press Inc., 2000.

Papolos, Demitri, and Janice Papolos. *The Bipolar Child*, 2nd ed. New York: Broadway Books, 2002.

PERIODICALS

American Psychiatric Association. "Practice Guideline for the Treatment of Patients with Bipolar Disorder (Revision)." *American Journal of Psychiatry* 149, no. 4. (April 2002): 1–50.

"Education and Your Bipolar Child." *Brown University Child and Adolescent Behavior Letter* 20, no. 7 (July 2004): 9.

"Lithium and Risk of Suicide." *The Lancet* (September 20, 2003): 969.

"Schizophrenia and Bipolar Disorder Could Have Similar Genetic Causes." *Genomics & Genetics Weekly* (September 26, 2003): 85.

KEY TERMS

Affective disorder—An emotional disorder involving abnormal highs and/or lows in mood. Now termed mood disorder.

Anticonvulsant—Drugs used to prevent convulsions or seizures. They often are prescribed in the treatment of epilepsy.

Antipsychotic drug—A class of drugs used to control psychotic symptoms in patients with psychotic disorders such as schizophrenia and delusional disorder. Antipsychotics include risperidone (Risperdal), haloperidol (Haldol), and chlorpromazine (Thorazine).

Benzodiazepine—One of a class of drugs that have a hypnotic and sedative action, used mainly as tranquilizers to control symptoms of anxiety. Diazepam (Valium), alprazolam (Xanax), and chlordiazepoxide (Librium) are all benzodiazepines.

***Diagnostic and Statistical Manual of Mental Disorders, Fourth Edition* (DSM-IV)**—This reference book, published by the American Psychiatric Association, is the diagnostic standard for most mental health professionals in the United States.

Electroconvulsive therapy (ECT)—A psychological treatment in which a series of controlled electrical impulses are delivered to the brain in order to induce a seizure within the brain. This type of therapy is used to treat major depression and severe mental illness that does not respond to medications.

Hyperthyroidism—A condition characterized by abnormal over-functioning of the thyroid glands. Patients are hypermetabolic, lose weight, are nervous, have muscular weakness and fatigue, sweat more, and have increased urination and bowel movements. Also called thyrotoxicosis.

Hypomania—A milder form of mania that is characteristic of bipolar II disorder.

Mania—An elevated or euphoric mood or irritable state that is characteristic of bipolar I disorder. This state is characterized by mental and physical hyperactivity, disorganization of behavior, and inappropriate elevation of mood.

Mixed mania—A mental state in which symptoms of both depression and mania occur simultaneously. Also called mixed state.

Neurotransmitter—A chemical messenger that transmits an impulse from one nerve cell to the next.

Psychomotor retardation—Slowed mental and physical processes characteristic of a bipolar depressive episode.

Sherman, Carl. "Bipolar's Clinical, Financial Impact Widely Missed. (Prevalence May Be Greater than Expected)." *Clinical Psychiatry News* (August 2002): 6.

ORGANIZATIONS

American Psychiatric Association. 1000 Wilson Blvd., Suite 1825, Arlington, VA 22209. Web site: <www.psych.org>.

American Psychological Association (APA). 750 First St. NE, Washington, DC 20002–4242. Web site: <www.apa.org>.

Child and Adolescent Bipolar Foundation (CABF). 1187 Wilmette Ave., PMB #331, Wilmette, IL 60091. Web site: <www.bpkids.org>.

Depression and Bipolar Support Alliance (DBSA). 730 N. Franklin St., Suite 501, Chicago, IL 60610. Web site: <www.dbsalliance.org>.

National Alliance for the Mentally Ill (NAMI). Colonial Place Three, 2107 Wilson Blvd., Ste. 300, Arlington, VA 22201–3042. Web site: <www.nami.org>.

National Institute of Mental Health (NIMH). Office of Communications, 6001 Executive Boulevard, Room 8184, MSC 9663, Bethesda, MD 20892–9663. Web site: <www.nimh.nih.gov>.

WEB SITES

U.S. Food and Drug Administration. "Antidepressant Use in Children, Adolescents, and Adults." Available online at <www.fda.gov/cder/drug/antidepressants/default.htm> (accessed November 9, 2004).

Paula Ford-Martin
Teresa Odle

Birth control *see* **Contraception**

Birth control pills *see* **Oral contraceptives**

Birth order

Definition

Birth order is the chronological order of sibling births in a **family**.

Description

Alfred Adler (1870–1937) was a pioneer in the study of birth order. His research suggested that the position a child had by the order of birth significantly affected the child's growth and personality. Research in the late twentieth century and early twenty-first century shows even greater influence, contributing to **intelligence**, career choice, and, to a certain degree, success in adulthood.

Being born first, last, or somewhere in the middle of itself is not of significance. What matters is how that birth order affects how a child is treated by parents and other siblings and how that child feels about it. Other factors also influence the child's socialization and the parents' expectations.

Birth spacing, gender, physical attributes, and being a twin also affect personality formation and the interpretation of birth order and behavior. These factors influence how parents treat children and how each child is viewed by the other siblings.

Birth spacing changes the dynamics of strict birth order, too. If there is a gap of five or more years between children, each child may be treated as an only child or as a firstborn. If there is a large gap between groups of children in a large family, each group may be treated as a separate birth order family. For example, if child 1, 2, and 3 are three years apart and there is a gap of six years before child 4 is born and child 5 and 6 follow in two year intervals, then child 1, 2, and 3 form a birth order grouping of firstborn, middle, and last, and child 4, 5, and 6 form another grouping of first, middle, and lastborn.

Gender also has a major impact on how a child is treated within the birth order arrangement. The firstborn of either gender, no matter where in the sibling order the child falls, will often be treated as a firstborn. For example if a family has two daughters then has two sons, the first daughter and the first son will be treated as firstborns. The daughter is the true firstborn, but the first son is the first child in the household to be treated with what the family perceives as maleness. Historically, this held true and usually contributed to older sisters not having a claim to inheritance because of their gender.

In addition, if there is only one daughter in a family of three boys, the daughter will often be treated as a first born no matter where in the birth order she is born. The simple fact that she is the only one of her sex allows her to take on the characteristics of a firstborn and be treated as such. This obviously also applies to one son in a household of daughters.

That sense of specialness also applies to children's physical attributes and conditions. If a child of any birth order has a serious medical problem or a physical or mental disability, that child rises either to firstborn status or lastborn status because parental attention is placed on this special child. Robust health and beauty can also skew birth order expectations. For example, if there are

two sons and the younger is bigger and more athletic, the younger may be treated as a firstborn because parental favor and expectations are higher for this child. Likewise, if the younger of two daughters is extremely pretty and her older sister is plain, the younger may either be treated as a favored lastborn or as a high-achieving firstborn.

Twins and other birth multiples also skew birth order predictions. Each twin or multiple grouping has its own birth rank. The firstborn twin usually takes on leadership roles for the twin pair. The secondborn usually is more compliant and willing to follow. For the single birth children born after twins or other multiples, birth order is skewed because the twins or multiples have become special children and, in the case of multiples, are their own birth order unit.

Birth order research focuses on five ordinal birth positions: firstborn, secondborn, middle, last, and only children.

Firstborns

In general, firstborn children have been found to be responsible, assertive, task-oriented, perfectionistic, and supporters of authority. Because they often look after their younger siblings, they get experience leading and mentoring others, often rising to leadership positions as adults. Nearly half of all U.S. presidents were firstborns; only four were lastborns. Studies have also linked firstborn children with higher academic achievement and possibly higher intelligence scores when compared to later-born children. This may be due to more exposure to adult language and greater interactions with parents. Firstborns often choose professions that require precision, such as careers in science, medicine, law, engineering, computer science, or accounting.

Firstborns can harbor some resentment toward siblings because parental attention has to be shared. They strive to hang onto parental affection by conforming, either to their parents' wishes, their teachers', or society's. If this does not bring the attention they want, some firstborns defy authority and misbehave or rebel.

Secondborns and middle children

Many secondborns are also middle children. They often report feeling inferior to older children because they do not possess their sibling's advanced abilities. Sometimes, they are very competitive with their firstborn sibling. Others choose to focus their energies in areas different from those in which their older sibling is already established. This competition with firstborns drives secondborns and middleborns to innovation, doing or being different from their older siblings in order to make themselves stand out in the family dynamic. In truth, they often are more competent at an earlier age than their older siblings because they have had their example to follow.

Middle children can feel forgotten or overlooked because of the attention or demands of either the first-borns or the lastborns. Some of these children never seem to find their place in the social order, and they try to rebel or misbehave in order to draw attention to themselves. Some of these troubled middle children bully younger siblings or children at school.

Other middle children capitalize on the injustice they feel as children and become trial lawyers or social activists because such roles allow them to fight against other social injustices. Some middleborns become very socially skilled because they have learned to negotiate and compromise daily with their siblings and their parents. Some of these children are often called the peace-makers of the household.

Middle children have also been found to succeed in team **sports**, and both they and lastborns have been found to be more socially adjusted if they come from large families.

Lastborns

Lastborns are generally considered to be the family "baby" throughout their lives. Because of nurturing from many older family members and the example of their siblings, lastborns from large families tend to develop strong social and coping skills and may even be able to reach some milestones earlier. As a group, they have been found to be the most successful socially and to have the highest **self-esteem** of all the birth positions.

Youngest children may feel weak and helpless because they compare themselves with older siblings who are able to do more things physically and socially. They may feel that they always have more growing up to do in order to have the privileges they see their older siblings have. Some lastborns develop self-esteem problems if older siblings or parents take power away from these last-borns so that they cannot make decisions or take responsibility. Because of this powerlessness, some lastborns may be grandiose, with big plans that never work out.

Some lastborns transfer this powerlessness into a personal asset by becoming the boss of the family, coyly eliciting or openly demanding their own way. Some families jump to and cater to these lastborns.

Other lastborns engage in **sibling rivalry** because of the injustices they think they experience because they are the youngest. Some ally with firstborns against middleborns.

Only children

Only children may demonstrate characteristics of firstborns and lastborns. Firstborns, after all, are only children until the first sibling is born. Only children grow up relating to adults in the family but have trouble relating to peers. However, this changes as they reach adulthood and get along well with adults.

Only children are achievement-oriented and most likely to attain academic success and attend college. They may also be creative. But only children can be pampered and spoiled as lastborns and can be self-centered. They may rely on service from others rather than their exert their own efforts. They sometimes please others if it suits them but may also be uncooperative. They can also be over-protected.

Some only children become hypercritical, not tolerating mistakes or failure in themselves or others. They can also transform this perfectionist tendency into rescuing behavior, agonizing over the problems of others and rushing to take over and solve everything without letting others help themselves.

Common problems

Sibling rivalry is a normal part of family life. All children become jealous of the love and attention that siblings receive from parents and other adults. When a new baby comes into the family, older children feel betrayed by their parents and may become angry, directing their anger first toward the parents and later toward the intruder who is usurping their position. Jealousy, resentment, and competition are most intense between siblings spaced less than three years apart. Although a certain amount of sibling rivalry is unavoidable, there are measures that parents can take to reduce its severity and its potential effects on their children.

An older child should be prepared for a new addition to the family by having the situation explained and being told in advance about who will take care of her while her mother is in the hospital having the baby. The child's regular routine should be disturbed as little as possible; it is preferable for the child to stay at home and under the care of the father or another close family member. If there is to be a new babysitter or other caretaker unknown to the child, it is helpful for them to meet at least once in advance. If sibling visits are allowed, the child should be taken to visit the mother and new baby in the hospital.

Once the new baby is home, it is normal for an older child to feel hurt and resentful at seeing the attention lavished on the newcomer by parents, other relatives, and family friends. It is not uncommon for the emotional turmoil of the experience to cause disturbances in eating or sleeping. Some children regress, temporarily losing such attainments as weaning, bowel and bladder control, or clear speech, in an attempt to regain lost parental attention by becoming babies again themselves.

There are a number of ways to ease the unavoidable jealousy of children whose lives have been disrupted by the arrival of a younger sibling. When friends or relatives visit to see the new baby, parents can make the older child feel better by cuddling him or giving him special attention, including a small present to offset the gifts received by the baby. The older child's self-esteem can be bolstered by involving him in the care of the newborn in modest ways, such as helping out when the baby is being diapered or dressed or helping push the stroller. The older child should be made to feel proud of the achievements and responsibilities that go along with his more advanced age—things the new baby cannot do yet because he or she is too young. Another way to make older children feel loved and appreciated is to set aside some quality time to spend alone with each of them on a regular basis. It is also important for parents to avoid overtly comparing their children to each other, and every effort should be made to avoid favoritism.

In general, the most stressful aspect of sibling rivalry is fighting. Physical, as opposed to verbal, fights usually peak before the age of five. It is important for parents not to take sides but rather to help children work out disagreements, calling for a "time out" for feelings to cool down, if necessary. Over-insistence that siblings share can also be harmful. Children need to retain a sense of individuality by developing boundaries with their siblings in terms of possessions, territory, and activities. Furthermore, it is especially difficult for very young children to share their possessions.

Parents should take time to praise cooperation and sharing between siblings as a means of positive reinforcement. The fact that siblings quarrel with each other does not necessarily mean that they will be inconsiderate, hostile, or aggressive in their dealings with others outside the family. The security of family often makes children feel free to express feelings and impulses they are unable to express in other settings.

Parental concerns

Firstborns

Firstborns often feel pressure to succeed or perform well, either by parents or through their own inner drives. They often are called on to take care of younger siblings or do chores because they are responsible. Firstborns also feel pressure to be good examples for their siblings.

Some parents are quick to punish firstborns for not measuring up. Others constantly correct firstborns because they think it will help these children succeed. If firstborns cannot meet these expectations or **fear** that they cannot, they often become depressed and sometimes resort to **suicide** to escape the **pain** they feel.

Parents need to realize that firstborns need not be perfect in order to succeed. They are already eager to please and criticism should be limited to broad strokes rather than focus on minor imperfections. Responsibilities should be meted out in small batches according to their age appropriate abilities. In addition, parents should acknowledge firstborns as people, not the products of their efforts.

When placed in leadership or mentoring roles with their younger siblings, some firstborns may demonstrate aggressive or domineering behavior. They may boss their brothers or sisters around or lord it over them. These behaviors can also transfer to the school setting, making these children uncooperative with their peers. Parents should monitor leadership behavior to make sure these children learn to lead with kindness while respecting other people's feelings.

Secondborns and middle children

Secondborns and middle children often feel invisible. Parents need to make a special effort to seek out their opinions in family discussions. Finding out what special talents or interests these children have and encouraging them through classes or events makes them feel like they matter and are as important as firstborns or lastborns. All of the children in family then feel special and loved as the unique individuals they are.

Lastborns

Youngest children are not usually very responsible because they have not been given the opportunity. Parents can foster responsibility and self- reliance by giving even the youngest child some responsibility, such as setting the table or putting clean clothing in their dresser drawers.

If lastborns are being bullied by older siblings, parents need to step in. Children need help developing strategies for working out difficulties. They can also benefit from hearing parents tell older siblings that it took time for them to do the things that lastborns are struggling to do.

Only children

Parents need to help their only children socialize with other children. They also need to help them accept imperfection in themselves and others by being tolerant of it themselves. In order to keep only children from being

KEY TERMS

Birth multiples—Children born in multiple births; e.g. twins, triplets, quads, etc.

Sibling rivalry—Competition among brothers and sisters in a nuclear family. It is considered to be an important influence in shaping the personalities of children who grow up in middle-class Western societies but less relevant in traditional African and Asian cultures.

rescuers, parents need to help these children develop patience and understanding of differences in others.

See also Sibling rivalry.

Resources

BOOKS

Isaacson, Cliff, and Kris Radish. *The Birth Order Effect: How to Better Understand Yourself and Others.* Avon, MA: Adams Media Corp., 2002.

Konig, Karl. *Brothers and Sisters: The Order of Birth in the Family.* Edinburgh, Scotland: Floris Books, 2002.

Krohn, Katherine E. *Everything You Need to Know about Birth Order.* New York: Rosen, 2000.

Leman, Kevin. *The Birth Order Book: Why You Are the Way You Are.* Grand Rapids, MI: Revell, 2004.

Richardson, Donald W. *Birth Order and You: Are You the Oldest, Middle, and Youngest Child?* Bellingham, WA: Self-Counsel Press, 2004.

PERIODICALS

"Birth Order May Affect Career Interests." *USA Today* 131, i. 2687 (August 2002): 11.

Renkl, Margaret. "Oldest, Youngest, or in Between: How Your Child's Birth Order Can Affect Her Personality—and What You Can Do to Influence Its Impact." *Parenting* 16, i. 5 (June 1, 2002): 82+.

Janie Franz

Birthmarks

Definition

Birthmarks are areas of discolored and raised spots found on the skin. Birthmarks are groups of malformed pigment cells or blood vessels.

Description

Vascular birthmarks are benign (noncancerous) skin growths comprised of rapidly growing or poorly formed blood vessels or lymph vessels. Found at birth (congenital) or developing later in life (acquired) anywhere on the body, they range from faint spots to dark swellings covering wide areas.

Birthmarks are most often found on the head or neck but can be anywhere on the body. The common appearing birthmark is a tiny red or purple mark. A specific group of birthmarks, called "strawberry spot," "port-wine stain," and "stork bite," are medically called hemangiomas. These birthmarks are essentially an overgrowth of blood vessel tissue in a specific area on the body.

Many birthmarks disappear without any special treatment, but some remain the same size or enlarge. In rare cases, the strawberry mark may cover large area of the face and body.

Demographics

About one in every three infants has a birthmark. Twice as many girls as boys have birthmarks. For appearance or cosmetic reasons, medical treatment may be necessary if the birthmark does not disappear on its own. Treatment for most birthmarks is delayed until the child is older.

About 10 in every 100 babies have vascular birthmarks. Skin angiomas, also called vascular nevi (marks), are overgrown blood vessel tissue (hemangiomas) or lymph vessel tissue (lymphangiomas) beneath the skin's surface. Hemangiomas are on the face and neck (60%), trunk (25%), or the arms and legs (15%). Congenital hemangiomas, 90 percent of which appear at birth or within the first month of life, grow quickly and disappear over time. They occur in 1–10 percent of full-term infants, and 25 percent of premature infants. About 65 percent are capillary hemangiomas (strawberry marks), 15 percent are cavernous (deep) hemangiomas, and the rest are mixtures.

Vascular malformations are poorly formed blood or lymph vessels that appear at birth. One type, the salmon patch (nevus simplex), is a pink mark comprised of dilated capillaries (also called a stork bite). It appears on the back of the neck in 40 percent of newborns and on the forehead and eyelids (also called an angel's kiss) in 20 percent. Stork bites appear in 70 percent of white and 60 percent of black newborns.

Fewer than 1 percent of newborns have port-wine stains (nevus flammeus), birthmarks. These vascular malformations of dilated capillaries appear in the upper and lower layers of the skin on the face, neck, arms, and legs.

Nevus flammeus are often permanent; these flat pink to red marks develop into dark purple bumpy areas in later life; 85 percent appear on only one side of the body.

Causes and symptoms

As of 2004 there were no known causes for congenital skin angiomas or birthmarks. Most birthmarks do not hurt; most do not cause any health problems and do not need treatment. Birthmarks may be an inherited weakness of vessel walls.

The birthmark is discoloration of the skin that starts before or just after birth. These marks can appear to be a red rash or lesion. Birthmarks tend to be different color from the skin. They are mostly flat, but some are raised, bumpy, and hairy. Many birthmarks fade or disappear altogether during the **preschool** years, but some never disappear completely.

Diagnosis

Patients are treated by pediatricians, dermatologists (skin disease specialists), plastic surgeons (doctors who specialize in correcting abnormalities of the appearance), and ophthalmologists (eye disease specialists), depending on the type and severity of the birthmark.

Angiomas and vascular malformations are not difficult to diagnose. The doctor takes a medical history and performs a physical examination, including visual inspection and palpation (feeling with the hands) of the marks. The skin is examined for discoloration, scarring, bleeding, infection, or ulceration. The type, location, size, number, and severity of the marks are recorded. The doctor may empty the mark of blood by gentle pressure. Biopsies or specialized **x rays** or scans of the abnormal vessels and their surrounding areas may confirm the diagnosis. Patients with port-wine stains near the eye may need skull x rays, **computed tomography** scans, and vision and central nervous system tests. Most insurance plans pay for diagnosis and treatment of these conditions.

Types of birthmarks

There are many types of birthmarks. Certain types of raised or flat red, pink, or bluish birthmarks need close watching by a qualified medical expert as the child grows. Description of common variations in skin color and birthmarks is as follows:

- Port-wine stains: These flat, pink, red, or purple colored birthmarks are caused by a concentration of dilated tiny blood vessels call capillaries. The stains usually occur on the head, face, and neck. They may be small, or they may cover large areas of the child's body. Port-wine stains do not change color when

gently pressed and do not disappear over time. They may become darker and may bleed when the child is older or as an adult. Skin-colored cosmetics will cover small port-wine stains. The most effective way of treating port-wine stains is with a special laser when the child is older.

- Stork bites or salmon patches (called angel kisses when occurring on forehead or eyelids): These small pink or red patches are often found on the baby's eyelids or forehead, between the eyes, on the upper lip, and back of the neck. The name comes from the marks on the back of the neck where, as the myth goes, a stork may have picked up the baby. This concentration of immature blood vessels is most visible when the baby is crying. Most of these fade and disappear.

- Strawberry hemangiomas: These bright or dark red, raised or swollen, bumpy areas look like a strawberry. Hemangiomas are a concentration of tiny, immature blood vessels. Most of these occur on the head. They may not appear at birth but often develop in the first two months. Strawberry hemangiomas are more common in premature babies and in girls. These birthmarks often grow in size for several months (they stop growing around the first birthday), then the birthmarks gradually begin to fade. By age five, the birthmarks fade in half the children affected, and they disappear by age nine.

- Mongolian spots: These blue or purple-colored splotches on the baby's lower back or buttocks occur on over 80 percent of African-American, Asian, and Indian babies. They also occur in dark-skinned babies of all races. The spots, a concentration of pigmented cells, usually disappear in the first four years of life.

Treatment

Treatment choices for skin angiomas and vascular malformations depend on their type, location, severity, and degree of disfigurement.

Watchful waiting

Birthmarks are regularly examined until they disappear or require treatment. This approach is appropriate for most hemangiomas, since many eventually shrink by themselves.

Complications

When birthmarks (hemangiomas) form in an area that can interfere with the baby's normal development (for example, blocking vision or causing difficulty breathing or hearing), treatment may be necessary. If the mark begins bleeding, parents should apply pressure firmly to control the bleeding. About 5 percent of

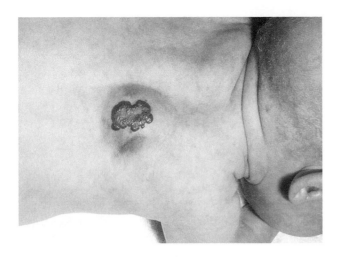

Strawberry nevus, commonly known as a strawberry mark, on the back of an infant. (© Mike Devlin/Photo Researchers, Inc.)

hemangiomas become ulcerated, especially if they are in an area that is under pressure or touched often.

Port-wine stains are on the forehead, sides of the face, or eyelids. They are occasionally linked with an increase of blood vessels in the brain or glaucoma. An increase in pressure in the eye can lead to blindness if not treated. Port-wine stains on the legs or arm may be linked to an overgrowth of that extremity.

Other complications, including congestive heart failure from large lesions, Kippel-Trenaunay-Weber syndrome, and Kasabach-Merrit syndrome, are rare.

Drugs

CORTICOSTEROIDS Parents may consider treatment for hemangiomas that do not shrink or fade by the time the child is four years old. The treatments include the use of high doses of steroids (either orally or injected into the lesion) to stop the growth. Steroids prevent the marks from growing; they do not make the birthmarks smaller. Other treatments include interferon alpha, laser therapy, and surgical removal.

INTERFERON ALPHA-2A This drug reduces cell growth in vascular marks that affect vision and that are unresponsive to corticosteroids. Given in daily injections under the skin, the response rate is 50 percent after seven months. Side effects include **fever**, chills, muscle and joint **pain**, vision disorders, low white and red blood cell counts, fatigue, elevated liver enzymes, **nausea**, blood clotting problems, and nerve damage.

ANTIBIOTICS Oral or topical (applied to the skin) **antibiotics** are prescribed for infected marks.

Surgery

Birthmarks may be removed by laser surgery. Lasers create intensive heat that destroys abnormal blood vessels beneath the skin, without damaging normal skin. Laser surgery is not usually painful but can be uncomfortable. Children are usually sedated or anesthetized. Healing occurs within two weeks. Side effects include bruising, skin discoloration, swelling, crusting, and minor bleeding.

In some cases, the birthmark can be surgically excised, or removed. Under local or general anesthesia, the skin is cut and vascular marks or their scars are removed. The cut is repaired with stitches or skin clips.

Cryosurgery is another technique used to remove small birthmarks. Vascular marks can be frozen with a substance that is sprayed onto the skin. **Wounds** heal with minimal scarring.

Birthmarks can also be treated by electrodesiccation. In this procedure, affected vessels are destroyed with the current from an electric needle.

Other treatments

Other treatments include the following:

- Sclerotherapy: Injection of a special solution causes blood clotting and shrinkage with little scarring. Side effects include stinging, swelling, bruising, scarring, muscle cramping, and allergic reactions. This treatment is used most commonly for spider angiomas.

- Embolization: A special material is injected into the vessel blocks blood flow, which helps control blood loss from a bleeding birthmark or reduces the size of inoperable growths. A serious side effect, **stroke**, can occur if a major blood vessel becomes blocked.

- Make-up: Special brands designed to cover birthmarks are sold. Two of these are Covermark and Derma blend.

- Cleaning and compression: Bleeding marks are cleaned with soap and water or hydrogen peroxide, and compressed with a sterile bandage for five to 10 minutes.

Prognosis

Many birthmarks fade or disappear before the child is school age. Some may never go away. Most of them are benign and do not need treatment. Babies with birthmarks are examined and diagnosed by the doctor. Those birthmarks that cause complications in normal childhood growth and development may require medical and surgical treatment.

KEY TERMS

Angioma—A tumor (such as a hemangioma or lymphangioma) that mainly consists of blood vessels or lymphatic vessels.

Benign—In medical usage, benign is the opposite of malignant. It describes an abnormal growth that is stable, treatable, and generally not life-threatening.

Capillaries—The tiniest blood vessels with the smallest diameter. These vessels receive blood from the arterioles and deliver blood to the venules. In the lungs, capillaries are located next to the alveoli so that they can pick up oxygen from inhaled air.

Corticosteroids—A group of hormones produced naturally by the adrenal gland or manufactured synthetically. They are often used to treat inflammation. Examples include cortisone and prednisone.

Cutaneous—Pertaining to the skin

Cutaneous angiolipomas—Benign growths consisting of fat cells and blood vessels just underneath the skin.

Hemangioma—A benign skin tumor composed of abnormal blood vessels.

Hereditary—Something which is inherited, that is passed down from parents to offspring. In biology and medicine, the word pertains to inherited genetic characteristics.

Incidence—The rate of development of a disease in a given population over time.

Kasabach-Merrit syndrome—A combination of rapidly enlarging hemangioma and thrombocytopenia; it is usually clinically evident during early infancy, but occasionally the onset is later. The hemangiomas are large and may increase in size rapidly and may cause severe anemia in infants.

Lymphangioma—A benign skin tumor composed of abnormal lymph vessels.

Lymphatic vessels—Part of the lymphatic system, these vessels connect lymph capillaries with the lymph nodes. They carry lymph, a thin, watery fluid resembling blood plasma and containing white blood cells. Also called lymphatic channels.

Nevus—Any pigmented blemish of the skin present at birth, including moles and various types of birthmarks.

Seizure—A sudden attack, spasm, or convulsion.

Subcutaneous—Referring to the area beneath the skin.

Syndrome—A group of signs and symptoms that collectively characterize a disease or disorder.

Ulcer—A site of damage to the skin or mucous membrane that is characterized by the formation of pus, death of tissue, and is frequently accompanied by an inflammatory reaction.

Vascular malformation—Abnormally formed blood or lymph vessels.

The various types of birthmarks have different prognoses:

- Capillary hemangiomas: Fewer than 10 percent need treatment. Without treatment, 50 percent disappear by age five; 70 percent by age seven; and 90 percent by age nine. No skin changes are found in half, while others have some discoloration, scarring, or wrinkling. From 30 to 90 percent respond to oral corticosteroids, and 45 percent respond to injected corticosteroids; 50 percent respond to interferon Alpha-2a. About 60 percent improve after laser surgery.

- Cavernous hemangiomas: Many do not disappear and are complicated by ulceration or infection. About 75 percent respond to laser surgery but have scarring.

- Spider angiomas: These fade in children but may recur. About 90 percent respond to sclerotherapy, electrodesiccation, or laser therapy.

- Cherry angiomas: These are easily removed by electrodesiccation.

- Lymphangiomas: These marks require surgery.

- Salmon patches on eyelid marks: These marks disappear by six to 12 months of age, and forehead marks fade by age six; however, 50 percent of stork bites on the neck persist into adulthood.

- Port-wine stains (flat birthmarks): These marks are easily covered with make-up. Treatment during infancy or childhood improves results. About 95 percent of the stains respond to FPDL surgery with minimal scarring; 25 percent will disappear, and

70 percent will partially disappear. For unknown reasons, 5 percent show no improvement.

Prevention

Birthmarks are congenital hemangiomas or vascular malformations and cannot be prevented.

Parental concerns

Though no treatment is needed in many of these cases, a child with a hemangiomas should be watched carefully by a doctor skilled in pediatric skin disorders. The hardest part for parents is to wait until the birthmarks begin to fade on their own or, in the case of a birthmark that does not fade, waiting until the child is old enough for surgical management.

When to call the doctor

Parents should report any birthmarks they notice to the child's pediatrician. They should call the pediatrician if they notice bleeding from the birthmark, if a sore develops on the birthmark, if the mark is growing larger.

Resources

BOOKS

Birthmarks: A Medical Dictionary, Bibliography, and Annotated Research Guide to Internet References. San Diego, CA: Icon Group International, 2004.

Thompson, June. *Spots, Birthmarks, and Rashes: The Complete Guide to Caring for Your Child's Skin.* Westport, CT: Firefly Books, 2003.

WEB SITES

"Birthmarks: Red." *MedlinePlus*, April 17, 2003. Available online at <www.nlm.nih.gov/medlineplua/ency/article/001440.htm> (accessed December 12, 2004).

Aliene S. Linwood, RN, DPA, FACHE

Bisexuality *see* **Homosexuality and Bisexuality**

Bites and stings

Definition

Humans can be injured by the bites or stings of many kinds of insects and animals. These range from the bites from a neighbor's dog or cat to bites from fellow humans and spiders to the stings from bees, wasps, snakes, and marine animals such as jellyfish and stingrays.

Description

Mammals

DOGS With more than 60 million pet dogs in the United States, plus thousands of strays, it is not surprising that an estimated 4.7 million Americans a year are bitten by a dog. Although most dog-bite injuries are minor, about 400,000 children seek medical attention for a dog bite every year, according to the Centers for Disease Control and Prevention. Of those injured, about 386,000 require emergency treatment and about a dozen die from their injuries. However, most of the injuries suffered by children seeking treatment in emergency rooms are of low severity and result in treatment and quick release from the hospital.

Children aged five to nine are most likely to be injured by dog bites. Males are more likely than females to require emergency treatment. About two-thirds of injuries to children aged four years or younger are to the head and neck.

Studies also show that most dog bites are from pets or other dogs known to the child who is bitten. In fact, more than half of the bites seen by emergency departments occur at home. Many of the bites result from attempting to break up fights between animals.

CATS Although cats are found in nearly one third of U.S. households, cat bites are far less common than dog bites. According to one study, cats inflict perhaps 400,000 harmful bites in the United States each year. The tissue damage caused by cat bites is usually limited but carries a high risk of infection. Whereas the infection rate for dog bite injuries is 15 to 20 percent, the infection rate for cat bites is 30 to 40 percent. Cat bites are also more likely to be provoked. A typical person who has been bitten is a young girl playing with a pet.

HUMANS Bites from mammals other than dogs and cats are uncommon, with one exception—human bites. There are approximately 70,000 human bites each year in the United States. Because the human mouth contains a multitude of potentially harmful microorganisms, human bites are more infectious than those of most other mammals.

Arthropods

Arthropods are invertebrates belonging to the phylum *Arthropoda*, the jointed-leg, spineless creatures of the world. *Arthropoda* include insects, arachnids (spiders), crustaceans, and other subgroups. There are more than 700,000 species in all. The list of arthropods that bite or sting humans is extensive and includes lice, bedbugs, fleas, mosquitoes, black flies, ants, chiggers, ticks, centipedes, scorpions, and other species. Spiders, ants, bees, and wasps are the four kinds of arthropod that most often bite people.

SPIDERS In the United States, only two kinds of venomous spider are truly dangerous: black widow spiders and brown recluse (violin or fiddle) spiders. The black widow, which is found in every state but Alaska, prefers dark, dry places, such as barns, garages, and outhouses, and also lives under rocks and logs. Disturbing a female black widow or its web may provoke a bite. Brown recluse spiders also prefer sheltered places, including clothing, and may bite if disturbed.

ANTS, BEES, AND WASPS Ants, bees, and wasps will sting to defend their nests or if they are disturbed. Ants sting more than 9.3 million people each year. Other hymenoptera account for more than 1 million stings annually. Species common to the United States include fire ants, honeybees, bumblebees, yellow jackets, bald-faced hornets, brown hornets, and paper wasps. The Africanized bee species, also called "killer bees," is as of 2004 found in the United States.

More than 50 Americans die each year after being stung by a bee or wasp. Almost all of those deaths are the result of allergic reactions to the sting and not of exposure to the venom itself.

Snakes

There are 20 species of venomous snakes in the United States. These snakes are found in every state except Maine, Alaska, and Hawaii. Each year about 8,000 Americans receive a venomous snakebite, but no more than about 15 die, mostly from rattlesnake bites.

The venomous snakes of the United States are divided into two families: the Crotalidae (pit vipers) and the Elapidae. Pit vipers, named after the small heat-sensing pit that lies between each eye and nostril, are responsible for about 99 percent of the venomous snakebites suffered by Americans. Rattlesnakes, copperheads, and cottonmouths (also called water moccasins) are pit vipers. This family of snakes delivers its venom through two long, hinged fangs in the upper jaw. Some pit vipers carry potent venom that can threaten the brain and spinal cord. The venom of others, such as the copperhead, is less harmful.

The Elapidae family includes two kinds of venomous coral snakes indigenous to the southern and western states. Because coral snakes are creatures that come out only at night, they almost never bite humans; they are held responsible for approximately 25 bites a year in the United States. Coral snakes also have short fangs and a small mouth, which lowers the risk of a bite actually forcing venom into the human body. However, their venom is highly poisonous.

Marine animals

Several varieties of marine animal may bite or sting. Jellyfish and stingrays are two kinds that pose a threat to people who live or vacation in coastal communities.

Causes and symptoms

Mammals

DOGS A typical dog bite results in a laceration, tear, puncture, or crush injury. Bites from large, powerful dogs may even cause **fractures** and dangerous internal injuries. Also, dogs trained to attack may bite repeatedly during a single episode. Infected bites usually cause **pain**, inflammation of the connective tissues, and a pus-filled discharge at the wound site within eight to 24 hours. Most infections are confined to the wound site, but many of the microorganisms in the mouths of dogs can cause systemic and possibly life-threatening infections. Examples are bacteremia and **meningitis**, especially severe in children with health conditions that increase their susceptibility to infection. **Rabies** is rare among pet dogs in the United States, most of which have been vaccinated against the disease. **Tetanus** is also rare but can be transmitted by a dog bite if the victim is not immunized.

CATS The mouths of cats and dogs contain many of the same microorganisms. Cat scratches and bites are also capable of transmitting the *Bartonella henselae* bacterium, which can lead to **cat-scratch disease**, an unpleasant but usually not life-threatening illness.

Cat bites are mostly found on the arms and hands. Sharp cat teeth typically leave behind a deep puncture wound that can reach muscles, tendons, and bones, which are vulnerable to infection because of their comparatively poor blood supply. This is why cat bites are much more likely to become infected than dog bites. Also, people are less inclined to view cat bites as dangerous enough to require immediate attention. The risk that infection has set in by the time a medical professional is consulted is, therefore, greater.

HUMANS Humans bites result from fights, sexual activity, medical and dental treatment, and seizures. Bites also may be sign of **child abuse**. Children often bite other children, but those bites are hardly ever severe. Human bites are capable of transmitting a wide range of dangerous diseases, including **hepatitis B**, syphilis, and **tuberculosis**.

Human bites fall into two categories: occlusional bites and clenched-fist injuries. Occlusional bites result from an actual bite and present a lower risk of infection. The clenched-fist injury happens when a fist hits a mouth during a fight and may lead to an infected hand.

Arthropods

SPIDERS As a rule, children rarely see a black widow bite them, nor do they feel the bite when it happens. The first (and possibly only) evidence that a child has been bitten may be a mild swelling of the injured area and two red puncture marks. Within a short time, however, some victims begin to experience severe **muscle cramps** and rigidity of the abdominal muscles. Other possible symptoms include excessive sweating, **nausea**, **vomiting**, headaches, and vertigo, as well as breathing, vision, and speech problems.

A brown recluse spider's bite can lead to necrotic arachnidism, in which the tissue in an area of up to several inches around the bite becomes necrotic (dies), producing an open sore that can take months or years to disappear. In most cases, however, the bite simply produces a hard, painful, itchy, and discolored area that heals without treatment in two to three days. The bite may also be accompanied by **fever**, chills, edema (an accumulation of excess tissue fluid), **nausea and vomiting**, **dizziness**, muscle and joint pain, and a rash.

BEES, WASPS AND ANTS The familiar symptoms of bee, wasp, and ant stings include pain, redness, swelling, and itchiness in the area of the sting. Multiple stings can have much more severe consequences, such as **anaphylaxis**, a life-threatening allergic reaction that occurs in children who are hypersensitive to the venom.

The fire ant sting usually produces immediate pain followed by a red, swollen area that disappears within 45 minutes. A blister or a red, swollen, itchy patch then develops. The blister may rupture and become infected.

Snakes

Venomous pit viper bites usually begin to swell within ten minutes and sometimes are painful. Other symptoms include skin blisters and discoloration, weakness, sweating, nausea, faintness, dizziness, bruising, and tender lymph nodes. Severe **poisoning** can also lead to **tingling** in the scalp, fingers, and toes, muscle contractions, an elevated heart rate, rapid breathing, large drops in body temperature and blood pressure, vomiting of blood, and coma.

Many pit viper and coral snake bites (20%) fail to poison their victim or introduce only a small amount of venom into the victim's body. The **wounds**, however, can still become infected by the harmful microorganisms that snakes carry in their mouths.

Coral snake bites are painful but may be hard to see. One to seven hours after the bite, the victim begins to experience the effects of the venom, which include tingling at the wound site, weakness, nausea, vomiting, excessive salivation, and irrational behavior. Major nerves of the body can become paralyzed for six to 14 days, causing double vision, difficulty swallowing and speaking, respiratory failure, and other problems. Six to eight weeks may be needed before normal muscular strength is regained.

Marine animals

JELLYFISH Jellyfish venom is delivered by barbs called nematocysts, which are located on the creature's tentacles and penetrate the skin of people who brush up against them. Instantly painful and itchy red lesions usually result. The pain can continue up to 48 hours. Severe cases may lead to skin necrosis, **muscle spasms and cramps**, vomiting, nausea, **diarrhea**, headaches, excessive sweating, and other symptoms. In rare instances, cardiorespiratory (heart/lung) failure may also occur.

STINGRAYS Tail spines are the delivery mechanism for stingray venom. Deep puncture wounds result that can cause an infection if pieces of spine become embedded in the wound. A typical stingray injury scenario involves a person who inadvertently steps on a resting stingray and is lashed in the ankle by its tail. Stingray venom produces immediate, excruciating pain that lasts several hours. Sometimes the victim suffers a severe reaction, including vomiting, diarrhea, hemorrhage (bleeding), a drop in blood pressure, and cardiac arrhythmia (disordered heart beat).

Diagnosis

Mammals

DOGS Gathering information on the circumstances of a dog attack is a crucial part of treatment. Medical professionals need to know:

• when the attack occurred (The chances of infection increase dramatically if the wound has been left untreated for more than eight hours.)

- what led to the attack (Unprovoked attacks are more likely to be associated with rabies.)
- the child's general health, including tetanus immunization history and information about **allergies** to medication and pre-existing health problems that may increase the risk of infection

A physical examination requires careful scrutiny of the wound, with special attention to possible bone, joint, ligament, muscle, tendon, nerve, or blood-vessel damage caused by deep punctures or severe crush injuries. Serious hand injuries should be evaluated by a specialized surgeon. Most of the time, laboratory tests for identifying the microorganisms in bite wounds are performed if infection is present. **X rays** and other diagnostic procedures may also be necessary.

CATS The diagnostic procedures used for dog bites also apply to cat bites.

HUMAN Testing the blood of a person who has been bitten for immunity to hepatitis B and other diseases is always necessary after a human bite. Ideally, the biter should be tested as well for the presence of transmissible disease. Physicians can advise if this is necessary if the biter is another small child. Medical professionals will also look for indications of child abuse when evaluating human bites.

Arthropods

SPIDERS Because bites from widow spiders and brown spiders require different treatment, capturing and identifying the spider helps to establish diagnosis.

Snakes

Diagnosis relies on a physical examination of the victim, information about the circumstances of the bite, and a look at the snake itself (if it can safely be killed and brought in for identification). Blood tests and urinalysis supply important data on the victim's condition. Chest x rays and electrocardiography (a procedure for measuring heart activity) may also be necessary.

Treatment

Mammals

DOGS Minor dog bites can be treated at home. The American Academy of Family Physicians recommends gently washing the wound with soap and water and then applying pressure to the injured area with a clean towel to stop the bleeding. The next step is to apply antibiotic ointment and a sterile bandage to the wound. To reduce swelling and fend off infection, ice should be applied and the injured area kept elevated above the level of the heart. The wound should be cleaned and covered with ointment twice a day until it heals.

Any dog bite that does not stop bleeding after 15 minutes of pressure must be seen by a medical professional. The same is true for bites that are deep or gaping; for bites to the head, hands, or feet; and for bites that may have broken a bone, damaged nerves, or caused a major injury of another kind. Bite victims must also watch for infection. A fever is a sign of infection, as are redness, swelling, warmth, increased tenderness, and pus at the wound site. Children with diabetes or **cancer** who have not had a tetanus shot in five years or who have a medical problem that can increase susceptibility to infection should seek medical treatment no matter how minor the bite appears.

Medical treatment of dog bites involves washing the wound with an anti-infective solution. Removal of dead and damaged tissue (under local, regional, or general anesthetic) may be required after the wound has been washed, and any child whose tetanus shots are not up-to-date should receive a booster injection. Some wounds are left open and allowed to heal on their own, while others require stitches (stitching may be delayed a few days if infection is a concern). Many emergency departments prescribe **antibiotics** for all people with dog bites, but some researchers suggest that antibiotics are usually unnecessary and should be limited to those whose injuries or other health problems make them likely candidates for infection. A follow-up visit after one or two days is generally required for anyone who has received bite treatment.

CATS Because of the high risk of infection, parents of children who are bitten by a cat should always call the child's doctor. Most cat scratches do not require professional medical treatment unless the wound appears infected or the scratched person has a weakened immune system.

Medical treatment for cat bites generally follows the procedures used for dog bites. Experts advise, however, that cat-bite wounds should always be left open to prevent infection. Persons who have been bitten by cats generally receive antibiotics as a preventive measure.

HUMANS Human bites should always be examined by a doctor. Such bites are usually treated with antibiotics and left open because of the high risk of infection. A person who has been bitten may also require immunization against hepatitis B and other diseases. This is usually not necessary if the biter is a child.

Arthropods

SPIDERS No spider bite should be ignored. The antidote for severe widow spider bites is a substance called antivenin, which contains antibodies taken from the blood serum of horses injected with spider venom. Doctors exercise caution in using antivenin, however, because it can trigger anaphylactic shock, a potentially deadly (though treatable) allergic reaction, and serum sickness, an inflammatory response that can give rise to joint pain, a fever, **rashes**, and other unpleasant, though rarely serious, consequences.

An antivenin for brown spider bites exists as well, but it is not readily available in the United States. The drug dapsone, used to treat leprosy, can sometimes stop the tissue death associated with a brown spider bite. Necrotic areas (areas of dead tissue) may need debridement (removal of dead and damaged tissue) and skin grafts. Pain medications, **antihistamines**, antibiotics, and tetanus shots are a few of the other treatments that are sometimes necessary after a bite from a brown spider or widow spider.

BEES, WASPS, AND ANTS Most stings can be treated at home. A stinger that is stuck in the skin can be scraped off with a blade, fingernail, credit card, or piece of paper (using tweezers may push more venom out of the venom sac and into the wound). The area should be cleaned and covered with an ice pack. Aspirin and other pain medications, oral antihistamines, and calamine lotion are good for treating minor symptoms. Putting meat tenderizer on the wound has no effect.

Persons who have been stung and experience an allergic reaction or who are at risk due to their medical history require immediate medical attention. The danger signs, which usually begin ten minutes after an individual is stung (though possibly not for several hours) include nausea, faintness, chest pain, abdominal cramps, diarrhea, and difficulty swallowing or breathing.

Snakes

Although most snakes are not venomous, any snakebite should immediately be examined at a hospital. While waiting for emergency help to arrive, the victim should wash the wound site with soap and water and then keep the injured area still and at a level lower than the heart. Ice should never be used on the wound site nor should attempts be made to suck out the venom. Making a cut at the wound site is also dangerous. It is important to stay calm and wait for emergency medical aid if it can

arrive quickly. Otherwise, the child should proceed directly to a hospital.

When the child arrives at a hospital, the medical staff must determine whether the bite was inflicted by a venomous snake and, if so, whether envenomation (venom is injected into the victim) occurred and how much venom the person has received. Patients may develop low blood pressure, abnormal blood clotting, or severe pain, all of which require aggressive treatment. Fortunately, the effects of some snake bites can be counteracted with antivenin. Minor rattlesnake envenomations can be successfully treated without antivenin, as can copperhead and watermoccasin bites. However, coral snake envenomations and the more dangerous rattlesnake envenomations require antivenin, sometimes in large amounts. Other treatment measures include antibiotics to prevent infection and a tetanus booster injection.

Marine animals

JELLYFISH Vinegar and other acidic substances are used to neutralize jellyfish nematocysts still clinging to the skin, which are then scraped off. Anesthetic ointments, antihistamine creams, and steroid lotions applied to the skin are sometimes beneficial. Other measures may be necessary to counter the many harmful effects of jellyfish stings, which, if severe, require emergency medical care.

STINGRAYS Stingray wounds should be washed with saltwater and then soaked in very hot water for 30 to 90 minutes to neutralize the venom. Afterwards, the wound should be examined by a doctor to ensure that no pieces of spine remain.

Prognosis

Mammals

Prompt treatment and recognizing that even apparently minor bites can have serious consequences are the keys to a good outcome after a mammal bite. Infected bites can be fatal if neglected. Surgery and **hospitalization** may be needed for severe bites.

Arthropods

SPIDERS Even without treatment, most children recover from black widow bites after two to three days. In the case of brown spider bites, the risk of death is greatest for children, though rare.

BEES, WASPS, AND ANTS The pain and other symptoms of a bee or wasp sting normally fade away after a few hours. Children who are allergic to such stings, however, can experience severe and occasionally fatal anaphylaxis (life-threatening allergic reaction to bites and stings).

Snakes

A snakebite victim's chances of survival are excellent if medical aid is obtained in time. Some bites, however, can result in amputation, permanent deformity, or loss of function in the injured area, although this is rare.

Marine animals

STINGRAYS Stingray venom kills its human victims on rare occasions.

Prevention

Mammals

DOGS The risk of a dog-bite injury can be reduced by avoiding sick or stray dogs, staying away from dogfights (children can get bitten when they try to separate the animals), and not behaving in ways that might provoke or upset dogs, such as wrestling with them or bothering them while they are sleeping, eating, or looking after their puppies. Infants and young children must never be left alone with a dog. Pit bulls, rottweilers, and German shepherds (responsible for nearly half of all fatal dog attacks in the United States in 2000) are potentially dangerous pets in households where children live or visit. For all breeds of dog, obedience training as well as spaying or neutering lessen the chances of **aggressive behavior**.

CATS Prevention involves warning children to stay away from strange cats and to avoid rough **play** and other behavior that can anger cats and cause them to bite.

Arthropods

SPIDERS Common-sense precautions include clearing webs out of garages, out buildings, and other places favored by venomous spiders; teaching children to keep their hands away from places where spiders may be lurking; and, when camping or vacationing, checking clothing, shoes, and sleeping areas.

BEES, WASPS, AND ANTS Children should avoid the nests of bees, wasps, and ants. When playing outside in an area where these insects are found, children also should avoid eating sweet food or wearing bright clothing, perfumes, or cosmetics that attract bees, wasps, and ants.

Emergency medical kits containing self-administrable epinephrine to counter anaphylactic shock are

Mosquito bite behind the ear of a girl. (© Deb Yeske/Visuals Unlimited.)

available for allergic children and should be carried by them at all times. Children who are suspected of being allergic should consult an allergist about shots that can reduce reactions to bee and wasp venom (venom immunotherapy). Venom immunotherapy in children leads to a significantly lower risk of reaction to stings up to ten to 20 years after treatment is stopped.

Snakes

Snakes should not be kept as pets. Measures such as mowing the lawn, keeping hedges trimmed, and removing brush from the yard also discourages snakes from living close to human dwellings. Tongs should be used to move brush, lumber, and firewood, to avoid exposing one's hands to snakes that might be lying underneath. Children should be prevented from playing in weedy, vacant lots and other places where snakes may live. Leather boots and long pants offer hikers and campers some protection from bites. Approaching a snake, even a dead one, can be dangerous since the venom of recently killed snakes may still be active.

Marine animals

JELLYFISH Prevention of jellyfish stings includes obeying posted warning signs at the beach. Also, jellyfish tentacles may be transparent and up to 120 feet (36.5 m) long; therefore, great caution must be exercised whenever a jellyfish is sighted nearby.

STINGRAYS Kicking the sand while walking through shallow areas that may be inhabited by stingrays will disturb the water, causing the animal to move before it can be stepped on.

KEY TERMS

Anaphylaxis—Also called anaphylactic shock; a severe allergic reaction characterized by airway constriction, tissue swelling, and lowered blood pressure.

Antibiotics—Drugs that are designed to kill or inhibit the growth of the bacteria that cause infections.

Antibody—A special protein made by the body's immune system as a defense against foreign material (bacteria, viruses, etc.) that enters the body. It is uniquely designed to attack and neutralize the specific antigen that triggered the immune response.

Antihistamine—A drug used to treat allergic conditions that blocks the effects of histamine, a substance in the body that causes itching, vascular changes, and mucus secretion when released by cells.

Arachnid—A large class of arthropods that includes spiders, scorpions, mites, and ticks.

Arachnidism—Poisoning resulting from the bite or sting of an arachnid.

Bacteremia—Bacterial infection of the blood.

Blood serum—A component of blood.

Immune system—The system of specialized organs, lymph nodes, and blood cells throughout the body that work together to defend the body against foreign invaders (bacteria, viruses, fungi, etc.).

Killer bees—Hybrids of African bees accidentally introduced into the wild in South and North America in 1956 and first reported in Texas in 1990. They were first imported by Brazilian scientists attempting to create a new hybrid bee to improve honey production.

Lymph nodes—Small, bean-shaped collections of tissue located throughout the lymphatic system. They produce cells and proteins that fight infection and filter lymph. Nodes are sometimes called lymph glands.

Pus—A thick, yellowish or greenish fluid composed of the remains of dead white blood cells, pathogens, and decomposed cellular debris. It is most often associated with bacterial infection.

Parental concerns

Children frequently play in areas where they can be exposed to stings and bites. Children who are sensitive to certain stings and bites are at risk for serious anaphylactic reactions.

See also Insect sting allergy.

Resources

BOOKS

Holve, Steve. "Envenomations." In *Cecil Textbook of Medicine*, 21st ed. Edited by Lee Goldman and J. Claude Bennett. Philadelphia: W.B. Saunders, 2000, pp. 2174–78.

"Overview of the 2002 Household Pet Survey." In *U.S. Pet Ownership and Demographics Sourcebook*. Schaumburg, IL: American Veterinary Medical Association, 2002.

Nagami, Pamela. *Bitten: True Medical Stories of Bites and Stings*. London: St. Martin's Press, 2004.

Royston, Angela. *Stings and Bites*. Oxford, UK: Heinemann Library, 2004.

Siverstein, Alvin, et al. *Bites and Stings*. Danbury, CT: Scholastic Library Publishing, 2002.

PERIODICALS

Graudins, A., et al. "Red-back spider (Latrodectus hasselti) antivenom prevents the toxicity of widow spider venoms." *Annals of Emergency Medicine* 37 (2001): 154–60.

Jarvis, R. M., et al. "Brown recluse spider bite to the eyelid." *Ophthalmology* 107 (2000): 1492–96.

Metry, D. W., and A. A. Hebert. "Insect and arachnid stings, bites, infestations, and repellents." *Pediatric Annals* 29 (2000): 39–48.

Sams, H. H. "Nineteen documented cases of Loxosceles reclusa envenomation." *Journal of the American Academy of Dermatology* 44 (2001): 603–08.

Sams, H. H., et al. "Necrotic arachnidism." *Journal of the American Academy of Dermatology* 44 (2001): 561–73.

ORGANIZATIONS

American Academy of Emergency Medicine. 611 East Wells Street, Milwaukee, WI 53202. Web site: <www.aaem.org>.

American Academy of Family Physicians. 11400 Tomahawk Creek Parkway, Leawood, KS 66211–2672. Web site: <www.aafp.org>.

American Medical Association. 515 N. State Street, Chicago, IL 60610. Web site: <www.ama-assn.org>.

Christine Kuehn Kelly

Biting *see* **Aggressive behavior**

Bladder anomalies *see* **Congenital bladder anomalies**

Bleeding disorders *see* **Coagulation disorders**

Blended family *see* **Stepfamilies**

Blood sugar tests

Definition

Blood sugar or plasma glucose tests are used to determine the concentration of glucose in blood. These tests are used to detect an increased blood glucose (**hyperglycemia**) or a decreased blood glucose (**hypoglycemia**).

Purpose

Blood glucose tests are used in a variety of situations, including the following:

- Screening persons for **diabetes mellitus**: The American Diabetes Association (ADA) recommends that a fasting plasma glucose (fasting blood sugar) be used to diagnose diabetes. If the person already has symptoms of diabetes, a blood glucose test without fasting, called a casual plasma glucose test, may be performed. In difficult diagnostic cases, a glucose challenge test called a two-hour oral glucose tolerance test is recommended. If the result of any of these three tests is abnormal, it must be confirmed with a second test performed on another day. The same test or a different test can be used, but the result of the second test must be abnormal as well in order to establish a diagnosis of diabetes.

- Blood glucose monitoring: Daily measurement of whole blood glucose identifies diabetics who require intervention to maintain their blood glucose within an acceptable range as determined by their physician. The Diabetes Control and Complications Trial (DCCT) demonstrated that persons with diabetes who maintained blood glucose and glycated hemoglobin (hemoglobin with glucose bound to it) at or near normal decreased their risk of complications by 50 to 75 percent. Based on results of this study, the American Diabetes Association (ADA) recommends routine glycated hemoglobin testing to measure long-term control of blood sugar.

- Diagnosis and differentiation of hypoglycemia: Low blood glucose may be associated with symptoms such as confusion, memory loss, and seizure. Demonstration that such symptoms are the result of hypoglycemia requires evidence of low blood glucose at the time of symptoms and reversal of the symptoms by glucose. In documented hypoglycemia, blood glucose tests are used along with measurements of insulin and C-peptide (a fragment of proinsulin) to differentiate between fasting and postprandial (after a meal) causes.

Description

The body uses glucose to produce the majority of the energy it needs to function. Glucose is absorbed from the gastrointestinal tract directly and is also derived from digestion of other dietary carbohydrates. It is also produced inside cells by the processes of glycogen breakdown (glycogenolysis) and reverse glycolysis (gluconeogenesis). Insulin is made by the pancreas and facilitates the movement of glucose from the blood and extracellular fluids into the cells. Insulin also promotes cellular production of lipids and glycogen and opposes the action of glucagons, which increases the formation of glucose by cells.

Diabetes may result from a lack of insulin or a subnormal response to insulin. There are three forms of diabetes: Type I or insulin dependent (IDDM), type II or noninsulin dependent (NIDDM), and gestational diabetes (GDM). Type I diabetes usually occurs in childhood and is associated with low or absent blood insulin and production of ketones even in the absence of stressed metabolic conditions. It is caused by autoantibodies to the islet cells in the pancreas that produce insulin, and persons must be given insulin to control blood glucose and prevent ketosis. Type II accounts for 85 percent or more of persons with diabetes. It usually occurs after age 40 and is usually associated with **obesity**. Persons who have a deficiency of insulin may require insulin to maintain glucose, but those who have a poor response to insulin may not. Ketosis does not develop under normal metabolic conditions but may occur with stress. Gestational diabetes is a form of glucose intolerance that first appears during pregnancy. It usually ends after delivery, but over a 10-year span approximately 30 to 40 percent of females with gestational diabetes go on to develop noninsulin dependent diabetes.

There are a variety of ways to measure a person's blood glucose.

Whole blood glucose tests

Whole blood glucose testing can be performed by a person in his or her home, or by a member of the healthcare team outside the laboratory. The test is usually performed using a drop of whole blood obtained by finger puncture. Care must be taken to wipe away the first drop of blood because this is diluted with tissue fluid. The second drop is applied to the dry reagent test strip or device.

Fasting plasma glucose test

The fasting plasma glucose test requires an eight-hour fast. The person must have nothing to eat or drink except water. The person's blood is usually collected by a nurse or phlebotomist by sticking a needle into a vein. Either serum, the liquid portion of the blood after it clots, or plasma may be used. Plasma is the liquid portion of unclotted blood that is collected. The ADA recommends a normal range for fasting plasma glucose of 55–109 mg/dL. A glucose level equal to greater than 126 mg/dL is indicative of diabetes. A fasting plasma glucose level of 110–125 gm/dL is referred to as "impaired fasting glucose."

Oral glucose tolerance test (OGTT)

The oral glucose tolerance test is done to see how well the body handles a standard amount of glucose. There are many variations of this test. A two-hour OGTT as recommended by the ADA is described below. The person must have at least 150 grams of carbohydrate each day, for at least three days before this test. The person must take nothing but water and abstain from **exercise** for 12 hours before the glucose is given. At 12 hours after the start of the fast, the person is given 75 grams of glucose to ingest in the form of a drink or standardized jelly beans. A healthcare provider draws a sample of venous blood two hours following the dose of glucose. The serum or plasma glucose is measured. A glucose concentration equal to or greater than 200 mg/dL is indicative of diabetes. A level below 140 mg/dL is considered normal. A level of 140–199 mg/dL is termed "impaired glucose tolerance."

The glycated (glycosylated) hemoglobin test is used to monitor the effectiveness of diabetes treatment. Glycated hemoglobin is a test that indicates how much glucose was in a person's blood during a two- to three-month window beginning about four weeks prior to sampling. The test is a measure of the time-averaged blood glucose over the 120-day life span of the red blood cells. The normal range for glycated hemoglobin measured as HbA_{1c} is 3 to 6 percent. Values above 8 percent indicate that a hyperglycemic episode occurred sometime during the window monitored by the test (two to three months beginning four weeks prior to the time of blood collection).

The ADA recommends that glycated hemoglobin testing be performed during a person's first diabetes evaluation, again after treatment is begun and glucose levels are stabilized, then repeated semiannually. If the person does not meet treatment goals, the test should be repeated quarterly.

A related blood test, fructosamine assay, measures the amount of albumin in the plasma that is bound to glucose. Albumin has a shorter half-life than red blood cells, and this test reflects the time-averaged blood glucose over a period of two to three weeks prior to sample collection.

Precautions

Diabetes must be diagnosed as early as possible. If left untreated, it results in progressive vascular disease that may damage the blood vessels, nerves, kidneys, heart, and other organs. Brain damage can occur from glucose levels below 40 mg/dL and coma from levels above 450 mg/dL. For this reason, plasma glucose levels below 40 mg/dL or above 450 mg/dL are commonly used as alert values. Point-of-care and home glucose monitors measure glucose in whole blood rather than plasma and are accurate generally within a range of glucose concentration between 40 and 450 mg/dL. In addition, whole blood glucose measurements are generally 10 percent lower than serum or plasma glucose.

Other endocrine disorders and several medications can cause both hyperglycemia and hypoglycemia. For this reason, abnormal glucose test results must be interpreted by a physician.

Glucose is a labile (affected by heat) substance; therefore, plasma or serum must be separated from the blood cells and refrigerated as soon as possible. Splenectomy can result in an increase and hemolytic anemia can result in a decrease in glycated hemoglobin.

Exercise, diet, anorexia, and **smoking** affect the results of the oral glucose tolerance test. Drugs that decrease tolerance to glucose and affect the test include steroids, **oral contraceptives**, estrogens, and thiazide diuretics.

Preparation

Blood glucose tests require either whole blood, serum, or plasma collected by vein puncture or finger puncture. No special preparation is required for a casual blood glucose test. An eight-hour fast is required for the fasting plasma or whole-blood glucose test. A 12-hour fast is required for the two-hour OGTT and three-hour OGTT tests. In addition, the person must abstain from exercise in the 12-hour fasting period. Medications known to affect carbohydrate metabolism should be discontinued three days prior to an OGTT test if possible, and the person must maintain a diet of at least 150 grams of carbohydrate per day for at least three days prior to the fast.

Aftercare

After the test or series of tests is completed (and with the approval of his or her doctor), the person should eat, drink, and take any medications that were stopped for the test.

The patient may feel discomfort when blood is drawn from a vein. Bruising may occur at the puncture site, or the person may feel dizzy or faint. Pressure should be applied to the puncture site until the bleeding stops to reduce bruising. Warm packs can also be placed over the puncture site to relieve discomfort.

Diabetic children learning how to monitor glucose levels with a blood test. (© *Roger Ressmeyer/Corbis.*)

Risks

The patient may experience weakness, fainting, sweating, or other reactions while fasting or during the test. If this occurs, he or she should immediately inform the physician or nurse.

Normal results

Normal values listed below are for children. Results may vary slightly from one laboratory to another depending upon the method of analysis used.

- fasting plasma glucose test: 55–109 mg/dL

- oral glucose tolerance test at two hours: less than 140 mg/dL

- glycated hemoglobin: 3–6 percent

- fructosamine: 1.6–2.7 mmol/L for adults (5% lower for children)

- gestational diabetes screening test: less than 140 mg/dL

- cerebrospinal glucose: 40–80 mg/dL

- serous fluid glucose: equal to plasma glucose

- synovial fluid glucose: within 10 mg/dL of the plasma glucose

- urine glucose (random semiquantitative): negative

For the diabetic person, the ADA recommends an ongoing blood glucose goal of less than or equal to 120 mg/dL.

The following results are suggestive of diabetes mellitus and must be confirmed with repeat testing:

- fasting plasma glucose test: greater than or equal to 126 mg/dL

- oral glucose tolerance test at two hours: equal to or greater than 200 mg/dL

- casual plasma glucose test (nonfasting, with symptoms): equal to or greater than 200 mg/dL

Parental concerns

The needle used to withdraw the blood only causes **pain** for a moment. If a child needs to take glucose tests

KEY TERMS

Diabetes mellitus—The clinical name for common diabetes. It is a chronic disease characterized by the inability of the body to produce or respond properly to insulin, a hormone required by the body to convert glucose to energy.

Glucose—A simple sugar that serves as the body's main source of energy.

Glycated hemoglobin—A test that measures the amount of hemoglobin bound to glucose. It is a measure of how much glucose has been in the blood during a two to three month period beginning approximately one month prior to sample collection.

regularly at home, the parent will need to keep track of the testing schedule and the results.

When to call a doctor

If the needle puncture site continues to bleed, or if hours or days later the site looks infected (red and swollen), then a doctor should be contacted.

See also Diabetes.

Resources

BOOKS

Chernecky, Cynthia C., and Barbara J. Berger. *Laboratory Tests and Diagnostic Procedures*, 3rd ed. Philadelphia: Saunders, 2001.

Henry, John B., ed. *Clinical Diagnosis and Management by Laboratory Methods*, 20th ed. Philadelphia: Saunders, 2001.

Kee, Joyce LeFever. *Handbook of Laboratory and Diagnostic Tests*, 4th ed. Upper Saddle River, NJ: Prentice Hall, 2001.

Wallach, Jacques. *Interpretation of Diagnostic Tests*, 7th ed. Philadelphia: Lippincott Williams & Wilkens, 2000.

ORGANIZATIONS

American Diabetes Association (ADA). National Service Center, 1660 Duke St., Alexandria, VA 22314. Web site: <www.diabetes.org/>.

Centers for Disease Control and Prevention (CDC). Division of Diabetes Translation, National Center for Chronic Disease Prevention and Health Promotion. TISB Mail Stop K-13, 4770 Buford Highway NE, Atlanta, GA 30341–3724. Web site: <www.cdc.gov/diabetes>.

National Diabetes Information Clearinghouse (NDIC). 1 Information Way, Bethesda, MD 20892–3560. Web site: <www.niddk.nih.gov/health/diabetes/ndic.htm>.

National Institute of Diabetes and Digestive and Kidney Diseases (NIDDK). National Institutes of Health, Building 31, Room 9A04, 31 Center Drive, MSC 2560, Bethesda, MD 208792–2560. Web site: <www.niddk.nih.gov>.

WEB SITES

"Glucose Test." *Medline Plus.* Available online at <www.nlm.nih.gov/medlineplus/ency/article/003482.htm< (accessed November 29, 2004).

Mark A. Best

Body piercing *see* **Piercing and tattoos**

Bonding

Definition

Bonding is the formation of a mutual emotional and psychological closeness between parents (or primary caregivers) and their newborn child. Babies usually bond with their parents in the minutes, hours, or days following birth.

Description

Bonding is essential for survival. The biological capacity to bond and form attachments is genetically determined. The drive to survive is basic in all species. Infants are defenseless and must depend on a caring adult for survival. The baby's primary dependence and the maternal response to this dependence causes bonding to develop.

Bonding and attachment are terms that describe the affectional relationships between parents and the infants. An increased awareness of the importance of bonding has led to significant improvements in routine birthing procedures and postpartum parent-infant contact. Bonding begins rapidly, shortly after birth, and reflects the feelings of parents toward the newborn; attachment involves reciprocal feelings between parent and infant and develops gradually over the first year. The focus of this entry is bonding in the newborn period. Attachment develops over the larger period of infancy and is treated in a separate entry.

Many parents, mothers in particular, begin bonding with their child before birth. The physical dependency the fetus has with the mother creates a basis for emotional and psychological bonding after birth. This attachment provides the foundation that allows babies to thrive in the world. When the umbilical cord is cut at birth, physical attachment to the mother ceases, and emotional and psychological bonding begins. A firm bond between mother and child affects all later development, and it influences how well children will react to new experiences, situations, and stresses.

Bonding research

American pediatricians John Kennell and Marshall Klaus pioneered scientific research on bonding in the 1970s. Working with infants in a neonatal intensive care unit, they noted that infants were taken away from their mothers immediately after birth for emergency medical procedures. These babies remained in the nursery for several weeks before being allowed to go home with their families. Although the babies did well in the hospital, a troubling percentage of them seemed not to prosper at home and were even victims of battering and abuse. Kennell and Klaus also noted the mothers of these babies were often uncomfortable with them, sometimes not believing that their babies had survived birth. Even mothers who had successfully raised previous infants have special difficulties when their children had been in the intensive care nursery. Kennell and Klaus surmised the separation immediately after birth interrupted a fundamental relationship between the mother and the new baby. They experimented with giving mothers of both premature and healthy full-term babies extra contact with their infants immediately after birth and in the few days following birth. Mothers with more access to their babies in the hospital developed better rapport with their infants, held them more comfortably, and smiled at and talked to them more often.

Gradually bonding research brought about widespread changes in hospital obstetrical practice in the United States. Fathers and **family** members often remain with the mother during labor and delivery. Mothers hold their infants immediately after birth, and babies often remain with their mothers throughout their hospital stay. Bonding research has also led to increased awareness of the natural capabilities of the infant at birth, and so it has encouraged many others to deliver their babies without anesthesia (which depresses mother and infant responsiveness).

Infancy

Emotionally and physically healthy mothers and fathers are attracted to their infant. They naturally feel a physical longing to smell, cuddle, and rock their infant. They look at their baby and communicate to the baby. In turn the infant responds with snuggling, babbling, smiling, sucking, and clinging. Usually, the parents' behaviors bring pleasure and nourishment to the infant, and

the infant's behaviors bring pleasures and satisfaction to the parents. This reciprocal positive maternal and paternal-infant interaction initiates attachment.

One important part in the parents' ability to bond with the infant after birth is the healthy, drug-free newborn is in a "quiet alert" state for 45 to 60 minutes after birth. Immediately after birth the newborn can see, can hear, will turn his head toward a spoken voice, and will move in rhythm to his mother's voice. Mothers and fathers who have the opportunity to interact with their newborns within an hour after birth bond with their baby quickly. The act of holding, rocking, laughing, singing, feeding, gazing, kissing, and other nurturing behaviors involved in caring for infants (and young children) are bonding experiences. The most important ways to create attachment is positive physical contact such as hugging, holding, and rocking. It should be no surprise that nurturing behaviors cause specific neurochemical actions in the brain. These actions lead to organization of brain systems responsible for attachment.

Physical changes occur in the mother after birth, such as hormonal increases triggered by the infant licking or sucking her nipples and increased blood flow to her breasts when she hears the infant cry. Instinctive behaviors triggered in the mother in response to the infant immediately after birth promote her bonding with the infant and thus support the infant's survival.

Toddlerhood

Bonding experiences lead to healthy relations for children in the earliest years of life. During the first three years of life, the human brain develops to 90 percent of adult size. The brain puts in place most of the systems and structures that are responsible for future emotional, behavioral, social, and physiological functioning. Bonding experiences must be present at certain critical times for the brain parts responsible for attachment to develop normally. These critical periods appear in the first year of life and are related to the capacity of the infant and parent or caregiver to develop a positive interactive relation. Problems with bonding and attachment can lead to a fragile biological and emotional foundation for later experiences.

Common problems

Any problem with bonding experiences can interfere with attachment capacities. When the interactive, reciprocal "dance" between the parent and infant is disrupted or becomes difficult, bonding experiences are difficult to maintain. Disruptions can occur because of medical problems with the infant or the parent, the environment, or the fit between the infant and the parent.

The infant's personality or **temperament** influences bonding. If an infant is difficult to comfort, is irritable, or unresponsive, the baby may have more difficulty developing a secure bond. Moreover, the infant's ability to take part in the maternal-infant interaction may be compromised because of a medical condition, such as **prematurity**, birth defect, or illness.

The parent's or caregiver's behavior can also hinder bonding. Critical, rejecting, and interfering parents have children who may avoid emotional intimacy. Abusive parents have children who become uncomfortable with intimacy and withdraw. The child's mother may be unresponsive to the child because of maternal depression, substance abuse, or overwhelming personal problems that interfere with her ability to be consistent and nurturing for the child.

The environment is also a factor. A major impediment to healthy bonding is **fear**. If an infant is distressed because of **pain**, pervasive threat, or a chaotic environment, the baby may have a difficult time engaging in a sympathetic care-giving relationship. Infants or children living amid domestic violence, in refugee shelters, in areas besieged by community violence, or in war zones are at risk for developing attachment problems.

The fit between the infant's temperament and capabilities and those of the mother and father is important. Some parents can bond with a calm infant but are overwhelmed by an irritable infant. Understanding each other's nonverbal cues and responding appropriately is essential to preserving the bonding experiences that build healthy attachments. Sometimes a style of communication and response familiar to a mother from one of her other children may not fit her new infant. The mutual frustration of being "out of sync" can undermine bonding.

Since the first phase of bonding takes place in the womb, researchers believe difficult and unwanted pregnancies and planned adoptions interfere with mother and infant bonding. Teenagers and immature mothers often conceal and reject their pregnancies. This behavior and feeling may result in **abandonment**, neglect, and the absence of bonding at birth. Often there is also an emotional detachment from a fetus that causes emotional or physical pain to the mother during pregnancy. Mothers may have difficulty bonding with an infant if prenatal testing suggests the child will have a birth defect or is likely to be mentally retarded and malformed. And babies planned for **adoption** at birth may be "given up" emotionally by the birth mother during pregnancy. Any or all of these circumstances can interfere with the infant-parent bonding process.

Mothers who develop secure bonds with their infants tend to spend time holding them and making eye contact. *(Photograph by Goujon/Jerrican. Photo Researchers, Inc.)*

Parental concerns

The birth of a premature infant is documented to be a time of stress and crisis for parents and infants. Among these stressors are perceived losses and grief from the early abrupt termination of pregnancy, feelings of guilt and failure in inability to carry the infant to term, uncertainty regarding the infant's future health and developmental potential, and immediate and long-term separation of the infant from the family.

Parental involvement in the care of sick or premature newborns is a major concern of many pediatricians and nursery staff. Touching, stroking, and talking, and, later, massaging are encouraged during frequent parental visits to the nursery. It is hoped that the emotional bonding of parents with low birth-weight infants will increase the baby's chance of doing well despite prematurity.

KEY TERMS

Attachment—A bond between an infant and a caregiver, usually its mother. Attachment is generally formed within the context of a family, providing the child with the necessary feelings of safety and nurturing at a time when the infant is growing and developing. This relationship between the infant and his caregiver serves as a model for all future relationships.

Because premature infants are sometimes seem fragile, parents may handle them less. Skin to skin contact is important to the growing infant, premature or full term. Lack of this contact may predispose the child to psychological problems as well as diminish opportunities for learning.

The practice of "kangaroo care," first introduced by two South American neonatologists, is a method of skin-to-skin contact to promote parent and infant bonding especially for premature infants. This method involves holding infants dressed only in a diaper and a hat between the mother's bare breasts or against the father's chest, similar to a kangaroo carrying their young. Through contact with their parents' skin, the babies are kept warm and allowed close interaction with their parents. This decreases some of the stressors associated with premature births and helps infants needing neonatal intensive care.

Parents who have experienced kangaroo care have expressed excitement and joy with the practice and many have felt like parents for the first time since their infant's birth. Infants have been observed in a restful **sleep** state while in the kangaroo position. As well, kangaroo care has been found to promote parent and infant bonding, breastfeeding, and early discharge for premature infants.

Kangaroo care is offered to stable babies who are less than 1,500 grams and are breathing on their own. Babies needing oxygen or nasal continuous positive airway pressure (CPAP) may also be eligible. Cardiopulmonary monitoring and oximetry may be continued during kangaroo care. The nurse remains nearby to monitor the infant as necessary.

See also Attachment between infant and caregiver.

Resources

BOOKS

Rhatigan, Pamela. *Soothe Your Baby the Natural Way: Bonding, Calming Rituals, Massage Techniques, Natural Remedies.* London: Hamlyn, 2005.

WEB SITES

"Bonding Period." *Birthing Naturally*, October 2003. Available online at <www.birthingnaturally.net/barp/bonding.html> (accessed December 14, 2004).

Perry, Bruce D. "Bonding and Attachment in Maltreated Children: Consequences of Emotional Neglect in Childhood." *Scholastic*. Available online at <http://teacher.scholastic.com/professional/bruceperry/bonding.htm> (accessed December 14, 2004).

Aliene S. Linwood, RN, DPA, FACHE

Bone cancer *see* **Sarcomas**
Bordetella pertussis infection *see* **Whooping cough**

Botulism

Definition

Botulism is an acute, progressive condition caused by botulinum toxin, a natural poison produced by the spore-forming bacteria *Clostridium botulinum*. Exposure to the botulinum toxin usually occurs from eating contaminated food although, in infants, it may be caused by specific types of clostridia obtained from soil or inhaled spores, causing growth of the bacteria in the infant's intestine. Botulinum toxin is a neurotoxin that blocks the ability of motor nerves to release acetylcholine, the neurotransmitter that relays nerve signals to muscles, a process that may result in unresponsive muscles, a condition known as flaccid paralysis. Breathing may be severely compromised in progressive botulism because of failure of the muscles that control the airway and breathing.

Description

Botulism occurs only rarely, but its high fatality rate makes it a great concern for those in the general public and in the medical community. Clinical descriptions of botulism reach as far back in history as ancient Rome and Greece. However, the relationship between contaminated food and botulism was not defined until the late 1700s. In 1793 the German physician, Justinius Kerner (1786–1862), deduced that a substance in spoiled sausages, which he called *wurstgift* (German for sausage poison), caused botulism. The toxin's origin and identity remained vague until Emile van Ermengem (1851–1932), a Belgian professor, isolated *Clostridium botulinum* in 1895 and identified it as the source of **food poisoning**.

Three types of botulism have been identified: food-borne, wound, and infant botulism. The main difference between types hinges on the route of exposure to the toxin. Food-borne botulism accounts for 25 percent of all botulism cases and can usually be traced to eating contaminated home-preserved food. Infant botulism accounts for 72 percent of all cases. About 98 percent of infants recover with proper treatment. Although domestic food poisoning is a problem worldwide, concern is growing regarding the use of botulism toxin in biological warfare. At the end of the twentieth century 17 countries were known to be developing biological weapons, including the culture of botulism toxins.

Transmission

Botulism is not spread from one individual to another, but through exposure to the deadly botulinum toxin, a natural poison produced by certain *Clostridium* bacteria that may be found in preserved, especially canned, foods and sometimes in the intestines of infants. Botulism spores can cause widespread illness if introduced into the environment.

Demographics

Botulism occurs worldwide, with 90 percent of the comparatively rare cases occurring in the United States. Approximately 110 cases of botulism are reported annually in the United States, with 50 percent of cases in California alone. Infant botulism accounts for 72 percent of all cases, far exceeding both food-borne and wound botulism. Food-borne botulism accounts for 25 percent of all cases, primarily due to eating contaminated home-preserved food.

Causes and symptoms

Toxins produced by the bacterium *Clostridium botulinum* are the main culprit in botulism. Other members of the *Clostridium* genus can produce botulinum toxin, namely *C. argentinense*, *C. butyricum*, and *C. baratii*, but these are minor sources. To grow, these bacteria require a low-acid, oxygen-free environment that is warm (40–120°F or 4.4–48.8°C) and moist. Lacking these conditions, the bacteria transform themselves into spores that, like plant seeds, can remain dormant for years. Clostridia and their spores exist all over the world, especially in soil and aquatic sediments. They do not threaten human or animal health until the spores encounter an environment that favors growth. The spores then germinate, and the growing bacteria produce the deadly botulism toxin.

Scientists have discovered that clostridia can produce at least seven types of botulism toxin, identified as A, B, C, D, E, F, and G. Humans are usually affected by A, B, E, and very rarely F; infants are affected by types A and B. Domesticated animals such as dogs, cattle, and mink are affected by botulism C toxin, which also affects birds and has caused massive die-offs in domestic bird flocks and wild waterfowl. Botulism D toxin can cause illness in cattle, and horses succumb to botulism A, B, and C toxin. There have been no confirmed cases of human or animal botulism linked to the G toxin.

In humans, botulinum toxin latches onto specific proteins in nerve endings and irreversibly destroys them. These proteins control the release of acetylcholine, a neurotransmitter that stimulates muscle cells. With acetylcholine release blocked, nerves are not able to stimulate muscles. Ironically, this action of the botulinum toxin has given it a beneficial niche in the world of medicine. Certain medical disorders are characterized by involuntary and uncontrollable muscle contractions. Medical researchers have discovered that injecting a strictly controlled dose of botulinum toxin into affected muscles inhibits excessive muscle contractions. The muscle is partially paralyzed and normal movement is retained.

Human botulism (caused by botulism toxins A, B, and E) may stem from contaminated food, wound contamination, or the intestinal botulism toxin found in infants. Each produces multiple symptoms as follows:

- Food-borne botulism. Food that has been improperly preserved or stored can harbor botulinum toxin-producing clostridia. Canned or jarred baby food has also been known to cause botulism. Symptoms of food-borne botulism typically appear within 18 to 36 hours of eating contaminated food, with extremes of four hours to eight days. Initial symptoms include blurred or double vision and difficulty swallowing and speaking. Possible gastrointestinal problems include **constipation**, **nausea**, and **vomiting**. As botulism progresses, the victim experiences weakness or paralysis, starting with the head muscles and progressing down the body. Breathing becomes increasingly difficult. Without medical care, respiratory failure and death are very likely.

- Infant botulism. Infant botulism was first described in 1976. Unlike adults, infants younger than 12 months are vulnerable to *C. botulinum* colonizing the intestine. Infants ingest spores in honey or simply by swallowing spore-containing dust or dirt. The spores germinate in the large intestine and, once colonized, toxin is produced and absorbed into the infant's body from the entire intestinal tract. The first symptoms include constipation, lethargy, and poor feeding. As infant botulism progresses, sucking and swallowing (thus eating) become difficult. A nursing mother will often notice her own breast engorgement as the first sign of her infant's illness. The baby suffers overall weakness and cannot control head movements. Because of the flaccid paralysis of the muscles, the baby appears floppy. Breathing is impaired, and death from respiratory failure is a very real danger.

- Wound botulism. Confirmed cases of wound botulism have been linked to trauma such as severe crush injuries to the extremities, surgery, and illegal drug use. Wound botulism occurs when *Clostridia* colonize an infected wound and produce botulinum toxin. The symptoms usually appear four to 18 days after an injury occurs and are similar to food-borne botulism, although gastrointestinal symptoms may be absent.

When to call the doctor

Infant botulism may be hard for parents to identify because the symptoms occur slowly. Parents should call the doctor or take the infant or child to emergency services as soon as the child shows symptoms such as weakness or listlessness, lethargy, irritability, and poor eating (or nursing) along with decreased bowel movements or constipation. An affected child may be so weak as to appear floppy and not in control of muscle movements, especially movement of the neck and head. Whether parents are aware of a possible source of the botulism toxin, the suggestive symptoms should not be ignored.

Diagnosis

Differential diagnosis of botulism can be complex because the symptoms mimic those of other diseases, especially diseases characterized by muscle weakness. Botulism must be differentiated from diseases such as the following:

- Guillain-Barré syndrome

- meningoencephalitis

- myasthenia gravis

- systemic poisoning or sepsis

- reactions to therapeutic drugs

- nervous system infection

- carbon monoxide or atropine intoxication

- severe allergic reactions to bee sting, shell fish, and other allergens

- failure to thrive

Sepsis is the most common initial diagnosis for actual infant botulism, and meningoencephalitis may also be the diagnosis if irritability and lethargy are pre-

sent. Infant botulism was at one time linked to 5 to 15 percent of cases of **sudden infant death syndrome** (SIDS, crib death) because of spores found in 4 to 15 percent of cases; however, a subsequent 10-year study did not find a significant influence of botulism on SIDS.

Laboratory tests are used to make a definitive diagnosis, but if botulism seems likely, treatment starts immediately without waiting for test results, which may take up to two days. Diagnostic tests focus on identifying the organism causing the illness. This may involve performing a culture on contaminated material from the suspect food or the nose or throat of the affected individual. In infant botulism, the infant's stool may be cultured to isolate the organism; this test may be performed by the state health department or the Centers for Disease Control (CDC). Culture results are available from the microbiology laboratory as soon as bacteria grow in a special plate incubated at temperatures at or above body temperature. The growth of *Clostridium* confirms the diagnosis. Sometimes the organism cultured is not *Clostridium* as suspected. The microbiology laboratory may use samples of the bacteria grown to perform other special techniques in order to help identify the causative organism.

While waiting for diagnostic test results, doctors ask about recently consumed food, possible open sores, recent activities and behavior, and other factors that may help to rule out other disease possibilities. A physical examination is done with an emphasis on the nervous system and muscle function. As part of this examination, imaging studies such as CT and MRI may be done and electrodiagnostic muscle function tests (electromyogram) or lumbar punctures may be ordered. Laboratory tests look for the presence of botulinum toxin or *Clostridia* in suspected foods and/or the child's blood serum, feces, or other specimens for traces of botulinum toxin or *Clostridia*. Magnesium levels may be measured, since magnesium increases the activity of *Clostridium*. Additional diagnostic tests may be done to rule out other diseases or conditions with similar symptoms.

Treatment

Drugs

Older children and adults with botulism are sometimes treated with an antitoxin derived from horse serum that is distributed by the Centers for Disease Control and Prevention. The antitoxin (effective against toxin types A, B, and E) inactivates only the botulinum toxin that is unattached to nerve endings. Early injection of the antitoxin, ideally within 24 hours of onset of symptoms, can preserve nerve endings, prevent progression of the disease, and reduce mortality.

Unfortunately, infants cannot receive the antitoxin used for adults. For them, human botulism immune globulin (BIG) is the preferred treatment. It is available in the United States through the Infant Botulism Treatment and Prevention Program in Berkeley, California. BIG neutralizes toxin types A, B, C, D, and E before they can bind to nerves. This antitoxin can provide protection against A and B toxins for approximately four months. Though many infants recover with supportive care, BIG cuts hospital stay in half and, therefore, reduces hospital costs by 50 percent as well.

Aside from the specific antitoxin, no therapeutic drugs are used to treat botulism. **Antibiotics** are not effective for preventing or treating botulism because the *Clostridium* group of toxins are not sensitive to them. In fact, antibiotic use is discouraged for infants because bacteria could potentially release more toxin into a baby's system as they are killed. Antibiotics can be used, however, to treat secondary respiratory tract and other infections.

Respiratory support

Treatment for infants usually requires them to be in an intensive care unit, involving intensive respiratory support and nasogastric tube feeding for weeks or even months. Once an infant can breathe unaided, physical therapy is initiated to help the child relearn how to suck and swallow. In older children and adults, a respirator is often required to assist breathing; a tracheostomy may be necessary in some cases.

Surgery

Surgery may be necessary to clean an infected wound (debridement) and remove the source of the bacteria producing the toxin. Antimicrobial therapy may be necessary.

Gastric lavage

When botulism in older children or adults is caused by food, it often is necessary to flush the gastrointestinal tract (gastric lavage). Often cathartic agents or enemas are used. It is important to avoid products that contain magnesium, since magnesium enhances the effect of the toxin.

Nutritional concerns

Parents should avoid feeding honey to infants younger than 12 months because it is one known source of botulism spores.

Prognosis

With medical intervention, botulism victims can recover completely, though it may be a very slow recovery. It takes weeks to months to recover from botulism, and

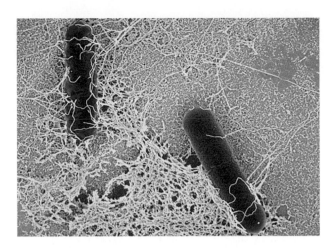

Electron micrograph of the *Clostridium botulinum* bacteria which cause botulism. *(Photograph by Gary Gaugler. Visuals Unlimited.)*

severe cases can take years before a total recovery is attained. Recovery depends on the nerve endings building new proteins to replace those destroyed by botulinum toxin.

Prevention

Vaccines have not been developed directed against botulism, which makes prevention of infant botulism or other forms of the disease difficult, since exposure to the botulinum toxic is typically unrecognized. Food safety is the surest prevention for botulism. Botulinum toxin cannot be seen, smelled, or tasted, so the wisest course is to discard any food that seems spoiled; avoid eating food from dented, rusty, or bulging cans; avoid refreezing meats once they have been thawed; and avoid buying broken containers of food or eating food that has been stored at room temperature or above for more than a few hours. People who like to can food at home must be diligent about using sterile equipment and following U.S. Department of Agriculture canning guidelines.

Infant botulism is difficult to prevent, because controlling what goes into an infant's mouth is often beyond control, especially in regard to airborne spores. One concrete preventative is to never feed honey to infants younger than 12 months as it is one known source of botulism spores. As infants begin eating solid foods, the same food precautions should be followed as for older children and adults.

Parental concerns

Because symptoms of infant botulism appear slowly, parents may be concerned that they will be missed or not found early. Normal watchfulness of the parents is sufficient, paying attention to any change in feeding, a decrease in bowel movements, or a lack of normal responses such

KEY TERMS

Acetylcholine—A chemical called a neurotransmitter that functions primarily to mediate activity of the nervous system and skeletal muscles.

Antitoxin—An antibody against an exotoxin, usually derived from horse serum.

Computed tomography (CT)—An imaging technique in which cross-sectional x rays of the body are compiled to create a three-dimensional image of the body's internal structures; also called computed axial tomography.

Culture—A test in which a sample of body fluid is placed on materials specially formulated to grow microorganisms. A culture is used to learn what type of bacterium is causing infection.

Electrooculography (EOG)—A diagnostic test that records the electrical activity of the muscles that control eye movement.

Flaccid paralysis—Paralysis characterized by limp, unresponsive muscles.

Lumbar puncture—A procedure in which the doctor inserts a small needle into the spinal cavity in the lower back to withdraw spinal fluid for testing. Also known as a spinal tap.

Magnetic resonance imaging (MRI)—An imaging technique that uses a large circular magnet and radio waves to generate signals from atoms in the body. These signals are used to construct detailed images of internal body structures and organs, including the brain.

Neurotoxin—A poison that acts directly on the central nervous system.

Neurotransmitter—A chemical messenger that transmits an impulse from one nerve cell to the next.

Sepsis—A severe systemic infection in which bacteria have entered the bloodstream or body tissues.

Spore—A dormant form assumed by some bacteria, such as anthrax, that enable the bacterium to survive high temperatures, dryness, and lack of nourishment for long periods of time. Under proper conditions, the spore may revert to the actively multiplying form of the bacteria. Also refers to the small, thick-walled reproductive structure of a fungus.

Toxin—A poisonous substance usually produced by a microorganism or plant.

Tracheostomy—A procedure in which a small opening is made in the neck and into the trachea or windpipe. A breathing tube is then placed through this opening.

---

as turning of the head and body movements. It may be helpful to remember how rare botulism is, how easy it is to assure food safety, and also that morbidity and mortality can be avoided with early recognition of the symptoms.

Resources

BOOKS

Rosaler, Maxine. *Botulism.* New York: Rosen Publishing Group, 2004.

PERIODICALS

Cadou, Stephanie G. "Diagnosing Infant Botulism." *The Nurse Practitioner* 26, no. 3 (March 2001): 76.

ORGANIZATIONS

Centers for Disease Control and Prevention. 1600 Clifton Rd., NE, Atlanta, GA 30333. Web site: <www.cdc.gov>.

L. Lee Culvert
Janie F. Franz

Braces, body *see* **Immobilization**
Braces, dental *see* **Orthodontics**

Brachial plexopathy, obstetric

Definition

Brachial plexopathy is any injury to the brachial plexus—the nerve bundles located on each side of the neck that give rise to the individual nerves controlling the muscles of the shoulders, arms, and hands.

Description

Brachial plexopathy occurs most often during birth, when an infant's neck and shoulders are stretched apart during passage through the birth canal. Injury to the brachial plexus is referred to by various names. Some names, such as obstetric Erb's palsy, refer to the specific region of the brachial plexus where the injury has occurred. Other more general names for the condition include:

- obstetric brachial plexus
- brachial plexus injury (BPI)
- brachial plexus palsy (BPP)
- brachial palsy in the neonate

Brachial plexus injuries

The nerves of the brachial plexus are the fifth through the eighth cervical nerves (C5, C6, C7, and C8) and the first thoracic nerve (T1). They run from nerve roots on each side of the upper spinal cord to regions beneath the collarbone where they branch out as the major nerves of the shoulders, arms, wrists, and hands.

Every brachial plexus injury is different, depending on the affected nerve or nerves and the extent and severity of the injury. There are four general types of injury, and an individual brachial plexopathy may include any or all of these injury types, on one or both (bilateral) sides of the body. The types are as follows:

- A stretch, praxis (damage), or traction (pulling or tension-creating) injury, in which the nerve has been overstretched and damaged but is not torn. Most brachial plexus injuries in newborns are of this type.
- A rupture, in which there has been a separation within a nerve. A single nerve may have more than one rupture.
- A neuroma, in which scar tissue has formed around a nerve injury. The scar tissue puts pressure on the nerve and interferes with nerve signal conduction to the muscles.
- An avulsion is the most severe form of brachial plexus injury. It is the detachment of a nerve from the spinal cord.

A minor brachial plexus injury can be a stretched nerve that results in a short-circuit in a few of the nerve fibers, causing temporary paralysis. A more severe injury may involve a complete disruption of the nerve, in which the nerve fibers around the injury become disorganized, all nerve function is lost, and scarring prevents the nerve from healing. Such an injury can result in permanent paralysis.

Obstetrical brachial plexopathy

Most injuries to the brachial plexus during birth involve the C5 and C6 nerve roots, affecting the movement of the shoulder, upper arm, and elbow. Limited shoulder motion can affect the function and strength of the hand. Obstetrical brachial plexopathies are classified according to the extent of the injury.

ERB'S PALSY Obstetric Erb's palsy is an injury in the upper brachial plexus involving C5 and C6 and sometimes C7. It usually affects the upper arm and the rotation of the lower arm. Erb's palsy is known also by the following names:

- Erb's paralysis
- Duchenne's paralysis
- Erb-Duchenne palsy or paralysis
- Duchenne-Erb syndrome or paralysis
- upper brachial plexus palsy or paralysis, Erb-Duchenne type

KLUMPKE'S PALSY Klumpke's palsy or Klumpke's paralysis is an injury to the lower brachial plexus: C7, C8, and sometimes T1. Children with Klumpke's palsy have normal use of the shoulder and elbow but weakness or paralysis in the hand and fingers. An infant also may have a drooping eyelid on the opposite side of the body from the affected hand.

TOTAL PLEXUS PALSY Also called Erb/Klumpke palsy, total plexus palsy involves all of the nerve roots of the brachial plexus to at least some extent. The entire upper extremity is affected.

Demographics

It is estimated that in North America between one and three of every 1,000 newborns are affected to some extent by brachial plexopathy. It appears to be less common than in the past, due to improvements in infant delivery methods and the increased use of cesarean sections (c-sections) to surgically remove the infant through the abdomen. However, some physicians are concerned that the late 1990s and early 2000s trend toward decreasing elective c-section deliveries will result in more cases of brachial plexopathy among newborns.

Erb's palsy is the most common type of obstetric brachial plexopathy. Total plexus palsy accounts for about 10 percent of obstetric brachial plexopathies and Klumpke's palsy accounts for less than 1 percent.

Causes and symptoms

Causes

Brachial plexopathy can result when the following events occur. An individual brachial plexopathy may include any or all of these injury types, on one or both (bilateral) sides of the body. The events are as follows:

- An infant's shoulder becomes stuck on the mother's pelvic bone during birth; the infant's neck may be stretched and the brachial plexus injured as the physician pulls on the baby to free it before circulatory or respiratory stress occurs.

- An infant's head and neck are pulled to one side while the shoulders pass through the birth canal.

- There is excessive stress on the infant's shoulders during a head-first delivery.

- There is pressure on the infant's raised arms during a breech (feet-first) delivery.

- An infant's shoulder is too large to fit easily through the birth canal (shoulder dystocia). An individual brachial plexopathy may include any or all of these injury types, on one or both (bilateral) sides of the body. (However, the association between brachial plexopathy and shoulder dystocia is controversial, with some studies indicating that 4 to 40 percent of shoulder dystocias result in brachial plexopathy and other studies finding no evidence of an association.)

Causes of brachial plexopathy, other than injuries during birth, include:

- any trauma or injury to the brachial plexus, such as might occur with vehicular accidents, **sports injuries**, puncture **wounds**, or surgery

- congenital abnormalities that affect the cervical ribs

- pressure from tumors in the region

- damage from radiation therapy

- exposure to some toxins, drugs, or chemicals

RISK FACTORS Although brachial plexus injuries can occur during any birth, there are particular risk factors. The highest rates of brachial plexus injury (7.8%) occur in newborns weighing over 10 lb (4.5 kg) who are born by assisted vaginal delivery to diabetic mothers. Premature and underdeveloped newborns are at a decreased risk for brachial plexopathy. Other risk factors for this injury are as follows:

- Some 50–70 percent of brachial plexus injuries occur in larger-than-average newborns, usually those over 7.7 lb (3.5 kg).

- About 44 percent of brachial plexopathies occur in newborns who experienced fetal distress.

- Breech deliveries increase the risk of brachial plexopathy by 175-fold, often causing bilateral injuries to the lower nerve roots of the brachial plexus.

- Prolonged labor and difficult or abnormal labor or delivery increase the risk of injury.

- Use of forceps or a vacuum device to deliver a baby increases risk.

- Injuries occur more frequently in births to mothers who have had several prior births.

- A mother who has had previous brachial-plexus-injured infants is at a 14-fold-increased risk of having another infant with brachial plexopathy.

Symptoms

The symptoms of brachial plexopathy vary greatly depending on the extent and severity of the damage. Some children with brachial plexopathy have the following limitations:

- They have no feeling or muscle control in the arm or hand.

- They can move their arm but have little control over the wrist and hand.

- They can use their hands normally but cannot use their shoulder or elbow muscles.

Typical symptoms that may be recognized at birth or shortly thereafter include the following:

- lack of spontaneous movement in the upper or lower arm or hand

- weakness in an arm

- weak or no grip

- no Moro reflex (a startled response when an infant's head drops suddenly, characterized by spreading the arms with the palms up and fingers flexed; as the reflex ends, the arms return to the body and the elbows flex and relax)

- weak or absent normal infant position with the arm flexed at the elbow and held against the body

- a limp or paralyzed arm

- lack of sensation in the arm or hand (a completely flaccid arm or part of an arm indicates an avulsion injury)

Other common symptoms of brachial plexopathy include:

- limited range-of-motion (ROM) in the arm or part of the arm

- sensation changes in the arm

- weakness in specific muscle groups

- inability to perform typical movements

- inability to bear weight in the arm

- neglect of the arm

- atypical positioning of the arm

- developmental delays

- torticollis (a shortened neck muscle, causing the head to tilt to one side)

Additional symptoms of brachial plexopathy include:

- arm **pain**

- facial paralysis on the affected side

- inability to sit up without assistance

- inability to crawl without a therapeutic device

Symptoms of Erb's palsy include:

- decreased abduction (turning outward) and external rotation of the shoulder

- decreased elbow flexion (bending)

- decreased supination (rotation of the forearm so that the palm of the hand is turned forward or upward)

- grasp reflex but no biceps reflex

- normal hand movement but abnormal Moro reflex

- sensory deficits

- paralysis of the diaphragm on the affected side in about 5 percent of Erb's palsy cases

Symptoms of total plexus palsy include:

- paralysis extending from the shoulder to the hand with no grasp reflex

- sensory loss

- Horner's syndrome (pupil contraction, receding eyeball, and sometimes inability to sweat on the affected side of the face) in about one-third of total plexus palsy cases

When to call the doctor

Although obstetric brachial plexopathy usually heals quite rapidly on its own, the infant may begin physical therapy within the first two weeks of life and should be evaluated by a specialist, such as a pediatric neurologist, by six weeks of age.

Diagnosis

A newborn lacking movement in an arm is examined first for **fractures** of the collarbone, ribs, humerus (the long bone of the upper arm, extending from the shoulder to the elbow), and even the femur (thighbone), as well as dislocations of the shoulder or elbow. Symptoms of such fractures and dislocations may be similar to those of brachial plexopathy and can cause infants to not move their arms. Those at risk for obstetric brachial plexopathy are also at risk for fractures and dislocations during birth. An infant who is not moving a fractured arm because of the pain will still exhibit a Moro reflex. However, when the infant is rolled from side to side, a brachial-plexopathy-affected arm may flop.

Brachial plexopathy is diagnosed by the following:

- an unpredictable or patchy pattern of sensory, motor, and reflex dysfunction in the arm

- **x rays** that rule out other causes for the symptoms

- a nerve conduction velocity (NCV) test detecting nerve damage (An electrode on the skin stimulates the nerve with a mild impulse and other electrodes record the resulting electrical impulse; the distance between the electrodes and the time the impulse takes to travel determines the conduction velocity; below-normal nerve conduction may indicate damage to the nerve.)

- electromyography (EMG) measures of the muscle response to nerve impulses (A needle electrode is inserted through the skin into the muscle and records the electrical activity of the muscle; EMG can reveal loss of nerve activity within one week of birth and can help determine which nerves are damaged.)

- magnetic resonance imaging (MRI; use magnets and radio waves to obtain images) of the brachial plexus determining the location and type of injury (MRI can be performed when the infant reaches two to three months of age.)

- computed tomography (CT) or computed axial tomography (CAT) scans performed at two to three months of age to reveal injury (CT scans use a thin, rotating x-ray beam to obtain an image as the x rays pass through body parts.)

- myelograms (x rays or CT scans taken after a dye is injected into the spinal fluid) revealing the fluid space surrounding the spinal cord in the neck (Although they may help to determine the location and type of nerve injury, myelograms generally have been replaced by MRI scans of the brachial plexus due to false positives and the invasiveness of procedure.)

Treatment

Nerve regeneration in newborns occurs at 1.8 mm. per day. Therefore, stretch or praxis injuries to the brachial plexus usually heal on their own within about three months, leading to complete recovery. However, many children with brachial plexopathy require treatment. Specialists who may become involved in a child's treatment include:

- physical therapists
- occupational therapists
- neurologists
- pediatric neurosurgeons
- orthopedic surgeons
- plastic surgeons

Physical therapy

Gentle massage and range-of-motion (ROM) exercises usually are initiated immediately, even in infants with very mild brachial plexopathy. Therapy regimes are individualized for each child, depending on the specific injury and its effects.

Treatment for brachial plexopathy may include a combination of exercises and focused physical, occupational, and aquatic therapies. Typically the therapist teaches the child's **family** to perform the following:

- position the infant properly
- never lift the child under the armpits
- perform passive range-of-motion (PROM) exercises on the infant
- assist with weight-bearing activities, even in a newborn
- help the infant avoid atypical movement patterns
- help thwart the infant's tendency to neglect the affected region
- detect muscle contractions even when no movement is evident
- help avoid tightening of the infant's muscles
- make adaptive equipment for the infant

At home parents may be instructed to do the following:

- perform ten repetitions of all prescribed PROMs two to three times daily
- begin gentle movements with the child's forearm rotated and the palm upward or forward (supination) to increase joint flexibility and muscle tone

- perform joint compression and weight-bearing exercises throughout the affected extremity
- practice aquatic exercises as prescribed
- practice tactile stimulation on the affected extremities, using textured materials, soft balls, vibration, and massage to increase sensory awareness
- actively involve the affected extremity in developmentally appropriate activities to increase strength and coordination, working first without the effects of gravity and later working against gravity
- place pillows or stuffed animals under the child's armpit or along side the affected arm during rest or **sleep** to obtain a sustained stretch

Play therapy

Play therapies are used to extend ROM from six months of age on in children with brachial plexopathy. General body activities include:

- any activity that forces the child to reach
- any activity that puts pressure on the affected arm or hand
- playing while lying on the stomach
- stacking empty boxes
- playing circle games
- playing "Simon says"
- "making angels" while lying on the floor
- throwing a beach ball overhead
- riding a tricycle or bicycle
- playing and walking in water
- climbing on play equipment
- climbing and sliding down a slide

Activities to increase hand coordination include:

- folding paper napkins
- copying and drawing basic shapes
- using scissors, paste, or toy tools
- painting
- writing on a chalkboard
- sewing cards
- playing with **toys** in the sink or tub
- playing with wooden puzzles, dominoes, Legos, or blocks

- stringing beads
- rolling dough
- playing in sand
- throwing a soft ball
- picking up and sorting small objects

Surgery

About ten percent of brachial plexus injuries in infants require surgery. Children with total plexus palsy who have not improved by three months of age and children with Erb's palsy who cannot strongly bend their elbow or raise their shoulder by six months of age are candidates for exploratory surgery to examine the nerve damage and perform possible nerve grafting. Surgeries are most successful if performed when the child is five to seven months of age. Surgeries are less likely to be successful if performed after 12 months of age.

Rupture injuries usually require surgery. Avulsion injuries require surgery to reattach the nerve root to the spinal cord. Surgeries that may be performed by a pediatric neurosurgeon include:

- neuroplastysurgery to repair the nerve, including stretching the nerve to relieve tension or reconnecting torn nerves
- neurolysis to destroy damaged nerve tissue or to loosen or remove scar tissue (neuroma) around the nerve
- nerve grafting by transplanting nerves from another part of the body, such as the ankle, to bridge a torn nerve or to reconnect the nerve root after an avulsion injury

Other types of surgery include:

- muscle surgery on a child aged 18 to 24 months if physical therapy has not restored shoulder rotation
- muscle or tendon transfer surgeries to restore function (For example, a child without elbow function might have a leg muscle transferred to the elbow and attached to the nerves.)
- muscle transfer surgeries in which the muscles are rearranged in an attempt to prevent permanent abnormalities
- plastic surgeries

A variety of other surgical procedures may be considered depending upon the specific situation. At least 90 percent of children improve following surgery. **Exercise** and massage are eventually reinitiated, depending on the type of surgery.

Other treatments

Other treatments for brachial plexopathy can be used. For example, various types of splints are available to position and support the extremity during activities and to increase weight-bearing ability. Also, casts are sometimes used to allow the nerves to heal. Finally, electrical stimulation, in conjunction with EMG, can deliver a small amount of electrical current to the muscle to prevent atrophy; it may be performed either by a therapist or at home. The child is examined regularly, both during and after treatment, for muscle recovery and proper joint development.

Prognosis

About 85 percent of infants with brachial plexopathy make a complete neurological recovery within three to six years. One study of 59 children found that 88 percent recovered by four months of age, 92 percent recovered by 12 months, and 93 percent recovered by 48 months. In another study of 28 infants with damage to the upper brachial plexus and 38 infants with total plexus palsy, 92 percent recovered spontaneously.

However, the prognosis for an individual brachial plexopathy depends on the location, severity, and extent of the damage and may be difficult to predict. In general, damage to the nerve sheath (outer covering) alone has a good prognosis. Praxis-type injuries, in which the nerve is damaged but not torn, usually improve within three months and eventually heal completely. Stretch injuries heal on their own, with 90 to 100 percent of function returning within one to two years. Severed nerves, particularly avulsion injuries in which the nerve is severed at the root, have poorer prognoses. In severe cases there may be permanent partial or total loss of nerve function in the affected nerves and weakness or paralysis of the arm may be permanent.

Erb's palsy has the best prognosis since, although shoulder, elbow, and forearm function may be affected, the hands and fingers are not affected. However, infants with Erb's palsy that involves C7 as well as C5 and C6 have a poorer prognosis. In addition Erb's palsy may lead to secondary deformities as the child grows. The most common problem is internal rotation contracture (permanent muscle contraction) of the shoulder.

Complete recovery from brachial plexopathy may be difficult to define. A Swedish study found that about 30 percent of children who had recovered the use of their shoulder, biceps, and hand by the age of three months still had disabilities at age five, including a weakened hand grip or difficulty dressing or running. The delay in normal functioning caused by brachial plexopathy and any muscle imbalances across a joint can have a major impact on the child's growing skeleton and can result in permanent muscular-skeletal abnormalities.

Long-term effects of brachial plexography may include:

- a weak shoulder girdle

- muscle atrophy

- joint contractures

- a bent elbow (called Erb Engram) with shoulder adduction (pulled in toward the body)

- impaired limb growth

- progressive bone deformities

Prevention

The primary prevention for obstetrical brachial plexopathy is the avoidance of a potentially difficult delivery by choosing **cesarean section**. Failure to anticipate a particularly large baby before delivery is an important risk factor. Some physicians suggest that women whose previous children had shoulder dystocia should be offered an elective cesarean delivery. However, cesarean deliveries also have risks associated with them, and it appears that increasing the frequency of c-sections would prevent few cases of brachial plexopathy since large-scale studies have shown that 3 percent of brachial plexus injuries occur during cesarean deliveries.

The use of an epidural (local) anesthetic during labor may contribute to the risk of brachial plexopathy since the anesthetic decreases the mother's ability to push during labor and may force the physician to use forceps or a vacuum device to pull the baby out.

Parental concerns

Promoting recovery

Although exercises required to treat brachial plexopathy in infants may be painful, they are essential for preventing much more serious pain and suffering as the child grows. In addition to performing prescribed massage and ROM exercises, parents should:

- always first offer objects or food to the child's affected side

- not allow the child to use compensatory movements, particularly those involving the trunk of the body

- have the child use the unaffected arm as a guide for the affected one so that the affected arm experiences what the unaffected arm is doing

Parents should help their child to become self-sufficient in the movements involved in the following daily tasks:

- toileting

- personal hygiene

- dressing

- performing simple household chores such as picking up toys, cleaning a room, or setting a table

Daily activities that increase ROM are essential even if the child is seeing a physical therapist. Parents should do the following:

- encourage a consistent daily routine and participation in activities

- try to incorporate therapy into daily play and other activities

- have the child participate in play activities that increase ROM for 15 to 30 minutes twice a day

- provide enjoyable and challenging activities

- encourage movement and use of affected joints

- encourage the child to focus on using the affected arm

- focus on the child's abilities rather than lack of abilities

- avoid doing something for the child simply because the child finds it difficult

- reward the child with verbal praise or a treat for attempting or initiating an activity

- allow the child enough time for each activity

Activities

Numerous activities have been found useful for promoting a child's recovery. Activities to increase shoulder flexibility include:

- placing and removing objects from a board or mirror

- popping bubbles

- rolling out dough with a rolling pin

- raising a dowel over the head

- playing basketball

Activities to increase shoulder abduction (movement of the arm away from the body) include playing bird or airplane and turning a jump rope.

Activities to increase elbow flexion (bending) include:

- bringing food items from hand to mouth

KEY TERMS

Abduction—Turning away from the body.

Adduction—Movement toward the body.

Avulsion—The forcible separation of a piece from the entire structure.

Brachial plexus—A group of lower neck and upper back spinal nerves supplying the arm, forearm and hand.

Cervical nerves—The eight pairs of nerves (C1C8) originating in the cervical (neck) region of the spinal cord.

Cesarean section—Delivery of a baby through an incision in the mother's abdomen instead of through the vagina; also called a C-section, Cesarean birth, or Cesarean delivery.

Computed tomography (CT)—An imaging technique in which cross-sectional x rays of the body are compiled to create a three-dimensional image of the body's internal structures; also called computed axial tomography.

Contracture—A tightening or shortening of muscles that prevents normal movement of the associated limb or other body part.

Dystocia—Failure to progress in labor, either because the cervix will not dilate (expand) further or because the head does not descend through the mother's pelvis after full dilation of the cervix.

Electromyography (EMG)—A diagnostic test that records the electrical activity of muscles. In the test, small electrodes are placed on or in the skin; the patterns of electrical activity are projected on a screen or over a loudspeaker. This procedure is used to test for muscle disorders, including muscular dystrophy.

Erb's palsy or paralysis—A condition caused by an injury to the upper brachial plexus, involving the cervical nerves C5, C6, and sometimes C7, affecting the upper arm and the rotation of the lower arm.

Flexion—The act of bending or condition of being bent.

Klumpke's palsy or paralysis—A condition caused by an injury to the lower brachial plexus, involving the cervical nerves C7 and C8, and sometimes the thoracic nerve T1, causing weakness or paralysis in the hands and fingers.

Magnetic resonance imaging (MRI)—An imaging technique that uses a large circular magnet and radio waves to generate signals from atoms in the body. These signals are used to construct detailed images of internal body structures and organs, including the brain.

Moro reflex—A startle response in a newborn, characterized by spreading the arms with the palms up and fingers flexed; the reflex usually disappears by two months of age.

Nerve condition velocity (NCV)—Technique for studying nerve or muscle disorders, measuring the speed at which nerves transmit signals.

Neurolysis—The destruction of nerve tissue or removal of scar tissue surrounding a nerve.

Neuroma—Scar tissue that forms around a nerve; a tumor derived from nerve tissue.

Neuroplasty—Surgery to repair nerves.

Palsy—Uncontrolable tremors.

Total plexus palsy—Erb/Klumpke palsy; a condition resulting from injury involving all of the brachial plexus nerves and affecting the entire upper extremity of the body.

- using big jacks or chew toys

- talking into a play microphone

- playing a musical instrument

Activities to increase elbow extension include **crawling** and reaching out for objects.

Activities to increase wrist extension include:

- shaking rattles

- pulling pegs from a pegboard

- knocking on a door

- playing drums or a xylophone

- banging with a hammer

- splashing water

- painting

If a child has no hand function, double sided Velcro can be placed around the hand and used to hold rattles and toys with Velcro attached to them. An older child can use a Velcro mitt and balls.

Support groups

There are numerous support groups across the United States for the families of children with Erb's palsy and other brachial plexopathies. Support groups offer encouragement and advice on the following topics:

• coping with pain and crying during therapy

• coping with daily routines

• play therapies and other activities

• sibling issues

• daycare and school

• social issues facing the child

Resources

BOOKS

Gilbert, Alain, ed. *Brachial Plexus Injuries.* London: Martin Dunitz, 2001.

PERIODICALS

Bavley, Alan. "Birth Injury Begins to Receive More Attention." *Kansas City Star* (May 7, 2000).

ORGANIZATIONS

Brachial Plexus Palsy Foundation. 210 Spring Haven Circle, Royersford, PA 19468. Web site: <http://membrane.com/bpp>.

Erb's Palsy Lawyers Network. Web site: <www.erbspalsy.com/index.htm>.

National Brachial Plexus/Erb's Palsy Association Inc. PO Box 23, Larsen, WI 54947. Web site: <www.nbpepa.org>.

National Institute of Arthritis and Musculoskeletal and Skin Diseases. National Institutes of Health, 1 AMS Circle, Bethesda, MD 20892–3675. Web site: <www.nih.gov/niams>.

United Brachial Plexus Network. 1610 Kent St., Kent, OH 44240. Web site: <www.ubpn.org>.

WEB SITES

"About Erb's Palsy." *The Erb's Palsy Lawyers Network*, 2004. Available online at <www.erbspalsy.com/about.htm> (December 24, 2004).

"Brachial Plexus." *Hyman-Newman Institute for Neurology and Neurosurgery.* Available online at <www.nyneurosurgery.org/brachial_intro.htm> (December 24, 2004).

"Brachial Plexus Birth Injury." *Pediatric Orthopedics*, 2000. Available online at <www.pediatric-orthopedics.com/Treatments/Brachial_Plexus/BrachialLink/Brachial_Lecture/brachial_lecture.html> (December 24, 2004).

"Erb's Palsy/Brachial Plexus Play Therapy Exercises." *United Brachial Plexus Network*, 2000. Available online at <www.ubpn.org/resources/playtherapy.html> (December 24, 2004).

"Frequently Asked Questions." *National Brachial Plexus/Erb's Palsy Association.* Available online at <www.nbpepa.org/faqs.htm> (December 24, 2004).

Stormet, Margaret. "Protocol for Treatment of Brachial Plexus/Erb's Palsy." *National Brachial Plexus/Erb's Palsy Association.* Available online at <www.nbpepa.org/protocol.htm> (December 24, 2004).

Margaret Alic, Ph.D.

Brain defects, congenital *see* **Congenital brain defects**

Breast development

Definition

A newborn baby has nipples, areolas, and the beginnings of breast tissue, but most of breast development occurs in two different periods of time in a woman's life: first in **puberty**, then during pregnancy. Breast development is a vital part of puberty in the human female. Interestingly, humans are the only mammals whose breasts develop before they are needed to serve their biological purpose—breastfeeding.

Description

The first stage of breast development begins at about six weeks of fetal development with a thickening called the mammary ridge or the milk line. By six months of development, this ridge extends all the way down to the groin, but then regresses. Solid columns of cells form from each breast bud, with each column becoming a separate sweat gland. Each of these has its own separate duct leading to the nipple. By the final months of fetal development, these columns have become hollow, and by the time a female infant is born, a nipple and the beginnings of the milk-duct system have formed.

As a girl approaches puberty, the first outward signs of breast development begin to appear. When the ovaries start to secrete estrogen, fat in the connective tissue begins to accumulate causing the breasts to enlarge and the duct system begins to grow. Breast development normally begins about one to two years before the men-

Breast development

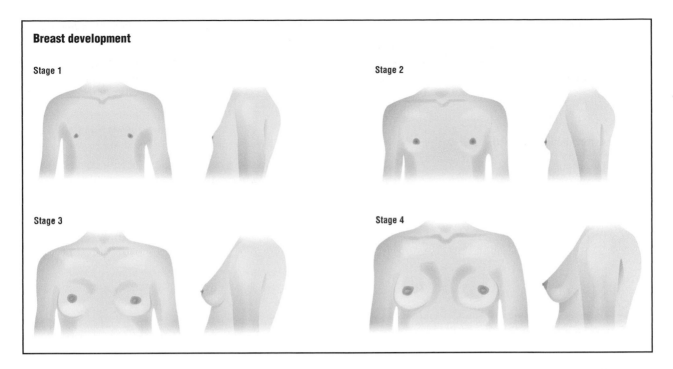

Stage 1 | Stage 2 | Stage 3 | Stage 4

The four stages of breast development. In Stage 1 shows the flat breasts of childhood. By Stage 2, breast buds are formed as milk ducts and fat tissue develop. In Stage 3, the breast become round and full, and the areola darkens. Stage 4 shows fully mature breasts. *(Illustration by GGS Information Services.)*

strual period begins. Usually these signs are accompanied by the appearance of pubic hair and hair under the arms.

Once ovulation and **menstruation** begin, the maturing of the breasts begins with the formation of secretory glands at the end of the milk ducts. The breasts and duct system continue to grow and mature with the development of many glands and lobules. The rate at which breasts grow varies significantly and is different for each young woman. Breast development occurs in five stages:

• Stage One: In preadolescence, the breasts are flat and only the tip of the nipple is raised.

• Stage Two: Buds appear, breast and nipple are raised, fat tissue begins to form and the areola (dark area of skin that surrounds the nipple) enlarges.

• Stage Three: Breasts are slightly larger with glandular breast tissue present. Initially this happens in a conical shape and later in a rounder shape. The areola begins to darken.

• Stage Four: The nipple and areola become raised and form a second mound above the rest of the breast. Menstruation typically starts within two years of reaching this stage, and some girls skip this stage completely.

• Stage Five: Mature adult breast is rounded and only the nipple is raised.

The entire process from the breast bud stage through stage five usually takes about three to five years, but for some girls it takes close to ten years. After these five stages, the breast is still not considered mature or fully developed. Only pregnancy brings about the fullness of breast growth and development.

Each month, women experience fluctuations in hormones that make up the normal menstrual cycle. Estrogen, which is produced by the ovaries in the first half of the menstrual cycle, stimulates the growth of milk ducts in the breasts. The increasing level of estrogen leads to ovulation halfway through the cycle, and then the hormone progesterone takes over in the second half of the cycle, stimulating the formation of the milk glands. These hormones are believed to be responsible for the cyclical changes such as the swelling, **pain**, and tenderness that many women experience in their breasts just before menstruation. Many women also experience changes in breast texture, with breasts feeling particularly lumpy. This, too, is related to the glands in the breast enlarging in preparation for a possible pregnancy. If pregnancy does not occur, the breasts return to normal size.

Common problems

Breast development can start in a girl as early as eight years or as late as 13 years. If a girl does not have breast buds or pubic hair, which is the first signs of puberty, by age 14, there may be other medical problems. Most girls begin menstruating between ages nine and 18, with an average around 12 years of age. Primary **amenorrhea** is the absence of any menstrual flow in a girl who has never menstruated by the age of 16. Primary amenorrhea is not considered to have occurred until a girl is beyond age 16, if she has undergone other normal changes that occur during puberty. Primary amenorrhea may occur with or without other signs of puberty, but this condition is rare in the United States occurring in only about 0.1 percent of all girls.

There are many possible causes of primary amenorrhea, including **malnutrition**, extreme **obesity**, genetic disorders, endocrine (hormonal) disorders, pituitary tumors, congenital abnormalities, **anorexia nervosa**, bulimia, and, of course, pregnancy. Emotional distress or crisis about being different from friends or **family** can occur.

Parental concerns

Parents should become concerned if their daughter shows no signs of breast development by age 14 and if by the age of 16, there has not been a menstrual period.

When to call the doctor

Parents should call their health provider if their daughter is older than 16 and has not yet begun menstruating.

See also Puberty.

Resources

BOOKS

Adams, G. R., and M. D. Berzonsky. *Blackwell Handbook of Adolescence (Blackwell Handbooks of Developmental Psychology)*. Malden, MA: Blackwell Publishing, 2003.

Hayward, C., et al. *Gender Differences at Puberty (Cambridge Studies on Child and Adolescent Health)*. Cambridge, MA: Harvard University Press, 2003.

Love, S., et al. *Dr. Susan Love's Breast Book*. New York: Perseus Book Groups, 2000.

ORGANIZATIONS

American College of Obstetricians and Gynecologists. 409 12th Street, SW, PO Box 96920, Washington, DC 20090. Web site: <www.acog.org>.

Association of Women's Health, Obstetric and Neonatal Nursing. 2000 L Street, NW, Suite 740, Washington, DC 20036. Web site: <www.awhonn.org>.

WEB SITES

"Amenorrhea-primary." *MedlinePlus*, May 11, 2004. Available online at <www.nlm.nih.gov/medlineplus/ency/article/001218.htm> (accessed December 7, 2004).

"Breast Health." *Breast Health*. Available online at <www.ohsuhealth.com/htaz/breast/breast_health_online_resources.cfm> (accessed December 7, 2004).

4Girls. Available online at <www.4girls.gov/> (accessed December 7, 2004).

Linda K. Bennington, RNC, MSN, CNS

Breastfeeding *see* **Lactation**

Breath holding spells

Definition

Breath holding spells are episodes of brief, involuntary cessations of breathing that occur in children in response to stimuli such as anger, frustration, **fear**, or injury.

Description

A breath holding spell (BHS) is a reflexive response that occurs in some healthy young children, usually between the ages of about eight months and two years. A typical breath holding spell lasts between two and 20 seconds. The child cries or gasps, forcibly exhales, stops breathing, and turns either blue (cyanotic form) or pale (pallid form). In a simple BHS the child may faint or briefly lose consciousness. If the child recovers before fainting, some physicians do not consider it to be a true breath holding spell. In a severe or complicated BHS, the child may have a small seizure while unconscious. The entire episode usually lasts less than one minute. The child regains consciousness and normal breathing, and color resume immediately.

The frequency of breath holding spells varies from several times a day to perhaps only once a year. About one-third of affected children have two to five spells daily whereas another one-third of affected children average one spell per month. It is not uncommon for a child with only sporadic or rare breath holding spells to have several in a single day.

Cyanotic form

About 60 percent of affected children have the cyanotic form of BHS, in which the skin and lips turn bluish. This type of breath holding spell also is called type 1, red-blue form, or cyanotic infantile syncope. It usually occurs when the child is angry or frustrated and may be a component of a temper tantrum.

Pallid form

About 20 percent of affected children have the pallid form of BHS in which the child turns pale. It also is called type 2, white breath-holding, reflex anoxic seizure, or pallid infantile syncope. The pallid form of BHS typically follows a frightening or painful experience.

An additional 20 percent of affected children have both types of breath holding spells at different times.

Demographics

Breath holding spells occur in about 5 percent of healthy children between the ages of six months and six years. They are most common between six and 18 months of age. Most affected children have had their first episode before the age of 18 months and almost all affected children have had an episode by the age of two. Breath holding spells are rare before six months of age. Although they are less common after the age of five, some children continue to have episodes until age six or seven.

Breath holding spells appear to occur equally among boys and girls. However, some studies have suggested that boys are more susceptible and that the average onset of BHS in boys is earlier (13–18 months) compared with girls (19–24 months). Studies have found no significant behavioral differences between children who have breath holding spells and those who do not. Nor is there a correlation between the frequency of spells and scores on behavioral profiles. Cyanotic breath holding spells typically begin when children are in a negative or oppositional phase and are starting to assert their independence. They typically end as the child learns to express emotions in words.

Causes and symptoms

Causes

Although the exact physiological mechanism of breath holding spells is not understood, they are an involuntary reflex caused by the interplay between the respiratory control center of the central nervous system, the autonomic nervous system, and the cardiopulmonary system.

CYANOTIC BHS Cyanotic BHS may be a component of a temper tantrum or a child's attempt to gain control over a situation. A cyanotic breath holding spell may also occur in response to the following:

• anger or frustration

• failure of the child to get its way

• a scolding or some other upsetting event

• **pain**

• being startled

• fear

• a confrontational situation

• a traumatic event

A breath holding spell is an involuntary reflex because it follows exhalation rather than inhalation. In a cyanotic BHS the long exhalation following crying causes breathing to stop. However, in some situations a child may learn how to trigger a cyanotic BHS. A child over the age of two with daily spells may have learned that intense crying or a temper tantrum can trigger a spell. If past breath holding spells have earned children lavish attention or enabled them to get their own way, the children may intentionally cause the spells to trigger an episode.

PALLID BHS Pallid breath holding spells are unpredictable. They usually occur in response to being startled, frightened, in pain, immunized, or injured, particularly after hitting the head.

In a pallid BHS the brain sends a signal via the vagus nerve that severely slows the heart rate, leading to a temporary cessation of breathing and loss of consciousness.

Risk factors

There appears to be a genetic component to at least some breath holding spells. About 25 percent of affected children—particularly those who experience pallid BHS—have a **family** history of BHS or fainting.

In some cases breath holding spells may be associated with anemia (a reduced number of red blood cells) caused by an iron deficiency, although this is controversial. Treatment may decrease the number of spells in some anemic children; however, treatment with iron increases the frequency of spells in children who are not anemic.

Symptoms

CYANOTIC BHS Once a parent or caregiver has witnessed a breath holding spell the symptoms are obvious. Children may do the following:

• cry vigorously for less than 30 seconds

• hyperventilate (over-breathe)

• have a pause in breathing followed by a long forced exhalation

• turn red in the face from anger

• stop breathing (apnea)

• have a strained face as if they are crying, although there is no sound

• turn bluish-purple, particularly in the face and around the lips, due to lack of oxygen in the brain.

The spell may end at this point and the child resumes breathing. Alternatively, the following may occur:

• The child may faint, become limp, or lose consciousness, usually for just a few seconds, due to a lack of oxygen reaching the brain.

• If breath holding lasts ten seconds or more, the unconscious child may experience muscle twitching, one or two jerky movements, back arching, body stiffening, or a true seizure.

• The child takes a deep breath and resumes normal breathing within 30 to 60 seconds.

• Consciousness and normal skin color return.

Most children recover completely within less than one minute after the start of the episode and resume normal activities. Some children may cry or scream for a period, and other children may fall asleep for an hour.

PALLID BHS In a pallid breath holding spell a child do the following:

• gasp and the lower jaw may quiver, but there is little or no crying

• experience a slowing heart rate or the heart may even stop briefly

• turn pale

• sweat

• stop breathing

• lose muscle strength and go limp

• faint or lose consciousness

• experience muscle twitching or body stiffness while unconscious

• have a seizure

Following these responses, the child's heart speeds up, breathing resumes on its own, and consciousness returns. The child usually recovers completely within one minute but may feel sleepy.

Seizures are much more likely with the pallid form than with the cyanotic form of BHS. Seizures during breath holding spells are more likely if breath holding lasts longer than usual. A child may vomit or urinate during a seizure.

When to call the doctor

Breath holding spells may have symptoms in common with various seizure disorders or other medical conditions. Therefore, a physician should be consulted if any of the following occurs:

• It is the first time a child has had a breath holding spell.

• The child is under six months of age, particularly if the spells occur during feeding or diaper changing.

• The child has a first breath holding spell at four-and-a-half years of age or older.

• The spells become more frequent.

• The spells become more severe.

• The pattern of the spells changes.

• The pallid form of BHS occurs frequently.

• The spells last more than one minute, with continuous body stiffening and relaxing.

Diagnosis

Diagnosis of breath holding spells usually is based on the medical history of children and their families and on complete physical and neurological examinations to rule out other causes. Breath holding spells usually are diagnosed in the following way:

- a child's history of breath holding spells
- the exact sequence of events, which can be written down or videotaped
- lack of incontinence
- lack of post-convulsion symptoms
- blood tests to determine if a child has iron-deficient anemia

In addition the physician inquire about the following:

- if the child has ever been diagnosed with a medical condition
- if there have been recent changes in the child's behavior that are cause for concern
- if there have been recent changes in the child's life such as moving, a new sibling, or divorce
- if the parents have concerns about how other people may be treating the child

Ruling out other causes

Medical conditions that may cause breath holding spells include the following:

- Rett syndrome, a rare genetic disorder affecting girls
- Batten disease, the juvenile form of a group of progressive neurological disorders known as neuronal ceroid lipofuscinoses
- Riley-Day syndrome, a rare genetic disorder
- familial dysautonomia, a rare genetic disorder that can cause involuntary breath holding spells in a child who is already seriously ill

Breath holding spells can be distinguished from epileptic seizures using the following criteria:

- BHS are provoked by an event or situation.
- BHS seizures are brief.
- Recovery from BHS is rapid.
- The change in skin color and loss of consciousness with BHS occur before any seizure-type jerking.
- With epilepsy, convulsions and muscle weakness precede the loss of skin color.
- An **electroencephalogram** (EEG) that records electrical activity in the brain is normal in all forms of BHS, whereas it may be abnormal with epilepsy.

An electrocardiogram (ECG, EKG) that records the electrical activity in the heart may be used to check for heart rhythm abnormalities, such as long QT syndrome, in children who have had a pallid breath holding spell. Children with long QT syndrome may have breath holding spells in response to exertion or excitement. However, because long QT syndrome is so serious, some physicians recommend that all children with breath holding spells have a baseline EKG.

Treatment

The primary treatment for BHS is to reassure the parent or caregiver that the spells are completely harmless and that they usually disappear by the age of two or two-and-a-half. The child may be put in bed to rest after recovering from the spell. The only treatment for cyanotic BHS is to not encourage or reward the behavior. It is possible that behavior therapy may help a child who suffers from frequent cyanotic spells.

If a child is anemic, iron (at 6 mg per kg [2.2 lb]) of body weight per day for at least three months) may reduce the frequency of breath-holding spells. If pallid breath holding spells are frequent and severe, a preventative anti-cholinergic medicine such as atropine sulfate may be prescribed, in consultation with a neurologist or cardiologist. The dosage is usually 0.1 mg of oral atropine three times daily. Anti-convulsive medications have no effect on breath holding spells.

Prognosis

There are no long-term effects of breath holding spells. Both types of BHS cease without treatment as the child's brain and body develops and matures. The cyanotic form usually peaks at about two years of age and is rare past the age of five. Both types of BHS disappear by the age of four or five in about 50 percent of affected children and in 90 percent of children by the age of six.

Up to 17 percent of children with pallid BHS will experience syncope (fainting spells) as adults, usually in response to fear, injury, or emotional stress. Children with cyanotic episodes are not at a greater risk for syncope as adults.

Prevention

As of 2004 there is no known prevention for pallid breath holding spells since the trigger for such spells is unpredictable. It sometimes may be possible to prevent or interrupt a cyanotic spell by doing the following:

- avoiding situations or events that may lead to **tantrums** or have caused previous breath holding spells

- distracting the child

- intervening in temper tantrums with soothing words and gestures

- encouraging the child to express emotion with words

- placing a cold cloth on the child's face, particularly within the first 15 seconds

Parenting strategies that may help avoid cyanotic BHS include the following:

- ensuring that the child gets plenty of rest, including daytime rest periods and adequate **sleep** at night

- not allowing the child to become too hungry, because hunger can contribute to frustration

- minimizing unnecessary frustration

- avoiding unnecessary discipline

- helping the child to learn other means of expressing anger and frustration

- maintaining a regular daily routine

- maintaining a calm home atmosphere

- allowing the child to make simple choices

- praising accomplishments and good behavior

- helping the child to feel secure

- helping the child to become more independent and self-confident

Parental concerns

Breath holding spells can be extremely frightening for parents, siblings, and caregivers. Families need to be reassured that BHS is not a harmful or dangerous event and that no treatment is needed. It is important that caregivers understand the cause of breath holding spells and the proper response.

During a breath holding spell parents should:

- Protect children from injury and prevent their arms, legs, and head from hitting something hard or sharp.

- Lay children down on their back or side, preferably on a padded surface such as a carpeted floor; this increases blood flow to the brain and helps prevent muscle jerking.

- Check for food in the mouth if the child ate just before a spell. Parents should not try to remove the food; rather the child's head should be turned to one side so that the food can come out on its own.

- Touch and talk to the child.

- Allow children to wake from the spell on their own.

- Time the spell with a watch.

Following a breath holding spell, parents should do the following:

- Acknowledge the child's behavior and emotions.

- Reassure any other children present that everything is okay and it is not their fault.

- Hug the child and walk away.

Parents should NOT do the following:

- overreact

- call 911 or use mouth-to-mouth resuscitation or **cardiopulmonary resuscitation** (CPR)

- place anything in the child's mouth which could cause **choking** or vomiting

- give the child any medications during the episode

- do anything that could reinforce the behavior, including paying undue attention to the child, making a fuss about the episode, or giving in to the child's demands

- try to keep children from all frustration by overprotecting or sheltering them

A parent who cannot watch a child having a breath holding spell without intervening should leave the room.

Parents who have difficulty dealing with a child's frequent breath holding spells may choose to seek counseling.

If a child does not begin breathing on his or her own within one minute, it is not a normal breath holding spell. The parent should call 911 or other emergency services and begin rescue breathing to maintain the child's air passage until help arrives.

Resources

PERIODICALS

Anderson, Jane, and Daniel Bluestone. "Breath-Holding Spells: Scary but not Serious." *Contemporary Pediatrics* 1 (January 1, 2000): 61.

DiMario, Francis J., Jr. "Prospective Study of Children with Cyanotic and Pallid Breath-Holding Spells." *Pediatrics* 197, no. 2 (February 2001): 26–59.

ORGANIZATIONS

American Academy of Pediatrics. 141 Northwest Point Boulevard, Elk Grove Village, IL 60007–1098. Web site: <www.aap.org>.

WEB SITES

Greene, Alan. "Breath Holding." *Dr. Green.com*, April 30, 2002. Available online at <www.drgreene.com/21_1039.html> (accessed December 20, 2004).

Grover, Geeta. "Breath Holding Spells." *The Pediatric Bulletin.* Available online at <http://home.coqui.net/myrna/breath.htm> (accessed December 20, 2004).

Heins, Marilyn. "Breath-Holding Spells." *ParenTips.* Available online at <www.parentkidsright.com/pt-breath.html> (accessed December 20, 2004).

Jennette, Robert. "Breath-Holding Spells in Children: How to Distinguish the Benign Type from Serious Conditions." *Postgraduate Medicine*, May 2002. Available online at <www.postgradmed.com/issues/2002/05_02/jennette.htm> (accessed December 20, 2004).

Terra, Richard P. "Breath-Holding Spells" *PeaceHealth*, July 19, 2004. Available online at <www.peacehealth.org/kbase/topic/mini/hw31827/overview.htm> (accessed December 20, 2004).

Margaret Alic, Ph.D.

Breech birth

Definition

Breech birth is the delivery of a fetus (unborn baby) in a bottom- or foot-first position. Between 3 to 4 percent of fetuses start labor in the breech position, which is a potentially dangerous situation.

Description

Throughout most of pregnancy the developing fetus is completely free to move around within the uterus. Between 32 and 36 weeks, however, the fetus becomes so large that movement is restricted. It is much harder for the fetus to turn over, so whatever position it has assumed by this point is likely to be the same position that he or she will be in when labor begins.

For reasons that are not fully understood, almost all unborn babies settle into a head down, or vertex, position. The fetus is upside down in the uterus, and the head will dilate the cervix (or vaginal opening) and lead the way during the birth process.

Some fetuses, however, present in a breech position. There are three breech positions: frank, complete, and incomplete. In a complete breech, the buttocks lead the way out of the uterus, and the legs are folded in front of the body. A frank breech baby also has his buttocks down, but his legs will stretch straight up with his feet by his head. An incomplete breech, also known as a footling breech, presents with one or both legs down so that the feet drop into the birth canal at delivery.

Of course, many babies are safely delivered from the breech position. There are certain factors that make a breech delivery more likely to be Successful; if ultrasound (a technique that uses sound waves to visualize the fetus) shows that the fetus is in the frank breech position, the fetus's chin is tucked on its chest, and the fetus is not big, it is more likely that an uncomplicated breech delivery is possible.

The biggest part of the fetus's body is usually its head. If the head fits through the mother's pelvis, then the rest of the fetus's body should slip out fairly easily. In addition, when the baby's head comes first, the soft bones of the skull "mold" to the shape of the birth canal during labor (which is what gives newborns that cone-headed appearance). If the fetus is born bottom first, it is possible that the body will fit through the mother's pelvis, but the baby's head will get stuck at the level of the chin. This condition, known as a entrapment, has the potential to cause serious injury to the fetus, and surgical intervention may be required to complete the birth.

There is also a possibility of umbilical cord prolapse with a breech birth. The baby continues to get its oxygen supply from its mother exclusively from the blood in the umbilical cord until the head is delivered and baby breathes on her own. In some cases of breech birth, part of the umbilical cord enters the birth canal before or with the baby's feet or buttocks and pressure on the cord cuts

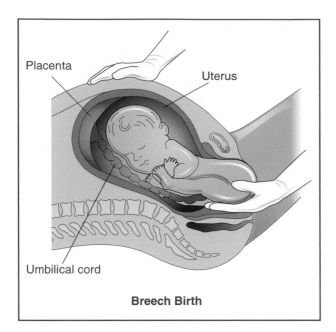

Placenta

Uterus

Umbilical cord

Breech Birth

Approximately 3–4% of babies will start labor in the breech (buttocks first) position. While this is a potentially dangerous situation, many full-term babies can be safely delivered from the breech position. *(Illustration by Electronic Illustrators Group.)*

off the blood and oxygen supply. This situation is known as cord prolapse.

Demographics

Breech presentation occurs in 3 to 4 percent of all births, and up to 95 percent of women with a breech fetus choose **cesarean section** for birth. The earlier a birth occurs in pregnancy, the higher the chances are that the fetus will be in a breech position. Twenty-five percent of premature infants born before 28 weeks are breech.

Causes and symptoms

The cause of breech birth is not known. Women with multiple gestations (i.e., **twins** or more) are more likely to have at least one fetus in a breech position simply due to space constraints in the womb. There are generally no identifiable symptoms of a breech fetus. However, some women may be able to detect the position of the fetus by where they feel the fetus kicking.

Diagnosis

A healthcare provider can often tell the position of the fetus by feeling it through the wall of the mother's abdomen. Another clue to the position is the location where the heartbeat is heard best. If the fetal heartbeat is

best heard below the level of the mother's navel, it is likely to be positioned head first. On the other hand, if the heartbeat is best heard above the level of the navel, it is likely to be breech. The most accurate way to determine breech position is using ultrasound.

Treatment

If a fetus is in the breech position in the last weeks of pregnancy, there are three possible courses of action: cesarean section (or c-section), attempted external cephalic version, or vaginal breech delivery.

Some women choose vaginal breech delivery. This should only be attempted if ultrasound shows that the fetus is in a favorable breech position. The frank breech position is the preferred position for successful vaginal breech birth, and the majority of breech fetuses are in this position. Most babies will do very well during a breech delivery, but there is a risk of fetal injury. Some providers may use forceps or a vacuum extraction device to help a breech baby out of the birth canal, a procedure known as assisted breech birth.

During an external cephalic version (also known as version), the obstetrician attempts to turn the fetus to a head first position before labor begins by manipulating the outside of the abdomen. The obstetrician places his or her hands on the mother's abdomen to feel the location of the unborn baby's buttocks and head. The buttocks are lifted up slightly and the doctor pushes on the baby's head to encourage him to perform a sideways somersault. It may take several tries before the fetus cooperates, but about half will eventually turn.

A version should only be done in a hospital, with an ultrasound machine used to guide the obstetrician in turning the fetus. The fetus should be monitored with a fetal monitor before and after the version. The mother is given medication to relax the uterus, minimize discomfort, and prevent premature contractions.

A version is not appropriate for every fetus who is in the breech position at the end of pregnancy. It can only be tried if there is one fetus in the uterus, if the placenta is not lying in front of the fetus, and if the umbilical cord does not appear to be wrapped around the fetus at any point.

Cesarean section is the most common way to deliver a breech baby and is the method recommended by the American College of Gynecology and Obstetrics if a version has failed. A c-section is performed by an obstetrician, who makes an incision in the lower abdomen through which the baby is delivered. Like any surgical procedure, c-section carries a risk of infection and hemorrhage. Postpartum recovery is also longer with

KEY TERMS

Complete breech—A breech position in which the baby is "sitting" bottom first on the cervix with legs crossed.

External cephalic version—Manual manipulation of the abdomen in order to turn a breech baby; also known as version.

Frank breech—A breech position where the baby is bottom first and his legs are extended upward so that his feet are near his head.

Incomplete breech—Also called a footling breech, in this position the baby has one or both feet down towards the pelvis so that his leg(s) are poised to deliver first.

Umbilical cord prolapse—A birth situation in which the umbilical cord, the structure that connects the placenta to the umbilicus of the fetus to deliver oxygen and nutrients, falls out of the uterus and becomes compressed, thus preventing the delivery of oxygen.

Vertex—The top of the head or highest point of the skull.

c-section than with vaginal delivery. However, in difficult breech presentations, or in cases where there are multiple fetuses and one or more are breech, it may be considered the best option for delivery.

Prognosis

Version is successful in turning a breech baby approximately 50 percent of the time. However, some babies who are successfully turned will turn back to the breech position after the procedure is done, particularly if version is attempted too early before the onset of labor.

Manipulations to deliver an entrapped head or stuck shoulder or arm can cause injury to the baby. Both entrapment and cord prolapse can be potentially fatal to an infant if delivery is delayed.

Among breech babies born after the full nine-month term, smaller babies usually do better. The exception to this is premature babies. C-section is generally the delivery mode of choice for premature babies due to the other risks these infants face (such as lung immaturity).

Prevention

There is no way to prevent a fetus from settling into the breech position at the end of pregnancy. A

woman who has had one breech fetus is at an increased risk for having another breech fetus in subsequent pregnancies.

See also Cesarean section; Childbirth.

Resources

BOOKS

Ford-Martin, Paula. *The Everything Pregnancy Book*, 2nd ed. Boston, MA: Adams Media, 2003.

Moore, Michele. *Cesarean Section.* Baltimore, MD: Johns Hopkins University Press, 2003.

PERIODICALS

Gaskin, Ina May. "The Undervalued Art of Vaginal Breech Birth." *Mothering* no. 125 (July-August 2004): 52–9.

Sachs, Jessica Snyder. "C-Sections by Choice." *Parenting* 18, no.2 (March 2004): 22.

ORGANIZATIONS

March of Dimes. 1275 Mamaroneck Avenue, White Plains, NY 10605. Web site: <www.marchofdimes.com>.

WEB SITES

"Breech Birth." Available online at <www.babycenter.com/refcap/pregnancy/childbirth/158.html> (accessed November 9, 2004).

Goer, Henci. "Scheduled cesareans: The best option for breech babies?" Available online at <www.parentsplace.com> (accessed November 9, 2004).

Amy Tuteur, MD
Paula Ford-Martin

Brittle bone disease *see* **Osteogenesis imperfecta**

Bronchiolitis

Definition

Bronchiolitis is a lung infection that affects children of any age; however, it is much more severe when it occurs in young infants.

Description

The bronchioles are small branches off of the more major bronchi or airway tubes that run through the lungs. When these bronchioles are infected, they become inflamed, and breathing may become difficult.

Bronchiolitis is a particularly important problem in babies who are born prematurely or who have other chronic medical illness. These children are at greatly increased risk of contracting bronchiolitis and of having a more severe course of the illness. Bronchiolitis is the most common reason that babies are hospitalized in the winter. Most cases of bronchiolitis occur between the months of December and May.

Demographics

Every year, 1–2 percent of all babies under 12 months of age require **hospitalization** due to bronchiolitis. At highest risk are boys, premature infants, infants living in urban locations, babies who have not been breastfed, and babies with chronic pulmonary, cardiac, or immune conditions.

Causes and symptoms

Most cases of bronchiolitis are caused by viruses, the most common of which is respiratory syncytial virus. Other common viral causes include parainfluenza, **influenza**, and adenovirus. Like most types of respiratory viruses, the viruses that cause bronchiolitis are usually contracted through breathing in infected droplets that are sprayed out by another ill individual during coughing or sneezing.

Most cases of bronchiolitis start with symptoms of a cold: sneezing, runny nose, fatigue, decreased appetite, **fever**. After two or three days of these symptoms, the bronchiole inflammation becomes severe enough to cause **cough**, wheezing, and rapid breathing.

Severely ill babies or children show signs of difficulty breathing. Their neck muscles and the muscles between their ribs will contract with each effort to breathe, and their chest may cave in as well. Smaller babies may make grunting sounds as they struggle to take in air. Babies will have difficulty nursing or taking bottles and may not be able to feed at all.

When to call the doctor

A doctor should always be called when a child appears to be in any respiratory distress. Fast breathing rates, wheezing, abnormal muscle contractions, or a blue cast to the lips or fingernails should all alert the parent that the child is having difficulty breathing and should be seen immediately by a healthcare provider.

Diagnosis

Initial diagnosis of respiratory distress is made based on clinical signs of difficulty breathing. A pulse oximeter or arterial blood gas measurement reveals the presence of decreased oxygen in the blood. Chest **x rays** may show characteristic patterns of lung involvement. Nasal swabs can be taken in order to identify the causative viral agent, although viral culture takes long enough that the patient is usually on the way to recovery by the time the viral agent has been identified.

Treatment

Treatment at home should consist of **acetaminophen** for fever and comfort (not aspirin, which has been implicated in **Reye's syndrome** in children), increased intake of liquids, and a cool water vaporizer. The utility of **asthma** medications, like bronchodilators, is as of 2004 still undecided.

Children who require hospitalization receive fluids intravenously and supplemental oxygen through a mask or nasal cannulae (small tubes into the openings of the nostrils). Ten percent of all hospitalized infants require mechanical ventilation. Children who are severely ill may be given antiviral medications, such as ribavirin, which is thought to shorten the length of illness and decrease its severity.

Prognosis

Most children recover uneventfully from bronchiolitis, although some studies have suggested that children who have had bronchiolitis may be at higher risk for reactive airway disease throughout the remainder of their lives.

Prevention

Bronchiolitis is spread the same way that most other respiratory viruses are communicated, through droplets and contact with infected nasal secretions. Good hand washing is paramount to prevention, as is keeping children out of public places while they are acutely ill and coughing and sneezing.

Parental concerns

A doctor should always be called when a child appears to be in any respiratory distress. Severe breathing difficulties need immediate medical treatment. Parent should educate their children about good personal hygiene to avoid spreading the germs that cause colds and bronchiolitis.

> ### KEY TERMS
>
> **Bronchiole**—Tubes in the lungs that carry air from the bronchi to lung tissues.

Resources

BOOKS

Goodman, Denise. "Inflammatory Disorders of the Small Airways." In *Nelson Textbook of Pediatrics*, edited by Richard E. Behrman et al. Philadelphia: Saunders, 2004.

Lazarus, Stephen. "Disorders of the Intrathoracic Airways." In *Textbook of Respiratory Medicine*, 3rd ed. Edited by John F. Murray and Jay A. Nadel. Philadelphia: Saunders, 2000.

Tristram, Debra A., and Robert C. Welliver. "Bronchiolitis." In *Principles and Practice of Pediatric Infectious Diseases*, 2nd ed. Edited by Sarah S. Long et al. St. Louis, MO: Elsevier, 2003.

PERIODICALS

Davison, C. "Efficacy of interventions for bronchiolitis in critically ill infants: a systematic review and meta-analysis." *Pediatric Critical Care Medicine* 5 (September 2004): 482–3.

Dayan, P. "Controversies in the management of children with bronchiolitis." *Center for Pediatric Emergency Medicine* 5 (March 2004): 41.

Steiner, R. W. "Treating acute bronchiolitis associated with RSV." *American Family Physician* 86 (January 2004): 325–30.

Rosalyn Carson-DeWitt, MD

Bronchitis

Definition

Bronchitis is an inflammation of the air passages between the nose and the lungs, including the windpipe or trachea and the larger air tubes of the lung that bring air in from the trachea (bronchi). Bronchitis can either be of brief duration (acute) or have a long course (chronic). Acute bronchitis is usually caused by a viral infection but can also be caused by a bacterial infection and can heal without complications. Chronic bronchitis is a sign of serious lung disease that may be slowed but cannot be cured. This form is found almost exclusively in adult smokers. Bronchitis in children is often misdiagnosed as **asthma**.

Description

Acute bronchitis is most prevalent in winter. It is most often caused by a viral infection and may be accompanied by a secondary bacterial infection. Acute bronchitis resolves within two weeks, although the **cough** may persist longer. Acute bronchitis, like any upper airway inflammatory process, can increase a child's likelihood of developing **pneumonia**.

Demographics

Acute bronchitis is one of the more common illnesses affecting **preschool** and school-age children. It is more commonly diagnosed among children under age five than any other age group. It occurs more often in young males. It can occur anytime but is more frequent during the winter months. In otherwise healthy children complications are few.

Causes and symptoms

Acute bronchitis usually begins with the symptoms of a cold, such as a runny nose, sneezing, and dry cough. However, the cough soon becomes deep and painful. Coughing brings up a greenish yellow phlegm or sputum. These symptoms may be accompanied by a **fever** of up to 102°F (38.8°C). Wheezing after coughing is common.

In uncomplicated acute bronchitis, the fever and most other symptoms, except the cough, disappear after three to five days. Coughing may continue for several weeks. Acute bronchitis is often complicated by a bacterial infection, in which case the fever and a general feeling of illness persist. To be cured, the bacterial infection should be treated with **antibiotics**. A cough that does not go away may be a sign of another problem such as asthma or pneumonia.

Physical findings of acute bronchitis vary with the age of the child, and the stage of the disease, but may include the following:

- runny nose
- dry, hacking unproductive cough that may change to a loose cough with increased mucus
- sore throat
- back and other muscle pains
- chills and low grade fever
- headache and general malaise (feeling unwell)

Diagnosis

Initial diagnosis of bronchitis is based on observing the child's symptoms and health history. The physician will listen to the child's chest with a stethoscope for specific sounds that indicate lung inflammation, such as moist rales and crackling, and wheezing, that indicate airway narrowing. Moist rales is a bubbling sound heard

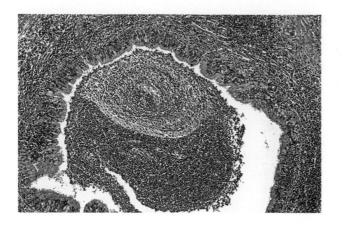

Light micrograph of a five-year-old revealing acute bronchitis, shown by a bronchial tube filled with pus. (*© Gladden Willis, M.D./Visuals Unlimited.*)

with a stethoscope that is caused by fluid secretion in the bronchial tubes.

A sputum culture may be performed, particularly if the sputum is green or has blood in it, to determine whether a bacterial infection is present and to identify the disease-causing organism so that an appropriate antibiotic can be selected. Normally, the patient will be asked to cough deeply then spit the material that comes up from the lungs (sputum) into a cup. This sample is then grown in the laboratory to determine which organisms are present. The results are available in two to three days.

Occasionally, in diagnosing a chronic lung disorder, the sample of sputum is collected using a procedure called a bronchoscopy. In this procedure, the patient is given a local anesthetic, and a tube is passed into the airways to collect a sputum sample.

To better determine what type of obstructive lung disease a patient has, the doctor may do a chest x ray and order blood tests. Other tests may be used to measure how effectively oxygen and carbon dioxide are exchanged in the lungs.

Treatment

When no secondary infection is present, acute bronchitis is treated in the same way as the **common cold**. Home care includes drinking plenty of fluids, resting, not **smoking**, increasing moisture in the air with a cool mist humidifier, and taking **acetaminophen** (Datril, Tylenol, Panadol) for fever and **pain**. Aspirin should not be given to children because of its association with the serious illness **Reye's syndrome**.

Cough suppressants are used only when the cough is dry and produces no sputum. If the patient is coughing up phlegm, the cough should be allowed to continue. The purpose of the cough is to bring up extra mucus and irritants from the lungs. When coughing is suppressed, the mucus accumulates in the plugged airways and can become a breeding ground for pneumonia bacteria.

Expectorant cough medicines, unlike cough suppressants, do not stop the cough. Instead they are used to thin the mucus in the lungs, making it easier to cough up. This type of cough medicine may be helpful to individuals suffering from bronchitis. People who are unsure about what type of medications are in over-the-counter cough syrups should ask their pharmacist for an explanation.

If a secondary bacterial infection is present, the infection is treated with an antibiotic. Patients need to take the entire amount of antibiotic prescribed. Stopping the antibiotic early can lead to a return of the infection. Tetracycline or ampicillin is often used to treat adults. Other possibilities include trimethoprim/sulfamethoxazole (Bactrim or Septra) and the newer erythromycin-like drugs, such as azithromycin (Zithromax) and clarithromycin (Biaxin). Children under age eight are usually given amoxicillin (Amoxil, Pentamox, Sumox, Trimox) because tetracycline discolors permanent teeth that have not yet come in.

For some children with acute bronchitis, doctors may prescribe medicines often used to treat asthma. These medicines can help open the bronchial tubes and clear out mucus. Bronchial dilators are usually given with an inhaler. An inhaler sprays the medicine right into the bronchial tree.

Prognosis

When treated, acute bronchitis normally resolves in one to two weeks without complications, although a cough may continue for several more weeks. The progression of chronic bronchitis, on the other hand, may be slowed, but an initial improvement in symptoms may be achieved.

Prevention

Parents should make sure their children are getting adequate **nutrition** and rest to boost their immunity during cold and flu season. Children should be taught to wash their hands regularly to avoid spreading bacteria and viruses. Other preventative steps include avoiding chemical and environmental irritants, such as air pollution. Immunizations against certain types of pneumonia (as well as **influenza**) are an important preventative measure for the very young or those children with chronic diseases.

KEY TERMS

Acute—Refers to a disease or symptom that has a sudden onset and lasts a relatively short period of time.

Bronchi—Singular, bronchus; the large tubular passages that carry air to the lung and allow air to be expelled from the lungs.

Chronic—Refers to a disease or condition that progresses slowly but persists or recurs over time.

Parental concerns

Parents should encourage fluids by frequent offers of small amounts of the child's favorite liquids. Humidifiers should produce moist air to keep mucus from drying and to make it easier for the child to breathe. The child should be checked for signs of **dehydration**, including daily weights. Acetaminophen is given for temperatures over 101°F (38.3°C). Quiet activity provides a diversion for the sick child.

In caring for a child with acute bronchitis, parents should make the following observations:

• Is there a decrease in coughing and mucus production?

• Does the child have periods of rest and sleep?

• Is the child's intake enough for his or her age?

• Has the child kept a normal body temperature for 24 hours?

Parents should be aware that there is a significant association between high levels of air pollution, smoking, and increased incidence of chronic bronchitis. Air pollutants aggravate chronic pulmonary disease in children and cause decreased pulmonary performance in exercising children and teenagers. Teenagers should be questioned and taught about the ill effects of smoking either tobacco or marijuana. Teenagers should also be questioned about industrial fumes or automobile exhaust exposure at school or work.

Resources

BOOKS

Acute Bronchitis: A Medical Dictionary, Bibliography, and Annotated Research Guide to Internet References. San Diego, CA: Icon Group International, 2004.

Bronchitis: A Medical Dictionary, Bibliography, and Annotated Research Guide to Internet References. San Diego, CA: Icon Group International, 2003.

Ivker, Robert S. *Sinus Survival: The Holistic Medical Treatment for Allergies, Bronchitis, Colds, and Sinus.* East Rutherford, NJ: Penguin Group, 2000.

Wright, Jill. *Asthma and Bronchitis.* Northfield, IL: How to Books, 2004.

ORGANIZATIONS

American Lung Association. 1740 Broadway, New York, NY 10019. Web site: <www.lungusa.org>.

National Heart, Lung, and Blood Institute. PO Box 30105, Bethesda, MD 20824–0105. Web site: <www.nhlbi.nih.gov>.

National Jewish Center for Immunology and Respiratory Medicine. 1400 Jackson St., Denver, CO 80206. Web site: <www.nationaljewish.org/main.html>.

WEB SITES

"Bronchitis." *MedlinePlus.* Available online at <www.nlm.nih.gov/medlineplus/bronchitis.html> (accessed December 17, 2004).

Aliene Linwood, RN, DPA, FACHE
Tish Davidson, AM

Bruises

Definition

Bruises, or ecchymoses, are a discoloration and tenderness of the skin or mucous membranes due to the leakage of blood from an injured blood vessel into the tissues. Purpura refers to bruising as the result of a disease condition. A very small bruise is called a petechia. These often appear as many tiny red dots clustered together and could indicate a serious problem.

Description

Bruises change colors over time in a predictable pattern, so that it is possible to estimate when an injury occurred by the color of the bruise. Initially, a bruise will be reddish, the color of the blood under the skin. After one to two days, the red blood cells begin to break down, and the bruise will darken to a blue or purplish color. This color fades to green at about day six. Around the eighth or ninth day, the skin over the bruised area will have a brown or yellowish appearance, and it will gradually fade back to its normal color.

Long periods of standing cause blood that collects in a bruise to seep through the tissues. Bruises are actually made of little pools of blood, so the blood in one place may flow toward the ground, and the bruise may appear in another location. For instance, bruising in the back of the abdomen may eventually appear in the groin; bruising in the thigh or the knee will work its way down to the ankle.

Demographics

All persons develop bruises at many times during their lives. The condition is entirely natural and normal.

Causes and symptoms

Healthy people may develop bruises from any injury that does not break through the skin. Vigorous **exercise** may also cause bruises due to bringing about small tears in blood vessels walls. In a condition known as purpura simplex, there is a tendency to bruise easily due to an increased fragility of the blood vessels. Bruises also develop easily in the elderly, because the skin and blood vessels have a tendency to become thinner and more fragile with aging, and there tends to be an increased use of medications that interfere with the blood clotting system. In the condition known as purpura senilis, the elderly develop bruises from minimal contact that may take up to several months to completely heal.

The use of nonsteroidal anti-inflammatories such as ibuprofen and naproxen sodium may lead to increased bruising. Aspirin, **antidepressants**, **asthma** medications, and cortisone medications also have this effect. The anticlotting medications also known as blood thinners, especially the drug warfarin (Coumadin), may be the cause of particularly severe bruising.

Sometimes bruises are linked with more serious illnesses. There are a number of diseases that cause excessive bleeding or bleeding from injuries too slight to have consequences in healthy people. An abnormal tendency to bleed may be due to hereditary bleeding disorders, certain prescription medications, diseases of the blood such as leukemia, and diseases that increase the fragility of blood vessels. If there are large areas of bruising or bruises develop very easily, this may herald a problem. Other causes that should be ruled out include liver disease, **alcoholism**, drug **addiction**, and acquired immune deficiency syndrome (**AIDS**). Bruising that occurs around the navel may indicate dangerous internal bleeding; bruising behind the ear, called Battle's sign, may be due to a skull fracture; and raised bruises may point to autoimmune disease.

When to call the doctor

A physician or healthcare professional should be consulted when accidents involve extensive bruising or when bruises do not heal in a timely manner (seven to 10 days). A physician should be called if bruises appear in unusual locations on the body such as on the back or around the eyes or wrists. Such injuries are often the result of abuse.

Diagnosis

Bruising is usually a minor problem that does not require a formal medical diagnosis. However, faced with extensive bruising, bruising with no apparent cause, or bruising in certain locations, a physician will pursue an evaluation that includes a number of blood tests. If the area of the bruise becomes hard, an x ray may be required.

Treatment

A bruise by itself usually requires no medical treatment. It is often recommended that ice packs be applied on and off during the first 24 hours after injury to reduce the bruising. After that, heat, especially moist heat, is recommended to increase the circulation and the healing of the injured tissues. Rest, elevation of the affected part, and compression with a bandage will also retard the accumulation of blood. Rarely, if a bruise is so large that the body cannot completely absorb it or if the site becomes infected, it may have to be surgically removed.

Several types of alternative treatments are often recommended to speed healing and to reduce the **pain** associated with bruises. Most of these treatments are topical in nature and frequently include vitamin K cream can be applied directly to the site of injury. Astringent herbs such as witch hazel, *Hamamelis virginiana*, can be used. This treatment will tighten the tissues and therefore diminish the bruising. The homeopathic remedy, *Arnica montana*, can be applied as a cream or gel to unbroken skin.

Oral homeopathic remedies may reduce bruising, pain, and swelling as well. *Arnica montana*, at 30 ml (1 oz), taken one to two times per day is highly recommended.

Prognosis

The blood under the skin which causes the discoloration of bruising should be totally reabsorbed by the body in three weeks or less. At that time, the skin color should have completely returned to normal.

Sometimes a bruise may become solid and increase in size instead of dissolving. This may indicate blood trapped in the tissues, which may need to be drained. This condition is referred to as a hematoma. Less

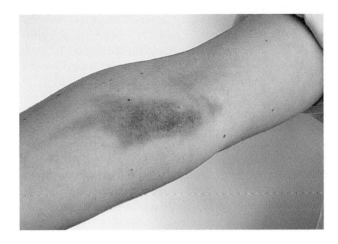

Bruised arm of a child. *(© Garo/Photo Researchers, Inc.)*

commonly, the body may develop calcium deposits at the injury site in a process called heterotopic ossification.

Prevention

Vitamin K promotes normal clotting in the blood and, therefore, may help reduce the tendency to bruise easily. Green leafy vegetables, alfalfa, broccoli, seaweed, and fish liver oils are good dietary sources of vitamin K. Other good foods to eat are those containing bioflavonoids, such as reddish-blue berries. These can assist in strengthening the connective tissue, which decreases the spread of blood and bruising. Zinc and vitamin C supplements are also recommended for this purpose.

Nutritional concerns

A balanced diet that includes green leafy vegetables and broccoli should provide a sufficient source of vitamin K. Vitamin C and zinc supplements are also helpful.

Parental concerns

Parents should provide a balanced diet for their children. They should also provide appropriate care for bruises that inevitably occur.

Resources

BOOKS

Gordon, Sharon, and Nanci Varquis. *Bruises.* New York: Scholastic Library Publishing, 2002.

Royston, Angela. *Bumps and Bruises.* Orlando, FL: Heinemann Library, 2004.

———— *Why Do Bruises Change Color?: And Other Questions about Blood.* Orlando, FL: Heinemann Library, 2003.

PERIODICALS

Baruch, M. B., and R. Beck-Little R. "A 12-year-old boy with multiple bruises and a dislocated knee but no reported injury." *Journal of Emergency Nursing* 30, no. 3 (2004): 213–5.

Gates, D. "Burgers or bruises? Being assaulted shouldn't be part of a nurse's aide's job." *American Journal of Nursing* 104, no. 9 (2004): 13–4.

Sibert, J., et al. "Bruising, coagulation disorder, and physical child abuse." *Blood Coagulation and Fibrinolysis* 15, no. Supplement 1 (2004): S33–9.

Yamagami, T., et al. "Clinical features of snowboarding injuries." *Journal of Orthopedic Science* 9, no. 3 (2004): 225–9.

ORGANIZATIONS

American Academy of Emergency Medicine. 611 East Wells Street, Milwaukee, WI 53202. Web site: <www.aaem.org/>.

American Academy of Family Physicians. 11400 Tomahawk Creek Parkway, Leawood, KS 66211–2672. Web site: <www.aafp.org/>.

American Academy of Pediatrics. 141 Northwest Point Boulevard, Elk Grove Village, IL 60007–1098. Web site: <www.aap.org/>.

American Academy of Physical Medicine and Rehabilitation. One IBM Plaza, Suite 2500, Chicago, IL 60611–3604. Web site: <www.aapmr.org/>.

American College of Emergency Physicians. PO Box 619911, Dallas, TX 75261–9911. Web site: <www.acep.org/>.

American College of Osteopathic Emergency Physicians. 142 E. Ontario Street, Suite 550, Chicago, IL 60611. Web site: <www.acoep.org/>.

American College of Sports Medicine. 401 W. Michigan St., Indianapolis, IN 46202–3233. Web site: <www.acsm.org/>.

WEB SITES

"Bruises." *MedlinePlus.* Available online at <www.nlm.nih.gov/medlineplus/bruises.html> (accessed December 7, 2004).

"Bruises/Contusions." *ForensicMD.* Available online at <www.forensicmed.co.uk/bruises.htm> (accessed December 7, 2004).

"Bruises, Ouch!" *University of Iowa Health Science Relations.* Available online at <www.vh.org/adult/patient/familymedicine/prose/bruises.html> (accessed December 7, 2004).

L. Fleming Fallon, Jr., MD, DrPH

Bruton's agammaglobulinemia

Definition

Bruton's agammaglobulinemia is a disorder that is present at birth (congenital) and is characterized by low or completely absent levels of immunoglobulins in the bloodstream. Bruton's agammaglobulinemia is also known as X-linked agammaglobulinemia (XLA).

Description

Children with XLA have very low, or completely absent, levels of immumoglobulins in their blood. Immunoglobulins are protein molecules in blood serum that function like antibodies. Without them, the body lacks a fully functioning immune system. Individuals with XLA are vulnerable to repeated, potentially fatal, bacterial infections.

Although persons with XLA carry the genes to produce immunoglobulins, a genetic defect on the X chromosome prevents their formation. This defect is not associated with the immunoglobulins themselves, but rather with the B cells in the bloodstream that ordinarily secrete the immunoglobulins.

B cells are a type of white blood cell. They are the sole producers of immunoglobulins in the body. B cells are produced in the bone marrow and carried to the spleen, lymph nodes, and other organs as they mature. The maturation process depends on an enzyme called Bruton's agammaglobulinemia tyrosine kinase (Btk). If Btk is missing or defective, the B cells cannot mature and cannot produce immunoglobulins.

The gene that controls the production of Btk is on the X chromosome. Certain changes (mutations) in this gene result in defective Btk. Males have one X and one Y chromosome (XY). Females have two X chromosomes (XX). The mother passes one of her two X chromosomes down to her child, and the father passes either an X or a Y chromosome to the child. The mutated gene that produces XLA is a recessive gene. This means that as long as one good copy is present, the disease will not occur. Boys only have one copy of the gene, because they only have one X chromosome. Girls have two copies of the gene. This means that for boys to have XLA they must only inherit one copy of the defective gene, but for girls to have the disease they have to inherit two copies, one from each parent. This is why diseases associated with X linked genes are usually much more common in boys than in girls. To date, no cases of XLA in girls have actually been reported.

Demographics

XLA occurs in one in every 50,000 to one in every 100,000 newborns. Males are overwhelmingly more likely to have it than girls. Children who have an affected relative are more likely to be at risk, because the defect causing the disorder is inherited.

Causes and symptoms

XLA is caused by a defect in the gene that controls the production of the enzyme Btk. This defect blocks B cells from maturing. Only mature B cells produce immunoglobulins. Because other portions of the immune system are functional, people with XLA can fight off some types of infection, such as fungal and most viral infections. Immunoglobulins, however, are vital for combating bacterial infections.

Infants with XLA usually do not show symptoms of the disorder during the first six months of life, because immunoglobulins from their mothers are circulating in their bloodstreams. Over time, their immunoglobulin levels begin to decrease because they cannot successfully produce their own. As the immunoglobulin levels decrease, the baby becomes increasingly vulnerable to bacterial infections.

Common symptoms of immunoglobulin deficiency usually appear after the infant is six months old. They include frequent ear and sinus infections, **pneumonia**, and **gastroenteritis**. Certain viruses, such as hepatitis and **polio** viruses, can also pose a threat. Children with XLA often have small tonsils and lymph nodes and may develop chronic skin infections. Approximately 20 percent of these children develop arthritis, possibly as a result of joint infections.

KEY TERMS

Antibody—A special protein made by the body's immune system as a defense against foreign material (bacteria, viruses, etc.) that enters the body. It is uniquely designed to attack and neutralize the specific antigen that triggered the immune response.

B cell—A type of white blood cell derived from bone marrow. B cells are sometimes called B lymphocytes. They secrete antibodies and have a number of other complex functions within the human immune system.

Bruton's agammaglobulinemia tyrosine kinase (Btk)—An enzyme vital for the maturation of B cells.

Carrier—A person who possesses a gene for an abnormal trait without showing signs of the disorder. The person may pass the abnormal gene on to offspring. Also refers to a person who has a particular disease agent present within his/her body, and can pass this agent on to others, but who displays no symptoms of infection.

Enzyme—A protein that catalyzes a biochemical reaction without changing its own structure or function.

Immunoglobulin G (IgG)— Immunoglobulin type gamma, the most common type found in the blood and tissue fluids.

Mutation—A permanent change in the genetic material that may alter a trait or characteristic of an individual, or manifest as disease. This change can be transmitted to offspring.

X chromosome—One of the two sex chromosomes (the other is Y) that determine a person's gender. Normal males have both an X and a Y chromosome, and normal females have two X chromosomes.

When to call the doctor

If a child has had many more infections, especially serious infections, than is normal for a child of his or her age there may be an immune system problem such as XLA and a doctor should be consulted.

Diagnosis

Frequent bacterial infections, a lack of mature B cells, and low-to-nonexistent levels of immunoglobulins point to a diagnosis of XLA. A sample of the child's blood serum can be analyzed for the presence of immunoglobulins by a technique called immunoelectrophoresis. To make a definitive diagnosis, the child's X chromosome is analyzed for defects in the Btk gene. Similar analysis can be used for prenatal diagnosis or to detect carriers of the defective gene.

Treatment

Treatment of XLA consists of regular intravenous doses of commercially prepared gamma globulin (sold under the trade names Gamimune or Gammagard) to ward off infections. **Antibiotics** are used to treat infections as they occur. Children with XLA must be treated promptly for even minor cuts and scrapes and taught to avoid crowds and people with active infections.

Prognosis

Prior to the era of gamma globulin and antibiotic treatment, approximately 90 percent of XLA individuals died before the age of eight. Early diagnosis and therapy in the early 2000s allows most individuals with XLA to reach adulthood and lead relatively normal lives. Infants who develop polio or persistent viral infections, however, have a poorer prognosis.

Prevention

There is no known way to prevent XLA. However, if an individual believes a **family** member may have XLA, it is possible to get genetic counseling prior to pregnancy to determine if the individual is a carrier of the gene. If the person is a carrier various options can be discussed.

Parental concerns

Children with XLA can have normal lives. Most medical care can be managed on an outpatient basis or even by home care. Special attention needs to be paid to the beginning of infections so that they can be treated promptly, but in general, children should be encouraged to participate in normal activities such as school and **play**. Usually, children with XLA are not given any vaccines containing live viruses (such as **measles**, **mumps**, or polio) because there is a small but dangerous risk that the child will actually get the disease that the vaccine was intended to prevent.

Resources

ORGANIZATIONS

Immune Deficiency Foundation. 40 W. Chesapeake Ave Suite 308 Towson, MD 21204. Web site: <www.primaryimmune.org>.

WEB SITES

Chin, Terry. "Agammaglobulinemia." Available online at <www.emedicine.com/ped/topic54.htm> (accessed October 27, 2004).

"X-Linked Agammaglobulinemia." *Children's Hospital and Health System.* Available online at <www.chw.org/display/PPF/DocID/2229/router.asp> (accessed October 27, 2004).

Tish Davidson, A.M.
Julia Barrett

Bulimia nervosa

Definition

Bulimia nervosa is a serious and sometimes life-threatening eating disorder affecting mainly young women. People with bulimia, known as bulimics, consume large amounts of food (binge) and then try to rid themselves of the food and calories (purge) by fasting, excessive **exercise**, **vomiting**, or using **laxatives**. The behavior often serves to reduce stress and relieve **anxiety**. Because bulimia results from an excessive concern with weight control and self-image and is often accompanied by depression, it is also considered to be a psychiatric illness.

Description

Bulimia nervosa is a serious health problem for over 2 million adolescent girls and young women in the United States. The bingeing and purging activity associated with this disorder can cause severe damage, even death, although the risk of death is not as high as for **anorexia nervosa**, an eating disorder that leads to excessive weight loss.

In rare instances, binge eating may cause the stomach to rupture. In the case of purging, heart failure can result due to loss of vital **minerals** such as potassium. Vomiting causes other serious problems, including acid-related scarring of the fingers (if used to induce vomiting) and damage to tooth enamel. In addition, the tube that delivers food from the mouth to the stomach (the esophagus) often becomes inflamed, and salivary glands can become swollen. Irregular menstrual periods can also result, and interest in sex may diminish.

Most bulimics find it difficult to stop their behavior without professional help. Many typically recognize that the behavior is not normal, but they feel helpless to control it. Some bulimics struggle with other compulsive, risky behaviors such as drug and alcohol abuse. Many also suffer from other psychiatric illnesses, including clinical depression, anxiety, and **obsessive-compulsive disorder** (OCD).

Bulimic behavior is often carried out in secrecy, accompanied by feelings of guilt or shame. Outwardly, many people with bulimia appear healthy and successful, while inside they have feelings of helplessness and low **self-esteem**.

Demographics

Most bulimics are females in their teens to early 20s. Males account for only 5 to 10 percent of all cases. People of all races develop the disorder, but most of those diagnosed are white.

Causes and symptoms

The cause of bulimia is as of 2004 unknown. Researchers believe that it may be caused by a combination of genetic and environmental factors. Bulimia tends to run in families. Research shows that certain brain chemicals, known as neurotransmitters, may function abnormally in acutely ill people with bulimia nervosa. Scientists also believe there may be a link between bulimia and other psychiatric problems, such as depression and OCD. Environmental influences include participation in work or **sports** that emphasize thinness, such as modeling, dancing, or gymnastics. **Family** pressures also may play a role. One study found that mothers who are extremely concerned about their daughters' physical attractiveness and weight may in part cause bulimia in them. In addition, girls with eating disorders tend to have fathers and brothers who criticize their weight. Bulimia tends to run in families.

According to the American Anorexia/Bulimia Association Inc., warning signs of bulimia include the following:

- eating large amounts of food uncontrollably (bingeing)
- vomiting, abusing laxatives or diuretics, or engaging in fasting, dieting, or vigorous exercise (purging)
- preoccupation with body weight
- using the bathroom frequently after meals
- depression or mood swings
- irregular menstrual periods

- onset of dental problems, swollen cheeks or glands, heartburn, or bloating

When to call the doctor

A healthcare professional should be consulted at the first sign of behaviors associated with bulimia.

Diagnosis

Bulimia is treated most successfully when diagnosed early. However, because the bulimic may deny there is a problem, getting medical help is often delayed. A complete physical examination in order to rule out other illnesses is the first step to diagnosis.

According to the American Psychiatric Association, a diagnosis of bulimia requires that a person have all of the following symptoms:

- recurrent episodes of binge eating (minimum average of two binge-eating episodes a week for at least three months)

- a feeling of lack of control over eating during the binges

- regular use of one or more of the following to prevent weight gain: self-induced vomiting, use of laxatives or diuretics, strict dieting or fasting, or vigorous exercise

- persistent over-concern with body shape and weight

Treatment

Early treatment is important; otherwise, bulimia may become chronic, with serious health consequences. A comprehensive treatment plan is called for in order to address the complex interaction of physical and psychological problems in bulimia. A combination of drug and behavioral therapies is commonly used.

Behavioral approaches include individual psychotherapy, group therapy, and **family therapy**. Cognitive-behavioral therapy, which teaches people how to change abnormal thoughts and behavior, is also used. **Nutrition** counseling and self-help groups are often helpful.

Antidepressants commonly used to treat bulimia include desipramine (Norpramin), imipramine (Tofranil), and fluoxetine (Prozac). These medications also may treat any co-existing depression.

In addition to professional treatment, family support plays an important role in helping the bulimic person. Encouragement and emotional support may convince the sick person to get help, stay with treatment, or try again

---

Bulimia nervosa

Criteria

1. Recurrent episodes of binge eating, which is characterized by 1) consumption of an amount of food that is definitely larger than most people would eat during a similar period of time and under similar circumstances AND 2) a sense of lack of control over eating during the episode.

2. Recurrent inappropriate compensatory behavior in order to prevent weight gain, such as self-induced vomiting; misuse of laxatives, diuretics, or enemas, or other medications; or fasting or excessive exercise.

3. Binge eating and compensatory behaviors both occur an average of twice a week for three months.

4. Self-evaluation is unduly influenced by body shape and weight.

5. The disturbance does not occur exclusively during episodes of anorexia nervosa.

Purging type: Regular episodes of self-induced vomiting or misuse of laxatives, diuretics, or enemas.

Nonpurging type: No regular episodes of self-induced vomiting or misuse of laxatives, diuretics, or enemas. Patient uses fasting or excessive exercise to avoid weight gain.

SOURCE: *Diagnostic and Statistical Manual of Mental Disorders IV.*

(Table by GGS Information Services.)

---

after a failure. Family members can help locate resources, such as eating disorder clinics in local hospitals or treatment programs in colleges designed for students.

Light therapy—exposure to bright, artificial light—may be useful in reducing bulimic episodes, especially during the dark winter months. Some feel that massage may prove helpful, putting people in touch with the reality of their own bodies and correcting misconceptions of body image. Hypnotherapy may help resolve unconscious issues that contribute to bulimic behavior.

Prognosis

Bulimia may become chronic and lead to serious health problems, including seizures, irregular heartbeat, and thin bones. In rare cases, it may be fatal. Timely therapy and medication can effectively manage the disorder and help the bulimic live a normal, productive, and fulfilling life.

Prevention

There is as of 2004 no known method for preventing bulimia. However, parents can promote healthy eating habits in their children and encourage them to embrace realistic, rather than overly thin, body images.

KEY TERMS

Binge—A pattern of eating marked by episodes of rapid consumption of large amounts of food; usually food that is high in calories.

Diuretics—A group of drugs that helps remove excess water from the body by increasing the amount lost by urination.

Neurotransmitters—Chemicals in the brain that transmit nerve impulses.

Obsessive-compulsive disorder—An anxiety disorder marked by the recurrence of intrusive or disturbing thoughts, impulses, images, or ideas (obsessions) accompanied by repeated attempts to supress these thoughts through the performance of certain irrational and ritualistic behaviors or mental acts (compulsions).

Purge—To rid the body of food and calories, commonly by vomiting or using laxatives.

Nutritional concerns

Abnormal food intake and purging may result in abnormal nutrition. Purging may lead to a loss of potassium and other essential metabolic ions. These can become life threatening.

Parental concerns

Parental remarks about body size and shape often trigger bulimia. Parents of bulimics must be supportive and participate in treatment if the condition is to be successfully treated.

See also Binge eating disorder.

Resources

BOOKS

Bendich, Adrianne, and David J. Goldstein. *Management of Eating Disorders and Obesity*, 2nd ed. Totawa, NJ: Humana Press, 2004.

Litt, Iris F. "Anorexia Nervosa and Bulimia." In *Nelson Textbook of Pediatrics*, 17th ed. Edited by Richard E. Behrman, et al. Philadelphia: Saunders, 2003, pp. 652–3.

Smith, Grainne. *Anorexia and Bulimia in the Family: One Parent's Practical Guide to Recovery*. New York: Wiley & Sons, 2004.

Walsh, B. Timothy. "Eating Disorders." In *Harrison's Principles of Internal Medicine*, 15th ed. Edited by Eugene Braunwald, et al. New York: McGraw Hill, 2001, pp. 486–90.

West, Delia Smith. "The Eating Disorders." In *Cecil Textbook of Medicine*, 22nd ed. Edited by Lee Goldman, et al. Philadelphia: Saunders, 2003, pp. 1326–35.

PERIODICALS

Burns, M., and N. Gavey. "Healthy weight at what cost? Bulimia and a discourse of weight control." *Journal of Health Psychology* 9, no. 4 (2004): 249–65.

Crow, S. J., et al. "Bulimia symptoms and other risk behaviors during pregnancy in women with bulimia nervosa." *International Journal of Eating Disorders* 36, no. 2 (2004): 220–3.

Hinney A., et al. "Genetic risk factors in eating disorders." *American Journal of Pharmacogenomics* 4, no. 4 (2004): 209–23.

Morad, M., I. Kandel, and J. Merrick. "Anorexia and bulimia in the family." *International Journal of Adolescent Medicine and Health* 16, no. 2 (2004): 89–90.

ORGANIZATIONS

American Academy of Family Physicians. 11400 Tomahawk Creek Parkway, Leawood, KS 66211–2672. Web site: <www.aafp.org/>.

American Academy of Pediatrics. 141 Northwest Point Boulevard, Elk Grove Village, IL 60007–1098. Web site: <www.aap.org/default.htm>.

American Psychiatric Association. 1400 K Street NW, Washington, DC 20005. Web site: <www.psych.org/>.

American Psychological Association. 750 First Street NW, Washington, DC, 20002–4242. Web site: <www.apa.org/>.

National Eating Disorders Organization (NEDO). 6655 South Yale Ave, Tulsa, OK 74136. Web site: <www.NationalEatingDisorders.org>.

WEB SITES

"Bulimia." *National Alliance for the Mentally Ill.* Available online at <www.nami.org/Template.cfm?Section=By_Illness&template=/ContentManagement/ContentDisplay.cfm&ContentID=7638> (accessed November 2, 2004).

"Bulimia." *National Library of Medicine.* Available online at <www.nlm.nih.gov/medlineplus/ency/article/000341.htm> (accessed November 2, 2004).

"Bulimia and Related Disorders." *Northern Arizona University.* Available online at <http://dana.ucc.nau.edu/~kdk2/bulimia.html> (accessed November 2, 2004).

"Bulimia Nervosa." *Internet Mental Health.* Available online at <www.mentalhealth.com/dis/p20-et02.html> (accessed November 2, 2004).

L. Fleming Fallon, Jr., MD, DrPH

Bullies

Definition

Bullies are aggressive children who repeatedly physically or emotionally abuse, torment, or victimize smaller, weaker, or younger children.

Description

Bullying usually involves an older or larger child or children victimizing a single child who is unable to defend himself or herself. Bullying is generally viewed as a form of harassment committed by a child or children who are older, stronger, or otherwise more powerful socially, upon weaker adolescents. Often, the power of the bully is dependent on the perception of the victim, with the bullied child often too intimidated to effectively resist the bully.

Although the stereotypical bully is male, girls engage in bullying behavior almost as often as boys. Their tactics differ, however, in that they are less visible. Boys who are bullies tend to resort to one-on-one physical aggression, while girls tend to bully as a group through social exclusion and the spreading of rumors. Girls who would never bully individually will often take part in group bullying activities.

Bullying begins at a very early age; it is not uncommon to find bullies in **preschool**. Until about age seven, bullies appear to choose their victims at random. After that, they single out specific children to torment on a regular basis. Nearly twice as much bullying goes on in grades two to four as in grades six to eight, and, as bullies grow older, they tend to use less physical abuse and more verbal abuse.

Bullies are often popular among their peers until about sixth grade. They average two or three friends, and other children seem to admire them for their physical toughness. By high school, however, their social acceptance diminishes to the point that their only "friends" are other bullies. Despite their unpopularity, bullies have relatively high **self-esteem**, perhaps because they process social information inaccurately.

For example, bullies attribute hostile intentions to people around them and therefore perceive provocation where it does not exist. "What are you staring at?" is a common opening line of bullies. For the bully, these perceived slights serve as justification for **aggressive behavior**.

Children who become the targets of bullies generally have a negative view of violence and go out of their way to avoid conflict. They tend to be "loners" who exhibit signs of vulnerability before being singled out by a bully. Being victimized leads these children, who already may lack self-esteem, to feel more anxious, thereby increasing their vulnerability to further bullying. Being the target of a bully leads to social isolation and rejection by peers, and victims tend to internalize others' negative views, further eroding their self-esteem. Although bullying actually lessens during **adolescence**, this is the period when peer rejection is most painful for victims.

Sometimes the victims of bullies are larger, stronger, or older than the bully but allow the bullying to continue because they are intimidated, do not believe in violence, or are taught non-violence by their parents.

Studies show that students who are gay or bisexual or are perceived as gay or bisexual experience an extremely high rate of bullying, not only by other students, but often by teachers and other school personnel. Also, bullying against gay and bisexual students is often ignored or sometimes encouraged by homophobic school staff members.

According to the American School Health Association, students who discover they are gay or bisexual often experience rejection, discrimination, isolation, and violence, and this fact makes it all the more important for teachers and administrators to be supportive and sensitive to them. Schools are obligated under federal law to protect students from discrimination and harassment, from other students as well as teachers and all other school employees. In 1996, a federal appeals court ruled that school officials can be held liable under the Equal Protection Clause of the U.S. Constitution for not protecting gay and bisexual students from harassment and discrimination. The ruling still stood as of 2004.

Extensive long-term research indicates that bullying is not a phase a child outgrows. In a study of more than 500 children, University of Michigan researchers discovered that children who were viewed as the most aggressive by their peers at age eight grew up to commit increasingly more serious crimes as adults. Other studies indicate that, as adults, bullies are far more likely to abuse their spouses and children.

Modern schools tend to discourage bullying with programs designed to teach students cooperation and train peers in bullying intervention techniques. However, some schools have a zero tolerance for violence so if two students are discovered in a fight, both are disciplined, often by suspension, even though one may be the bully and the other the victim.

Experts say that school violence often is rooted in bullying. While bullying is often verbal threats and harassment, it can get out of control and turn into violence, including the use of weapons.

Researchers who have studied bullying have concluded that up to 15 percent of children say they are regularly bullied, and it occurs most frequently at school in areas where there is inadequate or no adult supervision, such as the playground, hallways, cafeteria, and in classrooms before lessons start. Bullying usually starts in elementary school, peaks in middle school, and drops in high school. It does not disappear, however. Although boys are more often the perpetrators and victims of bullying, girls tend to bully in indirect ways, such as manipulating friendships, ostracizing classmates, and spreading malicious rumors. Boys who are regularly bullied tend to be more passive and physically weaker than the bullies. In middle school, girls who mature early are commonly victims of bullying, according to some findings.

Preschool

Bullying behavior can be seen as early as preschool. However, little data exists regarding the prevalence of bullying in preschool. Preschool-age children may bully others to get attention, show off, or to get another child's possessions, such as **toys**, clothing, or use of playground equipment. They may also be jealous of the children they are bullying or may be getting bullied themselves. Preschool bullying usually begins with name-calling and can escalate into physical violence if left unchecked. Preschool teachers are urged to intervene immediately to stop bullying and to teach acceptable behavior. If teachers or staff at a preschool do not do enough to stop bullying, parents should find another preschool.

School age

A 2001 report by the National Institute of Child Health and Human Development (NICHD) found that 17 percent of the respondents had been bullied sometimes or weekly; 19 percent had bullied others sometimes or weekly, and 6 percent had both bullied others and been bullied. The researchers estimated that 1.6 million children in grades six through 10 in the United States are bullied at least once a week and 1.7 million children bully others as frequently.

The survey, the first nationwide research on the problem in this country, questioned 15,686 public and private school students, grades six through 10, on their experiences with bullying. In a study of 6,500 middle school students in rural South Carolina, 23 percent said they had been bullied regularly during the previous three months, and 20 percent admitted bullying another child regularly during the same time.

Bullying appears to be rapidly increasing, according to statistics from the U.S. Department of Justice. Among sixth-grade students, rates of bullying rose from 10.5 percent in 1999 to 14.3 percent in 2001; among eighth-grade students victimization by bullies went from 5.5 percent in 1999 to 9.2 percent in 2001. In the tenth grade, bullying rose from 3.2 percent in 1999 to 4.6 percent in 2001, and among twelfth graders, it doubled from 1.2 percent in 1999 to 2.4 percent just two years later.

A bully's behavior does not exist in isolation. Rather, it may indicate the beginning of a generally antisocial and rule-breaking behavior pattern that can extend into adulthood. Programs to address the problem, therefore, must reduce opportunities and rewards for bullying behavior. The Olweus Bullying Prevention Program, developed, refined, and systematically evaluated in Norway in the mid-1980s, is the best-known initiative designed to reduce bullying among elementary, middle, and junior high school children. The strategy behind the program is to involve school staff, students, and parents in efforts to designed to develop awareness about bullying, improve peer relations, intervene to stop intimidation, develop clear rules against bullying behavior, and support and protect victims.

The program intervenes on three levels:

- School: Faculty and staff survey students anonymously to determine the nature and prevalence of the school's bullying problem, increase supervision of students during breaks, and conduct school-wide assemblies to discuss the issue. Teachers receive in-service training on how to implement the program.

- Classroom: Teachers and other school personnel introduce and enforce classroom rules against bullying, hold regular classroom meetings with students to discuss bullying, and meet with parents to encourage their participation.

- Individual: Staff intervention with bullies, victims, and their parents to ensures that the bullying stops.

The Bergen research showed that the program was highly effective among students in elementary, middle, and junior high schools: Bullying dropped by 50 percent or more during the program's two years. Behavior changes were more pronounced the longer the program was in effect. The school climate improved, and the rate of **antisocial behavior**, such as theft, vandalism, and **truancy**, declined during the two-year period.

Common problems

The NICHD study found that bullying has long-term and short-term psychological effects on both those who bully and those who are bullied. Victims experience loneliness and report having trouble making social and emotional adjustments, difficulty making friends, and poor relationships with classmates. Victims of bullying often suffer humiliation, insecurity, and a loss of self-esteem, and often develop a **fear** of going to school. The impact of frequent bullying often accompanies these victims into adulthood; they are at greater risk of suffering from depression and other mental health problems, including **schizophrenia**. In rare cases, they commit **suicide**.

Bullying behavior has been linked to other forms of antisocial behavior, such as vandalism, shoplifting, skipping and dropping out of school, fighting, and using alcohol and other drugs. Research suggests that bullying can lead to criminal behavior later in life: 60 percent of males who were bullies in grades six through nine were convicted of at least one crime as adults, compared with 23 percent of males who did not bully; 35 to 40 percent of these former bullies had three or more convictions by age 24, compared with 10 percent of those who did not bully.

The NICHD study found that those who bully and are bullied appear to be at greatest risk of experiencing the following: loneliness, trouble making friends, lack of success in school, and involvement in problem behaviors such as **smoking**, illegal drug use, and drinking.

Parental concerns

Parents should be aware of common signs that a child is being bullied. These include trouble sleeping, bedwetting, stomachaches, headaches, lack of appetite, fear of going to school, crying before or after school, lack of interest in social events, low self-esteem, unexplained loss of personal items and money, unexplained **bruises** and injuries, and **acting out** aggressively at home.

Parents should teach their children proper **communication skills** that they may need to seek assistance if they are being bullied, according to the Web site <www.bullying.org>. Other advice for parents from the Web site include:

- Be involved with the child's school and talk to other parents about the problem.
- Meet with school officials and make sure the school has an anti-bullying policy and that it is strictly enforced. If a child is being bullied, meet with school officials to find out what they are doing about it. If no action is being taken, demand that it be done.

KEY TERMS

Antisocial behavior—Behavior characterized by high levels of anger, aggression, manipulation, or violence.

Harassment—The persistent annoying, attacking, or bothering of another person.

Schizophrenia—A severe mental illness in which a person has difficulty distinguishing what is real from what is not real. It is often characterized by hallucinations, delusions, and withdrawal from people and social activities.

- Talk to the child's teacher or teachers to determine if they have seen any bullying problems in the classroom or playground.
- Talk to a school counselor and ask that person to discuss bullying with children.
- Report all verbal or physical threats against a child to school authorities and insist they take action. If they do not take action, report the problem to local police.

When to call the doctor

Bullying is violence. If both bullies and their victims are not offered help, there can be serious long-term consequences for both. Bullies and their victims may need professional counseling or psychological help. Parents should seek immediate help for children who are depressed or suicidal. Parents of bullies also need to seek psychological help for their child if the bullying continues for even a short period of time.

See also Antisocial behavior.

Resources
BOOKS
Coloroso, Barbara. *The Bully, the Bullied, and the Bystander: From Preschool to High School—How Parents and Teachers Can Help Break the Cycle of Violence.* New York: HarperResource, 2004.

Dorn, Michael. *Weakfish: Bullying Through the Eyes of a Child.* Macon, GA: Safe Havens International Inc., 2003.

Katch, Jane. *They Don't Like Me: Lessons on Bullying and Teasing from a Preschool Classroom.* Boston: Beacon Press, 2004.

Lee, Chris. *Preventing Bullying in Schools: A Guide for Teachers and Other Professionals.* London, UK: Paul Chapman Educational Publishing, 2004.

PERIODICALS

"Anti-Gay Bullying Widespread Among Teens." *Mental Health Weekly* (January 27, 2003): 6.

Dake, Joseph A., et al. "The Nature and Extent of Bullying at School." *Journal of School Health* (May 2003): 173–180.

Fink, Paul J. "Treating Bullies." *Clinical Psychiatry News* (December 2003): 5.

Jellinek, Michael S. "Treating Both Bullies and the Bullied." *Pediatric News* (June 2003): 10.

"Report Cites Harm to Bullies and Victims." *Health & Medicine Week* (September 29, 2003): 706.

ORGANIZATIONS

Bullying Prevention Program. Institute on Family and Neighborhood Life, Clemson University, 158 Poole Agricultural Center, Clemson, SC 29634. Web site: <www.stopbullyingnow.hrsa.gov/index.asp.>.

The Healthy Lesbian, Gay, and Bisexual Students Project. American Psychological Association Education Directorate, 750 First St. NE, Washington, DC 20002. Web site: <www.apa.org/ed/hlgb/>

WEB SITES

"Bullying." Available online at <www.bullying.org> (accessed October 12, 2004).

"Bullying, Harassment, School-based Violence." *The Safe Schools Coalition.* Available online at <www.safeschoolscoalition.org/RG-bullying_harassment_schoolbasedviolence.html> (accessed October 12, 2004).

Ken R. Wells

Bullying *see* **Bullies**

Burns

Definition

Burns are injuries to tissues that are caused by heat, friction, electricity, radiation, or chemicals.

Description

Burns are characterized by degree, based on the severity of the tissue damage. A first-degree burn causes redness and swelling in the outermost layers of skin (epidermis). A second-degree burn involves redness, swelling and blistering, and the damage may extend beneath the epidermis to deeper layers of skin (dermis). A third-degree burn, also called a full-thickness burn, destroys the entire depth of skin, causing significant scarring. Damage also may extend to the underlying fat, muscle, or bone.

Demographics

The severity of the burn is also judged by the amount of body surface area (BSA) involved. Healthcare workers use the "rule of nines" to determine the percentage of BSA affected in people more than 9 years of age: each arm with its hand is 9 percent of BSA; each leg with its foot is 18 percent; the front of the torso is 18 percent; the back of the torso, including the buttocks, is 18 percent; the head and neck are 9 percent; and the genital area (perineum) is 1 percent. This rule cannot be applied to a young child's body proportions, so BSA is estimated using the palm of a person's hand as a measure of 1 percent area.

The severity of the burn determines the type of treatment and also where the burned person should receive treatment. Minor burns may be treated at home or in a doctor's office. These are defined as first- or second-degree burns covering less than 15 percent of an adult's body or less than 10 percent of a child's body, or a third-degree burn on less than 2 percent BSA. Moderate burns should be treated at a hospital. These are defined as first- or second-degree burns covering 15 percent to 25 percent of an adult's body or 10 percent to 20 percent of a child's body, or a third-degree burn on 2 percent to 10 percent BSA. Critical, or major, burns are the most serious and should be treated in a specialized burn unit of a hospital. These are defined as first- or second-degree burns covering more than 25 percent of an adult's body or more than 20 percent of a child's body, or a third-degree burn on more than 10 percent BSA. In addition, burns involving the hands, feet, face, eyes, ears, or genitals are considered critical. Other factors influence the level of treatment needed, including associated injuries such as bone **fractures** and **smoke inhalation**, presence of a chronic disease, or a history of abuse. Also, children and the elderly are more vulnerable to complications from burn injuries and require more intensive care.

Causes and symptoms

Burns may be caused by even a brief encounter with heat greater than 120°F (49°C). The source of this heat may be the sun (causing a **sunburn**), hot liquids, steam, fire, electricity, friction (causing rug burns and rope burns), and chemicals (causing caustic burn upon contact).

Signs of a burn are localized redness, swelling, and **pain**. A severe burn will also blister. The skin may also peel, appear white or charred, and feel numb. A burn may trigger a **headache** and **fever**. Extensive burns may induce shock, the symptoms of which are faintness, weakness, rapid pulse and breathing, pale and clammy skin, and bluish lips and fingernails.

When to call the doctor

A physician or healthcare professional should be consulted whenever first or second degree burns cover more than 15 percent of a person's body surface area (BSA) or third degree burns involve more than 2 percent of a victim's BSA.

Diagnosis

A physician will diagnose a burn based on visual examination and will also ask the burned person or **family** members questions to determine the best treatment. He or she may also check for smoke inhalation, **carbon monoxide poisoning**, cyanide **poisoning**, other event-related trauma, or, if suspected, evidence of **child abuse**.

Treatment

Burn treatment consists of relieving pain, preventing infection, and maintaining body fluids, electrolytes, and calorie intake while the body heals. Treatment of chemical or electrical burns is slightly different from the treatment of thermal burns but the objectives are the same.

Thermal burn treatment

The first act of thermal burn treatment is to stop the burning process. This may be accomplished by letting cool water run over the burned area or by soaking it in cool (not cold) water. Ice should never be applied to a burn. Cool (not cold) wet compresses may provide some pain relief when applied to small areas of first- and second-degree burns. Butter, shortening, or similar salve should never be applied to the burn because these prevent heat from escaping and drive the burning process deeper into the skin.

If the burn is minor, it may be cleaned gently with soap and water. Blisters should not be broken. If the skin of the burned area is unbroken and it is not likely to be further irritated by pressure or friction, the burn should be left exposed to the air to promote healing. If the skin is broken or apt to be disturbed, the burned area should be coated lightly with an antibacterial ointment and covered with a sterile bandage. Aspirin, **acetaminophen**, or ibuprofen may be taken to ease pain and relieve inflammation. A doctor should be consulted if these signs of infection appear: increased warmth, redness, pain, or swelling; pus or similar drainage from the wound; swollen lymph nodes; or red streaks spreading away from the burn.

In situations in which a person has received moderate or critical burns, lifesaving measures take precedence over burn treatment, and emergency medical assistance must be called. A person with serious burns may stop breathing, and artificial respiration (also called mouth-to-mouth resuscitation or rescue breathing) should be administered immediately. Also, a person with burns covering more than 12 percent BSA is likely to go into shock; this condition may be prevented by laying the person flat and elevating the feet about 12 inches (30 cm). Burned arms and hands should also be raised higher than the person's heart.

In rescues, a blanket may be used to smother any flames as the person is removed from danger. The person whose clothing is on fire should "stop, drop, and roll" or be assisted in lying flat on the ground and rolling to put out the fire. Afterwards, only burned clothing that comes off easily should be removed; any clothing embedded in the burn should not be disturbed. Removing any smoldering apparel and covering the person with a light, cool, wet cloth, such as a sheet but not a blanket or towel, will stop the burning process.

At the hospital, the staff provide further medical treatment. A tube to aid breathing may be inserted if the person's airways or lungs have been damaged, as can happen during an explosion or a fire in an enclosed space. Also, because burns dramatically deplete the body of fluids, replacement fluids are administered intravenously. The person is also given **antibiotics** intravenously to prevent infection, and he or she may also receive a **tetanus** shot, depending on his or her immunization history. Once the burned area is cleaned and treated with antibiotic cream or ointment, it is covered in sterile bandages, which are changed two to three times a day. Surgical removal of dead tissue (debridement) also takes place. As the burns heal, thick, taut scabs (eschar) form, which the doctor may have to cut to improve blood flow to the more elastic healthy tissue beneath. The person will also undergo physical and occupational therapy to keep the burned areas from becoming inflexible and to minimize scarring.

In cases where the skin has been so damaged that it cannot properly heal, a skin graft is usually performed. A skin graft involves taking a piece of skin from an unburned portion of the person's body (autograft) and transplanting it to the burned area. When doctors cannot immediately use the individual's own skin, a temporary graft is performed using the skin of a human donor (allograft), either alive or dead, or the skin of an animal (xenograft), usually that of a pig.

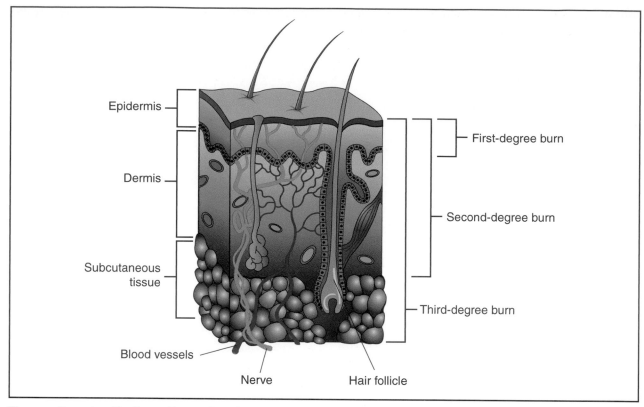

Epidermis

Dermis

Subcutaneous
tissue

Blood vessels

Nerve

Hair follicle

First-degree burn

Second-degree burn

Third-degree burn

There are three classifications of burns: first-degree, second-degree, and third-degree burns. *(Illustration by Electronic Illustrators Group.)*

The burn victim also may be placed in a hyperbaric chamber, if one is available. In a hyperbaric chamber (which can be a specialized room or enclosed space), the person is exposed to pure oxygen under high pressure, which can aid in healing. However, for this therapy to be effective, the burned individual must be placed in a chamber within 24 hours of being burned.

Chemical burn treatment

Burns from liquid chemicals must be rinsed with cool water for at least 15 minutes to stop the burning process. Any burn to the eye must be similarly flushed with water. In cases of burns from dry chemicals such as lime, the powder should be completely brushed away before the area is washed. Any clothing which may have absorbed the chemical should be removed. The burn should then be loosely covered with a sterile gauze pad and the person taken to the hospital for further treatment. A physician may be able to neutralize the offending chemical with another before treating the burn like a thermal burn of similar severity.

Electrical burn treatment

Before electrical burns are treated at the site of the accident, the power source must be disconnected if possi-

ble and the victim moved away from it to keep the person giving aid from being electrocuted. Lifesaving measures again take priority over burn treatment, so breathing must be checked and assisted if necessary. Electrical burns should be loosely covered with sterile gauze pads and the person taken to the hospital for further treatment.

Alternative treatment

In addition to the excellent treatment of burns provided by traditional medicine, some alternative approaches may be helpful as well. (Major burns should always be treated by a medical practitioner.) The homeopathic remedies *Cantharis* and *Causticum* can assist in burn healing. A number of botanical remedies, applied topically, can also help burns heal. These include aloe (*Aloe barbadensis*), oil of St. John's wort (*Hypericum perforatum*), calendula (*Calendula officinalis*), comfrey (*Symphytum officinale*), and tea tree oil (*Melaleuca* spp.). Supplementing the diet with vitamin C, vitamin E, and zinc also is beneficial for wound healing.

Prognosis

The prognosis is dependent upon the degree of the burn, the amount of body surface covered, whether critical body parts were affected, any additional injuries or complications like infection, and the promptness of medical treatment. Minor burns may heal in five to ten days with no scarring. Moderate burns may heal in ten to 14 days and may leave scarring. Critical or major burns take more than 14 days to heal and leave significant scarring. Scar tissue may limit mobility and functionality, but physical therapy may overcome these limitations. In some cases, additional surgery may be advisable to remove scar tissue and restore appearance.

Prevention

Burns are commonly received in residential fires. Properly placed and working smoke detectors in combination with rapid evacuation plans minimize a person's exposure to smoke and flames in the event of a fire. Children must be taught never to **play** with matches, lighters, fireworks, gasoline, and cleaning fluids.

Burns by scalding with hot water or other liquids may be prevented by setting the water heater thermostat no higher than 120°F (49°C), checking the temperature of bath water before getting into the tub, and turning pot handles on the stove out of the reach of children. Care should be used when removing covers from pans of steaming foods and when uncovering or opening foods heated in a microwave oven.

Thermal burns are often received from electrical appliances. Care should be exercised around stoves, space heaters, irons, and curling irons.

Sunburns may be avoided by the liberal use of a sunscreen containing either an opaque active ingredient such as zinc oxide or titanium dioxide or a nonopaque active ingredient such as PABA (para-aminobenzoic acid) or benzophenone. Hats, loose clothing, and umbrellas also provide protection, especially between 10 a.m. and 3 p.m. when the most damaging ultraviolet rays are present in direct sunlight.

Electrical burns may be prevented by covering unused electrical outlets with **safety** plugs and keeping electrical cords away from infants and toddlers who might chew on them. Persons should also seek shelter indoors during a thunderstorm to avoid being struck by lightning.

Chemical burns may be prevented by wearing protective clothing, including gloves and eyeshields. Chemical agents should always be used according to the manufacturer's instructions and properly stored when not in use.

Nutritional concerns

Adequate **nutrition**, including liquids and electrolytes, is essential when recovering from burns.

KEY TERMS

Debridement—The surgical removal of dead tissue and/or foreign bodies from a wound or cut.

Dermis—The basal layer of skin; it contains blood and lymphatic vessels, nerves, glands, and hair follicles.

Epidermis—The outermost layer of the human skin.

Shock—A medical emergency in which the organs and tissues of the body are not receiving an adequate flow of blood. This deprives the organs and tissues of oxygen and allows the build-up of waste products. Shock can be caused by certain diseases, serious injury, or blood loss.

Parental concerns

Parents should fire-proof their homes to protect small children. They should teach fire safety to their children from a very young age. Smoke detectors should be installed and tested at least twice each year. Parents are advised to discuss fire and escape routes (including alternates) from their home with their children. Holding a fire drill at night may be momentarily unpopular but may save lives and prevent serious injuries. Proper **childproofing** tools can prevent young children from being burned in the kitchen and bathroom.

Resources

BOOKS

Antoon, Alia Y., and Mary K. Donovan. "Burn Injuries." In *Nelson Textbook of Pediatrics*, 17th ed. Edited by Richard E. Behrman, et al. Philadelphia: Saunders, 2003, pp. 330–7.

Bosworth, Chrissie. *Burns Trauma: Management and Nursing Care*, 2nd ed. London: Whurr Publishers, 2002.

Demling, Robert H., and Jonathon D. Gates. "Medical Aspects of Trauma and Burn Care." In *Cecil Textbook of Medicine*, 22nd ed. Edited by Lee Goldman, et al. Philadelphia: Saunders, 2003, pp. 642–8.

Hall, Jesse B., and Gregory Schmidt. *Principles of Critical Care*, 3rd ed. New York: McGraw-Hill, 2004.

PERIODICALS

Collier, M. L., et al. "Home treadmill friction injuries: a five-year review." *Journal of Burn Care Rehabilitation* 25, no. 5 (2004): 441–4.

Patterson, D. R., et al. "Optimizing control of pain from severe burns: a literature review." *American Journal of Clinical Hypnosis* 47, no. 1 (2004): 43–54.

Rabbitts, A., et al. "Car radiator burns: a prevention issue." *Journal of Burn Care Rehabilitation* 25, no. 5 (2004): 452–5.

Stokes, D. J., et al. "The effect of burn injury on adolescents' autobiographical memory." *Behavior Research and Therapy* 42, no. 11 (2004): 1357–65.

ORGANIZATIONS

American Academy of Dermatology. 930 N. Meacham Road, PO Box 4014, Schaumburg, IL 60168–4014. Web site: <www.aad.org/>.

American Academy of Emergency Medicine. 611 East Wells Street, Milwaukee, WI 53202. Web site: <www.aaem.org/>.

American Academy of Family Physicians. 11400 Tomahawk Creek Parkway, Leawood, KS 66211–2672. Web site: <www.aafp.org/>.

American Academy of Pediatrics. 141 Northwest Point Boulevard, Elk Grove Village, IL 60007–1098. Web site: <www.aap.org/default.htm>.

American College of Emergency Physicians. PO Box 619911, Dallas, TX 75261–9911. Web site: <www.acep.org/>.

American College of Surgeons. 633 North St. Clair Street, Chicago, IL 60611–32311. Web site: <www.facs.org/>.

International Shrine Headquarters. 2900 Rocky Point Dr., Tampa, FL 33607–1460. Web site: <www.shrinershq.org/index.html>.

WEB SITES

"Burns." *KidsHealth.* Available online at <http://kidshealth.org/parent/firstaid_safe/emergencies/burns.html> (accessed December 7, 2004).

"Burns." *MedlinePlus.* Available online at <www.nlm.nih.gov/medlineplus/burns.html> (accessed December 7, 2004).

"Burns." *Merck Manual.* Available online at <www.merck.com/mmhe/sec24/ch289/ch289a.html> (accessed December 7, 2004).

"Burns: Taking Care of Burns." *American College of Family Physicians*, September 2002. Available online at <http://familydoctor.org/x2190.xml> (accessed December 7, 2004).

"Chemical Burns to the Skin." *University of Iowa Health Care.* Available online at <www.uihealthcare.com/topics/prepareemergencies/prep4904.html> (accessed December 7, 2004).

L. Fleming Fallon, Jr., MD, DrPH

Caffeine

Definition

Caffeine is a drug that stimulates the central nervous system.

Description

Caffeine is found naturally in coffee, tea, and chocolate. Colas and some other soft drinks contain it. Caffeine also comes in tablet and capsule forms and can be bought without a prescription. Over-the-counter caffeine brands include No Doz, Overtime, Pep-Back, Quick-Pep, Caffedrine, and Vivarin. Some **pain** relievers, medicines for migraine headaches, and **antihistamines** also contain caffeine.

General use

Caffeine makes people more alert, less drowsy, and improves coordination. Combined with certain pain relievers or medicines for treating migraine **headache**, caffeine makes those drugs work more quickly and effectively. Caffeine alone can also help relieve headaches. Antihistamines are sometimes combined with caffeine to counteract the drowsiness that those drugs cause. Caffeine is also sometimes used to treat other conditions, including breathing problems in newborns and in young babies after surgery.

Precautions

Caffeine cannot replace **sleep** and should not be used regularly for staying awake as the drug can lead to serious **sleep disorders**, like insomnia.

People who use large amounts of caffeine over long periods build up a tolerance to it. When that happens, they have to use more and more caffeine to get the same effects. Heavy caffeine use can also lead to dependence. If the person then stops using caffeine abruptly, withdrawal symptoms may occur. These can include throbbing headaches, fatigue, drowsiness, yawning, irritability, restlessness, **vomiting**, or runny nose. These symptoms can go on for as long as a week if caffeine is avoided. Then the symptoms usually disappear.

If taken too close to bedtime, caffeine can interfere with sleep. Even if it does not prevent a person from falling asleep, it may disturb sleep during the night.

The notion that caffeine helps people sober up after drinking too much alcohol is a myth. In fact, using caffeine and alcohol together is not a good idea. The combination can lead to an upset stomach, **nausea**, and vomiting.

Older people may be more sensitive to caffeine and thus more likely to have certain side effects, such as irritability, nervousness, **anxiety**, and sleep problems.

Children under the age of 12 should normally avoid caffeine.

Side effects

Although caffeine is used to treat headaches, regular consumption of large quantities of caffeine containing beverages can cause severe headaches.

Excess use of caffeine by children leads to decreased nighttime sleep, but increased daytime sleep.

Interactions

Certain drugs interfere with the breakdown of caffeine in the body. These include **oral contraceptives** that contain estrogen, the antiarrhythmia drug mexiletine (Mexitil), and the ulcer drug cimetidine (Tagamet).

Caffeine interferes with drugs that regulate heart rhythm, such as quinidine and propranolol (Inderal). Caffeine may also interfere with the body's absorption of iron. Anyone who takes iron supplements should take them at least an hour before or two hours after using caffeine.

Serious side effects are possible when caffeine is combined with certain drugs. For example, taking

KEY TERMS

Arrhythmia—Any deviation from a normal heart beat.

Central nervous system—Part of the nervous system consisting of the brain, cranial nerves, and spinal cord. The brain is the center of higher processes, such as thought and emotion and is responsible for the coordination and control of bodily activities and the interpretation of information from the senses. The cranial nerves and spinal cord link the brain to the peripheral nervous system, that is the nerves present in the rest of body.

Withdrawal symptoms—A group of physical and/or mental symptoms that may occur when a person suddenly stops using a drug or other substance upon which he or she has become dependent.

caffeine with the decongestant phenylpropanolamine can raise blood pressure. Very serious heart problems may occur if caffeine and monoamine oxidase (MAO) inhibitors are taken together. These drugs are used to treat Parkinson's disease, depression, and other psychiatric conditions. People who use these drugs should consult a pharmacist or physician about which drugs can interact with caffeine.

Because caffeine stimulates the nervous system, anyone taking other central nervous system (CNS) stimulants should be careful about using caffeine.

Parental concerns

Moderate amounts of caffeine are not normally associated with adverse effects. As a rule, a daily intake of 300 milligrams should not present a problem. The following list gives the estimated amount of caffeine in common foods, but actual concentrations may be higher or lower.

- coffee, 115 mg
- black tea, 40 mg
- cola and other soft drinks, 18 mg
- chocolate milk, 5 mg
- milk chocolate (1 ounce) 6 mg

Resources

BOOKS

Beers, Mark H., and Robert Berkow, eds. *The Merck Manual*, 2nd home ed. West Point, PA: Merck & Co., 2004.

Mcevoy, Gerald, et al. *AHFS Drug Information 2004*. Bethesda, MD: American Society of Healthsystems Pharmacists, 2004.

Siberry, George K., and Robert Iannone, eds. *The Harriet Lane Handbook*, 15th ed. Philadelphia: Mosby Publishing, 2000.

PERIODICALS

Hering-Hanit, R., and N. Gadoth. "Caffeine-induced headache in children and adolescents." *Cephalalgia* 23, no. 5 (June 2003): 332–5.

Pollak Charles P., and David Bright. "Caffeine consumption and weekly sleep patterns in U.S. seventh, eighth, and ninth graders." *Pediatrics* 111, no. 1 (January 2003): 42–6.

Steer, P. A., and D. J. Henderson-Smart. "Caffeine versus theophylline for apnea in preterm infants." *Cochrane Database of Systematic Review* 2 (2000): CD000273.

ORGANIZATIONS

Baylor College of Medicine USDA/ARS Children's Nutrition Research Center. 1100 Bates Street, Houston, TX 77030.

University of Minnesota Extension Service. Office of the Director, 240 Coffey Hall, 1420 Eckles Ave. St. Paul, MN 55108–6068.

WEB SITES

"Caffeine." *Center for the Evaluation of Risks to Human Reproduction*. Available online at <http://cerhr.niehs.nih.gov/genpub/topics/caffeine-ccae.html> (accessed October 16, 2004).

"Questions and Answers about Caffeine and Health." *International Food Information Council*. Available online at <www.ific.org/publications/qa/caffqa.cfm> (accessed October 16, 2004).

Nancy Ross-Flanigan
Samuel Uretsky, PharmD

C-section *see* **Cesarean section**

California Achievement Tests

Definition

The California Achievement Tests (CAT) are among the most widely used tests of basic academic skills for children from kindergarten through grade 12. The most recent edition of the CAT (the sixth) is also called *TerraNova, Second Edition* (or alternately, *TerraNova CAT*).

Purpose

The CAT is often administered to determine a child's readiness for promotion to a more advanced grade level and may also be used by schools to satisfy state or local testing requirements.

Description

First introduced in 1950, the CAT is a paper-and-pencil test for children from kindergarten through grade 12 that is designed to measure academic competency in a variety of areas. The test is available in six different forms: CAT Complete Battery, CAT Basic Battery, CAT Survey (grades two through 12 only), and CAT Plus.

- CAT Multiple Assessments. Uses multiple choice and open-ended test questions to assess reading/language arts, mathematics, science, and social studies skills.

- CAT Basic Multiple Assessments. Uses multiple choice and open-ended test questions to assess reading/language arts and mathematics skills.

- CAT Complete Battery. Uses multiple choice questions to assess reading/language arts, mathematics, science, and social studies skills.

- CAT Basic Battery. Uses multiple choice questions to assess reading/language arts and mathematics skills.

- CAT Survey. A shortened version of the complete battery, this form uses multiple choice questions to assess reading/language arts, mathematics, science, and social studies skills.

- CAT Plus. Add-on assessments that address the academic components of word analysis, vocabulary, language mechanics, spelling, and mathematics computation.

The CAT is a standardized test, meaning that norms were established during the design phase of the test by administering the test to a large, representative sample of the test population (in the case of the CAT, over 300,000 students). The test is given in a group, classroom setting, and can take anywhere from one-and-a-half to over five hours to complete depending on the test form and grade level. A teacher typically administers the CAT. When testing is complete, the test is sent back to the company that publishes the CAT (CTB/McGraw Hill) for scoring, and then scoring information is returned to the school in the form of individual test reports.

The test report includes a scale score, which is the basic measurement of how a child performs on the **assessment**, and a national percentile (NP), which reflects the percentage of students in the national norm group who have scores below the student's score (e.g., an NP of 80 means that 80 percent of students scored

---

---

lower than the student). The scale score may be derived one of two ways—a straight score determined by the total number of test items correct or through item-pattern scoring (also called item response theory, or IRT). Item-pattern scoring examines not only the number of correct responses, but also the difficulty level of the questions answered right and the interrelationship of the pattern of answers. Other scoring information may also be included in the test report depending on the scoring report format.

Preparation

For students who are unfamiliar with the mechanics of taking a standardized test, a practice test session given by a teacher shortly before the CAT testing session begins may be appropriate. Because the CAT is designed to be a measurement of a child's current educational achievement level, the test publisher recommends that no pre-test coaching or test study programs be used.

Parental concerns

Test anxiety can have a negative impact on a child's performance, so parents should attempt to take the stress off their child by making sure the child understands that it is the effort and attention they give the test, not the final score, that matters. Parents can also ensure that their children are well rested on the testing day and have a nutritious meal beforehand.

When test results are available, parents should schedule a meeting with their child's teacher to discuss the test's implications. Results from CAT testing can help parents and teachers identify academic strengths and weaknesses and develop strategies for capitalizing on the former and building skills in the latter.

Resources

BOOKS

CTB/McGraw Hill. *Terranova, 2nd ed. (California Achievement Tests, 6th ed.)* Available online at <www.ctb.com/mktg/terranova/tn_intro.jsp>.

Harris, Joseph. *What Every Parent Needs to Know About Standardized Tests.* New York: McGraw-Hill, 2001.

Paula Ford-Martin

Cancer

Definition

Cancer is a group of diseases characterized by uncontrolled growth of tissue cells in the body and the invasion by these cells into nearby tissue and migration to distant sites.

Description

Cancer results from alterations (mutations) in genes that make up DNA, the master molecule of the cell. Genes make proteins, which are the ultimate workhorses of the cells, responsible for the many processes that permit humans to breathe, think, and move, among other functions. Some of these proteins control the orderly growth, division, and reproduction of normal tissue cells. Gene mutations can produce faulty proteins, which in turn produce abnormal cells that no longer divide and reproduce in an orderly manner. These abnormal cells divide uncontrollably and eventually form a new growth known as a tumor or neoplasm. A healthy immune system can usually recognize neoplastic cells and destroy them before they divide. However, mutant cells may escape immune detection and become tumors or cancers.

Studies of the origins of cancer have shown that a combination of genetic influences and environmental causes over time triggers gene mutations, which may explain why most cancers are seen in adults of middle age or older (60%) and cancer is rare children. Many cancers have been shown to result from exposure to environmental toxins (carcinogens) and related alterations in DNA. Faulty DNA can also be inherited, predisposing an individual to develop cancer, although fewer than 10 percent of cancers are purely hereditary. Hereditary links have been shown in cancers of the breast, colon, ovaries, and uterus. Inherited physiological traits can also contribute to cancer, such as inheriting fair skin increasing the risk of skin cancer, but only if accompanied by prolonged exposure to intensive sunlight.

Tumors can be benign or malignant. A benign tumor is not cancer. It is slow growing, does not invade surrounding tissue, and once removed, does not usually recur. A malignant tumor is cancerous. It invades surrounding tissue and spreads to nearby or distant organs (metastasis). If the cancer cells have spread to surrounding tissue, even after the malignant tumor is removed, it will typically recur.

Cancer falls into several general categories:

- Carcinoma (90% of all cancer) are solid tumors arising in the layer of cells (epithelium) covering the body's surface and lining internal organs and glands. Adenocarcinomas develop in an organ or gland and squamous cell carcinomas originate in the skin.

- Melanoma originates in the skin, usually in pigment cells (melanocytes).

- Sarcoma is cancer of supporting tissue such as bone, muscle, and blood vessels.

- Leukemias and lymphomas are cancers of the blood and lymph glands.

- Gliomas are cancers of the nerve tissue.

The most common cancers affecting adults are cancer of the skin, lung, colon, breast, and prostate. Cancer of the kidneys, ovaries, uterus, pancreas, bladder, rectum, and the leukemias and lymphomas are among the 12 major cancers affecting Americans of all ages. Although children and adolescents do develop solid tumors, the most common high-risk cancers among children are:

- acute myeloid leukemia

- acute lymphoblastic leukemia

- neuroblastoma

- glioma

- sarcoma of bone (osteosarcoma) and soft tissue

Demographics

Childhood cancer is rare, occurring in about 14 in 100,000 children in the United States each year. However, in the entire U.S. population, one of every four deaths is from cancer, second only to deaths from heart disease. About 1.2 million cancer cases are diagnosed annually and more than 500,000 die, of whom 2,700 are children or adolescents.

Causes and symptoms

Genetic predisposition, environmental causes, and individual developmental problems are responsible for most childhood cancer. The presence of other disorders, such as **Down syndrome**, has also been shown to be associated with cancer in children. The major risk factors that apply to adult cancer are tobacco, alcohol, sexual and reproductive behavior, and occupation, none of which increases risk in children. Other well-known risk factors, such as **family** history, infectious agents, diet, environmental toxins, and pollution, can apply equally to children.

Tobacco

Approximately 80 to 90 percent of lung cancer cases occur in smokers. **Smoking** is also the leading cause of bladder cancer and has been shown to contribute to cancers of the upper respiratory tract, esophagus, larynx, kidney, pancreas, stomach, and possibly breast as well. Second-hand smoke (passive smoking) has been shown to increase cancer risk in children and adults who live with smokers.

Infectious agents

Cancer deaths worldwide can be traced to viruses, bacteria, or parasites. Epstein-Barr virus (EBV), for example, is associated with lymphoma, the hepatitis viruses are associated with liver cancer, HIV is associated with Kaposi's sarcoma, and the bacteria *Helicobacter pylori* is associated with stomach cancer.

Genetic predisposition

Certain cancers such as breast, colon, ovarian, and uterine cancer recur generation after generation in some families. Eye cancer (**retinoblastoma**), a type of colon cancer, and early-onset breast cancer have been shown to be linked to the inheritance of specific genes.

Environmental sources

Radiation is believed to cause 1 to 2 percent of all cancer deaths. Ultraviolet radiation from the sun accounts for a majority of melanoma deaths. Other sources of radiation are x-rays, radon gas, and ionizing radiation from nuclear material.

Pollution

Studies have established links between environmental toxins, such as asbestos, and cancer. Chlorination of water may account for a small rise in cancer risk. However, the main danger from pollutants occurs when toxic industrial chemicals are released into the surrounding environment. As of 2004 an estimated 1 percent of cancer deaths are believed to be due to air, land, and water pollution.

Cancer is a progressive disease that goes through several stages, each producing a number of symptoms.

Early symptoms can be produced by the growth of a solid tumor in an organ or gland. A growing tumor may press on nearby nerves, organs, and blood vessels, causing **pain** and pressure that may be the first warning signs of cancer. Other symptoms can include sores that do not heal, growths on the skin or below the skin, unusual bleeding, difficulty digesting food or swallowing, and changes in bowel or bladder function. **Fever** can be present as well as fatigue and weakness.

When to call the doctor

Despite the fact that there are hundreds of different types of cancer, each producing different symptoms, the American Cancer Society has established the following seven symptoms as possible warning signals of cancer:

- changes in the size, color, or shape of a wart or a mole
- a sore that does not heal
- persistent **cough**, hoarseness, or sore throat
- a lump or thickening in the breast or elsewhere
- unusual bleeding or discharge
- chronic indigestion or difficulty swallowing
- any change in bowel or bladder habits

Parents should report any such symptoms to the pediatrician along with unexplained fever or frequent infections. Vision problems, weight loss, lack of appetite, depression, swollen glands, paleness, or general weakness are other reasons for parents to consult the pediatrician. Generally, the earlier cancer is diagnosed and treated, the better the chance of a cure, although not all cancers have early symptoms.

Diagnosis

Diagnosis begins with a complete medical history, including family history of cancer, and a thorough physical examination. The doctor observes and palpates (applies pressure by touch) different parts of the body in order to identify any variations from normal size, feel, and texture of an organ or tissue. The doctor looks inside the mouth for abnormalities in color, moisture, surface texture, or the presence of any thickening or sores in the lips, tongue, gums, the roof of the mouth, or the throat. The doctor observes the front of the neck for swelling and may gently manipulate the neck and palpate the front and side surfaces of the thyroid gland at the base of the neck, looking for nodules or tenderness. The doctor also palpates the lymph nodes in the neck, under the arms, and in the groin, looking for enlargement. The skin is examined for sores that are slow to heal, especially those that bleed, ooze, or crust; irritated patches that may itch or hurt; and any change in the size of a wart or a mole.

In adolescent females, a pelvic exam may be conducted to detect cancers of the ovaries, uterus, cervix, and vagina. The doctor first looks for abnormal discharges or the presence of sores. Then the internal pelvic organs such as the uterus and ovaries are palpated (touched while applying gentle pressure) to detect abnormal masses. Breast examination evaluates unevenness, discoloration, or scaling; both breasts are palpated to feel for masses or lumps.

In adolescent males, inspection of the rectum and prostate may be included in the physical examination. The doctor inserts a gloved finger into the rectum and rotates it slowly to feel for growths, tumors, or other abnormalities. The testes are examined visually, looking for unevenness, swelling, or other abnormalities. The testicles are palpated to identify lumps, thickening or differences in size, weight, or firmness.

If an abnormality is detected on physical examination, or symptoms suggestive of cancer are noted, diagnostic tests will be performed. Laboratory studies of sputum, blood, urine, and stool can detect abnormalities that may confirm cancer. Sputum cytology involves the microscopic examination of phlegm that is coughed up from the lungs. Tumor markers, specific proteins released by certain types of cancer cells, can be detected by performing a test on venous blood. If leukemia or lymphoma is suspected, a complete blood count (CBC) with peripheral smear (differential) is done to evaluate the number, appearance, and maturity of red blood cells (RBCs) and white blood cells (WBCs) and to measure hemoglobin, hematocrit, and **platelet count**. A bone marrow biopsy may be done to determine what type of cells is present in the bone marrow. Blood chemistries will be done to help determine if liver or kidney problems are present. Blood chemistries are also useful in monitoring the effectiveness of treatment for all types of cancer and in following the course of the disease and detecting recurrences.

Diagnostic imaging techniques such as **computed tomography** (CT scans), **magnetic resonance imaging** (MRI), ultrasound, and fiberoptic scope examinations (such as colonoscopy or sigmoidoscopy) can help determine the location, size, and characteristics of a tumor even if it is deep within the body. Conventional **x rays** are often used for initial evaluation, because they are relatively cheap, painless, and easily accessible. In order to increase the information obtained from a conventional x ray, air or contrast media (such as barium or iodine) may be used to enhance the images.

The most definitive diagnostic test for cancer is a biopsy, which is the surgical removal of a piece of suspect tissue for staining and microscope examination (cytochemistry). By examining certain cell characteristics, abnormalities can be identified and the presence of specific types of cells can be diagnostic for certain cancers. The biopsy provides information about the type of cancer, its stage, the aggressiveness of the cancer in invading nearby tissue or organs, and the extent of metastases at diagnosis. The pathologist who evaluates cancer cells in biopsied tissue designates the cancer as being stage I, II, III, or IV, in terms of the degree of metastasis.

Newer molecular and cellular diagnostic testing, such as polymerase chain reaction (PCR), allows the molecular genetic analysis of tumors. Cytogenetic analysis of tumor chromosomes, for example, can identify structural abnormalities that may explain the unique origins of cancer in an individual child. Spectral karyotyping (SKY), an advanced method of screening chromosomes for numeric and structural abnormalities, is used to evaluate pediatric tumors. Gene sequences can also be evaluated in a method (comparative genomic hybridization) that compares samples from a tumor and normal tissue after both have been exposed to the same radioactive material. This method can determine gains and losses in DNA in the region of the tumor, detecting alterations that have caused the cancer. The developing science of proteomics studies specific proteins in cells and may someday be able to provide detailed assessment of cancer cells.

Treatment

The aim of cancer treatment is to remove or destroy all or as much of the primary tumor as possible and to prevent its recurrence or metastases. While devising a treatment plan for cancer, the likelihood of curing the cancer has to be weighed against the side effects of the treatment. If the cancer is highly aggressive and cure is not likely, treatment will be aimed at relieving symptoms and controlling the cancer for as long as possible.

Cancer treatment is always tailored to the individual. The treatment choice depends on the type and location of cancer, the extent to which it has already spread, and the age, sex, and general health status of the individual. The major types of treatment are: surgery, radiation, **chemotherapy**, immunotherapy, hormone therapy, and bone-marrow transplantation.

Advances in molecular biology and cancer genetics have contributed greatly to the development of therapies that provide cell-targeted treatment. Genetic testing uses molecular probes to identify gene mutations that have been linked to specific cancers. In the early 2000s ongoing research is focused on new treatment and prevention methods, including molecular-targeted therapies, virus therapy, immunotherapy, and drug therapy that stimulates the self-destruction of cancer cells (apoptosis).

Targeted molecular therapy, although as of 2004 still the subject of concentrated research, was being used effectively in pediatric study subjects where it has been shown to reduce the toxicity seen with conventional chemotherapy. Unlike chemotherapy, which treats all cells uniformly, targeted molecular therapy can focus on selected cells without affecting normal cells and tissues. This refinement frees children from some of the long-term toxic effects and complications that can negatively affect quality of life and survival even if the cancer is cured.

Surgery

Surgical removal of a solid tumor is most effective with small tumors confined to one area of the body. Surgery removes the tumor (tumor resection) and usually part of the surrounding tissue to ensure that no cancer cells remain in the area. Since cancer usually spreads via the lymphatic system, adjoining lymph nodes are sometimes removed as well. Surgery may also be preventive or prophylactic, removing an abnormal looking area of tissue that is likely to become malignant over time. During surgery biopsies may also be performed on tissue that may be affected by metastases. Surgery is not a typical treatment for leukemia or lymphoma, which arise in the circulatory system and lymphatic systems that extend throughout the body. Children with osteosarcoma (bone cancer) and other solid tumors are candidates for surgery, however.

Surgery may be performed in conjunction with radiation (cytoreductive surgery) or chemotherapy. The surgeon removes as much of the cancer as possible and the remaining area is treated with radiotherapy or chemotherapy or both. In advanced metastatic cancer when cure is unlikely, palliative surgery aims at reducing symptoms. Debulking surgery, for example, removes part of a tumor that is pressing on other organs and causing pain. In tumors that are dependent on hormones, one option is to remove organs that secrete the hormones.

Radiation therapy

Radiation kills tumor cells and is used alone when a tumor is in a poor location for surgery. More often, it is used in conjunction with surgery and chemotherapy. Radiation can be either external or internal. External radiation is aimed at the tumor from outside the body. In internal radiation (brachytherapy), radioactive liquid or

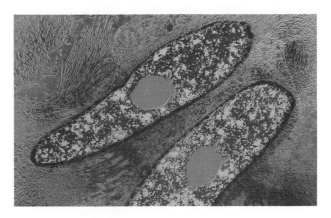

A transmission electron micrograph (TEM) of two spindle cell nuclei from a human sarcoma. Sarcomas are cancers of the connective tissue (bone, nerves, smooth muscle). *(Photograph by Dr. Brian Eyden. National Audubon Society Collection/Photo Researchers, Inc.)*

pellets are delivered to the cancerous site via a pill, injection, or insertion in a sealed container.

Chemotherapy

Chemotherapy is the administration of drugs that kill cancer cells (cytotoxic drugs). It destroys hard-to-detect cancer cells that have spread (metastasized) through the circulation or lymph system. Chemotherapeutic drugs are given orally or intravenously, either alone or in conjunction with surgery, radiation, or both. When chemotherapy is used before surgery or radiation, it is known as primary chemotherapy or neoadjuvant chemotherapy. Because the cancer cells have not yet been exposed to anti-cancer drugs, they are especially vulnerable, allowing neoadjuvant therapy to effectively reduce tumor size. However, the toxic effects of neoadjuvant chemotherapy may be severe, because normal cells are also destroyed. Chemotherapy may also make the body less tolerant of the side effects of other treatments such as radiation therapy. Adjuvant therapy is the more common type of chemotherapy, used to enhance the effectiveness of other treatments.

Immunotherapy

Immunotherapy uses the body's own immune system, specifically a type of disease-fighting white cell called T-cells, to destroy cancer cells. Tumor-specific proteins that are part of unique genetic mutations in pediatric cancer, for example, are believed to be ideal targets for anti-tumor immune processes. Various immunological agents are as of 2004 still in clinical trials and are not as of that year widely available, though initial results are promising. Monoclonal antibodies are used to

Common childhood cancers

Percentage of total childhood cancers	Type of cancer
39%	Leukemia (white blood cell cancer) and lymphoma (lymph system cancer)
20.7%	Brain cancers (brain and spinal cord tumors)
7.3%	Neuroblastoma (nerve cell cancer, most commonly in the adrenal gland)
6.1%	Wilms' tumor (kidney cancer that can metastasize to lung)
4.7%	Osteosarcoma (bone cancer) and Ewing's sarcoma (cancer in the bone shaft)
3.4%	Rhabdomyosarcoma (muscle tissue cancer, most often in head and neck)
2.9%	Retinoblastoma (malignant eye tumor)
16.4%	Germ cell cancer (ovarian or testicular cancers) and others

SOURCE: Margo Hoover-Regan. http://www.csupomona.edu/~cancerbio/pediatric%20cancer%20-%20Dr.%20Hoover-Regan.htm. Updated May 15, 2000.

(Table by GGS Information Services.)

fight cancer cells in much the same way as antibodies that are produced by the body's own immune system work to fight infection. Other substances are also being used experimentally. They include substances such as interferons, interleukins, growth factors, monoclonal antibodies, and vaccines. Unlike traditional vaccines, cancer vaccines do not prevent cancer but are designed to treat existing disease. They work by boosting the immune system and training immunized cells to destroy cancer cells.

Hormone therapy

Hormone therapy is standard treatment for cancers that are hormone-dependent and grow faster in the presence of specific hormones, such as cancer of the prostate, breast, and uterus. Hormone therapy blocks the production or action of these hormones, slowing growth of the tumor and extending survival for months or years.

Bone marrow transplantation

Bone marrow is the tissue within bone cavities that produces blood cells. Healthy bone marrow tissue constantly replenishes the blood supply and is essential to life. Sometimes drugs or radiation needed to destroy cancer cells also destroys bone marrow and only replacement with healthy cells counteracts this adverse effect. A bone marrow transplant involves removing marrow from a donor and transplanting blood-forming cells to a recipient.

While not a therapy in itself, bone marrow transplantation may allow a cancer patient to undergo aggressive therapy.

Many specialists work together to treat cancer patients. The oncologist is a physician who specializes in cancer care and usually coordinates the treatment plan, directing chemotherapy, hormone therapy, and any treatment that does not involve radiation or surgery. The radiation oncologist uses radiation to treat cancer, while the surgical oncologist performs surgery to diagnose or treat cancer. Gynecologist-oncologists and pediatric-oncologists, as their titles suggest, are physicians who treat women's and children's cancers. Radiologists read the x rays, ultrasound images, CT scans, and MRI images to help diagnose cancer. Hematologists specialize in disorders of the blood and bone marrow and are consulted in the evaluation of leukemia, lymphoma, and bone cancer.

Alternative treatment

A range of alternative treatments are available to help treat cancer that can be used in conjunction with, or separate from, surgery, chemotherapy, and radiation. Alternative treatment of cancer is a complicated arena and a trained complementary health practitioner should be consulted.

Although the effectiveness of complementary therapies such as acupuncture in alleviating cancer pain have not as of 2004 been clinically proven, many cancer patients find it safe and beneficial. Bodywork therapies such as massage and reflexology ease muscle tension and may alleviate side effects such as **nausea and vomiting**. Homeopathy and herbal remedies used in Chinese traditional herbal medicine also have been shown to alleviate some of the side effects of radiation and chemotherapy and are being recommended by many doctors.

Prognosis

Most cancers show good cure rates if detected and treated at early stages. The prognosis involves the type of cancer, its degree of invasiveness, and the extent of metastases at diagnosis. In addition, age, general health status, and response to treatment are important factors. Cancer deaths in children have shown consistent declines, decreasing between 1975 and 2000 from 50 in 1 million diagnosed to 25 in 1 million. However, cancer is the leading cause of death among children and adolescents, responsible for 2,700 deaths each year in the United States.

Prevention

Prevention of cancer means being aware of causes and risks, which involve a combination of genetic and environmental factors. Except for family history, specific genetic causes or an inherited predisposition are generally unknown in individuals until revealed in the diagnostic process. Known environmental causes can be avoided, however. A list of guidelines offered by nutritionists and epidemiologists from leading U.S. universities to reduce the risk of cancer includes some that may apply to children and adolescents:

- Eat plenty of vegetables and fruits, especially cruciferous vegetables such as broccoli, cauliflower, and cabbage.

- Decrease or avoid eating animal fats and red meats.

- Exercise vigorously for at least 20 minutes every day.

- Avoid excessive weight gain.

- Avoid tobacco (including second hand smoke).

- Avoid excessive amounts of alcohol.

- Avoid midday sun (between 11 a.m. and 3 p.m.) when rays are the strongest.

- Avoid risky sexual practices and multiple partners.

- Avoid known carcinogens in the environment or work place.

Certain drugs being used as of 2004 for treatment could also be suitable for prevention, at least prevention of recurrences. For example, the drug tamoxifen has been very effective against breast cancer and is in 2004 being used to prevent recurrence in breast cancer survivors. Similarly, retinoids derived from vitamin A are being tested for their ability to slow the progression of or to prevent head and neck cancers. Certain studies suggest that cancer incidence is lower in areas where soil and foods are rich in the mineral selenium.

Nutritional concerns

Certain foods, including many vegetables, fruits, and grains, are believed to offer protection against various cancers. In laboratory studies, **vitamins** such as A, C, and E, as well as beta-carotene found in carrots and isothiocyanate and dithiolthione compounds found in cruciferous vegetables, such as broccoli, cauliflower, and cabbage, have been shown to provide protection against certain types of cancer. Studies have shown that eating a diet rich in fiber as found in fruits, vegetables, and whole grains can reduce the risk of colon cancer.

Parental concerns

A diagnosis of childhood cancer raises many uncertainties and concerns for parents, including how to acquire the most effective therapy. Advances in molecular and cellular technologies have improved both the diagnosis and treatment of pediatric cancer and also carry with them the possibility of someday curing and

---

KEY TERMS

Benign—In medical usage, benign is the opposite of malignant. It describes an abnormal growth that is stable, treatable, and generally not life-threatening.

Biopsy—The surgical removal and microscopic examination of living tissue for diagnostic purposes or to follow the course of a disease. Most commonly the term refers to the collection and analysis of tissue from a suspected tumor to establish malignancy.

Bone marrow—The spongy tissue inside the large bones in the body that is responsible for making the red blood cells, most white blood cells, and platelets.

Carcinogenic—A substance that can cause cancer to develop.

Chemotherapy—Any treatment of an illness with chemical agents. The term is usually used to describe the treatment of cancer with drugs that inhibit cancer growth or destroy cancer cells.

Epithelium—The layer of cells that covers body surfaces, lines body cavities, and forms glands.

Hormone therapy—Treating cancers by changing the hormone balance of the body, instead of by using cell-killing drugs.

Immunotherapy—A mode of cancer treatment in which the immune system is stimulated to fight the cancer.

Malignant—Cells that have been altered such that they have lost normal control mechanisms and are capable of local invasion and spread to other areas of the body. Often used to describe a cancer.

Metastasis—A secondary tumor resulting from the spread of cancerous cells from the primary tumor to other parts of the body.

Radiation therapy—A cancer treatment that uses high-energy rays or particles to kill or weaken cancer cells. Radiation may be delivered externally or internally via surgically implanted pellets. Also called radiotherapy.

Sore—A wound, lesion, or ulcer on the skin.

Tumor—A growth of tissue resulting from the uncontrolled proliferation of cells.

---

preventing cancer in children. While cancer was at one time nearly always fatal in children, as of 2004 more than 75 percent of children diagnosed with cancer enjoyed disease-free survival. Targeted molecular therapy and immunotherapies are the ongoing focus of concentrated research, and studies using these cell-selective technologies in treating children have shown encouraging results, both in earlier responses and reduced toxicity and complications longer term. Parents can be assured of access to the current knowledge base in molecular biology and advanced treatment technologies that promise better outcomes.

See also Leukemias, acute; Leukemias, chronic.

Resources

BOOKS

Janes-Hodder, Honna, et al. *Childhood Cancer: A Parent's Guide to Solid Tumor Cancers*, 2nd ed. Cambridge, MA: O'Reilly Media Inc., 2002.

Woznick, Leigh A., and Carol D. Goodheart. *Living with Childhood Cancer: A Practical Guide to Help Families Cope*. Washington, DC: American Psychological Association (APA), 2002.

ORGANIZATIONS

American Cancer Society. 1599 Clifton Road, NE, Atlanta, GA 30329. Web site: <www.cancer.org>.

Cancer Research Institute (National Headquarters). 681 Fifth Avenue, New York, NY 10022. Web site: <www.cancerresearch.org>.

National Cancer Institute. 9000 Rockville Pike, Building 31, room 10A16, Bethesda, MD 20892. Web site: <wwwicic.nci.nih.gov>.

National Children's Cancer Society. 1015 Locust Suite 600, St. Louis, MO 63101. Web site: <www.nationalchildrenscancer society.com>.

WEB SITES

"Childhood Cancer." *Kid's Health*, 2004. Available online at <www.kidshealth.org/parent/medical/cancer/cancer.html> (accessed December 8, 2004).

L. Lee Culvert
Rosalyn Carson-DeWitt, MD
Teresa G. Odle

Candida infection *see* **Candidiasis**

▌Candidiasis

Definition

Candidiasis is an infection caused by a species of the yeast *Candida*, usually the *Candida albicans* fungus.

Candida is found on various parts of the bodies of almost all normal people but causes problems in only a few. Candidiasis can affect the skin, nails, and mucous membranes throughout the body including the mouth (thrush), esophagus, vagina (yeast infection), intestines, and lungs.

Description

Candida may cause yeast mouth infections (also known as thrush) in children with reduced immune function or in children taking certain **antibiotics**. Antibiotics may upset the balance of microorganisms in the body and allow an overgrowth of *Candida*. The use of inhaled steroids for the treatment of **asthma** has also been shown to cause oral candidiasis. Many infants acquire candidiasis from their mothers during the process of birth, when the baby comes in contact with naturally existing *Candida* found in the mother's vagina. Candidiasis is not considered harmful to infants unless it lasts more than several weeks after birth. These yeast mouth infections cause creamy white, curd-like patches on the tongue, inside of the mouth, and on the back of the throat. Under the whitish material, there are red lesions that may bleed.

Candida also may infect an infant's **diaper rash**, as it grows rapidly on irritated and moist skin. Children who suck their thumbs or other fingers may also develop candidiasis around their fingernails, causing redness on the nail edges.

Candida is a common cause of vaginal infections in adolescent girls, especially when the normal populations of the bacteria *Lactobacilli* have been reduced due to antibiotic use, allowing the overgrowth of *Candida*. A candidiasis infection in the vagina results in **itching**, burning, soreness, and a thick, white vaginal discharge.

Other risk factors for candidiasis include **obesity**, heat, and excessive sweating that result in the formation of moist skin areas where the yeast organism can grow.

In the early 2000s, several serious categories of candidiasis have become more common, due to overuse of antibiotics, the rise of **AIDS**, the increase in incidence of organ transplantations, the use of **chemotherapy** in **cancer** treatment, and the implantation of invasive devices (e.g., nasogastric tubes, catheters, and artificial joints and valves) into the body—all of which increase a patient's susceptibility to infection. Diabetics are especially susceptible to candidiasis, as they have high levels of sugar in their blood and urine and a low resistance to infection, both of which are conditions that favor the growth of yeast. Also known as invasive candidiasis, deep organ candidiasis is a serious systemic infection that can affect the esophagus, heart, blood, liver, spleen, kidneys, eyes, and skin. Like vaginal and oral candidiasis, it is an opportunistic disease that strikes when a child's resistance is lowered, often due to another illness. Children with granulocytopenia (deficiency of white blood cells) are particularly at risk for deep organ candidiasis. There are many diagnostic categories of deep organ candidiasis, depending on the tissues involved.

In the past candidiasis was referred to as moniliasis.

Demographics

Candidiasis is an extremely common infection. Thrush occurs in approximately 2–5 percent of healthy newborns and occurs in a slightly higher percentage of infants during their first year of life.

Over 1 million adult women and adolescent girls in the United States develop vaginal yeast infections each year. It is not life-threatening, but the condition can be uncomfortable and frustrating.

Causes and symptoms

Candidiasis is caused by a species of the yeast *Candida*, usually the *Candida albicans* fungus.

In oral candidiasis, the disease is characterized by whitish patches that appear on the tongue, inside of the cheeks, or on the palate. **Pain** or difficulty in swallowing may indicate a fungal infection in the throat, which is a potential complication of AIDS. Most adolescent girls with vaginal candidiasis experience severe vaginal itching and have a discharge that often looks like cottage cheese and has a sweet or bread-like odor. The vulva and vagina can be red, swollen, and painful. The infected skin in diaper rash that includes infection with *Candida* appears fiery red with areas that may have a raised red border.

Effects of deep organ or systematic candidiasis include **meningitis**, arthritis, fungemia (fungi in the blood, causing **fever** and possibly leading to sepsis), endocarditis (heart infection), endophthalmitis (infection and scarring in the eye that can affect vision), and renal or bladder bezoars (colonization and blockage of the urinary tract by *Candida*, which can cause urinary tract infections and kidney failure.

Diagnosis

Often clinical appearance and visual examination give a strong suggestion about the diagnosis. Generally, a doctor takes a sample of the vaginal discharge or swabs an area of oral or skin lesions, and then inspects this material under a microscope, where it is possible to see characteristic forms of yeasts at various stages in the lifecycle.

Fungal blood and stool cultures for detection of the *Candida* organism should be taken for patients suspected of having deep organ candidiasis. Tissue biopsy may be needed for a definitive diagnosis.

When to call the doctor

The doctor should be called if a child exhibits any symptoms of the various types of candidiasis.

Treatment

Treatment of candidiasis is primarily accomplished through the use of antifungal drugs. Oral candidiasis is usually treated with prescription lozenges or mouthwashes. Some of the most-used prescriptions are nystatin mouthwashes (Nilstat or Nitrostat) and clotrimazole lozenges. Skin infections can be treated with topical antifungal creams. Highly inflamed skin lesions can also be treated with corticosteroid creams.

For infants with oral candidiasis, pacifiers should be sterilized or discarded. Bottle nipples should be discarded and new ones used as the infant's mouth begins to heal.

The risk of diaper rash complicated with candidiasis can be reduced by preventing irritating **dermatitis** through the use of absorbent diapers and prevention of excessive exposure to urine or feces through frequent changing of diapers. The use of plastic pants that do not allow air circulation over the diaper area is not recommended. Children may still attend child care; however, childcare providers should follow good hygienic practices, including thorough hand washing and disposal of materials that may contain nasal and oral secretions of infected children, in order to prevent transmitting the infection to other children.

In most cases, vaginal candidiasis can be treated successfully with a variety of over-the-counter antifungal creams or suppositories, including Monistat, Gyne-Lotrimin, and Mycelex. However, infections often recur. If an adolescent girl has frequent recurrences, she should consult her doctor about prescription drugs such as Vagistat-1, Diflucan, and others.

The early 2000s increase in deep organ candidiasis has led to the creation of treatment guidelines, including, but not limited to, the following:

• Catheters should be removed from children with candidiasis.

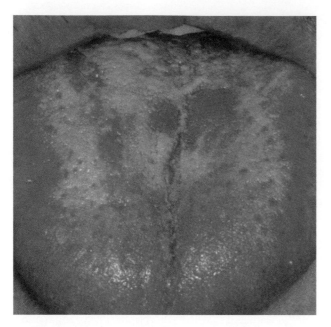

This patient's tongue is infected with candidiasis, or thrush.
(Photograph by Edward H. Gill, Custom Medical Stock Photo Inc.)

• Antifungal therapy may be used during chemotherapy to prevent candidiasis.

• Drugs should be prescribed based on a child's specific history and immune defense status (this is especially critical for children with AIDS). Stronger antifungal drugs, such as ketoconazole or fluconazole, may be necessary.

• Diabetes mellitus should be controlled with appropriate medication and dietary changes.

Alternative treatment

Home remedies for vaginal candidiasis include vinegar douches or insertion of a paste made from *Lactobacillus acidophilus* powder into the vagina. In theory, these remedies make the vagina more acidic and, therefore, less hospitable to the growth of *Candida*. Fresh garlic (*Allium sativum*) is believed to have antifungal action, so incorporating it into the diet or inserting a gauze-wrapped, peeled garlic clove into the vagina may be helpful. The insert should be changed twice daily. Some women report success with these remedies; however, they should try a conventional treatment if an alternative remedy is not effective.

Prognosis

Oral and skin candidiasis, though painful, are usually cured with the use of antifungal medications. However, in premature infants, in children with poor or compromised immune systems, or in children with deep organ or systematic infections, eradication of the infections may be more difficult to achieve. Mortality in low birth-weight premature infants with systemic candidiasis may reach 50 percent.

Prevention

Often candidiasis can be prevented through good sanitation procedures, such as keeping the body cool and dry, wearing natural fabric underclothes, changing underclothes frequently, wiping from front to back after bowel movements, and washing hands often. For children who are susceptible to candidiasis because of immune deficiencies, the regular use of antifungal drugs to prevent infections may be required.

Parental concerns

Parents need to practice good hygienic procedures as they care for their children, in order to prevent the development of candidiasis.

Resources

BOOKS

Martin, Jeanne Marie, and Rona P. Soltan. *Complete Candida Yeast Guidebook: Everything You Need to Know about Prevention, Treatment, and Diet.* New York: Prima Lifestyles, 2000.

The Official Patient's Sourcebook on Invasive Candidiasis. San Diego, CA: Icon Health Publications, 2002.

WEB SITES

Greenberg, Michael E. "Candidiasis." *eMedicine*, September 1, 2004. Available online at <www.emedicine.com/ped/topic312.htm> (accessed December 7, 2004).

Judith Sims
Richard H. Lampert

Canker sores

Definition

Canker sores (aphthous ulcers) are small shallow sores or ulcers that appear inside the lips, inside the cheeks, or on the gums. They begin as small, reddish swellings. Then they burst, and the rupture sores are covered with a white or yellow membrane. The edges of the sores are still red and look like a painful red halo. Without treatment, canker sores heal in two weeks or less.

Description

Canker sores occur inside the mouth, usually inside the lips, cheeks, or soft palate. They can also occur on or under the tongue and in the throat. Often, several canker sores appear at the same time and maybe in clusters. Canker sores appear as a whitish, round area with a red border. The sores are painful and sensitive to touch. The average canker sore is about 0.25 inch (0.6 cm) in size, although they can occasionally be larger. Canker sores are not infectious.

Demographics

Anyone can get canker sores, but they are most common among teenagers and people in their twenties. Females are slightly more likely to get canker sores than males. Some people have one or two episodes a year; others have almost continual problems. Females are likely to have canker sores during their premenstrual period.

Approximately 20 percent of the U.S. population is affected by recurring canker sores. That means as of 2004 some 56 million Americans suffer annually from these small but painful ulcers. Fortunately, certain safe, natural remedies are effective in treating canker sores.

Canker sores are sometimes mistaken as cold sores (also known as fever blisters). Cold sores are caused by the **herpes simplex** virus. The sores caused by this disease, also known as oral herpes, can occur anywhere on the body. Most commonly, herpes infection occurs on the outside of lips and much less often inside the mouth. Cold sores are infectious.

Causes and symptoms

There is some evidence that canker sores are due in part to nutritional deficiencies and a lack of vitamin B_{12}, **folic acid**, and iron. Gastrointestinal problems correlate with canker sores as well. Frequent recurrent canker sores may suggest a metabolic imbalance. The sores appear during times of stress or as a reaction to hormonal imbalances in women. Pregnancy causes remission. A tendency to get canker sores may be inherited.

As of 2004 data suggest that aphthous ulcers are a form of autoimmune disease. Other proposed causes for canker sores are trauma from toothbrush and toothpick scrapes (trauma), hormones, and **food allergies**.

Symptoms

The first symptom is a tingling or mildly painful **itching** sensation in the area where the sore will appear. After one to several days, a small red swelling appears. The sore is round and is a whitish color with a grayish colored center. Usually, there is a red ring of inflammation surrounding the sore. The main symptom is **pain**. Canker sores can be very painful, especially if they are touched repeatedly by the tongue or silverware.

When to call the doctor

Infants and children may have difficulty sleeping because of the pain. The doctor should be called for pain relief remedies or medication to help the child through this period. The doctor should be called if the child runs a fever, refuses to eat or drink, and if the child shows signs of **dehydration**.

Diagnosis

Canker sores are diagnosed by observation of the blister, which generally appears in the mouth or throat. Canker sores are bacterial infections and not contagious.

Recurrent canker sores may indicate a metabolic imbalance, dietary deficiency, stress, and a lack of rest. Children who have frequent canker sores may benefit from dietary supplements of B-complex vitamin or may undergo blood and **allergy tests** to see if some other underlying cause can be identified.

Treatment

Since canker sores heal by themselves, professional treatment is not usually necessary. Topical anesthetics

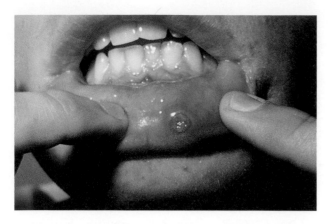

Apthous ulcer, or canker sore, on the inside of a patient's bottom lip. (© Lester V. Bergman/Corbis.)

may relieve the pain. The use of corticosteroid ointments sometimes speeds healing. If an ointment is used to treat a canker sore, the parent should first dry the sore. Next, a small amount of medicine should be put on a cotton swab and applied to the sore. The child should not have anything to drink or eat for 30 minutes to keep the medicine from washing away. Parents can also try preparations of tea tree oil, goldenseal, propolis, licorice, myrrh, and lysine, products with healing nutrients that are backed by research.

There are several treatments for reducing the pain and duration of the sores. The drugs frequently recommended are anti-inflammatory steroid mouthwashes, **analgesics**, and numbing ointments containing benzocaine.

The following treatments may be effective in relieving symptoms or shortening the duration of canker sores in their children.

- for pain relief in a prescription, 2 percent viscous lidocaine, applied with a cotton swab (Q-tip) several times daily

- prescription steroid ointment, Kenalog (triamcinolone) or Orabase; also tetracycline syrup or tetracycline capsules dissolved in water

- an anti-inflammatory ointment, Aphthasol, which is only modestly effective

- over-the-counter benzocaine preparations (Anbesol and Oragel); ointments such as Orabase or Zilactin-B to coat the ulcers and provide some protection and comfort

- for older children, zinc lozenges, taking vitamin C or vitamin B complex, using a sage and chamomile mouthwash, or taking lysine supplements

- tincture of propolis, available at health food stores, the "cement" made by honeybees to make their **hives** with remarkable antiseptic and healing properties

- for symptomatic relief of sores caused from food **allergies**, mixed equal amounts of milk of magnesia and Benadryl liquid, a teaspoon of which is swished by the child in his mouth for about one minute and then spat out, every four to six hours, to reduce pain

Alternative treatment

Alternative therapies for canker sores are meant to heal existing sores and prevent their recurrence. Several herbal remedies, including calendula (*Calendula officinalis*), myrrh (*Commiphora molmol*), and goldenseal (*Hydrastis canadensis*), may be helpful in treating existing sores. Compresses soaked in teas made from these herbs are applied directly to the sores. The tannic acid in a tea bag can also help dry up the sores when the wet tea bag is used as a compress. Taking dandelion (*Taraxacum officinale*) tea or capsules may help heal sores and prevent future outbreaks. Home remedies and herbal preparations may not be readily available as over-the-counter in forms suitable for pediatric patients. Since canker sores are often brought on by stress, stress-relieving techniques such as cuddling and rocking babies until they fall asleep may help relieve the stress associated with the severity of pain.

Prognosis

There is no cure for canker sores, and they occur more often with age. Treatments are to relieve symptoms or shorten the duration of the sore. If observation suggests a secondary infection, topical application of tetracycline to the lesion, three or four times daily, shortens healing to two to four days. Left untreated, canker sores can last as long as two weeks. Sores that persist for a longer time should be checked by a doctor.

Prevention

Children should avoid trauma, such as biting the inside of their mouth and tongue, or vigorous tooth brushing. Injury to the mucous membranes of the mouth and gums leaves places where bacteria can grow. This may make canker sores worse.

To decrease the incidence canker sores, parents may consider changing to a toothpaste free of sodium laurylsulfate.

Nutritional concerns

Eating certain foods can be painful to a child with canker sores. Parents should remove spicy foods and citrus fruit from the child's diet. These foods may aggravate the sores and cause unnecessary pain. Parents should encourage their children to eat yogurt with active lactobacillus cultures because it may prevent outbreaks.

Parental concerns

Parents are mainly concerned with the comfort of their babies and small children. They must also pay attention to the nutritional intake of infants and small children who may refuse to eat because of the pain from canker sores.

Resources

BOOKS

Parker, Philip M., et al. *Canker Sores: A Medical Dictionary, Bibliography, and Annotated Research Guide to Internet References.* Boulder, CO: netLibrary, 2003.

WEB SITES

"Canker Sores." *MedlinePlus*, January 13, 2003. Available online at <www.nlm.nih.gov/medlineplus/ency/article/000998.htm> (accessed December 14, 2004).

Aliene S. Linwood, RN, DPA, FACHE

Car sickness *see* **Motion sickness**

Carbohydrate intolerance

Definition

Carbohydrate intolerance is the inability of the small intestine to completely process the nutrient carbohydrate (a classification that includes sugars and starches) into a source of energy for the body. This is usually due to deficiency of an enzyme needed for digestion. **Lactose intolerance** is the inability to digest the sugar found in milk.

Description

Carbohydrates are the primary source of energy and, along with fats and proteins, one of the three major nutrients in the human diet. Carbohydrates are classified according to their structure, based on the number of basic sugar, or saccharide, units they contain.

A monosaccharide, called a simple sugar, is the simplest carbohydrate. Simple sugars include glucose (the form in which sugar circulates in the blood), fructose (found in fruit and honey), and galactose (produced by the digestion of milk). These simple sugars are important because they can be absorbed by the small intestine.

Two simple sugars linked together form a disaccharide. Disaccharide sugars present in the diet are maltose (a product of the digestion of starch), sucrose (table sugar), and lactose (the sugar in milk). These disaccharides must be broken down by enzymes into two simple sugars so that they can be absorbed by the intestine.

Polysaccharides are much more complex carbohydrates made up of many simple sugars. The most important polysaccharides are glycogen, which is stored in the liver, and cellulose (starch).

Digestion of sugars

Digestion of food begins in the mouth, moves on to the stomach, and then into the small intestine. Along the way, specific enzymes are needed to process different types of sugars. An enzyme is a substance that acts as a catalyst to produce chemical changes without being changed itself. The enzymes lactase, maltase, and isomaltase (or sucrase) are needed to break down the disaccharides; when one or more is inadequate, the result is carbohydrate intolerance.

Types of intolerance

Carbohydrate intolerance can be congenital, primary, or secondary. Congenital deficiency is caused by an enzyme defect present at birth. Alactasia is a very rare congenital condition and the result of a genetic defect that causes the complete absence of lactase, the enzyme needed to digest milk sugar. Primary deficiency is caused by an enzyme defect developed over time. The most common is lactose intolerance. Secondary deficiencies, often caused by a disease or disorder of the intestinal tract, disappear when the underlying cause is treated. Secondary deficiencies include protein deficiency, pancreatitis, **celiac disease**, short-bowel syndrome, and some intestinal infections. Chronic renal failure and certain medications also can cause secondary deficiencies.

Demographics

Lactose intolerance is widespread, affecting about 20 percent of American children and up to 70 percent of the world's adult population. Lactose intolerance is the most common of all enzyme deficiencies, and an estimated 30–50 million Americans have this condition. Some racial and ethnic populations are affected more than others. Lactose intolerance is found in as many as 75 percent of African Americans, Jewish Americans, Mexican Americans, and Native Americans, and in 90 percent or more of Asian Americans and some Mediterranean peoples. Descendants of Northern Europe usually do not develop the condition (incidence is less than 20 percent in these populations). Deficiencies in enzymes other than lactase are extremely rare.

Causes and symptoms

Causes

Enzymes play an important role in breaking down carbohydrates into forms that can pass through the intestine and be used by the body. Usually they are named by adding *ase* to the name of the substance they act on (for example, lactase is the enzyme needed to process lactose). In the mouth, cooked starch is broken down to a disaccharide by amylase, an enzyme in the saliva. The disaccharides maltose, sucrose, and lactose cannot be absorbed until they have been separated into simple sugar molecules by their corresponding enzymes present in the cells lining the intestinal tract. If this process is not completed, digestion is interrupted.

Although not common, a deficiency in the enzymes needed to digest lactose, maltose, and sucrose is sometimes present at birth. Intestinal lactase enzymes usually decrease naturally with age, but this occurs at varying degrees. Because of the uneven distribution of enzyme deficiency based on race and ethnic heritage, especially in lactose intolerance, genetics are believed to play a role in the cause of primary carbohydrate intolerance.

Digestive diseases such as celiac disease and tropical sprue (which affect absorption in the intestine), as well as intestinal infections and injuries, can reduce the amount of enzymes produced. In **cancer** patients, treatment with radiation therapy or **chemotherapy** may affect the cells in the intestine that normally secrete lactase, leading to intolerance.

Symptoms

The severity of the symptoms depends upon the extent of the enzyme deficiency, and ranges from a feeling of mild bloating to severe **diarrhea**. In the case of a lactase deficiency, undigested milk sugar remains in the intestine, which is then fermented by the normal intestinal bacteria. These bacteria produce gas, cramping, bloating, a "gurgly" feeling in the abdomen, and flatulence. In a growing child, the main symptoms are diarrhea and a failure to gain weight. Lactase deficiency causes gastrointestinal distress to begin about 30 minutes to two hours after eating or drinking foods containing lactose.

Food intolerances can be confused with **food allergies**, since the symptoms of **nausea**, cramps, bloating, and diarrhea are similar. Food intolerances involve an exaggerated or abnormal physical reaction to a food or food additive, and are not associated with an immune reaction. Food **allergies** involve an immune reaction.

Sugars that are not broken down into one of the simplest forms cause the body to push fluid into the intestines, which results in watery diarrhea (osmotic diarrhea). The diarrhea may sweep other nutrients out of the intestine before they can be absorbed, causing **malnutrition**.

When to call the doctor

If a child has the following symptoms, the parent should contact the child's pediatrician or gastroenterologist:

- abdominal **pain**, **vomiting**, or diarrhea that awakens the child during the night

- persistent or severe abdominal pain or diarrhea

- unexplained weight loss

- rectal bleeding

- blood or mucus in stools

- fever

Diagnosis

The doctor may recommend a lactose-free diet for two or three weeks to determine if lactose intolerance is causing the symptoms. During the lactose-free period, the child should avoid all products containing lactose. The parent and child are asked to record the intake of all foods and beverages and note when symptoms occur after eating or drinking.

To identify other problem-causing foods or beverages, it is helpful for the parent and child to keep a diary of symptoms for two or three weeks. The doctor can then review the diary with the parent and child to identify possible problem foods.

The diagnosis of carbohydrate or lactose intolerance is supported by the presence of symptoms related to the condition. In addition, the primary pediatrician or gastroenterologist may confirm the diagnosis after questioning the child (if old enough to provide an accurate history of symptoms) or parent about his or her physical health, performing a physical examination, and ordering laboratory tests to rule out other conditions that resemble carbohydrate intolerance.

When carbohydrate intolerance is suspected, the diagnosis can be confirmed using oral tolerance tests. The carbohydrate being investigated is given by mouth in liquid form. Several blood levels are measured and compared to normal values. This helps evaluate the individual's ability to digest the sugar.

To identify lactose intolerance in children and adults, the hydrogen breath test is used to measure the amount of hydrogen in the breath. The patient drinks a beverage containing lactose and the breath is analyzed at regular intervals. If undigested lactose in the large intestine (colon) is fermented by bacteria, various gases are produced. Hydrogen is absorbed from the intestines and carried by the bloodstream into the lungs, where it is exhaled. Normally, there is very little hydrogen detectable in the breath; therefore, its presence indicates faulty digestion of lactose.

When lactose intolerance is suspected in infants and young children, many pediatricians recommend simply changing from cow's milk to soy formula and watching for improvement. If needed, a stool sample can be tested for acidity. The inadequate digestion of lactose will result in an increase of acid in the waste matter excreted by the bowels and the presence of glucose.

Treatment

Carbohydrate intolerance caused by temporary intestinal diseases disappears when the condition is successfully treated. In primary conditions, no treatment exists to improve the body's ability to produce the enzymes, but symptoms can be controlled by diet.

An over-the-counter product marketed by the brand name Beano contains the enzyme alpha-galactosidase that works with the body's digestive system to break down complex carbohydrates into simple sugars that are easily digested. Beano is taken just before consuming gas-producing foods.

Nutritional concerns

Because there is wide variance in the degree of lactose intolerance, treatment should be tailored for the individual. Milk products should be avoided in young children who have signs of lactose intolerance. The child's doctor or a registered dietitian can help in making dietary adjustments and can advise when to start gradually reintroducing milk products, if applicable.

In infants, switching to soy-based formula may help. Special formulas, such as a glucose polymer-based formula, or a casein-based formula, may be recommended in infants with severe carbohydrate intolerance or when symptoms are severe.

Older children can adjust their intake of lactose, depending on how much and what they can tolerate. For some, a small glass of milk will not cause problems, while others may be able to handle ice cream or aged cheeses such as cheddar or Swiss, but not other dairy products. Generally, small amounts of lactose-containing foods eaten throughout the day are better tolerated than a large amount consumed all at once.

For those who are sensitive to even very small amounts of lactose, the lactase enzyme supplement is available without a prescription. The supplement is available in liquid form for use with milk. The addition of a few drops to a quart of milk will reduce the lactose content by 70 percent after 24 hours in the refrigerator. Heating the milk speeds the process, and doubling the amount of lactase liquid will result in milk that is 90 percent lactose free. Chewable lactase enzyme tablets are also available. Three to six tablets taken before a meal or snack will aid in the digestion of solid foods. Lactose-reduced milk and other products are also available in stores. Lactose-reduced milk contains the same nutrients as regular milk.

Because dairy products are an important source of calcium, people who reduce or severely limit their intake of these foods and beverages may need to consider other ways to consume an adequate amount of calcium. Taking calcium supplements or choosing other foods high in calcium may be needed to meet the recommended daily requirement of calcium. In addition, foods high in vitamin A, riboflavin, and vitamin B_{12} should be included in the daily diet to compensate for the nutrients normally found in cow's milk.

KEY TERMS

Alactasia—A rare inherited condition causing the lack of the enzyme needed to digest milk sugar.

Celiac disease—A disease, occurring in both children and adults, which is caused by a sensitivity to gluten, a protein found in grains. It results in chronic inflammation and shrinkage of the lining of the small intestine. Also called gluten enteropathy or nontropical sprue.

Cellulose—The primary substance composing the cell walls or fibers of all plant tissues.

Constipation—Difficult bowel movements caused by the infrequent production of hard stools.

Defecation—The act of having a bowel movement or the passage of feces through the anus.

Diarrhea—A loose, watery stool.

Digestion—The mechanical, chemical, and enzymatic process in which food is converted into the substances suitable for use by the body.

Enzyme—A protein that catalyzes a biochemical reaction without changing its own structure or function.

Feces—The solid waste, also called stool, that is left after food is digested. Feces form in the intestines and pass out of the body through the anus.

Gastroenterologist—A physician who specializes in diseases of the digestive system.

Hydrogen breath test—A test used to determine if a person is lactose intolerant or if abnormal bacteria are present in the colon.

Lactose—A sugar found in milk and milk products.

Metabolism—The sum of all chemical reactions that occur in the body resulting in growth, transformation of foodstuffs into energy, waste elimination, and other bodily functions. These include processes that break down substances to yield energy and processes that build up other substances necessary for life.

Nutrient—Substances in food that supply the body with the elements needed for metabolism. Examples of nutrients are vitamins, minerals, carbohydrates, fats, and proteins.

Peristalsis—Slow, rhythmic contractions of the muscles in a tubular organ, such as the intestines, that move the contents along.

Sugars—Those carbohydrates having the general composition of one part carbon, two parts hydrogen, and one part oxygen.

Alternative treatment

Alternative and complementary therapies include approaches that are considered to be outside the mainstream of traditional health care. The list of alternative treatments for carbohydrate intolerance includes aromatherapy, homeopathy, hydrotherapy, juice therapy, acupuncture, chiropractic, osteopathy, naturopathic medicine, and Chinese traditional herbal medicine.

Before learning or practicing any particular technique, it is important for the parent or caregiver and child to learn about the therapy, its safety and effectiveness, potential side effects, and the expertise and qualifications of the practitioner. Although some practices are beneficial, others may be harmful to certain patients.

Relaxation techniques and dietary supplements should not be used as a substitute for medical therapies prescribed by a doctor. Parents should discuss the alternative treatments with the child's doctor to determine the techniques and remedies that may be beneficial for the child.

Prognosis

Carbohydrate intolerance has a very low mortality rate. Newborns and infants have a higher risk of chronic diarrhea and malnutrition from carbohydrate intolerance. With good dietary management, children with carbohydrate intolerance can lead normal lives.

Prevention

Since the cause of the enzyme deficiency leading to carbohydrate intolerance is unknown, there is no way to prevent this condition.

Nutritional concerns

To help prevent or decrease the child's symptoms, parents can:

- help the child identify and avoid problematic foods

- work with a registered dietitian to facilitate specific dietary changes

- incorporate changes in the child's diet gradually, giving his or her body time to adjust

- establish set times for meals, and not permit the child to skip a meal

- encourage the child to drink at least eight glasses of water per day

- encourage the child to eat more slowly

- offer smaller, more frequent meals

Parental concerns

Parents should reinforce with the child that carbohydrate intolerance is not a life-threatening condition and that dietary changes can help reduce symptoms. They should remind the child that a few months may be needed before he or she notices substantial improvement in symptoms.

See also Lactose intolerance.

Resources

BOOKS

Macdonald, Ian. "Carbohydrates." In *Modern Nutrition in Health and Disease*, 9th ed. Maurice E. Shils, ed., et al. Philadelphia: Lippincott Williams & Wilkins, 1998.

Williams, Sue Rodwellm, and Eleanor Schlenker. *Essentials of Nutrition and Diet Therapy*, 8th ed. Philadelphia: C.V. Mosby, 2002.

ORGANIZATIONS

American College of Gastroenterology (ACG). P.O. Box 3099, Alexandria, VA 22302. (703) 820-7400. Web site: <www.acg.gi.org>.

American Gastroenterological Association. 4930 Del Ray Ave., Bethesda, MD 20814. (301) 654 2055. Web site: <www.gastro.org>.

International Foundation for Functional Gastrointestinal Disorders (IFFGD). P.O. Box 170864, Milwaukee, WI 53217-8076. (888) 964-2001. Web site: <www.iffgd.org>.

National Digestive Diseases Information Clearinghouse (NDDIC). 2 Information Way, Bethesda, MD 20892-3570. (800) 891-5389. Web site: <www.niddk.nih.gov>.

Karen Ericson, R.N.
Angela M. Costello

Carbon monoxide poisoning

Definition

Carbon monoxide (CO) **poisoning** occurs when carbon monoxide gas is inhaled. CO is a colorless, odorless, highly poisonous gas that is produced by incomplete combustion. It is found in automobile exhaust fumes, faulty stoves and heating systems, fires, and cigarette smoke. Other sources include wood-burning stoves, kerosene heaters, improperly ventilated water heaters and gas stoves, and blocked or poorly maintained chimney flues. CO interferes with the ability of the blood to carry oxygen. The result is **headache**, **nausea**, convulsions, and finally death by asphyxiation.

Description

Carbon monoxide, sometimes called coal gas, has been known as a toxic substance since the third century B.C. It was used for executions and suicides in early Rome.

Anyone who is exposed to CO becomes sick, and the entire body is involved in CO poisoning. A developing fetus can also be poisoned if a pregnant woman breathes CO gas. Infants, people with heart or lung disease, or those with anemia may be more seriously affected. People such as underground parking garage attendants who are exposed to car exhausts in a confined area are more likely to be poisoned by CO. Firemen also run a higher risk of inhaling CO.

Demographics

Carbon monoxide is the leading cause of accidental poisoning in the United States. Experts estimate that 1,500 Americans die each year from accidental exposure to CO and another 2,300 from intentional exposure (**suicide**). An additional 10,000 people seek medical attention after exposure to CO and recover.

Causes and symptoms

Normally when a person breathes fresh air into the lungs, the oxygen in the air binds with a molecule called hemoglobin (Hb) that is found in red blood cells. This process allows oxygen to be moved from the lungs to every part of the body. When the oxygen/hemoglobin complex reaches a muscle where it is needed, the oxygen is released. Because the oxygen binding process is reversible, hemoglobin can be used over and over again to pick up oxygen and move it throughout the body.

Inhaling carbon monoxide gas interferes with this oxygen transport system. In the lungs, CO competes with oxygen to bind with the hemoglobin molecule. Hemoglobin prefers CO to oxygen and accepts it more than 200 times more readily than it accepts oxygen. Not only does the hemoglobin prefer CO, it holds on to the CO much more tightly, forming a complex called carboxyhemoglobin (COHb). As a person breathes CO contaminated air, more and more oxygen transportation sites on the hemoglobin molecules become blocked by CO. Gradually, there are fewer and fewer sites available for oxygen. All cells need oxygen to live. When they do not get enough oxygen, cellular metabolism is disrupted and eventually cells begin to die.

The symptoms of CO poisoning and the speed with which they appear depend on the concentration of CO in the air and the rate and efficiency with which a person breathes. Heavy smokers can start off with up to 9 percent of their hemoglobin already bound to CO, which they regularly inhale in cigarette smoke. This makes them much more susceptible to environmental CO. The Occupational Safety and Health Administration (OSHA) has established a maximum permissible exposure level of 50 parts per million (ppm) over eight hours.

With exposure to 200 ppm for two to three hours, a person begins to experience headache, fatigue, nausea, and **dizziness**. These symptoms correspond to 15 to 25 percent COHb in the blood. When the concentration of COHb reaches 50 percent or more, death results in a very short time. Emergency room physicians have the most experience diagnosing and treating CO poisoning.

The symptoms of CO poisoning in order of increasing severity include the following:

• headache

• shortness of breath

• dizziness

• fatigue

• mental confusion and difficulty thinking

• loss of fine hand-eye coordination

• nausea and vomiting

• rapid heart rate

• hallucinations

• inability to execute voluntary movements accurately

• collapse

• lowered body temperature (hypothermia)

• coma

• convulsions

• seriously low blood pressure

• cardiac and respiratory failure

• death

In some cases, the skin, mucous membranes, and nails of a person with CO poisoning are cherry red or bright pink. Because the color change does not always occur, it is an unreliable symptom to count on for diagnosis.

Although most CO poisoning is acute, or sudden, it is possible to suffer from chronic CO poisoning. This condition exists when a person is exposed to low levels of the gas over a period of days to months. Symptoms are often vague and include (in order of frequency) fatigue, headache, dizziness, **sleep** disturbances, cardiac symptoms, apathy, nausea, and memory disturbances. Little is known about chronic CO poisoning, and it is often misdiagnosed.

When to call the doctor

A healthcare professional should be consulted whenever more than passing exposure to carbon monoxide is suspected. While waiting for help to arrive, a potentially affected person should be moved outdoors.

Diagnosis

The main reason to suspect CO poisoning is evidence that fuel is being burned in a confined area, for example, a car running inside a closed garage, a charcoal grill burning indoors, or an unvented kerosene heater in a workshop. Under these circumstances, one or more persons suffering from the symptoms listed above strongly suggests CO poisoning. In the absence of some concrete reason to suspect CO poisoning, the disorder is often misdiagnosed as migraine headache, **stroke**, psychiatric illness, **food poisoning**, alcohol poisoning, or heart disease.

Concrete confirmation of CO poisoning comes from a carboxyhemoglobin test. This blood test measures the amount of CO that is bound to hemoglobin in the body. Blood is drawn as soon after suspected exposure to CO as possible.

Other tests that are useful in determining the extent of CO poisoning include measurement of other arterial blood gases and pH; a complete blood count; measurement of other blood components such as sodium, potassium, bicarbonate, urea nitrogen, and lactic acid; an electrocardiogram (ECG); and a chest x ray.

Treatment

Immediate treatment for CO poisoning is to remove the victim from the source of carbon monoxide gas and into fresh air. If the victim is not breathing and has no pulse, **cardiopulmonary resuscitation** (CPR) should be started. Depending on the severity of the poisoning,

100 percent oxygen may be given with a tight fitting mask as soon as it is available.

Taken with other symptoms of CO poisoning, COHb levels of over 25 percent in healthy individuals, over 15 percent in people with a history of heart or lung disease, and over 10 percent in pregnant women usually indicate the need for **hospitalization**. In the hospital, fluids and electrolytes are given to correct imbalances that have arisen from the breakdown of cellular metabolism.

In severe cases of CO poisoning, individuals are given hyperbaric oxygen therapy. This treatment involves placing the person in a chamber in which the person breathes 100 percent oxygen at a pressure of more than one atmosphere (the normal pressure the atmosphere exerts at sea level). The increased pressure forces more oxygen into the blood. Hyperbaric facilities are specialized and are usually available only at larger hospitals.

Prognosis

The speed and degree of recovery from CO poisoning depends on the length of exposure to the gas and the concentration of carbon monoxide. The half-life of CO in normal room air is four to five hours, which means that in four to five hours half of the CO bound to hemoglobin will be replaced with oxygen. At normal atmospheric pressures, but breathing 100 percent oxygen, the half-life for the elimination of CO from the body is 50 to 70 minutes. In hyperbaric therapy at three atmospheres of pressure, the half-life is reduced to between 20 and 25 minutes.

Although the symptoms of CO poisoning may subside in a few hours, some affected persons show memory problems, fatigue, confusion, and mood changes for two to four weeks after their exposure to the gas.

Prevention

Carbon monoxide poisoning is preventable. Particular care should be paid to situations where fuel is burned in a confined area. Portable and permanently installed carbon monoxide detectors that sound a warning similar to smoke detectors are available for under $50. Specific actions that prevent CO poisoning include the following:

- Stop **smoking**. Smokers have less tolerance to environmental CO.

- Have heating systems and appliances installed by a qualified contractor to assure that they are properly vented and meet local building codes.

> **KEY TERMS**
>
> **Carboxyhemoglobin**—Hemoglobin that is bound to carbon monoxide instead of oxygen.
>
> **Hemoglobin**—An iron-containing pigment of red blood cells composed of four amino acid chains (alpha, beta, gamma, delta) that delivers oxygen from the lungs to the cells of the body and carries carbon dioxide from the cells to the lungs.
>
> **Hypothermia**—A serious condition in which body temperature falls below 95°F (35 °C). It is usually caused by prolonged exposure to the cold.
>
> **pH**—A measurement of the acidity or alkalinity of a solution. Based on a scale of 14, a pH of 7.0 is neutral. A pH below 7.0 is an acid; the lower the number, the stronger the acid. A pH above 7.0 is a base; the higher the number, the stronger the base. Blood pH is slightly alkaline (basic) with a normal range of 7.36–7.44.

- Inspect and properly maintain heating systems, chimneys, and appliances.

- Do not use a gas oven or stove to heat the home.

- Do not burn charcoal indoors.

- Make sure there is good ventilation if using a kerosene heater indoors.

- Do not leave cars or trucks running inside the garage.

- Keep car windows rolled up when stuck in heavy traffic, especially if inside a tunnel.

Parental concerns

Parents should not allow children to **play** in areas heated by kerosene space heaters or to use charcoal grills of any kind indoors.

Resources

BOOKS

Braunwald, Eugene, et al, eds. "Hypoxia and Cyanosis." In *Harrison's Principles of Internal Medicine*, 15th ed. New York: McGraw Hill, 2001, pp. 214–6.

Carbon Monoxide Poisoning: A Medical Dictionary, Bibliography, and Annotated Research Guide to Internet References. San Diego, CA: Icon Health Publications, 2004.

Penney, David G. *Carbon Monoxide Toxicity*. Lakeland, FL: CRC Press, 2000.

Robertson, William O. "Chronic Poisoning: Trace Metals and Others." In *Cecil Textbook of Medicine*, 22nd ed. Edited by Lee Goldman, et al. Philadelphia: Saunders, 2003, pp. 91–9.

PERIODICALS

Harper A., and J. Croft-Baker. "Carbon monoxide poisoning: undetected by both patients and their doctors." *Age and Ageing* 33, no. 2 (2004): 105–9.

Huffman, S. M. "Exposure to carbon monoxide from material handling equipment." *Journal of Occupational and Environmental Hygiene* 1, no. 5 (2004): D54–6.

Piantadosi C. A. "Carbon monoxide poisoning." *Undersea and Hyperbaric Medicine* 31, no. 1 (2004): 167–77.

Thomassen, O., G. Brattebo, M. Rostrup. "Carbon monoxide poisoning while using a small cooking stove in a tent." *American Journal of Emergency Medicine* 22, no. 3 (2004): 204–6.

Vacchiano, G., and R. Torino. "Carbon-monoxide poisoning, behavioral changes and suicide: an unusual industrial accident." *Journal of Clinical Forensic Medicine* 8, no. 2 (2004): 86–92.

ORGANIZATIONS

American Academy of Clinical Toxicology. 777 East Park Drive, PO Box 8820, Harrisburg, PA 17105–8820. Web site: <www.clintox.org/index.html>.

American Academy of Emergency Medicine. 611 East Wells Street, Milwaukee, WI 53202. Web site: <www.aaem.org/>.

American Academy of Family Physicians. 11400 Tomahawk Creek Parkway, Leawood, KS 66211–2672. Web site: <www.aafp.org/>.

American Academy of Pediatrics. 141 Northwest Point Boulevard, Elk Grove Village, IL 60007–1098. Web site: <www.aap.org/default.htm>.

American Association of Poison Control Centers. 3201 New Mexico Avenue NW, Washington, DC 20016. Web site: <www.aapcc.org/>.

American College of Emergency Physicians. PO Box 619911, Dallas, TX 75261–9911. Web site: <www.acep.org/>.

American College of Hyperbaric Medicine. PO Box 25914–130, Houston, Texas 77265. Web site: <www.hyperbaricmedicine.org/>.

American College of Occupational and Environmental Medicine. 55 West Seegers Road, Arlington Heights, IL 60005. Web site: <www.acoem.org/>.

American College of Osteopathic Emergency Physicians. 142 E. Ontario Street, Suite 550, Chicago, IL 60611. Web site: <www.acoep.org/>.

International Congress on Hyperbaric Medicine. 1592 Union Street, San Francisco, CA 94123. Web site: <www.ichm.net/>.

Undersea and Hyperbaric Medical Society. 10531 Metropolitan Ave, Kensington, MD 20895. Web site: <www.uhms.org/>.

WEB SITES

"A Guide to Prevent Carbon Monoxide Poisoning." *Industry Trade Group*. Available online at <www.carbon-monoxide-poisoning.com/> (accessed November 2, 2004).

"Carbon Monoxide Poisoning." *Centers for Disease Control and Prevention*. Available online at <www.cdc.gov/nceh/airpollution/carbonmonoxide/default.htm> (accessed November 2, 2004).

"Carbon Monoxide Poisoning." *National Library of Medicine*. Available online at <www.nlm.nih.gov/medlineplus/carbonmonoxidepoisoning.html> (accessed November 2, 2004).

OTHER

Carbon Monoxide Headquarters. *Wayne State University School of Medicine*. <www.phymac.med.wayne.edu/FacultyProfile/penney/COHQ/co1.htm> (accessed November 2, 2004).

L. Fleming Fallon Jr., MD, DrPH

Cardiopulmonary resuscitation

Definition

Cardiopulmonary resuscitation (CPR) is a procedure to support and maintain breathing and circulation for an infant, child, or adolescent who has stopped breathing (respiratory arrest) and/or whose heart has stopped (cardiac arrest).

Purpose

CPR is performed to restore and maintain breathing and circulation and to provide oxygen and blood flow to the heart, brain, and other vital organs. CPR can be performed by trained laypeople or healthcare professionals on infants, children, adolescents, and adults. CPR should be performed if an infant, child, or adolescent is unconscious and not breathing. Respiratory and cardiac arrest can be caused by allergic reactions, an ineffective heartbeat, asphyxiation, breathing passages that are blocked, **choking**, drowning, drug reactions or overdoses, electric shock, exposure to cold, severe shock, or trauma. In newborns, the most common cause of cardiopulmonary arrest is respiratory failure caused by **sudden infant death syndrome** (SIDS), airway obstruction (usually from inhalation of a foreign body), sepsis, neurologic disease, or drowning. Cardiac arrest in children over one year of age is most commonly caused by shock and/or respiratory failure resulting from an accident or injury.

Description

CPR is part of the emergency cardiac care system designed to save lives. Many deaths can be prevented by prompt recognition of cardiopulmonary arrest and notification of the emergency medical system (EMS), followed by early CPR, defibrillation (which delivers a brief electric shock to the heart in attempt to get the heart to beat normally), and advanced cardiac life support measures. When performed by a layperson, CPR is designed to support and maintain breathing and circulation until emergency medical personnel arrive and take over. When performed by healthcare personnel, it is used in conjunction with other basic and advanced life support measures.

CPR must be performed within four to six minutes after cessation of breathing to prevent brain damage or death. CPR consists of rescue breathing, which delivers oxygen to the victim's lungs, and external chest compressions, which help circulate blood through the heart to vital organs.

CPR technique differs for infants, children, and adolescents. The American Heart Association and the American Red Cross, the two organizations that provide CPR training and guidelines, distinguish infants, children, and adolescents for the purposes of CPR as follows:

- "Infant" includes neonates (those in the first 28 days of life) and extends to the age of one year.

- "Child" includes toddlers aged one year to children aged eight years.

- "Adult" includes children aged eight years and older.

Because infants and children under the age of eight have smaller upper and lower airways and faster heart rates than adults, CPR techniques are different for them than for older children and adults. Children and adolescents aged eight years and older have reached a body size that can be handled using adult CPR techniques and are thus classified as adults for delivery of CPR and life support. CPR is always begun after assessing the victim and contacting EMS.

Performing CPR on an infant

For an infant, the rescuer opens the airway using a gentle head tilt/chin lift or jaw thrust, places their mouth over the infant's mouth and nose then delivers gentle breaths so that the infant's chest rises with each breath. Chest compressions are delivered by placing two fingers of one hand over the lower half of the infant's sternum slightly below the nipple line and pressing down about one half inch to one inch. Compressions are delivered at a rate of 100 times per minute, giving five chest compressions followed by one rescue breath in successive cycles.

Performing CPR on a child aged one to eight

For a child aged one to eight years, the compression rate is the same—five compressions and one rescue breath. Rescue breaths are delivered using a mouth-to-mouth seal, instead of mouth-to-mouth-and-nose. Chest compressions are delivered by placing the heel of one hand over the lower half of the sternum and depressing about one to one and one half inches per compression.

Performing CPR on a child aged eight and older

For a child aged eight years and older, and for larger children under age eight, two hands are used for compressions, with the heel of one hand on the lower half of the sternum and the heel of the other hand on top of that hand. The chest is compressed about one and one half to two inches per compression. Rescue breaths are delivered with a mouth-to-mouth seal. The compression rate is 80 to 100 per minute delivered in cycles of 15 compressions followed by two rescue breaths.

Preparation

Before administering CPR to an infant or child, laypeople should participate in hands-on training. More than 5 million Americans annually receive training in CPR through American Heart Association and American Red Cross courses. In addition to courses taught by instructors, the American Heart Association also has an interactive video called *Learning System*, which is available at more than 500 healthcare institutions. Both organizations teach CPR the same way, but they use different terms. CPR training should be retaken every two to three years to maintain skill level.

Precautions

CPR should not be performed based on the overview contained in this article. To prevent disease transmission during CPR, face masks and face shields are available to prevent direct contact during rescue breathing.

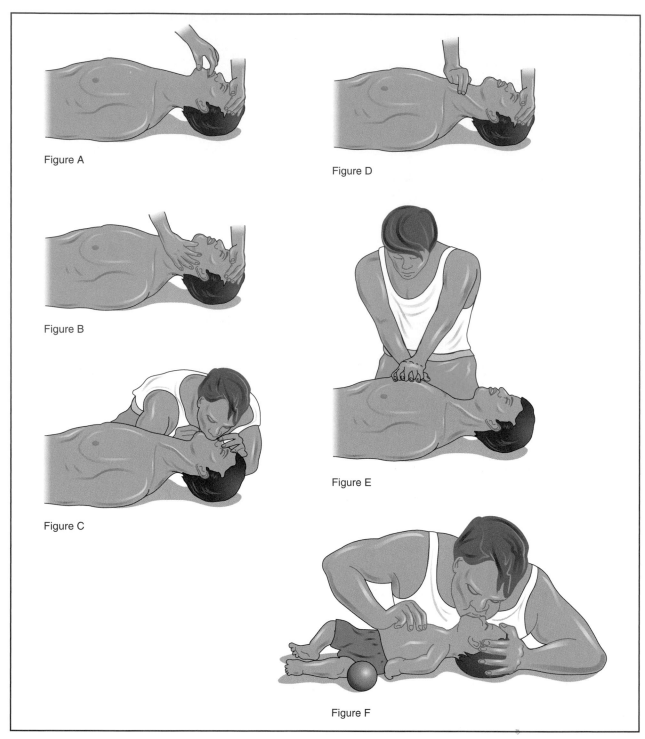

Figure A

Figure B

Figure C

Figure D

Figure E

Figure F

CPR in basic life support. Figure A: The victim should be flat on his back and his mouth should be checked for debris. Figure B: If the victim is unconscious, open airway, lift neck, and tilt head back. Figure C: If victim is not breathing, begin artificial breathing with four quick full breaths. Figure D: Check for carotid pulse. Figure E: If pulse is absent, begin artificial circulation by depressing sternum. Figure F: Mouth-to-mouth resuscitation of an infant. *(Illustration by Electronic Illustrators Group.)*

Aftercare

Emergency medical care is always necessary after CPR. Once a person's breathing and heartbeat have been restored, the rescuer should make the person comfortable and stay there until emergency medical personnel arrive. The rescuer can continue to reassure the person that help is coming and talk positively until professionals arrive and take over.

KEY TERMS

Cardiac arrest—Temporary or permanent cessation of the heartbeat.

Cardiopulmonary—Relating to the heart and lungs.

Defibrillation—A procedure to stop the type of irregular heart beat called ventricular fibrillation, usually by using electric shock.

Resuscitation—Bringing a person back to life or consciousness after he or she was apparently dead.

Ventricular fibrillation—An arrhythmia characterized by a very rapid, uncoordinated, ineffective series of contractions throughout the lower chambers of the heart. Unless stopped, these chaotic impulses are fatal.

Risks

CPR can cause injury to a person's ribs, liver, lungs, and heart. However, these risks must be accepted if CPR is necessary to save the person's life.

Normal results

In many cases, successful CPR results in restoration of consciousness and life. Barring other injuries, a revived person usually returns to normal functions within a few hours of being revived.

Abnormal results include injuries incurred during CPR and lack of success with CPR. Possible sites for injuries include a person's ribs, liver, lungs, and heart. Partially successful CPR may result in brain damage. Unsuccessful CPR results in death.

Parental concerns

Because most cardiopulmonary arrest in infants and children occurs in or around the home and results from SIDS, trauma, drowning, choking, or **poisoning**, all parents and child caregivers should consider becoming trained in CPR. Training is available at local schools and community centers.

Resources

BOOKS

Knoop, Kevin J., and Lawrence B. Stack. *Atlas of Emergency Medicine*, 2nd ed. New York: McGraw Hill, 2001.

Larmon, Baxter, et al. *Basic Life Support Skills*. Toronto, ON: Prentice Hall PTR, 2004.

PERIODICALS

Babbs, C. F., and V. Nadkarni. "Optimizing chest compression to rescue ventilation ratios during one-rescuer CPR by professionals and lay persons: children are not just little adults." *Resuscitation* 61, no. 2 (May 2004): 173–81

Kern, K. B., H. R. Halperin, and J. Field. "New guidelines for cardiopulmonary resuscitation and emergency cardiac care: changes in the management of cardiac arrest." *Journal of the American Medical Association* 285 (2001): 1267–69.

ORGANIZATIONS

American College of Emergency Physicians. PO Box 619911, Dallas, TX 75261–9911. Web site: <www.acep.org>.

American College of Osteopathic Emergency Physicians. 142 E. Ontario Street, Suite 550, Chicago, IL 60611. Web site: <www.acoep.org>.

American Heart Association, National Center. 7272 Greenville Avenue, Dallas, TX 75231. Web site: <www.americanheart.org>.

WEB SITES

"Cardiopulmonary Resuscitation." *American Heart Association,* 2004. Available online at <www.americanheart.org/presenter.jhtml?identifier=4479> (accessed October 29, 2004).

"CPR and Emergency Cardiovascular Care." *American Heart Association,* 2004. Available online at <www.americanheart.org/presenter.jhtml?identifier=3011764> (accessed October 29, 2004).

"Infant First Aid for Choking and CPR: An Illustrated Guide." *BabyCenter,* 2004. Available online at <www.babycenter.com/general/9298.html> (accessed October 29, 2004).

Jennifer E. Sisk, MA

Casts *see* **Immobilization**

Cat bite infection *see* **Animal bite infections**

CAT scan *see* **Computed tomography**

Cat's cry syndrome *see* **Cri du chat syndrome**

Cat-scratch disease

Definition

Cat scratch disease is an uncommon infection that typically results from a cat's scratch or bite. Most sufferers experience only moderate discomfort and find that their symptoms clear up without any lasting harm after a few weeks or months. Professional medical treatment is rarely needed.

Description

Cat-scratch disease (also called cat-scratch fever) is caused by the *Bartonella henselae* bacterium, which is found in cats around the world and is transmitted from cat to cat by fleas. Researchers have discovered that large numbers of North American cats carry antibodies for the disease (meaning that the cats have been infected at some point in their lives). Some parts of North America have much higher rates of cat infection than others, however. *Bartonella henselae* is uncommon or absent in cold climates, which fleas have difficulty tolerating, but prevalent in warm, humid places such as Memphis, Tennessee, where antibodies were found in 71 percent of the cats tested. The bacterium, which remains in a cat's bloodstream for several months after infection, seems to be harmless to most cats, and normally an infected cat will not display any symptoms. Kittens (cats younger than one year old) are more likely than adult cats to be carrying the infection.

Demographics

Bartonella henselae can infect people who are scratched or (more rarely) bitten or licked by a cat. It cannot be passed from person to person. Although cats are popular pets found in about 30 percent of American households, human infection appears to be rare. One study estimated that for every 100,000 Americans there are only 2.5 cases of cat-scratch disease each year. It is also unusual for more than one **family** member to become ill; a Florida investigation discovered multiple cases in only 3.5 percent of the families studied. Children and teenagers appear to be the most likely victims of cat-scratch disease, although the possibility exists that the disease may be more common among adults than previously thought.

Causes and symptoms

The first sign of cat-scratch disease may be a small blister at the site of a scratch or bite three to ten days after injury. The blister (which sometimes contains pus) often looks like an insect bite and is usually found on the hands, arms, or head. Within two weeks of the blister's appearance, lymph nodes near the site of injury become swollen. Often the infected person develops a fever or experiences fatigue or headaches. The symptoms usually disappear within a month, although the lymph nodes may remain swollen for several months. Hepatitis, **pneumonia**, and other dangerous complications can arise, but the likelihood of cat-scratch disease posing a serious threat to health is very small. **AIDS** patients and other immunocompromised people face the greatest risk of dangerous complications.

Occasionally, the symptoms of cat-scratch disease take the form of what is called Parinaud's oculoglandular syndrome. In such cases, a small sore develops on the palpebral conjunctiva (the membrane lining the inner eyelid) and is often accompanied by **conjunctivitis** (inflammation of the membrane) and swollen lymph nodes in front of the ear. Researchers suspect that the first step in the development of Parinaud's oculoglandular syndrome occurs when *Bartonella henselae* bacteria pass from a cat's saliva to its fur during grooming. Rubbing one's eyes after handling the cat then transmits the bacteria to the conjunctiva.

Diagnosis

A family doctor should be called whenever a cat scratch or bite fails to heal normally or is followed by a persistent fever or other unusual symptoms such as long-lasting bone or joint **pain**. The appearance of painful and swollen lymph nodes is another reason for consulting a doctor. When cat-scratch disease is suspected, the doctor will ask about a history of exposure to cats and look for evidence of a cat scratch or bite and swollen lymph nodes. A blood test for *Bartonella henselae* may be ordered to confirm the doctor's diagnosis.

Treatment

For otherwise healthy people, rest and over-the-counter medications for reducing fever and discomfort (such as **acetaminophen**) while waiting for the disease to run its course are usually all that is necessary. **Antibiotics** are prescribed in some cases, particularly when complications occur or the lymph nodes remain swollen and painful for more than two or three months, but there is no agreement among doctors about when and how they should be used. If a lymph node becomes very swollen and painful, the family doctor may decide to drain it.

Prognosis

Most people recover completely from a bout of cat-scratch disease. Further attacks are rare.

Prevention

Certain common-sense precautions can be taken to guard against the disease. Scratches and **bites** should be washed immediately with soap and water, and it is never a good idea to rub one's eyes after handling a cat without first washing one's hands. Children should be told not to **play** with stray cats or make cats angry. Immunocompromised people should avoid owning kittens, which are

KEY TERMS

Acetaminophen—A drug used for pain relief as well as to decrease fever. A common trade name for the drug is Tylenol.

Acquired immunodeficiency syndrome (AIDS)—An infectious disease caused by the human immunodeficiency virus (HIV). A person infected with HIV gradually loses immune function, becoming less able to resist other infections and certain cancers.

Antibiotics—Drugs that are designed to kill or inhibit the growth of the bacteria that cause infections.

Antibody—A special protein made by the body's immune system as a defense against foreign material (bacteria, viruses, etc.) that enters the body. It is uniquely designed to attack and neutralize the specific antigen that triggered the immune response.

Bacteria—Singluar, bacterium; tiny, one-celled forms of life that cause many diseases and infections.

Hepatitis—An inflammation of the liver, with accompanying liver cell damage or cell death, caused most frequently by viral infection, but also by certain drugs, chemicals, or poisons. May be either acute (of limited duration) or chronic (continuing). Symptoms include jaundice, nausea, vomiting, loss of appetite, tenderness in the right upper abdomen, aching muscles, and joint pain. In severe cases, liver failure may result.

Immune system—The system of specialized organs, lymph nodes, and blood cells throughout the body that work together to defend the body against foreign invaders (bacteria, viruses, fungi, etc.).

Immunocompromised—A state in which the immune system is suppressed or not functioning properly.

Lymph nodes—Small, bean-shaped collections of tissue located throughout the lymphatic system. They produce cells and proteins that fight infection and filter lymph. Nodes are sometimes called lymph glands.

Pneumonia—An infection in which the lungs become inflamed. It can be caused by nearly any class of organism known to cause human infections, including bacteria, viruses, fungi, and parasites.

Pus—A thick, yellowish or greenish fluid composed of the remains of dead white blood cells, pathogens, and decomposed cellular debris. It is most often associated with bacterial infection.

---

more likely than adult cats to be infectious. Because cat-scratch disease is usually not a life-threatening illness and people tend to form strong emotional bonds with their cats, doctors do not recommend getting rid of a cat suspected of carrying the disease.

Resources

BOOKS

Gerber, Michael A. "*Bartonella* species (Cat-Scratch Disease, Bacillary angiomatosis, Bacillary Peliosis)." In *Principles and Practice of Pediatric Infectious Diseases*, 2nd ed. Edited by Sarah S. Long et al. St. Louis, MO: Elsevier, 2003.

Stechenberg, Barbara W. "*Bartonella* species." In *Nelson Textbook of Pediatrics*. Edited by Richard E. Behrman et al. Philadelphia: Saunders, 2004.

BOOKS

Lex, Joseph R. "Catscratch Disease." *eMedicine*, December 30, 2003. Available online at <www.emedicine.com/emerg/topic84.htm> (accessed December 25, 2004).

Howard Baker
Rosalyn Carson-DeWitt, MD

Cavities, dental *see* **Tooth decay**

Celiac disease

Definition

Celiac disease is a disease of the digestive system in which the inside lining of the small intestine (mucosa) is damaged after eating wheat, rye, oats, or barley, resulting in interference with the absorption of nutrients from food.

Description

Celiac disease occurs when the body reacts abnormally to gluten, a protein found in grains, including wheat, rye, barley, and possibly oats. When someone with celiac disease eats foods containing gluten, that person's immune system causes an inflammatory response in the small intestine, which damages the tissues and results in impaired ability to absorb nutrients from foods (malabsorption). The inflammation and malabsorption create wide-ranging problems in many systems of the body. Since the body's own immune system causes the damage, celiac disease is classified as an autoimmune disorder.

Each person with celiac disease is affected differently. When food containing gluten reaches the small intestine, the immune system begins to attack a substance called gliadin, which is found in the gluten. The resulting inflammation causes damage to the delicate finger-like structures in the intestine, called villi, where food absorption actually takes place. This damage is referred to as villus atrophy. The patient may experience a number of symptoms related to the inflammation and the chemicals it releases, and/or the lack of ability to absorb nutrients from food, which can cause **malnutrition**.

Celiac disease is also called sprue, nontropical sprue, gluten sensitive enteropathy, and celiac sprue.

Demographics

Celiac disease may be discovered at any age, from infancy through adulthood. The disorder is more commonly found among white Europeans and in people of European descent. It is very unusual to find celiac disease in African or Asian people. The exact incidence of the disease is uncertain. Estimates vary from one in 5,000, to as many as one in every 300 individuals with this background. The prevalence of celiac disease seems to be different from one European country to another and between Europe and the United States. This discrepancy may be due to differences in diet and/or the possibility that the disease goes unrecognized in some areas. One study of random blood samples tested for celiac disease in the United States showed one in 250 testing positive. It is clearly underdiagnosed, probably because the symptoms are attributed to another problem, and physicians and laboratory technicians lack knowledge about celiac disease.

Because celiac disease has a hereditary influence or genetic component, close relatives (especially first-degree relatives, such as children, siblings, and parents) have a higher risk of being affected with the condition. The chance that a first-degree relative of someone with celiac disease has the disease is about 10 percent.

Causes and symptoms

The pattern of inheritance is complicated regarding this disease. The type of inheritance pattern that celiac disease follows is called multifactorial (caused by many factors, both genetic and environmental). Researchers think that several factors must exist in order for the disease to occur. The patient must have a genetic predisposition to develop the disorder. Then something in their environment acts as a stimulus, or

trigger, to their immune system, causing the disease to become active for the first time. For conditions with multifactorial inheritance, people without the genetic predisposition are less likely to develop the condition with exposure to the same triggers, or they may require more exposure to the stimulus before developing the disease than someone with a genetic predisposition. Stimuli that may provoke a reaction include surgery, especially gastrointestinal surgery; a change to a low fat diet, which includes an increased number of wheat-based foods; severe emotional stress; or a viral infection. The combination of genetic susceptibility and an outside agent leads to celiac disease.

The most commonly recognized symptoms of celiac disease relate to the improper absorption of food in the gastrointestinal system. Many patients with gastrointestinal symptoms will have **diarrhea** and fatty, greasy, unusually foul-smelling stools. The patient may complain of excessive gas (flatulence), distended abdomen, weight loss, and generalized weakness. Not all people have digestive system complications; some people only have irritability or depression. Irritability is one of the most common symptoms in children with celiac disease.

Not all individuals with celiac disease exhibit typical symptoms. As more is learned about celiac disease, it has become evident that the disease has many variations that may not produce typical symptoms. Unrecognized and therefore untreated celiac disease may cause or contribute to a variety of other conditions. The decreased ability to digest, absorb, and utilize food properly (malabsorption) may cause anemia (low red blood count from iron deficiency) or easy bruising from a lack of vitamin K. Poor mineral absorption may result in osteoporosis, or brittle bones, which may lead to bone **fractures**. Vitamin D levels may be insufficient and bring about a softening of bones (osteomalacia), which produces **pain** and bony deformities, such as flattening or bending. Defects in the tooth enamel, characteristic of celiac disease, may be recognized by dentists. Celiac disease may be discovered during medical tests performed to investigate **failure to thrive** in infants or lack of proper growth in children and adolescents. People with celiac disease may also experience **lactose intolerance** because they do not produce enough of the enzyme lactase, which breaks down the sugar in milk into a form the body can absorb. Other symptoms can include **muscle cramps**, fatigue, delayed growth, tingling or **numbness** in the legs (from nerve damage), pale sores in the mouth (called aphthus ulcers), tooth discoloration, or missed menstrual periods (due to severe weight loss).

A distinctive, painful skin rash, called **dermatitis** herpetiformis, may be the first sign of celiac disease in adults but rarely occurs in children with celiac disease.

Many disorders are associated with celiac disease, although the nature of the connection is unclear. One type of epilepsy is linked to celiac disease. Once their celiac disease is successfully treated, a significant number of these patients have fewer or no seizures. Patients with **alopecia** areata, a condition in which hair loss occurs in sharply defined areas, have been shown to have a higher risk of celiac disease than the general population. There appears to be a higher percentage of celiac disease among people with **Down syndrome**, but the link between the conditions was unknown as of 2004.

Several conditions attributed to a disorder of the immune system have been associated with celiac disease. People with insulin-dependent diabetes (type I) have a much higher incidence of celiac disease. One source estimates that as many as one in 20 insulin-dependent diabetics may have celiac disease. Patients with other conditions in which celiac disease may be more commonly found include those with juvenile chronic arthritis, some thyroid diseases, and IgA deficiency.

There is an increased risk of intestinal lymphoma, a type of **cancer**, in individuals with celiac disease. Successful treatment of the celiac disease seems to decrease the chance of developing lymphoma.

When to call the doctor

A doctor should be consulted when a child exhibits symptoms characteristic of this disease.

Diagnosis

Because of the variety of ways celiac disease can manifest itself, it is often not discovered promptly. Its symptoms are similar to many other conditions including **irritable bowel syndrome**, Crohn's disease, ulcerative colitis, diverticulosis, intestinal infections, chronic fatigue syndrome, and depression. The condition may persist without diagnosis for so long that the patient accepts a general feeling of illness as normal. This acceptance leads to further delay in identifying and treating the disorder. It is not unusual for the disease to be identified in the course of medical investigations for seemingly unrelated problems.

If celiac disease is suspected, based on symptoms, physical appearance, or delayed growth, a blood test should be ordered. This test looks for the antibodies to gluten (called antigliadin, anti-endomysium, and antireticulin) that the immune system produces in celiac disease. Antibodies are chemicals produced by the immune system in response to substances such as germs and other potentially harmful substances. Some experts advocate not just evaluating patients with symptoms, but using these blood studies as a screening test for high-risk individuals, such as those with relatives (especially first-degree relatives) known to have the disorder. An abnormal result points toward celiac disease, but further tests are needed to confirm the diagnosis. Because celiac disease affects the ability of the body to absorb nutrients from food, several tests may be ordered to look for nutritional deficiencies. For example, doctors may order a test of iron levels in the blood because low levels of iron (anemia) may accompany celiac disease. Doctors may also order a test for fat in the stool, since celiac disease prevents the body from absorbing fat from food.

If these tests are suspicious for celiac disease, the next step is a biopsy (surgical removal of a tiny piece of tissue) of the small intestine. This is usually done by a gastroenterologist, a physician who specializes in diagnosing and treating bowel disorders. It is generally performed in the office or in a hospital's outpatient department. The patient remains awake but is sedated. A narrow tube, called an endoscope, is passed through the mouth, down through the stomach, and into the small intestine. A small sample of tissue is taken and sent to the laboratory for analysis. If it shows a pattern of tissue damage characteristic of celiac disease, the diagnosis is established.

Treatment

The only treatment for celiac disease is a gluten-free diet (GFD). This diet is easy for the doctor to prescribe but may be difficult for a child to follow. For most people, adhering to this diet stops symptoms and prevents damage to the intestines. Damaged villi can be functional again in three to six months. This diet must be followed permanently, however. The fact that people had symptoms that were cured by the GFD is further evidence that the diagnosis was correct.

The physician will periodically recheck the level of antibody in the child's blood. After several months, the small intestine is biopsied again. If the diagnosis of celiac disease was correct (and the child followed the rigorous diet), healing of the intestine will be apparent. Most experts agree that it is necessary to follow these steps in order to be sure of an accurate diagnosis. Disorders other than celiac disease can cause a similar type of villus atrophy, especially in children under two years of age, so rechecking the intestine is especially important for very young children. If healing is evident, then gluten is reintroduced to the diet and a third biopsy is performed weeks to months later to see if the reintroduction of gluten results in villus atropy again. If the atrophy returns, the child has celiac disease, and a gluten-free diet should be continued for life.

A child with undiagnosed celiac disease may become very ill with severe diarrhea and malnutrition. Corticosteroids such as prednisone and intravenous (IV) fluids may be temporarily given while the child begins a GFD. Because celiac disease is diagnosed more quickly than in the past, corticosteroids are seldom required.

Nutritional concerns

Although there is no risk and much potential benefit to the use of GFD for treatment of celiac disease, the widespread use of gluten-containing grains in Western cultures makes adapting to a gluten-free diet challenging. Gluten is present in any product that contains wheat, rye, barley, or oats. It helps make bread rise and gives many foods a smooth, pleasing texture. In addition to the many obvious places gluten can be found in a normal diet, such as breads, cereals, and pasta, there are many hidden sources of gluten. Thickening agents, emulsifiers, fillers, flavor enhancers, and food stabilizers as well as products used in food packaging may contain gluten. Gluten may even be present on surfaces used for food preparation or cooking.

Fresh foods that have not been artificially processed, such as fruits, vegetables, and meats, are permitted as part of a GFD. Gluten-free foods can be found in health food stores and in some supermarkets. Mail-order food companies often have a selection of gluten-free products. Help in dietary planning is available from dieticians (healthcare professionals specializing in food and **nutrition**) or from support groups for individuals with celiac disease. There are many cookbooks on the market specifically for those on a GFD.

Prognosis

Treating celiac disease with a strict GFD is almost always completely effective. Gastrointestinal complaints and other symptoms are alleviated. Secondary complications, such as anemia and osteoporosis, resolve in almost all patients. People who have experienced lactose intolerance related to their celiac disease usually see those symptoms subside as well.

Once the diet has been followed for several years, individuals with celiac disease have similar mortality rates as the general population. However, about 10 percent of people with celiac disease develop a cancer involving the gastrointestinal tract (both carcinoma and lymphoma).

A few patients develop a refractory type of celiac disease, in which the GFD no longer seems effective. Once the diet has been thoroughly assessed to ensure no hidden sources of gluten are causing the problem, medications may be prescribed. Steroids or immunosuppressant drugs are often used to try to control the disease. It is unclear whether these efforts meet with much success.

Experts emphasize the need for lifelong adherence to the GFD to avoid the long-term complications of this disorder. They point out that although the disease may have symptom-free periods if the diet is not followed, silent damage continues to occur. Celiac disease cannot be outgrown or cured, according to medical authorities.

Prevention

There is no way to prevent celiac disease. However, the key to decreasing its impact on overall health is early diagnosis and strict adherence to the prescribed GFD.

Parental concerns

For parents used to preparing gluten-containing meals, searching for and cooking with gluten-free products may be difficult at first. Changing cooking habits will be easier if initially gluten-free recipes and food products are used. When they use any commercial food products, they must read carefully the list of ingredients. Although ingredients are listed in order of decreasing content, any product containing the smallest of amount of gluten must be avoided. Many food manufacturers are willing to provide additional information about their products. Most food labels contain addresses of the manufacturers and many include a toll-free telephone number. Some restaurants have ingredient lists for their products posted in the restaurant or available on request.

When a child with celiac disease eats at a friend's house, the friend's parent should be aware of the child's dietary limitations. The child may have to take lunch from home to eat at school, unless the school has a dietician who can ensure that gluten-free food is provided for the child.

Family support is important in ensuring acceptance of the diet. The child must not be made to feel that he/she is abnormal and a nuisance to the family. After the GFD is begun, the benefits to the child with celiac disease will initially be obvious and enthusiastically accepted. However, as the child gets older, the period of ill health may be forgotten, and the child may be reject the diet, especially during **adolescence**, when there is a desire for conformity. Unfortunately, in older children, the symptoms may not reappear immediately although intestinal damage is occurring. The child may interpret the delay

KEY TERMS

Antibody—A special protein made by the body's immune system as a defense against foreign material (bacteria, viruses, etc.) that enters the body. It is uniquely designed to attack and neutralize the specific antigen that triggered the immune response.

Antigen—A substance (usually a protein) identified as foreign by the body's immune system, triggering the release of antibodies as part of the body's immune response.

Gluten—A protein found in wheat, rye, barley, and oats.

Immune system—The system of specialized organs, lymph nodes, and blood cells throughout the body that work together to defend the body against foreign invaders (bacteria, viruses, fungi, etc.).

Villi—Tiny, finger-like projections that enable the small intestine to absorb nutrients from food.

in the return of symptoms as evidence that the child has recovered from celiac disease, but they have not, as celiac disease cannot be cured.

Resources

BOOKS

Icon Health Publications. *The Official Patient's Sourcebook on Celiac Disease*. San Diego, CA: Icon Health Publications, 2002.

Korn, Danna. *Kids with Celiac Disease*. Bethesda, MD: Woodbine House, 2001.

Kruszka, Bonnie J., and Richard S. Cihlar. *Eating Gluten-Free with Emily*. Bethesda, MD: Woodbine House, 2004.

Sanderson, Sheri L. *Incredible Edible Gluten-Free Food for Kids*. Bethesda, MD: Woodbine House, 2002.

ORGANIZATIONS

American Celiac Society. 58 Musano Court, West Orange, NJ 07052. Telephone: 201/325–8837.

Celiac Disease Foundation. 13251 Ventura Blvd., Suite 1, Studio City, CA 91604–1838. Web site: <http://celiac.org>.

Celiac Sprue Association/United State of America (CSA/USA). PO Box 31700, Omaha, NE 68131–0700. Web site: <www.csaceliacs.org>.

Gluten Intolerance Group of North America. PO Box 23053, Seattle, WA, 98102–0353. Web site: <www.gluten.net>.

National Center for Nutrition and Dietetics, American Dietetic Association. 216 West Jackson Boulevard, Suite 800, Chicago, IL 60606–6995. Telephone: 800/366–1655. Web site: <www.unl.edu2020/alpha/National_Center_for_Nutrition_and_Dietetics.html>.

ROCK: Raising Our Celiac Children. 216 West Jackson Boulevard, Suite 800, Chicago, IL 60606–6995. Telephone: 800/366–1655. Web site: <www.celiac.com/cgi-bin/webc.cgi/st_main.html?p_catid=8>.

WEB SITES

"Celiac Disease." *National Institute of Diabetes and Digestive and Kidney Diseases, National Institutes of Health*, 2004. Available online at <http://digestive.niddk.nih.gov/ddiseases/pubs/celiac/> (accessed October 25, 2004).

Celiac Disease and Diet Support Center. Available online at <www.celiac.com/> (accessed October 25, 2004).

OTHER

Gluten-Free Living, a bimonthly newsletter. PO Box 105, Hastings-on-Hudson, NY 10706. Available online at <www.glutenfreeliving.com/> (accessed October 25, 2004).

Judith Sims, MS
Amy Vance, MS, CGC

Cerebellar herniation *see* **Chiari malformation**

Cerebral palsy

Definition

Cerebral palsy (CP) is the term used for a group of nonprogressive disorders of movement and posture caused by abnormal development of, or damage to, motor control centers of the brain. CP is caused by events before, during, or after birth. The abnormalities of muscle control that define CP are often accompanied by other neurological and physical abnormalities.

Description

Voluntary movement (for example, walking, grasping, chewing) is primarily accomplished using skeletal muscles (muscles attached to bones). Control of the skeletal muscles originates in the cerebral cortex, the largest portion of the brain. Palsy means paralysis but may also be used to describe uncontrolled muscle movement. Therefore, cerebral palsy encompasses any disorder of abnormal movement and paralysis caused by abnormal function of the cerebral cortex. CP does not include conditions due to progressive disease or degeneration of the brain. For this reason, CP is also referred to as static (nonprogressive) encephalopathy (disease of the brain). Also excluded from CP are any disorders of muscle control that arise in the muscles themselves and/or in the peripheral nervous system (nerves outside the brain and spinal cord). CP is not a specific diagnosis but is more accurately considered a description of a broad but defined group of neurological and physical problems.v

Because CP is not one disorder, it is difficult to classify. It has been divided into four general types: spastic, athetoid, ataxic, and mixed. Another general categorization describes spastic, dyskinetic, and ataxic CP as follows:

- Spastic refers to diplegic impairment of either legs or arms, quadriplegic involving all four extremities, hemiplegic or one-sided involvement of arms and legs, or double hemiplegic impairment of both sides, arms and legs. **Spasticity** means having an increased stretch reflex.

- Dyskinetic refers to abnormal movements caused by inadequate regulation of muscle tone and coordination. The category includes athetoid or choreoathetoid CP; both are hyperkinetic forms of the disease.

- Ataxic refers to disturbances in coordination of voluntary movements; it includes mixed forms of CP, with mixed characteristics and symptoms.

Muscles that receive defective messages from the brain may be constantly contracted and tight (spastic), exhibit involuntary writhing movements (athetosis), or have difficulty with voluntary movement (dyskinesia). A lack of balance and coordination with unsteady movements (ataxia) may also be present. Spastic CP and mixed CP constitute the majority of cases. Effects on the muscles can range from mild weakness or partial paralysis (paresis) to complete loss of voluntary control of a muscle or group of muscles (plegia). CP is also designated by the number of limbs affected. For instance, affected muscles in one limb is monoplegia, both arms or both legs is diplegia, both limbs on one side of the body is hemiplegia, and in all four limbs is quadriplegia. Muscles of the trunk, neck, and head may be affected.

About 50 percent of all cases of CP diagnosed are in children who are born prematurely. Advances in the medical care of premature infants since the 1980s have dramatically increased the rate of survival of these fragile newborns. However, as gestational age at delivery and birth weight of a baby decrease, the risk for CP dramatically increases. A term pregnancy is delivered at 37–41 weeks gestation. The risk for CP in a preterm infant (32–37 weeks) is increased about five-fold over the risk for an infant born at term. Survivors of extremely preterm births (less than 28 weeks) face as much as a 50-fold increase in risk.

Two factors are involved in the risk for CP associated with **prematurity**. First, premature babies are at higher risk for various CP-associated medical complications, such as intracerebral hemorrhage, infection, and difficulty in breathing, to name a few. Second, the onset of premature labor may be induced, in part, by complications that have already caused neurologic damage in the fetus. A combination of both factors may play a role in some cases of CP. The tendency toward premature delivery runs in families, but genetic mechanisms are not fully clear.

An increase in multiple births in the early 2000s, especially in the United States, is associated with the increased use of fertility drugs. As the number of fetuses in a pregnancy increases, the risks for abnormal development and premature delivery also increase. **Twins**, for example, have four times the risk of developing CP as children from singleton pregnancies, owing to the fact that more twin pregnancies are delivered prematurely. The risk for CP in one of triplets is up to 18 times greater. Furthermore, evidence suggests that a baby from a pregnancy in which its twin died before birth is at increased risk for CP.

Although CP is the leading cause of disability in children, its incidence in the United States did not changed much between the 1980s and the early 2000s. Advances in medicine have decreased the incidence from some causes. Rh disease, for example, has been controlled by the advent of anti-Rh globulin; its administration to Rh-negative mothers has reduced one risk factor for CP. The risk has still increased from other causes, however, notably prematurity and multiple-birth pregnancies. The cause of most cases of CP remains unknown, but it has become clear in the early 2000s that birth difficulties are not to blame in most cases. Rather, developmental problems before birth, usually unknown and generally undiagnosable, are largely responsible. The rate of survival for preterm infants has leveled off in the early 2000s, and methods to improve the long-term health of these at-risk babies are being sought.

Demographics

Approximately 500,000 children and adults in the United States have CP, and it is newly diagnosed in about 6,000 infants and young children each year, representing about two to three children in 1,000 live births. No particular ethnic group seems to be at higher risk for CP. However, some low income families may be at higher risk due to poorer access to proper prenatal care and advanced medical services.

Causes and symptoms

CP can be caused by a number of different mechanisms at various times of life, ranging from several weeks after conception, through birth, to early childhood. In the twentieth century, it was accepted that most cases of CP were due to brain injuries received during a traumatic birth, a condition known as birth asphyxia. However, extensive research in the 1980s showed that only 5 to 10 percent of CP can be attributed to birth trauma. Other possible causes include abnormal development of the brain, prenatal factors that directly or indirectly damage neurons in the developing brain, premature birth, and brain injuries that occur in the first few years of life.

The causes of CP could be grouped into those that are genetic and those that are non-genetic, although most would fall somewhere in between. Grouping causes into those that occur during pregnancy (prenatal), those that happen around the time of birth (perinatal), and those that occur after birth (postnatal), is preferable. CP related to premature birth and multiple births is somewhat different and considered separately.

Prenatal causes

Although much was learned about human embryology in the last couple of decades of the twentieth century, a great deal remains unknown in the early 2000s. Studying prenatal human development is difficult because the embryo and fetus develop in a closed environment—the mother's womb. However, the development of a number of prenatal tests has opened a window on the process. Add to that more accurate and complete evaluations of newborns, especially those with problems, and a clearer picture of what can go wrong before birth is possible.

The complicated process of brain development before birth is susceptible to many chance errors that can result in abnormalities of varying degrees. Some of these errors will result in structural anomalies of the brain, while others may cause undetectable, but significant, abnormalities in how the cerebral cortex is wired. An abnormality in structure or wiring is sometimes hereditary but is most often due to chance or some unknown cause. The possible role genetics plays in a particular brain abnormality depends to some degree on the type of anomaly and the form of CP it causes.

Several maternal-fetal infections are known to increase the risk for CP, including **rubella** (German **measles**, now rare in the United States), cytomegalovirus (CMV), and **toxoplasmosis**. Each of these infec-

tions is considered a risk to the fetus only if the mother contracts it for the first time during that pregnancy. Even in those cases, most babies are born normal. Most women are immune to all three infections by the time they reach childbearing age, but a woman's immune status can be determined using the so-called TORCH (for toxoplasmosis, rubella, cytomegalovirus, and herpes) test before or during pregnancy.

Just as a **stroke** can occur in an adult and cause neurologic damage in an adult, so too can this type of event occur in the fetus. A burst blood vessel in the brain followed by uncontrolled bleeding (intracerebral hemorrhage) can cause a fetal stroke, or a clot (embolism) can obstruct a cerebral blood vessel. Infants who later develop CP, along with their mothers, are more likely than other mother-infant pairs to have **coagulation disorders** (coagulopathies) that put them at increased risk for bleeding episodes or blood clots. Certain coagulation disorders are inherited while others may be deficiencies in essential clotting factors or defects in the coagulation process.

Any substance that might affect fetal brain development, directly or indirectly, can increase the risk for CP. Likewise, any substance that increases the risk for premature delivery and low birth weight, such as alcohol, tobacco, or cocaine, among others, might indirectly increase the risk for CP. Links between a drug or other chemical exposure during pregnancy and a risk for CP are difficult to prove.

Because the fetus receives all nutrients and oxygen from blood that circulates through the placenta, anything that interferes with normal placental function might adversely affect development of the fetus, including the brain, or might increase the risk for premature delivery. Structural abnormalities of the placenta, premature detachment of the placenta from the uterine wall (abruption), and placental infections (chorioamnionitis) are thought to pose some risk for CP.

Certain conditions in the mother during pregnancy might pose a risk to fetal development leading to CP. Women with autoimmune anti-thyroid or anti-phospholipid (APA) antibodies are at slightly increased risk for CP in their children. A potentially important clue points toward high levels of cytokines in the maternal and fetal circulation as a possible risk for CP. Cytokines are proteins associated with inflammation, such as from infection or autoimmune disorders, and they may be toxic to neurons in the fetal brain.

Serious physical trauma to the mother during pregnancy could result in direct trauma to the fetus as well, or injuries to the mother could compromise the availability of nutrients and oxygen to the developing fetal brain.

Perinatal causes

Birth asphyxia that is significant enough to result in CP is uncommon in developed countries. An umbilical cord around the baby's neck (tight nuchal cord) and the cord delivered before the baby (prolapsed cord) are possible causes of birth asphyxia, as are bleeding and other complications associated with placental abruption and placenta previa (placenta lying over the cervix).

Infection in the mother is sometimes not passed to the fetus through the placenta but is transmitted to the baby during delivery. Any such infection, such as herpes, that results in serious illness in the newborn has the potential to produce some neurological damage.

Postnatal causes

The remaining 15 percent of CP cases are due to neurologic injury sustained after birth. CP that has a postnatal cause is sometimes referred to as acquired CP, but this is only accurate for those cases caused by infection or trauma.

Incompatibility between the Rh blood types of mother and child (mother Rh negative, baby Rh positive) can result in severe anemia in the baby (**erythroblastosis fetalis**). This may lead to other complications, including severe **jaundice**, which can cause CP. Rh disease in the newborn is rare in developed countries due to routine screening of maternal blood type and routine prevention of anti-Rh antibodies in Rh negative women after each birth of an Rh positive infant. The routine, effective treatment of jaundice due to other causes has also made it an infrequent cause of CP in developed countries.

Serious infections that affect the brain directly, such as **meningitis** and **encephalitis**, may cause irreversible damage to the brain, leading to CP. A **seizure disorder** early in life may cause CP or may be the product of a hidden problem that causes CP in addition to seizures. Unexplained (idiopathic) seizures are hereditary in only a small percentage of cases. Although rare in healthy infants born at or near term, intracerebral hemorrhage and brain embolism, like fetal stroke, are sometimes genetic.

Physical trauma to an infant or child resulting in brain injury, such as from abuse, accidents, or near drowning/suffocation, might cause CP. Likewise, ingestion of a toxic substance such as lead, mercury, other poisons, or certain chemicals could cause neurological damage. Accidental overdose of certain medications might also cause similar damage to the central nervous system.

Symptoms

The symptoms of CP and their severity are variable. Those who have CP may have only minor difficulty with **fine motor skills**, such as grasping and manipulating items with their hands. A severe form of CP could involve significant muscle problems in all four limbs, **mental retardation**, seizures, and difficulties with vision, speech, and hearing.

Although the defect in cerebral function that causes CP is not progressive, the symptoms of CP often change over time. Most of the symptoms relate in some way to the aberrant control of muscles. CP is categorized first by the type of movement/postural disturbance(s) present, rather than by a description of which limbs are affected. The severity of motor impairment is also a factor. Spastic diplegia, for example, refers to continuously tight muscles that have no voluntary control in both legs, while athetoid quadraparesis describes uncontrolled writhing movements and muscle weakness in all four limbs. These may describe CP symptoms generally but do not describe all people with CP. Spastic diplegia is seen in more individuals than is athetoid quadraparesis. CP can also be loosely categorized as mild, moderate, or severe, but these are subjective terms.

A muscle that is tensed and contracted is hypertonic, while excessively loose muscles are hypotonic. Spastic, hypertonic muscles can cause serious orthopedic problems, including curvature of the spine (**scoliosis**), hip dislocation, or contractures. A contracture is shortening of a muscle, aided sometimes by a weak-opposing force from a neighboring muscle. Contractures may become permanent, i.e., fixed, without some sort of intervention. Fixed contractures may cause postural abnormalities in the affected limbs. Clenched fists and contracted feet (equinus or equinovarus) are common in people with CP. Spasticity in the thighs causes them to turn in and cross at the knees, resulting in an unusual method of walking known as scissors gait. Any of the joints in the limbs may be stiff (immobilized) due to spasticity of the attached muscles.

Athetosis and dyskinesia often occur with spasticity but do not often occur alone. The same is true of ataxia. It is important to remember that mild CP or severe CP refers not only to the number of symptoms present but also to the level of involvement of any particular class of symptoms.

Other neurologically based symptoms may include the following:

- mental retardation/learning disabilities
- behavioral disorders
- seizure disorders
- visual impairment
- hearing loss
- speech impairment (dysarthria)
- abnormal sensation and perception

These problems may have a greater impact on a child's life than the physical impairments of CP, although not all children with CP are affected by other problems. Many infants and children with CP have growth impairment. About one third of individuals with CP have moderate-to-severe mental retardation, one third have mild mental retardation, and one third have normal **intelligence**.

When to call the doctor

Parents should seek medical advice when they notice what seems to be slow development in movement, speech, or cognitive ability in their young child. If a child does not acquire certain skills within a normal time frame, there may be some cause for concern. However, it is known that children progress at somewhat different rates, and a slow beginning is often followed by normal development.

Normal developmental milestones with typical ages for acquiring them, include the following:

- sits well unsupported at about six months (eight to ten months)

- babbles at about six months (up to eight months)

- crawls at about nine months (up to 12 months)

- finger feeds, holds bottle at about nine months (up to 12 months)

- walks alone at about 12 months (up to 15–18 months)

- uses one or two words other than dada/mama at about 12 months (up to 15 months)

- walks up and down steps at about 24 months (24 to 36 months)

- turns pages in books and removes shoes and socks at about 24 months (to 30 months)

Children do not consistently favor one hand over the other before 12 to 18 months of age, and doing so may be a sign that the child has difficulty using the other hand. This same preference for one side of the body may show up as asymmetric **crawling** or, later on, favoring one leg while climbing stairs. Because CP is nonprogressive, continued loss of previously acquired milestones may indicate that CP is not the cause of the problem; medical evaluation is needed to determine the cause.

Diagnosis

The signs of CP are not usually noticeable at birth. Children normally progress through a predictable set of developmental milestones through the first 18 months of life. Children with CP, however, tend to develop these skills more slowly because of their motor impairments,

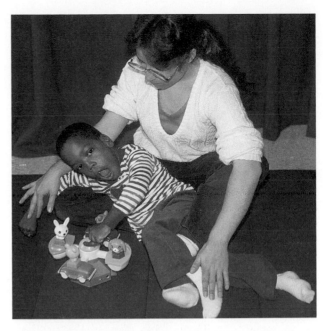

Young boy with cerebral palsy works with a physical therapist. (© Custom Medical Stock Photo, Inc.)

and delays in reaching milestones are usually the first symptoms of CP. Babies with more severe cases of CP are usually diagnosed earlier than others.

No one test is diagnostic for CP, but certain factors increase suspicion. The Apgar score measures a baby's condition immediately after birth. Babies who have low Apgar scores are at increased risk for CP. Presence of abnormal muscle tone or movements may indicate CP, as may the persistence of infantile reflexes. Imaging of the brain using ultrasound, **x rays**, MRI, and/or CT scans may reveal a structural anomaly. Some brain lesions associated with CP include scarring, cysts, expansion of the cerebral ventricles (**hydrocephalus**), abnormality of the area surrounding the ventricles (periventricular leukomalacia), areas of dead tissue (necrosis), and evidence of an intracerebral hemorrhage or blood clot. Blood and urine biochemical tests, as well as genetic tests, may be used to rule out other possible causes, including muscle and peripheral nerve diseases, mitochondrial and metabolic diseases, and other inherited disorders. Evaluations by a pediatric developmental specialist and a geneticist may be of benefit.

Treatment

Cerebral palsy cannot be cured, but many of the disabilities it causes can be managed through planning and timely care. Treatment for a child with CP depends on the severity, nature, and location of the primary muscular symptoms, as well as any associated problems that might be present. Optimal care of a child with mild CP may involve regular interaction with only a physical therapist and occupational therapist, whereas care for a more severely affected child may include visits to multiple medical specialists throughout life. With proper treatment and an effective plan, most people with CP can lead productive, happy lives.

Physical, occupational, and speech therapy

Spasticity, muscle weakness, coordination, ataxia, and scoliosis are all significant impairments that affect the posture and mobility of children and adults with CP. Physical and occupational therapists work with the patient and the **family** to maximize the patient's ability to move affected limbs, develop normal motor patterns, and maintain posture. Assistive technology, including wheelchairs, walkers, shoe inserts, crutches, and braces, are often required. A speech therapist and high-tech aids such as computer-controlled communication devices can make a tremendous difference in the life of those who have speech impairments.

Drug therapy

Before fixed contractures develop, muscle-relaxant drugs such as diazepam (Valium), dantrolene (Dantrium), and baclofen (Lioresal) may be prescribed. Botulinum toxin (Botox), a highly effective treatment, is injected directly into the affected muscles. Alcohol or phenol injections into the nerve controlling the muscle are another option. Multiple medications are available to control seizures, and athetosis can be treated using medications such as trihexyphenidyl HCl (Artane) and benztropine (Cogentin).

Surgery

Fixed contractures are usually treated with either serial casting or surgery. The most commonly used surgical procedures are tenotomy, tendon transfer, and dorsal rhizotomy. In tenotomy, tendons of the affected muscle are cut, and the limb is cast in a more normal position while the tendon regrows. Alternatively, tendon transfer involves cutting and reattaching a tendon at a different point on the bone to enhance the length and function of the muscle. A neurosurgeon performing dorsal rhizotomy carefully cuts selected nerve roots in the spinal cord to prevent them from stimulating the spastic muscles. Neurosurgical techniques in the brain such as implanting tiny electrodes directly into the cerebellum or cutting a portion of the hypothalamus have very specific uses and have had mixed results.

Prognosis

Cerebral palsy can affect every stage of maturation, from childhood through **adolescence** to adulthood. At each stage, those with CP, along with their

KEY TERMS

Asphyxia—Lack of oxygen.

Ataxia—A condition marked by impaired muscular coordination, most frequently resulting from disorders in the brain or spinal cord.

Athetosis—A condition marked by slow, writhing, involuntary muscle movements.

Cerebral palsy—A nonprogressive movement disability caused by abnormal development of or damage to motor control centers of the brain.

Coagulopathy—A disorder in which blood is either too slow or too quick to coagulate (clot).

Contracture—A tightening or shortening of muscles that prevents normal movement of the associated limb or other body part.

Cytokines—Chemicals made by the cells that act on other cells to stimulate or inhibit their function. They are important controllers of immune functions.

Diplegia—Paralysis affecting like parts on both sides the body, such as both arms or both legs.

Dorsal rhizotomy—A surgical procedure that cuts nerve roots to reduce spasticity in affected muscles.

Dyskinesia—Impaired ability to make voluntary movements.

Hemiplegia—Paralysis of one side of the body.

Hypotonia—Having reduced or diminished muscle tone or strength.

Quadriplegia—Paralysis of all four limbs and the trunk below the level of an associated injury to the spinal cord. Also called tetraplegia.

Serial casting—A series of casts designed to gradually move a limb into a more functional position.

Spastic—Refers to a condition in which the muscles are rigid, posture may be abnormal, and fine motor control is impaired.

Spasticity—Increased mucle tone, or stiffness, which leads to uncontrolled, awkward movements.

Static encephalopathy—A disease or disorder of the brain that does not get better or worse.

Tenotomy—A surgical procedure that cuts the tendon of a contracted muscle to allow lengthening.

caregivers, must strive to achieve and maintain the fullest range of experience and education consistent with their abilities. The advice and intervention of various professionals are crucial for many people with CP. Although CP itself is not considered a terminal disorder, it can affect a person's lifespan by increasing the risk for certain medical problems. People with mild cerebral palsy may have near-normal lifespan, but the lifespan of those with more severe forms may be shortened. However, over 90 percent of infants with CP survive into adulthood.

Prevention

Research in the early 2000s is focused on the possible benefits of recognizing and treating coagulopathies and inflammatory disorders in the prenatal and perinatal periods in order to reduce the incidence of CP and other congenital diseases. The use of magnesium sulfate in pregnant women with preeclampsia or threatened preterm delivery may reduce the risk of CP in very preterm infants. Finally, the risk of CP can be decreased through good maternal **nutrition**, avoidance of drugs and alcohol during pregnancy, and prevention or prompt treatment of infections.

Parental concerns

Parents of a child diagnosed with CP may not feel that they have the necessary expertise to coordinate the full range of care their child needs. Although knowledgeable and caring medical professionals are indispensable for developing a care plan, a potentially more important source of information and advice can be gained from other parents who have dealt with the same set of difficulties. Support groups for parents of children with CP can be significant sources of both practical advice and emotional support. Many cities have support groups that can be located through the United Cerebral Palsy Association, and most large medical centers have special multidisciplinary clinics for children with developmental disorders.

See also Febrile seizures; TORCH test; Seizure disorder.

Resources

BOOKS

Peacock, Judith. *Cerebral Palsy.* Mankato, MN: Capstone Press, 2000.

Pimm, Paul. *Living with Cerebral Palsy.* Austin, TX: Raintree Steck-Vaughn Publishers, 2000.

Pincus, Dion. *Everything You Need to Know about Cerebral Palsy.* New York: Rosen Publishing Group Inc., 2000.

ORGANIZATIONS

National Institute of Neurological Disorders and Stroke. 31 Center Drive, MSC 2540, Bldg. 31, Room 8806, Bethesda, MD 20814. Web site: <www.ninds.nih.gov>.

National Society of Genetic Counselors. 233 Canterbury Dr., Wallingford, PA 19086–6617. (610) 872–1192. http://www.nsgc.org/GeneticCounselingYou.asp.

United Cerebral Palsy Association Inc. (UCP). 1660 L St. NW, Suite 700, Washington, DC 20036–5602. Web site: <www.ucpa.org>.

WEB SITES

"Cerebral Palsy: Hope Through Research." *National Institute of Neurological Disorders and Stroke,* 2004. Available online at <www.ninds.nih.gov/health_and_medical/pubs/cerebral_palsyhtr.htm> (accessed November 29, 2004).

"NINDS Cerebral Palsy Information Page." *National Institute of Neurological Disorders and Stroke,* October 2004. Available online at <www.ninds.nih.gov/disorders/cerebral_palsy/cerebral_palsy.htm> (accessed November 29, 2004).

L. Lee Culvert
Scott J. Polzin, MS

Cerebrospinal fluid (CSF) analysis

Definition

Cerebrospinal fluid (CSF) analysis is a set of laboratory tests that examine a sample of the fluid surrounding the brain and spinal cord. This fluid is an ultrafiltrate of plasma. Plasma is the liquid portion of blood. CSF is clear and colorless. It contains glucose, electrolytes, amino acids, and other small molecules found in plasma, but it has very little protein and few cells. CSF protects the central nervous system from injury, cushions it from the surrounding bone structure, provides it with nutrients, and removes waste products by returning them to the blood.

CSF is withdrawn from the subarachnoid space through a needle by a procedure called a lumbar puncture or spinal tap. CSF analysis includes tests in clinical chemistry, hematology, immunology, and microbiology. Usually three or four tubes are collected. The first tube is used for chemical and/or serological analysis, and the last two tubes are used for hematology and microbiology tests. This method reduces the chances of a falsely elevated white cell count caused by a traumatic tap (bleeding into the subarachnoid space at the puncture site), and contamination of the bacterial culture by skin germs or flora.

Purpose

The purpose of a CSF analysis is to diagnose medical disorders that affect the central nervous system. Some of these conditions are as follows:

- **meningitis** and **encephalitis**, which may be viral, bacterial, fungal, or parasitic infections

- metastatic tumors (e.g., leukemia) and central nervous system tumors that shed cells into the CSF

- syphilis, a sexually transmitted bacterial disease

- bleeding (hemorrhaging) in the brain and spinal cord

- Guillain-Barré, a demyelinating disease involving peripheral sensory and motor nerves

Routine examination of CSF includes visual observation of color and clarity and tests for glucose, protein, lactate, lactate dehydrogenase, red blood cell count, white blood cell count with differential, syphilis serology (testing for antibodies indicative of syphilis), Gram stain, and bacterial culture. Further tests may need to be performed depending upon the results of initial tests and the presumptive diagnosis.

GROSS EXAMINATION Color and clarity are important diagnostic characteristics of CSF. Straw, pink, yellow, or amber pigments (xanthochromia) are abnormal and indicate the presence of bilirubin, hemoglobin, red blood cells, or increased protein. Turbidity (suspended particles) indicates an increased number of cells. Gross examination is an important aid to differentiating a subarachnoid hemorrhage from a traumatic tap. The latter is often associated with sequential clearing of CSF as it is collected; streaks of blood in an otherwise clear fluid; or a sample that clots.

GLUCOSE CSF glucose is normally approximately two-thirds of the fasting plasma glucose. A glucose level below 40 mg/dL is significant and occurs in bacterial and fungal meningitis and in malignancy.

PROTEIN Total protein levels in CSF are normally very low, and albumin makes up approximately two-thirds of the total. High levels are seen in many conditions, including bacterial and fungal meningitis, tumors, subarachnoid hemorrhage, and traumatic tap.

LACTATE The CSF lactate is used mainly to help differentiate bacterial and fungal meningitis, which cause increased lactate, from viral meningitis, which does not.

LACTATE DEHYDROGENASE This enzyme is elevated in bacterial and fungal meningitis, malignancy, and subarachnoid hemorrhage.

WHITE BLOOD CELL (WBC) COUNT The number of white blood cells in CSF is very low, usually necessitating a manual WBC count. An increase in WBCs may occur in many conditions, including infection (viral, bacterial, fungal, and parasitic), allergy, leukemia, hemorrhage, traumatic tap, encephalitis, and Guillain-Barré syndrome. The WBC differential helps to distinguish many of these causes. For example, viral infection is usually associated with an increase in lymphocytes, while bacterial and fungal infections are associated with an increase in polymorphonuclear leukocytes (neutrophils). The differential may also reveal eosinophils associated with allergy and ventricular shunts; macrophages with ingested bacteria (indicating meningitis), RBCs (indicating hemorrhage), or lipids (indicating possible cerebral infarction); blasts (immature cells) that indicate leukemia; and malignant cells characteristic of the tissue of origin. About 50 percent of metastatic cancers that infiltrate the central nervous system and about 10 percent of central nervous system tumors will shed cells into the CSF.

RED BLOOD CELL (RBC) COUNT While not normally found in CSF, RBCs will appear whenever bleeding has occurred. Red cells in CSF signal subarachnoid hemorrhage, **stroke**, or traumatic tap. Since white cells may enter the CSF in response to local infection, inflammation, or bleeding, the RBC count is used to correct the WBC count so that it reflects conditions other than hemorrhage or a traumatic tap. This is accomplished by counting RBCs and WBCs in both blood and CSF. The ratio of RBCs in CSF to blood is multiplied by the blood WBC count. This value is subtracted from the CSF WBC count to eliminate WBCs derived from hemorrhage or traumatic tap.

GRAM STAIN The Gram stain is performed on a sediment of the CSF and is positive in at least 60 percent of cases of bacterial meningitis. Culture is performed for both aerobic and anaerobic bacteria. In addition, other stains (e.g. the acid-fast stain for *Mycobacterium tuberculosis*, fungal culture, and rapid identification tests (tests for bacterial and fungal antigens) may be performed routinely.

SYPHILIS SEROLOGY Syphilis serology involves testing for antibodies that indicate neurosyphilis. The fluorescent treponemal antibody-absorption (FTA-ABS) test is often used and is positive in persons with active and treated syphilis. The test is used in conjunction with the VDRL test for nontreponemal antibodies, which is

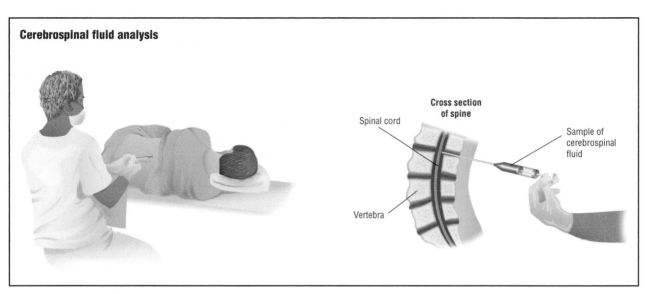

Cerebrospinal fluid analysis

Cross section
of spine

Spinal cord

Sample of
cerebrospinal
fluid

Vertebra

For cerebrospinal fluid collection, the health-care provider puts a syringe between the patient's vertebrae and pulls out a sample of the fluid surrounding the spinal cord. *(Illustration by GGS Information Services.)*

positive in most persons with active syphilis, but negative in treated cases.

Description

Lumbar puncture is performed by inserting the needle between the fourth and fifth lumbar vertebrae (L4-L5). This location is used because the spinal cord stops near L2, and a needle introduced below this level will miss the cord. In rare instances, such as a spinal fluid blockage in the middle of the back, a physician may perform a spinal tap in the cervical spine.

Precautions

In some circumstances, a lumbar puncture to withdraw a small amount of CSF for analysis may lead to serious complications. Lumbar punctures should be performed only with extreme caution and only if the benefits are thought to outweigh the risks. In people who have bleeding disorders, lumbar puncture can cause hemorrhage that can compress the spinal cord. If there is increased spinal column pressure, as may occur with a brain tumor and other conditions, removal of CSF can cause the brain to herniate, compressing the brain stem and other vital structures and leading to irreversible brain damage or death. Meningitis may be caused by bacteria introduced during the puncture. For this reason, aseptic technique must be followed strictly, and a lumbar puncture should never be performed at the site of a localized skin lesion.

Specimens should be handled with caution to avoid contamination with skin flora. They should be refrigerated if analysis cannot be performed immediately.

Aftercare

After the procedure, the site of the puncture is covered with a sterile bandage. The patient should remain lying for four to six hours after the lumbar puncture. Vital signs should be monitored every 15 minutes for four hours, then every 30 minutes for another four hours. The puncture site should be observed for signs of weeping or swelling for 24 hours. The neurological status of the patient should also be evaluated for such symptoms as **numbness** and/or tingling in the lower extremities.

Risks

The most common side effect after the removal of CSF is a **headache**. This occurs in up to 40 percent of children. It is caused by a decreased CSF pressure related to a small leak of CSF through the puncture site. These headaches usually are a dull **pain**, although some people report a throbbing sensation. A stiff neck and **nausea** may accompany the headache. Lumbar puncture headaches typically begin within two days after the procedure and persist from a few days to several weeks or months.

Normal results

The normal results include the following:

- gross appearance: normal CSF, clear and colorless

- CSF opening pressure: in children older than six to eight years, 90–180 mm H_2O; in infants and younger children, 10–100 mm H_2O

- specific gravity: 1.006–1.009

KEY TERMS

Demyelination—Disruption or destruction of the myelin sheath, leaving a bare nerve. It results in a slowing or stopping of the impulses that travel along that nerve.

Encephalitis—Inflammation of the brain, usually caused by a virus. The inflammation may interfere with normal brain function and may cause seizures, sleepiness, confusion, personality changes, weakness in one or more parts of the body, and even coma.

Guillain-Barré syndrome—Progressive and usually reversible paralysis or weakness of multiple muscles usually starting in the lower extremities and often ascending to the muscles involved in respiration. The syndrome is due to inflammation and loss of the myelin covering of the nerve fibers, often associated with an acute infection. Also called acute idiopathic polyneuritis.

Meningitis—An infection or inflammation of the membranes that cover the brain and spinal cord. It is usually caused by bacteria or a virus.

Multiple sclerosis—A progressive, autoimmune disease of the central nervous system characterized by damage to the myelin sheath that covers nerves. The disease, which causes progressive paralysis, is marked by periods of exacerbation and remission.

Spinal canal—The opening that runs through the center of the spinal column. The spinal cord passes through the spinal canal. Also called the vertebral canal.

Subarachnoid—Referring to the space underneath the arachnoid membrane, the middle of the three membranes that sheath the spinal cord and brain.

Treponeme—A term used to refer to any member of the genus *Treponema*, which is an anaerobic bacteria consisting of cells, 3–8 micrometers in length, with acute, regular, or irregular spirals and no obvious protoplasmic structure.

Vertebrae—Singular, vertebra. The individual bones of the spinal column that are stacked on top of each other. There is a hole in the center of each bone, through which the spinal cord passes.

- glucose: 40–80 mg/dL

- total protein: 15–45 mg/dL

- LD: 1/10 of serum level

- lactate: less than 35 mg/dL

- leukocytes (white blood cells): 0–6/microL (adults and children); up to 19/microL in infants; up to 30/microL (newborns)

- differential: 60–80 percent lymphocytes; up to 30 percent monocytes and macrophages; other cells 2 percent or less. Monocytes and macrophages are somewhat higher in neonates, and make up as much as 80 percent or more, with only 20 percent or less being lymphocytes.

- Gram stain: negative

- culture: sterile

- syphilis serology: negative

- red blood cell count: normally, none unless the needle passes though a blood vessel on route to the CSF

Parental concerns

If the child is anxious or uncooperative, a short-acting sedative may be given. Patients receive a local anesthetic to minimize any pain in the lower back from inserting the needle.

When to call the doctor

If the child does not respond to the parents, if the puncture site continues to leak a watery fluid, or the puncture site appears red and swollen, or has other signs of infection, then the doctor should be notified.

Resources

BOOKS

Braunwald, Eugene, ed., et al. "Approach to the Patient with Neurologic Disease." In *Harrison's Principles of Internal Medicine*, 15th ed. New York: McGraw-Hill, 2001.

Henry, J. B. *Clinical Diagnosis and Management by Laboratory Methods*, 20th ed. Philadelphia: Saunders, 2001.

Kee, Joyce LeFever. *Handbook of Laboratory and Diagnostic Tests*, 4th ed. Upper Saddle River, NJ: Prentice Hall, 2001.

Smith, Gregory P., and Carl R. Kieldsberg. *Cerebrospinal, Synovial, and Serous Body Fluids*. Philadelphia: Saunders Co., 2001.

Wallach, Jacques. *Interpretation of Diagnostic Tests*, 7th ed. Philadelphia: Lippincott Williams & Wilkens, 2000.

ORGANIZATIONS

National Institutes of Health. 9000 Rockville Pike, Bethesda, MD 20892. Web site: <www.nih.gov>.

Mark A. Best

Cerumen impaction

Definition

Cerumen impaction refers to the buildup of layers of earwax within the ear canal to the point of blocking the canal and putting pressure on the eardrum. Ironically, cerumen impaction is often caused by misguided attempts to remove earwax.

Description

Cerumen impaction develops when earwax accumulates in the inner part of the ear canal and blocks the eardrum. It does not happen under normal circumstances because the cerumen is produced by glands in the outer part of the ear canal; it is not produced in the inner part. Cerumen traps sand or dust particles before they reach the eardrum. It also protects the outer part of the ear canal because it repels water. The slow movement of the outer layer of skin of the ear canal carries cerumen toward the outer opening of the ear. As the older cerumen reaches the opening of the ear, it dries out and falls away.

Demographics

Cerumen impaction affects between 2 percent to 6 percent of the general population in the United States. It apparently affects males and females equally.

Causes and symptoms

Causes

Cerumen is most likely to become impacted when it is pushed against the eardrum by cotton-tipped applicators, hair pins, or other objects that people put in their ears, and when it is trapped against the eardrum by a hearing aid. Less common causes of cerumen impaction include overproduction of earwax by the glands in the ear canal or an abnormally narrow ear canal that tends to trap the wax.

Symptoms

The most important symptom of cerumen impaction is partial loss of hearing. Other symptoms are **itching**, tinnitus (noise or ringing in the ears), a sensation of fullness in the ear, and otalgia, or **pain** in the ear. The pain is caused by the pressure of several layers of impacted earwax against the ear drum.

In children younger than one year, cerumen impaction is sometimes discovered during a routine check-up when the doctor finds that the earwax is blocking his or her view of the eardrum. In these cases the cerumen must be removed so that the doctor can finish checking the child's ears and sense of hearing.

When to call the doctor

Impacted cerumen is not a medical emergency. **Family** care practitioners recommend that parents try to remove the impacted wax at home before calling the doctor. Several over-the-counter products are described below under the heading of Treatment. The way to use these products is to tilt the child's head to one side and fill the ear canal with the eardrops, using an eyedropper. Allow the drops to soak in for a few minutes and then treat the other ear if needed. This home treatment method may be repeated twice a day for three or four days.

Parents should, however, take the child to the doctor in the following circumstances:

- The child complains of **dizziness** or pain in the ear.
- The impaction does not improve after several days of treatment at home.
- The child has had a **myringotomy** or ear tube placement.
- The child has a history of discharges from the ear.

Diagnosis

The diagnosis of impacted cerumen is usually made by examining the ear canal and eardrum with an otoscope, an instrument with a light attached that allows the doctor to look into the canal.

Treatment

Irrigation is the most common method of removing impacted cerumen. It involves washing out the ear canal with water from a commercial irrigator or a syringe with a catheter attached. Although some doctors use Water Piks to remove cerumen, most do not recommend them because the stream of water is too forceful and may damage the eardrum. The doctor may add a small amount of alcohol, hydrogen peroxide, or other antiseptic. The water must be close to body temperature; if it is too cold or too warm, the child may feel dizzy or nauseated. After the ear has been irrigated, the doctor applies antibiotic ear drops to protect the ear from infection.

Irrigation should not be used to remove cerumen if the patient's eardrum is ruptured or missing; if the patient has a history of chronic **otitis media** (inflammation of the middle ear) or a myringotomy (cutting the eardrum to allow fluid to escape from the middle ear); or if the child has hearing in only one ear.

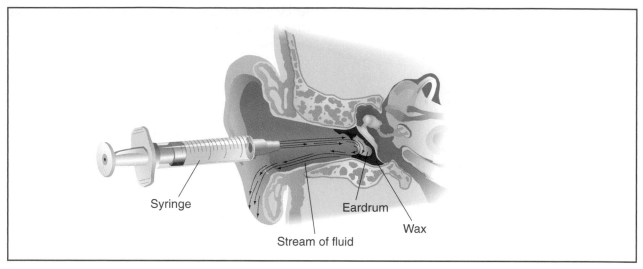

Ear wax is removed by flushing the ear canal with warm fluid. *(Illustration by Argosy, Inc.)*

If irrigation cannot be used or fails to remove the cerumen, the doctor can remove the wax with a vacuum device or a curette, which is a small scoop-shaped surgical instrument. Manual removal of the impaction is effective in 97 percent of children. The doctor holds the child's head steady with one hand while using the curette with the other hand to ease the impacted wax away from the sides of the ear canal. The doctor begins the removal in the area where the cerumen has already started to separate from the wall of the canal.

Some doctors prescribe special eardrops, such as Cerumenex, to soften the wax. The most common side effect of Cerumenex and similar products is an allergic skin reaction. Over-the-counter wax removal products include Debrox or Murine Ear Drops. A 3 percent solution of hydrogen peroxide may also be used. These products are less likely to irritate the skin of the ear.

Alternative treatment

One alternative method that is sometimes touted as a way to remove impacted cerumen is ear candling. Ear candling involves the insertion of a burning candle or a cone of wax-soaked linen or cotton into the affected ear. The person lies on his or her side with the affected ear uppermost. A collecting plate is placed on the ear to catch melted wax. The cone or candle is threaded through a hole in the plate into the ear canal and lit. A variation on this technique involves blowing herbal smoke into the ear through homemade pottery cones. Practitioners of ear candling claim that the heat from the burning candle or smoke creates a vacuum that draws out the impacted cerumen. Some also claim that ear candling improves hearing, relieves sinus infections, cures earache or swimmer's ear, stops tinnitus, or puri-

fies the mind. None of these claims is true, however. Ear candling is not recognized as an acceptable alternative practice by naturopaths, homeopaths, practitioners of Native American medicine, or any other authority on complementary and alternative medicine.

Ear candling is not only an ineffective way to remove impacted cerumen, it can actually damage the ear. According to a 1996 survey of 122 otolaryngologists (doctors who specialize in treating ear, nose, and throat disorders) in the Spokane area, the doctors reported 21 severe ear injuries resulting from ear candling, including 13 cases of external **burns**, seven cases of ear canal obstruction from melted candle wax, and one case of eardrum perforation. Ear candles cannot legally be sold as health devices in the United States because they do not have Food and Drug Administration (FDA) approval. A similar ban is in effect in Canada.

Prognosis

In most cases, impacted cerumen is successfully removed from the child's ear by irrigation or manual extraction with no lasting side effects. Irrigation can, however, lead to infection of the outer or the middle ear if the patient has a damaged or absent eardrum. Older children or adolescents who try to remove earwax themselves with hair pins or similar objects run the risk of perforating the ear drum or damaging the fragile skin covering the ear canal, causing bleeding and the risk of infection.

Prevention

The best method of cleaning the external ear is to wipe the outer opening with a damp washcloth folded over the index finger, without going into the ear canal itself. Two techniques have been recommended to prevent cerumen from reaccumulating in the ear. The patient may

KEY TERMS

Cerumen—The medical term for earwax.

Curette—Also spelled curet; a small loop or scoop-shaped surgical instrument with sharpened edges that can be used to remove tissue, growths, or debris.

Ear candling—An alternative method for removing impacted cerumen with a lighted hollow cone of paraffin or beeswax. It does not work and is not considered an acceptable treatment for any ear problem or disorder.

Impaction—A condition in which earwax has become tightly packed in the outer ear to the point that the external ear canal is blocked.

Irrigation—Cleansing a wound with large amounts of water and/or an antiseptic solution. Also refers to the technique of removing wax (cerumen) from the ear canal by flushing it with water.

Myringotomy—A surgical procedure in which an incision is made in the ear drum to allow fluid or pus to escape from the middle ear.

Otalgia—The medical term for pain in the ear. Impacted cerumen can sometimes cause otalgia.

Otitis media—Inflammation or infection of the middle ear space behind the eardrum. It commonly occurs in early childhood and is characterized by ear pain, fever, and hearing problems.

Tinnitus—A noise, ranging from faint ringing or thumping to roaring, that originates in the ear not in the environment.

place two or three drops of mineral oil into each ear once a week, allow it to remain for two or three minutes, and rinse it out with warm water; or place two drops of Domeboro otic solution in each ear once a week after showering.

Children who wear hearing aids should have their ears examined periodically for signs of cerumen accumulation.

Parents should teach children not to use cotton swabs or other objects to remove wax from the ear, and should advise older children and adolescents against experimenting with ear candling.

Parental concerns

Removal of impacted cerumen from children's ears is a routine procedure and should not ordinarily cause parents a great deal of concern. If the child has repeated

episodes of cerumen impaction, parents can discuss various preventive measures with the doctor.

See also Ear exam with an otoscope; Myringotomy and ear tubes; Otitis media.

Resources

BOOKS

"External Ear: Obstructions." Section 7, Chapter 83 in *The Merck Manual of Diagnosis and Therapy.* Edited by Mark H. Beers and Robert Berkow. Whitehouse Station, NJ: Merck Research Laboratories, 2002.

Jackler, Robert K., and Michael J. Kaplan. "Cerumen Impaction." In "Ear, Nose, & Throat," *Current Medical Diagnosis & Treatment 2001,* 40th ed. Edited by L. M Tierney, Jr., et al. New York: Lange Medical Books/ McGraw-Hill, 2001.

PERIODICALS

Ernst, E. "Ear Candles—A Triumph of Ignorance Over Science." *Journal of Laryngology and Otology* 118 (January 2004): 1–2.

Whatley, V. N., C. L. Dodds, and R. L. Paul. "Randomized Clinical Trial of Docusate, Triethanolamine Polypeptide, and Irrigation in Cerumen Removal in Children." *Archives of Pediatrics and Adolescent Medicine* 157 (December 2003): 1177–80.

ORGANIZATIONS

American Academy of Family Physicians (AAFP). 11400 Tomahawk Creek Parkway, Leawood, KS 66211–2672. Web site: <www.aafp.org>.

American Academy of Otolaryngology, Head and Neck Surgery Inc.

WEB SITES

"Cerumen Impaction." *FamilyPracticenotebook.com,* June 6, 2004. Available online at <www.fpnotebook.com/ ENT27.htm> (accessed November 29, 2004).

D'Alessandro, Donna, and Lindsay Huth. "Earwax (Cerumen)." *Virtual Children's Hospital,* April 2002. Available online at <www.vh.org/pediatric/patient/pediatrics/cqqa/ earwax.html> (accessed November 29, 2004).

OTHER

Health Canada/Santé Canada. *It's Your Health: Ear Candling.* Ottawa: Health Canada/Santé Canada, 2002.

Rebecca Frey, PhD

Cesarean section

Definition

A cesarean section (also referred to as c-section) is the birth of a fetus accomplished by performing a surgical incision through the maternal abdomen and uterus. It is one of the oldest surgical procedures known throughout history.

Purpose

Although Healthy People 2010 established a goal of a 15 percent rate for c-sections in the United States, the ideal rate has not been established. As of 2004, the average c-section rate is one out of every four births or approximately 26 percent of all births. A c-section allows safe and quick delivery of a baby when a vaginal delivery is not possible. The surgery is performed in the presence of a variety of maternal and fetal conditions with the most commonly accepted indications being complete placenta previa, cephalopelvic disproportion (CPD), placental abruption, active genital herpes, umbilical cord prolapse, failure to progress in labor or dystocia, proven nonreassuring fetal status, and benign and malignant tumors that obstruct the birth canal. Indications that are more controversial include breech presentation, previous c-section, major congenital anomalies, cervical cerclage, and severe Rh isoimmunization. C-sections have a higher maternal mortality rate than vaginal births with approximately 5.8 women per 100,000 live births dying, and half of these deaths are ascribed to the operation and a coexisting medical condition. Perinatal morbidity is associated with infections, reactions to anesthesia agents, blood clots, and bleeding.

Description

According to the United States Public Health Service, 35 percent of all c-sections are performed because the woman has had a previous c-section. The skin incision for a c-section is either transverse (Pfannenstiel) or vertical and does not indicate the type of incision made into the uterus. "Once a cesarean, always a cesarean," is a rule that originated with the classical, vertical uterine incision. It was believed that the resulting scar weakened the uterus wall and was at risk of rupture in subsequent deliveries. As of 2004, the incision is almost always made horizontally across the lower uterine segment, called a low transverse incision. This results in reduced blood loss and a decreased chance of rupture. This kind of incision allows many women to have a vaginal birth after a cesarean (VBAC).

Failure to progress and/or dystocia is the second most common reason for a c-section and represents about 30 percent of all cases. Uterine contractions may be weak or irregular, the cervix may not be dilating, or the mother's pelvic structure may not allow adequate passage for birth. When the baby's head is too large to fit through the pelvis, the condition is called cephalopelvic

disproportion (CPD). Failure to progress, however, can only be diagnosed with documentation of adequate contraction strength. The force of the contractions can be measured with an intrauterine pressure catheter (IUPC), which is a catheter that can be placed through the cervix into the uterus to measure uterine pressure during labor. Calculation of this force is determined by subtracting the baseline (resting) pressure from the peak pressure recorded for all contractions in a ten-minute period. This pressure calculation results in a force termed Montevideo units. A minimum of 200 Montevideo units are required before the forces of labor can be considered adequate. If the Montevideo units are less than this ten-minute sum and the fetal heart rate is reassuring, augmentation of labor with pitocin may be necessary.

Breech presentation occurs in about 3 percent of all births, and approximately 12 percent of c-sections are performed to deliver a baby in a breech presentation: buttocks or feet first. Breech presentations were still delivered vaginally in the 1970s, but with the advent of the malpractice climate, many doctors shied away from this practice, opting to perform a c-section. As a result, physicians who were being trained during that time period never learned how to manage a breech vaginal delivery. There was some change in this approach in the 1990s, and doctors are once again learning how to manage this situation; however, it is still uncertain whether this knowledge will be used in their practice.

Fetal distress or the more appropriate term, nonreassuring fetal heart rate, accounts for almost 9 percent of c-sections. With the introduction of **electronic fetal monitoring** (EFM) in the 1970s, doctors had more information for assessing fetal well-being. It was assumed that fetal monitoring would transmit signals of distress, thus, the EFM tracing became a legal document. There is still considerable debate as to what a non-reassuring FHR really is, but there are other parameters available to assist in this interpretation. When a fetus experiences stress, (oxygen deprivation) in utero, it may pass meconium (feces) into the amniotic fluid. The appearance of meconium in the fluid along with a questionable EFM tracing may indicate that a fetus is becoming compromised. At this point, if a woman is in early labor, a c-section may have to be performed. If, however, she is close to delivery, a vaginal delivery is often quicker. Oxygen deprivation may also be determined by testing the pH of a blood sample taken from the baby's scalp: a pH of 7.25-7.35 is normal; between 7.2 and 7.25 is suspicious; and below 7.2 is a sign of trouble. If the sample is equivocal, it can be repeated every 20 to 30 minutes.

The remaining 14 percent of c-sections occur secondary to other emergency situations, including the following:

- Umbilical cord prolapse: This situation occurs when the cord is the presenting part from the vagina. It becomes compressed and cuts off blood flow to the baby. The birth attendant must insert a hand into the vagina and relieve pressure on the cord until a c-section is performed.

- Placental abruption: The placenta separates from the uterine wall before the baby is born. If it is a complete abruption, the baby's blood flow will be cut off completely. The mother experiences severe **pain**, possible bleeding, and her abdomen feels rock hard. This situation demands an immediate c-section. Partial abruptions can occur without endangering the mother or the baby, but they need to be closely monitored. The risk of placental abruption is higher in multiple births and in women with high blood pressure.

- Placenta previa: With a complete previa, the placenta covers the cervix completely, and the mother may experience painless bleeding. With a complete previa, a c-section is mandatory as cervical dilation would cause bleeding. The baby is often in a transverse position in this case, which means it is lying horizontally across the pelvis. Women with partial previas will usually need a c-section due to bleeding problems, but those with marginal previas can often deliver vaginally.

- Active genital herpes: Any active herpetic lesions in the vaginal area can infect the baby as it passes through the birth canal. This is especially true for those with a primary outbreak, a first-time exposure.

- Mother's health status: A c-section may be necessary in women with pre-existing diseases, such as diabetes, **hypertension**, pregnancy induced hypertension (preeclampsia), autoimmune diseases such as lupus erythematosus, and blood incompatibilities. Each case must be evaluated on an individual basis in these instances to achieve the optimal outcome for baby and mother.

Precautions

There are some precautions any pregnant woman can follow to enhance her chances of preventing a c-section. These include the following:

- She should check her doctor's c-section rate to see if it is unnecessarily high. She can ask what his/her rate is and verify it by checking with the labor and delivery nurses at the hospital or with a **childbirth** educator.

- She should not stay on her back during labor. She can walk, rock, or use a hot shower or whirlpool.

- From the beginning, she should discuss with her doctor that she wants to avoid having a c-section if at all possible and enlist his opinion on how to achieve it.

- Studies show that women who go to the hospital early have a higher c-section rate than those who do not. Therefore, when labor starts, the woman should stay home for as long as she safely can. She should not go in if contractions are further apart than four to five minutes.

- She should use a midwife since studies show that they have a higher percentage of natural childbirths without surgical intervention than obstetricians do.

- She should hire a doula to assist during labor birth. Doulas have a lower c-section rate and can offer massage, different positions, and support alternatives during the difficult phases of labor.

- She should gather as much information as possible on hospital policies to educate herself and then discuss this information with her doctor or midwife. She should keep an open mind and stay informed.

Preparation

There is no perfect anesthesia for a c-section because every choice has its advantages and disadvantages. When a c-section becomes necessary and if it is not an emergency, the mother and her significant other should take part in the choice of anesthetic by being informed of risks and side effects. The anesthesia is usually a regional anesthetic (epidural or spinal), which makes her numb from below her breasts to her toes. In some cases, a general anesthetic will be administered if the regional does not work or if it is an emergency c-section. Every effort should be made to include the significant other in the preparations and recovery as well as the surgery if at all possible. An informed consent needs to be signed, and the physician should explain the surgery at that time. The mother may already have an intravenous (IV) line of fluid running into a vein in her arm. A catheter is inserted into her bladder to keep it drained and out of the way during surgery and the upper pubic area is usually shaved. Antacids are frequently administered to reduce the likelihood of damage to the lungs should aspiration of gastric contents occur. The abdominal area is then scrubbed and painted with betadine or another antiseptic solution. Drapes are placed over the surgical area to block a direct view of the procedure.

The type of skin incision, transverse or vertical, is determined by time factor, preference of mother, or physician preference. Two major locations of uterine incisions are the lower uterine segment and the upper segment of the body of the uterus (classical incision). The most common lower uterine segment incision is a transverse incision because the lower segment is the

Cesarean section

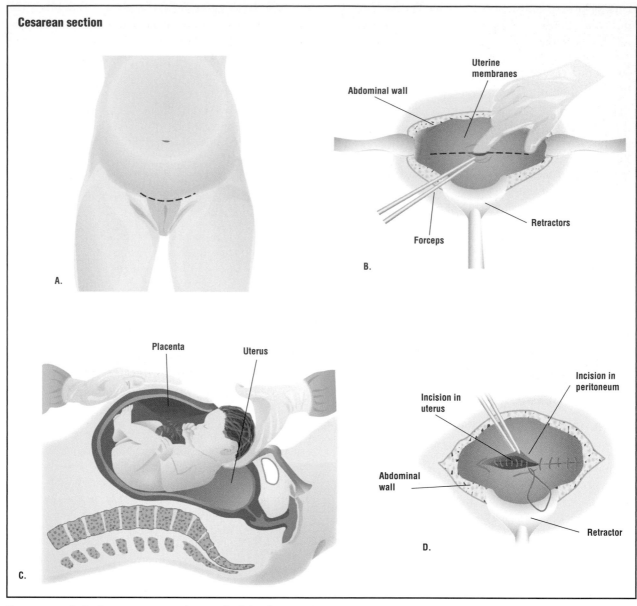

To remove a baby by cesarean section, an incision is made into the abdomen, usually just above the pubic hairline (A). The uterus is located and divided (B), allowing for delivery of the baby (C). After all the contents of the uterus are removed, the uterus is repaired and the rest of the layers of the abdominal wall are closed (D). *(Illustration by GGS Information Services.)*

thinnest part of the pregnant uterus and involves less blood loss. It is also easier to repair, heals well, is less likely to rupture during subsequent pregnancies and makes it possible for a woman to attempt a vaginal delivery in the future. The classical incision provides a larger opening than a low transverse incision and is used in emergency situations, such as placenta previa, preterm and macrosomic fetuses, abnormal presentation, and multiple births. With the classical incision, there is more bleeding and a greater risk of abdominal infection. This incision also creates a weaker scar, which places the woman at risk for uterine rupture in subsequent pregnancies.

Once the uterus is opened, the amniotic sac is ruptured and the baby is delivered. The time from the initial incision to birth is typically five to ten minutes. The umbilical cord is clamped and cut, and the newborn is given to the nursery personnel for evaluation. Cord blood is normally obtained for analysis of the infant's blood type and pH. The placenta is removed from the mother and her uterus is closed with suture. The abdominal area may be closed with suture or surgical staple. The time from birth through suturing may take 30 to 40 minutes. The entire surgical procedure may be performed in less than one hour. Physical contact or

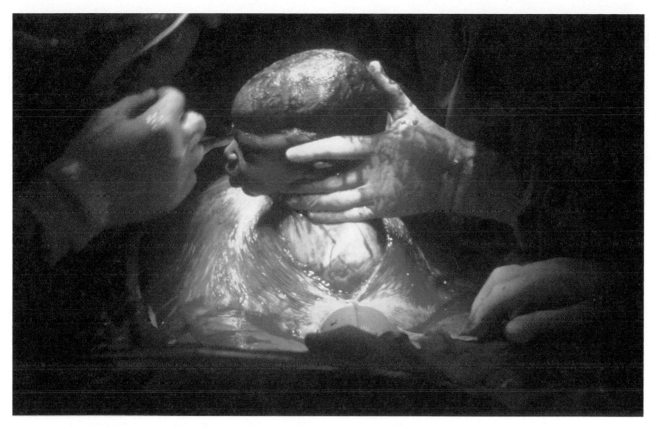

This baby is being delivered by cesarean section. *(Photograph by John Smith. Custom Medical Stock Photo Inc..)*

holding of the newborn may take place briefly while the mother is on the operating table if the baby is stable. The significant other can go with the baby to the nursery for the remainder of the operation.

Aftercare

Immediate postpartal care after a c-section is similar to post-operative care with the exception of palpating the fundus (top of the uterus) for firmness. If an epidural or spinal were used, Duramorph (a pain medication similar to morphine) is often administered through these catheters just prior to completion of surgery. It does very well in controlling pain but may cause **itching**, which can be managed. During recovery the mother is encouraged to turn, **cough**, and deep breathe to keep her lungs clear, and the neonate is usually brought to the mother to breastfeed if she so desires. The mother will be encouraged to get out of bed about eight to 24 hours after surgery. Walking stimulates the circulation to avoid formation of blood clots and promotes bowel movement. Once discharged home, the mother should limit stair climbing to once a day, and she should avoid lifting anything heavier than the baby. It is important to nap as often as the baby does and make arrangements for help

with the housework, meals, and care of other children. Driving may be resumed after two weeks, although some doctors recommend waiting for six weeks, which is the typical recovery period from major surgery.

Risks

The maternal death rate for c-section is less than 0.02 percent (5.8 per 100,000 live births), but that is four times the maternal death rate associated with vaginal delivery. The mother is at risk for increased bleeding from two incision sites and a c-section usually has twice as much blood loss as a vaginal delivery during surgery. Complications occur in less than 10 percent of cases, but these complications can include an infection of the incision, urinary tract, or tissue lining the uterus (endometritis). Less commonly, injury can occur to the surrounding organs, i.e., the bladder and bowel.

Normal results

The after-effects of a c-section vary, depending on the woman's age, physical fitness, and overall health. Following this procedure, a woman commonly experiences gas pains, incision pain, and uterine contractions,

KEY TERMS

Breech presentation—The condition in which the baby enters the birth canal with its buttocks or feet first.

Cephalopelvic disproportion—The condition in which the baby's head is too large to fit through the mother's pelvis.

Cervical cerclage—A procedure in which the cervix of the uterus is sewn closed, it is used in cases when the cervix starts to dilate too early in a pregnancy to allow the birth of a healthy baby.

Doula—A doula is someone who undergoes special training to enable them to support women during childbirth and into the postpartum period.

Dystocia—Failure to progress in labor, either because the cervix will not dilate (expand) further or because the head does not descend through the mother's pelvis after full dilation of the cervix.

Genital herpes—A life-long, recurrent sexually transmitted infection caused by the herpes simplex virus (HSV).

Perinatal—Referring to the period of time surrounding an infant's birth, from the last two months of pregnancy through the first 28 days of life.

Pitocin—A synthetic hormone that produces uterine contractions.

Placenta previa—A condition in which the placenta totally or partially covers the cervix, preventing vaginal delivery.

Placental abruption—An abnormal separation of the placenta from the uterus before the birth of the baby, with subsequent heavy uterine bleeding. Normally, the baby is born first and then the placenta is delivered within a half hour.

Postpartal—The six-week period following childbirth.

Rh blood incompatibility—Incompatibility between the blood of a mother and her baby due the absence of the Rh antigen in the red blood cells of one and its presence in the red blood cells of the other.

Umbilical cord prolapse—A birth situation in which the umbilical cord, the structure that connects the placenta to the umbilicus of the fetus to deliver oxygen and nutrients, falls out of the uterus and becomes compressed, thus preventing the delivery of oxygen.

which are also common with vaginal delivery. The hospital stay may be three to four days. Breastfeeding the baby is encouraged, taking care that it is in a position that keeps the baby from resting on the mother's incision. As the woman heals, she may gradually increase appropriate exercises to regain abdominal tone. Full recovery may be seen in four to six weeks.

The prognosis for a successful vaginal birth after a cesarean (VBAC) may be at least 75 percent, especially when the c-section involved a low transverse incision in the uterus, and there were no complications during or after delivery.

Of the hundreds of thousands of women in the United States who undergo a c-section each year, about 500 die from serious infections, hemorrhaging, or other complications. These deaths may be related to the health conditions that made the operation necessary and not simply to the operation itself.

Parental concerns

Undergoing a c-section may inflict psychological distress on the mother, beyond hormonal mood swings and postpartum depression. The woman may feel disappointment and a sense of failure for not experiencing a vaginal delivery. She may feel isolated if the father or birthing coach is not with her in the operating room or if she is treated by an unfamiliar doctor rather than by her own doctor or midwife. She may feel helpless from a loss of control over labor and delivery with no opportunity to actively participate. To overcome these feelings, the woman needs to understand why the c-section was crucial. It is important that she be able to verbalize an understanding that she could not control the events that made the c-section necessary and recognize the importance of preserving the health and safety of both herself and her child. Women who undergo a c-section should be encouraged to share their feelings with others. Hospitals can often recommend support groups for such mothers. Women should also be encouraged to seek professional help if negative emotions persist.

See also Apgar testing; Electronic fetal monitoring.

Resources

BOOKS

Olds, Sally et al. *Maternal-Newborn Nursing & Women's Health Care*, 7th ed. Saddle River, NJ: Prentice Hall, 2004.

ORGANIZATIONS

Association of Women's Health, Obstetric and Neonatal Nursing. 2000 L Street, NW, Suite 740, Washington, DC 20036. Web site: <www.awhonn.org>.

International Childbirth Education Association Inc. (ICEA). PO Box 20048, Minneapolis, MN 55420. Web site: <www.icea.org/info.htm>.

WEB SITES

"Cesarean Section." *MedlinePlus.* Available online at <www.nlm.nih.gov/medlineplus/cesareansection.html> (accessed December 7, 2004).

"Cesarean Section Homepage." *Childbirth.* Available online at <www.childbirth.org/section/section.html> (accessed December 7, 2004).

"C-Section." *March of Dimes.* Available online at <www.marchofdimes.com/pnhec/240_1031.asp> (accessed December 7, 2004).

Linda K. Bennington, RNC, MSN, CNS

Chalazion *see* **Styes and chalazia**

Charcot-Marie-Tooth disease

Definition

Charcot-Marie-Tooth disease (CMT) is the name of a group of inherited disorders of the nerves in the peripheral nervous system. These are the nerves throughout the body that communicate motor and sensory information to and from the spinal cord. CMT causes weakness and loss of sensation in the limbs.

Description

CMT is named for the three neurologists who first described the condition in the late 1800s. It is also known as hereditary motor and sensory neuropathy and is sometimes called peroneal muscular atrophy, referring to the muscles in the leg that are often affected. The age of onset of CMT can vary anywhere from young childhood to the 50s or 60s. Symptoms typically begin by the age of 20. For reasons unknown as of 2004, the severity in symptoms can also vary greatly, even among members of the same **family**.

Although CMT has been described for many years, it is only since the early 1990s that the genetic cause of many of the types of CMT have become known. There-

fore, knowledge about CMT increased dramatically shortly thereafter.

The peripheral nerves

CMT affects the peripheral nerves, those groups of nerve cells carrying information to and from the spinal cord. CMT decreases the ability of these nerves to carry motor commands to muscles, especially those furthest from the spinal cord located in the feet and hands. As a result, the muscles connected to these nerves eventually weaken. CMT also affects the sensory nerves that carry information from the limbs to the brain. Therefore, people with CMT also have sensory loss. This loss causes symptoms such as not being able to tell if something is hot or cold or having difficulties with balance.

There are two parts of the nerve that can be affected in CMT. A nerve can be likened to an electrical wire, in which the wire part is the axon of the nerve and the insulation surrounding it is the myelin sheath. The job of the myelin is to help messages travel very fast through the nerves.

CMT is usually classified depending by which part of the nerve is affected. Children who have problems with the myelin have CMT type 1 and children who have abnormalities of the axon have CMT type 2. Specialized testing of the nerves, called nerve conduction testing (NCV), can be performed to determine if CMT1 or CMT2 is present. These tests measure the speed at which messages travel through the nerves. In CMT1, the messages move too slowly, but in CMT2 the messages travel at the normal speed.

Demographics

Charcot-Marie-Tooth is the most common inherited neurological disorder, affecting approximately 150,000 Americans. It is the most common type of inherited neurological condition, occurring in approximately one in 2,500 people worldwide, in all races and ethnic groups.

Causes and symptoms

Genetic causes

CMT is caused by changes (mutations) in any one of a number of genes that carry the instructions on how to make the peripheral nerves. Genes contain the instructions for how the body grows and develops before and after a person is born. There are probably at least 15 different genes that can cause CMT. However, as of 2004, not all had been identified.

CMT types 1 and 2 can be broken down into subtypes based upon the gene that causes CMT. The subtypes are labeled by letters, so there is CMT1A, CMT1B, etc. Therefore, the gene with a mutation that causes CMT1A is different from the one that causes CMT1B.

Types of CMT

CMT1A The most common type of CMT, called CMT1A, is caused by a mutation in a gene called peripheral myelin protein 22 (PMP22) located on chromosome 17. The job of this gene is to make a protein (PMP22) that makes up part of the myelin. In most people who have CMT, the mutation that causes the condition is a duplication (doubling) of the PMP22 gene. Instead of having two copies of the PMP22 gene (one on each chromosome) there are three copies. It is not known how this extra copy of the PMP22 gene causes the observed symptoms. A small percentage of people with CMT1A do not have a duplication of the PMP22 gene, but rather they have a point mutation in the gene. A point mutation is like a typo in the gene that causes it to work incorrectly.

HEREDITY NEUROPATHY WITH LIABILITY TO PRESSURE PALSIES (HNPP) HNPP is a condition that is also caused by a mutation in the PMP22 gene. The mutation is a deletion. Therefore, there is only one copy of the PMP22 gene instead of two. People who have HNPP may have some of the signs of CMT. However, they also have episodes when they develop weakness and problems with sensation after compression of certain pressure points such as at the elbows or knee. Often these symptoms resolve after a few days or weeks, but sometimes they are permanent.

CMT1B Another type of CMT, called CMT1B, is caused by a mutation in a gene called myelin protein zero (MPZ), located on chromosome 1. The job of this gene is to make the layers of myelin stick together as they are wrapped around the axon. The mutations in this gene are point mutations because they involve a change (either deletion, substitution, or insertion) at one specific component of a gene.

CMTX Another type of CMT, called CMTX, is usually considered a subtype of CMT1 because it affects the myelin, but it has a different type of inheritance than type 1 or type 2. In CMTX, the CMT-causing gene is located on the X chromosome and is called connexin 32 (Cx32). The job of this gene is to code for a class of protein called connexins that form tunnels between the layers of myelin.

CMT2 There are at least five different genes that can cause CMT type 2. Therefore, CMT2 has subtypes A, B, C, D and E. As of early 2001, scientists have narrowed in on the location of most of the CMT2-causing genes. However, the specific genes and the mutations have not yet been found as of 2004 for most types. In the early 2000s, the gene for CMT2E was found. The gene is called neurofilament-light (NF-L). Because it has just been discovered, not much is known about how mutations in this gene cause CMT.

CMT3 In the past a condition called Dejerine-Sottas disease was referred to as CMT3. This is a severe type of CMT in which symptoms begin in infancy or early childhood. It is known as of 2004 that this is not a separate type of CMT; in fact, people who have onset in infancy or early childhood often have mutations in the PMP22 or MPZ genes. Children with type 3 CMT may not develop early motor skills such as walking until they are three or four years old.

CMT4 CMT4 is a rare type of CMT in which the nerve conduction tests have slow response results. However, it is classified differently from CMT1 because it is passed through families by a different pattern of inheritance. There are five different subtypes, and each has as of 2004 only been described in a few families. The symptoms in CMT4 are often severe and other symptoms such as deafness may be present. There are three different genes that have been associated with CMT4 as of early 2001. They are called MTMR2, EGR2, and NDRG1. More research is required to understand how mutations in these genes cause CMT.

Inheritance

Children with CMT have an increased risk for passing on the genes that cause the condition when they start a family of their own.

CMT1A and 1B, HNPP, and all of the subtypes of CMT2 have autosomal dominant inheritance. Autosomal refers to the first 22 pairs of chromosomes that are the same in males and females. Therefore, males and females are affected equally in these types. In a dominant condition, only one gene of a pair needs to have a mutation in order for a person to have symptoms of the condition. Therefore, individuals who have these types have a 50 percent, or one in two, chance of passing CMT on to each of their children. This chance is the same for each pregnancy and does not change based on previous children.

CMTX has X-linked inheritance. Since males only have one X chromosome, they only have one copy of the Cx32 gene. Thus, when a male has a mutation in his Cx32 gene, he will have CMT. However, females have two X chromosomes and, therefore, have two copies of the Cx32 gene. If they have a mutation in one copy of their Cx32 genes, they will only have mild to moderate symptoms of CMT that may go unnoticed. This is because their normal copy of the Cx32 gene does make normal myelin.

Females pass on one or the other of their X chromosomes to their children—sons or daughters. If a woman with a Cx32 mutation passes her normal X chromosome, she will have an unaffected son or daughter who will not pass CMT on to his or her children. If the woman passes the chromosome with Cx32 mutation on she will have an affected son or daughter, although the daughter will be mildly affected or have no symptoms. Therefore, a woman with a Cx32 mutation has a 50 percent, or a one in two, chance of passing the mutation to her children: a son will be affected, and a daughter may only have mild symptoms.

When males pass on an X chromosome, they have a daughter. When they pass on a Y chromosome, they have a son. Since the Cx32 mutation is on the X chromosome, a man with CMTX will always pass the Cx32 mutation on to his daughters. However, when he has a son, he passes on the Y chromosome, and the son will not be affected. Therefore, an affected male passes the Cx32 gene mutation on to all of his daughters, but to none of his sons.

CMT4 has autosomal recessive inheritance. Males and females are equally affected. In order for individuals to have CMT4, they must have a mutation in both of their CMT-causing genes, one inherited from each parent. The parents of an affected person are called carriers. They have one normal copy of the gene and one copy with a mutation. Carriers do not have symptoms of CMT. Two carrier parents have a 25 percent, or one in four, chance of passing CMT on to each of their children.

Symptoms

The onset of symptoms is highly variable, even among members of the same family. Symptoms usually progress very slowly over a person's lifetime. The main problems caused by CMT are weakness and loss of sensation mainly in the feet and hands. The first symptoms are usually problems with the feet such as high arches and problems with walking and running. Tripping while walking and sprained ankles are common. Muscle loss in the feet and calves leads to foot drop in which the foot does not lift high enough off the ground when walking. Complaints of cold legs are common, as are cramps in the legs, especially after **exercise**. Most children with CMT remain able to walk throughout their lives.

In many people, the fingers and hands eventually become affected. Muscle loss in the hands can make fine movements such as working buttons and zippers difficult. Some patients develop tremor in the upper limbs. Loss of sensation can cause problems such as **numbness** and the inability to feel if something is hot or cold.

Diagnosis

When CMT is suspected in a child, the diagnosis begins with a careful neurological exam to determine the extent and distribution of weakness. A thorough family history should be taken at this time to determine if other people in the family are affected. Testing may also be performed to rule out other causes of neuropathy.

A nerve conduction velocity test should be performed to measure how fast impulses travel through the nerves. This test may show characteristic features of CMT, but it is not diagnostic of CMT. Nerve conduction testing may be combined with electromyography (EMG), an electrical test of the muscles.

A nerve biopsy (removal of a small piece of the nerve) may be performed to look for changes characteristic of CMT. However, this testing is not diagnostic of CMT and is usually not necessary for making a diagnosis.

Definitive diagnosis of CMT is made only by genetic testing, usually performed by drawing a small amount of blood. As of early 2001, testing is available to detect mutations in PMP22, MPZ, Cx32 and EGR2. However, research is progressing rapidly and new testing is often made available every few months. All affected members of a family have the same type of CMT. Therefore, once a mutation is found in one affected member, it is possible to test other members who may have symptoms or are at risk of developing CMT.

Prenatal diagnosis

Testing during pregnancy to determine whether an unborn child is affected is possible if genetic testing in a family has identified a specific CMT-causing mutation. This can be done after ten to 12 weeks of pregnancy using a procedure called chorionic villus sampling (CVS). CVS involves removing a tiny piece of the placenta and examining the cells. Testing can also be done by **amniocentesis** after 16 weeks gestation by removing a small amount of the amniotic fluid surrounding the baby and analyzing the cells in the fluid. Each of these procedures has a small risk of miscarriage associated with it, and those who are interested in learning more should check with their doctor or genetic counselor. Couples interested in these options should obtain genetic

KEY TERMS

Axon—A long, threadlike projection that is part of a neuron (nerve cell).

Myelin—A fatty sheath surrounding nerves throughout the body that helps them conduct impulses more quickly.

Nerve condition velocity (NCV)—Technique for studying nerve or muscle disorders, measuring the speed at which nerves transmit signals.

Neuropathy—A disease or abnormality of the peripheral nerves (the nerves outside the brain and spinal cord). Major symptoms include weakness, numbness, paralysis, or pain in the affected area.

Peripheral nerves—Nerves outside the brain and spinal cord that provide the link between the body and the central nervous system.

counseling to carefully explore all of the benefits and limitations of these procedures.

Treatment

As of 2004, there was no cure for CMT. However, physical and occupational therapy are an important part of CMT treatment. Physical therapy is used to preserve range of motion and minimize deformity caused by muscle shortening, or contracture. Braces are sometimes used to improve control of the lower extremities and can help with balance. After wearing braces, children often find that they have more energy because they are using less energy to focus on their walking. Occupational therapy is used to provide devices and techniques that can assist tasks such as dressing, feeding, writing, and other routine activities of daily life. Substances such as **caffeine** and alcohol should be avoided if tremor is present. Voice-activated software can also help children who have problems with fine motor control.

It is very important that individuals with CMT avoid injury that causes them to be immobile for long periods of time. It is often difficult for people with CMT to return to their original strength after injury.

There is a long list of medications that should be avoided if possible by people diagnosed with CMT, such as the high blood pressure-reducing medication hydralazine (Apresoline), megadoses of vitamin A, B6, and D, and large intravenous doses of penicillin. Complete lists are available from the CMT support groups. Parents considering providing any of these medications to their children with CMT should weigh the risks and benefits with their physician.

Prognosis

The symptoms of CMT usually progress slowly over many years but do not usually shorten life expectancy. The majority of children with CMT do not need to use a wheelchair at any time during their lives. Most people with CMT are able to lead full and productive lives despite their physical challenges.

Prevention

As of 2004 there was no known way to prevent CMT. Genetic counseling for parents with CMT can help them understand the risk they face of having children with the disorder.

Parental concerns

The goal for children with CMT is to live as normal a life as possible. Along with seeing that children obtain proper healthcare from a specialist knowledgeable about the condition, parents can take the following precautions to help minimize problems:

- Children should be properly dressed in cold weather to avoid chilled hands and feet.

- The home should be designed to avoid the risk of falls, including installing handrails on steps, removing throw rugs, using nonskid bathmats, and arranging furniture so it does not block passage through rooms.

- Learning about CMT and discussing it with teachers, classmates, friends, and family members may help normalize the disorder and create support for the child.

Resources

ORGANIZATIONS

Charcot Marie Tooth Association (CMTA). 2700 Chestnut Parkway, Chester, PA 19013. Web site: <www.charcot-marie-tooth.org/site/content>.

CMT International. 1 Springbank Dr., St. Catherine's, ONT L2S2K1, Canada. Web site: <www.cmtint.org>.

Muscular Dystrophy Association. 3300 East Sunrise Dr., Tucson, AZ 85718. Web site: <www.mdausa.org>.

Neuropathy Association. 60 E. 42nd St., Suite 942, New York, NY 10165. Web site: <www.neuropathy.org>.

WEB SITES

"Charcot-Marie-Tooth Disease." *Health and Disease Information A to Z*, February 27, 2004. Available online at <www.hmc.psu.edu/healthinfo/c/cmt.htm> (accessed December 7, 2004).

"Charcot-Marie-Tooth Disorder Information Page." *NINDS Charcot-Marie-Tooth Disorder Information Page*, February 27, 2004. Available online at <www.ninds.nih.gov/health_and_medical/disorders/charcot_doc.htm> (accessed December 7, 2004).

Christine Kuehn Kelly

Charley horse *see* **Muscle spasms and cramps**

Chemotherapy

Definition

Chemotherapy, sometimes referred to as "chemo," is the treatment of **cancer** with anticancer drugs.

Purpose

The main purpose of chemotherapy is to kill cancer cells. It usually is used to treat patients with cancer that has spread from the place in the body where it originated (metastasized). Chemotherapy destroys cancer cells anywhere in the body. It even kills cells that have broken off from the main tumor and traveled through the blood or lymph systems to other parts of the body.

Chemotherapy can cure some types of cancer. In some cases, it is used to slow the growth of cancer cells or to keep the cancer from spreading to other parts of the body. Chemotherapy may be given before surgery or radiation therapy to shrink the tumor (neoadjuvant therapy). When a cancer has been removed by surgery or treated with radiation therapy, chemotherapy may be used to keep the cancer from coming back (adjuvant therapy).

Once a remission is achieved, consolidation chemotherapy, also called intensification chemotherapy, is given to sustain a remission. Maintenance chemotherapy is chemotherapy given in lower doses as a treatment to prolong a remission in certain types of cancer. Chemotherapy also can ease the symptoms of cancer (palliative chemotherapy), helping some patients have a better quality of life.

Description

Chemotherapy for the treatment of cancer began in the 1940s with the use of nitrogen mustard. More than 100 chemotherapy drugs are now available to treat cancer, and many more are being tested for their ability to destroy cancer cells.

Most chemotherapy drugs interfere with the ability of cells to grow or multiply. Although these drugs affect all cells in the body, many useful treatments are most effective against rapidly growing cells. Cancer cells grow more quickly than most other body cells. Other cells that grow fast are cells of the bone marrow that produce blood cells, cells in the stomach and intestines, and cells of the hair follicles. Therefore, the most common side effects of chemotherapy are linked to the treatment's effects on other fast-growing cells.

Types of chemotherapy drugs

Chemotherapy drugs are classified according to how they work. The main types of chemotherapy drugs are:

- Alkylating drugs—kill cancer cells by directly attacking DNA, the genetic material of the genes. Cyclophosphamide is an alkylating drug.

- Antimetabolites—interfere with the production of DNA and keep cells from growing and multiplying. An example of an antimetabolite is 5-fluorouracil (5-FU).

- Antitumor antibiotics—made from natural substances such as fungi in the soil. They interfere with important cell functions, including production of DNA and cell proteins. Doxorubicin and bleomycin belong to this group of chemotherapy drugs.

- Plant alkaloids—prevent cells from dividing normally. Vinblastine and vincristine are plant alkaloids obtained from the periwinkle plant.

- Steroid hormones—slow the growth of some cancers that depend on hormones. For example, tamoxifen is used to treat breast cancers whose growth depends on the hormone estrogen.

- Topoisomerase inhibitors—interfere with the action of topoisomerase enzymes, the enzymes that control the part of DNA needed to multiply. Etoposide belongs to this group.

Biological therapy

Biological therapy, also called immunotherapy, consists of treatment with substances that boost the body's own immune system against cancer. The body usually produces these substances in small amounts to fight diseases. These substances can be made in the laboratory and given to patients to destroy cancer cells, change the way the body reacts to a tumor, or help the body repair or make new cells destroyed by chemotherapy.

Combination chemotherapy

Chemotherapy usually is given in addition to other cancer treatments, such as surgery and radiation therapy. When given with other treatments, it is called adjuvant chemotherapy. An oncologist decides on the specific chemotherapy drug or combination of drugs that will work best for each patient. The use of two or more drugs together—combination chemotherapy—often works better than using a single drug. Scientific studies of different drug combinations help doctors learn the combinations that work best for each type of cancer. For example, research in 2003 found that a combination of chemotherapy and gene therapy stopped breast cancer and its metastasis (spread to other organs or parts of the body).

Clinical trials

Some patients may be eligible to participate in clinical trials, research programs conducted with patients to evaluate a new drug, medical treatment, device, or combination of treatments. The purpose of clinical trials is to find new and improved methods of treating different diseases and special conditions. More information is available at the National Institutes of Health's clinical trials Web site, <www.clinicaltrials.gov> or by calling (888) FIND-NLM, (888) 346-3656 or (301) 594-5983. Another resource is the National Cancer Institute's Web site, <www.cancer.gov/clinicaltrials>.

Precautions

There are many different types of chemotherapy drugs. Oncologists, doctors who specialize in treating cancer, determine the drugs that are best suited for each patient. This decision is based on the type and severity of cancer, location of the cancer, patient's age and health, and other drugs the patient takes. Some patients should not be treated with certain chemotherapy drugs. Age and other conditions may affect the drugs selected for treatment. Heart disease, kidney disease, and diabetes are conditions that may limit the choice of treatment drugs. In 2003, research revealed that **obesity** appears to reduce the effectiveness of high-dose chemotherapy. Researchers said further study was needed to determine the best dosage for obese patients receiving therapy.

How chemotherapy is given

Chemotherapy is administered in different ways, depending on the drugs to be given and the type of cancer.

Doctors determine the dose of chemotherapy drugs based on many factors, including the patient's height and weight.

Chemotherapy may be given by one or more of the following methods:

- orally (by mouth)
- injection
- through a catheter or port
- topically (via the skin)

Oral chemotherapy is given by mouth in the form of a pill, capsule, or liquid. This is the easiest method and can usually be done at home.

Intravenous (IV) chemotherapy is injected into a vein. A small needle is inserted into a vein on the hand or lower arm. The needle usually is attached to a small tube called a catheter, which delivers the drug to the needle from an IV bag or bottle.

Intramuscular (IM) chemotherapy is injected into a muscle. Chemotherapy given by intramuscular injection is absorbed into the blood more slowly than IV chemotherapy. Because of this, the effects of IM chemotherapy may last longer than chemotherapy given intravenously. Chemotherapy also may be injected subcutaneously (SQ or SC), which means under the skin. Injection of chemotherapy directly into the cancer is called intralesional (IL) injection.

Chemotherapy also may be given by a catheter or port permanently inserted into a central vein or body cavity. A port is a small reservoir or container that is placed in a vein or under the skin in the area where the drug will be given. These methods eliminate the need for repeated injections and may allow patients to spend less time in the hospital while receiving chemotherapy. A common location for a permanent catheter is the external jugular vein in the neck.

Intraperitoneal (IP) chemotherapy is administered into the abdominal cavity through a catheter or port. Chemotherapy given by catheter or port into the spinal fluid is called intrathecal (IT) administration. Catheters and ports also may be placed in the chest cavity, abdomen, bladder, or pelvis (intracavitary or IC catheter), depending on the location of the cancer to be treated.

Topical chemotherapy is given as a cream or ointment applied on the surface of the skin. This method is more common in treatment of certain types of skin cancers.

Treatment location and schedule

Patients may take chemotherapy at home, in the doctor's office, or as an inpatient or outpatient at the hospital. The choice of where to have chemotherapy depends on the drugs, delivery method, and sometimes the patient's and family's personal preferences. Most patients receive chemotherapy as an outpatient. Some patients stay in the hospital when first beginning chemotherapy, so their doctor can check for any side effects and change the dose if needed.

Frequency and length of chemotherapy treatment depends on the form of cancer, types of drugs, how the patient responds to the treatment, and the patient's health and ability to tolerate the drugs. Chemotherapy administration may take only a few minutes or as long as several hours. Chemotherapy may be given daily, weekly, or monthly. A rest period may follow a course of treatment before the next course begins, allowing new cells to grow and the patient to recover and regain strength. In combination chemotherapy, more than one drug may be given at a time, or the drugs may be given alternately, one following the other.

Maintaining the prescribed treatment schedule is essential to ensuring that the drugs work properly. The doctor should be contacted as soon as possible if a treatment session is missed, or a dose of the drug is skipped, for whatever reasons. Sometimes the doctor may need to delay a treatment based on the results of certain blood tests. Specific instructions will be provided if a treatment delay becomes necessary.

Preparation

TESTS A number of medical tests are done before chemotherapy is started. The results of **x rays**, other imaging tests, and tumor samples taken during biopsy or surgery will help the oncologist determine how much the cancer has spread.

Blood tests give the doctor important information about the function of the blood cells and levels of chemicals in the blood. A complete blood count (CBC) is commonly done before and regularly during treatment. The CBC shows the numbers of white blood cells, red blood cells, and platelets in the blood. Because chemotherapy affects the bone marrow, where blood cells are made, levels of these cells often drop during chemotherapy. The white blood cells and platelets are most likely to be affected by chemotherapy. A drop in the white blood cell count means the immune system cannot function properly. Low levels of platelets can cause a patient to bleed easily from a cut or other wound. A low red blood cell count can lead to anemia (deficiency of red blood cells) and fatigue.

INFORMED CONSENT Informed consent is an educational process between health care providers, patients, and/or their legal guardians. Before any procedure is performed or any form of medical care is provided, the patient and parents (if the patient is under age 18), are asked to sign a consent form, which provides permission for the child to receive chemotherapy treatment. The health care provider will review the informed consent form with the parents before they are asked to sign it. Before signing the form, the patient and parents should understand the nature and purpose of the treatment, its risks and benefits, and alternatives, including the option of not proceeding with the treatment. During the discussion about treatment, the health care providers are available to answer the patient's and parents' questions about the consent form or course of treatment.

PREPARING FOR THE TREATMENT When a chemotherapy treatment takes a long time, the patient may prepare for it by wearing comfortable clothes. Packing a book, favorite game, or an audiotape may help pass the time and ease the stress of receiving chemotherapy.

Usually parents stay with their child during the treatment. It is necessary to drive the child home (even if he or she is old enough to drive), since the medications taken to control **nausea** and the chemotherapy treatment itself can cause drowsiness.

ANTI-EMETIC DRUGS Sometimes, patients taking chemotherapy drugs known to cause nausea are given medications called anti-emetics before chemotherapy is administered. Anti-emetic drugs help to lessen feelings of nausea. Two anti-nausea medications that may be used are Kytril and Zofran. To decrease nausea from occurring just after a chemotherapy session, the child should not eat for about two hours before the treatment appointment.

Research published in 2003 revealed that taking melatonin, a natural hormone substance, may help improve chemotherapy's effectiveness and reduce the toxic effects of the drugs.

Aftercare

Tips for helping to control side effects after chemotherapy include:

- following any instructions given by the doctor or nurse
- taking all prescribed medications
- eating small amounts of bland foods
- maintaining good **nutrition** by getting enough calories, including protein in the diet, and taking a daily multivitamin (as recommended by the child's physician)

- drinking at least eight cups of fluids per day

- getting plenty of rest

- exercising regularly

Some patients find it helpful to breathe fresh air or get mild **exercise**, such as taking a walk.

Side effects and their severity are not indicators of how well the chemotherapy is working, since they vary greatly among patients and from drug to drug. Tests and exams can help determine the effectiveness of the chemotherapy.

Risks

Chemotherapy drugs are toxic to normal cells as well as cancer cells. A dose that will destroy cancer cells will probably cause damage to some normal cells. Doctors adjust doses to do the least amount of harm possible to normal cells. Side effects are temporary, and damaged non-cancerous cells will be replaced with healthy cells.

Some patients feel few or no side effects, and others may have more serious side effects. In some cases, a dose adjustment is all that is needed to reduce or stop a side effect. The types and severity of side effects depend on the chemotherapy drugs, dose, length of therapy, the body's reaction to the drug, and the child's overall health at the start of chemotherapy.

Some chemotherapy drugs have more side effects than others. Among the most common side effects are:

- fatigue

- **nausea and vomiting**

- loss of appetite

- **diarrhea**

- hair loss

- anemia

- infection

- easy bleeding or bruising

- sores in the mouth and throat

- neuropathy and other damage to the nervous system

- kidney damage

Fatigue (feeling tired and lacking energy) is the most common side effect of cancer and chemotherapy medications. Fatigue gradually goes away as the cancer responds to treatment. To help a child cope with fatigue, parents should plan rest periods, provide

nutritious meals to maintain energy and meet caloric needs, limit **caffeine**, and encourage exercise and activity.

Nausea and vomiting are common, but can usually be controlled by taking anti-nausea drugs; consuming adequate fluids; drinking fluids at least one hour before or after a meal; eating and drinking slowly, chewing food completely; eating smaller meals throughout the day; choosing high-carbohydrate, low-fat foods; and avoiding sweet, fried, or spicy foods. When vomiting episodes stop, the child may feel better after eating easy-to-digest and bland foods such as clear liquids, crackers, gelatin, and plain toast.

Loss of appetite may be due to nausea, changes in taste and smell, or the stress of undergoing cancer treatment. To help maintain the child's appetite, meals and snacks should be small rather than large. Food should be served when the child is hungry, and he or she should be offered favorite foods. It is recommended that children help select and prepare foods. Calories may be boosted by offering high-calorie and high-protein snacks and foods. Sometimes a feeding tube may be needed to maintain a child's weight or for children who cannot eat or drink.

If the child has diarrhea, high-fiber and high-fat foods, gassy foods, and carbonated beverages should be avoided. It is important for the child to continue drinking fluids throughout the day to avoid **dehydration** from diarrhea or vomiting.

Some chemotherapy drugs cause hair loss, but it is almost always temporary. The doctor can advise the parents and patients if hair loss is expected with the type of chemotherapy drug to be given. When hair loss occurs, it may begin after a few treatments, or several weeks after the first treatment. To care for the scalp and hair during chemotherapy, the child should use a mild shampoo and soft brush, and low heat for hair drying. The head should be protected from heat and sun with a hat or scarf. If desired, a wig or hair piece may be worn.

Low blood cell counts caused by the effect of chemotherapy on the bone marrow can lead to anemia, infections, and easy bleeding and bruising. Patients with anemia have too few red blood cells to deliver oxygen and nutrients to the body's tissues. Anemic patients feel tired and weak, are short of breath, and may have a rapid heartbeat. If red blood cell levels fall too low, a blood transfusion may be given.

Patients receiving chemotherapy are more likely to acquire infections because their infection-fighting white blood cells are reduced. It is important to take measures to avoid infections. When the white blood cell count drops too low, the doctor may prescribe medications called colony stimulating factors, which help white blood cells grow. Neupogen and Leukine are two colony stimulants that help fight infection. To reduce the risk of infection, thorough and frequent hand washing and safe food preparation are essential.

Platelets are blood cells that make the blood clot. When patients do not have enough platelets, they may bleed or bruise easily, even from small injuries. Patients with low blood platelets should take precautions to avoid injuries. Medicines such as aspirin and other **pain** relievers can affect platelets and slow down the clotting process.

Chemotherapy can cause irritation and dryness in the mouth and throat. Painful sores may form that can bleed and become infected. To help avoid mouth sores and irritation, the child should have a dental cleaning before chemotherapy begins, take care of the teeth and gums by brushing and flossing after every meal with a soft brush, rinse with a solution of baking soda and water, and avoid mouth washes or rinses that contain salt or alcohol. After use, the toothbrush should be rinsed thoroughly and stored in a dry place.

To help the child cope with a dry mouth, parents should encourage him or her to drink plenty of liquids. Popsicles or lollipops offer relief. Soft foods may be prepared, and dry foods may be moistened with sauce, butter, or gravy.

Tiredness, confusion, and depression can occur from chemotherapy's effect on certain central nervous system functions. The doctor should be notified if these symptoms occur.

Tests will be performed to monitor the effects of chemotherapy medications on the patient's kidneys and liver. Monitoring kidney and liver function helps to avoid potential damage or complications.

Normal results

The main goal of chemotherapy is to cure cancer. In fact, many cancers are cured by chemotherapy. Chemotherapy may be used in combination with surgery to keep a cancer from spreading to other parts of the body. Some widespread, fast-growing cancers are more difficult to treat. In these cases, chemotherapy may slow the growth of cancer cells.

The results of medical tests provide information so doctors can tell if the chemotherapy is working. Physical examination, blood tests, and x rays are used to check the effects of treatment on the cancer.

The possible outcomes of chemotherapy are:

- Complete remission or response. The cancer completely disappears; there is no evidence of disease. The course of chemotherapy is completed and the patient is tested regularly for a recurrence.

- Partial remission or response. The cancer shrinks in size but does not disappear. The same chemotherapy may be continued or a different combination of drugs may be given.

- Stabilization. The cancer does not grow or shrink. Other therapy options may be explored. A tumor may stay stabilized for many years.

- Progression. The cancer continues to grow. Other therapy options may be explored.

- A secondary malignancy may develop from the one being treated, and that second cancer may need additional chemotherapy or other treatment.

Parental concerns

Some important questions parents can ask about their child's course of chemotherapy include:

- What specific drugs will be given?

- How will the drugs be administered, and where will they be given?

- What are the potential benefits and risks of these drugs?

- What are some other possible treatments for the child's type of cancer?

- What is the standard care for the child's type of cancer?

- Are there any applicable clinical trials currently enrolling children?

- How many treatments will be needed? How long will they last?

- What are the potential side effects? When might they occur? How can they be treated or relieved? How serious are they likely to be? What side effects should be reported to the child's doctor?

- Can the child take other prescription or over-the-counter medications while receiving chemotherapy?

- What activities should be restricted or limited during the course of treatment?

- What is the long-term effect of chemotherapy?

Most school-age children can continue to go to school while receiving chemotherapy. However, the school schedule may need adjustment according to how the child feels and what side effects he or she experiences. During the cold and flu season, it may be best to keep the child home to prevent infection. If possible, treatments should be scheduled on a day when there is no school the next day, to provide time to recover.

To reduce the child's exposure to colds and illnesses and to help the child avoid infection:

• The child should avoid crowded areas, such as shopping malls.

• The child and entire **family** should be encouraged to wash hands frequently.

• People who are sick should be avoided, and they should be asked to refrain from visiting until they are healthy.

• The child should stay away from children who have recently received live virus vaccines such as chicken pox and oral **polio** since they may be contagious to people with a low blood cell count.

• Contact with animal litter boxes and waste, bird cages, and fish should be prevented.

• Contact with standing water, such as bird baths, flower vases, or humidifiers, should be prevented.

• Food must be safely prepared and cooked thoroughly to avoid food-borne illnesses.

• Parents should check with the child's doctor before scheduling immunizations, flu, or **pneumonia** vaccines.

Aspirin and products containing aspirin should be avoided, as they can affect platelet counts. Parents should check with the child's doctor before giving any **vitamins**, herbal supplements, and any over-the-counter medications.

The child's doctor should provide specific activity guidelines, including recommendations regarding the child's **sports** participation. Contact sports may be discouraged to reduce the risk of injury.

Treatment and care for a child with cancer can be costly, and some health insurance plans may not cover all expenses associated with a child's **hospitalization** or treatment. Help is available to cover medical expenses. The parents can discuss financial aid with the hospital. Some organizations provide financial assistance to children in need of chemotherapy or other cancer treatments.

Caring for a child with cancer is demanding. Support groups are available to help parents and caregivers cope with the challenges of providing care for children with special medical needs. It is important for parents to take care of themselves, too, by eating properly, exercis-

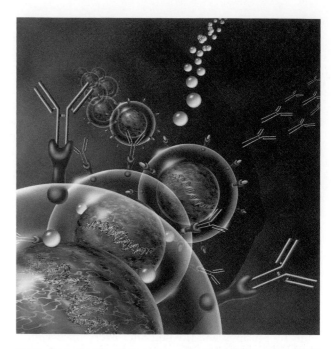

Illustration showing herceptin antibody, which inhibits DNA repair. When combined with chemotherapy (green balls), which damages DNA, the two inhibit the growth of cancer cells. (© *Art & Science/Custom Medical Stock Photo, Inc.*)

ing regularly, taking care of personal hygiene, keeping in contact with friends and family members for support, and managing stress by practicing relaxation techniques.

When to call the doctor

If a child has any of these symptoms, the parent or caregiver should call the child's doctor right away, as they could indicate an infection, blood clotting problem, or effect on the central nervous system:

• abdominal pain, vomiting, or diarrhea that awakens the child during the night

• persistent or severe abdominal pain, vomiting, or diarrhea

• unexplained weight loss

• fever

• chills or sweating

• frequent urgency to urinate, burning during urination, or change in color of urine

• rectal bleeding, or black or bloody bowel movements

• severe **cough** or sore throat

• redness, swelling, or tenderness, especially around a wound or sore

Adjuvant therapy—A treatment that is intended to aid primary treatment.

Alkaloid—A type of chemical commonly found in plants and often having medicinal properties.

Alkylating agent—A chemical that alters the composition of the genetic material of rapidly dividing cells, such as cancer cells, causing selective cell death; used as a chemotherapeutic agent.

Alopecia—The loss of hair, or baldness.

Anti-emetic—A preparation or medication that relieves nausea and vomiting. Cola syrup, ginger, and motion sickness medications are examples of antiemetics.

Antimetabolite—A drug or other substance that interferes with a cell's growth or ability to multiply.

Benign—In medical usage, benign is the opposite of malignant. It describes an abnormal growth that is stable, treatable, and generally not life-threatening.

Blood cell count—The number of red blood cells, white blood cells, and platelets in a sample of blood. Also called a complete blood count (CBC).

Bone marrow—The spongy tissue inside the large bones in the body that is responsible for making the red blood cells, most white blood cells, and platelets.

Catheter—A thin, hollow tube inserted into the body at specific points in order to inject or withdraw fluids from the body.

Chest x ray—Brief exposure of the chest to radiation to produce an image of the chest and its internal structures.

Infusion—Introduction of a substance directly into a vein or tissue by gravity flow.

Lymph nodes—Small, bean-shaped collections of tissue located throughout the lymphatic system. They produce cells and proteins that fight infection and filter lymph. Nodes are sometimes called lymph glands.

Malignant—Cells that have been altered such that they have lost normal control mechanisms and are capable of local invasion and spread to other areas of the body. Often used to describe a cancer.

Metastatic—The term used to describe a secondary cancer, or one that has spread from one area of the body to another.

Platelet—A cell-like particle in the blood that plays an important role in blood clotting. Platelets are activated when an injury causes a blood vessel to break. They change shape from round to spiny, "sticking" to the broken vessel wall and to each other to begin the clotting process. In addition to physically plugging breaks in blood vessel walls, platelets also release chemicals that promote clotting.

Radiation therapy—A cancer treatment that uses high-energy rays or particles to kill or weaken cancer cells. Radiation may be delivered externally or internally via surgically implanted pellets. Also called radiotherapy.

Red blood cells—Cells that carry hemoglobin (the molecule that transports oxygen) and help remove wastes from tissues throughout the body.

Remission—A disappearance of a disease and its symptoms. Complete remission means that all disease is gone. Partial remission means that the disease is significantly improved, but residual traces of the disease are still present. A remission may be due to treatment or may be spontaneous.

Tumor—A growth of tissue resulting from the uncontrolled proliferation of cells.

White blood cells—A group of several cell types that occur in the bloodstream and are essential for a properly functioning immune system; they fight infection.

- earaches, headaches, or stiff neck

- mouth sores, or blisters on the lips or skin

- sinus pain or pressure

- headaches

- changes in vision

- unexplained bleeding or bruising

- red spots under the skin

- confusion

- persistent depressed mood

- worsening overall health

Resources

BOOKS

Fischer, David A., et al. *The Cancer Chemotherapy Handbook.* London: C.V. Mosby, 2003.

McKay, Judith, and Nancee Hirano. *The Chemotherapy and Radiation Therapy Survivor's Guide,* 2nd ed. Oakland, CA: New Harbinger Publications, 1998.

Skeel, Roland T. K. *Handbook of Cancer Chemotherapy,* 6th ed. Philadelphia: Lippincott Williams & Wilkins, 2003.

PERIODICALS

"Chemotherapy and You: A Guide to Self-Help During Cancer Treatment." National Institutes of Health, National Cancer Institute. NIH Publication No. 03-1136, 2003.

"Gene Therapy and Chemotherapy Combine to Stop Breast Cancer and its Metastasis." *Gene Therapy Weekly* (Oct. 30, 2003): 2.

"Melatonin Improves the Efficacy of Chemotherapy and Quality of Life" *Biotech Week* (Sept. 10, 2003): 394.

"Obesity May Reduce Efficacy of High-Dose Chemotherapy." *Health Medicine Week* (Aug. 11, 2003): 385.

ORGANIZATIONS

American Cancer Society. 1599 Clifton Rd., NE, Atlanta, GA 30329-4251. (800) 227-2345 or (404) 320-3333. Web site:<www.cancer.org>.

Cancercare. (800) 813- 4673. Web site: <www.cancercare.org>.

National Cancer Institute. U.S. National Institutes of Health. Building 31, Room 10A31, 31 Center Drive, MSC 2580, Bethesda, MD 20892- 2580. (800) 422-6237. Web site: <www.cancer.gov>.

WEB SITES

CancerAnswers. Available online at: <www.canceranswers.com>.

Chemocare.com. Available online at: <www.chemocare.com>.

OncoLink. University of Pennsylvania Cancer Center. Available online at: <www.oncolink.upenn.edu>.

Planet Cancer. Available online at: <www.planetcancer.org>.

Toni Rizzo
Teresa G. Odle
Angela M. Costello

Chest physical therapy

Definition

Chest physical therapy is the term for a group of treatments designed to improve respiratory efficiency, promote expansion of the lungs, strengthen respiratory muscles, and eliminate secretions from the respiratory system.

Purpose

The purpose of chest physical therapy, also called chest physiotherapy, is to help patients breathe more freely and to get more oxygen into the body. Chest physical therapy includes postural drainage, chest percussion, chest vibration, turning, deep breathing exercises, and coughing. In the early 2000s, some newer devices, such as the positive expiratory pressure (PEP) valve and the flutter device, have been added to the various chest physical therapy techniques. Chest physical therapy is normally done in conjunction with other treatments to rid the airways of secretions. These other treatments include suctioning, nebulizer treatments, and the administering expectorant drugs.

Description

Good respiratory health is not possible without efficient clearance of secretions in the airway. In a healthy person, this is normally accomplished through two mechanisms: the mucociliary clearance system (MCS) and the ability to **cough**. There are many diseases and disabilities in children linked with poor lung health and an impaired ability to clear secretions. These include **cystic fibrosis**, **asthma**, **cerebral palsy**, **muscular dystrophy**, and various **immunodeficiency** disorders. When a child is unable to clear mucus, breathing becomes hard work. He or she must expend extra effort and energy in order to get oxygen. This difficulty can lead to a vicious cycle of recurrent episodes of inflammation, respiratory infections, lung damage, increased production of excess mucus, and possibly airway obstruction. Chest physical therapy is one way to reduce the risks of an inefficient clearance of airway secretions. Depending on the specific technique and health situation, chest physical therapy may be used on children from newborns to adolescents.

Various methods of chest physical therapy have been used since the early 1900s to help manage airway clearance disorders. The techniques have been refined since that time. The procedure may be performed by a respiratory therapist, a nurse, or a trained **family** member. However, chest physical therapy presents some challenges and requires skill and training in order to be safely and effectively performed.

Chest physical therapy is a method of clearing the airway of excess mucus. It is based on the theory that when various areas of the chest and back are percussed, shock waves are transmitted through the chest wall, loosening the airway secretions. If the child is positioned appropriately, the loosened secretions will then drain into the upper airways, where they can then be cleared using coughing and deep breathing techniques. The following techniques are all part of chest physical therapy.

Turning

Turning from side to side permits lung expansion. The child may turn on his or her own, or be turned by a caregiver. Turning should be done at a minimum of every two hours if the child is bedridden. The head of the bed can also be elevated in order to promote drainage.

Coughing

Coughing helps to break up secretions in the lungs so that the mucus can be expectorated or suctioned out if necessary. Patients sit upright and inhale deeply through the nose. They then exhale in short puffs or coughs. This procedure is repeated several times a day.

Deep breathing

Deep breathing helps expand the lungs and forces an improved distribution of the air into all sections of the lungs. The patient either sits in a chair or sits upright in bed and inhales then pushes the abdomen out to force maximum amounts of air into the lung. The abdomen is then contracted, and the patient exhales. Deep breathing exercises are done several times each day for short periods.

Because of the mind-body awareness required to perform coughing and deep breathing exercises, they are unsuitable for most children under the age of eight.

Postural drainage

Postural drainage uses the force of gravity to assist in effectively draining secretions from the smaller airways into the central airway where they can either be coughed up or suctioned out. The child is placed in a head- or chest-down position and is kept in this position for up to 15 minutes. To obtain the head-down positions, the use of a pillow, beanbag chair, or couch cushions can be helpful. Often, percussion and vibration are performed in conjunction with postural drainage.

Percussion

Percussion involves rhythmically striking the chest wall with cupped hands. It is also called cupping or clapping. The purpose of percussion is to break up thick secretions in the lungs so they can more easily be removed. Percussion is performed on each lung segment for one to two minutes at a time. Mechanical percussors are available and may be suitable for children over two years of age. The percussor is moved over one lobe of the lung for approximately five minutes, while the patient is encouraged to performing coughing and deep breathing techniques. This process is repeated until each segment of the lung is percussed.

Vibration

As with percussion, the purpose of vibration is to help break up lung secretions. Vibration can be either mechanical or manual. It is performed as the patient breathes deeply. When done manually, the person performing the vibration places his or her hands against the patient's chest and creates vibrations by quickly contracting and relaxing arm and shoulder muscles while the patient exhales. The procedure is repeated several times each day for about five exhalations.

Positive expiratory pressure (PEP)

PEP therapy has been extensively tested and is equivalent to standard chest physical therapy. It is an airway clearance method that is administered by applying a mechanical pressure device to the mouth. By breathing out with a moderate force through the resistance of the device, a positive pressure is created in the airways that helps to keep them open. This positive pressure permits airflow to reach beneath the areas of mucus obstruction and to move the mucus toward the larger airways where it can be expectorated. This technique may be suitable for alert, cooperative children over the age of four.

Flutter

The flutter valve is a hand-held mucus clearance device designed to combine positive expiratory pressure (PEP) with high frequency airway oscillations. The device looks like a pipe containing an inner cone that cradles a steel ball sealed with a perforated cover. Exhalation through the device results in a vibration of the airway walls, which in turn loosens secretions. It may be a suitable technique for children aged five years and over.

A child is considered to have responded positively to chest physical therapy if some, but not necessarily all, of the following changes occur:

- increased volume of sputum secretions
- changes in breath sounds
- improved chest x ray
- increased oxygenation of the blood as measured by arterial blood gas sampling
- the child's report of increased ease in breathing

Precautions

Chest physical therapy should not be performed on those children with the following:

- bleeding in the lungs
- head or neck injuries
- fractured ribs
- collapsed lungs
- acute asthma
- pulmonary embolism
- active hemorrhage
- some spinal injuries
- open **wounds** or burns

Preparation

The child should be taught about the necessity and rationale for chest physical therapy. It may be a challenge to get children to cooperate with the procedure. Providing a toy, watching a video, or giving a reward may be ways to encourage cooperation.

Aftercare

Many children may wish to perform **oral hygiene** measures after therapy to lessen the poor taste of the secretions they have expectorated.

Risks

The risks and complications associated with chest physical therapy are dependent upon the health of the child. Although chest physical therapy normally poses few problems, in some patients it may cause the following:

- oxygen deficiency if the head is kept lowered for drainage
- increased intracranial pressure
- temporary lowering of blood pressure
- bleeding in the lungs
- pain or injury to the ribs, muscles, or spine
- vomiting
- inhalation of secretions into the lungs
- heart irregularities

Parental concerns

Because chest physical therapy is often prescribed for childrven with chronic health problems, parents are

---

KEY TERMS

Coughing—In chest physical therapy, coughing is used to help break up secretions in the lungs so that the mucus can be suctioned out or expectorated. Patients sit upright and inhale deeply through the nose. They then exhale in short puffs or coughs.

Deep breathing—Deep breathing helps expand the lungs and forces better distribution of the air into all sections of the lung. The patient either sits in a chair or sits upright in bed and inhales, pushing the abdomen out to force maximum amounts of air into the lung. The abdomen is then contracted, and the patient exhales.

Mucociliary escalator—The coordinated action of tiny projections on the surfaces of cells lining the respiratory tract, which moves mucus up and out of the lungs.

Percussion—An assessment method in which the surface of the body is struck with the fingertips to obtain sounds that can be heard or vibrations that can be felt. It can determine the position, size, and consistency of an internal organ. It is performed over the chest to determine the presence of normal air content in the lungs, and over the abdomen to evaluate air in the loops of the intestine.

Postural drainage—The use of positioning to drain secretions from the bronchial tubes and lungs into the trachea or windpipe where they can either be coughed up or suctioned out.

Vibration—The treatment that is applied to help break up lung secretions. Vibration can be either mechanical or manual. It is performed as the patient breathes deeply. When done manually, the person performing the vibration places his or her hands against the patient's chest and creates vibrations by quickly contracting and relaxing arm and shoulder muscles while the patient exhales. The procedure is repeated several times each day for about five exhalations.

---

often required to learn the techniques so the procedure can be performed regularly at home. Many parents are fearful they might hurt their child or may perform the procedure incorrectly. They should be reassured that thousands of parents have learned how to perform chest physical therapy and do so safely and effectively.

Resources

PERIODICALS

"Maintaining Healthy Lungs: The Role of Airway Clearance Therapy." *The Exceptional Parent* 31 (August 2001): 126–33.

ORGANIZATIONS

Cystic Fibrosis Foundation. 6931 Arlington Road, Bethesda, MD 20814. Web site: <www.cff.org>.

WEB SITES

"Chest Physical Therapy." *Dr. Joseph F. Smith Medical Library*, 2003. Available online at <www.chclibrary.org/micromed/00042330.html> (accessed December 8, 2004).

"Cystic Fibrosis Center, Airway Clearance Center." *University of Wisconsin Medical School Department of Pediatrics*, 2004. Available online at <www.pediatrics.wisc.edu/patientcare/cf/acc.html> (December 8, 2004).

Deanna M. Swartout-Corbeil, RN
Tish Davidson A.M.

Chiari malformation

Definition

Chiari malformation is a congenital anomaly (a condition that is present at birth), in which parts of the brain protrude through the opening in the base of the skull into the spinal column.

Description

In order to explain the various components of Chiari malformation, it is helpful to describe a few parts of the brain and their functions. There are four major regions of the brain affected in Chiari malformation: the cerebellum, the brain stem, the ventricles, and the cerebrum. The cerebellum is located at the base of the skull and is divided into two parts or hemispheres with a third section that connects the hemispheres. Its main purpose is to coordinate body movements. The brain stem is located in front of the cerebellum and is composed of two parts. It regulates involuntary actions the body must conduct to survive, such as breathing, swallowing, and blinking the eyes. There are four ventricles in the brain. They are located above and in front of the cerebellum, and their function is to produce and circulate cerebrospinal fluid (CSF), the protective fluid that circulates through the brain and the spinal cord. The cerebrum is the largest part of the brain and is divided into two halves or hemispheres as well. It is located above the cerebellum and is responsible for the higher functions of the brain, such as thought. In Chiari malformation, one or more of these parts of the brain function improperly or are malformed. In addition to brain anomalies, Chiari malformation can also involve defects in the base of the skull and in the bony part of the spine.

There are four types of Chiari malformation. In Type I malformation, the lower portions of the cerebellum, known as the cerebellar tonsils, protrude through the opening in the skull known as the foramen magnum and into the spinal cord canal. It is often accompanied by a condition known as syringomyelia in which pockets of CSF form in the spinal cord. This type is usually diagnosed in **adolescence** or early adulthood when symptoms most commonly appear; however, with the availability of **magnetic resonance imaging** (MRI), many children are diagnosed at a much younger age.

Type II malformation, sometimes called Arnold Chiari malformation, is more severe than Type I and involves herniation of a more significant part of the cerebellum, part of the fourth ventricle, and parts of the brain stem. The brain tissues protrude farther into the spinal column than in Type I. These malformations are part of a larger syndrome seen in children with **spina bifida**, a condition in which the spine and spinal cord have not formed properly. Approximately 80–90 percent of children with Chiari malformation Type II also have **hydrocephalus**, a condition in which one or more of the ventricles becomes enlarged due to an accumulation of CSF. In these children, hydrocephalus is caused by obstruction of the fourth ventricle due to its herniation into the spinal column. Type II Chiari malformation may be diagnosed prenatally by ultrasound or shortly after birth during medical evaluation of the accompanying spina bifida.

In Type III malformation, parts of the cerebellum and the brain stem protrude into a spina bifida defect located at the base of the skull, on the neck. Type III malformation occurs rarely. Some neurologists do not consider it a Chiari malformation but rather a specific type of spina bifida called an encephalocervical meningocele.

Type IV malformation consists of an underdevelopment of the cerebrum and involves no herniation of brain tissue into the spinal area. As with Type III malformation, many neurologists do not consider this a Chiari malformation but rather cerebellar hypoplasia (underdevelopment). Both Type III and IV Chiari malformations are extremely rare, and this term is not often used in diagnosis of these conditions. The remainder of this entry only discusses Chiari malformation Types I and II.

Demographics

The true incidence of Chiari malformation is unknown. Some researchers believe that there may be far

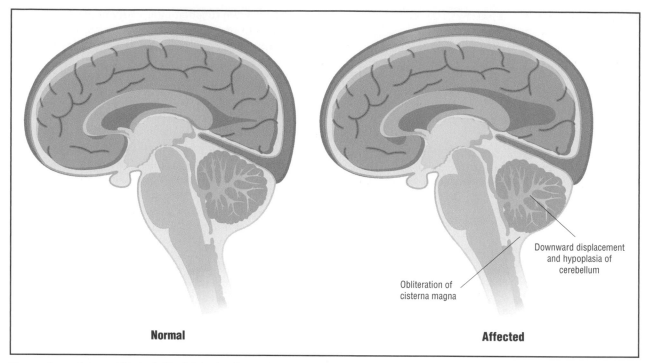

Comparison of normal brain (left) with brain affected by Arnold-Chiari malformation. *(Illustration by Argosy. Inc.)*

more cases of Type I malformation, in particular, than reported since many individuals with Type I malformation experience few if any symptoms. Most researchers agree that the rate of both Type I and Type II Chiari malformation is approximately 1 percent of all live births. Of those with Type I malformation, approximately 25 percent also have syringomyelia. However, the majority of all Chiari malformations are Type II and are almost exclusively associated with spina bifida defects. Spina bifida occurs in approximately one to two per 1,000 births. As access to imaging testing such as MRI has increased, so has the number of children diagnosed with Chiari malformation Type I. Therefore, the incidence of known Type I Chiari malformation is anticipated to increase.

Causes and symptoms

All Chiari malformations are present at birth, though symptoms may not begin until years later. The exact cause is unknown; however, it is suspected that, at some point during embryonic development, an increased pressure in the brain may cause brain structures to be displaced or moved into the spinal canal. Other possible causes for this malformation include exposure to harmful substances during fetal development or genetic factors. In general, there are several accepted theories of what may lead to problems that affect normal development of the brain: exposure to toxic or harmful substances; a lack of proper **vitamins** and nutrients in the mother's diet during pregnancy; infection; maternal use of prescription medi-

cation, illegal drugs, or alcohol; and genetic or familial factors. Chiari malformations are found in several known genetic disorders such as achondroplasia, Hadju-Cheney syndrome, and Klippel-Feil syndrome. Similarly, studies of families and identical **twins** with Chiari malformation show that the malformation occurs more often in these families than in families in which no member is affected. Another proposed cause for Chiari malformation is an abnormality in bone development. Chiari malformation may result because the cerebellum is of normal size, but the bones at the base of the skull are too small.

Symptoms of Chiari malformation vary according to the type of malformation. In Type I Chiari malformation, symptoms may begin anytime between infancy and early adulthood. Depending on when it is diagnosed, these symptoms may include blurred or double vision; involuntary eye movements; **headache**, usually at the base of the skull or upper neck which may become worse with coughing or straining; **scoliosis** or an abnormal curvature of the spine; **dizziness** and impaired muscle coordination; low muscle tone; alteration of the voice or a high-pitched cry; frequent respiratory tract infections, **vomiting** and difficulty swallowing; drop attacks (a sudden loss of muscle control that results in a collapse to the floor); and central cord syndrome, a pattern of reduced sensation and weakness in the arms.

Symptoms of Type II Chiari malformation include those that occur in Type I malformation. Victims may also exhibit vocal cord paralysis and episodes of apnea (a cessation of breathing sometimes requiring resuscitation). Type II malformation occurs almost exclusively with spina bifida, which causes symptoms that may include paralysis of the lower extremities (and less often, the upper limbs), and bowel and bladder dysfunction. If the child has hydrocephalus, these symptoms may worsen and can be fatal unless the hydrocephalus is treated.

Diagnosis

In some children Chiari malformation is evident at birth, especially Type II malformation. Type I malformations may have no symptoms for years. When symptoms are present, they may be very subtle. A complete medical history and physical exam will be conducted by the physician. If the doctor suspects a Chiari malformation, magnetic resonance imaging (MRI) is the most helpful diagnostic tool. MRI is a diagnostic procedure in which high-powered magnets, radio frequencies, and computers are used to produce detailed images of structures within the body. It is painless, noninvasive, and allows doctors to see the brain and spinal cord from several different angles. A **computed tomography** scan (CAT scan) may also be performed. In this imaging procedure, a combination of x ray and computer technology produces cross-sectional images of the body. This procedure is most helpful in assessing abnormalities of the skull and backbone associated with Chiari malformation. Ultrasonography (ultrasound) is also routinely used to evaluate the fetus before birth and in the period shortly after birth. Ultrasonography is a diagnostic procedure in which ultrasonic waves are used to visualize internal organs. This procedure is commonly used for diagnosis and follow-up care of hydrocephalus.

Prognosis

The prognosis for Chiari malformation varies depending on which type of malformation is present. For children and adolescents with Type I malformation, corrective surgery may be highly effective at relieving symptoms related to compression of the brain, such as vision problems; headaches; difficulties with balance, coordination, and swallowing; and frequent respiratory tract infections. Symptoms related to the fluid-filled sacs in the spine may be less responsive to surgery. Scoliosis will most likely stabilize and may improve in a significant portion of patients. Central cord syndrome, however, is less successfully corrected by surgery with only about one third of patients experiencing lasting improvement. Generally, in those with Type I Chiari malformation, younger children experience the most benefit from surgical interventions, and approximately 78 percent of all patients who have surgical procedures to correct the malformation have a better outcome than those who have no surgical intervention at all. Some patients may continue to experience neurological symptoms, but the long term prognosis for children with this type of Chiari malformation is excellent, including normal development and intellectual functioning.

The majority of all Chiari malformations are Type II. Children with Chiari II malformation have a much poorer prognosis than those with Type I malformation. Because of the associated conditions of spina bifida and hydrocephalus, these children are usually quite ill. Multiple surgeries are required, and almost 50 percent of these children die at an early age. Of those who survive, many have developmental delays and impaired intellectual functioning.

Prevention

Chiari malformation is a congenital anomaly, and no method of prevention is known.

Parental concerns

Chiari malformation can have a significant impact on both the child and the **family**. The full extent of problems associated with Chiari malformation may not be evident at birth, especially for children with Type I malformation. Children with Type I malformation may experience months of subtle but progressive symptoms before a diagnosis is made. Parents must play an active role in securing appropriate health care and an accurate diagnosis for their child. The symptoms of Chiari Type I malformation when observed individually may not seem significant. However, these symptoms form the basis of the initial diagnosis. Parents should document all unusual events their child experiences such as dizziness, headaches, slurred speech, fainting spells, and **numbness** or **pain** in the arms and legs. The first step for diagnosing Chiari malformation Type I is an accurate and detailed history and physical examination. Following this, an MRI is performed. The MRI usually provides a definitive diagnosis and helps determine if the child is a candidate for decompression surgery.

Medical treatment is a multidisciplinary team effort often involving the pediatrician, a neurosurgeon, a rhematologist, and a neurologist. Once diagnosed, the child and family face the prospect of surgery and recuperation. A child will typically be hospitalized for four to seven days after surgery. The prognosis for children with Chiari malformation Type I is very good. Over 70 percent of those who have surgery to correct Type I malformation experience a significant reduction in symptoms; however, there are some symptoms that may not resolve. There may be continued discomfort in the neck and lower head, and some muscle weakness may be permanent.

KEY TERMS

Brain stem—The part of the brain that is continuous with the spinal cord and controls most basic life functions. It is the last part of the brain that is destroyed by Alzheimer's disease.

Catheter—A thin, hollow tube inserted into the body at specific points in order to inject or withdraw fluids from the body.

Cerebellum—The part of the brain involved in the coordination of movement, walking, and balance.

Cerebrospinal fluid—The clear, normally colorless fluid that fills the brain cavities (ventricles), the sub-arachnoid space around the brain, and the spinal cord and acts as a shock absorber.

Cerebrum—The largest section of the brain, which is responsible for such higher functions as speech, thought, vision, and memory.

Computed tomography (CT)—An imaging technique in which cross-sectional x rays of the body are compiled to create a three-dimensional image of the body's internal structures; also called computed axial tomography.

Congenital—Present at birth.

Dura mater—The strongest and outermost of three membranes that protect the brain, spinal cord, and nerves of the cauda equina.

Embryonic—Early stages of life in the uterus.

Foramen magnum—The opening at the base of the skull, through which the spinal cord and the brain-stem pass.

Herniation—Bulging of tissue through opening in a membrane, muscle, or bone.

Hydrocephalus—An abnormal accumulation of cerebrospinal fluid within the brain. This accumulation can be harmful by pressing on brain structures, and damaging them.

Hypoplasia—An underdeveloped or incomplete tissue or organ usually due to a decrease in the number of cells.

Magnetic resonance imaging (MRI)—An imaging technique that uses a large circular magnet and radio waves to generate signals from atoms in the body. These signals are used to construct detailed images of internal body structures and organs, including the brain.

Neurologist—A doctor who specializes in disorders of the nervous system, including the brain, spinal cord, and nerves.

Neurosurgeon—Physician who performs surgery on the nervous system.

Rhematologist—A physician who specializes in the treatment of disorders of the connective tissue structures, such as the joints and related structures.

Scoliosis—An abnormal, side-to-side curvature of the spine.

Syringomyelia—Excessive fluid in the spinal cord.

Syrinx—A tubular fluid-filled cavity within the spine.

Ultrasonography—A medical test in which sound waves are directed against internal structures in the body. As sound waves bounce off the internal structure, they create an image on a video screen. Ultrasonography is often used to diagnose fetal abnormalities, gallstones, heart defects, and tumors. Also called ultrasound imaging.

Ventricles—Four cavities within the brain that produce and maintain the cerebrospinal fluid that cushions and protects the brain and spinal cord.

Many children may also experience a recurrence of symptoms within two years of surgery. For this reason, parents must continue follow-up treatment and care for at least two years following surgery. The availability of MRI technology has led to diagnosis of younger children with Type I malformation and improved the quality of life for these children. The earlier treatment can begin, the better outcome these children experience.

When discussing Chiari malformation and surgery with their child, parents should use words the child can understand. How illness and surgery are discussed depends on the age of the child. A younger child needs short simple answers, a school-aged child may understand more complicated explanations, and an adolescent will probably be present at all meetings with doctors and should be encouraged to talk to healthcare providers him- or herself. Regardless of the age of the child, mental health experts agree that children should be told about medical procedures and surgeries before they occur. Depending on the age of the child, parents may choose to talk to him a day before or weeks ahead. The child may have questions. Parents can answer them simply and honestly. While a younger child may ask many questions, an adolescent may be reluctant to appear ignorant and may not express his **fear** or confusion. Parents should encourage an adolescent to discuss all concerns and should be prepared to explain and reassure. Many doctors and children's hospitals have brochures to assist parents when discussing illness and surgery with their child.

Children with Chiari II malformation have a much poorer prognosis than those with Type I malformation and will usually be quite ill. Multiple surgeries are required, and many of these children die at an early age. All of these factors have a significant impact on the family. These children require multiple services, including surgery, physical and occupational therapy, and **special education**. Many have developmental delays and impaired intellectual functioning in addition to the physical limitations often caused by the accompanying spina bifida. Parents may need support services in addition to the team of healthcare providers. Many parents find it helpful to participate in a support group of other families of children with special needs. Most states and children's hospitals offer these services and know of organizations in the area that may help these families. Parents can work closely with the hospital's social work department to learn more about available resources.

See also Hydrocephalus; Spina bifida.

Resources

BOOKS

Behrman, Richard E., Robert M. Kliegman, and Hal B. Jenson, eds. *Nelson Textbook of Pediatrics*, 16th ed. Philadelphia: W. B. Saunders Company, 2000.

Parker, James N., et al. *The Official Parent's Sourcebook on Chiari Malformation.* Boulder, CO: netLibrary, 2003.

Rudolph, Colin D., and Abraham M. Rudolph, eds. *Rudolph's Pediatrics*, 21st ed. New York: McGraw-Hill, 2003.

WEB SITES

"Chiari Malformation Presentation." *Hyman-Newman Institute for Neurology and Neurosurgery.* Available online at <http://neurosurgery.org/ chiari_presentation.htm> (accessed July 29, 2004).

Incesu, Lutfi, Anil Khosia, and Michael R. Aiello. "Chiari II Malformation." Available online at <www.emedicine.com/RADIO/topic150.htm> (accessed October 25, 2004).

Siddiqi, Nasir H., and Fred J. Laine. "Chiari I Malformation." *The American Association of Neurological Surgeons/ Congress of Neurological Surgeons*, March 15, 2004. Available online at <www.emedicine.com/RADIO/ topic149.htm> (accessed October 25, 2004).

Deborah L. Nurmi, MS

Chickenpox

Definition

Chickenpox (also called varicella) is a common, extremely infectious, rash-producing childhood disease that also affects adults on occasion.

Description

Chickenpox is caused by the varicella-zoster virus (a member of the herpes virus family), which is spread through the air or by direct contact with an infected person. It produces an itchy, blistery rash that typically lasts about a week and is sometimes accompanied by a **fever** or other symptoms. A single attack of chickenpox almost always brings lifelong immunity against the disease. Because the symptoms of chickenpox are easily recognized and in most cases merely unpleasant rather than dangerous, treatment can almost always be carried out at home. Severe complications can develop, however, and professional medical attention is essential in some circumstances.

Once someone has been infected with the virus, an incubation period of about 10 to 21 days passes before symptoms begin. The period during which infected people are able to spread the disease is believed to start one or two days before the rash breaks out and to continue until all the blisters have formed scabs, which usually happens four to seven days after the rash breaks out but may be longer in adolescents and adults. For this reason, doctors recommend keeping children with chickenpox away from school for about a week. It is not necessary, however, to wait until all the scabs have fallen off.

Prior to the use of the varicella vaccine, chickenpox was a typical part of growing up for most children in the industrialized world. The disease can strike at any age, but throughout the twentieth century by ages nine or ten about 80 to 90 percent of American children had already been infected. U.S. children living in rural areas and many foreign-born children were less likely to be immune. Study results reported by the Centers for Disease Control and Prevention (CDC) indicate that more than 90 percent of American adults are immune to the chickenpox virus. Adults, however, are much more likely than children to suffer dangerous complications. More than half of all chickenpox deaths occur among adults.

Demographics

Before the varicella vaccine (Varivax) was released for use in 1995, nearly all of the 4 million children born each year in the United States contracted chickenpox, resulting in **hospitalization** in five of every 1,000 cases and 100 deaths. Because almost every case of chickenpox, no matter how mild, leads to lifelong protection against further attacks, adults account for less than 5 percent of all cases in the United States.

Causes and symptoms

A case of chickenpox usually starts without warning or with only a mild fever and a slight feeling of unwellness. Within a few hours or days small red spots begin to appear on the scalp, neck, or upper half of the trunk. After another 12 to 24 hours the spots typically become itchy, fluid-filled bumps called vesicles, which continue to appear in crops for the next two to five days. In any area of skin, lesions of a variety of stages can be seen. These blisters can spread to cover much of the skin, and in some cases also may be found inside the mouth, nose, ears, vagina, or rectum. Some people develop only a few blisters, but in most cases the number reaches 250 to 500. The blisters soon begin to form scabs and fall off. Scarring usually does not occur unless the blisters have been scratched and become infected. Occasionally a minor and temporary darkening of the skin (called hyperpigmentation) is noticed around some of the blisters. The degree of itchiness can range from barely noticeable to extreme. Some chickenpox sufferers also have headaches, abdominal **pain**, or a fever. Full recovery usually takes five to ten days after the first symptoms appear. Again, the most severe cases of the disease tend to be found among older children and adults.

Although for most people chickenpox is no more than a matter of a few days' discomfort, some groups are at risk for developing complications, the most common of which are bacterial infections of the blisters, **pneumonia**, **dehydration**, **encephalitis**, and hepatitis. Some of the groups at greater risk are:

- Infants: Complications occur much more often among children younger than one year old than among older children. The threat is greatest to newborns, who are more at risk of death from chickenpox than any other group. Under certain circumstances, children born to mothers who contract chickenpox just prior to delivery face an increased possibility of dangerous consequences, including brain damage and death. If the infection occurs during early pregnancy, there is a small (less than 5%) risk of congenital abnormalities.

- Immunocompromised children: Children whose immune systems have been weakened by a genetic disorder, disease, or medical treatment usually experience the most severe symptoms of any group. They have the second-highest rate of death from chickenpox.

- Adults and children 15 and older: Among this group, the typical symptoms of chickenpox tend to strike with greater force, and the risk of complications is much higher than among young children.

Immediate medical help should always be sought when anyone in these high-risk groups contracts the disease.

Diagnosis

Where children are concerned, especially those with recent exposure to the disease, diagnosis can usually be made at home, by a school nurse, or by a doctor over the telephone if the child's parent or caregiver is unsure that the disease is chickenpox.

Treatment

With children, treatment usually takes place in the home and focuses on reducing discomfort and fever. Because chickenpox is a viral disease, **antibiotics** are ineffective against it.

Applying wet compresses or bathing the child in cool or lukewarm water once a day can help the itch. Adding four to eight ounces of baking soda or one or two cups of oatmeal to the bath is a good idea (oatmeal bath packets are sold by pharmacies). Only mild soap should be used in the bath. Patting, not rubbing, is recommended for drying the child off, to prevent irritating the blisters. Calamine lotion (and some other kinds of lotions) also reduces itchiness. Because scratching can cause blisters to become infected and lead to scarring, the child's nails should be cut short. Of course, older children need to be warned not to scratch. For babies, light mittens or socks on the hands can help guard against scratching.

If mouth blisters make eating or drinking an unpleasant experience, cold drinks and soft, bland foods can ease the child's discomfort. Painful genital blisters can be treated with an anesthetic cream recommended by a doctor or pharmacist. Antibiotics often are prescribed if blisters become infected.

Fever and discomfort can be reduced by **acetaminophen** or another medication that does not contain aspirin. Aspirin and any medications that contain aspirin or other salicylates must not be used with chickenpox, for they appear to increase the chances of developing **Reye's syndrome**. The best idea is for a parent to consult a doctor or pharmacist to confirm which medications are safe.

Immunocompromised chickenpox sufferers are sometimes given an antiviral drug called acyclovir (Zovirax). Studies have shown that Zovirax also lessens the symptoms of otherwise healthy children and adults who contract chickenpox, but the notion that it should be

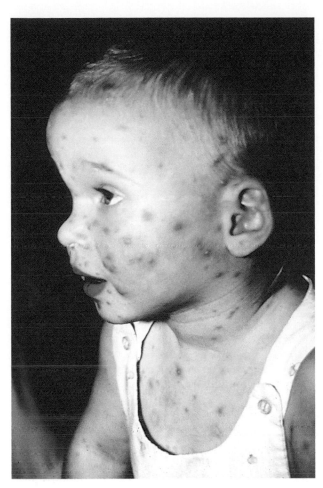

Child with chickenpox on the face and chest. *(Photograph by John D. Cunningham. Visuals Unlimited.)*

used to treat the disease among the general population, especially in children, is controversial.

Prognosis

Most cases of chickenpox run their course within a week without causing lasting harm. However, there is one long-term consequence of chickenpox that strikes about 20 percent of the population, particularly people 50 and older. Like all herpes viruses, the varicella-zoster virus never leaves the body after an episode of chickenpox. It lies dormant in the nerve cells, where it may be reactivated years later by disease or age-related weakening of the immune system. The result is shingles (also called herpes zoster), a painful nerve inflammation, accompanied by a rash that usually affects the trunk or the face for ten days or more. Especially in the elderly, pain, called postherpetic neuralgia, may persist at the site of the shingles for months or years. As of 2004, two relatively newer drugs for treatment of shingles are valacyclovir (Valtrex) and famciclovir (Famvir), both of which

stop the replication of herpes zoster when administered within 72 hours of appearance of the rash. The effectiveness of these two drugs in immunocompromised patients has not been established, and Famvir was not recommended for patients under 18 years.

Prevention

A substance known as varicella-zoster immune globulin (VZIG), which reduces the severity of chickenpox symptoms, is as of 2004 available to treat immunocompromised children and others at high risk of developing complications. It is administered by injection within 96 hours of known or suspected exposure to the disease and is not useful after that. VZIG is produced as a gamma globulin from blood of recently infected individuals.

A vaccine for chickenpox became available in the United States in 1995 under the name Varivax. Varivax is a live, attenuated (weakened) virus vaccine. It has been proven to be 85 percent effective for preventing all cases of chickenpox and close to 100 percent effective in preventing severe cases. Side effects are normally limited to occasional soreness or redness at the injection site. CDC guidelines state that the vaccine should be given to all children (with the exception of certain high-risk groups) at 12 to 18 months of age, preferably when they receive their measles-mumps-rubella vaccine. For older children, up to age 12, the CDC recommends **vaccination** when a reliable determination that the child in question has already had chickenpox cannot be made. Vaccination also is recommended for any older child or adult considered susceptible to the disease, particularly those, such as healthcare workers and women of childbearing age, who face a greater likelihood of severe illness or transmitting infection. A single dose of the vaccine was once thought sufficient for children up to age 12; older children and adults received a second dose four to eight weeks later. However, an outbreak at a daycare center in 2000 brought concern in the medical community about a second vaccination for younger children, since many of the affected children had been vaccinated. Researchers began recommending a second vaccination in 2002. In 1997, the cost of two adult doses of the vaccine in the United States was about $80. Although this cost was not always covered by health insurance plans, children up to age 18 without access to the appropriate coverage could be vaccinated free of charge through the federal Vaccines for Children program. Varivax is not given to patients who already have overt signs of the disease. It was once thought unsafe for children with chronic kidney disease, but a 2003 report said the vaccination was safe in these children. The finding is important, since even chickenpox can be a serious complication in children who must undergo a kidney transplant.

KEY TERMS

Acetaminophen—A drug used for pain relief as well as to decrease fever. A common trade name for the drug is Tylenol.

Acyclovir—An antiviral drug, available under the trade name Zovirax, used for combating chickenpox and other herpes viruses.

Dehydration—An excessive loss of water from the body. It may follow vomiting, prolonged diarrhea, or excessive sweating.

Encephalitis—Inflammation of the brain, usually caused by a virus. The inflammation may interfere with normal brain function and may cause seizures, sleepiness, confusion, personality changes, weakness in one or more parts of the body, and even coma.

Hepatitis—An inflammation of the liver, with accompanying liver cell damage or cell death, caused most frequently by viral infection, but also by certain drugs, chemicals, or poisons. May be either acute (of limited duration) or chronic (continuing). Symptoms include jaundice, nausea, vomiting, loss of appetite, tenderness in the right upper abdomen, aching muscles, and joint pain. In severe cases, liver failure may result.

Immune system—The system of specialized organs, lymph nodes, and blood cells throughout the body that work together to defend the body against foreign invaders (bacteria, viruses, fungi, etc.).

Immunocompromised—A state in which the immune system is suppressed or not functioning properly.

Pneumonia—An infection in which the lungs become inflamed. It can be caused by nearly any class of organism known to cause human infections, including bacteria, viruses, fungi, and parasites.

Pus—A thick, yellowish or greenish fluid composed of the remains of dead white blood cells, pathogens, and decomposed cellular debris. It is most often associated with bacterial infection.

Reye's syndrome—A serious, life-threatening illness in children, usually developing after a bout of flu or chickenpox, and often associated with the use of aspirin. Symptoms include uncontrollable vomiting, often with lethargy, memory loss, disorientation, or delirium. Swelling of the brain may cause seizures, coma, and in severe cases, death.

Salicylates—A group of drugs that includes aspirin and related compounds. Salicylates are used to relieve pain, reduce inflammation, and lower fever.

Shingles—An disease caused by an infection with the *Herpes zoster* virus, the same virus that causes chickenpox. Symptoms of shingles include pain and blisters along one nerve, usually on the face, chest, stomach, or back.

Trunk—That part of the body that does not include the head, arms, and legs. Also called the torso.

Varicella zoster—The virus that causes chickenpox (varicella).

Varicella-zoster immune globulin—A substance that can reduce the severity of chickenpox symptoms.

Varivax—The brand name for varicella virus vaccine live, an immunizing agent used to prevent infection by the *Herpes (Varicella) zoster* virus. The vaccine works by causing the body to produce its own protection (antibodies) against the virus.

Virus—A small infectious agent consisting of a core of genetic material (DNA or RNA) surrounded by a shell of protein. A virus needs a living cell to reproduce.

The vaccine also is not recommended for pregnant women, and women should delay pregnancy for three months following a complete vaccination. The vaccine is useful when given early after exposure to chickenpox and, if given in the midst of the incubation period, it can be preventative. The Infectious Diseases Society of America stated in 2000 that immunization is recommended for all adults who have never had chickenpox.

While there was initial concern regarding the vaccine's safety and effectiveness when first released, the vaccination is in the early 2000s gaining acceptance as numerous states require it for admittance into daycare or public school. In 2000, 59 percent of toddlers in the United States were immunized; up from 43.2 percent in 1998. A study published in 2001 indicates that the varicella vaccine is highly effective when used in clinical practice. Although evidence has not ruled out a booster shot later in life, all research addressing the vaccine's effectiveness throughout its six-year use indicates that chickenpox may be the first human herpes virus to be wiped out. Although initial concerns questioned if the vaccination might make shingles more likely, studies are beginning in the early 2000s to show the effectiveness of the vaccine in reducing cases of that disease.

Parental concerns

A doctor should be called immediately if any of the following occur:

- The child's fever goes above 102°F (38.9°C) or takes more than four days to disappear.

- The child's blisters appear infected. Signs of infection include leakage of pus from the blisters or excessive redness, warmth, tenderness, or swelling around the blisters.

- The child seems nervous, confused, unresponsive, or unusually sleepy; complains of a stiff neck or severe **headache**; shows signs of poor balance or has trouble walking; finds bright lights hard to look at; is having breathing problems or is coughing a lot; is complaining of chest pain; is **vomiting** repeatedly; or is having convulsions. These may be signs of Reye's syndrome or encephalitis, two rare but potentially dangerous conditions.

Resources

BOOKS

Arvin, Ann M. "Varicella-zoster Virus." In *Principles and Practice of Pediatric Infectious Diseases*, 2nd ed. Edited by Sarah S. Long et al. St. Louis, MO: Elsevier, 2003.

Myers, Martin G., et al. "Varicella-Zoster Virus." In *Nelson Textbook of Pediatrics*. Edited by Richard E. Behrman et al. Philadelphia: Saunders, 2004.

PERIODICALS

Arvin, Ann M. "Varicella Vaccine: The First Six Years." *New England Journal of Medicine* (March 2001).

"Chickenpox Vaccine OK for Pediatric Patients." *Vaccine Weekly* (January 22, 2003): 25.

Henderson, C. W. "Chickenpox Immunization Confirmed Effective in Adults." *Vaccine Weekly* (September 2000): 22.

"Study: Two Vaccines Work Best." *Vaccine Weekly* (January 8, 2003): 14.

ORGANIZATIONS

Centers for Disease Control and Prevention. 1600 Clifton Rd., NE, Atlanta, GA 30333. Web site: <www.cdc.gov>.

WEB SITES

"Chickenpox." *MedlinePlus.* Available online at <www.nlm.nih.gov/medlineplus/chickenpox.html> (accessed December 25, 2004).

Beth A. Kapes
Teresa G. Odle
Rosalyn Carson-DeWitt, MD

Chickenpox vaccine

Definition

Chickenpox vaccine or varicella zoster vaccine (VZV) is an injection that protects children from contracting chickenpox (varicella), one of the most common childhood diseases.

Description

VZV consists of living but attenuated (weakened) varicella zoster, the virus that causes chickenpox. The weakened virus induces a child's immune system to develop antibodies against the varicella virus without causing the disease. Thus it prevents children from contracting chickenpox. Prior to the introduction of VZV, approximately 4 million Americans contracted chickenpox each year, and 95 percent of children contracted the disease before the age of 18. The vaccine first became available in the United States in 1995 and is produced by Merck & Company under the trade name Varivax.

Vaccine development

A sample of the varicella zoster virus was isolated from the blood of a three-year-old Japanese boy in 1972. A Japanese researcher, Michiaki Takahashi, attenuated the virus by growing it in various animal and human cell cultures. He then tested it on children and found that it was effective in preventing chickenpox. This "Oka" varicella strain, named after the original infected child, was licensed by Merck in 1981 and used to develop Varivax. The vaccine was clinically tested for safety and effectiveness.

Producing sufficient quantities of the vaccine to immunize all children against chickenpox has proven to be a major obstacle. Weakened viruses for vaccines are grown in cell cultures. However unlike other weakened viruses, varicella zoster remains in the cell rather than being secreted from the cell and collected from the culture medium. Thus the infected cells must be collected and broken open by ultrasound. The released virus is extremely sensitive to heat caused by ultrasound, and Merck scientists had to determine the precise conditions for opening the cells and releasing the virus unharmed. The company built a new production facility for Varivax that uses robots to strictly control the ultrasound procedure.

In addition to the live attenuated varicella virus, Varivax contains:

- bovine (cow) albumin or serum

- sodium ethylenediamine tetraacidic acid (EDTA)

- gelatin

- monosodium glutamate

- protein from the human cell line MRC-5

- neomycin, an antibiotic

- phosphate buffers

- sodium chloride

- sucrose

Effectiveness

VZV is considered to be safe and 70 to 90 percent effective. Vaccinated children who do contract chickenpox usually have milder symptoms. The vaccine also prevents chickenpox in children exposed to the virus three to five days prior to **vaccination**.

The Centers for Disease Control and Prevention (CDC), the American Academy of Pediatrics, and the American Academy of Family Physicians all recommend that healthy children be vaccinated against chickenpox. In 2001 child-care facilities and public schools began phasing in a varicella vaccination requirement for enrollment. By 2002, some 81 percent of American children had been vaccinated with VZV, and the CDC determined that the number of chickenpox cases had declined substantially. The CDC expects that widespread childhood vaccination against chickenpox will further reduce the incidence of the virus in the general population. This, in turn, will reduce the incidence of chickenpox among those who cannot receive VZV, including children who are most at risk for serious complications from the disease.

Breakthrough infections

As of 2004 it was unclear whether VZV provided life-long immunity to chickenpox. The U.S. Food and Drug Administration (FDA) required Merck to follow several thousand children for 15 years, to determine the long-term effects of the vaccine and whether additional booster shots of VZV would be necessary. It is possible that vaccinated children obtain booster immune effects through repeated contact with the virus from infected children.

Early evidence suggested that the rate of breakthrough chickenpox infections (infections in previously vaccinated children) was about 2 percent annually and that the likelihood of such infections did not increase with time after vaccination. Breakthrough infections in vaccinated children usually are very mild. They last only a few days and there are fewer than 50 lesions on the child's body and little or no **fever**. It is not clear whether breakthrough chickenpox infections are less contagious than infections in unvaccinated children.

Some physicians remain reluctant to vaccinate against an usually mild childhood disease such as chickenpox. Some also are concerned that vaccinated children may contract chickenpox as adults when it can be a much more serious disease with a 20 percent higher risk of death.

Shingles

Although children who have had chickenpox are immune to the disease and cannot contract it a second time, the varicella zoster virus can remain inactive in the human body. These dormant viruses are concentrated in nerve cells near the spinal cord and may reactivate in adults, causing the disease herpes zoster or shingles. The reactivated virus further infects nerve cells, causing severe **pain**, burning, or **itching**. Shingles usually occurs in people over the age of 50 and may be associated with a weakening immune system.

It is not known whether the weakened virus used for VZV can remain dormant in the body, eventually causing shingles in the same way that the naturally occurring varicella virus can. In 1998 the CDC found 2.6 cases of post-vaccination herpes zoster for every 100,000 distributed doses of VZV. In contrast there were 68 cases of herpes zoster in healthy children under age 20, following natural infection with varicella. However, as of 2004, it is too early to determine whether vaccinated children are more or less likely to develop shingles in adulthood as compared with adults who were naturally infected with chickenpox as children.

A 2002 study indicated that exposure to varicella is much higher in adults living with children and that such exposure substantially boosts immunity against shingles. The authors of the study predicted that mass vaccination against varicella will create an epidemic of herpes zoster, affecting as many as 50 percent of those who were between the ages of ten and 44 at the time that the vaccine was introduced.

General use

Consequences of chickenpox

Chickenpox is highly contagious and easily transmitted among children through personal contact, coughing, or sneezing. The disease is characterized by red spots on the face, chest, back, and other body parts. These spots fill with fluid, rupture, and crust over. Symptoms of chickenpox may not appear for as long as two to three weeks following infection. The virus is contagious from one or two days before the first rash appears until the blisters have formed complete scabs and no new rash has appeared for 24 hours. This may take from five days to two weeks. Thus the varicella virus can spread very rapidly within families and among groups of children in school and daycare.

In most instances chickenpox is not a serious disease, although the itchy lesions and fever and other mild flu-like symptoms may cause a week or two of discomfort. However the disease can have serious complications. Scratching the pox can cause bacterial infection that can lead to permanent scars. In rare cases chickenpox can lead to the following:

- muscle aches
- sore throat
- ear infections
- **pneumonia**
- arthritis
- neurological symptoms, including shakiness
- **encephalitis**, an inflammation of the brain

In the United States more children die of chickenpox than of any other disease that can be prevented by a vaccine. Prior to the introduction of VZV, there were about 100 deaths and 12,000 hospitalizations annually as a result of chickenpox infections. Approximately 40 percent of the deaths and 60 percent of the hospitalizations occurred in children under age ten. Teenagers and adults, as well as children with leukemia or other cancers or with impaired immune systems, are at particular risk for severe chickenpox and its complications. Babies whose mothers contracted chickenpox during pregnancy are at risk for multiple birth defects. Babies whose mothers contract chickenpox shortly before or after giving birth are at risk of developing a severe form of the disease. As many as 5 percent of these babies die. Most high-risk children and non-immune adults contract chickenpox from unvaccinated children.

Children with chickenpox miss an average of five to six days of school and their parents miss an average of three to four days of work while caring for them. The CDC estimates that, including direct medical costs and indirect societal costs, $5.40 is saved for every $1.00 spent on childhood VZV immunization.

Vaccine administration

It is recommended that babies receive a single-dose injection of Varivax between the ages of 12 and 18 months, usually at the same time that they receive their first **measles**, **mumps**, and **rubella** (MMR) vaccine. Children and adolescents who have not already had chickenpox can be vaccinated at any time. However, adolescents aged 13 or older, as well as adults, require two doses of Varivax, four to eight weeks apart, to obtain the same level of immunity as children under 13. The reason for this is not known.

VZV usually is covered by health insurance. In the United States the Vaccines for Children program covers the cost of chickenpox vaccination for children without health insurance and for specific other groups of children, including Native Americans.

Precautions

In rare instances it is possible to contract the weakened vaccine strain of varicella from a recently vaccinated child.

Healthy children

Children on long-term steroids for any reason, including **asthma**, should consult their physician about the timing of the vaccination. Children should not receive VZV if the following applies:

- They are allergic to gelatin or the antibiotic neomycin.
- They have had a serious reaction to a previous varicella vaccination.
- They are taking aspirin or other salicylates that have the remote possibility of causing Reye's syndrome.

In addition, infants under one year and pregnant teenagers should not receive VZV. Females should not become pregnant within one month of receiving VZV.

Children at high risk for severe chickenpox or its complications, including newborns and premature infants exposed to chickenpox after birth, often are given varicella-zoster immune globulin (VZIG). VZIG is made from the blood serum of people with high antibody levels against the varicella virus. It must be administered within 96 hours of exposure to chickenpox, and it results in a passive immunity against the disease for about three months.

Additional CDC precautions for administrating VZV pertain to the following groups of children:

- those with a family history of immunodeficiency
- those who have had a blood transfusion or received other blood or serum products within the past five months

• those who have received antibody-containing products, including VZIG or other immune globulin, within the past 11 months

Children with medical conditions

Medical conditions that preclude vaccination against chickenpox include active, untreated **tuberculosis** and any other moderate or serious illness. Moreover, children with weakened immune systems should not receive a live virus vaccine such as VZV. This restriction applies to children who have the following situations:

• They have leukemia or other cancers.

• They have had **cancer** treatments, including radiation or drugs.

• They have received organ transplants or hematopoietic stem cell transplants.

• They have a weakened immune system due to HIV/ AIDS.

Children with leukemia in remission or HIV-infected children with normal immune function may be eligible for VZV. However, chickenpox can cause serious complications in HIV-infected children with compromised immune systems. Therefore, the National Institute of Allergy and Infectious Diseases (NIAID) and the National Institute of Child Health and Human Development (NICHD) are as of 2004 sponsoring a clinical study of the safety and effectiveness of Varivax in HIV-infected children. In the initial phase of the study, HIV-infected children who were without symptoms tolerated Varivax well. Since shingles is very common in HIV-infected children, the NIAID and NICHD also launched a clinical study to determine whether Varivax can prevent shingles in HIV-infected children who have had chickenpox.

Side effects

Reactions to VZV are usually mild and may include:

• pain, rash, hardness, and/or swelling at the injection site in about 20 percent of children and about one in three adolescents

• small chickenpox lesions one to two weeks after vaccination

• generalized mild **rashes** or small bumps up to a month after vaccination in 1–4 percent of VZV recipients

Moderate or severe reactions to VSV have been reported very rarely. These reactions include: high fever or seizures one to six weeks after vaccination in fewer than one out of 1,000 children; pneumonia; and **anaphylaxis**, an allergic reaction that may include weakness, wheezing, breathing difficulties, **hives**, a fast heart rate, **dizziness**, or behavior changes, within a few minutes to a few hours after the injection. Other reactions, such as a low blood count or brain involvement, including encephalitis, occur so rarely that they may not be associated with VZV.

Following the distribution of the first 10 million doses of VZV, it was determined that severe reactions occurred with a frequency of approximately one in 50,000. This is far lower than the risks associated with chickenpox. There is no evidence that healthy children who have had chickenpox or who received VZV previously are at a greater for adverse effects from an additional dose of Varivax.

The National Vaccine Injury Compensation Program helps pay for medical expenses resulting from vaccine reactions. In case of a serious reaction to VZV, parents should do the following:

• A doctor should be consulted immediately.

• The date, time, and type of reaction should be recorded.

• Medical personnel or the local health department should file a Vaccine Adverse Event Report.

Interactions

VZV is not known to interact with any foods or drugs. However, **antiviral drugs** for treating herpes viruses, including acyclovir or valacyclovir, should not be administered within 24 hours of Varivax, because these drugs can reduce the effectiveness of the vaccine.

Parental concerns

Most children are afraid of injections; however, there are simple methods for easing a child's **fear**. Prior to the vaccination, parents should do the following:

• Tell children that they will be getting a shot and that it will feel like a prick; however, it will only sting for a few seconds.

• Explain to children that the shot will prevent them from becoming sick.

• Have older siblings comfort and reassure a younger child.

• Bring along the child's favorite toy or blanket.

• Never threaten children by telling them they will get a shot.

• Read the vaccination information statement (VIS) and ask the medical practitioner questions.

During the vaccination, parents should follow these steps:

- Hold the child.
- Make eye contact with the child and smile.
- Talk softly and comfort the child.
- Distract the child by pointing out pictures or objects or by using a hand puppet.
- Sing or tell the child a story.
- Have the child tell a story.
- Teach the child how to focus on something other than the shot.
- Help the child to take deep breaths.
- Allow the child to cry.
- Stay calm.

Parents may choose to use a comforting restraint method while the child is receiving the injection. These methods enable the parent to control and steady the child's arm while not holding the child down. With toddlers, the positions are as follows:

- The child is held on the parent's lap.
- The child's arm is behind the parent's back, held under the parent's arm.
- The parent's arm and hand control the child's other arm.
- The child's feet are held between the parent's thighs and steadied with the parent's other arm.

With older children, the parent and child can assume the following positions:

- The child is held on the parent's lap or stands in front of the seated parent.
- The parent's arms embrace the child.
- The child's legs are between the parent's legs.

Following the vaccination, parents should do the following:

- Hold and caress or breastfeed the child.
- Talk soothingly and reassuringly.
- Hug and praise the child for doing well.
- Review the VIS for possible side effects.
- Use a cool, wet cloth to reduce soreness or swelling at the injection site.
- Check the child for rashes over the next few days.

KEY TERMS

Antibody—A special protein made by the body's immune system as a defense against foreign material (bacteria, viruses, etc.) that enters the body. It is uniquely designed to attack and neutralize the specific antigen that triggered the immune response.

Booster shot—An additional dose of a vaccine to maintain immunity to the disease.

Breakthrough infection—A disease that is contracted despite a successful vaccination against it.

Herpes zoster virus—Acute inflammatory virus that attacks the nerve cells on the root of each spinal nerve with skin eruptions along a sensory nerve ending. It causes chickenpox and shingles. Also called varicella zoster virus.

Immunity—Ability to resist the effects of agents, such as bacteria and viruses, that cause disease.

Varicella zoster—The virus that causes chickenpox (varicella).

Varicella-zoster immune globulin—A substance that can reduce the severity of chickenpox symptoms.

In addition, parents should anticipate that their children may eat less during the first 24 hours after the injection, and they should receive plenty of fluids. The medical practitioner may suggest a non-aspirin-containing pain reliever.

Resources

BOOKS

Atkinson, William, and Charles (Skip) Wolfe, eds. *Epidemiology and Prevention of Vaccine-Preventable Diseases*, 7th ed. Atlanta, GA: National Immunization Program, Centers for Disease Control and Prevention, 2003.

PERIODICALS

Brisson, M., et al. "Exposure to Varicella Boosts Immunity to Herpes-Zoster: Implications for Mass Vaccination Against Chickenpox." *Vaccine* 20 (June 7, 2002): 2500–07.

ORGANIZATIONS

National Immunization Program. NIP Public Inquiries, Mailstop E-05, 1600 Clifton Rd. NE, Atlanta, GA 30333. Web site: <www.cdc.gov/nip>.

National Vaccine Information Center. 421-E Church St., Vienna, VA 22180. Web site: <www.909shot.com>.

WEB SITES

"Guide to Contraindications to Vaccinations." *National Immunization Program*, May 18, 2004. Available online at <www.cdc.gov/nip/recs/contraindications.htm> (accessed December 20, 2004).

"Varicella Vaccine (Chickenpox)." *National Immunization Program*, December 20, 2001. Available online at <www.cdc.gov/nip/vaccine/varicella/faqs-gen-vaccine.htm> (accessed December 20, 2004).

Margaret Alic, Ph.D.

Child abandonment *see* **Abandonment**

Child abuse

Definition

Child abuse is the blanket term for four types of child mistreatment: physical abuse, sexual abuse, emotional abuse, and neglect.

Description

Prevalence of abuse

Child abuse was once viewed as a minor social problem affecting only a handful of U.S. children. However, in the late 1990s and early 2000s it has received close attention from the media, law enforcement, and the helping professions, and with increased public and professional awareness has come a sharp rise in the number of reported cases. Because abuse is often hidden from view and its victims too young or fearful to speak out, however, experts suggest that its true prevalence is possibly much greater than the official data indicate. An estimated 896,000 children across the country were victims of abuse or neglect in 2002, according to national data released by the U.S. Department of Health and Human Services (HHS) in April 2004. Parents were the abusers in 77 percent of the confirmed cases, other relatives in 11 percent. Sexual abuse was more likely to be committed by males, whereas females were responsible for the majority of neglect cases. The data show that child protective service agencies received about 2,600,000 reports of possible maltreatment in 2002. About 1,400 children died of abuse or neglect, a rate of 1.98 children per 100,000 children in the population. In many cases children are the victims of more than one type of abuse. The abusers can be parents or other **family** members, caretakers such as teachers and **babysitters**, acquaintances (including other children), and (in rare instances) strangers.

Although experts are quick to point out that abuse occurs among all social, ethnic, and income groups, reported cases usually involve poor families with little education. Young mothers, **single-parent families**, and parental alcohol or drug abuse are also common in reported cases. Statistics show that more than 90 percent of abusing parents have neither psychotic nor criminal personalities. Rather they tend to be lonely, unhappy, angry, young, and single parents who do not plan their pregnancies, have little or no knowledge of child development, and have unrealistic expectations for child behavior. From 10 percent to perhaps as many as 40 percent of abusive parents were themselves physically abused as children, but most abused children do not grow up to be abusive parents.

Types of abuse

PHYSICAL ABUSE Physical abuse is the non-accidental infliction of physical injury to a child. The abuser is usually a family member or other caretaker and is more likely to be male. One fourth of the confirmed cases of child abuse in the United States involve physical abuse. A rare form of physical abuse is **Munchausen syndrome** by proxy, in which a caretaker (most often the mother) seeks attention by making the child sick or appear to be sick.

EMOTIONAL ABUSE Emotional abuse is the rejecting, ignoring, criticizing, isolating, or terrorizing of children, all of which have the effect of eroding their **self-esteem**. Emotional abuse usually expresses itself in verbal attacks involving rejection, scapegoating, belittlement, and so forth. Because it often accompanies other types of abuse and is difficult to prove, it is rarely reported and accounts for only about 6 percent of the confirmed cases.

SEXUAL ABUSE Psychologists define child sexual abuse as any activity with a child, before the age of legal consent, that is for the sexual gratification of an adult or a significantly older child. It includes, among other things, sexual touching and penetration, persuading a child to expose his or her sexual organs, and allowing a child to view pornography. In most cases the child is related to or knows the abuser, and about one in five abusers are themselves underage. Sexual abuse accounts for 12 to 15 percent of confirmed abuse cases. In multiple surveys, 20 to 25 percent of females and 10 to 15 percent of males report that they were sexually abused by age 18.

NEGLECT Neglect, the failure to satisfy a child's basic needs, can assume many forms. Physical neglect is

392

the failure (beyond the constraints imposed by poverty) to provide adequate food, clothing, shelter, or supervision. Emotional neglect is the failure to satisfy a child's normal emotional needs, or behavior that damages a child's normal emotional and psychological development (such as permitting drug abuse in the home). Failing to see that a child receives proper schooling or medical care is also considered neglect. Slightly more than half of all reported abuse cases involve neglect.

Infancy and toddlerhood

Infants who are premature, mentally retarded, or have physical handicaps are more likely to provoke abuse from their caregiver than are infants without such problems. Similarly, nonhandicapped infants who are nonrhythmic (that is, have uneven **sleep** and eating patterns) are more likely to be abused. It appears that the child's tendency to learn slowly, to be less coordinated, or less affectionate—rather than any physical problem—that promotes abuse. Infants, because of their fragility, are more susceptible to injury from physical **discipline** than older children. Infants are especially susceptible to **head injury** from shaking or being thrown. A baby can be fatally injured by being thrown even onto a soft mattress. The baby's brain hits the back of the skull if the child is thrown with even mild force and intracranial bleeding can result.

Shaken baby syndrome (SBS) is the leading cause of death in child abuse cases in the United States. The syndrome results from injuries caused by someone vigorously shaking an infant, usually for five to 20 seconds, which causes brain damage. In some cases, the shaking is accompanied by a final impact to the baby's head against a bed, chair, or other surface. Although SBS is occasionally seen in children up to four years of age, the vast majority of incidents occur in infants who are younger than one year; the average age of victims is between three and eight months. Approximately 60 percent of shaken babies are male, and children of families who live at or below the poverty level are at an increased risk for SBS (and any other type of child abuse).

Preschool

Typically, abused children show developmental delays by **preschool** age. It is unclear whether these delays occur due to cumulative neurological damage or due to inadequate stimulation and uncertainty in the child about the learning environment and the absence of positive parental interactions that would stimulate language and motor processes. These delays, in concert with their parents' higher-than-normal expectations for their children's self-care and self-control abilities, may

provoke additional abuse. Abused preschoolers respond to peers and other adults with more aggression and anger than do non-abused children. A coercive cycle frequently develops in which parents and children mutually control one another with threats of negative behavior.

School age

School-aged children who are abused typically have problems academically and have poorer grades and performance on standardized achievement tests. Studies of abused children's intellectual performance find lower scores in both verbal and math and visual-spatial areas. Abused children also tend to be distracted and overactive, making school a very difficult environment for them. With their peers, abused children are often more aggressive and more likely to be socially rejected than nonabused children. Less mature socially, abused children show difficulty in developing trusting relationships with others. The anger that is often instilled in such children is likely to be incorporated into their personality structures. Carrying an extra load of anger makes it difficult for them to control their behavior and increases their risk for resorting to violent action. To control their fears, children who live with violence may repress feelings. This defensive maneuver takes its toll in their immediate lives and can lead to further pathological development. It can interfere with their ability to relate to others in meaningful ways and to feel empathy. Individuals who cannot empathize with others' feelings are less likely to curb their own aggression and more likely to become insensitive to brutality in general.

As adolescents, abused children are more likely to be in contact with the juvenile justice system than nonabused children of comparable family constellation and income level. Many of these children are labeled "ungovernable" for committing offenses such as **running away** and **truancy**. A higher proportion of abused than nonabused delinquent youth are also involved in crimes of assault. Follow-up studies on abused children in later **adolescence** show that in addition to having problems with the law, they are also more likely to be substance abusers or to have emotional disturbances such as depression.

Common problems

Physical abuse

The usual physical abuse scenario involves a parent who loses control and lashes out at a child. The trigger may be normal child behavior such as crying or dirtying a diaper. Unlike nonabusive parents, who may become angry at or upset with their children from time to time

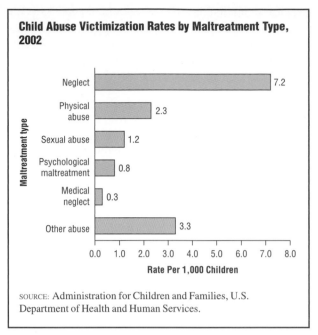

Child Abuse Victimization Rates by Maltreatment Type, 2002

Neglect — 7.2
Physical abuse — 2.3
Sexual abuse — 1.2
Psychological maltreatment — 0.8
Medical neglect — 0.3
Other abuse — 3.3

Maltreatment type / Rate Per 1,000 Children

SOURCE: Administration for Children and Families, U.S. Department of Health and Human Services.

This graph of 2002 data on child abuse in the United States shows that neglect is by far the most common type of abuse. *(Graph by GGS Information Services.)*

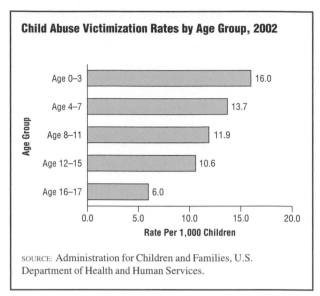

Child Abuse Victimization Rates by Age Group, 2002

Age 0–3 — 16.0
Age 4–7 — 13.7
Age 8–11 — 11.9
Age 12–15 — 10.6
Age 16–17 — 6.0

Age Group / Rate Per 1,000 Children

SOURCE: Administration for Children and Families, U.S. Department of Health and Human Services.

This graph of 2002 data on child abuse in the United States shows that younger children are more likely to be vicims of abuse than older children. *(Graph by GGS Information Services.)*

but are genuinely loving, abusive parents tend to harbor deep-rooted negative feelings toward their children. Unexplained or suspicious **bruises** or other marks on the skin are typical signs of physical abuse, as are **burns**. Skull and other bone **fractures** are often seen in young abused children, and in fact, head injuries are the leading cause of death from abuse. Children less than one year old are particularly vulnerable to injury from shaken baby syndrome. Physical abuse also causes a wide variety of behavioral changes in children.

Emotional abuse

Emotional abuse can happen in many settings: at home, at school, on **sports** teams, and so on. Some of the possible symptoms include loss of self-esteem, sleep disturbances, headaches or stomach aches, school avoidance, and running away from home.

Sexual abuse

The two prerequisites for this form of maltreatment are sexual arousal towards children and the willingness to act on this arousal. Factors that may contribute to this willingness include alcohol or drug abuse, poor impulse control, and a belief that the sexual behaviors are acceptable and not harmful to the child. The chances of abuse are higher if the child is developmentally handicapped or vulnerable in some other way. Genital or anal injuries or abnormalities (including the presence of **sexually trans-**

mitted diseases) can be signs of sexual abuse, but often there is no physical evidence for a doctor to find. In fact, physical examinations of children in cases of suspected sexual abuse supply grounds for further suspicion only 15 to 20 percent of the time. **Anxiety**, poor academic performance, and suicidal conduct are some of the behavioral signs of sexual abuse but are also found in children suffering other kinds of stress. Excessive **masturbation** and other unusually sexualized kinds of behavior are more closely associated with sexual abuse itself.

Neglect

Many cases of neglect occur because the parent experiences strong negative feelings toward the child. At other times, the parent may truly care about the child but lacks the ability or strength to adequately provide for the child's needs because handicapped by depression, drug abuse, **mental retardation**, or some other problem. Neglected children often do not receive adequate nourishment or emotional and mental stimulation. As a result, their physical, social, emotional, and mental development is hindered. They may, for instance, be underweight, develop language skills less quickly than other children, and seem emotionally needy.

Parental concerns

When children reach age three, parents should begin teaching them about "bad touches" and about confiding in a suitable adult if they are touched or treated in a way that makes them uneasy. Parents also need to exercise caution in hiring babysitters and other caretakers. Anyone who suspects abuse should immediately report those suspicions to the police or their local child protection services agency, which is usually listed in the blue pages of the telephone book under Rehabilitative Services or Child and Family Services, or in the yellow pages. Round-the-clock crisis counseling for children and adults is offered by the Childhelp USA/IOF Foresters National Child Abuse Hotline. The National Committee to Prevent Child Abuse is an excellent source of information on the many support groups and other organizations that help abused and at-risk children and their families. One of these organizations, National Parents Anonymous, sponsors 2,100 local self-help groups throughout the United States, Canada, and Europe. Telephone numbers for its local groups are listed in the white pages of the telephone book under Parents Anonymous or can be obtained by calling the national headquarters.

When to call the doctor

Physical signs of abuse may include bruises, especially those in different stages of healing, bruises in the shape of an object, such as fingers, a ring, or a belt buckle; unexplained burns, black eyes, or broken bones; vaginal or rectal bleeding, **pain**, **itching**, swelling or discharge; a vacant stare or dazed appearance; frequent attempts to run away; and sexual promiscuity.

Behavioral signs of child abuse include: low self esteem; flinching or ducking from motion or people moving towards them; eating disorders or loss of appetite; self mutilation such as "cutting," biting oneself or pulling out hair; unusual habits like rocking, sucking cloth; extreme changes in behavioral patterns; poor interpersonal relationships or a lack of self-confidence; clinginess, withdrawal or aggressiveness; regressing to infantile behavior such as bedwetting, **thumb sucking** or excessive crying; recurrent **nightmares**, disturbed sleep patterns, or a sudden **fear** of the dark; unexplained fear of a particular person; unusual knowledge of sexual matters; acting much younger or older than chronological age; frequent **lying**, or a fall in grades at school; and depression.

It is important to remember that some of these symptoms of child abuse can be normal manifestations of **play** and activity. Other symptoms could be the result of a traumatic event that is not necessarily abuse, such as **divorce**. Still, others are definitely "red flag" symptoms of abuse. If any physical signs of abuse appear, get medical help immediately. Talk frankly with the doctor and share any concerns about possible abuse. If there is physical proof of abuse, get a doctor's report in writing. Any behavioral signs of abuse are cause for concern to a good parent,

KEY TERMS

Munchausen syndrome by proxy—A form of abuse in which a parent induces symptoms of disease in a child.

Nonrhythmic—Having uneven sleep and eating patterns.

Shaken baby syndrome—Injuries caused by someone vigorously shaking an infant, usually for five to twenty seconds, which causes brain damage.

teacher, or caregiver. A good first move is to open and nurture trusting lines of communication. The parent should increase the time spent with the child and increase the attention given to the child. The parent should show more interest in the child's life and ask more questions. The parent needs to assure the child of the parent's unqualified love and support, and make sure the children know that the parent wants them to feel happy and confident. Children need to know that no matter what has happened, their parents will always love them.

Resources

BOOKS

Browne, Kevin, et al. *Early Prediction and Prevention of Child Abuse: A Handbook.* Hoboken, NJ: John Wiley & Sons, 2002.

Crosson-Tower, Cynthia. *Understanding Child Abuse and Neglect,* 6th ed. Upper Saddle River, NJ: Allyn & Bacon, 2004.

Richardson, Sue, and Heather Bacon. *Creative Response to Child Sexual Abuse: Challenges and Dilemmas.* London: Jessica Kingsley Publishers, 2003.

PERIODICALS

Bechtel, Kirsten, et al. "Characteristics that Distinguish Accidental from Abusive Injury in Hospitalized Young Children with Head Trauma." *Pediatrics* 114 (July 2004): 165–69.

Bensley, Lillian, et al. "Community Responses and Perceived Barriers to Responding to Child Maltreatment." *Journal of Community Health* 29 (April 2004): 141–53.

Brunk, Doug. "Complete Physical Key When Abuse Suspected: History May Be Unreliable." *Family Practice News* (April 1, 2004): 82.

———. "The True Incidence of U.S. Child Abuse Deaths Unknown: Fragmented Surveillance System Blamed." *Family Practice News* (April 1, 2004): 82.

Fritz, Gregory K. "A Child Psychiatrist's Dream: Ending Child Abuse." *The Brown University Child and Adolescent Behavior Letter* 20 (September 2004): 8.

ORGANIZATIONS

National Clearinghouse on Child Abuse and Neglect Information. 330 C St., SW, Washington, DC 20447. Web site: <www.nccanch.acf.hhs.gov>.

National Council on Child Abuse and Family Violence. 1025 Connecticut Ave. NW, Suite 1012, Washington, DC 20036. Web site: <www.nccafv.org>.

WEB SITES

"Child Maltreatment 2002: Summary of Key Findings." *National Clearinghouse on Child Abuse and Neglect Information*, April 2004. Available online at <http://nccanch.acf.hhs.gov/pubs/factsheets/canstats.pdf> (accessed November 9, 2004).

"Recognizing Child Abuse: What Parents Should Know." *Prevent Child Abuse America*, 2004. Available online at <www.preventchildabuse.org/learn_more/parents/recognizing_abuse.pdf> (accessed November 9, 2004).

Howard Baker, RN
Ken R. Wells

Child care *see* **Day care**

Child custody laws

Definition

Child custody laws are federal and state laws that govern a parent's legal authority to make decisions affecting a child (legal custody) and to maintain physical control over the child (physical custody). Child custody laws also pertain to the visitation rights of the non-custodial parent.

Purpose

Child custody laws exist to provide a legal structure for relationships between children and their divorced parents. Ideally, divorced parents should work together to have an amicable relationship and shared custody, but bitterness between divorced spouses and tendencies to involve children in marital and **divorce** disputes require child custody laws. Child custody laws help to define the **family** situation in terms of the best interests of the child or children involved in the divorce. Child custody laws can also be applied in cases when unmarried parents claim custody based on a biological relationship, when grandparents dispute the competence of the child's parents, and when same-sex couples with adopted children separate. In some cases, custody may be granted to an individual or individuals not related (e.g., foster parents).

Description

In the United States, responsibilities for a child's care and decision-making related to that care are governed by federal and state laws. In general, custody laws and custody decisions favor continued and frequent contact between the child and both parents, as well as an ongoing role for both parents in the raising of their children. However, custody decisions are strongly influenced by the circumstances of each individual case, the welfare of the involved child or children, and the perceived effect of each parent on the child.

In almost all custody cases, courts consider a value called the "best interests of the child" as the highest priority when rendering a custody decision. The best interests of a child are determined by considering a number of factors, including the following:

- child's age, sex, and mental/physical health
- mental and physical health of both parents
- child's established lifestyle (home, school, church, etc.)
- lifestyle of both parents, including any history of child abuse
- emotional bonds between each parent and child, and the ability of each parent to provide emotional support and guidance
- ability of each parent to provide physical necessities (e.g., food, home, clothing, healthcare)
- impact of change on the child
- ability and willingness of each parent to encourage a healthy relationship and communication between the child and the other parent
- child's preferences

Most courts use the above factors to determine which parent can provide the child with a stable home environment and continuity of lifestyle.

Child custody laws address several different types of parenting situations and custody circumstances. For the purposes of custody, legal definitions of parenthood are as follows:

- Biological parents: The mother and father responsible for conception and birth of the child.

- Stepparent: A non-biological parent who marries or cohabitates with a biological parent.

- Stepchild: A non-biological child brought into the family by marriage or cohabitation with the biological parent.

- Custodial parent: The parent awarded primary custody by a court during divorce proceedings.

- Non-custodial parent: The parent awarded part-time custody or visitation rights by a court during divorce proceedings.

Custody decisions involve physical and legal custody. Physical custody refers to the responsibility of taking care of the children (food, clothing, housing, etc.). Legal custody refers to the responsibility for decisions that affect the child's interests (medical, educational, and religious decisions, etc.). In 20 states, custody is divided into physical custody and legal custody; in the remaining states, physical and legal custody are not considered separately, and the term "custody" refers to both responsibilities. In states that do not distinguish between physical and legal custody, the term "custody" implies both types of responsibilities. Custody decisions by a court of law designate joint custody between two parents or primary custody for one parent (the custodial parent) and visitation rights for the non-custodial parent. Custody decisions are described as follows:

- Joint physical custody: Children split their time between parents, spending a substantial amount of time with each parent.

- Joint legal custody: Parents share in decision-making regarding medical, educational, and religious issues involving the children.

- Joint legal and physical custody: Parents share both time and decision-making responsibilities.

- Primary (sole) custody: One parent is designated the primary physical and legal custodian of the child or children, and the other parent is granted visitation rights.

Courts in every state are willing to order joint legal custody; however, about half the states are reluctant to order joint physical custody unless both parents agree to it, the child's lifestyle is not substantially disrupted (e.g., parents live within the same school district), and parents appear to be able to effectively and amicably cooperate with each other regarding their children. Two states (New Mexico and New Hampshire) require joint custody to be awarded, except when the children's best interests or a parent's health or **safety** are compromised.

Primary or sole custody is usually awarded when parents live a significant distance from one another,

when one parent can provide clear benefits for the child over the other parent, or when one parent is deemed unfit to care for the child. In some cases, neither parent is judged fit to retain custody, usually due to substance abuse problems, mental health issues, or prolonged absence or incarceration. In such cases, an individual or individuals other than the parents are granted custody or given a temporary guardianship or **foster care** arrangement by a court. In general, courts would prefer that a child remain with family members than be placed in foster care.

Common problems

Unfortunately, children are often involved in divorce and custody battles and, as a result, may suffer from psychological and emotional damage that will require counseling and therapy. In some cases, a child has the legal right to choose which parent he/she wants to live with. However, placing the responsibility of making such a decision on the child can cause internal conflict and emotional stress related to feeling that they have to choose one parent over the other. Parents should make every effort to keep bitter feelings between themselves and not involve children in their divorce conflict. Having the child attend regular therapy or counseling sessions can help the child's adjustment to the divorce and changes in the living situation. Group therapy with other children in similar circumstances can be especially helpful.

Although child custody laws were established to protect the best interests of the child, final custody decisions are not always best for the child. In some cases, the parent with the best legal representation, not necessarily the parent who will provide the best care, wins custody. Parents may misrepresent their ability to properly care for children or provide false information about the other parent in order to win custody. An independent custody evaluator, usually appointed by the court, can help by conducting psychological evaluations of both parents and children to determine the custody arrangement that will be in the best interests of the children.

Parental concerns

In the early 2000s one parent often lives out of state for a variety of reasons, including employment, extended family relationships, and standard of living. All states and the District of Columbia follow the Uniform Child Custody Jurisdiction Act, which sets standards for when a court can determine custody and when a court must defer to an existing determination from another state. In general, a state court can decide custody about a child if the state is the child's home state; the child has significant connections with individuals (grandparents, doctors, teachers) in the state concerning the child's care, protection, and personal relationships; the child is in the state and has been either abandoned or is in danger of being abused or neglected if sent back to the other state; or no other state can meet one of the above three tests; or a state can meet at least one of the tests but has declined to make a custody decision. Parents who wrongfully remove or retain a child in order to create a home state or significant connections will usually be denied custody. In cases where more than one state meets the above standards, the law requires that only one state award custody. The Uniform Child Custody Jurisdiction Act has helped establish consistency in the treatment of custody decisions and helped solve problems created by kidnapping or disagreements over custody between parents living in different states.

Divorce and custody battles can create stress and worries for parents. In making custody decisions, courts look for responsible parents who are actively involved in the children's lives. Liberal, unrestricted visitation for the non-custodial parent is often based on the relationship with children and the degree of involvement in the children's everyday activities.

During the twentieth century, custody laws often mandated that custody be automatically given to mothers, especially for younger children. In the early 2000s, in most states, this ruling has been rejected or revised, and no state as of 2004 required that a child be awarded to the mother without regard for the fitness of both parents as primary caregivers. Fathers who desire physical custody should not assume that gender stereotypes will result in a mother automatically being given custody. As of 2004, when both mother and father often work full-time, parents enter a custody case as equals with regard to physical custody. Parents who present themselves as flexible and willing to assume physical custody are more likely to be granted custody.

Parents in same-sex relationships may have concerns regarding custody issues due to their sexual orientation. However, in a few states, including Alaska, California, New Jersey, New Mexico, Pennsylvania, and the District of Columbia, a parent's sexual orientation cannot in and of itself prevent a parent from being given custody or visitation rights. However, gay and lesbian parents may still be denied custody or visitation because many judges may be motivated by personal or community prejudices. Stepparents may face a similar situation, since stepparents, unless they legally adopt a stepchild, have no legal rights with regard to custody or visitation. In cases in which a stepparent may provide a more stable environment for a child than the biological parents,

judges may still favor biological parents due to personal and societal beliefs about what constitutes a "normal" family.

Resources

BOOKS

Ahrons, C. *We're Still Family: What Grown Children Have to Say about their Parents' Divorce.* New York: Harper Collins, 2004.

Boland, M. L. *Your Right to Child Custody, Visitation, and Support.* Naperville, IL: Sphinx Publishing, 2000.

Watnik, W. *Child Custody Made Simple.* Claremont, CA: Single Parent Press, 2003.

WEB SITES

Child Custody Organization. Available online at <www.childcustody.org> (accessed December 20, 2004).

"Divorce and Child Custody." *Nolo Law for All.* Available online at <www.nolo.com/lawcenter/ency/index.cfm/catID/272E58B9-BFE3-4B3E-835B37AAE3180FCD> (accessed December 20, 2004).

Father's Custody Center. Available online at <www.fatherscustody.org/> (accessed December 20, 2004).

Jennifer E. Sisk, M.A.

Childbirth

Definition

Childbirth is formally divided by the medical field into three stages. The first stage is labor, which has three phases: early, active, and transitional. The first stage ends with complete dilatation (opening) of the cervix. The second stage is delivery, which involves pushing and the actual birth of the baby. The third stage is delivery of the placenta or afterbirth.

Description

A full-term pregnancy is considered to be 280 days, nine calendar months or ten lunar months calculated from the first day of the last menstrual period. This is a fairly arbitrary number that may, in fact, vary with genetic differences and depends on a normal menstrual cycle, which varies considerably from woman to woman. The average actual length from conception to birth is estimated as 267 days. Childbirth is a natural process,

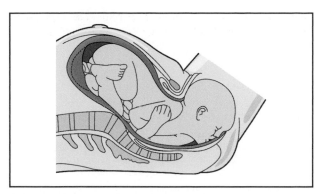

Childbirth in stage 2. The baby's head is crowning and about to emerge from the vagina. *(Illustration by Hans & Cassidy.)*

and it, too, varies among women. Despite what the obstetrical texts say about what to expect, there are many variations that make each woman's experience hers alone. The whole process averages about 14 hours for first-time mothers and about eight hours for mothers in their subsequent pregnancies.

Labor can be described in terms of a series of stages.

First stage of labor

During the first stage of labor, the cervix dilates (opens) from 0 to 10 centimeters (cm). This stage has an early, or latent, phase, an active phase, and a transitional phase. The latent phase usually lasts the longest and is the least intense phase of labor. This phase is characterized by dilatation (opening) of the cervix to 3–4 cm along with the thinning out of the cervix (effacement). It can take place over a period of days without being noticed or over a period of two to six hours with distinctive contractions. Most women are relatively comfortable during the latent phase, and walking around is encouraged, since it naturally stimulates the process.

With the initiation of labor, the muscular wall of the uterus begins to contract causing the cervix to open (dilatation) and thin out (efface). For a first-time mother the cervix must completely efface before dilatation continues. Effacement is reported in percentages as 50 percent or 100 percent, which is completely thinned out. The amniotic sac may or may not break during labor, and the birth attendant may rupture the bag with an amniohook, which looks a little like a large crochet hook. There is no **pain** involved with the breaking the bag of waters, although the contractions may intensify. During a contraction, the infant experiences pressure that pushes it against the cervix to assist with the dilatation. During this first phase, a woman's contractions typically increase in frequency and duration. Periodic vaginal exams are performed by the physician or nurse to determine progress. As pain and discomfort increase, however, the woman may be tempted to request pain medication. The administration of pain medication or anesthetics should be delayed until the active phase of labor begins, at which point the medication will not act to slow down or stop the labor.

The active phase of labor is usually shorter than the first, lasting an average of two to four hours. The contractions are more intense and accomplishing more in less time. They may be three to four minutes apart lasting 40–60 seconds even though the pattern may not be regular. During the active phase, dilatation continues to 7 cm. Relaxing between contractions is essential for coping because these contractions are more intense. Breathing exercises learned in childbirth classes can help the woman cope with the discomfort experienced during this phase. Pain medication offered at this point consists of either a short-term medication, such as Nubain or Stadol, or long-term such as epidural anesthesia.

The transitional phase continues dilation 7–10 cm. It is the most exhausting and demanding phase of labor. The contractions become very strong, are two to three minutes apart, and last 60–90 seconds. It may feel as if the contractions never stop, and there is no time to relax between them. Dilatation of the final 3 cm to 10 cm takes, on average, 15 minutes to an hour. Strong rectal pressure, with or without an urge to push or move the bowels, may cause the woman to grunt involuntarily. If it is a natural labor and delivery, the laboring woman at this phase becomes very inwardly focused and can lose control. It is important to breathe with her through contractions as this keeps her attention on what she needs to do.

Second stage of labor

Up to this point, the woman may feels as if her participation is small, because all she has done is breathe. Active involvement can now begin along with some emotional relief that it is almost over. Without anesthesia, there is often an overwhelming urge to push, and the mother gets a second wind. The baby's head is through the cervix and on its way down the birth canal. The uterine contractions get stronger, and the infant passes along the vagina helped by contractions of the uterus and the mother's pushing. If an epidural anesthetic is being used, many practitioners recommend decreasing the dosage so the mother has better control of her pushing. Research has shown, however, that the contractions will continue to push the baby down the birth canal without mother's help. If a woman is numb from an epidural, she cannot push effectively, and it is usually better to let the contractions work alone. This is called "laboring down."

When the top of the baby's head appears at the opening of the vagina, the birth is nearing completion. First

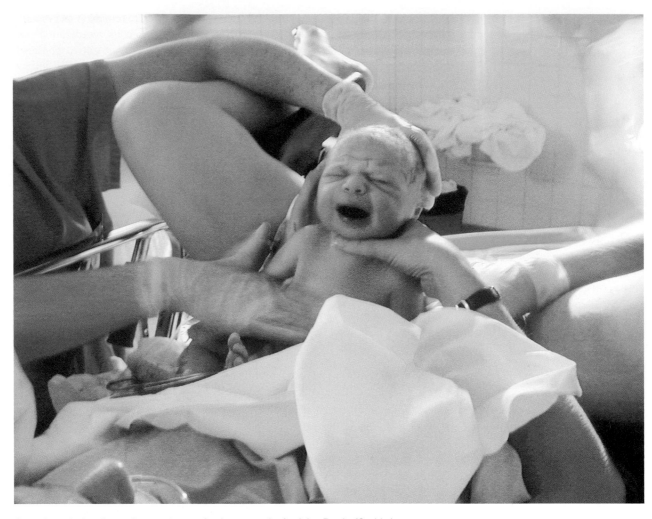

A newborn baby sits crying on the mother's stomach. (© Jules Perrier/Corbis.)

the head passes under the pubic bone. It fills the lower vagina and stretches the perineum (the tissues between the vagina and the rectum). This position is called "crowning," since only the crown of the head is visible. When the entire head is out, the shoulders follow. The attending practitioner suctions the baby's mouth and nose to ease the baby's first breath. The rest of the baby usually slips out easily, and the umbilical cord is cut.

Episiotomy

Many practitioners argue that it is better to cut the perineum than to let it tear. This cut is called an episiotomy. In reality, it is more difficult to repair a straight cut than a small tear in much the same way it is harder to put together a puzzle with straight edges; it is more difficult to match evenly and can result in vaginal discomfort once healed. Instead, the perineum can be massaged and gently stretched to prevent tearing as the baby's head

crowns. There is also less pain associated with a tear than an episiotomy. If the woman has not had an epidural or pudendal block, she will get a local anesthetic to numb the area for repair.

Third stage

In the final stage of labor, the placenta is expelled by the continuing uterine contractions. The placenta is pancake shaped and about 10 cm (25 cm) in diameter. During pregnancy, it is attached to the wall of the uterus and served to exchange needed nourishment from the mother to the fetus and simultaneously to remove waste products from the fetus. Generally, there is a rise in the uterus due to a contraction and a gush of blood as the placenta is expelled. The placenta should be examined to make sure it is intact. Retained placenta can cause severe uterine bleeding after delivery, and it must be removed.

Breech presentation

Approximately 4 percent of babies present in the breech position when labor begins. In this presentation, the baby's bottom is the presenting part instead of the head, which is called a vertex presentation. Using a technique called a version, an obstetrician may attempt to turn the baby to a head down position. This is only successful approximately half the time, and there are possible complications with the procedure, such as umbilical cord entanglement and separation of the placenta. However, some practitioners are very successful with versions, and it does make a vaginal delivery safer.

The risks of vaginal delivery with breech presentation are much higher than with a head-first (vertex) presentation. The mother and attending practitioner need to weigh the risks to make a decision on whether to deliver via a **cesarean section** or attempt a vaginal birth. The degree of risk depends to a great extent on which one of the three types of breech presentations it is. In a frank breech the baby's legs are folded up against its body. This is the most common breech presentation and the safest for vaginal delivery. The others include complete breech, in which the baby's legs are crossed under and in front of the body, and footling breech, in which one leg or both legs are positioned to enter the birth canal. Neither of these is considered safe enough for a vaginal delivery.

Even with a complete breech, there are other factors to consider for a vaginal birth. An ultrasound examination should be done to determine that the baby's head is not too large and that it is tilted forward (flexed) rather than back (hyperextended). Fetal monitoring and close observation of the progress of labor are also important. A slowing of labor or any indication of difficulty in the body passing through the pelvis should be an indication that it is safer to consider a cesarean section.

Forceps delivery

Although not used as much in the early 2000s as in earlier times, forceps can be used if the baby's head is very low in the birth canal. Also, if there is some sudden change in the maternal-fetal status, the doctor may opt for a forceps delivery if it would be faster than a cesarean section. Forceps are spoon-shaped devices that can be placed around the baby's head while the doctor gently pulls the baby out of the vagina.

Before placing the forceps around the baby's head, pain medication or anesthesia may be given to the mother. The doctor may use a catheter to empty the mother's bladder and may clean the perineal area with soapy water. Often an episiotomy is done before a for-ceps birth, although tears can still occur. The use of forceps can cause vaginal lacerations in the mother.

Half of the forceps are slid into the vagina and around the side of the baby's head to gently grasp the head. When both forceps are in place, the doctor pulls on them to help the baby through the birth canal during a uterine contraction. The frequency of forceps delivery varies from one hospital to the next, depending on the experience of staff and the types of anesthesia offered at the hospital. Some obstetricians accept the need for a forceps delivery as a way to avoid cesarean birth while other obstetrical services do not use forceps at all. Complications from forceps deliveries can occur, such as nerve damage or temporary **bruises** to the baby's face. When used by an experienced physician, forceps can save the life of a baby in distress.

Vacuum-assisted birth

This method of delivering a baby was developed as a gentler alternative to forceps. Similar to forceps deliveries, vacuum-assisted births can only be used with a fully dilated cervix and a well-descended head. In this procedure, a device called a vacuum extractor is used by placing a large rubber or plastic cup against the baby's head. A pump then creates suction that gently pulls on the cup to ease the baby out the birth canal. The force of the suction may cause a bruise or swelling on the baby's head, but it resolves in a day or two.

The vacuum extractor is less likely to injure the mother than forceps, and it allows more space for the baby to pass through the pelvis. There can be problems in maintaining the suction during the vacuum-assisted birth, however, so forceps might be a better choice if the delivery needs to be expedited.

Cesarean sections

A cesarean section, also called a c-section, is a surgical procedure in which an incision is made through a woman's abdomen and uterus to deliver her baby. This procedure is performed whenever abnormal conditions complicate labor and vaginal delivery that threaten the life or health of the mother or the baby. The procedure is performed in the United States on nearly one in every four women resulting in more than 900,000 babies each year being delivered by c-section. The procedure is often used in women who have had a previous c-section, but if the incision on the uterus is not vertical, the woman can try a vaginal birth after cesarean (VBAC).

Dysfunctional labor is commonly caused by one of the three following conditions: maternal structural abnormalities; abnormal fetal presentations; failure to progress. Non-reassuring fetal heart rate tracings represent a condition in which the fetus may not be tolerating labor and oxygen deprivation can occur. Other conditions which might indicate a need for c-section include: vaginal herpes, **hypertension** (high blood pressure), and uncontrolled diabetes in the mother.

Causes and symptoms

Childbirth usually begins spontaneously, but it may be started by artificial means if the pregnancy continues past 41 weeks gestation. There are three signs that labor may be starting: rhythmical contractions of the uterus; leaking of the bag of waters (amniotic sac); and bloody show. The importance of the sign of contractions is in the rhythm and not the contractions. True labor contractions may start once every ten or 15 minutes or even at longer intervals, but gradually the interval decreases until they come every three to four minutes. The most important thing a woman can do at this phase is to remain relaxed. The bag of waters may leak slowly or may suddenly burst, and there is a gush of fluid. There is no pain when the water breaks, although it may be startling. If contractions are not ongoing prior to this, they are likely to start soon after. If they do not, it may be necessary to stimulate labor as the womb is now open to possible infection. The bloody show is a slight discharge of blood and mucus. It usually occurs after the cervix has started to dilate slightly and the mucus plug that keeps the cervix sealed from potential pathogens becomes dislodged.

Diagnosis

The diagnosis of true labor can only be determined by a vaginal exam to determine if the cervix has changed in dilatation (opening). True labor is determined by whether the contractions are, in fact, changing the cervix. If a woman is experiencing contractions and makes no cervical change, then this is false labor. Dilatation is measured in centimeters and it goes from zero to ten centimeters, which is complete dilatation. Although the woman having the contractions may feel like she is really experiencing labor, true labor is determined by cervical change. Many women may experience Braxton-Hicks contractions (practice contractions) in preparation for true labor, and these can become uncomfortable at times, which prevents the woman from resting. A warm bath or warm drink may help her to relax and **sleep**. Inevitably she will wake up in true labor with effective contractions. Palpating contractions as they occur can assist in determining whether they are strong. A very strong contraction cannot be indented and will feel as hard as the forehead. A moderate contraction will palpate like the

feel of the chin and an easy contraction feels like the end of the nose. If the contractions can be indented, they probably do not constitute true labor.

Electronic fetal monitoring

Electronic fetal monitoring (EFM) involves the use of an electronic fetal heart rate (FHR) monitor to record the baby's heart rate. The FHR is picked up by means of an ultrasound transducer and the movement of the heart valves. Elastic belts are used to hold sensors against the pregnant woman's abdomen. The sensors are connected to the monitor and detect the baby's heart rate as well as the uterine contractions. The monitor then records the FHR and the contractions as a pattern on a strip of paper, called a tracing. Electronic fetal monitoring is frequently used during labor to assess fetal well-being. EFM can be used either externally or internally. Internal monitoring does not use ultrasound, is more accurate than electronic monitoring, and provides continuous monitoring for the high-risk mother. An internal monitor requires that the bag of waters be broken and that the woman is at least two to three centimeters dilated. It is used in high-risk situations or when it is difficult to obtain an accurate FHR tracing.

Telemetry monitoring has been available since the early 1990s but is not used in many hospitals as of 2004. Telemetry uses radio waves transmitted from an instrument on the mother's thigh, which allows the mother to remain mobile. It provides continuous monitoring and does not require the patient to be in bed continuously.

Besides EFM and telemetry, which is usually continuous, there is intermittent monitoring using a hand-held Doppler to assess the FHR. This method gives the mother freedom of movement during labor. Prior to electronic gadgetry a special stethoscope was used, called a fetoscope, which is rarely seen as of 2004 because it requires more skill to use. Research on the use of intermittent monitoring and continuous monitoring found no difference in fetal outcomes with intermittent monitoring. The use of continuous monitoring does result in a higher c-section rate partly because the tracing can be misinterpreted or because the mother usually requires more interventions when she cannot be mobile.

Treatment

Many women choose some type of pain relief during childbirth, ranging from relaxation and imagery to drugs. The specific choice may depend on what is available, the woman's preferences, her doctor's recommendations, and how the labor is proceeding. All drugs have some risks and some advantages.

Regional anesthetics

Regional anesthetics include epidurals and spinals. With this procedure, medication is injected into the space surrounding the spinal nerves. Depending on the type of medications used, this type of anesthesia can block nerve signals, causing temporary pain relief or a loss of sensation from the waist down. An epidural or spinal block can provide complete pain relief during cesarean birth.

An epidural is placed with the woman lying on her side or sitting up in bed with the back rounded to allow more space between the vertebrae. Her back is scrubbed with antiseptic, and a local anesthetic is injected in the skin to numb the site. The needle is inserted between two vertebrae and through the tough tissue in front of the spinal column. A catheter is put in place that allows continuous doses of anesthetic to be given.

This type of anesthesia provides complete pain relief and can help conserve a woman's energy, since she can relax or even sleep during labor. This type of anesthesia does require an IV and fetal monitor. It may be harder for a woman to bear down when it comes time to push, although the amount of anesthesia can be adjusted as this stage nears.

Spinal anesthesia operates on the same principle as epidural anesthesia and is used primarily in cases of c-section delivery. It is administered in the same way as an epidural, but the catheter is not left in place following the surgery. The amount of anesthetic injected is large, since it must be injected at one time. Spinals provide quick and strong anesthesia and allow for major abdominal surgery with almost no pain.

Narcotics

Short-acting narcotics can ease pain and not interfere with a woman's ability to push. However, they can cause sedation, **dizziness**, **nausea**, and **vomiting**. Narcotics cross the placenta and can affect the baby.

Natural childbirth and preparation for childbirth

There are several methods available to prepare for childbirth. The one selected often depends on what is available through the healthcare provider. Overall, **family** involvement is receiving increased attention by the healthcare systems, and the majority of hospitals now offer birthing rooms and maternity centers to accommodate the entire family.

Lamaze, or Lamaze-Pavlov, is the most commonly used method in the United States as of 2004. It became the first popular natural childbirth method in the 1960s.

KEY TERMS

Amniotic sac—The membranous sac that contains the fetus and the amniotic fluid during pregnancy.

Breech birth—Birth of a baby bottom-first, instead of the usual head-first delivery. This can add to labor and delivery problems because the baby's bottom doesn't mold a passage through the birth canal as well as does the head.

Cervix—A small, cylindrical structure about an inch or so long and less than an inch around that makes up the lower part and neck of the uterus. The cervix separates the body and cavity of the uterus from the vagina.

Embryo—In humans, the developing individual from the time of implantation to about the end of the second month after conception. From the third month to the point of delivery, the individual is called a fetus.

Gestation—The period from conception to birth, during which the developing fetus is carried in the uterus.

Perineum—The area between the opening of the vagina and the anus in a woman, or the area between the scrotum and the anus in a man.

Placenta—The organ that provides oxygen and nutrition from the mother to the unborn baby during pregnancy. The placenta is attached to the wall of the uterus and leads to the unborn baby via the umbilical cord.

Vertex—The top of the head or highest point of the skull.

Various breathing techniques, cleansing breath, panting and blowing, are used for different phases together with the use of a focal point to enable the laboring woman to maintain control. A partner helps by coaching the mother throughout the birthing process.

The Read method, named for Dr. Grantly Dick-Read (who published his book *Childbirth Without Fear* in 1944) involves primarily remaining relaxed and breathing normally. Dr. Dick-Read promoted this method in the 1930s to help mothers deal with apprehension and tension associated with childbirth. He emphasized the practice of tensing and relaxing muscles so that complete relaxation occurs between contractions in labor. This action also serves to promote good oxygenation to the muscles.

The Bradley method is called father-coached childbirth, because it focuses on the father serving as the coach throughout the process. It encourages normal activities during the first stages of labor without interventions and focuses on breathing and relaxation.

HypnoBirthing is becoming increasingly popular in the United States in the early 2000s and has proven to be quite effective. Based upon the work of Grantly Dick-Read, it teaches the mother to understand and release the fear-tension-pain syndrome, which so often is the cause of pain and discomfort during labor. When people are afraid, their bodies divert blood and oxygen from non-essential defense organs to large muscle groups in their extremities. Unfortunately, the body considers the uterus to be a non-essential organ. HypnoBirthing explores the myth that pain is a necessary accompaniment to a normal birthing. When a laboring woman's mind is free of **fear**, the muscles in her body, including her uterine muscles, relax, thus facilitating an easier, stress-free birth. In many cases, first stage labor shortens, which diminishes fatigue during labor leaving the mother stronger for pushing. The founder of HypnoBirthing, Marie Mongan, promotes the philosophy that eliminating fear allows the woman's body to work like it is supposed to.

The LeBoyer method stresses a relaxed delivery in a quiet, dimly lit room. It strives to avoid overstimulation of the baby and to foster mother-child **bonding** by placing the baby on the mother's abdomen and having the mother massage him or her immediately after the birth. This is followed by the father giving the baby a warm bath.

See also Apgar testing; Electronic fetal monitoring; Cesarean section.

Resources

BOOKS

Murkoff, H. I., et al. *What to Expect When You're Expecting*, 3rd ed. New York: Workman Publishing, 2002.

Olds, Sally, et al. *Maternal-Newborn Nursing & Women's Health Care*, 7th ed. Saddle River, NJ: Prentice Hall, 2004.

Simkin, Penny, et al. *The Labor Progress Handbook*. Ann Arbor, MI: Blackwell Publishing, 2000.

Simkin, Penny. *Pregnancy, Childbirth, and the Newborn, Revised and Updated: The Complete Guide*. Minnetonka, MN: Meadowbrook Press, 2001.

ORGANIZATIONS

American Academy of Husband-Coached Childbirth. PO Box 5224, Sherman Oaks, CA 91413–5224. Web site: <www.bradleybirth.com/>.

Childbirth Enhancement Foundation. 1004 George Avenue, Rockledge, Fl 32955. Web site: <www.cefcares.org/>.

HypnoBirthing Institute. PO Box 810, Epsom, NH 03234. Web site: <www.joes.com/home/HYPNOBIRTHING/>.

International Association of Parents and Professionals for Safe Alternatives in Childbirth. Rte. 1, Box 646, Marble Hill, MO 63764. Web site: <www.napsac.org/default.htm>.

International Childbirth Education Association. PO Box 20048, Minneapolis, MN 55420. Web site: <www.icea.org/>.

Lamaze International. 2025 M Street, Suite 800, Washington DC 20036–3309. Web site: <www.lamaze-childbirth.com/>.

Linda K. Bennington, MSN, CNS

Childhood Vaccine Injury Act

Definition

The Childhood Vaccine Injury Act established a federal program for compensating victims of vaccine-related injuries or death.

Purpose

During the early 1980s childhood immunization programs fell into chaos. Vaccine manufacturers and healthcare providers were overwhelmed with liability lawsuits from parents who believed that their children had been harmed by the **DTP vaccine**, which protects against **diphtheria**, **tetanus**, and pertussis (**whooping cough**). Companies that developed and produced vaccines halted or threatened to halt production and serious vaccine shortages developed. Childhood immunization rates fell.

To address this problem, physicians, public health agencies, the pharmaceutical industry, government representatives, and the parent-founded and -operated National Vaccine Information Center called for a no-fault alternative to litigation for resolving vaccine injury claims.

In response the U.S. Congress passed the Childhood Vaccine Injury Act of 1986 (PL 99-660). The purpose of the act was to do the following:

- establish the National Vaccine Injury Compensation Program (VICP) as a no-fault alternative to suits against vaccine manufacturers and healthcare providers

- provide victims with an accessible and efficient means of obtaining compensation

- reduce the costs of litigation

- ensure adequate supplies of vaccine

- stabilize the cost of vaccines

- help prevent vaccine injuries through education and a vaccine adverse event reporting system (VAERS)

- create incentives for developing safer vaccines

The Childhood Vaccine Injury Act was part of an initiative to immunize all children against potentially life-threatening diseases. The act was amended several times after its original passage.

Description

In addition to establishing the VICP, the Childhood Vaccine Injury Act requires that **vaccination** records be included in a patient's permanent medical record and that they include the following:

- date of vaccine administration

- vaccine manufacturer and lot number

- name, address, and title of the healthcare provider

The act also requires that doctors report all adverse events occurring within 30 days of vaccination to the VAERS. About 12,000 vaccine-related adverse reactions are reported annually; however, it is estimated that less than 10 percent of doctors file such reports.

The Vaccine Injury Compensation Program (VICP)

The VICP took effect on October 1, 1988. The program is administered jointly by the Division of Vaccine Injury Compensation within the Health Resources and Services Administration (HRSA) of the U.S. Department of Health and Human Services (HHS), by the U.S. Court of Federal Claims, and by the U.S. Department of Justice (DOJ). A nine-member Advisory Commission on Childhood Vaccines oversees the VICP. This commission performs the following services:

- recommends improvements to the program

- proposes changes to the Vaccine Injury Table that specifies qualifying vaccines and injuries or deaths

- proposes legislation

- proposes new, safer vaccines for inclusion in the VICP

- collects information about vaccine-related injuries from federal, state, and local immunization programs

- revises vaccine information statements

- revises adverse reaction reporting requirements

Vaccine Injury Table

The VICP applies to all vaccines recommended by the U.S. Centers for Disease Control and Prevention (CDC) for routine administration to children. However, to qualify for compensation, the petitioner must prove one of the following:

- that an injury occurred that is specified in the Vaccine Injury Table

- that a vaccine significantly aggravated a pre-existing condition

- that a vaccine caused a condition

As of August 26, 2002, the Vaccine Injury Table included the following vaccines:

- DTP for diphtheria, tetanus, and pertussis, as well as other tetanus- and pertussis-containing vaccines

- MMR for **measles**, **mumps**, and **rubella** (German measles), as well as other measles- and rubella-containing vaccines

- OPV and IPV for **polio**, including cases in which polio was contracted from a child vaccinated with OPV

- hepatitis B

- Hib conjugate vaccines for haemophilus influenzae type B that causes meningitis

- varicella (chickenpox)

- pneumococcal conjugate vaccines

- live, oral, rhesus-based rotavirus vaccines for **gastroenteritis**, administered on or before August 26, 2002 (This vaccine was administered routinely only between October 1, 1998 and October 15, 1999.)

- new vaccines

These vaccines are covered regardless of whether they were administered individually or in combination or whether they were administered by public or private healthcare providers. When a new vaccine is added to the Vaccine Injury Table, coverage is retroactive for eight years. When the CDC recommends a new vaccine for routine administration to children, it may be automatically added to the table. Claims can be filed for other vaccines; however, the claimant must prove that the injury was caused by the vaccine. Since this can be very difficult to prove, most VICP claims fall within the Vaccine Injury Table.

The Vaccine Injury Table contains guidelines for evaluating whether the injury or death was vaccine-related. For example, a claim that a child's seizures were triggered by a vaccine must include proof that the child's first seizure occurred within three days of the vaccine administration.

Furthermore, claims for vaccine-related injuries are only valid if the effects continued for at least six months following the vaccination or resulted in **hospitalization** or surgical intervention. The claim must be filed within 36 months of the appearance of the first symptoms. Claims for vaccine-related deaths must be filed within 24 months of the death or within 48 months of the onset of the injury that caused the death.

VICP procedures

Claims must be filed through the VICP before civil litigation can be pursued. Claims can be filed by the injured individual or by a parent, legal guardian, or trustee on behalf of a child or incapacitated victim. The procedural steps are as follows:

• A claimant files a petition for compensation with the U.S. Court of Federal Claims in Washington, DC, and with the secretary of HHS, along with a $150-filing fee.

• A physician from within the Division of Vaccine Injury Compensation reviews the petition and makes a recommendation.

• The physician's recommendation is included in a report filed with the court by the DOJ.

• Hearings are held before a "special master," an attorney appointed by the court judges; a DOJ attorney represents the HHS position; hearings usually last one or two days.

• The special master decides whether the claimant should be compensated.

• A hearing determines the amount of compensation.

• Decisions may be appealed first to a judge of the court, then to the Federal Circuit Court of Appeals, and finally to the Supreme Court.

Although claimants are not required to be represented by an attorney, most petitioners find that they need one. The law provides for compensation for reasonable attorney fees and costs, regardless of the outcome of the claim. An attorney filing a VICP petition must be a member of the bar of the U.S. Court of Federal Claims.

When the victim is a child, the following medical records must accompany the original petition to the court and the HHS secretary:

• all prenatal and birth records and newborn hospital records

• all medical records prior to and including vaccination records

• all post-injury hospital/emergency treatment records

• all post-injury outpatient records

• the VAERS form, if available

• long-term records, including school records, reports, and evaluations, and educational and psychological testing results

• police/ambulance records

• death and autopsy records

Compensation

Compensation for a vaccine-related injury may include the following:

• past and future non-reimbursable medical and custodial care and rehabilitation costs

• a maximum of $250,000 for **pain**, suffering, and emotional distress

• lost earnings or potential lost earnings

• reasonable attorney's fees and costs

Compensation for approved claims have averaged $824,462. The highest compensation award was for $9.13 million. Compensation for a vaccine-related death is limited to $250,000 for the deceased's estate plus attorney's fees and costs. Compensation is paid from the Vaccine Injury Compensation Trust Fund that is funded by a 75-cent excise tax on every purchased dose of a covered vaccine.

Petitions cannot be filed under VICP if a civil action for damages related to a vaccine injury is pending or if damages have been awarded by a court or in a settlement against the manufacturer or vaccine administrator. Civil litigation cannot be pursued if the petitioner accepts an award under the VICP.

Victims may file a civil suit against a vaccine manufacturer or the vaccine administrator given the following:

• The VICP petition is dismissed or ruled non-compensable.

KEY TERMS

Autism—A developmental disability that appears early in life, in which normal brain development is disrupted and social and communication skills are retarded, sometimes severely.

Thimerosal—A mercury-containing preservative used in some vaccines.

Vaccine—A substance prepared from a weakened or killed microorganism which, when injected, helps the body to form antibodies that will prevent infection by the natural microorganism.

Vaccine Adverse Event Reporting System (VAERS)—A federal government program for reporting adverse reactions to the administration of a vaccine.

Vaccine Injury Compensation Program (VICP)—A program through which victims of vaccine-induced injury or death can be awarded financial compensation.

Vaccine Injury Table—The guidelines by which claims to the VICP are evaluated; includes the vaccines, injuries or other conditions, and the allowable time periods for coverage by the VCIP.

- The VICP compensation offer is rejected by the claimant.

- The vaccine is not covered by VICP.

Common problems

Some lawyers and parents argue that there are serious problems with the VICP. They claim the following:

- The VICP is much too complicated and time-consuming.

- Victims are not necessarily able to recover damages.

- The VICP does not consider the emotional and psychological effects of a vaccine-related injury on the child's **family**.

- The VICP greatly underestimates the amount of legal work required for a reasonable chance of a successful claim.

- There is no real difference between the VICP and civil litigation except that the defendant is the U.S. Government rather than the vaccine manufacturer.

- The death-benefit limit of $250,000 does not take into account instances in which prolonged hospitalization preceded death.

- The death-benefit limit does not take into account an adult, family wage earner with a vaccine-related injury or death resulting from exposure to a newly-vaccinated child. (However, a claimant affected by the death benefit limitation may file a civil suit.)

Parental concerns

Outcomes

Between 1988 and 2004, 6,506 petitions were filed with the VICP, of which 4,246 were claims for **autism** resulting from the mercury-containing vaccine preservative thimerosal. Between 1989 and 2004, 140 of the thimerosal claims were dismissed and the rest of these claims were found to be not compensable. Of the non-autism/thimerosal claims, 916 were dismissed and 680 were compensated. Between 1990 and 2004, the government paid out over $588 million in compensation, fees, and costs for 676 claims. Nearly $10 million were paid out for attorney fees.

The VCIP has been credited with helping to stabilize the American vaccine market by providing the following services:

- providing a faster and easier method for resolving claims

- providing liability protection to vaccine manufacturers and healthcare providers

- encouraging research and development of new, safer vaccines

See also Chickenpox vaccine; Hepatitis B vaccine; Meningitis vaccine.

Resources

PERIODICALS

Bridges, Sarah. "A Child's Severe Reaction to a Vaccine Alters Life." *Washington Post* August 3, 2003: W12.

"Pediatrics Information Center Urges Parents to Vaccinate Safely." *Health & Medicine Week* September 24, 2001: 9.

ORGANIZATIONS

National Vaccine Information Center. 421-E Church St., Vienna, VA 22180. Web site: <www.909shot.com>.

National Vaccine Injury Compensation Program.*Health Resources and Services Administration, U.S. Department of Health and Human Services*, Parklawn Building, Room 16C 17, 5600 Fishers Lane, Rockville, MD 20857. Web site: <www.hrsa.gov/osp/vicp/vicp.html>.

WEB SITES

"Commonly Asked Questions about the National Vaccine Injury Compensation Program." *Health Resources and Services Administration, Office of Special Programs*, December 18, 2002. Available online at <www.hrsa.gov/osp/vicp/qanda.htm> (accessed December 8, 2004).

"National Vaccine Injury Compensation Program Fact Sheet." *Health Resources and Services Administration, Office of Special Programs*, November 2002. Available online at <www.hrsa.gov/osp/vicp/fact_sheet.htm> (accessed December 8, 2004).

"National Vaccine Injury Compensation Program: Special Programs Bureau." *Health Resources and Services Administration*, November 2002. Available online at <www.hrsa.gov/osp/vicp/dvicprog.htm> (accessed December 8, 2004).

"Post-1988 Monthly Statistics Report." *National Vaccine Injury Compensation Program*, August, 13, 2004. Available online at <www.hrsa.gov/osp/vicp/monthly_stats_post.htm> (accessed December 8, 2004).

"The Vaccine Injury Compensation Program." *National Vaccine Information Center*. Available online at <www.909shot.com/Issues/Comp_Summary.htm> (accessed December 8, 2004).

Margaret Alic, PhD

Childproofing

Definition

About 2 million children are injured or killed by hazards in the home each year. Many of these incidents are preventable simply by taking precautions and by using simple, relatively inexpensive child **safety** products widely available. The practice of altering an environment in order to maximize the safety of small children is called childproofing.

Description

According to the National Safety Council, more than 20,000 accidental deaths and approximately 25 million accidental injuries occur each year to those under the age of 25. Most of these events occur in the home. The leading causes of injuries to children at home are **burns**, drowning, **poisoning**, cuts, and falls. Safety experts state that most of these accidents are preventable with planning and foresight.

Pediatricians advise parents to begin thinking about home safety when their children are around six months old. As soon as the child is even slightly mobile, childproofing the home is a wise practice. The following suggestions are common precautions that may be taken to avoid accidents in the home.

In the kitchen

The kitchen is one of the most potentially dangerous rooms in the household. In order to avoid the possible hazards, parents should follow these guidelines:

- Always buy the least hazardous products possible and keep toxic items out of sight, out of reach, and under lock and key.

- Post the numbers of the doctor, hospital, emergency service, and poison-control center on or near telephone.

- Teach children never to run with sharp implements (such as knives). Store knives in a secured drawer, in slotted knife blocks, or in trays attached to the wall, out of reach.

- Remove stove knobs or put covers over the burners when the stove is not in use.

- Never transfer household products to a container that once held food. Use the original containers.

- Never store snacks over the stove where a child might be tempted to try to reach them.

In the bathroom

The bathroom also contains a variety of potential dangers for children. These measures may help prevent accidental injuries in this room:

- Unplug electrical appliances when not in use and store them in a locked cabinet or drawer.

- Place nonslip mats or decals in the tub or shower and place a padded spout cover on the faucet.

- To prevent scald burns, set the temperature on the hot-water heater to a maximum of 120°F (49°C).

- Install safety locks on the medicine cabinet to prevent children from reaching prescriptions, **vitamins**, soaps, and other toxic substances. All medications should have child-resistant caps.

- Keep razors and scissors stored in a locked cabinet.

- Install toilet locks to prevent the lid from being lifted by young children. Children can easily fall into the toilet and may drown in as little as 1 in (2.5 cm) of water.

In children's rooms

Each child's room poses certain dangers, and the following are steps to assure children's safety in their bedrooms:

- Keep unopened windows locked and move furniture away from windows. Consider putting guards even on ground-floor windows. Though screens offer the illusion of safety, they are not strong enough to prevent a child from falling through the window.

- Make certain toy boxes are either without a lid or have a feature that prevents the lid from closing on a child's head or fingers.

- Make sure baby furniture meets current safety standards. There should be no sharp edges, and crib slats should be no more than 2.5 inches (6 cm) apart. If the distance is wider than this, a child may be caught or strangled between the bars.

- The crib mattress should fit snugly within the crib frame, with no more than two fingers' distance between the mattress and the crib railing, to avoid strangulation.

- Consider securing heavier pieces of furniture to walls, as children are often injured by pulling heavy furniture down on top of themselves.

In the living room

The living room can be dangerous for children. The following are some safety measures to take:

- Cover all unused electrical outlets with safety plugs.

- Pad sharp tables, and remove glass-topped tables, if possible.

- Pad the corners on a raised hearth or cover the edges with heat-resistant padding.

- Place a protective screen around the fireplace, and never leave children unsupervised when the fireplace is in use.

Hallways and stairs

Hallways and steps can be dangerous for **family** members. The following are some measures to take to make them less so:

- Install a smoke detector on every level of the home, as well as in the hallways outside every sleeping area. Change the batteries yearly.

- Use a carbon monoxide detector outside each sleeping area and near appliances which burn fuel.

- Teach children to use the handrail on stairways and to walk, not run, on the steps. Keep stairways cleared of all objects.

- Use safety gates that screw to the wall at the tops of stairways.

In the yard

The property around the house poses some dangers for children. Here are some steps parents can take to make the yard a safer place:

- Check to see if any plants in the yard are poisonous, and remove them or isolate them with fencing.

- Remove rotting or loose branches from trees promptly.

- Inspect gates and fences regularly to be certain there are no rusty nails or splintered wood.

- If there is a pool, it should be fenced, and all windows and doors providing access to the pool area should be locked. Alarms may be placed on these doors, to alert adults if children do slip into the pool area. Install a phone or keep a charged, waterproof cordless phone near the pool with emergency numbers posted on it.

In the garage

The garage can be a lethal place for small children. Here are some steps to take to secure it for the whole family:

- Petroleum products and any other poisonous substances should be stored up high, in appropriate containers, and locked.

- Garage doors should have electric openers that have an automatic reversing mechanism to prevent the door from closing on a child.

Child safety devices

The following child safety devices can help prevent injuries to young children and are commonly available in stores:

- Safety latches and locks. Latches and locks that are easy to install and use but sturdy enough to withstand pulls and tugs from children are good choices. Safety latches do not guarantee protection, but they can make it more difficult for children to reach dangerous substances.

- Safety gates. Safety gates can help to keep children away from stairs or rooms that contain hazards. Gates that cannot be dislodged easily by a child, but that adults can open and close without difficulty are best. Newer safety gates that meet safety standards have a certification seal from the Juvenile Products Manufacturers Association (JPMA). Check older gates to be sure they do not have V-shapes large enough for a child's head and neck to fit into.

- Door knob covers and door locks. These devices help prevent children from entering rooms with possible hazards. Be certain that the door knob cover is sturdy enough so that it does not break but will still permit a door to be opened quickly by an adult in the case of an emergency.

- Anti-scald devices. These devices help regulate water temperature in order to prevent burns from water that is too hot.

- Smoke detectors. Used on every level of the home and especially near bedroom areas, smoke detectors should be checked monthly to make certain they are working.

- Window guards. To help prevent falls from windows, decks, and balconies, install window guards. However, remember that adults should be able to open at least one window in every room easily in case of fire.

- Corner and edge bumpers. Devices like corner and edge bumpers can be used on sharp edges to prevent injuries from falls.

- Outlet covers. Outlet covers should be inserted in all unused outlets as a way to prevent electrocution or electrical shock. Make sure they cannot be easily removed and that they are large enough so as not to pose a **choking** hazard for young children.

- Carbon monoxide detectors. Parents should place carbon monoxide detectors near all sleeping areas in the home, especially if the house uses gas or oil heat or if it has an attached garage.

- Door stops and door holders. These aid in preventing finger and hand injuries by preventing small fingers and hands from being pinched in doors or hinges.

Common problems

One of the most common childproofing challenges in a home is making certain that **toys** are age-appropriate and that they are in good working order. It can be difficult to keep toys that are geared for an older child away from a younger sibling, but parents should make an attempt to do so. The primary hazard presented by toys meant for older children is the possibility that a smaller child will choke on smaller parts. Parents can instruct their older children why it is important to keep these types of toys away from their siblings who can possibly be harmed by them.

Parents should also be aware if any toy or equipment made for children has been recalled by the manufacturer. This information is easily obtained by checking the Consumer Product Safety Commission (CPSC) recall list (available online at <www.cpsc.gov/cpscpub/prerel/prerel.html>).

Parental concerns

Parents are responsible for providing a safe home environment for their children. However, no amount of childproofing can replace vigilant supervision as a means of maintaining child safety. On the other hand, taking these simple and common sense precautions can help prevent many potential accidents.

See also Safety.

Resources

BOOKS
Lansky, Vicki. *Baby Proofing Basics*. Minnetonka, MN: Book Peddlers, 2002.

PERIODICALS
Townsend, Lindsey. "Keeping Your Child Safe at Home." *Pediatrics for Parents* (October 2003): 4–6.

ORGANIZATIONS
Consumer Product Safety Commission. U.S. Consumer Product Safety Commission, Washington, DC 20207–0001. Web site: <www.cpsc.gov>.

National Safety Council. 1121 Spring Lake Drive, Itasca, IL 60143–3201. Web site: <www.nsc.org>.

WEB SITES
"Childproofing Your Home: 12 Safety Devices to Protect Your Children." *Consumer Product Safety Commission.* Available online at <www.cpsc.gov/cpscpub/pubs/grand/12steps/12steps.html> (accessed October 25, 2004).

Deanna M. Swartout-Corbeil, RN

Children's Apperception Test

Definition

The Children's Apperception Test (CAT) is a projective personality test used to assess individual variations in children's responses to standardized stimuli presented in the form of pictures of animals (CAT-A) or humans (CAT-H) in common social situations. In a supplement to the CAT—the CAT-S—the stimuli include pictures of children in common **family** situations such as prolonged illnesses, births, deaths, and separations from parental figures.

Purpose

The CAT is used to assess personality, level of maturity, and, often, psychological health. The theory is that a child's responses to a series of **drawings** of animals or humans in familiar situations are likely to reveal significant aspects of a child's personality. Some of these dimensions of personality include level of reality testing and judgment, control and regulation of drives, defenses, conflicts, and level of autonomy.

Description

The CAT, developed by psychiatrist and psychologist Leopold Bellak and Sonya Sorel Bellak and first published in 1949, is based on the picture-story test called the **Thematic Apperception Test** (TAT). The TAT, created by psychologist Henry A. Murray for children (ten years old and older) as well as adults, uses a standard series of 31 picture cards in assessing perception of interpersonal relationships. The cards, which portray humans in a variety of common situations, are used to stimulate stories or descriptions (orally or in writing) about relationships or social situations and can help identify dominant drives, emotions, sentiments, conflicts and complexes. The examiner summarizes and interprets the stories in light of certain common psychological themes.

In creating the original CAT, animal figures were used instead of the human figures depicted in the TAT because it was assumed that children from three to ten years of age would identify more easily with drawings of animals. The original CAT consisted of ten cards depicting animal (CAT-A) figures in human social settings. The Bellaks later developed the CAT-H, which included human figures, for use in children who, for a variety of reasons, identified more closely with human rather than animal figures. A supplement to the CAT (the CAT-S), which included pictures of children in common family situations, was created to elicit specific rather than universal responses.

Like the TAT and the Rorschach inkblot test, the CAT is a type of personality **assessment** instrument known as a projective test. The term projective refers to a concept originated by Sigmund Freud. In Freud's theory, unconscious motives control much of human behavior. Projection is a psychological mechanism by which a person unconsciously projects inner feelings onto the external world, then imagines those feelings are being expressed by the external world toward him or herself.

As opposed to cognitive tests, which use intellectual and logical problems to measure what an individual knows about the world, projective assessments such as the CAT are designed to be open-ended and to encourage free expression of thoughts and feelings, thereby revealing how an individual thinks and feels.

Administration

The CAT, which takes 20–45 minutes to administer, is conducted by a trained professional—psychiatrist, psychologist, social worker, teacher or specially trained pediatrician—in a clinical, research, or educational setting. The test may be used directly in therapy or as a **play** technique in other settings.

After carefully establishing rapport with the child, the examiner shows the child one card after another in a particular sequence (although fewer than ten cards may be used at the examiner's discretion) and encourages the child to tell a story—with a beginning, middle, and end—about the characters. The examiner may ask the child to describe, for example, what led up to the scene depicted, the emotions of the characters, and what might happen in the future.

Scoring

In a projective test such as the CAT, there is no right or wrong answer. Thus there is no numerical score or scale for the test. The test administrator records the essence of each of the stories told and indicates the presence or absence of certain thematic elements on the form provided. As in the TAT, each story is carefully analyzed to uncover the child's underlying needs, conflicts, emotions, attitudes, and response patterns. The CAT's creators suggest a series of ten variables to consider when interpreting the results. These variables include the story's major theme, the major character's needs, drives, anxieties, conflicts, fears, and the child's conception of the external world.

Reliability and validity

Although responses in projective tests are believed to reflect personality characteristics, many experts have called into question the reliability, validity, and hence, usefulness of these tests as diagnostic techniques.

The CAT, as well as other projective measures, has been criticized for its lack of a standardized method of administration as well as the lack of standard norms for interpretation. Studies of the interactions between examiners and test subjects have found, for example, that the race, gender, and social class of both participants influence the stories that are told as well as the way the stories are interpreted by the examiner.

KEY TERMS

Apperception—The process of understanding through linkage with previous experience.

Projective test—A type of psychological test that assesses a person's thinking patterns, observational ability, feelings, and attitudes on the basis of responses to ambiguous test materials. Projective tests are often used to evaluate patients with personality disorders.

Rorschach test—A well-known projective test in which subjects are asked to describe a series of black or colored inkblots. The inkblots allow the patient to project his or her interpretations, which can be used to diagnose particular disorders. Also known as the Rorschach Psychodiagnostic Test.

Suggested uses

The CAT, which is designed for use in clinical, educational, and research settings, provides the examiner with a source of data, based on the child's perceptions and imagination, for use in better understanding the child's current needs, motives, emotions, and conflicts, both conscious and unconscious. Its use in clinical assessment is generally part of a larger battery of tests and interview data.

Parental concerns

Although it can provide useful information about a child's personality, the CAT, as a projective measure, relies heavily on the interpretations of the test administrator and is often referred to as an assessment tool rather than a test.

In addition to questioning the general reliability and validity of all projective tests, some experts maintain that cultural and language differences among children tested may affect CAT test performance and may produce inaccurate test results.

Parents need to keep in mind that **psychological tests** such as the CAT, which should be administered only by well-trained professionals, are only one element of a child's psychological assessment. These tools should never be used as the sole basis for a diagnosis. A detailed review of psychological, medical, educational, or other relevant history are required to lay the foundation for interpreting the results of any psychological measurement.

Resources

BOOKS

McCoy, Dorothy. *The Ultimate Guide to Personality Tests.* Inglewood, CA: Champion Press, 2005.

Paul, Annie Murphy. *The Cult of Personality: How Personality Tests Are Leading Us to Miseducate Our Children, Mismanage Our Companies, and Misunderstand Ourselves.* Riverside, NJ: Simon & Schuster, 2004.

PERIODICALS

Camara, W. J., et al. "Psychological test usage: implications in professional psychology." *Professional Psychology: Research and Practice* 31 (2000): 141–54.

Kamphaus, R. W., et al. "Current trends in psychological testing of children." *Professional Psychology: Research and Practice* 31 (2000): 155–64.

ORGANIZATIONS

American Psychological Association Committee on Psychological Tests and Assessments. 750 First St., NE, Washington, DC 20002–4242. Web site: <www.apa.org/psychnet>.

ERIC Clearinghouse on Assessment and Evaluation. O'Boyle Hall, Department of Education, Catholic University of America, Washington, DC 20064. Web site: <www.ericae.net>.

Genevieve Slomski, Ph.D.

Choking

Definition

Choking is a condition caused by inhalation of a foreign object that partially or fully blocks the airway.

Description

Choking is a major cause of respiratory emergencies and cardiac arrest in infants and children. Choking occurs when a foreign object, such as food, buttons, coins, or toy parts, are inhaled and partially or completely block the airway, preventing adequate breathing. In many cases of choking, particularly in adults, the individual actively coughs and is able to expel the foreign object with no assistance or medical attention. However, children and infants are at increased risk of choking and foreign body airway obstruction due to immature airway and dental anatomy, distraction and **play** during eating, and a natural tendency to put objects into their mouths.

A 1995 study of the characteristics of objects known to commonly cause choking deaths in children found that round objects are most dangerous. For example, a small ball or marble can completely seal a child's or infant's trachea (windpipe). Round or cylindrical foods, hard candy, chewing gum, and balloons also present choking hazards. In infants, choking usually results from inhalation of small objects (coins, small **toys**, deflated balloons, buttons) that they place in their mouths.

Demographics

Each year, more than 17,000 infants and children are treated in hospital emergency departments for choking-related incidents, and more than 80 percent of these occur in children aged four years and younger. Airway obstruction death and injury are especially prevalent in children under age four due to anatomy (small airway), natural curiosity and tendency to put objects in their mouths, and incomplete chewing. According to statistics from the Centers for Disease Control and Prevention, choking rates in 2001 were highest in infants.

Causes and symptoms

Choking is a major cause of death for children under three and is a hazard for older children as well. Young children naturally explore the world with their mouths, and they will readily put in their mouths anything that fits. If a small object slips back into the throat and blocks the trachea, the child may become unable to breathe, and unless the child is helped to eject the object quickly, the child may asphyxiate and die. Food is also a choking hazard, especially for children under three who do not know how to chew food thoroughly.

According to statistics from the Centers for Disease Control and Prevention, of the 17,000 or so cases of pediatric choking in 2001, 60 percent were related to food, 31 percent were related to non-food substances, and 9 percent were related to undetermined objects. Of the food-related choking incidents, 19 percent resulted from candy or gum. Of the choking incidents resulting from non-food objects, 13 percent were related to coins.

Food-related choking usually occurs because infants and young children do not chew their food well, and larger pieces can become stuck in their throat. The following foods have been identified by the American Academy of Pediatrics as presenting choking hazards:

- hot dogs
- hard candy
- chewing gum
- nuts and seeds
- chunks of meat or cheese
- whole grapes
- popcorn
- chunks of peanut butter
- raw vegetables
- raisins

The following objects have been identified as presenting choking hazards:

- coins
- buttons
- marbles
- small balls
- deflated balloons
- watch batteries
- jewelry
- ball point pen caps and paper clips
- arts and crafts supplies
- small toys and toys with small detachable parts

When to call the doctor

All infants, children, and adolescents who have a choking incident should see a doctor, since complications can occur even if the object causing the choking is successfully expelled. Sometimes, pieces can be aspirated into the lungs, and even though breathing returns to normal, wheezing, chest **pain**, persistent **cough**, and **pneumonia** can develop within a few days due to the foreign body in the lung. Foreign bodies may require removal by bronchoscopy or surgery.

Vomiting may occur after being treated with the **Heimlich maneuver**. All infants and children who experience a choking episode severe enough to require the Heimlich maneuver should be taken to the hospital emergency room to be examined for airway injuries.

Diagnosis

Choking is diagnosed by observation of the choking victim. Children able to actively cough should be watched to make sure they expel the object on their own and that their airways do not become blocked. Indications that a choking victim's airway is blocked include the following:

- inability to cough, cry, or speak

- blue or purple face color from lack of oxygen

- grabbing at throat

- weak cough and labored breathing that produces a high-pitched noise

- all of the above, followed by loss of consciousness

When the actual choking incident is not observed, choking can be diagnosed by observing the above symptoms. For children, infants, and adolescents who are unconscious, choking and foreign body obstruction can be diagnosed by attempting to give rescue breaths. If a breath administered to the victim does not inflate the chest, rescuers should assume that the airway is blocked and take steps to clear the airway.

Treatment

An emergency choking incident is treated using the Heimlich maneuver, usually administered by parents, caregivers and teachers, or bystanders. Children who have a choking incident that requires the Heimlich maneuver should be examined by a physician for potential injuries to their airway and aftereffects of oxygen deprivation.

The Heimlich maneuver is used when a child is choking on a foreign object to the extent that he/she cannot breathe. Oxygen deprivation from a foreign body airway obstruction can result in permanent brain damage or death in four minutes or less. Using the Heimlich maneuver can save a choking victim's life. The Heimlich maneuver is not performed on infants under one year of age; rather, a series of back blows and chest thrusts are used to attempt to dislodge the foreign object.

If the foreign body cannot be expelled from the child's airway using the Heimlich maneuver, cardiac and/or respiratory arrest may occur, and the child may stop breathing. If this happens, **cardiopulmonary resuscitation** (CPR) is performed to restore and maintain breathing and circulation and to provide oxygen and blood flow to the heart, brain, and other vital organs. CPR can be performed by trained laypeople or healthcare professionals on infants, children, adolescents, and adults. CPR should be performed if an infant, child, or adolescent is unconscious and not breathing.

Prognosis

Incorrectly applied, the Heimlich maneuver can break bones or damage internal organs. Following the Heimlich maneuver, dysphagia (swallowing difficulty) and obstructive pulmonary edema (fluid accumulation in the lungs) may occur and require medical treatment.

In many cases the foreign material is dislodged from the throat, and the choking victim suffers no permanent effects of the episode. If the foreign material is not removed, the choking victim may suffer permanent brain damage from lack of oxygen or may die.

Prevention

Choking is easily preventable by taking the following steps:

- supervising infants and children while they eat and play

- childproofing play areas by removing small objects

- cutting foods into very small pieces

- avoiding serving foods listed above as choking hazards to children under age four

- monitoring older children to make sure they do not give younger children hazardous foods or objects

- following age and **safety** guidelines on toys

- learning CPR and the Heimlich maneuver

- not letting children and infants play with coins

Parental concerns

Because most choking incidents occur in the home, all parents and infant/child caregivers should be trained in the Heimlich maneuver. Training is available through the American Red Cross and American Heart Association at local schools, YMCAs, and community centers.

The likelihood of choking incidents can be reduced by closely supervising infants and children while they eat and play. Most choking incidents are associated with food items, especially hot dogs, candies, grapes, nuts, popcorn, and carrots. Common non-food items that present choking hazards include deflated balloons, buttons, coins, small balls, small toys, and toy parts. All toys should be examined to make sure they are age-appropriate and do not have loose parts.

Resources

BOOKS

Basic Life Support for Healthcare Providers. Dallas, TX. American Heart Association, 2001.

PERIODICALS

Centers for Disease Control and Prevention. "Nonfatal Choking-Related Episodes among Children—United States, 2001." *Journal of the American Medical Association* 288 (November 20, 2002): 2400–02.

Vikle, Gary M., et al. "Airway Obstruction in Children Aged Less than Five Years: The Prehospital Experience." *Prehospital Emergency Care* 8 (2004): 196–99.

ORGANIZATIONS

American Heart Association. 7320 Greenville Ave., Dallas, TX 75231. Web site: <www.americanheart.org>.

The Heimlich Institute. 311 Straight St., Cincinnati, OH 45219–9957. Web site: <www.heimlichinstitute.org>.

WEB SITES

"Choking Episodes among Children." *National Center for Injury Prevention and Control.* Available online at <www.cdc.gov/ncipc/duip/spotlite/choking.htm> (accessed December 8, 2004).

"Heimlich Maneuver." *American Heart Association*, 2004. Available online at <www.americanheart.org/presenter.jhtml?identifier=4605> (accessed December 8, 2004).

"Infant First Aid for Choking and CPR: An Illustrated Guide." *BabyCenter*, 2004. Available online at <www.babycenter.com/general/9298.html> (accessed December 8, 2004).

National Safe Kids Campaign. Available online at <www.safekids.org> (accessed December 8, 2004).

Jennifer E. Sisk, M.A.

Cholesterol, high

Definition

High cholesterol (hypercholesterolemia or hyperlipidemia) refers to the presence of higher than normal amounts of total cholesterol circulating in the bloodstream. Cholesterol is a fatty substance (lipid) that is essential to the body as protection for the walls of the vasculature (veins and arteries) and linings of body organs, a component in the manufacture of hormones, and a factor in the digestion of consumed fats in foods. It is manufactured in the liver and carried throughout the body in the bloodstream. Cholesterol is also a component of animal tissue and can be consumed in products such as meat, eggs, fish, milk, and milk products such as butter and cheese. Elevated cholesterol levels can result in the accumulation of fatty deposits on blood vessel walls, narrowing veins and arteries and impeding blood flow to the heart, brain, and other organs.

Description

Cholesterol has both a good form and a bad form that add up to total cholesterol when measured together. The body needs cholesterol to produce bile acids that help digest fats ingested in food, make hormones, protect cell walls, and participate in other processes that help maintain health. Ironically, cholesterol can also be a problem, if too much is manufactured by the liver or consumed through the diet and not metabolized or used. The utilization of fat in the body, or fat metabolism, is a complex process, complicated even more by abnormally high levels of cholesterol found circulating in the blood. Although high cholesterol is not often found in young children, it may begin to develop in adolescents or young adults either as an inherited condition or through unhealthy eating habits and can continue into adulthood, creating potentially serious health problems. High cholesterol levels and fatty deposits in veins and arteries (atherosclerosis) have been found during autopsies of children who have died of accidents and other causes.

The liver metabolizes cholesterol, including the cholesterol obtained from foods in the diet. The components of cholesterol are then carried into the bloodstream bound to the surface of certain lipoproteins. Low-density lipoproteins or LDLs carry about 75 percent of the cholesterol into the blood and high-density lipoproteins carry the other 25 percent. LDL is the lipoprotein known as bad cholesterol because it consists primarily of cholesterol and is most associated with the development of vascular disease. Cholesterol is not the major part of HDL, the so-called good cholesterol, and the presence of higher amounts of HDL in the blood actually helps reduce the more harmful LDL levels. Another lipoprotein, very low-density lipoprotein (VLDL), carries harmful fats known as triglycerides but does not carry a significant amount of cholesterol. Triglycerides are also measured as part of a lipid profile and high levels are associated with vascular disease and heart disease. Cholesterol levels in blood serum vary considerably from day to day and even from one time of a day to another related to the consumption of fats in the diet.

High LDL (low-density lipoprotein) is a major precursor of vascular disease and heart disease. This form of cholesterol combines with triglycerides, cellular waste, calcium, and scar tissue to form a waxy deposit (plaque) on the inner walls of large and medium-sized arteries, causing a condition called hardening of the arteries (atherosclerosis or arteriosclerosis). Plaque typically builds up as people get older, more in some people than others depending on lifestyle (diet, **exercise**, alcohol consumption, and **smoking**) and heredity. The result may be a narrowing (stenosis) or blockage of blood vessels, interrupting the essential flow of blood and oxygen to the heart, brain, abdominal organs, and peripheral circulation to the arms and legs. Eventually this can lead to heart attack or **stroke**, permanent damage to the heart or brain, and life-threatening complications.

The population as a whole is at some risk of developing high LDL cholesterol. Specific risk factors include a **family** history of high cholesterol, **obesity**, coronary artery disease (atherosclerosis), stroke, **alcoholism**, diabetes, high blood pressure, and lack of regular exercise. The chances of developing high cholesterol increase after the age of 45. One of the primary causes of high LDL cholesterol is a combination of too much fat and sugar in the diet, especially through the consumption of fast foods and refined or packaged foods, a problem that has been especially true in the United States since the

advent of manufactured foods. A renewed interest in whole foods may help to alter the prevalence of high cholesterol and vascular disease.

An increased serum cholesterol may be found in familial hyperlipidemia or hypercholesterolemia, underactive thyroid (**hypothyroidism**), untreated diabetes, a high-fat diet, pregnancy, heart attack, stress, and certain liver conditions (cirrhosis). A decreased level may be found in liver dysfunction, overactive thyroid (**hyperthyroidism**), malabsorption, **malnutrition**, or advanced **cancer**, among other conditions.

Although high cholesterol has been shown to be a risk factor for developing atherosclerosis in adults, with associated increased morbidity and mortality, studies have not indicated that high cholesterol in children and adolescents is related to the development of specific illness or increasing mortality in adulthood. There is strong evidence in numerous research studies, however, that a family history of high cholesterol, atherosclerosis, heart attack, or stroke increases the risk of a child developing high cholesterol levels.

High cholesterol is often diagnosed and treated by general practitioners or family practice physicians. In some cases, the condition is treated by an endocrinologist or cardiologist. Pediatricians will generally refer affected children to the appropriate specialist.

Demographics

The U.S. Food and Drug Administration (FDA) estimates that 90 million American adults, roughly half the adult population, have elevated cholesterol levels. This estimate does not indicate that as many children are candidates for high cholesterol levels; however, about 2 percent of the U.S. population has a family history of hypercholesterolemia in parents or grandparents, and this history is the most common predictor of high cholesterol levels in children and adolescents. Before **puberty**, average total and LDL cholesterol levels are higher in girls than in boys. Both LDL and HDL levels are higher in non-Hispanic black children than in non-Hispanic whites and Mexican-American children.

Causes and symptoms

The causes of high cholesterol may be genetic or hereditary factors in the manufacture of cholesterol by the liver or in fat metabolism, a diet high in saturated fats and trans-fatty acids, obesity, alcoholism, smoking, and lack of exercise.

There are no readily apparent symptoms that indicate high cholesterol, high LDL, high triglycerides, or low HDL. Obesity is a general indication of possible high cholesterol levels. Labored breathing or general feelings of sluggishness and lack of energy may warrant examination by a physician and testing of cholesterol. Families or individuals who regularly consume a high-fat diet consisting of animal products, fast foods, and refined foods may also benefit from being tested for abnormal cholesterol levels.

When to call the doctor

Excess weight may be the only sign of possible high cholesterol in children. It is wise for parents to consult a physician if a child is consistently overweight and diet or exercise does not seem to make a significant difference. Sluggishness may also be noted if a child's veins and arteries are consistently filled with higher than normal amounts of fatty substances that are not being metabolized by the body.

Diagnosis

Total serum cholesterol is the cholesterol most often measured and reported in medical office tests, home tests, and blood cholesterol screening clinics; people who quote their cholesterol level as high may be talking about a total cholesterol of over 200mg/dL. A definitive diagnosis of high cholesterol, however, ideally includes measuring LDL, HDL, total cholesterol, and triglyceride levels, as well as the cholesterol to HDL ratio. This combination of tests performed in the clinical laboratory is called a lipid panel or lipid profile. Most physicians want to know the results of a lipid panel before diagnosing high cholesterol and recommending treatment. Screening for lipid levels in all children is not usually recommended. It is recommended that children whose parents have a total cholesterol level over 200mg/dL or whose family history includes heart disease or stroke in either parents or grandparents have a cholesterol screening performed. If the fasting blood level of cholesterol is 170 to 199 mg/dL, total cholesterol should be repeated and the two tests averaged. A final result of 200 mg/dL or over indicates that the entire lipid panel should be done to determine if hyperlipidemia is present.

In most adults the recommended levels for cholesterol and triglycerides, measured as milligrams per deciliter (mg/dL) of blood, are: total cholesterol, less than 200; LDL, less than 130; HDL, more than 35; triglycerides, 30–200; and cholesterol to HDL ratio, four to one. However, the recommended cholesterol levels may vary from person to person, depending on other risk factors such as a family history of heart disease or stroke or the presence of **hypertension**, diabetes, advanced age, alcoholism, or smoking.

The physician may recommend nuclear magnetic resonance (NMR) lipoprofile testing for individuals whose lipid measurements, history, and risk factors are not diagnostic, that is they are not revealing why an individual has coronary artery disease. Doctors have always been puzzled by why some people develop heart disease while others with identical HDL and LDL levels do not. Research studies in the early 2000s indicate that it may be due to the size of the cholesterol particles in the bloodstream. Nuclear magnetic resonance (NMR) lipoprofile exposes a blood sample to a magnetic field to determine the size of the cholesterol particles. Particle size also can be determined by a centrifugation test, in which blood samples are spun very quickly to allow particles to separate and move at different distances. The smaller the particles, the greater the chance of developing heart disease. It allows physicians to treat patients who have normal or close to normal results from a lipid panel but abnormal particle size.

Treatment

The primary goal of cholesterol treatment is to lower LDL to under 160 mg/dL in people without heart disease and who are at lower risk of developing it. The goal in people with higher risk factors for heart disease is less than 130 mg/dL. In patients who already have heart disease, the goal is under 100 mg/dL, according to FDA guidelines. Also, since low HDL levels increase the risk of developing heart disease, the goal for all individuals is to maintain an HDL of more than 35 mg/dL. These values apply to children and adolescents as well as adults.

First-line treatment of high cholesterol for all ages includes diet, exercise, and weight loss. The National Cholesterol Education Program recommends that children over age two eat a variety of foods for healthy development and ideal weight, consuming no more than 30 percent total fat in the diet and no more than 10 percent saturated fat as in animal foods. The American Heart Association Step 2 diet has been tested as a diet-alone treatment and in conjunction with drug therapy for children with high cholesterol, with good results. Regular exercise through aerobic activity is recommended.

In addition to diet and exercise, a variety of prescription medicines are available to help reduce cholesterol levels in the blood; these medications may not always be recommended for children, except for those whose parents or grandparents have high cholesterol and coronary artery disease. A class of drugs called statins is known to help lower LDL in combination with dietary changes and exercise, and studies have shown that they have no adverse effects in children. A class of drugs called fibric acid derivatives is sometimes recommended to lower triglycerides and raise HDL. Doctors decide which drug is most effective for an individual based on the cause and the severity of the cholesterol problem and other health conditions that may be present, as well as possible side effects of the drug. Diet and exercise remain important factors in reducing elevated cholesterol levels, even if drug therapy is prescribed.

Alternative treatment

Alternative treatment of high cholesterol may include high doses of garlic, niacin, soy protein, algae, or other fatty acids, and the Chinese medicine supplement Cholestin (a red yeast fermented with rice).

GARLIC A number of clinical studies have indicated that garlic can offer modest reductions in cholesterol. A 1997 study by **nutrition** researchers at Pennsylvania State University found that men who took garlic capsules for five months reduced their total cholesterol by 7 percent and LDL by 12 percent. Another study showed that seven cloves of fresh garlic a day significantly reduced LDL, as did a daily dose of four garlic extract pills.

CHOLESTIN Cholestin has been available since 1997 as a cholesterol-lowering dietary supplement. It is a processed form of red yeast fermented with rice, a traditional herbal remedy used for centuries in China. Two studies released in 1998 showed Cholestin lowered LDL cholesterol by 20 to 30 percent. It also appeared to raise HDL and lower triglyceride levels. Although the supplement contains hundreds of compounds, the major active LDL-lowering ingredient is lovastatin, a chemical also found in the prescription drug Mevacor. The product is available as a dietary supplement, not a drug; its actual mechanism is not known. No serious side effects have been reported, but minor side effects, including bloating and heartburn, have been noted.

OTHER TREATMENTS A study released in 1999 indicated that blue-green algae contains polyunsaturated fatty acids that lower cholesterol. The algae, known as *Aphanizomenon flos-aquae* (AFA) is available as an over-the-counter dietary supplement. Flax seed oil is another source of fatty acids known to reduce cholesterol levels. Niacin, also known as nicotinic acid or vitamin B3, has been shown to reduce LDL levels by 10 to 20 percent and raise HDL levels by 15 to 35 percent. It also reduces triglycerides. Because an extremely high dose of niacin is needed to treat cholesterol problems, it should only be taken under a doctor's supervision to monitor possible toxic side effects. Niacin can also cause flushing when taken in high doses. Soy protein with high levels of isoflavones also has been shown to reduce LDL levels by up to 10 percent. In 2003, a Cuban research study revealed that policosanol, a substance made from sugar

cane wax or beeswax, lowered LDL cholesterol nearly 27 percent in study subjects.

Nutritional concerns

Several specific diet options have been shown to be beneficial for reducing cholesterol. A vegetarian diet provides up to 100 percent more fiber and up to 50 percent less cholesterol from food than a meat-based diet. A balanced vegetarian diet consists of at least six servings of whole grain foods, three or more servings of green leafy vegetables, two to four servings of fruit, two to four servings of legumes (protein source), and one or two servings of non-fat dairy products daily. The macrobiotic diet is similar, with brown rice being a staple, but with the addition of other protein sources such as fish and fowl, tofu, and other soy products (miso, tempeh). The low glycemic or diabetic diet is known to raise the HDL (good cholesterol) level by as much as 20 percent in three weeks. Low glycemic foods promote a slow but steady rise in blood glucose levels following a meal, which increases the level of HDL. They also lower total cholesterol and triglycerides. Low glycemic foods include certain fruits, vegetables, beans, and whole grains. Processed (packaged foods) and refined foods (white flour products, white rice) and refined sugars (white sugar, brown sugar, molasses, and products made with them) should be avoided in all diets. Soy protein can be added to the daily diet to help replace animal sources of protein and reduce cholesterol; a diet containing 62 mg of isoflavones in soy protein is recommended and can be incorporated into other diet regimens, including vegetarian, macrobiotic, and low glycemic.

Prognosis

High cholesterol is one of the key risk factors for heart disease and has been shown to be treatable. Left untreated, high levels of LDL and total cholesterol can lead to the formation of plaque, the narrowing of blood vessels, vascular disease, and subsequent heart attacks and stroke.

Prevention

Since a large number of people with high cholesterol are overweight, a healthy diet and regular exercise are probably the most beneficial ways to control cholesterol levels. Exercise is an extremely important part of burning calories obtained by eating fats and helps maintain lower bad cholesterol and higher levels of good cholesterol. Exercise should consist of 20 to 30 minutes of vigorous aerobic exercise at least three times a week. Exercises that cause the heart to beat faster include fast

KEY TERMS

Atherosclerosis—A disease process whereby plaques of fatty substances are deposited inside arteries, reducing the inside diameter of the vessels and eventually causing damage to the tissues located beyond the site of the blockage.

Fatty acid—The primary component of lipids (fats) in the body. The body requires some, called essential fatty acids, to form membranes and synthesize important compounds.

Glycemic—The presence of glucose in the blood.

Hypertension—Abnormally high arterial blood pressure, which if left untreated can lead to heart disease and stroke.

Legumes—A family of plants, including beans, peas, and lentils, that bear edible seeds in pods. These seeds are high in protein, fiber, and other nutrients.

Lipids—Organic compounds not soluble in water, but soluble in fat solvents such as alcohol. Lipids are stored in the body as energy reserves and are also important components of cell membranes. Commonly known as fats.

Polyunsaturated fat—A non-animal oil or fatty acid rich in unsaturated chemical bonds. This type of fat is not associated with the formation of cholesterol in the blood.

Trans-fatty acid—A type of fat created by hydrogenating polyunsaturated oils. This changes the double bond on the carbon atom from a cis configuration to a trans configuration, making the fatty acid saturated, and a greater health concern. For example, stick margarines are known to contain more trans-fatty acids than liquid oils.

walking, bicycling, jogging, roller skating, swimming, and walking up stairs.

Nutritional concerns

In general, the nutritional goals for preventing high levels of cholesterol are to substantially reduce or eliminate foods high in animal fat, including meat, shellfish, eggs, and dairy products. The use of polyunsaturated fats in cooking is also recommended, including cold pressed oils such as olive oil, canola oil, and sesame oil. Many vegetable oils are hydrogenated or extracted at high temperatures and are best avoided. Trans-fatty acids found in solid shortenings, most margarines, and hydrogenated oils or products containing them should also be avoided because they are known to increase levels of LDL.

Parental concerns

Parents need not be concerned about high cholesterol levels in their children unless the child is obese or there is a family history of high cholesterol, heart attack, or stroke. Parents who have cholesterol levels over 200 mg/dL themselves may want to have their children's cholesterol levels tested. Much information is available from public health sources and family physicians about diet and exercise recommendations to help people of all ages reduce the risk of vascular disease and related illnesses, such as heart disease and stroke.

Resources

BOOKS

Bratman, Steven, and David Kroll. *Natural Pharmacist: Natural Treatments for High Cholesterol.* Roseville, CA: Prima Publishing, 2000.

PERIODICALS

"Eating a Vegetarian Diet that Includes Cholesterol-lowering Foods May Lower Lipid Levels as Much as Some Medications." *Environmental Nutrition* (March 2003): 8.

Sage, Katie. "Cut Cholesterol with Policosanol: This Supplement Worked Better than a Low-fat Diet in One Study." *Natural Health* (March 2003): 32.

ORGANIZATIONS

National Cholesterol Education Program. NHLBI Information Center, PO Box 30105, Bethesda, MD 20824–0105. Web site: <www.nhlbi.nih.gov>.

WEB SITES

"Cholesterol." *MedlinePlus.* Available online at <www.nlm.nih.gov/medlineplus/cholesterol.html> (accessed December 8, 2004).

L. Lee Culvert
Ken R. Wells
Teresa G. Odle

Chordee *see* **Hypospadias**

Chorea *see* **Movement disorders**

Circumcision

Definition

The surgical removal of the foreskin of the penis in a male or the prepuce of a clitoris in a female.

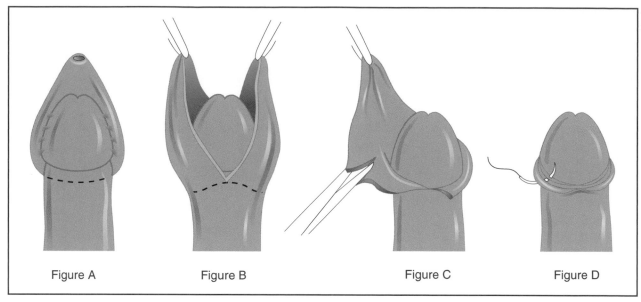

A typical circumcision procedure involves the following steps: **Figure A: The surgeon makes an incision around the foreskin. Figure B: The foreskin is then freed from the skin covering the penile shaft. Figure C: The surgeon cuts the foreskin to the initial incision, lifting the foreskin from the mucous membrane. Figure D: The surgeon sutures the top edge of the skin that covers the penile shaft and the mucous membrane.** *(Illustration by Electronic Illustrators Group.)*

Purpose

In the United States, circumcision in infant boys is performed for social, medical, cultural, or religious reasons. Once a routine operation urged by pediatricians and obstetricians for newborns in the middle of the twentieth century, circumcision has become an elective option that parents make for their sons on an individual basis. Families who practice Judaism or Islam may select to have their sons circumcised as a religious practice. Others may elect circumcision for medical reasons.

Female circumcision (also known as female genital mutilation) is usually performed for cultural and social reasons by **family** members and others who are not members of the medical profession, with no anesthesia. Not only is the prepuce of the clitoris removed but often the vaginal opening is sewn to make it smaller. This practice is supposed to ensure the virginity of a bride on her wedding day. It also prevents the woman from achieving sexual pleasure during coitus. Female circumcision is illegal in most countries of the world. It is considered by most people to be a human rights violation.

Though the incidence of male circumcision has decreased from 90 percent in 1979 to 60 percent in 2002, it is still the most common surgical procedure in the United States. Circumcision rates are much lower for the rest of the industrialized world. In Britain, it is only performed for religious practices or to correct a specific medical condition of the penis.

Parents may choose circumcision because they believe the surgery protects against infections of the urinary tract and the foreskin, prevents **cancer**, lowers the risk of getting **sexually transmitted diseases**, and prevents phimosis (a tightening of the foreskin that may close the opening of the penis). Though studies indicate that uncircumcised boys under the age of five are 20 times more likely than circumcised boys to have urinary tract infections (UTIs), the rate of incidence of UTIs is quite low. There are also indications that circumcised men are less likely to suffer from penile cancer, inflammation of the penis, or have many sexually transmitted diseases. Here again, the rate of incidence is low. Good hygiene usually prevents most infections of the penis. Phimosis and penile cancer are very rare, even in men who have not been circumcised. Education and good safe-sex practices can prevent sexually transmitted diseases in ways that a surgical procedure cannot because these are diseases acquired through risky behaviors.

With these factors in mind, the American Academy of Pediatrics issued a policy pronouncement that states although there is existing scientific evidence that support the medical benefits of circumcision, the benefits are not strong enough to recommended circumcision as a routine practice.

Description

The foreskin of the penis safeguards the sensitivity of the glans and shields it from irritation by urine, feces, and foreign materials. It also protects the urinary opening against infection and accidental injury.

Despite a long-standing belief that infants do not experience serious **pain** from circumcision, most authorities in the early 2000s believe that some form of local anesthesia is necessary. The physician injects local anesthesia at the base of the penis or under the skin around the penis (subcutaneous ring block). Both anesthetics block key nerves. EMLA cream, a topical formula of several anesthetics, can also be used.

In circumcision of infant boys, the foreskin is pulled tightly into a specially designed clamp. Pressure is applied and the foreskin pulls away from the broadened tip of the penis. Pressure from the clamp stops bleeding from blood vessels that supplied the foreskin. In older boys or adults, an incision is made around the base of the foreskin, the foreskin is pulled back, and then it is cut away from the tip of the penis. Stitches are usually used to close the skin edges.

After circumcision, the wound should be washed daily. An antibiotic ointment or petroleum jelly may be applied to the site. If there is an incision, a wound dressing will be present and should be changed each time the diaper is changed. Sometimes a plastic ring is used instead of a bandage. The ring usually falls off in five to eight days. The penis heals in seven to 10 days.

Infants who undergo circumcision may be fussy for some hours afterward, so parents should be prepared for crying, feeding problems, and **sleep** problems. Generally these go away within a day. In older boys, the penis may be painful, but the pain goes away gradually. A topical anesthetic ointment or spray may be used to relieve this temporary discomfort. There may also be a bruise on the penis, which typically goes away with no particular attention.

The clitoral prepuce of infant girls is drawn up and away from the body before being removed. In this procedure, the clitoris is also frequently removed. The vaginal opening may be partially closed. Healing is slower in girls than for boys. Most female circumcisions are performed under unhygienic conditions using primitive, homemade implement such as rusty razor blades and thorns. Infections are common.

Risks

Complications following newborn circumcision appear in one out of every 500 procedures. Most complications are minor. Bleeding occurs in half of the complications and is usually easy to control. Infections are rare and present with **fever** and signs of inflammation. Uneven healing of skin may lead to laterally curving erections in adulthood.

KEY TERMS

Foreskin—A covering fold of skin over the tip of the penis.

Glans penis—The cone-shaped tip of the penis.

Hernia—A rupture in the wall of a body cavity, through which an organ may protrude.

Hydrocele—A collection of fluid between two layers of tissue surrounding the testicle; the most common cause of painless scrotal swelling.

Hypospadias—A congenital abnormality of the penis in which the urethral opening is located on the underside of the penis rather than at its tip.

Phimosis—A tightening of the foreskin that may close the opening of the penis.

Prepuce—A fold of skin, such as the foreskin of the penis or the skin that surrounds the clitoris.

There may be injuries to the body of the penis that may be difficult to repair. In 2000, there were reports that the surgical clamps used in circumcision were at fault in over 100 injuries reported between July 1996 and January 2000. In nearly all cases, the clamps were assumed to be in working order but had been repaired with replacement parts that were not of the manufacturer's specifications. Physicians were urged to inspect the clamps before use and ensure that their dimensions fit the infant's body parts.

Circumcised girls have a high incidence of infertility and sexual dysfunction as adults. Most experience infections immediately after the procedure.

Normal results

Among boys who are circumcised, most have no penile, urologic, or sexual dysfunction as adults. A majority of girls who are circumcised experience urologic, reproductive, and sexual dysfunction as adults.

Parental concerns

The only medical justification for male circumcision is to correct a health problem or condition. There are no medical justifications for female circumcision. The only other justification for male or female circumcision is religious or cultural. Leaders of the vast majority of religions throughout the world condemn any form of female circumcision.

Resources

BOOKS

Darby, Robert. *A Surgical Temptation: The Demonization of the Foreskin and the Rise of Circumcision in Britain.* Chicago: University of Chicago Press, 2005.

Elder, Jack S. "Anomalies of the Penis and Urethra." In *Nelson Textbook of Pediatrics*, 17th ed. Edited by Richard E. Behrman, et al. Philadelphia: Saunders, 2003, pp. 1812–6.

Fleiss, Paul M., and Frederick Hodges. *What Your Doctor May Not Tell You about Circumcision: Untold Facts on America's Most Widely Performed—and Most Unnecessary Surgery.* New York: Warner Books, 2002.

Gollaher, David L. *Circumcision: A History of the World's Most Controversial Surgery.* New York: Basic Books, 2000.

Lewis, Joseph, et al. *In the Name of Humanity: Speaking Out against Circumcision.* San Diego, CA: Book Tree, 2003.

PERIODICALS

Adelman, W. P., and A. Joffe. "Controversies in male adolescent health: varicocele, circumcision, and testicular self-examination." *Current Opinions in Pediatrics* 16, no. 4 (2004): 363–7.

Campbell, C. C. "Care of women with female circumcision." *Journal of Midwifery and Women's Health* 49, no. 4 (2004): 364–5.

Essen, B., and S. Johnsdotter. "Female genital mutilation in the West: traditional circumcision versus genital cosmetic surgery." *Acta Obstetrics and Gynecology of Scandinavia* 83, no. 7 (2004): 611–3.

Hiss, J., A. Horowitz, and T. Kahana. "Fatal hemorrhage following male ritual circumcision." *Journal of Clinical Forensic Medicine* 7, no. 1 (2000): 32–4.

ORGANIZATIONS

American Academy of Family Physicians. 11400 Tomahawk Creek Parkway, Leawood, KS 66211–2672. Web site: <www.aafp.org/>.

American Academy of Pediatrics. 141 Northwest Point Boulevard, Elk Grove Village, IL 60007–1098. Web site: <www.aap.org/>.

American College of Surgeons. 633 North St. Clair Street, Chicago, IL 60611–32311. Web site: <www.facs.org/>.

American Medical Association. 515 N. State Street, Chicago, IL 60610. Web site: <www.ama-assn.org/>.

American Urological Association. 1120 North Charles Street, Baltimore, MD 21201. Web site: <www.auanet.org/index_hi.cfm>.

WEB SITES

"Circumcision." *Circumcision Information Resource Pages.* Available online at <www.cirp.org/> (accessed November 2, 2004).

"Circumcision." Available online at *Circumcision Resource Center.* Available online at <www.circumcision.org/> (accessed November 2, 2004).

"Circumcision." *Mothers Against Circumcision.* Available online at <www.mothersagainstcirc.org> (accessed November 2, 2004).

"Doctors Opposing Circumcision." *University of Washington.* Available online at <http://faculty.washington.edu/gcd/DOC/> (accessed November 2, 2004).

L. Fleming Fallon Jr., MD, DrPH

Cleft lip and palate

Definition

A cleft lip and/or palate is a birth defect (congenital) of the upper part of the mouth. A cleft lip creates an opening in the upper lip between the mouth and nose and a cleft palate occurs when the roof of the mouth has not joined completely.

Description

Cleft means split or separated. During the first months of pregnancy, separate areas of the face—such as bony and muscular parts, mouth, and throat, develop individually and then join together. If some parts do not join properly the result is a cleft, the type and severity of which can vary. During the fifth through ninth weeks of pregnancy genetic and environmental factors are most likely to affect lip and palate development. Cleft palate occurs when the right and left segments of the palate fail to join properly. The back of the palate (toward the throat) is called the soft palate, and the front section (toward the mouth opening) is known as the hard palate. A cleft palate can range from just an opening at the back of the soft palate to a nearly complete separation of the roof of the mouth (soft and hard palate). In some cases, an infant with a cleft palate may also have a small lower jaw and have difficulty breathing. This condition is called Pierre Robin sequence.

Cleft lip occurs when the lip elements fail to come together during fetal development, thus creating an opening in the upper lip between the mouth and nose. The lip looks split. A cleft lip may be complete, meaning that

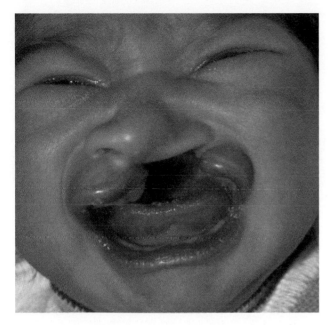

Infant with a unilateral cleft lip and palate. *(Custom Medical Stock Photo Inc.)*

there is complete separation in one or both sides of the lip extending up and into the nose, or it may be incomplete, in which case there is only a notch in the fleshy portion of the lip. The incomplete cleft lip results in less facial distortion because the connected parts of muscle and tissue have a stabilizing effect. In a complete cleft lip, the muscles pull away from the center of the face, resulting in distortion of the nose and mouth. A cleft on one side is called a unilateral cleft. If a cleft occurs on both sides, it is called a bilateral cleft.

Demographics

Over 5,000 infants are born each year in the United States with a cleft lip or palate (about one in every 700 births). Cleft lip without cleft palate is the third most common congenital malformation among newborns in the United States and is estimated to occur roughly twice as often in males than in females. Cleft palate without cleft lip is fifth most common, and it affects roughly twice as many girls as boys. Clefts may affect the left or right side of the mouth only (unilateral) or both sides (bilateral). Left-side clefts represent 70 percent of all unilateral clefts. In the United States, clefting seems to be at least in part related to ethnicity, occurring most often among Asians, Latinos, and Native Americans (one in 500), next most often among persons of European ethnicity (one in 700), and least often among persons of African ethnicity (one in 1,000).

Causes and symptoms

The causes of clefts are as of 2004 still poorly understood. Most scientists believe that clefting occurs as a result of a combination of genetic and environmental factors. In the United States and western Europe, researchers report that a **family** history of facial clefts is present in approximately 40 percent of all cases. The likelihood of a baby being born with a facial cleft increases if a first-degree relative (mother, father, or sibling) has a cleft. Mothers who abuse alcohol and drugs, lack **vitamins** (especially **folic acid**) during the first weeks of pregnancy, or have diabetes are more likely to have a child with facial clefts.

Clefts may occur alone or with other abnormalities that may be hidden or obvious. Up to 13 percent of infants with cleft lip or palate have other birth defects. Some cases involve genetic syndromes that may result in specific problems for the infant and may have a high risk of affecting others in the family. For this reason, newborns with clefts should be thoroughly examined by a specialized physician soon after birth.

When to call the doctor

Families with a history of cleft lip or palate or any other syndrome or condition associated with clefting should discuss the chances of recurrence with a genetic counselor.

Diagnosis

Because clefting causes specific physical manifestations, it is easy to diagnose. Although some types of clefts can be detected during pregnancy by an ultrasound test, many are not discovered until birth.

Treatment

A cleft lip and/or palate can be repaired with corrective surgery, performed in a hospital under general anesthesia. Generally, within the first few days following birth of an infant with a facial cleft, a team is assembled to prepare a plan for treatment of the cleft. The treatment team usually includes representatives from several medical or psychological specialties, including pediatrics, plastic surgery, otolaryngology, orthodontia, prosthodontics, oral surgery, speech and language pathology, audiology, nursing, and psychology. It is common for one team member to coordinate service and communication between the team members and the family.

Surgical repair of a cleft lip is carried out at about three to four months of age. The whole emphasis in repairing the lip is on the muscle repair in order to mold the distorted front central section of the upper gum

Cleft lip repair

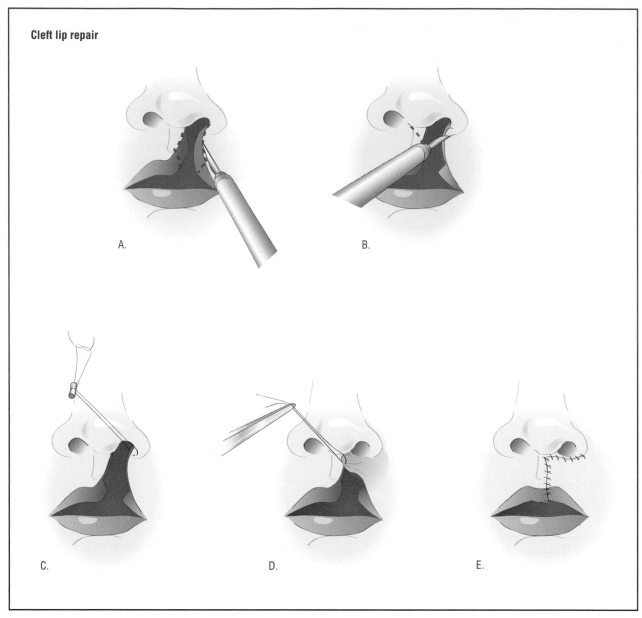

A.

B.

C.

D.

E.

Cleft lip repair. The edges of the cleft between the lip and nose are cut (A and B). The bottom of the nostril is formed with suture (C). The upper part of the lip tissue is closed (D), and the stitches are extended down to close the opening entirely (E). *(Illustration by Argosy, Inc.)*

containing the four upper front teeth (premaxilla) back into its proper position. Cleft lip often requires only one reconstructive surgery, especially if the cleft is unilateral. The surgeon makes an incision on each side of the cleft from the lip to the nostril, drawing the two sides of the cleft together and suturing them together. Bilateral cleft lips are usually repaired in two surgeries, about a month apart. The first surgery is performed when a baby is between six and 10 weeks old and usually requires a one-night stay in the hospital.

Cleft palate can require several surgical procedures during the course of a child's first 18 years. The first surgery to repair the palate usually occurs when the infant is between six and 12 months old. It usually involves palatal lengthening and drawing tissue from either side of the mouth to rebuild the palate. The procedure usually requires two or three nights in the hospital, the first night in the intensive care unit. The purpose of this surgery is to create a functional palate, reduce the chances that fluid will develop in the middle ears, and help the proper development of the child's teeth and facial bones. In addition, the functional palate helps the child's speech development and feeding abilities. In both types of surgery, the necessity for more operations depends on the skill of the surgeon as well as the severity of the cleft, its shape, and the thickness of available tissue that can be used to create the palate. About 20 percent of children with a cleft palate require further surgical procedures to help improve their speech. Additional surgeries may also improve the appearance of the lip and nose, close openings between the mouth and nose, help breathing, and stabilize and realign the jaw.

Nutritional concerns

Infants with cleft lip or cleft soft palate generally have few feeding problems. However, when the cleft involves the hard palate, the infant is usually not able to suck efficiently. For these infants, caregivers must experiment with various feeding techniques, such as special nipples or alternate feeding positions. The infant with a cleft should be held in a nearly sitting position during feeding to prevent the breast or formula milk from flowing back into the nose. In addition, the infant should be burped frequently, approximately every three or four minutes. The sucking reflex is strong in all infants and should be encouraged in infants with facial clefts even if the sucking is inefficient, since the reflex seems to help the later development of speech. It is important to keep the cleft clean and not to allow formula, mucus, or other matter to collect in the cleft.

Prognosis

Both cleft lip and cleft palate are treatable birth defects. Most children born with either or both of these conditions undergo reconstructive surgery while they are still infants to correct the defect and significantly improve facial appearance. With advances in surgical techniques and with more complete repair of facial clefts, about 80 percent of affected children have normal speech development by the time they enter school. Continuation of speech therapy results in continuous improvement for most common speech problems.

Prevention

While little is known about how to prevent clefts, researchers from the California Birth Defects Monitoring Program found that women considering pregnancy may be able to reduce the risk of facial clefts (and possibly other birth defects) in their offspring by taking a multivitamin containing folic acid for one month prior to becoming pregnant. Other studies have shown that

---

KEY TERMS

Bilateral cleft lip—A cleft that occurs on both sides of the lip.

Cleft—An elongated opening or slit in an organ.

Complete cleft—A cleft that extends through the entire affected mouth structure.

Congenital—Present at birth.

Palatal lengthening (palatal pushback)—A surgical procedure in which tissue from the front part of the mouth is moved back to lengthen it.

Palate—The roof of the mouth.

Premaxilla—The front central section of the upper gum, containing the four upper front teeth.

Unilateral cleft—A cleft that occurs on only the right or left side of the lip.

---

fetuses with certain predisposing genes may be at increased risk for cleft palate if their mothers smoke. Because some types of medications (for example some drugs used to treat epilepsy) have been linked to increased risk of clefts, women who take medications for chronic illnesses should check with their doctors before they become pregnant.

Parental concerns

Parents of a newborn baby with a cleft lip or palate are often confused and afraid of the impact the defect will have on their child's life. These feelings can be alleviated by learning about the cleft and treatment options. They also must communicate what they are learning about clefts to family, siblings, and friends. It is important for people who come into contact with the child to realize that a cleft is not a wound, although it may give the impression that it is tender or sore. Parents can help others understand that the cleft does not hurt and that it will be repaired. To ensure normal psychological and speech development, parents should interact with their infant as they would with any newborn in the family and should encourage others to do the same.

As the child with a cleft grows and develops, he or she will certainly experience many good and bad reactions from adults and children. Other children may tease the child or use the term "harelip." It may be helpful for parents of a child with a facial cleft to meet with his classmates and teachers to explain the history of the term

---

harelip. Although a facial cleft was once referred to as a harelip to reflect its similarity to the mouth of a rabbit, the term is considered insulting today. Educating adults and children about cleft lip and palate is the best way to relieve others' **anxiety** about the defect and lessen any negative psychological effects that bad reactions might have on the child.

See also Language development.

Resources

BOOKS

Bzoch, Kenneth R. *Communicative Disorders Related to Cleft and Lip Palate.* Austin, TX: PRO-ED Inc., 2004.

Golding-Kushner, Karen J. *Therapy Techniques for Cleft Palate Speech and Related Disorders.* San Diego, CA: Singular Publishing Group Inc., 2001.

Gruman-Trinkner, Carrie, and Blaise Winter. *Your Cleft-Affected Child: The Complete Book of Information, Resources, and Hope.* Berkeley, CA: Publishers Group West, 2001.

Wysznski, Diego I. *Cleft Lip and Palate: From Origin to Treatment.* Oxford, UK: Oxford University Press, 2002.

PERIODICALS

Caniklioglu, M. C. "Use of a nickel titanium palatal expander in cleft-palate cases." *Journal of Clinical Orthodontics* 38, no. 7 (July 2004): 374–77.

Chapman, K. L. "Is presurgery and early postsurgery performance related to speech and language outcomes at 3 years of age for children with cleft palate?" *Clinical Linguistics and Phonetics* 18, no. 4–5 (June-August 2004): 235–57.

Hermann, N. V., et al. "Early craniofacial morphology and growth in children with bilateral complete cleft lip and palate." *Cleft Palate and Craniofacial Journal* 41, no. 4 (July 2004): 104–05.

Mulliken, J. B. "The changing faces of children with cleft lip and palate." *New England Journal of Medicine* 351, no. 8 (August 2004): 745–47.

Smith, A. S., et al. "Prenatal diagnosis of cleft lip and cleft palate using MRI." *American Journal of Roentgenology* 183, no. 1 (July 2004): 229–35.

Van Lierde, K. M., et al. "Vocal quality characteristics in children with cleft palate: a multiparameter approach." *Journal of Voice* 18, no. 3 (September 2004): 354–62.

Whitehill, T. L., and C. H. Chau. "Single-word intelligibility in speakers with repaired cleft palate." *Clinical Linguistics and Phonetics* 18, no. 4–5 (June-August 2004): 341–55.

ORGANIZATIONS

About Face USA. PO Box 969, Batavia, IL 60510–0969. Web site: <www.aboutfaceusa.org/default.htm>.

American Cleft Palate: Craniofacial Association (ACPCA)/ Cleft Palate Foundation (CPF). 1504 East Franklin Street, Suite 102, Chapel Hill, NC 27514–2820. Web site: <www.cleftline.org>.

American Speech-Language-Hearing Association. 10801 Rockville Pike, Rockville, MD 20852. Web site: <www.asha.org>.

Children's Craniofacial Association (CCA). 13140 Coit Road, Suite 307, Dallas, Texas 75240. Web site: <www.ccakids.org/default.htm>.

WEB SITES

"Cleft Lip and Palate Resource." *Wide Smiles.* Available online at <www.widesmiles.org> (accessed November 16, 2004).

March of Dimes Homepage. Available online at <www.modimes.org/> (accessed November 15, 2004).

Monique Laberge, Ph.D.

Clotting disorders *see* **Coagulation disorders**

Clubfoot

Definition

Clubfoot is a condition in which one or both feet are twisted into an abnormal position at birth. The condition is also known as talipes.

Description

True clubfoot is characterized by abnormal bone formation in the foot. There are four variations of clubfoot: talipes varus, talipes valgus, talipes equines, and talipes calcaneus. In talipes varus, the most common form of clubfoot, the foot generally turns inward so that the leg and foot look somewhat like the letter J (when looking at the left foot head-on). In talipes valgus, the foot rotates outward like the letter L. In talipes equinus, the foot points downward, similar to that of a toe dancer. In talipes calcaneus, the foot points upward, with the heel pointing down.

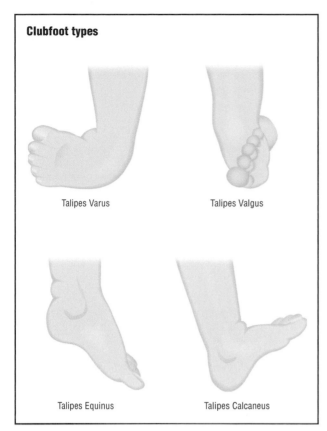

Clubfoot types

Talipes Varus

Talipes Valgus

Talipes Equinus

Talipes Calcaneus

The four varieties of clubfoot. Talipes varus is by far the most common type. *(Illustration by GGS Information Services.)*

Clubfoot can affect one foot or both feet. Sometimes the feet of an infant appear abnormal at birth because of the intrauterine position of the fetus prior to birth. If there is no anatomic abnormality of the bone, this is not true clubfoot, and the problem can usually be corrected by applying special braces or casts to straighten the foot.

True clubfoot is usually obvious at birth because a clubfoot has a typical appearance of pointing downward and being twisted inwards. Since the condition starts in the first trimester of pregnancy, the abnormality is quite well established at birth, and the foot is often very rigid. Uncorrected clubfoot in an adult causes only part of the foot, usually the outer edge or the heel or the toes, to touch the ground. For a person with clubfoot, walking becomes difficult or impossible.

Demographics

The ratio of males to females with clubfoot is 2.5 to 1. The incidence of clubfoot varies only slightly. In the United States, the incidence is approximately one in every 1,000 live births. A 1980 Danish study reported an overall incidence of 1.2 in every 1,000 children. By 1994, that number had doubled to 2.41 in every 1,000 live births. No reason was offered for the increase.

A **family** history of clubfoot has been reported in 24.4 percent of families in a single study. These findings suggest the potential role of one or more genes being responsible for clubfoot.

Causes and symptoms

Experts do not agree on the precise cause of clubfoot. Some experts feel that clubfoot may begin early in pregnancy, probably in the 10th to 12th weeks of gestation. The exact genetic mechanism of inheritance has been extensively investigated using family studies and other epidemiological methods. As of 2004, no definitive conclusions had been reached, although a Mendelian pattern of inheritance is suspected. This may be due to the interaction of several different inheritance patterns, different patterns of development appearing as the same condition, or a complex interaction between genetic and environmental factors. The MSX1 gene has been associated with clubfoot in animal studies. But, as of 2004, these findings had not been replicated in humans.

Several environmental causes have been proposed for clubfoot. Many obstetricians feel that intrauterine crowding causes clubfoot. This theory is supported by a significantly higher incidence of clubfoot among **twins** compared to singleton births. Intrauterine exposure to the drug misoprostol has been linked with clubfoot. Misoprostol is commonly used when trying, usually unsuccessfully, to induce abortion in Brazil and in other countries in South and Central America. Researchers in Norway have reported that males who are in the printing trades have significantly more offspring with clubfoot than men in other occupations. For unknown reasons, **amniocentesis**, a prenatal test, has also been associated with clubfoot. The infants of mothers who smoke during pregnancy have a greater chance of being born with clubfoot than are offspring of women who do not smoke.

The physical appearance of a clubfoot may vary. However, at birth, an affected foot usually turns inward and points downward. It resists realignment. The calf muscle may be smaller and less well developed than normal. One or both feet may be affected.

When to call the doctor

An pediatrician should be consulted at birth, the usual time clubfoot is initially diagnosed. While there is no immediate urgency, the condition should be evaluated by a pediatrician or an orthopedic surgeon in the first weeks of life so that treatment can be started.

Diagnosis

Clubfoot is diagnosed by physician inspection. This is most often completed immediately after birth. Clubfoot may be suspected during the latter stages of pregnancy, especially in a mother of shorter or smaller than normal stature, a large fetus, or multiple infants.

Treatment

Clubfoot is corrected by casting or surgery. To have the best chances for successful resolution without resorting to surgery, treatment as soon after birth as possible. The Ponseti method of stretching and casting has been used with increasing success since the 1990s. The Ponseti method requires that a doctor stretch the child's affected foot toward its anatomically correct position and hold it in place with a cast. The foot is realigned and a new cast applied weekly for several weeks. Once the correct position has been achieved, a brace must be worn during periods of **sleep** to maintain the correction. To be successful, the method requires active parental involvement.

When casting and bracing are not successful, surgery may be required to realign the tendons, ligaments, and joints in the foot and ankle. Such a procedure is usually completed between nine and 12 months of age. After surgery, a cast holds the foot in the desired position.

Prognosis

The prognosis for successfully treating clubfoot is good at this time. Persons with clubfoot that is corrected by surgery may notice some increased stiffness in their affected feet as they age. A corrected clubfoot is often a shoe size smaller than normal and may be somewhat less flexible. The calf muscles in an affected clubfoot leg may be slightly smaller than an unaffected leg. However, without treatment, clubfoot will result in a functional disability.

Prevention

At the present time, there is no way to prevent clubfoot. Pregnant women can reduce the risk of clubfoot by refraining from **smoking**.

Parental concerns

Parents of an infant with clubfoot should be prepared to participate in treatment for two or more years. They should seek prompt treatment from a qualified health care provider.

Resources

BOOKS

Hall, Judith G. "Single Gene and Chromosomal Disorders." In *Cecil Textbook of Medicine*, 22nd ed. Edited by Lee Goldman, et al. Philadelphia: Saunders, 2003, pp. 191–7.

Hassold, Terry, and Stuart Schwartz. "Chromosome Disorders." In *Harrison's Principles of Internal Medicine*, 15th ed. Edited by Eugene Braunwald, et al., New York: McGraw Hill, 2001, pp. 396–403.

Thompson, George H. "Talipes Equinovarus (Clubfoot)." In *Nelson Textbook of Pediatrics*, 17th ed. Edited by Richard E. Behrman, et al. Philadelphia: Saunders, 2003, pp. 2256–7.

PERIODICALS

Gigante, C., et al. "Sonographic assessment of clubfoot." *Journal of Clinical Ultrasound* 32, no. 5 (2004): 235–42.

Ippolito, E., et al. "The influence of treatment on the pathology of club foot. CT study at maturity." *Journal of Bone and Joint Surgery of Britain* 86, no. 4 (2004): 574–89.

Mammen, L., and C. B. Benson. "Outcome of fetuses with clubfeet diagnosed by prenatal sonography." *Journal of Ultrasound Medicine* 23, no. 4 (2004): 497–500.

Noonan, K. J., et al. "Leg length discrepancy in unilateral congenital clubfoot following surgical treatment." *Iowa Orthopedic Journal* 24, no. 1 (2004): 60–64.

Papavasiliou, V. A., and A. V. Papavasiliou. "A novel surgical option for the operative treatment of clubfoot." *Acta Orthopedica Belgium* 70, no. 2 (2004): 155–61.

ORGANIZATIONS

American Academy of Orthopedic Surgeons. 6300 North River Road, Rosemont, Illinois 60018–4262. Web site: <www.aaos.org/>.

American Academy of Pediatrics. 141 Northwest Point Boulevard, Elk Grove Village, IL 60007–1098. Web site: <www.aap.org/default.htm>.

March of Dimes. 1275 Mamaroneck Avenue, White Plains, NY 10605. Web site: <www.modimes.org/>.

National Easter Seal Society. 230 W. Monroe St., Suite 1800, Chicago, IL 60606–4802. Web site: <www.easterseals.org/>.

National Organization for Rare Disorders (NORD). PO Box 8923, New Fairfield, CT 06812–8923. Web site: <www.rarediseases.org/>.

WEB SITES

"Clubfoot and Other Deformities." *March of Dimes.* Available online at <www.marchofdimes.com/professionals/681_1211.asp> (accessed November 16, 2004).

Patel, Minoo, and John Herzenberg. "Clubfoot." *eMedicine.* Available online at <www.emedicine.com/orthoped/topic598.htm> (accessed November 16, 2004).

Ponseti, Ignacia. "Treatment of Congenital Clubfoot." *Virtual Children's Hospital, University of Iowa.* Available online at <www.vh.org/pediatric/provider/orthopaedics/Clubfoot/Clubfoot.html> (accessed November 16, 2004).

Schopler, Steven A. "Clubfoot." *Southern California Orthopedic Institute*, 2004. Available online at <www.scoi.com/clubfoot.htm> (accessed November 16, 2004).

Shriners Hospitals for Children. "Help for Patients with Clubfoot." *Houston Shriners Hospital.* Available online at <www.shrinershq.org/patientedu/clubfoot2.html> (accessed November 16, 2004).

L. Fleming Fallon Jr., MD, DrPH

CMV *see* **Cytomegalovirus infection**

CO poisoning *see* **Carbon monoxide poisoning**

Coagulation disorders

Definition

Coagulation disorders (coagulopathies) are disruptions in the body's ability to control blood clotting, an essential function of the body designed to prevent blood loss. The most commonly known coagulation disorder is **hemophilia**, a condition in which a critical component of blood coagulation is missing, causing individuals to bleed for long periods of time before clotting occurs. There are numerous other coagulation disorders stemming from a variety of causes.

Description

Coagulation, or clotting, is a complex process (called the coagulation cascade) that involves 12 coagulation factors (designated by Roman numerals as factors I through XII) found in blood plasma and several other blood components. The factors include prothrombin, thrombin, and fibrin. Each has a precise role in coagulation. Besides the factors, which are all proteins, plasma (the fluid component of the blood) carries a number of other proteins that regulate bleeding. Platelets, tiny colorless cells in the blood, initiate contraction of damaged blood vessels so that less blood is lost. They also help plug damaged blood vessels and work with other constituents in plasma to accelerate blood clotting. A deficiency in clotting factors or a disorder that affects platelet production or one of the many steps in the entire process can disrupt clotting and severely complicate blood loss from injury, **childbirth**, surgery, and specific diseases or conditions in which bleeding can occur.

Coagulation disorders arise from different causes and involve different complications. Some common coagulation disorders are:

- Hemophilia or hemophilia A (factor VIII deficiency) is an inherited coagulation disorder, affecting about 20,000 Americans. This genetic disorder is carried by females but most often affects male offspring. It is characterized by spontaneous musculoskeletal bleeding. Christmas disease or hemophilia B (factor IX deficiency) is less common than hemophilia A with similar symptoms. Factor IX is produced in the liver and is dependent on interaction with vitamin K in order to function properly. Deficiency in the vitamin can affect the clotting factor's performance as well as deficiency in the factor itself.

- Disseminated intravascular coagulation, also known as consumption coagulopathy, is not a disease in itself but a clinical emergency that occurs as a result of other diseases and conditions. This condition accelerates clotting, which ironically can result in hemorrhage when the clotting factors are exhausted.

- Thrombocytopenia, the most common cause of coagulation disorder, is characterized by reduced numbers of circulating platelets in the blood. This disease also includes idiopathic thrombocytopenia.

- Von Willebrand's disease, a hereditary disorder with prolonged bleeding time, is due to a clotting factor deficiency and impaired platelet function. It is the most common inherited coagulation disorder.

- Hypoprothrombinemia is a congenital deficiency of clotting factors that can lead to hemorrhage.

- Other coagulation disorders include factor XI deficiency (hemophilia C), and factor VII deficiency. Hemophilia C afflicts one in 100,000 people and is the second most common bleeding disorder among women. Factor VII is also called serum prothrombin conversion accelerator (SPCA) deficiency. One in 500,000 people may be afflicted with this disorder that is often diagnosed in newborns because of bleeding into the brain as a result of traumatic delivery.

Demographics

Hemophilia, or hemophilia A (factor VIII deficiency) affects about 20,000 Americans and one out of every 5000 males worldwide; Christmas disease, or hemophilia B, is less common than hemophilia A. Von Willebrand's disease affects both males and females and is often diagnosed in children. Thrombocytopenia is the most common coagulation disorder. Factor XI deficiency, or hemophilia C, afflicts one in 100,000 people and is the second most common bleeding disorder among women; it occurs more frequently among certain ethnic groups, with an incidence of about one in 10,000 among Ashkenazi Jews. A deficiency of factor VII, also called serum prothrombin conversion accelerator (SPCA) deficiency, affects one in 500,000 people and is often diagnosed in newborns.

Causes and symptoms

Some coagulation disorders present symptoms such as severe bruising. Others show no apparent symptoms but carry the threat of severe internal bleeding.

Hemophilia

Because of its hereditary nature, hemophilia A may be suspected before symptoms occur. Some signs of hemophilia A are numerous large, deep **bruises** and painful, swollen joints caused by internal bleeding. Individuals with hemophilia do not bleed faster, just longer. A person with mild hemophilia may first discover the disorder with prolonged bleeding following a surgical procedure or injury. If there is bleeding into the neck, head, or digestive tract, or bleeding from an injury, emergency measures may be required. Bleeding can be spontaneous, occurring with no obvious trauma.

Mild and severe hemophilia A are inherited through a complex genetic system that passes a recessive gene on the female chromosome. Women usually do not show signs of hemophilia but are carriers of the disease. Each male child of the carrier has a 50 percent chance of having hemophilia, and each female child has a 50 percent chance of passing the gene on.

Christmas disease

Christmas disease, or hemophilia B, is also hereditary but less common than hemophilia A. The severity of Christmas disease varies from mild to severe, although mild cases are more common. The severity depends on the degree of deficiency of factor IX. Hemophilia B symptoms are similar to those of hemophilia A, including numerous, large, and deep bruises and prolonged bleeding. The more dangerous symptoms are those that represent possible internal bleeding, such as swelling of joints or bleeding into internal organs upon trauma. Hemophilia most often occurs in families with a known history of the disease, but occasionally, new cases occur in families with no apparent history.

Disseminated intravascular coagulation

Disseminated intravascular coagulation (DIC) occurs when the malfunction of clotting factors causes platelets to form clots in small blood vessels throughout the body. This action leads to depletion of clotting factors and platelets, which are then not available at a site of injury where clotting is needed. When DIC occurs, the individual bleeds abnormally even though there is no history of coagulation abnormality. Symptoms may include minute spots of hemorrhage on the skin, and purple patches or hematomas caused by bleeding under the skin. Bleeding may occur at a surgical site or intravenous injection (IV) sites. Related symptoms include **vomiting**; seizures; shortness of breath; severe **pain** in the back, muscles, abdomen, or chest; and, if prolonged or uncorrected, shock and coma or death.

Not inherited and not a disease, DIC results from vascular complications during pregnancy or delivery, surgery, overwhelming infections, acute leukemia, metastatic **cancer**, extensive **burns**, liver disease, pancreatitis, trauma, snakebites, and other causes. As of 2004 it was not precisely understood why or how these various disorders lead to uncontrolled intravascular coagulation. What the underlying causes of DIC have in common is a dysfunction that involves proteins, platelets, or other clotting factors and processes. For example, uterine tissue can enter the mother's circulation during prolonged labor, introducing foreign proteins into the blood, or the venom of some exotic snakes can activate one of the clotting factors. Severe head trauma can expose blood to brain tissue. Regardless of the specific cause of DIC, the results are a malfunction of thrombin (an enzyme) and prothrombin (a glycoprotein), which activate the fibrinolytic system, releasing clotting factors in the blood. DIC can alternate from hemorrhage to thrombosis, and both can exist, which further complicates diagnosis and treatment.

Thrombocytopenia

Thrombocytopenia may be acquired or congenital (existing at birth). It represents a defective or decreased production of platelets. Symptoms include sudden onset of small bruises or spots of hemorrhage on the skin or bleeding into mucous membranes (such as nosebleeds). The disorder may also be evident as blood in vomit or stools, bleeding during surgery, or heavy menstrual flow.

Some patients show none of these symptoms but complain of fatigue and general weakness. There are several causes of thrombocytopenia, which is more commonly acquired as a result of another disorder. Common underlying disorders include leukemia, drug toxicity, or aplastic anemia, all of which lead to decreased or defective production of platelets in the bone marrow. Other diseases may destroy platelets outside the marrow. These include severe infection, disseminated intravascular coagulation, and cirrhosis of the liver. The idiopathic form most commonly occurs in children and is most likely the result of production of antibodies that cause destruction of platelets in the spleen and to a lesser extent the liver.

Von Willebrand's disease is caused by a defect in the von Willebrand clotting factor, often accompanied by a deficiency of factor VIII as well. It is a hereditary disorder that affects both males and females. In rare cases, it may be acquired. Symptoms include easy bruising, bleeding in small cuts that stops and starts, abnormal bleeding after surgery, and abnormally heavy menstrual bleeding. Nosebleeds and blood in the stool with a black, tarlike appearance are also signs of von Willebrand's disease.

Hypoprothrombinemia

Hypoprothrombinemia is an inherited or acquired deficiency in prothrombin, or factor II, a glycoprotein formed and stored in the liver. Prothrombin, under the right conditions, is converted to thrombin, which activates fibrin and begins the process of coagulation. Some individuals may show no symptoms, and others may suffer severe hemorrhaging. Easy bruising, profuse nosebleeds, postpartum hemorrhage, excessively prolonged or heavy menstrual bleeding, and postsurgical hemorrhage may also result. Acquired hypoprothrombinemia usually arises from a vitamin K deficiency caused by liver disease, newborn hemorrhagic disease, or other causes.

Other coagulation disorders

Factor XI deficiency, or hemophilia C, is a bleeding disorder that occurs among certain ethnic groups. Nearly 50 percent of individuals with this disorder experience no symptoms, but others may notice blood in their urine, nosebleeds, or bruising. Some factor XI deficiencies may result in bleeding long after an injury, and some women experience prolonged bleeding after childbirth. A deficiency of factor VII may cause varying levels of bleeding severity in those affected. Women may experience heavy menstrual bleeding, bleeding from the gums or nose, bleeding deep within the skin, and episodes of bleeding into the stomach, intestines, and urinary tract. Bleeding into the joints is rare but may also occur in some individuals.

When to call the doctor

Coagulation disorders are usually discovered when an injury or surgery initiates bleeding and the bleeding does not stop. Any signs of prolonged bleeding, even from a small cut, should be reported to a physician or emergency service. Bleeding under the skin (hematoma), which looks like a severe bruise, should also be reported and medical care sought. The sooner bleeding is controlled the better. A diagnostic work up is indicated to reveal any coagulopathy that exists, whether inherited or acquired.

Diagnosis

Diagnostic blood tests are performed in the clinical laboratory, including assays of the specific clotting factors, to help detect various coagulation disorders. Measured parameters are compared with known normal values to detect deficiencies or defects. Additionally, a choice of hundreds of diagnostic tests can be ordered by the physician to identify causative conditions, deficiencies, or diseases underlying the coagulopathy. Physicians also complete a medical history and physical examination. If acquired coagulation disorders are suspected, information such as prior or current diseases and medications are important to help determine the cause of the blood disorder. Each possible coagulopathy has specific criteria for diagnosis, including the following:

- Hemophilia A is diagnosed with laboratory tests that can detect the presence of clotting factor VIII, factor IX, and others, as well as the presence or absence of clotting factor inhibitors. Christmas disease involves an investigation of bleeding and clotting times, as well as determining factor IX deficiency. Other tests may include prothrombin time and thromboplastic generation. Gene carriers for both forms of hemophilia can be detected through DNA studies in conjunction with results from factor VIII assays.

- As of 2004 there was no one test or group of tests that can reliably diagnose DIC because it is a clinical event that occurs without warning, arising from another event such as surgery, childbirth, snakebite, and certain disease conditions. Diagnosis usually requires a number of laboratory tests that measure concentrations of platelets and fibrinogen in the blood along with measuring prothrombin time. Other supportive data include measuring levels of factors V and VIII, fibrinogen, hemoglobin, and platelets, any of which may be diminished or entirely depleted. Serial tests may also be recommended, because a single coagulation parameter measured at any one moment may not reveal the rapidly progressive intravascular process.

- Tests for thrombocytopenia include coagulation tests that may reveal a decreased **platelet count** and prolonged bleeding time. Other coagulation factors may be measured. If these tests indicate that platelet destruction is causing the disorder, the physician may order a bone marrow biopsy.

- Von Willebrand's disease is diagnosed by ordering laboratory tests that reveal a prolonged bleeding time, absent or reduced levels of factor VIII, and a normal platelet count. Other tests are likely be done to confirm a diagnosis.

- Hypothrombinemia is diagnosed based on **family** history and the use of tests that measure vitamin K deficiency, deficiency of prothrombin, and measurements of clotting factors V, VII, IX, and X.

- Factor XI deficiency is determined by measuring the specific coagulation factor as well as other coagulation tests including prothrombin time and clotting time. It is diagnosed most often after injury-related bleeding.

Treatment

In mild coagulopathies, treatment may involve the use of drugs that stimulate the release of deficient clotting factors. In severe cases, bleeding may only stop if the clotting factor that is missing is replaced through infusion of human blood components containing concentrated amounts of specific clotting factors. These may be prepared in the form of fresh frozen plasma or cryoprecipitate. Cryoprecipitate was invented in 1965 to replace the need for whole plasma transfusions, which introduced more volume than needed and carried the threat of exposure to hepatitis or AIDs. More sensitive testing methods have virtually eliminated this risk. Commercial preparations of freeze-dried clotting factors have also made it possible for people to infuse themselves as directed by their physicians. This aspect of self-care made life easier for those with coagulation problems; in every other respect as of 2004, bleeding or coagulation disorders should not be self-managed. Comprehensive care addresses children's needs by providing various types of counseling to help deal with the psychosocial aspects of diseases such as von Willebrand's and hemophilia.

With mild bleeding episodes in persons afflicted with hemophilia A, infusions of a drug called desmopressin (DDAVP) may be administered. Severe bleeding episodes require transfusions of human blood clotting factors. Hemophiliacs are encouraged to receive physical therapy to help damaged joints and to **exercise** through non-contact **sports** such as swimming, bicycle riding, or walking, to avoid injury that may lead to bleeding.

Christmas disease is treated similarly to hemophilia A, with a mix of synthetic products and human blood products to provide coagulation factors as needed. Superficial **wounds** can be cleaned and bandaged. When hemophiliac children are to receive immunizations, parents should inform medical personnel in advance so that bleeding problems can be avoided. These children should probably not receive intramuscular injections.

When disseminated intravascular coagulation occurs, progression can be rapid, and treatment is complicated by the large variety of possible underlying causes. If at all possible, the physician first treats the underlying disorder. If the patient is not already bleeding, this supportive treatment may correct DIC. However, if bleeding is already occurring, a combination of transfused blood, platelets, fresh frozen plasma, or other blood products may be needed. Heparin, an anticoagulant, has been controversial in treating DIC, but it is often used as a last resort to stop hemorrhage. However, heparin has not proven useful in treating patients with DIC resulting from heat stroke, exotic snakebites, trauma, incompatible transfusions, and acute problems resulting from obstetrical complications.

Secondary acquired thrombocytopenia is best alleviated by treating the underlying cause or disorder. The specific treatment may depend on the underlying cause. Sometimes, corticosteroids or immune globulin may be given to improve platelet production.

Von Willebrand's disease is treated by several methods to reduce bleeding time and to replace factor VIII, which then replaces the von Willebrand factor. This may include infusion of cryoprecipitate or fresh frozen plasma. Desmopressin may also help raise levels of the von Willebrand factor.

Hypoprothrombinemia may be treated with concentrates of prothrombin. Vitamin K may also be given to stimulate coagulation, and in bleeding episodes, fresh plasma products may be transfused.

Factor XI (hemophilia C) deficiency is most often treated with plasma, since there are no commercially available concentrates of factor XI in the United States. Factor VII deficiency may be treated with prothrombin complex concentrates; as of 2004 factor VII is not licensed in the United States.

Prognosis

The prognosis for individuals with mild forms of coagulation disorders is normally good. Many people can lead normal lives and achieve normal life

KEY TERMS

Clotting factors—Substances in the blood, also known as coagulation factors, that act in sequence to stop bleeding by triggering the formation of a clot. Each clotting factor is designated with a Roman numeral I through XIII.

Coagulopathy—A disorder in which blood is either too slow or too quick to coagulate (clot).

Enzyme—A protein that catalyzes a biochemical reaction without changing its own structure or function.

Hemorrhage—Severe, massive bleeding that is difficult to control. The bleeding may be internal or external.

Heparin—An organic acid that occurs naturally in the body and prevents blood clots. Heparin is also made synthetically and can be given as an anticoagulant treatment.

Idiopathic—Refers to a disease or condition of unknown origin.

Metastatic—The term used to describe a secondary cancer, or one that has spread from one area of the body to another.

Thrombosis—The formation of a blood clot in a vein or artery that may obstruct local blood flow or may dislodge, travel downstream, and obstruct blood flow at a remote location. The clot or thrombus may lead to infarction, or death of tissue, due to a blocked blood supply.

expectancy. Without treatment of bleeding episodes, severe muscle and joint pain and eventually permanent damage can occur. Any incident that causes blood to collect in the head, neck, or digestive system can be very serious and requires immediate attention. DIC is an emergency situation that can be severe enough to cause stroke, coma, and death. The prognosis depends on early intervention and treatment of the underlying condition. Hemorrhage from a coagulation disorder, particularly into the brain or digestive track, can prove fatal.

Prevention

Inherited disorders cannot be prevented; they must be managed when detected. Acquired bleeding disorders are caused by a variety of conditions, some related to other diseases. There is no single prevention method although treatment of the underlying disorder or disease may prevent episodes of bleeding and subsequent coagu-

lation problems. Episodes of bleeding can be prevented by avoiding injury. People who have hemophilia A or B and other bleeding disorders are advised to avoid activities and contact sports that can cause severe injury.

Parental concerns

Knowledge that a child has an inherited or acquired coagulation disorder that may lead to potentially dangerous bleeding episodes is of great concern to parents. Effective management of coagulation disorders by physicians can help the child to lead a relatively normal life with some cautions about avoiding injury. Counseling is available to help children handle the psychosocial aspects of living with a coagulation disorder.

See also Hemophilia.

Resources

BOOKS

The 2002 Official Patient's Sourcebook on Hemophilia. San Diego, CA: Icon Group International, 2002.

Berntorp, Erik, et al. *Textbook on Hemophilia.* Oxford, UK: Blackwell Publishing, 2005.

Kroll, Michael H. *Manual of Coagulation Disorders.* Oxford, UK: Blackwell Publishing, 2001

McDougald, Monroe. *Hemophilia Care in the New Millennium.* Secaucus, NJ: Kluwer Academic Publishers, 2001.

Willett, Edward. *Hemophilia.* Berkeley Heights, NJ: Enslow Publishers, 2001.

ORGANIZATIONS

National Heart, Lung, and Blood Institute. PO Box 30105, Bethesda, MD 20824-0105. Web site: <www.nhlbi.nih.gov>.

National Hemophilia Foundation. 116 West 32nd St., 11th Floor, New York, NY 10001. Web site: <www.hemophilia.org>.

L. Lee Culvert
Teresa Norris, RN

Coarctation of the aorta

Definition

Coarctation of the aorta (COA) is a congenital heart defect that develops in the fetus. It involves a constricture of the aorta, the main artery that delivers blood from the left ventricle of the heart to the rest of the body. In a constricture or coarctation, the sides (walls) of the aorta press together abnormally, impeding the flow of blood. COA can produce symptoms of congestive heart failure or high blood pressure (**hypertension**) as early as the first week of life or may produce no symptoms until later in life.

Description

In the fetus, blood from the heart to the lungs is delivered into the aorta through a short blood vessel called the ductus arteriosis. This duct or shunt normally closes at birth or shortly after. In symptomatic children with COA, the descending aorta receives blood from the right side of the heart through the ductus arteriosus, an abnormal condition often accompanying other heart abnormalities such as a duct that does not close normally (**patent ductus arteriosus** or PDA), mitral valve defects, and other types of **congenital heart disease**. In asymptomatic children with COA, the descending aorta receives left ventricle blood through the ascending aorta; these children have fewer, if any, associated cardiac abnormalities. Approximately 10 percent of newborns with congenital heart disease have symptomatic coarctation of the aorta. About 85 percent of all children and adults with COA have a double aortic valve (bicuspid aortic valve) in the heart.

Blood normally leaves the heart by way of the left ventricle and is distributed to the body through the arteries. The aortic arch is the first artery to carry blood as it leaves the heart. Other arteries to the head and arms branch off the aortic arch. Constriction of the aorta, as in COA, produces resistance to the flow of blood, resulting in raising the blood pressure above the narrowing and reducing blood pressure below or downstream from the narrowing. High blood pressure (hypertension) affects parts of the body supplied by arteries that branch off the aortic arch above the narrowing. By contrast, most of the lower body does not receive enough blood supply. To compensate for this, the heart works harder, and blood pressure rises.

About half of all infants with COA are diagnosed within the first three months of life. Frequently, other congenital cardiac complications are also present. Thirty percent of infants with **Turner syndrome**, for example, also have coarctation. Evidence exists that at least some cases of coarctation may be inherited.

Demographics

Coarctation of the aorta is present in about 8 to 10 percent of infants born with other congenital heart defects, occurring approximately twice as many males as females.

Causes and symptoms

COA is congenital, that is it develops while the baby is in the womb and may appear in newborns along with other signs of congenital heart disease. Among the consequences of COA is an enlargement of the left ventricle (ventricular hypertrophy) in response to increased back-pressure of the blood and the demand for more blood by the lower body. Symptoms in infants may include shortness of breath (dyspnea), difficulty in feeding, and poor weight gain. Children can also have no symptoms at all at birth (asymptomatic) and develop mild symptoms as older children. The older child with COA may display fatigue, shortness of breath, or a feeling of weakness or lameness in the legs.

When to call the doctor

COA is typically diagnosed within the first three months of life because of circulatory problems that produce symptoms. Some children have surgery, and some children are managed with drug therapy alone. Parents learn to recognize symptoms of high blood pressure or insufficient blood supply to the lower extremities. Medical attention is needed at the first sign of shortness of breath. Even when a child has had surgery or is on medication, the doctor should be contacted when any abnormal symptoms arise, such as shortness of breath, difficulty in feeding (with infants), and poor weight gain. Older children generally have fewer symptoms but may appear to be easily fatigued or to experience shortness of breath or weakness or lameness in their legs.

Diagnosis

Physical examination may reveal a pale child with some degree of dyspnea. On examination of the heart rhythm using a stethoscope, infants with coarctation of the aorta usually have an abnormal "gallop" heart rhythm, and 50 percent of children also have **heart murmurs**. Sometimes excessive arterial pulses can be seen in the arteries of the neck (carotid and suprasternal notch arteries), indicating increased pressure in these arteries, while the major artery of the legs (femoral artery) may have a weak pulse or none can be detected. The systolic pressure is higher in the arms than in the legs. Enlargement of the heart can be seen in x rays and congestion of the blood vessels in the lungs. Similar symptoms may be seen in older children and adults. A 10 mm Hg (mercury) pressure difference between the upper and lower extremities is diagnostic for coarctation of the aorta. For some individuals, the systolic pressure difference is observed only during **exercise**. Infants frequently have an abnormal electrocardiogram (ECG) that indicates that the right or both ventricles are enlarged, while in older children the ECG may be normal or show that the left ventricle is enlarged. The site and the extent of coarctation may also be detected using color-flow Doppler ultrasonography (echocardiology).

Asymptomatic children may have a normal heart size or only slight enlargement. Differences in blood pressure between the arms and legs may be noted. Hypertension is less likely and, if noted, may be less marked than in symptomatic children with other heart defects. The bicuspid aortic valve is usually present. Color-flow Doppler studies may show a reduced blood flow below the coarctation.

Treatment

The goal of treatment in children is to reopen the ductus arteriosus and restore blood flow to the descending aorta. Congestive heart failure may be treated simultaneously with anticongestive medications. Drug therapy is used first to treat hypertension and heart failure in children and adults who have coarctation of the aorta. Surgery may be required for infants who have severe coarctation of the aorta and is usually recommended for those who have associated cardiac defects or those infants who do not respond to drug therapy. Surgery may also be indicated for infants whose early symptoms do not indicate immediate surgery but who develop severe hypertension during the first several months of life. Older children and adults are advised to avoid vigorous exercise prior to surgical correction of the coarctation. Surgery may involve resection of the coarctation segment or opening and patching the aorta where the coarctation occurred. Balloon angioplasty is sometimes performed on infants who are not ideal candidates for repair surgery because of higher risk; this procedure involves passing a catheter with an attached deflated balloon through the femoral artery in the groin and inflating the balloon to open the coarctation segment of the aorta. Recoarctation can occur in some individuals, even after corrective surgery. Recurrence is higher with balloon angioplasty than with repair surgery.

Prognosis

Approximately half of all infants diagnosed with coarctation of the aorta have no other cardiac defects and respond well to medical management, growing and developing normally. These infants are generally asymptomatic and will eventually outgrow the condition after several years of life. Although hypertension may increase for several months early in life, it eventually decreases as the circulatory system develops and vessels become larger.

Symptomatic children who have other heart defects generally respond well to repair surgery, and COA symptoms are reduced. The mortality rate for COA infants is about 5 percent. The average life span of children who have coarctation of the aorta is 34 years of age, reduced primarily due to complications and to the presence of other heart problems. The most common complications following repair surgery are postoperative renal failure and recoarctation. Complications in children who have not had surgery are hypertension, aortic rupture, intracranial bleeding, and congestive heart failure. Undetected or untreated COA can also lead to early adulthood death due to congestive heart failure, systemic hypertension, coronary artery disease, and aortic aneurysm. Women who have an uncorrected coarctation of the aorta have a mortality rate of 10 percent during pregnancy and a 90 percent rate of complications.

Parental concerns

Because congenital coarctation of the aorta is unpredicted, parents may be unprepared for the diagnosis and need careful, sensitive medical explanation by the pediatrician or surgeon. The birth of a child with this condition may raise parents' concerns about their child's ability to lead a normal life. If COA is detected, with or without the child's presenting symptoms, medical and surgical treatment usually corrects the condition and reduces symptoms. Over half of children overcome the condition and grow and develop normally without severe restrictions. Children who have other heart problems may have the repair surgery and other procedures to reduce symptoms and improve blood flow and with continued drug therapy and some restrictions on activity can lead relatively normal lives into adulthood.

See also Congenital heart disease; Patent ductus arteriosus.

Resources

BOOKS

Congenital Heart Disease: A Medical Dictionary, Bibliography, and Annotated Research Guide to Internet References. San Diego, CA: Icon Group International, 2004.

Corno, Antonio. *Congenital Heart Defects: Decision Making for Surgery.* Milan, Italy: Springer Italia Sri, 2005.

Everett, Allen, et al. *Illustrated Field Guide to Congenital Heart Disease and Repair.* Charlottesville, VA: Scientific Software Solutions, 2004.

Fogel, Mark. *Ventricular Function in Congenital Heart Disease.* Oxford, UK: Blackwell Publishing, 2004.

KEY TERMS

Aneurysm—A weakened area in the wall of a blood vessel which causes an outpouching or bulge. Aneurysms may be fatal if these weak areas burst, resulting in uncontrollable bleeding.

Angioplasty—A medical procedure in which a catheter, or thin tube, is threaded through blood vessels. The catheter is used to place a balloon or stent (a small metal rod) at a narrowed or blocked area and expand it mechanically.

Aorta—The main artery located above the heart that pumps oxygenated blood out into the body. The aorta is the largest artery in the body.

Dyspnea—Difficulty in breathing, usually associated with heart or lung diseases.

Electrocardiagram (ECG, EKG)—A record of the electrical activity of the heart, with each wave being labeled as P, Q, R, S, and T waves. It is often used in the diagnosis of cases of abnormal cardiac rhythm and myocardial damage.

Hypertension—Abnormally high arterial blood pressure, which if left untreated can lead to heart disease and stroke.

Patent ductus arteriosus—A congenital defect in which the temporary blood vessel connecting the left pulmonary artery to the aorta in the fetus doesn't close after birth.

Turner syndrome—A chromosome abnormality characterized by short stature and ovarian failure caused by an absent X chromosome. It occurs only in females.

Jonas, Richard A. *Comprehensive Surgical Management of Congenital Heart Disease.* Oxford, UK: Oxford University Press, 2004.

Smith, Audrey, et al. *A Practical Atlas of Congenital Heart Disease.* New York: Springer, 2003.

ORGANIZATIONS

American Heart Association. 7320 Greenville Ave., Dallas, TX 75231. Web site: <www.americanheart.org>.

WEB SITES

"Children: Heart Disease and Health." *American Heart Association*, 2004. Available online at <www.americanheart.org> (accessed January 5, 2005).

L. Lee Culvert
John T. Lohr, PhD

Cocaine *see* **Stimulant drugs**

Cochlear implants

Definition

A cochlear implant is a surgical treatment for hearing loss that works like an artificial human cochlea in the inner ear, helping to send sound from the ear to the brain. It is different from a hearing aid, which simply amplifies sound.

Purpose

A cochlear implant bypasses damaged hair cells in the child's cochlea and helps establish some degree of hearing by stimulating the hearing (auditory) nerve directly.

Description

Hearing loss is caused by a number of different problems that occur either in the auditory nerve or in parts of the middle or inner ear. The most common type of deafness is caused by damaged hair cells in the cochlea. The cochlea is a fluid-filled canal in the inner ear that is shaped like a snail shell. Inside are thousands of tiny hairs called cilia. As sound vibrates the fluid in the cochlea, the cilia move. This movement stimulates the auditory nerve and sends messages about sound to the brain. When these hair cells stop functioning, the auditory nerve is not stimulated, and the child cannot hear. Hair cells can be destroyed by many things, including infection, trauma, loud noise, aging, and birth defects.

The first piece of a cochlear implant is the microphone. It is usually worn behind the ear, and it picks up sound and sends it along a wire to a speech processor. The speech processor is usually worn in a small shoulder pouch, pocket, or on a belt. The processor boosts the sound, filters out background noise, and turns the sound into digital signals. Then it sends these digital signals to a transmitter worn behind the ear. A magnet holds the transmitter in place through its attraction to the receiver-stimulator, a part of the device that is surgically attached beneath the skin in the skull. The receiver picks up digital information forwarded by the transmitter and converts it into electrical impulses. These electrical impulses flow through electrodes contained in a narrow, flexible tube that has been threaded into the cochlea during surgery and stimulate the auditory nerve. The auditory nerve carries the electrical impulses to the brain, which interprets them as sound.

Despite the benefits that the implant appears to offer, some hearing specialists and members of the deaf community still believe that the benefits may not outweigh the risks and limitations of the device. Because the device must be surgically implanted, it carries some surgical risk. Also, it is impossible to be certain how well any individual child will respond to the implant. After getting an implant, some people say they feel alienated from the deaf community, while at the same time not feeling fully a part of the hearing world.

The sounds heard through an implant are different from those sounds heard normally, and have been described as artificial or "robot-like." This is because the implant's limited number of electrodes cannot hope to match the complexity of a human's 15,000 hair cells. Cochlear implants are, however, becoming more advanced and providing even better sound resolution.

Surgical procedure

During the procedure, the surgeon makes an incision behind the ear and opens the mastoid bone (the ridge on the skull behind the ear) leading into the middle ear. The surgeon then places the receiver-stimulator into a well made in the bone and gently threads the electrodes into the cochlea. This operation takes between an hour-and-a-half and five hours. It is performed using general anesthesia.

Precautions

Because the implants are controversial, very expensive, and have uncertain results, the United States Food and Drug Administration (FDA) has limited the implants to people for whom the following is true:

• individuals who get no significant benefit from hearing aids

• individuals who are at least 12 months old

• individuals with severe to profound hearing loss

Preparation

Before a child gets an implant, specialists at an implant clinic conduct a careful evaluation, including extensive hearing tests to determine how well the child can hear.

First, candidates undergo a trial with a powerful hearing aid. If the hearing aid cannot improve hearing enough, a physician then performs a physical examination and orders a scan of the inner ear, because some patients with a scarred cochlea are not good candidates for cochlear implants. A doctor may also order a psychological exam to better understand the person's expectations. Patients and their families need to be highly motivated and have a realistic understanding of what an implant can and cannot do.

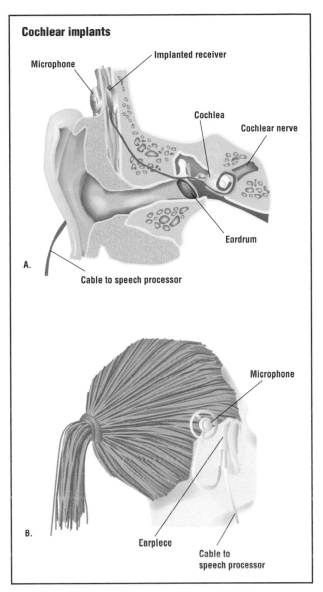

A cochlear implant has a microphone outside the ear that transmits sounds to an implanted receiver. In turn, the receiver transmits electrical impulses to the cochlea and cochlear nerve, which is stimulated in normal hearing. *(Illustration by GGS Information Services.)*

Aftercare

The child may remain in the hospital for a day or two after the surgery, although with improving technology and techniques some children may go home the same day. After about a month, the surgical **wounds** will have healed, and the child returns to the implant clinic to be fitted with the external parts of the device (the speech processor, microphone, and transmitter). A clinician tunes the speech processor and sets levels of stimulation for each electrode from soft to loud.

The child is then trained in how to interpret the sounds heard through the device. The length of the training varies from days to years, depending on how well the child can interpret the sounds heard. With the new approval for using cochlear implants in children as young as 12 months of age, the toddler may not be trained specifically to interpret the sounds in the same way an older child would. The specific therapy that is recommended is highly dependent on the age of the child.

Risks

As with all operations, there are a few risks of surgery. These include the following:

• dizziness

• facial paralysis (which is rare and usually temporary)

• infection at the incision site

Scientists are not sure about the long-term effects of electrical stimulation on the nervous system. It is also possible that the implant's internal components may be damaged by a blow to the head. This may cause the device to stop working. In general the failure rate of the implants is only 1 percent after one year.

Parental concerns

There is increasing debate about the use of cochlear implants in infants. This is considered by some to be desirable because, if the implantation is done before a

child has begun to significantly acquire language, there is some evidence that the child may be able to develop at a pace similar to hearing children of the same age. Making a decision about whether or not a child, especially a very young one, should have a cochlear implant can be very difficult. The child's doctor may be able to provide parents with resources or put them in contact with other parents who have had to make the same decision whom they can consult.

See also Hearing impairment.

Resources

BOOKS

Christiansen, John B., and Irene W. Leigh. *Cochlear Implants in Children: Ethics and Choices.* Washington DC: Gallaudet University Press, 2002.

Chute, Patrician M., and Mary Ellen Nevins. *The Parents' Guide to Cochlear Implants.* Washington DC: Gallaudet University Press. 2002.

PERIODICALS

Barker, Brittan A., and Bruce J. Tomblin. "Bimodal Speech Perception in Infant Hearing Aid and Cochlear Implant Users." *Archives of Otolaryngology—Head & Neck Surgery* 130 (May 2004): 582–87.

Chin, Steven B. "Children's Consonant Inventories after Extended Cochlear Implant Use." *Journal of Speech, Language, and Hearing Research* 46 (August 2003): 849–63.

Conor, Carol McDonald, and Teresa A. Zwolan. "Examining Multiple Sources of Influence on the Reading Comprehension Skills of Children Who Use Cochlear Implants." *Journal of Speech, Language, and Hearing Research* 47 (June 2004): 509–27.

ORGANIZATIONS

American Society for Deaf Children. PO Box 3355 Gettysburg, PA 17325. Web site: <www.deafchildren.org>.

Tish Davidson, A.M.
Carol A. Turkington

Codeine *see* **Narcotic drugs**

Cognitive development

Definition

Cognitive development is the construction of thought processes, including remembering, problem solving, and decision-making, from childhood through **adolescence** to adulthood.

Description

It was once believed that infants lacked the ability to think or form complex ideas and remained without cognition until they learned language. It is now known that babies are aware of their surroundings and interested in exploration from the time they are born. From birth, babies begin to actively learn. They gather, sort, and process information from around them, using the data to develop perception and thinking skills.

Cognitive development refers to how a person perceives, thinks, and gains understanding of his or her world through the interaction of genetic and learned factors. Among the areas of cognitive development are information processing, **intelligence**, reasoning, **language development**, and memory.

Historically, the cognitive development of children has been studied in a variety of ways. The oldest is through intelligence tests, such as the widely used Stanford Binet Intelligence Quotient (IQ) test first adopted for use in the United States by psychologist Lewis Terman (1877–1956) in 1916 from a French model pioneered in 1905. IQ scoring is based on the concept of "mental age," according to which the scores of a child of average intelligence match his or her age, while a gifted child's performance is comparable to that of an older child, and a slow learner's scores are similar to those of a younger child. IQ tests are widely used in the United States, but they have come under increasing criticism for defining intelligence too narrowly and for being biased with regard to race and gender.

In contrast to the emphasis placed on a child's native abilities by intelligence testing, learning theory grew out of work by behaviorist researchers such as John Watson (1878–1958) and B. F. Skinner (1904–1990), who argued that children are completely malleable. Learning theory focuses on the role of environmental factors in shaping the intelligence of children, especially on a child's ability to learn by having certain behaviors rewarded and others discouraged.

Piaget's theory of cognitive development

The most well-known and influential theory of cognitive development is that of French psychologist Jean Piaget (1896–1980). Piaget's theory, first published in 1952, grew out of decades of extensive observation of children, including his own, in their natural environments as opposed to the laboratory experiments of the behaviorists. Although Piaget was interested in how children reacted to their environment, he proposed a more active role for them than that suggested by learning theory. He envisioned a child's knowledge as composed of schemas, basic units of knowledge used to organize past experiences and serve as a basis for understanding new ones.

Schemas are continually being modified by two complementary processes that Piaget termed assimilation and accommodation. Assimilation refers to the process of taking in new information by incorporating it into an existing schema. In other words, people assimilate new experiences by relating them to things they already know. On the other hand, accommodation is what happens when the schema itself changes to accommodate new knowledge. According to Piaget, cognitive development involves an ongoing attempt to achieve a balance between assimilation and accommodation that he termed equilibration.

At the center of Piaget's theory is the principle that cognitive development occurs in a series of four distinct, universal stages, each characterized by increasingly sophisticated and abstract levels of thought. These stages always occur in the same order, and each builds on what was learned in the previous stage. They are as follows:

- Sensorimotor stage (infancy): In this period, which has six sub-stages, intelligence is demonstrated through motor activity without the use of symbols. Knowledge of the world is limited, but developing, because it is based on physical interactions and experiences. Children acquire object permanence at about seven months of age (memory). Physical development (mobility) allows the child to begin developing new intellectual abilities. Some symbolic (language) abilities are developed at the end of this stage.

- Pre-operational stage (toddlerhood and early childhood): In this period, which has two sub stages, intelligence is demonstrated through the use of symbols, language use matures, and memory and imagination are developed, but thinking is done in a non-logical, non-reversible manner. Egocentric thinking predominates.

- Concrete operational stage (elementary and early adolescence): In this stage, characterized by seven types of conservation (number, length, liquid, mass, weight, area, and volume), intelligence is demonstrated through logical and systematic manipulation of symbols related to concrete objects. Operational thinking develops (mental actions that are reversible). Egocentric thought diminishes.

- Formal operational stage (adolescence and adulthood): In this stage, intelligence is demonstrated through the logical use of symbols related to abstract concepts.

Early in the period there is a return to egocentric thought. Only 35 percent of high school graduates in industrialized countries obtain formal operations; many people do not think formally during adulthood.

The most significant alternative to the work of Piaget has been the information-processing approach, which uses the computer as a model to provide new insight into how the human mind receives, stores, retrieves, and uses information. Researchers using information-processing theory to study cognitive development in children have focused on areas such as the gradual improvements in children's ability to take in information and focus selectively on certain parts of it and their increasing attention spans and capacity for memory storage. For example, researchers have found that the superior memory skills of older children are due in part to memorization strategies, such as repeating items in order to memorize them or dividing them into categories.

Infancy

As soon as they are born, infants begin learning to use their senses to explore the world around them. Most newborns can focus on and follow moving objects, distinguish the pitch and volume of sound, see all colors and distinguish their hue and brightness, and start anticipating events, such as sucking at the sight of a nipple. By three months old, infants can recognize faces; imitate the facial expressions of others, such as smiling and frowning; and respond to familiar sounds.

At six months of age, babies are just beginning to understand how the world around them works. They imitate sounds, enjoy hearing their own voice, recognize parents, **fear** strangers, distinguish between animate and inanimate objects, and base distance on the size of an object. They also realize that if they drop an object, they can pick it up again. At four to seven months, babies can recognize their names.

By nine months, infants can imitate gestures and actions, experiment with the physical properties of objects, understand simple words such as "no," and understand that an object still exists even when they cannot see it. They also begin to test parental responses to their behavior, such as throwing food on the floor. They remember the reaction and test the parents again to see if they get the same reaction.

At 12 months of age, babies can follow a fast moving object; can speak two to fours words, including "mama" and "papa"; imitate animal sounds; associate names with objects; develop attachments to objects, such as a toy or blanket; and experience **separation anxiety** when away from their parents. By 18 months of age,

babies are able to understand about 10–50 words; identify body parts; feel a sense of ownership by using the word "my" with certain people or objects; and can follow directions that involve two different tasks, such as picking up **toys** and putting them in a box.

Toddlerhood

Between 18 months to three years of age, toddlers have reached the "sensorimotor" stage of Piaget's theory of cognitive development that involves rudimentary thought. For instance, they understand the permanence of objects and people, visually follow the displacement of objects, and begin to use instruments and tools. Toddlers start to strive for more independence, which can present challenges to parents concerned for their **safety**. They also understand **discipline** and what behavior is appropriate and inappropriate, and they understand the concepts of words like "please" and "thank you."

Two-year-olds should be able to understand 100 to 150 words and start adding about ten new words per day. Toddlers also have a better understanding of emotions, such as love, trust, and fear. They begin to understand some of the ordinary aspects of everyday life, such as shopping for food, telling time, and being read to.

Preschool

Preschoolers, ages three to six, should be at the "preoperational" stage of Piaget's cognitive development theory, meaning they are using their imagery and memory skills. They should be conditioned to learning and memorizing, and their view of the world is normally very self-centered. Preschoolers usually have also developed their social interaction skills, such as playing and cooperating with other children their own age. It is normal for preschoolers to test the limits of their cognitive abilities, and they learn negative concepts and actions, such as talking back to adults, **lying**, and bullying. Other cognitive development in preschoolers are developing an increased attention span, learning to read, and developing structured routines, such as doing household chores.

School age

Younger school-age children, six to 12 years old, should be at the "concrete operations" stage of Piaget's cognitive development theory, characterized by the ability to use logical and coherent actions in thinking and solving problems. They understand the concepts of permanence and conservation by learning that volume, weight, and numbers may remain constant despite changes in outward appearance. These children should be able to build on past experiences, using them to explain why some things happen. Their attention span should increase with age, from being able to focus on a task for about 15 minutes at age six to an hour by age nine.

Adolescents, ages 12 through 18, should be at the "formal operations" stage of Piaget's cognitive development theory. It is characterized by an increased independence for thinking through problems and situations. Adolescents should be able to understand pure abstractions, such as philosophy and higher math concepts. During this age, children should be able to learn and apply general information needed to adapt to specific situations. They should also be able to learn specific information and skills necessary for an occupation. A major component of the passage through adolescence is a cognitive transition. Compared to children, adolescents think in ways that are more advanced, more efficient, and generally more complex. This ability can be seen in five ways.

First, during adolescence individuals become better able than children to think about what is possible, instead of limiting their thought to what is real. Whereas children's thinking is oriented to the here and now—that is, to things and events that they can observe directly—adolescents are able to consider what they observe against a backdrop of what is possible; they can think hypothetically.

Second, during the passage into adolescence, individuals become better able to think about abstract ideas. For example, adolescents find it easier than children to comprehend the sorts of higher-order, abstract logic inherent in puns, proverbs, metaphors, and analogies. The adolescent's greater facility with abstract thinking also permits the application of advanced reasoning and logical processes to social and ideological matters. This is clearly seen in the adolescent's increased facility and interest in thinking about interpersonal relationships, politics, philosophy, religion, and morality.

Third, during adolescence individuals begin thinking more often about the process of thinking itself, or metacognition. As a result, adolescents may display increased introspection and self-consciousness. Although improvements in metacognitive abilities provide important intellectual advantages, one potentially negative byproduct of these advances is the tendency for adolescents to develop a sort of egocentrism, or intense preoccupation with the self.

A fourth change in cognition is that thinking tends to become multidimensional, rather than limited to a single issue. Whereas children tend to think about things one aspect at a time, adolescents can see things through more complicated lenses. Adolescents describe themselves and others in more differentiated and complicated terms and find it easier to look at problems from multiple perspectives. Being able to understand that people's personalities are not one-sided or that

Cognitive development

Age	Activity
One month	Watches person when spoken to.
Two months	Smiles at familiar person talking. Begins to follow moving person with eyes.
Four months	Shows interest in bottle, breast, familiar toy, or new surroundings.
Five months	Smiles at own image in mirror. Looks for fallen objects.
Six months	May stick out tongue in imitation. Laughs at peekaboo game. Vocalizes at mirror image. May act shy around strangers.
Seven months	Responds to own name. Tries to establish contact with a person by cough or other noise.
Eight months	Reaches for toys out of reach. Responds to "no."
Nine months	Shows likes and dislikes. May try to prevent face-washing or other activity that is disliked. Shows excitement and interest in foods or toys that are well-liked.
Ten months	Starts to understand some words. Waves bye-bye. Holds out arm or leg for dressing.
Eleven months	Repeats performance that is laughed at. Likes repetitive play. Shows interest in books.
Twelve months	May understand some "where is…?" questions. May kiss on request.
Fifteen months	Asks for objects by pointing. Starting to feed self. Negativism begins.
Eighteen months	Points to familiar objects when asked "where is…?" Mimics familiar adult activities. Know some body parts. Obeys two or three simple orders.
Two years	Names a few familiar objects. Draws with crayons. Obeys found simple orders. Participates in parallel play.
Two and a half years	Names several common objects. Begins to take interest in sex organs. Gives full names. Helps to put things away. Peak of negativism.
Three years	Constantly asks questions. May count to 10. Begins to draw specific objects. Dresses and undresses doll. Participates in cooperative play. Talks about things that have happened.
Four years	May make up silly words and stories. Beginning to draw pictures that represent familiar things. Pretends to read and write. May recognize a few common words, such as own name.
Five years	Can recognize and reproduce many shapes, letters, and numbers. Tells long stories. Begins to understand the difference between real events and make-believe ones. Asks meaning of words.

SOURCE: *Miller-Keane Encyclopedia and Dictionary of Medicine, Nursing, and Allied Health, 5th ed.* and Child Development Institute, http://www.childdevelopmentinfo.com.

(Table by GGS Information Services.)

social situations can have different interpretations depending on one's point of view permits the adolescent to have far more sophisticated and complicated relationships with other people.

Finally, adolescents are more likely than children to see things as relative, rather than absolute. Children tend to see things in absolute terms—in black and white. Adolescents, in contrast, tend to see things as relative. They are more likely to question others' assertions and less likely to accept facts as absolute truths. This increase in relativism can be particularly exasperating to parents, who may feel that their adolescent children question everything just for the sake of argument. Difficulties often arise, for example, when adolescents begin seeing their parents' values as excessively relative.

Common problems

Cognitive impairment is the general loss or lack of development of cognitive abilities, particularly **autism** and learning disabilities. The National Institutes of Mental Health (NIMH) describes learning disabilities as a disorder that affects people's ability to either interpret what they see and hear or to link information from different parts of the brain. These limitations can show up in many ways, such as specific difficulties with spoken and written language, coordination, self-control, or attention. Such difficulties extend to schoolwork and can impede learning to read or write or to do math. A child who has a learning disability may have other conditions, such as hearing problems or serious emotional disturbance. However, learning disabilities are not caused by these conditions, nor are they caused by environmental influences such as cultural differences or inappropriate instruction.

Parental concerns

As of 2004 it is widely accepted that a child's intellectual ability is determined by a combination of heredity and environment. Thus, although a child's genetic inheritance is unchangeable, there are definite ways that parents can enhance their child's intellectual development through environmental factors. They can provide stimulating learning materials and experiences from an early age, read to and talk with their children, and help children explore the world around them. As children mature, parents can both challenge and support the child's talents. Although a supportive environment in early childhood provides a clear advantage for children, it is possible to make up for early losses in cognitive development if a supportive environment is provided at some later period, in contrast to early

disruptions in physical development, which are often irreversible.

When to call the doctor

If, by age three, a child has problems understanding simple directions or is perplexed when asked to do something simple, the parents or primary caregiver should consult a physician or pediatrician. The child may have a delay in cognitive development. Parents should also consult a healthcare professional if, after age three, their child's cognitive development appears to be significantly slower than their peers.

Resources

BOOKS

Bjorklund, David F. *Children's Thinking: Cognitive Development and Individual Differences.* Stamford, CT: Wadsworth Publishing, 2004.

Pica, Rae. *Your Active Child: How to Boost Physical, Emotional, and Cognitive Development Through Age-Appropriate Activity.* New York: McGraw-Hill, 2003.

Thornton, Stephanie. *Growing Minds: An Introduction to Children's Cognitive Development.* New York: Palgrave Macmillan, 2003.

Wadsworth, Barry J. *Piaget's Theory of Cognitive and Affective Development: Foundations of Constructivism,* 5th ed. Upper Saddle River, NJ: Allyn & Bacon, 2003.

PERIODICALS

Blumberg, Fran. C., and Lori M. Sokol. "Boys' and Girls' Use of Cognitive Strategy when Learning to Play Video Games." *The Journal of General Psychology* (April 2004): 151–58.

Dahl, Ronald. "Risk-Taking and Thrill-Seeking." *Behavioral Healthcare Tomorrow* (June 2004): SS6–SS7.

Li, Xiaoming, and Melissa S. Atkins. "Early Childhood Computer Experience and Cognitive and Motor Development." *Pediatrics* (June 2004): 1715–22.

Thurber, Christopher A. "I Am. Therefore, I Think: Explanations of Cognitive Development." *Camping Magazine* (July-August 2003): 36–41.

Wacharasin, Chintana, et al. "Factors Affecting Toddler Cognitive Development in Low-Income Families: Implications for Practitioners." *Infants & Young Children* (April-June 2003): 175–81.

Zinner, Susan. "The Role of Cognitive Development in Pediatric Medical Decision-Making." *Global Virtue Ethics Review* (January 2004): N/A.

ORGANIZATIONS

Cognitive Development Society. University of North Carolina, PO 3270, Chapel Hill, NC 27599. Web site: <www.cogdevsoc.org>.

National Academy of Child & Adolescent Psychiatry. 3615 Wisconsin Ave. NW, Washington, DC 20016. Web site: <www.aacap.org>.

WEB SITES

Developmental Psychology: Cognitive Development, 2004. Available online at <www.psy.pdx.edu/PsiCafe/Areas/Developmental/CogDev-Child/index.htm> (accessed November 9, 2004).

Piaget's Theory of Cognitive Development, 2003. Available online at <http://chiron.valdosta.edu/whuitt/col/cogsys/piaget.html> (accessed November 9, 2004).

Ken R. Wells

Cohabitation *see* **Stepfamilies**

Cold sore

Definition

Cold sores are small red blisters, filled with clear fluid, that form on the lip and around the mouth. Rarely, they form on the roof of the mouth. Cold sores are caused by the **herpes simplex** virus type 1 (HSV-1), which lives inside nerve tissue. Despite their name, cold sores have nothing to do with colds. The herpes simplex virus type 1 should not be confused with the herpes simplex virus type 2 (HSV-2), which most often causes genital herpes.

Description

There are eight different kinds of human herpes viruses. Only two of these, herpes simplex types 1 and 2, can cause cold sores. It is commonly believed that herpes simplex virus type 1 infects above the waist and herpes simplex virus type 2 infects below the waist. This is not true. Both herpes virus type 1 and type 2 can cause herpes lesions on the lips or genitals, but recurrent cold sores are almost always type 1.

The sores can appear within days or weeks or even years following the first exposure to the virus. The first time symptoms appear they are usually more intense than later outbreaks. For example, some children experience more **pain** at the blister site or even flu-like symptoms, including swollen glands, **fever**, or **sore throat**. Medical names for cold sores include oral herpes, labial herpes, herpes labialis, and herpes febrilis.

Transmission

Herpes simplex virus is transmitted by infected body fluids (such as saliva) when they contact breaks in another person's skin or mucous membranes. Newborns may become infected during delivery through an infected birth canal. HSV-1 can be passed to children by parents, nurses, and caregivers who fail to practice careful hand washing. Children with **burns**, eczema, or **diaper rash** or those who are immunosuppressed are highly susceptible to the herpes virus.

VIRUS VERSUS BACTERIA Viruses behave differently than bacteria. While bacteria are independent and can reproduce on their own, viruses enter human cells and force them to make more viruses. The infected human cell dies and releases thousands of new viruses. The cell death and resulting tissue damage causes the cold sores. In addition, the herpes virus can infect a cell, and instead of making the cell produce new viruses, it hides inside the cell and waits. The herpes virus hides in the nervous system. This action is called latency. A latent virus can wait inside the nervous system for days, months, or even years. At some future time, the virus "awakens" and causes the cell to produce thousands of new viruses that cause an active infection.

Latent and active infection is understood by considering the cold sore cycle. The first infection is the primary infection. The primary infection is controlled by the body's immune system and the sores heal. Between active infections, the virus is latent. At some point in the future, latent viruses become activated and once again cause sores or recurrent infections. Although it is unknown what triggers latent virus to activate, several conditions bring on infections. These include stress, illness, fever, fatigue, exposure to sunlight, **menstruation**, and diet.

Demographics

The herpes simplex virus is widespread in children. Thirty-five percent of five-year olds carry HSV-1 antibodies. A primary infection commonly occurs by the time a child reaches age five. These viral infections are more common in lower socioeconomic groups.

Nearly 80 percent of the general population carry the herpes simplex virus that causes cold sores, and 60 million have outbreaks once or more in a year. Most infants and children harbor the herpes virus before age ten. Interestingly enough, only 20 percent to 25 percent of those carrying the virus ever gets symptoms (break out in cold sores).

Causes and symptoms

While anyone can have the herpes virus infection, not everyone will show symptoms. The first symptoms of herpes occur within two to 20 days after contact with an infected person. Symptoms of the primary infection are usually more severe than those of recurrent infections. The primary infection can cause symptoms like other viral infections, including fatigue, **headache**, fever, and swollen lymph nodes in the neck.

Typically, 50 to 80 percent of children with oral herpes experience a prodrome (symptoms of oncoming disease) of pain, burning, **itching**, or tingling at the site where blisters will form. This prodrome stage may last a few hours or one to two days. The herpes infection prodrome occurs in both the primary infection and recurrent infections.

In 95 percent of the patients with cold sores, the blisters occur at the outer edge of the lips, which is called the vermillion border. Less often, blisters form on the nose, chin, or cheek. Following the prodrome, the disease process is rapid. First, small red bumps appear. These quickly form fluid-filled blisters.

Causes of cold sores in children

Infants are most likely to get a cold sore because someone with an active virus kisses them. The cause can even be a kiss from someone who did not have a visible sore but had the virus in his or her saliva. A baby may also get the herpes virus passing through the birth canal if the mother has genital herpes.

Once a child gets the virus, it stays in his body permanently, hiding in nerve cells near the ear. In some children, the virus lies dormant and never causes harm. In others, it periodically wakes up and triggers cold sores. Nobody knows what stirs the virus into action, but stress, fever, colds, and **sunburn** encourage outbreaks. Rich foods such as chocolate, **food allergies**, or hormonal changes may also cause outbreaks in children and adolescents.

Symptoms of cold sores in infants

The first symptoms of cold sores in infants are swollen gums and sore mouth. A few days later, there is a cluster of small blisters on or near the lips that turn into a shallow, painful sore. The breakout is often accompanied with fever and swollen lymph glands in the neck. In a few days the sore will crust and slowly disappear. The whole flare-up lasts about seven to ten days. The next time the infant has an outbreak the blister is the first symptom, not the swollen gums and painful mouth. If not treated, recurring outbreaks may last longer.

Stages of cold sores in children and adolescents

Cold sores, untreated, can last up to 14 days. Children often feel the tingling at the site before the sore appears. Parents should begin the treatment at the first sign of tingling or redness, which can reduce the time to two to four days. Beginning treatment after the blister appears can also significantly reduce the time and degree of pain. The following describes the stages of a cold sore:

- Day 1: Prodrome (tingle) stage: Before a blister appears, the child usually feels a tingling, itching, or burning sensation beneath the skin, usually around the mouth or the base of the nose. This is the best time to start treatment.

- Days 2 to 3: The blister or blisters appear. Children usually have one or several blisters on or around the moth, most often at the border of the lip and the skin on the face. Cold sores occasionally occur on the roof of the mouth.

- Day 4: Ulcer or weeping stage: The blister opens, revealing a reddish area. The child is most contagious and in the most pain at this point.

- Days 5 to 8: Crusting stage: The blisters dry up, and a crust forms which is yellow or brown in color. Children should be told not to pick at this crust.

- Days 9 to 14: Healing stage: A series of scabs form over the sore, each smaller than the previous one until the cold sore is healed.

When to call the doctor

The HSV-1 virus can cause ocular herpes, a serious eye infection affecting the cornea (the clear window) of the eye, which can threaten vision and needs immediate medical attention and treatment. When a baby or child has a cold sore, parents should do all they can to keep them from touching their eyes. If a painful sore appears on the child's eyelid, eye surface, or on the end of his nose, call the pediatrician right away. The child may need **antiviral drugs** to keep the infection from scarring the cornea. Ocular herpes can weaken vision and even cause blindness.

Some children have a serious primary (first episode) herpes infection called gingivostomatitis, which causes fever, swollen lymph glands, and several blisters inside the mouth and on the lips and tongue that may form large, open sores. These painful sores may last up to three weeks and can make eating and drinking difficult. Because of this problem, young children with gingivostomatitis are at risk for **dehydration**. Children with this condition should be seen by a doctor.

Most infants have protection for at least six months from HSV-1 by antibodies they received from their mothers. But if a newborn gets a cold sore, the pediatrician should be called right away.

If the immune system of children is compromised because of **cancer** treatment or **AIDS**, they could have more serious problems with the herpes virus. Parents should let the doctor know if these health conditions exist.

Children with a history of frequent herpes flare-ups who spend time skiing or on the beach should call a doctor for a prescription for starting oral anti-herpes medication (pills) before such outings and then using sunscreen while they are outside. These precautions can prevent most outbreaks.

Diagnosis

Cold sores are diagnosed by review of symptoms, physical examination, and history. The diagnosis is confirmed by various viral tests. A Tzanck or Papanicolau smear may be done. A positive smear cannot distinguish between varicella zoster virus and HSV-1, and a negative smear does not rule out HSV infection. Tissue culture provides a more reliable method of diagnosis. Cells killed by the herpes virus have a certain appearance under the microscope. Laboratory blood test looks for the virus or to confirm the presence of antibodies that fight the virus.

Approximately 85 percent of active herpes infections are without symptoms. When the symptoms do appear, they have the following sequence:

- burning, itching, or tingling at the site before the sore appears

- clusters of fluid-filled vesicles ulcerate, dry, and crust

- lesions dry and crust within seven to ten days

- usually one or two lesions present on the lips, tongue, gingival, or buccal mucosa

- puritis (itching) and pain

Treatment

There is no cure for herpes virus infections. Antiviral drugs are available that have some effect on lessening the symptoms and decreasing the length of herpes outbreaks. There is evidence that some may also prevent future outbreaks. These antiviral drugs work by interfering with the reproduction of the viruses and are most effective when taken as early in the infection as possible. For the best results, drug treatment should begin during the prodrome stage before blisters are visible. Depending on the length of the outbreak, drug treatment could continue for up to ten days.

Antiviral pills such as acyclovir (Zovirax), famciclovir, (Famvir), and valacyclovir (Valtrex) can cancel an outbreak and help prevent recurrent outbreaks. Acyclovir (Zovirax) is the drug of choice for herpes infection and can be given intravenously or taken by mouth. A liquid form for children is also available. Acyclovir is effective in treating both the primary infection and recurrent outbreaks. When taken by mouth, acyclovir reduces the frequency of herpes outbreaks.

Antiviral creams Zovirax and Denavir should be applied within the first 24 hours of feeling the tingling or discomfort, before the plaster erupts. The duration of the outbreak can be shortened by a day or two. Antiviral creams are not as effective as the pills.

During an outbreak, sores should be washed once or twice a day with warm, soapy water, and gently patted dry. Over-the-counter lip products that contain the chemical phenol (such as Blistex Medicated Lip Ointment) and numbing ointments (Anbesol) help to relieve cold sores. A bandage over the sores protects them and prevents spreading the virus to other sites on the lips or face.

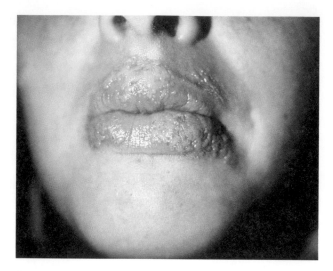

Close-up view of a cold sore, caused by herpes simplex virus, on a patient's mouth. (© *Kenneth Greer/Visuals Unlimited.*)

Acetaminophen (Tylenol) or ibuprofen (Motrin, Advil) may be necessary to reduce pain and fever.

Alternative treatment

Cold sores in infants and children will go away on their own, but there are measures that will help the child feel better:

- To ease the pain, apply ice to the sore, or if the doctor approves, give the baby a mild pain reliever, such as ibuprofen or acetaminophen. (Do not give aspirin to a baby; it could trigger Reye's syndrome. This is a rare but potentially life-threatening illness.) Choices for pain relief include medication, ointments, or mouth rinses recommended by the pediatrician. Parents may also use Oragel, an ointment often used for **canker sores** or teething.

- Avoid giving the child spicy, salty, or sour foods, and foods with acid (oranges and grapefruits), which can irritate the open sore.

- Apply a water-based zinc ointment such as Desitin. It helps dry out the sore so it can heal faster.

- Extra **sleep** and plenty of liquids to drink can help.

Adolescents can learn to manage their own outbreaks. They can take the following steps:

- Use over-the-counter pain relievers, such as acetaminophen (Tylenol) or ibuprofen (Motrin, Advil).

- Avoid squeezing or picking the blister.

- Apply ice to ease the pain.

- Acidophilus pills may be helpful in treating cold sores. L-lysine is an amino acid widely advertised to treat cold sores. Conflicting medical opinions exist about its effectiveness.

Nutritional concerns

If children are prone to recurrent viral infections, parents should review their eating habits. The children should avoid foods and drinks that are proven suppressors of immunity (foods high in sugar, **caffeine**, and alcohol content) and have regular meals with plenty of fresh vegetables and fruits and whole-grain products. Some foods may be increased or reduced for specific types of viral infections. For herpes, foods containing the amino acid arginine (nuts and seeds) need to be reduced, and those containing the amino acid lysine (yogurt and cottage cheese) need to be increased. Immune system health in children can also benefit from a wide range of **vitamins** and **minerals** as nutritional supplements. Vitamin B complex and vitamins A, C, and E are the most important supplements.

Prognosis

Anyone can become infected with the herpes virus. Once infected, the virus remains latent in the body for life. It lives in nerve cells where the immune system cannot find it. The herpes virus lies dormant in the nerves of the face and is reactivated by sunburn, a recent viral illness (cold or flu), and periods of stress. Cold sores spread from person to person by direct skin-to-skin contact.

The highest risk for spreading the virus is the time period beginning with the blisters and ending with scab formation. However, infected people need not have visible blisters to spread the infection since the virus may be present in the saliva without obvious oral lesions.

Most children experience fewer than two recurrent outbreaks of cold sores each year; some have frequent outbreaks and others never experience outbreaks. Most blisters form in the same area each time and are triggered by the same reasons (such as stress, sun exposure, etc.).

Prevention

Cold sores are contagious. As of 2004 there were no herpes vaccines available, although herpes vaccines were in research and development. Avoiding close contact with people shedding the virus is the best way to prevent primary herpes. Several practices can reduce reoccurring cold sores and the spread of virus:

- Parents should teach children not to share drinks, food, or eating utensils, and not to exchange kisses with someone with mouth sores.

- When parents have an outbreak, they should avoid kissing their children (and other adults).

- Parents should be watchful of infected children and not allow them to share **toys** that may be put into the mouth. Toys that have been in the child's mouth should be disinfected before other children **play** with them.

- Parents should be especially careful with infants; they should not kiss the eyes or lips of a baby who is under six months old. The child's eyes and genitals are particularly susceptible to the herpes virus. They should keep the child from picking at a cold sore as much as possible.

- To keep from spreading the infection to other parts of the child's body or giving the virus to someone else, parents and caregivers should wash their hands and the child's hands often, especially after feedings and diaper changes.

- The child should be protected from the sun, since exposure to sunlight can trigger an outbreak. If the child is outside on a sunny day, generously apply sunscreen and lip balm that contains sun block before prolonged exposure to the sun. Sun block should be used during both winter and summer months, to help prevent cold cores. Wearing a hat with a large brim is also helpful.

- Parents should wear gloves when applying ointment to a child's sore. They should remove gloves and wash hands before and after changing diapers.

- Antibiotic ointments may be used to treat secondary bacterial infection of lesions. Parent should avoid using steroid creams or gels on a suspected herpes infection because these agents could make the infection worse.

- Parents should maintain good general health. A healthy diet, plenty of sleep, and **exercise** help to minimize the chance of getting a cold or the flu, which may bring on cold sores. Also, good general health keeps the immune system strong; this helps to keep the virus in check and prevents outbreaks.

Parental concerns

The child with a herpes infection is usually miserable and needs generous cuddling and comfort in spite of the infection. Parents of children who get cold sores should be aware of early symptoms and be ready to treat the sore in the first couple days. They should also keep in mind the prevention tips mentioned above. Parents should call the child's pediatrician if the child has not had a cold sore before, especially in the case of babies.

KEY TERMS

Antiviral drug—A medication that can destroy viruses and help treat illnesses caused by them.

Contagious—The movement of disease between people. All contagious disease is infectious, but not all infections are contagious.

Herpetic gingivostomatitis—A severe oral infection that affects children under five years of age; vesicles and ulcerations, edematous throat, enlarged painful cervical lymph nodes occur; chills, fever, malaise, bed breath, and drooling.

Latent virus—A nonactive virus that is in a dormant state within a cell. The herpes virus is latent in the nervous system.

Oral lesions—A single infected sore in the skin around the mouth or mucus membrane inside of the oral cavity.

Prodrome—Early symptoms that warn of the beginning of disease. For example, the herpes prodrome consists of pain, burning, tingling, or itching at a site before blisters are visible while the migraine prodrome consists of visual disturbances.

Recurrence—The return of an active infection following a period of latency.

Reye's syndrome—A serious, life-threatening illness in children, usually developing after a bout of flu or chickenpox, and often associated with the use of aspirin. Symptoms include uncontrollable vomiting, often with lethargy, memory loss, disorientation, or delirium. Swelling of the brain may cause seizures, coma, and in severe cases, death.

Secretion—A substance, such as saliva or mucus, that is produced and given off by a cell or a gland.

Resources

BOOKS

Health and Healing the Natural Way: Energize Your Life. Pleasantville, New York: The Reader's Digest Association, Inc., 2000.

Parker, Philip M., et al. *Cold Sores: A Medical Dictionary, Bibliography, and Annotated Research Guide to Internet References.* Boulder, CO: netLibrary, 2003.

PERIODICALS

Novatnack, Ellen, and Steven Shchweon. "Herpes: A bigger problem than you think." *RN Magazine* 65 (June 2002): 31–37.

WEB SITES

"Herpes labialis (oral Herpes simplex)." *MedlinePlus,* July 12, 2004. Available online at <www.nlm.nih.gov/

medlineplus/ency/article/000606.htm> (accessed December 14, 2004).

Aliene S. Linwood, RN, DPA, FACHE
Belinda Rowland, PhD

Colds *see* **Common cold**

Colic

Definition

Colic is defined as when a baby cries for longer than three hours every day for more than three days a week. It is the extreme end of normal crying behavior. The condition is harmless, even though it is distressing for parents or caregivers.

Description

Almost all babies go through a fussy period, but when crying lasts longer than about three hours a day and is not caused by a specific medical problem, it is considered colic. Pediatricians will tell parents that babies do not exhibit colic symptoms until around three weeks of age, but there are many parents who would disagree. The physician may also tell the parents that it will be at its worst around six weeks of age and then usually stops around three or four months of age. Some parents might disagree with that, too. It can be acknowledged as a relatively short period of time in a baby's life, but it seems like an eternity to the parents. It frequently, but not always, starts at the same time of day, and for most babies that is in the evening. The inconsolable crying begins suddenly; the legs may be drawn up, and the belly distended. The hands may be clenched. It seems as if it goes on forever and winds down when the baby is exhausted or when gas or stool is passed. Some babies continue crying for longer than three hours.

Demographics

Anywhere from 20 to 25 percent of babies cry enough to meet the definition of colic. There are approximately 4 million babies born every year in the United States, so that means almost a million babies have symptoms of colic.

Causes and symptoms

The baby with colic tends to be unusually sensitive to stimulation. Some babies experience greater discomfort from intestinal gas. Some cry from hunger. Some cry from overfeeding. **Fear**, frustration, or even excitement can lead to abdominal discomfort and colic. The situation may become a viscous cycle: the people caring for the baby become worried, anxious, or depressed, and the baby can sense their emotions and cries more. There are two theories regarding the cause of colic, and the first is that it is due to an immature nervous system. The majority of babies with colic can be classified with this condition to some degree. A small percentage of babies with colic may have milk **allergies**, reflux, and silent reflux. Formula changes or changes in diet for the breastfeeding mother can contribute to the problem. One recent study noted that the babies of mothers who smoke have a higher incidence of colic. The culprit is likely nicotine, which increases blood levels of a gut protein involved in digestion, according to Brown University epidemiologist Edmond Shenassa. This situation could result in painful cramping that makes babies cry.

When to call the doctor

Parents should call the pediatrician if they are concerned. A careful physical exam is prudent to insure the baby does not have a medical problem that needs attention. It is imperative not to misdiagnose a serious condition and call it colic. Should the behavior pattern of crying suddenly change and be associated with **fever**, **vomiting**, **diarrhea**, or other abnormal symptoms, parents should call the doctor immediately.

Diagnosis

Diagnosis occurs mostly by elimination. If the physical exam demonstrates nothing else is wrong, the pediatrician may diagnose colic by the parent's description of the crying.

Treatment

Parents should remember that colic is a benign condition, and the only treatment is through a matter of experimentation and observation. If a trigger for colic can be identified, that is a big start. Possible triggers include:

- Foods: Avoid stimulants such as **caffeine** and chocolate if breastfeeding.

- Formula: Switching formula works for some babies but is not at all helpful for others.

- Medicine: Medication that a breastfeeding mother takes may affect the baby.

- Feeding: If a bottle feeding takes less than 20 minutes, the hole in the nipple may be too large. Avoid overfeeding the infant or feeding too quickly.

Other strategies that can be tried include:

- movement and vibration
- using an infant swing
- rocking in a rocking chair
- going for a car ride
- holding the baby close in an upright position
- swaddling in a blanket

Nutritional concerns

The primary nutritional concerns are related to the breastfeeding mother's diet by avoiding the intake of stimulants. For those who are bottle feeding, a switch in the formula may be beneficial.

Prognosis

Colic is a benign condition. The infant outgrows it. Moreover, in spite of apparent abdominal **pain**, colicky infants eat well and gain weight normally.

Prevention

Very little can be done to prevent colic, other than trying to discover triggers that cause the baby to cry and to not smoke.

Parental concerns

It is natural for parents to be concerned when a baby cries, and their concern only heightens if it seems they can do nothing to stop the crying. Once a physical exam has been performed and medical causes have been ruled out, parents can accept the fact that the baby has colic and try to work with it the best way possible. They may want to take breaks from the baby by dividing childcare between them. A parent can be more loving to a baby when the parent has a chance to refresh.

See also Crying and fussing in an infant.

Resources

BOOKS

Seidel, Henry M., et al. *Primary Care of the Newborn*, 3rd ed. St. Louis, MO: Mosby, 2001.

WEB SITES

What Is Colic? Available online at <www.colichelp.com/> (accessed December 8, 2004).

"Your Colicky Baby." *Kids Health for Parents.* Available online at <http://kidshealth.org/parent/growth/growing/colic.html> (accessed December 8, 2004).

Linda K. Bennington, MSN, CNS

Color blindness

Definition

Color blindness is an abnormal condition characterized by the inability to clearly distinguish different colors of the spectrum. The difficulties can range from mild to severe. It is a misleading term because people with color blindness are not blind. Rather, they tend to see colors in a limited range of hues; a rare few may not see colors at all.

Description

Normal color vision requires the use of specialized receptor cells called cones, which are located in the retina of the eye. There are three types of cones, red, blue, and green, which enable people to see a wide spectrum of colors. An abnormality, or deficiency, of any of the types of cones will result in abnormal color vision.

There are three basic variants of color blindness. Red/green color blindness is the most common deficiency, affecting 8 percent of Caucasian males and 0.5 percent of Caucasian females. The prevalence varies with culture.

Blue color blindness is an inability to distinguish both blue and yellow, which are seen as white or gray. It is quite rare and has equal prevalence in males and females. It is common for young children to have blue/green confusion that becomes less pronounced in adulthood. Blue color deficiency often appears in people who have physical disorders such as liver disease or **diabetes mellitus**.

A total inability to distinguish colors (achromatopsia) is exceedingly rare. These affected individuals view the world in shades of gray. They frequently have poor visual acuity and are extremely sensitive to light (photophobia), which causes them to squint in ordinary light.

Demographics

Researchers studying red/green color blindness in the United Kingdom reported an average prevalence of only 4.7 percent in one group. Only 1 percent of Eskimo males are color blind. Approximately 2.9 percent of boys from Saudi Arabia and 3.7 percent from India were found to have deficient color vision. Red/green color blindness may slightly increase an affected person's chances of contracting leprosy. Pre-term infants exhibit an increased prevalence of blue color blindness. Achromatopsia has a prevalence of about one in 33,000 in the United States and affects males and females equally.

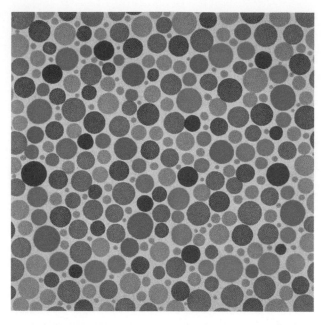

Common test used to detect red-green color blindness. Those with normal color vision should see the number 68. *(© Lester V. Bergman/Corbis.)*

Causes and symptoms

Red/green and blue color blindness appear to be located on at least two different gene locations. The majority of affected individuals are males. Females are carriers but are not normally affected. This indicates that the X chromosome is one of the locations for color blindness. Male offspring of females who carry the altered gene have a 50 percent chance of being color-blind. The rare female that has red/green color blindness, or rarer still, blue color blindness, indicates there is an involvement of another gene. As of 2004, the location of this gene was not yet identified.

Achromatopsia, the complete inability to distinguish color, is an autosomal recessive disease of the retina. Thus, both parents have one copy of the altered gene but do not have the disease. Each of their children has a 25 percent chance of not having the gene, a 50 percent chance of having one altered gene (and, like the parents, being unaffected), and a 25 percent risk of having both the altered gene and the condition. In 1997, the achromatopsia gene was discovered to reside on chromosome 2.

The inability to correctly identify colors is the only sign of color blindness. It is important to note that people with red/green or blue varieties of color blindness use other cues such as color saturation and object shape or location to distinguish colors. They can often distinguish red or green if they can visually compare the colors. However, most have difficulty accurately identifying colors without any other references. Most people with

any impairment in color vision learn colors, as do other young children. These individuals often reach **adolescence** before their visual deficiency is identified.

Color blindness is sometimes acquired. Chronic illnesses that can lead to color blindness include Alzheimer's disease, diabetes mellitus, glaucoma, leukemia, liver disease, chronic **alcoholism**, macular degeneration, multiple sclerosis, Parkinson's disease, **sickle cell anemia**, and retinitis pigmentosa. Accidents or strokes that damage the retina or affect particular areas of the brain eye can lead to color blindness. Some medications such as **antibiotics**, barbiturates, anti-tuberculosis drugs, high blood pressure medications, and several medications used to treat nervous disorders and psychological problems may cause color blindness. Industrial or environmental chemicals such as carbon monoxide, carbon disulfide, fertilizers, styrene, and some containing lead can cause loss of color vision. Occasionally, changes can occur in the affected person's capacity to see colors after age 60.

When to call the doctor

An ophthalmologist should be consulted at the time color blindness is first suspected.

Diagnosis

There are several tests available to identify problems associated with color vision. The most commonly used is the American Optical/Hardy, Rand, and Ritter Pseudoisochromatic Test. It is composed of several discs filled with colored dots of different sizes and colors. A person with normal color vision looking at a test item sees a number that is clearly located somewhere in the center of a circle of variously colored dots. A color-blind person is not able to distinguish the number.

The Ishihara Test is comprised of eight plates that are similar to the American Optical Pseudoisochromatic Test plates. The individual being tested looks for numbers among the various colored dots on each test plate. Some plates distinguish between red/green and blue color blindness. Individuals with normal color vision perceive one number. Those with red/green color deficiency see a different number. Those with blue color vision see yet a different number.

A third analytical tool is the Titmus II Vision Tester Color Perception Test. The subject looks into a stereoscopic machine. The test stimulus most often used in professional offices contains six different designs or numbers on a black background, framed in a yellow border. Titmus II can test one eye at a time. However, its value is limited because it can only identify red/green deficiencies and is not highly accurate.

Treatment

As of 2004 there is no treatment or cure for color blindness. Most color vision deficient persons compensate well for their abnormality and usually rely on color cues and details that are not consciously evident to persons with typical color vision.

Inherited color blindness cannot be prevented. In the case of some types of acquired color deficiency, if the cause of the problem is removed, the condition may improve with time. But for most people with acquired color blindness, the damage is usually permanent.

Prognosis

Color blindness that is inherited is present in both eyes and remains constant over an individual's entire life. Some cases of acquired color vision loss are not severe, may appear in only one eye, and last for only a short time. Other cases tend to become worse with time.

Prevention

There is no way to prevent genetic color blindness. There is no way to prevent acquired color blindness that is associated with Alzheimer's disease, diabetes mellitus, leukemia, liver disease, macular degeneration, multiple sclerosis, Parkinson's disease, sickle cell anemia, and retinitis pigmentosa.

Some forms of acquired color blindness may be prevented. Limiting use of alcohol and drugs such as antibiotics, barbiturates, anti-tuberculosis drugs, high blood pressure medications, and several medications used to treat nervous disorders and psychological problems to levels that are required for therapeutic benefit may limit acquired color blindness.

Parental concerns

Parents can inquire about other **family** members who have experienced color blindness. If such family members exist, parents can have their children tested for color perception at an early age. Screening for color perception is usually performed in grade school.

Resources

BOOKS

Color Blindness: A Medical Dictionary, Bibliography, and Annotated Research Guide to Internet Resources. San Diego, CA: Icon Group International, 2003.

Fay, Aaron, and Frederick A. Jokobiec. "Diseases of the Visual System." In *Cecil Textbook of Medicine,* 22nd ed. Edited by Lee Goldman, et al. Philadelphia: Saunders, 2003, pp. 2406–19.

> ## KEY TERMS
>
> **Achromatopsia**—The inability to distinguish any colors.
>
> **Cones**—Receptor cells, located in the retina of the eye, that allow the perception of colors.
>
> **Photophobia**—An extreme sensitivity to light.
>
> **Retina**—The inner, light-sensitive layer of the eye containing rods and cones. The retina transforms the image it receives into electrical signals that are sent to the brain via the optic nerve.
>
> **Rods**—Photoreceptors, located in the retina of the eye, that are highly sensitive to low levels of light.

Olitsky, Scott, and Leonard B. Nelson. "Disorders of Vision." In *Nelson Textbook of Pediatrics,* 17th ed. Edited by Richard E. Behrman, et al. Philadelphia: Saunders, 2003, pp. 2087–9.

Wiggs, Janey L. "Color Vision." In *Ophthalmology,* edited by Myron Yanoff and Jay S. Duker. St. Louis, MO: Mosby, 2000.

PERIODICALS

Abadi, R. V. "Effects of Color Blindness." *Ophthalmic and Physiological Optics* 24, no. 3 (2004): 252–57.

Atchison, D. A., et al. "Traffic Signal Color Recognition Is a Problem for Both Protan and Deutan Color-vision Deficients." *Human Factors* 45, no. 3 (2003): 495–503.

Dick, F., et al. "Is Color Vision Impairment Associated with Cognitive Impairment in Solvent Exposed Workers?" *Occupational and Environmental Medicine* 61, no. 1 (2004): 76–78.

Tagarelli, A., et al. "Color Blindness in Everyday Life and Car Driving." *Acta Ophthalmology Scandinavia* 52, no. 4 (2004): 436–42.

ORGANIZATIONS

American Academy of Family Physicians. 11400 Tomahawk Creek Parkway, Leawood, KS 66211–2672. Web site: <www.aafp.org/>.

American Academy of Pediatrics. 141 Northwest Point Boulevard, Elk Grove Village, IL 60007–1098. Web site: <www.aap.org/default.htm>.

WEB SITES

"Color Blindness: More Prevalent Among Males." *Howard Hughes Medical Institute.* Available online at <www.hhmi.org/senses/b130.html> (accessed November 16, 2004).

Rutherford, Kim. "What Is Color Blindness?" *KidsHealth for Kids*. Available online at <http://kidshealth.org/kid/talk/qa/color_blind.html>(accessed November 16, 2004).

Waggoner, Terrace L. *Ishihara Test for Color Blindness*. Available online at <www.toledo-bend.com/colorblind/Ishihara.html>(accessed November 16, 2004).

L. Fleming Fallon Jr., MD, DrPH

Common cold

Definition

The common cold, also called a rhinovirus or corona-virus infection, is a viral infection of the upper respiratory system, including the nose, throat, sinuses, eustachian tubes, trachea, larynx, and bronchial tubes. Over 200 different viruses can cause a cold. Almost all colds clear up in less than two weeks without complications.

Description

Cold season in the United States begins in early autumn and extends through early spring. Although it is not true that getting wet or being in a draft causes a cold (a person has to come in contact with the virus to catch a cold), certain conditions may lead to increased susceptibility. These include:

• fatigue and overwork

• emotional stress

• poor nutrition

• smoking

• living or working in crowded conditions

Although most colds resolve on their own without complications, they are a leading cause of visits to the doctor and of time lost from work and school. Treating symptoms of the common cold has given rise in the United States to a multi-million dollar industry in over-the-counter medications.

Colds make the upper respiratory system less resistant to bacterial infection. Secondary bacterial infection may lead to middle ear infection (**otitis media**), **bronchitis**, **pneumonia**, sinus infection, or **strep throat**. People with chronic lung disease, **asthma**, diabetes, or a weakened immune system are more likely to develop these complications.

Transmission

People with colds are contagious during the first two to four days of the infection. Colds pass from person to person in several ways. When an infected person coughs, sneezes, or speaks, tiny fluid droplets containing the virus are expelled. If these are breathed in by other people, the virus may establish itself in their noses and airways.

Colds may also be passed through direct contact. If a person with a cold touches his runny nose or watery eyes, then shakes hands with another person, some of the virus is transferred to the uninfected person. If that person then touches his mouth, nose, or eyes, the virus is transferred to an environment where it can reproduce and cause a cold.

In addition, cold viruses can be spread through inanimate objects (door knobs, telephones, **toys**) that become contaminated with the virus. This is a common method of transmission in childcare centers. If a child with a cold touches his runny nose, then plays with a toy, some of the virus may be transferred to the toy. When another child plays with the toy a short time later, he may pick up some of the virus on his hands. The second child then touches his contaminated hands to his eyes, nose, or mouth and transfers some of the cold virus to himself.

Demographics

Colds are the most common illness to strike any part of the body, with over one billion colds in the United States each year. Anyone can get a cold, although preschool and grade school children catch them more frequently than adolescents and adults. Children average six to ten colds a year. In families with children in school, the number can be as high as 12 per year. Women, especially those aged 20 to 30 years old, have more colds than men, possibly because of their closer contact with children. Individuals older than 60 usually have fewer than one cold per year. Repeated exposure to viruses causing colds creates partial immunity.

Causes and symptoms

Colds are caused by more than 200 different viruses. The most common groups are rhinoviruses and corona-viruses. Different groups of viruses are more infectious at different seasons of the year, but knowing the exact virus causing the cold is not important in treatment.

Once acquired, the cold virus attaches itself to the lining of the nasal passages and sinuses. This condition causes the infected cells to release a chemical called histamine. Histamine increases the blood flow to the infected cells, causing swelling, congestion, and increased mucus production. Within one to three days the infected person begins to show cold symptoms.

The first cold symptoms are a tickle in the throat, runny nose, and sneezing. The initial discharge from the nose is clear and thin. Later it changes to a thick yellow or greenish discharge. Most adults do not develop a **fever** when they catch a cold. Young children may develop a low fever of up to 102°F (38.9°C).

In addition to a runny nose and fever, signs of a cold include coughing, sneezing, nasal congestion, **headache**, muscle ache, chills, **sore throat**, hoarseness, watery eyes, tiredness, and lack of appetite. The **cough** that accompanies a cold is usually intermittent and dry.

Most people begin to feel better four to five days after their cold symptoms become noticeable. All symptoms are generally gone within ten days, except for a dry cough that may linger for up to three weeks.

When to call the doctor

Colds make people more susceptible to bacterial infections such as strep throat, middle ear infections, and sinus infections. People who have colds that do not begin to improve within a week or who experience chest **pain**, fever for more than a few days, difficulty breathing, bluish lips or fingernails, a cough that brings up greenish-yellow or grayish sputum, skin rash, swollen glands, or whitish spots on the tonsils or throat should consult a doctor to see to determine if they have acquired a secondary bacterial infection that needs to be treated with an antibiotic.

Children who have chronic lung disease, diabetes, or a weakened immune system—either from diseases such as **AIDS** or leukemia or as the result of medications, (corticosteroids, **chemotherapy** drugs)—should consult their doctor if they get a cold. Children with these health problems are more likely to get a secondary infection. For children with asthma, colds are a common trigger of asthma symptoms.

Diagnosis

Colds are diagnosed by observing a child's symptoms. There are no laboratory tests as of 2004 for detecting the cold virus. However, a doctor may do a **throat culture** or blood test to rule out a secondary infection.

Influenza is sometimes confused with a cold, but flu causes much more severe symptoms, as well as a fever. **Allergies** to molds or pollens also can make the nose run. Allergies are usually more persistent than the common cold. An allergist can do tests to determine if the cold-like symptoms are being caused by an allergic reaction. Also, some people get a runny nose when they go outside in winter and breathe cold air. This type of runny nose is not a symptom of a cold.

Treatment

There are no medicines that will cure the common cold. Given time, the body's immune system makes antibodies to fight the infection, and the cold is resolved without any inter-vention. **Antibiotics** are useless against a cold. However, there are many products that have been developed by pharmaceutical companies in the United States designed to relieve cold symptoms. These products usually contain **antihistamines**, **decongestants**, and/or pain relievers.

Antihistamines block the action of the chemical histamine that is produced when the cold virus invades the cells lining the nasal passages. Histamine increases blood flow and causes the cells to swell. Antihistamines are taken to relieve the symptoms of sneezing, runny nose, itchy eyes, and congestion. Side effects are dry mouth and drowsiness, especially with the first few doses. Antihistamines should not be taken by people who are driving or operating dangerous equipment. Some people have allergic reactions to antihistamines. Common over-the-counter antihistamines are Chlor-Trimeton, Dimetapp, Tavist, and Actifed. The generic name for two common antihistamines are chlorpheniramine and diphenhydramine.

Decongestants work to constrict the blood flow to the vessels in the nose. They can shrink the tissue, reduce congestion, and open inflamed nasal passages, making breathing easier. Decongestants can make people feel jittery or keep them from sleeping. They should not be used by people with heart disease, high blood pressure, or glaucoma. Some common decongestants are Neo-Synepherine, Novafed, and Sudafed. The generic names of common decongestants include phenylephrine, phenylpropanolamine, pseudoephedrine, and in nasal sprays naphazoline, oxymetazoline, and xylometazoline.

Many over-the-counter medications are combinations of both antihistamines and decongestants; an ache and pain reliever, such as **acetaminophen** (Datril, Tylenol, Panadol) or ibuprofen (Advil, Nuprin, Motrin, Medipren); and a cough suppressant (dextromethorphan). Common combination medications include Tylenol Cold and Flu, Triaminic, Sudafed Plus, and Tavist D. Aspirin should not be given to children with a cold because of its association with a risk of **Reye's syndrome**.

Nasal sprays and nose drops are other products promoted for reducing nasal congestion. These usually contain a decongestant, but the decongestant in the nasal preparations can act more quickly and strongly than ones found in pills or liquids because it is applied directly in the nose. Congestion returns after a few hours. People can become dependent on nasal sprays and nose drops. If used for a long time, users may suffer withdrawal symptoms when these products are discontinued. The label on the preparation should be checked for recommendations on length and frequency of use, since nasal sprays and nose drops should not be used for more than a few days.

People react differently to different cold medications and may find some more helpful than others. A medication may be effective initially then lose some of its effectiveness. Children sometimes react differently than adults. Over-the-counter cold remedies should not be given to infants without consulting a doctor first.

Care should be taken not to exceed the recommended dosages, especially when combination medications or nasal sprays are taken. These medicines do not shorten or cure a cold; at best they can only help a person feel more comfortable.

In addition to the optional use of over-the-counter cold remedies, there are some self-care steps that can be taken to ease discomfort. These include:

- drinking plenty of fluids, but avoiding acidic juices, which may irritate the throat

- gargling with warm salt water—made by adding one teaspoon of salt to 8 oz of water—for a sore throat

- avoiding second-hand smoke

- getting plenty of rest

- using a cool-mist room humidifier to ease congestion and sore throat

- rubbing Vaseline or other lubricant under the nose to prevent irritation from frequent nose blowing

- for babies too young to blow their noses, the mucus should be suctioned gently with an infant nasal aspirator (It may be necessary to soften the mucus first with a few drops of salt water.)

Alternative treatment

Alternative practitioners emphasize that people get colds because their immune systems are weak. They point out that everyone is exposed to cold viruses, but not everyone gets every cold. The difference seems to be in the ability of the immune system to fight infection. Prevention focuses on strengthening the immune system by eating a healthy diet low in sugars and high in fresh fruits and vegetables, practicing meditation or using other means to reduce stress, and getting regular moderate **exercise**.

Once cold symptoms appear, some naturopathic practitioners believe the symptoms should be allowed to run their course without interference. Others suggest the following:

- Aromatherapy remedy: Inhaling a steaming mixture of lemon oil, thyme oil, eucalyptus, and tea tree oil (*Melaleuca* spp.).

- Ayurvedic medicinal remedy: Gargling with a mixture of water, salt, and turmeric powder or astringents, such

Rhinovirus, cause of the common cold, magnified. *(© 1991 CHSP. Custom Medical Stock Photo, Inc.)*

as alum, sumac, sage, and bayberry to ease a sore throat.

- Herbal remedies: Taking coneflower (*Echinacea* spp.) or goldenseal (*Hydrastis canadensis*). Other useful herbs to reduce symptoms are yarrow (*Achillea millefolium*), eyebright (*Euphrasia officinalis*), garlic (*Allium sativum*), and onions (*Allium cepa*).

- Homeopathic remedies: Microdoses of *Viscue album*, *Natrum muriaticum*, *Allium cepa*, or *Nux vomica*.

- Chinese traditional medicinal remedies: Taking yin chiao (sometimes transliterated as yinquiao) tablets that contain honeysuckle and forsythia when symptoms appear as well as using natural herb loquat syrup for cough and sinus congestion.

- Nutritional therapy: The use of zinc lozenges every two hours along with high doses of vitamin C as well as eliminating dairy products for the duration of the cold.

Prognosis

Given time, the body produces antibodies to cure itself of a cold. Most colds last a week to ten days. Most people start feeling better within four or five days. Occasionally a cold will lead to a secondary bacterial infection that causes strep throat, bronchitis, pneumonia, sinus infection, or a middle ear infection. These conditions usually clear up rapidly when treated with an antibiotic.

Prevention

It is not possible to prevent colds because the viruses that cause colds are common and highly infectious. However, there are some steps individuals can take to reduce their spread. These include:

- washing hands well and frequently, especially after touching the nose or before handling food

- using instant hand sanitizers, which are antiseptics and not antibiotics

- covering the mouth and nose when sneezing

- disposing of used tissues properly

- avoiding close contact with someone who has a cold during the first two to four days of their infection

- not sharing food, eating utensils, or cups

- using paper towels rather than shared cloth towels

- avoiding crowded places where cold germs can spread

- eating a healthy diet and getting adequate sleep

- using a daycare facility with six or fewer children, to dramatically reduce germ contact

Parental concerns

The over-use of antibiotics has led to the development of antibiotic-resistant stains of bacteria. For these bacteria, antibiotics may be ineffective. Therefore, parents should not press the doctor to prescribe antibiotics when their children only have a cold.

Also, a parent should not give a child aspirin during a cold, because aspirin has been linked to the development of Reye's syndrome in children recovering from viral illnesses, especially influenza (flu) or **chickenpox**. Reye's syndrome can lead to permanent brain damage or death.

Resources

BOOKS

Royston, Angela. *Colds (It's Catching)* Oxford, UK: Heinemann Library, 2001.

Silverstein, Alvin. *Common Colds.* Minneapolis, MN: Sagebrush Corp., 2001.

Judith Sims
Tish Davidson, A.M.

Common variable immunodeficiency

Definition

Common variable **immunodeficiency** (CVID) is a disorder of the immune system characterized by low levels of specific immunoglobulins, antibodies produced by the immune system to fight infection or disease. In CVID, immunoglobulin G (IgG) antibodies, one of several classes of antibodies, are either absent or produced in lower than normal numbers. Children who have this disorder are subject to recurring infections and may not respond appropriately to immunization. In some children, levels of the four types of IgG may be out of balance, a condition that has been associated with autoimmune diseases.

Description

The function of the immune system is to respond to organisms and substances that invade the body, such as bacteria, viruses, fungi, parasites, and toxins, by producing antibodies against them. Antibodies are specific proteins (immunoglobulins) manufactured by the immune system to bind to corresponding molecules (antigens) on the cell surfaces of foreign organisms in an attempt to make them harmless. This antigen/antibody reaction is the body's way of protecting itself from invasion and possible illness. Immunodeficiency means that the immune system is deficient in one or more of its components and is unable to respond effectively to disease-producing organisms that invade the body. IgG antibodies, the specific immunoglobulins absent or reduced in CVID, are targeted at bacterial organisms, viruses, and certain toxins.

Individuals with CVID will typically have frequent infections, especially repeat infections caused by the same organism. Recurring infections are an indication that the immune system is not responding normally and that immunity to reinfection has not developed. Surprisingly, people with CVID will usually have a normal number of B cells, the type of white blood cells (B-cell lymphocytes) that make antibodies to fight infection. However, the B cells will either be lacking one of the necessary IgG antibodies (IgG subclasses IgG1, IgG2, IgG3, and IgG4) on their surfaces or will have reduced amounts of one or more subclasses, making the B cells incapable of responding appropriately to microorganisms. Although the total IgG level may be normal, the imbalance in the types of IgG antibodies makes the B cells unprepared to fight all types of infection. The toxin associated with **tetanus**, for example, is attacked by IgG1 and IgG3 antibodies; reduced percentages of either immunoglobulin subclass on a child's cells will leave the child unprotected against that specific toxin. Similarly, frequent sinus infections may result from deficiencies of IgG2 and IgG3.

CVID may include deficiencies in other immunoglobulins as well, such as IgA and IgM deficiencies, although these deficiencies are more frequently associated with a group of other primary immunoglobulin deficiencies (agammaglobulinemia, **severe combined immunodeficiency**, and others). Other components of the immune system may be normal in CVID. T-cell lymphocytes, the type of white cells responsible for cellular immunity, are usually manufactured at normal levels in the same individuals who have CVID, although certain cell signal components may be lacking.

Autoimmune diseases such as autoimmune hemolytic anemia (AIHA), immune thrombocytopenia purpura (ITP), rheumatoid arthritis, autoimmune thyroiditis, and systemic lupus erythematosus are sometimes associated with CVID. These conditions develop in CVID as a result of the production of autoantibodies (antibodies directed against the body's own tissue). The term variable applies to this range of possible complications, which also includes gastrointestinal disorders as well as certain cancers, such as lymphomas and leukemias.

Demographics

Common variable immunodeficiency is believed to affect one in 50,000 to 200,000 individuals although it is not always diagnosed, and exact numbers of cases in the population cannot be accurately determined.

Causes and symptoms

The cause of common variable immunodeficiency was as of 2004 not known, although some forms seem to be inherited. The group of deficiencies is believed to be heterogeneous, that is, having widely varying characteristics among those affected.

CVID usually appears in children after the age of ten. The primary symptom is the presence of recurring infections that tend to be chronic rather than acute. Most children have had at least one episode of **pneumonia** caused by *Streptococcus pneumoniae*. Some children may also have frequent digestive disturbances and **diarrhea** that can lead to improper absorption of nutrients and malnourishment, occurring most commonly in IgA deficiency.

When to call the doctor

Young children and teenagers who are having recurrent infections, particularly infections of the same type such as frequent upper respiratory infection or chronic chest symptoms, ear infections, **sinusitis**, **asthma**, or pneumonia should be evaluated by a pediatrician or **family** practitioner.

Diagnosis

Children are typically diagnosed after age ten, but some immunoglobulin subclass deficiencies appear between ages one and three and are diagnosed after repeat cases of sinusitis, pneumonia, bacteremia, bronchiectasis, or diarrhea and malabsorption. A history of the child's illnesses and immunizations will be obtained, and the doctor will determine the child's general pattern of growth and development. Diagnostic testing may include routine blood tests such as a complete blood count (CBC) and differential (peripheral blood smear) to evaluate overall health and determine the type and number of red cells, white cells, and platelets in the blood. B lymphocytes and T lymphocytes may be quantified. An erythrocyte sedimentation rate (ESR) may be done to determine if inflammation is present. Blood chemistries may be performed to evaluate overall organ system functioning. If immunodeficiency is suspected, the primary diagnostic test that will distinguish common variable immunodeficiency from other types of immune system dysfunction is a reduced level of IgG immunoglobulins or IgG antibody subclasses, despite a relatively normal number of B cells. Serum immunoglobulin levels are measured in the clinical laboratory by a procedure called electrophoresis. This procedure both quantifies the amount of each antibody present and identifies the various classes and subclasses of antibodies. Deficiencies may be noted in one class or subclass or in combinations of IgG, IgM and IgA antibodies. Genetic testing may be done to rule out other types of immunodeficiency disease.

Not all children who have repeat infections are immunodeficient. Doctors tell the difference by evaluating the child's history and development. A normal child who most likely does not need further examination or diagnostic testing will have the following characteristics:

- no history of deep infection at multiple sites, even though repeat upper respiratory infections or ear infections may occur

- overall normal growth and body functions

- generally good health and normal functioning between infections

- no known family history of immune system deficiencies

The type of organism causing repeat infection can be a clue to which immunoglobulins are deficient. Therefore, when infection is present in suspected cases of common variable immunodeficiency, it may be important to identify the bacteria or virus causing the illness. Diagnostic tests may include performing a culture on material from the nose, throat, a wound, blood, or urine of the affected child.

Treatment

As of 2004 no specific treatment cured common variable immunodeficiency; each child is treated according to the individual clinical condition, the symptoms presented, and the antibody subclasses shown to be absent or deficient. Treatment is aimed generally at boosting the body's immune response and preventing or controlling infections. Immune serum, obtained from donated blood that contains adequate levels of IgG antibodies, may sometimes be transfused as a source of antibodies to boost the immune response, even though it may not contain all the antibodies the child needs and may lack antibodies specific for some of the recurring infections. The preferred treatment is to give immunoglobulins intravenously (immunoglobulin intravenous therapy or IVIG) or intramuscularly (IMIG) if specific antibody deficiencies are found; this is not usually done to boost IgA levels, however, because of the possible presence of anti-IgA antibodies that could cause an unwanted reaction. Immunization against frequent infection can be achieved in some children by administering polysaccharide-protein conjugate vaccines shown to improve immune response in certain types of infection. **Antibiotics** are used routinely at the first sign of an infection to help eliminate infectious organisms.

Alternative treatment

Several nutritional supplements are reported to help build the immune system. These include garlic (contains the essential trace element germanium), essential fatty acids (abundant in flax seed oil, evening primrose oil, and fish oils), sea vegetables such as kelp, acidophilus to supply natural bacteria in the digestive tract, and **vitamins** A and C, both powerful antioxidants that improve immune function and increase resistance to infection. Zinc is another nutrient essential to immune system functioning. Green drinks made with young barley are believed to cleanse the blood and supply chlorophyll and nutrients for tissue repair. Alcohol, medications, drugs, coffee, and other **caffeine** drinks should be avoided. Stress is known to produce biochemicals that reduce white blood cell functioning; therefore, it is important for the child to get sufficient **sleep** and reduce stress to help improve immune system functioning. Therapeutic massage, **yoga**, and other types of stress reduction programs are available in most communities.

Prognosis

Regular medical observation, treatment of symptoms, and appropriate immune system boosting usually produces a good result in children with common variable immunodeficiency. In some children, delayed maturation of certain IgG subclasses will make the condition a temporary one that corrects itself as more typical levels of the IgG antibodies develop. In other children, prognosis is related to the immune system's ability to produce specific antibodies. Individuals with common variable immunodeficiency usually have a normal life span although a variety of complications can occur, including autoimmune, gastrointestinal, granulomatous, and malignant conditions as a result of progressive immune deficiency.

Prevention

The disorder cannot be prevented, but parents can take precautions to prevent the recurrent infections commonly associated with immunodeficiency. For example, practicing good hygiene and providing optimum **nutrition** are important for helping children avoid contact with infectious organisms and to develop resistance against them. Avoiding crowds and staying away from other children or relatives who have active infections is another important way to avoid challenges to the immune system.

Nutritional concerns

Maintaining a healthy immune system requires essential nutrients that can be provided through a good

KEY TERMS

Antibody—A special protein made by the body's immune system as a defense against foreign material (bacteria, viruses, etc.) that enters the body. It is uniquely designed to attack and neutralize the specific antigen that triggered the immune response.

Antigen—A substance (usually a protein) identified as foreign by the body's immune system, triggering the release of antibodies as part of the body's immune response.

Bacteria—Singular, bacterium; tiny, one-celled forms of life that cause many diseases and infections.

Culture—A test in which a sample of body fluid is placed on materials specially formulated to grow microorganisms. A culture is used to learn what type of bacterium is causing infection.

Immunization—A process or procedure that protects the body against an infectious disease by stimulating the production of antibodies. A vaccination is a type of immunization.

Immunoglobulin G (IgG)—Immunoglobulin type gamma, the most common type found in the blood and tissue fluids.

Vaccination—Another word for immunization.

Vaccine—A substance prepared from a weakened or killed microorganism which, when injected, helps the body to form antibodies that will prevent infection by the natural microorganism.

Virus—A small infectious agent consisting of a core of genetic material (DNA or RNA) surrounded by a shell of protein. A virus needs a living cell to reproduce.

diet and regular supplementation. A diet to improve immune system functioning includes fresh fruits and vegetables, as many eaten raw as possible to provide necessary enzymes; whole grain cereals, brown rice, and whole grain pasta for essential vitamins, **minerals**, and fiber; and non-meat sources of protein such as nuts, seeds, tofu, legumes (beans), and eggs. Fish, fowl, and lean meats can be consumed in small amounts. Sweets, especially if sweetened with refined sugars, should be reduced or avoided altogether. Vitamin supplements should include vitamins A, C, and E, which are all valuable parts of the body's defense system, helping to increase the production of healthy white blood cells and to fight infection.

Parental concerns

Parents are aware that school-age children and teenagers are in frequent contact with their peers in school and at **play**, and infections commonly spread. In this situation, when infection occurs frequently, it is important to remember that not all children or teens who have repeat infections are immunodeficient and that the pediatrician or family practitioner will have specific criteria and diagnostic tests to rule out common variable immunodeficiency.

See also Immunodeficiency syndromes; HIV infection and AIDS.

Resources

BOOKS

Sompayrac, Lauren. *How the Immune System Works.* Oxford, UK: Blackwell, 2003.

ORGANIZATIONS

Centers for Disease Control and Prevention. 1600 Clifton Road, Atlanta, GA 30333. Web site: <www.cdc.gov>.

WEB SITES

"Understanding the Immune System." *Science behind the News.* Available online at <http://press2.nci.nih.gov/sciencebehind/immune/immune.00htm> (accessed December 8, 2004).

L. Lee Culvert
John T. Lohr, PhD

Communication skills

Definition

Communication is the process by which information is exchanged between individuals. It requires a shared understanding of symbol systems, such as language and mathematics.

Description

Communication is much more than words going from one person's mouth to another's ear. In addition to the words, messages are transferred by the tone and quality of voice, eye contact, physical closeness, visual cues, and overall body language.

Experts in child development agree that all babies develop skills for spoken and written language according to a specific developmental schedule, regardless of which language the child is exposed to. Although the milestones follow one another in roughly the same sequence, there is significant variability from child to child on when the first word is spoken and the first sentence is composed.

Language employs symbols—words, gestures, or spoken sounds—to represent objects and ideas. Communication of language begins with spoken sounds combined with gestures, relying on two different types of skills. Children first learn to receive communications by listening to and understanding what they hear (supported by accompanying gestures); next, they experiment with expressing themselves through speaking and gesturing. Speech begins as repetitive syllables, followed by words, phrases, and sentences. Later, children learn to read and write. Many children begin speaking significantly earlier or later than the milestone dates. Parents should avoid attaching too much significance to deviations from the average. When a child's deviation from the average milestones of development causes the parents concern, a pediatrician or other professional may be contacted for advice.

Infancy

Touch can be a positive, encouraging communication technique from birth through adulthood. In infancy messages of love, security, and comfort are transferred through holding, cuddling, gentle stroking, and patting. Infants cannot understand the meaning of words they hear, but they can feel, interpret, and respond to gentle, loving supportive hands caring for them.

The development of language in infants follows this progression: crying, babbling, cooing, single words (mama and daddy), and simple names of some objects.

Toddlerhood

Toddlers one and two years of age experience the world through the physical senses. **Language development** for toddlers includes: using two-word combinations, taking turns speaking and listening, using the word no frequently, and using gestures to express needs and desires.

Preschool

Preschool children from three to five years of age develop further. They expand their word combinations and are able to speak in sentences, use correct grammatical patterns, use pronouns, articulate sounds clearly, and rapidly increase their working vocabulary. Preschool children may also understand words they do not use themselves.

School-age

School-age children and adolescents appreciate giving and receiving hugs as well as getting a reassuring pat on the back or a gentle hand resting on their hand. Asking permission from a child is recommended for any contact beyond a casual touch.

School-age children six to 11 years of age learn to communicate their own thoughts, as well as understand viewpoints of others. They can understand words with multiple meanings, however, words describing what they have not experienced are not thoroughly understood. School-age children have expanding vocabularies, enabling them to describe ideas, thoughts, and feelings. Their conversational skills refine.

Adolescents 12 years of age and older are able to communicate theories and explain them like adults would. Adolescents are able to talk about and understand most adult ideas.

Privacy is sometimes necessary for good communication. Space should be available for private conversations away from roommates, friends, certain **family** members, and visitors. This is especially important when communicating with adolescents. There may be sensitive topics adolescents will not want to discuss with parents present, or will only want to discuss with one parent.

Messages must be received for communication to be complete. Listening is an essential part of communication. Children and parents need to develop active listening skills to be effective listeners. As children enter the teen years, reflective communication skills are invaluable for them and for their parents. Active listening skills involve the following:

- paying attention without distractions and maintaining eye contact

- clarifying through reflecting what is heard (This involves using similar words to express back to the speaker what was understood about the content of the message.)

- showing empathy by identifying with the other's feelings

- listening with an open mind in order to understand another person's point of view

Children's receptive communication skills are more advanced than their verbal communication skills. They understand more than people often expect, based on their verbal skills. Effective parents talk with their children, not to them. To engage children in conversation, parents can ask open-ended questions and not judge what their children say.

Visual communication

People communicate with eyes as well as ears. Communication occurs with cues of body language and facial expression. Eye contact is a communication connector. Making eye contact helps confirm attention and interest between the individuals communicating.

Some people are visual learners. They learn best when they can see or read instructions, demonstrations, diagrams, or information. Using various methods of presenting and shaping information increases understanding. Photographs, videotapes, dolls, computer programs, charts, and graphs can as effectively communicate information as written or spoken words can.

Tone of voice

Because infants' conception of verbal language is limited, their impressions are based on tone and quality of voice. Infants are able to discriminate parental voices from those of strangers and are more responsive to familiar voices. Soft, smooth voice quality is more comforting and soothing to infants than loud, startling, harsh voices. Infants can sense their caregiver's emotional state by the person's tone of voice. Awareness of infant's sensitivity to these messages is gained by watching their body language. They are relaxed when they hear a calm, happy caregiver and tense and rigid when they hear an angry, frustrated, or frightened one.

Verbal communication extends beyond words. Audible sounds transfer meaning. In addition, tone or attitude communicates sometimes a different meaning than the words used. Effective communicators do not send mixed messages. They say what they mean without sarcasm or equivocation.

Body language

Open body stance and positioning invite communication and interaction, whereas a closed body stance and positioning impedes communication. Using an open body posture improves communication with children. Both parents and children learn to read each other's body language.

Timing

Recognizing the right time to communicate is a skill. A distraught child whose parents have left for work is not ready to hear a story. The time will be more productive and the information better received if the child has a chance to make an emotional transition.

Common problems

Parents should strive to make words and intended meanings match when communication with their children. Children who are given mixed messages are confused and uncertain. Sometimes parents unwittingly attempt to control their children with double or mixed messages; doing so is unhealthy for their relationship to one another.

There are various kinds of spoken language problems, delays, and disabilities. In general, experts distinguish between those children who are slow in developing spoken language (**language delay**) and those who have difficulty achieving a milestone of spoken language (**language disorders**). Language disorders include **stuttering**; articulation disorders, such as substituting one sound for another (tandy for candy); omitting a sound (canny for candy); or distorting a sound (shlip for slip). Voice disorders include inappropriate pitch, volume, or quality. The causes for language problems have been linked to hearing, nerve, and muscle disorders; **head injury**; viral diseases; **mental retardation**; drug abuse; and cleft lips or palate.

Parental concerns

In the past, most parents, pediatricians, and educators recommended giving a child time to outgrow a difficulty with spoken language. From the late 1990s, research had shown that early speech and language disorders could lead to later difficulties in learning to read, write, and spell. Thus, many professionals recommended evaluation by a speech-language pathologist for toddlers who displayed language delay. However, not all speech-language specialists agree on early evaluation and therapy. Researchers have found that about two-thirds of children who were not talking at age two showed continued delays until age three, and one half were still behind the typical language development schedule at age four. But by kindergarten, only one-fourth of those children had not caught up with their peers.

See also Language development.

Resources

BOOKS

DeVito, Joseph A. *Human Communication.* Old Tappan, NJ: Allyn & Bacon Inc., 2005.

Nixon, Caroline. *Primary Communication Box: Reading Activities and Puzzles for Younger Learners.* Cambridge, UK: Cambridge University Press, 2005.

Segrin, Chris, et al. *Family Communication.* Mahwah, NJ: Lawrence Erlbaum Associates, 2005.

Aliene S. Linwood, RN, DPA, FACHE

Computed tomography

Definition

Computed tomography (CT), formerly referred to as computerized axial tomography (CAT), is a common diagnostic imaging procedure that uses **x rays** to generate images (slices) of the anatomy.

Purpose

Computed tomography (CT) is an x-ray imaging procedure used for a variety of clinical applications. CT is used for spine and head imaging, gastrointestinal imaging, vascular imaging (e.g., detection of blood clots), **cancer** staging and radiotherapy treatment planning, screening for cancers and heart disease, rapid imaging of trauma, imaging of musculoskeletal disorders, detection of signs of infectious disease, and guidance of certain interventional procedures (e.g., biopsies). CT is the preferred imaging exam for diagnosing several types of cancers, and along with the chest x ray, CT is the most commonly performed procedure for imaging the chest. CT is also used to perform noninvasive angiographic imaging to assess the large blood vessels.

CT may be performed on newborns, infants, children, and adolescents. In children, CT is most frequently used in the hospital emergency department to evaluate the effects of trauma, especially to the head, face, brain, and spine, and to diagnose or rule out **appendicitis** and other abdominal disorders because a scan can be completed in less than 20 seconds. Chest CT examinations are used to assess complications from infectious diseases, such as **pneumonia** and **tuberculosis**, inflammation of the airways, and birth defects. CT scans of the pelvic area are used to image ovarian cysts and tumors, bladder abnormalities, urinary tract stones, kidney disease, and bone disease. Head CT scans are used to examine the brain and sinuses. For children with cancer, CT is used to assist in treatment planning and to monitor cancer progression and response to treatment. For children requiring complex surgeries (e.g., brain, spine), CT is often used to produce images of the anatomy that help surgeons plan the surgery. Newer CT scanners, called multislice or multidetector CT, are used to rapidly image newborns to assess congenital heart defects.

Description

CT is performed using a specialized scanner, an x-ray system, a patient table, and a computer workstation. The CT scanner is shaped like a large square with a hole in the center or round like a doughnut. X rays are produced in the form of a beam that rotates around the patient. During a CT scan, the patient table is moved through the center hole as x-ray beams pass through the patient's body. The x rays are converted into a series of black-and-white images, each of which represents a "slice" of the anatomy.

CT scans are conducted by a technologist with specialized training in x rays and CT imaging. During scanning, the technologist operates the CT scanner using a computer located in an adjacent room. Because movement during the scan can cause inaccurate images, the technologist instructs the patient via an intercom system to hold their breath and not move during the x rays. The scan itself may only take five to 15 minutes, but total examination time may be up to 30 minutes, since the patient must be prepped and positioned. Abdominal CT scans usually require that the child drink a solution that contains a dye, called oral contrast, that shows up on the CT images to help better define internal organs. For pelvic scans, contrast material may be delivered via the rectum. Some CT scans also require the injection of contrast material into the vein to help define the blood vessels and surrounding tissue.

The images from CT examination are called slices because they are acquired in very small (millimeter-size) sections of the body. The image slices are displayed on a computer monitor for viewing or printed as a film. A radiologist interprets the x-ray images produced during the CT examination. For emergency CT scans, images are interpreted immediately so that the child can be treated as soon as possible. For non-urgent outpatient CT scans, the radiologist interprets the images and sends a report to the referring physician within a few days.

For emergency situations, CT scans are performed in a hospital radiology department in conjunction with

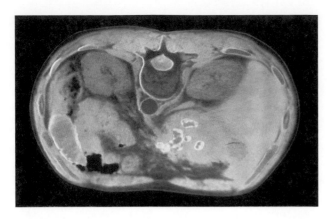

False color computed tomography scan through the abdomen, showing the liver (larger yellow organ) and spleen (smaller yellow organ). The abdominal aorta is colored red and located above the spine and between the kidneys. *(Photo Researchers, Inc.)*

the emergency department. For non-urgent conditions, CT scans can be performed on an outpatient basis in a hospital radiology department or outpatient imaging center. In small hospitals or hospitals in rural areas, a CT scanner may not be permanently located in the hospital; rather, a mobile imaging service will be contracted to bring a specially designed trailer with CT equipment to the hospital on prescheduled days.

Precautions

CT scans expose the child to radiation, and overuse of CT scanning has received attention from organizations that regulate medical radiation exposure. Although no side effects have been linked to radiation exposure from CT imaging, the Food and Drug Administration has issued guidance to physicians regarding levels of radiation during pediatric CT examinations. New CT scanners have preset imaging features that allow scanning at the lowest radiation dose for the child's weight and age.

Oral contrast may be unpleasant tasting, although chocolate, vanilla, and fruit flavors may be available. Injected contrast can cause sensations of heat or cold through the body. Some children may have allergic reactions to the contrast material, although severe reactions are rare. Parents should inform CT staff if their child has ever had a reaction to any medication, contrast material, or anesthesia. Because contrast material may contain iodine, sensitivity to contrast material may occur if the child has other **allergies** to iodine or seafood, and CT staff should be informed if the child has such allergies. Also, because CT contrast material can affect kidney function, parents should notify CT staff if their child has kidney disease.

Preparation

Abdominal CT examinations usually require fasting for at least 12 hours before the scan. If the intestines will also be imaged, a laxative before the scan is required. Parents should alert CT staff if children are diabetic and taking insulin, since **hypoglycemia** can occur with missed meals.

Before the CT scan, the patient has to change into a hospital gown. When oral contrast is necessary, patients need to arrive at least one hour before the scan to drink the contrast solution. During the scan, the child is asked to lie on the CT table. Positioning devices, such as head cradles or knee rests, may be used. For very young or very active children, foam or Velcro restraints may be used to minimize movement during imaging. Or sedation may be used if children cannot remain still. After positioning the child, the technologist inserts an intravenous catheter to inject contrast material.

CT scanners may frighten young children, so prior to the imaging examination, the basic procedure should be explained to help reduce **fear**. Some radiology departments offer special patient education booklets for children that help explain imaging procedures.

Aftercare

No special aftercare is required following CT scans, unless sedation or general anesthesia was used during the scan. In these cases, children are required to remain in a supervised recovery area for an hour or more following the procedure to be monitored for reactions to anesthesia. If injected contrast material is used, some minor first aid (small bandage, **pain** relief) for the injection site may be necessary.

Risks

Radiation exposure is a risk during CT examinations. However, the radiation from a CT scan is usually less than that from regular x rays, and the benefits of the examination far outweigh the minor radiation dose received during the scan.

Some children may have reactions to anesthesia or sedation, including headaches, shivering, or **vomiting**. Rarely, severe anaphylactic reactions can occur that require emergency treatment.

Parental concerns

Younger children may be frightened of the CT scanner, and a parent or other **family** member may be required to be present in the scanning room. To help alleviate fear, taking the child into the CT room to see the

KEY TERMS

Anaphylaxis—Also called anaphylactic shock; a severe allergic reaction characterized by airway constriction, tissue swelling, and lowered blood pressure.

Radiologist—A medical doctor specially trained in radiology, the branch of medicine concerned with radioactive substances and their use for the diagnosis and treatment of disease.

equipment prior to the procedure may be helpful. To reduce risk of radiation exposure, anyone remaining in the scanning room during x-ray delivery will have to wear a lead apron on shield.

Resources

BOOKS

Margolis, Simeon, et al. *The Johns Hopkins Consumer Guide to Medical Tests: What You Can Expect, How You Should Prepare, What Your Results Mean.* New York: Rebus Inc., 2002.

Medical Tests: A Practical Guide to Common Tests. Boston, MA: Harvard Health Publications, 2004.

Segen, J. C., et al. *The Patient's Guide to Medical Tests: Everything You Need to Know about the Tests Your Doctor Prescribes.* New York: Facts on File, 2002.

Shannon, Joyce Brennfleck. *Medical Tests Sourcebook: Basic Consumer Health Information about Medical Tests.* Detroit, MI: Omnigraphics, 2004.

PERIODICALS

Harvey, D. "Evaluating Pediatric Trauma: Imaging vs. Lab Tests." *Radiology Today* 5 (August 2, 2004): 14–16.

ORGANIZATIONS

American College of Emergency Physicians. 2121 K St., NW, Suite 325, Washington, DC 20037. Web site: <www.acep.org>.

American College of Radiology. 1891 Preston White Dr., Reston, VA 20191. Web site: <www.acr.org>.

Radiological Society of North America. 820 Jorie Blvd., Oak Brook, IL 60523–2251. Web site: <www.rsna.org/>.

WEB SITES

"CT Scan." *Emedicine*, November 1, 2004. Available online at <www.emedicinehealth.com/Articles/11618-1.asp> (accessed December 21, 2004).

"Pediatric CT (Computerized Tomography)." *Radiology Info. The Radiology Information Source for Patients.* Available online at <http://www.radiologyinfo.com/content/pedia-ct.htm> (accessed December 21, 2004).

Jennifer Sisk, MA

Concussion

Definition

Concussion is a trauma-induced change in mental status, with confusion and amnesia, and with or without a brief loss of consciousness.

Description

A concussion occurs when the head hits or is hit by an object, or when the brain is jarred against the skull with sufficient force to cause temporary loss of function in the higher centers of the brain. The injured person may remain conscious or lose consciousness briefly and is disoriented for some minutes after the blow.

Demographics

According to the Centers for Disease Control and Prevention, approximately 300,000 people sustain mild to moderate sports-related brain injuries each year, most of them young men between 16 and 25 years of age.

The risk of concussion from football is extremely high, especially at the high school level. Studies show that approximately one in five players suffer concussion or more serious brain injury during their brief high-school careers. The rate at the collegiate level is approximately one in 20. Rates for hockey players are not known as certainly but are believed to be similar.

Causes and symptoms

Causes

Most concussions are caused by motor vehicle accidents and **sports injuries**. In motor vehicle accidents, concussion can occur without an actual blow to the head. Instead, concussion occurs because the skull suddenly decelerates or stops, which causes the brain to be jarred against the skull. Contact **sports**, especially football, hockey, and boxing, are among those most likely to lead to concussion. Other significant causes include falls, collisions, or blows due to bicycling, horseback riding, skiing, and soccer.

Concussion and lasting brain damage is an especially significant risk for boxers, since the goal of the sport is, in fact, to deliver a concussion to the opponent. For this reason, the American Academy of Neurology has called for a ban on boxing. Repeated concussions over months or years can cause cumulative **head injury**. The cumulative brain injuries suffered by most boxers can lead to permanent brain damage. Multiple blows to the head can cause punch-drunk syndrome or dementia pugilistica, as evidenced by Muhammad Ali, whose Parkinson's is a result of his career in the ring.

Young children are likely to suffer concussions from falls or collisions on the playground or around the home. **Child abuse** is, unfortunately, another common cause of concussion.

Symptoms

Symptoms of concussion include the following:

• headache

• disorientation as to time, date, or place

• confusion

• dizziness

• vacant stare or confused expression

• incoherent or incomprehensible speech

• lack of coordination or weakness

• amnesia for the events immediately preceding the blow

• nausea or **vomiting**

• double vision

• ringing in the ears

These symptoms may last from several minutes to several hours. More severe or longer-lasting symptoms may indicate more severe brain injury. The person with a concussion may or may not lose consciousness from the blow; if he does lose consciousness, it will be for several minutes at the most. Prolonged unconsciousness indicates more severe brain injury.

The severity of concussion is graded on a three-point scale, used as a basis for treatment decisions.

• Grade 1: no loss of consciousness, transient confusion, and other symptoms that resolve within 15 minutes

• Grade 2: no loss of consciousness, transient confusion, and other symptoms that require more than 15 minutes to resolve

• Grade 3: loss of consciousness for any period

Days or weeks after the accident, the person may show signs of the following:

• headache

• poor attention and concentration

• memory difficulties

• anxiety

• depression

• sleep disturbances

• light and noise intolerance

The occurrence of such symptoms is called "post-concussion syndrome."

When to call the doctor

A doctor should be consulted whenever a head injury causes any of the symptoms noted above.

Diagnosis

It is very important for those attending an individual with a concussion to pay close attention to the person's symptoms and progression immediately after the accident. The duration of unconsciousness and degree of confusion are very important indicators of the severity of the injury and help guide the diagnostic process and treatment decisions.

A doctor, nurse, or emergency medical technician may make an immediate **assessment** based on the severity of the symptoms; a **neurologic exam** of the pupils, coordination, and sensation, and brief tests of orientation, memory, and concentration. Those with very mild concussions may not need to be hospitalized or have expensive diagnostic tests. Questionable or more severe cases may require **computed tomography** scan (CT) or **magnetic resonance imaging** (MRI) scans to look for brain injury.

Treatment

The symptoms of concussion usually clear quickly and without lasting effect, if no further injury is sustained during the healing process. Guidelines for returning to sports activities are based on the severity of the concussion.

A grade 1 concussion can usually be treated with rest and continued observation alone. The person may return to sports activities that same day, but only after examination by a trained professional, and after all symptoms have completely resolved. If the person sustains a second concussion of any severity that same day, he or she should not be allowed to continue contact sports until he or she has been symptom-free, during both rest and activity, for one week.

A person with a grade 2 concussion must discontinue sports activity for the day, should be evaluated by a trained professional, and should be observed closely throughout the day to make sure that all symptoms have completely cleared. Worsening of symptoms or continuation of any symptoms beyond one week indicates the need for a CT or MRI scan. Return to contact sports should only occur after one week with no symptoms, both at rest and during activity, and following examination by a physician. Following a second grade 2 concussion, the person should remain symptom-free for two weeks before resuming contact sports.

A person with a grade 3 concussion (involving any loss of consciousness, no matter how brief) should be examined by a medical professional either on the scene or in an emergency room. More severe symptoms may warrant a CT or MRI scan, along with a thorough neurological and physical exam. The person should be hospitalized if any abnormalities are found or if confusion persists. Prolonged unconsciousness and worsening symptoms require urgent neurosurgical evaluation or transfer to a trauma center. Following discharge from professional care, the person is closely monitored for neurological symptoms that may arise or worsen. If headaches or other symptoms worsen or last longer than one week, a CT or MRI scan should be performed. Contact sports are avoided for one week following unconsciousness of only seconds, and for two weeks for unconsciousness of a minute or more. A person receiving a second grade 3 concussion should avoid contact sports for at least a month after all symptoms have cleared and then engage in the sport only with the approval of a physician. If signs of brain swelling or bleeding are seen on a CT or MRI scan, the athlete should not return to the sport for the rest of the season, or even indefinitely.

For someone who has sustained a concussion of any severity, it is critically important that he or she avoid the possibility of another blow to the head until well after all symptoms have cleared to prevent second-impact syndrome. The guidelines above are designed to minimize the risk of this syndrome.

Prognosis

Concussion usually leaves no lasting neurological problems. Nonetheless, symptoms of **post-concussion syndrome** may last for weeks or even months.

Studies of concussion in contact sports have shown that the risk of sustaining a second concussion is even

greater than it was for the first if the person continues to engage in the sport.

While concussion usually resolves on its own without lasting effect, it can set the stage for a much more serious condition. Second impact syndrome occurs when a person with a concussion, even a very mild one, suffers a second blow before fully recovering from the first. The brain swelling and increased intracranial pressure can lead to a potentially fatal result. More than 20 such cases have been reported since the syndrome was first described in 1984.

Prevention

Many cases of concussion can be prevented by using appropriate protective equipment. This includes seat belts and air bags in automobiles and helmets in all contact sports. Helmets should also be worn while bicycling, skiing, or horseback riding. Soccer players should avoid heading the ball when it is kicked at high velocity from close range. The surfaces immediately below and surrounding playground equipment should be covered with soft material, either sand or special matting.

Parental concerns

The value of high-contact sports such as boxing, football, or hockey should be weighed against the high risk of brain injury during a young person's participation in the sport. Steering a child's general enthusiasm for sports into activities less apt to produce head impacts may reduce the likelihood of brain injury. Children participating in any contact sport or activity that can cause brain injury should always wear a helmet.

Resources

BOOKS

Hergenroeder, Albert C., and Joseph N. Chorley. "Head and Neck Injuries." In *Nelson Textbook of Pediatrics*, 17th ed. Edited by Richard E. Behrman, et al. Philadelphia: Saunders, 2003, pp. 2313–4.

Hodge, Charles J. "Head Injury." In *Cecil Textbook of Medicine*, 22nd ed. Edited by Lee Goldman, et al. Philadelphia: Saunders, 2003, pp. 2241–2.

Parker, Rolland S. *Concussive Brain Trauma: Neurobehavioral Impairment and Maladaptation.* Lakeland, FL: CRC Press, 2000.

Ropper, Allan H. "Traumatic Injuries of the Head and Spine." In *Harrison's Principles of Internal Medicine*, 15th ed. Edited by Eugene Braunwald, et al. New York: McGraw Hill, 2001, pp. 2434–41.

KEY TERMS

Amnesia—A general medical term for loss of memory that is not due to ordinary forgetfulness. Amnesia can be caused by head injuries, brain disease, or epilepsy, as well as by dissociation. Includes: 1) Anterograde amnesia: inability to retain the memory of events occurring after the time of the injury or disease which brought about the amnesic state. 2) Retrograde amnesia: inability to recall the memory of events which occurred prior to the time of the injury or disease which brought about the amnesic state.

Parkinson's disease—A slowly progressive disease that destroys nerve cells in the basal ganglia and thus causes loss of dopamine, a chemical that aids in transmission of nerve signals (neurotransmitter). Parkinson's is characterized by shaking in resting muscles, a stooping posture, slurred speech, muscular stiffness, and weakness.

PERIODICALS

Iverson, G. L., et al. "Cumulative effects of concussion in amateur athletes." *Brain Injury* 18, no. 5 (2004): 433–43.

Lovell, M., et al. "Return to play following sports-related concussion." *Clinics in Sports Medicine* 23, no. 3 (2004): 421–41.

Ryan, L. M., and D. L. Warden. "Post concussion syndrome." *International Review of Psychiatry* 15, no. 4 (2004): 310–6.

Wisniewski, J. F., et al. "Incidence of cerebral concussions associated with type of mouth guard used in college football." *Dental Traumatology* 20, no. 3 (2004): 143–9.

ORGANIZATIONS

American Academy of Emergency Medicine. 611 East Wells Street, Milwaukee, WI 53202. Web site: <www.aaem.org/>.

American Academy of Family Physicians. 11400 Tomahawk Creek Parkway, Leawood, KS 66211–2672. Web site: <www.aafp.org/>.

American Academy of Neurology. 1080 Montreal Avenue, St. Paul, MN 55116. Web site: <www.aan.com/>.

American Academy of Pediatrics. 141 Northwest Point Boulevard, Elk Grove Village, IL 60007–1098. Web site: <www.aap.org/default.htm>.

American College of Emergency Physicians. PO Box 619911, Dallas, TX 75261–9911. Web site: <www.acep.org/>.

Brain Injury Association. 105 North Alfred Street, Alexandria, VA 22314. Web site: <www.biausa.org/Sportsfs.htm>.

International Brain Injury Association. 1150 South Washington Street, Suite 210, Alexandria, VA 22314. Web site: <www.internationalbrain.org/>.

WEB SITES

"Concussion." *American Academy of Family Physicians.* Available online at <www.aafp.org/afp/990901ap/990901e.html> (accessed December 8, 2004).

"Concussion." *University of Missouri School of Medicine.* Available online at <www.muhealth.org/~neuromedicine/concussion.shtml> (accessed December 8, 2004).

"Facts about Concussion and Brain Injury and Where to Get Help" *Centers for Disease Control and Prevention.* Available online at <www.cdc.gov/doc.do?id=0900f3ec8000d38c> (accessed December 8, 2004).

"Head Injury." *MedlinePlus.* Available online at <www.nlm.nih.gov/medlineplus/ency/article/000028.htm> (accessed December 8, 2004).

L. Fleming Fallon, Jr., MD, DrPH

Condom

Definition

A condom is a device, usually made of latex, used to avoid pregnancy and/or **sexually transmitted diseases** such as gonorrhea, syphilis, and human **immunodeficiency** virus (HIV). Condoms are also known as prophylactics, as well as the popular slang term "rubbers." There are male and female versions of condoms.

Description

Condoms were originally used as a contraceptive to prevent unwanted pregnancies. In the early 2000s, however, condoms are just as important as a device for preventing the spread of sexually transmitted diseases (STDs), especially **HIV**, the virus that causes acquired immune deficiency syndrome (AIDS).

Male condoms have been in use in varied forms for at least three thousand years. Female condoms are relatively new, first being approved in Europe in 1992 and by the U.S. Food and Drug Administration (FDA) in the United States in 1993. An improved female condom became available in Europe in 2002. As of mid-2004, it was under review by the FDA but had not been approved for use in the United States.

Male condoms, by far the most popular, consist of a disposable one-time-use tube-shaped piece of thin latex rubber or lambskin. The condom is unrolled over the erect penis before sexual intercourse. The tip of the condom usually has an open space to collect and hold the semen. The condom is a barrier that prevents sperm from entering a woman's uterus. It is also used in anal sex by males with females and other males to prevent transmission of STDs.

Male condoms are available in a wide variety of sizes, styles, textures, colors, and even flavors. Condoms are also recommended for use on a male when oral sex is being performed on him.

Condoms are about 85 percent effective in preventing pregnancies. That means that out of 100 females whose partners use condoms, 15 will still become pregnant during the first year of use, according to the nonprofit advocacy group Planned Parenthood. Unwanted pregnancies usually occur because the condom is not used properly or breaks during intercourse.

More protection against pregnancy is possible if a spermicide is used along with a condom. Spermicide is a pharmaceutical substance used to kill sperm, especially in conjunction with a birth-control device such as a condom or diaphragm. Spermicides come in foam, cream, gel, suppository, or as a thin film. The most common spermicide is called nonoxynol-9, and many condoms come with it already applied as a lubricant.

However, spermicides alone do not kill HIV or other sexually transmitted viruses and do not prevent the spread of HIV and other STDs. Also, nonoxynol 9 can irritate vaginal tissue and thus increase the risk of getting an STD. In anal sex, especially between two males, spermicides also can irritate the rectum, increasing the risk of getting HIV. Spermicides are specifically discouraged for use by gay or bisexual males for anal sex.

Latex condoms are also recommended over condoms made from other materials, especially lambskin, because they are thicker and stronger and have less risk of breakage during sex. Non-latex condoms do not prevent the spread of STDs, including HIV, and should not be used by gay or bisexual men or men who have HIV or other sexually transmitted diseases.

Condoms are available over-the-counter, meaning they do not require a prescription, and there are no age restrictions on purchasing condoms. They are available at a variety of locations, including drug stores, convenience stores, supermarkets, and **family** planning clinics. They are also available for purchase on the Internet.

How to use a male condom

PUTTING IT ON Many people, especially teens, are misinformed or uninformed on how to properly use a condom. In a 2001 study of youths ages 15 to 21, researchers found 33 to 50 percent of youth said it was important for the condom to fit tightly, leaving no air space at the tip, and that petroleum jelly, such as Vaseline, is a good lubricant. Another 20 percent said lambskin condoms offer better protection against HIV than latex condoms. All three beliefs are false.

For pleasure, ease, and effectiveness, both partners should know the correct way to put on and use a condom. Put the condom on before the penis touches the vulva, rectum, or mouth. Men leak fluids from their penises before and after ejaculation that can cause pregnancy and carry STDs. Use a condom only once and use a new one for each erection.

Condoms usually come rolled in a ring shape and are individually sealed in an aluminum foil, cardboard, or plastic pack. Carefully open the package to insure the condom does not tear. Do not use a condom if it is torn, brittle, stiff, or sticky.

To properly put on a male condom, follow these steps:

- Put several drops of lubricant inside the condom.

- Pull back the foreskin of an uncircumcised penis before putting on the condom.

- Place the rolled condom over the tip of the erect penis. Leave a half-inch (1 cm) of space at the tip to collect semen. Pinch the air out of the tip with one hand while placing it on the penis.

- Unroll the condom over the penis with the other hand, rolling it all the way down to the base of the penis. Smooth out any air bubbles since they can cause condoms to break.

- Lubricate the outside of the condom.

TAKING IT OFF To properly remove a male condom, follow these steps:

- Remove the penis from the vagina, rectum, or mouth soon after ejaculation and before the penis becomes soft.

- Hold the condom at the base of the penis while pulling out to prevent semen from leaking or spilling.

- Throw the condom away. It is not recommended that it be flushed down a toilet.

Female condom

The female condom is a seven-inch (17-cm) polyurethane pouch that fits into the vagina. It collects semen

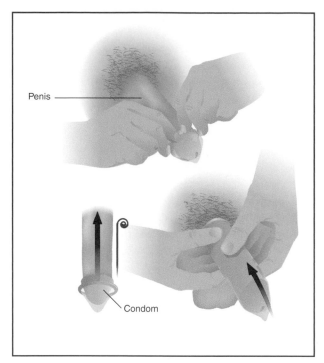

Penis

Condom

A condom is most effective when it is placed on the penis correctly without trapping air between the penis and the condom. *(Illustration by Argosy, Inc.)*

before, during, and after ejaculation, keeping semen from entering the uterus, thus protecting against pregnancy. In one year of use, it is 79 percent effective in preventing pregnancies. It also reduces the risk of many STDs, including HIV.

There is a flexible ring at the closed end of the thin, soft pouch of the female condom. A slightly larger ring is at the open end. The ring at the closed end holds the condom in place in the vagina. The ring at the open end rests outside the vagina. When the condom is in place during sexual intercourse, there is no contact of the vagina and cervix with the skin of the penis or with secretions from the penis. It can be inserted up to eight hours before sex.

To insert the female condom, follow these steps:

• Find a comfortable position, such as standing with one foot on a chair, squatting with knees apart, or lying down with legs bent and knees apart.

• Hold the condom with the open end hanging down. Squeeze the inner ring with a thumb and middle finger.

• With the inner ring squeezed together, insert the ring into the vagina and push the inner ring and pouch into the vagina past the pubic bone.

• When inserted properly, the outer ring will hang down slightly outside the vagina.

• Adding a water-based lubricant to the inside of the condom or to the penis may be helpful.

There are no age restrictions and no prescription is needed to purchase female condoms. They can be used only once, and each costs $2.50 to $5.

School age

In a 2001 study by the Youth Risk Behavior Surveillance System, nearly 46 percent of American high school students reported they had had sexual intercourse at least once. Nearly 7 percent of students surveyed said they had engaged in their first sexual intercourse before age 13.

Of these sexually active students, 42 percent reported they did not use a condom the last time they had sex. Nationwide, male students (65.1%) were significantly more likely than female students (51.3%) to report condom use. This significant sex difference was identified for white and black students and students in grades 10, 11, and 12. Overall, black students (67.1%) were significantly more likely than white and Hispanic students (56.8% and 53.5%, respectively) to report condom use. This significant ethnic difference was identified for both female and male students.

Students in grades 9, 10, and 11 (67.5%, 60.1%, and 58.9%, respectively) were significantly more likely than students in grade 12 (49.3%) to report condom use, and students in grade 9 (67.5%) were significantly more likely than students in grade 11 (58.9%) to report condom use. The 2001 survey was published in the October 2002 issue of the *Journal of School Health*.

Common problems

The most common problems associated with condoms are breakage during use and improper knowledge on how to use condoms. These problems can lead to pregnancy and sexually transmitted diseases, especially HIV.

Parental concerns

Parents of adolescents often are concerned that distribution of condoms leads to increased sexual activity. However, a study of 4,100 high school students published in the June 2003 issue of the *American Journal of Public Health* found that students who had access at school to condoms and instructions on their proper use were no more likely to have sexual intercourse than students at schools without condom distribution programs.

When to call the doctor

It is not well known nor publicized, but having a condom break or leak while having sex is not necessarily

KEY TERMS

Antiretroviral drugs—Several classes of drugs that are used to treat HIV.

Contraceptive—A device or medication designed to prevent pregnancy by either suppressing ovulation, preventing sperm from passing through the cervix to fertilize an egg, or preventing implantation of a fertilized egg.

Diaphragm—The thin layer of muscle that separates the chest cavity containing the lungs and heart from the abdominal cavity containing the intestines and digestive organs. This term is also used for a dome-shaped device used to cover the back of a woman's vagina during intercourse in order to prevent pregnancy.

Ejaculation—The process by which semen (made up in part of prostatic fluid) is ejected by the erect penis.

Polyurethane—A type of synthetic plastic.

Prophylaxis—Protection against or prevention of a disease. Antibiotic prophylaxis is the use of antibiotics to prevent a possible infection.

Rubbers—A slang name for condoms.

Semen—The thick, whitish liquid released from the penis on ejaculation. It contains sperm and other secretions.

Spermicide—A substance that kills sperm. Also called a spermatocide.

Uncircumcised—Not having had the foreskin of the penis removed.

Uterus—The female reproductive organ that contains and nourishes a fetus from implantation until birth. Also called the womb.

Vulva—The external genital organs of a woman, including the outer and inner lips, clitoris, and opening of the vagina.

---

ment with antiretroviral drugs, which usually prevents the virus from taking hold, according to the CDC. The treatment must begin within 72 hours after exposure but is more effective if begun within 24 hours of exposure. The exposed person should contact a physician immediately or go to the nearest hospital emergency room. The CDC does not have data on the effectiveness of PEP treatment on persons other than healthcare workers.

Pregnancy can also be prevented should a condom break or leak during sex. Emergency contraceptive pills (ECP), also called "morning-after pills," have been available since 1997. The pills have high levels of regular birth control hormones and are effective in preventing pregnancies following unprotected sex 75 to 94 percent of the time. They should be taken within 72 hours of unprotected sex.

As of August 2004, there were two ECPs available: Preven and Plan B. However, 11 brands of regular oral contraceptive pills in varying regimens can be effective in preventing post-sex pregnancies. Prescriptions are required for ECPs except in Washington State, where they can be dispensed without a prescription by selected pharmacies, doctors' offices, and hospital emergency rooms.

There are often financial, legal, and social barriers to persons under 18 getting ECPs. The group Advocates for Youth recommends young women always keep ECPs on hand (in advance) so they can be used as soon as possible following unprotected sex, such as when a condom breaks during sexual intercourse.

Resources

BOOKS

Condoms: A Medical Dictionary, Bibliography, and Annotated Research Guide to Internet References. San Diego, CA: Icon Group International Inc., 2003.

Female Condoms: A Medical Dictionary, Bibliography, and Annotated Research Guide to Internet References. San Diego, CA: Icon Group International Inc., 2004.

Richardson, Justin, and Mark A. Schuster. *Everything You Never Wanted Your Kids to Know about Sex, but Were Afraid They'd Ask: The Secrets to Surviving Your Child's Sexual Development from Birth to the Teens.* New York: Crown Publishers, 2003.

PERIODICALS

"Condom Availability has Positive Impact on Teen Health." *The Brown University Child and Adolescent Behavior Letter* (July 2003): 4.

"Condom Errors are Common." *Men's Fitness* (February 2003): 55.

---

a health disaster, even if the condom wearer has HIV. The risk of HIV transmission during vaginal sex between a female and a male who has the virus is low, estimated at one-tenth to one-fifth of a percent, according to the Centers for Disease Control and Prevention. The risk for a single exposure through anal sex is estimated at one tenth of a percent to 3 percent, according to the CDC.

Once exposed to the virus, the person can begin a therapy called post-exposure prophylaxis (PEP). The newly exposed person must begin four weeks of treat-

"Condom Failure Depends on Experience of the User and Frequency of Use." *Obesity, Fitness & Wellness Week* (July 31, 2004): 80.

Eisenberg, Maria E. "The Association of Campus Resources for Gay, Lesbian, and Bisexual Students with College Students' Condom Use." *Journal of American College Health* (November 2002): 109–116.

Jancin, Bruce. "Despite Guidelines, U.S. Condom Use Still Low." *Clinical Psychiatry News* (January 2004): 66.

"Teens Often Misinformed about Proper Condom Use." *Contraceptive Technology Update* (January 2002): 9–10.

ORGANIZATIONS

Advocates for Youth. 2000 M St. NW, Suite 750, Washington, DC 20036. Web site: <www.advocatesforyouth.org>.

Planned Parenthood Federation of America Inc. 434 W. 33rd St., New York, NY 10001. Web site: <www.plannedparenthood.org>.

WEB SITES

"Male Latex Condoms and Sexually Transmitted Diseases." *Centers for Disease Control and Prevention*, January 23, 2003. Available online at <www.cdc.gov/hiv/pubs/facts/condoms.htm> (accessed November 9, 2004).

"Teens and Condoms." Available online at <www.avert.org/teencondoms.htm> (accessed November 9, 2004.).

Ken R. Wells

Conduct disorder

Definition

Conduct disorder (CD) is a behavioral and emotional disorder of childhood and **adolescence**. Children with conduct disorder act inappropriately, infringe on the rights of others, and violate the behavioral expectations of others.

Description

Children and adolescents with conduct disorder act out aggressively and express anger inappropriately. They engage in a variety of antisocial and destructive acts, including violence towards people and animals, destruction of property, **lying**, **stealing**, **truancy**, and **running away** from home. They often begin using and abusing drugs and alcohol and having sex at an early age. Irritability, temper **tantrums**, and low **self-esteem** are common personality traits of children with CD.

Demographics

Conduct disorder is present in approximately 6–16 percent of boys and 2–9 percent of girls under the age of 18. The incidence of CD increases with age. Girls tend to develop CD later in life (age 12 or older) than boys. Up to 40 percent of children with conduct disorder grow into adults with **antisocial personality disorder**.

Causes and symptoms

There are two subtypes of CD, one beginning in childhood (childhood onset) and the other in adolescence (adolescent onset). Research suggests that this disease may be caused by one or more of the following factors:

- poor parent-child relationships
- dysfunctional families
- inconsistent or inappropriate parenting habits
- substance abuse
- physical and/or emotional abuse
- poor relationships with other children
- cognitive problems leading to school failures
- brain damage
- biological defects

Difficulty in school is an early sign of potential conduct disorder problems. While the child's IQ may be in the normal range, he or she can have trouble with verbal and abstract reasoning skills and may lag behind classmates, and consequently feel as if he/she does not "fit in." The frustration and loss of self-esteem resulting from this academic and social inadequacy can trigger the development of CD.

A dysfunctional home environment can be another major contributor to CD. An emotionally, physically, or sexually abusive household member; a **family** history of antisocial personality disorder; or parental **alcoholism** or substance abuse can damage a child's self-perception and put him or her on a path toward negative or **aggressive behavior**. Other less obvious environmental factors can also play a part in the development of conduct disorder; several long-term studies have found an association between maternal **smoking** during pregnancy and the development of CD in offspring.

Other conditions that may cause or co-exist with conduct disorder include **head injury**, substance abuse disorder, major depressive disorder, and **attention deficit hyperactivity disorder** (ADHD). Fifty to seventy-five percent of children diagnosed with CD also have ADHD, a disorder characterized by a persistent pattern of inattention and/or hyperactivity.

CD is defined as a repetitive behavioral pattern of violating the rights of others or societal norms. Three of the following criteria or symptoms are required over the previous 12 months for a diagnosis of CD (one of the three must have occurred in the past six months):

- bullies, threatens, or intimidates others

- picks fights

- has used a dangerous weapon

- has been physically cruel to people

- has been physically cruel to animals

- has stolen while confronting a victim (for example, mugging or extortion)

- has forced someone into sexual activity

- has deliberately set a fire with the intention of causing damage

- has deliberately destroyed property of others

- has broken into someone else's house or car

- frequently lies to get something or to avoid obligations

- has stolen without confronting a victim or breaking and entering (e.g., shoplifting or forgery)

- stays out at night; breaks curfew (beginning before 13 years of age)

- has run away from home overnight at least twice (or once for a lengthy period)

- is often truant from school (beginning before 13 years of age)

When to call the doctor

When symptoms of conduct disorder are present, a child should be taken to his or her health care provider as soon as possible for evaluation and possible referral to a mental health care professional. If a child or teen diagnosed with conduct disorder reveals at any time that he/she has had recent thoughts of self-injury or **suicide**, or if he/she demonstrates behavior that compromises personal **safety** or the safety of others, professional assistance from a mental health care provider or care facility should be sought immediately.

Diagnosis

Conduct disorder may be diagnosed by a family physician or pediatrician, social worker, school counselor, psychiatrist, or psychologist. Diagnosis may require psychiatric expertise to rule out such conditions as **oppositional defiant disorder**, **bipolar disorder**, or ADHD.

A comprehensive evaluation of the child should ideally include interviews with the child and parents, a full social and medical history, review of educational records, a cognitive evaluation, and a psychiatric exam.

One or more clinical inventories or scales may be used to assess the child for conduct disorder, including the Youth Self-Report, the Overt Aggression Scale (OAS), Behavioral **Assessment** System for Children (BASC), Child Behavior Checklist (CBCL), the Nisonger Child Behavior Rating Form (N-CBRF), Clinical Global Impressions scale (CGI), and Diagnostic Interview Schedule for Children (DISC). The tests are verbal and/or written and are administered in both hospital and outpatient settings.

Treatment

Treating conduct disorder requires an approach that addresses both the child and his/her environment. Behavioral therapy and psychotherapy can help a child with CD to control his/her anger and develop new coping techniques. Social skills training can help a child improve his/her relationship with peers.

Family group therapy may also be effective in some cases. Parents should be counseled on how to set appropriate limits with their child and be consistent and realistic when disciplining. A parental skills training program may be recommended. If an abusive home life is at the root of the conduct problem, every effort should be made to move the child into a more supportive environment.

For children with coexisting ADHD, substance abuse, depression, **anxiety**, or **learning disorders**, treating these conditions first is preferred, and may result in a significant improvement in behavior. In all cases of CD, treatment should begin when symptoms first appear. Several studies have shown **methylphenidate** (Ritalin) to be a useful drug for both ADHD and CD in some children.

When aggressive behavior is severe, mood stabilizing medication, including lithium (Cibalith-S, Eskalith, Lithobid, Lithonate, Lithotabs), and carbamazepine (Tegretol, Carbatrol, Epitol) may be an appropriate option for treating the aggressive symptoms. However, placing the child into a structured setting or treatment program such as a psychiatric hospital may be just as beneficial for easing aggression as medication.

Prognosis

Follow-up studies of conduct-disordered children have shown a high incidence of antisocial personality disorder, affective illnesses, and chronic criminal behavior in adulthood. However, proper treatment of co-existing disorders, early identification and intervention, and long-term support may improve the outlook significantly.

Conduct disorder that first occurs in adolescence is thought to have a statistically better prognosis than childhood-onset conduct disorder. Adolescents with CD tend to have better relationships with their peers and are less likely to develop antisocial personality disorder in adulthood than those with childhood-onset CD. There is also less of a gender gap in adolescent-onset conduct disorder, as girls approach boys in CD incidence. Childhood-onset CD is much more common among boys.

Prevention

A supportive, nurturing, and structured home environment is believed to be the best defense against conduct disorder. Children with learning disabilities and/or difficulties in school should get immediate and appropriate academic assistance. Addressing these problems when they first appear helps to prevent the frustration and low self-esteem that may lead to CD later on.

Parental concerns

A child with conduct disorder can have a tremendous impact on the home environment and on the physical and emotional welfare of siblings and others sharing the household. While seeking help for their child with CD, parents must remain sensitive to the needs of their other children and adjust household routines accordingly. This may mean avoiding leaving siblings alone together, getting assistance with childcare, or even seeking residential or hospital treatment for the conduct disordered child if the safety and well-being of other family members is in jeopardy.

See also Aggression; Oppositional defiant disorder.

Resources

BOOKS

Diagnostic and Statistical Manual of Mental Disorders, 4th edition, text revision *(DSM-IV-TR).* Washington, DC: American Psychiatric Press, Inc., 2000.

Eddy, J. Mark. *Conduct Disorders: The Latest Assessment and Treatment Strategies.* Kansas City, MO: Compact Clinicals, 2003.

PERIODICALS

Black, Susan. "New Remedies for High School Violence." *Education Digest.* 69, no.3 (November 2003): 43.

"Conduct Disorder and Oppositional Defiant Disorder: Trends and Treatment." *The Brown University Child and Adolescent Psychopharmacology Update.* 6, no.8 (August 2004): 1+.

ORGANIZATIONS

The American Academy of Child and Adolescent Psychiatry. 3615 Wisconsin Ave., N.W., Washington, D.C. 20016. (202) 966–7300. Web site: <www.aacap.org>.

WEB SITES

Goodman, Robin and Anita Gurian. "About Conduct Disorder." *NYU Child Study Center.* Available online at: <www.aboutourkids.org/aboutour/articles/about_conduct.html> (accessed September 12, 2004).

Paula Ford-Martin

Congenital adrenal hyperplasia

Definition

Congenital adrenal hyperplasia (CAH) is a genetic disorder characterized by a deficiency in the hormones cortisol and aldosterone and an over-production of the hormone androgen. CAH is present at birth and affects the sexual development of the child.

Description

Congenital adrenal hyperplasia (CAH) is a form of adrenal insufficiency in which 21-hydroxylase, the enzyme that produces two important adrenal steroid hormones, cortisol and aldosterone, is deficient. Because cortisol production is impeded, the adrenal gland over-produces androgens (male steroid hormones). CAH affects both females and males. Females with CAH are born with an enlarged clitoris and normal internal reproductive tract structures. Males have normal genitals at birth. CAH causes abnormal growth for both sexes; those affected will be tall as children but short as adults because of early bone maturation. Females develop male characteristics, and males experience premature sexual development.

In its most severe form, called salt-wasting (or salt-losing) CAH, where there is a total or near total deficiency of the 21-hydroxylase enzyme, a life-threatening adrenal crisis can occur if the disorder is untreated. Adrenal crisis can cause **dehydration**, shock, and death within 14 days of birth. There is also a milder form of CAH in which children have partial 21-hydroxylase enzyme deficiencies (simple virilizing form). Another type of CAH is characterized by only a slight deficiency in production of the 21-hydroxylase enzyme (nonclassic or late-onset form), in which symptoms occurs later in childhood or during young **adolescence**.

CAH is also called adrenogenital syndrome or 21-hydroxylase deficiency.

Demographics

CAH, a genetic disorder, is the most common adrenal gland disorder in infants and children, occurring in one in 10,000 total births worldwide.

Causes and symptoms

CAH is an inherited recessive disorder, which means that a child must inherit one copy of the defective gene from each parent who is a carrier; when two carriers have children, each pregnancy carries a 25 percent risk of producing an affected child. CAH is related to the deficiency of 21-hydroxylase, an enzyme that is required to transform cholesterol into cortisol. The 21-hydroxylase gene is made by a gene located on the short arm of chromosome 6. This gene is located in an area of the chromosome that contains many other important genes whose products control immune function. Various mutations of the 21-hydroxylase gene result in various degrees of CAH (salt-losing form, simple-virilizing form, and the nonclassic form). When 21-hydroxylase is deficient, this leads to a hyperfunction and increased size (hyperplasia) of the adrenals.

In females, CAH produces an enlarged clitoris at birth, with the urethral opening at the base (ambiguous genitalia, appearing more male than female) and masculinization of features as the child grows, such as deepening of the voice, facial hair, and failure to menstruate or abnormal periods at **puberty**. The internal structures of the reproductive tract, including the ovaries, uterus, and fallopian tubes, are normal. Females with severe CAH may be mistaken for males at birth. In males, the genitals are normal at birth, but the child becomes muscular, the penis enlarges, pubic hair appears, and the voice deepens long before normal puberty, sometimes as early as two to three years of age. At puberty, the testes are small.

In the severe salt-wasting form of CAH, newborns may develop symptoms shortly after birth, including **vomiting**, dehydration, electrolyte (a compound such as sodium or calcium that separates to form ions when dissolved in water) changes, and cardiac arrhythmias. If not treated, this form of CAH can result in death within one to six weeks after birth.

In the mild form of CAH, which occurs in late childhood or early adulthood, symptoms include premature development of pubic hair, irregular menstrual periods, unwanted body hair, or severe **acne**. However, sometimes there are no symptoms, and children affected are diagnosed because of an affected relative.

When to call the doctor

Many cases of CAH will be detected at birth, but in milder cases, symptoms may not develop until later, at which time medical care should be obtained. For children with more severe cases of CAH, regular medical care is necessary to achieve desired treatment results.

Diagnosis

CAH is diagnosed by a careful examination of the genitals and blood and urine tests that measure the hormones produced by the adrenal gland. A number of states in the United States perform a hormonal test (a heel prick blood test) for CAH and other inherited diseases within a few days of birth. In questionable cases, genetic testing can provide a definitive diagnosis. For some forms of CAH, prenatal diagnosis is possible through chronic villus sampling in the first trimester and by measuring certain hormones in the amniotic fluid during the second trimester.

Treatment

The goal of treatment for CAH is to return the androgen levels to normal. This is usually accomplished through drug therapy, although surgery may be an alternative for children with little or no enzyme activity. Life-long treatment for CAH is required.

Drug therapy consists of use of a cortisol-like steroid medications called glucocorticoids. Oral hydrocortisone is prescribed for younger children, and prednisone or dexamethasone is prescribed for older children. Side effects of steroids include stunted growth. Steroid

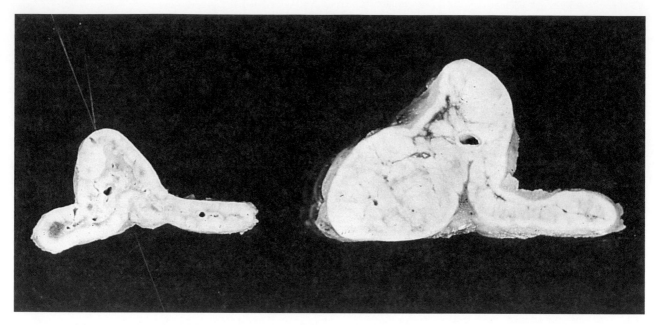

Adrenal cortical hyperplasia. The adrenal on the left is normal, the right shows hyperplasia. *(Photo Researchers, Inc.)*

therapy should not be suddenly stopped, since adrenal insufficiency will result. Treatment results must be monitored carefully, because of large individual variations in enzyme deficiency in children with CAH.

For children with salt-wasting CAH, fludrocortisone (Florinef), which acts like aldosterone (the missing hormone), is also prescribed. Infants and small children may also receive salt tablets, while older children are encouraged to eat salty foods. Serum electrolytes must be checked frequently, especially for children with salt-wasting CAH, to assure that normal levels of sodium and potassium are maintained.

Medical therapy achieves hormonal balance most of the time, but at times appropriate levels can be hard to maintain. CAH patients may have periods of fluctuating hormonal control that lead to increases in the dose of steroids prescribed. Sometimes these doses can become excessive as needs later decrease, leading to growth inhibition.

Increased doses may also be required when the child has a **fever** or a serious injury (a broken bone). If children are vomiting their oral medicine, have severe **diarrhea**, are unconscious, or cannot take anything by mouth before surgery, they may need to receive their medications by injections.

Children with CAH should see a pediatric endocrinologist frequently. The endocrinologist will assess height, weight, and blood pressure, and order an annual x ray of the wrist (to assess bone age), as well as assess blood hormone levels. If they require medical treatment, CAH children with the milder form of the disorder are usually effectively treated with hydrocortisone or prednisone.

Females with CAH who have masculine external genitalia require surgery to reconstruct the clitoris and/or vagina. This is usually performed when the child is an infant. However, some doctors and parents believe that the best time for vaginal surgery is during adolescence.

An experimental type of drug therapy—a three-drug combination, with an androgen blocking agent (flutamide), an aromatase inhibitor (testolactone), and low dose hydrocortisone—was as of 2004 being studied by physicians at the National Institutes of Health. Preliminary results are encouraging, but it will be many years before the **safety** and effectiveness of this therapy is fully known.

Adrenalectomy, a surgical procedure to remove the adrenal glands, is a more radical treatment for CAH. It was widely used before the advent of steroids. In the early 2000s, it is recommended for CAH children with little or no enzyme activity and can be accomplished by laparoscopy. This is a minimally invasive type of surgery done through one or more small one-inch (2.5 cm) incisions and a laparoscope, an instrument with a fiber-optic light containing a tube with openings for surgical instruments. Adrenalectomy is followed by hormone therapy, but in lower doses than CAH patients not treated surgically receive.

KEY TERMS

Adrenal glands—A pair of endocrine glands (glands that secrete hormones directly into the bloodstream) that are located on top of the kidneys. The outer tissue of the glands (cortex) produces several steroid hormones, while the inner tissue (medulla) produces the hormones epinephrine (adrenaline) and norepinephrine.

Aldosterone—A hormone secreted by the adrenal glands that is important for maintaining salt and water balance in the body.

Androgens—Hormones (specifically testosterone) responsible for male sex characteristics.

Congenital—Present at birth.

Cortisol—A steroid hormone secreted by the adrenal cortex that is important for maintenance of body fluids, electrolytes, and blood sugar levels. Also called hydrocortisone.

Hormone—A chemical messenger secreted by a gland or organ and released into the bloodstream. It travels via the bloodstream to distant cells where it exerts an effect.

Hyperplasia—A condition where cells, such as those making up the prostate gland, rapidly divide abnormally and cause the organ to become enlarged.

Steroids—Hormones, including aldosterone, cortisol, and androgens, that are derived from cholesterol and that share a four-ring structural characteristic.

Prognosis

CAH can be controlled and successfully treated in most patients as long as they remain on drug therapy.

Prevention

Prenatal therapy, in which a pregnant woman at risk for a second CAH child is given dexamethasone to decrease secretion of androgens by the adrenal glands of the female fetus, has been in use since 1994. This therapy is started in the first trimester when fetal adrenal production of androgens begins but before prenatal diagnosis is done that would provide definitive information about the sex of the fetus and its disease status. This means that a number of fetuses are exposed to unnecessary steroid treatment in order to prevent the development of male-like genitals in female fetuses with CAH. Several hundred children have undergone this treatment with no major adverse effects, but its long-term risks are unknown. Since there is very little data on the effectiveness and safety of prenatal therapy, it should only be offered to patients who clearly understand the risks and benefits and who are capable of complying with strict monitoring and follow-up throughout pregnancy and after the child is born.

Parental concerns

Parents with a **family** history of CAH or who have a child with CAH should seek genetic counseling. Genetic testing during pregnancy can provide information on the risk of having a child with CAH.

Because children with CAH may not always be able to administer their own treatment (because they are too young or they are unconscious), parents are encouraged to make sure that the child with CAH wears a medical identification bracelet or necklace (Medic-Alert) stating that the child takes glucocorticoids and possibly Florinef. This notifies medical personnel to administer stress doses of medicines if needed.

When taking a child with CAH for emergency care, parents are advised to refer to the condition by its full name rather than CAH. This is because this rare disease could be confused with another condition that shares the same initials: chronic active hepatitis. The parents should inform medical personnel if the child has salt-wasting CAH. It is also recommended that parents have a letter or information prepared concerning CAH and care needed so that this can be given to a new doctors who may treat the child.

Parents should be sensitive to the psychological aspects of the disease and obtain counseling for children with CAH. Topics of concern might include an understanding of the disease, the life-long requirement for medication, genital surgery, and sexuality.

Resources

BOOKS

Congenital Adrenal Hyperplasia: A Medical Dictionary, Bibliography, and Annotated Research Guide. San Diego, CA: Icon Group International, 2004.

PERIODICALS

Gmyrek, Glenn A., et al. "Bilateral Laparoscopic Adrenalectomy as a Treatment for Classic Congenital Adrenal Hyperplasia Attributable to 21-Hydroxylase Deficiency." *Pediatrics* 109 (February 2002): 28.

ORGANIZATIONS

American Academy of Pediatrics. 141 Northwest Point Blvd., Elk Grove Village, IL 60007–1098. Web site: <www.aap.org/>.

National Adrenal Diseases Foundation. 510 Northern Blvd., Great Neck, NY 11021. Web site: <www.medhelp.org/nadf/>.

WEB SITES

"Congenital Adrenal Hyperplasia Due to 21-Hydroxylase Deficiency: A Guide for Patients and Their Families." *Johns Hopkins Children's Center.* Available online at <www.hopkinsmedicine.org/pediatricendocrinology/cah/> (accessed December 8, 2004).

Judith Sims
Jennifer Sisk

Congenital amputation

Definition

Congenital amputation is the absence of a limb or part of a limb at birth.

Description

There are different types of congenital amputation birth defects. An infant with congenital amputation may be missing an entire limb or just a portion of a limb. The complete absence of a limb leaving a stump is called transverse deficiency, or amelia. When a specific part of a limb is missing, for example, when the fibula bone in the lower leg is missing, but the rest of the leg is intact, it is called a longitudinal deficiency. The condition in which only a mid-portion of a limb is missing, as when the hands or feet are attached directly to the trunk, is known as phocomelia.

Congenital amputation may be the result of the constriction of fibrous bands within the membrane that surrounds the developing fetus (amniotic band syndrome), the exposure to substances known to cause birth defects (teratogenic agents), genetic factors, or other, unknown, causes.

Demographics

An estimated one in 2,000 babies is born with all or part of a limb missing. This number includes everything from a missing part of a finger to the absence of both arms and both legs. Congenital amputation is the least common form of amputation. There have been occasional periods in history where the frequency of congenital amputations has increased. For example, in the 1960s many pregnant women were given tranquilizers containing the drug thali-domide. The result was the "thalidomide tragedy" during which there was a drastic increase in the number of babies born with deformations of the limbs. In this case, the birth defect usually presented itself as very small, deformed versions of normal limbs. Subsequently, birth defects as a result of exposure to Agent Orange, the U.S. defoliant used in Vietnam, and radiation exposure near the site of the Chernobyl disaster in Russia have left numerous children with malformed or absent limbs.

Causes and symptoms

Most of the time, the cause of congenital amputations is unknown. According to the March of Dimes, most birth defects have one or more genetic factors and one or more environmental factors, but what the actual factors are in any given case is often difficult, if not impossible, to pinpoint. Most birth defects occur in the first three months of pregnancy when the organs of the fetus are forming.

During the crucial first weeks, frequently before a woman is aware she is pregnant, the developing fetus is most susceptible to substances that can cause birth defects (teratogens). Exposure to teratogens can cause congenital amputation. Congenital amputation can also be caused by genetic factors. In some cases, tight amniotic bands may constrict the developing fetus, preventing a limb from forming properly, if at all. It is estimated that amniotic band syndrome occurs in between one in 12,000 and one in 15,000 live births. It is not known what makes the amniotic bands behave in this way in some instances and not in others.

When to call the doctor

Many congenital amputations are not discovered until the birth of the baby. At that time the doctor overseeing the delivery can give the parents helpful resources and refer them to the appropriate medical professionals to begin to discuss possible treatment paths and to help the parents cope effectively. If the abnormality is discovered before the birth, the obstetrician can help the parents decide what steps should be taken, and parents can begin to plan to meet the special needs their child will have.

Diagnosis

Ultrasound examinations may reveal the absence of a limb in some developing fetuses, but routine ultrasounds may not pick up signs of more subtle defects. However, if a doctor suspects that the fetus is at risk for developing a limb deficiency (for example, if the mother has been exposed to radiation), a more detailed ultrasound examination may be performed.

Treatment

If a problem with amniotic band constriction is detected early enough, it may be possible to correct the bands before there is significant damage to limb development. There have been cases in which physicians have detected amniotic band constriction and performed minimally invasive surgery that freed constricting amniotic bands and preserved the affected limbs. This procedure, however, is not commonly available.

Successful treatment of a child with congenital amputation involves an entire medical team, including a pediatrician, an orthopedist, a psychiatrist or psychologist, a prosthetist (an expert in making artificial limbs, or prosthetics), a social worker, and occupational and physical therapists. There is controversy over whether it is considered sound practice to fit the child early with a functional prosthesis. Some experts believe that this leads to more normal development and less wasting away (atrophy) of the muscles of the limbs. However, some parents and physicians believe that the child should be allowed to learn to **play** and perform tasks without a prosthesis, if possible. This is thought to help build a child's positive self-image because it does not reinforce the idea that the child is missing something that should be replaced. Also, many children reject prosthetic devices and do not want to wear them. When the child is older, he or she can be involved in decisions concerning whether to be fitted for a prosthesis.

Prognosis

A congenital limb deficiency has a profound effect on the life of the child and his or her parents. Children have been found to be extraordinarily good at learning to accomplish tasks using the means they have available and finding ways to compensate for their disability. Parents can help their child by encouraging persistence, allowing the child to do normal activities for him or herself, and not becoming frustrated and doing them for the child. Occupational therapy can help the child learn to accomplish tasks that are more complex if the child encounters difficulties. Prosthetic devices are increasingly sophisticated. Some experts believe that early fitting of a prosthesis enhances acceptance of the prosthesis by the child and parents.

Prevention

There is no known way to prevent congenital amputations, but the prevention of birth defects in general begins with the well being of the mother before and during pregnancy. Prenatal care should be clear and comprehensive, so that the mother understands both her genetic

risks and her environmental risks. Several disciplines in alternative therapy also recommend various supplements and **vitamins** that may reduce the chances of birth defects. Studies have suggested that a multivitamin including **folic acid** may reduce birth defects, including congenital abnormalities. **Smoking**, drinking alcohol, using recreational drugs or drugs not prescribed by a physician and having a poor diet while pregnant may increase the risk of congenital abnormalities. Daily, heavy exposure to chemicals is also thought to be especially dangerous for gestating women.

Parental concerns

Raising a child with one or more congenital amputations can be challenging. The way in which the child thinks of him or herself is dependent on the way in which the parents treat the child and the ways in which the parents introduce the child to others. Parents should be careful to treat the child as they would any other and not to expect any less from him or her. Children with congenital amputations are remarkably good at compensating for their disability. They are not mentally disabled in any way, and less should not be expected from them in an educational setting because of their disability. Lowered expectations can have a detrimental effect on the child's self-image.

Parents also need to be careful about how they respond to questions and comments about their child's disability when their child is present, always keeping in mind that the child can hear their answers and comments. The way in which the parent feels about the child's disability has a very strong impact on how the child feels about it.

Resources

BOOKS

Klein, Stanley D., and John D. Kemp, eds. *Reflections from a Different Journey: What Adults with Disabilities Wish All Parents Knew.* New York: McGraw-Hill, 2004.

Smith, Douglas G., Michael, John W. and John H. Bowker, eds. *Atlas of Amputations and Limb Deficiencies: Surgical, Prosthetic, and Rehabilitation Principles.* Rosemont, IL: American Academy of Orthopedic Surgeons, 2004.

ORGANIZATIONS

March of Dimes Birth Defects Foundation. 1275 Mamaroneck Ave., White Plains, NY 10605. Web site: <www.modimes.org>.

Tish Davidson, A.M.
Jeffrey P. Larson, RPT

Congenital bladder anomalies

Definition

The two most common congenital bladder abnormalities are exstrophy and congenital diverticula. An exstrophic bladder is one that is open to the outside and turned inside out, so that its inside is visible at birth, protruding from the lower abdomen. A diverticulum is an extension of a hollow organ, usually shaped like a pouch with a narrow opening.

Description

During fetal development, folds enclose tissues and organs and eventually fuse at the edges to form sealed compartments. Both in the front and the back, folds eventually become major body structures. In the back, the entire spinal column folds in like a pipe wrapped in a pillow. In the front, the entire lower urinary system is folded in.

Exstrophy of the bladder represents a failure of this folding process to complete itself, so the organs form with more or less of their front side missing and remain open to the outside. At the same time, the front of the pelvic bone is widely separated. The abdominal wall is open, too. In fact, the defect often extends all the way to the penis in the male or splits the clitoris in the female.

A congenital bladder diverticulum represents an area of weakness in the bladder wall through which extrudes some of the lining of the bladder. (A small balloon squeezed in a fist will create diverticula-like effect between the fingers.) Bladder diverticula may be multiple, and they often occur at the ureterovesical junction (the entrance of the upper urinary system into the bladder). In this location, they may cause urine to reflux into the ureter and kidney, leading to infection and possible kidney damage.

Demographics

Exstrophy is rare, occurring once in approximately 40,000 births.

Causes and symptoms

As with many birth defects, the causes are not well known. Lack of prenatal care and **nutrition** has been linked to many birth defects; however, beyond the avoidance of known teratogens (anything that can cause a birth defect), there is little prevention possible. Diverticula are more common and less serious.

If left untreated, the person with bladder exstrophy will have no control over urination and is more likely than others to develop bladder **cancer**. Diverticula, particularly if it causes urine reflux, may lead to chronic infection and its subsequent consequences.

Diagnosis

A major consideration with congenital abnormalities is that they tend to be multiple. Further, each one is unique in its extent and severity. Exstrophy can involve the rectum and large bowel and coexist with hernias. The obvious bladder exstrophy seen at birth will prompt immediate action and a search for other anomalies.

Diverticula are not visible and will be detected only if they cause trouble. They are usually found in an examination for the cause of recurring urinary infections. **X rays** of the urinary system or a cystoscopy (examination with a telescope-like instrument) will identify them. Often, the two procedures are done together: a urologist performs the cystoscopy, then a radiologist instills a contrast agent into the bladder and takes x rays.

Treatment

Surgery is necessary and can usually produce successful results. If possible, the surgery must be performed within 48 hours of birth. Prior to surgery, the exposed organs must be protected and all related defects identified and managed. Delay in the surgery leads to the frequent need to divert the urine into the bowel because the partially repaired bladder cannot control the flow. After surgery, the likelihood of infection requires monitoring.

After surgery, ongoing precautions to reduce frequency of infection may have to be used. Cranberry juice has the ability to keep bacteria from adhering to the membranes and can help prevent infection whenever there is increased risk. There are botanical and homeopathic treatments available; however, consultation by a trained practitioner is recommended before treatment.

Prognosis

With immediate surgery, three-fourths of all people can be successfully repaired. They will have control of their urine and no long-term consequences. The rate of infection is greater for those with congenital bladder anomalies, since any abnormality in the urinary system predisposes it to invasion by bacteria.

Prevention

Birth defects often have no precisely identified cause; therefore, prevention is limited to general measures such as early and continuous prenatal care, appropriate nutrition, and a healthy lifestyle.

Parental concerns

Parents must monitor the urinary output of their newborn children for the first few days of life. Parents of children with bladder diverticula should be aware of prevention and treatment practices for urinary tract infections.

See also Cystitis.

Resources

BOOKS

Asplin, John R., and Fredric L. Coe. "Hereditary Tubular Disorders." In *Harrison's Principles of Internal Medicine*, 15th ed. Edited by Eugene Braunwald et al. New York: McGraw-Hill, 2001, pp. 1598–1605.

Elder, Jack S. "Anomalies of the Bladder." In *Nelson Textbook of Pediatrics*, 17th ed. Edited by Richard E. Behrman, et al. Philadelphia: Saunders, 2003, pp. 1804–5.

Guay-Woodford, Lisa M. "Anomalies of the urinary tract." In *Cecil Textbook of Medicine*, 22nd ed. Edited by Lee Goldman et al. Philadelphia: Saunders, 2003, pp. 772–4.

Tanagho, Emil A., and Jack W. McAnich. *Smith's General Urology*. New York: McGraw-Hill, 2003.

PERIODICALS

Caire, J. T., et al. "MRI of fetal genitourinary anomalies." *American Journal of Roentgenology* 181, no. 5 (2003): 1381–5.

Carr, M. C. "Prenatal management of urogenital disorders." *Urology Clinics of North America* 31, no. 3 (2004): 389–97.

KEY TERMS

Congenital—Present at birth.

Cystoscopy—A diagnostic procedure in which a hollow lighted tube (cystoscope) is used to look inside the bladder and the urethra.

Diverticulum—Plural, diverticula; an outpouching in a tubular organ caused when the inner, lining layer bulges out (herniates) through the outer, muscular layer. Diverticula are present most often in the colon (large intestine), but are also found in the bladder.

Exstrophy—A congenital condition in which a hollow organ, such as the bladder, is turned inside out, establishing contact between the organ and the outside of the body.

Radiologist—A medical doctor specially trained in radiology, the branch of medicine concerned with radioactive substances and their use for the diagnosis and treatment of disease.

Teratogen—Any drug, chemical, maternal disease, or exposure that can cause physical or functional defects in an exposed embryo or fetus.

Ureter—The tube that carries urine from the kidney to the bladder; each kidney has one ureter.

Ureterovesical junction—The point where the ureter joins the bladder.

Urologist—A physician who specializes in the anatomy, physiology, diseases, and care of the urinary tract (in men and women) and male reproductive tract.

Greenwell, T. J., et al. "Pregnancy after lower urinary tract reconstruction for congenital abnormalities." *British Journal of Urology International* 92, no. 7 (2004): 773–7.

Tsuchiya, M., et al. "Ultrasound screening for renal and urinary tract anomalies in healthy infants." *Pediatrics International* 45, no. 5 (2003): 617–23.

ORGANIZATIONS

American Academy of Family Physicians. 11400 Tomahawk Creek Parkway, Leawood, KS 66211–2672. Web site: <www.aafp.org/>.

American Academy of Pediatrics. 141 Northwest Point Blvd., Elk Grove Village, IL 60007–1098. Web site: <www.aap.org/default.htm>.

American Foundation for Urologic Disease. 1128 North Charles St., Baltimore, MD 21201. Web site: <www.afud.org/>.

*American Urological Association.*1000 Corporate Boulevard Linthicum, MD 21090. Web site: <www.auanet.org>.

WEB SITES

"Bladder Anomalies." *eMedicine.* Available online at <www.emedicine.com/ped/topic1402.htm> (accessed December 21, 2004).

"Pediatric Urologic Problems>" *Department of Urology/ Mount Sinai School of Medicine.* Available online at <www.mssm.edu/urology/patient_care/ pediatric_urologic_problems.shtml> (accessed December 21, 2004).

L. Fleming Fallon, Jr., MD, DrPH

Congenital brain defects

Definition

Congenital brain defects are a group of disorders of brain development that are present at birth.

Description

Brain development begins shortly after conception and continues throughout the growth of a fetus. A complex genetic program coordinates the formation, growth, and migration of billions of neurons, or nerve cells, and their development into discrete, interacting brain regions. Interruption of this program, especially early in development, can cause structural defects in the brain. In addition, normal brain formation requires proper development of the surrounding skull, and skull defects may lead to brain malformation. Congenital brain defects may be caused by inherited genetic defects, spontaneous mutations within the genes of the embryo, or effects on the embryo due to the mother's infection, trauma, or drug use.

Early in fetal development, a flat strip of tissue along the back of the fetus rolls up to form a tube. This so-called neural tube develops into the spinal cord, and at one end, the brain. Closure of the tube is required for subsequent development of the tissue within. Many different types of brain defects are caused by improper closure of this neural tube. One such congenital brain anomaly, anencephaly (literally "without brain") results when the topmost portion of the tube fails to close and the brain does not develop. Anencephaly is the most common severe malformation seen in stillborn births. It is about four times more common in females than males.

Anencephaly is sometimes seen to run in families, and for parents who have conceived one anencephalic fetus, the risk of a second is as high as 5 percent. Fewer than half of babies with anencephaly are born alive, and survival beyond the first month is rare.

Another congenital brain defect, encephalocele, is a protrusion of part of the brain through a defect in the skull. The most common site for encephalocele is along the front-to-back midline of the skull, usually at the rear, although frontal encephaloceles are more common among Asians. Pressure within the skull pushes out cranial tissue. The protective layer over the brain, the meninges, grows to cover the protrusion, as does skin in some cases. Defects in skull closure are thought to cause some cases of encephalocele, while defects in neural tube closure may cause others. Encephaloceles may be small and contain little or no brain tissue or may be quite large and contain a significant portion of the brain.

Failure of neural-tube closure below the level of the brain prevents full development of the surrounding vertebral bones and leads to **spina bifida**, or a divided spinal column. Incomplete closure causes protrusion of the spinal cord and meninges, called meningomyelocele. Some cases of spina bifida are accompanied by another defect at the base of the brain, known as the Arnold-Chiari malformation or Chiari II malformation. For reasons that are unclear as of 2004, part of the cerebellum is displaced downward into the spinal column. Symptoms may be present at birth or delayed until early childhood.

The Dandy-Walker malformation is a brain defect marked by incomplete formation or absence of the central section of the cerebellum and the growth of cysts within the lowest of the brain's ventricles. The ventricles are fluid-filled cavities within the brain, through which cerebrospinal fluid (CSF) normally circulates. The cysts may block the exit of the fluid, causing **hydrocephalus**. Symptoms may be present at birth or delayed until early childhood.

Soon after closure of the neural tube, the brain divides into two halves, or hemispheres. Failure of division is termed holoprosencephaly (literally "whole forebrain"). Holoprosencephaly is almost always accompanied by facial and cranial deformities along the midline of the head, including **cleft lip**, **cleft palate**, fused eye sockets and a single eye (cyclopia), and deformities of the limbs, heart, gastrointestinal tract, and other internal organs. Most infants are either stillborn or die soon after birth. Survivors suffer from severe neurological impairments.

The normal ridges and valleys of the mature brain are formed after cells from the inside of the developing brain migrate to the outside and multiply. When these cells fail to migrate, the surface remains smooth, a condition called lissencephaly ("smooth brain"). Lissencephaly is often associated with facial abnormalities including a small jaw, a high forehead, a short nose, and low-set ears.

If damaged during growth, especially within the first 20 weeks, brain tissue may stop growing, while tissue around it continues to form. This causes an abnormal cleft or groove to appear on the surface of the brain, called schizencephaly (literally "split brain"). This cleft should not be confused with the normal wrinkled brain surface, nor should the name be mistaken for **schizophrenia**, a mental disorder. Generalized destruction of tissue or lack of brain development may lead to hydranencephaly, in which cerebrospinal fluid fills much of the space normally occupied by the brain. Hydranencephaly is distinct from hydrocephalus, in which CSF accumulates within a normally-formed brain, putting pressure on it and possibly causing skull expansion.

Excessive brain size is termed megalencephaly (literally "big brain"). Megalencephaly is defined as any brain size above the 98th percentile within the population. Some cases are familial and may be entirely benign. Others are due to metabolic or neurologic disease. The opposite condition, microcephaly, may be caused by failure of the brain to develop or by intrauterine infection, drug toxicity, or brain trauma.

Demographics

Researchers estimate that central nervous system anomalies, congenital brain defects included, occur in approximately 15 of every 10,000 live births. Some congenital brain defects, such as those associated with spina bifida have a higher prevalence, affecting as many as two to three per 1,000 live births. In general, birth defects of the brain are not more prevalent in one gender; however, specific defects such as anencephaly, affect girls four times more often than boys, and in families who have conceived one child with anencephaly, the risk to another pregnancy increases nearly 5 percent.

Causes and symptoms

Causes

Congenital brain defects may have genetic, infectious, toxic, or traumatic causes. In most cases, no certain cause can be identified.

GENETIC CAUSES Some brain defects are caused by trisomy, the inclusion of a third copy of a chromosome normally occurring in pairs. Most trisomies occur because of improper division of the chromosomes during formation of eggs or sperm. Trisomy of chromosome 9 can cause some cases of Dandy-Walker and Chiari II malformation. Some cases of holoprosencephaly are caused by trisomy of chromosome 13, while others are due to abnormalities in chromosomes 7 or 18. Individual gene defects, either inherited or spontaneous, are responsible for other cases of congenital brain malformations.

DRUGS Drugs known to cause congenital brain defects when used by the mother during critical developmental periods include:

- anticonvulsant drugs
- retinoic acid and tretinoin
- warfarin
- alcohol
- cocaine

OTHER Other causes of congenital brain defects include:

- intrauterine infections, including cytomegalovirus, **rubella**, **herpes simplex**, and varicella zoster
- maternal diabetes mellitus
- maternal phenylketonuria
- fetal trauma

Symptoms

Besides the features listed above, symptoms of congenital brain defects may include:

- Chiari II malformation: Impaired swallowing and gag reflex, loss of the breathing reflex, facial paralysis, uncontrolled eye movements (**nystagmus**), impaired balance and gait.
- Dandy-Walker malformation: Symptoms of hydrocephalus, lack of muscle tone or floppiness, seizures, **spasticity**, deafness, irritability, visual impairment, deterioration of consciousness, paralysis.
- Lissencephaly: Lack of muscle tone, seizures, **developmental delay**, spasticity, cerebral palsy.
- Hydranencephaly: Irritability, spasticity, seizures, temperature oscillations.
- Megalencephaly due to neurological or metabolic disease: **Mental retardation**, seizures.

Diagnosis

Congenital brain defects are diagnosed either from direct physical examination or imaging studies

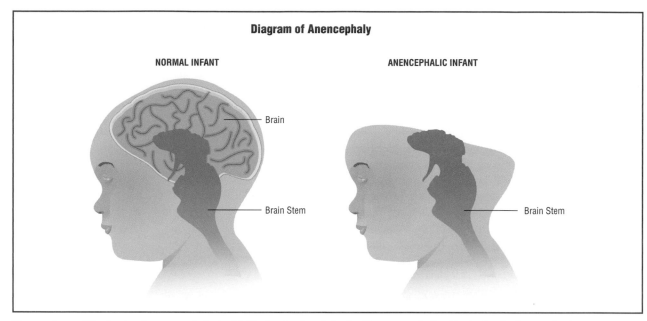

Diagram of Anencephaly

NORMAL INFANT

Brain

Brain Stem

ANENCEPHALIC INFANT

Brain Stem

Comparison of the brain of a normal infant with the brain of an infant with anencephaly. *(Illustration by Argosy, Inc.)*

including **computed tomography** scans (CT) and **magnetic resonance imaging** (MRI). Electroencephalography (EEG) may be used to reveal characteristic abnormalities.

Prenatal diagnosis of neural tube defects causing anencephaly or meningomyelocele is possible through ultrasound examination and maternal blood testing for alpha-fetoprotein, which is almost always elevated. Ultrasound can also be used to diagnose Dandy-Walker and Chiari II malformations. **Amniocentesis** may reveal trisomies or other chromosomal abnormalities.

Treatment

Spina bifida may be treated with surgery to close the open portion of the spinal cord. Surgery for encephalocele is possible only if there is a minimal amount of brain tissue protruding. Malformations associated with hydrocephalus (Dandy-Walker, Chiari II, and some cases of hydranencephaly) may be treated by installation of a drainage shunt for cerebrospinal fluid. Drugs may be used to treat some symptoms of brain defects, including seizures and spasticity or muscle rigidity.

Prognosis

Most congenital brain defects carry a very poor prognosis. Surgical treatment of meningomyelocele and encephalocele may be successful, with lasting neurological deficiencies that vary in severity. Early treatment of hydrocephalus may prevent more severe brain damage.

Prevention

Some cases of congenital brain defects can be prevented with good maternal **nutrition**, including **folic acid** supplements. Folic acid is a vitamin that has been shown to reduce the incidence of neural tube defects. The Centers for Disease Control and Prevention recommends that all women of childbearing age consume 0.4 mg of folic acid daily to prevent neural tube defects. All over-the-counter multivitamins contain this amount of folic acid. Pregnant women should avoid exposure to infection, especially during the first trimester. Abstention from drugs and alcohol during pregnancy may reduce risk. Genetic counseling is advisable for parents who have had one child with anencephaly, since the likelihood of having another is increased.

Parental concerns

Some congenital brain anomalies, such as anencephaly, are not compatible with life, and fetuses affected by them will die. Many more brain anomalies are not lethal. Most congenital brain anomalies, however, will impact mental functioning, development, and, in some cases, physical mobility. When functions of the brain are severely limited, the child may be placed on a life support system. If the essential tasks of the brain are not impaired, the child will most likely face brain dysfunction, including any or all of the following: memory and language problems, neuromotor functioning problems, and behavioral and social problems. It is important that the child's abilities are accurately assessed and that an appropriate plan of treatment is developed. A multidisci-

KEY TERMS

Amniocentesis—A procedure performed at 16-18 weeks of pregnancy in which a needle is inserted through a woman's abdomen into her uterus to draw out a small sample of the amniotic fluid from around the baby for analysis. Either the fluid itself or cells from the fluid can be used for a variety of tests to obtain information about genetic disorders and other medical conditions in the fetus.

Cerebrospinal fluid—The clear, normally colorless fluid that fills the brain cavities (ventricles), the subarachnoid space around the brain, and the spinal cord and acts as a shock absorber.

Congenital—Present at birth.

Fetus—In humans, the developing organism from the end of the eighth week to the moment of birth. Until the end of the eighth week the developing organism is called an embryo.

Spasticity—Increased mucle tone, or stiffness, which leads to uncontrolled, awkward movements.

plinary team approach to the medical, educational, and emotional needs of the child is imperative. The treatment team for these children often includes neurologists, surgeons, nurses, physical and occupational therapists, educators, and social workers, all coordinated by the primary physician.

Many children with congenital brain anomalies, such as Chiari I malformation and nearly 50 percent of those affected by hydrocephalus, have normal intellectual functioning, and some have unimpaired physical mobility. These children, however, still require medical management and benefit from a multidisciplinary healthcare team. Many face multiple surgical procedures and hospital admissions. It is important to prepare children for these medical treatments and surgeries. Children's hospitals, local school systems, and state governments can assist parents in finding the support and resources they need.

See also Chiara malformation; Spina bifida.

Resources

BOOKS

Moore, Keith L., et al. *Before We Are Born: Essentials of Embryology and Birth Defects*. Kent, UK: Elsevier—Health Sciences Division, 2002.

WEB SITES

"Congenital Birth Defects." *Dr. Joseph F. Smith Medical Library*. Available online at <www.chclibrary.org/micromed/00043570.html> (accessed December 8, 2004).

"Congenital Birth Defects." *Principal Health News*. Available online at <www.principalhealthnews.com/topic/topic100586649> (accessed December 8, 2004).

Richard Robinson
Deborah L. Nurmi, MS

Congenital heart disease

Definition

Congenital heart disease, or congenital heart defect, includes a variety of structural problems of the heart or its major blood vessels, which are present at birth.

Description

The heart, which is completely developed about eight weeks after conception, is one of the earliest organs to completely develop. Congenital heart defects occur when the heart or blood vessels near the heart do not develop properly before birth. Some infants are born with mild types of congenital heart defects, but most need surgery in order to survive. In some cases, the defect may be mild and unnoticed at birth, then diagnosed later in life.

Research is ongoing, and at least 35 congenital heart or cardiovascular defects have been identified. Each defect is defined by its location and severity. Most congenital cardiovascular defects obstruct the flow of blood in the heart or nearby blood vessels, or cause an abnormal flow of blood through the heart. Rarer congenital cardiovascular defects occur when the newborn has only one ventricle (lower chamber), when the pulmonary artery (leading to the lungs) and the aorta (the largest artery that brings blood to the body) come out of the same ventricle, or when one side of the heart is not completely formed.

Patent ductus arteriosus

Ductus arteriosus refers to an open passageway—or temporary blood vessel (ductus)—that carries blood from the heart via the pulmonary artery to the aorta before birth. This passageway allows blood to bypass the lungs, which are not yet functional in the fetus. The ductus should close spontaneously in the first few hours after birth. When it does not close in the newborn, some of the blood that should flow through the aorta returns to the lungs. **Patent ductus arteriosus** is common in premature babies, but rare in full-term babies. It has been associated with mothers who had German **measles** (**rubella**) while pregnant. Patent ductus arteriosus accounts for 6–11 percent of all cases of congenital cardiovascular defects in the United States.

Hypoplastic left heart syndrome

Although rare, hypoplastic left heart syndrome, a condition in which the left side of the heart is underdeveloped, is the most serious congenital cardiovascular defect. With this syndrome, blood returning from the lungs must flow through an opening or hole in the wall between the atria, called an **atrial septal defect**. The right ventricle pumps blood into the pulmonary artery and blood reaches the aorta through a patent ductus arteriosus (see description in the previous section). In hypoplastic left heart syndrome, the baby seems normal at birth, but as the ductus closes, blood cannot reach the aorta and circulation fails. If left untreated, hypoplastic left heart syndrome is always fatal.

Heart rhythm problems

An arrhythmia is an abnormal heart beat. Normally, the heart beats at 50–150 beats per minute, depending on the child's age. Bradycardia is an irregularly slow heart rhythm, and tachycardia is an irregularly fast heart rhythm. Both conditions reduce the heart's pumping ability.

Obstruction defects

When heart valves, arteries, or veins are narrowed, they partially or completely block the flow of blood. The most common obstruction defects are pulmonary valve stenosis, aortic valve stenosis, and **coarctation of the aorta**. Coarctation of the aorta accounts for 8–11 percent of all cases of congenital cardiovascular defects in the United States.

Stenosis is a narrowing of the valves or arteries. In pulmonary stenosis, the pulmonary valve does not open properly, forcing the right ventricle to work harder. In aortic stenosis, the improperly formed aortic valve is narrowed. As the left ventricle works harder to pump blood through the body, it becomes enlarged. In coarctation of the aorta, the aorta is constricted, reducing the flow of blood to the lower part of the body and increasing blood pressure in the upper body.

Bicuspid aortic valve and subaortic stenosis are less common obstruction defects. A bicuspid aortic valve has only two flaps instead of three, which can lead to stenosis in adulthood. Subaortic stenosis is a narrowing of the left ventricle below the aortic valve that limits the flow of blood from the left ventricle.

Septal defects

When a baby is born with a hole in the septum (the wall separating the right and left sides of the heart), blood leaks from the left side of the heart to the right. A major leakage can lead to enlargement of the heart and failing circulation. The most common types of septal defects are atrial septal defect, an opening between the two upper heart chambers (atria), and ventricular septal defect, an opening between the two lower heart chambers (ventricles). Atrial septal defects account for 4–10 percent of all cases of congenital cardiovascular defects in the United States; ventricular septal defects account for about 14–16 percent.

Two variations of septal defects include atrioventricular canal defect and Eisenmenger's complex. Atrioventricular canal defect (also called endocardial cushion defect or atrioventricular septal defect) is a large hole in the septum, accompanied by abnormal tricuspid and mitral valves that are not formed as individual valves. Instead, a single large valve crosses the defect. The defect allows oxygen-rich blood from the lungs to flow from the left side of the heart to the right side of the heart and back again to the lungs. The heart must work harder to accommodate this extra blood and may become enlarged. Eisenmenger's complex is a ventricular septal defect coupled with pulmonary high blood pressure, an enlarged right ventricle, and sometimes an aorta that is not positioned correctly. With this syndrome, blood flows abnormally from the right side of the heart to the left.

Cyanotic defects

Heart disorders that cause a decreased, inadequate amount of oxygen in blood pumped to the body are called cyanotic defects. Cyanotic defects result in a blue discoloration of the skin due to low oxygen levels. Cyanotic defects include truncus arteriosus, total anomalous pulmonary venous return, **tetralogy of Fallot**, **transposition of the great arteries**, tricuspid atresia, and pulmonary atresia.

Truncus arteriosus is a complex malformation in which only one artery comes from the heart and forms the aorta and pulmonary artery. Total anomalous pulmonary venous return is a condition in which the pulmonary veins that bring oxygen-rich blood from the lungs back to the heart are not connected to the left atrium. Instead, the pulmonary veins drain through abnormal connections to the right atrium.

Nine to fourteen percent of cases of congenital cardiovascular defects in the United States are tetralogy of Fallot, which includes four defects. The major defects are a large hole (ventricular septal defect) between the ventricles, which allows oxygen-poor blood to mix with oxygen-rich blood, and narrowing at or beneath the pulmonary valve. The other defects are an overly muscular right ventricle and an aorta that lies over the ventricular septal defect.

In transposition (reversal of position) of the great arteries, the positions of the pulmonary artery and the aorta are reversed, causing oxygen-rich blood to re-circulate to the lungs while oxygen-poor blood goes to the rest of the body. Transposition of the great arteries comprises 10–14 percent of congenital cardiovascular defect cases in the United States.

In tricuspid atresia, the baby lacks a triscupid valve and blood cannot flow properly from the right atrium to the right ventricle. In pulmonary atresia, the baby lacks a pulmonary valve and blood cannot flow properly from the right ventricle into the pulmonary artery and on to the lungs.

Other defects

Ebstein's anomaly is a rare congenital syndrome that causes malformed tricuspid valve leaflets, which allow blood to leak between the right ventricle and the right atrium. This condition may cause a hole in the wall between the left and right atrium, called an atrial septal defect. Treatment often involves repairing the tricuspid valve. Ebstein's anomaly may be associated with maternal use of the psychiatric drug lithium during pregnancy.

Brugada syndrome is another rare congenital cardiovascular defect that appears in adulthood and may cause sudden death if untreated. Symptoms, which include rapid, uneven heart beat, often appear at night. Scientists believe that Brugada syndrome is caused by mutations in the gene SCN5A, which involves cardiac sodium channels.

Infants born with DiGeorge sequence can have heart defects such as a malformed aortic arch and tetralogy of Fallot. Researchers believe DiGeorge sequence most often is caused by mutations in genes in the region 22q11.

Marfan syndrome is a connective tissue disorder that causes tears in the aorta. Since the disease also causes excessive bone growth, most Marfan syndrome patients are over 6 ft (1.8 m) tall. In athletes and others, it can lead to sudden death. Researchers believe the defect responsible for Marfan's syndrome is found in gene FBN1 on chromosome 15.

Heart muscle abnormalities may lead to congestive heart failure. In heart failure, the heart does not pump blood well enough for the body to get the nourishment it needs for normal function and activity. When the heart does not function properly, fluid can build up in the lungs, causing difficult breathing. Fluid can also build up in the rest of the body, causing swelling.

Demographics

About 44,000 infants (about eight of every 1,000 infants or 1 percent of live births) are born every year with congenital cardiovascular defects, the most common birth defect. It is the number one cause of death from birth defects during the first year of life. Nearly twice as many children die from congenital cardiovascular defects in the United States than from all forms of childhood cancers combined. Most of these children can benefit from surgical treatment, even if the defect is severe. Overall, the mortality rate from congenital cardiovascular defects has significantly declined in the past few decades. About one million adults (over age 20) with cardiovascular defects are currently living in the United States.

Causes and symptoms

Causes

In most cases, the causes of congenital cardiovascular defects are unknown. Genetic and environmental factors, and lifestyle habits can all be involved. However, only a few genes have been discovered that have been linked to the presence of heart defects. The likelihood of having a child with a congenital cardiovascular defect increases if the mother or father, another child, or another relative had congenital cardiovascular defects, or there is a **family** history of sudden death.

Women with diabetes and **phenylketonuria** (an inherited liver condition also called PKU) are at higher risk of having children with congenital heart defects. Many cases of congenital cardiovascular defects result from the mother's excessive use of alcohol or history of taking illegal drugs, such as cocaine, while pregnant. The mother's exposure to certain prescription drugs such as anticonvulsant and dermatologic medications during pregnancy also can cause congenital cardiovascular defects. Her exposure to industrial chemicals, solvents, and ionizing radiation (x ray) also increases the risk of having children with congenital heart defects.

The occurrence of some infections during pregnancy, including viral infections such as rubella (German measles), can cause congenital cardiovascular defects. In addition, there are many genetic conditions, such as **Down syndrome** or Turner's syndrome, which affect multiple organs and can cause congenital cardiovascular defects. Children with oral clefts are 16 times more likely to have a congenital cardiovascular defect than the normal population, although the reason for this association is unknown.

Symptoms

General symptoms of congenital cardiovascular defects include:

- shortness of breath or rapid breathing

- difficulty feeding in infancy

- sweating

- cyanosis (bluish discoloration of the skin, lips, and fingernails)

- heart murmur

- respiratory infections that recur excessively

- poor weight gain in infants

- stunted growth

- underdeveloped limbs and muscles

Some infants and children have no signs or symptoms of congenital cardiovascular defects.

Symptoms of specific types of congenital cardiovascular defects are as follows:

- Patent ductus arteriosus—quick tiring, slow growth, susceptibility to **pneumonia**, and rapid breathing. If the ductus is small, there are no symptoms.

- Hypoplastic left heart syndrome—ashen color, rapid and difficult breathing, and inability to eat.

- Abnormal heart rhythm—feeling of skipped heart beats, **dizziness**, lightheadedness, fainting, shortness of breath, and fatigue.

- Obstruction defects: cyanosis (skin that is discolored blue)—chest **pain**, unusual fatigue or quick tiring, dizziness or fainting, and high blood pressure.

- Septal defects—difficulty breathing, stunted growth, and high blood pressure. Sometimes there are no symptoms.

- Cyanotic defects: cyanosis—sudden rapid breathing or unconsciousness, and shortness of breath and fainting during **exercise**.

- Congestive heart failure—difficulty breathing, swelling, quick tiring, and feeding problems in infants.

When to call the doctor

The parent or caregiver should call the child's pediatrician or cardiologist when the child has these symptoms or conditions:

- infant who has feeding problems, difficulty sucking, or **vomiting** more than two or three feedings per day

- poor weight gain in young children

- swelling in the ankles or feet

- swollen abdomen

- poor exercise tolerance

- recurrent chest colds and respiratory infections

- abnormal blood pressure

- signs of infection including **sore throat**, general body aches or **fever**

The parent or caregiver should seek emergency treatment by calling 911 in most areas when the child has these symptoms or conditions:

- bluish skin tone

- bluish coloration around the lips, fingernail beds, and tongue

- breathing difficulties or rapid breathing

- dizziness or fainting

- uncontrolled coughing or coughing with blood

- irregular heart beats or palpitations (abnormal heart beats that feel like fluttering in the chest)

- chest pain (rare in children)

Diagnosis

Severe congenital cardiovascular defect is diagnosed in infancy and usually becomes evident shortly after birth. However, significant cardiovascular defects may be found anytime during childhood. In a few cases, a cardiovascular defect is not detected until the child is a teenager or adult.

The medical and family history help the physician determine if the child has any conditions or disorders that might contribute to or cause the cardiovascular defect. A family history of cardiovascular defects might suggest a genetic predisposition to the disease.

During the physical exam, the child's blood pressure is measured, and a stethoscope is used to listen to sounds made by the heart and blood flowing through the arteries. Some **heart murmurs** (abnormal heart sounds) can indicate a congenital heart defect. The child's pulse, reflexes, and height and weight are checked and recorded. The child's blood oxygen level can be measured using a pulse oximeter, a sensor placed on the fingertip or earlobe. Internal organs are palpated, or felt, to determine if they are enlarged.

Blood and urine tests are performed to detect the presence of any abnormal substances that may indicate congenital cardiovascular defects.

Echocardiography and cardiac **magnetic resonance imaging** (MRI) may be used to confirm congenital cardiovascular defects when suggested by the child's symptoms and physical exam results.

An echocardiogram (echo) uses ultrasound, or high-frequency sound waves, to display an image of the heart's internal structures. It can be used to detect valve and other heart problems. A Doppler echo uses sound waves to measure blood flow. Fetal echocardiography is used to diagnose congenital cardiovascular defects in utero, usually after 20 weeks of pregnancy. Between 10 and 14 weeks of pregnancy, physicians may use an ultrasound to look for a thickness at the nuchal translucency, a pocket of fluid in back of the embryo's neck, which may indicate a cardiac defect in 55 percent of cases.

Cardiac MRI, a scanning method that uses magnetic fields and radio waves to create three-dimensional images of the heart, can help physicians evaluate congenital cardiovascular defects, but is not always necessary. MRI reveals how blood flows through the heart and how the heart is working. Physicians also may use a chest x ray to look at the size, shape, and location of the heart and lungs.

An electrocardiogram (ECG, EKG) helps the physician evaluate the electrical activity of the heart. During an EKG, small electrode patches are attached to the skin on the chest and connected to a computer that measures the heart's electrical impulses and records them in a zig-zag patter on a moving strip of paper.

Stress tests may be performed to provide information about how the heart responds to stress. The test may involve actual exercise or a medication that simulates exercise. Increasing levels of exercise difficulty are monitored while the electrocardiogram, heart rate, and blood pressure are recorded.

Special monitors may be used to evaluate an abnormal heart rhythm. Ambulatory monitors are small portable electrocardiograph machines that record the heart's rhythm. Each type of monitor has unique features related to length of recording time and ability to send the recordings over the phone.

In some cases, these tests are not conclusive enough to confirm the diagnosis of congenital cardiovascular defects. More invasive diagnostic procedures, such as angiography and cardiac catheterization, may be performed to show the type and severity of heart disease. These procedures should be performed by a specially trained physician and diagnostic team in a well-equipped heart center.

During catheterization, a long, slender tube, called a catheter, is inserted into a vein or artery and slowly directed to the heart using x-ray guidance. To better view the heart and blood vessels, contrast material (dye) is injected through the catheter and viewed and recorded on an x-ray video as it moves through the heart. This imaging technique is called angiography. In some cases, blood vessel blockages or narrowed areas may be treated during the catheterization procedure using a specialized balloon tip or other device at the end of the catheter. When treatment is performed as part of a catheterization procedure, it is referred to as an interventional procedure.

Treatment

Treatment should be provided by a pediatric cardiologist, a specialist trained to diagnose and treat congenital cardiovascular defects.

Medications

Medications used to treat congenital cardiovascular defects include diuretics, which aid the child in excreting water and salts, and Digoxin, which strengthens the contraction of the heart, slows the heartbeat, and removes fluid from tissues. A potassium supplement may be prescribed along with diuretics, which remove potassium from the body along with excess fluid. Heart rate control drugs and antiarrhythmic drugs may be prescribed to treat irregular heart rhythms. Other medications may include anticoagulants (blood thinners) to reduce the risk of blood clots and **stroke**, ACE inhibitors to decrease artery constriction and improve blood flow, and inotropes to strengthen the heart's contractions.

Electrical therapy and implantable devices

If medications are not effective in controlling a child's heart rate, cardioversion may be required. In this procedure, an electrical shock is delivered to the chest wall to synchronize the heart and allow the normal rhythm to restart. A permanent pacemaker or implantable cardioverter defibrillator (ICD) is sometimes needed to regulate the child's heart rhythm. A pacemaker is a device that sends small electrical impulses to the heart

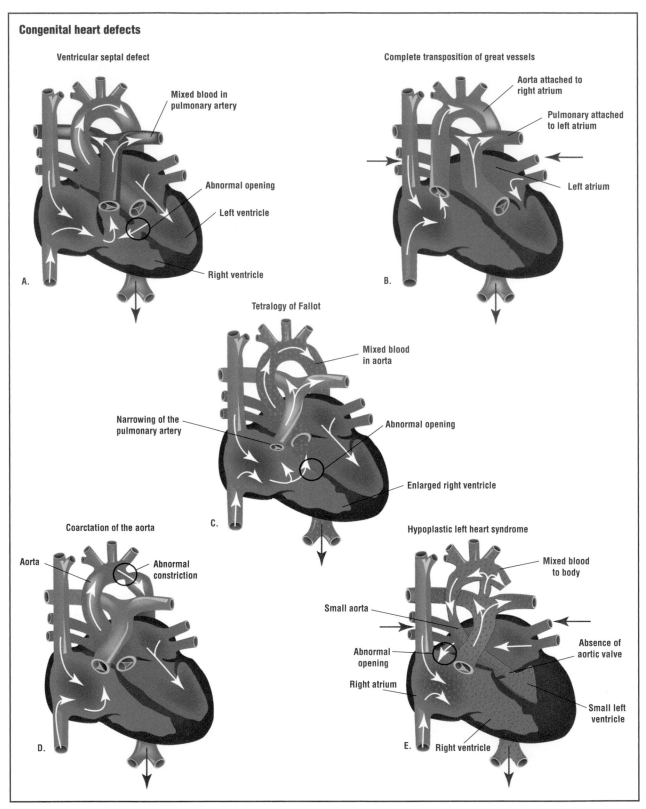

Congenital heart defects

Ventricular septal defect

Mixed blood in pulmonary artery

Abnormal opening

Left ventricle

Right ventricle

A.

Complete transposition of great vessels

Aorta attached to right atrium

Pulmonary attached to left atrium

Left atrium

B.

Tetralogy of Fallot

Mixed blood in aorta

Narrowing of the pulmonary artery

Abnormal opening

Enlarged right ventricle

C.

Coarctation of the aorta

Aorta

Abnormal constriction

D.

Hypoplastic left heart syndrome

Mixed blood to body

Small aorta

Absence of aortic valve

Abnormal opening

Right atrium

Small left ventricle

E. Right ventricle

The most common types of congenital heart defects are ventricular septal defect (A), complete transposition of the great vessels (B), tetralogy of Fallot (C), coarctation of the aorta (D), and hypoplastic left heart syndrome (E). *(Illustration by GGS Information Services.)*

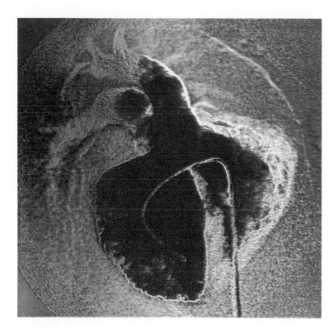

An angiogram of a ventricular septal defect, a congenital heart disease that causes a hole in the center wall of the heart, which normally completely divides the two ventricles, or lower chambers. *(Photograph by Simon Fraser/Science Photo Library/Photo Researchers, Inc.)*

muscle to maintain a suitable heart rate. An ICD is a device used primarily to treat ventricular tachycardia and ventricular fibrillation, two life-threatening heart rhythms. The ICD constantly monitors the heart rhythm. When a very rapid, abnormal heart rhythm is detected, the ICD delivers energy to the heart muscle to cause it to regain a normal rhythm.

Interventional procedures

Catheter-based procedures may be performed to open stenotic valves or vessels, widen the septal opening between the atria, or close abnormal vessels or certain septal defects. During catheterization, a long, slender tube called a catheter is inserted into a vein or artery and slowly directed to the heart, using x-ray guidance. Blood vessel blockages or stenotic valves may be treated during the catheterization procedure using a specialized balloon tip or other device at the end of the catheter. The balloon is rapidly inflated and deflated to open or widen the area. In older patients, a stent (metal mesh tube) can be positioned to act as a scaffold and hold the area open. Several closure devices such as coils, patches, or umbrella-like devices, have been developed that can be inserted through the catheter and are designed to close the defect.

Surgery

The goal of surgery is to repair the defect as much as possible, restore circulation to as close to normal as pos-

sible, reduce symptoms, improve survival, and improve quality of life. Sometimes, multiple surgical procedures are necessary. Surgery for most congenital cardiovascular defects has low risk of death (less than 2 percent), compared to 80–100 percent in the 1940s. Surgical procedures used to treat congenital cardiovascular defects include:

• arterial switch

• balloon atrial septostomy

• balloon valvuloplasty

• Damus-Kaye-Stansel procedure

• Fontan procedure

• pulmonary artery banding

• Ross procedure

• shunt procedure

• venous switch or intra-atrial baffle

Arterial switch, to correct transposition of the great arteries, involves connecting the aorta to the left ventricle and connecting the pulmonary artery to the right ventricle. Balloon atrial septostomy, also done to correct transposition of the great arteries, enlarges the atrial opening during heart catheterization. Balloon valvuloplasty uses a balloon-tipped catheter to open a narrowed heart valve, improving the flow of blood in pulmonary stenosis. It is sometimes used to treat aortic stenosis. Transposition of the great arteries also can be corrected by the Damus-Kaye-Stansel procedure, in which the pulmonary artery is cut in two and connected to the ascending aorta and the farthest section of the right ventricle.

For tricuspid atresia and pulmonary atresia, the Fontan procedure connects the right atrium to the pulmonary artery directly or with a conduit, and the atrial defect is closed. Pulmonary artery banding, narrowing the pulmonary artery with a band to reduce blood flow and pressure in the lungs, is used for ventricular septal defect, atrioventricular canal defect, and tricuspid atresia. The band can be removed at a later time, and the defect corrected with open-heart surgery.

To correct aortic stenosis, the Ross procedure grafts the pulmonary artery to the aorta. For tetralogy of Fallot, tricuspid atresia, or pulmonary atresia, the shunt procedure creates a passage between blood vessels, sending blood into parts of the body that need it. For transposition of the great arteries, venous switch creates a tunnel inside the atria to re-direct oxygen-rich blood to the right ventricle and aorta, and venous blood to the left ventricle and pulmonary artery.

When all other options fail, some patients may need a heart transplant. A heart transplant involves replacing the child's heart with a healthy heart from a donor who has died or been declared brain dead. The child's eligibility for a transplant depends on the results of blood tests and other factors related to his or her health and potential for survival.

Nutritional concerns

Infants and children with congenital cardiovascular defects tend to gain weight more slowly. An 8-oz to 1 lb (225–450 g) weight gain in a month may be acceptable. The physician will monitor the child's weight gain and advise the parents of the goal weight gain and any necessary dietary changes. The most common reason for poor growth among children with congenital cardiovascular defects is that they do not consume enough calories or nutrients. Some other factors that may interfere with growth include:

• rapid heart beat and increased breathing rate

• poor appetite

• decreased food intake due to rapid breathing and fatigue

• frequent respiratory infections

• poor absorption of nutrients from the digestive tract

• decreased oxygen in the blood

For infants with congenital cardiovascular defects, **nutrition** supplements may need to be added to regular formula or breast milk. Sometimes additional feedings are required with the aid of a nasogastric tube to provide enough calories and promote weight gain. The nasogastric tube is placed in the baby's nose and passes to the stomach. Formula or breast milk is delivered through the tube. Breastfeeding may not be possible right after birth, depending on the child's condition. A breast pump may be used to maintain the mother's milk supply during times when the baby cannot nurse.

Babies with congenital cardiovascular defects tire quickly during feedings, making frequent feedings necessary. Feedings should be on-demand and may need to be as often as every two hours in the first few months. Some babies have difficulty feeding from a regular bottle nipple; parents may need to try different brands. If medications are prescribed, they should be given before a feeding. Medications should not be mixed in the formula or breast milk unless the doctor advises otherwise.

The pediatrician will advise when solid foods can be started, usually around six months of age. Fat should not be restricted in the diet, especially in the first two years. High-calorie foods and snacks can play an important role in providing good nutrition and helping the child grow at a healthy rate.

Follow-up care

Children with congenital cardiovascular defects require lifelong monitoring, even after successful surgery. Along with routine medical care and standard immunizations, periodic heart check-ups are necessary. Usually, heart check-up appointments are scheduled more frequently just after the diagnosis or after surgery. Additional immunizations, such as the **influenza** vaccine, may be recommended.

Medical identification

A medical identification bracelet or necklace should be worn to alert all health care providers of the child's heart condition in cases of emergency.

Prognosis

The outlook for children with congenital cardiovascular defects has improved markedly since the 1980s. Many types of congenital cardiovascular defects that were once fatal can be treated successfully. Most children with congenital cardiovascular defects grow up to be healthy adults. Children with complex heart disease may continue to need special medical attention throughout **adolescence** and into adulthood for survival and to maintain a good quality of life.

Research on diagnosing cardiovascular defects when the fetus is in the womb may lead to future treatment to correct these conditions before birth. Promising new prevention methods and treatments include genetic screening and the cultivation of cardiac tissue in the laboratory that could be used to repair congenital cardiovascular defects. As scientists continue to advance the study of genetics, they also will better understand the genetic causes of many congenital cardiovascular defects.

Prevention

Congenital cardiovascular defects cannot be prevented. However, to protect patients with congenital cardiovascular defects from heart infections (endocarditis), the American Heart Association recommends regular dental check-ups to prevent infections of the mouth as well as the preventive use of **antibiotics**. Preventive antibiotics should be taken before surgery, invasive tests or procedures, and dental work. A 2003 study reported that preventive antibiotics are underused in people with congenital cardiovascular defects, possibly because they

KEY TERMS

Aneurysm—A weakened area in the wall of a blood vessel which causes an outpouching or bulge. Aneurysms may be fatal if these weak areas burst, resulting in uncontrollable bleeding.

Aorta—The main artery located above the heart that pumps oxygenated blood out into the body. The aorta is the largest artery in the body.

Arteriosclerosis—A chronic condition characterized by thickening, loss of leasticity, and hardening of the arteries and the build-up of plaque on the arterial walls. Arteriosclerosis can slow or impair blood circulation. It includes atherosclerosis, but the two terms are often used synonymously.

Artery—A blood vessel that carries blood away from the heart to the cells, tissues, and organs of the body.

Atrial—Referring to the upper chambers of the heart.

Bacterial endocarditis—An infection caused by bacteria that enter the bloodstream and settle in the heart lining, a heart valve, or a blood vessel. People with congenital cardiovascular defects have an increased risk of developing bacterial endocarditis, so preventive antibiotics are prescribed before surgery, invasive tests or procedures, and dental work to reduce this risk.

Coarctation of the aorta—A congenital defect in which severe narrowing or constriction of the aorta obstructs the flow of blood.

Congenital—Present at birth.

Cyanotic—Marked by a bluish tinge to the skin that occurs when the blood oxygen level drops too low. It is one of the types of congenital heart disease.

Ductus—The blood vessel that joins the pulmonary artery and the aorta. When the ductus does not close at birth, it causes a type of congenital heart disease called patent ductus arteriosus.

Echocardiogram—A record of the internal structures of the heart obtained from beams of ultrasonic waves directed through the wall of the chest.

Electrocardiagram (ECG, EKG)—A record of the electrical activity of the heart, with each wave being labeled as P, Q, R, S, and T waves. It is often used in the diagnosis of cases of abnormal cardiac rhythm and myocardial damage.

Hypertension—Abnormally high arterial blood pressure, which if left untreated can lead to heart disease and stroke.

Hypoplastic—Refers to incomplete or underdeveloped tissues or organs. Hypoplastic left heart syndrome is the most serious type of congenital heart disease.

Nuchal translucency—A pocket of fluid at the back of an embryo's neck, visible via ultrasound. When this pocket of fluid is thickened, it may indicate that the infant will be born with a congenital cardiovascular defect.

Renal artery stenosis—A disorder in which the arteries that supply blood to the kidneys are narrowed or constricted.

Septal—Relating to the septum, the thin muscle wall dividing the right and left sides of the heart. Holes in the septum are called septal defects.

Stenosis—A condition in which an opening or passageway in the body is narrowed or constricted.

Ventricles—The lower pumping chambers of the heart. The ventricles push blood to the lungs and the rest of the body.

do not understand their increased risk of developing bacterial endocarditis.

Parental concerns

If the child needs surgery, it is important for him or her to be as healthy as possible for the operation. If the child has a fever, **cough**, or cold, the parent should inform the surgical team to determine if the procedure should be delayed. The medical team can help parents prepare the child for surgery, and provide information on how to explain the procedure, based on the child's age, ability to understand, and emotions. The child usually stays in the hospital from five to seven days after surgery and returns to normal activities within four to six weeks.

Most children with congenital cardiovascular defects can be fully active and are encouraged to exercise. A scientific statement by the American Heart Association advises children and teens with genetic heart disease to seek advice from their doctors about the types of physical activities that are safe. The statement was intended to help doctors counsel patients who have an increased risk of sudden cardiac death during physical activity. With some congenital cardiovascular defects, certain athletic activities such as competitive **sports** may be limited, depending on the child's diagnosis and medical condition. Since a child with congenital cardiovascular defects may tire easily, frequent breaks and rest periods should be encouraged, as needed, during activities. Parents should obtain a doctor's note to explain their child's specific exercise limitations. This information should be shared with all teachers and coaches.

Even though most children with congenital cardiovascular defects do not have any mental limitations, some children with congenital cardiovascular defects have developmental delays or other learning difficulties. Therefore, community and school-based resources are important for these children to achieve optimum functioning.

A child with a congenital cardiovascular defect has a greater adulthood risk of having a child with a cardiovascular defect. The frequency of disease increases from less than 1 percent in the general population to 2–20 percent when a parent is affected. Defects such as coarctation of the aorta and aortic valve stenosis have the greatest risk of occurring in the child's offspring. Genetic counseling and further testing, such as chromosome analysis before pregnancy or **amniocentesis** during pregnancy, may be recommended in adults with congenital cardiovascular defects.

Treatment and care for a child with congenital cardiovascular defects can be costly, and some health insurance plans may not cover all the expenses associated with a child's **hospitalization** or surgery. Help is available to cover medical expenses. The parents can discuss financial aid with the hospital. Some organizations, including The Heart of a Child Foundation and Little Hearts on the Mend Fund, provide financial assistance to children in need of heart surgery.

Caring for a child with congenital cardiovascular defects is demanding. Support groups are available to help parents and caregivers cope with these challenges. It is important for parents to take care of themselves, too, by eating properly, exercising regularly, taking care of personal hygiene, keeping in contact with friends and family members for support, and managing stress by practicing relaxation techniques.

See also Atrial septal defect.

Resources

BOOKS

Friedman, William F., and John S. Child. "Disorders of the Cardiovascular System." In *Harrison's Principles of Internal Medicine*. Dennis L. Kasper, et al. New York: McGraw Hill, July, 2004.

"If Your Child Has A Congenital Heart Defect." In *Heart Diseases and Disorders Sourcebook.*, 2nd ed. Karen Bellenir and Peter D. Dresser, eds. Detroit: Omnigraphics, Inc., 2000.

McGoon, Michael D., ed. and Bernard J. Gersh, MD.*Mayo Clinic Heart Book: The Ultimate Guide to Heart Health.* 2nd ed. New York: William Morrow and Co., Inc., 2000.

Topol, Eric J., MD. "Pediatric and Congenital Heart Diseases." In *Cleveland Clinic Heart Book: The Definitive Guide for the Entire Family from the Nation's Leading Heart Center*. New York: Hyperion, 2000.

Trout, Darrell, and Ellen Welch.*Surviving with Heart: Taking Charge of Your Heart Care*. Colorado: Fulcrum Publishing, 2002.

Wild, C. L., and M. J. Neary. *Heart Defects in Children: What Every Parent Should Know*. Minneapolis, MN: Chronimed Publishing, 2000.

PERIODICALS

"AEP Underused for Congenital Heart Disease Patients." *Heart Disease Weekly* (Aug. 31, 2003): 23.

"New Insight Offered into the Genetics of Congenital Heart Disease." *Heart Disease Weekly* (Oct. 12, 2003): 3.

ORGANIZATIONS

Adult Congenital Heart Association (ACHA). 1500 Sunday Dr., Suite 102, Raleigh NC 27607-5151. (919) 861-4547. Web site: <www.achaheart.org>.

American College of Cardiology. Heart House. 9111 Old Georgetown Rd., Bethesda, MD 20814-1699. (800) 253-4636 ext. 694 or (301) 897-5400. Web site: <www.acc.org>.

American Heart Association. 7320 Greenville Ave., Dallas, TX 75231-4596. (214) 373-6300 or (800) 242-8721. Web site: <www.americanheart.org/children>.

Children's Heart Services. P.O. Box 8275, Bartlett, IL 60108-8275. (630) 415-0282. Web site: <www.childrensheartservices.org>.

The Cleveland Clinic Heart Center. The Cleveland Clinic Foundation, 9500 Euclid Ave., F25, Cleveland, Ohio, 44195. (800) 223-2273 ext. 46697 or (216) 444-6697. Web site: <www.clevelandclinic.org/heartcenter>.

Congenital Heart Disease Information and Resources. 1561 Clark Dr., Yardley, PA 19067. Web site: <www.tchin.org>.

The Heart of a Child Foundation and Little Hearts on the Mend Fund. Provides financial assistance to children in need of heart surgery. 26710 Fond Du Lac Rd., Rancho Palos

Verdes, CA 90275. (310) 375-6617. Web sites: <www.heartofachild.org> and <www.littleheartsonthemend.org>.

Heart Support of America. 4873 N. Broadway, Knoxville, TN 37918. Web site: <www.heartsupport.com>.

International Children's Heart Foundation. 1750 Madison, Suite 100, Memphis, TN 38104. (877) 869-4243. Web site: <www.babyhearts.com>.

Mended Little Hearts. Support program for parents of children with cardiovascular defects. (888)-HEART99. Web site: <www.mendedhearts.org/MLH/mlh.htm>.

National Heart, Lung and Blood Institute. P.O. Box 30105, Bethesda, MD 20824-0105. (301) 251-1222. Web site: <www.nhlbi.nih.gov>.

Texas Heart Institute. Heart Information Service. P.O. Box 20345, Houston, TX 77225-0345. Web site: <www.tmc.edu/thi>.

WEB SITES

HeartCenterOnline. Available online at: <www.heartcenteronline.com>.

The Heart: An Online Exploration. Developed by The Franklin Institute Science Museum with support from Unisys Corporation. The Franklin Institute Science Museum. 222 N. 20th St., Philadelphia, PA, 19103. (215) 448-1200. Available online at: <http://sln2.fi.edu/biosci/heart.html>.

Heart Information Network. Available online at: <www.heartinfo.org>.

Melissa Knopper
Teresa G. Odle
Angela M. Costello

Congenital hip dysplasia

Definition

Congenital hip dysplasia is a condition of abnormal development of the hip, resulting in hip joint instability and potential dislocation of the thigh bone from the socket in the pelvis. This condition has been in the early 2000s been termed developmental hip dysplasia, because it often develops over the first few weeks, months, or years of life.

Description

Congenital hip dysplasia is a disorder in children that is either present at birth or shortly thereafter. During gestation, the infant's hip should be developing with the head of the thigh bone (femur) sitting perfectly centered in its shallow socket (acetabulum). The acetabulum should cover the head of the femur as if it were a ball sitting inside of a cup. In the event of congenital hip dysplasia, the development of the acetabulum in an infant allows the femoral head to ride upward out of the joint socket, especially when the infant begins to walk.

Demographics

In the United States, approximately 1.5 percent of all infants have congenital hip dysplasia. Though the worldwide incidence of congenital hip dysplasia varies, researchers estimate the global incidence to be approximately 1 percent.

Clinical studies show a familial tendency toward hip dysplasia with a greater chance of this hip abnormality in the first born compared to the second or third child. Infants with siblings who have been diagnosed with congenital hip dysplasia or who have parents with the defect are at an increased risk. Females are affected four to eight times more than males, and in children with congenital hip dysplasia, the left leg in more often affected. This disorder is found in many cultures around the world. However, statistics show that infants in colder climates have a higher incidence. It is speculated that this increase may be due to the practice of swaddling which can place the infant's legs in an extreme straightened or adducted position, forcing the hips closer together. The incidence of congenital hip dysplasia is also higher in infants born by cesarean and in breech position births.

Causes and symptoms

Hormonal changes within the mother during pregnancy result in increased ligament looseness or laxity and are thought to possibly cross over the placenta and cause the baby to have lax ligaments while still in the womb. Other symptoms of complete dislocation include a shortening of the leg and limited ability to abduct the leg, or move it outward.

Diagnosis

Because the abnormalities of this hip problem often vary, a thorough physical examination is necessary for an accurate diagnosis of congenital hip dysplasia. The hip disorder can be diagnosed by moving the hip to determine if the head of the femur is moving in and out of the hip joint. One specific method, called the Ortolani test, begins with each of the examiner's hands around the infant's knees, with the second and third fingers pointing down the child's thigh. With the legs abducted (moved apart), the examiner may be able to hear a distinct clicking sound, called a hip click, with motion. If symptoms are present with a noted increase in abduction, the test is considered positive for hip joint instability. It is important to note this test is only valid a few weeks after birth.

The Barlow method is another test performed with the infant's hip brought together with knees in full bent position. The examiner's middle finger is placed over the outside of the hipbone while the thumb is placed on the inner side of the knee. The hip is abducted to where it can be felt if the hip is sliding out and then back in the joint. In older babies, if there is a lack of range of motion in one hip or even both hips, it is possible that the movement is blocked because the hip has dislocated and the muscles have contracted in that position. Also in older infants, hip dislocation may be present if one leg looks shorter than the other.

X-ray films can be helpful in detecting abnormal findings of the hip joint. **X rays** may also be helpful in finding the proper positioning of the hip joint for treatment. Ultrasound has been noted as a safe and effective tool for the diagnosis of congenital hip dysplasia. Ultrasound has advantages over x rays, as several positions are noted during the ultrasound procedure. This is in contrast to only one position observed during the x ray.

Treatment

The objective of treatment is to replace the head of the femur into the acetabulum and, by applying constant pressure, to enlarge and deepen the socket. In the past, stabilization was achieved by placing rolled cotton diapers or a pillow between the thighs. The child may be dressed in two or three diapers, called double or triple diapering. Both these techniques keep the knees in a frog-like position. In the early 2000s, the Pavlik harness and von Rosen splint are commonly used in infants up to the age of six months to spread the legs apart and force the head of the femur into the acetabulum. A stiff shell cast, called a splint, may be also used to achieve the same purpose. In some cases, older children between six to 18 months old may need surgery to reposition the joint. Also at this age, the use of closed manipulation may be applied successfully, by moving the leg around manually to replace the joint. Operations are performed to reduce the dislocation of the hip and to repair a defect in the acetabulum. A cast is applied after the operation to hold the head of the femur in the correct position. As of 2004 the use of a home traction program was more common. However, after the child is eight years of age, surgical procedures are primarily done for **pain** reduction

measures only. Total hip surgeries may be inevitable later in adulthood.

Alternative treatment

Nonsurgical treatments include **exercise** programs, orthosis (a force system, often involving braces), and medications. A physical therapist may develop a program that includes strengthening, range-of-motion exercises, pain control, and functional activities. Chiropractic medicine may be helpful, especially the procedures of closed manipulations, to reduce the dislocated hip joint.

Prognosis

Unless corrected soon after birth, congenital hip dysplasia can cause a characteristic limp or waddling gait in children. If left untreated, the child will have difficulty walking and may experience life-long pain. If diagnosed early, congenital hip dysplasia treatment is highly effective. Children who have received casting, bracing, or surgery, usually go on to have normal hip and leg development. In individuals for whom the diagnosis is made later, the prognosis is not as positive. These children may require more extensive surgery. After surgery, however, the prognosis for normal development of the hip and leg is excellent.

Prevention

Prevention includes proper prenatal care to determine the position of the baby in the womb. This may be helpful in preparing for possible breech births associated with hip problems. Avoiding excessive and prolonged infant hip adduction, or forcing the legs in a straight position close together for periods of time (as in swaddling) may help prevent strain on the hip joints. Early diagnosis remains an important part of prevention of congenital hip dysplasia.

Parental concerns

It is important for infants suspected of having congenital hip dysplasia to receive regular physical examinations. Since this disorder of the hip is progressive and early detection and treatment are essential, the American Academy of Pediatrics has suggested guidelines for examination and treatment of children suspected of having development hip dysplasia. They suggest referral to a pediatric orthopedist if an infant has a positive Ortolani or Barlow test. For infants with mild hip clicks, they suggest the child be seen by the regular pediatrician in two weeks for follow up since most benign hip clicks will resolve within that time period. If signs of hip dysplasia

KEY TERMS

Abduction—Turning away from the body.

Acetabulum—The large cup-shaped cavity at the junction of pelvis and femur (thigh bone).

Adduction—Movement toward the body.

Bracing—Using orthopedic devices to hold joints or limbs in place.

Dislocation—The displacement of bones at a joint or the displacement of any part of the body from its normal position.

Dysplasia—Abnormal changes in cells.

Femur—The thigh bone.

Orthosis—An external device, such as a splint or a brace, that prevents or assists movement.

Placenta—The organ that provides oxygen and nutrition from the mother to the unborn baby during pregnancy. The placenta is attached to the wall of the uterus and leads to the unborn baby via the umbilical cord.

Splint—A thin piece of rigid or flexible material that is used to restrain, support, or immobilize a part of the body while healing takes place.

---

are still present after two weeks, it is recommended that the child be seen by a pediatric orthopedist. If double or triple diapering is recommended by the pediatrician after the initial newborn exam, it is imperative that parents follow up with their pediatrician for a more extensive examination of the hips soon after the newborn comes home.

Resources

BOOKS

Rudolph, Colin D., and Abraham M. Rudolph, eds. *Rudolph's Pediatrics*, 21st ed. New York: McGraw-Hill, 2003.

ORGANIZATIONS

March of Dimes Birth Defects Foundation. 1275 Mamaroneck Ave., White Plains, NY 10605. Web site: <www.modimes.org>.

WEB SITES

American Academy of Pediatrics, Committee on Quality Improvement, Subcommittee on Developmental Dysplasia of the Hip. "Clinical Practice Guideline: Early Detection of Developmental Dysplasia of the Hip (AC0001)." *Pediatrics* 105, no. 4 (April 2000): 896–905. Available online at <www.aap.org/policy/ac0001.htm> (accessed December 8, 2004).

Norton, Karen I., and Sandra A. Mitre. "Developmental Dysplasia of the Hip." *eMedicine*, April 22, 2003. Available online at <www.emedicine.com/radio/topic212.htm> (accessed December 8, 2004).

Jeffrey P. Larson, RPT
Deborah L. Nurmi, MS

Congenital hypothyroidism *see* **Hypothyroidism**

Congenital megacolon *see* **Hirschsprung's disease**

Congenital thymic hypoplasia *see* **DiGeorge syndrome**

Congenital ureter anomalies

Definition

The ureter drains urine from the kidney into the bladder. Not simply a tube, the ureter is an active organ that propels urine forward by muscular action. It has a valve at its bottom end that prevents urine from flowing backward into the kidney. Normally there is one ureter on each side of the body for each kidney. However, among the many abnormalities of ureteral development, duplication is quite common. Ureters may also be malformed in a variety of ways—some harmful, others not.

Description

There are many different types of ureter anomalies. Ureters can be duplicated completely or partially, they can be in the wrong place, they can be deformed, and they can end in the wrong place. The trouble these abnormalities bring is directly related to their effect on the flow of urine. As long as urine flows normally through them, and only in one direction, no harm is done. A description of ureter anomalies follows.

Duplication of ureters is quite common, either in part or completely. Kidneys are sometimes duplicated as well. Someone may have four kidneys and four ureters or two kidneys, half of each drained by a separate ureter, or a single kidney with two, three, or four ureters attached. As long as urine can flow easily in the correct direction, such malformations may never be detected. If, however, one of the ureters has a dead end, a stricture or stenosis (narrowing), or a leaky ureterovesical valve (between the ureter and bladder), infection is the likely result.

Stricture or stenosis of a ureter prevents urine from flowing freely. Whenever flow is obstructed in the body—urine, bile, mucus, or any other liquid—infection follows. Ureters can be obstructed anywhere along their course, though the ureterovesical valve is the most common place.

A ureter may have an ectopic (out-of-place) orifice (opening): it may enter the bladder, or even another structure, where it does not belong and therefore lack an adequate valve to control reflux.

The primary ureter, or a duplicate, may not even reach the bladder, but rather terminate in a dead end. Urine will stagnate there and eventually cause infection.

A ureter can be perfectly normal but in the wrong place, such as behind the vena cava (retrocaval ureter), the large vein in the middle of the abdomen. In this case the ureter may be pinched by the vena cava so that flow is hindered. Other abnormal locations may also lead to compression and impaired flow.

Besides infection, urine that backs up causes the ureter and the kidney to expand or dilate. Eventually, the kidney stops functioning because of the back pressure. This condition is called hydronephrosis (a kidney swollen with urine).

Demographics

The urogenital system is more likely than any other organ system to have birth defects, and they can occur in endless variety. Congenital ureter anomalies affect as many as one in every 160 individuals.

Causes and symptoms

In general, the causes of birth defects are multiple and often as of 2004 unknown. Furthermore, the precise cause of specific birth defects has only rarely been identified. Such is the case with congenital ureteral anomalies.

Practically the only symptom generated by ureteral abnormalities is urinary tract infection. A lower tract infection, in the bladder, is called **cystitis**. In children it may cause **fever** and systemic symptoms, but in adults it causes only cloudy, burning, and frequent urine. Upper tract infections, by contrast, can be serious for both adults and children, causing high fevers, back **pain**, severe generalized discomfort, and even leading to kidney failure or septicemia (infection spreading throughout the body by way of the blood stream).

In rare cases, urine from an ectopic ureter will bypass the bladder and dribble out of the bottom somewhere, through a natural orifice like the vagina or a completely separate unnatural opening.

KEY TERMS

Congenital—Present at birth.

Contrast agent—Also called a contrast medium, this is usually a barium or iodine dye that is injected into the area under investigation. The dye makes the interior body parts more visible on an x-ray film.

Cystoscopy—A diagnostic procedure in which a hollow lighted tube (cystoscope) is used to look inside the bladder and the urethra.

Ectopic—Out of place or located away from the normal position.

Retrocaval ureter—A ureter that is located behind the vena cava blood vessel.

Septicemia—A systemic infection due to the presence of bacteria and their toxins in the bloodstream. Septicemia is sometimes called blood poisoning.

Ureterovesical valve—A sphincter (an opening controlled by a circular muscle), located where the ureter enters the bladder, that keeps urine from flowing backward toward the kidney.

Urogenital—Refers to both the urinary system and the sexual organs, which form together in the developing embryo.

Diagnosis

For children experiencing serious or recurrent urinary tract infections, the pediatrician will search for underlying abnormalities. Cystoscopy (looking into the bladder with a thin telescope-like instrument) and **x rays** with a contrast agent to illuminate the urinary system will usually identify the defect. **Computed tomography** scans (CT) and **magnetic resonance imaging** (MRI) may provide additional information. Urine cultures to identify the infecting germs will be repeated frequently until the problem is corrected.

Treatment

Sometimes the recurring infections caused by flow abnormalities can be treated with repeated and changing courses of **antibiotics**. Over time, the infecting germs develop resistance to most treatments, especially the safer ones. If it can be done safely, it is better to repair the defect surgically. Urologists have various approaches to urine drainage that range from simply reimplanting a ureter into the bladder, in such a way that an effective valve is created, to building a new bladder out of a piece of bowel.

Alternative treatment

There are botanical and homeopathic treatments available for urinary tract infection. None can take the place of correcting a problem that is occurring because of a malformed or dysfunctional organ system. Once correction of the cause is addressed and there is unimpeded flow of urine, adequate fluid intake can contribute to prevention of future infections.

Prognosis

As long as damage to the kidneys from infection or back pressure has not become significant, the surgical repair of troublesome ureteral defects produces excellent long-term results in the great majority of cases. Monitoring for recurrent infections is always a good idea, and occasional checking of kidney function will detect hidden ongoing damage.

Prevention

The cause of congenital ureter anomalies is not known. There is no prevention.

Resources

BOOKS

Colberg, John W. "Urologic Abnormalities of the Genitourinary Tract." Chapter 21, section 16, in *Rudolph's Pediatrics*, 21st ed. Edited by Colin D. Rudolph and Abraham M. Rudolph. New York: McGraw-Hill, 2003, pp. 1735–39.

Joffre, F., et al. *Radiological Imaging of the Ureter*. Secaucus, NJ: Springer, 2003.

ORGANIZATIONS

American Association of Clinical Urologists. 1111 N. Plaza Dr., Suite 550, Schaumberg, IL 60173. Web site: <www.aacu.web.org/>.

WEB SITES

"Congenital Ureter Anomalies." *Dr. Joseph F. Smith Medical Library*. Available online at <www.chclibrary.org/micromed/00043640.html> (accessed December 9, 2004).

"Genitourinary Tract." *Pediatrics.* Available online at <http://pediatrics.aappublications.org/cgi/collection/gynourinary_tract> (accessed December 9, 2004).

J. Ricker Polsdorfer, MD
Deborah L. Nurmi, MS

Conjunctivitis

Definition

Conjuctivitis is an inflammation resulting in redness of the lining of the white part of the eye and the underside of the eyelid (conjunctiva) that can be caused by infection, allergic reaction, or physical agents like infrared or ultraviolet light.

Description

Conjunctivitis is the inflammation of the conjunctiva, a thin, delicate membrane that covers the eyeball and lines the eyelid. Conjunctivitis is an extremely common eye disease because the conjunctiva is continually exposed to microorganisms and environmental agents that can cause infections or allergic reactions. Conjunctivitis can be acute or chronic depending on how long the condition lasts, the severity of symptoms, and the type of organism or agent involved. It can affect one or both eyes and, if caused by infection, can be very easily transmitted to others during close physical contact, particularly among children in a school or daycare setting. Other names for conjunctivitis include pink eye and red eye.

Demographics

Conjunctivitis is the most common eye infection of childhood. It occurs so frequently that records are not kept, so exact demographic information has not been amassed.

Causes and symptoms

Conjunctivitis may be caused by a viral infection, such as a cold; acute respiratory infection; or other disease such as **measles**, **herpes simplex**, or herpes zoster. Symptoms include mild to severe discomfort in one or both eyes; redness; swelling of the eyelids; and watery, yellow, or green discharge. Symptoms may last anywhere from several days to two weeks. Infection with an adenovirus, however, may also cause a significant amount of pus-like discharge and a scratchy, foreign-body-sensation in the eye. These symptoms may be accompanied by swelling and tenderness of the lymph nodes near the ear.

Bacterial conjunctivitis can occur in adults and children and is caused by organisms such as *Staphylococcus*, *Streptococcus*, and *Hemophilus*. Symptoms of bacterial conjunctivitis include a pus-like discharge and crusty eyelids after awakening. Redness of the conjunctiva can be mild to severe and may be accompanied by swelling.

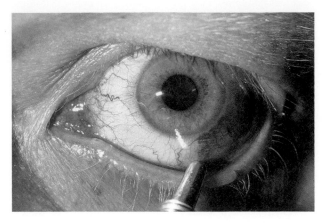

An antibotic eye ointment is applied to relieve bacterial conjunctivitis. *(© T. Bannor/Custom Stock Medical Photo, Inc.)*

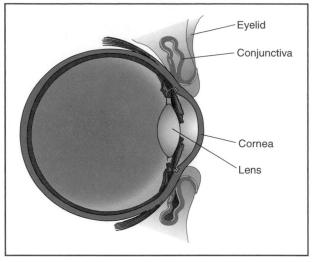

Eyelid

Conjunctiva

Cornea

Lens

Conjunctivitis is the inflammation of the conjunctiva, a thin, delicate membrane that covers the eyeball and lines the eyelid. It may be caused by a viral infection, such as a cold or acute respiratory infection, or by such diseases as measles, herpes simplex, or herpes zoster. *(Illustration by Electronic Illustrators Group.)*

Persons with symptoms of conjunctivitis who are sexually active may possibly be infected with the bacteria that cause either gonorrhea or chlamydia. There may be large amounts of pus-like discharge, and symptoms may include intolerance to light (photophobia), watery mucus discharge, and tenderness in the lymph nodes near the ear that may persist for up to three months.

Conjunctivitis may also be caused by environmental hazards, such as wind, smoke, dust, and allergic reactions caused by pollen, dust, or grass. Symptoms range from **itching** and redness to a mucus discharge. Persons who wear **contact lenses** may develop allergic conjunctivitis caused by various eye solutions used and the foreign proteins contained in them.

Other less common causes of conjunctivitis include exposure to sun lamps or the electrical arcs used during welding and problems with inadequate drainage of the tear ducts.

Diagnosis

An accurate diagnosis of conjunctivitis centers on taking a patient's history to learn what symptoms are being experienced, when symptoms began, and other predisposing factors, such as upper respiratory complaints, **allergies**, **sexually transmitted diseases**, herpes simplex infections, and exposure to persons with pink eye. It may be helpful to learn whether an aspect of an individual's occupation may be the cause, for example, welding. Diagnostic tests are usually not indicated unless initial treatment fails or an infection with gonorrhea or chlamydia is suspected. In such cases, the discharge may be cultured and tested to determine the organism responsible for causing the condition.

Treatment

The treatment of conjunctivitis depends on what caused the condition. In all cases, warm compresses applied to the affected eye several times a day may help to reduce discomfort.

Conjunctivitis due to a viral infection, particularly those due to adenoviruses, are usually treated by applying warm compresses to the affected area and using topical antibiotic ointments to prevent secondary bacterial infections.

Viral conjunctivitis caused by herpes simplex should be referred to an ophthalmologist. Topical steroids are commonly prescribed in combination with antiviral therapy.

In cases of bacterial conjunctivitis, a physician may prescribe an antibiotic eye ointment or eye drops containing sodium sulfacetamide (Sulamyd) to be applied daily for seven to 14 days. If, after 72 hours, the condition does not improve, a physician or primary care provider should be notified, because the bacteria involved may be resistant to the antibiotic used or the cause may not be bacterial.

For cases of conjunctivitis caused by a gonococcal organism, a physician may prescribe an intramuscular injection of ceftriaxone (Rocephin) and a topical antibiotic ointment containing erythromycin or bactracin to be applied four times daily for two to three weeks. Sexual partners should also be treated.

With accompanying chlamydia infection, a topical antibiotic ointment containing erythromycin (Ilotycin) may be prescribed to be applied one to two times daily. In addition, oral erythromycin or tetracycline therapy

KEY TERMS

Adenovirus—A type of virus that can cause upper respiratory tract infections.

Chlamydia—The most common bacterial sexually transmitted disease in the United States. It often accompanies gonorrhea and is known for its lack of evident symptoms in the majority of women.

Gonococcal—Refers to the bacterium *Neisseria gonorrheae*. This bacterium causes gonorrhea, a sexually transmitted infection of the genitals and urinary tract. The gonococcal organism may occasionally affect the eye, causing blindness if not treated.

Herpes simplex virus—A virus that can cause fever and blistering on the skin and mucous membranes. Herpes simplex 1 infections usually occur on the face (cold sores) and herpes simplex 2 infections usually occur in the genital region.

Herpes zoster virus—Acute inflammatory virus that attacks the nerve cells on the root of each spinal nerve with skin eruptions along a sensory nerve ending. It causes chickenpox and shingles. Also called varicella zoster virus.

Staphylococcus—Any of several species of spherical bacteria that occur in groups of four or in irregular clusters. They can infect various parts of the body, especially the skin and mucous membranes.

Streptococcus—Plural, streptococci. Any of several species of spherical bacteria that form pairs or chains. They cause a wide variety of infections including scarlet fever, tonsillitis, and pneumonia.

may be indicated for three to four weeks. Again, sexual partners should also be treated.

Allergic conjunctivitis can be treated by removing the allergic substance from a person's environment, if possible; by applying cool compresses to the eye; and by administering eye drops four to six times daily for four days. Also, the antihistamine diphenhydramine hydrochloride (Benadryl) may help to relieve itchy eyes.

Prognosis

If treated properly, the prognosis for conjunctivitis is good. Conjunctivitis caused by an allergic reaction should clear up once the allergen is removed. However, allergic conjunctivitis will likely recur if the individual again comes into contact with the particular allergen. Conjunctivitis caused by bacteria or a virus, if treated properly, is usually resolved in ten to 14 days. If there is no relief of symptoms in 48 to 72 hours, or there is moderate to severe eye **pain**, changes in vision, or the conjunctivitis is suspected to be caused by herpes simplex, a physician should be notified immediately. If untreated or if treatment fails and is not corrected, conjunctivitis may cause visual impairment by spreading to other parts of the eye, such as the cornea.

Prevention

Conjunctivitis can, in many cases, be prevented, or at least the course of the disease can be shortened by following these simple practices:

- frequently washing hands with antiseptic soap and using single-use towels while the disease continues

- avoiding chemical irritants and known allergens

- in an area where welding occurs, using the proper protective eye wear and screens to prevent damaging the eyes

- using a clean tissue to remove discharge from eyes and washing hands to prevent the spread of infection

- if medication is prescribed, finishing the course of **antibiotics**, as directed, to make sure that the infection is cleared up and does not recur

- avoiding close contact, such as vigorous physical activities, with other persons until symptoms resolve

Resources

BOOKS

"Disorder of the Conjunctiva." In *Nelson Textbook of Pediatrics.* Edited by Richard E. Behrman et al. Philadelphia: Saunders, 2004.

Weiss, Avery H. "Conjunctivitis Beyond the Neonatal Period." In *Principles and Practice of Pediatric Infectious Diseases*, 2nd ed. Edited by Sarah S. Long et al. St. Louis, MO: Elsevier, 2003.

WEB SITES

Silverman, Michael A., et al. "Conjunctivitis." *eMedicine*, October 12, 2004. Available online at <www.emedicine.com/emerg/topic110.htm> (accessed December 25, 2004).

Lisa Papp, RN
Rosalyn Carson-DeWitt, MD

Constipation

Definition

Constipation is an acute or chronic condition in which bowel movements occur less often than usual or consist of hard, dry stools that are painful or difficult to pass. Although constipation is a relative term, with normal patterns of bowel movements varying widely from person to person, generally an adult who has not had a bowel movement in three days or a child who has not had a bowel movement in four days is considered constipated. Infants who are still exclusively breastfed may go seven days without a stool.

Description

The colon (the large intestine) absorbs water while forming waste products (the stool) from digested food. Muscle contractions in the colon (peristalsis) push the stool toward the rectum. By the time the stool reaches the rectum, it is solid because most of the water has been absorbed. However, hard, dry stools and constipation occur when too much water is absorbed by the colon from the stool, which can result from the muscle of the colon contracting too slowly. Constipation is also referred to as irregularity of bowels or lack of regular bowel movements.

Constipation can occur at any age and is more common among individuals who resist the urge to move their bowels at their body's signal. This often happens when children start school or enter daycare. They may feel shy about asking permission to use the bathroom, they may be involved in more enjoyable activities and may not want to stop, or they may be rushed when using the bathroom and not have time to complete the bowel movement. Once constipation has developed and bowel movements become painful or more difficult, the child will attempt to go even less often, and the constipation will worsen.

Although this condition is rarely serious, it can lead to the following:

- tearing of the mucosal membrane of the anus (especially in children), which can cause bleeding and the development of an anal fissure

- bowel obstruction

- chronic constipation

- hemorrhoids (a mass of dilated veins in swollen tissue around the anus)

- hernia (a protrusion of an organ through a tear in the muscle wall)

- spastic colitis (**irritable bowel syndrome**, a condition characterized by alternating periods of **diarrhea** and constipation)

- laxative dependency

Less commonly, chronic constipation may be a symptom of colorectal **cancer**, depression, diabetes, diverticulosis (small pouches in the muscles of the large intestine), **lead poisoning**, or Parkinson's disease (in adults) and should be investigated by a doctor.

Demographics

Constipation is a common complaint in children, occurring in up to 10 percent of youngsters. It accounts for approximately 3 percent of pediatric outpatient visits and 25 percent of visits to a pediatric gastroenterologist.

Causes and symptoms

Constipation usually results from not getting enough **exercise**, not drinking enough fluids (especially water), delays in going to the bathroom when there is the urge to defecate, or from a diet that does not include an adequate amount of fiber-rich foods such as beans, bran cereals, fruits, raw vegetables, rice, and whole-grain breads. Eating too many dairy products such as milk, cheese, yogurt, and ice cream may also result in harder stools. Constipation in children often occurs when they hold back bowel movements for various reasons, such as when they are not ready for **toilet training** or are afraid of toilet training.

Other less common causes of constipation include anal fissure (a tear or crack in the lining of the anus); chronic kidney failure; colon or rectal cancer; depression; hypercalcemia (abnormally high levels of calcium in the blood); **hypothyroidism** (underactive thyroid gland); illness requiring complete bed rest; and irritable bowel syndrome. Stress and travel can also contribute to constipation, as well as other changes in bowel habits.

Constipation can also be a side effect of the use of the following medications, many of which are not commonly used by children:

- aluminum salts in antacids

- antihistamines

- antipsychotic drugs

- aspirin

- belladonna (*Atopa belladonna,* a source of atropine, a medication used to relieve spasms and dilate the pupils of the eye)

- beta blockers (medications used to stabilize irregular heartbeat, lower high blood pressure, and reduce chest **pain**)

- blood pressure medications

- calcium channel blockers (medication prescribed to treat high blood pressure, chest pain, some types of irregular heartbeat and **stroke**, and some non-cardiac diseases)

- diuretics (drugs that promote the formation and secretion of urine)

- iron or calcium supplements

- narcotics (potentially addictive drugs that relieve pain and cause mood changes)

- tricyclic **antidepressants** (medications prescribed to treat chronic pain, depression, headaches, and other illnesses)

A child who is constipated may feel bloated, have a **headache**, swollen abdomen, or pass rock-like feces; or strain, bleed, or feel pain during bowel movements. A constipated baby may strain, cry, draw the legs toward the abdomen, or arch the back when having a bowel movement. Newborns and young infants may also strain, turn red in the face, grunt and draw legs up when passing normal, soft stool. If the stool is not hard (rabbit pellet in consistency), then these infants are not considered constipated.

When to call the doctor

Most people become constipated once in a while, but a doctor should be contacted if significant changes in bowel patterns last for more than a week or if symptoms continue more than three weeks after increasing activity and fiber and fluid intake.

In addition, a doctor should be called if an infant younger than two months is constipated, or if an infant (except those that are exclusively breastfed) goes three days without a stool. If **vomiting** or irritability is also present, then the doctor should be called immediately. A doctor should also be consulted if a child is holding back bowel movements (in order to resist toilet training) or whenever constipation occurs after starting a new prescription, vitamin, or mineral supplement or is accompanied by blood in the stools, changes in bowel patterns, **fever**, and rectal or abdominal pain.

Diagnosis

The child's symptoms and medical history help a primary care physician to diagnose constipation. The doctor uses his fingers to see if there is a hardened mass in the abdomen and may perform a rectal examination.

Other diagnostic procedures include a barium enema, which reveals blockage inside the intestine; laboratory analysis of blood and stool samples for internal bleeding or other symptoms of systemic disease; and a sigmoidoscopy (examination of the sigmoid area of the colon with a flexible tube equipped with a magnifying lens).

Treatment

Constipation is usually a temporary problem in children and no cause for concern. A child with constipation should be instructed to drink an adequate amount of water each day (six to eight glasses), exercise on a regular basis, and eat a diet high in soluble and insoluble fibers. Soluble fibers include pectin, flax, and gums; insoluble fibers include psyllium and brans from grains like wheat and oats. Fresh fruits and vegetables contain both soluble and insoluble fibers. Dietary fiber intake should be increased gradually, along with an increase in water consumption, in order to produce soft, bulky stools.

Constipation in infants may be treated by the following:

- if over two months of age, feeding the infant 2–4 ounces (60–120 ml) of fruit juice (grape, pear, apple, cherry, or prune) twice a day

- if over four months of age and the infant has begun solid foods, feeding the baby foods with high fiber content (such as peas, beans, apricots, prunes, peaches, pears, plums, and spinach) twice a day

If changes in diet and activity fail to relieve occasional constipation, an over-the-counter laxative may be used for a few days. Preparations that soften stools or add bulk (bran, psyllium) work more slowly but are safer than Epsom salts and other harsh **laxatives** or herbal laxatives containing senna (*Cassia senna*) or buckthorn (*Rhamnus purshianna*), which can harm the nerves and lining of the colon. A child who is experiencing abdominal pain, **nausea**, or vomiting should not use a laxative. Laxatives should not be used for a long period, because the child can become dependent on them.

A warm-water or mineral oil enema can relieve constipation in children with severe or stubborn cases of constipation. However, laxatives or enemas should not be given to children without instruction from a doctor.

If a child has an impacted bowel, the doctor can insert a gloved finger into the rectum and gently dislodge the hardened feces.

Alternative treatment

Castor oil, applied topically to the abdomen and covered by a heat source (a heating pad or hot water

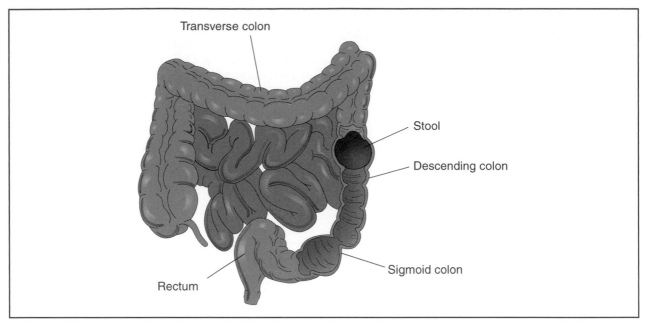

Transverse colon

Stool

Descending colon

Sigmoid colon

Rectum

Constipation is an acute or chronic condition in which bowel movements occur less often than usual or consist of hard, dry stools that are painful or difficult to pass. *(Illustration by Electronic Illustrators Group.)*

bottle) can help relieve constipation when used nightly for 20 to 30 minutes.

Acupressure

This needleless form of acupuncture is said to relax the abdomen, ease discomfort, and stimulate regular bowel movements when diet and exercise fail to do so. After lying down, the child closes his or her eyes and takes a deep breath. For two minutes, the child or parent applies gentle fingertip pressure to a point about 2.5 in (14 cm) below the navel.

Acupressure can also be applied to the outer edges of one elbow crease and maintained for 30 seconds before pressing the crease of the other elbow. This should be done three times a day to relieve constipation.

Aromatherapy

Six drops of rosemary (*Rosmarinus officinalis*) and six drops of thyme (*Thymus* spp.) diluted by one ounce of almond oil, olive oil, or another carrier oil can relieve constipation when used to massage the abdomen.

Herbal therapy

A variety of herbal therapies can be useful in the treatment of constipation. Several herbs, including chamomile (*Matricaria recutita*), dandelion (*Taraxacum mongolicum*), and burdock (*Arctium lappa*), act as bitters, stimulating the movement of the digestive and excretory systems.

Homeopathy

Homeopathy also can offer assistance with constipation. There are acute remedies for constipation that can be found in one of the many home remedy books on homeopathic medicine. A constitutional prescription also can help rebalance someone who is struggling with chronic constipation.

Massage

Massaging the leg from knee to hip in the morning, at night, and before trying to move the bowels is said to relieve constipation. There is also a specific Swedish massage technique that can help relieve constipation.

Yoga

The knee-chest position, said to relieve gas and stimulate abdominal organs, involves the following:

• standing straight with arms at the sides

• lifting the right knee toward the chest

• grasping the right ankle with the left hand

• pulling the leg as close to the chest as possible

• holding the position for about eight seconds

• repeating these steps with the left leg

The cobra position, which can be repeated as many as four time a day, involves the following:

- lying on the stomach with legs together
- placing the palms just below the shoulders, holding elbows close to the body
- inhaling, then lifting the head (face forward) and chest off the floor
- keeping the navel in contact with the floor
- looking as far upward as possible
- holding this position for three to six seconds
- exhaling and lowering the chest

Prognosis

Changes in diet and exercise can often eliminate constipation. However, childhood constipation can sometimes be difficult to treat when a child, after having a painful experience, makes a decision to resist and delay going to the bathroom. These cases often require prolonged support, explanation, and medical treatment.

Prevention

Avoiding constipation by making lifestyle changes is easier than treating it. Most American adults only consume between 11 to 18 grams of fiber a day, but to prevent constipation, consumption of 30 to 35 grams of fiber (an amount equal to five servings of fruits and vegetables, and a large bowl of high-fiber cereal) and between six and eight glasses of water each day can generally prevent constipation. A suggested goal for dietary fiber intake during childhood and **adolescence** is consumption in grams equivalent to the age of the child plus 5 grams per day.

Sitting on the toilet for 10 minutes at the same time every day, preferably after a meal, can induce regular bowel movements. This may not become effective for a few months, and it is important to defecate whenever necessary.

Fiber supplements containing psyllium (*Plantago psyllium*) usually become effective within about 48 hours and can be used every day without causing dependency. Powdered flaxseed (*Linium usitatissimum*) works the same way. Insoluble fiber, like wheat or oat bran, is as effective as psyllium but may give the child gas at first.

Parental concerns

Constipation can be a frustrating problem for both children and their parents. Parents need to work closely

---

with the doctor to determine why the child is constipated and to develop an appropriate treatment strategy.

Resources

BOOKS

Bernard, H. *The Homoeopathic Treatment of Constipation.* New Delhi, India: B. Jain Publishers Pvt. Limited, 2003.

Peiken, Steven R. *Gastrointestinal Health: The Proven Nutritional Program to Prevent, Cure, or Alleviate Irritable Bowel Syndrome (IBS), Ulcers, Gas, Constipation, Heartburn, and Many Other Digestive Disorders.* London: Harper Trade, 2005.

Whorton, James C. *Inner Hygiene: Constipation and the Pursuit of Health in Modern Society.* Collingdale, PA. DIANE Publishing Co., 2003.

WEB SITES

"Constipation." *MedlinePlus.* Available online at <www.nlm.nih.gov/medlineplus/constipation.html> (accessed December 9, 2004).

Judith Sims
Maureen Haggerty

Contact dermatitis

Definition

Contact **dermatitis** is the name for any skin inflammation that occurs when the skin's surface comes in contact with a substance originating outside the body. There are two major categories of contact dermatitis, irritant and allergic. Irritant dermatitis is essentially a direct injury to the skin, caused by such compounds as acids, alkalis, phenol, and detergents. The immune system is not involved in irritant dermatitis, and the person's skin is damaged without prior sensitization.

In allergic dermatitis, however, the patient's skin reacts to a substance to which it has become sensitized. A third type of dermatitis, photo contact dermatitis, is triggered by exposure of the skin to light following the application of certain cosmetics or chemicals. Photo contact dermatitis may be either irritant or allergic.

Description

Contact dermatitis may be either an acute or chronic skin disorder. In general, allergic contact dermatitis is more severe and acute in its onset than irritant contact dermatitis. In irritant contact dermatitis, the rash is usually limited to the area that was exposed to the substance, whereas in allergic contact dermatitis, the rash often spreads beyond the area directly exposed to the allergen. Irritant contact dermatitis most commonly affects the hands, while allergic contact dermatitis may be found on almost any part of the body, including the armpits and genitals. Allergic contact dermatitis is more likely to involve swelling of the skin and the development of small fluid-filled blisters than irritant contact dermatitis.

Photo contact dermatitis is usually limited to the area of skin exposed to direct light. If the substance that was applied to the skin was changed to an irritant by light exposure, the primary symptom is a burning sensation resembling **sunburn**. If the substance was changed to an allergen, the primary sensation is **itching**.

Demographics

Contact dermatitis is a common complaint in people of all ages, in part because of the large number of potential irritants and allergens in the contemporary environment. One textbook on contact dermatitis runs to over 1,100 pages of descriptions of the various manufactured products and other substances that can cause these skin reactions.

In the United States, contact dermatitis ranks among the top 10 reasons for visits to primary care doctors and accounts for 7 percent of all visits to dermatologists. Every year between 10 and 50 million Americans in all age groups develop an allergic rash following contact with **poison ivy** or **poison oak**.

About 20 percent of children in the general United States population develop allergic contact dermatitis at some point prior to **adolescence**. Between 20 percent and 35 percent of healthy children react to one or more allergens on standard patch tests. Children of parents with allergic contact dermatitis have a 60 percent greater chance of having a positive reaction on a patch test themselves.

Contact dermatitis is more likely to affect Caucasians than African, Asian, or Native Americans. People with fair skin and red hair are particularly susceptible to contact dermatitis.

With regard to sex, girls are twice as likely as boys to develop both irritant and allergic skin reactions.

Causes and symptoms

Irritant contact dermatitis

Irritant contact dermatitis (ICD) is the more commonly reported of the two kinds of contact dermatitis, and is seen in about 80 percent of cases. It can be caused by soaps, detergents, solvents, adhesives, fiberglass, and other substances that are able to directly injure the skin by breaking or removing the protective layers of the upper epidermis. Irritants remove lipids, which are fatty substances that help to maintain the integrity of skin cells; irritants also damage the skin's ability to hold water. A common form of irritant contact dermatitis in infants is **diaper rash**, which develops when the protective epidermal layer of the baby's skin is damaged by long periods of contact with fecal matter and urine.

Most attacks of ICD are slight and confined to the hands and forearms but can affect any part of the body that comes in contact with an irritating substance. The symptoms can take many forms: redness, itching, crusting, swelling, blistering, oozing, dryness, scaling, thickening of the skin, and a feeling of warmth at the site of contact. In extreme cases, severe blistering can occur and open sores can form. Jobs that require frequent skin exposure to water, such as hairdressing and food preparation, can make the skin more susceptible to ICD.

Thin, moist, or already damaged skin is more susceptible to ICD than thick, dry, or intact skin.

Allergic contact dermatitis

Allergic contact dermatitis (ACD) results when repeated exposure to an allergen (an allergy-causing substance) triggers an immune response that inflames the skin. There are two phases in the development of ACD: an induction phase, in which the allergen penetrates the epidermis and is processed by an antigen-presenting cell; and an elicitation phase, in which the sensitized person has a second exposure to the allergen, which produces an inflammatory response several hours or days after the second exposure. Sensitivity to the specific allergen is often lifelong.

Tens of thousands of drugs, pesticides, cosmetics, food additives, commercial chemicals, and other substances have been identified as potential allergens. Fewer than 30, however, are responsible for the majority of ACD cases. Common culprits include poison ivy, poison oak, and **poison sumac**; fragrances and preservatives in cosmetics and personal care products, such latex items as gloves and condoms; and formaldehyde. Many people find that they are allergic to the nickel in inexpensive jewelry; some adolescents find that they are allergic to the metal alloys used in orthodontic braces. ACD is usually confined to the area of skin that comes in contact with the allergen. Symptoms range from mild to severe and resemble those of ICD.

Photo contact dermatitis

In photo contact dermatitis, certain substances undergo chemical changes as a result of exposure to light that transform them into either irritants or allergens. Aftershave lotions, **sunscreens**, and certain topical sulfa drugs may be changed into allergens, while coal tar and certain oils used in manufacturing may become irritants after light exposure.

When to call the doctor

Contact dermatitis is not a medical emergency. It can often be treated at home once the irritant or allergen has been identified. A visit to the doctor may be necessary, however, in order to identify the cause(s) as well as obtain specific recommendations for treatment.

Diagnosis

Diagnosis of contact dermatitis begins with a physical examination and asking the patient questions about his or her health and daily activities. When contact dermatitis is suspected, the doctor attempts to learn as much as possible about the child or adolescent's school, **sports** participation, hobbies, favorite jewelry, use of medications and cosmetics—anything that might shed light on the source of the problem. The doctor will ask when the symptoms started, whether this is the first time they occurred, whether the rash is spreading, whether the primary sensation is itching or burning, and how severe the itching or burning feels.

In some cases, an examination of the home or school may be undertaken; in one interesting case, the doctors discovered that a rash on the back of the child's thighs was an allergic reaction to nickel in the metal parts of the chairs in the child's school. If the dermatitis is mild, responds well to treatment, and does not recur, ordinarily the investigation is at an end. More difficult cases require patch testing to identify the specific allergen.

Two methods of patch testing are used in the early 2000s. The most widely used method, the Finn chamber method, employs a multiwell aluminum patch. Each well is filled with a small amount of the allergen being tested and the patch is taped to normal skin on the patient's upper back. After 48 hours, the patch is removed and an initial reading is taken. A second reading is made a few days later.

The second method of patch testing involves applying a small amount of the test substance to directly to normal skin and covering it with a dressing that keeps air out and keeps the test substance in (occlusive dressing). After 48 hours, the dressing is taken off to see if a reaction has occurred. Identifying the allergen may require repeated testing, can take weeks or months, and is not always successful. Moreover, patch testing works only with ACD, though it is considered an essential step in ruling out ICD.

In a few cases, the doctor may take a skin biopsy in order to rule out certain infectious skin diseases.

Treatment

The best treatment for contact dermatitis is to identify the allergen or irritating substance and avoid further contact with it. If the culprit is, for instance, a cosmetic, avoidance is a simple matter, but in some situations, avoidance may be impossible or force the sufferer to make drastic changes in his or her life. Barrier creams and such protective clothing as gloves, masks, and long-sleeved shirts are coping devices to reduce the chance of contact dermatitis when avoidance is impossible, though they are not always effective.

For the symptoms themselves, treatments in mild cases include cool compresses and nonprescription lotions and ointments. Diaper rash is often treated by applying various emollient preparations that restore lipids to the child's skin. In older children and adolescents, more severe cases of contact dermatitis are treated with corticosteroids applied to the skin or taken orally. Contact dermatitis that leads to a bacterial skin infection is treated with **antibiotics**. Although **antihistamines** do not cure contact dermatitis, the doctor may prescribe them to relieve severe itching.

Alternative treatment

Herbal remedies have been used for centuries to treat skin disorders including contact dermatitis. An experienced herbalist can recommend the remedies that will be most effective for an individual's condition. Among the herbs often recommended are the following:

- Burdock (*Arctium lappa*) minimizes inflammation and boosts the immune system. It is taken internally as a tea or tincture (a concentrated herbal extract prepared with alcohol).

• Calendula (*Calendula officinalis*) is a natural antiseptic and anti-inflammatory agent. It is applied topically in a lotion, ointment, or oil to the affected area.

• Aloe (*Aloe barbadensis*) gel soothes skin irritations. The gel is applied topically to the affected area.

A homeopath treating a patient with contact dermatitis will do a thorough investigation of the individual's history and exposures before prescribing a remedy. One homeopathic remedy commonly prescribed to relieve the itching associated with contact dermatitis is *Rhus toxicodendron*, which is taken internally three to four times daily.

Poison ivy, poison oak, and poison sumac are common culprits in cases of allergic contact dermatitis. Within fifteen minutes of exposure to these plants, rash development may be prevented by washing the area with soap and water. The leaves of jewelweed (*Impatiens* spp.), which often grows near poison ivy, may neutralize the poison-ivy allergen if rubbed on the skin right after contact. Several topical remedies may help relieve the itching associated with allergic contact dermatitis, including the juice of plantain leaves (*Plantago major*); a paste made of equal parts of green clay and goldenseal root (*Hydrastis canadensis*); a paste made of salt, water, clay, and peppermint (*Mentha piperita*) oil; and calamine lotion.

Prognosis

If the offending substance is promptly identified and avoided, the chances of a rapid and complete recovery are excellent. Otherwise, symptom management—not cure—is the best doctors can offer. Sensitivity to allergens is typically lifelong. For a few people, contact dermatitis becomes a chronic and disabling condition that can have a profound effect on quality of life.

Prevention

Avoidance or substitution of known or suspected allergens or irritating substances is the best prevention. If avoidance is difficult, barrier creams and protective clothing can be tried. Skin that comes in contact with an offending substance should be thoroughly washed as soon as possible.

Parental concerns

Parents should be concerned primarily with identifying the cause(s) of a child or adolescent's contact dermatitis, as treatment is often ineffective until the offending substance can be removed or avoided. Most cases of contact dermatitis are mild and can be treated without disrupting the child's school routine or severely affecting his or her quality of life. In some cases, parents may find

---

KEY TERMS

Antibiotics—Drugs that are designed to kill or inhibit the growth of the bacteria that cause infections.

Corticosteroids—A group of hormones produced naturally by the adrenal gland or manufactured synthetically. They are often used to treat inflammation. Examples include cortisone and prednisone.

Dermatologist—A physician that specializes in diseases and disorders of the skin.

Epidermis—The outermost layer of the human skin.

Immune response—A physiological response of the body controlled by the immune system that involves the production of antibodies to fight off specific foreign substances or agents (antigens).

Lipids—Organic compounds not soluble in water, but soluble in fat solvents such as alcohol. Lipids are stored in the body as energy reserves and are also important components of cell membranes. Commonly known as fats.

Topical—Not ingested; applied to the outside of the body, for example to the skin, eye, or mouth.

---

it helpful to consult a dermatologist to identify the specific causes and to suggest products that can be substituted for those that are causing the skin reactions.

See also Diaper rash; Poison ivy, oak, and sumac; Rashes.

Resources

BOOKS

"Contact Dermatitis." Section 10, Chapter 111 in *The Merck Manual of Diagnosis and Therapy*, edited by Mark H. Beers, and Robert Berkow. Whitehouse Station, NJ: Merck Research Laboratories, 2002.

Pelletier, Kenneth R. "CAM Therapies for Specific Conditions: Eczema." Part II, in *The Best Alternative Medicine*. New York: Simon & Schuster, 2002.

PERIODICALS

Atherton, D. J. "A Review of the Pathophysiology, Prevention, and Treatment of Irritant Diaper Dermatitis." *Current Medical Research and Opinion* 20 (May 2004): 645–49.

Duarte, I., et al. "Contact Dermatitis in Adolescents." *American Journal of Contact Dermatitis* 14 (December 2003): 200–02.

Kutting, B., et al. "Allergic Contact Dermatitis in Children: Strategies of Prevention and Risk Management." *European Journal of Dermatology* 14 (March-April 2004): 80–5.

Samimi, S. S., et al. "A Diagnostic Pearl: The School Chair Sign." *Cutis* 74 (July 2004): 27–8.

Shaw, D. W., et al. "Allergic Contact Dermatitis from Tacrolimus." *Journal of the American Academy of Dermatology* 50 (June 2004): 962–65.

Sood, A., et al. "Contact Dermatitis to a Limb Prosthesis." *American Journal of Contact Dermatitis* 14 (September 2003): 169–71.

ORGANIZATIONS

American Academy of Dermatology (AAD). PO Box 4014, Schaumburg, IL 60168–4014. Web site: <www.aad.org>.

National Institute of Arthritis and Musculoskeletal and Skin Diseases (NIAMS). 1 AMS Circle, Bethesda, MD 20892–3675. Web site: <www.niams.nih.gov>.

WEB SITES

Crowe, Mark A.. "Contact Dermatitis." *eMedicine*, September 1, 2004. Available online at <www.emedicine.com/ped/topic2569.htm> (accessed November 16, 2004).

OTHER

American Academy of Dermatology (AAD) Public Resources. *Allergic Contact Rashes.* Schaumburg, IL: AAD, 2003.

Howard Baker

Contact lenses *see* **Eyeglasses and contact lenses**

Contraception

Definition

Contraception (birth control) prevents pregnancy by interfering with the normal process of ovulation, fertilization, and implantation. There are different kinds of birth control that act at different points in the process.

Purpose

Every month a woman's body begins the process that can potentially lead to pregnancy. An egg (ovum) matures, the mucus that is secreted by the cervix (a cylindrical-shaped organ at the lower end of the uterus) changes to be more inviting to sperm, and the lining of the uterus grows in preparation for receiving a fertilized egg. Any woman who wants to prevent pregnancy must use a reliable form of birth control. Birth control (contraception) is designed to interfere with the normal process and prevent the pregnancy that could result. There are different kinds of birth control that act at different points in the process, from ovulation through fertilization to implantation. Each method has its own side effects and risks. Some methods are more reliable than others.

Although there are many different types of birth control, they can be divided into a few groups based on how they work. These groups include:

- Hormonal methods: These use medications (hormones) to prevent ovulation. Hormonal methods include birth control pills (**oral contraceptives**), Depo Provera injections, and Norplant.

- Barrier methods: These methods work by preventing the sperm from getting to and fertilizing the egg. Barrier methods include male **condom** and female condom, diaphragm, and cervical cap. The condom is the only form of birth control that also protects against **sexually transmitted diseases**, including human **immunodeficiency** virus (HIV) that causes acquired immune deficiency syndrome (AIDS).

- Spermicides: These medications kill sperm on contact. Most spermicides contain nonoxynyl-9. Spermicides come in many different forms such as jelly, foam, tablets, and even a transparent film. All are placed in the vagina. Spermicides work best when they are used at the same time as a barrier method.

- Intrauterine devices (IUDs): These devices are inserted into the uterus, where they stay from one to ten years. An IUD prevents the fertilized egg from implanting in the lining of the uterus and may have other effects as well.

- Tubal ligation: This medical procedure is a permanent form of contraception for women. Each fallopian tube is either tied or burned closed. The sperm cannot reach the egg, and the egg cannot travel to the uterus.

- Vasectomy: This medical procedure is a the male form of sterilization and should be considered permanent. In vasectomy, the vas defrens, the tiny tubes that carry the sperm into the semen, are cut and tied off.

Unfortunately, there is no perfect form of birth control. Only abstinence (not having sexual intercourse) protects against unwanted pregnancy with 100 percent reliability. The failure rates, or the rates at which pregnancy occurs, for most forms of birth control are quite low. However, some forms of birth control are more difficult or inconvenient to use than others. In actual practice, the birth control methods that are more difficult or inconvenient have much higher failure rates, because they are not used faithfully.

Description

All forms of birth control have one feature in common. They are only effective if used faithfully. Birth control pills work only if taken every day; the diaphragm is effective only if used during every episode of sexual intercourse. The same is true for condoms and the cervical cap. Some methods are automatically working every day, no matter what. These methods include Depo Provera, Norplant, the IUD, and tubal sterilization.

There are many different ways to use birth control. They can be divided into several groups:

- By mouth (oral): Birth control pills must be taken by mouth every day.

- Injected: Depo Provera is a hormonal medication that is given by injection every three months.

- Implanted: Norplant is a long-acting hormonal form of birth control that is implanted under the skin of the upper arm.

- Vaginal: Spermicides and barrier methods work in the vagina.

- Intra-uterine: The IUD is inserted into the uterus.

- Surgical: Tubal sterilization is a form of surgery. A doctor must perform the procedure in a hospital or surgical clinic. Many women need general anesthesia.

The methods of birth control differ from each other regarding when they are used. Some methods of birth control must be used specifically at the time of sexual intercourse (condoms, diaphragm, cervical cap, spermicides). All other methods of birth control must be working all the time to provide protection (hormonal methods, IUDs, tubal sterilization).

Condoms and spermicides

Condoms are about 85 percent effective in preventing pregnancies. That means that out of 100 females whose partners use condoms, 15 will still become pregnant during the first year of use, according to the nonprofit advocacy group Planned Parenthood. Unwanted pregnancies usually occur because the condom is not attached or used properly or breaks during intercourse. More protection against pregnancy is possible if a spermicide is used along with a condom. Spermicide is a pharmaceutical substance used to kill sperm, especially in conjunction with a birth-control device such as a condom or diaphragm. Spermicides come in foam, cream, gel, suppository, or as a thin film. The most common spermicide is called nonoxynol-9, and many condoms come with it already applied as a lubricant. However, spermicides do not kill HIV or other sexually transmitted viruses and do not prevent the spread of HIV and other STDs. Also, nonoxynol-9 can irritate vaginal tissue and thus increase the risk of getting an STD. In anal sex, especially between two males, spermicides also can irritate the rectum, increasing the risk of getting HIV. Spermicides are specifically discouraged for use by gay or bisexual males for anal sex.

Latex condoms are also recommended over condoms made from other materials, especially lambskin, because they are thicker and stronger and have less risk of breakage during sex. Non-latex condoms do not prevent the spread of STDs, including HIV, and should not be used by gay or bisexual men or men who have HIV or other sexually transmitted diseases. Condoms are available over-the-counter, meaning they do not require a prescription, and there are no age restrictions on purchasing condoms. They are available at a variety of locations, including drug stores, convenience stores, supermarkets, and **family** planning clinics. They are also available for purchase on the Internet.

FEMALE CONDOM   The female condom is a seven-inch polyurethane pouch that fits into the vagina. It collects semen before, during, and after ejaculation, keeping semen from entering the uterus through the cervix and thus protecting against pregnancy. In one year of use, it is 79 percent effective in preventing pregnancies. It also reduces the risk of many STDs, including HIV. There is a flexible ring at the closed end of the thin, soft pouch of the female condom. A slightly larger ring is at the open end. The ring at the closed end holds the condom in place in the vagina. The ring at the open end rests outside the vagina. When the condom is in place during sexual intercourse, there is no contact of the vagina and cervix with the skin of the penis or with secretions from the penis. It can be inserted up to eight hours before sex.

Precautions

There are risks associated with some forms of birth control. Some of the risks of each method are:

- Birth control pills: The hormone (estrogen) in birth control pills can increase the risk of heart attack in women over forty who smoke.

- IUD: This device can increase the risk of serious pelvic infection. The IUD can also injure the uterus by poking into or through the uterine wall. Surgery might be needed to fix this injury.

Various types of contraception, including birth control pills, condoms, and diaphram. *(Photograph by Michael Keller. The Stock Market.)*

- Tubal sterilization: "Tying the tubes" is a surgical procedure and has all the risks of any other surgery, including the risks of anesthesia, infection, and bleeding.

- Condom: The most common problems associated with condoms are breakage during use and improper technique in using condoms. These can lead to pregnancy and sexually transmitted diseases, especially HIV.

Preparation

No specific preparation is needed before using contraception. However, a woman must be sure that she is not already pregnant before using a hormonal method or having an IUD placed.

Risks

Many methods of birth control have side effects. Knowing the side effects can help a woman to deter-

mine which method of birth control is right for her. There is no perfect form of birth control. Every method has a small failure rate and side effects. Some methods carry additional risks. However, every method of birth control has fewer risks than pregnancy. The risks include:

- Hormonal methods: The hormones in birth control pills, Depo Provera, and Norplant can cause changes in menstrual periods, changes in mood, weight gain, **acne**, and headaches. In addition, once a woman stops using Depo Provera or Norplant, she may go many months before she begins ovulating again.

- Barrier methods: A woman must insert the diaphragm in just the right way to be sure that it works properly. Some women get more urinary tract infections if they use a diaphragm because the diaphragm can press against the urethra, the tube that connects the bladder to the outside.

Contraception

Type of contraceptive	Description	Use	Failure rate per 100 women in one year
Abstinence	Refraining from intercourse, anal sex, and oral sex	Universally applicable. Also prevents spread of sexually transmitted diseases	0
Birth control pill	Prescription pill containing estrogen and progestin that suppresses ovulation	Must be taken daily, regardless of the frequency of intercourse	1-2
Cervical cap with spermicide	Soft rubber cup that fits around the cervix, obtained by prescription	Inserted before intercourse. May be difficult to insert	17-23, depending on type
Condom, female	Lubricated sheath that is inserted into the vagina. Similar in shape to the male condom, with a flexible ring	Applied immediately before intercourse, for single use	21
Condom, male	Latex or polyurethane sheath placed over erect penis, widely available in drugstores	Applied immediately before intercourse, for single use. Best protection against sexually transmitted diseases	11
Depo-Provera injection	Injection that inhibits ovulation, obtained by prescription	Injections performed at a doctor's office, once every three months	Less than 1
Diaphragm with spermicide	Dome-shaped rubber disk that covers the cervix, obtained by prescription	Inserted before intercourse and left in place at least six hours after	17
Douching	Use an over-the-counter feminine douche immediately after intercourse in an effort to wash out the sperm	Sperm travel quickly to the cervix, making this an ineffective method of birth control	40
IUD (intrauterine device)	T-shaped device inserted in the uterus during a visit to the doctor	Can remain in place for up to one or 10 years, depending on type	Less than 1
Morning-after pill (emergency contraceptive)	Pills similar to regular birth control pills, obtained by prescription	Must be taken within 72 hours of unprotected intercourse	80% reduction in pregnancy risk
Patch	Adhesive patch worn on the skin that releases hormones preventing ovulation. Obtained by prescription	New patch is applied once a week for three weeks, followed by one week without the patch	1-2
Periodic abstinence	Refraining from intercourse when conception is likely	Requires regular menstrual cycles and close monitoring of body functions pertaining to ovulation	20
Spermicide alone	A foam, cream, jelly, film, or suppository, or tablet containing nonoxynol-9	Depending on product, inserted between five and 90 minutes before intercourse; usually left in place at least six to eight hours after	20-50, depending on product
Withdrawal	Having intercourse, but removing the male penis before ejaculation	Not recommended for teens, and some seminal fluid leaks before ejaculation, making it an ineffective method of birth control	27

SOURCE: Food and Drug Administration, December 2003; Planned Parenthood, March 2004; kidshealth.org, September 2001.

(Table by GGS Information Services.)

- Spermicides: Some women and men are allergic to spermicides or find them irritating to the skin.

- IUD: The device is a foreign object that stays inside the uterus, and the uterus tries to get it out. A woman may have heavier menstrual periods and more menstrual cramping with an IUD in place.

- Tubal ligation: Some women report increased menstrual discomfort after this surgery. It is not known if this side effect is related to the tubal ligation itself.

Parental concerns

Nearly 60 percent of sexually active girls under age 18 would discontinue at least some reproductive health services if their parents were informed that they were seeking contraceptive services, according to a study published in the August 14, 2002 issue of the *Journal of the American Medical Association (JAMA)*. If parental notification would cause the majority of minor girls to stop seeking reproductive health services or to use less effective methods of contraception, the rates of teen pregnancies and STD infections would substantially increase,

KEY TERMS

Fallopian tubes—The pair of narrow tubes leading from a woman's ovaries to the uterus. After an egg is released from the ovary during ovulation, fertilization (the union of sperm and egg) normally occurs in the fallopian tubes.

Fertilization—The joining of the sperm and the egg; conception.

Implantation—The process in which the fertilized egg embeds itself in the wall of the uterus.

Ovulation—The monthly process by which an ovarian follicle ruptures releasing a mature egg cell.

Carol Ford of the Adolescent Medicine Program at the University of North Carolina–Chapel Hill and Abigail English of the Center for Adolescent Health & the Law state in an accompanying *JAMA* editorial. Although there is widespread consensus that communication between adolescents and their parents about sexual decision-making is important, there is no reason that confidential reproductive health care and efforts to improve communication between parents and their adolescent children cannot occur simultaneously, these authors suggest.

Parents of adolescents often are concerned that distribution of contraceptives leads to increased sexual activity. However, a study of 4,100 high school students published in the June 2003 issue of the *American Journal of Public Health* found that students who had access at school to condoms and instructions on their proper use were no more likely to have sexual intercourse than students at schools without condom distribution programs.

See also Condom.

Resources

BOOKS

Birth Control Pills: A Medical Dictionary, Bibliography, and Annotated Research Guide to Internet References. San Diego, CA: Icon Health Publications, 2003.

Peacock, Judith. *Birth Control and Protection: Choices for Teens.* Santa Rosa, CA: LifeMatters, 2000.

Whitney, Leon Fradley. *Birth Control Today: A Practical Approach to Intelligent Family Planning.* Temecula, CA: Textbook Publishers, 2003.

PERIODICALS

"Give Teens More Info to Bridge Information Gap." *Contraceptive Technology Update* 25(September 2004): 106–07.

Sullivan, Michele G. "Teens View Hormonal Contraception as Unsafe." *Internal Medicine News* 37 (July 15, 2004): 24.

"Teens Face Obstacles When Obtaining EC (Emergency Contraceptives)." *Contraceptive Technology Update* 25 (April 2004): 41–2.

Tucker, Miriam E. "Newer Contraceptives Give Teens More Options." *OB GYN News* 38 (August 1, 2003): 9.

ORGANIZATIONS

Advocates for Youth. 2000 M St. NW, Suite 750, Washington, DC 20036. Web site <www.advocatesforyouth.org>.

Planned Parenthood Federation of America Inc. 434 W. 33rd St., New York, NY 10001. Web site: <www.plannedparenthood.org>.

WEB SITES

"Teens and Condoms." *Avert.org*, August 13, 2004. Available online at <www.avert.org/teencondoms.htm> (accessed November 23, 2004).

Amy B. Tuteur
Ken R. Wells

Cooley's anemia *see* **Thalassemia**

Corneal abrasion

Definition

A corneal abrasion occurs when there is a loss of cells from the epithelium or surface of the cornea. It is usually due to trauma but may occur without trauma such as with the overuse of **contact lenses**.

Description

The cornea is the clear curved structure found at the front of the eye. It is comprised of three layers and the membranes that separate these layers. It is very difficult to penetrate past the epithelium or top layer of the cornea. The cornea is normally devoid of blood vessels yet has many sensory nerves. When any trauma to the corneal epithelium occurs, cells are lost or destroyed and **pain** is immediately sensed. When a corneal abrasion occurs, the conjunctiva, or the white of the eye, turns red, as new blood vessels form and those present enlarge, in an attempt to increase blood flow to the eye as it attempts to bring to the eye those cells needed for the healing of the cornea.

A corneal abrasion heals by the movement of neighboring epithelial cells, which slide over the wounded area, and through a cell division process called mitosis, which fill in the abraded area with new epithelial cells. Within two to three days of trauma to the cornea, these new cells start to adhere to the underlying membrane of the epithelium, called the basement membrane and within seven to eight days the abraded area usually heals completely without scarring. But if a corneal abrasion is deep and penetrates the next layer of the cornea, then scarring is possible and complete healing of the abrasion may be delayed as long as three months.

Demographics

Corneal abrasions account for 10 percent of ocular emergency care. The incidence of non-penetrating injuries to the eye, which includes corneal abrasions, is 1.57 percent per year. More males are treated for corneal abrasions than are females.

Causes and symptoms

Common causes of corneal abrasions include fingernails, make-up implements, paper cuts, plant material, including tree branches, animal scratches, cigarettes, inverted eyelashes, and blunt trauma, such as that with a knife or with scissors. Children are most likely to get a corneal abrasion while playing, while adults are more likely to sustain an abrasion in the workplace. Ultraviolet radiation such as that which occurs with a welder's flash or use of a sunlamp, can also cause an abrasion, as well as misuse and mishandling of contact lenses. When a missile type object causes an abrasion, the object can become embedded in the cornea or penetrate the eye.

Pain, irritation, tearing, red eye, twitching of the eye, decreased vision, and sensitivity to bright lights are common complaints that accompany a corneal abrasion. If there is significant swelling of the cornea, then vision may be decreased. If there is inflammation inside the eye, a dull ache may be felt inside the eye. Very rarely, **nausea** is experienced due to the pain associated with a corneal abrasion. The only symptom in a nonverbal patient, such as an infant, may be that the child is fussier than usual.

When to call the doctor

Any redness or foreign body sensation, especially if only one eye is affected, should be evaluated promptly for a corneal abrasion. If a corneal abrasion is not treated appropriately, scarring and ulceration of the corneal are possible. A corneal abrasion should be treated by a healthcare practitioner capable of evaluating eye conditions. **Herpes simplex**, recurrent corneal erosion (RCE), and acanthamoeba infections are other conditions that can mimic a corneal abrasion but which require very different treatments.

Diagnosis

The individual with a corneal abrasion will usually report a known trauma to the eye area.

To diagnose a corneal abrasion, a topical anesthetic with a yellow dye called flourescein is placed into the eye. Under blue cobalt light, the part of the cornea abraded will be stained by the dye and is easily seen by the examiner. The area and depth of the abrasion can be easily seen under a special microscope called a slit lamp biomicroscope. If a microscope is not available, then a blue light called a Burton lamp may be used.

Usually the anesthetic drop will relieve the ocular pain immediately. If a dull aching sensation persists after this instillation then a co-existing iritis, or inflammation of the iris, also called a uveitis, may also be present. When a biomicroscope is available, the eye is checked for infection or inflammation. The eyelids are everted (turned out) to check for any foreign bodies. These areas may also be rinsed with saline to remove any small foreign body that may be a source of the abrasion.

If any of the instilled dye leaks into the eye, then the cornea has been perforated and a small projectile may be inside the eye. Other testing, such as **x rays**, must be done to rule out foreign bodies inside the eye. Since metal is the most common material seen in penetrating injuries, an MRI is not usually done. If the cornea has been perforated, then the patient is referred to a corneal specialist for surgery.

If an infection is suspected or if an abrasion does not heal, then swabbing of the eye for microscopic culture may be done to definitively establish the organism involved.

Treatment

If the corneal abrasion is very small and superficial, then the application of mild antibiotic drops three to four times a day for a few days to a week is sufficient to prevent an infection. At bedtime, an antibiotic ointment, which will remain on the eye longer, may be necessary for deep abrasions. When an infection is present, then specially compounded fortified **antibiotics**, formulated specifically for the organism that caused the infection, are prescribed topically. For those with very minor abrasions, instillation of non-preserved lubricating drops a few times a day for a few days may be all that is required.

The pain of a corneal abrasion can be treated with drugs such as homatropine which keep the eye in a dilated state and stop the spasm of the iris, a major cause of discomfort for the individual with a corneal abrasion. Nonsteroidal drops, called NSAIDs, may also be prescribed for a few days to relieve the pain. In some instances, oral **analgesics** may be prescribed, but children under 12 should not be given aspirin. If the area is large and there is no underlying viral infection, then a mild steroid to decrease future scarring and treat an associated iritis may also be needed. Topical anesthetics are never prescribed because they delay and interfere with the healing process.

For many years the standard treatment for a corneal abrasion included patching. Patching can decrease blinking, which was thought to speed the healing process. But patching is as of 2004 no longer done routinely because it decreases the amount of oxygen that gets to the cornea. Patching is never done for contact lens patients, whose eyes are at a greater risk of a *Pseudomonas* infection, nor when the cause of an abrasion is due to vegetative matter, such as a tree branch. Organisms can thrive in these types of environment. Patching is also not done for patients who are monocular (have one good eye), if the better eye has the abrasion, nor for patients for whom depth perception is important, as this is lost when only one eye is used. Controlled studies have demonstrated that patching a corneal abrasion does not improve healing either in children or adults and that patching of an eye may make walking difficult.

For the contact lens wearer with a corneal abrasion, contact lens wear must be discontinued for at least one week and glasses must be worn. Patients who wear contact lenses are given antibiotics that act on the bacteria that are ubiquitous in the eye of the contact lens wearer. The eye must be evaluated by an eye-care practitioner prior to reinstituting contact lens wear.

For the patient with a large abrasion and without an infection, and who does not wear contact lenses, a bandage contact lens approved for extended overnight wear may be worn. The pressure of the contact lens may comfort the patient, and the antibiotics are absorbed by the contact lens, giving the eye continuous 24 hour protection from a potential bacterial infection.

Treatment of a corneal abrasion with over-the-counter (OTC) drugs advertised to decrease redness should not be used to self treat corneal abrasions. These drugs

act by constricting the blood vessels in the eye, decreasing the blood supply to the eye and delaying healing. Also, the preservatives in these drops may irritate the cornea.

Except for a very mild abrasion, the doctor may require daily follow-up examination to ensure that the abrasion is healing. This is especially important if vegetative matter is the cause of the abrasion. Those who have been patched must be re-evaluated within 24 hours to see if the symptoms have improved.

Prognosis

Corneal abrasions usually heal within a week, but complications can occur. A secondary infection and scarring can result if the abrasion is not treated. Up to 50 percent of those with a corneal abrasion develop a uveitis or inflammation inside the eye.

Approximately 10 to 25 percent of those with corneal abrasions will develop recurrent corneal erosion (RCE) a condition in which the epithelium of the cornea pulls off because it did not heal properly or completely. This can happen weeks, months, or years after the initial trauma. Usually the patient either awakens with sharp pain or is bothered by a foreign body sensation that is worse in the morning. This erosion is usually treated conservatively with lubricating drops and hypertonic saline ointment for a month or more, although some patient need a debridement of the cornea or laser treatment. Oral doxycycline and topical steroids have been shown to help with the restructuring of the cornea with a RCE.

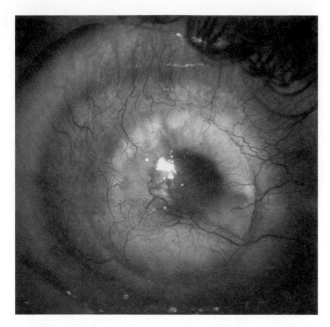

A close-up view of an abrasion on patient's cornea. *(Photograph by Dennis R. Cain. Custom Medical Stock Photo, Inc.)*

The probability of corneal ulcer development from a corneal abrasion increases tenfold in contact lens wearers for those who use extended wear contacts, over those who remove their contacts as night. This risk may be decreased for those wearing the new silicone contact lenses.

Prevention

Prevention of a traumatic injury or an accident is not possible, but for those types of abrasions caused by chronic trauma, such as with contact lenses, the likelihood of abrasions and subsequent ulcers can be reduced by proper contact lens wear and care. It is important that children and adolescents who wear contact lenses have glasses to wear and that glasses are worn every day to give the eyes a chance to breathe. The contact lenses should be replaced and cared for as recommended by an eye care practitioner.

For those who engage in welding, eye protection, including the use of helmets, decreases the incidence a corneal abrasions caused by welding **burns**.

Parental concerns

Rarely do corneal abrasion lead to loss of vision, but any trauma to the eye must be evaluated by a healthcare practitioner for the possibility of an abrasion. When an abrasion is present, then it is imperative that prescribed treatment, including cessation of contact lenses and use of prescribed drops be followed. If the corneal abrasion is due to contact lens abuse, then the consequences of further misuse of contact lenses must be thoroughly discussed with the eye care practitioner.

Resources

BOOKS

Hersch, Peter S., et al. "Anterior Segment Trauma" in *Principles and Practice of Ophthalmology*, edited by Daniel M. Albert, et al. Philadelphia: Saunders, 2000.

Scoper, Stephen V. "Corneal Abrasions, Lacerations, and Perforations" in *Current Ocular Therapy*, Vol. 5, edited by Frederick T. Fraunfelder. Philadelphia: Saunders, 2000.

PERIODICALS

Karpecki, Paul M. "The Effort to Cure Recurrent Erosions." *Review of Optometry* (July 15, 2002): 76–77

Michael, Jeffery G., et al. "Management of Corneal Abrasion in Children: A Randomized Clinical Trial." *Annals of Emergency Medicine* 40 (July 2002): 67–72.

Rittichier, Kristine K., et al. "Are Signs and Symptoms Associated with Persistent Corneal Abrasions in Children?" *Archives of Pediatrics and Adolescent Medicine* 154 (April 2000): 370–74.

Trad, Michael J. "Pressure Patching Indicated in Few Cases of Traumatic Corneal Abrasions." *Primary Care Optometry News* 9 (September 2004): 36–37.

Martha Reilly, OD

Cough

Definition

A cough is a forceful release of air from the lungs that can be heard. Coughing protects the respiratory system by clearing it of irritants and secretions.

Description

While people can generally cough voluntarily, a true cough is usually a reflex triggered when an irritant stimulates one or more of the cough receptors found at different points in the respiratory system. These receptors then send a message to the cough center in the brain, which in turn tells the body to cough. A cough begins with a deep breath in, at which point the opening between the vocal cords at the upper part of the larynx (glottis) shuts, trapping the air in the lungs. As the diaphragm and other muscles involved in breathing press against the lungs, the glottis suddenly opens, producing an explosive outflow of air at speeds greater than 100 miles (160 km) per hour.

In normal situations, most people cough once or twice an hour during the day to clear the airway of irritants. However, when the level of irritants in the air is high or when the respiratory system becomes infected, coughing may become frequent and prolonged. It may interfere with **exercise** or **sleep**, and it may also cause distress if accompanied by **dizziness**, chest **pain**, or breathlessness. In the majority of cases, frequent coughing lasts one to two weeks and tapers off as the irritant or infection subsides. If a cough lasts more than three weeks it is considered a chronic cough, and physicians try to determine a cause beyond an acute infection or irritant.

Coughs are generally described as either dry or productive. A dry cough does not bring up a mixture of mucus, irritants, and other substances from the lungs (sputum), while a productive cough does. In the case of a bacterial infection, the sputum brought up in a productive cough may be greenish, gray, or brown. In the case of an allergy or viral infection it may be clear or white. In the most serious conditions, the sputum may contain blood.

Demographics

Formal statistics on coughs are not maintained. Virtually all persons will experience coughs several times each year throughout their lives.

Causes and symptoms

In the majority of cases, coughs are caused by respiratory infections, including the following:

- colds or **influenza**, the most common causes of coughs

- **bronchitis**, an inflammation of the mucous membranes of the bronchial tubes

- croup, a viral inflammation of the larynx, windpipe, and bronchial passages that produces a bark-like cough in children

- whooping cough, a bacterial infection accompanied by the high-pitched cough for which it is named

- **pneumonia**, a potentially serious bacterial infection that produces discolored or bloody mucus

---

KEY TERMS

Antitussive—A drug used to suppress coughing.

Expectorant—A drug that promotes the discharge of mucus from respiratory system.

Gastroesophageal reflux—The backflow of stomach contents into the esophagus.

Glottis—The opening between the vocal cords at the upper part of the larynx.

Larynx—Also known as the voice box, the larynx is the part of the airway that lies between the pharynx and the trachea. It is composed of cartilage that contains the apparatus for voice production—the vocal cords and the muscles and ligaments that move the cords.

Sputum—The substance that is coughed up from the lungs and spit out through the mouth. It is usually a mixture of saliva and mucus, but may contain blood or pus in patients with lung abscess or other diseases of the lungs.

- **tuberculosis**, another serious bacterial infection that produces bloody sputum

- fungal infections, such as aspergillosis, histoplasmosis, and cryptococcosis

Environmental pollutants, such as cigarette smoke, dust, or smog, can also cause a cough. In the case of cigarette smokers, the nicotine present in the smoke paralyzes the hairs (cilia) that regularly flush mucus from the respiratory system. The mucus then builds up, forcing the body to remove it by coughing. Post-nasal drip, the irritating trickle of mucus from the nasal passages into the throat caused by **allergies** or **sinusitis**, can also result in a cough. Some chronic conditions, such as **asthma**, chronic bronchitis, emphysema, and **cystic fibrosis**, are characterized in part by a cough. A condition in which stomach acid backs up into the esophagus (gastroesophageal reflux) can cause coughing, especially when a person is lying down. A cough can also be a side-effect of medications that are administered via an inhaler. It can be a side-effect of beta-blockers and ACE inhibitors, which are drugs used for treating high blood pressure.

When to call the doctor

A physician or other healthcare provider should be called when a cough does not subside after three or four

---

days. Individuals such as smokers, who have chronic coughs, should consult a doctor if the nature of their cough changes or they produce blood when they cough.

Diagnosis

To determine the cause of a cough, a physician should take an exact medical history and perform an exam. Information regarding the duration of the cough, what other symptoms may accompany it, and what environmental factors may influence it aid the doctor in his or her diagnosis. The appearance of the sputum also helps determine what type of infection, if any, may be involved. The doctor may even observe the sputum microscopically for the presence of bacteria and white blood cells. Chest **x rays** may help indicate the presence and extent of such infections as pneumonia or tuberculosis. If these actions are not enough to determine the cause of the cough, a bronchoscopy or laryngoscopy may be ordered. These tests use slender tubular instruments to inspect the interior of the bronchi and larynx.

Treatment

Treatment of a cough generally involves addressing the condition causing it. An acute infection such as pneumonia may require **antibiotics**, an asthma-induced cough may be treated with the use of bronchodilators, or an antihistamine may be administered in the case of an allergy. Physicians prefer not to suppress a productive cough, since it aids the body in clearing respiratory system of infective agents and irritants. However, cough medicines may be given if the person cannot rest because of the cough or if the cough is not productive, as is the case with most coughs associated with colds or flu. The two types of drugs used to treat coughs are antitussives and **expectorants**.

Antitussives

Antitussives are drugs that suppress a cough. Narcotics—primarily codeine—are used as antitussives and work by depressing the cough center in the brain. However, they can cause such side effects as drowsiness, **nausea**, and **constipation**. Dextromethorphan, the primary ingredient in many over-the-counter cough remedies, also depresses the brain's cough center but without the side effects associated with narcotics. Demulcents relieve coughing by coating irritated passageways.

Expectorants

Expectorants are drugs that thin mucus in order to make it easier to cough up. Guaifenesin and terpin hydrate are the primary ingredients in most over-the-counter expectorants. However, some studies have shown that in acute infections, simply increasing fluid intake has the same thinning effect as taking expectorants.

Coughs due to bacterial or viral upper respiratory infections may be effectively treated with botanical and homeopathic therapies. The choice of remedy will vary and be specific to the type of cough the person has. Some combination over-the-counter herbal and homeopathic cough formulas can be very effective for cough relief. Lingering coughs or coughing up blood should be treated by a trained practitioner.

Many health practitioners advise increasing fluids and breathing in warm, humidified air as ways of loosening chest congestion. Others recommend hot tea flavored with honey as a temporary home remedy for coughs caused by colds or flu. Various **vitamins**, such as vitamin C, or **minerals**, such as zinc, may be helpful in preventing or treating conditions (including colds and flu) that lead to coughs. Avoiding of mucus-producing foods can be effective in healing a cough condition. These mucus-producing foods can vary, based on individual intolerance, but dairy products are a major mucus-producing food for most people.

Prognosis

Because the majority of coughs are related to the **common cold** or influenza, most will end in seven to 21 days. The outcome of coughs due to a more serious underlying disease depends on the pathology of that disease.

Prevention

It is important to identify and treat the underlying disease and origin of the cough. It is helpful to avoid cigarette smoke and coming in direct contact with people experiencing cold or flu symptoms. Hands should be washed frequently during episodes of upper-respiratory illnesses.

Nutritional concerns

Persons with coughs should be sure to maintain balanced and healthy diets.

Parental concerns

Parents of children under the age of five should closely monitor their children when they have a cough. Parents of children over five years of age must accept the fact that their children are likely to acquire coughs and related illnesses from schoolmates. They should remain vigilant and consider having their children seen by a physician if the cough does not resolve after five to seven days.

See also Common cold.

Resources

BOOKS

Boat, Thomas F. "Talipes Chronic or Recurrent Respiratory Symptoms." In *Nelson Textbook of Pediatrics*, 17th ed. Edited by Richard E. Behrman et al., Philadelphia: Saunders, 2003, pp. 1401–44.

Hanley, Michael E., and Carolyn Welsh. *Current Diagnosis & Treatment in Pulmonary Medicine.* New York: McGraw-Hill, 2003.

Weinberger, Steven E. *Principles of Pulmonary Medicine.* Little Rock, AR: Elsevier, 2003.

Weinberger, Steven E., and Eugene Braunwald. "Cough and Hemoptysis." In *Harrison's Principles of Internal Medicine*, 15th ed. Edited by Eugene Braunwald et al. New York: McGraw-Hill, 2001, pp. 203–6.

PERIODICALS

Chow, P. Y., et al. "Chronic cough in children." *Singapore Medical Journal* 45, no. 10 (2004): 462–9.

Franco, E., et al. "Pertussis vaccination for adolescents and adults." *Expert Opinion on Biological Therapy* 4, no. 10 (2004): 1669–76.

ORGANIZATIONS

American Academy of Family Physicians. 11400 Tomahawk Creek Parkway, Leawood, KS 66211–2672. Web site: <www.aafp.org/>.

American Academy of Pediatrics. 141 Northwest Point Blvd., Elk Grove Village, IL 60007–1098. Web site: <www.aap.org/default.htm>.

American College of Physicians. 190 N Independence Mall West, Philadelphia, PA 19106–1572. Web site: <www.acponline.org/>.

American Lung Association. 1740 Broadway, New York, NY 10019. Web site: <www.lungusa.org>.

WEB SITES

"Cough." *Brigham Young University*, October 26, 2000. Available online at <www.byu.edu/shc/library/common/cough.html> (accessed January 5, 2005).

"Cough." *MedlinePlus.* Available online at <www.nlm.nih.gov/medlineplus/cough.html> (accessed January 5, 2005).

Holmes, Robert L., and Clare T. Fadden. "Evaluation of the Patient with Chronic Cough." *American Academy of*

Family Practice, May 1, 2004. Available online at <www.aafp.org/afp/971001ap/cough.html> (accessed January 5, 2005).

L. Fleming Fallon, Jr., MD, DrPH

Cough suppressants

Definition

Cough suppressants are medicines that prevent or stop a person from coughing.

Description

Cough suppressants act on the center in the brain that controls the cough reflex. They are meant to be used only to relieve dry, hacking coughs associated with colds and flu. They should not be used to treat coughs that bring up mucus or the chronic coughs associated with **smoking**, **asthma**, emphysema, or other lung problems.

The most effective cough suppressants are narcotics. Heroin, which is not approved for medicinal use in the United States, and codeine have been widely used to stop coughs. These compounds, in addition to relieving coughs, also relieve **pain**, cause sedation, and are addictive. The most popular drug in this class is dextromethorphan, which is quite safe and is available without prescription. Dextromethorphan is an ingredient in most over-the-counter cough preparations:

- Vicks Formula 44
- Drixoral Cough Liquid Caps
- Sucrets Cough Control
- Benylin DM

The letters DM in a product's name normally indicates the presence of dextromethorphan, but it is always best to read the ingredients. Dextromethorphan works best in liquid formulations but is also available in capsules, lozenges, and tablets.

General use

Dextromethorphan is used for the temporary relief of coughs caused by minor throat and bronchial irritation such as may occur with common colds or with inhaled irritants. Dextromethorphan is most effective in the treatment of chronic, nonproductive cough.

Dextromethorphan has been reported to be effective in reversing some of the adverse effects of methotrexate, a drug that has found use in many conditions including **cancer**, **psoriasis**, and some types of arthritis.

Precautions

Lozenges containing dextromethorphan hydrobromide should not be used in children younger than six years of age. Liquid-filled capsules containing the drug should not be used in children younger than 12 years of age.

Dextromethorphan is not meant to be used for coughs associated with asthma, chronic **bronchitis**, or other lung conditions. It should not be used for coughs that produce mucus.

A lingering cough could be a sign of a serious medical condition. Patients with a cough that lasts more than seven days or is associated with **fever**, rash, **sore throat**, or lasting **headache** should have medical attention. Parents should call a physician as soon as possible if their child has these symptoms.

Side effects

Dextromethorphan rarely causes side effects but has been reported to cause **dizziness**, drowsiness, and stomach upset. There have been rare reports of **vomiting** caused by dextromethorphan.

Although dextromethorphan is very safe, it can cause problems when taken in too large a dose. In overdose, dextromethorphan can cause extreme dizziness, shallow breathing, and coma.

Interactions

Dextromethorphan has no clinically significant interactions with medications that are likely to be given to children. However, dextromethorphan should not be used in combination with narcotic **analgesics** such as meperidine or codeine, since dextromethorphan will increase the side effects of the analgesic.

Parental concerns

Lozenges containing dextromethorphan hydrobromide should not be used in children younger than six years of age. Liquid-filled capsules containing the drug should not be used in children younger than 12 years of

---

KEY TERMS

Chronic—Refers to a disease or condition that progresses slowly but persists or recurs over time.

Narcotic—A drug derived from opium or compounds similar to opium. Such drugs are potent pain relievers and can affect mood and behavior. Long-term use of narcotics can lead to dependence and tolerance. Also known as a narcotic analgesic.

Nonproductive—A cough in which no mucus is coughed up, also called dry cough.

---

age. Doses must be measured carefully. Measuring teaspoons should be used in place of household teaspoons.

Adolescent behavior must be observed, since some multi-ingredient over-the-counter cough remedies have become drugs of abuse. While these products are not addictive, they are toxic when misused.

See also Expectorants.

Resources

BOOKS

Beers, Mark H., and Robert Berkow, eds. *The Merck Manual*, 2nd home ed. West Point, PA: Merck & Co., 2004.

Mcevoy, Gerald, et al. *AHFS Drug Information 2004*. Bethesda, MD: American Society of Healthsystems Pharmacists, 2004.

Siberry, George K., and Robert Iannone, eds. *The Harriet Lane Handbook*, 15th ed. Philadelphia: Mosby Publishing, 2000.

PERIODICALS

Baker, S. D., and D. J. Borys. "A possible trend suggesting increased abuse from Coricidin exposures reported to the Texas Poison Network: comparing 1998 to 1999." *Veterinary and Human Toxicology* 44, no. 3 (June 2002): 169–71.

Kirages, Thomas J., Harsh P. Sulé, and Mark B. Mycyk. "Severe manifestations of coricidin intoxication." *American Journal of Emergency Medicine* 21, no. 6 (October 2003): 473–5.

Schroeder, Knut, and T. Fahey. "Over-the-counter medications for acute cough in children and adults in ambulatory settings." *Cochrane Database of Systematic Reviews* 3 (2001): CD001831.

ORGANIZATIONS

American Academy of Emergency Medicine. 555 East Wells Street, Suite 1100, Milwaukee, WI 53202–3823. Web site: <www.aaem.org>.

American Academy of Pediatrics. 141 Northwest Point Boulevard, Elk Grove Village, IL 60007–1098. Web site: <www.aap.org>.

WEB SITES

"Drug Information." *MedlinePlus.* Available online at <www.nlm.nih.gov/medlineplus/druginfo/uspdi/202187.html> (accessed October 17, 2004).

"Over-the-Counter Drug Products." *Center for Drug Evaluation and Research.* Available online at <www.fda.gov/cder/Offices/OTC/default.htm> (accessed October 17, 2004).

"Prescription Drug Abuse." *MedlinePlus* Available online at <www.nlm.nih.gov/medlineplus/prescriptiondrugabuse.html> (accessed October 17, 2004).

Nancy Ross-Flanigan
Samuel Uretsky, PharmD

CPR *see* **Cardiopulmonary resuscitation**

Cradle cap *see* **Seborrheic dermatitis**

Cramps, menstrual *see* **Dysmenorrhea**

Craniosynostosis

Definition

Craniosynostosis is one of a diverse group of deformities in the head and facial bones called craniofacial anomalies. An infant or child with craniosynostosis has improperly fused or joined bones (sutures) in the skull. ("Cranio" means skull; "synostosis" means fused bones.) When children with craniosynostosis also show other body deformities, their condition is called syndromic craniosynostosis. Primary craniosynostosis occurs when one or more of an infant's sutures (where skull bones meet) fuse prematurely. Secondary craniosynostosis results when one or more of an infant's sutures fuse prematurely as a result of lack of proper brain growth.

Description

A baby's skull is often thought of as a single piece of bone. However, it is actually made up of several bones that fit together like a jigsaw puzzle. These areas meet at what are called sutures. Sutures allow a growing baby's brain to expand. The four sutures come together at the fontanel, or "soft spot" in a baby's head. Eventually the sutures stop growing, and the cranial bones fuse.

Sometimes a suture is fused too early, however, preventing a growing child's brain from expanding. This condition can cause the brain to grow more rapidly in another area of the skull. The result is an abnormally shaped skull. Sometimes this happens before birth (congenital), or sometimes it occurs as the baby develops after birth.

There are four sutures of the skull that may be affected by craniosynostosis:

- Metopic: This suture extends from the top of the head down the middle of the forehead to the nose.

- Coronal: This suture extends from each ear to the fontanelle.

- Sagittal: This suture extends from the front of the head to the back, down the middle of the top to the head.

- Lambdoidal: This suture extends across the back of the head.

Types

The form of craniosynostosis depends on the suture or sutures that are affected.

Plagiocephaly (unicoronal synostosis)

Plagiocephaly is the most common form of craniosynostosis. It occurs in approximately one out of every 2,500 births. Plagiocephaly involves early fusion of either the right or left side of the coronal suture, the suture that extends from each ear over the top of the head to the fontanelle. The forehead and brow of a child with plagiocephaly look as if they have been pushed back or flattened because the forehead and brow have stopped their normal growth.

Brachycephaly (bicoronal synostosis)

Brachycephaly, which means "short headed," occurs when the right and left coronal sutures close prematurely. Brachycephaly results in an abnormally broad head with a high forehead. It is often associated with other craniofacial abnormalities, including Crouzon syndrome, Apert syndrome, Pfeiffer syndrome, and Saethre-Chotzen syndrome. It also is associated with **Down syndrome** (trisomy 21).

Trigonocephaly

This type of craniosynostosis involves fusion of the metopic suture that runs from the top of the head toward the nose, which can create a ridge running down the forehead and gives the front of the head a wedge-shaped effect. The eyes also may be close together.

Scaphocephaly (sagittal craniosynostosis)

This early fusion involves the sagittal suture that runs from front to back on the top of the skull. The result can be a long, narrow skull.

Positional nonsyndromic plagiocephaly (positional molding)

Positional nonsyndromic plagiocephaly is a form of craniosynostosis. In 1992, the American Academy of Pediatrics recommended that infants **sleep** on their backs to reduce the risk of **sudden infant death syndrome** (SIDS). This successfully reduced the number of infants with SIDS, but also increased the number of infants suffering from positional plagiocephaly due to back sleeping. An infant with positional nonsyndromic plagiocephaly has a flattened skull at the back of the head. This condition is also commonly called positional molding or deformational plagiocephaly.

Demographics

Craniosynostosis occurs in one out of 2,000 live births in the United States. It affects males twice as often as females. Of those affected, 2–8 percent have primary craniosynostosis and the remaining cases are secondary craniosynostosis. Plagiocephaly is the most common form of craniosynostosis. It occurs in approximately one out of every 2,500 live births. Sagittal craniosynostosis is the most common type of single suture craniosynostosis. It is estimated to occur in one in 4,000 to 8,500 live births. Although sagittal craniosynostosis mostly occurs by chance, about 2–6 percent of cases are considered to be inherited.

Frequencies of the types of craniosynostosis based on suture classification include: sagittal (50–58%); coronal (20–29%); metopic (4–10%); and lambdoid (2–4%).

Causes and symptoms

As of 2004 the exact cause of craniosynostosis is not understood. Many scientists believe it is the result of a defect in the ossification (bone formation) in the bones of the skull. Craniosynostosis usually occurs by chance (sporadic). In some families, however, it is inherited.

Genetic abnormalities such as craniosynostosis are described by the type of chromosome that carries the abnormal gene and whether the gene is recessive or dominant. The autosomal chromosomes are the nonsex chromosomes.

Autosomal recessive

In order for a child to inherit an autosomal recessive abnormality, both parents have to be carriers of the abnormal gene. When both parents are carriers, there is a 25 percent chance that each child born will inherit the abnormal gene and develop craniosynostosis. The child also has a 50 percent chance of inheriting the abnormal gene and becoming a carrier. Males and females are affected equally.

Autosomal dominant

When one parent has the abnormal gene and the other parent has normal genes, craniosynostosis can still result. That is because the abnormal gene dominates the normal gene. For an autosomal dominant disorder when one parent is a carrier of the abnormal gene, there is a 50 percent chance each child born will inherit the abnormal gene. Males and females are affected equally.

Other genetic syndromes, such as Crouzon syndrome, Apert syndrome, and Pfeiffer syndrome, are associated with craniosynostosis. All have different patterns of inheritance and chances of recurrence.

The physical symptoms of craniosynostosis depend on the sutures affected. Since other syndromes are associated with craniosynostosis, other symptoms may also be present, including the following:

- Endocrine disorders: **Hyperthyroidism** (overactivity of the thyroid gland), **vitamin D deficiency**, renal osteodystrophy (defective bone development), hypercalcemia (high levels of calcium in the blood), and rickets (weakened bones resulting from vitamin D deficiency).

- Hematologic disorders: Bone marrow diseases including sickle cell disease, and thalassemia.

- Inadequate growth of brain: Microcephaly (abnormal smallness of head), and **hydrocephalus** (abnormal buildup of cerebrospinal fluid in the head).

When to call the doctor

Craniosynostosis is a progressive condition that must be treated. The skull and facial asymmetry associated with craniosynostosis are frequently observed by an infant's pediatrician or **family** physician. Parents may also observe the condition.

Diagnosis

Craniosynostosis may be present at birth or may be observed later when a child has delays in neurological development. It often may be diagnosed by physical examination alone. Craniosynostosis may be suspected

KEY TERMS

Anomaly—Something that is different from what is normal or expected. Also an unusual or irregular structure.

Apert syndrome—A craniofacial abnormality characterized by abnormal head shape, small upper jaw, and fusion of fingers and toes.

Asymmetrical—Unbalanced, disproportionate, or unequal.

Brachycephaly—An abnormal thickening and widening of the skull.

Chromosome—A microscopic thread-like structure found within each cell of the human body and consisting of a complex of proteins and DNA. Humans have 46 chromosomes arranged into 23 pairs. Chromosomes contain the genetic information necessary to direct the development and functioning of all cells and systems in the body. They pass on hereditary traits from parents to child (like eye color) and determine whether the child will be male or female.

Computed tomography (CT)—An imaging technique in which cross-sectional x rays of the body are compiled to create a three-dimensional image of the body's internal structures; also called computed axial tomography.

Coronal suture—Skull suture that lies behind the forehead area, across the head from left side to the right side.

Craniosynostosis—A premature closure of one or more of the joints (fissures) between the bones of the skull, which causes an abnormally shaped skull.

Crouzon syndrome—A disorder characterized by malformations of the skull and face.

Deformational plagiocephaly (positional molding)—A form of craniosynostosis in which the head is misshapen, the result of constant pressure to the same area of the head.

Fontanelle—One of several "soft spots" on the skull where the developing bones of the skull have yet to fuse.

Lambdoidal suture—The suture between the two parietal bones and the occipital bone in the skull.

Metopic suture—Suture extending from the top of the head down the middle of the forehead to the nose.

Pfeiffer syndrome—This condition includes craniosynostosis, shallow eye sockets, underdevelopment of the midface, short thumbs and big toes, and possible webbing of hands and feet.

Plagiocephaly—A form of craniosynostosis that involves fusion of the right or left side of coronal suture.

Sagittal suture—The suture between the two parietal bones in the top of the skull.

Scaphocephaly—An abnormally long and narrow skull.

Suture—A "seam" that joins two surfaces together, such as is found between the bones of the skull. Also refers to stitching together the torn or cut edges of tissue.

Trigonocephaly—An abnormal development of the skull characterized by a triangular shaped forehead.

when an infant has an abnormally shaped head or a small bony ridge along the skull in various locations. The condition may also be suspected if a baby's fontanel (soft spot) closes off earlier than expected. The physician will do a complete physical exam and take a complete prenatal and birth history of the child, including position in the uterus. Family history of craniosynostosis or other craniofacial abnormalities also will be discussed.

Since craniosynostosis may be associated with other neurological and muscular disorders, such as Crouzon syndrome, Apert syndrome, or Pfeiffer syndrome, the physician will also discuss whether there have been any delays in the child's developmental progression.

If craniosynostosis is suspected, an x ray or a CT scan of the child's skull will be taken. In addition, DNA testing can help identify the gene mutations that can cause the condition. Mutations in what are called fibroblast growth factor receptors (FGR1, 2, and 3) and the transcription factor TWIST are responsible for several types of craniosynostosis.

Treatment

For most children with craniosynostosis, facial and skull deformity will be obvious and may be expected to worsen as the child grows. Surgical management by experienced neurosurgeons (brain surgeons) and orthopedic (bone) surgeons will be necessary in most cases. It usually is performed between the ages of six and ten months.

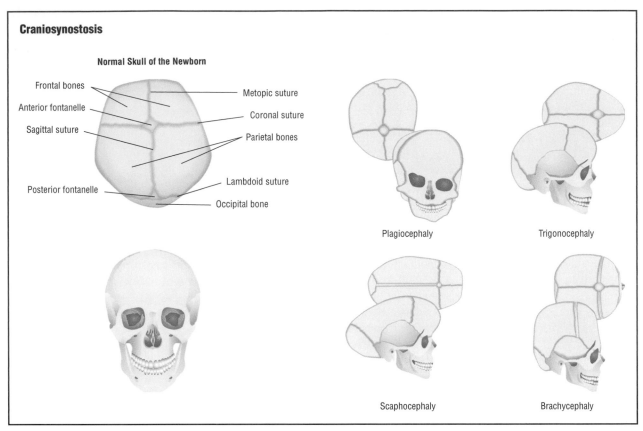

Craniosynostosis

Normal Skull of the Newborn

Frontal bones

Anterior fontanelle

Sagittal suture

Posterior fontanelle

Metopic suture

Coronal suture

Parietal bones

Lambdoid suture

Occipital bone

Plagiocephaly

Trigonocephaly

Scaphocephaly

Brachycephaly

Illustration of a normal skull (left) and those with the four types of of craniosynostosis. Plagiocephaly, in which one side of the coronal suture closes prematurely, is the most common type. *(Illustration by GGS Information Services.)*

Surgery involves releasing the fused sutures and reshaping the bone of the skull and eye orbit. The fused sutures are excised (removed), and the skull reshaped and replaced with a variety of materials. Surgery usually lasts for three to seven hours, and several days of **hospitalization** are necessary to monitor and treat any complications of the surgery. When more severe deformities are present, repeat surgery of the skull and eye sockets may be necessary. This will help release and advance the child's mid-face.

In the early 2000s, newer, less invasive techniques are being developed using endoscopes. Endoscopes are narrow tubes that are inserted into the brain through narrow incisions (cuts). They allow surgeons to visualize the brain and pass tiny surgical instruments through the tube to perform surgery to re-open the sutures and allow the brain to grow normally.

Children born with co-existing craniofacial conditions, such as Apert syndrome, which affects the growth of the jaw, may benefit from a technique called mandibular bone lengthening or distraction osteogenesis. This technique was first used in Russia to treat bone problems

in the leg and has now been used successfully to correct deformities of the jaw.

Positional plagiocephaly (positional molding, deformational plagiocephaly)

Positional plagiocephaly, the result of an infant's back sleeping position, can be treated by varying the infant's sleeping position from back to side sleeping, and providing tummy **play** time. A wedge-shaped foam pillow sold at many baby stores may help position the infant for side sleeping. The child may also be repositioned in the crib or the crib's location changed. When positional molding is identified at less than three months of age, repositioning is usually successful in stopping the plagiocephaly and reversing the flattening. If the flattening is severe or the condition is not caught until an infant is older, a helmet may be necessary. The helmet is specifically made for the infant by an orthotic specialist, a person who creates devices that provide more normal functioning for impaired people. The infant may wear the helmet for up to 23 hours daily, removing it only during baths. Average length of treatment is three to six months. The helmet gently redirects the skull's growth and is most successful when the skull is most pliable, from about three months to about six months. The plagiocephaly will be monitored throughout this time, and the helmet adjusted as the child grows.

Prognosis

It is important to detect and treat craniosynostosis early. Untreated craniosynostosis will remain the same or worsen as a child grows and can affect a child's mental and physical development. Associated neuromuscular conditions also may affect the child's development. A child with craniosynostosis will require ongoing medical evaluations to ensure that the brain, skull, and facial bones are developing properly.

Prevention

As of 2004 there was no known prevention for craniosynostosis. Nothing that parents did or did not do causes the condition. The exception is positional plagiocephaly, which results from an infant being put to sleep on the back. This can be prevented by varying the infant's sleeping position from back to side sleeping, and providing tummy play time. A wedge-shaped foam pillow sold at many baby stores may help position the infant for side sleeping.

Parents who have an increased likelihood of carrying the genes that result in craniosynostosis may seek genetic counseling to better understand inheritance patterns and chances for reoccurrence.

Parental concerns

The physical symptoms of an asymmetrical face and head seen when a child has craniosynostosis are readily apparent and may cause the child embarrassment. The pressure a growing brain exerts on a fused suture also can cause a delay in development or, rarely, permanent brain damage. In addition, several conditions exist along with craniosynostosis and need to be evaluated.

A child needs to be carefully evaluated when craniosynostosis is present to distinguish between positional plagiocephaly, caused by back sleeping, and other forms of craniosynostosis. Positional plagiocephaly can be treated by repositioning the infant and perhaps by having the infant wear a helmet. Craniosynostosis must be treated by surgery. The differential diagnosis and treatment of posterior plagiocephaly is a challenging aspect of craniofacial surgery.

Resources

PERIODICALS

Coumoul, Xavier, and Deng Chu-Xia. "Roles of FGF receptors in mammalian development and congenital diseases." *Birth Defects Research Part C: Embryo Today: Reviews* 69 (2003): 286–304.

Jimenez, David, et al. "Endoscopy-assisted wide-vertex craniectomy, barrel stave osteotomies, and postoperative helmet molding therapy in the management of sagittal suture craniosynostosis." *Journal of Neurosurgery (Pediatrics 5)* 100 (2002): 407–17.

Kabbani, H., and T. S. Raghuveer. "Craniosynostosis." *American Family Physician* 69 (June 15, 2004): 2863–70.

Panchal, Jayesh, and Venus Uttchin. "Management of Craniosynostosis." *Plastic & Reconstructive Surgery* 111 (May 2003): 2032–49.

ORGANIZATIONS

Crouzon Support Network. PO Box 1272, Edmonds, WA 98020. Web site: <www.crouzon.org/>.

FACES: The National Craniofacial Association. PO Box 11082, Chattanooga, TN 37401. Web site: <www.faces-cranio.org/>.

National Association for Rare Disorders. 55 Kenosia Avenue, PO Box 1968, Danbury, CT 06813–1968. Web site: <www.rarediseases.org/info/contact.html>.

WEB SITES

"Autosomal dominant." *MedlinePlus*, June 15, 2003. Available online at <www.nlm.nih.gov/medlineplus/ency/article/002049.htm> (accessed December 9, 2004).

"Autosomal recessive." *MedlinePlus*, June 15, 2003. Available online at <www.nlm.nih.gov/medlineplus/ency/article/002052.htm> (accessed December 9, 2004).

"Craniofacial Anomalies." *The Children's Hospital of Philadelphia*, 2002. Available online at <www.chop.edu/consumer/your_child/condition_section_index.jsp?id=9703> (accessed December 9, 2004).

"Craniosynostosis: A new less, invasion treatment." *Craniosynostosis Net*, July 15, 2003. Available online at <www.craniosynostosis.net/about.html> (accessed December 9, 2004).

"NINDS Craniosynostosis Information Page." *National Institute of Neurological Disorders and Stroke*, 2004. Available online at <www.ninds.nih.gov/health_and_medical/disorders/craniosytosis_doc.htm> (accessed December 9, 2004)

Christine Kuehn Kelly

Crawling

Definition

Crawling is a slow creeping mode of locomotion, consisting of forward motion with weight supported by the infant's hands (or forearms) and knees. It is the primary means of mobility in infants.

Description

Crawling is the primary form of mobility achieved by infants before they learn to walk. It is the baby's first method of getting around efficiently on his or her own. In the traditional crawl, babies start by learning to balance on their hands and knees. Then they figure out how to move forward and backward by pushing off with their knees. At the same time they are strengthening the muscles that will soon enable them to walk.

Most babies learn to crawl between six and ten months. Some babies opt for another method of locomotion around this time, like bottom shuffling (scooting around on their bottom, using a hand behind and a foot in front to propel them), slithering on their stomach, or rolling across the room. Five percent of babies skip crawling altogether and move directly to pulling, standing, and walking. Parents should not worry about the infant's style; getting mobile is more important than how the baby does it.

Babies have a primitive crawling reflex at birth, which is instinctively activated when they are on their abdomens. Their legs flex, and they move forward, raising their heads to free them for motion. However, this reflex disappears during the early weeks of life, and true crawling does occur until six months, normally around the same time that an infant is able to sit up alone for extended periods of time. Learning to crawl occurs gradually and is usually complete by the time the baby is nine to ten months old.

Infancy

For most babies, creeping, wriggling, or slithering forward on the stomach comes before crawling, typically by the age of seven months. Infants also find that they can cover a distance simply by rolling from place to place. Especially on smooth floors, it is easy for them to move forward using only their arms or elbows and pulling their legs along, which are held out straight behind them. Infants can also get around while remaining in a seated position and pulling themselves with one or both arms, a form of mobility sometimes called hitching or bottom shuffling. From the infant's perspective, it has

several advantages over crawling: it can leave one arm free, it allows better visibility, and the baby is already in a sitting position when she reaches her destination. Often, these alternate means of mobility are so convenient the child never learns to crawl, advancing directly to pulling herself upright and learning to walk. This is normal and not a cause for concern.

In creeping the infant is prone, with the abdomen touching the floor, and the head and shoulders supported with the weight borne on the elbows. The body is pulled along by movements of the arms, and the legs drag. The leg movements may resemble swimming or kicking.

Crawling is a more advanced locomotion than creeping. The trunk is above the floor, but parallel to it. The infant uses both his hands and knees in propelling himself forward. Not all infants follow this pattern of hitching, creeping, and crawling. Different children use different means of locomotion and may even skip a stage. (Skipping is especially likely if an infant is sick or for some other reason is unable to practice moving about).

Learning to crawl involves gradual trial-and-error attempts. When infants first get up on their hands and knees, they make modest attempts at movement, rocking or swaying in the direction they want to go. When they try to move, their balance is unstable, and they have trouble coordinating their movements, often moving an arm or leg and toppling over. One source of difficulty comes from the fact that neurological control over the arms and shoulders develops faster than control of the legs. For this reason once the infant is finally able to make real progress, he or she often moves backward, because it is easier to push harder with the hands and arms than with the feet. Although parents can provide temporary support by firmly placing their hands against the baby's feet, propelling them into forward motion despite themselves, backwards crawling typically persists for several weeks until the infant's coordination develops. Infants with greater strength in their hands, arms, and shoulders than in their legs and feet may learn to grasp, pull-up, and stand before crawling.

After crawling, the next stage is learning to walk. To that end, an infant soon begins pulling up on everything within reach. Once he or she gets the feel of balancing on the legs, an infant is ready to stand on his own and walk while holding onto furniture.

Common problems

Infant safety

Accidents are a leading cause of death in children from one to 24 months of age. They are second only to acute infections as a cause of acute morbidity and doctor visits. Most accidents in infancy occur because parents either underestimate or overestimate the child's ability. Parents need to learn about their infant's developmental progress to use appropriate **childproofing** measures.

Parental concerns

To encourage crawling, parents can place **toys** and other desirable objects just beyond the baby's reach. They can also use billows, boxes, and sofa cushions to create obstacles courses for the baby to negotiate. This kind of **play** improves the baby's agility and speed.

Once an infant can crawl, the parent needs to provide a safe, roomy area for exploration. The baby is at the beginning of one of the most intense periods of educational development of her life and needs to satisfy her natural curiosity and her enormous capacity to learn by exploring. Rather than restrict her to a small area, it is recommended that parents childproof the home and keep it that way for the next two to three years. The greatest dangers to an inquisitive infant include uncovered electrical outlets; ungated stairways; and household cleaners, medications, and other potentially toxic substances. Other childproofing precautions include removing or securely anchoring lightweight furniture; hiding or securing electrical cords that could be pulled on; keeping valuable items or small objects that could be swallowed out of the baby's reach; keeping crib bars raised high; and strapping the infant securely into high chairs, car seats, and strollers.

When to call the doctor

If a child has not shown an interest in getting mobile by some means, figured out how move his harms and legs together in a coordinated motion, or learned to use both arms and both legs equally by one year of age, par-

Infant crawling on the hands and knees. Most infants learn to crawl between six and eight months of age. *(© Jim Craigmyle/ Corbis.)*

ents may want to discuss the matter with their pediatrician.

See also Gross motor skills.

Resources

BOOKS

Greene, Alan. *From First Kicks to First Steps: Nurturing Your Baby's Development from Pregnancy through the First Year of Life.* New York: McGraw-Hill, 2004.

Lerner, Claire, et al. *Bringing Up Baby: Three Steps to Making Good Decisions in Your Child's First Years.* Washington, DC: Zero to Three Press, 2005.

WEB SITES

"Developmental Milestones: Crawling." *Baby Center.* Available online at <www.babycenter.com/refcap/6501.html> (accessed December 14, 2004).

Aliene S. Linwood, RN, DPA, FACHE

Creativity

Definition

Creativity is the ability to think up and design new inventions, produce works of art, solve problems in new ways, or develop an idea based on an original, novel, or unconventional approach.

Description

Creativity is the ability to see something in a new way, to see and solve problems no one else may know exists, and to engage in mental and physical experiences that are new, unique, or different. Creativity is a critical aspect of a person's life, starting from inside the womb onward through adulthood.

Although many people equate creativity with **intelligence**, the two terms are not synonymous, and it is not necessary to have a genius-level IQ in order to be creative. While creative people do tend to have average or above-average scores on IQ tests, beyond an IQ of about 120 there is little correlation between intelligence and creativity. Researchers have found environment to be more important than heredity in influencing creativity, and a child's creativity can be either strongly encouraged or discouraged by early experiences at home and in school.

Standard intelligence tests measure convergent thinking, which is the ability to come up with a single correct answer. However, creativity involves divergent thinking, which is the ability to come up with new and unusual answers.

Creative individuals tend to share certain characteristics, including a tendency to be more impulsive or spontaneous than others. Nonconformity (not going along with the majority) can also be a sign of creativity. Many creative individuals are naturally unafraid of experimenting with new things; furthermore, creative people are often less susceptible to **peer pressure**, perhaps because they also tend to be self-reliant and unafraid to voice their true feelings even if those go against conventional wisdom.

Creativity in childhood is typically assessed through paper-and-pencil measures such as the Torrance Test of Creative Thinking. These tests are designed to measure divergent thinking, such as fluency, flexibility, originality, and elaboration. Signification criticisms have been raised about these tests as measures of creativity. First is the general problem that there are no universally accepted definitions of creativity. Second, critics of creativity tests argue that these tests do not measure creativity per se but instead reflect the specific abilities that are assessed by the tests. Third, the scores on these tests often depend partly on speed, which is not necessarily a criterion for creativity. A final consistent concern relates to the scoring of creativity tests, which by definition are somewhat subjective. Thus, the reliability of such tests is commonly questioned.

Infancy

Scientific research in the late twentieth century revealed how the quality of interaction with unborn infants affects their later development of creative abilities. From birth to 18 months, infants can be encouraged to engage in creativity by playing with a variety of safe household materials, such as margarine tubs, empty boxes, and large empty spools. Parents and caregivers can encourage experimentation by showing excitement and interest in what babies do.

Parents can encouraged infants to develop creativity by singing to the infant and playing music, moving the infant's hands to music, hanging a colorful mobile over the crib, placing pictures and photos where the baby can focus on them, and playing sound games with infants, such making up nonsense words or using rhyming words when talking to them.

Toddlerhood

From ages 18 months to four years, toddlers have progressively better hand and eye coordination. Caregivers should give them opportunities to develop this coordination by allowing them to draw with water-based paints, with chalk, and with crayons. Toddlers also can develop their creativity by pasting, tearing, cutting, printing, modeling with clay or play dough, or working with various materials to create collage, and for the older child, experimenting with fabric, tie dye, batik, printing, and simple woodwork.

From around 12 months, children may begin to imitate things that adults do. Real fantasy **play** begins at around ages 18 to 21 months. This should not prevent caregivers from playing imaginatively from a younger age, since fantasy play is linked to creativity. Studies have shown that children with very active fantasies tend to have personality traits that contribute to creativity—originality, spontaneity, verbal fluency, and a higher degree of flexibility in adapting to new situations.

Children who fantasize a lot have unusually good inner resources for amusing themselves. Parents can provide materials that lend themselves to fantasy play (dressing-up clothes, dolls, housecleaning sets, and stuffed animals), play pretending games with their children, and make suggestions and encourage new ideas when toddlers play alone.

Adults should start involving toddlers with creative activities as soon as they feel the child will enjoy them. Adults need to remember that young toddlers are not skillful enough to consciously produce works of art. At 18 months they may be more ready for creative play and even at this age, they may spend no more than five minutes of concentration on any one activity.

Preschool

Preschoolers can use the same materials as toddlers but can use them in more complex ways. By age five, many children start drawing recognizable objects. By age six, they are usually interested in explaining their art works. They also like to tell stories and can make books of their stories, including drawing pictures to accompany the writing.

At this age fantasy play becomes more complex. Preschoolers often direct each other on what to do or say as they play "Let's pretend." Play is a critical part of developing creativity, according to Mary Mindess, a child psychology professor at Lesley University in Cambridge, Massachusetts. "Play allows children to construct meaning for themselves," Mindess stated in an article in the August 2001 newsletter *The Brown University Child and Adolescent Behavior Letter*. "Two children may share an experience, but each will process the experience differently. Very often during play, children take things they see in real life, or things they imagine they experience—like something they read in a book or saw on television—and make meaning of it," she wrote. As an example, she cites Mark Twain's stories about Tom Sawyer and Huckleberry Finn as good role-playing examples. "They include many examples of play," she wrote. "If, as in a scene in *The Adventures of Tom Sawyer*, a child pretends to be a riverboat captain, there's a lot more to that role-playing than simply knowing what a captain does and some basic boat terminology. There are feelings that accompany the role-playing: mainly, the power of being captain and the satisfaction in the ability to make decisions."

School age

Early school-age children, six to nine years, incorporate lots of fantasy into their play, including action games with superheroes. Children of this age group spend much of their time daydreaming. Some daydreams become "real" as children begin to act them out in stories and plays.

Many researchers believe that in order to foster creativity in schools, education should be based on the discovery of knowledge and the development of critical attitudes, rather than on the passive absorption of knowledge. They believe this applies whether the class is in art, history, science, or humanities. However, most school teaching in the United States is based on the child's ability to memorize. The highest marks are often given to those who merely studied their lessons well. The pupil whose creative side is more developed may be considered a disruptive member of the class.

For this reason some educators decided to encourage creativity outside the school system. Science clubs are open to the young, in different countries, in which students can unleash their ideas and imagination. Student science fairs are also useful in developing creativity.

In the United States, children who participate in the nationwide invention contest organized by the *Weekly Reader* do not have to submit a model. A drawing or a photograph is sufficient to enter the contest, the purpose of which is to stimulate creative thinking among all the students in a class, all becoming involved in the process of invention either individually or in small groups. The class then chooses the best invention that will be presented later at the level of the national contest.

At ages nine to 12, children's creativity is greatly affected by peer influence. They increase the amount of detail and use of symbols in **drawings**. They also have expanded their individual creative differences and begin to develop their own set of creative values.

Teenagers are highly critical of the products they make and ideas they have. They try to express themselves creatively in a more adult-like way. Their creativity is influenced by their individual differences, physically, mentally, emotionally, and socially. In most high schools, classes that stress creativity, such as art, music, writing, and drama are electives and many may not be required. For many adolescents, high school is their last opportunity to take these creative classes.

Also, teens become more self-aware and self-conscious. This focus often causes them to conform to their peers, which stifles their creativity and makes their thoughts less flexible. Flexibility refers to the ability to consider various alternatives at the same time.

Common problems

Rewards or incentives appear to interfere with creativity and reduce children's flexibility of thought. Studies show that any constraints such as structured instructions reduce creative flexibility in children. Many parents and teachers do not understand that children who are creative are often involved in imaginary play and are motivated by internal rather than external factors.

Parental concerns

Environment appears to play a greater role than heredity in the development of creativity: identical **twins** reared apart show greater differences in creativity than in intellectual ability. **Family** environments with certain characteristics have been found to be more conducive to creativity than others. One of these characteristics is a relaxed parental attitude rather than one that is overly anxious or authoritarian.

On the whole, the families of creative children **discipline** them without rigid restrictions, teaching them respect for values above rules. Similarly, they emphasize achievement rather than grades. The parents in such homes generally lead active, fulfilling lives themselves and have many interests. Finally, they reinforce creativity in their children by a general attitude of respect and confidence toward them and by actively encouraging creative pursuits and praising the results. It has been found that creativity in both children and adults is affected by positive reinforcement.

Positive reinforcement has also been shown to boost fifth graders' scores on creativity tests, help sixth graders write more original stories, and lead college students to produce novel word associations. Studies have also found that positively reinforcing one kind of creative activity encourages original thinking in other areas as well.

Just as certain actions and attitudes on the part of parents can encourage creativity, others have been found to discourage it. Devising restrictive guidelines or instructions for an activity reduces its potential as a creative experience. Unrestricted, imaginative play is central to creativity in children—exposure to new objects and activities stimulates the senses, reinforces exploratory impulses, and results in the openness to new experiences and ideas that foster creative thinking. In addition, anything that takes the focus away from the creative act itself and toward something external to it can be damaging. For example, knowing that one's efforts are going to be evaluated tends to restrict the creative impulse, as does knowing of the possibility of a prize or other reward.

Schools as well as families can encourage creativity by offering children activities that give them an active role in their own learning, allow them freedom to explore within a loosely structured framework, and encourage them to participate in creative activities for the sheer enjoyment of it rather than for external rewards.

When to call the doctor

Several studies have shown relationships sometimes exist between creativity and mental illness, including depression, **schizophrenia**, and **attention-deficit hyperactivity disorder** (ADHD).

For decades, scientists have known that eminently creative individuals have a much higher rate of manic depression or **bipolar disorder** than does the general population. But few controlled studies have been done to build the link between mental illness and creativity. One study that does support such a link was presented at the 2002 annual meeting of the American Psychiatric Association by Stanford University researchers Connie Strong and Terence Ketter. Using personality and **temperament** tests, they found healthy artists to be more similar in personality to individuals with manic depression than to healthy people in the general population.

While creativity itself is not a sign of mental illness, parents should be aware that there is a much higher degree of mental illness, especially depression and bipolar disorder, in creative children than in their less creative peers.

Resources

BOOKS

Bruce, Tina. *Cultivating Creativity in Babies, Toddlers, & Young Children.* London: Hodder & Stoughton, 2004.

Einon, Dorothy. *Creative Child: Recognize and Stimulate Your Child's Natural Talent.* Hauppauge, NY: Barron's Educational Series, 2002.

Fisher, Robert, and Mary Williams. *Unlocking Creativity: A Teacher's Guide to Creativity Across the Curriculum.* London: Taylor & Francis, 2004.

Runco, Mark A., and Robert S. Albert. *Theories of Creativity.* Cresskill, NJ: Hampton Press, 2004.

PERIODICALS

"Biological Basis for Creativity Linked to Mental Illness." *Mental Health Weekly Digest* (October 27, 2003): 4.

Carruthers, Peter. "Human Creativity: Its Cognitive Basis, Its Evolution, and Its Connection with Childhood Pretence." *British Journal for the Philosophy of Science* (June 2002): 225–49.

Mindess, Mary. "Play: The New Dirty Word." *The Brown University Child and Adolescent Behavior Letter* (August 2001): 1.

Talsma, Julia. "Encourage Creative Process to Spur Innovation: Dr. Kelman Outlines Three Elements of Creativity: Inspiration, Insight, Intuition." *Ophthalmology Times* (June 15, 2003): 50.

Tecco, Betsy Dru. "Unleash Your Creativity! When You Take the Time to be Creative, a World of Possibilities Unfolds." *Current Health 2.* (December 2003): 14–18.;

Underwood, Anne. "Real Rhapsody in Blue: A Quirky Phenomenon that Scientists Once Dismissed Could Help Explain the Creativity of the Human Brain." *Newsweek* (December 1, 2003): 67.

ORGANIZATIONS
American Creativity Association. PO Box 5856, Philadelphia, PA 19128. Web site: <www.amcreativityassoc.org>.

WEB SITES
Fowler, Lynda K. "Encouraging Creativity in Children." *Ohio State University Extension*, 2004. Available online at <www.ohioline.osu.edu/flm97/fs06.html> (accessed November 23, 2004).

"Good Times Being Creative." *National Network for Child Care*, February 2004. Available online at <www.nncc.org/Series/good.time.creat.html> (accessed November 23, 2004).

Ken R. Wells

Cretinism *see* **Hypothyroidism**

Cri du chat syndrome

Definition

Cri du chat (a French phrase that means "cry of the cat") syndrome is a group of symptoms that result when a piece of chromosomal material is missing (deleted) from a particular region on chromosome 5. Children born with this chromosomal deletion have a characteristic mewing cat-like cry as infants that is thought to be caused by abnormal development of the larynx (organ in the throat responsible for voice production). They also have unusual facial features, poor muscle tone (**hypotonia**), small head size (microcephaly), and **mental retardation**.

Description

Jerome Lejeune first described cri du chat syndrome in 1963. Cri du chat syndrome is also called 5p minus syndrome or chromosome 5p deletion syndrome because it is caused by a deletion, or removal, of genetic material from chromosome 5. The deletion that causes cri du chat syndrome occurs on the short or p arm of chromosome 5. This deleted genetic material is vital for normal development. Absence of this material results in the features associated with cri du chat syndrome.

A high-pitched mewing cry during infancy is a classic feature of cri du chat. Infants with cri du chat also typically have low birth weight, slow growth, a small head (microcephaly), and poor muscle tone (hypotonia). Infants with cri du chat may also have congenital heart defects, language difficulties, delayed motor skill development, **scoliosis**, and varying degrees of mental retardation. Behavioral problems such as hyperactivity may also develop as the child matures.

Demographics

It has been estimated that cri du chat syndrome occurs in one of every 50,000 live births. According to the 5p minus Society, approximately 50 to 60 children are born with cri du chat syndrome in the United States each year. The syndrome can occur in all races and in both sexes.

Causes and symptoms

Cri du chat is the result of a chromosome abnormality—a deleted piece of chromosomal material on chromosome 5. In 90 percent of children with cri du chat syndrome, the deletion is sporadic. This means that it happens randomly and is not hereditary. If a child has cri du chat due to a sporadic deletion, the chance the parents could have another child with cri du chat is 1 percent. In approximately 10 percent of children with cri du chat, there is a hereditary chromosomal rearrangement that causes the deletion. If a parent has this rearrangement, the risk for their having a child with cri du chat is greater than 1 percent.

An abnormal larynx causes the unusual cat-like cry made by infants that is a hallmark feature of the syndrome. As children with cri du chat get older, the cat-like cry becomes less noticeable. This can make the diagnosis more difficult in older children. In addition to the cat-like cry, individuals with cri du chat also have unusual facial features. These facial differences can be very subtle or more obvious. Microcephaly (small head size) is common. During infancy many children with cri du chat do not gain weight or grow normally. Approximately 30 percent of infants with cri du chat have a congenital heart defect. Hypotonia (poor muscle tone) is also common, leading to problems with eating and slow, but normal development. Mental retardation is present in all children with cri du chat, but the degree of mental retardation varies between children.

When to call the doctor

A doctor should be consulted if a child exhibits symptoms typical of cri du chat syndrome.

Diagnosis

During infancy, the diagnosis of cri du chat syndrome is strongly suspected if the characteristic cat-like cry is heard. If a child has this unusual cry or other features seen in cri du chat syndrome, chromosome testing should be performed. Chromosome analysis provides the definitive diagnosis of cri du chat syndrome and can be performed from a blood test. Chromosome analysis, also called karyotyping, involves staining the chromosomes and examining them under a microscope. In some cases the deletion of material from chromosome 5 can be easily seen. In other cases, further testing must be performed. Fluorescence in-situ hybridization (FISH) is a special technique that detects very small deletions. The majority of the deletions that cause cri du chat syndrome can be identified using the FISH technique.

Treatment

As of 2004, there is no cure for cri du chat syndrome. Treatment consists of supportive care and developmental therapy.

Prognosis

Individuals with cri du chat have a 10 percent mortality during infancy due to complications associated with congenital heart defects, hypotonia, and feeding difficulties. Once these problems are controlled, most individuals with cri du chat syndrome have a normal lifespan. The extent of mental retardation and other symptoms depends on the site of the chromosomal deletions, with larger deletions resulting in more serious symptoms. With extensive early intervention and special schooling, many cri du chat children can develop adequate social, motor, and language skills.

Prevention

As of 2004, cri du chat syndrome had no known prevention.

Parental concerns

Cri du chat syndrome can be detected before birth if the mother undergoes **amniocentesis** testing or chorionic villus sampling (CVS). This testing would only be recommended if the mother or father is known to have a chromosome rearrangement, or if they already have a child with cri du chat syndrome.

Families may wish to seek counseling regarding the effects of the syndrome on relationships within the **family**. Many people respond with guilt, **fear**, or blame when a genetic disorder is diagnosed in the family, or they may overprotect the affected member. Support groups are often good sources of information about cri du chat syndrome; they can offer helpful suggestions about living with it as well as emotional support.

KEY TERMS

Amniocentesis—A procedure performed at 16–18 weeks of pregnancy in which a needle is inserted through a woman's abdomen into her uterus to draw out a small sample of the amniotic fluid from around the baby for analysis. Either the fluid itself or cells from the fluid can be used for a variety of tests to obtain information about genetic disorders and other medical conditions in the fetus.

Chorionic villus sampling—A procedure performed at 10 to 12 weeks of pregnancy in which a needle is inserted either through the mother's vagina or abdominal wall into the placenta to withdraw a small amount of chorionic membrane from around the early embryo. The amniotic fluid can be examined for signs of chromosome abnormalities or other genetic diseases.

Chromosome—A microscopic thread-like structure found within each cell of the human body and consisting of a complex of proteins and DNA. Humans have 46 chromosomes arranged into 23 pairs. Chromosomes contain the genetic information necessary to direct the development and functioning of all cells and systems in the body. They pass on hereditary traits from parents to child (like eye color) and determine whether the child will be male or female.

Congenital—Present at birth.

Deletion—The absence of genetic material that is normally found in a chromosome. Often, the genetic material is missing due to an error in replication of an egg or sperm cell.

Hypotonia—Having reduced or diminished muscle tone or strength.

Karyotyping—A laboratory test used to study an individual's chromosome make-up. Chromosomes are separated from cells, stained, and arranged in order from largest to smallest so that their number and structure can be studied under a microscope.

Microcephaly—An abnormally small head.

ResourcesBooks

Key, Doneen. *Do You Want to Take Her Home?: Trials and Tribulations of Living Life as a Handicapped Person Due to Multiple Birth Defects.* Lancaster, CA: Empire Publishing, 2001.

Moore, Keith L., et al. *Before We Are Born: Essentials of Embryology and Birth Defects.* Kent, UK: Elsevier—Health Sciences Division, 2002.

ORGANIZATIONS

5p- Society. 7108 Katella Ave. #502, Stanton, CA 90680. Web Site: <www.fivepminus.org>.

Alliance of Genetic Support Groups. 4301 Connecticut Ave. NW, Suite 404, Washington, DC 20008. Web site: <www.geneticalliance.org>.

Cri du Chat Society. Department of Human Genetics, Box 33, MCV Station, Richmond VA 23298. Telephone: 804/786-9632.

Cri du Chat Syndrome Support Group. Web site: <www.cridchat.u-net.com>.

National Organization for Rare Disorders (NORD). PO Box 8923, New Fairfield, CT 06812-8923. Web site: <www.rarediseases.org>.

WEB SITES

"Cri du chat syndrome." *Medline Plus.* Available online at <www.nlm.nih.gov/medlineplus/ency/article/001593.htm> (accessed November 16, 2004).

Judith Sims
Holly Ann Ishmael, M.S.

Crib death *see* **Sudden infant death syndrome**

Cromolyn *see* **Antiasthmatic drugs**

Crossed eyes *see* **Strabismus**

Croup

Definition

Croup is one of the most common respiratory illnesses in children. It is an inflammation of the larynx and the trachea. When a child has croup, that portion of the airway just below the vocal cords narrows and becomes swollen, making breathing both noisy and labored.

Description

Croup is a broad term describing a group of illnesses that affect the larynx, trachea, and bronchi. The key symptom is a harsh, barking **cough**. One of the most common respiratory illnesses in children, croup is frequently noted in infants and children and can have a variety of causes. Before the days of **antibiotics** and immunizations, croup was a dreaded and often deadly disease usually caused by the **diphtheria** bacteria. Though in the early 2000s cases of croup are normally mild, it can still be dangerous. Croup affects the vocal cords and the area just below, the voice box, or larynx, and the windpipe, or trachea. The lower breathing passages (bronchi) may also be affected. Swelling of these areas causes the airway to narrow, which makes breathing difficult. It is also sometimes called laryngotracheitis, a medical term describing the inflammation of the trachea and larynx.

The characteristic symptoms of croup can be better understood by knowing the anatomic makeup of a child's larynx. Small children typically have quite a narrow larynx, so even a slight decrease in the airway's radius may lead to a large decrease in the air flow, leading to the symptoms of croup.

There are two primary types of croup: viral and spasmodic. Viral croup is caused by a viral infection in the trachea and larynx. It often starts with a cold that over time develops into a barking cough. When the child's airway becomes increasingly swollen and more mucus is secreted, it becomes more challenging to breathe. Breathing gets increasingly noisy, and a condition known as **stridor** may occur. (Stridor is a sign of respiratory obstruction that presents as a high-pitched, coarse, musical sound that occurs during breathing.) Children with viral croup usually have a low-grade temperature, but a few may have fevers up to 104°F (40°C). As breathing requires more effort, the child may stop eating and drinking. The child may also become too fatigued to even cough. If the airway continues to swell, it may approach a point at which the child can no longer breathe. Stridor is fairly common with a mild case of croup, especially if the child is active or crying. However, if a child has stridor at rest, the child may have severe croup. Symptoms are usually worse at night. The symptoms peak between 24 and 48 hours and usually resolve within one week.

Spasmodic croup is usually precipitated by an allergy or mild upper respiratory infection. It can be quite alarming, both because of the noise of the cough and because it usually comes on suddenly in the middle of the night. A child may go to **sleep** with a mild cold and wake up a few hours later, gasping for air. In addition, the child may have a cough that sounds like a seal barking, and will have a hoarse voice. Children with spasmodic croup normally do not have a **fever**.

Spasmodic croup can sometimes be difficult to differentiate from viral croup. Although spasmodic croup is associated with the same viruses that cause viral croup, spasmodic croup tends to recur and may be an indication of some type of allergic reaction instead of a direct infection.

Transmission

The viruses causing croup are highly contagious and easily transmitted between individuals through sneezing and coughing. It is usually transmitted via the respiratory route, entering through the nose and nasopharynx.

Demographics

Croup accounts for about 15 percent of all respiratory tract infections in children seen by physicians. It typically is seen in late fall and winter, and primarily occurs in children aged six months to three years. It has an annual peak incidence of 50 new cases per 1,000 children during the second year of life. Males are twice as likely as females to get the disease. The incidence decreases significantly after age six.

Causes and symptoms

Croup is most commonly brought on by a viral infection. The parainfluenza viruses (types 1, 2, and 3) are the most frequent causes of croup, accounting for approximately 75 percent of all cases diagnosed. Human parainfluenza virus 1 (HPIV-1) is the most common cause. Croup may also be caused by **influenza** A and B, adenovirus, **measles**, and respiratory syncytial virus (RSV). Other possible causes of croup are bacteria, inhaled irritants, **allergies**, and acid reflux.

The following are usually true of viral croup:

- It commonly occurs in individuals between the ages six months to six years.

- Stridor, and the classic barking cough are usually present.

- The child may have a fever.

- Wheezing may be present.

- It usually lasts two to seven days.

The following items are characteristic of spasmodic croup:

- The symptoms come on suddenly, often in the middle of the night.

- Stridor occurs along with the barking cough.

- It typically lasts two to four hours.

When to call the doctor

Most cases of croup can be safely managed at home, but parents should call their child's doctor for advice, even if it is in the middle of the night. Call 911 for emergency help if any of the following is true:

- The croup is possibly caused by an inhaled object or by an insect sting.

- The child is drooling.

- The child has blue lips or skin.

- The child has a very high fever.

- The child is very anxious, has rapid breathing, and/or is struggling to get a breath.

- The child insists on sitting up or complains of a **sore throat** and is drooling. This is a possible indication that he or she may have a disease called **epiglottitis**, which is potentially life-threatening.

- The child makes a whistling sound that gets louder with each breath.

- The child has stridor when resting.

Diagnosis

The diagnosis of croup is usually made based on the description of symptoms by the parent, as well as a physical examination. Sometimes other studies, such as **x rays**, may be required. The doctor may note chest retractions with breathing and may hear wheezing and decreased breath sounds when listening to the chest with a stethoscope. Sometimes a foreign object or narrowing of the trachea is seen on a neck x ray.

Treatment

The most important part of treating patients with croup is maintaining an open airway. If a child wakes up in the middle of the night with croup, he or she should be taken to the bathroom. The door should be closed and the shower turned on to allow the bathroom to steam up. The parent should then sit in the steamy bathroom with the child. The moist, warm air should assist the child in breathing within 15 to 20 minutes, though the child will still have the barking cough. For the rest of that night and for two to three nights following, a humidifier or cold-water vaporizer should be placed in the child's room. If another attack of croup recurs that night or the next, the steam treatment should be repeated. If the steam does not work, sometimes taking the child outside, where he or she can inhale the cool, moist night air will be enough to improve breathing. Though a study in the early 2000s cast some doubt on the efficacy of using steam or mist, it does seem to be helpful for most children with croup. Parents may also give **acetaminophen** to reduce fevers

and increase the child's comfort level. Cough medicines should usually be avoided.

Several other treatments are possible if the croup is severe enough to warrant the child's being seen by a physician. Aerosolized racemic epinephrine as well as oral dexamethasone (a steroid) may be used to help shrink the upper airway swelling. A bacterial infection will require antibiotics. If the airway becomes increasingly obstructed, the child may require intubation (the placing of a tube through the nose or mouth through the larynx into the main air passage to the lungs.) If the patient is dehydrated, intravenous fluids will be administered.

Prognosis

Croup is normally a self-limiting disease with an excellent prognosis. Only a few who are diagnosed require **hospitalization**, and less than 5 percent require intubation. If proper airway management is maintained, death is rare. There is some speculation that children with a history of croup may be at a higher risk for developing **asthma**, but the evidence was not clear as of 2004.

Prevention

The best way to prevent croup is to prevent the causative infections. Parents should practice excellent hand washing, especially during the cold and flu season, and avoid close contact with anyone who has a respiratory infection.

Parental concerns

The onset of croup can be frightening, especially when it comes on suddenly. Parents can help their child by not panicking or appearing anxious, as this may increase anxiety in the child, which can worsen symptoms. If they are at all unsure about how their child is responding to home treatment, parents should not hesitate to seek medical advice or treatment, no matter the time of day or night.

See also Influenza.

Resources

PERIODICALS

Colletti, James E. "Myth: Cool Mist Is an Effective Therapy in the Management of Croup." *Canadian Journal of Emergency Medicine* 6 (September 2004): 5, 357–9.

Knutson, Doug, and Ann Aring. "Viral Croup." *American Family Physician* 69 (February 1, 2004): 3, 535–40.

KEY TERMS

Epiglottitis—Inflammation of the epiglottis, most often caused by a bacterial infection. The epiglottis is a piece of cartilage behind the tongue that closes the opening to the windpipe when a person swallows. An inflamed epiglottis can swell and close off the windpipe, thus causing the patient to suffocate. Also called supraglottitis.

Larynx—Also known as the voice box, the larynx is the part of the airway that lies between the pharynx and the trachea. It is composed of cartilage that contains the apparatus for voice production–the vocal cords and the muscles and ligaments that move the cords.

Retractions—Tugging-in between the ribs when breathing in.

Stridor—A term used to describe noisy breathing in general and to refer specifically to a high-pitched crowing sound associated with croup, respiratory infection, and airway obstruction.

Trachea—The windpipe. A tube composed of cartilage and membrane that extends from below the voice box into the chest where it splits into two branches, the bronchi, that lead to each lung.

"Patient Education Guide: What to Do When Your Child Has Croup." *Journal of Respiratory Diseases* 23 (March 2002): 23, 192–5.

ORGANIZATIONS
American Academy of Pediatrics. 141 Northwest Point Boulevard, Elk Grove Village, IL 60007–1098. Web site: <www.aap.org>.

WEB SITES
"Croup." *MedlinePlus.* Available online at <www.nlm.nih.gov/medlineplus/ency/article/000959.htm> (accessed January 11, 2005).

Deanna M. Swartout-Corbeil, RN

Crying and fussing in an infant

Definition

All babies cry and fuss. Many infants spend a considerable amount of time being fussy. Young infants cry between one and five hours out of 24. Crying is important for babies; it is the baby's first way of communicating and an important way to release tension. Constant crying, though, can be a symptom of **colic** or a sign that something else is wrong.

Description

The baby's cry is a perfect signal of life. It has three features:

- The newborn's cry is automatic and reflexive. The infant senses a need, which triggers a sudden inspiration of air followed by a forceful expelling of that air through vocal cords, which vibrate to produce the sound called a cry.

- The baby's cry is disturbing, even ear-piercing, loud enough to catch the caregiver's attention but not so disturbing as to make the listener want to avoid the sound altogether.

- Third, the cry can be personalized as both the sender and the listener learn ways to make the signal more precise. Each baby's cry is as unique as his or her fingerprints.

Infancy

Crying in infants is a normal, healthy means of expression and communication. The average six-week-old baby cries for two-and-a-half hours every day. Infants cry because they are hungry, uncomfortable, in **pain**, overstimulated, tired, or just bored. A new mother can distinguish her infant's crying from that of other babies within three days, and some fathers can make this distinction as well. A hungry cry begins softly and then becomes loud and rhythmic; an angry cry is similar to a hungry cry but louder. A cry of pain has a distinctive pattern, beginning with a single shriek followed by a short silence and then continuous loud wailing. Neglected or abused infants have a high-pitched cry that is difficult for adults to tolerate. This cry is characteristic of babies born to crack-addicted mothers and has been linked to abnormalities in the central nervous system. An infant's crying patterns and ability to be comforted are important indicators of **temperament**, both in infancy and even in later years.

The most common way to comfort a crying infant is to hold him or her close to the chest. Some infants are soothed by the motion of a cradle, rocking chair, stroller, swing, or automobile. Sucking on a pacifier is another comfort. Other methods include a warm bath, a massage, music, or some background noise, such as the sound of a hair dryer, a washing machine, or fan. There are also special recordings that reproduce sounds similar to those the infant heard while in the mother's womb. Some infants are hypersensitive to stimuli, and their crying will get worse if they receive any more than a minimum of comforting, such as parental holding or cuddling. A sign of healthy emotional development is the degree to which an infant learns to comfort him- or herself, either with the aid of an object such as a stuffed toy or blanket, or by certain patterns of behavior, such as sucking on a thumb.

Another cause of excessive crying is hypersensitivity. Hypersensitive infants cry in response to new experiences that do not normally upset other babies; ordinary comforting measures, such as holding, rocking, feeding, or swaddling do not work and may even make the crying worse. Hypersensitivity can be a matter of temperament, and it may be influenced by the behavior and attitude of the parents. Some children get into the habit of excessive crying as a way of demanding parental attention. The parents of such children may be overprotective, not giving them the chance to develop independence and resourcefulness by solving problems on their own.

Common problem

Many new parents are not prepared for the amount of time a newborn spends crying. Infants typically cry an average of two hours of every 24 for the first seven weeks of life. The duration peaks at about six or seven weeks. Almost all infants have a period during the day when they are fussy. New parents need to recognize this as normal and not worry. Parents might use this fussy time for bathing or playing with the infant. The most typical time for fussy times is between 6 p.m. and 11 p.m., often when parents are tired and less able to tolerate crying.

A common cause of persistent crying in infants is colic, which is caused by gastrointestinal distress. Colicky infants may have a hard abdomen, get red in the face, and curl their legs up. Often times the colic begins in the evening after the baby's last meal before bedtime. Rocking or walking around with the baby held up against the shoulder can sometimes soothe the infant. Holding the infant face-down across the lap puts pressure on the belly that can sometimes ease the distress.

Among the most common physical reasons for excessive crying are earaches, viral illnesses, and other causes of low grade **fever**. Teething also causes increased crying. Medical attention may be necessary if an infant is crying more than usual or if the cries themselves sound different, for example, the cries are weaker or more high-pitched than usual.

Different kinds of cries

As parents get to know their baby, they become experts in understanding the baby's cries. Cries are the baby's form of communication. Following are several common reasons babies cry:

- Hunger: If three or four hours have passed since the last feeding, if the infant has just awakened, or if he or she had just had a full diaper and begins to cry, the baby is probably hungry. Most babies eat six to ten times in a 24-hour period. For at least the first three months, babies usually wake for night feedings.

- Tiredness: The baby has decreased activity, loses interest in people and **toys**, rubs eyes, looks glazed, and yawns. If the infant cries, he or she may just need to take a nap.

- Discomfort: If babies are uncomfortable, too wet, too hot, or too cold, they will squirm or arch their back when crying, as they try to get away from the source of discomfort. The distress of gas or indigestion can cause the baby to cry, as can wet or soiled diapers and uncomfortable positions. Parents should try to find the source of the child's distress and solve the problem.

- Pain: A sudden shrill cry followed by a brief silence and then more crying communicates pain. The parents should examine the baby carefully to locate the source of pain and remove it.

- Overstimulation: When overtired or overstimulated, babies cry to release tension. If the room is noisy and people are trying to get the baby's attention, the baby may close his eyes, turn his head away, and cry. The parent should find a quiet, dark room and hold the baby until he or she is calmer.

- Illness: When babies are sick, they may cry in a weak, moaning way. If the baby seems ill, parents should take their temperature and call the healthcare provider.

- Frustration: Some babies cry out of frustration because they cannot do what they want to do. Sometimes they want a toy but cannot control their arms and hands enough to reach it. Taking note of the baby's attention to an object and putting it within reach may solve the problem.

- Loneliness: Babies who fall asleep feeding and are placed in a crib may wake soon afterwards crying. These babies are signaling that they miss the warmth of their parent's embrace and do not like being alone. A baby seeking such comfort may calm down simply with the assuring sight of mother, hearing her voice, feeling her touch, cuddling, or being offered something to suck.

- Worry or **fear**: When the baby suddenly finds himself in the arms of a stranger and cannot see the parent, the baby may begin to cry. Some babies need more time than others to warm up to someone new.

- Boredom: If the baby has been left to **play** while a parent is busy with another task, boredom may set in. The child is not tired, hungry, or uncomfortable, but starts a whiny, fussy cry. A new position or different toy may help.

Parental concerns

Responding to baby's cry is biologically correct. Mothers are biologically programmed to give a nurturing response to their newborn's cries and not to restrain themselves. Biological changes take place in a mother's body in response to their infant's cry. On hearing the baby cry, the blood flow to the mother's breast increases, with a biological urge to nurse. The act of breastfeeding itself causes a surge of prolactin. Hormones that cause a mother's milk to let down brings feelings of relaxation and pleasure; it is a pleasant release from the tension built up by the baby's cry. These biological responses help mothers to connect with and meet their babies' needs.

New parents sometimes feel guilty when their babies cry. It is not the parent's fault that babies cry. Parents should be responsive to their babies and try to help them feel secure in their world. The parent's job is to create a sympathetic environment that lessens the baby's need to cry, to offer a set of caring and relaxed arms so the baby does not need to cry, and to do as much detective work to figure out why the baby is crying as possible.

There are many times when parents cannot tell why their baby is crying. Some things to try include:

- Hold the baby. No matter the reason for the baby's crying, holding offers security and may calm the baby.

- Breastfeed. Nursing the baby is as much for comfort as food. Most babies calm easily when offered the breast.

- Provide motion. Babies enjoy repetitive, rhythmic motion such as rocking, swinging, swaying, and jiggling. Many parents sway when they are holding a fussy baby because it soothes the baby.

- Turn on some white noise. The womb was a noisy place. Sometimes the baby can be calmed by white noise that is continuous and uniform, such as that of a heartbeat, the rain, static between radio stations, and the vacuum cleaner. Some alarm clocks even have a white noise.

KEY TERMS

Diagnosis—The art or act of identifying a disease from its signs and symptoms.

Hormone—A chemical messenger secreted by a gland or organ and released into the bloodstream. It travels via the bloodstream to distant cells where it exerts an effect.

Hypersensitivity—A condition characterized by an excessive response by the body to a foreign substance. In hypersensitive individuals even a tiny amount of allergen can cause a severe allergic reaction.

Swaddling—To wrap the infant securely in clothing or blankets; to provide comfort and control.

- Let music soothe the baby. Soft, peaceful music calms some babies.

- Give the baby a massage. Babies love to be touched and stroked, so a massage is one way to calm a fussy baby. A variation of massage is the baby pat; many babies love a gentle rhythmic pat on their backs or bottoms.

- Swaddle the baby. During the first three or four months of life, many babies feel comforted if they are held tightly in a way the reminds them of the womb.

- Distract the baby. Sometimes a new activity or change of scenery is calming. Maybe a walk outside, a dance with a song, or a splashy bath can be helpful in turning a fussy baby into a happy one.

- Let the baby have something to suck on. The most natural pacifier is mother's breast, but pacifiers and teething rings also may work. It is important for everything to be clean that goes into the baby's mouth.

When to call the doctor

Parents should call the healthcare provider if there are concerns about why the baby continues to cry. It is important not to misdiagnose a serious condition and call it colic. If the baby's behavior or crying pattern changes suddenly or if the crying is associated with fever, forceful **vomiting**, **diarrhea**, bloody stools, or other abnormal spasms or symptoms, call the doctor immediately. Parents should not hesitate to seek help immediately if they feel overwhelmed and are afraid that they will hurt or neglect their baby.

See also Colic.

Resources

BOOKS

Jones, Sandy. *Comforting Your Crying Baby: Why Your Baby Is Crying and What You Can Do about It.* New York: Innova Publishing, 2005.

Lester, Barry M. *Why My Baby Is Crying: The Parent's Survival Guide to Copying with Crying Problems and Colic.* London: Harper Information, 2005.

Nelson, Judith Kay. *Crying, Caregiving, and Connection: An Attachment Perspective.* Florence, KY: Brunner-Routledge, 2005.

WEB SITES

Nissi, Jan. "Crying: Age 3 and Younger." *PeaceHealth*, March 3, 2003. Available online at <www.peacehealth.org/kbase/topic/symptom/crybb/overview.htm> (accessed December 14, 2004).

Aliene S. Linwood, RN, DPA, FACHE

Cryptochidism *see* **Undescended testes**

CT scan *see* **Computed tomography**

Custody laws *see* **Child custody laws**

Cuts *see* **Wounds**

Cyclic vomiting syndrome

Definition

First described in 1882, cyclic **vomiting** syndrome (CVS) is a rare idiopathic disorder characterized by recurring periods of vomiting in an otherwise normal child. The word, idiopathic, means that the origin of the disorder is unknown. The syndrome is sometimes called abdominal migraine because it may be caused by some of the same mechanisms in the central nervous system that cause migraine headaches.

Description

Children with cyclic vomiting syndrome have bouts of severe **nausea and vomiting** that may last for hours or days. In some cases the vomiting is so severe that the child is unable to go to school for several days. The episodes alternate with periods of normal digestive functioning.

The bouts of vomiting that characterize CVS usually begin at the same time of day as previous episodes, last about the same length of time, and have the same symptoms. The most common pattern is severe **nausea** and vomiting that begins late at night or early in the morning. The child may vomit as often as six to 12 times an hour over a period of one to five days, although cases have been reported in which the episode lasts for ten days. The vomited material may contain blood or bile as well as mucus or watery fluid.

In addition to the vomiting, the child may have a **headache**, low-grade **fever**, **dizziness**, **pain** in the abdomen, heavy drooling, and **diarrhea**. Some children also become unusually sensitive to light, while others may be unable to walk or talk.

Demographics

Children between the ages of three and seven years are most susceptible to CVS, although it can appear at any time from infancy to adulthood. The average age of patients at onset is 5.2 years, but CVS has been diagnosed in patients as old as 73.

The frequency of cyclic vomiting syndrome in the general population is not known for certain as of the early 2000s, but it is thought that the disorder is probably underdiagnosed because other diseases and disorders can also cause periods of acute nausea and vomiting. Some researchers think that as many as one child in 50 may have CVS.

CVS appears to affect all races and ethnic groups equally. The female-to-male ratio has been reported as 11 to nine.

Causes and symptoms

Causes

The cause of CVS is as of 2004 a mystery. Similarities to migraine suggest a common cause, but no firm evidence has been found. It is known, however, that 82 percent of patients with CVS have a **family** history of migraine compared to 14 percent of control subjects. Patients can usually identify some factor that precedes an attack. Common triggers of CVS episodes include the following:

- stress and excitement
- certain foods, particularly chocolate and cheese
- bacterial or viral infections, particularly colds, sinus infections, and influenza
- hot and humid weather

- **motion sickness**

- lack of sleep

- menstruation

In the summer of 2003, two teams of researchers in Italy and the United States reported that some cases of CVS appear to be caused by a DNA mutation that affects the proper functioning of the mitochondria (energy generators) in human cells and that this mutation is inherited from the mother. Further research is needed, however, in order to determine whether other genetic factors are involved in CVS.

Symptoms

Vomiting associated with CVS can be protracted and lead to such complications as **dehydration**; erosion of tooth enamel leading to **tooth decay**; unbalanced blood electrolyte levels; and tearing, burning, or bleeding of the esophagus (swallowing tube). Between attacks, however, the child has no sign of any illness.

CVS has four distinct stages or phases:

- Prodrome: A warning symptom (or group of symptoms) appears just before an acute attack of an illness. Patients with CVS often feel pain in the abdomen a few minutes or hours before the vomiting starts. Adults with CVS often have **anxiety** or panic attacks as a prodrome.

- Episode phase: The patient is actively nauseated and vomiting and cannot keep down any food or medications given by mouth. He or she may also feel drowsy, dizzy, or exhausted.

- Recovery phase: The vomiting stops and the child's normal appetite and level of energy return.

- Symptom-free interval.

When to call the doctor

The vomiting and other symptoms associated with CVS are so severe that parents will usually call the doctor during the first episode, before a pattern has been identified. It may take several episodes of the disorder before the parents or the doctor notice a pattern.

Diagnosis

The most important and difficult aspect of diagnosing CVS is to make sure there is not an acute and life-threatening event in progress. So many different diseases can cause vomiting—from bowel obstruction to epilepsy—that an accurate and timely diagnosis is critical. Because there is no way to prove the diagnosis of CVS, the physician must instead disprove every other diagnosis. This process, which is known as a diagnosis of exclusion, can be tedious, expensive, exhausting, and involve almost every system in the body. The first episode of cyclic vomiting syndrome may be diagnosed as stomach flu when nothing more serious turns up. Only after several episodes and several fruitless searches for a cause will a physician normally consider the diagnosis of CVS.

A careful history-taking is critical to making the correct diagnosis of CVS. A family history of migraine, particularly on the mother's side of the family, should alert the doctor to the possibility that the patient has CVS. The doctor may also order blood tests for metabolic screening or imaging studies of the kidneys, gall bladder, small bowel, or sinuses in order to rule out endocrine disorders, gastrointestinal disorders, kidney disease, and chronic **sinusitis**.

In some cases, the doctor may refer the patient to a psychiatrist for evaluation in order to rule out depression, anxiety disorders, or an eating disorder.

Treatment

There is no permanent cure for cyclic vomiting syndrome as of the early 2000s. Doctors as of 2004 recommend a combination of several strategies for managing the disorder:

- Avoidance of known dietary or stress-related triggers: Such triggers as hot weather or automobile transportation, however, may be difficult or impossible to avoid.

- Prophylactic treatment with medications: Prophylactic treatment refers to therapy that is given to prevent a disease. This approach is recommended for children with CVS who have 10 to 12 episodes per year or have episodes of vomiting lasting longer than three days. Several different medications have given good results in small trials. The antimigraine drugs amitriptyline (Elavil) and cyproheptadine (Periactin) performed well for children in one study group. Propranolol (Inderal) is sometimes effective for children with CVS, and erythromycin helped several patients in one study—not because it is an antibiotic but because it irritates the stomach and encourages it to move its contents forward instead of in reverse.

- Abortive treatment: Abortive treatment is therapy given to stop an attack of CVS after it has begun. Drugs that have been found to work well as abortive agents are ondansetron (Zofran, an antinausea drug) and sumatriptan (Imitrex, an antimigraine drug). These drugs can be given intravenously, and sumatriptan is also available as a nasal solution.

- Supportive care: Supportive care for episodes of CVS includes such antinausea drugs as diphenhydramine (Benadryl) or chlorpromazine (Largactil), and intravenous fluids when necessary.

Another medication that has been reported to be successful in treating children with CVS is dexmedetomidine (Precedex), which was originally developed to sedate patients on respirators in intensive care settings. The researchers found that dexmedetomidine relieved the anxiety as well as the nausea associated with CVS.

Alternative treatment

Constitutional homeopathic medicine can work well in treating CVS because it addresses the person's overall health, not just the treatment of acute symptoms.

Stress management techniques may be helpful for older children or teenagers in preventing episodes of CVS triggered by emotional or psychological stress. These techniques may include the relaxation response developed by Herbert Benson, meditation, and biofeedback.

Weekly outpatient acupuncture treatments are also helpful to some children with CVS.

Nutritional concerns

Avoiding dehydration is the primary nutritional concern during episodes of cyclic vomiting syndrome. In most cases the child will bring up water that is offered during the acute phase of an attack even though he or she may be very thirsty. About 50 percent of children require an intravenous infusion of glucose and water to prevent dehydration.

Some children have a normal appetite for food soon after the vomiting stops, while others may take several days to return to a full diet. Parents should offer the child clear liquids first to prevent dehydration and gradually reintroduce solid foods as the child's appetite improves.

Prognosis

The average duration of cyclic vomiting syndrome is 2.5 to 5.5 years. Some children, however, continue to have episodes of the disorder into adulthood. About 60 percent of children diagnosed with CVS eventually develop migraine headaches in **adolescence** or early adulthood. If the more severe complications of prolonged vomiting can be successfully prevented or managed, however, most patients can lead normal lives between acute attacks.

Prevention

Some episodes of vomiting may be prevented by avoiding specific triggers or by taking prophylactic medications. As the cause of the disorder is as of 2004 not yet fully understood, however, there is no way to prevent CVS as a whole.

Parental concerns

Cyclic vomiting syndrome can be a heavy emotional and financial burden on the families of affected children. Episodes of CVS are often upsetting or downright frightening to other family members, in addition to the fact that they often spoil family outings or vacations when they are triggered by excitement or motion sickness. Moreover, CVS can interfere with a child's schooling; most children diagnosed with the disorder miss an average of 20 school days per year and may require tutoring or **home schooling**.

See also Dehydration; Motion sickness; Nausea and vomiting.

Resources

PERIODICALS

Boles, R. G., et al. "Maternal Inheritance in Cyclic Vomiting Syndrome with Neuromuscular Disease." *American Journal of Medical Genetics* 120A (August 1, 2003): 474–82.

Cupini, L. M., et al. "Cyclic Vomiting Syndrome, Migraine, and Epilepsy: A Common Underlying Disorder?" *Headache* 43 (April 2003): 106–07.

Khasawinah, T. A., et al. "Preliminary Experience with Dexmedetomidine in the Treatment of Cyclic Vomiting Syndrome." *American Journal of Therapeutics* 10 (July–August 2003): 303–07.

Li, B. U., and L. Misiewicz. "Cyclic Vomiting Syndrome: A Brain-Gut Disorder." *Gastroenterology Clinics of North America* 32 (September 2003): 997–1019.

Salpietro, C. D., et al. "A Mitochondrial DNA Mutation (A3243G mtDNA) in a Family with Cyclic Vomiting." *European Journal of Pediatrics* 162 (October 2003): 727–28.

ORGANIZATIONS

Cyclic Vomiting Syndrome Association in the United States and Canada (CVSA—USA/Canada). 3585 Cedar Hill Road, NW, Canal Winchester, OH 43110. Web site: <www.cvsaonline.org>.

National Organization for Rare Disorders Inc. (NORD). 55 Kenosia Avenue, PO Box 1968, Danbury, CT 06813. Web site: <www.rarediseases.org>.

KEY TERMS

Abdominal migraine—Another term that is sometimes used for cyclic vomiting syndrome (CVS).

Idiopathic—Refers to a disease or condition of unknown origin.

Mitochondria—Spherical or rod-shaped structures of the cell. Mitochondria contain genetic material (DNA and RNA) and are responsible for converting food to energy.

Prodrome—Early symptoms that warn of the beginning of disease. For example, the herpes prodrome consists of pain, burning, tingling, or itching at a site before blisters are visible while the migraine prodrome consists of visual disturbances.

Prophylactic—Preventing the spread or occurrence of disease or infection.

WEB SITES

"Cyclic Vomiting Syndrome." Available online at <http://digestive.niddk.nih.gov/ddiseases/pubs/cvs/index.htm> (accessed November 16, 2004).

Sundaram, Shikha, and B. UK Li. "Cyclic Vomiting Syndrome." *eMedicine*, August 10, 2002. Available online at <www.emedicine.com/ped/topic2910.htm> (accessed November 16, 2004).

J. Ricker Polsdorfer, MD

Cystic fibrosis

Definition

Cystic fibrosis (CF) is an inherited disease that affects the lungs, digestive system, sweat glands, and male fertility. Its name derives from the fibrous scar tissue that develops in the pancreas, one of the principal organs affected by the disease.

Description

Cystic fibrosis affects the body's ability to move salt and water in and out of cells. This defect causes the lungs and pancreas to secrete thick mucus, blocking passageways and preventing proper function.

Many of the symptoms of CF can be treated with drugs or nutritional supplements. Close attention to and prompt treatment of respiratory and digestive complications have dramatically increased the expected life span of a person with CF. While in the 1970s, most children with CF died by age two, in the early 2000s about half of all people with CF live past age 31. That median age is expected to grow as new treatments are developed, and it is estimated that a person born in 1998 with CF has a median expected life span of 40 years.

Demographics

CF affects approximately 30,000 children and young adults in the United States, and about 3,000 babies are born with CF every year. CF primarily affects people of white northern-European descent; rates are much lower in non-white populations.

Causes and symptoms

Causes

Cystic fibrosis is a genetic disease, meaning it is caused by a defect in the person's genes. Genes, found in the nucleus of all the body's cells, control cell function by serving as the blueprint for the production of proteins. Proteins carry out a wide variety of functions within cells. The gene that, when defective, causes CF is called the CFTR gene, which stands for cystic fibrosis transmembrane conductance regulator. A simple defect in this gene leads to all the consequences of CF. There are over 500 known defects in the CFTR gene that can cause CF. However, 70 percent of all people with a defective CFTR gene have the same defect, known as delta-F508.

Much as sentences are composed of long strings of words, each made of letters; genes can be thought of as long strings of chemical words, each made of chemical letters, called nucleotides. Just as a sentence can be changed by rearranging its letters, genes can be mutated, or changed, by changes in the sequence of their nucleotide letters. The gene defects in CF are called point mutations, meaning that the gene is mutated only at one small spot along its length. In other words, the delta-F508 mutation is a loss of one "letter" out of thousands within the CFTR gene. As a result, the CFTR protein made from its blueprint is made incorrectly and cannot perform its function properly.

The CFTR protein helps to produce mucus. Mucus is a complex mixture of salts, water, sugars, and proteins that cleanses, lubricates, and protects many passageways in the body, including those in the lungs and pancreas. The role of the CFTR protein is to allow chloride ions to exit the mucus-producing cells. When the chloride ions leave these cells, water follows, thinning the mucus. In this way, the CFTR protein helps to keep mucus from becoming thick and sluggish, thus allowing the mucus to be moved steadily along the passageways to aid in cleansing.

In CF, the CFTR protein cannot allow chloride ions out of the mucus-producing cells. With less chloride leaving, less water leaves, and the mucus becomes thick and sticky. It can no longer move freely through the passageways, so they become clogged. In the pancreas, clogged passageways prevent secretion of digestive enzymes into the intestine, causing serious impairment of digestion—especially of fat—which may lead to **malnutrition**. Mucus in the lungs may plug the airways, preventing good air exchange and, ultimately, leading to emphysema. The mucus is also a rich source of nutrients for bacteria, leading to frequent infections.

INHERITANCE OF CYSTIC FIBROSIS Each person actually has two copies of each gene, including the CFTR gene, in each of their body cells. During sperm and egg production, however, these two copies separate, so that each sperm or egg contains only one copy of each gene. When sperm and egg unite, the newly created cell once again has two copies of each gene.

The two gene copies may be the same or they may be slightly different. For the CFTR gene, for instance, a person may have two normal copies, or one normal and one mutated copy, or two mutated copies. A person with two mutated copies will develop cystic fibrosis. A person with one mutated copy is said to be a carrier. A carrier will not have symptoms of CF but can pass on the mutated CFTR gene to his/her children.

When two carriers have children, they have a one-in-four chance of having a child with CF each time they conceive. They have a two-in-four chance of having a child who is a carrier, and a one-in-four chance of having a child with two normal CFTR genes.

Approximately one in every 25 Americans of northern-European descent is a carrier of the mutated CF gene, while only one in 17,000 African Americans and one in 30,000 Asian Americans are carriers. Since carriers are symptom-free, very few people know if they are carriers unless there is a **family** history of the disease. Two white Americans with no family history of CF have a one in 2,500 chance of having a child with CF.

It may seem puzzling that a mutated gene with such harmful consequences would remain so common; one might guess that the high mortality of CF would quickly lead to loss of the mutated gene from the population. Some researchers in the early 2000s believe the reason

for the persistence of the CF gene is that carriers, those with only one copy of the gene, are protected from the full effects of cholera, a microorganism that infects the intestine, causing intense **diarrhea** and eventual death by **dehydration**. It is believed that having one copy of the CF gene is enough to prevent the full effects of cholera infection, while not enough to cause the symptoms of CF. This so-called "heterozygote advantage" is seen in some other genetic disorders, including sickle-cell anemia.

Symptoms

The most severe effects of cystic fibrosis are seen in two body systems: the gastrointestinal (digestive) system and the respiratory tract from the nose to the lungs. CF also affects the sweat glands and male fertility. Symptoms develop gradually, with gastrointestinal symptoms often the first to appear.

GASTROINTESTINAL SYSTEM Approximately 10 to 15 percent of babies who inherit CF have meconium **ileus** at birth. Meconium is the first dark stool that a baby passes after birth; ileus is an obstruction of the digestive tract. The meconium of a newborn with meconium ileus is thickened and sticky, due to the presence of thickened mucus from the intestinal glands. Meconium ileus causes abdominal swelling and **vomiting** and often requires surgery immediately after birth. Presence of meconium ileus is considered highly indicative of CF. Borderline cases may be misdiagnosed, however, and attributed instead to milk allergy.

Other abdominal symptoms are caused by the inability of the pancreas to supply digestive enzymes to the intestine. During normal digestion, as food passes from the stomach into the small intestine, it is mixed with pancreatic secretions that help to break down the nutrients for absorption. While the intestines themselves also provide some digestive enzymes, the pancreas is the major source of enzymes for the digestion of all types of foods, especially fats and proteins.

In CF, thick mucus blocks the pancreatic duct, which is eventually closed off completely by scar tissue formation, leading to a condition known as pancreatic insufficiency. Without pancreatic enzymes, large amounts of undigested food pass into the large intestine. Bacterial action on this rich food source can cause gas and abdominal swelling. The large amount of fat remaining in the feces makes it bulky, oily, and foul-smelling.

Because nutrients are only poorly digested and absorbed, the person with CF is often ravenously hungry, underweight, and shorter than expected for his age. When CF is not treated for a longer period, a child may develop symptoms of malnutrition, including anemia, bloating, and, paradoxically, appetite loss.

Diabetes becomes increasingly likely as a person with CF ages. Scarring of the pancreas slowly destroys those pancreatic cells which produce insulin, producing type I, or insulin-dependent diabetes.

Gallstones affect approximately 10 percent of adults with CF. Liver problems are less common but can be caused by the buildup of fat within the liver. Complications of liver enlargement may include internal hemorrhaging, accumulation of abdominal fluid (ascites), spleen enlargement, and liver failure.

Other gastrointestinal symptoms can include a prolapsed rectum, in which part of the rectal lining protrudes through the anus; intestinal obstruction; and rarely, intussusception, in which part of the intestinal tube slips over an adjoining part, cutting off blood supply.

Somewhat less than 10 percent of people with CF do not have gastrointestinal symptoms. Most of these people do not have the delta-F508 mutation but a different one, which presumably allows at least some of their CFTR proteins to function normally in the pancreas.

RESPIRATORY TRACT The respiratory tract includes the nose, the throat, the trachea (or windpipe), the bronchi (which branch off from the trachea within each lung), the smaller bronchioles, and the blind sacs called alveoli, in which gas exchange takes place between air and blood.

Swelling of the sinuses within the nose is common in people with CF. This usually shows up on an x ray and may aid the diagnosis of CF. However, this swelling, called pansinusitis, rarely causes problems and does not usually require treatment.

Nasal polyps, or growths, affect about one in five people with CF. These growths are not cancerous and do not require removal unless they become annoying. While nasal polyps appear in older people without CF, especially those with **allergies**, they are rare in children without CF.

The lungs are the site of the most life-threatening effects of CF. The production of a thick, sticky mucus increases the likelihood of infection, decreases the ability to protect against infection, causes inflammation and swelling, decreases the functional capacity of the lungs, and may lead to emphysema. People with CF live with chronic populations of bacteria in their lungs, and lung infection is the major cause of death for those with CF.

The bronchioles and bronchi normally produce a thin, clear mucus that traps foreign particles including bacteria and viruses. Tiny hair-like projections on the surface of these passageways slowly sweep the mucus along, out of the lungs and up the trachea to the back of the throat, where it may be swallowed or coughed up. This "mucociliary escalator" is one of the principal defenses against lung infection.

The thickened mucus of CF prevents easy movement out of the lungs and increases the irritation and inflammation of lung tissue. This inflammation swells the passageways, partially closing them down, further hampering the movement of mucus. A person with CF is likely to **cough** more frequently and more vigorously as the lungs attempt to clean themselves out.

At the same time, infection becomes more likely since the mucus is a rich source of nutrients. **Bronchitis**, **bronchiolitis**, and **pneumonia** are frequent in CF. The most common infecting organisms are the bacteria *Staphylococcus aureus, Haemophilus influenzae*, and *Pseudomonas aeruginosa*. A small percentage of people with CF have infections caused by *Burkholderia cepacia*, a bacterium which was resistant to most **antibiotics** as of 2004. (*Burkholderia cepacia* was formerly known as *Pseudomonas cepacia*.) The fungus *Aspergillus fumigatus* may infect older children and adults.

The body's response to infection is to increase mucus production; white blood cells fighting the infection thicken the mucus even further as they break down and release their cell contents. These white blood cells also provoke more inflammation, continuing the downward spiral that marks untreated CF.

As mucus accumulates, it can plug up the smaller passageways in the lungs, decreasing functional lung volume. Getting enough air can become difficult; tiredness, shortness of breath, and intolerance of **exercise** become more common. Because air passes obstructions more easily during inhalation than during exhalation, over time, air becomes trapped in the smallest chambers of the lungs, the alveoli. As millions of alveoli gradually expand, the chest takes on the enlarged, barrel-shaped appearance typical of emphysema.

For unknown reasons, recurrent respiratory infections lead to digital clubbing, in which the last joint of the fingers and toes becomes slightly enlarged.

SWEAT GLANDS The CFTR protein helps to regulate the amount of salt in sweat. People with CF have sweat that is much saltier than normal, and measuring the saltiness of a person's sweat is the most important diagnostic test for CF. Parents may notice that their infants taste salty when they kiss them. Excess salt loss is not usually a problem except during prolonged exercise or heat. While most older children and adults with

CF compensate for this extra salt loss by eating more salty foods, infants and young children are in danger of suffering its effects (such as heat prostration), especially during summer. Heat prostration is marked by lethargy, weakness, and loss of appetite and should be treated as an emergency condition.

FERTILITY Some 98 percent of men with CF are sterile, due to complete obstruction or absence of the vas deferens (the tube carrying sperm out of the testes). While boys and men with CF form normal sperm and have normal levels of sex hormones, sperm are unable to leave the testes, and fertilization is not possible. Most women with CF are fertile, though they often have more trouble getting pregnant than women without CF. In both boys and girls, **puberty** is often delayed, most likely due to the effects of poor **nutrition** or chronic lung infection. Women with good lung health usually have no problems with pregnancy, while those with ongoing lung infection often do poorly.

Diagnosis

The decision to test a child for cystic fibrosis may be triggered by concerns about recurring gastrointestinal or respiratory symptoms or salty sweat. A child born with meconium ileus will be tested before leaving the hospital. Families with a history of CF may wish to have all children tested, especially if there is a child who already has the disease. Some hospitals require routine screening of newborns for CF.

Sweat test

The **sweat test** is both the easiest and most accurate test for CF. In this test, a small amount of the drug pilocarpine is placed on the skin. A very small electrical current is then applied to the area, which drives the pilocarpine into the skin. The drug stimulates sweating in the treated area. The sweat is absorbed onto a piece of filter paper and is then analyzed for its salt content. A person with CF will have salt concentrations that are 1.5 to 2 times greater than normal. The test can be done on persons of any age, including newborns, and its results can be determined within an hour. Virtually every person who has CF will test positively on it, and virtually everyone who does not will test negatively.

Genetic testing

The discovery of the CFTR gene in 1989 allowed the development of an accurate genetic test for CF. Genes from a small blood or tissue sample are analyzed for specific mutations; presence of two copies of the mutated gene confirms the diagnosis of CF in all but a very few cases. However, since there are so many different possible mutations and since testing for all of them would be too expensive and time-consuming, a negative gene test cannot rule out the possibility of CF.

Couples planning a family may decide to have themselves tested if one or both have a family history of CF. Prenatal genetic testing is possible through **amniocentesis**. Many couples who already have one child with CF decide to undergo prenatal screening in subsequent pregnancies and use the results to determine whether to terminate the pregnancy. Siblings in these families are also usually tested, to determine if they will develop CF and to determine if they are carriers, to aid in their own family planning. If the sibling has no symptoms, determining his carrier status is often delayed until his teen years or later, when he is closer to needing the information to make decisions.

Newborn screening

Some states in the early 2000s require screening of newborns for CF, using a test known as the IRT test. This blood test measures the level of immunoreactive trypsinogen, which is generally higher in babies with CF than those without it. This test gives many false positive results immediately after birth and so requires a second test several weeks later. A second positive result is usually followed by a sweat test.

Treatment

As of 2004 there was no cure for CF. However, treatment advanced during the last quarter of the twentieth century, increasing both the life span and the quality of life for most people affected by CF. Early diagnosis is important to prevent malnutrition and infection from weakening the young child. With proper management, many people with CF engage in the full range of school and **sports** activities.

Nutrition

People with CF usually require high-calorie diets and vitamin supplements. Height, weight, and growth of a person with CF are monitored regularly. Most people with CF need to take pancreatic enzymes to supplement or replace the inadequate secretions of the pancreas. Tablets containing pancreatic enzymes are taken with every meal; depending on the size of the tablet and the meal, as many as 20 tablets may be needed. Because of incomplete absorption even with pancreatic enzymes, a person with CF needs to take in about 30 percent more food than a person without CF. Low-fat diets are not recommended except in special circumstances, since fat is a source of both essential fatty acids and abundant calories.

Some people with CF cannot absorb enough nutrients from the foods they eat, even with specialized diets and enzymes. For these people, tube feeding is an option. Nutrients can be introduced directly into the stomach through a tube inserted either through the nose (a nasogastric tube) or through the abdominal wall (a gastrostomy tube). A jejunostomy tube, inserted into the small intestine, is also an option. Tube feeding can provide nutrition at any time, including at night while the person is sleeping, allowing constant intake of high-quality nutrients. The feeding tube may be removed during the day, allowing normal meals to be taken.

Respiratory health

The key to maintaining respiratory health in a person with CF is regular monitoring and early treatment. Lung function tests are done frequently to track changes in functional lung volume and respiratory effort. Sputum samples are analyzed to determine the types of bacteria present in the lungs. Chest x-rays are usually taken at least once a year. Lung scans, using a radioactive gas, can show closed off areas not seen on the x ray. Circulation in the lungs may be monitored by injection of a radioactive substance into the bloodstream.

People with CF live with chronic bacterial colonization; that is, their lungs are constantly host to several species of bacteria. Good general health, especially good nutrition, can keep the immune system healthy, which decreases the frequency with which these colonies begin an infection or attack on the lung tissue. Exercise is another important way to maintain health, and people with CF are encouraged to maintain a program of regular exercise.

In addition, clearing mucus from the lungs helps to prevent infection, and mucus control is an important aspect of CF management. Postural drainage is used to allow gravity to aid the mucociliary escalator. For this technique, the person with CF lies on a tilted surface with head downward, alternately on the stomach, back, or side, depending on the section of lung to be drained. An assistant thumps the rib cage to help loosen the secretions. A device called a flutter offers another way to loosen secretions: it consists of a stainless steel ball in a tube. When a person exhales through it, the ball vibrates, sending vibrations back through the air in the lungs. Some special breathing techniques may also help clear the lungs.

Several drugs are available to prevent the airways from becoming clogged with mucus. Bronchodilators and theophyllines open up the airways; steroids reduce inflammation; and mucolytics loosen secretions. Acetylcysteine (Mucomyst) has been used as a mucolytic during the 1980s and 1990s but is not prescribe frequently in the early 2000s, while DNase (Pulmozyme) is a newer product gaining in popularity. DNase breaks down the DNA from dead white blood cells and bacteria found in thick mucus.

People with CF may pick up bacteria from other CF patients. This is especially true of *Burkholderia cepacia*, which is not usually found in people without CF. While the ideal recommendation from a health standpoint might be to avoid contact with others who have CF, this is not usually practical (since CF clinics are a major site of care), nor does it meet the psychological and social needs of many people with CF. At a minimum, CF centers recommend avoiding prolonged close contact between people with CF and scrupulous hygiene, including frequent hand washing. Some CF clinics schedule appointments on different days for those with and without *B. cepacia* colonies.

Some doctors choose to prescribe antibiotics only during infection, while others prefer long-term antibiotic treatment against *S. aureus*. The choice of antibiotic depends on the particular organism or organisms found. Some antibiotics are given as aerosols directly into the lungs. Antibiotic treatment may be prolonged and aggressive.

Supplemental oxygen may be needed as lung disease progresses. Respiratory failure may develop, requiring temporary use of a ventilator to perform the work of breathing.

Lung transplantation has become increasingly common for people with CF, although the number of people who receive lungs was as of 2004 much lower than those who want them. Transplantation is not a cure, however, and has been likened to trading one disease for another. Long-term immunosuppression is required, increasing the likelihood of other types of infection. About 50 percent of adults and more than 80 percent of children who receive lung transplants live longer than two years. Liver transplants are also done for CF patients whose livers have been damaged by fibrosis.

Long-term use of ibuprofen has been shown to help some people with CF, presumably by reducing inflammation in the lungs. Close medical supervision is necessary, however, since the effective dose is high and not everyone benefits. Ibuprofen at the required doses interferes with kidney function and, together with aminoglycoside antibiotics, may cause kidney failure.

A number of experimental treatments were as of 2004 the subject of much research. Some evidence indicates that aminoglycoside antibiotics may help overcome the genetic defect in some CF mutations, allowing the protein to be made normally. While promising, these results would apply to only about 5 percent of those with CF.

Gene therapy is the most ambitious approach to curing CF. In this set of techniques, non-defective copies of the CFTR gene are delivered to affected cells, where they are taken up and used to create the CFTR protein. While elegant and simple in theory, gene therapy has met with a large number of difficulties in trials, including immune resistance, very short duration of the introduced gene, and inadequately widespread delivery.

Prognosis

People with CF may lead relatively normal lives, with the control of symptoms. The possible effect of pregnancy on the health of a woman with CF requires careful consideration before she and her partner begin a family; as do issues of longevity, and the children's status as carriers. Although most men with CF are functionally sterile, new procedures for removing sperm from the testes are being tried and may offer more men the chance to become fathers.

Approximately half of people with CF live past the age of 30. Because of better and earlier treatment, a person born in 2004 with CF is expected, on average, to live to age 40.

Prevention

Adults with a family history of cystic fibrosis may obtain a genetic test of their carrier status for purposes of family planning. Prenatal testing is also available. There is no known way to prevent development of CF in a person with two defective gene copies.

Resources

BOOKS

Boat, Thomas F. "Cystic Fibrosis." In *Nelson Textbook of Pediatrics.* Edited by Richard E. Behrman et al. Philadelphia: Saunders, 2004.

Boucher, R. C., et al "Cystic Fibrosis." In *Textbook of Respiratory Medicine*, 3rd ed. Edited by John F. Murray and Jay A. Nadel. Philadelphia: Saunders, 2000.

ORGANIZATIONS

Cystic Fibrosis Foundation. 6931 Arlington Road, Bethesda, MD 20814. Web site: <www.cff.org>.

WEB SITES

CysticFibrosis.com. Available online at <http://www.cysticfibrosis.com> (accessed December 26, 2004).

Richard Robinson
Rosalyn Carson-DeWitt, MD

Cystitis

Definition

Cystitis is inflammation of the urinary bladder. Urethritis is an inflammation of the urethra, which is the tube that connects the bladder with the exterior of the body. Sometimes cystitis and urethritis are referred to collectively as a lower urinary tract infection (UTI). Infection of the upper urinary tract involves the spread of bacteria to the kidney and is called pyelonephritis.

Description

Cystitis in women

Cystitis is a common female problem. It is estimated that 50 percent of adult women experience at least one episode of dysuria (painful urination); half of these people have a bacterial UTI. Between 2 percent and 5 percent of women's visits to primary care physicians are for UTI symptoms. About 90 percent of UTIs in women are uncomplicated but recurrent.

Cystitis in men

UTIs are uncommon in younger and middle-aged men but may occur as complications of bacterial infections of the kidney or prostate gland.

Cystitis in children

In children, cystitis often is caused by congenital abnormalities (present at birth) of the urinary tract. **Vesicoureteral reflux** is a condition in which the child cannot completely empty the bladder. The condition allows urine to remain in or flow backward (reflux) into the partially empty bladder. In addition, cystitis can also be caused by wiping forward instead of backward after a bowel movement, especially in girls that are newly toilet trained.

Demographics

The frequency of bladder infections in humans varies significantly according to age and sex. The male/female ratio of UTIs in children younger than 12 months is four to one because of the high rate of birth defects in the urinary tract of male infants. Urinary tract infections are fairly common in young girls. In adult life, the male/female ratio of UTIs is one to 50. After age 50, however, the incidence among males increases due to prostate disorders.

Causes and symptoms

The causes of cystitis vary according to gender because of the differences in anatomical structure of the urinary tract.

Females

Most bladder infections in women are so-called ascending infections, which means they are caused by disease agents traveling upward through the urethra to the bladder. The relative shortness of the female urethra (1.2 to 2 inches [3-5 cm] in length for adults) facilitates bacteria gaining entry to the bladder and multiplying there. The most common bacteria associated with UTIs in women (including teens) are: *Escherichia coli* (approximately 80% of cases), *Staphylococcus saprophyticus*, *Klebsiella*, *Enterobacter*, and *Proteus* species. Risk factors for UTIs in women include:

- sexual intercourse (The risk of infection increases if the woman has multiple partners.)

- use of a diaphragm for contraception

- an abnormally short urethra

- diabetes or chronic **dehydration**

- the absence of a specific enzyme (fucosyltransferase) in vaginal secretions (The lack of this enzyme makes it easier for the vagina to harbor bacteria that cause UTIs.)

- inadequate personal hygiene (Bacteria from fecal matter or vaginal discharges can enter the female urethra because its opening is very close to the vagina and anus.)

- history of previous UTIs (About 80 percent of women with cystitis develop recurrences within two years.)

The early symptoms of cystitis in women are dysuria (**pain** on urination); urgency (a sudden strong desire to urinate); and increased frequency of urination. About 50 percent of females experience **fever**, pain in the lower back or flanks, **nausea and vomiting**, or shaking chills. These symptoms indicate pyelonephritis (spread of the infection to the upper urinary tract).

Males

Most UTIs in adult males are complications of kidney or prostate infections. They usually are associated with a tumor or kidney stones that block the flow of urine and often are persistent infections caused by drug-resistant organisms. UTIs in men are most likely to be caused by *E. coli* or another gram-negative bacterium. Risk factors for UTIs in men include lack of **circumcision** and urinary catheterization. The longer the period of catheterization, the higher the risk of contracting a UTI.

The symptoms of cystitis and pyelonephritis in men are the same as in women.

Children

In children, cystitis causes pain and tenderness in the lower abdomen, frequent urination, blood in the urine, and fever. However, some foods, including citrus juices, **caffeine**, and carbonated beverages, can irritate the lower urinary tract and mimic the symptoms of an infection.

Hemorrhagic cystitis

Hemorrhagic cystitis, which is marked by large quantities of blood in the urine, is caused by an acute bacterial infection of the bladder. In some cases, hemorrhagic cystitis is a side effect of radiation therapy or treatment with cyclophosphamide. Hemorrhagic cystitis in children is associated with adenovirus type 11.

When to call the doctor

A doctor or other healthcare provider should be contacted whenever urination becomes painful or the voided urine is cloudy or bloody, or when a child complains of pain when voiding urine.

Diagnosis

When cystitis is suspected, the doctor first examines a person's abdomen and lower back, to evaluate unusual enlargements of the kidneys or swelling of the bladder. In small children, the doctor checks for fever, abdominal masses, and a swollen bladder.

The next step in diagnosis is collection of a urine sample. The procedure involves voiding into a cup, so small children may be catheterized to collect a sample. Laboratory testing of urine samples as of the early 2000s can be performed with dipsticks that indicate immune system responses to infection, as well as with microscopic analysis of samples. Normal human urine is sterile. The presence of bacteria or pus in the urine usually indicates infection. The presence of hematuria (blood in the urine) may indicate acute UTIs, kidney disease, kidney stones, inflammation of the prostate (in men), endometriosis (in women), or **cancer** of the urinary tract. In some cases, blood in the urine results from athletic training, particularly in runners.

Other tests

Women and children with recurrent UTIs can be given ultrasound exams of the kidneys and bladder together with a voiding cystourethrogram to test for structural abnormalities. (A cystourethrogram is an x-ray test in which an iodine dye is used to better view the urinary bladder and urethra.) In some cases, **computed tomography** scans (CT scans) can be used to evaluate people for possible cancers in the urinary tract.

Treatment

Medications

Uncomplicated cystitis is treated with **antibiotics**. These include penicillin, ampicillin, and amoxicillin; sulfisoxazole or sulfamethoxazole; trimethoprim; nitrofurantoin; cephalosporins; or fluoroquinolones. (Fluoroquinolones generally are not used in children under 18 years of age.) A 2003 study showed that fluoroquinolone was preferred over amoxicillin, however, for uncomplicated cystitis in young women. Treatment for women is short-term; most women respond within three days. Men and children do not respond as well to short-term treatment and require seven to 10 days of oral antibiotics for uncomplicated UTIs.

Persons of either gender may be given phenazopyridine or flavoxate to relieve painful urination.

Trimethoprim and nitrofurantoin are preferred for treating recurrent UTIs in women.

Individuals with pyelonephritis can be treated with oral antibiotics or intramuscular doses of cephalosporins. Medications are given for ten to 14 days and sometimes longer. If the person requires **hospitalization** because of high fever and dehydration caused by **vomiting**, antibiotics can be given intravenously.

Surgery

A minority of women with complicated UTIs may require surgical treatment to prevent recurrent infections. Surgery also is used to treat reflux problems (movement of the urine backward) or other structural abnormalities in children and anatomical abnormalities in adult males.

Alternative treatment

Alternative treatment for cystitis may emphasize eliminating all sugar from the diet and drinking lots of water. Drinking unsweetened cranberry juice not only adds fluid but also is thought to help prevent cystitis by making it more difficult for bacteria to cling to the bladder wall. A variety of herbal therapies also are recommended. Generally, the recommended herbs are antimicrobials, such as garlic (*Allium sativum*), goldenseal (*Hydrastis canadensis*), and bearberry (*Arctostaphylos uva-ursi*); and/or demulcents that soothe and coat the urinary tract, including corn silk and marsh mallow (*Althaea officinalis*).

Homeopathic medicine also can be effective in treating cystitis. Choosing the correct remedy based on the individual's symptoms is always key to the success of this type of treatment. Acupuncture and Chinese traditional herbal medicine can also be helpful in treating acute and chronic cases of cystitis.

Prognosis

The prognosis for recovery from uncomplicated cystitis is excellent.

Prevention

Females

Women and teens with two or more UTIs within a six-month period sometimes are given prophylactic treatment, usually nitrofurantoin or trimethoprim for three to six months. In some cases the woman is advised to take an antibiotic tablet following sexual intercourse.

Other preventive measures for women include drinking large amounts of fluid; voiding frequently, particularly after intercourse; and proper cleansing of the area around the urethra. Children with UTIs should be encouraged to drink plenty of fluids and wipe themselves properly after a bowel movement.

In 2003, clinical trials in humans tested a possible vaccine for recurrent urinary tract infections. The vaccine was administered via a vaginal suppository.

Nutritional concerns

Many experts recommend that people with a UTI should drink cranberry juice, which contains hippuric acid that tends to lower the pH (acidify) of urine. This change reduces the ability of bacteria to thrive, thus helping to cure a UTI.

Parental concerns

Parents should monitor the urine of their young children. Older children should be encouraged to discuss episodes of painful urination with their parents or other knowledgeable persons.

Resources

BOOKS

Davis, Ira D., and Ellis D. Avner. "Lower Urinary Tract Causes of Hematuria." In *Nelson Textbook of Pediatrics*, 17th ed. Edited by Richard E. Behrman et al. Philadelphia: Saunders, 2003, pp. 2256–7.

Potts, Jeanette M. *Essential Urology: A Guide to Clinical Practice*. Totowa, NJ: Humana Press, 2004.

Stamm, Walter. "Urinary tract infections and pyelonephritis." In *Harrison's Principles of Internal Medicine*, 15th ed. Edited by Eugene Braunwald et al. New York: McGraw-Hill, 2001, pp. 1620–6.

Urinary Tract Infections: A Medical Dictionary, Bibliography, and Annotated Research Guide to Internet References. San Diego, CA: ICON Health Publications, 2004.

PERIODICALS

Meria, P., et al. "Encrusted cystitis and pyelitis in children: an unusual condition with potentially severe consequences." *Urology* 64, no. 3 (2004): 569–73.

Tsakiri, A., et al. "Eosinophilic cystitis induced by penicillin." *International Urology and Nephrology* 36, no. 2 (2004): 159–61.

ORGANIZATIONS

American Foundation for Urologic Disease. 1128 North Charles St., Baltimore, MD 21201. Web site: <www.afud.org/>.

American Urological Association. 1120 North Charles St., Baltimore, MD 21201. Web site: <www.auanet.org>.

L. Fleming Fallon, Jr., MD, DrPH

Cytomegalovirus infection

Definition

Cytomegalovirus (CMV) is a virus related to the group of herpes viruses. Infection with CMV can cause

---

> ## KEY TERMS
>
> **Bacteriuria**—The presence of bacteria in the urine.
>
> **Dysuria**—Painful or difficult urination.
>
> **Hematuria**—The presence of blood in the urine.
>
> **Pyelonephritis**—An inflammation of the kidney and upper urinary tract, usually caused by a bacterial infection. In its most serious form, complications can include high blood pressure (hypertension) and renal failure.
>
> **Urethritis**—Inflammation of the urethra, the tube through which the urine moves from the bladder to the outside of the body.

---

no symptoms or can be the source of serious illness in people with weak immune systems. CMV infection is also an important cause of birth defects.

Description

CMV is an extremely common organism worldwide. It is believed that about 85 percent of the adults in the United States have been infected by CMV at some point in their lives. CMV is found in almost all of the body's organs. It is also found in body fluids, including semen, saliva, urine, feces, breast milk, blood, and secretions of the cervix (the narrow, lower section of the uterus).

CMV is also able to cross the placenta (the organ that provides oxygen and nutrients to the unborn baby in the uterus). Because CMV can cross the placental barrier, initial infection in a pregnant woman can lead to infection of the developing baby.

Demographics

In the United States, about 40 to 60 percent of all adults in the middle- and upper-socioeconomic classes show antibody proof of prior infection with CMV; antibody proof is as high as 80 percent in adults in the lower socioeconomic class. Worldwide, about 0.2 to 2.2 percent of all babies are born with congenital CMV infection. Of those babies born with congenital CMV infection, about 10 percent to 20 percent ultimately suffer form **hearing impairment**, eye damage, or problems with intellectual or motor function.

Causes and symptoms

CMV is passed between people through contact with body fluids. CMV also can be passed through sexual contact. Babies can be born infected with CMV, either becoming infected in the uterus (congenital infection) or during birth (from infected cervical secretions).

Like other herpes viruses, CMV remains inactive (dormant) within the body for life after the initial infection. Some of the more serious types of CMV infections occur in people who have been harboring the dormant virus, only to have it reactivate when their immune system is stressed. Immune systems may be weakened because of **cancer chemotherapy**, medications given after organ transplantation, or diseases that significantly lower immune resistance like acquired **immunodeficiency** syndrome (**AIDS**).

In a healthy person, initial CMV infection often occurs without symptoms and is rarely noticed. Occasionally, a first-time infection with CMV may cause a mild illness called mononucleosis. Symptoms include swollen glands, liver, and spleen; **fever**; increased white blood cells; **headache**; fatigue; and **sore throat**. About 8 percent of all mononucleosis cases are due to CMV infection. A similar infection, though slightly more serious, may occur two to four weeks after receiving a blood transfusion containing CMV.

In people with weakened immune systems, CMV infection can cause more serious and potentially life-threatening illnesses. These illnesses include **pneumonia** and inflammations of the liver (hepatitis), brain (**encephalitis**), esophagus (esophagitis), large intestine (colitis), and retina of the eye (retinitis).

Babies who contract CMV from their mothers during birth rarely develop any illness from these infections. Infants born prematurely who become CMV infected during birth have a greater chance of complications, including pneumonia, hepatitis, decreased blood platelets.

However, an unborn baby is at great risk for serious problems when the mother becomes infected with CMV for the first time while pregnant. About 10 percent of these babies will be born with obvious problems, including **prematurity**, lung problems, an enlarged liver and spleen, **jaundice**, anemia, low birth weight, small head size, and inflammation of the retina. About 90 percent of these babies may appear perfectly normal at birth. Unfortunately, about 20 percent later develop severe hearing impairments and **mental retardation**. A 2003 report found that pregnant women 25 years of age and older who are immune to CMV are much less likely to pass the virus to their babies than younger women who have never been exposed to CMV.

Diagnosis

Body fluids or tissues can be tested to reveal CMV infection. However, this information is not always particularly helpful because CMV stays dormant in the cells for life. Tests to look for special immune cells (antibodies) that are directed specifically against CMV are useful in proving that a person has been infected with CMV. However, these tests do not give any information regarding when the CMV infection first occurred.

Treatment

Ganciclovir and foscarnet are antiviral medications that have been used to treat patients with weak immune systems who develop a serious illness from CMV (including retinitis). As of 1998, research was still being done to try to find useful drugs to treat newborn babies

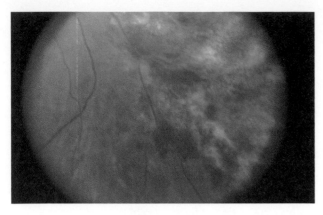

An infected retina caused by a cytomegalovirus. *(Photograph by Paula Ihnat. Custom Medical Stock Photo, Inc.)*

suffering from congenital infection with CMV. **Antiviral drugs** are not used to treat CMV infection in otherwise healthy patients because the drugs have significant side effects that outweigh their benefits. In 2003, researchers in Europe announced a new compound that appeared to be highly effective against CMV infections. The new drug acted earlier in the viral replication of the infection and showed promise; however, clinical trials were continuing.

Prognosis

Prognosis in healthy people with CMV infection is excellent. About 0.1 percent of all newborn babies have serious damage from CMV infection occurring while they were developing in the uterus. About 50 percent of all transplant patients develop severe illnesses due to reactivation of dormant CMV infection. These illnesses have a high rate of serious complications and death.

Prevention

Prevention of CMV infection in the normal, healthy person involves good hand washing. Blood products can be screened or treated to insure that they do not contain CMV. In 2003, a new high-dose prophylactic (preventive) treatment was being tested to reduce CMV risk in stem cell transplant recipients.

Resources

BOOKS

"Cytomegalovirus Infection." In *Obstetrics: Normal and Problem Pregnancies.* Edited by Steven G. Gabbe. London: Churchill Livingstone, 2002.

Pass, Robert F. "Cytomegalovirus." In *Principles and Practice of Pediatric Infectious Diseases*, 2nd ed. Edited by Sarah S. Long et al. St. Louis, MO: Elsevier, 2003.

Stagno, Sergio. "Cytomegalovirus." In *Nelson Textbook of Pediatrics.* Edited by Richard E. Behrman et al. Philadelphia: Saunders, 2004.

PERIODICALS

Fowler, Karen B., Sergio Stagno, and Robert F. Pass. "Maternal Immunity and Prevention of Congenital Cytomegalovirus Infection." *Journal of the American Medical Association* (February 26, 2003): 1008.

"High-Dose Acyclovir May Reduce Cytomegalovirus Infection Risk." *Virus Weekly* (July 15, 2003): 16.

"Novel Compound Highly Effective Against Cytomegalovirus Infection." *AIDS Weekly* (November 25, 2003): 17.

ORGANIZATIONS

Centers for Disease Control and Prevention. 1600 Clifton Rd., NE, Atlanta, GA 30333. Web site: <www.cdc.gov>.

March of Dimes Birth Defects Foundation. 1275 Mamaroneck Ave., White Plains, NY 10605. Web site: <www.modimes.org>.

Rosalyn Carson-DeWitt, MD
Teresa G. Odle